ENGLISH COINS
1180-1551

LORD STEWARTBY

SPINK & SON LTD
LONDON
2009

English Coins 1180-1551

© Lord Stewartby
2009

Typeset by Design to Print UK Ltd,
9 & 10 Riverview Business Park, Forest Row, East Sussex RH18 5DW
www.designtoprintuk.com

Printed and bound in Malta
by Gutenberg Press Ltd

The contents of this book, including the numbering system and illustrations,
are protected by copyright.

All rights are reserved. No part of this publication may be reproduced, stored in a
retrieval system, or transmitted, in any form or by any means, electronic, mechanical,
photocopying, recording or otherwise, without the prior permission of
Spink & Son Ltd.

ISBN 10: 1-902040-89-9 (softback)
ISBN 13: 978-1-902040-89-9 (softback)

ISBN 10: 1-902040-91-0 (hardback)
ISBN 13: 978-1-902040-91-2 (hardback)

Mixed Sources
Product group from well-managed
forests, and other controlled sources
www.fsc.org Cert no. TT-CoC-002424
© 1996 Forest Stewardship Council

The paper used for this book is FSC-certified and
totally chlorine-free. FSC (the Forest Stewardship
Council) is an international network to promote
responsible management of the world's forests.

In Memoriam

Christopher Blunt 1904 – 1987

Philip Grierson 1910 – 2006

CONTENTS

Synopsis...vi

Preface..xi

Introduction..1

Chapter 1, 1180-1247
   The Short Cross Coinage.......................................13

Chapter 2, 1247-1278
   The Long Cross Coinage..72

Chapter 3, 1279-1343
   Edward I – Edward III..108

Chapter 4, 1344-1351
   Edward III..184

Chapter 5, 1351-1411
   Edward III – Henry IV..199

Chapter 6, 1412-1464
   Henry IV – Edward IV..269

Chapter 7, 1464-1526
   Edward IV – Henry VIII..338

Chapter 8, 1526-1544
   Henry VIII..452

Chapter 9, 1544-1551
   Debasement, Henry VIII – Edward VI................475

Epilogue..533

Bibliography...535

Index..547

Key to Plates..553

SYNOPSIS OF CHAPTERS I – IX

I: 1180-1247 13
    Classification 21
        Class I 22
        Class II 28
        Class III 32
        Class IV 32
        Class V 37
        Class VI 43
        Class VII 49
        Class VIII 55
    Rhuddlan 57
    Ireland 60
    Imitations 62
    Mint Output 63
    Calendar 1180-1247 65
    Lists – Pennies 1180-1247, and Fractions (1222 only) 67
        Rhuddlan, Ireland 71

II: 1247-1278 72
    Classification 77
        Class I 79
        Class II 80
        Class III 82
            Moneyers of the Provincial Mints 85
        Class IV 87
        Class V 88
        Classes VI and VII 96
    Ireland 97
    Imitations 98
    Gold Pennies 99
    Mint Output 101
    Calendar 1247-1278 103
    Lists
        Gold Pennies, from 1257 104
        Silver Pennies, 1247-1278 105
        Ireland 107

III: 1279-1343 108
    Classification and Arrangement 113
        Groats 115
        Pence 117
            Group I 117
            Group II 119
            Group III 120
            Group IV 123
            Group V 125
            Groups VI, VII and VIII 126

vi

Synopsis

	Group IX	129
	Group X	131
	Groups XI – XIV	138
	Group XV	142
Halfpence, 1280-1335		145
Farthings, 1279-1335		148
Halfpence and Farthings, 1335-1343		151
English Coins of Berwick-upon-Tweed		153
Class I		154
Class II		154
Classes III and IV		155
Classes V-VII		156
Class VIII		157
Ireland		158
Class I		159
Classes II-IV		161
Edward III		162
Imitations		163
Mint Output		164
Calendar 1279-1343		168
Lists		
Groats 1279-81		170
Pence 1279-1343		170
Halfpence 1280-1335		177
Farthings 1279-1335		178
Halfpence and Farthings 1335-1343		179
Berwick-upon-Tweed:	Pence	179
"	Halfpence	180
"	Farthings	181
Ireland:	Pence	181
"	Halfpence	182
"	Farthings	183

IV: 1344-1351 184
    Classification 186
        Gold Coins 186
        Pence 188
        Halfpence and Farthings 193
    Berwick-upon-Tweed 193
    Mint Output 194
    Calendar 1344-1351 195
    Lists
        Gold 1344-1351 195
        Silver 1344-1351 196
        Berwick 198

V: 1351-1411 199
    Classification 206
        The Pre-Treaty Period, 1351-61 208
            Group A 212

Synopsis

        Groups B and C 213
        Group D 215
        Group E 216
        Group F 217
        Group G 218
    The Treaty Period, 1361-69 223
        Treaty A Group (1361) 225
        Treaty B Group (1361-69) 226
    Edward III, Post-Treaty Period, 1369-77 230
    Richard II (1377-99) – Structure 233
        Richard II, First Period (1377-c.1390) 236
        Richard II, Second Period (c.1390-1399) 239
    Henry IV, Heavy Coinage, 1399-1411 243
Mint Accounts 248
Calendar 1351-1411 250
Weights 1351-1411 252
Lists
    Nobles 1351-1411 252
    Half-nobles 1351-1411 255
    Quarter-nobles 1351-1411 257
    Groats 1351-1411 259
    Halfgroats 1351-1411 262
    Pennies 1351-1411 264
    Halfpence 1351-1411 267
    Farthings 1351-1411 268

VI: 1412-1464 269
    Classification 1412-1422 (Henry IV-V) 276
        Henry IV, Light Coinage (1412-13) 278
        Henry V (1413-1422) 284
    Classification and Chronology, 1422-1464 290
        Henry VI, Annulet Group (I) 293
        Henry VI, Rosette, Pinecone and Leaf-Mascle Groups (II-IV) 298
        Henry VI, Trefoiled Groups (V-VII) 304
        Pelleted Groups of Henry VI (VIII-XI) and Edward IV (Type I) 308
        Edward IV, Heavy Coinage, Types II-IV, with Mintmark Rose 312
Mint Accounts, 1411-1464 315
Calendar 1412-1464 317
Weights, 1412-1464 318
Lists
    Nobles 1412-1464 318
    Half-nobles 1412-1464 320
    Quarter-nobles 1412-1464 322
    Groats 1412-1464 323
    Halfgroats 1412-1464 327
    Pennies 1412-1464 330
    Halfpence 1412-1464 334
    Farthings 1412-1464 336

SYNOPSIS

- **VII:** 1464-1526 338
  - Edward IV Light Coinage – Classification and Chronology 348
    - Edward IV, Early Light Coinage (Types V and VI), 1464-6 351
    - Edward IV, First Reign, Types VII-XI 356
    - Henry VI, Second Reign (1470-1) and Edward IV, type XII 361
    - Edward IV, Annulet Series, Types XIII-XV 364
    - Edward IV, Second Cross Series, Types XVI-XX 366
    - Edward IV, Type XXI, Mintmark Cinquefoil 369
  - Ecclesiastical Issues of Edward IV's Light Coinage 370
    - Canterbury, 1464-1483 371
    - York, 1464-1483 373
    - Durham, 1464-1483 375
  - Edward IV-V, Type XXII (1483), and Richard III (1483-5) 376
  - Henry VII – Structure and Classification 382
    - Henry VII, Group I 385
    - Henry VII, Group II 388
    - Henry VII, Group IIIA and IIIB 393
    - Henry VII, Group IIIC, Mintmark Pansy-Anchor 398
    - Henry VII, Transition to Profile Portrait Types (IIIc-V) 401
    - Last Issues of Henry VII and the First Coinage of Henry VIII 407
  - Ecclesiastical Mints from c.1505 412
  - Mint Accounts 415
  - Calendar 1464-1526 418
  - Weights 1464-1526 420
  - Lists
    - Sovereigns 1489-1526 421
    - Ryals 1465-1526 421
    - Half-ryals 1465-1470 423
    - Quarter-ryals 1465-1470 424
    - Angels 1465-1526 424
    - Angelets 1465-1526 428
    - Shillings 1504 430
    - Groats 1464-1526 430
    - Halfgroats 1464-1526 438
    - Pence 1464-1526 443
    - Halfpence 1464-1526 449
    - Farthings 1464-1526 451

- **VIII:** 1526-1544 452
  - Fine Gold 455
  - Crown Gold 457
  - Tower Mint Silver Coins 459
  - Ecclesiastical Mints 463
  - Mint Accounts 466
  - Calendar 1526-1544 467
  - Weights and Fineness, 1526-1544 468
  - Lists
    - Sovereigns 1526-1544 469
    - Angels and Angelets 1526-1544 469

Synopsis

George Nobles and Half-nobles from 1526	470
Crowns 1526-1544	470
Halfcrowns 1526-1544	471
London Groats and Halfgroats, 1526-1544	471
London Small Silver 1526-1544	472
Canterbury from 1526	472
York from 1526	473
Durham pence from 1526	474

IX: 1544-1551 475
    Arrangement and Classification 481
    Henry Gold and First Coins in Edward's Name 485
        Sovereigns and Half-Sovereigns of Henry's Type 486
        Angels and Fractions 490
        Crowns and Halfcrowns of Henry's Type 490
    Henry Silver and First Coins in Edward's Name 492
        Testons 493
        Groats 495
        Halfgroats 501
        Small Silver 503
    Edward Sovereigns and Fractions, 1549-1550 504
    Southwark Edward Gold, 1551 506
    Edward Shillings 1549-1551 507
    Dublin 512
    Mint Accounts, 1544-1551 514
    Calendar 1544-1551 517
    Weights and Fineness, 1544-1551 518
    Lists
        Sovereigns of 20s. 1544-1547 519
        Half-Sovereigns (King Enthroned) 1544-1551 520
        Angels and Fractions, 1544-1545 521
        Crowns 1545-1551 521
        Halfcrowns 1545-1551 522
        Edward Sovereigns and Fractions 1549-1550 523
        Southwark Gold 1551 524
        Testons 1544-1547 524
        Groats 1544-1551 525
        Halfgroats 1544-1551 528
        Pence 1544-1551 529
        Halfpence 1544-1551 531
        Farthings from 1544 531
        Shillings 1549-1551 531

PREFACE

Although this book was not written until 1994 – 2007, it had been in contemplation for more than forty years previously and much of the preparatory work was done during that time. Its production had to wait until I had more time to devote to it, but the delay has had the beneficial consequence of enabling me to take into consideration the material contained in many important works that have appeared in recent years, most notably the *New History of the Royal Mint* and the *Sylloge* of the Schneider collection of English gold coins. The twentieth century was a period of intense activity in English numismatics, and it seems timely to attempt a conspectus of the subject in light of our state of knowledge at the turn of the millennium.

My aim has been to provide a general historical survey combined with a classified description of the coins. As such, I hope the book will serve the needs both of the historian and general user and of those with a more particular interest in numismatics. It is not primarily about the administration of coinage, the behaviour of mints or the content of the currency except insofar as these are directly germane (as they often are) to the study of the coins themselves. The technical parts of the book have largely been distilled from highly detailed monographs and articles which, in my experience, often make it difficult even for students of the series to obtain an overall view. This I have therefore tried to provide, hoping that the discussion and basic information included will prove useful to the specialist as well as constituting a general introduction to an increasingly complex subject. A book of this kind could have been annotated almost without limit, but at the cost of putting its completion at risk. Instead the bibliography has been expanded to an extent that the reader should find in it the sources of nearly all matters covered in the text, relevant items being readily identifiable. Because of the complexity of the material, the Synopsis may be found the most accessible point of reference for the coins.

Each chapter contains an introductory section covering the historical background and an overview of the coinage of the period. This is followed by sections on the classification and technical numismatics of the series and a summary of the mint accounts. The detailed lists then appended include a general description of design and legend, together with enough of the detail that differentiates one type, class or variety from another to enable identification to be made according to the relevant classification. For this purpose the lists need to be used in conjunction with the explanatory text. No attempt is made to include every minor variant from the norm, although many of the main varieties are noted, especially when they may assist in identification. In a few series (such as Short Cross coins of the 1220s and 1230s, or Edwardian sterlings of the early 1300s) even the experienced student may find it necessary to have recourse to the specialist monographs in order to take identification beyond the main classes or sub-classes; but it has nevertheless seemed to me worthwhile to summarize here the features by which further subdivision has been defined, so as to make clear the nature of the evidence on which sequence and chronology are founded. Mules are usually noted under the type or class of the later die. Wherever practicable I have retained the traditional numbering of classes, including often the use of Roman numerals. In recent years these have sometimes been converted to Arabic numbers, but Roman are preferable, both to avoid confusion with other figures (e.g. in hoard lists or for plate numbers), and also for convenience because they can be used free-standing, without the need to add 'type' or 'group'.

Inscriptions, normally in Gothic script on the coins, are represented by Italics. Capitals are used to indicate Roman letters (notably E, H, M, N) and lower case their

Gothic equivalents. 'Left' and 'right' are from the spectator's view; when referring to the representation of the king, the heraldic convention is used – 'dexter' means the king's right (= spectator's left) and 'sinister' his left. Except in relation to a shield of arms the quarters on the reverse of silver coins are taken in circular order, e.g. *Civi* in first quarter, *tas* in second, etc.

Where appropriate, the entry for each coin in the Key to the Plates consists of two parts: first, the generic category of which it is representative, e.g. 'Pre-Treaty halfgroat' (this should enable any coin to be given a number for general reference); and second (in brackets), a more detailed reference for the particular specimen illustrated, e.g. '(group C)'. Locations of the coins featured on the plates are listed at the end, and I am greatly indebted to their owners/curators for permission to illustrate them and for assistance in making them available.

In respect of the text also my debt to others is great. Mr. Jeffrey North, Mr. Peter Woodhead and Dr. Martin Allen have all read large parts of the text, and their comments have been invaluable. The historical sections have benefited from the guidance of Prof. Christopher Brooke, Dr. Maurice Keen and Dr. Christopher Challis. Over the years members of staff of the coin rooms of the British Museum, the Ashmolean Museum and the Fitzwilliam Museum have responded to my endless enquiries, as have many students, dealers and collectors. Because they are so numerous, I hope they will accept a collective expression of thanks. However, I must be specific in recording my gratitude to those to whom I have referred particular sections of the book – Mr. Joseph Bispham, Mr. Robin Davis, Mr. Glenn Gittoes, Mr. David Greenhalgh, Dr. Eric Harris, Mr. Timothy Webb Ware, and Mr. and Mrs. Paul Withers; and in particular to Mr. Ronald Churchill and Mr. Robert Thomas for showing me, in advance of publication, the results of their work on the Long Cross coinage of Henry III, and so enabling me to incorporate the substance of their classification in this book.

In the preparation of the volume I have been much assisted by Mrs. Theresa Mitchell, who created an exemplary text from my disorderly manuscript; by Miss Helen Bone and Mr. Andrew Williams through their adroit construction of the plates; by Miss Henrietta Webb, with her elegant line-drawings; and by Mr. Philip Skingley and the staff of Messrs. Spink who have afforded me every facility in bringing the book to publication.

Since the 1950s I was fortunate enough to have enjoyed the encouragement and collaboration of Christopher Blunt and Philip Grierson. Much of what I know about the workings of medieval coinage was learnt from them. I hope that they would have felt this volume to be an appropriate fruit of their instruction and example.

Jesus College
Cambridge.
July 2008

I.S.

INTRODUCTION

The period from 1180 to 1551 covers the age of the sterling and the age of the groat, the two principal eras in English monetary history of the later middle ages. In 1180 Henry II reorganised the control and production of the coinage in ways which endured for generations and brought the English penny an international reputation for soundness and reliability. Indeed, the term sterling, which was in common use for the English penny from the twelfth century onwards, was derived from a word meaning fixed or stable, qualities that could not be attributed to many of the foreign coinages of the time. In the fourteenth century, belatedly in comparison with most of continental Europe, England at last adopted the use of larger denominations, based in silver on the groat, or great penny, of fourpence and in gold on the noble, or half-mark, of 6s. 8d. In the sixteenth century the noble, or 'angel' as it later became known, gradually gave way to a pound-based system of gold coins, but the most significant break with medieval habits took place in 1551. In that year, in the process of reconstituting the currency after the chaos of Henry VIII's debasement, the groat ceased after two hundred years to be a regular or central element of the coinage, a silver crown (5s.) and halfcrown made their first appearance and all mints outside London except York were closed. In terms of technical numismatics there is also a coherence in the timespan covered by this book. Prior to the reign of Henry II the designs of the coinage were altered at frequent intervals, and there is usually little difficulty in establishing its structure. At the other end the Tudor age saw the introduction of portraiture, Roman lettering, dates and other features that render the task of arranging and understanding the material much more straightforward. In between these limits, however, the process is more complex, dependent upon the close observation of minor developments in design and detail, and with reliable evidence for chronology often lacking.

For the purposes of this book the term 'English coins' means those struck under the authority of the English crown for currency in England. It thus excludes coins minted at London for currency in Ireland or Aquitaine as well as issues made by English rulers on continental standards in their French possessions. Conversely, it includes coins struck to the English standard in Ireland and at Calais which were designed to circulate in England and are related to or form an integral part of the English series. The English monetary system differed markedly from those of the Continent, where unitary states had not yet come into being and minting was fragmented. Although from an early period there were extensive coinages for the kings of France and the emperors in Germany, independent issues by lesser rulers survived alongside them. In England, however, there had been a single royal coinage since the tenth century and minting in the names and under the control of feudal lords took place only during the Civil War of the Stephen period after central authority collapsed in the 1140s. Minting rights granted by successive kings had been enjoyed by leading figures in the church since at least the eighth century, but from the time of Alfred onwards their coins were of the same type as the king's even if, especially in the late middle ages, often marked with symbols or initials that identify the ecclesiastical authority under which they were issued.

Another important contrast between the English coinage and that of continental Europe was in the stability of its weight and its high level of fineness. Although between the thirteenth century and the debasement of the 1540s the English penny lost just over half its weight, the process of reduction, which took place slowly and in modest stages, was a consequence of the rise in the values of the precious metals as the demand for them increased with the growth of commerce; it was not the result of a deliberate policy of raising revenue by debasement to accommodate growing expenditure by the crown. Elsewhere in Europe, however, monetary discipline was often lacking and debasement rapid. In England, on the other hand, recoinages took place at extended intervals, effectively when renewal of an ageing currency in poor condition had become unavoidable. Before the fourteenth century such recoinages, in 1180, 1247 and 1279, involved no material alteration of the weight or format of the coin, which remained on the standard introduced during the Norman period. There were also two partial recoinages, in 1205 and 1300, the first prompted by the need to replace old coin that had lost weight as a result of illicit clipping, the second a response to an influx of inferior continental imitations. From the mid-fourteenth century, however, it became necessary to adjust the weights of the coins

MINTS OF THE STERLING RECOINAGES, HENRY II – EDWARD I

	1180	1205	1248	1280	1300
London	x	x	x	x	x
Bristol			x	x	x
Bury St. Edmunds		x	x	x	x
Canterbury		x	x	x	x
Carlisle	x	x	x		
Chester				x	x
Chichester		x			
Durham		x		x	x
Exeter	x	x	x		x
Gloucester			x		
Hereford			x		
Ilchester			x		
Ipswich		x			
Kingston-upon-Hull					x
Lincoln	x	x	x	x	
Lynn		x			
Newcastle			x	x	x
Northampton	x	x	x		
Norwich		x	x		
Oxford	x	x	x		
Rochester		x			
Shrewsbury			x		
Wallingford			x		
Wilton	x		x		
Winchester	x	x	x		
Worcester	x				
York	x	x	x	x	x

from time to time so as to align their intrinsic value to current market levels. During the bimetallic period from Edward III onwards this process was complicated by fluctuations in the relative purchasing power of gold and silver, which could result in a shortage of supplies of whichever metal was undervalued. The major recoinages of 1351, 1412, 1464 and 1526 all therefore attempted to set new prices for gold and silver at levels which would attract bullion or old coin to the mints without making one metal more attractive than the other, as happened, for example, when gold predominated in the 1390s or silver in the 1450s. In each of these cases the misalignment of the metals was an important component in precipitating the subsequent recoinage. In respect of gold there was greater need to reflect conditions on the international market, but weight reductions in the silver coinage normally did little more than bring the official weight standard into line with the level to which the old currency had sunk as a result of wear and clipping.

In the late Saxon and Norman periods the currency had been reminted every few years, evidently for some fiscal purpose. This process of *renovatio* had required an extensive network of regional and local mints of which there were often as many as sixty or seventy in frequent if not continuous activity. Henry II's first recoinage, in 1158, replaced the *renovatio* system, which could not be made to function properly during the troubled 1140s. Henceforth each coin type was to remain unchanged for an extended period, and much of the purpose of the lesser mints thus disappeared. Fewer than half of those active in the first half of the twelfth century remained in use after 1158, and in the recoinage of 1180 the number was down to ten. When that recoinage was completed several regional mints continued to operate intermittently through the 1180s and 1190s, but after the partial renovation of 1205, in which sixteen mints participated, coinage was confined, for more than a century, to London and Canterbury, with modest contributions from ecclesiastical mints at Bury St. Edmunds and Durham. Only one attempt was made to revive other royal mints, at York and Winchester in 1218, and that proved unsuccessful.

In 1247, 1280 and 1300 national coverage was again achieved by opening regional mints for the purpose of recoinage. Apart from London, only York features in each of the five recoinages of the sterling era, although Canterbury and Bury only failed to do so because Henry II had excluded all ecclesiastical franchises in 1180. The list of 1180 mints includes a reasonable geographic spread, although the absence of any in East Anglia, Kent or Sussex is notable, the more so since all the six mints reopened in 1205 were in this prosperous region. In 1247, however, four of them had disappeared, and instead there was a new focus on the western counties, from Shropshire to Somerset. This saw the revival of Bristol, of growing economic importance in the late middle ages. After 1300 there were never again so many mints commissioned for a recoinage. This was partly because the recoinage did not need to be complete – since types were not changed old coin, if in a tolerable state (and sometimes even if not), could remain in circulation almost indefinitely; but it also reflects broadening economic activity, the growth of commerce and travel, and a resultant lessening of the need for regional exchange. The only additional royal mint in England that contributed to Edward III's reformed coinage was York in 1353-5. In 1411/2 no new mints were added. Indeed, Calais, where since the 1360s, until it closed for lack of bullion in 1404, there had been what was effectively a branch of the Tower mint to service the wool staple, was left dormant for a further ten years; and when it was revived in 1422 this was because of new supplies of silver and gold from foreign trade rather than as a delayed response to the weight reduction at the end of Henry IV's reign. At about the same time there were plans to support the growing production of coin by opening mints at York and Bristol, but the former alone materialised and then for one year only. Mints at York and Bristol were, however, both brought into play for

Introduction

Edward IV's recoinage in 1464 and survived briefly beyond the restoration of Henry VI in 1470/1, but the involvement of two other 1464 mints, at Coventry and Norwich, was only transitory. While Norwich, centre of an East Anglia made rich by wool, had last had a mint under Henry III, Coventry was the only place in the central midlands ever to have had one after the twelfth century, and its very short spell of activity suggests that it was scarcely needed. Although York was briefly revived by Richard III in 1484 and under Henry VII a few years later, the only other exception to the rule that, after Edward IV until the debasement of the 1540s, royal coinage was confined to the Tower was a small issue by Henry VIII at Tournai soon after its capture in 1513. When the hammered coinage was finally demonetized in 1696, the selection of regional mints to carry it out – Bristol, Chester, Exeter, Norwich and York – would not have seemed out of place four hundred years before.

From the early thirteenth century the number of mints operated wholly or partly under ecclesiastical license were few but of increasing importance. While Canterbury, York and Durham reflected their eminent status in the hierarchy of the church, the abbeys of Bury St. Edmunds and Reading owed their privilege to royal favour. However, minting at Bury, which had been extensive in the early fourteenth century, came to an end early in the reign of Edward III, but the mint at Reading which seemed set to replace it was only active for a few years and on a very limited scale. The Canterbury mint, in which the archbishop had long been a junior partner with the crown, was also closed before 1351, but it was revived, partly for political reasons and without royal participation, by Edward IV in the 1460s. After the closure of Calais in the 1440s there would in any case have been a stronger practical case for a mint to be available at Canterbury to serve the Kentish ports. From this time onwards until the 1530s it assumed a leading position in the production of halfgroats.

At York the archbishop's rights were exercised more continuously, although until the reign of Henry VII his mint was limited to the striking of pence. Before Edward III a mint could only be operated for the archbishop in his palace when there was also a mint in the king's castle, but in 1331 and subsequently the opposite was the case. Thus, when a royal mint was active for two years in the 1350s, the archbishop's mint was suspended for the duration. Thereafter York came to provide the bulk of the country's need for pence for a century and a half; but for some unexplained reason it then ceased to mint pence under Henry VII and Henry VIII until the 1530s, switching instead to halfgroats and halfpence and even, in a famous episode, to groats for Cardinal Wolsey. Durham owed its ecclesiastical mint to the fact that since Norman times the diocese of Durham had been, in feudal terminology, a County Palatine, in which the bishop enjoyed quasi-regal secular powers. His minting right was frequently exercised, and for much of the fifteenth century more or less continuously. Halfpence were authorised under Edward IV, during whose reign the mint was operating on a large scale, but otherwise Durham produced pence only.

When a bishop died the temporalities of his see reverted to the crown until a successor was installed. Since the king enjoyed the revenues during a vacancy, he was often in no hurry to make an appointment. This process had a useful numismatic consequence in that dies issued to York or Durham during a *sede vacante* period would usually lack the normal episcopal marks – quatrefoil or keys at York, heraldic mark or initials at Durham. Dies without special marks may however also refer to a period when a bishop had been suspended from office as the result of a quarrel with the king, like for example that between Edward I and Bishop Bek in 1302 and 1305. Although coins from such unmarked dies may provide a fixed chronological point in the series, some of the attributions that have been based on this evidence are, or may be, the result of error, when the appropriate marks were accidentally omitted, or if unmarked dies in stock at London were dispatched for convenience. Except in respect of their special marks the dies used at the episcopal mints were usually identical with those made for the Tower or other royal mints, but there were several periods, sometimes extending for many years, when dies were made locally, the most notable being at York during the reign of Richard II and at Durham under Edward IV.

Throughout the middle ages, and for some generations afterwards, English coins were hand-produced by what is termed the hammered method. In the sixteenth century experiments with machinery were made in several countries including England but for technical reasons and because of resistance by the moneyers the hammered process was not replaced until the seventeenth. Blanks were cut or punched out of a sheet of metal and placed between an upper and a lower die. The upper die, or trussel, was an iron cylinder with the reverse design imprinted in steel or hardened iron on its lower end. The lower die (the staple, standard, or pile) carried the obverse type on the face of a shorter cylinder with a spike underneath by which it was secured in a wooden anvil. The trussel was held in the hand, or with tongs or withy, and hit, sometimes repeatedly, by the hammerman. Since it received the direct impact of the blow, the trussel's life was likely to be shorter than that of the standard, which was cushioned by the softer metal of the blank. Sets of dies therefore often consisted of one pile and two trussels, as is evidenced not only from various mint records but also by surviving coins. For instance, under Henry III and Edward I the abbot of Bury St. Edmunds was granted only one set at a time, which had to be returned before the next set was issued; there is no known case of a Bury reverse die at this period being combined with more than a single obverse, while each obverse is normally found combined with two reverses. At Durham, however, where in the pre-Yorkist era the bishop was allowed three sets at any time, he did not usually exchange all three simultaneously; and the resulting die-chain is often valuable in establishing a sequence of varieties. At the Tower and other royal mints there was no overall limitation on the number of dies in concurrent use, this depending upon the volume of coinage at the time. Once coinage was underway, new dies would normally be supplied as needed, not in predetermined numbers or sets. At times of heavy minting the number of reverse dies was sometimes three or four times greater than the number of obverses, with the latter retained in use to a point where they could no longer impart a satisfactory impression on a coin.

Very high output was sometimes obtained from a single obverse die in the later middle ages. In 1353-5, at the royal mint in York (where the ratio of obverse to reverse dies was 1:3), the average was around 90,000. But although this was exceptional, under Edward I and II average output was over 30,000 coins per obverse die, and higher numbers have been estimated for Shrewsbury during the 1249-50 recoinage and for Bury St. Edmunds in the 1280s and 1290s. Where the die-ratio was 1:2 the average output of reverse dies would of course have been half the figure for obverses. Averages, however, result from the aggregation of higher and lower numbers from individual dies, some of which, from the perceived state of their products, may have been heavily overused or discarded early through cracking, breakage, shortage of bullion, or whatever. Several medieval dies, mostly of the fourteenth century, are preserved in the Public Record Office, the Royal Mint and the British Museum. Many of the trussels show the effect of repeated hammering, becoming flattened and cracked, and bent over at the sides, and so eventually unusable, while lower dies would often survive much longer. Die-output figures from the fifteenth century are few, but tend to be much lower than from the thirteenth or fourteenth, both in England and elsewhere. A figure of c. 12,000 for obverses of gold angels of Edward IV has been estimated by Webb Ware, and averages below this seem likely in other cases on the basis of known mint output and observed numbers of dies among surviving coins. Presumably there were technological reasons to account for at least part of the reduction in die-output as against earlier periods. Skill shortage seems also to have been a factor on some occasions. When the Tower mint was reopened by Henry IV in 1411, this followed a span of more than ten years in which little or no coin had been produced, and the frequency of broken letter punches on coins of the next few years points to a loss of technical experience.

At times of heavy coinage dies were mass-produced. The designs were relatively simple, at least for silver coin, and remained largely unchanged for long periods. Like other major coin types that had gained an international currency, from the 'owls' of Athens to Venetian ducats, and in contrast to the less stable coinages of areas like France and the Low Countries, where debasement could generate frequent changes in denominations and values, the reputation of English money acted as a disincentive to innovation in design. The crowned head on sterlings was never a portrait of a particular monarch; bearded until 1278, beardless thereafter, until late in the reign of Henry VII it took no account of the actual appearance of the ruler, and the long curls of hair from the 1270s onwards were unaltered regardless of contemporary fashion. The head was simply a pictorial representation of English royal authority. On silver reverses the uninspiring combination of a plain cross with groups of large pellets, which served the utilitarian purpose of identifying an English coin, endured for three hundred years. It was eventually replaced by a shield with the royal coat of arms under Henry VII, in which the three lions (heraldically 'leopards') of England were quartered with the lilies of France. Otherwise heraldry, popular on the Continent for the convenient recognition of different issuers, played no significant role on English silver, being confined in the pre-Tudor age to various episcopal and other symbols.

On gold there was greater scope for display. The reverses of the first gold coins of Edward III in 1344 set a pattern that lasted for more than a hundred years: the design of what is called the royal cross, an elaborate Gothic composition adapted from French coins of Philip the Fair (1285-1314), incorporates lions, fleurs-de-lis, crowns and floreate cross-ends. Their obverses included the only imaginative heraldic types on English medieval gold, the splendid mantled lion on Edward's florin a match for anything produced abroad. Very soon, however, with the arrival of the noble and its half, with the striking image of a large king standing in a small ship, English gold coins took on a more solid aspect, subordinating fancy to dependability. Updating of the design by Edward IV, with his rose-noble in an explicit Yorkist idiom in 1465, and its replacement by the restored Henry VI in 1470 with St. Michael on the angel-noble, provide us with the most overt examples of the influence of domestic politics on English medieval coin types. Although aspects of the Gothic style that had prevailed in western Christendom for three hundred years lingered on into the sixteenth century, the adoption of personal portraiture on coinage of the Tudor era was the most direct example of a response to the classical and humanistic currents of the Renaissance. Even so, it was not for more than forty years to be accompanied on English coins by the Roman script which had long provided a more legible caption to the portraits of ambitious Italian princes. There was, however, also a new theme, that of the power and grandeur of the Tudor monarchy, which even the austere Henry VII took care to foster, and of which his magnificent new gold sovereign was the embodiment.

Before 1279, for three hundred years, all English coins had carried the name of the moneyer responsible for their issue, with an abbreviation of the name of the mint. Otherwise inscriptions were traditionally in Latin. The normal form on the obverse was the name and title(s) of the king: at its simplest, *Henricus Rex*, but from the Edwardian era onwards longer, if more abbreviated, such as *Edward(us) Dei Gra(tia) Rex Angl(ie) & Franc(ie) D(omi)n(u)s Hyb(ernie)* – Edward by the Grace of God King of England and France, Lord of Ireland (whereas in France or Scotland the title was king of the French or Scots, in England he was king not of the people but of the country). To the inconvenience of numismatists endeavouring to distinguish between the coins of Edwards I, II and III or Henries IV, V, and VI, regnal numerals were not used until the introduction of Henry VII's portrait coinage – the only exception to this being *III* or *Terci(us)* on the new type of Henry III from 1247, to distinguish it from the preceding issues of his reign which still carried the unchanged name and type of Henry II's coinage of 1180. On reverses of groats and halfgroats there are two circles of inscription, the inner one with the mint name, the outer with the motto *Posui Deum Adiutorem Meum.* The small silver has the mint name only. The place name (in the genitive, when long enough) is preceded by *Civitas* for a city (i.e. the see of a bishop) or *Villa* for a town: thus, *Civitas London, Eboraci* (York), etc., *Villa Novi Castri* (Newcastle), *Calisie*, etc. Abbreviation is normally indicated by an apostrophe ('), contraction sometimes by a horizontal line above the relevant letters.

Except for Henry III's gold coin, which used the same moneyer-plus-mint formula as the contemporary silver, mint names never appeared on English medieval gold, although mint initials were occasionally used, notably at the recoinage mints in 1465. Calais nobles were normally differentiated from those of London by a pennant from the mast. Like the larger silver, gold was inscribed with talismanic religious texts on the reverse. These remained unchanged until the introduction of the angel and angelet called for new mottoes referring to the Cross which replaced the figure of the king in the ship. New gold coins under Henry VIII were also an occasion to use new legends, but the greatest variety of readings is to be found on the portrait gold coins and base silver shillings of Edward VI in 1549-51. These years also saw the introduction of dates on English and French coins, although they had long been in use in many areas of the Continent. At this period, and on occasions earlier, the inscriptions are sometimes transposed, with the motto surrounding the king's head or other prominent type and the royal titles on the subordinate side, thus often leading to confusion as to which side of the coin should be described as the obverse.

Almost all extant medieval coins have survived either by inclusion in a hoard hidden for safety but never recovered by its owner, or as a result of accidental loss. Both sources are important for numismatists, since although hoarded coins are by far the more numerous and the structure of hoards provides essential evidence for chronology, there are several periods from which few hoards have been discovered, whereas casual losses occurred continuously. Thus, coins of the last years before a recoinage are often rare, partly for economic reasons as output declined (as with silver in the late fourteenth century), but also because they had little opportunity to be hoarded before the currency was reminted. In such circumstances, as for example in the 1270s, single finds may produce important varieties unknown from hoards. By including many coins of lower value they also provide a general counterweight to the evidence of hoards, which tend to consist of larger denominations. Since the 1970s metal detectors have brought to light considerable numbers of minor coins, thereby greatly extending our knowledge of medieval halfpence and farthings. The discovery of medieval hoards also continues apace, especially from areas and periods that experienced unsettled conditions – most notably the Edwardian wars in Scotland.

Introduction

The literature on hoards from the British Isles is extensive. Although frequently inaccurate, Thompson's pioneering *Inventory* remains a basic sourcebook, supplemented and updated by Allen's recent listing of English hoards which has the advantage of being arranged chronologically by date of deposit. In the present work a selected list is given of the more significant hoards whose contents are recorded in sufficient detail to enable comparisons to be made of the relative numbers of coins of different periods, mints or types.

Documentary evidence for English coinage is abundant from the thirteenth century onwards. The third edition of Ruding's *Annals* is the only general work devoted to the subject, but although published in 1840 it remains of value as a source. Mint accounts have been published by Blunt and Brand for Henry III, by Crump and Johnson for Edward I-III, and by Stokes for the period from 1377 to 1550. Those for the gold coinage have been set out in convenient detail by Woodhead. Challis has produced extended tables for the debasement period, and his lists in the *New History of the Royal Mint* incorporate these and other corrections and additions for the whole period. Mints and moneyers feature frequently in the Pipe Rolls and other official rolls from Henry II to Henry III, providing important chronological data for the arrangement of the Short Cross and Long Cross series. Our knowledge of the structure of the coinage thereafter is founded upon a series of mint indentures of which the essential details are included by Challis in his summary calendar in the *New History*. The earliest of these indentures, dating from Edward I's recoinage (1279), set a pattern that was followed for centuries, if with increasing detail about the terms on which the mintmaster was authorised to undertake the coinage. The indenture was a commercial contract between king and master, and as such it had to be renewed or replaced at the beginning of each reign, upon a change of master or warden, or when weights, values, fineness or business terms were altered. Sometimes it would specify the proportion in which different denominations were meant to be struck from each pound of gold or silver; while masters preferred to mint most economically, which meant concentrating on the larger coins, the crown had a continuing duty, even if it was not always honoured, to provide an adequate supply of smaller change, and was sometimes willing to allow the master higher charges per pound of silver for minting it into halfpence or farthings.

The pound by value contained twenty shillings of twelve pence each, or 240 pence (denoted by d., for *denarius)* in total. Weights of coins were not individually stated, but were expressed as the sum to be struck from each pound weight. For example, 45 nobles of 6s. 8d., making £15, were to be coined from a pound of gold in 1351, and 300 pence or their equivalent (£1 5s.) from a pound of silver. These figures resulted in an intended average weight of 120 gr. Troy for a noble, and 18 gr. for a penny or 72 gr. for a groat. Medieval indentures normally included provision both for an absolute upper and lower weight for individual coins and for a small margin, known as a tolerance or remedy, above or below the intended average weight, within which a certain proportion of the coins should fall. Until the reign of Henry VIII the fineness of all gold coin was 23 carats 3½ grains (99.48 per cent), with only half a grain of alloy. Sterling silver was 92.5 per cent fine, expressed as 11 oz. 2 dwt. Weight and fineness were to be tested periodically by weighing and analysing a small sample of the mint's output over a specified period. This process was known as a trial of the pyx, since the coins in question were placed in a locked box (or 'pyx'), with elaborate arrangements for security, pending the next trial. Although trials were originally ordained to be held quarterly, the interval between them in practice was usually several years.

Merchants bringing bullion or foreign coin to the mint did not receive the full equivalent amount in English money, since deductions were made for expenses and for the king's profit (known as seignorage). Thus in 1351 there were charges of 2s. per pound for gold and 8d. per pound for silver to cover the master's costs, 7s. 3d. and 6d. per pound respectively for seignorage. So the merchant would get £15 less 9s. 3d. = £14 10s. 9d. per pound for his gold and £1 5s. less 1s. 2d. = £1 3s. 10d. for his silver. Short of a weight reduction, the only way in which the mint price could be made more attractive was to reduce the deductions for king and master, and this tended to happen when supplies dried up. The master was responsible for carrying out the work of the mint in accordance with the terms of his indenture, and the warden, who represented the interests of the crown, had to ensure that he did so.

The form of the mint accounts varies somewhat from period to period. Sometimes they record the weight of bullion purchased and the amounts of coin issued, sometimes one or other of the two. Bullion purchased was measured by weight expressed either in pounds, ounces and pennyweights (with twelve ounces to the pound and twenty pennyweights to the ounce) or in pounds, shillings and pence, both systems thus providing a division of the pound into 240ths. The Tower pound, which contained 5,400 grains (240 pennyweights of 22.5 gr.), was in 1526 replaced in mint accounting by the Troy pound of 5,760 grains (pennyweight 24 gr.). When mintage charges varied for different denominations or sources of silver, separate accounts were kept for each. The Exchequer year ran to Michaelmas (29 September) and from Edward I onwards mint accounts were often (but far from always) made up to the same date.

The lists of coins appended to each chapter in this book include an attempted assessment of rarity, which although often unscientific is important for the proper understanding of any series. 'Extremely rare' (ER) implies that known specimens are very few, not more than single figures. 'Very rare' (VR) indicates an item that might exist in perhaps ten or fifteen examples and would be difficult for a collector to obtain. 'Rare' is vaguer – something that would appear on the market from time to time but would be much less abundant than most comparable types or varieties. This whole area is notoriously difficult and subjective. Where a series has been intensively studied a reasonably accurate record may exist of the numbers of each type or variety in existence. In other cases the degree of rarity has to be impressionistic, based to a large degree on experience of the numismatic market. There may, however, be a considerable difference between rarity as perceived by a dealer or collector, and as evident from the number of extant specimens. An extreme example of this is the early gold noble of Edward IV: the British Museum acquired dozens of specimens from the Fishpool hoard, but in market terms the coin is a great rarity, with only a very small number in private hands. Another difficulty is that perceived rarity depends in part on how material the variety may be. Where the difference from other coins in the series is very minor, a variety of which eight or ten examples might exist may barely justify being labelled VR, since very few students or collectors would be conscious of or concerned about its separate existence. Conversely, for important items ER and VR are sometimes used less strictly than is implied above.

Wherever practicable the broad structure of traditional classifications has been retained. Good examples of the way in which adjustments and additions have been made to the original surveys by subsequent students are to be seen in the *Sylloge* volumes by Mass on the Short Cross series and by North on Edwardian sterlings, both of which have been the subject of intensive attention in recent years. They are also both series in which most of the classes and groups are the invention of modern numismatists, based on the use of particular punches, and not the result of deliberate variation of features or mintmarks by medieval moneyers, as became the practice in the fifteenth century. That cases where it has been necessary to substitute a new scheme of arrangement (e.g. for pence of Henry V) are few is testimony to the remarkable achievements of those pioneers in English numismatics whose work has proved to be so soundly based.

During the nineteenth century advances in the study of English coinage of the later middle ages had consisted chiefly of establishing its general structure. The outlines were taking shape, but there was little definition within them. Although Edward Burns in *The Coinage of Scotland* (1887) had developed many of the analytical techniques familiar to modern students, his innovative methodology was not to be applied systematically to the English series until many years later. The principal progress made by English scholars during the first half of the twentieth century were, from the historical perspective, in the more critical use of documentary sources, and on the technical side in the detailed study of lettering and other individual features of the dies. These two strands were brought together most effectively by the brothers H.B. Earle Fox and J. Shirley Fox in their account of the Edwardian sterling coinage between 1279 and 1351, which set new standards in the treatment of both these types of evidence. An important aspect of the Foxes' work (later developed for different series by Lawrence, Whitton, Blunt and others) was the arrangement of the material in a numerical classification by classes and sub-classes, the lack of which in the pre-analytical era had rendered the detailed recording of the contents of hoards a difficult and often impracticable task.

The analytical process was based on the way in which coin dies were manufactured in the later middle ages. Elements of design, such as crown, face or hair, and the letters of the inscription were stamped into the die with separate punches. Since punches were liable to break, and in any case wore out eventually with repeated use, they were periodically replaced. From 1351 each letter was normally put in by a single punch, and the complex ones (for example *e, h, m* or *R*) were more susceptible to damage. Sometimes a whole new letter fount would be introduced, but more often particular punches were replaced individually, thus enabling a detailed sequence of dies, or groups of dies, to be constructed (punch 1, punch 1 broken, punch 2, and so on).

One of the most sophisticated analyses of letter forms was Brooke's work on the reign of Henry V. In this he argued that the use of broken letter punches was deliberate, creating a range of successive varieties that he interpreted as privy marks for the purpose of the pyx. Lawrence had developed similar arguments in relation to various marks on the coinage of Edward III, and the privy-marking theory came to play a central role in late medieval numismatics for many years. However, whether broken letters were ever used deliberately as marks of difference is very doubtful. The two main occasions of their occurrence can both be explained by technical factors: the new light coinage from 1411/12 followed a period when the mint had been closed for lack of bullion and skilled craftsmen had left, while in the coinage of the 1490s the introduction of mannered lettering involved the use of intricate punches liable to fracture.

From 1361 onwards indentures contained a provision that the master should have a 'privee signe' on his coins to enable them to be identified subsequently – not as Brooke and Lawrence had supposed, to distinguish the products of each three-monthly pyx period. Among the most obvious examples of a master's privy sign is the small cinquefoil that occurs on most of the coins struck under Lewys John for Henry V. But at other times the recognition of what may have constituted a master's sign cannot reliably be made, and it would be wrong to assume that the provision was always carried out. In the Yorkist period and subsequently increased significance was undoubtedly attached to the symbol placed at the head of the inscription and commonly known as a mintmark or (especially when a distinction is to be drawn between it and a symbol placed elsewhere) as an initial mark.

Introduction

Previously the mark had normally been some form of cross. Under Henry VI the initial mark had not been the most prominent form of symbol, a greater range of marks (annulets, mascles, rosettes, leaves, etc.) appearing within the inscriptions, but from the 1460s greater variety was introduced into the mintmark itself. The alteration of one mintmark to another (as happened, for example, c. 1475 when all existing dies in current use, with mintmark annulet, were withdrawn and reissued with a new mark by punching a cross over the annulet) makes it clear that such marks served some important administrative purpose. Presumably they had to do with internal controls at the mint. Observed patterns of die use seem to imply that they are more likely to have been related to the security or record of the dies themselves than to the identification of the coins struck from them. Otherwise it is difficult to account for the frequency of what numismatists call mules, that is coins struck from an obverse die of one group and a reverse die of another. Because lower dies lasted longer, mules most often combine an earlier obverse with a later reverse, but there are plenty of cases in which mules exist both ways between two groups of dies, showing that there must have been an overlap between their respective periods of availability. The only conclusion that can be drawn from this is that moneyers were not concerned to ensure that die-pairings produced what are called 'true' coins (as opposed to mules) with consistent features on both sides. There are even cases, such as the Annulet-Trefoil Calais halfgroats of Henry VI, where dies were made for both obverses and reverses of a particular variety, but may never have been used together, since only mules, and no true coins, are known of the type. Whatever dies were at hand might be used, and some of them remained in use or available for several years – mules between dies of non-adjacent groups are not unduly rare. Occasionally old dies were brought back into service after a long interval: two of the most striking examples are halfgroats of 1399/1400 from old obverse dies of Edward III, and another halfgroat combining dies of Henry V and Richard II.

By the 1960s basic analysis of the coinage of most reigns had been undertaken and much of the subsequent work has been aimed at refinement of the detail. More attention has also been accorded to the evidence of hoards and mint accounts. Comparison of the contents of different hoards has produced a better understanding of their relative chronology. From the thirteenth century onwards the circulation in currency of coins of different classes (and mints) was thorough enough to mean that hoards generally provide a useful indication of the relative quantities in which they had been struck. When such proportions are calibrated against outputs recorded in the accounts they can assist towards an absolute dating of the issues involved. These techniques have not yet been generally applied, but where they have been they have often resulted in amendments to long established chronological assumptions. By way of example it has now been shown by Webb Ware that the introduction of mintmark cinquefoil under Edward IV, which Blunt and Whitton dated to 1480, should be brought back to c. 1475, with implications for the whole of the coinage of Edward's second reign.

The structure of a series can be fully understood only when a thorough die-analysis has been done, and the pattern of production related to the mint accounts. A case in point concerns one of the major *cruces* of fifteenth-century coinage, the interpretation of the rare Edwardian coins on which mintmark sun-and-rose dimidiated has been altered to boar's head, the personal badge of Richard III. Traditionally these coins were attributed to the short reign of Edward V, at the point when Richard assumed the protectorship, before removing his young nephew a few weeks later. Die-analysis, however, demonstrates that the boar's head was added only after Richard had taken the crown, and the same alteration can be seen to have been made to the earliest coins in Richard's own name, from dies on which the original mintmark had also been the sun-and-rose. For many series no comparable die-studies have yet been made, but when that happens further such surprises may well emerge.

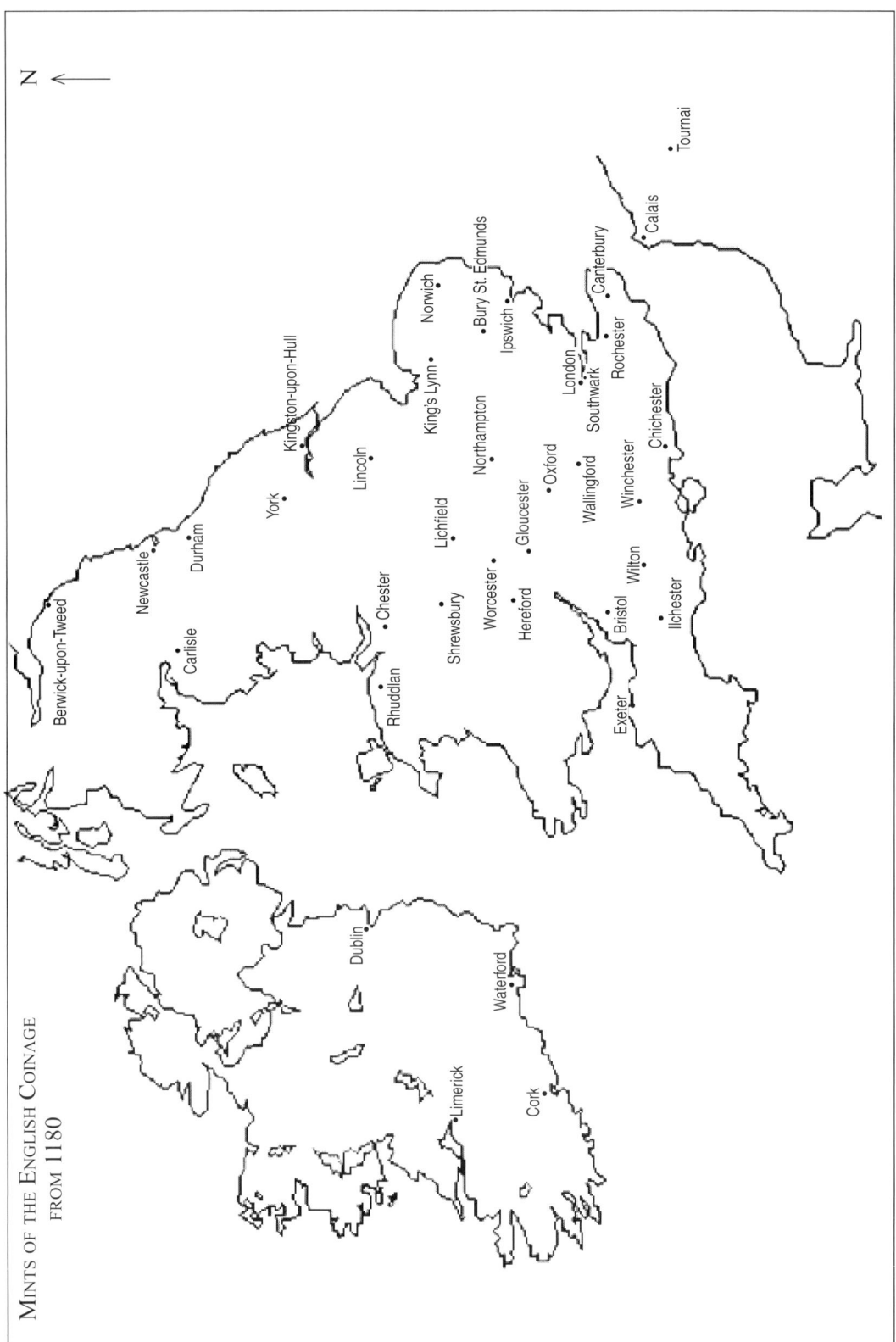

CHAPTER I

1180 - 1247
The Short Cross Coinage

After the chaos of the Stephen period, when the throne was in dispute and central administration disintegrated in many parts of the country under conditions of intermittent civil war, it was fortunate for England that the new king, Henry II (1154-89), was a ruler of exceptional ability and energy who set about the wholesale reconstruction of royal government. His first recoinage, in 1158, did little more than replace the miscellany of official and irregular issues, which had proliferated in the previous twenty years, with a uniform currency in his own name. This coinage, however, perpetuated many of the shortcomings of the late Norman period, and deficiencies of execution meant that the names of moneyer and mint were seldom fully legible. Although Henry reduced the number of mints and gradually withdrew ecclesiastical privileges as opportunity offered, further reform was needed both to bring the coinage under tighter central control and to improve the general condition of the currency. Both these aims were achieved by Henry's second recoinage in 1180.

The design of the new pennies of 1180 did not differ greatly from that of their predecessors. A facing or near-facing bust of the king, holding a sceptre, and surrounded by his name and title, had been used for most of the types of the late Norman period as well as for Henry II's own first coinage. The head was now, however, enclosed within a linear circle, with the inscription outside it interrupted only by hand and sceptre and no longer by the bust itself – an arrangement that gives a tidier appearance overall. A new form of crown was also introduced, consisting of a row of pearls surmounted by a single cross pommy in the centre. Most noticeably, the king is now seen with a realistic beard – his pre-1180 coins had shown him beardless, in the manner of all his predecessors on their coins since the Conquest, regardless of the reality.

On the reverse was the traditional cross, within a beaded border and surrounded by the names of moneyer and mint (e.g. *Clement on Winc*). The central cross, now with small crosses pommy in each angle, was of voided form (with double limbs), lending itself more readily to the division of pennies into halves and quarters than the solid crosses of most previous types. An unsuccessful attempt to introduce round halfpence and farthings into the currency was to be made in 1222, but small change continued to be supplied by cut fractions for another hundred years after Henry II's reform. As in the Saxon and Norman periods mint names were abbreviated for lack of space, but their identification is usually unambiguous. The use of the preposition *on* (i.e. 'at') dates back to the beginning of the eleventh century but, being now purely formulaic, might with advantage have been dropped. The number of moneyer names from the previous coinage that recur in the recoinage of 1180 is in single figures, and some of those with commoner names are not necessarily the same individuals. The general discontinuity of officials at this time was the consequence of a major administrative reorganisation which accompanied the recoinage. Some pre-Conquest personal names are still found, such as Asketil, Edric, Lefwine or Osber, but Norman forms now overwhelmingly predominate – Alains, Henries, Iohans, Ricards, Walters, Willems and so on, throughout the country. A few of these occur repeatedly, so that, when two moneyers at the same mint shared a Christian name, initials or abbreviations of surnames to distinguish them were now needed more frequently than in earlier coinages.

In general appearance the pennies of Henry II's second recoinage were a great improvement on those of the previous eighty years. They were more evenly struck, on carefully rounded blanks, and in both respects compare very favourably with the earlier English coinage of the twelfth century. When the chronicles refer to England's *nova moneta formae rotundae*, they are in particular drawing a contrast with the roughly made pennies of the pre-1180 coinage, often of irregular shape and sometimes more nearly square than round. Unfortunately the achievements of 1180 were not fully sustained. After the recoinage the dies were often less tidily engraved, there was some degradation of design and striking tended to become less careful. When a partial renovation of the coinage was undertaken by King John in 1205, there was a return to the high standards of 1180, but again there was a decline thereafter. In all essentials, including Henry's own name, the coin-type adopted in 1180 remained unchanged for sixty-seven years. When it was eventually replaced in 1247, the voided cross on the reverse was extended to the edge of the coin, as a result of which the coins of 1180-1247 have long been known to numismatists as the Short Cross type, and their successors as the Long Cross type.

Decisions taken at the king's council in Oxford early in 1180 about the projected recoinage may have included the new administrative arrangements relating to exchange. In the Norman period and before, the moneyers were responsible both for making the coin and for changing it. Under Henry II's reform the two functions were separated, the role of the moneyer was confined to responsibility for manufacture, and the number of mints was greatly reduced. In the next few years there are several references to the new offence of exchanging contrary to the assize. Occasionally exchangers also acted as moneyers, but only by specific arrangement. The king henceforward took his profit from coinage either as seignorage direct from the exchange or as rent for farming it. Thirty-one mints had participated in the English coinage of 1158-1180, at least eight of them during the original recoinage only. Between 1180 and 1247 the total number was twenty, fifteen of which were active in the first phase (1180-1204) and sixteen in the second (1205-47). Of the ten contributors to the 1180 recoinage all but two feature again before 1205, along with five others added after the death of Henry II. However, while all sixteen mints of the second phase took part in the renovation of 1205-7, only six of them continued thereafter or later reappeared. On the face of it these figures seem to suggest that a fundamental reduction in the number of mints operating did not occur for a generation after Henry II's recoinage; but this impression is somewhat misleading. After the recoinage only London, and from 1189 Canterbury, coined on a substantial scale up to 1205, with regular but limited support from York. Carlisle, Durham, Exeter, Lichfield, Lincoln, Northampton, Norwich, Shrewsbury, Winchester and Worcester contributed occasionally, but in several cases only briefly. Compared with the 1160s and 1170s, this represented a major step towards centralization, albeit a transitional stage in the process.

Practical arrangements for the replacement of the currency took some time to prepare. Richard of Ilchester, bishop of Winchester, who had recently reorganised the Norman exchequer, went to France on official business in March 1180, and when he returned in the summer he brought back the king's exchangers from Tours and Le Mans. According to Ralph de Diceto, Philip Aimery of Tours assumed the management of the recoinage, and he was one of twelve special exchangers named in the Pipe Roll who received their first payments for the period from the end of August until 6 October. There is record also of payments made from September to melters (*fusores*) at Winchester, Exeter and York. Several chronicles record that only the new money was to pass from Martinmas (11 November), and it is from this date, after a five week interval, that payment to specified exchangers recommenced. For most mints there are records of two exchangers then operating until Easter 1181 or thereabouts, but only one for the remainder of the 1180/1 exchequer year. Lincoln and Worcester now feature in the list. The inference is that the most intensive phase of reminting fell within the last quarter of 1180 and the first quarter of 1181. In the 1181/2 Pipe Roll there are only four references to salaries for exchangers, one each at London, Northampton and Worcester until Easter 1182, and one for the whole year at Winchester. Thereafter, although most of the recoinage mints continued to function from time to time on a more limited scale, there were no more separately funded exchangers, and the recoinage must already have been complete some time previously. In 1185/6 the sheriff of Cumberland was fined for allowing old money to remain current, but except in remote areas it had long since disappeared.

Movements of treasure round the country for the king's needs were routine in the twelfth century, particularly between London and the Treasury at Winchester. But in 1180 and the next two years there are many more references than usual, the destinations involving most of the mint towns of the recoinage, and some of them stated to have been for the purpose of priming mints or exchanges. Of the first group of recoinage mints, London, Winchester, Northampton, York, Exeter and Wilton, exchanges were attached to all except the last which, as a royal borough, evidently had a mint for the king's own convenience. Exchanges also accompanied three of the second wave of mints, Lincoln, Oxford and Worcester, the only omission being Carlisle, which had a local source of silver from the Cumbrian mines. There are references to treasure being sent during the recoinage to Nottingham to make an exchange, although there was never a mint there after the Norman period. The network of mints in 1180 differs from that of the 1158 recoinage in a number of respects, some of them quite surprising. In 1180 the most westerly mint south of Carlisle and north of Exeter was Worcester, whereas in 1158 there had been six in the western border counties from Cheshire to Somerset. Newcastle had had a prominent mint in the pre-1180 coinage, but now no longer features; and apart from London there is a complete blank in the south-east. Although there was an exchange at Norwich the lack of any mint in prosperous East Anglia in the 1180s is remarkable, especially since Norwich, Thetford, Ipswich and Bury St. Edmunds had all had active mints through much of Henry II's first coinage. The reduction in the number of mints to ten (the lowest total for any of the six recoinages from 1158 to 1300) was clearly part of the king's policy to exert more direct control. This policy also had the effect of excluding all the ecclesiastical mints for the rest of the reign, even the major establishment shared between king and archbishop at Canterbury.

With the death of Henry II in 1189 Richard I inherited an efficient and prosperous realm, but his priorities were to be very different from those of his father. Although himself also an energetic administrator, Richard paid little attention to affairs in England except to the extent that his kingdom could provide him with resources to pursue his interests abroad. In a reign of almost ten years Richard was in England for less than six months in all, first between August and December 1189, shortly after his accession, and again from March to May 1194 after his release from imprisonment. On the former occasion he was mainly concerned, apart from his coronation, with raising money for the Third Crusade, and on the latter with his recoronation by the new archbishop of Canterbury. This was the Justiciar, Hubert Walter, distinguished lawyer and fellow crusader, to whom Richard had entrusted responsibility for secular as well as church affairs. The king was again in need of money, partly to defray the ransom of £100,000 due to the Emperor Henry VI, into whose hands he had fallen in 1192 on his return from the Holy Land, but also in order to meet expenditure in his continental possessions. For the last five years of his reign he was occupied in restoring the structure of his French empire. Ironically, his habitual need of funds was to cost him his life when, having heard that a vassal was in possession of newly discovered treasure, he was fatally wounded in attempting to obtain it.

The most interesting numismatic development of Richard's reign, the revival of episcopal minting rights, was at least in part a result of his need for money. His grant of a die to the bishop of Coventry in November 1189 resulted in the only occurrence of a mint at Lichfield in the history of English coinage. This grant was undoubtedly due to the close personal association between Richard and Bishop Hugh de Nonant. Much involved in the politics of the time, the bishop was buying other privileges from the king in 1189 and must have been seen by him as a valuable fund-raiser. The archbishop of Canterbury was granted dies shortly afterwards, sharing the profits of the mint with the king according to a time-honoured arrangement. Canterbury immediately resumed a major role in the coinage, frequently exceeding London's output during the thirteenth century. At Durham the bishop's minting rights had been withdrawn during the pre-1180 coinage, but the mint was reopened during the vacancy that followed the death of Bishop Hugh du Puiset in 1195 and was allowed to continue after the appointment of his successor. The absence of ecclesiastical mints from the recoinage of 1180 had, however, presumably been part of a deliberate policy of Henry II to restrict the financial privileges of the church. Several minting rights had already lapsed earlier in his reign, but the new administrative structure of 1180, whereby a mint could not normally operate without an exchange, had meant in effect that Henry could invalidate those minting rights that were still in being merely by failing to grant the right to a separate exchange.

Lichfield's mint did not survive long. Several royal mints that had participated in the recoinage also ceased activity in Richard's reign – Lincoln and Worcester early, then Exeter, and in due course the more important mint at Winchester. The only replacements were Norwich and a temporary establishment at Shrewsbury connected with a new local mine. Of the 1180 regional mints only Carlisle and York remained operational through the 1190s or beyond. With the reduction in the number of mints went a change in the control of the exchanges which, evidently as the result of an initiative by Hubert Walter, were amalgamated into the Exchange of All England (*Cambium Totius Anglie*), now a permanent department of government accountable to the exchequer. A profit of £400 was recorded from the *Cambium* in 1192/3. Northampton's exchange was separately farmed in that year, which suggests that the *Cambium Totius Anglie* was in effect the authority responsible for London and Canterbury. In 1197 and again in 1200 it was farmed out for two years at a time, but from 1202 it was again accounting profits directly to the crown.

The unexpected accession of the capricious King John, as a result of his brother's sudden death in 1199, had left the administration of the realm, which remained in the competent hands of Hubert Walter, largely undisturbed. In his first few years the new king concerned himself chiefly with his territories in France most of which, by a combination of ill-fortune and incompetence, he had by 1204 contrived to lose. The renovation of the coinage undertaken in 1205 was one of a number of initiatives that show his attention now directed more towards affairs at home. This year proved to be a turning point in the reign. The death of Hubert Walter in July 1205 set in train a series of events that led England into one of the gravest constitutional crises in its history, and ultimately to civil war. The politics of these troubled years were to leave an impact on the coinage at many points.

By the beginning of the thirteenth century the currency was again in a poor state. Badly struck coins of irregular shape were an invitation to the clipper. Already in Richard's reign there is record of money received by the exchequer from the chattels of clippers. In ordering payment from the royal treasury of 70 marks, destined to go abroad, in the summer of 1204, it was necessary to specify that it should be made in larger and sounder pennies (*grossioribus et fortioribus*). Although the potential revenue must have been an attraction, a main reason for John's renovation of 1205 was the respectable one of restoring the condition of the circulating medium. On 9 November 1204 at Guildford the king issued a writ to all sheriffs originating the reform. No one was to have clipped coin after 13 January 1205. After that date it was to be bored through, and if its owner lived in a town it should be confiscated. An assize made on 26 January suggests, as might have been expected, that the exchange of deficient money had not proved feasible in so short a time because new mints and exchanges had not yet been set up to handle it. Old money lacking no more than thirty pence in the pound could now remain current, but below that standard it was to be bored through. The possessor of any pennies minted since the previous Christmas and found clipped was to be attached as a thief. Pennies were to be made up to the full standard, and should have an outer circle. Exchange was only to be made at the king's or the archbishop of Canterbury's exchange. Jews, goldsmiths and foreign merchants were liable to heavy penalties in addition to confiscation. The Pipe Roll for 1204/5 contains references to certain Jews paying fines well in excess of the value of their defective coin.

How great an increase in minting took place in 1205 can be seen from the exchange accounts. In the twenty-one months from April 1203 to January 1205 profits of £378 were accounted from the *Cambium Totius Anglie*. For the next twelve months the exchange of London alone produced £710 6s. 9d. Apart from London, Canterbury was the only mint in operation at the beginning of 1205; the exchange relating to both the king's and the archbishop's coinage was farmed in January 1205 for twelve months to Hubert Walter. As other mints were opened, their exchanges were also put out to farm. On the evidence of the coins, seven regional mints were opened in the spring or early summer, in approximate order of importance, Winchester, York, Lincoln, Exeter, Norwich, Durham and Chichester. Seven more followed shortly afterwards – Ipswich, Northampton, Lynn, Oxford, Rochester, Carlisle and Bury St. Edmunds. In April the bishop of Chichester, Simon FitzRobert, was granted one die, alongside two for the king, and an order for their delivery was made in May. As had been the case with Hugh de Nonant at Lichfield, Bishop Simon's involvement in the financial affairs of government (he was also known as Simon de Camera) was no doubt the cause of this exceptional privilege to the see of Chichester. Abbot Samson of Bury, where the traditional right of minting had not been exercised since before 1180, was granted his die in June. The same month saw the commencement of the farm of the mint and exchange of Northampton. There is no record of farms of exchanges attached to any of the recoinage mints extending beyond September 1207. By that date the renovation was complete. Early in October 1207 the king issued a writ to all the moneyers, die-keepers and other officials of the recoinage mints charging them to seal up their dies and report with them at Westminster later in the month.

The list of mints commissioned in 1205, which differs in a number of cases from that of 1180, reveals a strong bias towards the ports and trading towns of eastern and southern England. Since in 1205 the currency was being upgraded rather than replaced, this new concentration towards the North Sea and the Channel indicates where the problem of clipped coin was greatest and where it was most important for English money to be of acceptable standard. Winchester, York, Lincoln, Northampton, Exeter, Oxford and Carlisle feature in both the Short Cross recoinages. Two mints of 1180 do not reappear in 1205, Wilton and Worcester. The former had one more contribution to make, in 1248, but Worcester did not, and no other western mint was opened in 1205 instead. Canterbury and Durham, having been revived in the 1190s, played their part in John's recoinage after missing Henry II's. The other additions in 1205 were all in the south-east, Lynn and

Norwich in Norfolk, Bury and Ipswich in Suffolk, Rochester in Kent and Chichester in Sussex. Of these six mints, only Norwich had operated in the Short Cross period before 1205. Lynn (later King's Lynn) had been established as a free borough through a charter obtained from the king in 1204 by John de Gray, bishop of Norwich; an outlet for the fenland abbeys at the mouth of the Wash, it now made its only appearance in the English coinage.

That John's partial renovation of 1205 involved a larger network of mints than Henry's full recoinage in 1180 was chiefly due to the inclusion of the four in which ecclesiastics enjoyed part or all of the profits – Bury St. Edmunds, Canterbury, Chichester and Durham. John's approach to ecclesiastical privilege differed from his father's, although with similar intent. When an incumbent died his policy was to defer a new appointment for as long as possible so that the revenues of the see would accrue to the crown. The indirect consequences of this, however, were highly damaging to John's own interests, alienating in turn the English church, the Pope, the king of France and his own leading subjects. Following a dispute over the succession at Canterbury Stephen Langton was elected to the archbishopric in the presence of the Pope. John's refusal to recognize Langton led the Pope to place England under an interdict in March 1208. The king had also quarrelled with his half-brother, Geoffrey Plantagenet, Archbishop of York, who fled abroad in 1207, and in April 1208 Bishop Philip of Durham died, so that the temporalities of these two sees were also in John's hands at the time. Archbishop Walter de Gray was not installed at York until late in 1215, while Durham remained vacant until 1217.

Failure to come to terms with Langton resulted in excommunication of the king in 1209. John's support in 1213 for his German nephew, the Emperor Otto IV, against his rival Frederick of Hohenstaufen, prompted Philip II of France to plan an invasion of England. Eventually, in May 1213, John was forced to accept the Pope's terms, to reinstate the clergy and to restore the losses of the church. Langton returned from exile in July 1213 but the interdict was not lifted until the following year. At this time John was in France campaigning for his remaining continental possessions, but his defeat at Bouvines in July 1214 settled the issue and put an end to Otto's rule. Unrest quickly developed in England and rebellion broke out in April and May, 1215. The concessions of Magna Carta, which John signed on 15 June, failed to satisfy the barons and they invited Prince Louis of France to accept the English throne. Louis arrived in May 1216, proceeding to London which had been the stronghold of the rebels since the previous May. In the south east, only Dover under the Justiciar, Hubert de Burgh, held out for the king. John's strength lay in the north, and it was as he travelled up from Lynn with his court and army that the final disaster of his reign befell him. His treasure and baggage were engulfed and lost in the estuary of the Wash while the king himself, seized by a fever, managed to reach Newark where he died in October 1216. Soon after the nine year old Henry III had been crowned at Gloucester, Louis had to escape to France. William Marshall, Earl of Pembroke, and Hubert de Burgh gradually succeeded in containing the rebels. Louis returned in April 1217 but in May the rebels were decisively beaten in the streets of Lincoln and although reinforcements were sent over to Louis as late as August 1217, they were cut off by de Burgh and peace was finally concluded at the Treaty of Lambeth in September. Order was almost immediately restored to the administration, but it was not until 1224 that the last of the baronial strongholds was surrendered.

With the closure of the regional mints in 1207, coinage had continued only at London, Canterbury and Durham. In the dislocation of John's later years minting was for a time restricted to London alone. At Canterbury there was a hiatus in the coinage for several years from c.1208, and mint accounts show that it did not resume until 1214. Although

The Short Cross Coinage

the king had taken the whole of the profits of the Canterbury exchange, along with the other temporalities of the see, after Hubert Walter's death, with the imposition of the interdict he presumably decided that it was simpler to close the establishment altogether and concentrate minting in London, even though an exchange was brought into operation for a time at the Kentish port of Sandwich. With the loss of London to the rebels in 1215/16 John established a base at Canterbury, and this may explain the occurrence of a small group of Canterbury coins of distinctive style which find no parallel in the London series.

Following Bishop Philip's death the king's receivers at Durham accounted for profits from the exchange between June 1208 and November 1212, but the amounts were so small that minting can only have been occasional. After an interval of nine years a new bishop, Richard Marsh, was elected in June 1217. Three dies were sent to Durham in June 1218, after the archbishop of York had notified the Exchequer of the names of the relevant officials; but the bishop's coinage cannot have lasted long since the coins are rare and after this momentary revival Durham disappeared from the scene for the remainder of the Short Cross period. Coinage at Bury St. Edmunds did not survive the renovation. When the aged Abbot Samson died in 1211 John refused to confirm Hugh Northwold, who had been elected by the monks, but after the papal commissioners had given judgement in Hugh's favour in March 1215 the king reluctantly accepted the appointment during the Magna Carta negotiations. The abbot's rights were quickly confirmed and his mint resumed activity during the final year of the reign, thus initiating a period of more than a century during which coinage took place at Bury more or less continuously.

At the beginning of the reign of Henry III there were thus only the three mints in operation, at London, Canterbury and Bury. In 1217 a short-lived attempt was made to resume coinage at York and Winchester, and the reopening of the bishop's mint at Durham in 1218 brought the number of mints up to six. In 1218 these six were placed under the authority of Pembroke's son, William Marshall junior, but the three additions were soon closed again and Bury was subsequently exempted from Marshall's jurisdiction. Recoinages apart, the brief revival of York and Winchester in 1217/18 proved to be the last occasion for more than a hundred years on which minting took place outside London and Canterbury, Bury and Durham. Centralization was now complete. During the rest of the Short Cross coinage, with Durham remaining closed until the 1250s, Bury thus had the only mint in the country after the dominant pairing of London and Canterbury. In 1221, however, the abbot was prohibited from competing for the business of merchants who would otherwise have gone to the king's exchange at London. This evidently proved difficult to enforce, since two years later the exchange at Bury was taken over by the keepers of the London exchange in return for an annual payment of £20 although the abbot retained the right to have his own silver minted. This arrangement had been due to last until the king came of age (as Henry so declared himself in 1227), but the normal operation of the Bury mint and exchange was not restored until late in 1229, after the appointment of Abbot Hugh's successor, Richard de Insula. The restriction on Bury was reflected in a notification of 1223 to the continental trading towns of Ypres, Arras, St. Omer and Ghent that silver was in future to be exchanged only at London and Canterbury. In 1226 the Bury exchange returned a small profit to the crown, but it is unclear whether the coin involved had been locally minted.

From the reign of Henry III we have extensive references to moneyers in the records, and these provide an essential key to the chronology of successive varieties of coin. Full lists of moneyers and other mint officials were enrolled in 1217/18, 1221/2 and 1222/3, and in later years there are regular notices of the appointment or replacement of individual moneyers. Extra moneyers had been recruited at London and Canterbury for John's renovation, but otherwise the normal complement from the 1190s onwards until the late 1230s was seven or eight at Canterbury and three or four at London. Nicholas of St. Albans, who had had a long career as a mintmaster in Denmark, was appointed moneyer at both mints in 1237, two Canterbury moneyers being compensated for surrendering their dies to him. Nicholas thus became the only royal moneyer in the last years of the Short Cross coinage, although two other names are also found at Canterbury representing the archbishop's interests, and one for the abbot at Bury. In 1240-1, however, Nicholas's appointment came under challenge. He was summoned to the Exchequer in November 1240, together with the Canterbury officials and the Flemish merchants with whom they dealt, and in January 1241 his authority at London and Canterbury was questioned. But in 1242 his appointment was confirmed, with the farm of the foundries of the two mints, and the coin series does not suggest any interruption in his activity at this period.

The last thirty years of the Short Cross coinage, under Henry III, saw a major increase in the volume of currency. The exploitation of new silver mines in central Europe in the twelfth century had stimulated the development of international trade. From the late twelfth century the activity of mints in north-west Europe expanded, and although prices rose the greater availability of coin contributed to the growth of urban centres with increasing dependence on a money economy. Because English coin had maintained a high intrinsic standard for generations it gained a strong reputation on the Continent where most of the local currencies had suffered from debasement of weight or fineness or both. As a result a broad sterling area developed in northern Europe and beyond. Until the loss of most of the English territories in northern France in 1204, Short Cross coins were extensively used across the channel and more sterling hoards of this period have been found in Normandy, Maine, Anjou and Brittany than in England itself. In the thirteenth century English sterlings increasingly found their way to Germany, where their types were imitated by local issuers, and onward towards the Mediterranean. Important hoards composed largely of sterlings have been found as far afield as Ribe in Denmark, Montpellier in the south of France and Naxos in the Aegean. With the larger sums of money now in frequent use throughout Europe, it is curious that until the second half of the thirteenth century no state north of the Alps was to follow the example of Venice, which had introduced a larger silver coin, the *grosso*, in 1202. Gold was not yet in general use for commercial purposes in northern Europe.

Closer to home, the English sterling had an impact throughout the British Isles. In Ireland John was the first English king to bring the local currency onto the English standard, with a recoinage undertaken not long after the renovation in England. Although there is no mention in the English records of coinage at Rhuddlan castle in North Wales, the coins suggest that a mint was established there at some time in the 1180s, and continued to operate for perhaps some thirty years, until late in the reign of John. Coins had occasionally been struck in South Wales by the Norman kings, but this was the only period in the middle ages when a sustained coinage took place in Wales in the name of the English crown, even if not under its authority. In Scotland a new type was introduced by William the Lion (1165-1214) in 1195, reproducing the short voided cross on the reverse, but with stars instead of crosses pommy in the angles. These stars (or later mullets), coupled with a profile portrait, were to become a characteristic feature of Scottish coins for nearly two hundred years, differentiating them at a glance from the English coins with which they remained interchangeable in currency until the middle of the fourteenth century.

The Short Cross Coinage

Classification

Until the middle of the nineteenth century there was fierce debate as to whether the Short Cross coinage should be attributed to Henry II or to Henry III (1216-72). The issue was complicated by the absence of any English coins in the names of Richard I (1189-99) or John (1199-1216), although there were coins of Richard from his French possessions and coins of John from Ireland. This difficulty, however, was more apparent than real, since the immobilisation of coin-types and their attendant inscriptions had been standard practice on the Continent since Carolingian times, Charlemagne's own name continuing to appear on derivative issues until the eleventh century. The convention was that the name of the originator of the coinage, like the type, would remain unchanged so long as the issue lasted, regardless of a change of ruler, on the basis that it was not the new ruler's coinage but the extension of a predecessor's. When Richard I acceded to the English throne many of the coins of his territories in France still carried the names of eleventh-century counts of Anjou or Le Mans. In England, therefore, Richard and John were merely continuing their father's coinage. The renovation of 1205 was not a replacement of it and so did not qualify for a change of type or name. In Ireland, however, when John introduced the first new coinage on the English standard, a new type and his own name as its originator were required.

The Short Cross Question, as it had come to be known, was finally solved by Longstaffe in 1863. Longstaffe compared the names of moneyers on the coins with references to them in the Pipe Rolls and concluded as a result that the Short Cross coinage constituted a continuous series from Henry II to Henry III. In the following year a great hoard of Short Cross pennies was found at Eccles in Lancashire and the material from this that came available to John Evans enabled him to confirm Longstaffe's main conclusions and to work out a classification which was to remain in use for fifty years. The next great discovery was the Colchester hoard of 1902. Containing nearly 11,000 coins, this greatly increased the number of specimens available, and was thereby largely responsible for a revival of interest which led to the publication by Lawrence in 1915 of a new study of the Short Cross series. Evans had divided the coinage into five classes. Basically, his class I covered the recoinage; class II, the long period following, until the renovation of 1205; classes III and IV, the 1205 recoinage and its aftermath; and class V, the later issues, from about the beginning of the reign of Henry III. Lawrence's scheme was in many ways similar to Evans's; but he split the old class II into three new classes (II, III, and IV); retained two classes (now numbered V and VI) for the years from 1205 (although fundamentally altering the division between the two from that used by Evans to separate his III and IV); and, having retained Evans class V (now renumbered as VII), added a new class at the end (VIII) which Evans had not separated from his class III, even though its late position had been correctly recognised by Longstaffe. Although subject to considerable refinement by subsequent students, this eight-class structure has stood the test of time, and in terms of the main classes only a small minority of Short Cross coins would not still be classified in the same way as Lawrence had done nearly a century ago. Intensive research in subsequent years by Mass (classes I and II), Allen (III and V), Brand (IV and V), Stewart (VI and VII), Gittoes (VI and VII), North (VII and VIII) and Jones (VIII) has resulted in more detailed analysis of the coins by sub-classes, and much of the fruits of this work was conveniently incorporated by Mass in the Sylloge of his collection.

ENGLISH SHORT CROSS MINTS AND CLASSES

	1158-1180	I	II	III	IV	V	VI	VII	VIII	Long Cross
London	x	x	x	x	x	x	x	x	x	x
Exeter	x	x		x		x				x
Northampton	x	x		x	x	x				x
Wilton	x	x								x
Winchester	x	x		x	x	x	x			x
York	x	x	x	x	x	x	x			x
Carlisle	x	x		x	x	x				x
Lincoln	x	x	x			x				x
Oxford	x	x				x				x
Worcester		x	x							
Lichfield			x							
Canterbury	x		x	x	x	x	x	x	x	x
Durham	x				x	x	x	x		x
Norwich	x				x	x				x
Shrewsbury	x				x					x
Bury St. Edmunds	x					x	x	x	x	x
Chichester						x				
Ipswich	x					x				
Lynn						x				
Rochester						x				

Class I

As in the pre-1180 coinage of Henry II, the bust on early Short Cross coins, by virtue of showing more curls of hair on the sinister side, gives the appearance of being turned slightly to the spectator's left. This is the common feature of class I, which represents the coinage of the 1180s. Class I was divided by Lawrence into three parts: Ia, from six mints, consists of the earliest varieties of the new coinage, with considerable fluidity in type and lettering; Ib, with the design now standardised, spans the bulk of the recoinage and a period beyond, with all ten mints in action; and Ic, in which the activity of most of the provincial mints tails off, is a coarser extension of Ib running to the end of the reign. Cut halfpennies and farthings appear to be unusually abundant in class I, particularly in Ia, perhaps because the exchange of new coins for old at the start of the recoinage often required payment of sums including fractions of a penny when old coins were short of weight, or more generally because of a need to replace the supply of fractions when the old currency was withdrawn.

Although Ia constitutes only a very small proportion of class I, it includes a wide variety of experimental features, as die-sinkers felt their way towards a suitable format. Mass has defined five sub-divisions based on lettering and features of design. The common characteristic throughout is the presentation of the head, and in particular of the hair which consists of irregular clusters of curls rather than the 2-5 pattern which became standard with class Ib. The face is easier to observe than to describe, being often narrower than in Ib, less evenly composed and more obviously turned to the left, especially in the earlier varieties. Some dies of Ia1 and a few of Ia2 have what Mass describes as a wild or primitive look, with high cheekbones and staring eyes. There are extensive die-interchanges between (not always adjacent) sub-divisions of class Ia as modifications of design and lettering followed in rapid succession during the early stages of the recoinage.

The defining feature of Ia1 is an unusual form of border outside the inscription, consisting of a linear circle adorned with large pellets at intervals. If this 'dot-dash' border was conceived as a deterrent to clipping, it cannot have proved very successful since it is not always easy to see, unless the coin is on a full flan and the striking well centred. A few early dies of London, Winchester and Northampton have a large cross patty, instead of the normal cross pommy, as the sceptre-head or the central ornament in the crown. The earliest coins also sometimes show variety in the treatment of the drapery, with a semi-circular collar or a line or two of drapery around the shoulder on the sinister side, a feature carried over from the pre-1180 coinage. In Ia2 the dot-and-dash border is replaced by a beaded circle, the standard form henceforward. In other respects Ia2 shares many of the characteristics of Ia1, notably in the lettering. Although rounded *c* and *e* are sometimes found in Ia1 and Ia2, both these early varieties normally have a Roman *E* and often an open square *C*; *m* is of the uncial (rounded) style. In many cases these three letters thus briefly retained the forms that had been in use before 1180. Another letter common to Ia1 and Ia2 is an *N* that lacks a serif at the base of its second upright. Dies of Ia1 usually, and of Ia2 exceptionally, have only *x* of *Re/x* behind the sceptre which itself is often at a much flatter angle than was to become the norm. Prior to 1180 there had usually been no obverse stops, and the large pellet that occurs before *Rex* on most dies of the recoinage (Ia and Ib) was therefore one of the minor innovations of the new type. On a few reverse dies of Ia1 and Ia2 the stops by *on* (otherwise standard until class VII) are omitted. Although Ia1/2 mules are frequent, examples of the converse combination are very few.

Lawrence defined his class Ia by the presence of square *E* and *C*. However, in showing that the Ia style of portrait continued after square letters had disappeared, Mass has argued persuasively that the whole early complex of dies should be classed together as Ia since they are confined to the six original mints of the recoinage before the addition of four more mints in Ib. Some coins previously described as Ib would accordingly fall within the widened Ia. Thus, while the first two phases of Ia are defined by both epigraphy and portraiture (Ia1-2 and Ia3-4), the final phase is distinguished from Ib by the portrait alone (Ia5).

The rounded *m* and Roman *E* survived temporarily into Ia3 (a variety largely confined to reverses), but the square *C* did not. The new *c* which defines Ia3, and the new *e*, when introduced soon afterwards, are rounded and their fronts are closed by two semicircular ('half-moon') serifs. Ia4, which has the same rounded *e* and *c*, is defined by obverse dies with a seriffed *X* and was labelled Ia* by Brand and Jones. When *M* occurs, it is of the Roman form from now onwards. Finally there are coins, still with a bust of Ia style and irregular groups of curls, which have no seriffed *X* or square *E* or *C* (the rounded form of these letters now no longer having half-moon fronts): in the past they would have been classed as early Ib but have now been renamed Ia5. These coins are considerably less rare than those of the previous sub-divisions, and constitute a third or more of all the coins of the class Ia complex as now defined. Unless they show a distinctive letter form, reverse dies of Ia3, 4 and 5 are not separately distinguishable. One reverse die of Ib1 for Ricard of Exeter gives the appearance of having square *E* and *C* in the mint name; this is due not to muling, but to the reading having been altered from *Lund* to *Exec*.

LETTER FORMS IN CLASS Ia

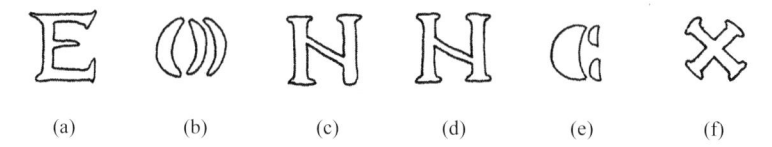

(a) (b) (c) (d) (e) (f)

(a) Square Roman *E*, Ia1-3; (b) Round *m*, Ia1-3; (c) *N* with three serifs, Ia1-2 (and Ib2-Ic); (d) *N* with four serifs, Ia3-Ib1; (e) Rounded *C* fronted by 'half-moons', Ia3-5; (f) *X* with serifs, Ia4.

In Ia3-Ia5 the letter *N* (sometimes reversed in Ia3 and Ia4) has four serifs, and the continuation of this letter after the end of class Ia provides a means of identifying the first phase of class Ib. In Ib the portrait has settled down, with two curls to dexter and five to sinister. This is the classic issue of the recoinage, with all ten mints contributing. The earlier coins (Ib1), still with the four-serif *N*, have the portrait sharply drawn and are among the most handsome of the Short Cross series. Later issues of Ib can also be identified by the letter *N*, which now reverts to a three-serif form similar to that of Ia1-2. This new sub-division (Ib2) is generally coarser in style than Ib1, the lettering less sharp and the portrait less well defined, with thickening curls.

Coins of the final phase of class I, represented by Ic during which most of the regional mints were less active, are altogether rougher in style than those of the main recoinage. As Lawrence observed, the pellet before *R/ex* is normally no longer found. This does not provide an absolute division between Ib and Ic, since a small proportion of coins whose features are otherwise those of Ib also lack the stop, just as a few of Ic still retain it. The head of Ic is broader and more loosely composed; the dies are more carelessly engraved, without the sharp definition of Ib, and the curls are now less consistent in number and arrangement. Lettering is thicker and coarser. The *N* still has three serifs.

The progress of the recoinage and its aftermath can be observed from the numbers of mints and moneyers operating in the various stages of class I. The broad statistics are these: in Ia there was a total of forty-one moneyers at six mints; in Ib sixty-six moneyers at ten mints; and in Ic twenty-three moneyers at nine mints. The five varieties making up the Ia complex are very tightly linked. Only three of the moneyers in Ia1-4 appear to have ceased within that period – Iohan at Wilton almost immediately (Ia1), Henri at Winchester in Ia2, and Henri Pi at London in Ia4. Only three other moneyers in Ia1-4 failed to register in Ia5, while continuing into Ib - Iordan of Exeter, Filip of Northampton and Willelm of York. Conversely, only two new moneyers arrived in Ia5 - Roger at Exeter and Reinier at Winchester. These figures emphasize the short duration of class Ia. The opening of four new mints in class Ib1, at Carlisle, Lincoln, Oxford and Worcester, added nineteen moneyers to the list. There were also five new moneyers at London, one each at Northampton and Exeter, and one (-ustin), known only from a recently discovered cut halfpenny of uncertain mint, lifting the total in Ib1 to sixty-four. That Ib1 had seen the full flood of the recoinage is evident from the figures for Ib2, by which time more than half of the Ib1 moneyers had disappeared - ten gone at London, five each at York and Oxford, four each at Winchester and Exeter, three each at Northampton and Lincoln, and one at Wilton. Against this exodus there was only a single new arrival in Ib2, Hugo at Lincoln. Thereafter the decline was more gradual. Of the twenty-seven moneyers of Ib2, twenty continued into Ic, London having lost three in Ib2, Lincoln two, and Northampton and Wilton one each (the latter mint thus closed before Ic). Only at London are any new names found in class Ic (Gefrei and Gilebert). Of the nine mints known for class Ic, all except Oxford are found in one or more of the classes from II to IV, but most of them (Exeter, Northampton, Carlisle, Lincoln and Worcester) only occasionally, and on a very small scale.

The Short Cross Coinage

Moneyers of Short Cross Class I

	Ia1-4	Ia5	Ib1	Ib2	Ic	II-IV
LONDON						
Aimer	x	x	x			x
Alain	x	x	x			
Alain V	x	x	x			
Fil Aimer	x	x				
Henri	x	x	x			x
Henri Pi	x					
Iefrei	x	x	x			
Iohan	x	x	x	x		
Pieres	x	x	x	x	x	
Pieres M	x	x	x	x		
Randul	x	x	x			
Reinald	x	x	x			
Willelm	x	x	x			
Raul			x	x	x	x
Alward			x			
Davi			x	x	x	
Godard			x			
Osber			x	x		
Gefrei					x	
Gilebert					x	
CARLISLE						
Alain			x	x	x	x
EXETER						
Asketil	x	x	x			
Iordan	x		x	x		
Osber	x	x	x			
Roger		x	x	x	x	
Raul			x			
Ricard			x	x	x	x
LINCOLN						
Edmund			x	x	x	x
Girard			x			

1180–1247

Lincoln (Cont)	Ia1-4	Ia5	Ib1	Ib2	Ic	II-IV
Lefwine			x	x	x	x
Rodbert			x	x		
Walter			x			
Willelm			x	x	x	x
Will D.F.			x			
Hugo				x		

Northampton						
Filip	x		x	x		
Hugo	x	x	x			
Raul	x	x	x	x	x	
Reinald	x	x	x	x	x	
Walter	x	x	x	x	x	x
Willelm	x	x	x			x
Simund			x			

Oxford						
Asketil			x			
Iefrei			x			
Rodbert			x			
Rodbt F.B.			x			
Sagar			x			
Owein			x	x	x	
Ricard			x	x	x	

Wilton						
Iohan	x					
Osber	x	x	x	x		
Rodbert	x	x	x			

Winchester						
Adam	x	x	x	x	x	x
Clement	x	x	x			
Gocelm	x	x	x	x	x	x
Henri	x					
Osber	x	x	x			x
Rodbert	x	x	x			
Reinier		x	x			

The Short Cross Coinage

	Ia1-4	Ia5	Ib1	Ib2	Ic	II-IV
WORCESTER						
Edrich			x			
Godwine			x	x	x	
Osber			x	x	x	x
Oslac			x			
YORK						
Alain	x	x	x			
Efrard	x	x	x	x	x	x
Gerard	x	x	x			
Hugo	x	x	x	x	x	x
Hunfrei	x	x	x			
Isac	x	x	x			
Turkil	x	x	x	x	x	x
Willelm	x		x			
UNCERTAIN						
(-)ustin			x			

References to several of the class I moneyers occur in the records. At London both Henries (Anglicus and Pineferding) were charged with exchanging offences, in the latter case perhaps explaining his early removal as a moneyer. Alain of Carlisle features only for an offence of selling wine, but one of those found guilty of exchanging contrary to the assize (and savagely punished for it) was the moneyer Edrich of Worcester, whose wife was charged ten marks in 1181/2 to have his chattels. Four of five persons named in John's reign as having received money from the Treasury in connection with the York exchange under Henry II had been York moneyers during the recoinage – William FitzSirici, Hugh FitzLefwine, Turkil de Bredegate and Ebrard Bradex. These four also appeared (1190/1) in a list of a number of prominent York citizens fined in connection with the slaughter of the Jews. Ironically, one of their colleagues at the York mint in 1180 had the Jewish name Isac. Ebrard had also stood surety for another class I York moneyer, Gerard FitzLefwine, who had committed coinage offences. One name that does not appear on coins of class I is Walter of Oxford, since in 1182/3 Walter the Linendraper accounted for five marks for having been unwilling to make the king's money.

Four of those paid as special exchangers also worked as London moneyers. Aimer (FitzPhilippi) was one, while Peter Melekin and Geoffrey Joismeri may be presumed to have been the Pieres M. and Iefrei of the coins. Most notably there is Philip Aimer himself whose name appears as Fil Aimer on dies of later Ia – a curious signature since Fil Aimer would normally mean son of Aimer and there was no other London moneyer called Filipe so as to need the surname. On the evidence of numbers of dies used Fil Aimer appears to have been the dominant moneyer in the Ia4 period; his name is found only on coins of Ia3-5, according well with the arrival of Philip in the summer of 1180, although indicating that his office as moneyer was much briefer than as exchanger.

In the absence of mint accounts there is no clear indication of exactly when the new coinage began to be struck, although it was presumably before the appointment of special exchangers at the end of August 1180. In this connection the mint of Wilton is of interest. Three Winchester obverse dies (two of Ia1, one of Ia2) were also used by Rodbert at Wilton. One of Rodbert's Wilton reverses (Ia2) is also a Winchester die, with *Win* altered to *Wilt*. Osber (or Osbern, or Osbert) was also a moneyer at both these mints (he continued at Winchester until class IVa), incurring a debt for rent at Winchester in 1183/4 which was eventually paid off by the borough of Wilton ten years later. Brand and Jones argued that a serious fire in July 1180, which destroyed much of Winchester including the mint, provided an explanation for the transfer of dies from Winchester to Wilton, and if the recoinage began as early as June this could be so. However, their contention that the mint at Wilton was opened as a substitute for Winchester because of the emergency is not sustainable. A third moneyer, Iohan, is now known, from a coin of Ia1, and Rodbert also used an unaltered Wilton reverse die of Ia1 (i.e., earlier than the reverse he brought from Winchester). The mint at Wilton must therefore have been opened with two moneyers at the start of the recoinage, but following Iohan's rapid departure it seems then to have been operated periodically as a branch of the Winchester mint to meet the king's needs, and managed by two of his Winchester moneyers. Minting at Wilton continued into Ib2, long after Winchester was in full production. Winchester, rather than London, may have been the administrative centre of the recoinage: in the 1180 Pipe Roll there is record of dies sent from Winchester via Oxford to Northampton, and then back to Winchester.

If the new coinage had begun in June, before the Winchester fire, the new arrangements for exchange would need to have been in place before the special appointments at the end of August. We do not have any explicit evidence to judge whether this was so. Mass has calculated that the total number of obverse dies used in class Ia may have been around 200, more than double the number of Va dies used in the first five or six months of the 1205 renovation. Although the 1180 recoinage was much more comprehensive, the use of so many dies does suggest that the new type had been in issue for some months before the autumn. Worcester, one of the four new mints of class Ib, first had a special exchanger from November 1180, by which date Ib must have replaced Ia. It is evident that the end of the main recoinage took place during the currency of Ib1, since so many of the moneyers of Ib1 had retired before the introduction of Ib2. This would imply that Ib2 may not have begun before 1182/3. All the class I mints except Wilton survived beyond Ib, but there is a lack of evidence as to when Ib2 was replaced by Ic. Both Ib2 and Ic are abundant, and Allen's suggested date of c. 1185 for the end of class Ib is unlikely to be too late. Apart from Wilton, the only recoinage mint that did not continue even briefly into Richard's reign was Oxford; its coins of Ic are so rare that it presumably ceased work well before 1189.

Class II

While Lawrence deserves credit for having identified a small but distinct group of coins falling between his classes I and III, his description of class II and choice of illustrations for it created serious difficulties of interpretation for subsequent students. Part of the problem was caused by Lawrence's 'IIb', described as often having colons beside *on*, a variety which Brand eventually showed to belong within early class IV. This left Lawrence's 'IIa' which Mass has now defined more precisely and which does indeed constitute a short but separate phase of the coinage at about the beginning of the reign of Richard I. Although struck by seventeen moneyers, at six mints, class II is much the rarest of the eight Lawrence classes, and the dies cannot have been available for more than a few months at most, in or about the winter of 1189/90. The chronological significance of the class arises from it containing the only known coins of the mint of Lichfield and the earliest post-1180 coins of Canterbury, each as a result of charters granted by the new king late in 1189.

The head of class II, as now defined, is characterised by an absence of hair on the cheeks, between side curls and beard. The bust is frequently set low down, without neck or collar, or with only traces of them. The eyes are usually shown as large pellets, although annulets are sometimes found, and the upper lip tends to be heavier than in Ic. The crown has five pearls in the band, as opposed to seven commonly in class III – the single seven-pearl die of class II is of the moneyer Raul whose career, so far as we know, did not extend into class III. Lettering is also a valuable diagnostic feature of class II, notably the N which now again has four serifs and is often much broader than in class Ic. The wide D has a thin, rounded loop; the back of the e is a thick crescent with the front neatly closed. There is no stop before *Rex*, but an occasional die (Canterbury, Worcester) has a pellet in *henri.cus*. The letter X is either (i) a small angled cross pommy or (ii) one of a variety of more normal plain forms, and this provides a basis for sub-division of the class. The pommy X occurs on dies of London, Lincoln, York and Lichfield, a plain X at London, Canterbury and Worcester. Use of both types of X at London but not at the newly revived mint of Canterbury suggested that the X pommy was the first form of the letter in class II, available for the one die sent to Lichfield whose charter was granted three weeks earlier than Canterbury's. On most of the obverses of Lincoln and York this X is found alone beneath the sceptre (*Re/x*), an arrangement not noted on any London die.

LETTER FORMS IN CLASS II

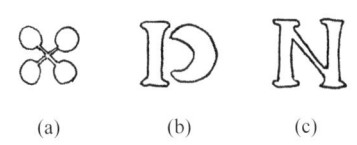

(a)   (b)   (c)

(a) X pommy, IIi; (b) D with round loop; (c) Four-serif N.

A considerable problem in defining the features of class II, as Mass observed, is that there is a lack of consistency between mints. Coins of London and Canterbury, accounting for the great majority of the material, differ in some important respects from those of Lichfield, Lincoln, Worcester and York, all of which are very rare. At the two main mints the beard consists of a cluster of long whiskers protruding from the chin in all directions. The curls are small and thin, but vary in their disposition – often two on each side, vertically, or sometimes a larger bunch, but always separated from the beard. At the four lesser mints the beard is less luxuriant, consisting of shorter hairs or even (especially at Lincoln) of tiny pellets; and a cluster of tiny curls is more usual than the 2-2 pattern.

As in class Ic, Raul of London was the dominant moneyer in class II, although even his coins are quite rare. The names of two of the other four London moneyers, Aimer and Willem, had not featured since Ib1, and two, Ricard and Stivene, were new. Unfamiliarity with their names probably led to some early, experimental spellings – Heimer, Ricad, and Stievene or Estevene. The four class II moneyers at Canterbury, Menir (not Meinir as later), Reinald, Roberd and Ulard all began careers that were to extend into class IV or beyond. Me(i)nir was presumably Mainer 'the rich', founder of the almshouse in Stour Street.

1180–1247

Moneyers of Short Cross Classes II-IV

	I	II	IIIa	IIIb	IVa	IVb	IVc	V
London								
Aimer	x	x	x	x	x			
Raul	x	x						
Ricard		x	x	x	x	x	x	x
Stivene		x	x	x	x	x		
Willelm		x	x	x	x	x	x	x
Fulke					x	x	x	x
Henri	x				x	x	x	x
Canterbury								
Meinir		x	x	x	x	x		
Reinald		x	x	x	x	x		
Ulard		x	x	x	x	x		
Roberd		x	x	x	x	x	x	x
Goldwine			x	x	x	x	x	x
Hernaud						x	x	x
Hue						x	x	x
Ioan						x	x	x
Samuel						x	x	x
Simon						x	x	x
Carlisle								
Alein	x			x	x	x		
Durham								
Adam					x			
Alein					x	x		
Pires						x		x
Exeter								
Ricard	x			x				x
Lichfield								
Ioan		x						
Lincoln								
Edmund	x	x						
Lefwine	x	x						
Willelm	x	x						

The Short Cross Coinage

	I	II	IIIa	IIIb	IVa	IVb	IVc	V
NORTHAMPTON								
Waltier	x		x	x				
Roberd				x				x
Giferei					x			
NOR								
Randul					x	x	x	
Willelm	x				x	x		
NORWICH								
Iohan						x		x
SHREWSBURY								
Ive					x	x		
Reinald					x	x		
Willem					x			
WINCHESTER								
Adam	x		x	x				x
Gocelm	x			x				
Osbern	x			x	x			
Willelm				x	x			
Pires					x			
WORCESTER								
Osbern	x	x						
YORK								
Everard	x	x	x	x	x			
Hugo/Hue	x	x	x	x	x			
Turkil	x	x	x	x	x			
Davi					x	x	x	x
Nicole					x	x	x	x

The three moneyers each of Lincoln and York had all been operating in the later stages of class I and their occurrence in class II may be seen as an extension of their continued activity after the end of the recoinage. This was, however, to be the last contribution of Lincoln until the renovation of 1205. At York a change in spelling from Efrard (as in class I) to Everard, as he became for the remainder of his career, took place during class

II. Apart from the exceptional appearance of Lichfield, the curiosity among the lesser class II mints is Worcester which had been a relatively minor participant in class I and was not to be revived hereafter. The absence from class II of more significant mints, which reappear in class III or IV, such as Winchester, Northampton, Exeter and Carlisle, must be due to the very short duration of class II when no new dies happened to be needed for them.

Class III

The curious bristly chins and bare cheeks of class II were soon replaced by a more normal arrangement, with a neater beard of small strokes, normally curved, running downwards from the curls of hair. This new style of bust is the defining feature of class III, differentiating it also from class IV in which the beard is indicated by pellets. Lawrence proposed a rough subdivision of class III according to the size of bust, his IIIa having a head filling the greater part of the field and IIIb a smaller one. This distinction having proved difficult to apply, Allen has now shown that the representation of the hair produces a more valid definition. On earlier dies (IIIa) there are many small curls on both sides, as on most coins of the preceding class. This variety is quite scarce. Later and more plentiful coins (IIIb) have fewer and thicker curls (looking forward to class IVa); usually there are two or three large curls on each side, often with smaller curls inside them or occasionally above or below, and pellets are sometimes found in the lower curls – a late feature, which also occurs in early class IV. Most coins of class III have seven pearls in the band of the crown, although a few (mostly in IIIa) still have five as in class II. Also as in the previous class, the eyes often have a blobbed appearance, although open forms gradually occur more frequently. All in all, the busts of class III are in detail almost infinitely variable.

Class III lettering continues the process of widening, as already begun in class II; *A* and *N* are often very broad. Space was sometimes saved by dropping a letter from the name of the moneyer (e.g. Willem, Waltir) or of the mint, but also now by ligation, most notably the *n* and *d* of *Lund*. Misspellings, rare before class III, now occur quite often.

Of the lesser mints of class II only York now remained in operation. Four class I mints, however, reappear in class III. Mules between classes I and III have been found at Carlisle which had not featured in class II, and also at York which had. At Winchester IIIa is represented only by the new moneyer Adam, although in IIIb Gocelm and Osbern return together with the new name Willelm. In 1193/4 and 1194/5 the farmers of the Winchester mint are shown as Richard Fusor and William the moneyer. Class I moneyers also resumed at Carlisle (now spelt Alein), Exeter and Northampton; except for Waltir at Northampton, who had one of IIIa, the earliest new dies at these three mints were of IIIb. Roberd in IIIb has been traditionally attributed to Northampton, but this is not certain since both his dies read only *Nor*. All the class III moneyers at London, Canterbury and York struck both sub-classes, the only new name being Goldwine at Canterbury. At York, Hugo of classes I-II has now become Hue.

Although much more plentiful than class II, coins of class III are relatively uncommon. Those of York are rare, and of Carlisle, Exeter and Northampton very rare. In 1192/3 the sheriff of Northampton accounted for 62½ marks for the farm of the exchange for fifteen months, a sum difficult to reconcile with the rarity of the coins of this mint in both classes III and IV. Class III must date from 1190 and perhaps the next three years or so, but not much longer, if its relative scarcity is measured against the abundance of class IV.

Class IV

The coins of class IV, which constitute the issues of most of the reign of Richard I and of the first five years of John's, have a strong claim to be regarded as the ugliest ever produced under the authority of the English crown. The face is variable in form and size, sometimes narrowing towards the chin as in earlier classes, but often later broad and shapeless. In many cases the lower part of the face sinks into the collar and so loses all definition of chin or neck. Annulet eyes give it a staring expression and the beard of pellets adds to its coarse and uncouth appearance. The pellets, few or many, which are scattered haphazardly over the lower face, are the defining feature of the class. For much of class IV the band of the crown consists of seven conjoined pearls, as in later class III, but in due course this was replaced by a row of five pellets separately spaced but connected by a thin line. Lettering is loose and carelessly rendered. Although individual letters such as *A* and *N* are still very broad, their component strokes are generally thinner than in class III and finished with exaggerated serifs. A curious feature of the class is that some letters, especially the final letter of the mint signature, are left incomplete through lack of space, or replaced by a single upright. This latter device caused difficulty to early students of the series, and led to the identification of imaginary mints such as Chichester (from *CI* for the *EV* of York) or I(lchester). The ligation of letters also becomes more frequent, as do misspellings on both sides, now almost a norm; and odd dies of two Canterbury moneyers, Goldwine and Reinald, have a London mint signature.

Class IV, the last of the first phase of the Short Cross coinage, was one of only two of his new classes that Lawrence did not attempt to subdivide, although like the other one, class VIII, which comes at the end of the second phase, it ran for several years and successive stages in its development can be identified. Brand proposed a tripartite division into IVa, IVb and IVc, based on bust and lettering, and this has been generally adopted. Obverses of the rare class IVc are easily recognised by the reversal of the letter *S*, which continued into Va. The division between the very abundant classes IVa and IVb depends chiefly on the number and disposition of the side curls, but although most coins can be readily assigned to one or the other by this means there are some exceptions to the normal pattern.

In class IVa the standard arrangement is of two, three or four thick curls each side, in the manner of class IIIb. There are, however, several dies with more curls, or with unevenness between the two sides. It is also arguable that a few obverses with a single curl each side, normally a characteristic of IVb, belong within IVa, perhaps in its early stages, but the evidence for this awaits exposition. A rare but undoubted early feature, however, is a pellet within the lower curls as had occurred on some late dies of IIIb. Brand showed that Lawrence's class 'IIb', with shaped face, pellet beard and colons by on in the reverse inscription, properly belongs in the period of class IVa. This colon variety, to which Brand applied the label IVa*, is only known at the four major mints. Of the fourteen moneyers at these mints who struck both IIIb and IVa, twelve are also known with colon reverses; the only exceptions are Aimer of London and Osbern of Winchester both of whose careers ended with IVa. However, since none of the five new moneyers at any of these mints, whose coins begin during IVa, is known with colon reverses, the colon dies may come quite early within IVa, before their appointments, even if not at the very beginning of the class.

Hair represented by a single curl each side, or by two in parallel, is the principal distinguishing feature of class IVb. The face itself in this phase of the class is often grotesque, spotty, large, and square or shapeless, without definition below the curls. The eyes are sometimes shown as pellets instead of annulets, and an extra fold of drapery may be added beside the collar. As before, the band of the crown normally consists of seven pearls, run together, although more or fewer sometimes occur. Late in IVb the new form, with five pearls separately spaced, appears and this continues into IVc. On a few dies with this crown the single curl is replaced by several thinner curves, a rare exception to the normal pattern for IVb.

Lettering is at its worst in IVb, loosely and inaccurately punched, and misspelling abounds. Uprights often protrude beyond their serifs. The letter S acquires an almost circular outline, causing in one instance a confusion with C which led Lawrence to postulate an obverse die-link between Shrewsbury and Canterbury. A colon sometimes follows the mint name. Small points are occasionally added in the quarters on IVb reverses. Another rare feature, on a few late reverse dies of London and Canterbury, is a crude pommy form of initial cross, consisting of four pellets loosely combined. Although this cross foreshadows the cross pommy of class Va, it is very different in appearance and was not maintained in class IVc.

LETTER FORMS IN CLASS IV

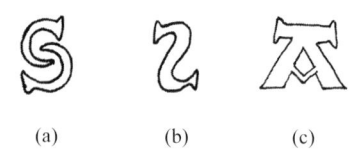

(a) Circular S, IVb; (b) Reversed S, IVc; (c) A with chevron bar, IVc.

Apart from the reversed S which defines it, class IVc resembles late IVb in many respects. The face is still large, ugly and spotty; the crown with five spaced pearls continues; and so does the single curl each side for the hair (with the same variant of several curves). On the other hand, epigraphy improves. Misspellings are rare and letter forms less carelessly rendered. On a few dies the A has a central bar, at first a chevron, later straight as was to become normal in class V.

Only the three main mints at London, Canterbury and York were active in all three subdivisions of class IV. Of the three other mints that came through from class III, Winchester closed during IVa, but Carlisle survived into IVb, while the situation at Northampton is unclear because of ambiguity in the attribution of coins reading *Nor* as between Northampton and Norwich. Apart from Norwich the only additional mints in IVa and IVb were Durham and Shrewsbury, both now appearing for the first time in the Short Cross coinage. Only four mints are recorded for the brief class IVc, London, Canterbury, York and '*No*', but it is possible that other IVb mints remained active at this period though without IVc dies – particularly Durham which received its next new dies early in class V.

At London the careers of Aimer and Stivene came to an end during class IV, while Fulke and Henri began in IVa. Ricard and Fulke, active throughout the class, are mentioned in the Pipe Roll for 1201/02. At Canterbury there was a substantial change of personnel in IVb: only Roberd of the original class II team continued after IVb, but the departures of Meinir, Reinald and Ulard were more than offset by the addition, relatively late in IVb, of five new names, so that Canterbury had seven moneyers in IVc (and going into class V), against only four at London. York's three class I moneyers are last found in IVa, Davi and Nicole taking their places, from IVa through class V. Everard's name appears in a group of four persons fined in 1200/01 for misbehaviour relating to the mint and he may be presumed to have ceased operations by that date. In the IVa-b period Carlisle retained its single moneyer Alein, but at both Durham and Shrewsbury three names are found.

The Short Cross Coinage

The *Nor* moneyers are problematic. Northampton's two class III moneyers did not survive into class IV. Instead there is Giferei in IVa, with an explicit mint signature (*Nora*). In 1197/8 Geoffrey FitzWalter (perhaps referring to the Northampton moneyer Walter of classes I and III) accounted for £10 to be relieved of his duties at the mint, which explains why his coins are of IVa only. Allen has suggested that the Northampton mint may have been closed at this point, in which case the two *Nor* moneyers, Randul and Willem, who shared obverse dies in both IVa and IVb, could be attributable to Norwich. In favour of Northampton for these two, whether or not they were the same individuals as Raul and Willem of Northampton in class I, is the material activity known for this mint in the 1180s and 1190s. On the other hand the keepers of the London exchange provided £100 between 1194 and 1196 to support the exchange at Norwich, which may be an indication that a mint was established there during the period of class IVa. The only pre-1205 coin safely attributable to Norwich reads *Norw* and is by Iohan, a productive moneyer in class V. The reverse of this coin is of convincing class IV style, but its obverse is abnormal, with a profusion of small curls running all round the face. For this reason it has sometimes been dismissed as an imitation, but it has nothing in common with the known imitative series. In class V Norwich (from Va) participated earlier than Northampton (Vb), which could suggest that Randul (with the reading *No*), the only relevant moneyer operating immediately before the recoinage (in class IVc), is more likely to have been working at Norwich.

Although Shrewsbury had had an active mint in the tenth and eleventh centuries, its importance then declined, and after 1100 its output was occasional. It had participated briefly and modestly in the 1158 recoinage but not in that of 1180. In 1194, however, a recently discovered silver mine at Carreghova, just beyond the Welsh border, led to a revival of coinage at Shrewsbury. The Pipe Roll records that the burgesses of the town were paid for the cost of a building for the mint and money was also sent to purchase the mine and finance the exchange. The first account for the mine ran from June 1194 and the mint was probably opened at about the same time. The same person served as keeper of the exchange at Shrewsbury and as custodian of the mine. While the latest entries in the rolls relating to the mine occur in 1195, the mint may have continued beyond this, although never on any substantial scale to judge by the rarity of the coins. Three names of moneyers are found. The first and much the rarest of them was Willem, known only by coins of early class IVa from a single reverse die. Also in IVa, although probably later, there are coins of Reinald and Ive, and these two continued into IVb; in both sub-classes there is only one reverse die recorded of each moneyer. Since their IVb obverse dies have large annulet eyes and the IVc-style crown with five separated pearls, it may be supposed that the Shrewsbury mint did not close early in IVb. With IVb Reinald becomes Reinaud, a change which had also occurred (during IVa) in the case of the Canterbury moneyer of this name.

Bishop Hugh du Puiset (1153-95) had enjoyed the profits of a moneyer at Durham for part of Henry II's first coinage, but some years before 1180 the privilege had been withdrawn. According to Roger of Howden it was restored by Richard I in 1196 for Hugh's successor, Philip of Poitou, after a long interval during which it had not been permitted to his predecessors. There is, however, an entry in the Chancellor's Roll recording that the receivers of the see from April to December 1195, during the vacancy after Hugh's death, accounted for expenditure *ad cambium faciendum* which indicates at least that an exchange was in preparation or existence before Philip obtained the temporalities. There are three moneyer names at Durham in class IV – Adam (IVa), Alein (IVa and b) and Pires (IVb), each operating singly. Alein was perhaps the same person as Alein at Carlisle if Willelm's combined responsibility for the mints of Carlisle and Newcastle in the pre-1180 coinage is any precedent. No coins are known of Durham in class IVc, but

1180–1247

Short Cross Class V Moneyers of Ongoing Mints

	IV	Va1	Va2	'Vb/a'	Vb1	Vb2	Vb3	Vc	VI
London									
Fulke	x	x	x	x	x	x			
Henri	x	x	x	x					
Ricard	x	x	x	x	x	x			
Willelm	x	x	x	x	x	x	x		
Rener			o	x	x	x	x		
Ricard T			o	x	x				
Willelm B			o	x	x	x	x		
Adam				x	x	x	x		
Beneit				x	x	x	x		
Ilger				x	x	x	x	x	
Ricard B				x	x	x	x		
Willelm L				x	x	x	x		
Willelm T				x	x	x	x		
Abel								x	x
Rauf								x	x
Walter								x	x
Canterbury									
Arnaud, Hern-	x	o	x	x	x	x	x	x	
Coldwine	x	x	x	x	x	x	x	x	
Hue	x	o	x	x	x	x	x	x	
Iohan	x	x	x	x	x	x	x	x	x
Roberd	x	x	x	x	x	x	x	x	x
Samuel	x	x	x	x	x	x	x	x	x
Simon	x	x	x	x	x	x	x	x	x
Iohan B						x	x	x	
Iohan M						x	x	x	
Bury St Edmunds									
Fulke					x	x		x	
Durham									
Pieres	x		x		x	x		x	x

o – obverse only

The Short Cross Coinage

P(i)eres continued to coin intermittently until early class VII. Durham dies of IVa either have English spellings with *R* (*Duro, Dura*), or Latin with *N* (*Dunol*) which continued in IVb. Since no reverse die has been noted as paired with more than a single obverse, the issue of new dies evidently required surrender of the old. All Durham coins of class IV are rare, those of Adam and Pires extremely so.

Class IV may be dated from c. 1194 until 1204. Of the three sub-classes IVc is so much the rarest that it can hardly have begun more than a year before the renovation. Without figures for mint output in the relevant years it is difficult to judge at all accurately when IVb succeeded IVa; but the division between the two is unlikely to have been far removed, one way or the other, from the change of reign in 1199.

Class V

Lawrence's definition of his class V, covering the 1205 renovation and its aftermath, has proved well founded, together with his tripartite subdivision of it. Subsequent work, notably by Brand and Allen, has suggested some refinement but the basic structure remains undisturbed. In general, coins of class V are smaller and neater than those of earlier classes, and their dies more carefully and consistently engraved. The beard is now again represented by strokes instead of pellets, and throughout the class the band of the crown is normally shown as five large pearls. The scarce class Va, distinguished by a reversed *S* and initial cross pommy, belongs to the early months of 1205, when the new coinage was getting under way. In addition to London and Canterbury, seven provincial mints were brought into action soon enough to receive dies of Va. Class Vb, with normal *S* and cross patty, saw the full list of sixteen mints in operation; more than sixty moneyers were involved in this phase of the coinage, which represents the peak of the output of the regional mints in 1205-7. Class V ends with a variety similar to Vb but with the letter *X* in the form of a flat saltire, composed of four wedges (Vc). Five of the regional mints had closed too soon to receive dies of class Vc, and the others must have followed not long afterwards, since their coins of Vc are scarce or rare. A large majority of class Vc, which continued in issue for perhaps three years after the closure of the recoinage mints, thus consists of coins of London and Canterbury.

Most of the coins of class Va have an initial cross pommy on the reverse and this, together with the letter *S* reversed as in class IVc, defined the sub-class in the Lawrence classification. There is also however a small transitional group of dies (Va1), pre-dating normal Va, which have the initial cross patty on the reverse. These were accordingly often regarded as Va/Vb mules, until Allen demonstrated that the introduction of the cross pommy did not occur until just after the transition from class IV to class V, as defined by the change from pellets to whiskers in the beard. Except for the bust, which has a beard of small strokes, neatly arranged, as is characteristic of class V, these coins from the fourteen obverse dies noted of Va1 might have been regarded as an extension of class IVc. There is no identifiable difference between reverse dies of IVc and early Va1, and die-links between the two confirm the new and correct positioning of Va1.

Class Va1 is found only at London and Canterbury, but is known of all the eleven moneyers of these mints who had been active in class IVc. The hair of class Va1 is represented either (A) by clusters of small crescent curls, or occasionally (B) by small circular curls (not containing pellets) which Mass calls 'ringlets'. A few of those with hair A have large round eyes as in IVc. Normally the sceptre divides *R/ex* in the traditional way, although */Rex* all behind the sceptre is once found and one highly aberrant London die has the sceptre to the right, breaking the inscription *h/enricus.Re/x*. Dies with hair

B have only been found paired with reverses having the initial cross pommy, and have accordingly been labelled Va1/Va2 mules by Mass; but a few coins with hair A also have cross pommy reverses, and it therefore seems possible that the new form of reverse cross was introduced at about the same time as the ringlet hair and thus before the start of Va2. The sceptre-right die and dies with hair B have a regular *S*, followed by a stop before *Rex*. Because of this *S*, the latter have in the past been described as Vb/Va mules, just as coins of Va1 with the initial cross patty were thought to be Va/Vb mules; but the *S* itself is plain, unlike the normal *S* in Vb which has a pellet on its waist.

All the varieties of Va1 are very rare. The dies belong to a very early and brief experimental phase, when individual features of inscription and portrait had not settled down into a standard form for the recoinage, and regional mints were not yet ready. The strange aspect of some of the busts of Va1 is reminiscent of the early stages of class Ia, at the outset of the 1180 recoinage. The die-sinkers may even have had coins of class I before them, since with more curls to sinister the head sometimes gives the appearance of being turned slightly to the spectator's left, and a pellet before *R/ex* is another characteristic of Ia and Ib. Each of these features also occurs occasionally in early Va2.

The recoinage proper began with the traditional class Va, now Allen's Va2, with reversed *S* and cross pommy. Allen drew the line between obverses of Va1 and Va2 on the basis of the absence (Va1) or presence (Va2) of small pellets within some or all of the curls. Throughout Va2 two main curls are shown each side of the head, sometimes with a smaller third one below on one or both sides. Allen divided obverses of Va2 into three styles; the first of these (group A), which is rare, has busts resembling those of Va1 with ringlet hair, except for the pellets in the curls. The neat face of group A dies is set well above the collar and the curls are small. Winchester is the only new mint known to have received an obverse die of group A (notable for having the head slightly turned as in class I) and so may be assumed to have been the first of the regional mints to be activated. Canterbury's sole die of group A and three of London's five have a stop before *R/ex* as in late Va1.

Group B dies are the classic representatives of Va2, with broad portraits and large, round curls. All the Va2 regional mints received dies of group B, but Winchester again, as with group A, was the only one of them to use a die of the third group. At this point the portrait settled down, with a thinner, more pointed and symmetrical face (C) which continued into and throughout class Vb and thus immediately identifies the majority of the recoinage issues. In class Vb the earlier dies (Vb1) have the same flat-topped *R* as had been used in class Va2, but on the more extensive Vb2 there is a new *R* with a rounded top. Where an *R* is present on the reverse, occasional mules between Vb1 and Vb2 can be identified. A late variant of Vb2 is distinguished by eyes consisting of a broken loop, the dexter eye U-shaped, the sinister one inverted. Brand was not convinced that the broken-eye coins, which he described as Vb3, constituted the concluding issue of class Vb, and this view receives support from patterns of die-linkage at certain mints (notably Ipswich). Three mints – Bury, Durham and York – produced coins of Vb2 and Vc but none of Vb3 and this, together with reverse die-links between Vb2 and Vc noted at Canterbury and Winchester, suggests that dies of Vb2 and Vb3 were both available towards the end of class Vb.

The Short Cross Coinage

LETTER FORMS AND POMMY CROSS IN CLASS V

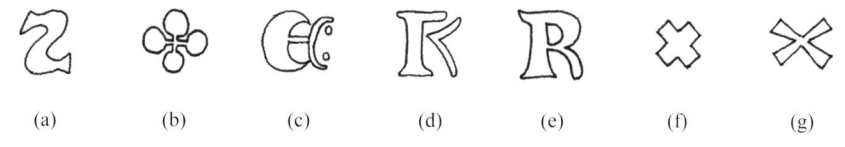

(a) (b) (c) (d) (e) (f) (g)

a) Reversed *S*, Va; (b) Cross pommy, Va; (c) Ornamented *e*, Va-b;
(d) Flat-topped *R* of Vb1; (e) Round-topped *R* of Vb2-Vc;
(f) Plain *X*, Va-b; (g) *X* of wedges, Vc.

Most of the coins with the new *X* of class Vc have a portrait with a broader and more rounded chin than is normally found in class Vb, and this can be a useful pointer to classification when the *X* itself is unclear. The eyes of Vc are also indicative, since they are rarely round as in Vb2, but more usually oval and with pointed ends, or often even solid. Although Vc was defined by Lawrence as having the *X* in the form of a St. Andrews cross, this letter is more properly regarded as a cross of four wedges (which vary somewhat in form), since a plain saltire, more like a St. Andrews cross, is found in the variety immediately following Vc which is now classed as VIa1.

Various features of Va2 gradually faded out as class V progressed. The third curl is still found quite often in Vb1 but only rarely in Vb2 and virtually never thereafter. The division of *Re/x* (often with pellets beside the *X*) is not rare in either Vb1 or Vb2, but except for one abnormal die of Vc it is not found after Vb2. Several early class V dies (chiefly obverses) show ornamental letters – the most prominent being *e* and *c* with added points at their fronts and *R* with a long, pellet-ended tail. These occur mainly in Va2, but they are still occasionally found in Vb1. Curiously, their only appearance in Vb2 is on an obverse die at Chichester, the only such occurrence at a provincial mint in any subclass. The lettering of class V is tidy and well-formed. *A* is generally barred from Va2 onwards. Normally there is no stop on the obverse, and just the two by *on* on the reverse, although colons occasionally appear in Vb. Spelling errors are rare throughout class V, but several cases have been identified of incorrect mint signatures. Thus obverse die-links reveal that two Vb1 reverse dies in the name of Andreu with Canterbury and London signatures were actually used at Lincoln and Winchester respectively.

More than half the total of obverse dies recorded at all mints in every variety of class V were used at London or Canterbury; and the dominance of their joint role in the recoinage may be illustrated by the fact that their coins of Va+Vb in hoards outnumber those of all other mints combined. London began in class V with its four moneyers from class IVc, losing Henri(k) at the end of Va, but adding nine new names for a total of twelve in both Vb1 and Vb2. These numbers exclude Arnaud (of Canterbury) and Iohan (of Canterbury and elsewhere), each known for a single die of Vb1 with a London mint signature, on the grounds that the mint names are presumably the result of error. The three remaining London moneyers from class IV had all gone before Vc, in which Abel, Rauf and Walter appear for the first time. This trio, plus Ilger who had arrived in Vb1, provided the full complement at London throughout class Vc and the earlier part of class VI.

Canterbury's seven class IV moneyers also remained in office for the recoinage, all continuing through to class Vc. The only additions were two more Iohans, distinguished by their initials B and M, who lifted the team to nine in Vb2-Vc. Having used almost as many obverse dies of Va and Vb as at London, Canterbury is recorded for less than a quarter of the London total in Vc. As Canterbury coins do not occur in the early stages of class VI, the likelihood is that the mint was inactive for some years at this period, probably as a result of the Interdict of March 1208 which was not lifted until 1213.

During the course of Va2 London and Canterbury were joined by seven other mints. Four of these, Winchester, Lincoln, Norwich and York, were the next largest contributors to the recoinage. All of them remained active long enough to receive dies of Vc, although York is known only from a single Vc obverse die and must already have been slowing since it was the only substantial mint not to have used dies of Vb3. The two most distant new mints in Va2 were Exeter and Durham. Exeter, as usual, owed its involvement more to geography than to size, and ceased before Vc. The single-moneyer mint for the bishop of Durham continued to be served by the pre-1205 moneyer Pieres. Durham used more obverse dies (seven) of Vc than any other mint apart from London, Canterbury and Winchester, consistently with its activity having extended, if intermittently, beyond the closure of the regional mints.

Winchester names nine moneyers during class V, of whom at least six must have been in office concurrently during Vb1 and Vb2. Adam is the only name among them that had figured at Winchester in the 1190s (class III). On the evidence both of die numbers and totals in hoards, Winchester was by far the most prolific of the new mints, and the only one responsible for more than ten per cent of the recoinage. Lincoln was a four-moneyer mint in Va2, but three new moneyers also used an obverse die of Va2 during the production of Vb (cases of Vb moneyers using old Va2 obverse dies are also found at London, Norwich and York). Although Lincoln was prominent in the early stages of the recoinage, only two of its moneyers remained active after Vb1. Norwich had the normal complement for a medium-sized regional mint of three names, one of which (Iohan) had first occurred in class IVb. York, with Davi and Nicole continuing from class IV, had four moneyers in both Vb1 and Vb2.

No coins of Chichester are known from an obverse die with the reversed *S* of Va2, but this mint was opened early enough to receive reverse dies for its three original moneyers, Pieres, Rauf and Simon, with the cross pommy. Those of Pieres and Simon (like others of Simon of Canterbury) have a normal *S*, indicating that the cross pommy was retained slightly longer than the reversed *S*. The inference of this is that the 'Vb/Va' mules, at the head of the Chichester series, are only mules in terms of modern classification and not in the sense of coins struck from heterogeneous dies. This probably also explains why so-called 'Vb/Va' mules at other mints are often less rare than Va/Vb mules, despite the usual tendency of mules to have the reverse of the later variety. Chichester had four moneyers in total, but Simon was evidently replaced by Willelm in Vb2. Two Chichester coins of Vc have recently come to light, a sub-class not previously recorded for this mint.

Northampton was the most active of the new regional mints in Vb1. It may, however, have had only two moneyers operating concurrently, since Roberd (a name found earlier, in class III) ends in Vb2 when Roberd T begins; only Adam survived into Vb3 and Vc. Ipswich also runs from Vb1 to Vc, and with only two moneyers; its Vc coins are very common in consequence of a large group of them contained in the hoard found nearby at Sudbourne. Although their output was evidently lower, and ended before Vc, Oxford and Lynn each had three moneyers. The two smallest royal mints were Rochester, with two moneyers, and Carlisle, with one. Neither of these is known for Vb3 or Vc. Rochester received one obverse die of Vb1, perhaps from stock, but most of their coins are of Vb2 and these two may therefore have been the last of the new mints to have opened, as well as being among the first to close. The Carlisle moneyer was now Tomas, son of his predecessor Alan; as appears from entries in subsequent rolls, thirty marks for the farm of the Carlisle exchange were originally recorded in the name of Alan FitzAlan but the sum was eventually settled by Tomas.

The Short Cross Coinage

Like Durham, the abbot's mint at Bury was entitled to a single moneyer, but the right had not been exercised since before 1180. Abbot Samson's dies were granted on 12 June 1205 and his moneyer Fulke, or Folke, began to coin in Vb1. His coins of Vb1 and Vb2 are not rare, but only one obverse die is known of Vc, during which the mint ceased to operate. Possibly this was related to the closure of the regional mints, but it could have been an indirect consequence of the Interdict, since no further coinage took place at Bury until after the confirmation of Abbot Hugh in 1215. During the recoinage the pattern of die-linking at Bury suggests that the usual arrangement of one obverse and two reverse dies being issued against surrender of the previous set did not apply.

At Ipswich the names of the two moneyers, Alisandre and Iohan, coincide suggestively with those of the farmers of the exchange, Alexander and John Prikehurt. At Chichester the position was less straightforward. This was the only mint with two or more moneyers in the recoinage where the moneyers do not seem to have shared obverse dies. In April 1205 the bishop had been granted one die to be current with two for the king. The engraver was informed in May that three dies should be at Chichester, and in July instructions were issued that the bishop should have the dies without delay. Of the four moneyers named on coins of this mint Pieres and Rauf coined from Vb1 (or 'Vb1/Va') to Vb3, but Simon only from 'Vb1/Va' to Vb2 and Willelm only in Vb2 and 3. Since the quota of dies for Chichester was three, it appears that Simon and Willelm operated in succession. These two happen to share names with the farmers, Simon FitzRobert who had the exchange and the king's two dies for a year from August 1205, and then William Toht who still owed for them three years later. The fact that Simon was also the bishop does not preclude the possibility that he may have acted both as farmer and as moneyer.

Class Va may be dated with confidence to the first half of 1205. The assize of 26 January provided that any pennies minted since the previous Christmas and found clipped should be bored through, and their owner attached as a thief. If this implies that such coins must have been easily recognisable, the introduction of the distinctive cross pommy in Va2 could perhaps have been designed for the purpose. In that case the few dies of Va1 might belong to the weeks following the announcement of the reform on 9 November 1204. In June 1205 the abbot of Bury was granted his die and the mint and exchange of Northampton were put to farm. Since no dies of Va2 went to either of these mints, Vb1 must have been current by about this time. However, dies of Va2 were probably still available at least until May, on the evidence of the transitional dies, with cross pommy but normal S, made for Chichester.

Allen recorded 388 obverse dies of Vb2 and Vb3 against 150 of Vb1. This suggests that Vb2 must have replaced Vb1 late in 1205 or early in 1206. This is, incidentally, consistent with the activity of Simon of Chichester, if his term as moneyer finished along with his farm at the beginning of August 1206, because two of the five obverse dies that he used are of Vb2. The Pipe Roll for 1209/10 records receipt of net profits of £110 from operation of the exchange of Lincoln during the seventh and eighth years of the reign (1205/7). Six of the twenty-five obverse dies used at Lincoln were of Vc, which must have been current in the first half of 1207. Class Vb2, or the majority of it, thus belongs to 1206. None of the separate farms runs beyond September 1207, by which time the recoinage was presumably complete, rounded off by the conference of moneyers and mint workers in the following month.

Only eight of the thirteen mints of the recoinage (apart from London, Canterbury and Durham which continued beyond it) struck class Vc, and the work of the other five (Carlisle, Exeter, Lynn, Oxford and Rochester) may have ended in 1206. A period of between twelve and eighteen months for lesser mints would accord with the pattern of other recoinages. Class Vc remained in issue for a few years after the end of the recoinage.

1180–1247

SHORT CROSS MONEYERS OF CLASS V RECOINAGE MINTS

	IV	Va1	Va2	'Vb/a'	Vb1	Vb2	Vb3	Vc
CARLISLE								
Tomas					x	x		
CHICHISTER								
Pieres				x	x	x	x	
Rauf				x	x	x	x	x
Simon				x	x	x		
Willelm						x	x	x
EXETER								
Gileberd			x		x	x	x	
Iohan			x		x	x	x	
Ricard			x		x	x	x	
IPSWICH								
Alisandre					x	x	x	x
Iohan					x	x	x	x
LINCOLN								
Alain			x					
Andreu			x		x	x	x	x
Iohan			x					
Ricard			x	x				
Rauf			o		x			
Tomas			o		x			
Hue			o			x	x	x
LYNN								
Iohan					x	x	x	
Nicole					x	x	x	
Willelm					x	x	x	
NORTHAMPTON								
Roberd	x				x	x		
Adam					x	x	x	x
Roberd T						x		
NORWICH								
Iohan	x		x		x	x	x	x
Renald, -aud			x		x	x	x	x
Gifrei			o		x	x	x	x

42

The Short Cross Coinage

	IV	Va1	Va2	'Vb/a'	Vb1	Vb2	Vb3	Vc
OXFORD								
Ailwine					x	x	x	
Henri					x	x		
Miles					x	x	x	
ROCHESTER								
Hunfrei					o	x		
Alisandre						x		
WINCHESTER								
Adam	x		x		x	x	x	x
Henri			x					
Iohan			x	x	x	x		x
Miles			x		x	x	x	x
Ricard			x		x	x		
Andreu					x	x	x	x
Lukas					x	x	x	x
Bartelme						x	x	x
Rauf						x	x	x
YORK								
Davi	x		x		x	x		
Nicole	x		x		x	x		x
Tomas			o		x	x		
Renaud					x	x		

o – obverse only

Although Canterbury probably closed during 1208, London's output remained at a high level. There is little evidence on which to estimate when VIa replaced Vc. In the Naxos hoard London coins of Vc were marginally more numerous than those of VIa, perhaps pointing to the introduction of class VI c. 1210 if output remained at around the same level.

Class VI

Although class VI ran for only about seven years, from c.1210 to 1217, it contains a great diversity of coins which are classed together more because of belonging to the same period, between classes V and VII, than of any consistency in style of portrait or lettering. In recognizing this, Lawrence improved on the Evans classification, which had divided the coins of classes V plus VI into his classes III and IV according to whether they had two or three curls each side of the head; and the captions to his plates, VIa, b and c, give an indication of what he (correctly) regarded as early, middle and late examples of the class. He did not, however, define his subdivisions in the text, and his table of moneyers gives two columns only, for VIa and VIb. Subsequent work by Brand and Stewart has served to refine the classification, while leaving a need for further detailed study of dies in order to achieve greater precision in establishing boundaries between one subdivision and another, and to account for various apparent abnormalities.

In outline, class VIa is an extension of class Vc in general appearance, but with new versions of the letter X; VIb has taller lettering, with increasingly coarse forms of bust; VIc is of finer style, and sees the revival of three curls and ornamental lettering; and VId is a rare final sub-class defined by a further change of lettering. In addition there is a small and anomalous group of coins, confined to Canterbury and labelled VIx, which stands outside the regular series and appears to belong to the period of VIc. With this exception, London coined throughout the class. Of the ongoing mints, Canterbury resumed during VIb and Bury early in VIc. Durham is found only in VIa. Two royal mints, at York and Winchester, were reactivated in VIc, but quickly closed again.

The new forms of X which differentiate coins of class VIa from those of late class V are: first, a flat saltire, consisting of two thin strokes (VIa1); then a plain cross with rounded ends, resembling a quatrefoil (VIa2). This quatrefoil X is found throughout class VI (and beyond), except in VIa1. Under Lawrence's scheme coins of class VIa1 would generally have been regarded as belonging to class Vc, and indeed their X is more truly a St. Andrews cross than the wedge-limbed cross that preceded it. Thus class VIa1 might have been labelled Vc2 or Vd, but Brand's observation that in class VIa the pearls in the crown are normally smaller than in class Vc provides a further point of differentiation from late class V and this arrangement has the advantage of reserving to class V only those varieties represented in the recoinage. The workmanship of class VIa is generally coarse. Lettering is heavy and misspellings relatively frequent in contrast to the discipline of class V. Occasional obverses are found omitting letters (*henrius, henricu*), with /*Rex* behind the sceptre, or even the garbled *henricur/sRx*. Some reverses have loosely formed circles of large pellets. In VIa1 London coins are abundant of all four moneyers who had been active in late class V. Coins of VIa2 are much rarer, especially of Durham which at this time received its last dies until class VII.

LETTER FORMS IN EARLY CLASS VI

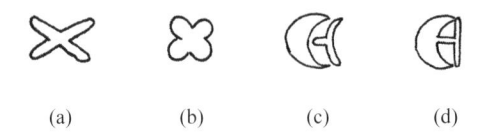

(a)   (b)   (c)   (d)

(a) Saltire X, VIa1; (b) Normal X, VIa2 onwards; (c) Crescent-and-spur *e*, VIa; (d) Compact *e*, VIb.

Soon after the quatrefoil X was introduced other epigraphical changes were made. Lettering becomes taller and thinner (VIb), the N often being notably long and narrow. At first (VIb1) the face tends to remain rounded as in VIa, but classic examples of VIb are easily recognized by their tall, thin bust, with the head often grotesquely elongated although less crudely executed (VIb2). As before, there are two curls each side, usually in VIb2 placed high up towards the crown. The whiskers are thick and tend to radiate from the jaw (as opposed to the downward strokes of VIa). Brand regarded round-faced coins of VIb1, which is confined to London, as the third and last subdivision of VIa, but the new lettering offers a more reliable basis for defining the start of VIb. The most convenient criterion for separating early VIb from VIa2 is the letter *e*. In VIa, as in Vc, the *e* is formed of a thick crescent with

MONEYERS OF SHORT CROSS CLASS VI

	V	VIa1	VIa2	VIb1	VIb2	VIc1	VIx	VIc2	VIc3	VId	VII
LONDON											
Abel	x	x	x	x	x	x		x	x	x	x
Ilger	x	x	x	x	x	x		x	x	x	x
Rauf	x	x	x	x	x	x		x	x	x	x
Walter	x	x	x	x	x	x					
CANTERBURY											
Iohan	x			x	x	x	x	x	x	x	x
Robert	x			x							
Samuel	x			x	x			x	x	x	x
Simon	x			x	x			x	x	x	x
Henri				x	x			x	x	r	x
Hiun, Iun				x	x	x		x	x	x	x
Roger				x	x	x		x	x	x	x
Walter				x	x	x		x	x	x	x
Arnold						o	x				
Salemun						o	x				x
Tomas										x	x
BURY ST EDMUNDS											
Rauf						x		x	x	x	x
DURHAM											
Pieres	x		x								x
WINCHESTER											
Henri	x							x			
YORK											
Tomas	x							x			
Iohan								x			
Peres								x			
Wilam								x			

o – obverse only; r – reverse only

a large spur providing the centre bar and curved front; the new *e* of VIb is rounder and more compact. Although struck only at London, class VIb1 constitutes a substantive phase of the coinage. It shows a range of bust styles, transitional from VIa2 to transitional to VIb2, but the main issue is distinct and is crudely designed. Pellets are frequently omitted from the curls. The lettering is remarkably varied in size and includes some of the largest letters in the series. During VIb the letter *A*, hitherto squat and squarish, becomes more elegant, its limbs angled to a point, below a wider top-bar. Later coins frequently have a stop before *R/ex*. Mistakes in the inscriptions are more frequent than at any time other than class IV. An obverse die used by Rauf and Ilger reads *hnericus Rex/x*. One London die of Walter reads *Lei*, while several others have *Wlater*, suggesting the systematic perpetuation of an error.

Canterbury resumed minting in VIb2 and its coins are plentiful. Of the eight Canterbury moneyers of class VIb, Iohan, Robert, Samuel and Simon have names that had occurred in the recoinage and may well have been the same individuals, but the other four were certainly new (Henri, Hiun, Roger and Walter). All the moneyers except Robert, who departed during VIb2, continued into class VII. Just before the end of VIb2 Robert's place was filled by Roger, but Canterbury did not regain its normal complement of eight moneyers until Tomas obtained his first die in VId.

The long, whiskery faces of many late coins of VIb2 are so ugly that with VIc a conscious attempt seems to have been made to upgrade the appearance of the portrait. The faces of class VIc tend to be more triangular in outline than the oblong or rectangular heads of preceding varieties. Often the face is punched into the die so as to stand out within the beard, which consists of finer strokes, no longer radiating from the chin. New eyes are tear-shaped, with indented pupils at the rounded inner end. The mouth is often clearly open. Class VIc begins with coins (VIc1) having two curls each side, and some other features inherited from VIb2; VIc2 and VIc3, both with three curls each side, have respectively ornamental and undecorated lettering. Of the three subdivisions, VIc2 is much the most abundant. The Bury mint, revived in VIc1 for the first time since class V, now became a regular contributor to the coinage. The few known coins of York, and the even fewer of Winchester, are all of VIc3. Of the four York moneyers Tomas was perhaps the same as the Tomas in Vb (Vc being so rare at this mint). Yet again, as on the two previous occasions in the Short Cross period when minting was reactivated at Winchester (in Ia and Va), a moneyer named Henri put in the briefest of appearances. A Brian is mentioned as his colleague in the rolls, but no coins with this name have been found.

The two-curl coins of VIc1 exhibit some variety of portrait, but always of a more natural shape than in VIb2 and with the new distinctive eyes. The nostrils are often indicated by small points alongside the lower nose – a feature also to be noted in VIb2. Lettering is still tall and plain, but the curved fronts of *c* and *e* are tending to lengthen. The stop before *R/ex* is still much in evidence in VIc1, although decreasingly so thereafter. Inscriptions are more accurately rendered in class VIc, with ligation of letters now less frequent.

At London Abel, Ilger and Rauf remained in office into class VII, but VIc1 is the last variety recorded for Walter, and this confirms its position following VIb. Obverses of VIc1 are occasionally found in combination with reverses having the ornamental lettering of VIc2, and this also demonstrates the sequence. Although one London obverse die (used by all three moneyers) has been noted combining two curls with ornamental letters, the virtually simultaneous change to three curls and the elaborate letter fount of VIc2 seems to have been a further deliberate step in the process of improvement. The portraits continue to be variable in shape, but the addition of the third curl (usually very small, and without a pellet inside it) does give the head more balance and the whole effect is undoubtedly a great advance on the coarse portraits of VIa and VIb. This impression is enhanced by the general elegance of the lettering, which is neater and more shapely than before, quite apart from the decorated forms. The most exotic ornamental letters are *A* and *T* with twisted shanks, and *e*, *c* and *G* with pellets added within their frontal crescents. Less evident, and sometimes overlooked, are *h* and *R* with curled tails, or letters with a thin extra stroke parallel to an upright. Almost all the letters used (except, evidently, *M*, *S* and *W*, where width or shape are not so conducive to decoration) are sometimes ornamented, but the number of such actually found on any one die may be one or many. Mules (either way) with VIc3, which are not particularly rare, usually involve VIc2 dies with few and less obviously ornamented letters. Although the very rare VIc1/c2 mules sometimes also have only a single ornamental letter on the reverse, it is likely that the more elaborate forms came relatively early in VIc2 and that, as the use of ornamental letters was gradually discontinued, they did not last as long as the more unobtrusive ones.

Letter Forms in Later Class VI

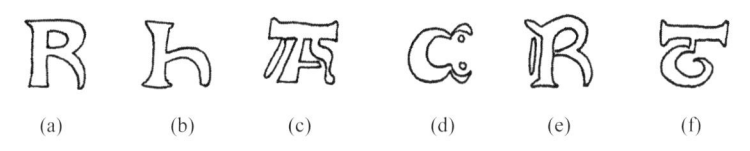

(a) and (b) *R* and *h* of VIx; (c)-(f) Ornamental *A*, *C*, *R*, and *T* of VIc2;

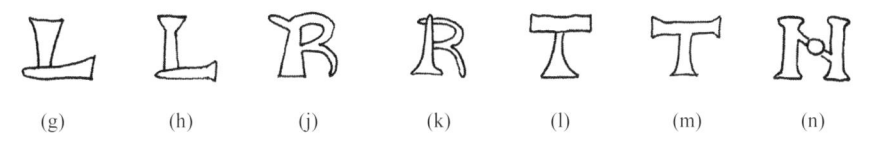

(g), (j) and (l) *L*, *R* and *T* of VIc3; (h), (k) and (m), *L*, *R* and *T* of VId; (n) Pellet-barred *N*, VId.

Coins of VIc3, without ornamental letters, are much scarcer than those of VIc2 which in other respects they closely resemble. Their lettering is the same as the undecorated forms in VIc2. The long stroke in letters such as *L*, *R* and *T* is a wedge with hollowed sides, flared outwards at the wide end. Brand regarded the next variety, class VId, as a subset of VIc3 but, apart from the pellet-barred *N* which is the most characteristic (but not invariable) feature of VId dies, there are differences in lettering which enable mules between VIc3 and VId (and between VId and VIIa) to be identified. The letters of VId are tall and well formed. The uprights of *L*, *R* and *T* are nail-shaped, made with a narrow bar, pointed at one end, and with a serif at the head. The *c* and *e* of VId are also often distinctive, with extended curly fronts. Although a stop before *R/ex* is still occasionally found in VIc3, it has disappeared altogether by VId. On reverses of VId, while a stop each side of *on* does still occur, sometimes only the first stop is found or, more commonly (and looking forward to class VII), neither.

As in VIc, the bust of VId is normally tall and large, with two big and one small curl each side, but a broader face with only two curls is found on three obverse dies and a very neat and compact one, foreshadowing some of early class VII, on three others.

Only fifteen obverse dies of VId have been noted in all, and the coins are all rare. One mule (by Samuel) has been found with an obverse of VIc2, underlining the shortness of the currency of dies of VIc3. Mules (both ways) between VIc3 and VId are most frequently found of Canterbury, and in VId more than twice as many coins are known of Canterbury as of London. Tomas at Canterbury, sworn in December 1217, was the only new moneyer in class VId.

There remains the one very rare and exceptional Canterbury variety (VIx), evidently belonging to the period of later class VI. Obverse dies of VIx must have been based on a model from early class V, since the division *Re/x* is not otherwise found after class V and the VIx bust is large, with round eyes, two curls and a pellet on the chin, recalling some of the well-made portraits from early in the recoinage. Connecting VIx with a later period, however, are the use of points beside the nose to indicate the nostrils, as in VIb and VIc1; the names of the moneyers; and, more concretely, the existence of mules (by Arnold, Iohan and Salemun) from obverse dies of VIc1. Such mules can be identified by the peculiar lettering of VIx on their reverse dies. The letters are large and well-formed, with several distinctive characteristics. The back of the *h* is lower and flatter than in regular class VI; the right side of *R* has a carefully shaped waist; *X* is square and plain. Six names of moneyers are found in class VIx. Four of these are well attested Canterbury moneyers of class VI (Iun, Iohan, Roger and Waltier); one, Salemun (spelt *Salemum* on his VIx die), succeeded his father Samuel early in class VII; and Arnold (a name found early in class V, more usually as Arnaud), could perhaps be the Ernaldus who is recorded in the rolls of 1217/18 and later as *custos cuneorum* to the moneyer Roger. With one exception, each of the moneyers is represented by a single reverse die; the exception is Iun of whom a second reverse is found paired only with one obverse die each of VIc2 and VIc3, as if it had been put aside during the VIx period and only brought into use later. Because of their curious style, coins of class VIx were long regarded as imitations; but the consistency of the dies, the mules with VIc and the representative run of personal names confirm their status as official, if somewhat irregular, products of the Canterbury mint. The most likely context for their issue is the disruption caused by the Baron's War of 1215-7.

A chronology for the subdivisions of class VI can be deduced from the representation of the various mints. Class VIa, missing Canterbury, must be attributed to the period of the interdict and, as noted under class V, may have begun c. 1210. The last record of profits from the Durham exchange, during the vacancy following the death of Bishop Philip in 1208, occurs in 1211/12 and the 39,000 pennies struck during that year, which the figures imply, were probably from the three Durham obverse dies of VIa2. The introduction of class VIb1, again lacking at Canterbury, may be dated to the year 1212/13. This mint resumed activity in March 1214 with VIb2, which was presumably already underway at London by that date, because London coins of this variety are many times more plentiful than those of Canterbury. The relative scarcity of these Canterbury coins suggests that VIb2 ended in 1214/15. On this basis, the start of class VIc would fall within the last year or two of John, consistently with the reappearance in VIc1 of Bury, with the new moneyer Rauf, following the confirmation of the abbot's minting rights in June 1215. This allows the abnormal VIx, muled by three Canterbury moneyers with obverses of VIc1, to be placed during the civil war of 1215/16, when London was in rebel hands and the king was in Kent, using Canterbury as his base. Class VIc2 may be dated to 1217 (or conceivably from the end of 1216). In this case the improved appearance of these coins may have been an initiative of the new administration after John's death. Henry III was only nine years old at his accession, but the bearded head is not anomalous if, like Richard's and John's, these coins are still seen as a continuation of the coinage of Henry II. The dies of VIc3 delivered to the king's moneyers at York and Winchester in December 1217 establish a date for this scarce variety, and the rarer VId presumably also belongs to the winter of 1217/18. In May 1218 the archbishop of York had still not received his dies, and it looks as if the early closure of the royal mint may have meant that he never did so.

Class VII

More than half of all surviving Short Cross coins belong to Lawrence's class VII, much the longest, as well as the largest, class in this series. This abundance is partly due to the two major hoards having been buried in the 1230s, but the period of some twenty-five years from 1217 to c.1242, during which class VII was in issue, was also one of high mint output that led to a considerable increase in the volume of currency. The arrangement of this extensive material presents problems, since there are few obvious features to provide a guide to sequence or subdivision of the kind available for earlier classes. While the beginning and end of the careers of individual moneyers, as recorded in the rolls, are useful in establishing what sort of coins were being struck at certain dates, the general sameness of appearance of many of the issues of the 1220s and 1230s, in the long middle phase of class VII, is a limiting factor in deriving a scheme of classification for them. Although the earliest coins of class VII differ sharply from class VI, as do the latest from class VIII, there is no such clear definition in between. Thus, the boundaries of class VII are unambiguous, but within the class appearance changes gradually over a long period, so that there is little affinity between late coins and those struck more than twenty years earlier. There are, however, a few general features common to the great majority of examples of class VII. The face is more rounded than in classes V, VI and VIII, and is usually set low down with little or no collar. Curls are usually 3-3, with the third and lowest very small. On the reverse the traditional stops by *on*, almost invariable in preceding classes, are now omitted. Beyond these points, uniformity is hard to find.

Lawrence used three columns, for VIIa, b and c, in his lists of moneyers, but he did not label his illustrations in the same way, as he had done for classes V and VI, and he made no attempt to describe the characteristics on which he based his sub-classes. A broad division into three phases may, however, be made along the following lines: class VIIa consists of carefully struck coins, with neat portrait and lettering, including most notably the *A* with its limbs meeting in a point beneath a top-bar; in class VIIb the lettering is less tidy, with *A* now rectangular (as an *H* with a top-bar), and the general design and execution are coarser; and in class VIIc everything tends to be larger, the size of the coins, the degenerate face and in particular the height of the letters. Class VIIa occupied a relatively short phase, of no more than five years or so, and class VIIc perhaps a similar period at the end, leaving class VIIb to fill the long middle phase from the early 1220s to the mid-1230s.

A major advance in the study of class VII was made in 1988 by North, who put forward a scheme of subdivision into eleven principal varieties. North's table recording the varieties known for each moneyer is broadly consistent with what is known of their dates of arrival and departure, and he has attempted the daunting task of providing a framework for sequence and chronology in this most complex of classes. But it is in the nature of the material that there is often a lack of clear definition between one variety and the next and the classification is therefore often somewhat subjective and difficult to apply in practice, even for those familiar with the series. North used Roman letter suffixes (VIIaA, etc.) for his varieties in order not to impose too rigid a chronology on what he regarded as only a preliminary examination of the series; but Mass, in adopting

1180–1247

Moneyers of Short Cross Class VII

	VI	VIIa1	VIIa2	VIIa3	VIIb1	VIIb2	VIIb3	VIIb4	VIIc1	VIIc2	VIIc3	VIII
London												
Abel	x	x	x	x								
Ilger	x	x	x	x	x	x						
Rau(l)f	x	x	x	x	x	x						
Elis				x	x							
Terri				x	x							
Adam						x	x	x	x	x		
Ledulf						x	x	x	x			
Ricard						x	x	x				
Giffrei						x	x	x	x			
Nichole									x	x	x	x
Canterbury												
Henri	x	x	x	x	x	x	x	x	x	x		
Ioan	x	x	x	x	x	x	x	x	x			
Iun	x	x	x	x	x							
Roger	x	x	x	x	x	x	x	x				
Samuel	x	x	x	x								
Simon	x	x	x	x	x	x						
Tomas	x	x	x	x	x	x	x	x				
Walter	x	x	x									
Roger of R		x	x	x	x	x	x					
Salemun	x			x	x							
Ioan Chic					x	x	x	x	x	x	x	x
Osmund					x	x	x	x	x	x		
Willem						x	x	x	x	x	x	x
Willem Ta						x	x	x	x			
Ioan F.R.						x	x	x	x			
Robert								x	x			
Nichole									x	x	x	x
Robert Vi									x			
Durham												
Pieres	x	x										

The Short Cross Coinage

	VI	VIIa1	VIIa2	VIIa3	VIIb1	VIIb2	VIIb3	VIIb4	VIIc1	VIIc2	VIIc3	VIII
BURY ST EDMUNDS												
Rauf	x	x	x									
Willelm			x	x								
Norman				x	x	x						
Simund						x	x	x	x	x		
Ioan										x	x	x

the North arrangement (with some minor adjustments) for his *Sylloge*, showed sufficient confidence in its structure to replace letters with numbers, and this format has been used in the present context. There remain, however, several areas where further work is needed before a clear sequence can be established with confidence.

LETTER *A* IN CLASS VII

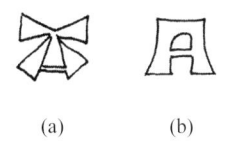

(a)   (b)

(a) Pointed *A*, VIIa; (b) Squarer *A*, VIIb-c.

Class VIIa includes coins of widely differing style and appearance, united only by the continued use of the angled Roman *A* as in earlier classes. Unfortunately, however, this letter does not appear on obverses and, although it occurs in the mint names of Bury and Canterbury, the dies of three London moneyers, Ilger, Elis and Terri, whose output belongs to the period of both VIIa and VIIb, contain no *A* and can only be divided between the two by comparison of other features, such as the eyes. North identified four phases in class VIIa labelled A-D, and these were converted into VIIa1-3 by Mass.

The earliest coins of the class can be identified from the rare mules that exist both ways with class VId. Most of such mules are of a variety showing a small and very neat bust, or on reverse dies a finely grained inner circle. Since the two class VII obverse dies used at Durham are of this variety, it is conveniently known as the Durham type. The lettering on this type is unusually small, with the tiny *e* and *c* consisting of a circular body with a small frontal crescent. The *c* is also sometimes used in place of *e*, or reversed to form a *D*. In VIIa1 (= North B) the letter *A* normally has a wide top-bar consisting of two wedges, giving it a waist in the middle. Related to the Durham type are some coins with a bust and some letters slightly larger, including an *S* with prominently curved serifs. These coins are also classed as VIIa1 since they share with the Durham type a beard of tiny strokes which differentiates them from VIIa2. In VIIa1 the eyes are tear-shaped (no. 1) in the manner of late class VI. The nose is neat with realistic nostrils.

Eye Punches in Class VII (after North)

1. Tear-shaped: VIIa1-3, VIIb1; 2. Thin annulet: VIIa3, VIIb1, VIIc3;
3. Thick oval: VIIa3; 4. Fractured: VIIb2-3; 5. Thick annulet: VIIb4, VIIc1-2;
6. Irregular annulet: VIIc2; 7. Pellet in annulet: VIIc2; 8. Solid: VIIc2.

The more prominent beard of VIIa2 (= North A) consists of longer, vertical bristles, leading Eaglen to refer to it as the 'Hapsburg chin'. The face is now rounder, and a little larger overall, still with realistic nose and tear-shaped eyes. Letter forms are more varied, with some larger, but still mostly with the curved-serif *S*. Class VIIa2 is more plentiful than VIIa1, but most of the coins of VIIa belong to VIIa3, the amalgamation of North's C and D proposed by Mass on the ground that D evolves from C in a way that does not assist a precise division between the two. Nevertheless, North's separation of his C and D remains valid in many respects. Obverses of VIIa3 have a larger face, with the beard less clearly marked, degenerating into a crude, squarish portrait in North's VIIaD. Another guide to the evolution of the portrait is the eyes, which in North's C are at first realistic, being tear-shaped as before, but then small, thin annulets (2); and in D they are usually of a new, thick oval form (3). Throughout VIIa3 the nose is normally thin and pointed, with the nostrils also pointed. Lettering is generally larger, with *e* widening. Later versions of the VIIa letter *A* sometimes have the limbs still angled but no longer meeting at the apex.

In this account the VIIa material has been described according to the subdivisions defined by North and Mass, but there are signs that this arrangement may, in some respects, be in need of revision. Thus a different picture emerges if a division in the early part of VIIa is made according to the circles on the reverse, at first neatly grained, later composed of coarse pellets. The two moneyers (apart from Pieres at Durham) who ceased working early in VIIa were Walter at Canterbury and Rauf at Bury. Yet Walter and Rauf are recorded by North and Mass for both of their first two subdivisions of VIIa, as is Roger of Rochester, Walter's successor. At the one-moneyer mint of Bury the sequence is undoubtedly Rauf, Willelm, Norman. Rauf's coins of class VII, which have grained circles, are very rare and the allocation of his two obverse dies to separate subdivisions looks awkward in view of the relatively heavy output at Bury in the early years of Henry III. Adopting a sequence based on grained and pelleted circles would give a more coherent result: at Bury Rauf (grained circles only) is followed by Willelm (grained and pelleted), and then by Norman (pelleted only); at Canterbury Walter (grained and pelleted) was replaced by Roger of R (pelleted only).

Many coins of VIIa have small pellets in the curls, but in the last phase of VIIa3 (North D) they are usually omitted. On the odd die of VIIa1 only two curls are found each side, as occasionally in VId. A few dies in VIIa1 and 2 exhibit ornamental letters, less extravagantly decorated than in VIc but similar in form. The most obvious are *e* and *c* with a small point at each end of their fronts. *R* with a curled tail, *N* reversed and *D* or *B* with a thin second upright are also found. Although reverse dies of VIIa, as in the rest of class VII, are usually without stops, for a relatively brief period in VIIa3 (North D) there was a sudden outbreak of stopping. This sometimes consists of a pellet or two placed

The Short Cross Coinage

apparently at random, but a format found on the coins of several moneyers has six small points, two each flanking the initial cross and *on*, and two others inserted in the middle of the names of moneyer and mint (e.g., *.hen.ri.on.Can.te.*).

Durham's rare coins of VIIa1 are the last issues from this mint until the 1250s. The long-serving Pieres was still in office. The archbishop of York was ordered to receive the oath of the bishop's moneyer and die-keepers and to report their names to the exchequer, which may explain why the dies sent to Winchester and York in December 1217 were of VIc3 while those of Durham, whose mint had been commissioned at the same time, were sent in the following June, and were of VIIa1. As with VIc coins of York, some Durham pence of VIIa exhibit a collared edge.

At London class VII began with the three moneyers from late class VI, Abel, Ilger the Goldsmith and Radulf de Frowik. The last two continued into VIIb, but the coinage of Abel who had retired before 1222 ceases in VIIa3 (North C), and that of Terri (Terricus le Chaungeor), his replacement, begins before the end of VIIa3 (North D). Elis (Elias of Worcester) had been presented on 9 July 1218, but an entry in 1220/1 records that the existing trio had refused to admit him, which would account for his coins not being found until VIIa3 (North C).

In February and March 1222 Ilger, Rauf, Elis and Terri were supplied with dies for halfpence and farthings as well as pennies. Until recently, in the absence of actual specimens, it seemed doubtful whether these dies had ever been used. The first known halfpenny was published in 1989, since when further halfpence and some farthings have gradually come to light. All four moneyers are now recorded for one or both of the fractional denominations. Raulf's halfpenny is of importance in showing a pointed *A* and so placing the issue of fractions within late class VIIa rather than early in VIIb. In design and general appearance these small coins are miniature versions of pence of late class VIIa3 (North D), except that a pellet within a crescent is placed before the moneyer's name instead of a cross.

The eight Canterbury moneyers of class VId all survived into class VIIa, but in January 1218 Samuel is recorded as having been succeeded by his son Salomon (*Salemun* on the coins) and Walter, who retired to take the cross, was replaced by Roger of Rochester (*Roger of R* on the coins, to distinguish him from Roger of Ipswich already in office). Walter, the two Rogers and Eudo Chic were the archbishop's moneyers at this period. Eudo is not a name found on the coins, but despite the divergence of name there is a case for regarding him as the same person as Hiun, or Iun (the only moneyer's name at this period which does not feature in the records), who coined from VIb to early VIIb. Eudo's successor in 1221/2 was a member of the same prominent burgess-family, Ioan Chic, whose coins begin at the moment when Iun's cease. In the case of Samuel and Salemun the entry for January 1218 shows Salemun's name over an erasure in the roll but it looks as if the alteration may have been made later since Samuel's coins continue until near the end of VIIa3 (North D) and Salemun's do not start until then. Based on the references to moneyers in the rolls, Allen has suggested the following dates for the divisions of VIIa: VIIa1, 1217/8 or 1218; VIIa2, 1218 – c. 1220; and VIIa3, c. 1220 – 1222.

At Bury, Rauf remained in office briefly. His coins of VIIa are extremely rare, from one pair of dies in each of VIIa1 and 2. Rauf's successor was Willelm, whose coins are of VIIa2 and 3 (North C), he in turn giving way in VIIa3 to Norman. In the roll of the King's Treasurer's Remembrancer for 1217/18 the Bury moneyer is given as Willelm, but in that of the Lord Treasurer's Remembrancer for the same year his name has been crossed through and Norman's inserted above it. This emendation also may have been made at a date later than 1218, as six pairs of dies used by Willelm suggest a tenure of several months at least. Eighteen of Norman's twenty obverse dies are of VIIa3, but only one each of VIIb1 and VIIb2, suggesting that the two latter varieties were current during the years 1223-9 while the mint at Bury was under restraint.

Class VIIb as a whole incorporates the long series of coins occupying a stretch of some fourteen years (from 1222 to c. 1236) between VIIa and VIIc, distinguished from the former by having a rectangular instead of a pointed *A*, and from the latter by their smaller lettering. There is sometimes a pellet in the reverse inscription, most commonly after the third letter of the mint, or at the end. The busts of VIIb are very varied, but on most the face is set low down with an open mouth and little or no collar or chin. Since the letters tend to be less compact than in VIIa, the cross on the crown usually points to the centre, or even the left side, of the wider *e*, a useful diagnostic indicator of the new sub-class in the case of the three London moneyers who lack an *A*.

North's four subdivisions of VIIb (A-D) have been used unchanged by Mass, with the labels VIIb1-4. A few early dies of VIIb1 still have a normal Roman *M* (one of these was the only VIIb1 die of Norman at Bury), but this was soon replaced by *H* which continued in use for the remainder of class VII. In VIIb1, a large group which lacks distinctive features, the face is sometimes more oblong, with a square chin. The eyes are either (1) shaped, as in VIIa, or (2) small annulets, and there are no pellets in the curls. VIIb2 is more easily recognized: the two readiest characteristics are a pellet on the chin and the use of the old punch for shaped eyes in a fractured state (4). It is also the only part of VIIb in which small points are often found in the curls. Although the bust of VIIb2 is usually similar to the rest of VIIb, a smaller and neater version also occurs, with a pointed (and pelleted) chin.

Classes VIIb1 and 2 were current from 1222 until beyond 1230. At Canterbury VIIb1 is the first variety struck both for Ioan Chic, who replaced Iun in 1221/2, and for Osmund Polre of whom it is recorded in the Fine Roll for 1225/6 that he was not to have a die that had been granted to him. New moneyers in VIIb2 were Willem and Willem Ta at Canterbury and Adam, Ledulf and Ricard at London. Willem the Tailor replaced Simon Chic, whose last coins are also of VIIb2, in April 1230. Adam of Bentley, Ricard de Neketon and Ledulf the Teuton are also first recorded in 1230, presumably as replacements for Elis and Terri, whose last coins are of VIIb1, and for Ilger and Raulf who end with VIIb2 (in which Ilger seems to have been for some time the dominant London moneyer). On this basis VIIb2 must have begun c. 1229. In the Eccles hoard there were a few coins of Adam, Ricard and Willem Ta, but none of Ledulf, suggesting that the hoard may have been deposited during the course of 1230. None of the coins from Eccles in the British Museum is of a later variety than VIIb2, which could have continued for another year or two. Eccles also contained a few early coins of Simund of Bury, who must therefore have replaced Norman in 1229/30.

In VIIb3 and 4 the portrait is large and rather crude. There is no pellet on the chin (sometimes, indeed, no chin at all) and no points in the curls. VIIb3 still has the fractured eyes (4) of VIIb2, but in VIIb4 these were replaced by thick annulets (5). Coins of VIIb4 can be distinguished from those of VIIb1 with annulet eyes by changes in lettering. Most notably, the upright of *R* in VIIb4 is nearly straight, with a thin serif at the foot; in VIIb1 it was more wedge-shaped. Another typical letter found often in VIIb3 and b4 is a very small *S*.

Class VIIb3 saw the arrival of Giffrei at London and Ioan F.R. (FitzRobert) at Canterbury. The only new name in VIIb4 was Robert at Canterbury, who was appointed in place of Tomas Valentine in 1235. Since three Canterbury moneyers whose last coins are of early VIIc were either dead by 1237 (Ioan = John Turte) or lost their dies to Nicholas of St. Albans in the same year (Robert and Willem Ta), class VIIb must have come to an end by c. 1236. Suggested dates of c. 1232-4 and c. 1234-6 for VIIb3 and 4 take account of these changes of moneyer and the relative quantities of the post-Eccles varieties of class VIIb.

Coins of class VIIc are distinguished by having much taller lettering than had been used before in this class. The very tall *V*, and *c* and *e* with long curved fronts (especially in VIIc1), are typical. Stops on the reverse are rarely found. The bust is large and the style often degenerate, especially in the later stages. North's three divisions are based largely upon variations of detail. In VIIc1 there are no points in the curls, and the eyes (5) are thick annulets (often looking slightly squashed). In VIIc2 the face is usually of rather better style, and the chin and beard are more pronounced. The eyes are varied: either annulets (5, 6); or the same containing small points as pupils (7); or blobs (8), which may be the result of the previous punch having filled up. There are small points in the curls on most dies of VIIc2, and sometimes a pellet on the chin. A chevron-barred *A* is found on a few coins of VIIc1 and 2. The last and rarest variety of VIIc has portraits with a pointed beard (not unlike some coins of class VIII), heavy brows, annulet eyes (2) and small points in all the curls (VIIc3). The nose is long and plain. In VIIc3 there is a distinctive *N*, tall and narrow, and the initial cross, sometimes preceded by a stop, is very thick. Obverses of VIIc3 are very occasionally found muled with reverses of early class VIII.

At Canterbury VIIc1 was produced by ten moneyers, VIIc2 by six, and VIIc3 by only the three who continued into class VIII. VIIc1 was the last variety struck by Ioan, Robert and Willem Ta. It is also the only one known of Robert Vi, a name found on a single reverse die; this name is unattested in the rolls as a moneyer, but a Kentish writ of June 1237 refers to Robert the Vintner of Canterbury, who is a possible candidate. Three more Canterbury moneyers, Henri, Ioan F.R. and Osmund departed during VIIc2. At London Ledulf survived into VIIc1, Adam and Giffrei into VIIc2. Thus the only royal moneyer in the rare VIIc3 (c. 1242) was Nicholas of St. Albans, whose earliest coins are of VIIc1, and whose sole responsibility for London and Canterbury (except for the archbishop's two moneyers, Ioan Chic and Willem) was confirmed in 1242. The relatively abundant coins of VIIc1 may be attributed to the late 1230s (say, c. 1236 to c. 1240). VIIc2 cannot have begun later than c. 1240 since it was the last variety of Ioan F. R. who died in or before 1240/1. At Bury Simund was replaced during VIIc2 by Ioan, who was to continue in office into the Long Cross period. Ioan's Bury coins of class VII, being too late for the Colchester hoard, were of considerable rarity until the discovery of the Naxos hoard.

Class VIII

Until 1969-71, when 274 examples from the Naxos hoard reached the London market, coins of class VIII were distinctly rare in English collections, although more than a hundred in total had come to light abroad in the hoards from Ribe and Gisors. Because the Naxos hoard extends beyond 1247 and so covers the whole of class VIII, its contents are of particular importance for measuring the relative numbers of different mints, moneyers and sub-classes. The existence of a concluding class of the Short Cross series, characterized by a revival of the initial cross pommy, had not been recognised by Evans, but its position was correctly demonstrated by Lawrence. Subsequent work by Elmore Jones defined the three principal phases of the class, and more recently North described their features in greater detail. Although the Jones designation of varieties as VIIIA (with initial cross patty) and VIIIB1-3 (with cross pommy) has been in use for more than fifty years, North's suggestion that it should be replaced by VIIIa (combining VIIIA and VIIIB1), VIIIb (B2) and VIIIc (B3) more sensibly reflects the structure of the class and deserves to be adopted generally, as it has been in the Mass *Sylloge*.

MONEYERS OF SHORT CROSS CLASS VIII

	VII	VIIIa	VIIIb	VIIIc	LongCross
LONDON					
Nichole	x	x	x	x	x
CANTERBURY					
Iohan	x		x	x	x
Nichole	x		x	x	x
Willelm	x		x	x	x
BURY ST EDMUNDS					
Io(h)an	x	x	x	x	x

In respect of portraiture, epigraphy, punctuation and, on the overwhelming majority of specimens, the initial cross pommy, class VIII differs fundamentally from its predecessor. Its introduction has been associated, plausibly but unprovably, with the presentation of a new die-cutter, one Richard Abel, in 1242, the year in which Nicholas of St. Albans assumed his new and exceptional appointment at London and Canterbury. The pointed face on most coins of class VIII looks back more towards classes V and VI than to the broad chinless heads of class VII, and the use of the cross pommy could also suggest that the new appearance owed something to the availability of models from the 1205 recoinage.

Class VIIIa, as now defined, consists of the very rare early coins with large, plain lettering. The X is composed of a transverse stroke, with two bent wedges above right and below left, and, being asymmetrical, is not truly of the curule shape as it is often described. The letters are tall, but more disciplined than in VIIc and with straight sided uprights; c and e are round and open, with shapely serifs (which can give the e a closed appearance, but without a frontal stroke), the barred A is angled but not pointed, and the upper loop of R is as wide as its tail. This lettering is found on VIIIa London reverse dies with two forms of initial cross, (i) an elegant cross patty, and (ii) a neat cross pommy. The extremely rare cross patty coins (Jones VIIIA) are in other respects very similar to those with the same lettering but cross pommy (Jones VIIIB1), and the patty cross must have been very quickly replaced. The attempt by Mass to separate obverse dies with VIIIa lettering also into two subdivisions is, however, not wholly persuasive. The neat portrait of VIIIa has two curls each side enclosing large pellets, and the tidy beard consists of small hairs. Eyes are usually annulets, sometimes between two curved eyelids. Some obverses have a stop before R/ex and, except on the earliest reverses, there is usually a triple colon before on. No VIIIa coins of Canterbury are known, and at Bury the only pair of VIIIa dies has the pommy form of cross.

LETTER X IN CLASS VIII

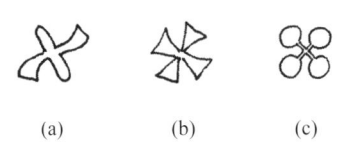

(a) (b) (c)

(a) X of VIIIa with two bent wedges; (b) X of four wedges, VIIIb; (c) X pommy, VIIIc.

The Short Cross Coinage

With the more plentiful class VIIIb, lettering is again the most obvious distinguishing feature, making the identification of VIIIa/b mules straightforward. The letters of VIIIb are shorter, with concave uprights, closed *c* and *e*, and an *X* consisting of four wedges. Sometimes the wedges are bent, and arranged so as to give the appearance of a shape not unlike the *X* of VIIIa. A Gothic *n*, once noted in VIIIa, occurs on several VIIIb dies. The initial cross is now almost always pommy, although the patty form is found on one freak London die while on another an original patty cross seems to have been altered by superimposing a cross pommy. Stops before *R/ex* and *on*, though not invariable, are now customary, most frequently in the form of a triple colon. The face in VIIIb is more sharply angled, with the strokes of the beard seeming to grow inwards from a clear outline; there is often a pellet on the chin. The portrait is generally of good style, although some degradation occurs. Thus the annulet eyes (no longer with eyelids) sometimes become blobs. Curls are still crescents around large pellets, usually two each side, but sometimes with an extra half curl by the crown, or occasionally one and a half curls or three.

The final stage of the Short Cross series is represented by some of its least attractive members, often carelessly struck from dies of degenerate style. In class VIIIc the face is large and coarse, with two thick curls, a bulbous nose, heavy lips and eyes usually solid. Lettering is slightly taller than in VIIIb, but noticeably coarser and thicker, with individual letters occasionally omitted. *X* is now, like the initial cross on the reverse, a cross pommy; sometimes it is very large. Gothic *n* is less rare in VIIIc than previously. Stops occur as in VIIIb, still with the triple colon preponderating. Class VIIIc accounts for around two-thirds of the coins of class VIII as a whole, and its inception cannot be dated later than 1244.

At all three mints the same moneyers occur in class VIII as in late class VIIc. London, with Nichole as sole moneyer, was the only mint to strike all the varieties of class VIII. These include extremely rare VIIc/VIIIa mules with both patty and pommy initial crosses, and only slightly less rare mules from VIIIa obverses with reverses of VIIIb. Canterbury does not appear to have received any dies of VIIIa, and its VIIc/VIII mule thus has an VIIIb reverse. Nichole's Canterbury coins in the Naxos hoard were only marginally more abundant than the aggregate of those of the archbishop's two moneyers, Iohan and Willelm, both of whose coins of VIIIb are rare. An obverse die-link (VIIIb) between coins by Nichole with the London and Canterbury signatures seems more likely to be the result of a reverse die incorrectly delivered than of movement of Nichole's equipment between the two mints for which he was responsible.

Bury's John is the rarest of the class VIII moneyers, and perhaps the only one who struck more coins of VIIIb than of VIIIc. On his single reverse die of VIIIa he is still *Ioan*, but the smaller lettering of VIIIb and VIIIc allowed room for *Iohan*. The mint signature in VIIIb and VIIIc is normally shown as *Sant Ed*, with a triple colon between the two words and *Ed* ligated.

Rhuddlan

The Norman castle of Rhuddlan, long held by the earls of Chester, stood on the river Clwyd about four miles upstream from the port of Rhyl. For more than seventy years from 1167 Rhuddlan was almost continuously under control of the princes of Gwynedd. Although taken by King John in 1211 it was recaptured by Llywelyn ap Iorwerth in 1213 and remained in Welsh hands until ceded to Henry III in 1241 by Dafydd ap Llywelyn. Norman coins of the *Paxs* type with the mint name *Rudili* have generally been taken to indicate a brief issue from Rhuddlan in the late 1080s. The attribution to Rhuddlan of the much more extensive irregular issues of Short Cross type, a century and more later, reading *Rula(n)*, has recently been corroborated by finds made at Llanfaes, Anglesey, in 1992 in which they amounted to about eight per cent. of the total of Short Cross coins from all mints, as well as being less worn as would befit the products of a nearby source.

Although all the Short Cross coins of Rhuddlan are from locally made dies, they follow the general design of the English series, and enough of the details of the regular coinage, to enable successive varieties to be loosely related to it. Hoard evidence indicates that they span a period of perhaps some thirty years around the turn of the century. Nothing is known of the authority under which the Rhuddlan coinage was struck, but it may perhaps have been an independent venture of the local princes. The series began during the time of Dafydd ap Owain, who held the area until 1195 and was married to a half-sister of Henry II. The coins are of good weight and fineness and, if unofficial, were clearly designed to be acceptable within the English currency. The biggest mystery is how a modest but sustained supply of silver became available for a generation or more. There was some trade through the north coast of Wales, but not evidently such as would have attracted silver bullion or foreign coin on any scale. Welsh silver mining is mainly associated with areas further south, notably in Cardiganshire, which was to feed a mint at Aberystwyth in the seventeenth century. But it is notable that the 1190s saw the reestablishment, after a long interval, of a mint at Shrewsbury to coin local silver, and a possible explanation of the activity of a mint at Rhuddlan may be some undocumented source of newly mined silver in North Wales at this period.

Brand divided the coins of Rhuddlan into five classes, labelling them by small Roman numerals to avoid confusion with the classes of the English series. In classes i and ii the hair is indicated by curved lines, as on English coins of classes I-IV, and in classes iii-v by circular curls as introduced in the recoinage of 1205, from English class V onwards. Further subdivision is provided by reference to details of lettering, the crown, the initial cross on the reverse and the names of the four moneyers who held office in succession. The crown of nine pellets in classes i and ii has no parallel in the English series. It is formed of a normal band of five pearls, with an additional central pellet in the cross above. In summary and subject to a few exceptions, these features occur follows:

FEATURES OF SHORT CROSS CLASSES AT RHUDDLAN

Class	Moneyers	Hair	Crown	Cross	N	C
i	Halli	Curved	9 pellets	Patty	Reversed	*c*
ii	Halli,	"	"	Pommy	"	*e*
	Tomas	"	"	Pommy	"	*e*
	Simon(d)	"	"	Patty	"	*e*
iii	Simon(d)	Circular	8 pellets	Pommy	Normal	*c*
iv	Simod	"	"	Pommy	Normal or reversed	*e*
v	Henricus	"	"	Patty	Normal	*c*

The first of the Rhuddlan moneyers was Halli, who was responsible for all the coins of class i. This class is a reasonably competent copy of English class Ib, mainstay of the 1180 recoinage. As on the prototype, there is normally a stop before *R/ex*. The curls begin with the 2-5 pattern typical of Ib; thereafter there are clusters of five each side. The dies are literate, although *N* is reversed on both sides. One exceptional coin has normal *N*, reversed *S*, no obverse stop, an eight-pellet crown and the opposite of the usual arrangement of the hair (5-2); although this piece differs in so many respects from the normal coins of class i it probably belongs to the same period but represents the work of a different die-cutter. While the earliest hoard in which Halli's coins of class i occur is that from Aston (c. 1193), in the neighbouring county of Cheshire, it is quite possible that the Rhuddlan series began in the 1180s, not long after the English recoinage. Halli's successor Tomas was already represented in a parcel from the Lisieux hoard which also ended with English coins of class IIIb and in the Wainfleet hoard deposited c.1195.

Obverses of class ii retain many of the characteristics of class i including the nine-pellet crown, reversed *N* and usual stop; but *c* acquires a central bar to become an *e*. Despite this, they are generally well made and literate, although one (iic) reads *hnerieus*. The wide eyes of class i are now replaced by pellets, the curls are thicker, and the moustache is prominent. But the most remarkable feature of the class ii coins of Halli and Tomas is the initial cross pommy on the reverse, some years before this form was first used in the English series. In connection with the Eccles and Colchester hoards Evans and Grueber had correctly attributed the coins of Halli and Tomas, and some of Simond, to the period before 1205. However, the presence of a cross pommy on so many of the coins of Rhuddlan misled Lawrence into supposing that they all belonged around the time when class VII gave way to his newly designated class VIII, and suggesting an historical context in homage done to Henry III by Llywelyn's son David. The occurrence of the cross pommy in class ii was probably due to no more than the convenience of a new engraver who needed a cross of this kind anyway for the central design.

That a different die-sinker was involved at this point is also evident from the last two reverse dies in Halli's name, which have the cross pommy in conjunction with a retrograde inscription (iia). These are the earliest reverses of class ii and first occur combined with the last obverse die of class i. Like these i/ii mules, Halli's true coins of class ii are also very rare, for he was soon replaced by Tomas. Three forms of initial cross pommy are found on Tomas's dies, which often lack the stop after *on*. The earliest cross is small and free-standing, on coins described by Brand as iib; this was followed by a larger version of which the bottom pellet is incorporated into the dotted inner circle (iic); and the last is similar but has an extra small pellet added in the centre (iid), as in the nine-pellet crown. The latest coins of the class, in the name of the third moneyer, Simon(d), revert to an initial cross patty (iie). The first of his two class ii obverse dies had already been used by Tomas.

Simond's coins of class ii are rare, but his later coins, which show the influence of the 1205 recoinage, are the least scarce of the Rhuddlan issues. Their earliest hoard context is Newry, which ended with English class V. The head of class iii, with its rounded curls, is clearly modelled on the recoinage type, although the revival of the cross pommy at this point does not necessarily reflect the use of this form for the first time in English class Va. Apart from the head, more minor features also distinguish class iii from its predecessors. The crown loses its extra pellet, *N* is no longer reversed and the stop before *R/ex* disappears. One or both stops on the reverse are more often than not omitted. The letter *c* is now itself again, open and usually with small serifs. One development on English coins from 1204/5 onwards, the addition of a bar to the letter *A*, was not reflected in the Rhuddlan series, which retained an open *A* throughout. Two early transitional varieties of class iii retain features of class ii: one (iiib), except for an eight-pellet crown, still has a class ii style of bust, with crescent side curls, and a stop before *R/ex;* the other (iiia), although looking much more like a normal coin of class iii, has not lost the ninth pellet from the crown. Most of the regular coins of the class (iiic) are struck from a single obverse die (with a pellet in *henri.cus*), which appears to have been recut quite drastically more than once.

The last coins of Simod (as he is now spelt), although also based on English class V and retaining the cross pommy, were allocated by Brand to a separate class (iv), on the grounds that they are much cruder than those of class iii and, more specifically, revert to the practice of class ii in using *e* for *c*. The head is more solidly drawn than in class iii, rather in the manner of bust B of English class Va. One of the two obverse dies of class iv reads *Ri/ex*; on the other, which is also found with a reverse of Henricus, the *N* is reversed. The two reverse dies of class iv are very curious: the inscription reads backwards, but the individual letters are not reversed.

Simond's successor Henricus, last and rarest of the Rhuddlan moneyers, reverted to an initial cross patty on the reverse (class v), although on his die that was used with a class iv obverse it is more of a blob than a cross. Stops by *on* are also restored. The coarsest obverse has a stop before *R/ex*; another reads *Rc/x*. Although the crude busts on the three class v obverses bear some resemblance to English class VI or VII, it is doubtful whether this indicates a date much later than class V. If Henricus had had a career extending into the 1220s, his coins might have been expected to be more plentiful. In the absence of more precise hoard evidence it is impossible to judge whether the series came to an end before, during or after the English occupation of 1211-3.

Ireland

According to the St. Albans chroniclers, Roger of Wendover and Matthew Paris, King John visited Ireland in the summer of 1210 in support of John de Gray, bishop of Norwich, whom he had appointed as his Justiciar in Ireland; de Gray had brought the penny of Ireland up to the English weight standard and provided for round halfpennies and farthings to be made. The king had ordered that the use of this money should be general in England as well as in Ireland, and the penny of either realm was to be acceptable in his treasuries without distinction – a revealing comment on the underlying motive for John's Irish recoinage.

In the 1190s, before his accession to the English throne, John had had an extensive coinage as Lord of Ireland, consisting of small coins equivalent in weight to a half and a quarter of the English penny. As seen from an English perspective, these have generally been described as halfpence and farthings, but this is not how they were conceived in Ireland. Since the Carolingian period the penny, or denier, had undergone debasement almost everywhere in Europe, except in England, losing weight or fineness. In Ireland, as in parts of Germany, the loss of weight had resulted in coins known as bracteates, on flans so thin that they could effectively be struck on only one side. John's Irish 'halfpennies', therefore, are evidently pennies on an Irish standard, influenced by the low weight of the bracteates and conveniently equivalent to half the sterling standard. The existence of these coins of John's lordship explains why, when pence on the English standard were later introduced, they were accompanied by round halfpence and farthings, recognising the habits of Irish people already familiar with coins of lower value. It is notable that, although John's royal halfpence and farthings did not circulate in England, their existence as round coins was of sufficient interest to qualify for mention in the chronicles.

Being a new coinage, and not as in England an extension of his predecessors', the Irish issues of John's reign qualified for a new type in John's own name. The king's head and crown are more realistically rendered than on English coins of the period. The designs on both sides are framed in triangles (perhaps an allusion to the supposed shape of the island). On the reverse is a sun of six wavy rays cupped in a crescent moon, with a small star in each corner of the triangle. The sun and moon were favoured badges of the Plantagenets; they had been prominently displayed, flanking the figure of the king, on the Great Seal of Richard I, supposedly deriving from the Counts of Toulouse, from whom his mother, Eleanor of Aquitaine, was descended. The minting of round halfpennies and farthings had of course rendered it unnecessary to produce fractions by cutting pennies, and this may have contributed to the decision not to use the voided cross of the English Short Cross type on the Irish reverse. The triangle on each side divided the inscription into three segments, *Ioha/nnes/Re*(sceptre)*x* and, e.g., *Robe/rd on/Dive*. From Edward I until Henry VIII the kings of England described themselves on their Irish coins correctly as lords of Ireland; but John (whose official documents were apt to refer to Ireland as a *regnum*) used his English royal title on the coins, as Henry III was also to do. Lawrence noted that the letter *X* on John's Irish pennies was formed of four wedges like that used in the contemporary English class Vc. On the fractions the reverse design is modified, the halfpence having a cross potent instead of a sun above the crescent and the farthings a sun alone.

The three mints of the triangle coinage were Dublin, Limerick and Waterford, all of which had participated in John's earlier Irish issues. A large majority of the triangle pennies carries the name of Roberd at Dublin, perhaps to be identified with Robert of Bedford, later bishop of Lismore, who is stated in the Irish Pipe Roll for 1210/11 to have paid a fine of a tun of wine for renouncing the office of *custos cuneorum*, a phrase that in the thirteenth century sometimes means moneyer as well as keeper of dies. At the head of the Dublin series, to judge by their superior workmanship, come a few coins with the name Iohan on the reverse, so rare that it is legitimate to wonder whether their dies could have been prepared as patterns with reference to de Gray's name, or even to the king's, rather than for the use of an ephemeral moneyer at the inauguration of the coinage. Changes in the design of the crown on halfpence suggest that, late in the Dublin coinage, Roberd was followed by a moneyer Willem, possibly without an overlap. Being absent from the Newry hoard, Willem's coins are very rare, as are others, also late, on which the name is Wilelm P. At Limerick the names are Willem and Wace, evidently in that order; at Waterford Willem only, his pennies very crude. Halfpence are known of all three mints, and of all moneyers except Iohan and Wilelm P., but farthings only of Dublin, by Roberd and Willem. Except for Roberd's halfpence, all the fractions are very rare. Halfpence show that the activity of Limerick and Waterford came late in the coinage, and again this is confirmed by the absence of coins of these mints from the Newry hoard. Dolley wondered whether the two names at Limerick might both have represented the same William Wace who was appointed bishop of Waterford in 1223 or indeed whether the four Williams named in the late stages of the coinage were all separate individuals.

There is no reason to doubt Wendover's association of this Irish coinage with the period of de Gray's authority. De Gray had been appointed Justiciar in June 1208, but the earliest record of his actual presence in Ireland is in January 1209. Dolley argued that a reference in the Close Roll for 1205 to *denarii Hiberniae* being sent from Northampton to Exeter, destined for France, related to John's new penny coinage, and accordingly proposed that this had been introduced in Dublin at the same time as the recoinage in England. This entry, however, is one of a series between 1204 and 1207 in which the usual phrase is *denarii ex thesauro Hiberniae*, referring to John's recourse to Ireland for finance after the loss of territories in France. When Henry III extended his new coinage to Ireland in 1251, he did not do so until the English recoinage was complete, and it is likely that John would have done the same. In November 1207 John ordered that his coin and no other should be current throughout Ireland but it is not necessary to interpret this as meaning that his new coinage was already in issue, or at least in contemplation, before de Gray's arrival since coins had been struck in Ireland by other issuers in the relatively recent past and, in any case, imported foreign coin should, as in England, be reminted. The finds from Newry and Sudbourne might have helped to fix the date of the introduction of the triangle coinage but unfortunately no record was made of either hoard. The length of the whole issue seems unlikely to have exceeded the two or three years that was the normal duration of a recoinage. If Robert of Bedford was the Dublin moneyer Roberd, replaced in 1210/11 by Willem late in the coinage, outside limits for the whole issue might be 1207/8 to c.1211/12.

Imitations

The high regard in which English coins were held on the Continent resulted in active imitation by foreign mints from early in the thirteenth century. Short Cross imitations range from accurate copies of English coins to adaptations and derivatives which clearly advertise their continental origin by inscription or elements of design. Most of the copies belong to the first quarter of the century, and most of the derivative types to the second.

The best of the copies have often been mistaken for authentic English issues, those of finer style resembling genuine coins of class V, and coarser examples having been taken for coins of those classes (VI and VIII) which, like themselves, have a bust roughly modelled on that of the recoinage type. The occurrence in Lawrence's lists under classes V, VI and VIII of moneyer names unverified by subsequent students can in many cases be explained by reference to imitations. Some of these copies are the work of highly skilled professional moneyers, capable of reproducing faithfully almost every detail. Others of good style, however, are betrayed by misspellings or odd letter forms (e.g. quite frequently *e* for *c* or a cross pommy *x*). Among the more emphatic clues to irregular origin are obverse die-links between reverses with different mint names (e.g. Rener of London with Davi of York), a recurrent feature in imitative series; and obvious deficiencies of weight or fineness. Most of the good copies weigh about the same as English coins, but some are up to 10 or 15 per cent. light. Few reach the sterling standard of fineness, silver content being usually between 80 and 90 per cent.

Imitation of the Short Cross type in Germany appears to have begun shortly after the start of the recoinage of 1205. There are very few copies based on classes I to IV, not surprisingly since the original issues of 1180 were old and mostly worn by the turn of the century while coins of classes II to IV are generally unattractive and poorly struck. The neat and well made coins of class V, however, provided ideal models for imitation. Most of the copies carry names of moneyers only found in class V, and many other features confirm the identity of their prototypes – a pointed bust, initial cross pommy, open *C*, pellet-centred *S*, division of *Re/x* and so on.

For these reasons six out of eight main groups of copies identified in a recent study clearly belong to the period of the recoinage or soon afterwards, but on the basis of a coin naming the Canterbury moneyer Henri, whose career began in class VIb, one of the other two groups must be dated, or at least have extended, after 1214. The remaining group includes dies not only in the names of the VIb moneyers Henri and Iun, but one based on the class VII moneyer Elis (*Leis*) which points to continuation of the series into the 1220s. This group also contains coins from several dies with the inscription *Londe Civitas* which were once thought to be official English issues without a moneyer's

The Short Cross Coinage

name, by analogy with the earliest Long Cross coins in 1247. Their identity is, however, established beyond doubt by a cinquefoil which forms the central ornament in the crown on many of the obverse dies of the group. This was the armorial device of the lords of Lippe, and was later to feature on Short Cross coins bearing the name of Bernhard III of Lippe (1229-65) or of his mint of Lemgo.

Like the *Londe Civitas* and related group from Lippe, it is likely that most of the other good Short Cross copies originated in Westphalia. Some of them are even overstruck on local German coins such as the *Kolnerpfennig* (seated bishop and cathedral), which were of a standard similar to the sterling – a practice which is difficult to explain except on the assumption that, since foreign coin was not permitted to circulate in England, foreign merchants arriving with sterling-type coins could thereby avoid the need for exchange or reminting. As evidenced by several hoards from France, English coins were increasingly acceptable abroad from the end of the twelfth century, and from John's reign there are records of extensive transactions with the Hanseatic merchants of the Netherlands and the Rhine.

A subsidy of 6,000 marks provided in 1207 by John to his nephew Otto, as king of the Romans, may have increased the familiarity of English coin in Germany and, more particularly, have influenced the adoption of the Short Cross type for an imperial coinage, mainly from Dortmund, issued by Otto IV (1209-18) and his successor Frederick II (1218-50). Most of the explicit German issues with some version of the Short Cross type, however, belong to the 1230s and 1240s, from a wide range of issuers, from the bishops of Munster (especially), the Archbishop of Cologne (at Herford), the counts of Swalenberg and Arnsberg, and several lesser figures. By the 1230s the issue of unacknowledged copies appears to have come to an end – a single exception with the name of the London moneyer Ledulf, appointed in 1230, is the only chronological outlier.

Sterlings of John's Irish triangle type, which circulated as part of the English currency, were not entirely neglected by German imitators. The few straight copies that were produced are not deceptive since they omit the moon below the sun on the reverse. Curiously, they do not seem to have been struck until many years after the issue of the originals, since the only recorded hoard provenances date from the 1260s (Brussels and Hildesheim). In the 1230s, however, an adaptation of the type had been struck by the bishop of Osnabruck, who enclosed the city's emblem of a Catherine wheel in an Irish triangle.

Mint Output

Mint accounts for London and Canterbury survive from most of the reign of Henry III. Prior to that there are fragmentary records of the direct profits of the *Cambium Totius Anglie* (CTA) or of the arrangements for its farm. The latter do not of course provide reliable information about amounts of coin struck, only about what may have been expected. Most of the mints were farmed out during John's renovation.

The Pipe Rolls, containing accounts of the keepers of the exchange of London and Canterbury, and certain other records yield extensive information about mint output from 1220 onwards. Silver purchased by the exchange was immediately passed to the mint to be coined. Seignorage assessed on silver purchased was charged at the rate of six pence in the pound, so that grossing up the stated profits of exchanging produces totals for mint output. The calculations are based on an assumption that 242 pence were struck from the pound of silver at this period. Figures so derived tally closely with some other records surviving in the Public Record Office relating to purchases of silver by the exchanges, amounts of coin minted and payments to keepers of the dies at the rate of one shilling for every hundred pounds struck. Where appropriate, Canterbury figures have been increased by 60 per cent to allow for the fact that the king's share excluded the three-eighths of the profits due to the archbishop. Separate accounts were normally rendered for London and Canterbury, but from 1225 to 1229 they were combined. The Close Rolls include detailed Canterbury figures from 1220 to 1222 which show that output was much higher from April to September than in the winter months and illustrate the seasonal nature of cross-channel trade at this period. Until 1242 Canterbury's output regularly exceeded London's, but in four of the five remaining years of the Short Cross coinage this position was reversed.

The earliest record of exchange profit relates to the first year of the new CTA, 1192/3, when £400 was returned, implying a minimum output of £16,000. A few years later (c.1197) London's output would have reached £16,700 and Canterbury's £21,200, perhaps indicating typical levels in the later years of Richard I. Farms of mint and exchange during John's recoinage, for twelve months from the summer of 1205, ranged from £200 for York and £160 (and a dole of Auxerre wine) for Winchester to £40 for Northampton and Oxford and £20 for Chichester. During the period of London's monopoly after 1208 output remained high. The fifteen months from March 1211 to December 1212 yielded exchange profits of £781 14s., equivalent to coinage of at least £31,000.

In total we have figures for almost twenty out of the last twenty-seven years of the Short Cross coinage, showing known aggregate output for London and Canterbury of some £667,000, equivalent to annual averages of £33,000 or 8 million pennies. In 1223-5 and 1229-34 the exchange was farmed. The few figures from the 1220s suggest lower average output than in the 1230s and 1240s; but even so the total Short Cross issues in the reign of Henry III must have been in excess of three-quarters of a million pounds, or in the order of two hundred million pence, and largely a reflection of growing continental demand for English wool.

	LONDON £	COMBINED £	CANTERBURY £
July 1220 – Nov. 1222	9,088		34,310
March 1225 – July 1226		21,881	
July 1226 – Mar. 1229		23,510	
July 1234 – July 1235	17,975		20,420
July 1235 – July 1236	18,732		28,534
July 1236 – July 1237	19,323		34,050
July 1237 – Feb. 1238	7,775		12,726
Feb. 1238 – Feb. 1239	10,944		17,831
Feb. 1239 – Feb. 1240	9,615		24,768
Feb. 1240 – Feb. 1241	21,756		29,155
Feb. 1241 – Feb. 1242	12,483		14,828
Feb. 1242 – Feb. 1243	23,321		16,932
Feb. 1243 – Feb. 1244	37,937		35,109
Feb. 1244 – Feb. 1245	29,497		19,025
Feb. 1245 – Apr. 1246	24,920		28,600
Apr. 1246 – Nov. 1247	38,985		27,200

The Short Cross Coinage

Calendar 1180 – 1247

1180   Council at Oxford resolved upon recoinage.
         Richard of Ilchester to France (5 March – July/August); returned with exchangers.
         Winchester mint damaged by fire (July).
         Treasure sent from Winchester to London, Northampton and Exeter for new coinage. Payments to special exchangers for 29 Aug.– 6 Oct. and from 11 Nov. onwards. New money alone to be current after Martinmas (11 Nov.).

1181   Philip Aimer sent home (May).
         Treasure to Worcester and Nottingham for exchanges (Pipe Roll 1180/1).

1182   Last payments to special exchangers (three to Easter, one to Michaelmas).

1189   Death of Henry II (6 July). Richard I crowned 3 Sept.; abroad from Dec.
         York: Geoffrey Plantagenet elected archbishop (10 Aug.).
         Bury: abbot's charter confirmed right to mint and die.
         Lichfield: grant of die to Bp. Hugh de Nonant of Coventry (12 Nov.).
         Canterbury: three dies granted to Abp. Baldwin (1 Dec.).

1193   Northampton exchange farmed (1192/3).

1194   Richard I in England for two months (13 March – 12 May).
         Shrewsbury mint and exchange opened; first account for Carreghova mine from 24 June.

1195   Winchester: exchange farmed (1193/5?).
         Durham: death of Bp. Hugh du Puiset (3 Mar.); king's receivers accounted for profits of mines and exchange (April – c. Dec.).
         Short Cross type introduced in Scotland by William the Lion.

1196   Durham: Bp. Philip of Poitiers elected (Nov. 1195/Jan. 1196; consecrated 20 April 1197).
         Norwich: £100 paid for maintaining exchange (1194-6).

1198   Northampton: Geoffrey FitzWalter paid to be relieved of office of moneyer (1197/8).

1199   Death of Richard I (6 April); John crowned 27 May.
         Bury: right to mint and die confirmed.

1201   York: Everard Bradex and others fined for malpractice (1200/1).

1204   Prohibition of clipped money from 13 Jan. 1205 (9 Nov.).

1205   Assize to regulate exchange of clipped money (26 Jan.).
         Chichester: grant of die to Bp. Simon FitzRobert (28 April); order for delivery 17 May; farm of king's dies from 1 Aug. (27 June).
         Bury: abbot's die and exchange granted (12 June).
         Northampton: exchange and four dies farmed for one year from 24 June.
         Canterbury: Abp. Hubert Walter died 12/13 July; succession disputed.

1206   Lincoln: accounts rendered for profit of exchange in 1204/5 and 1205/6.

1207   Canterbury: Pope Innocent III consecrated Abp. Stephen Langton (June); rejected by king.
         York: Abp. Geoffrey fled after quarrel with king.
         Writ (7 Oct.) to convene conference of moneyers at Westminster on 24 Oct.
         Ireland: King's coin alone to be current.

1208   England placed under papal interdict (23 March).
         Durham: death of Bp. Philip of Poitou (22 April).
         Ireland: John de Gray, bishop of Norwich, Justiciar (June).

1209   King John excommunicated (Oct.).

1210	John visited Ireland (June – Aug.).
1211	Dublin: Robert of Bedford fined for renouncing custody of the dies (1210/11).
	Bury: death of Abbot Samson (30 Dec.).
1212	John's expedition to North Wales.
	York: death of Abp. Geoffrey (18 Dec.).
1213	Philip II of France threatened to invade England.
	Rhuddlan castle fell to Llywelyn ap Iorwerth.
	Canterbury: Abp. Langton installed (temporalities 1 June).
1214	Interdict lifted (2 July).
	John defeated at Bouvines (27 July).
	Canterbury mint accounts resumed (9 March).
1215	Bury: Abbot Hugh de Northwold confirmed (11 March), accepted by John (9 June); minting rights confirmed (19 July).
	Magna Carta (15 June); king in Kent (Sept. – Dec.).
	York: Abp. Walter de Gray translated from Worcester (temporalities 19 Feb. 1216).
1216	Invasion by Prince Louis of France in May; claim abandoned in Sept.
	Death of John (18 Oct.); Henry III crowned (28 Oct.).
1217	Return of Louis (22 April); king in Kent (April – May); Treaty of Lambeth (11 Sept.).
	Durham: Bp. Richard Marsh elected (temporalities 29 June).
	Winchester: dies received on 1 Dec.
	York: dies received on 3 Dec.
	Canterbury: list of moneyers sworn on 6 Dec. includes Tomas de Valentina.
1218	York: archbishop to have dies (9 May).
	Durham: Abp. of York to notify names of officials to Exchequer; three dies sent to bishop (22 June).
	London: Elias of Worcester presented as moneyer (9 July).
	Canterbury: Salomon replaced Samuel, Roger of Rochester replaced Walter de Hee (list of 20 Jan.).
	Bury: Norman Ruffus replaced William of the Monastery as moneyer.
1221	London: three moneyers decline to admit Elias (1220/1).
	Bury: abbot not to compete with king's exchange at London (1 May).
1222	Round halfpence and farthings authorised (21 Feb.) from 18 April; dies issued 17 Feb.and 31 March.
	London: Elias and Terric le Chaungeor listed as moneyers (1221/2).
	Canterbury: John Chiche listed as moneyer vice Eudo Chiche.
1223	Bury: abbot restricted to coinage for own use.
	Letters patent announce that exchange is confined to London and Canterbury (10 Feb.).
1226	Canterbury: Osmund Polre fined to take Salemun's (?) die, but John Turte has it.
	Bury: exchange profits recorded in Pipe Roll.
1227	Henry III declared himself of age.
1228	Canterbury: Abp. Langton died (9 July).
1229	Bury: restriction on abbot's coinage discontinued; Hugh appointed bishop of Ely, succeeded by Abbot Richard de Insula (elected 5 June).
	Canterbury: Abp. Richard Grant appointed (temporalities 24 March).
1230	London: Adam of Bentley, Ricard de Neketon and Ledulf the Teuton appointed moneyers, replacing Ilger the Goldsmith, Radulf de Frowik and Terric le Chaungeor.
	Canterbury: William the Tailor took die of Simon Chiche deceased (April).

The Short Cross Coinage

1231 Canterbury: death of Abp. Grant (3 Aug.).
1232 Henry III assumed personal rule.
1233 Bury: death of Richard de Insula (29 Aug.).
Canterbury: Abp. Edmund of Abingdon (temp. 4 Feb.).
1234 Bury: Henry of Rushbrook elected abbot (2 Feb.).
1235 Canterbury: Robert of Canterbury took die of Tomas de Valencen deceased (Nov.)
London: Ricard de Neketon dead; Richard Bachelor fined to have his place (9 April).
1237 Nicholas of St. Albans sworn as moneyer for London and Canterbury (30 June); William the Tailor and Robert of Canterbury given 100s. per annum to relinquish dies (24 June); John Turte dead (by March).
1240 Canterbury: death of Abp. Edmund (16 Nov.).
1241 Canterbury: Abp. Boniface elected (temporalities post 27 Feb. 1244); John FitzRobert's die surrendered (14 Feb.).
Exchequer challenge to appointment of Nicholas of St. Albans at London and Canterbury (1240/1).
1242 Richard Abel presented as die-cutter (Michaelmas term) until 2 Feb. 1243.
Farm of foundries at London and Canterbury to Nicholas of St. Albans confirmed (by 3 May).
1247 Council of Oxford (April) decided on reform of coinage; letters patent (27 July); new (Long Cross) coinage introduced (1 Nov.).

PENNIES (1180 – 1247)
AND FRACTIONS (1222 ONLY)

Penny, wt. 22.3 gr. (1.44g.); halfpenny and farthing (both class VIIa only), 11.2 gr. (0.72g.) and 5.6 gr. (0.36 g.)

PENCE

Obv. Bearded bust of king facing, with pearled diadem or crown; dexter hand holding sceptre; linear inner circle; *henricus Rex* (sceptre usually breaks *R/ex*). Rev. Within a beaded border a short voided cross, the ends pommy; a small cross pommy in each quarter; around, name of moneyer *.on.* mint, preceded by a cross patty or (in classes Va and VIII) a cross pommy.

Class I (1180-9). Facing bust appears to be turned slightly to spectator's left (with more curls to sinister than to dexter). Five pearls in the crown. Style gradually becomes standardised and, latterly, coarser. London, Carlisle (*Cardu*, Ib and Ic only), Exeter, Lincoln (*Nico*, Ib and Ic only), Northampton, Oxford (Ib and Ic only), Wilton (Ia and Ib only), Winchester, Worcester (*Wiric*, Ib and Ic only), and York (*Everwi*).

Ia. Experimental early issues, with inconsistent numbers of curls. Often square *C* and *E* and round *m* on earlier varieties (Ia1-3). *N* sometimes reversely barred in Ia3 and 4. Usually stop before *Rex*; some early rev. dies lack stops by *on*. All quite rare except Ia5. London, Exeter (rare), Northampton, Wilton (rare), Winchester and York.

Ia1. Linear outer circle, with spaced pellets. *N* with three serifs. Usually *Re/x*.

Ia2. Normal beaded outer circle (henceforward). *N* with three serifs. *Re/x* (rarely) or *R/ex*.
Ia3. New rounded *c* fronted by half-moons; *e* similar, or square. *N* with four serifs. *R/ex* henceforward. Obv. dies of Ia3 are much rarer than revs.
Ia4. *X* with serifs; no square letters. *N* with four serifs (sometimes reversed); *c* and *e* with half-moons.
Ia5. Curls 2-3 to 6-9; bust as on earlier varieties. No square letters or serif *X*; *c*, *e* and *N* as in Ia4.
Ib. Settled portrait, with curls 2-5. Normally stop before *R/ex*. Mints of Ia plus Carlisle, Lincoln, Oxford and Worcester.
Ib1. *N* with four serifs. Neat lettering.
Ib2. *N* with three serifs; thicker letters. Looser curls. Also rare Ib1/2 mules.
Ic. Broader bust, curls less regular. Coarser style. *N* with three serifs. Normally no stop before *R/ex*. Mints of Ib, less Wilton; Carlisle, Exeter, Northampton and Worcester are all rare, Oxford VR.
Class II (1189/90). Facing head with no hair on cheeks (between curls and beard); small, thin curls, 2-2 or in clusters; bust set low, with little or no neck or collar; normally five pearls in crown; often pellet eyes. London and Canterbury dies have long whiskers on chin; other mints, shorter hairs or tiny pellets. Wide *N* with four serifs; *D* with round loop. On early dies (i), a cross pommy *X*; later (ii) normal *X*. Sometimes *Re/x* (Lincoln and York). Also some VR mules Ic/II and II/Ic. London (i, ii), Canterbury (ii only, rare), Lichfield (*Lihefl*; one pair of dies, i, ER), Lincoln (i only, VR), Worcester (ii only, ER), York (i only, VR).
Class III (1190-c.1193). Beard of curved lines from curls to chin; usually seven pearls in band of crown; blob eyes except on some later dies. *N* with four serifs. Wide letters; ligation begins. London, Canterbury, Carlisle (Ic/III mule and IIIb only, VR), Exeter (IIIb only, VR), Northampton (VR), Winchester, York (rare; also ER Ic/III mule).
IIIa (Allen IIIab1). Many small, wiry side curls in clusters each side; whiskers neat, thin and tiny. Some have five pearls in crown. Scarcer than IIIb.
IIIb (Allen IIIab2). Two or three principal curls each side, often enclosing smaller curls, and sometimes with extra curls above or below; some late dies have pellets in lower curls. Beard less regular; whiskers often thicker.
Class IV (c.1194-1204). Beard consists of pellets randomly distributed about the lower face; coarse bust; usually annulet eyes. Wide letters (*A*, *N*, etc.). Ligation and misspellings frequent. London, Canterbury, Carlisle (rare; IVa, b only), Durham (*Dur*, *Duno*; rare; IVa, b only), Northampton or Norwich (all VR), Shrewsbury (*Salop*; rare; IVa, b only), Winchester (IVa only) and York.
IVa. Normally two, three or four thick curls each side; sometimes pellets in lower curls. Face with pointed or rounded chin. Crown of seven pearls. Colon stops (by *on*) on some rare early rev. dies (Lawrence 'IIb', Brand 'IVa*'): London, Canterbury, Winchester (VR) and York only.
IVb Normally a single curl, or two in parallel, each side. Crown usually of seven pearls, but of five spaced pearls on later dies (sometimes with several curls). Rev. initial cross occasionally crude pommy.
IVc. Letter *S* reversed. Crown with five spaced pearls on a thin line. Usually single curls as in IVb. Four mints only (London, Canterbury, *No* and York); all rare.

The Short Cross Coinage

Class V (1205-c.1210). Smaller coins from carefully made dies of good style, with neater portrait (beard of small strokes) and regular lettering. Normally five large pearls in band of crown. Occasional ornamented letters (Va2-b2). London, Canterbury, Bury St. Edmunds (*Sadmu, Sed*, etc.; Vb, c only), Carlisle (Vb only), Chichester (*Cices*; Vb/a and Vb only), Durham (*Dure*), Exeter (Va, b only), Ipswich (*Gipe*; Vb, c only), Lincoln (*Nicole*), Lynn (*Lene*; Vb only), Northampton (Vb, c only), Norwich, Oxford (Vb only), Rochester (*Rove*; Vb only), Winchester, York.

Va. Usually letter S reversed and initial cross pommy.
Va1. Experimental portraits. *R/ex*. London and Canterbury only; all VR.
   A. Side curls curved lines. Initial cross patty (also mules with cross pommy, Va1/2). Var. has sceptre to right, and forward *S* followed by stop.
   B. 'Ringlet' side curls (small annulets without pellets in centre). Initial cross pommy. *S* reversed, or normal *S* followed by stop.
Va2. Reversed *S* (except on a few very late rev. dies); initial cross always pommy. Two or three curls each side, enclosing pellets. Three bust types: A, as Va1(B) but with small points in the curls; B, broad portraits with large round curls; C, with thinner, pointed face. *R/ex* or *Re/x*. London, Canterbury plus seven mints; Durham and Exeter are rare; Chichester, 'Vb1/Va' mules only (VR).
Vb. Normal *S*, usually with central pellet; initial cross patty. *R/ex*, or *Re/x* (often with pellets by *x*). London, Canterbury plus fourteen mints; Lynn rare.
Vb1. Flat-topped *R*. Two round curls each side, often with small third curl below. Also mules 'Vb1/a2' and (VR) Va2/b1.
Vb2. Round-topped *R*. Curls normally 2-2.
Vb3. Broken eyes. Curls 2-2. *R/ex* only.
Vc. *X* as flat saltire of four wedges. Rounder bust; curls 2-2; eyes usually oval, often solid. Normally *R/ex*. London, Canterbury plus seven mints; Bury, Northampton and York are rare.

Class VI (c.1210-1217/8). Coins of variable style, loosely developed from class V. Normally five small pearls in crown. Curls 2-2 (to VIc1) or 3-3 (from VIc2). *X* in *R/ex* is quatrefoil (except VIa1). Initial cross patty. London (all except VIx), Canterbury (from VIb2, including VIx), Bury (*Santad*, etc.; from VIc1), Durham (VIa2 only), Winchester (VIc3 only), York (VIc3 only).

VIa. Similar to Vc except for letter *X*. Curls 2-2. Five (usually small) pearls in crown. Small face, chin usually rounded. Heavy lettering, with crescent-and-spur *e* as in Vc.
VIa1. Flat saltire *X*. London only.
VIa2. Quatrefoil *X* henceforward. London and Durham (rare) only.
VIb. Taller lettering, with new (rounder) *e*. Stop before *R/ex* increasingly found. Curls 2-2. Coarse whiskers. Eyes often blobs.
VIb1. Face and chin rounded, as in VIa. London only.
VIb2. Narrow, elongated face; curls high up; usually pellet on chin. Coarse style. London and Canterbury only.
VIc. Face more naturally shaped, with rounded or pointed chin, and finer whiskers; open tear-shaped eyes. Large pearls in crown. Some have stop before *R/ex* (decreasingly after VIc1).
VIc1. Curls 2-2. Large, plain lettering; *c* and *e* with longer fronts. London, Canterbury, Bury.
VIx. Canterbury only. Large face based on class Va-b; curls 2-2. Special lettering. *Re/x*. VR; also ER mules VIc/VIx (usually with obv. of VIc1).

VIc2.   Curls 3-3 (ER var. has 2-2). Ornamental letters. Also rare mules VIc1/2. London, Canterbury, Bury.

VIc3.   Curls 3-3. No ornamental letters. Also mules VIc2/3 and 3/2. Mints as VIc2 plus Winchester (ER) and York (VR).

VId.   New lettering with slender uprights; often pellet-barred *N*. No stop before *R/ex*; stops on rev. variable. Bust usually large, with curls 3-3 (rarely 2-2). Rare; also rare mules VIc2/d (ER), VIc3/d and VId/c3. London, Canterbury, Bury.

Class VII (1217/8-c.1242). Face generally more rounded than in classes V and VI, and set low down; curls usually 3-3 and enclosing pellets. Normally no stops by *on*. London, Canterbury and Bury throughout class; Durham VIIa1 only. Also halfpence and farthings of London in VIIa only.

VIIa.   (1217/8-1222). Carefully struck coins; neat portrait and lettering (with pointed *A*). Some ornamental letters (VR) in VIIa1 and 2. Circles on rev. at first neatly grained, later of coarse pellets.

VIIa1. (North B). Small, neat lettering (*A* with wide top bar). Bust often very small. Beard of tiny strokes; tear-shaped eyes (no. 1). Also VR mules VIIa1/VId (Canterbury only) and VId/VIIa.

VIIa2. (North A). Rounder face, with prominent chin and bristly beard of long vertical whiskers; shaped eyes (1). Some larger letters (*S* usually with crescent serifs, as occasionally in VIIa1).

VIIa3. (North C and D). Larger face, becoming squarer; beard less clearly marked. Eyes in C shaped (1) or annulets (2); in D, oval (3). Larger lettering. Multiple stops (up to six) on some rev. dies (D).

VIIb.   (1222-c.1236). Coarser work; the face set low, with open mouth and little or no chin. Rectangular *A*; *H* for *M*, except on earliest dies. Lettering still small but less compact (cross on crown usually points to centre or left of *e*). Odd single stops on some revs.

VIIb1. Eyes shaped (1), or annulets (2). No pellets in curls. *R* has wedge-shaped upright.

VIIb2. Fractured eye punch (4). Pellet on chin. Often pellets in curls. Sometimes a small bust with pointed chin.

VIIb3. Large crude face; no pellet on chin. No pellets in curls. Fractured eyes (4).

VIIb4. As 3, but eyes thick annulets (5). *R* with nearly straight-sided upright and thin serif.

VIIc.   (c.1236-c.1242). Large, degenerate face. Tall lettering. Occasional stops on rev. Chevron-barred *A* sometimes in VIIc1 and 2.

VIIc1. No points in curls. Thick annulet eyes (5).

VIIc2. Points in curls on most dies; neater portrait; sometimes a pellet on the chin. Eyes annulets (5, 6), sometimes with pupils (7), or blobs (8).

VIIc3. Points in curls; annulet eyes (2); heavy brows; long, plain nose; beard more pointed. Tall, narrow *N*. Thick initial cross. Also ER mules VIIc3/VIII.

Class VIII (c.1242-1247). Tapered face. Initial cross pommy (except VIIIai). Stops (single, colon or triple) frequent, especially before *R/ex* and *on*. Some have Gothic *n*. London, Canterbury (VIIIb and c only), Bury (*Sant Ed*).

VIIIa. Tall, plain lettering; *X* with bent arms; open round *c* and *e*. Eyes usually annulets, sometimes between two eyelids. Curls 2-2. Two varieties of reverse – i (Jones VIIIA): Initial cross patty, London only; also mules VIIc/VIIIa, all ER. ii (Jones VIIIB1): Initial cross pommy (henceforward), London (VR) and Bury (ER) only.

The Short Cross Coinage

VIIIb. (Jones VIIIB2). Short letters, hollowed uprights, *c* and *e* closed, *X* of four wedges. Angled face of fair style, with clear outline. Eyes annulets (or blobs). Curls vary. Also mules of London, VIIIa/b (VR), and Canterbury, VIIc/VIIIb (ER).

VIIIc. (Jones VIIIB3). Thick letters with *X* pommy. Degenerate bust, of coarse style; bulbous nose; usually solid eyes; two thick curls. Often carelessly struck.

HALFPENCE AND FARTHINGS (1222 only) resemble pence of late VIIa, except for crescent-and-pellet instead of cross before rev. inscription. London only. ER.

RHUDDLAN
PENCE ONLY (1180s –1210s?)

Four moneyers consecutively. Local dies. *Rula(n)*.

Halli. Brand class i – Head based on English class I, with crescent curls. Extra pellet in crown. *N* reversed. Initial cross patty.

Class iia – As i but *e* for *c*; *N* reversed. Initial cross pommy. Rev. legend retrograde. VR (also ER i/iia mule).

Tomas. Class ii – *e* for *c*. Initial cross pommy of three forms: iib, normal; iic, bottom pellet in inner circle; iid, as iic but with extra central pellet. Stop after *on* often omitted.

Simon(d). Class iie – as ii of Tomas, but rev. cross patty. Rare.

Class iii – Head based on English class V, with broken annulet curls and normal crown (iiic). Normal *N* and *C*. Rare early vars. have old curls (iiib) or crown with extra pellet (iiia). Rev. cross pommy. One or both stops by *on* usually omitted.

Class iv – Two crude obv. dies as class iii but with round chin and *e* for *c*; one has *Ri/ex,* the other *N* reversed. Rev. initial cross pommy; legend retrograde, no stops, *Simod*. VR.

Henricus. Class v – Crude head (three dies). Rev. cross patty; stops by *on*. VR (also ER mule iv/v).

IRELAND
PENCE (C. 1207/8-11?)

Weight and standard as in England. Obv. Crowned head of king in triangle, sceptre in dexter hand; a quatrefoil to right. *Ioha//nnes//Re/x*. Rev. Within a triangle, six-rayed sun in a crescent moon; a small star in each angle. Inscription in three segments, a cross potent above each.

Dublin (*Diveli*): Iohan, ER; Roberd; Willem, VR; Wilelm P., VR.

Limerick (*Lime*): Willem, VR; Wace, ER.

Waterford (*Vat*): Willem, ER.

Round halfpence (all moneyers except Iohan and Wilelm P.) and farthings (Dublin only, Roberd and Willem), of similar type, were not current in England.

CHAPTER II

1247 - 1278

THE LONG CROSS COINAGE

The reform of the coinage in 1247 was one of the more effective initiatives of an increasingly disordered reign. Henry III was ill-equipped for the responsibilities of kingship. Although cultured and devout, his approach to the administration of government was confused and his foreign policy unrealistic. He was also insensitive to the aspirations of his barons, who were looking to consolidate the gains of Magna Carta and to exercise some control over an exasperating king and his foreign advisers. Henry rebuilt the abbey church at Westminster of Edward the Confessor, whom he revered, but his lavish tastes left him permanently short of money. Until 1258 he remained generally in control of affairs, but that year saw the first major constitutional crisis of his reign. The death in 1250 of the Emperor Frederick II, who had held the kingdoms of Germany and Sicily, had led Henry's brother, Richard of Cornwall, to put himself forward as a candidate for the first, while the king sought the second for his younger son Edmund. At the same time Henry was encouraged by associates of his queen, Eleanor of Provence, to pursue his claims in France. In due course he was obliged to treat for peace with Louis IX and to come to terms with his own disaffected nobility. By the Provisions of Oxford and Westminster in 1258-9 Henry conceded administrative reform, but the settlement did not hold and in 1264 civil war broke out. The king was captured by the forces of his brother-in-law, Simon de Montfort, at Lewes in May 1264 and for more than a year government was in effect conducted by de Montfort in the king's name. By including in the process both knights from the shires and burgesses from the towns, de Montfort is often credited with having laid the foundations of the English parliamentary system. In August 1265, however, he was killed at the Battle of Evesham. As a result of the settlement that followed, the king's son Edward assumed responsibility for government while the involvement of Henry himself in public affairs virtually ceased during the last years of his life.

None of these events, although of lasting importance in the development of the English constitution, had much impact on the growing prosperity of the kingdom. Largely thanks to the wool trade, the balance of payments remained in healthy surplus, generating an abundant supply of silver to the English mints, as it had done in the later Short Cross period. By the 1240s, however, much of the currency was in a decrepit state. No previous type of English coin had remained current for so long. Some of it still survived from the recoinage of Henry II in the 1180s, and a larger element which went back to the renovation of 1205 was already elderly. Added to the cumulative effects of wear and tear was the opportunity for clipping presented by the poor striking of so many pennies of the later Short Cross period. Matthew Paris records that consideration was given at the Council of Oxford in 1247 as to whether the coinage should be debased in fineness or reduced in weight, which suggests that the potential for profit from a new coinage may have been an important motive; but it was certainly true that the bad condition of the currency had rendered a recoinage necessary. To counter the threat of clipping, the king therefore ordered a new type to be introduced on which the cross was to extend to the edge of the reverse. No coin would be acceptable if any part of the cross had been clipped away. Another advantage of the new type was that the long voided cross made it easier to cut pennies into halves and quarters – although this contributed to further postponement of their replacement by round halfpence and farthings. An unintended consequence, however, of the extended cross was to reduce the room available for the inscription. Now there was barely space for three letters in each of the four segments, and this led to the frequent linking of two or three consecutive letters (or even of a letter and a limb of the cross), which can sometimes make the name of mint or moneyer difficult to read. Furthermore, because of the omission of a small cross before the moneyer's name, as had been used since time immemorial, it is not always immediately apparent where the inscription begins.

EXAMPLE OF LIGATION OF LETTERS

WAL TER ONC ANT

Wal/ter/onC/ant

Three chronicles illustrated their record of the recoinage with drawings of the new type in the margin. Although the long cross on the reverse was its defining characteristic, the obverse design also differed in a number of respects from the pre-1247 type: the circle within the legend was now beaded, but the most significant change was that there was no sceptre to accompany the king's head, which was thus surrounded by an unbroken inscription. This included, for the only time in English coinage before the sixteenth century, a regnal numeral, *henricus Rex (Anglie) Terci'(us)*, or later *III'*, emphasizing that this was a new coinage of the present king rather than a continuation of the coinage of his grandfather Henry II. A sceptre had featured on all coins since the later years of Henry I and it may well now have been deliberately omitted in order further to differentiate the obverses of the new coins from those that were being withdrawn. That this was the case is suggested by the fact that in 1250, almost as soon as the recoinage was complete, a sceptre was again incorporated into the design. Thereafter the obverse type remained unchanged in its essentials for the rest of the reign. However, not long after Edward's accession the curls which had been depicted in various stylized forms since the 1180s were replaced by more realistic locks of hair; but since these early coins of Edward's reign (1272-1307) were no more than a continuation of his father's issues, Henry's name (and numeral) remained, immobilized in the same way as had been that of Henry II throughout the Short Cross coinage.

The first official notice of the new coinage records a grant made by the king in June 1247 to Richard of Cornwall under which profits were to be shared equally between them for five years. Richard is reputed to have been the richest man in England and it is evident from an entry six weeks later that an essential element of his contribution would be the provision of finance. In consideration of a loan of ten thousand marks (equivalent to 1.6 million pence) Richard was now to have his share of the profits extended to twelve years. The first of the new coins were issued in November 1247. As in all recoinages of the later middle ages, minting was resumed at London slightly sooner than elsewhere. Nicholas of St. Albans, who had held a monopoly of the royal coinage for the previous five years, remained in charge at London and Canterbury at the outset, but the earliest variety, which carries no mint name, was confined to London. When Canterbury and then Bury, the two other mints of Short Cross class VIII, soon joined in, the legend had to be modified slightly so as to include an abbreviated place-name. This was, however, only a temporary solution since the need for a network of mints around the country and the enlistment of many more moneyers must, as in 1180 and 1205, have been evident from the start, and the moneyer-plus-mint formula was soon restored. Eight new mint-names then appear. A writ issued in February 1248 for the opening of mints at Lincoln, Northampton, Winchester, Norwich and Exeter required their moneyers and other officials to report for swearing in at the Exchequer in early March. All these mints began to coin in this phase, as did Gloucester, Oxford and York. Writs have not been found for these three, but one dated July, relating to the archbishop's mint, implies that by then a royal mint at York had already been authorised.

Before the end of 1248 the crowding of the obverse inscription was eased by substituting the Roman numeral *III* for *Terci* and the names of a second tranche of regional mints are found with the new type. Instructions had been issued in October 1248 to the bailiffs of nine more towns to prepare for the recoinage. As with the February mints, four trustworthy and prudent men were to be elected by each town to serve as moneyers, four others as keepers of the dies, two goldsmiths as assayers and one as clerk – all these to report to the Exchequer in the first week of November. The towns in question were Bristol, Carlisle, Hereford, Ilchester, Newcastle, Nottingham, Shrewsbury, Wallingford and Wilton. No coins are known of Nottingham, but mints were put into operation at the other eight. All five of the February mints had participated in both the 1180 and 1205 recoinages, as had Oxford and York, but only Carlisle of those authorised in October. Wilton had contributed in 1180, while Hereford, Ilchester, Newcastle and Wallingford had not done so since the first coinage of Henry II. The relative importance of individual towns was changing. Most noteworthy are the departure of Ipswich, which had had a substantial mint up to the twelfth century, and the return of Bristol, now of increasing commercial influence.

More is known from official records about the moneyers of the Long Cross coinage than those of earlier periods, and this body of evidence has now been systematically surveyed by Churchill. References to the appointment or replacement of many of the London and Canterbury moneyers occur in the Pipe, Patent, Close or Memoranda Rolls, and a manuscript in the British Museum (Hargrave 313) records the names of all the officials at the sixteen royal mints opened for the recoinage in 1248-50. Prior to the 1240s moneyers evidently had some direct concern with the issue of coins bearing their own names, but under Henry III they seem to have functioned usually as sole or joint contractors. All the regional mints commissioned in 1248 had four moneyers in office, regardless of the volume of coinage expected. At London Nicole was in sole charge until the recoinage was well under way. He was then joined by three others, but a regular complement of six London moneyers was not established until the middle of the 1250s. At Canterbury the number was also raised to six at this time, excluding one accredited to the archbishop (who shared premises with the royal moneyers, as obverse die-links demonstrate). No attempt was made any longer to identify the coins of moneyers with the same name, as had been done in earlier coinages, the omission of initials being another casualty of the shortage of space caused by the extension of the limbs of the cross. Thus there is no means of differentiating the coins of the two Williams at Wilton, or of the Roberts and Williams at Canterbury in the 1250s. The office of moneyer was increasingly seen as a source of income for royal officials with other duties rather than as an active commitment to the production of coin.

In the later 1250s the senior official at London was William of Gloucester, the king's goldsmith. In 1257, in addition to his role as moneyer, he was appointed warden of the exchanges of London and Canterbury as well as being entrusted with responsibility for the gold coinage introduced in that year. In 1260 the king set up a judicial enquiry into the affairs of the mint, apparently because of disputes between the moneyers, but partly perhaps because the coinage was proving more profitable to the moneyers than to the king. In the upshot, from January 1262 William ceased to hold the office of warden, which was accountable for the king's profit, and from this date wardens began to account to the crown for profits of the mint foundry as well as for the seignorage. At some point in the 1260s the role of moneyer at London seems to have reverted to a monopoly, in the hands of Reginald of Canterbury, with only one moneyer at a time at each of the other mints also. By the end of the Long Cross coinage the name of the moneyer had thus become redundant and its removal from the reverse in Edward's reform of 1279 was no more than a recognition of the different system of control already in place.

The recoinage must have been a highly lucrative exercise for the moneyers and correspondingly unattractive to holders of old coin, which was received at the exchange by weight and not by tale. In addition to the king's seignorage of 6d. in the pound, 10d. was deducted to cover the traditional minting charge of 6d. plus 4d. to compensate for the supposedly inferior quality of the old money. An examination made at the Exchequer in March 1248 had shown that, although the new coin was not more than 6d. less than pure, the old coin was 10d. short and this valuation was to be applied to all old money submitted for exchange; but since modern assay indicates the old coin to have been of similar sterling fineness to the new it seems that the deficiency was due to loss of weight, already allowed for in the terms of the exchange. Owners of Short Cross coin wanting immediate exchange would thus in effect have been charged twice for the shortfall, although subject to some delay they retained the right to pay for their own assay in order to obtain a better rate.

During the Long Cross period the main mints themselves were usually farmed out to the moneyers but, as in the later Short Cross period, the amounts struck at London and Canterbury can be calculated from the profits of the Exchange at 6d. in the pound on purchases of silver. Between 1247 and 1278 these two mints between them coined nearly £1.4 million, or around 340 million pence. In the full flood of the recoinage, the thirty-two months from November 1247 to July 1250, London struck £190,000 and Canterbury £100,000. Thereafter there was a gradual decline in output, although the two main mints continued to coin on a considerable scale throughout the 1250s and 1260s. For nine years from 1252 Canterbury's output exceeded that of London, as it had done in the 1220s and 1230s, but the position was reversed thereafter. During the second half of 1264 the mint at Canterbury may have been closed altogether, perhaps as a consequence of the king's captivity. After 1270 its output fell away sharply, with further periods of inactivity in 1272/3 and 1274/8. From December 1270 until the end of the Long Cross coinage in November 1278, while Canterbury contributed less than £2,000 in total, London produced over £100,000, perhaps around half of it during the last six months. Coinage at Bury was maintained throughout the period and, although not continuous in the same sense as at the major mints, it is represented in all the main classes. The bishops of Durham, not having had their own dies since 1218, did not obtain them again until 1253, after the recoinage was over. From this date onwards Durham features as a regular if sometimes intermittent mint, like Bury, but its role remained a very minor one during the Long Cross period and as yet gave no promise that it would outpace Bury under the Edwards.

Although none of the seventeen regional mints commissioned in 1248 was in operation for as long as two years, by the time that their work was completed they had produced collectively nearly half of the total output during the recoinage. In the Hilary Term of 1250 (January - February) the Lord Treasurer's Remembrancer recorded that the mint-towns were to restore the assays provided to them, the sheriffs were to return the dies to the Exchequer without delay, and the moneyers and other mint officials were to report and answer for their activities at various dates from April to June. All the recoinage mints were probably closed at about the same time. In July warrants were issued to the sheriffs to collect outstanding monies owed by moneyers and other officials of each of them. By a fortunate chance a detailed account relating to one of the provincial mints has survived. In the Shrewsbury Borough Records is a roll recording the number of assays made, and their dates, between 2 February 1249 and 9 February 1250. In all 231 separate assays were made and £7,227 of coin minted, monthly totals ranging from £929 in July to £161 in November. Brand's analysis of 304 coins of Shrewsbury revealed that 37 obverse dies and 86 reverses had been used in their production. On the assumption that very few of the original dies were not represented in the sample, average output would have been around 45,000 coins per obverse and approaching 20,000 per reverse die.

The recoinage figures show the currency of England at the time of the recoinage to have been well in excess of half a million pounds sterling, or approaching 150 million silver pennies. Handling large sums of money in a single denomination of relatively modest value would often have been inconvenient and it is perhaps surprising, in view of its prosperity, that England was slow to adopt the use of larger coins which came into being elsewhere to help finance the commercial expansion of Europe in the thirteenth century. Although the Venetians had been producing their *grosso* since 1202, their old *denaro* had shrunk so much that the *grosso* of twenty-four *denari* weighed little more than 2g., equivalent to less than 2d. English. The French *gros tournois*, introduced in 1266, was a much larger coin, but an English groat did not appear until 1279 and only became established in the second half of the fourteenth century. Certain pieces with the English Long Cross sterling type but on larger flans have occasionally been described as double pennies; but the names of Canterbury moneyers and signs of gilding suggest that they might have been made as souvenirs related to the shrine of St. Thomas. When major sums were involved silver ingots weighing a mark or more were sometimes used. With the greater supply of newly mined silver to thirteenth-century Europe, and before gold coinage had become generally available in the fourteenth century, the use of such ingots for substantial payments was increasingly frequent. Ingots were often produced and authenticated at official mints; one of the few surviving examples, made in London in 1278, carries impressions from coin dies of the last months of the Long Cross coinage.

First of the major European gold coins of the later middle ages were the florins of Florence, introduced in 1252. It is true that the Emperor Frederick II had struck a magnificent gold *augustale* of classical style in 1231, but this was a political gesture, and confined to mints in the south of Italy, an area where, as in Sicily and southern Spain, familiarity with gold coinage had been maintained through Muslim influence. Only five years after the arrival of the florin, Henry III was in 1257 the first to essay a gold coinage in northern Europe, but it was struck partly for presentation purposes, and perhaps also to convert a store of gold into more negotiable form, although attempts to introduce it into currency did not succeed. Late in his reign Louis IX (1226-70) made a similar experiment, with his *écu d'or*, but it was no more successful than Henry's, and a regular French gold coinage was only established under Philip IV (1285-1315) towards the end of the century.

By the middle of the thirteenth century the English sterling had an established reputation in northern Europe and the new Long Cross type soon became familiar in neighbouring lands. Within a few years recoinages had been carried out in Ireland and Scotland, and the use and imitation of English Long Cross sterlings had become widespread on the Continent. Although Richard of Cornwall's contract in 1247 had covered England, Ireland and Wales the recoinage was at first confined to England. No mint operated in medieval Wales after Rhuddlan in the Short Cross period, and the nearest sources of new coin in 1248 were Shrewsbury, Hereford, Gloucester and Bristol. In 1251, however, a recoinage was organized in Ireland where the new coins, while continuing with the distinctive triangular frame on the obverse, reproduced the English long cross on the reverse and quickly became integrated with English money in the sterling currency area. After a little over two years the Dublin mint was closed. Its only other contribution to the Long Cross coinage was a very limited issue in 1276-8.

The Long Cross Coinage

In Scotland a recoinage was launched in 1250, involving fifteen mints mostly situated in the lowland areas of the east and south. While retaining the traditional profile bust and stars in the quarters of the reverse, the new Scottish coins copied the English long voided cross, so assisting the continued interchangeability of the two coinages in both countries. Berwick, the border town at the mouth of the Tweed, now became the principal Scottish mint, displacing Roxburgh further up the river. The later Long Cross issues from Scotland differ more obviously from their predecessors than do their English counterparts, and can thus provide a useful reference point for the relative chronology of hoards buried from the mid-1260s onwards.

Classification

Long Cross pennies of the period from 1247 to the 1260s are the most abundant of all English medieval coins as a result of the discovery in 1908 of a vast hoard in a house on the Rue d'Assaut in the ancient quarter of Brussels. Buried c. 1264, this consisted of about 150,000 silver coins of which the British portion, purchased *in toto* by the firm of A.H. Baldwin, amounted originally to more than 80,000. However, Long Cross coins have

MINTS AND CLASSES OF THE LONG CROSS COINAGE

	I	II	III	IV	V	VI	VII
London	x	x	x	x	x	x	x
Canterbury	x	x	x	x	x		
Bury St. Edmunds	x	x	x	x	x	x	x
Exeter		x	x				
Gloucester		x	x				
Lincoln		x	x				
Northampton		x	x				
Norwich		x	x				
Oxford		x	x				
Winchester		x	x				
York royal		x	x				
Bristol			x				
Carlisle			x				
Hereford			x				
Ilchester			x				
Newcastle			x				
Shrewsbury			x				
Wallingford			x				
Wilton			x				
York, abp.			x				
Durham					x	x	x
Dublin					x		x

been less frequently encountered than the Edwardian sterlings that followed, since a group of several tens of thousands of coins from the Brussels hoard had until recently remained largely intact. The largest English hoard of the period was that found at Colchester in 1969, containing 14,000 coins. Of these some 11,300 were regular issues from English mints ending c. 1256, with a later addition of a group straight from the Bury mint in the 1270s. There were also 289 English coins struck in Dublin, 489 of the contemporary Scottish Long Cross type, and a few continental imitations. Perversely, the existence of such a huge quantity of material resulted in relative neglect of the Long Cross series during the twentieth century, because of the great labour involved in sorting, identifying and recording it. But Archibald's detailed report (2001) on the Colchester hoard has provided new impetus to the subject, and work on producing a catalogue of the Brussels residue by Churchill and Thomas is now nearing completion. Unfortunately, no list of the English portion of the Brussels hoard was made before selections were taken from it, with the result that some of the rarer items are underrepresented in what remains.

In the nineteenth century no serious attempt had been made to provide a classification of the Long Cross coinage, the arrangement of which was confused by misunderstanding of the significance of the types without sceptre. Because there is a sceptre on the preceding Short Cross coinage, but not on the new Edwardian type from 1279, it was long thought that the sceptred Long Cross types came first, and this was supposedly corroborated by the existence of sceptreless coins without a moneyer's name, a feature of the subsequent Edwardian series. Before the appearance of the Brussels hoard Lawrence and others had already begun to work out a revised scheme and in 1913-15 he published his new arrangement of the coinage, with three main divisions and consisting of seven classes, three without sceptre followed by four with. The first division comprises the sceptreless classes I-III, which cover the recoinage of 1247-50; the second division consists of the main sceptred series, the brief transitional class IV followed by the extensive class V, representing the coinage of the 1250s and 1260s; and classes VI and VII, differentiated from the previous sceptred issues by their new style of portrait, constitute a limited third division belonging to the 1270s. In classes I-V the hair is represented by two crescents on each side, enclosing pellets, but the Edwardian classes VI and VII have more realistic locks as were to become standard from 1279 onwards. There are several distinct groupings within the inconveniently long class V; indeed, the term type would have been more appropriate than class in the Long Cross series, since Lawrence's classes differ from each other in design or obverse inscription or both in a way that Short Cross classes do not.

NORMAL OBVERSE FEATURES OF MAIN LONG CROSS CLASSES

CLASS	READING	LIGATION	SCEPTRE	HAIR
Ia	*henricus Rex*	None	No	Crescent curls
Ib	*henricus Rex Ang*	nr, An	No	"
II	*henricus Rex Terci*	nr, er	No	"
III	*henricus Rex III*	nr, enr	No	"
IV	*henricus/Rex/III*	nr	Yes	"
V	*henricus Rex/III*	nr	Yes	"
VI	*henricus Rex/III*	en	Yes	Long wide locks
VII	*henricus Rex/III*	en	Yes	Shorter neat locks

The Long Cross Coinage

Very little has been published on the series since Lawrence, whose classification has in its essentials stood the test of time. Working on the Brussels material in the 1970s Davis produced some refinements to the subdivision of the Lawrence classes, and these were incorporated in his privately produced catalogues of the Long Cross coins in the British Museum and the Royal Mint; but only his division of class II, according to the letter *X*, has been formally published. More recently, important work has been carried out on the whole series by Churchill and Thomas, and the content of this chapter is largely based on the results of their study. In respect of the recoinage issues they have identified the star mintmark before *henricus* as a significant indicator of sequence within classes II, III and IV. Although there are occasional variants, the normal forms of star are shown in summary in the following table.

No.	Description	Classes
1	Crude spiky star within a crescent.	Ia, Ib
2	Spiky star without crescent.	IIa
3	Solid, neat six-pointed star, usually with horizontal axis.	IIb-IIIbc
4	Thinner six-rayed star with vertical axis, ends rounded.	IIIbc-IIId
5	Eight-rayed star with rounded limbs.	IIId, IV

STAR INITIAL MARKS ON LONG CROSS CLASSES I - IV

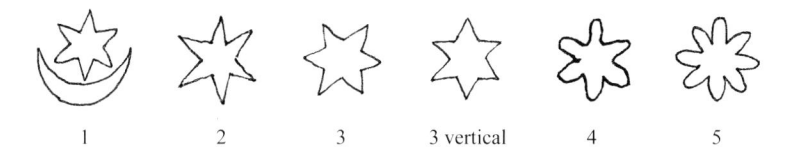

Class I

The first class of the new Long Cross coinage is exceptional in the English series prior to 1279 in omitting the moneyer's name, as a consequence of the king's name and title running continously from obverse to reverse. Since all coinage for the king at London and Canterbury was initially by Nicole, and Ion was the sole moneyer at Bury St. Edmunds, there was at the outset little reason to add a personal name. On the earliest variety of all the inscription reads *henricus Rex/Anglie Terci*, without a mint name either. These very rare coins must belong to the first weeks of the new coinage at London, before Canterbury and Bury were brought into play, but as soon as dies were needed for the two other mints the inscription was rearranged so as to include the first syllable of a mint name, thus *henricus Rex Ang/lie Terci Lon* (or *Can*, or *Aed*). Lawrence originally described these coins with a mint signature as class I and, as if by afterthought, the very rare *henricus Rex* variety as class I*; but on the plate illustrating Lawrence and Brooke's report of the 1912 Steppingley find the labels Ia and Ib are used, and these have been found more convenient by subsequent students.

In the first four classes the obverse inscription begins at the top of the coin, preceded by an initial mark consisting in class I of a crescent enclosing a star (or sun), the device already used, much more prominently, on the reverse of the English sterlings struck for John in Ireland. The star in this mark is rather crudely executed; it usually has six points, but occasionally five or even seven. The crown of class I (and until class IV) is composed of a flat band with a pellet at each end and a trefoil, or fleur, of pellets in the centre. In class Ia the face is rounded, with a beard of small strokes or pellets and a fringe of five small dots below the crown. Some early dies also show lines above, apparently indicating the top of the head within the circlet of the crown. In class Ib the face is usually longer, with a beard represented by two or three rows of dots, although a beard of strokes is still occasionally found. Later Ib dies have a fringe of three dots, the norm thereafter. Another feature of class Ia discontinued during Ib is a small point within the groups of pellets on the reverse, although before disappearing altogether the point is sometimes evident in one quarter only.

On the earliest coins of Ia there is no ligation of letters on either side, but later reverses (including most of those involved in Ib/Ia mules) have *An* and *er* joined. In Ib more letters were accommodated on the obverse by dropping Ia's usual colon before *Rex* (although a single stop often occurs) and by joining *nr* and *An*. Reverse dies of Ib often have an apostrophe contraction mark after *Terci'*.

One example of the Bury coin of Ib was known in the eighteenth century, but the Brussels hoard produced only two more. There were also, however, two in the much smaller Colchester hoard, perhaps influenced by the proximity of the find to the local mint. All are from a single pair of dies. Class Ib is also quite scarce of Canterbury, although much less rare than at Bury. London coins of Ib are reasonably plentiful, and there are rare mules both ways between Ia and Ib, which incidentally serve to confirm the London origin of class Ia. Although Ib/II mules are quite common, there are no mules between classes I and II that involve dies of Ia.

Class II

It is perhaps surprising that it should have been thought more important to retain the king's numeral than the name of his realm, but by the dropping of *Anglie* his title, now reduced to *Rex Terci'*, could be accommodated on the obverse alone (class II). Even if this new format had not been anticipated at the outset, it would soon have been prompted by the wish to identify on the reverse the new mints and moneyers engaged in the recoinage. Although the writs for the first of the new mints were not issued until February, reverse dies of class II will first have been issued very early in 1248 at the latest, and perhaps even before the end of 1247, since one carries the name of the Canterbury moneyer Ion who was replaced in January/February. Apart from the inscriptions, the only design change from class I was minor, although it facilitated the inclusion of *Terci*, which needs more space than *Ang*: in class II a star alone, without a crescent, is now found ahead of the obverse legend (this continued until the inscription was rearranged in class V as a result of the addition of the sceptre). As in class Ib, the face of class II is typically long and narrow, especially in IIb, although a throwback to the broader face of Ia is occasionally found. Other occasional echoes of class I include a five-point fringe below the crown instead of the now more normal three points, and an extra point between the pellets on some early reverses.

LETTERS *X* AND *R* IN LONG CROSS CLASSES I – III

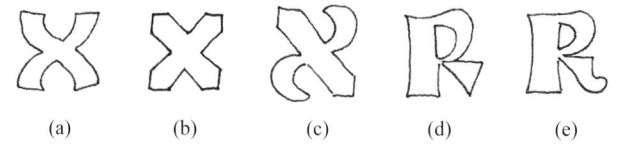

(a)   (b)   (c)   (d)   (e)

(a) X1, curule, Ia-IIb1; (b) X2, plain, IIb2-Va; (c) X3, hooked, IIIab;
(d) Wedge-tailed *R*, I-IIIc (and Vb-c); (e) Ball-tailed *R*, IIId-Va.

The Long Cross Coinage

Lawrence did not sub-divide class II, but Davis showed that two forms of the letter *X* were used during the class, while Churchill and Thomas (CT) have now emphasized the significance of the mintmark star. Davis used the label IIa for obverse dies that have the same *X* with curled limbs (X1) as is found in class I, and IIb for those which have a plain form with pointed ends (X2) that continues to feature through class III and beyond. Churchill and Thomas, however, have argued that division of the class into IIa and IIb should follow the two versions of the star, their IIa having the thin and spiky star 2 (which is rather like that within the crescent in class I, and again may have five or six points), and their IIb having the new and more solid star 3, the two lower points of which frequently straddle the top of the central ornament in the crown. They then split CT IIb into IIb1, which combines the new star with the old *X*, and IIb2 with new star and new *X*. This arrangement transfers some coins of Davis IIa to CT IIb1 with some potential uncertainty as to the precise identity of coins described as IIa unless it is stated which classification has been used. There is, however, logic in the CT subdivision of the class (which has been adopted here), since CT IIa was struck only at London, Canterbury and Bury, and so constitutes a distinct phase of the coinage before any of the regional mints were opened. Furthermore, there is a close relationship between CT IIb1 and IIb2 in that, with immaterial exceptions if any, the new regional mints that were opened in rapid succession in the spring of 1248 received obverse dies of one or the other of them, but not of both. Thus Winchester, Lincoln and Northampton received dies of IIb1, Exeter, Gloucester, Norwich, Oxford and York, of IIb2. Although both varieties of CT IIb were struck at each of the three ongoing mints, the relative scarcity of IIb1 at the major mint of Canterbury is consistent with it having been succeeded soon by IIb2.

SUBDIVISION OF CLASS II

CT	Davis	Star	*X*
IIa	IIa	2	curled
IIb1	IIa	3	curled
IIb2	IIb	3	plain

At the beginning of class II some of the new moneyer-signed reverse dies may have been issued to London and Canterbury without matching *Terci* obverses. Perhaps Ib obverse dies remained in stock, or even briefly continued to be produced before *Terci* replaced *Ang* since, whereas only a single IIa/Ib mule (of London) has been found, there are relatively plentiful Ib/II mules of Nicole at both mints. There are also comparable coins in the names of the two archiepiscopal moneyers who had been in office at the end of the Short Cross coinage, Ion and Willem, both extremely rare. Ion was John Chiche who is recorded as having been replaced as moneyer to the archbishop by Gilbert Bonnington in the Hilary Term of 1248. This situation is reflected in their extant coins, because Ion did not survive to sign coins of true class II, while Gilbert's own coinage begins with Ib/II mules (also extremely rare). Early reverse dies of class II often include an intrusive *e*, e.g. *Nic/ole/on e/Can*.

The Ib coins of Bury St. Edmunds are so rare that it is no surprise to find that new dies were not issued to the Ion (also a late Short Cross moneyer) at this mint during the Ib/II phase. In the Long Cross coinage his name first occurs on true coins of class II, and continues thereafter until early class V. Eaglen attributes the Bury coins of both classes I and II to Abbot Henry who died in June 1248. At Canterbury the trio of moneyers, Nicole, Gilbert and Willem, remained in place for the rest of the recoinage and beyond (although coins of CT IIa by Willem have not yet been noted). The first new moneyer at London was Henry Frowik, recorded in the Memoranda Roll for 1248 as having been appointed in the Easter Term; his earliest coins are of IIIa1 – pointing to a likely date for the transition from class II to III during, or very soon after, the second quarter of 1248. Of the eight provincial mints that struck both classes II and III, their coins of class III are much the more numerous: in the Colchester hoard those of class II from these mints were outnumbered, collectively, by those of class III by fifteen to one. Class II coins of the provincial mints are all quite rare, especially those of Norwich.

Long Cross Moneyers of Classes II and III at Ongoing Mints

	Short Cross	Ia	Ib	Ib/II	IIa	IIb1	IIb2	IIIa	IIIab	IIIb	IIIbc	IIIc	IIId	IV
London														
No Name		x	x											
Nicole	x			x	x	x	x	x	x	x	x	x	x	x
Henri								x	x	x	x	x	x	x
Davi												x	x	x
Ricard												m	x	x
Canterbury														
No Name			x											
Nicole	x			x	x	x	x	x	x	x	x	x	x	x
Ion	x			x										x
Gilbert				x	x	x	x	x	x	x	x	x	x	x
Willem	x			x		x	x	x	x	x	x	x	x	x
Bury														
No Name			x											
Ion	x				x	x	x	x	x	x	x	x	x	x

m – IIIc/d mule only.

Class III

The coins of the eight new mints ordered in October 1248 all belong to class III, chiefly distinguished from class II by the use of the Roman figure *III* instead of *Terci'* to make the obverse legend less compressed. Lawrence subdivided class III into three, basically according to the form of the bust. By his definition, IIIa has the long, narrow face of class II; IIIb, a broader and rounder bust; and IIIc, a shorter, pointed face with lines below to indicate the neck. In IIIa and IIIb the eyes are almond-shaped (their outline often indicated by two curves), and there are no points between the upper and lower curls; instead of the usual pellets, a notable variant of the IIIa head, on two London obverse dies, has a beard of fine strokes reminiscent of class I. In IIIc the eyes consist of an annulet enclosing a pellet, the curls of the hair tend to become more s-shaped, and there is usually a small point between them. As a general but not invariable rule, coins of IIIa and IIIb have a single stop after *Rex*, those of IIIc a colon. On early reverse dies of class III the letters *on*, if in the same segment, are often separate, as they had been in class II, but before long they came more frequently to be joined.

Although the divisions between sub-classes are not absolute and are sometimes difficult to apply in individual cases, the Lawrence classification remains convenient for descriptive purposes. Nevertheless, subsequent work has resulted in a number of refinements, and one significant adjustment, to the Lawrence scheme. Changes often developed with a degree of gradualism, and in recognising this Davis added the labels IIIab and IIIbc to designate coins transitional between two consecutive sub-classes and combining features of each of them. Also, closer examination of the coins generally classed as Lawrence IIIc suggests that there are two points in the series at which it is appropriate to introduce new sub-divisions. The first of these comes early in the class and has been labelled IIIa2 by Churchill and Thomas. Although this variety exhibits some characteristics similar to those of IIIc, and does not have much in common with regular IIIa (henceforth called IIIa1), its approximate position in the series is indicated by reverse die-links that have been found with IIb, IIIa1 and IIIab. The other addition belongs at the end of class III, where some coins, hitherto treated as of late class IIIc, are given their own designation as IIId, recognising a distinct change of style that looks forward to class IV.

The earliest coins of class III, those of IIIa1 with faces characteristic of class II, are known of all the class II mints but not of any of the eight mints authorised in October 1248, which feature only in class III (from IIIab1 onwards). Excluding for a moment consideration of the new sub-class IIIa2, which stands somewhat apart from the main sequence, there is a gradual evolution of the portrait in class III. Thus, the narrow face of IIIa1 was not suddenly replaced by the rounder shape of IIIb, and there are intermediate versions which show a face broader than in class II but less rounded than in IIIb. This intermediate style (IIIab) occurs at all mints and is the earliest variety recorded from most of the October mints. There are two versions of this variety, IIIab1 and IIIab2, distinguished by the letter *X*. Throughout class III the *X* is usually of the plain form (X2) introduced in IIb2, but the variant IIIab2 has an elaborate hooked form of *X* with the forward limb plain and the other represented by two tight crescents (X3); this composite *X* has only been noted at the ongoing mints plus Gloucester, Northampton and Winchester. As in IIIa1, the beard of IIIab is composed of four or five small pellets (or occasionally three) either side of a slightly larger central pellet; in IIIb there are usually three large pellets each side of the chin. Following IIIb come the coins of IIIbc with certain features transitional to IIIc, such as mintmark star 4, a smaller and more pointed face, or vestigial lines of the neck beneath, but such coins have not been noted of all the provincial mints. Through class III and beyond the letters *nr* in *henricus* are joined, but in IIIbc there is often the triple link of *enr*. The star 3 mintmark, as introduced in IIb1, continued in use for the rest of class II and in class III up to and including IIIb and a few coins of IIIbc. It was then replaced by a thinner star (4), with rounded ends and six limbs of which two are frequently on a vertical axis. Star 4 occurs on most coins of IIIbc, on all those still classed as IIIc, and on most of those now described as IIId.

In commenting on the diagnostic features of his divisions of class III, Lawrence did not say that a colon after *Rex* occurs on all coins of IIIc, or that it is never found elsewhere in the class; but those assumptions are implicit in Brooke's summary and have sometimes caused problems of identification. In fact, some coins of IIIc have one stop or none, while a colon instead of a single stop is sometimes found on coins towards the beginning of the class – giving rise to descriptions such as 'IIIc, but with face of IIIa'. Many such coins actually belong to the new IIIa2. A key feature of IIIa2 is that the lower points of the star 3 mintmark do not straddle the central ornament of the crown, but two of its points are vertical at 0° and 180°. Most of these coins have a colon after *Rex*; their face is small, often with lines for the neck and a rough beard containing pellets and strokes such as to give the king's face a coarse appearance. Because of their colon and necklines coins of IIIa2 have usually hitherto been described as of IIIc, but they may be distinguished from IIIc not only by virtue of their having star 3 but also because of their almondy, non-annulet eyes.

Most coins of class III, including all those of the recoinage mints, continue to use a wedge-tailed *R*; near the end of the class, however, this was replaced by a neat ball-tailed form of the letter which continued in use through class IV and into early class V. This new *R* is one of the main means of identifying coins of the newly defined sub-class IIId (called 'IIIc late' by Davis), but they do also have generally neater and more elegant lettering, and resemble class IV in other ways – in their tightly grained circles, and frequently in the style and shape of the portrait, which has a more rounded face. During IIId star 4 was replaced by the last of the star punches, with eight blunt-ended rays (star 5), which is a feature of class IV.

Churchill and Thomas have identified four groups of coins that would have been described by Lawrence as belonging to his IIIc. First, there is the variety now labelled IIIa2; this variety is virtually confined to London, Canterbury, Bury and the eight February mints, although Ilchester (like the archbishop's mint at York), exceptionally, seems to have been issued with an odd die of IIIa2 in the first batch. The second and third of the four groups include most of the coins that belong to traditional IIIc, and the fourth is the late variety herein described as IIId, the introduction of which marks a break in the numismatic series.

Although IIIc was the sub-class in issue when the provincial recoinage came to an end, it is not recorded for all the regional mints. No IIIc coins have been found of Exeter, Wallingford or York royal, but whether these closed slightly earlier than other mints, or simply did not need further dies prior to closure, we cannot tell. The same applies to some others, of which IIIc coins are rare – notably Bristol, Carlisle, Hereford, Ilchester and Northampton.

There is considerable variety in the appearance of the busts in the issues described here as IIIc. At first, in the second of the four CT groups, the head is crudely drawn, and of rather coarse and irregular appearance. All the coins of the provincial mints are of this variety (here IIIc1). Later, the portrait shows considerable improvement, with the face usually rounded, but sometimes with a more pointed chin (here IIIc2). Observing that this later variety, the third of the CT groups, is only found at the ongoing mints, and so belongs to the post-provincial phase, Churchill and Thomas have labelled it 'IIId1'; but the distinction between these two varieties is not easy to describe and for the purposes of this book the later variety has therefore been left within IIIc (i.e., as part of what Davis had called 'IIIc early').

As most of the recoinage consisted of coins of class III, they are naturally very common. London and Canterbury each coined almost as much in the first twelve months, from November 1247, as in the following year, but overall 1249 saw the peak of recoinage activity after the second wave of regional mints had been brought into operation. IIIa, which probably includes the first Bury coins of Abbot Edmund appointed in September, must have begun, and was perhaps complete, during 1248, too early for the second list of eight mints which opened with what we now call IIIab (apart from the one IIIa2 die at Ilchester). Shrewsbury began to mint in February 1249, but it is possible that some of the larger mints in the second wave may have received dies and commenced minting slightly

The Long Cross Coinage

earlier than this. Most of the regional mints probably closed, like Shrewsbury, in the early months of 1250.

At Canterbury and Bury the class II names continued unchanged through class III. In the Trinity term (May-June) of 1250 four additional moneyers were sworn, David of Enfield and Richard Bonaventure for London, William Cokyn and John Terri for Canterbury. Coins of this William are indistinguishable from those of his long-standing Canterbury namesake, but the other names provide useful evidence for dating. Davi struck London coins of IIIc and IIId, but since his IIIc coins are much fewer than those of IIId it seems that IIIc was coming to an end in the summer of 1250. With *R*s in his name Ricard's earliest coins have sometimes been seen as IIIc/d mules. Ion at Canterbury, however, is not recorded until class IV, which implies that it was some time before dies were made for him.

Dies for the archbishop of York were authorised in July 1248. Five names are found on York coins of class III, the four names of the royal moneyers who commenced in class II and the unlisted Tomas in class III only. Although Tomas began later, his coins are much more plentiful than those of any of the other four York moneyers and it is safe to assume that he was working for the archbishop. His earliest coins, however, are not of class II (or IIIa1), as might have been expected if he had started in 1248, but of class IIIa2. The explanation for this delay is evident from a writ issued in the following summer to the sheriff of York arranging for replacements to be appointed for the archbishop's die-keeper who was incapacitated. There are no obverse die-links between Tomas and the other York moneyers, as there probably would have been if he had been working alongside the royal team.

Moneyers of the Provincial Mints

In most cases the names of mints and moneyers as given in the Hargrave manuscript list tally exactly with those on the coins. Of the eight mints which began with class II, the list omits Northampton but gives Norwich twice (once with Northampton's four moneyers). At Lincoln two Williams are listed, one of them perhaps an error for Walter of whom there are coins of classes II and III. Two Williams were also listed at Wilton, but there is no means of distinguishing their coins. The only substitution was evidently at Bristol where from IIIb a rare moneyer called Roger occurs in addition to the four listed names, perhaps as a replacement for Henri who had produced IIIb but is the only listed moneyer at this mint not known to have struck either IIIbc or IIIc.

A remarkable feature of the list is the very limited number of Christian names of moneyers and other mint officials. Among the moneyers there were Ions at eight mints (conveniently, since the short name allowed a longer mint signature), Willems at seven, Ricards at five, Henries and Walters at four each, and Adams, Roberts, Rogers and Huges at three each - nine names accounting for forty out of sixty-three in all. Singletons tend to occur at lesser mints - three at Ilchester, two each at Shrewsbury and at Wallingford, where Clement (1259) and Alisandre (1260) each later became mayor of the borough. Several other recoinage moneyers, a number of whom were members of rich and powerful local families, are known to have served at one time or another in the office of mayor or bailiff.

In class II the three mints, Winchester, Lincoln and Northampton, that received obverse dies of IIb1 were probably the earliest of the regional mints to commence operations in 1248. The other class II mints, Exeter, Gloucester, Norwich, Oxford and York royal, began with dies of IIb2. Six of these eight mints continued in production up to IIIc inclusive. The activity of the class III-only mints began during the currency of IIIab dies and was concentrated in the IIIb phase, but much reduced in IIIc.

85

1247–1278

The moneyers of the class II+III mints were:

Exeter (*Eccetre*)
  Ion (Iohannes de Egestone)
  Philip (Phillipus Tinctor)
  Robert (Robertus Picon)
  Walter (Walterus Okestone)

Gloucester (*Glouce*)
  Ion (Iohannes filius Simonis)
  Lucas (Lucas Cornubiae)
  Ricard (Ricardus le Francois)
  Roger (Rogerius Emcpse)

Lincoln (*Lincoln*)
  Ion (Iohannes de Luda)
  Ricard (Ricardus de Ponte)
  Walter (unlisted)
  Willem (Willelmus de Paris, or W. Brand)

Northampton (*Norha*)
  Lucas (Lucas Parmentarius)
  Philip, or Phelip (Philippus filius Roberti)
  Tomas (Thomas Rinne)
  Willem (Willelmus de Gangy)

Norwich (*Nor(t)wiz or -wis*)
  Huge (Hugo le Brunham)
  Iacob (Iacobus Coccus)
  Ion (Iohannes Martun)
  Willem (Willelmus de Hapesburge)

Oxford (*Oxonfo, Oxone*)
  Adam (Adam Feteplace)
  Gefrei (Gaufridus de Scocwille)
  Henri (Henricus Simeone)
  Willem (Willelmus Sarsorius)

Winchester (*Winche*)
  Huge (Hugo Silvester)
  Iordan (Iordanus Drapparius)
  Nicole (Nicholaus Cupping)
  Willem (Willelmus Prior)

York royal (*Everwic*)
  Alain, Alein (Alanus filius Sansonis)
  Ieremie (Geremias de Bedegate)
  Ion (Iohannes de Seleby)
  Rener (Raynerius Taliator)

The moneyers of the class III-only mints were:

Bristol (*Brustov*)
  Elis (Elyas de Aby)
  Henri (Henricus Langbord)
  Iacob (Iacobus Laware)
  Walter (Walterus de Paris)
  Roger (unlisted)

Carlisle (*Carlel*)
  Adam (Adam Caperun)
  Ion (Iohannes de Boltone)
  Robert, -erd (Robertus de Chilay)
  Willem (Willelmus de Thiparun)

Hereford (*Heref*)
  Henri (Henricus Hathefet)
  Ricard (Ricardus Mamworthe)
  Roger (Rogerius le Mercer)
  Walter (Walterus Siward)

Ilchester (*Ivelce*)
  Huge (Hugo le Rus)
  Ierveis (Gervasius Gris)
  Randulf (Radulfus Fardein)
  Stephe (Stephanus le Rus)

Newcastle (*Newecas or Nev-*)
  Adam (Adam de Blakedone)
  Henri (Henricus de Karlel)
  Ion (Iohannes de Papede)
  Roger (Rogerius filius Willelmi)

Shrewsbury (*Sroseb*)
  Lorenz (Laurentius Cox)
  Nicole (Nicholaus filius Ivonis)
  Peris (Petrus filius Clementis)
  Ricard (Ricardus Pride)

The Long Cross Coinage

Wallingford (*Wali*)
    Alisandre (Alexander de Stanes)
    Clement (Clemens Clericus)
    Ricard (Ricardus Blaune)
    Robert (Robertus Pecok)

Wilton (*Wiltone*)
    Huge (Hugo Goldrun)
    Ion (Iohannes Berte)
    Willem (Willelmus filius Radulfi,
    and W. Manger)

York episcopal (*Everw*)
    Tomas (not listed)

REGIONAL RECOINAGE MINTS OF 1248–50

	IIb1	IIb2	IIIa	IIIab	IIIb	IIIbc	IIIc
Winchester	x		x	x	x	x	x
Lincoln	x		x	x	x	x	x
Northampton	x		x	x	x	x	x
Exeter		x	x	x	x		
Gloucester		x	x	x	x		x
Norwich		x	x	x	x	x	x
Oxford		x	x	x	x	x	x
York royal		x	x	x	x	x	
Bristol				x	x	x	x
Carlisle				x	x	x	x
Hereford				x	x		x
Ilchester			x	x	x	x	x
Newcastle				x	x		x
Shrewsbury				x	x	x	x
Wallingford				x	x		
Wilton				x	x	x	x
York abp.			x	x	x	x	x

Class IV

The earliest coins with the sceptre are of class IV, a rare transitional type on which for the last time the inscription still begins at the top, preceded by a star. The legend is thus divided in three places, by the initial star, by the king's hand (and annulet sceptre-end) after *henricus*, and by the sceptre-head after *Rex*, with the numeral *III* between sceptre-head and star. This arrangement reduced the available space and so required a new fount of lettering, smaller than in class III, which contributes to the generally neat and handsome appearance of the coins of class IV. Some features of late class III continued, such as the colon before *III*, round eyes, query-shaped curls and punch 5 for the initial star, but others underwent change. Thus, although many coins of class IV have pellets between the curls, as before, a few show thin crescents outside them as often found in the early stages of class V. The principal development, however, was in the ornaments on the band of the crown. On London coins of the class three varieties are found. As Lawrence noted, the earliest has the old style of crown, with the central ornament pommy and large pellets at each end (IVa), while a late form has a fleur-de-lis flanked by two half fleurs (IVb). There is, however, also an intermediate version on which the central lis of IVb is accompanied by pellets at the ends (IVab). Although the labels given to these three varieties are convenient for notation, they are not equivalent to the principal subdivisions of the more abundant classes: indeed, all the class IV coins of Canterbury and Bury are of IVab, but this is the rarest variety at London.

VARIETIES OF CROWN IN LONG CROSS CLASS IV

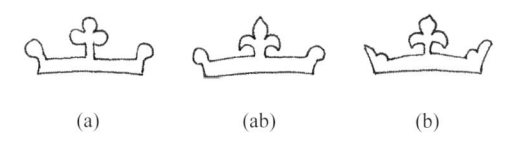

(a)   (ab)   (b)

(a) Pommy central ornament with end-pellets; (ab) Central lis with end-pellets; (b) Central lis with half-lis at ends.

The only new moneyer in class IV was Ion at Canterbury. In 1250 the London moneyers stood surety for John Terri of Canterbury when he was accused of issuing false money; but since Ion (or *Iohs*, or in Vg sometimes *Iohanes*) continued to coin until late class V the accusation was presumably found to be baseless. However, this episode could perhaps have led to some delay and so account for the fact that Ion's coins do not begin in class IIIc-d, like those of Davi and Ricard, the two London moneyers appointed at the same time. Class IV may, on the evidence of rarity, be accorded a period of no more than weeks, during the later part of 1250.

Class V
Before the end of 1250 the design of the Long Cross coinage was again altered and now settled into the form that it was to retain until the 1270s. Class V, a refinement of class IV, with the legend starting to the right of the sceptre-head (as it had done in the Short Cross coinage), and so ending less awkwardly with *III'* instead of *Rex* behind the sceptre, is by far the largest of the Lawrence classes. As befits a series of coins that continued in issue for more than twenty years, class V exhibits a number of changes in letter forms, crown and other details, enabling a sequence of varieties to be defined. Lawrence divided the class into eight or nine sub-classes (Va-Vh or Vi). These sub-classes can be dated with varying degrees of precision on the basis of moneyers' names, and belong to two main and two minor phases. The very plentiful coins of the first phase, which spans more than half of the 1250s, are of three sub-classes, Va, Vb and Vc, characterized by what Lawrence called their 'high crown'. After these, evidently c. 1257, was a short phase in which two rare and abnormal varieties appeared (Vd and Ve), exhibiting different styles of bust, and crowns with small and carefully shaped fleurs-de-lis. The abundant coins of the third phase (Vf and Vg), which ran from the later 1250s well into the 1260s, are similar in general aspect to those of the first phase, except for having a 'low crown' with a very short central fleur. Finally, there are degenerate versions of Vg, which Lawrence classed as Vh or Vi, belonging to the last years of Henry III and beyond. In early class V the bishop's mint at Durham was reopened after an interval of more than thirty years.

The Long Cross Coinage

Coins were also struck at Dublin in 1251-4 for the purpose of recoinage in Ireland; they are cognate with coins from English mints of the first phase of class V, and were the responsibility of the two London moneyers Davi and Ricard.

The high crown of Va-Vc has a tall central fleur pommy which rises through the dotted circle to divide the king's name between *e* and *n*. Lawrence defined Va and Vb as having round eyes, Va with a ball-tailed *R* as in classes IIId-IV, and Vb with a new, wedge-tailed *R*. His Vc has new eyes with an oval outline. In Va the face tends to be shorter (as in class IV) than in Vb-c. The chin pellet is prominent in Va, less so thereafter. There are usually small crescents outside the curls; and in Vc there are sometimes pellets between the curls and a row of small dots along the outline of the beard. In this phase a stop is often found after *III'*, and rarely (in Va only) before *Rex*. Some coins of Va show the neat class IV letter fount but larger punches were generally used in this phase thereafter. Since the start of the Long Cross coinage the *A* had normally been plain, but during early class V a more elaborate form was introduced, with its first limb indented. This new *A* is occasionally double-barred, as (in Vc) *N* may be also. *N* and *R* are ligated (although one Va London die omits *N* altogether). During class Va the plain *X* that had been normal since class IIb (X2) was replaced by a composite letter having its first limb straight with concave sides and the other made up of two small curved wedges (X4). This new curled *X* remained in use through Vb and Vc.

Although Lawrence's arrangement of the sub-classes of this phase provides a serviceable scheme for descriptive purposes, and in many cases is indicative of sequence, there were periods of overlap – for example, when the Va and Vb forms of the letter *R* were both in use (occasionally even on the same die). There is thus no simple point of transition either from Va to Vb or from Vb to Vc, such as would permit a precise chronology to be constructed. Nevertheless, some further subdivision has been attempted, although the labels used can give a misleading impression of the structure since some are chronological while others are not, and some apply to thousands of coins but others only to the products of a single die. Thus a few London coins of Va and Vb, in each case from one obverse die only, have half-fleurs instead of pellets at the ends of the crown, in the manner of IVb; these were called Va1 and Vb1 by Davis. A rarer and more remarkable variant of the Va crown is found on a Canterbury die which has a double band adorned with pellets somewhat as in Ve, and this has been labelled Va4 by Churchill and Thomas. Normal coins of class Va are designated Va2 or Va3 according to whether they have the plain letter X2 or X4 with crescent wedges. The commoner variety at London and Bury is Va3, but at Canterbury Va2. Normal coins of class Vb are sometimes called Vb2, although this is the only substantive variety. In Vc Churchill and Thomas have introduced an apparently sequential subdivision: the scarce Vc1 with ball-tailed R2; Vc2, the most abundant, with wedge-tailed R1; and Vc3 with an abnormal central ornament in the crown, consisting of three pellets with or without short stalks.

In the Long Cross coinage Bury was only issued with one pair of dies at a time. In Va the mint-name, hitherto (except in Ib) *S. Edmund*, becomes more often *Seint Ed*. The last variety produced by Ion was Va. His successor at Bury, Randulf le Blund, was presented at the Exchequer in the spring of 1252, and struck all sub-classes from Vb to Vf with the exception of Ve. His first coins have the wedged *R* of Vb on the obverse but an *R* with an unusually long tail, ending in a pellet, on the reverse, in consequence of which they have sometimes been classified as Vb/Va mules; however, the *R* on the reverse is not the same as the normal ball-tailed letter of Va, and there can be little doubt that the two dies involved were made about the same time, during the course of Vb. His own longer name reduced Randulf's mint signature to *S. Ed*.

LETTERING IN LONG CROSS CLASS V

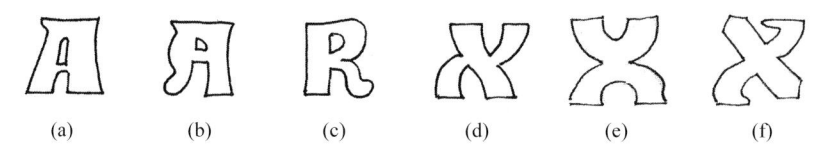

(a) Plain *A*, Va (and earlier); (b) Ornate *A*, Va onwards; (c) Hunched *R*, Vd onwards; (d) X4, with crescent wedges, Va-c; (e) X5, curule, Vd-g; (f) X6, hooked, Vg onwards.

The first Long Cross moneyer at Durham was Ricard, whose coins are of Va, Vb and Vc. Walter Kirkham, the new bishop, had received his temporalities in October 1249, and dies were authorised for him late in 1250; but it was not until June 1253 that his minting rights were confirmed. Three pairs of dies were duly delivered to the bishop's attorney, but since they were of class Va it may be that they had already been made sometime earlier. The next batch of Durham dies consisted of three pairs of class Vb, which Churchill and Thomas identify with the new ones involved when there was a complete exchange of dies in December 1253. Of Vc, however, eight obverse and eleven reverse dies have been noted in the Durham material from Brussels, suggesting that on at least one occasion Durham received sets of dies consisting of one obverse and two reverses.

If Vb dies were sent to the bishop of Durham in December 1253, it would be natural to assume that Vc was not introduced until 1254, but these dates are not readily compatible with other evidence. Nicholas of St. Albans is mentioned in the Patent Roll as deceased by March 1253. In May 1255 the London die formerly held by him was granted to William of Gloucester, whose coins begin with Vc2. As measured by his representation in the Colchester hoard, Nicole's London output in Vc was only around seven per cent of his figure for Va+b, whereas his colleagues Henri and Ricard each had more coins of Vc in the hoard than of Va+b, confirming that the end of Nicole's coinage fell very early in the currency of Vc. If the date for Nicole's death is correctly recorded, it would suggest that dies of Vc, substantially the largest of the three sub-classes of this phase, may have been first supplied late in 1252 (or very early in 1253). Beside William, other moneyer names that first appear in class Vc are Walter from Vc2 and Ion from Vc3 at London, and Robert from Vc2 and Walter from Vc3 at Canterbury. Coins of Robert and the London Walter were present in the Colchester hoard, of the other two not. Several Roberts are mentioned as Canterbury moneyers in the years 1255-7, but the earliest of them was granted his die at Easter 1255. Walter of Brussels is first recorded as having received his die at London for life in October 1256, along with five others, four of whom had already been in office as moneyers before that date. The last member of the consortium was John Hardel, whose name was added to the other five in one of the rolls, perhaps between the Easter term of 1256, when the arrangement was authorised, and October when Letters Patent were issued. Since Vc London coins of Walter entered the Colchester hoard but Ion's did not, the first part of the hoard may have been closed during the second half of 1256. No date of appointment is known for Walter at Canterbury (possibly because he was a moneyer for the archbishop), but a Walter Adrian, moneyer, witnessed the accounts of the Canterbury exchange from June 1256 to December 1258. Although not present in Colchester, Canterbury Vc coins by Walter are reasonably plentiful, implying that Vc may have lasted into 1257. The continuation of the name Nicole at Canterbury beyond Vc, after the death of Nicholas of St. Albans, is explained by the farm of a die for life to one Nicholas de Hadlo early in 1256.

The Long Cross Coinage

MONEYERS OF LONG CROSS CLASSES IV TO VII

	IV	Va	Vb	Vc	Vd	Ve	Vf	Vg	Vh	Vi	VI	VII
LONDON												
Nicole	x	x	x	x								
Davi	x	x	x	x	x	x	x					
Henri	x	x	x	x	x	x	x	x				
Ricard	x	x	x	x	x	x	x	x				
Willem				x	x	x	x	x				
Walter				x	x	x	x	x				
Iohs, Ion				x	x	x	x	x				
Thomas								x				
Robert								x				
Renaud								x	x	x	x	x
Phelip												x
CANTERBURY												
Nicole	x	x	x	x	x	x	x	x				
Gilbert	x	x	x	x	m	x	x	x				
Willem	x	x	x	x	x	x	x	x				
Ioh(s), Ion	x	x	x	x	x	m	x	x				
Robert				x	x	x	x	x	x			
Walter				x	x	x	x	x				
Ambroci								x				
Alein								x	x			
Ricard								x	x			
Roger								x				
BURY												
Ion	x	x										
Randulf			x	x	x		x					
Renaud								x				
Stephane								x				
Iohs, Ion								x	x	x	x	x
Ioce												x
DURHAM												
Ricard		x	x	x								
Roger								x				
Willem								x				
Roberd											x	x

m – mules only.

There follows one of the stranger episodes in English coinage of the sterling era, involving the rare coins of classes Vd and Ve, which constitute the second phase of class V. In the Long Cross coinage up to Vc there had usually been a degree of continuity between the features of one class or sub-class and the next. Class Vd, however, differs conspicuously from its predecessor. Although the basic design of the coins was unaltered, new punches were used for all its main elements. There were three distinct forms of head, all of them materially different from what had gone before. On the reverse the twin limbs of the voided cross are thinner, and further apart. A new fount of lettering was introduced, rather tall, with plain uprights (slightly indented at their ends), a more angular *R* with a hunched tail, *N* often reversed, *h* sometimes with outturned tail, and a more symmetrical curule *X*. There is less ligation of letters, *nr* never being joined when the *N* is reversed, and *on* being often separate. Several unusual spellings also occur in Vd: Robert became Roberd, and Davi*d*, Nic*h*ole and Willem*e* each gained a letter, while Ioh(s) and Rand(ulf) were shortened, and their mints became *Kan* and *Beri*. On a few London reverses there is a colon before the moneyer's name. All ongoing moneyers are represented by true coins of the sub-class, except that no Vd Canterbury reverse die in Gilbert's name has been noted.

The first of the three Vd heads is of rough work, and often very crude (Vd1). It is not to be wondered that such curious coins have sometimes been suspected of being the work of continental imitators. The second and third busts, however, are of much finer style and, together with the many abnormalities of Vd, suggest the work of a literate if idiosyncratic engraver. The head of Vd2 is large but tidy, with a rounded chin and little neck, and a crown with squat central ornament. In Vd3, of fine style, the head is mostly smaller, leaving room for a longer neck. In Vd2 and Vd3 the band of the crown sometimes appears to consist of two thin lines. Canterbury used dies of all three varieties. Vd1 has only been found at Canterbury, sometimes with very crude reverse dies, including one with a large lis after the *K* of *Kan*. London coins are of Vd2 and Vd3, Bury of Vd3 only. The distinctive epigraphy and other features assist in the identification of mules involving dies of Vd. The most usual combination is Vc3/Vd. There are also coins from Vd obverses paired with 'normal' reverses which have usually been assumed to be of Vc, although most of them are probably Vd/e or later, as reverse dies of mules tend to be. Since Vc/d mules are relatively numerous of both London and Canterbury, there seems to have been no interruption in the actual production of coin, and we can only speculate as to why the normal evolution of design was dislocated at this point.

After the oddities of Vd, a step towards normality was taken in the form of Ve, which also belongs to the second phase. This is much the rarest and most ephemeral of the main varieties of class V. Although rather larger, the face resembles that of Vd, but the crown is wider and its double band is prominently decorated with a row of four pearls. This experimental style seems, however, to have found little more favour than the single pearled-crown die in Va, since Ve is known only from one obverse die at London and two at Canterbury. Some lettering of Vd continues in Ve, although without the reversed *N*. Ligation of *nr* is resumed, and spelling reverts to normal (apparent exceptions to this being presumably Ve/d mules).

Even since the Brussels find, coins of Vd, including mules, are all relatively rare. No moneyers are known to have begun or ended their careers with coins of either Vd or Ve. The second phase of class V as a whole was thus short-lived, and may be dated c. 1257. Although this would fall within the vacancy at Bury between the death of Abbot Edmund on 31 December 1256 and the grant of temporalities to his successor in January 1258, there is little difficulty in attributing Rand's coins of Vd to 1257, in accordance with

London-Canterbury chronology, since the account for this period records payment of the moneyer's annual fee for two years – and the prior's and convent's right to operate the mint during a vacancy was later acknowledged in discussion of a case that arose in 1281.

CROWNS IN LONG CROSS CLASS V

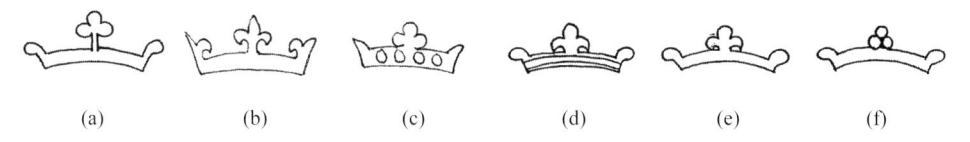

(a) (b) (c) (d) (e) (f)

(a) High crown, Va-c2; (b) Fleured crown of Vd; (c) Pelleted crown of Ve; (d) Double-banded crown of Vf; (e) Low crown, Vg; (f) Trefoiled crown, Vh.

Although not reaching the peaks of the early 1250s, mint output after the recoinage remained at a high level into and through the 1260s, with Canterbury's exceeding London's for a few years from the mid-1250s. Coins of the third phase of class V are accordingly very common (Vf and Vg). In general appearance they much more closely resemble those of the first phase than of the second. They can, however, be simply distinguished from the coins of Va-c by their new 'low crown' on which the central fleur is small, flat and stalkless, and although still pointing between *e* and *n* it scarcely protrudes beyond the beaded circle. In Vf this crown has two thin bands, in Vg a single thicker one. Also, whereas Va-c have crescents outside the curls, in Vf and Vg pellets are liberally scattered around the curls and beard. The style of lettering is similar to that of Va-c, although often with the tail of *h* turned outwards as first found in Vd. X5, the curule *X* of Vd, also continues into Vf and early Vg. Most coins of Vg, however, have a new *X* with one straight limb and the other curved with prominent inward serifs (X6). A triple colon is sometimes found before *henricus*, more commonly in Vf than in Vg. In Vf the letters of *on* are usually separate, but in Vg ligation is again the norm.

Class Vf is the last to bear the names of Randulf of Bury and Davi of London, but no name at Canterbury begins or ends in this sub-class. If the Bury coins of Vd are correctly attributed to the vacancy in 1257, Randulf's Vf die might date from early 1258 after Abbot Simon had received his temporalities. Later the same year (in the Trinity term) a new Bury moneyer, Reginald FitzHenry, was appointed, whose name (as *Renaud*) appears only on scarce coins of Vg. Class Vf, which although not rare is much less abundant than Vg, may thus be dated 1257-8.

Class Vg lasted for ten years or more. Except for Nicole and Davi, all the Vc London moneyers continued in operation into Vg. Several new names now appear: Thomas, Robert and Renaud at London; Ambroci, Alein and Ricard at Canterbury; Renaud, Stephane and Ion at Bury; and Roger and Willem at Durham. Of these eleven new moneyers in Vg we know the dates of appointment of only five, but an idea of the relative position of the others can be gained from comparing the structure of successive hoards. After Renaud at Bury, whose appointment in the summer of 1258 must have come very early in Vg, the next new moneyer was Thomas at London, who took the die held previously by David of Enfield in May 1260 (although David may of course have ceased to coin well before that date). This was Thomas of Weseham, the king's surgeon, who was compensated in the following year for surrender of the die, which he can only have used for a very short time since his coins are of the greatest rarity (only two or three in Brussels). At Canterbury in February 1261 Ambrose the clerk (*Ambroci*) was to have in his name, on behalf of himself and another, the die of Robert Attewaterlok, but this arrangement was not implemented and in January 1262 he took a die jointly with Robert Polre, his appointment, exceptionally, being for a period of one year only. Whereas Ambroci was represented in Brussels, but not heavily, the hoard contained no Bury coins at all of John de Burnedisse appointed in January 1265. The last known appointment of a Vg moneyer was that of Richard le Specer, archbishop's moneyer at Canterbury, in April 1268.

Nothing is known of a Robert at London, but since his coins are extremely rare it is possible that the mint name was an error for Canterbury. Renaud at London was Reginald de Cantuaria, succeeded by Philip de Cambio in 1278, but the date when he took up office is not known. This is particularly unfortunate since for perhaps fifteen years he was overwhelmingly the most productive moneyer in the country. More than a hundred London coins of Renaud were present in the Brussels hoard but he was probably not appointed more than a year or so before the hoard was buried. Bury's Renaud was followed by an even rarer Brussels moneyer, Stephane, who was presumably appointed not long before the burial of the hoard but very soon replaced by the post-Brussels Ion at the beginning of 1265. Another Vg moneyer represented sparingly in the hoard was Roger at Durham. The bishop's mint was evidently closed for a time in the later 1250s, since there are no coins between Ricard's in Vc and Roger's in Vg; perhaps it was reopened following the appointment of Bishop Robert Stichill in late 1260. The absence from Brussels of any Bury coins of Ion argues against putting the closure of the hoard later than the winter of 1264/5. On the other hand, it would be difficult to date its burial much before 1264, since coins of Vg by moneyers such as Willem at London and Robert at Canterbury are so abundant that the hoard needs to have been buried late enough to account for the very large volume of their Vg output.

The relative dating of successive hoards of the later Long Cross period can be measured by the increasing proportion of coins in Renaud's name, indicating dates of burial progressively later than that of Brussels. The latest pre-Renaud hoard is Hornchurch, which cannot have been closed before 1260 since it contained a London coin of Thomas (but none yet of Canterbury by Ambroci or Alein). In approximate chronological sequence there are then four English hoards, each consisting of a few hundred coins, from Palmer's Green (mid-1260s), Tower Hill and Coventry (late 1260s) and Steppingley (c. 1270). Of the post-Brussels moneyers, Ricard at Canterbury, appointed in 1268, is not represented in hoards earlier than Coventry and Steppingley, in each of which coins of Renaud comprised a fifth or more of the English total. These two hoards also contained enough coins of the unidentified Alein (whose career had begun in time for him to have a modest representation in Brussels) to indicate that he continued to be productive during the second half of the 1260s. Since Alein did not share obverse dies with Ambroci in Vg, and he is also known in Vh, he seems likely to have been appointed after Ambroci's term of office was completed. There is no hoard provenance for a coin of the Willem who presumably followed Roger at Durham at some point in the post-Brussels period.

The fourth and final phase of class V is ill-defined. At a late stage in the class the central fleur of the crown came to be replaced by three pellets, usually in trefoil, and sometimes joined to the band by short stalks. In his text Lawrence described all coins with the three-pellet crown as Vh, but there is considerable variety among them. With a large, rounded head the early coins of Vh are, except for their crown, virtually indistinguishable from Vg. Later examples of Vh are from dies more coarsely executed: the bust is narrower, with thick eyes and a short iron for the nose and mouth, and the pellets in the crown are

The Long Cross Coinage

larger. In his table of moneyers Lawrence included a column headed Vi, in which the only entry was for Renaud of London, although in his list of coins of Bury he gives readings for both Vh (*Ioh's*) and Vi (*Ions*), the latter noted as of very coarse work. If the Vi label is reserved for the crudest versions, on which the head is very roughly executed and the lettering is large (usually resulting in the need for the triple link *enr*), no Canterbury coin has been found that qualifies. Lawrence's nominees, Renaud of London and Ion of Bury, remain the only candidates.

It has sometimes been thought that coins with the pelleted crown of Vh were present in the Brussels hoard, but there is no clear evidence to that effect, and the coins of Ricard at Canterbury would suggest otherwise. Richard le Specer was sworn of his office in April 1268 but was dead before September 1271 when his die was reassigned. Since he is known for both Vg and Vh, the transition from the fleured to the pelleted crown should presumably be dated c. 1269/70. However, it could also be that there was some overlap between the two, in which case some Vh coins might belong before that date. While Renaud at London and Ion at Bury are each the sole Vh moneyer of their respective mints, a few Vh coins have been noted of other Vg Canterbury moneyers beside Ricard. Hoard evidence does not indicate that many moneyers were still active at Canterbury towards 1270. Against thirty-four Canterbury coins of Vg in the Coventry hoard there were only two of this mint of Vh (Ricard and Robert), and all but two of the forty-six London coins of Renaud in the hoard were listed as of Vg, which illustrates how scarce were the Vh coins even of its most prolific moneyer before the age of metal detectors.

Until recently the Canterbury coins of Vh by Ricard were thought to be the last products of this mint from the Long Cross period, but the discovery of two Vh coins in the name of Roger has now altered the picture and posed some new questions. The situation at Canterbury in the early 1270s is confused. From the death of Archbishop Boniface in July 1270 until late 1272, when the king himself died and the Dominican scholar Robert Kilwardby was appointed to the see, its revenues were in the hands of the crown. So when the moneyer Richard le Specer died, Henry granted his die in September 1271 to John Digge for life, for a fine of fifty marks. In June 1275 Roger le Assaur was sworn in as moneyer to Archbishop Robert, an order was issued for him to be supplied with three dies in his name, and John Digge was instructed to deliver to him the keys of the Canterbury exchange. A footnote to this entry records that shortly afterwards Digge had returned to the archbishop one of three dies that he held by concession of Henry III, but in respect of his transgression in having improperly retained the other two dies during the vacancy of the see (i.e. July 1270 to October 1272) and subsequently, he put himself at the mercy of the archbishop. During the last two years of Henry III (1270-2) £643 was minted at Canterbury, but how much of this was in Ricard's name we do not know. No minting is recorded at Canterbury in 1272/3, but £1,074 was produced between November 1273 and June 1274, after which there is no record that the mint was active again until 1278. It might have been expected that coin would have been struck with John's name after Ricard's death, in 1271/2 or in 1273/4, but no coin that could be dated after 1270 is known of a Ion at Canterbury. Instead, there are now the Vh coins by Roger who is not known to have been in office until after the closure of the mint from June 1274 onwards. It is difficult to see when Roger's coins could have been struck, unless the irregularities which Digge admitted had involved a die or dies intended for Roger at an earlier date; but this requires some sort of assumption (for which there is no documentation) such as that Roger had been meant to succeed Ion before the mint closed in 1274, and that the appointment in 1275 was an attempt to regularize the position (as an assayer Roger might well have had previous connection with the mint). The next occasion when the accounts record coinage at Canterbury was in April 1278, but this would mean that Roger would have had to wait nearly three years before he had an opportunity to put his dies to work, and at a time when the other three mints were all using dies of class VII.

Classes VI and VII

The two Edwardian classes that conclude the Long Cross series are unmistakable: with flowing locks of hair replacing the conventional curls that had been a feature of English coins since 1180, these coins foreshadow the new form of bust which from 1279 was to become standard on English silver coins of the late middle ages. Class VI has a very coarsely executed head, with large blobbed eyes, and a low crown with small fleurs and a fringe of four pellets beneath it. The face of class VII is more carefully drawn, with shorter hair, almond eyes, and a more shapely crown with taller fleurs; although there is some variety in the style of bust, no clear sequential pattern has yet been established within class VII. Until the discovery of the Colchester hoard in 1969 class VI was represented only by two unique coins, by Ion of Bury and by a new moneyer Roberd at Durham. The 1916 coins of Bury from the same pair of dies in Colchester must have reached the hoard in a payment undisturbed since leaving the mint. London (Renaud) is as yet recorded in class VI only from a cut halfpenny. In class VII there are coins of London with the names Renaud and Phelip, of Durham by Robert and of Bury by Ion and Ioce. The main variation in classes VI and VII relates to the inscriptions. The compact crowns of classes VI and VII do not intrude into the legend, and the separation of *e* and *n* in *henricus* (with resultant ligation of *nr*), which had been normal in class V, was no longer needed. In class VI and usually in class VII the *e* and *n* are joined instead. The Bury coin of class VI has the second and third *n* on the reverse of Gothic form, and a similar letter is also found on a London class VII obverse die of Renaud. The same shape inverted served for *u* (instead of the normal *v*) in Renaud's name and in Lund on Phelip's dies; this letter is also found occasionally on the obverse in *henricus*.

In the Easter Term of 1278 Renaud was succeeded in office at London by Philip de Cambio and a new moneyer was also sworn for Bury, Ioceus the goldsmith replacing John. Phelip's are the only coins of class VII of any mint that are not of great rarity. The London mint accounts show an average monthly amount of £800 of silver coined between November 1272 and June 1275, but whether or not this rate was maintained during the next two years, it seems likely that most of the £60,000 recorded between June 1275 and November 1278 would have been struck after Phelip's appointment in May 1278, because his coins of class VII, though scarce, are so much more numerous than Renaud's. It is not obvious what caused such an increase in mint activity during the last six months of the coinage, but it may have been related to some irregularity, since in 1279 Phelip and his assayer were tried and executed for adding too much alloy to the silver. In promoting the need for his new coinage Edward I was anxious to emphasise the deficiencies of the old, and in November 1278 large numbers of Jews were hanged for clipping (perhaps an extra source of silver for the mint). Analysis of Phelip's coins shows that they contained slightly more alloy than those of his predecessors, but they still seem to have reached a minimum of 92.5 per cent. fineness, the standard of sterling silver, and his exemplary punishment was probably part of the campaign to justify the recoinage. The one surviving English silver ingot of this period, stamped with Phelip's dies, falls marginally short of the sterling standard.

The only silver known to have been minted at Canterbury during the Long Cross period after 1274 was £810 (nearly 200,000 coins) between April and November 1278,

The Long Cross Coinage

during the currency of class VII. Even if swiftly followed by a recoinage, one might have expected the odd survivor from an issue of such size. Yet no Canterbury coin is known of class VII. For this reason, improbable as it may seem, the possibility that it was Roger's dies of class Vh that were used in 1278 cannot, on the basis of evidence currently available, be absolutely excluded. In June 1278 the archbishop resigned his see to become cardinal bishop of Porto, and for the period from July to November the Canterbury mint accordingly accounted to the crown.

The lack of a secure date for Roger's coin complicates the chronology of the coinage at other mints. In the case of Durham, the Foxes argued that new dies would not have been issued to the bishop after the death of Henry III until Edward I had returned to England for his coronation in August 1274; because Bishop Robert Stichill had then recently died, the first grant of minting rights in the new reign would have been to Bishop Robert de Insula who received his temporalities in November 1274. As neither Vh nor Vi is known of Durham, class VI by the new moneyer Roberd may have followed a period when the mint was closed. But when class VI was struck, within the bracket 1274-8, is impossible to say; conceivably, if Vh continued into the mid-1270s or beyond, class VI could have fallen later within that bracket than has generally been assumed. Similar considerations apply to the dating of classes Vh to VII at London and Bury.

Ireland

During the winter of 1250/1 the Irish Treasury was still having to send old coin to London and Canterbury for reminting. In the following May, partly for convenience, but also no doubt with a view to the potential profit, Richard of Cornwall received a specific grant of rights to coinage in Ireland for twelve years from September 1251. Roger of Haverhull was appointed warden of the exchange throughout Ireland and master of the mint, which was to be established in Dublin castle, with exchanges in Dublin, Limerick and Carrickfergus. The first account for expenses runs from October 1251. Closure of the mint was eventually ordered in January 1254, with the dies to be returned to London. No coinage took place in Ireland during the next twenty years, but in 1275 Stephen of Fulburn, recently appointed Bishop of Waterford and Treasurer of Ireland, was to take dies to Ireland for a new coinage which materialised in the following year. Richard Olof, a prominent Dublin citizen, held the Irish mint from June 1276 until May 1279, shortly before the Edwardian recoinage was launched, and coins were again struck there during those years. Since no recoinage was yet being undertaken, the revival of the mint at this period is curious – perhaps it was one of the conditions attaching to Stephen's appointment.

£43,000 was minted at Dublin in the years 1251-4. Unlike those struck for John in Ireland, Dublin sterlings of this period follow the current English reverse design. One of the factors influencing this may have been that, without round halfpence and farthings as there had been in John's time, a voided cross served the utilitarian purpose of facilitating the production of cut fractions. The new pennies did however retain the distinctive triangle around the bust on the obverse. In general appearance they otherwise coincide with early sceptred issues from the English mints, often having a tall central fleur in the crown as in class Va-c. There is considerable variation in their smaller details. For example, the crown may have pellets added on the band (recalling rare varieties in the English series), and the eyes may be oval or round. Some dies show shoulder lines, pellets before *henricus* or elsewhere in the inscription, a wireline inner triangle, or a hexafoil instead of the usual cinquefoil to the right of the bust. From a study of more than two thousand Dublin specimens of class V, mostly from the Brussels hoard, Seaby counted 154 obverse and 345 reverse dies. Since most of them are represented by many specimens, they are likely to include almost all the dies originally used, especially in the case of obverses which on average must have struck approaching 70,000 coins each. The Dublin moneyers of this coinage were Ricard and Davi, whose coins appear to have been struck in a proportion of seven to three, or perhaps two to one. As a similar ratio applies to London coins of early class V with the same two names, Richard Bonaventure and David of Enfield appear to have been awarded the Dublin contract on terms equivalent to those of their partnership in England.

No mint accounts survive for Richard Olof's Dublin coinage of 1276-9. All five specimens on record are from different dies and, as with the class VII coins of Durham and Bury, their great rarity probably underrepresents the size of the original issue. With their more realistic hair they have an obvious parallel in the English Long Cross coins of the Edwardian years, and although the busts differ somewhat from the English style the presence of a Gothic *u* on some of the dies provides an undoubted association with class VII.

Imitations

Continental imitations of the Long Cross type are much more abundant than their Short Cross predecessors. Partly this is due to their presence in thousands in the Brussels hoard, but the scale of their production was of a different order of magnitude from anything previously encountered. At least forty-eight obverse dies have been noted among copies of the Irish triangle type alone. As in the Short Cross period foreign mints produced a whole range of imitations, from close copies of the Long Cross type to free adaptations of it, and from the skilled work of professional craftsmen to the rough and inarticulate. In the earlier years the most active issuer was again Bernhard of Lippe whose sterlings, mostly struck at Lemgo and Blomberg, were often differentiated by a cinquefoil in the crown or on the centre of the reverse, and included some that carried the name of Widekind, the legendary local hero, or in due course of Bernhard himself. Related by style and die-links to these overtly imitative pieces are others, anonymous and without a cinquefoil, carrying the names of London moneyers such as Nicole and Henri. The Scottish design also was copied in Westphalia, by the counts of Schwalenberg and Sternberg. Although the Long Cross type continued to be imitated in Germany for many years, the focus of imitation gradually shifted westwards beyond the Rhine, and a hoard found in 1914 at Slype in the west of Flanders confirms the evidence of Brussels for widespread use of English coins and their copies in the area of modern Belgium during the 1260s. In fact, unlike their Edwardian successors, Long Cross imitations have not been much found in English hoards, and there was clearly an active market for them on the Continent. The popularity of English Long Cross coins abroad was no doubt chiefly due to commerce, but it may have been assisted by the largesse distributed in northern Europe in the 1250s by Richard of Cornwall in furtherance of his imperial ambitions. Late in the period imitation spread northwards. More than half the coins in the late thirteenth century hoard from Haarlo in the Netherlands consisted of English and other coins of the Long Cross type. Some of the late imitations bear the mint name of Kuinre, a lost castle on the Zuider Zee. Others, strongly represented in the 1887 find from Ribnitz in Mecklenburg, even have the reading *Civitas London*, suggesting that the type may have continued to be copied after the Edwardian recoinage of 1279. Many of the later imitations

The Long Cross Coinage

are small and light, indicating local products issued without any real expectation of being accepted as substitutes for English originals.

Identification of the most deceptive Long Cross copies presents greater problems than in the Short Cross and Edwardian periods because the regular Long Cross series has not hitherto been studied to the same degree of detail, so as to establish what was the official norm. The more accurate and literate copies no doubt include some that have not yet been recognised for what they are. The most obvious physical clues are weight and fineness, although deficiencies of technique, such as off-centre striking, can also be relevant. While some imitations fall into a weight range that overlaps that of the official coinage, many are measurably light, and their metal tends to fall below the sterling standard. As in the Short Cross series, however, there are also a few cases of German coins of good standard overstruck with the English types, presumably to save the mint charges that they would otherwise face on arrival in England. Several of the unusual readings recorded in Lawrence's lists must have been based on copies, and many imitations betray their origin by errors in their inscriptions – considerably more so than in the Edwardian series. Some are so blundered as to be incomprehensible. That this is particularly the case with reverses is probably due in part to the limited variability of the obverse legend, but mainly to the large number of unfamiliar reverse readings, complicated by their segmentation and the use of ligated letters. Some post-Brussels imitations carry the name of the late London moneyer Renaud, but most names on Long Cross imitations are otherwise copied from those first found in the recoinage and the early 1250s, up to class Vc. Proportionately, Nicole's name appears on imitations even more frequently than it does in the official series.

North's preliminary study of the Long Cross imitations and Archibald's report on the Colchester hoard (which contained thirty imitations based on the English type and three on the Irish) illustrate the wide variety that is to be found in the material. A few obverses can be related to originals of classes I and II but most, naturally, reproduce features of the abundant classes III and V. The sceptred imitations usually show the high crown of Va-c rather than the later low crown. Useful details for the recognition of unofficial work are the crown and eyes, and more complicated letters such as *S* and *X*. Characteristically for an imitative series, die-pairing was promiscuous. Obverse die-links are found between different English 'mints', while Irish obverses are used with English reverse readings and *vice versa*. Reverses carrying the names of recoinage mints were combined indiscriminately with sceptreless and sceptred obverses, the perverse results of which (such as a 'class V' coin in the name of Rener of York or one of 'class III' naming Davi of Dublin) sometimes confused earlier students of the series.

Coins of English class Vd have often been regarded as imitations since some of them look out of place in an official series. Yet they do exhibit features of a regular issue: weight and fineness are up to standard; all the late Vc moneyers at both London and Canterbury are represented, but no others; there is none of the habitual indiscipline in the pairing of dies such as one expects to find in an imitative series; and no die-links have been noted with undoubted imitations. Despite their anomalies, therefore, the coins labelled Vd by Lawrence must retain their status in the official canon.

Gold Pennies

Although England had its own gold coinage only momentarily during the thirteenth century, there is ample evidence for the availability of foreign gold coin and Henry III was himself a keen accumulator of it. While much of the king's treasure was in gold leaf, he also had many bezants (the *hyperpyra* of Constantinople), some *oboli* and *denarii de Musc'* or *Murc'* (Arabic dinars and double-dinars from Murcia in Spain), and even a few of the *augustali* of Frederick II. In the ten years to 1253 Henry had gathered more than two thousand marks of gold in the Wardrobe alone. Instead of his projected crusade, however, he had to use this treasure for his Gascon expedition of 1253-4. Immediately thereafter he began to build up a second treasure, no doubt with further foreign adventures in mind, but because of his recurrent financial difficulties it soon had to be diverted to domestic use. The gold leaf probably provided the material for his own gold coinage of 1257 the production of which he entrusted to his goldsmith, William of Gloucester.

Of the weight of two sterlings, and of purest gold, Henry's new coin was to be current for 20d., in line with the prevailing rate of exchange of 10:1 between gold and silver. In fact, undamaged specimens weigh marginally more than two silver pennies, perhaps because of the addition of a small amount of alloy, the two-pennyweight in the coins being their pure gold content rather than their total weight. In August 1257 the king commanded the Lord Mayor of London and the sheriffs to proclaim that the gold money that he had had made should be current in the City as elsewhere at 20d. This suggests that the new coin may already have been in existence and have met some resistance. When in November the king asked leading citizens of London for their opinion as to its usefulness, they replied that it would be inconvenient to the poor and that it would lower the value of gold if dispersed into so many hands, as was already happening with the price of gold leaf. In the light of this the king provided that no one should be compelled to take the gold penny, and that the Exchange would buy back any such coin at $19^{1}/_{2}$d. Later, however, the price of gold must have risen, since on three occasions between 1265 and 1270 the king is recorded as having bought gold pennies at 2s. each. These were to be paid into the Wardrobe for his use as offerings on feast days. That two of the extant examples come from Italy is also a reminder that Henry was always under obligation to the Pope.

The design of the gold penny is much more delicately executed than that of the silver coins of the period. The king in his robes sits on a decorated throne, holding a lis-headed sceptre in his right hand and an orb in his left. Below his feet the floor is diapered. Evans compared the tiny crowned head, with broad forehead and realistic hair, with that on the effigy of Henry III in Westminster Abbey, and although the features are too small for it to be regarded as a proper portrait more effort does seem to have been made here to reflect Henry's actual appearance than with the normal stereotype of kingship on English medieval silver. This was the first occasion on which the enthroned figure of a ruler appeared on a western gold coin, owing its choice perhaps to the king's veneration for Edward the Confessor who had used this 'sovereign' type on one of his issues of silver pennies two hundred years before. The reverse type incorporates the long voided cross of the silver penny, but the three pellets in each angle are reduced in size and a large rose is placed between them. On the obverse the inscription follows that of the contemporary silver but, being broken by the cross above the orb and by the throne and figure below, the name is shortened to *h/enric'*. Seven coins are recorded, from four pairs of dies. Their obverses differ mainly in the degree of beading on the throne, and the reverses in the arrangement of the inscription *Willem on Lund(en)*. The letters are more elegantly made than on the silver, and from a smaller fount in order to allow more space for the design. There is no ligation of the letters, and some elaborate forms are found on individual dies – a Gothic *n*, a cross-barred Roman *N*, an ornamental *E* and an *L* with flourished ending.

Whether the use of several pairs of dies, each exhibiting some variation of design, indicates more than a limited period of minting, it is hard to judge. Since three of the

The Long Cross Coinage

recorded specimens are each unique there could well have been more dies used than we yet know. On the other hand, the Wardrobe accounts of 1259-61 see Henry selling some of his stock unfavourably at prices based on gold:silver ratios of less than 10:1, which argues against his gold coinage then being still in production.

Mint Output

The accounts for London and Canterbury in the Long Cross period follow the same format as described earlier under Henry III pre-1247, and are apparently complete. So far as volume is concerned, the pattern in 1247-1278 differs in two important respects from the late Short Cross period: first, the recoinage of 1247-50 lifted totals well above the high levels of the mid-1240s, to which they did not revert for a few years afterwards; second, from 1270 output declined (ceasing altogether at Canterbury in 1274), until a recovery at London in the late 1270s produced an unexpected flurry shortly before the Long Cross coinage was terminated.

Of the provincial mints opened for the recoinage there are preserved, in addition to the actual mintage at Shrewsbury, figures for die-keepers' fees at ten other mints. These fees were paid at the rate of one shilling per £100 minted, and from them output totals may be calculated. These have been compared with the numbers of each of the different mints in the Colchester hoard, which broadly coincide with the proportions suggested by the fees (enabling approximate estimates to be made for the other seven mints that participated in the recoinage). The implied output figures based on fees are as follows:

Lincoln	£36,300	Gloucester	£22,200
Northampton	£28,200	York royal	£21,200
Oxford	£28,200	Exeter	£17,700
Winchester	£25,000	Newcastle	£13,300
Norwich	£24,200	Wilton	£9,500

Estimated figures for the other seven mints are:

Bristol	c.£12,000	Carlisle	c.£5,000
York (abp.)	c.£11,000	Ilchester	c.£5,000
Hereford	c.£7,000	Wallingford	c.£5,000
Bury St. Edmunds	c.£17,000		

There are also actual mint output totals for:

| Shrewsbury, Feb. 1249 – Feb. 1250 | £7,227 |
| Dublin, Oct. 1251 – Sept. 1254 | £43,239 |

Principal mints:	London £	Canterbury £
Nov. 1247 – Nov. 1248	73,013	40,258
Nov. 1248 – Nov. 1249	80,559	41,703
Nov. 1249 – July 1250	35,939	18,394
July 1250 – May 1252	69,569	37,519
May 1252 – Nov. 1254	84,526	90,159
Nov. 1254 – July 1256	51,689	66,408
July 1256 – June 1257	28,566	32,733
June – Oct. 1257	9,244	14,236
Oct. 1257 – Dec. 1258	28,294	34,882
Dec. 1258 – Nov. 1259	19,250	32,412
Nov. 1259 – Mar. 1261	26,745	31,636
Mar. – Dec. 1261	24,107	36,763
Dec. 1261 – Jan. 1262	2,158	640
Jan. 1262 – Jan. 1263	26,381	24,209
Jan. 1263 – Jan. 1264	34,910	18,837
Jan. – July 1264	6,613	820
July 1264 – July 1265	5,435	
Jan. – Nov. 1265		14,876
July – Nov. 1265	16,074	
Nov. 1265 – July 1266	19,172	12,126
July 1266 – Dec. 1270	70,982	26,002
Dec. 1270 – Nov. 1272	18,756	643
Nov. 1272 – Nov. 1273	6,599	
Nov. 1273 – June 1274	10,315	1,074
June 1274 – June 1275	7,960	
June 1275 – Nov. 1278	60,663	
April – July 1278		355
July – Nov. 1278		455

The Long Cross Coinage

Calendar 1247 - 1278

1247   Grant to Richard, Earl of Cornwall, of half profits of recoinage for five years (13 June), extended to twelve years from 1 November, in consideration of 10,000 mark loan (27 July).

    Bury: abbot's die authorised (6 Dec.), writ for delivery, 26 Dec.

1248   Writ for mints at Lincoln, Northampton, Winchester, Norwich and Exeter (26 Feb.); officials to report to Exchequer in March.

    Pyx trial (12 March), ingots assayed for Canterbury, Bury, all five February mints, plus Ilchester.

    William Hardel, warden of the exchange, to superintend withdrawal of old coin (27 April). Foreign workmen to be recruited (16 July).

    Canterbury: Gilbert Bonnington appointed archbishop's moneyer *vice* John Chiche (Jan./Feb.).

    London: Henry Frowik sworn as *custos* (May).

    York: dies granted to Archbishop Walter de Gray (20 July).

    Writ for mints at Bristol, Carlisle, Hereford, Ilchester, Newcastle, (Nottingham,) Shrewsbury, Wallingford and Wilton (10 Oct.); officials to report 1-8 Nov.

    Bury: Abbot Henry d. 19 June; succeeded by Edmund of Walpole 17 Sept.

1249   Durham: Bishop Nicholas resigned (2 Feb.); Walter Kirkham appointed (temporalities 20 Oct.).

    York: replacements ordered for archbishop's incapacitated die-keeper.

1250   Orders for closure of recoinage mints (Hilary term, 23 Jan. – 12 Feb.).

    London: Richard Bonaventure and David of Enfield appointed moneyers (May/June).

    Canterbury: William Cokyn and John Terri appointed moneyers (May/June).

    Durham: dies ordered for Bishop Walter (Michaelmas term, Oct./Nov.).

    Long Cross recoinage undertaken in Scotland.

1251   Grant (8 May) to Richard of Cornwall to make new money in Ireland from 15 Aug.; Roger of Havershull appointed warden of exchange for Ireland (17 Sept.); first Irish mint account runs from 14 Oct.

1252   Bury: Randulf le Blund presented as moneyer (Easter term).

1253   Nicholas of St. Albans dead (*ante* 6 March).

    Durham: dies restored to Bp. Walter (June). Three pairs exchanged in Dec.

1254   Closure of Dublin mint ordered (8 Jan.); dies to be returned to London.

1255   Canterbury: dies granted on farm for 100s. p.a. to Robert de Cantuaria (29 April) and Robert de Cambio (14 Nov.).

    London: die of Nicholas granted to William of Gloucester (8 May).

1256   Canterbury: grant of dies for life at 100s. p.a. to Nicholas de Hadlo (10 Jan.), John Terri (12 April) and William Cokyn (12 April).

    London: grant of dies for life at 100s. p.a. (25 Oct.) to Henry Frowik, Richard Bonaventure, David of Enfield, Walter de Brussel, William of Gloucester and John Hardel.

    Bury: Abbot Edmund d. 31 Dec.

1257   Gold penny ordered to be current for 20d. in the City of London (16 Aug.)

    Canterbury: die granted to Robert de Cantuaria junior (27 Jan.), which die to William of Gloucester (1 Oct.) on Robert's decease.

1258   Bury: Abbot Simon of Luton appointed (temporalities 12 Jan.); Reginald FitzHenry appointed moneyer (May/June).

    King conceded Provisions of Oxford.

1247–1278

1259 Treaty of Paris: Henry III agreed terms with Louis IX.
1260 London: David's die granted to Thomas of Weseham, king's surgeon (27 May).
 Durham: Bp. Walter d. 9 Aug.; Robert Stichill appointed (Sept.; temporalities 5 Dec.).
 Judicial enquiry into mint disputes.
1261 London: Thomas compensated for withdrawal of die (July ?)
 Canterbury: Ambrose the clerk appointed moneyer (Feb.) for one year.
1262 Reform of financial administration, salaries for moneyers. William of Gloucester replaced as warden.
 Canterbury: Ambrose to share die with Robert Polre (Jan.).
1264 Battle of Lewes (14 May); king surrendered to Simon de Montfort.
 No coinage at Canterbury, July - Dec.
1265 Bury: John de Burnedisse appointed moneyer (29 Jan.).
 Battle of Evesham (4 Aug); de Montfort killed.
1267 London: William of Gloucester's privileges confirmed.
1268 Canterbury: Richard le Specer appointed archbishop's moneyer (19 April).
1270 Canterbury: Abp. Boniface of Savoy (since 1244) d. 18 July.
1271 Canterbury: die of Richard le Specer, lately deceased, granted for life to John Digge (23 Sept.).
1272 Henry III d. 16 Nov.; Edward I abroad.
 Canterbury: Abp. Robert Kilwardby appointed (temporalities 12 Dec.).
1274 Durham: Bp. Robert Stichill d. 4 Aug.; Robert of Holy Island appointed (temporalities 8 Nov.). No mention of mint in account for vacancy (20 Aug. – 12 Nov.).
 Edward I returned to England (crowned 19 Aug.).
 No coinage at Canterbury, June 1274 - April 1278.
1275 Canterbury: Roger le Assaur appointed archbishop's moneyer (27 June), three dies ordered.
 Provision for dies to be taken to Ireland (Feb.- March).
1276 Dublin: Richard Olof moneyer (from 8 June).
1278 London: Philip de Cambio appointed moneyer (18 May) to succeed Reginald de Cantuaria; mint account closed 29 Nov.
 Bury: Joceus de Kyrketone goldsmith replaced John as moneyer (May).
 Canterbury: Archbishop Robert resigned (5 June); his last account closed 7 July. Mint accounted profit to king, 7 July - 20 Nov. 1278.

GOLD PENNIES, FROM 1257

Wt. c. 45.5gr. (2.95g.). Valued at 20d., 1257; 24d. from 1265.
 Obv. Figure of king seated facing on ornamented throne, with sceptre and orb. *h/enric/Rex III*, with varied stops by *III*. Rev. Long voided cross with rose between three points in each angle. *Willem on Lund(e)(n)*. Some unusual letters, including Gothic *n*. ER.

The Long Cross Coinage

SILVER PENNIES 1247 – 1278

ENGLISH MINTS

Obv. type: Crowned facing head, with beard (normally indicated by pellets); except in classes VI and VII the hair is represented by two crescents enclosing pellets each side and a row of dots below the crown; classes IV-VII show sceptre in king's right hand. *henricus Rex* etc., *nr* usually joined. Rev. Long voided cross with a small point in the centre and three large pellets in each angle; names of mint and moneyer (except class I), with frequent ligation of letters. Mint signature of Bury St. Edmunds is normally *S. Edmund* (II – V) or *Se(i)nt Ed* (V – VII), or abbreviated.

CLASSES I - III, without sceptre

I (end of 1247). Crescent and star before king's name. No moneyer's name.

Ia.   *henricus(:)Rex*, no letters joined. Five pellets below crown. Round face. Beard of short strokes or pellets. Rev. *Ang/lie/Ter/ci'*. Some rev. dies have no letters joined; otherwise, *An* and *er* joined. A small point between the groups of pellets. London only (no mint name). VR.

Ib.   *henricus Rex An(g), nr* and *An* joined. Some have stop before and/or after *Rex*. Thinner face, with beard of pellets (rarely strokes). Five or three pellets below crown. Rev. *lie/Ter/ci'/Lon* (etc.), *er* joined, mostly with a stop after *ci'*. Some have extra points between pellets. London: *Lon, Lun*; also VR mules Ia/b and Ib/a. Canterbury: *Can*, rare. Bury St. Edmunds: *Aed*, ER.

II (1248). *henricus Rex Terci'* (var. *Terc*); usually *nr* and *er* joined. Star at top, before king's name. Face mostly long and thin, with pellet beard. Five or (normally) three pellets below crown. Rev. names of moneyer and mint (henceforward); letters *on* normally unjoined. Occasionally an extra point between pellets on early dies. At first rev. dies of class II were extensively used with Ib obvs. at London and Canterbury.

IIa.   Mintmark star 2, curled *X* (X1). The face tends to be broader than in IIb. London, Canterbury, Bury.

IIb1.   Star 3, curled *X* (previously part of Davis IIa). London, Canterbury, Bury; plus Winchester, Lincoln and Northampton.

IIb2.   Star 3, plain *X* (X2). London, Canterbury, Bury; plus Exeter, Gloucester, Norwich (VR), Oxford and York royal.

III (1248-50). *henricus Rex III', nr* joined; *X* normally plain (X2). Star at top. Three pellets below crown (henceforward). Beard with inner row of small pellets; ER var. has beard of strokes. Wedge-tailed *R* except in IIId. London, Canterbury and Bury; plus seventeen recoinage mints.

IIIa1.   Faces as in class II (mostly long and pointed). Beard of four or five pellets, rarely three, each side of chin pellet; or occasionally a beard of strokes. Eyes usually slightly almond-shaped. No pellets between upper and lower curls. Star 3, usually straddling central ornament of crown, with two points on horizontal axis. Normally a single pellet stop after *Rex*.

IIIa2.   Smaller face, with rough beard, and necklines often indicated. No pellets between curls. Almondy eyes. Normally a colon after *Rex*. Star 3 with two points on vertical axis (at 0° and 180°).

IIIab.   As IIIa1, but broader bust, transitional between IIIa and IIIb. Plain *X* (X2, IIIab1), or hooked with second stroke consisting of two crescents (X3, IIIab2).

IIIb. Rounder and broader face, with little or no indication of neck. Beard usually includes three large pellets each side of chin. Still no pellets beween curls. Star 3. Usually a pellet after *Rex*.

IIIbc. As IIIb, but with features of IIIc (e.g. traces of neck, pellets between curls, more pointed face). Ligation of *enr* frequent. Star 3 (rare) or 4.

IIIc. Shorter, pointed face, with lines indicating neck; round eyes. Hair crescents often have outward-curling ends. Star 4. Usually a colon after *Rex*, and pellet between curls. Wedge-tailed *R* as previously. Earlier coins (IIIc1) have coarser bust. Later dies show a more finely drawn portrait (IIIc2, CT IIId1; confined to ongoing mints).

IIId Finely grained circles. New ball-tailed *R*. Bust with rounded face often resembles class IV. (CT IIId2). Star 4 or (rarely) 5. London, Canterbury and Bury only.

CLASSES IV - V, with sceptre and stylized curls

IV (1250). Star 5 at top; *henricus/Rex/:III'*, divided by sceptre; *nr* joined. Smaller lettering. Round eyes. Normally pellets between curls. Hair crescents often with curled ends, and sometimes with small crescents outside them. All rare. IVa. Crown with pommy central fleur and pellets at each end; London only. IVab. Crown with fleur-de-lis central ornament and pellets at ends; London (ER), Canterbury, Bury. IVb. Crown with central lis and half-lis at ends; London only.

V. Inscription *henricus Rex/III'* (with *nr* normally joined, except in Vd), beginning after sceptre-head (300°).

First Phase (Va-Vc), 1250-7. London, Canterbury, Bury, Durham (*Durh*); see also Dublin. 'High crown', with tall central fleur pommy (as in classes I-IVa), and pellets at each end (or rarely half-lis, in Va1 and Vb1). Normally small crescents outside curls. Often a stop after *III*. *A* occasionally double-barred.

Va. Round eyes. Prominent pellet on chin. Ball-tailed R2. *X* plain (X2) in Va2, or later with second limb of two crescent wedges (X4) in Va3. Canterbury var. has pelleted crown (Va4, ER).

Vb. Round eyes; head usually larger than in Va; chin pellet less prominent. Wedge-tailed R1; X4.

Vc. As Vb, but almond-shaped eyes. Some have pellets between curls. CT divide Vc into Vc1 with ball-tailed R2, Vc2 with wedged R1, and Vc3 with three pellets (sometimes with stalks) instead of central fleur of crown. *N* occasionally double-barred. Also muled both ways with Vd.

Second Phase (Vd and Ve), c. 1257. London, Canterbury (*Kan* in Vd), Bury (Vd only, *Beri*). Special crowns. Pellets between curls. Tall lettering, with curule *X* (X5); *on* normally separate.

Vd. Arched crown band, with fleured ornaments. Three varieties of head: 1, crude style; 2, large but tidy head, rounded chin, little neck, with crown band sometimes doubled; 3, as 2, but small head and longer neck. Rev. cross widely voided. New lettering; *N* often reversed; hunch-tailed *R*; *en* or *nr* sometimes joined (but not when *N* is reversed), but generally little ligation. Unusual spellings occur of moneyers' names and mints (*Kan, Beri*). All rare or VR; also mules Vc3/d, and Vd/c (ER).

Ve. Crown with pearled band. *nr* joined. All VR; also mules Ve/c (ER), Vd/e, and Ve/d (ER).

Third Phase (Vf and Vg), 1257-late 1260s. London, Canterbury, Bury, Durham (Vg only). 'Low crown', with small flat central fleur. Normal lettering; *h* often has out-turned tail; *nr* joined. Usually extra pellets in field.

The Long Cross Coinage

Vf. Crown with double band. Curule *X*. Many have triple colon before *henricus*. Also rare mules Vd/f.

Vg. Crown with single thick band. *X* curule (X5) or, later, with first limb straight, second curled and hooked (X6). Early dies sometimes have triple colon before *henricus*.

Fourth Phase (Vh and Vi), from c. 1270. London, Canterbury (Vh only), Bury. Coarser versions of Vg, with three pellets (usually in triangle) instead of central fleur of crown.

Vh. Earlier coins have large, broad head as in Vg, with small pellets (sometimes with short stalks) in crown. Later the head is narrower and coarser, with larger pellets on the crown; thick blobbed eyes; short nose and mouth. Sometimes colon after *henricus* or moneyer's name. Rare; VR at Bury (*Ioh's*).

Vi. Roughly executed head. Large letters, mostly with *enr* joined. Very crude work. There is no absolute dividing line between Vh and Vi. London rare, Bury (*Ions*) ER.

CLASSES VI and VII (1270s), with sceptre and realistic hair

VI. Crude face with large almond-shaped eyes and long wide locks of hair. Low crown with fleured ornaments, and four pellets below. Lis-headed sceptre. Inscription as in class V, but *en* joined. London (ER), Bury (*Seint Ed*, with Gothic *n*), Durham (*Durh*, ER).

VII. New neat bust with tight curls of hair, and oval eyes. Shaped crown with neat fleurs; fringe of four pellets below. Usually *en* joined but *nr* not. Some dies have Gothic *n* or *u*. London, Bury (*Sent Edm*, ER), Durham (*Dure*, ER).

IRELAND

Dublin only (*Diveli*), 1251-4 and 1276-8. Cf. English classes V and VII. Many detailed varieties. Obv. Crowned facing head within a triangle, with sceptre in king's right hand; *henri* (*enr* ligated)/*cus R/ex/ III*'. Rev. Long Cross type as at mints in England.

V. Crescent curls. Pierced cinquefoil, or rarely hexafoil, in right corner of triangle. Davi, Ricard.

VII. Realistic locks of hair. Cinquefoil (of five separate pellets around a central one) in corner of triangle. Roman *v* or Gothic *u*. Ricard only. ER.

CHAPTER III

1279 - 1343
Edward I – Edward III

For more than a hundred years after the death of Henry III the English throne was occupied by three generations of his descendants, all named Edward and so posing some questions of regnal attribution for numismatists. Edward I (1272-1307) instituted a major recoinage in 1279, which set the pattern for more than fifty years, throughout the rest of his own reign and that of Edward II (1307-27), until economic conditions and a shortage of silver led to new initiatives under Edward III (1327-77) in the 1330s and 1340s. The three Edwards were rulers of very different calibre and disposition, but one feature common to all their reigns was frequent involvement in external military campaigns. After returning from his Crusade in 1274, the formidable and ambitious Edward I, with years of government experience gained during his father's lifetime, devoted his energies to legal and administrative reform, of which a new coinage was a natural component. But from the late 1270s he had also become engaged in the subjugation of Wales, and campaigns in France and Scotland followed in the 1290s. Problems with the Scottish war clouded his later years, and contributed to the difficulties of his ineffectual son. Dependent upon unreliable favourites, defeated at Bannockburn in 1314, and unable to command the respect essential for royal government, Edward II's reign of twenty years came to an ignominious end when he was deposed in 1327 by the agency of his own French Queen Isabella, and reputedly murdered not long afterwards. Assuming personal rule in 1330, at the age of eighteen, Edward III quickly showed himself to have his grandfather's energy and ability, although he was more politically adroit than Edward I and in consequence on better terms with his magnates. After warfare had been successfully resumed in Scotland, Edward III became increasingly concerned with affairs in France, where the feudal homage that the English king owed to the king of France for his duchy of Gascony had long complicated their relationship. In 1336, responding to a Scottish appeal for help, Philip VI invaded Gascony, and in the following year declared Aquitaine confiscate. Edward III, grandson of Philip IV through his mother, then retaliated by laying claim to the French throne, as being nearer in line of succession than Philip VI (who was a grandson of Philip III), at the same time promising a return to the good government of St. Louis and an end to the debasement of the coinage which had earned Philip IV the name of 'le faux monnayeur'. France was invaded in 1339 and in the following year, which with the English naval victory at Sluys saw the first major encounter of the Hundred Years' War, Edward formally assumed the title of King of France. The costs of foreign war were again heavy, and throughout the Edwardian period the crown's need to raise finance increased the leverage that the nobility, knights and burgesses could exert when assenting to taxation, so contributing to the development of the Parliamentary system. Ironically, while Edward I had left the crown in debt, the less enterprising Edward II bequeathed a healthy exchequer to his successor; but financial constraints soon reappeared, and with them an increasing parliamentary concern over matters relating to coinage and currency.

Of all medieval English coins the pennies of Edward I and II are the most frequently encountered. The balance of payments was still favourable and in the 1280s and 1300s great quantities of silver passed through the mints. The campaigns against the Scots from the 1290s onwards led to the loss of many hoards in Scotland and the north of England, so that new finds are of almost annual occurrence. Without a native gold coinage or a successful equivalent to the continental *gros*, large payments or accumulations of treasure in England involved huge quantities of coin. The greatest hoard of the period on record, from the bank of the river Dove at Tutbury in Staffordshire in 1831, was said to have contained at least a hundred thousand Edwardian sterlings. Although many of these were probably melted down, eight thousand more appeared in the 1877 find at Montrave in Fife, twelve thousand at Aberdeen in 1886 (a group still substantially intact) and the supply continues. The Aberdeen hoard and more recent Scottish finds such as those from Renfrew (1963), Loch Doon (1966) and Ednam (1996) are of particular value in demonstrating the proportions of different varieties according to modern classification.

Documentary evidence is also unusually plentiful for this period, allowing important insights into medieval coinage policy and mint practice. Edward I's recoinage was undertaken in 1279-81, during which time the reminting of old currency resulted in the issue of more than £300,000 in the first two years at London alone, supplemented in 1280 by Canterbury and a number of temporary mints opened for the purpose in the regions. During the recoinage a groat of fourpence was introduced, the first multiple of the silver penny in the English coinage, but having failed to win public acceptance it was soon discontinued and the denomination was not to become an established part of the system until 1351. More enduring were the round fractions which now became a regular feature of the English currency for the first time, farthings from 1279, halfpence a year later. In order to make the smallest coin easier to handle, extra alloy was at first added, but this experiment was discontinued after about a year, from which time onwards the farthing was struck from fine silver and at the weight of approximately one quarter of a penny.

After the closure of the regional mints in 1281, output continued to be substantial for the rest of the 1280s but in the 1290s it declined sharply in face of the infiltration of the English currency by continental imitations. This led to the demonetization of foreign coins in 1300 and to a partial renovation of the currency (like that of 1205), again supported by regional mints. The volume of coinage was still at a high level for much of the next ten years, but after 1310 there was another marked (although more gradual) reduction in the amount of bullion reaching the mints. Economic historians debate to what extent this was the result of military and diplomatic expenditure as well as economic and monetary factors, but the fact of it is undoubted and by the mid-1320s the activity of the English mints had almost ceased. The Edwardian penny coinage of 1279 to 1335 thus falls into two main phases, separated by the renovation of 1300, during each of which there was a comparable pattern of heavy output followed by declining volume. In 1335, partly in order to provide a higher mint price for silver but also in response to a shortage of small change, the weight and the fineness of halfpence and farthings were both slightly reduced and the export of precious metal was forbidden. This resulted in the minting of pence becoming relatively uneconomic but in increased output of the fractions, particularly halfpence. With the start of the Hundred Years' War in 1337 Edward III was in need of revenue to maintain an army on the Continent and to provide subventions to his allies. Export duties were increased and the king imposed a royal monopoly on the sale of wool; but reform of the coinage was becoming urgent. In 1344 the weight of the English penny, for the first time in the later middle ages, was materially reduced, and a regular gold coinage was initiated.

By 1279 a considerable proportion of the money in circulation was more than twenty-five years old, and the most recent issues were claimed to have fallen below the requisite standard of fineness. If the great recoinage was justified by the state of the currency, Edward I was also concerned to improve the control and accountability of his officials. A clear division of responsibility was drawn between the wardens, who reported directly to the king, and the master-workers, or masters, who entered into a commercial contract to run the mints as a manufacturing business. Thus the wardens had to check the honesty of the masters and their staff, and were responsible for exchanging old coin for new, the purchase of bullion, the issue of coin and the king's profit. The masters were responsible for the production of coin to the correct weight and fineness, for which they had to recruit and manage a substantial body of workmen and clerical staff. These new arrangements no longer required individual moneyers at each mint to be named on their coins, and thus in recording only their mint of origin the new coins of 1279 broke with a tradition of centuries. They also departed from the practice of the previous hundred years of having a voided cross on the reverse, since the addition of round farthings in 1279 and round halfpence in 1280 removed the need to produce fractional denominations by the physical division of pence into halves and quarters. Edward's new penny, being the work of professional continental workmen, also differed in general aspect from its predecessors, with clearer lettering and a neater portrait. It was to set the pattern for the design of the English silver coinage for the next two hundred years.

The new coinage took several months to plan and launch. Two wardens were appointed in January 1279, Gregory de Rokesley, the mayor of London and a leading merchant, and Orlandino de Podio, an Italian banker. In March William and Peter de Turnemire from Marseilles were appointed master-workers, and a third (and senior) partner, Hubert Alion from Asti, was added in April. The wardens' account runs from 28 April and they were sworn in on 17 May when dies were first delivered. In June the king sent good old coins to ten cities to prime the exchanges, and the first exchange of new money took place in August. The archbishop was authorised to receive his share of the profits of the Canterbury mint in June, but the mint was still sealed up in August and although Canterbury dies were ready in November the mint was still in need of preparatory work. Writs for the supply of dies to the bishop of Durham and to the abbey of Bury St. Edmunds were issued in November, but complications in the latter case delayed the opening of the Bury mint until the following summer. In December 1279 the king entered into a new indenture with William de Turnemire, effective from 8 January 1280, covering the mints of London, Canterbury, Bristol and York. London was to have as many furnaces as possible, Bristol and York twelve each and Canterbury eight including three for the archbishop. This was the earliest contract of its kind, and spelt out the minting charges applicable to each denomination. On sterlings and groats the master was allowed 7d. per pound of silver, 3¼d. being for labour costs, 1¼d. for loss of silver in the fire, 1½d. for remedy and 1d. for his own fees and expenses. The king was to have 12d. but if the new groats could be made more economically, the savings were also to go to the crown. Farthings were more expensive to make, so the master would get 10½d., financed by the addition of extra alloy. Pence were struck at 243d. to the pound, but from January 1280 to February 1281 this was increased to 245d., the additional twopence going to the king because of the extra costs of replacing the currency. Also, slightly higher rates, ranging from 244d. to 250d. per pound, are shown in the mint accounts from 1308/9 for halfpence and farthings.

London was usually by far the largest and most important mint throughout the period. Except in the 1290s Canterbury played a significant, and increasingly active, supporting role, even outperforming London between 1314 and 1320. The ecclesiastical establishments at Durham and Bury St. Edmunds were the only other mints operating in England most of the time, but although they provided some northward extension of facilities for coinage and their output made a useful addition to the currency as a whole, their existence was due more to political than to commercial considerations. Between

Edward I – Edward III

1279 and 1299 London issued nearly £700,000 in pence alone, and in the next twenty-five years a similar amount. The equivalent figures for Canterbury were £220,000 in the first period and just over twice as much in the second. In hoards buried in the 1320s or 1330s London coins tend to account for some 50 per cent. or more of the total and Canterbury coins for between 25 and 30 per cent. More than half of the remaining 20-25 per cent. would consist of coins of Durham and Bury, with the balance from the provincial mints of 1280 and 1300. Chronologically, the average proportions would be about a quarter from the first twenty years and three-quarters from 1300 onwards, the bias in favour of more recent issues, when compared with the respective volumes of mint output during those periods, reflecting the natural wastage of earlier coins from circulation through loss, melting, export or (as in 1300) reminting.

The mint accounts for this period are of unusual interest since the charge for mintage of English silver was higher than that for foreign silver (described as coming from Bruges, Brussels or Ghent, or as Baudekin silver), so that the warden had to separate the two in his record of bullion purchased. With the reminting of old domestic currency during the recoinage, English silver heavily outscored foreign at London until April 1281; but in the middle of 1281 foreign silver overtook English and by the later 1280s their original positions had been reversed. At Canterbury, which serviced the Channel ports, the prominence of English silver in 1280 was less marked than at London, and after 1281 this mint relied almost entirely on foreign silver up to 1290. Thereafter supplies from either source dwindled to the point where the mint at Canterbury had to close from 1294 until the end of 1299. Although London continued to operate throughout the 1290s it was on a much reduced scale, with more of the silver tending to be of English origin in the second half of the decade. The renovation of 1300 involved the issue of around 50 million new pence, more than a quarter of them from the additional mints operating in the regions. Thereafter activity was relatively subdued for three years before a huge increase of output based on foreign silver took place from 1304. Under Edward II minting declined until in 1323 Canterbury again had to close and London was reduced to a trickle. Although a few pence were again struck at Canterbury at the beginning of Edward III's reign, between 1328 and 1331, the mint then ceased to function until the reduction of the weight standard in 1344. Presumably because the archbishop had a share in the profits, Canterbury was not authorised to strike halfpence and farthings which were normally reserved to royal mints, and this enabled London to remain in business through the 1320s and 1330s.

Groats are not identified in the London accounts but most if not all of them belong to the recoinage period. For the fractions, however, the higher rates of mintage caused them to be separately recorded. Farthings and halfpence accounted for between five and ten per cent. of the sums issued during the original recoinage, but considerably less thereafter, with farthings continuing to outnumber halfpence by a large margin. After the turn of the century little silver was struck into halfpence until 1335, although there was a steady if modest issue of farthings even in the later years when no other denomination was coined at all. The recoinage mints produced halfpence and farthings in 1280, when they were needed as part of a complete reconstruction of the currency, but not in 1300 when the renovation had a more limited objective.

Four of the regional mints were brought into operation both in 1280 and in 1300: Bristol, Chester, Newcastle and York. Lincoln contributed in 1280 as it had done in all previous recoinages, but not thereafter. Instead, a new royal mint was opened in 1300 beyond the river Humber, at Kingston-upon-Hull, before the royal mint at York – this had alarmed the archbishop, who feared that his ancient right of coinage, only exercisable when the king had his mint at York, might thereby be circumvented. Also in 1300 Exeter, a regular participant in pre-Edwardian recoinages but missing in 1280, was added in the south-west. Ireland was served by the reopening of a mint in Dublin for both recoinages, assisted by Waterford in the earlier one. Their coins are basically of the English type but are instantly recognisable by the traditional triangular frame enclosing the portrait. Coinage also took place in the 1290s, on a very limited scale, at Dublin, Waterford and Cork, but after the 1300 renovation the only further occasion in the Edwardian period on which coins were struck in Ireland was in 1339 during the debased issues of halfpence and farthings.

The declining output of the English mints during the 1290s was in large part due to the influx of foreign coin, although war with France, rebellion in Wales and trouble with Scotland did not help. Continental sterlings yielded a double profit to the bearer, since they not only avoided mint charges for conversion into English coin but they were also often of inferior silver. Several attempts were made in the 1280s and 1290s to confiscate foreign coins but, to judge from the contents of hoards, with only limited success. Most of these had some variant of the English type. Those with the facing portrait bare-headed, or 'polled', were known as pollards, and others with a chaplet of roses (*croket*) were called *rosarii*, or crockards. By the Statute of Stepney in May 1299 the king forbad the export of English or the import of foreign coin. Crockards and pollards already in the country were to pass only for a halfpenny each from Christmas 1299, and then to be completely demonetized at Easter 1300. Another problem was the recurrent evil of clipping, leading Edward to take harsh measures against the Jews who were supposedly its chief exponents. The recoinage of 1300 was thus aimed at restoring the quality of the currency by the reminting of native coin, which had suffered loss of weight, as well as of the baser foreign money.

In order to maintain the interchangeability of English and Scottish coins in both countries, Alexander III had carried out a thorough recoinage of earlier issues in Scotland c. 1280. Although individual mints are not named on the new Scottish sterlings, different combinations of mullets and stars in the quarters of the reverse cross indicate that a network of regional mints was brought into action to carry through the exercise as quickly as possible. No records survive from the Scottish recoinage, but it is evident from the workmanship of the coins that foreign craftsmen were recruited as in England. Scottish coins were also struck in the name of John Balliol, whom Edward had placed on the throne in 1292 and summarily removed four years later. His mint at Berwick-upon-Tweed, however, although no longer available to the Scots, was soon commissioned to produce English coin, and continued to do so until the Scots recaptured the town in 1318. English coinage at Berwick was later revived for a few years after the town was recovered under Edward III in 1333. With one brief exception early in the reign of Edward II, the English coins of Berwick were struck from local dies, and do not conform to the pattern of the regular English series. Apart from Berwick under English rule there was no active mint north of Tweed between 1296 and 1318. When Robert Bruce regained control of Berwick in that year, he commissioned a new issue of Scottish coins, but within a few years supplies of silver to the English mints dried up and the scarcity of Bruce's coins points to a similar situation in the north. During the later years of the thirteenth century English coins had come to form a large part of the currency of Scotland, and they continued to do so in the first half of the fourteenth century. But whereas in England the renovation of 1300 had removed most of the crockards and pollards as well as many earlier Edwardian coins that had suffered from clipping, the lack of mints in Scotland during the Wars of Independence allowed more coins of the 1280s and 1290s, English and continental, to remain in circulation than in England. Fourteenth-century hoards from Scotland thus normally contain a relatively higher proportion of pre-1300 issues than do those from England.

Edward I – Edward III

Classification and Arrangement

The study of thousands of Edwardian pence has enabled successive generations of students to refine the classification of the series to the most intricate detail, so that the position of individual dies in the sequence can often be determined with a high degree of precision. Originally it was thought that differences in the length of the king's name indicated successive reigns – *Edw* for Edward I, *Edwardus* for Edward III, and intermediate forms for Edward II, an arrangement which appeared to be consistent with the occurrence on their coins of the personal marks of successive bishops of Durham. It is, of course, anachronistic to suppose that medieval administrators would have thought in such terms, and they were in any case unconcerned to distinguish between the coins of successive kings of the same name. But while this theory has long since been abandoned in its crude form, it does in fact contain an element of logic since most Edwardian pence up to 1300 read *Edw*, longer forms then followed until 1344 and, although *Edw* returns in 1344-51, *Edwardus* did not appear until 1351. The first scientific classification was the work of Edward Burns who, with reference to the contents of the Montrave hoard, defined fifty varieties in a sequence still broadly accepted today. This remarkable achievement was confirmed and amplified in a classic monograph by the brothers H.B. Earle Fox and J. Shirley-Fox, which brought extensive documentary evidence to bear on the numismatic material and enabled an absolute chronology to be more accurately established. The Fox scheme consists of fifteen groups spanning the whole coinage from 1279 to 1344. Group I contains the early coins of London struck in 1279 before the opening of additional mints, and groups II and III cover the recoinage issues in which ten mints participated. Groups IV and V include the abundant coins of the next ten years, with groups VI-VIII representing the diminished output of the 1290s. Coins of the seven mints opened for the recoinage of 1300 belong almost entirely to group IX. The very extensive group X (1300-10) covers the heavy output from the remainder of the reign of Edward I and the first years of Edward II, and groups XI to XVc the period of declining volume up to the early 1320s, after which few pence were struck until 1344. The last of the issues at the old weight, in the early years of Edward III, belong to the very rare group XVd.

The Fox groups are chiefly based on the progression of punches used for lettering, crown, hair and other features, and do not for the most part represent deliberate differences to mark new batches of dies (one of the rare exceptions to this being group VII with its distinctive rosette on the breast). Indeed, the boundary between one group and the next is often arbitrary, depending upon which feature is given preference. To the mint personnel of the time the groups now defined by modern numismatists would have been irrelevant, and mules between groups or sub-groups would have been the natural result of some dies lasting longer than others. But they are invaluable today in demonstrating the sequence of issue of the dies, and have enabled subsequent work to reveal the anatomy of the coinage in minute particular, even if the degree of granularity to which analysis of the series has now been taken requires a practised eye to follow and goes beyond what is needed except for the most specialist purpose. With the exception of groups VI and VII, where the sequence remains uncertain, the broad arrangement of the Fox groups has not been challenged. North's *Sylloge* of the series conveniently incorporates the many detailed divisions and sub-divisions that have been made by subsequent students, and is an indispensable guide to the state of modern knowledge of this complex series. While most of the Fox groups have thus now been sub-divided in a greater degree of detail, some of them have required a rearrangement of the sequence of varieties within them. Although the rare groups VI and VII still pose unresolved problems, others, notably groups IV, VIII and X, have been internally reorganised. The last of these, representing the enormous output of the first decade of the fourteenth century, is much the most complicated, and has now been divided into a Primary and a Secondary phase, each subdivided into six main varieties and many lesser ones based on inscription, lettering and forms of crown. A simple division of the material between the thirteenth and the fourteenth centuries may be drawn on the basis of the depiction of the crown: up to group IX, which covers the recoinage of 1300, the end fleurs had normally been shown with all three foils visible (trifoliate), but very soon after the introduction of group X a more realistic (bifoliate) form was adopted, showing only two of them, and this was almost invariable thenceforward.

The task of constructing an absolute chronology for successive groups and sub-groups can be approached from a number of angles: the proportions of different varieties in hoards, documentary evidence, and the activity of individual mints. One of the most important of these, as recognised long ago, was the bishop's mint at Durham. After the death in June 1283 of Robert of Holy Island, who had held the see since 1274, personal marks of his successors were placed on Durham dies, and these provide several convenient fixed points for dating. The coins of Antony Bek (1283-1311), which run from group IVb to XIa, are identified by the cross moline from his arms, briefly at first in one quarter of the reverse cross, but thereafter placed before the inscription. It is entirely in keeping with Bek's presumptuous character that he should have been the one to initiate this practice. His relations with Edward I were not always straightforward, and growing difficulties between them from 1300 led to the confiscation of his temporalities by the king in 1302-3 and again in 1305-7. Bek's successor was the monk Richard Kellawe (1311-16), promoted from the cathedral chapter in the exceptional circumstances of 1311, when the king's authority was under challenge from the Lords Ordainers. Not being armigerous, Kellawe had his reverse dies (from XIa to XIII) marked with a bishop's crozier, or pastoral staff, at the upper end of the cross, but Louis de Beaumont (1317-33), sponsored by his cousin Queen Isabella, returned to armorial usage, with a lion and fleurs-de-lis (recognising his French royal lineage) instead of an initial cross on his coins from group XIII to XVc. The heraldic charge of Bishop Richard de Bury (1333-45), the king's former tutor, was a cinquefoil, which is not found on Durham coins; but early Durham pennies of Edward III (XVd) with a small crown in a panel in the centre of the reverse may belong to his episcopate, even if the origin of the mark is unexplained. The Foxes attempted to construct a chronological model in order to fit certain varieties at Durham without a bishop's mark into periods of Bek's suspension or of *sede vacante* (notably that after Kellawe's death). But it is now clear that such unmarked varieties occur at too many separate points in the series for all of them to be explained in this manner, and unmarked dies must from time to time have been sent to Durham through error or idleness, or perhaps simply for expediency. Some of Bek's later obverse dies have a plain initial cross altered to moline, as if dies held in stock were altered to meet an order from Durham. Thus although it is usually a fair assumption that Durham dies with the mark of a particular bishop belong to his episcopacy, sometimes they continued to be used during the subsequent vacancy, while those without a mark may, but do not necessarily, belong to a period when the see was temporarily vacant or its privileges withdrawn. Durham coins occur of all groups from II to XV with the exception of group VIII. This could indicate that the mint was inactive during the second half of the 1290s, like Canterbury, but when supplies of silver were very sparse old dies might have remained serviceable for a while. The bishop was entitled to three sets of dies at any time, and usually would not wait until all three needed to be exchanged for new. One consequence of this is a number of remarkable mules, such as those combining Bek's cross moline with Kellawe's crozier

Edward I – Edward III

(XIa). A Beaumont obverse muled with a London reverse (XVc) shows that dies were sometimes issued incorrectly, a phenomenon also illustrated by a sole 'Canterbury' coin of group X, die-linked to London, in a cluster of London coins in the Mayfield hoard.

PERSONAL MARKS OF THE BISHOPS OF DURHAM UNDER EDWARD I AND II

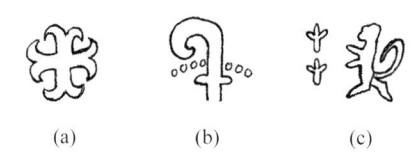

(a)   (b)   (c)

(a) Bek's cross moline, IV-XI; (b) Kellawe's crozier, XI-XIII;
(c) Beaumont's lion and lis, XIII-XV.

Coins of Durham generally outnumber those of Bury St. Edmunds in hoards by around three to one, reflecting the respective number of dies allocated to the bishop and the abbot – an allocation that itself may have owed more to market forces than to ecclesiastical rank. Although the writ for a new set of Bury dies was issued in November 1279 there was delay in its implementation. The abbot asked for a standard of silver to be supplied and for guidance about how many pence were to be struck from a pound. The king's council eventually decided not to send a standard and to pass instructions by word of mouth. Alone in the Edwardian series, early coins of Bury still carry the name of the moneyer, Robert of Hadleigh, and this peculiarity may also have contributed to the delay, since his first coins were not minted until the end of June 1280. Bury's pence continued to carry Robert's name for several years, and its eventual replacement by the mint name is presumably to be associated with the appointment of Robert's successor in 1287. The existence of rare coins of this mint of group VIII may be due to the fact that, since the abbot was only entitled to one set of dies at a time, he needed replacements more frequently than the bishop of Durham. An order for a new set for Bury as late as 1340, like a similar order for Durham dies in 1336, shows that an ecclesiastical mint, lacking the right to coin fractions, might still have occasion to strike pence after they had ceased to be an economic proposition at London. However, in 1338 the abbot of Reading was, exceptionally, provided with dies for the smaller denominations, a right that he continued to enjoy when the minting of pence was resumed after the weight reduction of 1344.

Groats

It is clear from the number of dies and varieties that groats must have been struck in reasonable quantity, but although they might have been found more convenient for saving than sterlings very few have been found in hoards and as a result they are rare today. Many surviving specimens show signs of having been mounted, and they do not seem to have been fully accepted into normal currency. Since charges for the minting of groats were at the same rate per pound as for pence, they are not shown separately in the accounts and their period of issue is thus not accurately known. A reference in Turnemire's December 1279 contract indicates that the extent of any possible savings from minting the larger coin was not yet known; but this does not necessarily imply that at that date none had yet been struck, since the groat had been included in the original specification for the new coinage.

Edward's groat was a handsome coin and broadly, if not in detail, established the design for this denomination until the reign of Henry VII. The portrait is no larger – indeed, it is sometimes smaller – than that on pence, but the greater space available enabled it to be enclosed in a tressure of four arcs (or quadrilobe), with the addition of small floral ornaments in the spandrels, beside the head, and often on the breast. Two concentric circles of inscription on the reverse (a format only previously used on the odd occasion in the Saxon and Norman periods) are divided, as on pence, by a long cross with pellets in the angles, but the cross is more ornamental, with foliate ends, than on the smaller silver or indeed than on later groats until the Tudors. Although Turnmire was authorised to strike the groat throughout the kingdom, the only mint that actually produced it was London, the name of which, in the unusual form *Londonia Civi*, occupies the inner circle of inscription. The outer continues the king's titles from the obverse, thus reading in full *Edwardus Di Gra Rex Angl/Dns hibn e Dux Aqut*. Except for a trial type penny of 1279 with *Dei Gra,* this was the first occurrence of either *Dei Gratia* or the Aquitainian title on an English coin, although both had long been used on the Great Seal. Stops between words are colons of two or more usually three pellets, and abbreviation marks, abnormally, are often found as marks of contraction within words (*D'i, Dn's*), as well as after them.

Clear points of correspondence between groats and pennies are difficult to find, and this has led to differing views about the sequence of issue of the various types. Fox illustrated seven specimens and associated them with pence of groups I to IV. North also divided them into seven varieties, but differently arranged. Allen's recent study is based on 59 groats, from 29 obverse dies of which thirteen are represented by a single example. Such a high proportion of singletons implies that many other dies were used, and the discovery of new specimens providing currently unrecorded die-combinations might well result in the need for some rearrangement. But for the time being North's classification may be used for descriptive purposes, even if the order is unclear at several points.

North placed his variety a, with normal colon stops, at the head of the series, partly because of some resemblance between the small neat face and that on pence of Ic to IIa. This is the least rare variety of the groats. No reverse die-links have been found between a and any other variety. However, a possible link between a and b is the form of the crown on two dies of variety a, which has an upper band of crescents supporting the intermediate jewels, somewhat in the manner of variety b. Groats with the ornate crown of variety b, of which five obverses have been noted, share reverse dies with the much rarer variety c, represented by a single obverse die. The portraits on b and c resemble those on early pence of group III, and this connection is borne out by the drapery on the c die which is a broken ellipse as on pence of IIIa. Links with other (probably later) varieties are found in a groat combining an obverse of b with a reverse of e, and another with the c obverse and a reverse of f. Variety e, also found muled with an f reverse, has a large, oval face like that on pence of IIIc-d, and on some dies the late *S* has a swollen centre as on pence from IIIf and IIIg onwards.

Variety f, with the late *S*, has three pellets below the bust (as on the earliest Dublin pence of Edward I), instead of the usual rosette, and its reverses are identifiable by the reading *hbin'* and, on most dies, by a pellet on the bar of the *N* in *Dns* (as on certain pence of group IIIe). Obverses of f have either the usual form of triple quadrilobe, with a thick band in the middle between two thin dotted lines, or a double tressure with the outer line omitted. The latter form is also found on a coin from a curious die, unknown to Fox but labelled g by North, on which the crown has bifoliate side fleurs, the trefoils in the spandrels are composed of three annulets, and the inscription ends *Ang* followed by two annulets, instead of *Angl*. This die is paired with a normal f reverse, and the face punch together with the double tressure links it closely to that variety.

There remains one variety, North d, which not only differs materially from the others in elements of its design but has not been found connected with any other through reverse die-links or mules. The trefoils in the spandrels, which on other varieties are often almost circular, are here formed of three spread leaves, and there are slipped trefoils in the reverse cross-ends. *N* in *Dns* is reversed, a form otherwise only found occasionally in variety a. But if variety d stands outside the rest of the series, several features such as the spearhead jewels in the crown and the late *S* argue that it cannot be the earliest. Fox described it last, and if any variety represents an issue of groats later than the general period of pence of groups II and III, this rare type perhaps has a claim for consideration. However, halfpence and farthings, the other new denominations of the recoinage, were suspended in 1281, and it may be that the issue of groats ceased about the same time.

Pence

Despite the addition of greater and lesser denominations under Edward I, the penny continued to constitute the core of the currency throughout the recoinage and for many years beyond.

Group I

What is presumably the first coin in Edward's name is a unique penny which was probably designed as a pattern or trial piece but which shows considerable wear from circulation. It retains the long voided cross on the reverse from the pre-1279 coinage, but with rosettes (reminiscent of those on Henry's gold penny) instead of groups of three pellets in the angles. In the omission of a mint name it also has a parallel with the earliest coins of 1247, but instead of continuing the royal titles from obverse to reverse as the first Long Cross pence had done (and as is found on Edward's own groats) the reverse repeats the king's name, now in full, and adds *Dei Gra*, which was not to be introduced on the normal penny series until Edward III's reign. Although the bust is undraped, and the crown consists of a band surmounted by three strawberry leaves, the design of the obverse generally resembles that subsequently adopted. The trial reverse, however, was entirely superseded. A plain single cross was introduced on the regular series, with a reversion to the three pellets of the preceding coinage; and the early recognition of the need to reopen provincial mints for the recoinage must have led to the decision to place mint names on the reverse (now *Civitas London, Villa Bristollie*, etc.), as had happened almost immediately in the renovation of 1247.

Coins of Fox group I were struck only at London. The earliest regular type of the new coinage, described by Fox as Ia, has an obverse inscription generally similar to that on the trial type, with *Rex* in full, and with lettering from the same fount, including the Gothic *n* and a characteristic *R* of which the tail is formed by a wedge with concave sides. But there are a number of differences: Ia has *Edw* not *Ed, hyb* not *hybe*, and it lacks the stops found on the trial die. On Ia dies the crown has either a forked central fleur (with upturned side petals) and bifoliate side fleurs, or a normal lis in the centre and trifoliate side fleurs, as is standard on all groups from I to IX. The portrait is usually distinctive, with the hair closer than on most later varieties; the fringe below the crown is occasionally omitted. One of the face punches used in Ia was the same as that on the trial die. Drapery is shown by two wedges that sometimes meet. Reverses have the same large lettering as on the obverse except that *N* is Roman (and occasionally double-barred).

Coins struck from both dies of Ia are very rare, but the dies were more extensively combined with those of Ic, so that Ia/c and Ic/a mules are rather less rare. The (relatively few) Ia dies must have remained in use for a time after Ic dies had become available.

The next types, Ib and Ic, have much smaller, neat lettering with Roman N, often reversed. Like Ia, they still have *Rex* in full, which in the nineteenth century misled some numismatists into attributing them to Edward III. Reverses of Ib and Ic are indistinguishable, but the single Ib obverse die is unique in the regular Edwardian series in reading *Ed, Anglie* in full and *hibn* (a form otherwise only found on groats). Clearly this die belongs to the early experimental phase at the outset of the new coinage, and the same is probably true of certain abnormal readings in Ic which include rare varieties with *Re, Rx* or the transposition *Angl Rex*. The Ib die has a colon after *Rex*, and some early Ic dies also include colons (very rarely) or pellets in the legend. Henceforward, although contraction marks remain normal, punctuation becomes exceptional. On the Ib die the portrait is immediately recognisable from the undraped bust (Ib has this, as well as the abbreviation to *Ed*, in common with the trial type). The hair is wider than in Ia and the eyes more prominent, two features which, with some variation, are characteristic also of Ic and Id.

With Id the inscription settles down to the standard form which continued unaltered until group X: *Edw R Angl Dns hyb*, the shortening of *Rex* to *R* being a result of the larger size of lettering which was to persist throughout the 1280s. The composite crowns of Ic and Id have a thick, plain band, not shaped to the ornaments. These are usually two pearls (i.e. rounded), but a (pointed) spearhead is sometimes found in the dexter position, and in Ic the sinister pearl is often omitted altogether. Mules between Ic and Id were unknown to the Foxes, which led them to suggest that the two might have been parallel issues. However, the mules between Ia and Ic and the close relationship between Id and early group II suggest that Id did follow Ic in a normal sequence. Mules between Ic and Id have now been noted, but they are exceptionally rare for two consecutive varieties, so as to suggest that, for some administrative reason, Id dies may not have been issued until those of Ic had generally been withdrawn. Ic/a mules have occasionally been mistaken for Ic/d but the (larger) letter founts of Ia and Id may be reliably distinguished from each other by the form of the *A*, which in Ia has a top bar consisting of two wedges sloping slightly downwards.

DISTINCTIVE LETTERS *A* IN GROUP I

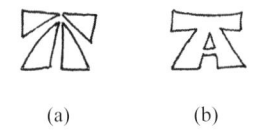

(a)   (b)

(a) Large *A* of Ia; (b) Large *A* of Id.

A few Id dies have an annulet on the breast, a mark only otherwise recorded early in group X. In the absence of any other explanation of this exceptional feature, Fox tentatively suggested that it might indicate a London issue on behalf of Reading abbey, which had enjoyed active royal patronage from time to time. In its foundation charter of 1125 the abbot had been granted the right to a moneyer at London, and he was to have a mint at Reading itself between 1338 and 1351. Although Edward I is recorded as having taken an interest in the affairs of the abbey in the 1270s, there is no documentary evidence for the exercise of its minting right in this reign, and the attribution can only be regarded as speculative.

All the dies used between May 1279, when dies were first delivered to the keepers of the exchange, and August, when the first exchange of new money took place, were probably of group I. Dies for Canterbury were ready on 15 November. Since the earliest coins of Canterbury are of group IIa, but extremely rare, IIa dies must have been in use at London at least some weeks previously, indicating the transition from Id to IIa c. October 1279.

CROWN FEATURES IN GROUPS I AND II

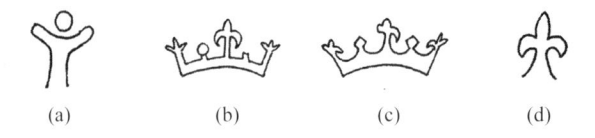

(a) Exceptional centre ornament in Ia; (b) Crown with plain band, Ic;
(c) Crown of IIa, with shaped band and damaged dexter foil of central fleur;
(d) Central fleur of IIb crown.

Group II

After Id the Foxes placed, as group II, the common pence with a small face above a long neck, among which the mint names of Bristol, Canterbury, Durham and York occur in addition to London, as other mints were brought into commission for the recoinage in January 1280. There is, however, a variety intermediate between the two on which the face is put in from any one of the three larger punches used in Id (and accordingly with little neck), but surmounted by a new form of crown the band of which is now shaped to the ornaments. This intermediate variety, having everything except the shaped crown in common with Id, could equally well have been designated Ie. But because of its new crown, and also perhaps because it includes the earliest coins of Canterbury and York, mints which according to the Fox arrangement had opened in group II, this variety has been labelled IIa by modern students, requiring the normal coins of group II to be described as IIb. The IIa crown, like that in IIb, has spearhead ornaments but it differs from the IIb crown in having the central fleur less tall and usually with its dexter foil broken. The letter *N* is usually reversed in IIa, and in IIb it is almost invariably so; but because a reversed *N* is also occasionally found in Id, and a normal *N* in IIa, there is no unequivocal means of identifying mules between these two sub-groups.

London coins of IIa, which belong to the autumn of 1279, are plentiful. But those of Canterbury and York (which were known to Burns and Fox but regarded by them as mules with group I obverses) are extremely rare, suggesting that the first dies for these two mints were made only just before IIb replaced IIa. This would point to a first distribution of IIb dies before the end of 1279, perhaps even within the first batch of dies made for Canterbury in November. No coins of IIa are recorded of Bristol or Durham. However, transitional coins (IIab), with the IIa crown plus the face and drapery of IIb, are known of Bristol as well as London, suggesting that Bristol may have received its first dies very soon after Canterbury and York.

Group IIb continued during the early part of 1280 under the Turnemire contract from January, but gave way to group III during the spring or early summer.

Mints of the Edwardian Recoinage, 1279-81

	Ia	b	c	d	IIa	b	IIIa	b	c	d	e	f	g	IV
London	x	x	x	x	x	x	x	x	x	x		x	x	x
Canterbury					x	x		x	x	x		x	x	x
Bury									x	x			x	x
Durham					x			x	x		x		x	x
Bristol						x		x	x	x		x	x	
Chester													x	
Lincoln									x	x		x	x	
Newcastle											x			
York royal						x	x		x	x		x	x	
York episcopal											x	x		

Group III

Seven sub-divisions of group III, a to g, were differentiated by Fox and these have remained in use broadly as originally proposed, although not without some problems of definition in detail. This large group covers most of the recoinage, in which Lincoln, Newcastle and Chester were added to the royal mints of group IIb, a new mint for the archbishop was opened at York, and the abbot's at Bury St. Edmunds was revived. Group III may be dated to 1280-2. The table shows the differing periods of activity of the various mints: after IIIa, which is from a small batch of dies supplied only to London, IIIb comes from all the mints of group II; Bury and Lincoln were added in IIIc, York episcopal and Newcastle in IIIe, and Chester in IIIg. Newcastle did not receive dies later than IIIe, nor the two York mints any later than IIIf. The other three recoinage mints, Bristol, Lincoln, and Chester end with IIIg. According to the monastic records of Bury, the first of the new coins (IIIc) were minted there in June 1280. Less precisely, a keeper of dies was sent to Lincoln, the other new mint of IIIc, between May and October. In August the king authorised two dies for William Wickwane, who as archbishop of York was always robust in defence of the privileges of his see, and cash was sent to Newcastle as a float for the exchange, providing a pointer to the date of IIIe. The exchange at Chester received its float early in December 1280, which suggests that IIIg dies may then already have been available. The latest entry relating to the Newcastle exchange is in May 1281 and to those of Lincoln and Chester in July. The recoinage mints were apparently closed in the summer of 1281 and their wardens rendered final accounts in September and October. At a guess, group III may have replaced group II in April or May of 1280, since IIIc was in issue by June and the duration of IIIa and IIIb was relatively short. IIIe (and by implication IIId at the southern mints) dates from August 1280, and IIIg followed IIIf before the end of the year. Group III outlasted the activity of the recoinage mints, and on the evidence of the quantities of Canterbury coins of successive groups in hoards, measured against the mint accounts, Allen has suggested that IIIg was not replaced by IVa until well into 1282.

Most coins of group III have a well-centred, youthful head, with narrow face, and the abbreviation marks are normally small crescents; but it is difficult to point to any universal characteristic of the group. The first two varieties, however, are easily distinguished by their crown and drapery. IIIa and IIIb both have pearls, as in group I, as intermediate ornaments in the crown, of which the side fleurs are occasionally bifoliate. On IIIa the drapery is shown as a broken ellipse (a curved line with hooked ends), and on IIIb as a segment of a circle. Both varieties, and particularly IIIa which is confined to London, are much scarcer than later sub-groups. All five mints of IIb contributed to IIIb and rare mules of all of them exist between IIb and early III, as may be identified by the style of lettering on their reverses. In IIb the Roman N is almost invariably reversed, the uprights are plain and the A is broad with the feet often slightly arched. In early III the uprights have hollowed sides, N is never reversed and the A is narrower, with flat feet. The R of IIb, with crescent tail, also differs from that of IIIb, which has a wedge. IIb/III mules have been noted of London, Bristol and Canterbury, and IIIb/II mules of London, Bristol, Durham and York. The existence of IIIb/II as well as IIIa/II London mules confirms the impression that IIIa dies were only available for a very short period.

LETTERS *I* AND *A* IN LATE GROUP II AND EARLY GROUP III

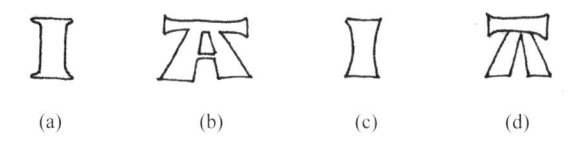

(a) (b) (c) (d)

(a) and (b), *I* and *A* of late II; (c) and (d), *I* and *A* of early III.

The arrangement of IIIc, IIId and IIIe is less straightforward. All have spearheads in the crown (the normal ornaments henceforward) and the end fleurs are straight-sided. In their original monograph the Foxes described a variety with a long, narrow face and low crown, confined to the northern mints at Durham, Newcastle and York, as IIId, and its southern counterpart as IIIe; but in 1917 they reversed the order of the two, and this later designation, which makes the northern variety IIIe and the southern IIId, is the one generally in current use. Their reason for doing this was perhaps that, as they always recognised, IIIc "gradually merges into" IIId (as it is now called), the distinction between the two being that, in their words, the drapery of IIIc is "composed of a single curved band ... broader on one side of the bust than on the other" while that of IIId is "made of two triangular pieces". A majority of the common pence of IIIc and IIId can be attributed to one or other of the two varieties according to these criteria, but many individual specimens remain doubtful since the distinction between the hollowed band of IIIc and the two wedges of IIId, if they overlap, is often far from clear. Although Archibald has usefully suggested that coins with an earlier form of *h*, with crescent tail, should be described as IIIc, regardless of the drapery, and those on which the tail of the *h* turns outwards as IIId, there remains no absolute dividing line between the varieties and the description IIIcd may still need to be applied in the case of ambiguous examples. Burns also distinguished a rare early transitional variety (now called IIIbc) at London and Canterbury, with the pearl crown of IIIb but the drapery of IIIc. There is some variety of bust in regular IIIc and IIId, substantial sub-groups which saw the first contributions from Lincoln and Bury St. Edmunds. The Bury moneyer's name is first shown as *Robertus de hadl'*, but this form was soon replaced by *Robert de hadeleie* which then became the norm.

VARIETIES OF DRAPERY IN GROUP III

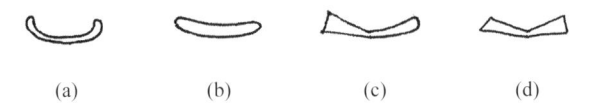

(a) Broken ellipse, IIIa; (b) Segment of circle, IIIb; (c) Curved band with one side thicker, IIIc; (d) Two triangular wedges, IIId (and onwards).

Newcastle, which makes its only appearance in the recoinage in IIIe, is of most interest in respect of the singular reverse type of its halfpence, which have one large pellet, instead of the normal group of three smaller ones, in each angle of the cross. Most of the recoinage pence from the archbishop's mint at York are also of IIIe, the first of the long series up to the time of Henry VII to be distinguished from the king's by a quatrefoil on the centre of the reverse cross (perhaps representing the handle of the key of St. Peter). Some of them also have a small cross or quatrefoil on the king's breast. Later obverse dies of IIIe show the sinister hair punch broken (with a nick at the bottom), and some of these, from all the northern mints, also have a pellet-barred *N*. The peculiarities of IIIe dies, delivered only to Durham, Newcastle and the two mints at York, are evidence of the separate organization established for the northern mints under Peter de Turnemire, described in August 1280 as the king's master moneyer of York.

DISTINCTIVE LETTER FORMS IN GROUP III

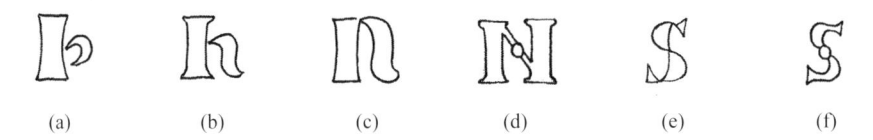

(a) Crescent-tailed *h*, IIIc; (b) *h* with tail turned outwards, IIId;
(c) Gothic *n*, IIIf York; (d) Pellet-barred *N*, IIIe; (e) Early *S*, of crescent and wedges;
(f) Late *S*, with swollen centre, from IIIf onwards.

Sub-groups IIIf and IIIg are readily distinguished from earlier varieties by the form of the crown. Although several punches were used, they all show the outer petals of the side fleurs curved outwards, giving a much more spread outline than the compact, straight-sided crowns of IIIc-e. Obverse dies of IIIf have a broad face with a characteristic large nose, and the letter *S* of a new form with a swelling in the middle. Coins of IIIf are generally scarce, and the fact that no examples of this variety have been found of Durham or Bury also suggests a limited duration. The only IIIf dies made for York have Gothic *n*, an exceptional feature at this period. These IIIf pence of York are extremely rare, especially those with the archbishop's quatrefoil. Since the York reverse dies have the earlier, waisted form of *S* they may be IIIf/e mules (some IIIf coins of other mints with the early *S* on the reverse could be IIIf/d, f/e or f/g mules, but no York coins are known of IIIg). There is also, however, a York coin from a IIIe obverse but with the late *S* on the reverse, and so evidently a IIIe/f mule. In the much more abundant IIIg the face is smaller, with a smiling expression, and the *S* may be either of the early or of the late form. Because the late *S* continues into groups IV and V some students (including Burns) have supposed that IIIg, in which many dies still have the early *S* (and at least one has a pellet-barred *N* as in IIIe), preceded IIIf. On the other hand, the last occurrence (until 1300) of both York mints is not in IIIg but in IIIf, and if IIIg had intervened between IIIe and IIIf, it might have been expected that some new dies would have been made for York during the currency of the plentiful IIIg, which included extensive issues from the recoinage mints of Bristol and Lincoln as well as the whole of the output of Chester. As Chester used only two of the three crown punches found in IIIg, it may have closed before Bristol and Lincoln, where all three occur. It is, however, possible that at this stage (and at others) there was some overlap in the use of punches and in the issue of dies which we now associate with consecutive sub-groups. In addition to the regular group III coins of Bury St. Edmunds there is one variety from anomalous dies with Gothic *n*, the spelling *hib*, a coarse crown and a peculiar portrait with bushy hair. Fox regarded this coin as the earliest of the series, made from local dies, and illustrative of events related to the dispute between the abbot and the king about the reopening of the mint. However, its spread crown, Gothic *n* and comma stops could all be seen as features relating it to the IIIf-g period.

USUAL ABBREVIATION MARKS IN GROUPS II–IV

(a)   (b)   (c)

(a) Wedge, II; (b) Crescent, III; (c) Comma, IV.

Throughout group III the normal abbreviation marks are small crescents (sometimes solid like half-moons), and these crescents provide a useful distinguishing feature in contrast to the wedges of group II and the very large commas of groups IV and V. Unfortunately, however, there are a number of exceptions to the rule. Commas are sometimes found in IIIb and IIIg, and also rarely in the other sub-groups except IIIe. Although large commas, as in group IV, do sometimes occur, mainly in IIIg but also on the (abnormal) York dies of IIIf, they are very rare in group III.

Group IV

It is difficult to express in words the characteristics common to coins of Fox group IV, which constitutes the issues of most of the 1280s, after closure of the recoinage mints. The continuing mints were London and Canterbury, Durham and Bury. Between September 1281 and July 1290 London issued £317,000 in pence and Canterbury £161,000. Appropriately, London coins of group IV are about twice as abundant as those of Canterbury. Fox sub-divided this large group into five varieties, IVa to IVe. The last two of these are easily defined by the addition of prominent pellets, but the bulk of the group consists of coins described by Fox as IVa, IVb and IVc, and these have been the subject of various attempts at classification since the original study by Burns. The definitions of the three sub-groups included here are based on the work of North, and in some respects cut across the arrangements of previous writers. There are many small variations of the hair, the face and the crown, which is generally broad with spread side-fleurs as in late group III. As in previous groups the *c* and *e* are open, but often more conspicuously so than on earlier types. *S* with swollen waist follows the form found in late group III. An unbarred *A* occurs on many coins, particularly later in the group. The one almost universal feature of group IV is the large comma abbreviation marks, although even these do not provide an absolute definition of the group in view of their occasional use near the end of group III.

Early coins of the group, those covered by the IVa label, are so varied that detailed sub-division is highly complex. For most practical purposes it is convenient to divide them into two broad categories, Early and Late. In Early IVa the face and late crowns of IIIg continue, and the hair is short. Letters in this phase have straight-sided uprights, with prominent serifs, and the commas are large. Late IVa has a new oval face, a taller crown and longer hair. Letters are thicker, and latterly concave-sided, and sometimes include a very large *S* or an unbarred *A*. Early coins of Bury revert to the *Robertus* reading, not used since IIIc, but during Late IVa the normal version of the moneyer's name with *hadeleie* in full was resumed.

North defines IVb primarily by reference to the crown with a tall central fleur and a straight-limbed sinister side fleur, the outer foil of which gradually breaks away to give a bifoliate appearance. The oval, smiling face is flanked by bushier hair, and the letter fount now usually has uprights with concave sides. Durham's last unmarked coins at this period are found in IVb, followed by the first with the cross moline mark for Bishop Antony Bek whose temporalities were granted in September 1283. Bek's earliest reverse dies have the cross moline displacing the pellets in the *Civi* quarter of the cross, but this type was soon discontinued in favour of a cross moline before the inscription on both sides of the coin, a usage which continued until group IX and required the reverse legend to be split *Civ/itas/Dur/eme*.

DEFECTIVE CROWNS IN GROUP IV

(a)   (b)

(a) IVb, straight sinister fleur, with outer foil breaking; (b) IVc, nicked band by dexter fleur.

In IVc the face is longer and the hair bushier, but the simplest diagnostic feature is a new crown, with the sinister fleur turned inwards and at the dexter end a small but distinct nick in the band between spearhead and side fleur (this nicked crown remained in use through IVd but was replaced early in IVe). Lettering in IVc includes both straight and hollowed uprights, and unbarred *A* now sometimes again occurs. The one Bury die attributed to IVc, and thus evidently the last to be used with a Robert reverse, reads *Dn* for *Dns*.

Mules between IVa, b and c are not readily discernible, since there are no sufficiently consistent variations of lettering between them to separate their reverse dies. With London and Canterbury coins of IVd and IVe, however, the situation changes. IVd has a pellet before the start of each inscription, while IVe normally has a row of three pellets on the breast and on reverses a pellet within the inscription (usually before *Lon* or *tor*). These pellets enable mules in both directions between IVc and IVd and between IVd and IVe to be identified. No Bury coin of IVd has been found. The extremely rare IVd penny of Durham has a pellet between the cross moline and *Edw* on the obverse but none on the reverse. However, the coins of Bury and Durham associated with IVe lack pellets on the breast and (with one possible exception at Durham) in the reverse legend. Their attribution rests on the similarity of the portrait to that on most IVe coins of London and Canterbury, which has what Burns described as 'ropy' hair consisting of separate thick strands. By this token there are also a few London and Canterbury coins, from IVe reverses but without pellets on the breast, the obverses of which may nevertheless be regarded as belonging to IVe. Their position is also confirmed by the use of a new crown punch, introduced early in IVe, which has the side fleurs bent outwards almost horizontally. The rare IVe coins of Bury (one of which has a double-barred *N*) carry the mint name on the reverse for the first time – *Villa S Edmudi*, with a mark of contraction above the *S*. Those of Durham, almost equally rare, have a composite cross moline both sides, made up of a small plain cross with added annulets: Fox attributed this variety to IVc, presumably because of its lack of pellets, but the ropy hair and wide crown place it beyond doubt with IVe. Another Durham reverse die apparently of this period is found only with later obverses (Vb, VIb and VIIb), but its lettering is too large for group VI or VII, the cross moline appears to be composite (and unlike the very large form on Vb dies), and there is a faint pellet before *tas*, which would assist an association with IVe.

Group IV, begun probably in 1282, continued in issue for many years. Most of the Durham coins of IVb exhibit the cross moline mark of Bishop Bek from September 1283. The rarity of unmarked Durham pence of IVb, probably attributable to the end of Bishop Robert's episcopacy or to the *sede vacante* following his death in June, renders it likely that IVb did not replace IVa until well into 1283. At Bury Robert of Hadleigh's coins end with the single die of IVc and those of his successor, now with the mint signature, begin with IVe, which must therefore have been in issue when Richard of Lothbury was admitted as moneyer at the end of November 1287. This would accord with an end date for group IV of c.1289, when the supply of bullion was in marked decline.

Group V

The pence of this scarce group may be identified at a glance by their unusually large flans, very tall lettering and large initial crosses. There is also normally a single pellet on the breast. The crown is from a new punch with the side fleurs widely splayed. An earlier and rarer variety, Va, known only of London and Canterbury, retains the normal-sized face of IVe, although with bushier hair, and its position is confirmed by London mules both ways with IVe. In Vb the face is long and narrow, with a tapering chin, and the hair is tighter. The eyes are often almond-shaped as in groups VI and VII. London and Canterbury Vb/a mules are not unduly rare, and can be recognized by the form of the letter *c*. In Va the size of the *c* is normal (for the group), and the serifs are triangular; in Vb the *c* is very large, its back rounded and the serifs thin. The initial cross moline on the rare Durham coins of Vb is much larger than in any other group, and the letter *M* is now again correctly formed, with a *v* between the uprights instead of a wedge as in groups III and IV. A Durham Vb/VI mule from the Montrave hoard enabled Burns to define the transition between the early groups belonging to the 1280s (with large lettering from Id to V), and the small-lettered series of the 1290s (groups VI-IX). Bury coins of Vb are also rare, and include for the first time a variety with the uncontracted reading *Edmundi*.

Letter C in Group V

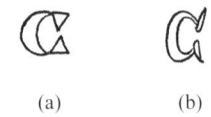

(a) *C* of Va, with triangular serifs; (b) Large *C* of Vb, with thin serifs.

Totals of bullion struck reduced sharply in the late 1280s, falling below £1,000 annually at Canterbury from 1290. Since group V is the last before the recoinage of 1300 (group IX) in which coins of Canterbury are not either very rare or absent, the group may be dated c. 1289/90 (and perhaps a little beyond).

English Mints of Groups IV–VIII, 1281-99

	IVa	b	c	d	e	Va	b	VIa	b	VIIa	b	VIIIa	b	c
London	x	x	x	x	x	x	x	x	x	x	x	x	x	x
Canterbury	x	x	x	x	x	x	x	m	x	x				
Bury (Robert de H)	x	x	x											
" (Villa S.E.)					x		x			x	x		x	x
Durham, plain cross	x	x												
" , moline (Bek)		x	x	x	x		x		x		x			

m – VI/V mule only.

Groups VI, VII and VIII

Group V was followed by a series of types with much smaller lettering, and usually on smaller flans, which constitute the coinage of the 1290s. The volume of bullion reaching the English mints during these years was in decline, and increasingly affected by the intrusion of continental imitations. The coins are in consequence considerably scarcer than those of the 1280s. Fox defined three groups, VI, VII and VIII in which London, although now much less active, was the only mint still producing more than a minimal output. Between July 1290 and September 1294 Canterbury issued only £2,500, and from 1294 to November 1299 the mint was closed. Canterbury coins of group VII are of considerable rarity; only one has been found to represent group VI; and none are known at all of group VIII which must accordingly belong to the later 1290s when the mint was idle. The ecclesiastical mints also struggled to remain active after 1290. Durham coins, although recorded in groups VI and VII, are distinctly rare (the latter extremely so), while none are known of group VIII. Bury coins exist of all three groups, but all are rare, especially those of group VII. Altogether, VI and VII are the rarest groups of Edward I's reign.

Edward I – Edward III

Letter Forms in Groups VI–VIII

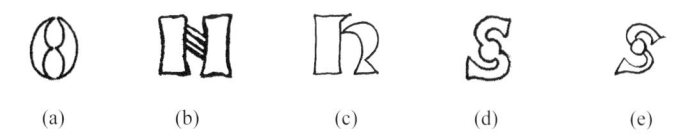

(a) Waisted *O*, VIb; (b) Double-barred *N*, VII; (c) Notched *h*, VIII;
(d) Normal *S*, VIIIa; (e) Top-tilted *S*, VIIIb (and IXa).

Coins of group VI being of smaller module (but compensatingly thicker) than those of group V, their letter fount, which includes neat, closed *c* and *e*, and *N* with concave sides, is accordingly of much reduced size. Early coins (VIa1), confined to London, have a large and distinctive oval face, with almond eyes. The crown is similar to that of group V, and often shows a small nick in the band beside the central fleur. The initial cross is nearly plain and there are usually no marks of abbreviation. Except for a single pair of dies of finer execution (VIa2), with thick initial cross patty and straight-sided *N*, workmanship in VIa tends to be coarse, in contrast to that of the main division of the group (VIb), the dies of which are very carefully made. The face of VIb is smaller, with pellet eyes, and usually set above a taller neck and bust. The initial cross is now more clearly patty and crescent abbreviation marks are the norm. New letter forms often seen in VIb include a barred *A* and a waisted *O*. Double-barred *N* (as commonly in group VII) is also occasionally found in VIb. One large London obverse has the extended reading *Edwa* with a colon to fill space after *hyb*, while another reads *hyb'n*. Durham and Bury pence of VIb are rare, and Canterbury was unknown for the whole group until the appearance of a VIb/Vb mule in 1977. At Bury the smaller lettering of group VI permitted the abbreviation of *Sancti* to be extended from *S* to *Sci*, although curiously the *N* was again dropped from the final segment.

Flawed Crowns in Groups VI–VIII

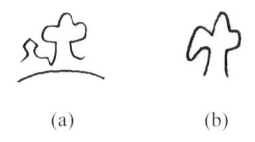

(a) Crown with nicked band, VI and VIIa; (b) Crown with damaged fleur, VIIIa-b.

Group VII is chiefly distinguished by a rose on the breast, although this does not feature on cognate coins of Durham or Bury, and is occasionally omitted even at London and Canterbury (a pattern of omission reminiscent of that of the three pellets on the breast in IVe). The rose does, however, occur on some rare coins of this period struck in Ireland. Group VII shares a number of features with group VI – small dies and flans, closed *c* and *e*, and *N* now normally double-barred. However, the initial cross is larger and of a fuller patty form and abbreviation marks are commas. The main subdivision, VIIa, has the same broad, antler-like crown as VI, but the hair is shorter and the face rather square. The eyes are almond-shaped as in VIa. Canterbury coins of VIIa are rare; those of Bury, which have a contraction mark above *Sci*, extremely so. London coins with a rose on the breast are also found with a different portrait (VIIb). The hair is larger and bushier, and the crown, with a tall central fleur, has less spread side fleurs. No Bury coins can be associated with this variety, but some very rare pence of Canterbury and Durham, although without the rose, exhibit certain of the same features as the VIIb coins of London and presumably belong with them. The portrait on those of Canterbury is similar in general appearance to that at London, with possibly the same punch for the face, but the style is coarser. The one Durham obverse die does use the London VIIb punches for crown and hair, but the lettering is larger than anything found on other VIIb dies, although not dissimilar to that on the 'IVe' reverse die combined with this obverse. From detailed analysis of coins of group VII Greenhalgh distinguished seven separate varieties and, on the evidence of a worsening flaw in the upright punch for the letter I and of a nick in the crown band between the central fleur and the dexter jewel, proposed that dies conforming to the Fox description of VIIb (his VIIi-iii) preceded those of Fox VIIa (his VIIiv-vii).

Although group VIII may be presumed to have continued in issue for a period of five years or so, albeit at a time of low activity, there is very little variety to be observed. The group is defined as much by negative as by positive features. Thus there is no ornament on the breast as usually in groups VII and IX, the almond eyes of VIa and VII are no longer found, and *N* is only very occasionally double-barred. The crown is similar to that of VIIb, with a tall central fleur the sinister foil of which is usually damaged. As Burns observed, coins of this group have a characteristic form of the letter *h*, with an indentation in the outside of its back. This notched *h* provides a useful means of distinguishing coins of group VIII from some early examples of IXa without a star on the breast. Another peculiarity of the group is that abbreviation marks, small crescents or sharp commas, are frequently found after the *h* as well as the *B* of *hyb*.

Fox designated supposedly earlier and later illustrated examples as VIIIa and VIIIb, but this classification has not proved satisfactory and a new arrangement with three subdivisions was adopted by North, reversing the Fox order. North's VIIIa is distinguished from VIIIb by having a normal integral *S*, with a slightly swollen centre, while in VIIIb the *S* has a larger swelling and its top is tilted forward. Before the end of VIIIa the sinister jewel in the crown had been replaced with a small pellet, and this was the normal form in VIIIb. In VIIIb the neck and drapery are often thicker, and some later coins are of rather rough execution. The new VIIIc is a variant of VIIIb on which the band of the crown punch is more prominently curved to give a higher arch outline than usual. London is the only mint of which all three subdivisions are found, none of them particularly rare. The rare Bury coins, of VIIIa and VIIIb, have the reading *Vila*. Of Durham, like Canterbury, there are no group VIII pence at all, and if any were struck in the later 1290s they would have been from dies of VI or VII.

The sequence of varieties in the early 1290s remains difficult to establish, and the evidence is in some respects ambiguous. Fox regarded group VI as the first of the small-lettered series, but Burns had placed his variety A31 (equivalent to Fox VII) before A32 (Fox VI), despite the fact that the Vb/VIb Durham mule was a cardinal item in his arrangement. Canterbury coins of VIIa and VIIb are not exceptionally rare, so that the existence of only a single coin of this mint from a group VI obverse die might be taken to indicate that group VI was in issue at the time (1293/4) when output at Canterbury was dwindling to nothing, while group VII belonged to the years immediately preceding (1290-3), when Canterbury was still minting albeit on a modest scale. London coins of group VII are about four times as plentiful as those of Canterbury, which is roughly in line with their relative volumes of production in those three years. However, there are no known mules at any mint between groups V and VII whereas, in addition to the Durham V/VI mule, there are VI/V mules of both London (VIa/Vb) and Canterbury (VIb/Vb) which constitute a powerful argument for placing VI rather

Edward I – Edward III

than VII as the immediate successor to group V. It is possible that there was some overlap in the use of dies of the two groups, or that dies were not all used in the same sequence as they were made. The same may also have been the case with individual punches. The coins of groups VI and VII have here been described and listed in the Fox sequence, without an implication that this is necessarily correct. Both these groups, however, may be dated to the first half of the 1290s, when output was much reduced but with Canterbury still in operation. Group VIII would then run from 1294 or 1295 to 1299.

Group IX

Fox divided the coins of this extensive group into an earlier series (IXa), of large module, and the main issues of the 1300 recoinage, which are from smaller dies on more compact flans (IXb). North has added the designation IXc for a rare and final variety, the dies of which are more often found muled with IXb or early X than paired with each other. A common feature of pence of group IX is a star on the breast but it is far from automatic and all main varieties of all mints are also frequently found without it. Since the incidence of the star does not fit any obvious chronological pattern the simplest explanation of its uneven occurrence would be some connection with the manufacture or distribution of dies at a period of greatly increased output.

It is not clear exactly when group IX replaced group VIII. London began converting continental sterlings before Michaelmas 1299, as the accounts for the previous twelve months include more than £13,000 from foreign silver, perhaps still from group VIII dies because Canterbury, which resumes early in group IX, did not reopen until the November. Instructions to open additional mints (excluding Chester, which was an afterthought) were given on 29 March 1300, and their accounts run from April (Kingston, including York royal), May (Bristol), June (Exeter and Newcastle) and July (Chester). The crockards and pollards were called in from May 1299, cried down to halfpence at Christmas 1299, and demonetized at Easter 1300, by which time London and Canterbury had been actively reminting them for several months. Before the end of 1300 all the extra mints except Newcastle were closed. Bristol's accounts run to October, Chester's to November, Exeter's and Kingston's to December. The mint of the erudite Archbishop Thomas Corbridge at York was probably active only briefly, since his coins are relatively rare; he had had difficulty in obtaining his dies, which were only granted on 28 June and not delivered until the end of July, after all the other new mints had opened their accounts. The great majority of the coins of group IX must have been struck during 1300, although with London and Canterbury using dies of group IXa before the end of 1299, and with some dies of IXb (and IXc) remaining in use at the ongoing mints beyond the end of 1300, as evidenced in particular by the abundant mules with X at London and Newcastle.

Coins of IXa still have the top-tilted *S* of VIIIb but, when without the star, are most readily distinguished from those of group VIII by a new *h* without the notched back. Like the rest of group IX, they also tend to have very prominent pellet eyes. An early variety of IXa, often of rather rough workmanship and described by North as IXa1, has a large, plain initial cross and the VIIIb crown with tall central fleur. Coins of more refined work but otherwise similar, except for having a small, neat cross patty as in IXb and a new crown, are labelled IXa2. In IXa1 the letters may have either straight or concave uprights, but for the rest of group IX they are always straight-sided. Contractive marks are often found in IXa1 (but never after *h* of *hyb* as in VIII), rarely in IXa2. Canterbury and Durham mints are known for both varieties of IXa. For the last time, the Durham coins still have a cross moline on both sides.

In the summer of 1300 the bishop of Durham was having to obtain replacement dies every

MINTS OF THE 1300 RENOVATION

	VIII	IXa1	a2	IXb1	b2	IXc	X
London	x	x	x	x	x		x
Canterbury		x	x	x	x	m	x
Bury	x		x	x	x	x	x
Durham, moline (Bek)		x	x	x	x		x
" , plain cross				x	x	m	x
Bristol				x	x		
Chester				x			
Exeter				x	x		
Kingston				x	x		
Newcastle				x	x	m	x
York royal				x	x		
York episcopal				x			

m – mules (with IXb or X) only.

week or so, and the king complained to his warden that dies recently sent to Durham lasted only a few days because the metal was too soft. There is also some numismatic evidence of difficulty in providing the bishop's dies. First, a few irregular dies, evidently of local manufacture, were used at Durham in late IXa and early IXb (the two sub-groups being distinguished, as with London-made dies, by their size, and by the presence or absence of a cross moline on the reverse). These local dies have crude portraits and the lettering includes an open *e* which assists in the identification of the reverses. Perhaps the needs of the bishop, who was increasingly in dispute with the king from early in 1300, may have been given a low priority at or about the beginning of the recoinage when the new royal mints had to be supplied. New IXb dies must, however, have soon arrived from London since the local IXb dies are as often as not paired with regular dies. The second curious feature of group IXb at Durham is that coins with a plain initial cross outnumber those with Bek's cross moline by about three to one. Since Bek did not lose control of his mint until 1302, these plain cross coins cannot be associated with a period of suspended temporalities and it looks as if at some stage undifferentiated dies were supplied to Durham either accidentally or in order to avoid the delay in altering them or preparing new marked ones.

LETTERS AND CROWNS IN GROUP IX

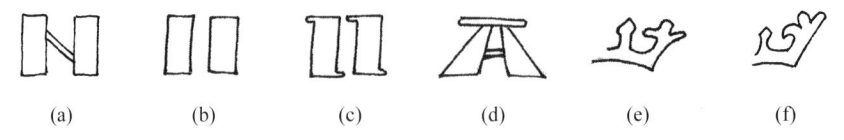

(a) (b) (c) (d) (e) (f)

(a-c), *N*s in IXb; Roman (A), Unbarred (B) and Pothook (C); (d) Barred *A*, IXc;
(e) Crown 1, IXb (also IXa2); (f) Crown 2, IXb.

The reduction in module associated with IXb may have been related to the need to produce large numbers of new dies for the recoinage, involving the operation of seven additional mints. Smaller dies required shorter lettering (with unbarred *A*), while to save space *Vill* was used instead of *Villa*, and the cross moline was dropped from Durham reverses. There is considerable variety among the extensive issues of IXb. North's subdivision of IXb is based on the two crown punches used, one (IXb1) with splayed fleurs being the same as used in IXa2, the other (IXb2) with the sinister fleur almost straight-sided. IXb1 and IXb2 are not however consecutive varieties, since both crown punches were for a period in use together and crown 1 continued after crown 2 had been put aside: thus the last two mints of IXb to be opened, Chester and York archiepiscopal, only used dies with the splayed crown, whereas the other mints all had both. As Allen has shown, IXb may be subdivided in a more sequential fashion by reference to three styles of the letter *N*. The first style (A) is normal Roman: this is found at the four old mints plus Kingston, Bristol and Newcastle. With style B, *N* Roman but unbarred, Exeter and York royal are added. The most usual *N* on IXb dies (C), found at all mints, is of the so-called 'pothook' form, consisting of two uprights with serifs extending only to the left at the top and to the right at the bottom. Crown 1 is found on IXb dies with all three styles of *N*, but crown 2 only with styles B and C.

Survival rates for IXb coins of the regional mints correspond satisfactorily with the output recorded in the accounts. Thus coins of Bristol, Newcastle (including IXb/X mules) and York royal are the most abundant. Much fewer are those of Exeter and Kingston, while Chester's are quite rare. At most mints star-marked coins substantially outnumber the unmarked, but not at Canterbury, Durham or Newcastle.

At the end of group IX a few dies (IXc) were made of unusual style, with larger and cruder lettering (including a distinctive barred *A*) and abnormal portraits (with crown 1). They have contraction marks and a Roman *N*, reminiscent of early dies of IXb. But their late position, evident from mules with early X, is confirmed by their being confined to mints which continued into group X. Oddly, the only mint of which true IXc coins are known is Bury, where the obverse die reads *Ew* for *Edw*. No Bury coins occur of the earliest varieties of group X, and it seems that IXc dies were issued at about the same time as others of the next group. This would account for the absence of any IXc dies at London, as well as the existence of IXc/X mules at Canterbury and Newcastle and X/IXc mules at Durham. Reverses of IXc are also known of these three mints combined with IXb obverses.

Regular dies of group IXb must also for a time have been available alongside dies of early group X. Differences between the two groups which are significant to modern numismatists were irrelevant to the mint officials who distributed them from stock at the time. Thus, Newcastle received proportionately far more reverse dies of group X than obverses, so that IXb/X mules of this mint are considerably more plentiful than true coins of either group IX or X. Conversely, X/IXb mules are very common of London, where a IXb/X mule is perhaps unique. Rare IXb/X mules are also known of Canterbury and Durham. At all four mints where such mules occur the IXb obverse has crown 1.

Group X

In hoards buried in the 1320s or later pence of group X normally comprise between forty and fifty per cent. of the total. This great volume of coinage represents the huge output of the mints during the first decade of the fourteenth century. Between 1300/01 and 1309/10 London minted £480,000 of pence and Canterbury £250,000. The Foxes dated group X to the five years 1302-7, largely on the grounds that Durham coins with a plain initial cross of IXb and early X should be attributed to the period of Bishop Bek's suspended temporalities in 1302-3, and those of late varieties of X to the second suspension in 1305-7. However, the Newcastle accounts for 1300-2 show that 27 per cent. of its total output was struck in June - September 1300, 59 per cent. between Michaelmas 1300 and 1301 and 14 per cent. in the following year. Since Newcastle IXb/X mules account for about half of the surviving coins of this mint of groups IX and X, but true coins of IXb and of early X only for about a quarter each, it is clear that Newcastle reverse dies of group X must have been available by September 1300 or very soon thereafter. At the other end of the group, the coins of Durham show that the last dies delivered to Bek, who died in March 1311, were of XIa, suggesting that group X probably came to an end in 1310. A ten year span for group X, as indicated by this evidence, is easier to reconcile with the volume of coinage recorded in the mint accounts than is the narrower dating suggested by the Foxes.

Not surprisingly for such an extensive issue, the coins of group X exhibit considerable variety of detail. Minor variations and errors in the inscriptions are relatively frequent. Extension of the king's name beyond the traditional *Edw* of groups Id to IX sometimes led to contraction of *hyb* to *hb*, *hy* or *h* and other letters are occasionally omitted. On reverse dies mis-spellings or corrections are not uncommon, suggestive of carelessness or second thoughts: thus, for example, *Dondon, Cantas, Casto*r or *Duaeme*, and *Vill* over *Civi* or *Dur* over *Lon*. Group X lettering is generally concave, providing a sharp stylistic contrast with that of IXb at the beginning, but less so with that of group XI at the end since straight uprights were introduced on some late dies in group X. The boundary between groups X and XI is therefore not now defined by the change from hollowed to straight-sided letters but only by the introduction of the characteristic new crown of group XI. The Foxes divided their group X into six sub-groups, Xa to Xf, but intensive work on the series during the last forty years has shown that substantial revision to the structure is needed. Much of the variety within the group is the result of damage to or the replacement of individual punches. From the observation of such features a detailed sequence can be established for the manufacture of particular groups of dies. Any taxonomic scheme is thus to some extent arbitrary, since divisions based on spelling or forms of lettering will overlap those based on punches for face, hair or crown. Post-Fox arrangements have involved a major subdivision of the group, into a Primary phase consisting chiefly of the varieties labelled Xa and Xb by Fox, and a Secondary phase covering the rest of the group and broadly coinciding with the aggregate of Fox varieties Xc to Xf. Wood's analysis of the group, as adopted in the North *Sylloge*, has resulted in the definition of six main types within each phase. In subdivision of the Primary phase primacy is given to variations in the obverse inscription, in the Secondary phase to successive crown punches. In each phase there is further subdivision according to changes in other elements, yielding a total of twenty-three separate varieties in all. The Primary phase has been referred to in some recent literature as 'Xab' and the Secondary phase as 'Xcf' but, apart from the unsuitability of retaining reference to the discarded Fox arrangement, these labels are not themselves accurate since some of the coins now seen as belonging to the Primary phase would not have been labelled Xa or Xb according to Fox. In the present context, therefore, P and S are used to represent the Primary and Secondary phases, with in each case the addition of the same numerical suffixes, 1-6, for the individual types, as used by Wood and North. Throughout the group, as can be seen from (sometimes slight) changes in letter forms, there is frequent muling between dies of adjacent, or nearly adjacent, varieties.

The Primary phase accounts for less than twenty per cent. of the surviving coins of group X. This is consistent with the relatively lower output of the royal mints in the years 1301-4, immediately following the recoinage, compared with a vastly increased rate of coinage from 1304/5 onwards. At both London and Canterbury output in the five years from 1304/5 to 1308/9 was more than six times greater than during the four years from 1300/1 to 1303/4.

Edward I – Edward III

These proportions are consistent with a starting date for the Secondary phase of group X of c. 1305. A similar pattern pertained at the ecclesiastical mints, with Durham and Bury coins of the Primary phase much scarcer than those of the Secondary phase. Newcastle, the only other group X mint, did not receive dies later than type P3 (reverse only). This probably means that P3 continued in issue at least until September 1302, when Newcastle's last account closed, although the output of the mint in 1301/2 was so much less than in the previous year that it might have ceased production before September. Based on the relative numbers of the several varieties of group X contained in hoards, and on their calibration against the figures for mint output, an approximate chronology would be as follows:

P1-3	late 1300 – c. 1303	S3-4	c. 1307-9
P4-6	c. 1303-5	S5	c. 1309-10
S1	c. 1305-6	S6	1310
S2	c. 1306-7		

Durham coins of group X present greater problems than was evident when the Foxes were writing. Bek's dispute with the king, which began in 1300, culminated in the suspension of his temporalities on 1 July 1302, but it is now known that his moneyer continued to coin at least until the end of July and as late as September 1302 Edward I was telling his representative that he could not give him instructions until the matter had been discussed in Parliament. In the event Bek's temporalities were restored in July 1303. But from some time in 1305 they were again suspended. After Edward's death the mint and other of Bek's privileges were once more restored to him (July 1307). These events are not easily reconciled with the numismatic material. As in group IX there are Durham coins of group X both with Bek's cross moline and with a plain initial cross, but which if any of the latter can be attributed to the interruptions in the bishop's access to his dies in 1302-3 and 1305-7 is difficult to determine. The lack of moline dies before type P5 and of plain cross dies in types P4-6 is the opposite of what might have been expected, while plain cross coins in all types of the Secondary phase are rarer than the molines, which hardly argues for the displacement of moline by plain cross dies from 1305 to 1307. The Foxes suggested that moline dies of their Xe and Xf altered from plain cross indicated the resumption of minting by Bek in 1307, after a period of the king's receivership; an alternative explanation could be that normal London dies were sometimes sent to Durham, in emergency, by oversight, or from disregard of the correct procedure, and that some of them were 'corrected' by converting the cross from plain to moline.

MINTS AND TYPES OF GROUP X, PRIMARY PHASE (XP)

	P1a	P1b	P2	P3a	P3b	P4	P5	P6
London	m	m	x	x	x	x	x	x
Canterbury	x	x	x	x	x	x	x	x
Bury				x	x	x	x	x
Durham, plain cross			x	x				
" , moline (Bek)							x	
Newcastle	x	x	x	m				

m – mules only.

Like Burns, Fox correctly recognised that coins with the king's name lengthened to *Edward R* (Xa) or *Edwar R* (Xb) came early in group X, and in that order. However, although these two types constitute at least ninety per cent of the coins of the Primary phase, subsequent work has revealed a more complicated pattern at this period, including a number of varieties with other obverse readings. Wood has defined six main and several subordinate divisions of the Primary series. He identifies a scarce variety reading *Edwar R* (P1) as the first of the group, earlier than the abundant *Edward* coins (P2 and P3); and another reading *Edwr'R'* (P4) as intermediate between those with *Edward* and the normal *Edwar* type (P5). Lastly, he identified a few transitional coins (P6) which read *Edwa R* as became normal in the Secondary series. The first three varieties of the Primary phase are very frequently muled with reverse dies of group IX, but such muling virtually ceases from type P4 onwards.

The earliest coins reading *Edwar R* (P1) may be differentiated most simply from the bulk of Fox Xb (P5), with the same reading, by the crown. This is either trifoliate (P1a), from revived use of the crown 2 punch of IXb; or (apparently as a result of recutting the same punch) bifoliate with the sinister fleur turned inwards and claw-shaped (P1b). The central fleur of this crown is short, with the side petals spread outwards almost horizontally, whereas the new crown punch which replaced it during the *Edward* series, and which accordingly occurs on most of the *Edwar R* coins of P5, has a taller central fleur with curled petals, and bolder side fleurs of true bifoliate shape. Type P1 is known only of London, Canterbury and Newcastle; it is rare with either form of crown, particularly the trifoliate, which at London is only recorded on X/IXb mules. A variant reading *Edwr R* is very occasionally found on coins attributable to P1 but, apart from differences of crown and lettering, their lack of contraction marks immediately distinguishes them from P4.

Fox Xa, consisting of the well-known coins reading *Edward* in full, is here represented by types P2 and P3, and includes the earliest group X coins of Durham and Bury, and the last of Newcastle. Wood distinguished an earlier 'large letter issue' (P2), followed by a 'small letter issue' (P3), the change of fount taking place shortly before the flat bifoliate crown of P1b was replaced by a new and taller crown which continued into the later stages of the Primary phase. He labelled the small-letter type with the old crown 3a, and with the taller crown 3b. A characteristic letter form on many dies of P2 and P3 is the *W* formed of two overlapping *V*s; and another, introduced late in P3, is an *S* with a break in its upper back. One London die of P3a has an annulet on the breast, like the Id coins speculatively attributed to the abbot of Reading; another, of 3b, has three large pellets (or filled annulets?), one on the breast and the others beside the bust, an arrangement not otherwise found on Edwardian coins but reminiscent of jetons of the period which commonly have large pellets above the shoulders. The Durham series (plain cross only) resumes with types P2 and P3a, sometimes muled with dies of group IX. One Durham obverse of P3a reads, exceptionally, *Rex* in full. No Durham coins are known of P3b, and there are no further plain cross coins of this mint until the Secondary phase. The first group X coins of Bury are of type P3, those of 3a being extremely rare. From Newcastle there are true coins of type P2, but although the last reverse dies used at this mint have the smaller lettering of P3a, they are only found as P2/3a mules.

Die-sinkers must have found the *Edward* reading uncomfortably long, since P3 was followed by a small batch of dies with the trial reading *Edwr'R'* (P4) before the regular form of Fox Xb, *Edwar R* (P5) was adopted. P4, in which the overlapping *W* is still often used, is scarce of London and Canterbury, rare of Bury, and still absent from Durham (perhaps reflecting the confiscation of 1302-3). It was soon superseded by the standard *Edwar* coins of P5, the most abundant type in the Primary complex. Dies were again delivered to Durham, but now all with Bek's cross moline. Finally, there is a rare variety (P6), again absent at Durham, on which the king's name is shortened to *Edwa*, but which differs from early coins of the Secondary phase in retaining the tall crown of P3b-P5. Characteristic letters on this variety are a serpentine *S* and a stub-tailed *R*, both of which continued into the Secondary phase.

LETTER FORMS IN GROUP X, PRIMARY PHASE (XP)

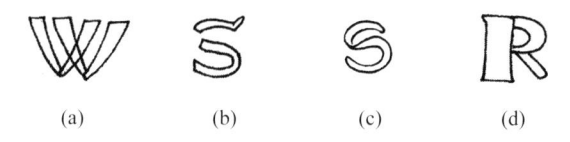

(a)   (b)   (c)   (d)

(a) Overlapping *W*, P2-4; (b) Broken *S*, late P3-early P5;
(c) Serpentine *S*, P6-S2; (d) Stub-tailed *R*, P6 and onward.

The Primary phase was a period of experiment both in the spelling and in the punctuation of the obverse inscription. Abbreviation of *hyb* is particularly common with the longest forms of the king's name. In P2 and P3 there is usually an apostrophe after *hyb* (occasionally also after the *h*), and often after *Angl*. In later varieties the same features do occur, but in P4 and early P5 there are contractive marks after all words except *Dns*, while normal pence of P5 are commonly without marks at all. Also in P5 a pellet or colon, or pellet with comma, is sometimes found after *hyb*.

The remainder of group X was classified by the Foxes in four sub-groups, Xc to Xf, but subsequent students have found their definitions imprecise and the arrangement itself unworkable. A new system has therefore been developed for the Secondary series, corresponding more to that of Burns. This classification is based primarily on the five forms of crown, with further subdivision according to changes in the face, hair and lettering. In its most detailed form, as defined by Wood and incorporated in North's *Sylloge*, it comprises thirteen separate varieties, divided between six main types (S1-6), with further subdivisions of three of them. The characteristics of the five crowns are best understood from the figures, but the features which most usefully assist in their identification are as follows:

Crown 1 (S1) - The sinister foil of the central fleur is larger than the dexter, and the outline of the (straight-sided) dexter fleur is less rounded than on the other punches. Intermediate ornaments are small spearheads.

Crown 2 (S2) - Broad, well-shaped central fleur. Dexter side fleur leans out more widely than in crown 1, and is slightly curved. The ornaments are vestigial at best, and the dexter one disappears on later dies.

Crown 3 (S3 and S6) - Tall central fleur, with the side foils high up (the dexter foil breaks, to give an asymmetrical appearance: cf crown 1 in this respect). Ornaments spearheads, the dexter one tilted inwards.

Crown 4 (S4) - Neat, symmetrical central fleur (with foils lower than on crown 3); sinister side fleur has hooked inner foil. Dexter ornament tilted inwards (cf crown 3), but is closer to side fleur than to central fleur.

Crown 5 (S5) - Tall central fleur (of which the sinister foil becomes damaged). A wide gap between dexter ornament (which tilts outwards) and side fleur which leans widely away (and which loses most of its inner foil on later dies).

CROWNS OF GROUP X, SECONDARY PHASE (XS)

In a number of respects the secondaries differ materially from the primaries. The king's name is now almost invariably reduced to *Edwa*, *Edwar* only occurring on a few individual dies. Within the obverse inscription there are no contractive marks and very few cases of other forms of stops. However, stops after *hyb* (colon, triple colon or a comma above a pellet), although rarely found in S1 and S2, occur again with increasing frequency later in the group.

MINTS AND TYPES OF GROUP X, SECONDARY PHASE (XS)

	S1a	S1b	S2	S3a	S3b	S4	S5a	S5b	S6
London	x	x	x	x	x	x	x	x	x
Canterbury	x	x	x	x	x	x	x	x	x
Bury		x	x	x	x	x	x	x	x
Durham, plain cross		x	x	x	x		x		
" , moline (Bek)		x	x	x	x	x	x	x	

Coins of type S1 have the same oval face and short hair as in the late Primary phase, being distinguished from type P6 only by the new crown 1. They are very common, amounting to nearly twenty per cent of all coins of group X. Before the obverse reading became standardised as *Edwa R Angl Dns hyb* (S1b) there are some very rare early dies (S1a), recorded only at London and Canterbury, which read *Edwar R Ang* or *Edwa R Ang*. Most of these *Ang* dies have the thick lettering of late P5, from which their reverses are often indistinguishable. With a single anomalous exception (S3b), one of the London *Edwar R Ang* dies is the last in group X to have been found muled with a reverse of IXb. Lettering in S1 varies, but includes a new angular *G*, while retaining the stub-tailed *R* and serpentine *S* of the last of the primaries. Uprights are less hollowed than in the Primary phase, so that, for example, *N* becomes a wider and more solid letter. The Durham plain cross coin of S1b is of great rarity.

Crown 2, by which type S2 is identified, accompanies a new portrait with a larger face, a pointed chin and bushier hair. On later dies crown 2 loses its dexter ornament. Terminal stops are more abundant than in S1. On many coins of S2 some letters are damaged, including *e* fractured at the base and *h* with a crescent tail and a wedge-shaped upright (the inner side of the base being broken away to form a point). This fount with broken letters is commonly described as 'Mayfield' lettering, from the die-linked group in that hoard which exhibited it. Coins of S2 are very plentiful, representing more than twenty per cent of group X as a whole.

Edward I – Edward III

Type S3 consists of coins with the commonest form of crown, no. 3, accounting for about a third of all coins of group X. From this point onwards the letter *W* normally consists of two adjacent *V*s. Two distinct forms of lettering divide the coins with crown 3, S3a having the same 'Mayfield' form as in most of S2, with its broken letters, and S3b a new fount in which the *e* is broad, with a rounded back, *h* consists of a thick upright with hollowed sides and a tail which curls outwards, and *o* is usually broken at one end. Also, some straight-sided letters now begin to appear occasionally. Several different hair punches were used in S3, and early in S3a the face punch of S2 broke at the bottom, to give the appearance of a cleft chin, this leading to its replacement by a long and narrow face which is found on most coins of S3a and some of S3b. This narrow face in its turn gave way during S3b to a new head known as the 'classic' bust. The face of this is in low relief, with the eyes prominently outlined, and the chin is again more pointed; below the head are two split wedges, suggesting hollowed drapery, and the neck punch (which remained in use until group XIV or later) has a small circular depression below the dexter jawline. S3a includes a few obverse dies at London, Canterbury and Durham with the longer form *Edwar*. In S3b there is an even rarer variety, a London mule with a IXb reverse, this abnormal survival of an old die having had the unfortunate consequence of misleading the Foxes into regarding the obverse as belonging to an earlier part of group X than the late position which it actually occupies.

LETTERING IN GROUP X, SECONDRY PHASE (XS)

(a)   (b)   (c)   (d)   (e)

(a) and (b) 'Mayfield' letters, broken *e* and *h*, S2-3; (c-e) New lettering of S3b, (c) Rounded, whole *e*, (d) *h* with outturned tail, and (e) Broken *O*.

With the same lettering and classic bust as in S3b some dies have the new crown 4. Coins with this crown, of type S4, are quite rare. They are known of all four mints, but no Durham example has been found with the plain cross.

The crown 4 punch cannot have long remained in use before being replaced. Type S5, with the new crown 5, is common, but much less so than S1, S2 or S3. Terminal stopping is now much more frequent than hitherto. Two principal sub-divisions of S5 may be distinguished by the size of the flans as well as by lettering and the initial cross. Earlier coins, S5a, are of the same module as previous sub-groups, with large lettering and a delicately shaped cross patty with hollowed arms. Some coins still have the classic bust, but later examples of S5a (to judge by damage to the central fleur of the crown) have a new and smaller face. In S5b the coins are generally smaller, with a corresponding reduction in the size of the lettering, which is squat and dumpy. The thicker and coarser initial cross of S5b, which corresponds to the Fox description of Xf, is characteristic.

Finally, there is a very rare type (S6), not known of Durham, which resembles S5b except for having crown punch no. 3 brought back into use, and a new small *s*. These coins, like most of S5 (and as sometimes also from S3b onwards), have straight-sided uprights on the reverse, but they are probably not to be considered X/XI mules as they have sometimes been described.

Groups XI - XIV

These four groups cover the coinage of the second decade of the thirteenth century. From 1310 onwards the mint accounts show a material reduction in the volume of coinage. The only exception to this decline seems to have been at Bury St. Edmunds where surviving material indicates that output after group XIII was relatively stronger than it had been previously. In the nine years from October 1311 to September 1319 London coined £92,000 of pence and Canterbury £126,000. Nearly a third of these totals was produced in 1313/4, from which year Canterbury's output consistently exceeded London's until 1320/1. Very little was minted in 1315/6, a contributory factor perhaps being the famine that the country suffered in that year.

MINTS OF GROUPS XI – XIV

	XIa1	XIa2	XIa3	XIb1	XIb2	XIb3	XIc	XId	XII	XIII	XIV
London	x	x	x	x	x	x	m		x	x	x
Canterbury	x	x	x	x	x	x	x	x	x	x	x
Bury	x	x	x	x	x	x	x		x	x	x
Durham, no marks	x										x
moline (Bek)	x	x									
crozier (Kellawe)		x	x	x	x	x	x		x	x	
lion & lis (Beaumont)										x	x

m – mules with XIb3 only.

Durham's output was also lower in the 1310s than the 1300s, but this mint provides important chronological evidence for the period. Bek died in March 1311, his successor Kellawe, first granted dies in June 1311, died in October 1316, and Beaumont received his first dies in June or July 1317. Coins with Bek's cross moline cease in sub-group XIa; those with Kellawe's crozier run from XIa to XIII; and Beaumont's lion and lis are found on pence from late group XIII to XVc. Receivers for the bishopric recorded that modest profits had been made by the mint during both the vacancies, between Bek and Kellawe (March – May 1311) and between Kellawe and Beaumont (October 1316 – May 1317); but the dies issued and used during these periods are indistinguishable from those of the deceased bishop since in neither case are there unmarked Durham coins at the appropriate point in the series.

CROWNS OF GROUPS XI – XV

| XI | XIIa | XIII | XIV | XV |

From group XI onwards each group is defined primarily by a new punch for the crown. These crowns are more distinctive than those of group X, which perhaps explains why, unlike their predecessors, they were each used by the Foxes to designate a separate group.

Edward I – Edward III

In group XI the crown has a bold spearhead as the sinister ornament but the dexter one is malformed and generally appears as a small hook facing outwards, usually detached from its stalk. On a few early coins of London and Canterbury the dexter ornament is intact, but other features of the group XI crown enable it to be identified without difficulty. In particular, the central and sinister fleurs have well-formed side foils which bend slightly outwards at the lower end. The Foxes divided group XI into three varieties according to certain changes in the lettering: *c* and *e* having rounded backs in XIa, but pointed backs in XIb; and XIc being distinguished by a very curious form of the letter *A*, consisting of an upright second limb with a horizontal wedge at the top left and a diagonal wedge supplying the left limb. In group XI and later groups the lettering is generally straight-sided, a simple (if approximate) means of identifying pence of Edward II's reign. *Edwa R* remains the normal reading in group XI, but *Edwar R* is also found with increasing frequency. Terminal stopping occurs on a few obverse dies of group XI, but less often than in the later stages of group X. Colons are, however, occasionally found also on reverse dies of group XI, most notably before *Vil* on the London-made dies supplied to Berwick at this period.

LETTERING IN GROUP XI

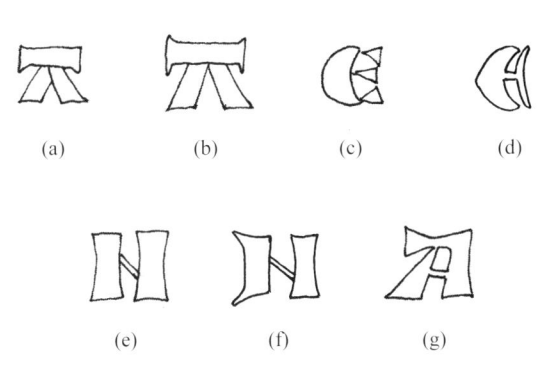

(a)   (b)   (c)   (d)

(e)   (f)   (g)

(a) Squat *A*, XIa1; (b) Lanky *A*, XIa2; (c) Open *e*, XIa3; (d) Pointed *e*, XIb;
(e) *N* without serifs, XIb2; (f) Square *N* with serifs, XIb3; (g) Asymmetrical *A*, XIc.

North has retained the basic Fox sub-groups while noting that XIa and XIb each contain three further epigraphical sub-divisions. Die-interchanges between different varieties are frequent. XIa begins with small letters as in late group X, including a stub-tailed *R*, squat *A* and sometimes *S* with the top tilted forwards. This variety (North XIa1) includes the few early examples of the group with the crown still undamaged. The commoner type (XIa2) has larger lettering with a scroll-tailed *R* and an *A* with longer legs. Last comes the rare variety (XIa3), to which the Berwick dies belong, distinguished by the open *c* and *e*, formed of a crescent with two or three wedges added but no curved closing stroke at the front.

In XIb the early dies (North XIb1) have lettering similar, except for the closed and pointed-backed c and e, to later XIa, and they may further be identified by the prominent outline of the eyes. Next comes a very common variety (XIb2) on which the lettering is tall and narrow, especially *N* without serifs and with the uprights slightly concave (this letter leading Mayhew to use the designation XIN for the variety in listing the Upperkirkgate hoard). New and smaller letter punches, including a square *N* with bold serifs, were introduced late in the sub-group (XIb3), together with a smaller face which remained in use throughout groups XII and XIII. Whether the rare dies with the distinctive asymmetrical *A* of XIc deserve to be regarded as a separate sub-group is doubtful; at London and Canterbury they are more often found muled with dies of XIb2 or 3 than as true coins, and they probably came into use alongside dies of XIb3.

London coins of group XI are more plentiful than those of Canterbury, which accords with the mint accounts of 1311/12. At Durham the last coins of Bek are of XIa1 and XIa2, and the earliest of Kellawe of XIa2. There are also Durham pence of XIa without episcopal marks. These plain cross coins were previously regarded as belonging to the *sede vacante* following Bek's death in March 1311, but since they are of XIa1, and not XIa2, and since there are also dies of both XIa1 and XIa2 with a plain cross altered to moline, it is more likely that they constitute another case of the inadvertent supply of unmarked dies to Durham. Kellawe's obverse dies are also unmarked, but his reverse dies, with the cross terminating in a crozier at the top, can also be identified, on worn coins, by a knop on the shaft of the cross below the crozier head, within the dotted circle, and by the (Latin) spelling *Dunelm* instead of Bek's *Dureme*. Among the greatest curiosities in the Durham series are some very rare moline/crozier mules (XIa2), combining a worn and rusty Bek obverse with strong new Kellawe reverses. A converse mule, Kellawe/Bek, has also been identified, but the obverse (naturally plain for Kellawe) has the open *e* of XIa3, and the coin therefore appears to be too late for the vacancy in 1311. From the Durham evidence it is however clear that XIa2 was in issue during the first half of 1311, at the end of Bek's episcopate and the beginning of Kellawe's.

In the 1958 hoard from Whittonstall, near Durham, which contained in all more than five hundred coins of group X, eighteen out of the eighty-nine group XI coins of Durham were of Kellawe, but of London and Canterbury there were respectively only eleven and four coins of group XI. This hoard must have been buried during 1311, and the very low representation of the latest group from the southern mints argues for group XI having begun not much before the end of 1310. London coins of group X are about four times as plentiful in hoards as those of group XI, indicating on the basis of relative bullion volumes an end date for group XI of c.1314. Such a calculation is inherently imprecise, but it receives support from the fact that in groups XII and XIII London coins are outnumbered by those of Canterbury, and this is consistent with the bullion figures for the two mints from 1314 onwards.

Some indication of Canterbury's growing relative importance may already be detected at the end of group XI. More dies of XIc seem to have been used at Canterbury than at London (one of the results of this being the existence of XII/XIc and XIII/XIc mules of Canterbury). There are also a few Canterbury obverse dies of this period which generally resemble XIb except for having crown 3 from group X, Secondary type S3 (a punch that had already once been brought back into use, in type S6). North labels this variety XId, indicating a position late in group XI, since reverse dies paired with it are of XIb3 or XIc. However, he also notes that the initial cross is not of the usual thick form of group XI, but is composed of four wedges in the manner of group XIII, and Mahyew has associated the variety with the latter group. In 1313/4 Canterbury output slightly exceeded that of London, in 1314/5 greatly so. Signs of additional activity at Canterbury at the close of group XI would thus corroborate the suggested date of c.1314 for the replacement of the group.

Group XII, substantially the rarest of Edward II's groups, is distinguished by a composite crown with a large central fleur whose broad side foils are usually pointing upwards, giving a general appearance more like a strawberry leaf than a fleur-de-lis. The normal version of this crown, described by North as XIIa, has diamond-shaped petals, often slightly indented, and the intermediate ornaments, if any, are single pellets or a trefoil of small pellets. This variety is recorded of all four mints, Canterbury being the least rare. North also distinguished two extremely rare minor varieties (XIIb and c), confined to London and Bury, with similar but different crowns and an initial cross patty composed of thin wedges. In XIIb the central fleur is cruciform, with the petals diamond-shaped but thinner than in XIIa, the ornaments are spearheads, and the lettering is larger. XIIc has tiny heart-shaped petals and ornaments.

Coins of XIIb and XIIc have certain features in common with group XIII, notably the initial cross. In XIIc there is a new letter *R*, as in XIII, with straight-sided upright and a wide serif at the foot. Also, a Bury obverse of XIIc has been noted with the same broken-backed *e* punch as is found in late XIII and early XIV. Although group XII may be dated c.1314, from the conclusion of group XI, and belongs to a time when Canterbury had overtaken London in volume of output, it is not clear whether the group as a whole occupied only the very brief period which its rarity would suggest, and the possibility exists that some late dies with the crown of XII could have been made during the period of group XIII.

Durham coins of group XII, unknown to the Foxes at the time of their monograph, have Kellawe's crozier and a plain obverse cross as on his coins of group XI. So do most of the reasonably plentiful Durham pence of group XIII, but there are also rare coins in this group of his successor Beaumont. Group XIII therefore probably began not later than 1315 and must still have been in issue in 1317. In group XIII Canterbury coins again outnumber those of London, as they continue to do for the rest of the active period (to XVc). Bury's contribution was, however, still limited, as it had been since XIb.

Group XIII is defined by a crown with the central fleur straight-sided, likened by the Foxes to a Greek double-headed axe; the ornaments are arrow-heads. There is a small nick in the outside of the sinister fleur, which then disintegrates and is rather haphazardly 'repaired' on several dies. North wondered whether this could be the crown of group XI recut, with the broken dexter ornament replaced: if so, it might explain why the side fleur failed so soon. Most dies of group XIII have an elegant initial cross patty, composed of four thin wedges, as already found on the rare coins of XIIb and XIIc. Late coins may be identified by the punch for the letter *e* which breaks away at the lower back. Group XIII is the last in which *Edwa R*, instead of *Edwar R,* still occurs on a few dies. Another very occasional feature is a colon (after *hyb* at Canterbury, or *tas* at Durham).

The crown of group XIV has a tall central fleur, but is most easily distinguished from that of group XIII in having no ornaments on the intermediate spikes, and in being paired with a new and larger punch for the face, with a prominent pointed chin, and aptly described by the Foxes as having a "curious enigmatical smile, and leering eyes". Small stops in the obverse inscription, first found on rare Bury coins of group XIII, also occur in group XIV, on a few dies of all mints except Canterbury. Early coins of group XIV still have the broken backed *e* of late group XIII, and a few also have the thin initial cross but this was soon replaced by a thicker cross. Coins of group XIV are more plentiful of all four mints than group XIII, particularly those of Bury which are no longer rare. Beaumont's coins of group XIII, however, are rare, so that group XIV may have begun in the second half of 1317. An extremely rare Durham coin of group XIV with the broken *e* has the thin, plain initial cross instead of Beaumont's lion and lis, and the same obverse die, in a very worn state, is also recorded with a reverse of XVc; neither of these coins, sometimes described as 'London'/ Durham mules, can be connected with the *sede vacante* period of 1316/7, since group XIII was still current at that time. As Canterbury and London coins of group XV are about equally abundant as those of group XIV, the mint output figures, in which more than half of the bullion recorded at both mints between 1317 and 1324 was struck before Michaelmas 1319, suggest that group XV was already in issue by that date.

Group XV

In 1319/20 Canterbury's output still exceeded London's, but the position was reversed in the following year. In the three years from Michaelmas 1321 London managed to issue only £3,600 in pence while Canterbury, after production had fallen to £1,100 in 1322/3, then lay idle for the rest of the reign of Edward II. London continued to mint farthings throughout the 1320s, but in the four years to 1327/8 pence and halfpence featured only in one account each, and in negligible quantities. The penny coinage of this period is represented by Fox group XV, the first three subdivisions of which (XVa, b and c) belong substantially to the five years from 1319, and the fourth (XVd), which is very rare, to the reign of Edward III, from 1328/9 onwards, when the minting of pence was revived but the volume of output remained insignificant.

MINTS OF GROUP XV

	XVa	XVb	XVc	XVd1	XVd2	XVd3
London	x	x	x	x		
Canterbury	x	x	x	x	x	
Bury	x	x	x	x		
Durham, lion & lis (Beaumont)	x	x	x			
", crown (de Bury)						x
", no marks			x			
York episcopal					x	
Reading						x

Pence of group XV are identified by a smaller and flatter crown than in groups XIII and XIV, having a well-formed central fleur with stalk-like ornaments in between, of which the dexter one is tilted outwards. During XVc the punch for the sinister fleur of the crown appears to have been broken or filed down. Early dies of this group (XVa) continue to show the lettering and smiling face of group XIV; but they are scarce except at Canterbury (in accordance with the mint accounts up to 1320), being soon replaced by XVb with a much smaller face and, consequently, the crown often set well below the dotted circle. Another new face punch marks the change to XVc. This is similar in size to that of XIV - XVa, but the eyes are rounder and the expression unsmiling. Coins of XVc may also be distinguished from those of XVa by changes in lettering. In XVa the e has an angular back and the tail of the h turns outwards. During XVb some smaller letters were introduced, but in XVc there is a new h with a crescent tail and a very tall e with a flattened back.

LETTER FORMS IN GROUPS XIII-XV

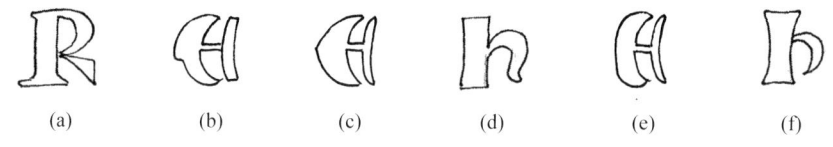

(a) New R with wide serif, XIIc and XIII; (b) Broken-backed e, late XIII-early XIV;
(c) Pointed e, XVa; (d) h with outturned tail, XVa; (e) Tall e with straight back, XVc;
(f) Crescent-tailed h, XVc.

Edward I – Edward III

At London and Canterbury pence of both XVb and XVc are more plentiful than those of XVa, indicating a date for the introduction of XVb perhaps as early as 1319; and in XVc London is at last catching up with Canterbury, as the account for 1320/1 suggests it should be. Bury coins of this period are scarce, those of XVb being the least uncommon. Beaumont's coinage at Durham continued on a reasonable scale, although XVa is only known from one obverse die. As in group XIV Beaumont's lion is flanked by one or two lis, in the latter case either one above the other in front or one in front and one behind. Durham pence with obverse initial cross, although very rare, are known of both XVb and XVc. The Foxes thought that the latter might represent an issue of the brief vacancy between Beaumont's death in September 1333 and the grant of temporalities to Richard de Bury in the December. But no coinage is recorded in the accounts for the vacancy and London-made dies at that date would in any case have been of XVd. These Durham coins of group XV without Beaumont's lion must again be 'London'/Durham mules, particularly since the converse combination exists in the form of a Beaumont obverse coupled with a London signed reverse (although whether such 'London' coins were actually struck there could only be established if the reverse die were found to be paired also with normal London obverses). Another curious Durham mule, XVI/XVc, links a reverse of the 1320s with an obverse of the 1340s, and unless purely accidental the use of such an old die might have been intended to avoid a reverse with de Bury's mark after his death in April 1345.

In XVc obverse stops feature only (on two dies each) at Bury St. Edmunds and Durham. Although rare dies of XIII and XIV at Bury and of XIV at Durham are also found with stops, it is possible that the stopped dies of XVc of these two mints belong to a period after 1323-4, when dies were no longer being made for London and Canterbury, since small pellet stops were to be a normal feature of most obverse dies of XVd of all mints. Very small issues from the ecclesiastical mints in exercise of privilege might still take place when pence were no longer being minted for the king, as later analogy shows.

The only pence of Edward III struck at London and Canterbury prior to 1344 are of XVd. This rare sub-group includes coins not only of Durham and Bury but also, remarkably, of York and Reading. The £61 of pence in the London account for October 1326 to February 1327 would have been of XVc, since no new dies were issued under Edward II after 1324. In 1329-30 London struck £453 in pence, and Canterbury resumed minting between 1328 and 1331. Most of London's pence feature in the account for February-September 1329. Of Canterbury's total of £783, however, only £145 was struck in the year to September 1329, the majority belonging, after an interval of fifteen months, to a second spell between January and September 1331.

Somewhat surprisingly, William Melton, Archbishop of York, was successful in an application for dies in 1331, even though, as the barons of the exchequer pointed out, Edward I had only allowed the privilege to be exercised, in 1280 and 1300, when there was also a royal mint in the city. Melton, however, a financial expert, had formerly been a confidant of the king's father and grandfather and carried considerable influence at court. This was the first occasion in the later middle ages when coinage was authorised at York for the archbishop alone, although it was to become the normal pattern for the next two hundred years. Writs for his dies were issued in April and July 1331, and the mint was established in August. In March 1334 Richard of Snoweshill, warden of the mint and exchange in August–September 1331, and thereafter the archbishop's receiver until 1333, received quittance for his accounts. Although the number of surviving York pence of XVd could indicate a more extended issue than at the southern mints, it is uncertain whether the mint remained in operation as late as 1333 or 1334. However, a reference in

December 1336 to the archbishop's receipt of £842 of 'our new money' might relate to coin recently minted at York.

In January 1328 a new die was ordered for the abbot of Bury, the old one (perhaps one of the two XVc dies with stops) having been destroyed in a riot. Another order in 1329 records that the abbot had not yet exercised his right of coinage in the new reign, so he cannot have received the new die much before the revival of the Canterbury mint. A further die was ordered for Bury in 1340, suggesting that the previous one may have remained available for occasional use throughout the 1330s; but no second variety of Bury coin is on record and it is not known whether any were struck so late. In November 1338, however, the abbot of Reading had been granted the right to strike pence, halfpence and farthings and dies for each denomination were ordered. The first pre-1344 Reading penny was not discovered until 1999. Like the halfpenny, it has a scallop shell, from the arms of the abbey, in one quarter of the reverse.

Although a Roman *N* is found on a few dies that can be associated with XVd on other grounds, the use of a Gothic *n* is the simplest diagnostic criterion for the sub-group. Woodhead's analysis has established that the earliest XVd pence were without special marks (XVd1), followed by a batch of dies (XVd2) with a pellet in the centre of the initial cross and three extra points within the group of pellets in the *tas* quarter of the reverse. All the London pence and some of Canterbury belong to the unmarked XVd1, which must have been in issue during 1329 and 1330, while most of those of Canterbury and all those of York are of XVd2 from dies supplied in 1331 (or after). The sequence of varieties is confirmed by Canterbury mules: XVd1 is muled both ways with XVc, while a XVd2 reverse was later used with a group XVI obverse. At this mint at least, the survival of XVc dies into the XVd period is demonstrated, but they could in theory have survived for use beyond 1327 at London and Durham also.

After the abbatial mints of Reading and Bury, London is the rarest of the XVd mints. All five London coins recorded by Woodhead are from different dies, suggesting that higher output may have been expected than actually occurred. At York also five obverse dies have been noted, but all these are known from more than one example, and a total of twenty-six or more specimens makes this possibly the most prolific of the XVd mints. After York, the next least rare XVd mint is Durham, with fifteen survivors noted from three pairs of dies. The inclusion in the recent Cambridge find of two of the rarest mints of XVd, London and Bury, prompts the thought that the higher proportions of extant coins of the two northern mints, relative to those of London and Canterbury, may have resulted from unrecorded Scottish hoards of the late Edwardian period.

LETTERS OF GROUP XVd

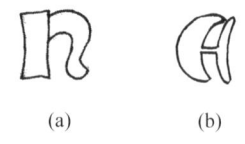

(a)   (b)

(a) Gothic *n*; (b) Defective *e*.

The orders for new dies for Durham in 1336 and Bury in 1340 show that coinage was still expected to occur at ecclesiastical mints on occasions long after pence had ceased to be struck at London or Canterbury. The unique Reading penny is of particular importance, not only in proving that this did actually happen, but also for showing us what a penny of the late 1330s looked like (XVd3). It has no extra points on the reverse, and so demonstrates that a coin of XVd without such marks need not belong to the period before XVd2 was introduced in 1331. The single pair of dies known of Bury may well have been those ordered in 1329, since the lettering is similar to that on Bury coins of XVc; they can therefore be attributed to XVd1. In the case of the Durham coins, however, there has long been dispute about their attribution, whether to Beaumont before 1333 or to de Bury later. These coins have no episcopal mark on the obverse, but their reverse dies, with the new reading *Dune/lmi*, have a lozenge in the centre of the cross containing a tiny crown (facing right or left, but never upright). The meaning of this symbol is unclear and it has no obvious link with either bishop. Observing that the Durham dies lacked the characteristics of XVd2, Woodhead preferred to date them no later than 1330, in Beaumont's lifetime. But others have pointed to the difficulty of assuming that Beaumont, having used the lion and lis on all his obverse dies since group XIII, should suddenly switch to a different mark, on the other side of the coin, late in his episcopate. A small epigraphical feature may also point to a later dating. The Durham dies show the letter *e* weak, or defective, at the bottom, as is perhaps also seen on the Reading obverse die and on one or two XVd2 dies of Canterbury and York. This would suggest that the Durham dies may have been those ordered for de Bury in 1336, and so attributable to XVd3.

Considering how few dies of XVd are recorded, there is more variety among them than might have been expected. One London reverse has a Roman *N* in *Lon*, and in XVd2 there are one Canterbury and two York obverses with Roman *N*s. The Bury reverse has Gothic *m* and *n*, but the three Durham reverses all have a Roman *M* and two of them Roman *N* as well. The most interesting variant is a York obverse with a small point in each angle of the initial cross which, as the Foxes noted, is a form found on Snoweshill's sign manual.

Halfpence, 1280 - 1335

Halfpence were first issued in August 1280. By September 1281 a total of £5,000 had been struck at London, but there is then no further mention of halfpence until 1285. A revival from 1285/6 to 1290/1 involved the minting of some £1,500 in halfpence over the six years, but only half that amount was produced in the next seven years, to 1298. No halfpence were struck in the two years to September 1300. Although £370 was accounted in 1300/1, thereafter halfpence were only produced intermittently and on a negligible scale until the reduction of the standard in 1335, only twice exceeding £100 in a single year, and frequently with none at all, particularly in the years after 1320. Halfpence of group III, representing the considerable output of 1280-1, are common, but those of later groups, until the reign of Edward III, are mostly scarce or rare. The only occasion on which mints in England other than London struck halfpence was during the original recoinage, when Bristol, Lincoln, Newcastle and York participated. No fractional coins were struck at any of the ecclesiastical mints during this period.

It is not possible to construct a classification for the halfpennies (or farthings) comparable to that which has been evolved for pence for the simple reason that, whereas the penny series is a continuum with for the most part a smooth development from one group or sub-group to the next, the minting of the fractions was irregular and intermittent.

Dies and punches were taken up or put aside as occasion arose, and so came to be used in combinations that sometimes defy the normal rules of numismatic taxonomy. The Withers arrangement concentrates on punches for the crown and face, recognising that these do not always produce a picture consistent with the testimony of the lettering. Although there are various points of contact between the fractions and the pennies, it therefore has to be accepted that the nature of the material is not such as to allow them all to be fitted into the same tidy structure.

In the case of group III there is sufficient correspondence of detail between pence and halfpence for the classification of the halfpence to be related to that of the pence at least to the extent of identifying earlier and later varieties. The earlier have waisted (composite) *S*, barred *A* and inward-turned side fleurs as on pence of IIIc-e. A few rare early examples of London (IIIbc) have a thin curved line of drapery (but with two small curved wedges above it) comparable to that on pence of IIIb, and they have often been classified as such although the crown has spearhead ornaments which do not appear on group III pence before IIIc. Difficulties in distinguishing between the 'hollowed' drapery of IIIc and the wedges of IIId or IIIe are even greater for halfpence than for pence, because of their smaller size and lesser definition, and the designation IIIcd is therefore generally used. There is little variety in these coins, apart from the face which is sometimes from a punch similar to that on the IIIbc halfpence, but often from a larger one. Bristol and Lincoln contributed to the production of IIIcd halfpence, although those of Lincoln are rare.

Halfpence were also struck at Newcastle and York. The dies for these were evidently made at York, along with those for the northern pence of IIIe, since they show some features which differ from the southern halfpence of IIIcd. Most notably, the rare Newcastle halfpenny has a variant of the normal reverse type (unique in the late medieval series) in which the group of three small pellets in each angle of the cross is replaced by a single large one. The lettering on Newcastle reverse dies includes the pellet-barred *N* that occurs on some pence of IIIe, and its large size required shortening the inscription to *Novicastri* only, by the omission of *Villa*. Large lettering also occurs on some of the halfpenny dies used at York.

Late group III halfpence, of London and Bristol only, are associated with the period of IIIg pence by a crown with splayed side-fleurs. They also have lettering slightly larger than in IIIcd, usually with *A* unbarred and the late *S*. If Chester received dies for halfpence they would presumably have been of this kind, but none has yet been found.

The lack of any halfpence that can be related to the early stages of group IV accords with the absence of any record of their having been struck between October 1281 and May 1285. Some very rare halfpence with three pellets on the breast and one before *Lon* correspond to pence of IVe. A similar reverse, except that the *S* is waisted, is found with an unmarked obverse and North has labelled this IVd, although technically it might perhaps be described as a IVc/e mule. However, other halfpence now described as IVc, without extra marks, resemble those of IIIg except for having lettering and crown from smaller punches. No halfpence attributable to group V have been found, and mules between groups IV and VI suggest that none may have been struck.

Halfpence of the 1290s present equivalent difficulties of arrangement to those of the pence of groups VI to VIII. To group VI are assigned halfpence with neat lettering, including closed *c* and *e* and integral *S*. The head is small, with short hair, and the central fleur of the crown is often damaged. Halfpence associated with group VII have a broader face with almond eyes; lettering is larger, often with double-barred *N* as on pence, a composite *S*, and the *c* and *e* open. London halfpence of group VII do not show the rose on breast found on group VII pence, but the rose does feature on extremely rare halfpence

Edward I – Edward III

of Dublin. The crown in group VII appears to be from the same punch as that of group VI, but before the damage to the central fleur. So here again, as with the pence, there are possible problems of sequence in the VI-VII period. Unfortunately die-linking in the 1290s was too random to be of much help. While there are mules both ways between IV and VI, a IV/VII mule has also been noted; and there are various interchanges between groups VI, VII and VIII.

The last of the pre-1300 halfpence have a taller and narrower crown, and are associated with pence of group VIII by their dumpy initial cross patty and by the characteristic letter *h* with notched back; *c* and *e* are again closed and *N* is normally single-barred. One halfpenny reads *Edwa*, as on a very rare penny of the same group. Mules with reverses of VI can be identified by the letter *O* which is often waisted on halfpence, as on pence, of group VI. Since halfpence were not struck at London in the two years to September 1300, the absence of any that can be associated with pence of group IX, or with the recoinage mints opened in 1299, is only to have been expected.

The silver coined into halfpence in 1300/1 is represented by rare coins (XP; North 'Xab') with a long narrow face and other affinities to the Primary pence of group X. Lettering is hollow-sided, and the lengthening of *Edw R to Edwar R* leads to a crowded inscription. This is the normal reading on pence of group X, type P5 (Fox Xb), but many of these halfpence, as the accounts demonstrate, must date from the early part of the Primary phase. The fuller reading *Edward* of the pence of types P2-3 (Fox Xa) could not have been fitted onto a halfpenny die, and the use of a trifoliate crown (1) on most of the XP halfpence suggests that irons for this revived issue were made at the outset of group X. However, a new, bifoliate punch (crown 2) is also found on a few of these Primary halfpence.

CROWNS ON HALFPENCE OF GROUP Xh

1   2   3

From this point onwards Edwardian halfpence cease to have a relationship with successive issues of pence. The Irish title, *Dns hyb*, was dropped in favour of giving the king's complete Latin name: *Edwardus Rex A (-Angli)*. The general appearance of bust and lettering is still that of group X and remains so for thirty years or more, since a number of the original punches continued in use until the 1330s. These include crown punches 1 and 2 from the XP issue, to which was added a revival of the old punch from group VIII with trifoliate dexter fleur (crown 3), distinguished by having a central fleur of 'battle-axe' shape (i.e. with straight sides) instead of the elegant lis of crown 1. All three punches survived to be used for early dies of the 1335 issue and are therefore of little use for establishing relative chronology. A variety with crown 2 reading *Rex An* closely resembles the Berwick coins from London-made dies of Blunt class V (equivalent to pence of early group XI and dated c.1312), but otherwise there are few clues as to date or sequence. Since very small quantities of halfpence, if any, were struck in most years after 1300, relatively few new dies would have been needed during this time and the lack of new punches with features related to pence of groups XI to XV causes no surprise. The whole series is here labelled Xh in order to indicate that, although the basic association is with group X, the halfpence stand outside the detailed classification applicable to the pence and their issue extended into the period of subsequent groups.

Farthings, 1279 - 1335

Farthings were struck on a larger scale and more consistently than halfpence throughout most of this period. The mint accounts show more than five times as many farthings as halfpence struck at London between January 1280 and September 1281, leaving out of consideration any farthings struck in 1279. After the lack of entries for fractions in the first half of the 1280s, £1,500 was minted in farthings from 1285/6 to 1290/1, very slightly more by value than in halfpence during this period, but with farthings coming to predominate in the later years. Very few fractions were produced in 1291-3, but the next seven years again saw substantial issues of farthings, although on a declining trend. Unlike halfpence, of which few were struck in the 1290s, some farthings were minted at London in 1299/1300; but after the renovation of that year the production of farthings increased sharply. More than £1,000 worth was struck each year from 1300/01 to 1305/06, and annual output remained at several hundred pounds during the first half of the reign of Edward II. From 1319/20 the figures for farthings were lower (while halfpence had almost disappeared), but there was an increase in the late 1320s and early 1330s, under Edward III, when farthings were the only denomination in regular production. Like halfpence, farthings were struck at provincial mints in the recoinage of 1279-81, but outside London only otherwise at Berwick and in Ireland.

Four main divisions, based on type and inscription, are readily evident in the farthing series, each containing coins that can be related to several groups of pence. Type A is, except in the inscriptions, a miniature version of the early pence, and includes all the larger farthings struck to a higher weight with extra alloy in 1279-80. A memorandum written in the first half of 1279 concerning the new coinage, and preserved in the *Red Book of the Exchequer*, noted that the number of farthings struck to the pound would be "seysante cink souz e wit deners", i.e. 65s. 8d., or 788 pieces (taking souz and deners to have their numerical meanings of twelves and units, in the common medieval manner). These coins would thus weigh 6.85 gr., but their silver content was little more than three-quarters of this. All farthings of the three subsequent types were struck from fine silver at the normal weight of approximately one quarter of the penny and are accordingly of reduced module. The second and third types, B and C, which are associated respectively with pence of groups IIId-e to VII, and of VIII to IXb, have no inner circle and a larger bust, reaching to the bottom of the coin, which divides the inscription. The fourth type (D), which belongs to the period of pence of groups X to XVd, reverts to the basic penny design like the first type but of course at the smaller format.

The heavy farthings of type A accompanied pence of groups I, II and early III. The obverse inscription is *Edwardus Rex* and the London mint-signature is given in adjectival form (as often used on the Continent), *Londoniensis*. An extremely rare early variant reading, *Londriensis*, may be compared with the reference in the *Red Book* memorandum to the new fractions as *Lundreis*. The portrait on the earliest farthings (A1) is comparable to that on pence of Ia, although the small size led to the crown being modified by the omission of intermediate ornaments and the use of bifoliate side fleurs. On most there is a colon before *Rex*, and the *N*s are Roman and reversed. *A*, with drooping top, resembles that on Ia pence. A later variety (A2) with trifoliate crown, normal *A*, and smaller letters is associated with Ic pence, and so also confined to London. In A2 there is occasionally an extra line above (indicating the top of the head?) or below the main band of the crown. Neither of these group I varieties is particularly rare, and although no separate figures for farthings are given in the mint accounts before 1280 it is clear that they were minted in some quantity, as they would need to have been during the early months of the recoinage.

Farthings of the period of group II pence (A3), although of the same basic type, have a smaller, narrow face (like that on IIb pence) and a larger crown (its base almost straight), now with intermediate jewels. The lettering is small, with a neat initial cross, and the colon no longer occurs on the obverse. The last of the heavy farthings (A4) accompanied the early pence of group III and, like them, have a broader portrait than in group II, with the base of the crown more arched. The initial cross and lettering are larger and less neat, with *N* no longer reversed. The output of farthings at London continued on a considerable scale during 1280, but those related to groups II and early III are today quite scarce. Farthings of these varieties were also struck at Bristol and York (using the normal forms of mint signature), but they are very rare. The absence of A4 farthings from Lincoln, whose pence began with IIIc in the summer of 1280, may be seen as confirmation that the heavy farthings were discontinued relatively early in group III.

The design of type B may have been introduced in order to differentiate the new lighter farthings of sterling silver not only from their heavier if baser predecessors, but also from the new round halfpennies which first appeared in August 1280. Their inscription, reduced to eight letters divided by the bust, is *E R An/glie*, representing perhaps a further attempt to differ as much as possible from what had gone before. On the earliest London farthing of type B the bust is set high up, within the inscription as in type A, but the normal arrangement shows it extending nearly to the lower edge of the coin. Most of the London farthings of type B belong to the period of the recoinage, or a little later, constituting the extensive output of this denomination recorded in the accounts for 1280-1. Fox had supposed that all the type B farthings of group III (B1), of both London and the provincial mints, belonged to the IIIg period, because "they resemble the Chester type more than any other type of penny, and may be taken to be contemporary with it". This attribution also misled Fox into connecting the introduction of sterling silver farthings with reductions in the rates of Turnemire's remuneration for minting the different denominations recorded in the accounts as effective from Christmas 1280. But the Newcastle farthing, unknown until recently, is important in demonstrating that many of the type B farthings associated with group III must be attributed to the period of pence of IIId and IIIe (and so be dated from the summer of 1280), since IIIe is the only sub-group in which pence of Newcastle occur. Accordingly, North has attributed type B farthings of group III with a straight-sided crown to IIId (southern) or IIIe (northern), and only those with a spread crown (like that on late group III pence), which are confined to London, to IIIg. These are the last London farthings to carry the *Londoniensis* reading. All the farthings from the provincial mints are rare, those of Lincoln perhaps the least so. The Newcastle coin, unlike the halfpenny, has the normal triple pellet reverse type, although it follows the halfpenny in reading *Novicastri* only. No halfpence or farthings are known of Chester. It seems likely that by late 1280, when this mint was opened, farthing dies may no longer have been sent outside London, which would explain why the last farthings of Bristol, of which there are IIIg halfpence, are of IIId.

In view of the lack of reference to fractions in the mint accounts from 1281 to 1285 and the relatively modest issues recorded for the late 1280s, farthings attributable to the period of group IV pence should not be common and, as with the halfpence, would belong to the later years of the decade, during the currency of pence of IVd and IVe. Rare London coins (B2), of neat style with a square initial cross, and now reading *Civitas London*, have been associated with this period, while others (B3) with a crude, taller crown (too wide for the head) and plainer initial cross are tentatively assigned to group V, even though they are found muled with old *Londoniensis* reverses. Those of B3 might represent at least some of the increased output of farthings recorded in the accounts ended July 1290 and September 1291.

The last of the *Anglie* farthings (B4) probably belong to the period of groups VI and VII, encompassing the marked revival of farthing output in 1293/4. The face is larger, often with almond eyes as on pence of these groups. The hair consists of thick strands, spread more widely, with the dexter inner strand often angular.

Although the general design of type B remained unchanged for the rest of the 1290s, a material and clearly deliberate alteration was made in the inscription a few years before the end of the century, *Anglie* being replaced by *Angl Dn*. This new type (C) includes some varieties of crown and portrait, but the general association of these scarce farthings is undoubtedly with pence of groups VIII and IX. From 1293/4 to 1297/8 nearly £900 on average was minted into farthings annually, but much less was struck in the next two years, and most of the type C farthings must therefore fall in the period of group VIII. The decline in output to £190 in 1299/1300 reflects the concentration of the London mint on pence during the recoinage, and it is notable that none of the other mints in 1300 coined fractions as had been the case with the provincial mints of 1280. North has defined three sub-divisions of the type C farthings. The earliest (here C1) has a tall, coarse crown with bushy hair seeming to emerge almost horizontally from underneath it. On variety C2 the crown is neater and flatter, with short, compact hair, and on C3 there is a low, splayed crown with the hair less compact. Lettering is slightly incurved on C1, straight-sided on C2 and C3, the latter with pronounced serifs. C1 and C2 would be associated with group VIII or IXa, and C3 with IXb, its late position being confirmed by a mule with a reverse of group X. North has noted that the crown and hair punches of C3 were also used later on some halfpence of XP and Xh.

CROWNS OF FARTHINGS OF GROUP Xq

1   2   3

With the advent of group X the design of the farthings was again aligned with that of the pence (type D), although their smaller size, as well as their different style, immediately distinguishes them from the heavy farthings of 1279-80. As with the halves of Xh which continued up to 1335, the quarters of this series (here described as Xq) remained in issue for the same period. Again they bear a general resemblance to pence of group X but for the most part without particular features to associate them with individual sub-divisions of group X or with later groups. Like the halfpence of Xh, the Xq farthings use the inscription *Edwardus Rex*, often with part of *Anglie*, rather than the fuller but more abbreviated titles on the pence. North, largely following the work of Harris, Purvey and Woodhead, defines three main subdivisions of Xq based on differences in the crown

Edward I – Edward III

(which has no intermediate ornaments). The very large issues of farthings from 1300 to 1306 must be represented by the abundant coins of the earliest of these subdivisions. A strange and extremely rare variety, perhaps associated with the introduction of type D, has the inscription starting at 180°. The first crown is very flat, with a low spread central lis, and surmounting a large, oval face as on early group X pence. These Xq1 coins usually read *Rex* alone, but occasionally *Rex A*. On the next two varieties the face is smaller, beneath a taller crown. On farthings of Xq2, which usually read *Rex An*, the fleurs have wedge-shaped petals, and the face has prominent pellet eyes. This variety probably accompanied pence of late group X to group XI or later, when output was still at a relatively high level. The dies of the Blunt class V farthing of Berwick, which can be dated c.1312 because the associated Berwick pence belong to group XIa, are made from the same irons as those for London farthings of Xq2. The crown of Xq3 has curious side-fleurs: the dexter one curls in to touch the band, but the sinister one is v-shaped. On Xq3 farthings the face is spade-shaped, with a pointed chin. An initial cross composed of four wedges on some specimens of Xq3 suggests an association with pence of XIII-XIV, and thus a date in the middle or later 1310s. Farthings of Xq3 must have remained in production throughout the 1320s and up to the debasement of 1335, a period when most of the available bullion was minted into coins of this denomination. The minting of pence had almost ceased from 1324 (and halfpence had not been struck in quantity since 1301) so that in several of the years between 1325 and 1335 only farthings were coined.

Halfpence and Farthings, 1335 - 1343

The failure of the main mints, in the face of foreign competition, to attract any material amount of silver during the XVd period eventually led to a decision to lower the weight and fineness of halfpence and farthings, with effect from May 1335. The standard was reduced from 11.1 oz. to 10 oz. of fine silver (i.e. from 92.5 to 83.3 per cent.) and more coins were to be struck from the pound: 504 halfpence or 1016 farthings, so making the new farthing slightly lighter than half of a halfpenny because of the greater cost of minting the smallest coin. A pound by value of full-weight pence would thus give enough silver to produce £1 3s. in new halfpence, and a small profit after charges. But the new standard was not designed to cause the reminting of existing currency (some of which would already have lost the equivalent of the potential profit in circulation), so much as to prevent the drain of good English coin abroad and to provide some new bullion for the London mint. In the event, relatively little silver was forthcoming until 1341/2 although there was regular, if modest, production of both denominations in the earlier years. The pattern of output, however, differed between the two, with the emphasis at first on farthings and later on halfpence. Of the total of £5,600 struck in farthings, £2,000 was accounted in the first seventeen months, to September 1336, with the rate declining thereafter, to an annual average of £300 in the last three years. Less silver was struck in halfpence than in farthings in each accounting period up to 1337/8, whereas almost four fifths of the halfpenny total of £27,700 was produced between October 1341 and the end of 1343. Accounts for this coinage run to 15 December 1343, when the mint ceased production in anticipation of the new coinage to be introduced at the revised standard in the following month.

Apart from London, the only royal mints to take part in the halfpenny and farthing coinage of 1335-43 were the outposts at Dublin and Berwick. York, Durham and Bury were not authorised to coin fractions, and any coinage that took place there after

1335 would have been pence in continuation of group XVd, and so now relatively unprofitable. It was no doubt because of this that, when the abbot of Reading received his grant of dies in 1338, he was given the exceptional right for an ecclesiastic of coining halfpence and farthings. In 1339 dies for halfpence and farthings were also sent to Dublin. Although extremely rare, and evidently in both cases the product of very small mintage, halfpence have survived of both Reading and Dublin and these provide valuable evidence for the chronology of the London series. Berwick, as usual, followed an independent course, but appropriately neither coins nor mint accounts (from 1333 to 1342) include pence for this period.

The defining characteristic of the fractional coins of this period, here described as XVe, is a star in the inscription on both sides, presumably designed to differentiate the lighter and baser issues at a glance from their heavier and finer predecessors. On the basis of some 250 specimens from the Stanwix hoard, Woodhead has divided the XVe London halfpence into five classes, according to the crown punches used, but the simplest division is into an earlier issue (XVe1) with the star before the mint name, and a much larger one (XVe2) with the star after it. XVe1 includes coins with all the three crown punches (Woodhead classes 1-3) that had been used in the pre-1335 series (Xh). Halfpence of XVe1 with crown 1, the old trifoliate punch first used at the beginning of group X (c. 1300), are extremely rare. Some of those with the bifoliate crown 2 (also rare) have a Gothic *n* on one or both dies, possibly suggesting the work of the engraver of the penny dies of XVd. Most XVe1 halfpence have crown 3, the larger trifoliate punch, which shows damage and recutting during this class; Gothic *n* is again occasionally found. The abundant halfpence of XVe2 mostly have a new bifoliate crown (4), but a few show the old crowns 1 or 2. About a third of the XVe2 halfpence have reverses with the pellets separate in the normal way, but on the majority of reverse dies the pellets are conjoined, as trefoils. A few XVe2 reverses with conjoined pellets have the star before *Civi* instead of after *don*, and one or two others have the star before *Lon* or no star at all. In XVe1 the star is neat and has six points; in XVe2 it normally has eight small points, sometimes resembling a small rosette. Most obverses of XVe1 read *An*; *Ang* occurs on some of XVe1 and on all of XVe2 (on many of which the *G* is from an abnormally large punch).

Few as they are, the scallop-marked halfpence of Reading fit into the same pattern. Those of XVe1 (with crown 3) have the star after *Villa*, and of XVe2 the star after *Rading*. When dies were first made for Reading in 1338 XVe1 must therefore have still been current. The use of crowns 1 and 2 and the star between *Civitas* and *Dublinie* on Irish halfpence, the dies for which were ordered in 1338, also show their relationship to London coins of XVe1. If the Stanwix figures are representative, suggesting that only about one in eight of the London halfpence were of XVe1, the mintage figures would point to the transition between XVe1 and XVe2 falling within the account for 1338/9. Most of the XVe2 halfpence belong to the period of heavy output from 1341/2; and it may be noted that the proportion of XVe halfpence with conjoined pellets in Stanwix, about 60 per cent., approximately coincides with the proportion that bullion minted into halfpence in 1342 and 1343 bears to the whole output of the XVe period.

Although the number of XVe farthings struck at London was approaching 20 per cent. of the number of halfpence, their survival rate is much lower and they are relatively rare today. In several respects the two principal varieties follow those of the halfpence: thus XVe1 farthings have the reverse star before *Lon*, and read *A* or *An*, while XVe2 obverses read *Ang* (with the large *G*), and the star usually follows *don*. The low crown of XVe1 (like that in Xq) was replaced by a taller punch in XVe2. As on halfpence, the pellets

Edward I – Edward III

on later farthings are usually joined. A transition in the farthing series from XVe1 to XVe2 c.1339 would accord with their respective survival rates since (in contrast to the equivalent halfpence) farthings of XVe1 are much the more numerous and the minting of farthings fell to insignificant levels after 1339/40. No Reading farthings of group XVe are yet known, but in view of the great rarity of the XVe halfpence of this mint, and the existence of Reading farthings in group XVI, it is quite likely that they were struck.

English Coins of Berwick-upon-Tweed

The port of Berwick, at the mouth of Tweed, was raised to the status of a royal burgh by David I of Scotland, in whose reign (1124-53) coins were first minted there. During the second half of the thirteenth century Berwick became the most important Scottish mint, largely as a result of converting into domestic coin the foreign silver received in payment for wool from southern Scotland. Having deposed John Balliol, his own appointee to the Scottish throne, in July 1296, Edward I proceeded to capture and sack Berwick. Following the Scottish victory at Stirling Bridge in 1297, the Scots reoccupied the town, but without taking the castle which remained in English hands. In 1298 the town was evacuated by the Scots and thereafter both town and castle remained in possession of the English until they were recovered, during Bruce's campaigns, in 1318. In 1333 Berwick was again taken by the English who then held it continuously, except for a short period in the summer of 1355, until 1461. Although mint names are generally lacking from Scottish coins of the period, it is likely that Berwick remained the most active mint in the 1280s and under John Balliol, and that the facilities required for coinage would have been available to Edward on his arrival in 1296.

A considerable amount of new material has appeared since 1931 when Blunt's basic study of the English coins of Berwick was published, and this has been conveniently collated by North and Withers. Blunt divided the series into eight main classes, attributing his classes I-IV to Edward I, V-VII to Edward II, and VIII to Edward III. Class I consists of coins of fine style which Blunt regarded as the first English issue, of 1296-7. Coins of class II are from very crude dies (extensively muled with obverses of class I) and Blunt considered these to be issues of the beleaguered English commander to pay his castle garrison in the winter of 1297-8. Under his scheme classes III and IV would represent the regular series resumed from 1298, extending through the period of the 1300 renovation in England and beyond, and so alongside the English coinage of Fox groups IX and X. Class V, the only Berwick issue struck from London-made dies, accords with Fox group XIa, and Blunt associated this with the visit of Edward II who passed the winter of 1310/11 at Berwick. The cruder coins of classes VI and VII would then have been the work of local die-sinkers up to 1318. Finally, there are coins with a bear's head in one or two quarters of the reverse (Blunt class VIII), which belong to Edward III's reign, after 1333. Some adjustments need to be made to this broad arrangement in the light of subsequent research, but Blunt's original architecture has not been greatly disturbed. However, the earlier stages in particular still want confirmation from hoard evidence, which is generally lacking for the late 1290s and the early 1300s; there remains uncertainty regarding the attribution of some of the coarser varieties as between classes II and VII; and the sequence of the bear's head types has been reversed. In the case of halfpence and farthings there is also sometimes a problem in relating their features closely to those of the pennies.

Class I

By analogy with the regular English series, the trifoliate crown and the reading *Edw R* serve to place the pence of class I before 1300. They are from well-made dies, in general appearance more akin to Fox groups III and IV than to the London issues of the 1290s (Fox VI - VIII) but clearly the work of professional craftsmen. A characteristic feature of these, like all other Berwick coins before class V except for the crude class II, is the use of a square Roman *E* on the reverse. Obverses of class I pence often have contraction marks, a feature which, along with a comparable style of bust, helps to associate a few halfpence with class I. There are also extremely rare farthings, reading *Edwardus Rex* or *Edwardus Angl*, which have more stylistic affinity with class I than with class III.

Of class I pence seventeen obverse dies have been noted. Blunt classed those with *hyb* as Ia and others with the curious reading *hyd* as Ib. Since eight dies read *hyd* it is hardly to be seen as a normal accidental error. Wood has observed that, in addition to this difference of spelling, class I obverse dies may be divided according to the form of bust, five having a wide face with a bulbous nose and a pellet on the chin, the rest a narrower face with the nose and chin pointed and thinner. The implications of this are difficult to interpret, since all four combinations of spelling and bust are found, and all four are also known from mules with reverses of class II. One of the two Ib wide-face dies, with the odd reading *Ed R*, is only recorded on a I/II mule.

Class II

Berwick pence of class II, by contrast, are of uncouth appearance, and certainly not the work of experienced engravers. The *e* is Gothic on both sides, there are sometimes small points as stops, and the initial cross is plain and often rather dumpy. The largest sub-class, IIa, has a crude crown (usually bifoliate) the ornaments of which, like the eyes, are supplied by large pellets. Lettering is poorly formed and there is some variation in the inscriptions. A few obverse dies read *Edwa* and one *hybe*. The mint name is usually spelt with double *R*. Eleven obverse dies have been noted of IIa, and mules with class I obverses are not unduly rare. Dies of class IIb are of better style, with a bifoliate crown, tidy bust and simple, rather solid, lettering which enables extremely rare Ia/IIb mules to be identified. IIb obverses all read *Edw*; and the reverses differ from most of those of IIa in having a single *R* in the mint name.

The rare coins described by Blunt as class IIc have a bifoliate crown (the band of which is pointed upwards in the centre), the reading *Edwa*, and sometimes a pellet on the breast – all features associated with later classes. They are much cruder than IIb, and being unconnected with other varieties by die-links they have sometimes been regarded as imitations or local copies. Withers has placed them with the last of the Berwick coins of Edward II, around the time of class VII, but whether they belong to the 1290s or to the 1310s, or to some other as yet unrecognised phase of coarse workmanship, cannot be determined in the light of present knowledge.

There are no mules between pence of classes II and III, which suggests that the unskilled workmen of class II and their equipment were replaced when more expert die-sinkers were again available. Blunt's view that class II should be associated with the winter of 1297/8 is an interesting hypothesis but difficult to substantiate. Even leaving aside IIc, there are more than a dozen class II obverse dies and, including the abundant I/II mules, coins of class II are at least as plentiful as those of class I, suggesting a much more substantial issue than would have been necessary for a few months in an isolated castle. Class II could thus have continued in issue for some time after the town was recovered by the English. Alternatively it might constitute the revival of English minting in 1298, following an interval while the town had been lost, and before the return of regular mint personnel, a situation which would be consistent with the worn or damaged condition of the obverse dies evident from most of the I/II mules.

It is not surprising that coins of class II have sometimes been attributed to class VII and *vice versa*, since they are the two classes to which coins of cruder workmanship belong. There is particular difficulty in respect of the fractions, in view of their lack of close correspondence with the pennies. The halfpenny with thick oval eyes attributed by Blunt to class II is a case in point. A die very similar to the reverse of this coin has recently been found muled with an orthodox class V obverse, raising the question whether the supposed class II halfpence ought to be dated later than 1300. Among the farthings there are two of coarse work. The obverse of one has pellets in the crown, suggestive of class II. The other, reading legibly *Edwa R Angl Dn*, might be a candidate for the class VII period.

Classes III and IV

Pence of the next two classes, III and IV, revert to the general style of class I – notably, some early IIIa coins have a portrait resembling the wider face of class I and the same punch for the crown; but they may immediately be distinguished from it by the reading *Edwa* instead of *Edw*, and they lack the contraction marks commonly found in class I. The most obvious difference between classes III and IV is in the form of the letters *V* and *W*: in class IV a marked serif is added to the right wedge of the *V* and to both outer wedges of the *W*, a convenient pointer to the identity of III/IV mules, which are not particularly rare. As in class I the *e* is open Gothic on the obverse, Roman (*E*) on the reverse. Subdivisions of classes III and IV are based on the crown and the letter *N*. In III and IVa the crown is trifoliate, in IVb and IVc bifoliate. IIIa, IVa and IVb have a Gothic *n* in *Dns*, IIIb and IVc a Roman *N* (sometimes pellet-barred in IIIb). Since these permutations do not appear to represent deliberate differentiation, the sub-classes are not necessarily to be taken as indicating absolute sequence within each class. Thus both IIIa and IIIb obverses are muled with reverses of IV, while the only converse mule is IVa/IIIa, an identification confirmed by the unusual reverse inscription which in IIIa sometimes begins *Wil/la B* instead of the normal *Vill/a Be*. Pence of class IV are the commonest of the Berwick series, and with class III they probably belong to the early years of the fourteenth century when output was very high at the main English mints (Fox group X). Except for a few early coins of IVa, there is a pellet on the breast in class IV, perhaps influenced by the star breastmark in Fox group IX (1300). Other reflections of the southern idiom are the regular use of *Edwa* from III onwards and the adoption of a bifoliate crown after IVa.

LETTER *V* AT BERWICK UNDER EDWARD I

(a)   (b)

(a) Normal *V*, classes I and III; (b) *V* with wide serif, class IV.

Both halfpence and farthings are recorded of class III, the IIIb halfpence being the least rare examples of this denomination for the mint. The halfpenny with Gothic *n* (IIIa), however, which reads *hb*, is very rare. Unlike the farthings attributed to class I, the extremely rare class III farthing has an obverse inscription (*Edwa R* ...) corresponding to that on pence and halfpence. One halfpenny, somewhat resembling those of IIIb but with a longer neck and different crown, has a small star on the breast, pointing to a date not earlier than 1300, and a pellet on the breast is found on others; although the peculiar *V* and *W* of class IV pence are not reproduced on any known fractions, the breastmark on these coins, and their differences of portraiture, may indicate a connection with class IV rather than class IIIb. There are also some very rare farthings, of crude style and with circular eyes, and sometimes with a pellet visible on the breast, which probably relate to class IV.

Classes V-VII

All three denominations unquestionably again appear in class V, although the halfpenny is very rare and the farthing extremely so. Blunt's association of this class with Edward II's visit in 1310/11 now needs revision in the light of more detailed sub-division of Fox group XI. The Berwick pence from London-made dies are of the last (and rare) variety of XIa with open c and e (North XIa3), which on the basis of the Durham evidence is probably not to be dated before late 1311 or 1312. Thus, although the king's visit may have played a part in causing dies to be sent to Berwick from London, it does not now seem likely that dies or punches could have been brought up with the royal party. The Berwick pence show all the features of group XI, including the broken dexter ornament in the crown and the two forms *Edwa* and *Edwar* (the latter much the rarer), while the colon which appears before *Vil* (allowing only these three letters in the first quarter) may be compared with a colon after *tas* on a few reverse dies of XIa3 from other mints.

Class V halfpence and farthings also have a colon before *Villa*, but in other respects they conform with London coins of Xh and Xq2. The halfpence have the old bifoliate crown 2, introduced early in group X, and the short form *An* consistent with it. The farthings revert to the reading *Edwardus Rex*, the letter *e* with angular back being of a form found on London farthings associated with group XI.

Blunt's idea that London tools were brought north to Berwick with Edward II led to his view that a pair of class V penny dies, on which the portrait is crude, with squinting eyes, were the work of a local die-sinker using London letter punches. He used the label V* to denote this rare variety (reading *Edwa R*), but it is in fact from an old and worn London-made obverse die of normal class V, on which the face and hair have been recut. The same is true of the obverse of the variety described by Blunt as class VI, reading *Edwar R*, on which the (trifoliate) crown as well as the face and hair has been renewed, this being coupled with new reverse dies copying class V. In view of this the description class VI needs to be redefined to cover all the coins from recut obverse dies of class V, together with reverses copied from class V. On some class VI reverses the colon before *Villa* is reproduced, but the lettering is coarse (with closed *e*), and on one die the inscription is retrograde. There are mules both ways between classes V and VI.

With the return to local die-cutting, foreshadowed by renovation of the class V dies, the standard of workmanship deteriorated markedly. Berwick was evidently unable to call upon anyone of equivalent competence to the producers of the coins of classes I,

III and IV. The last pence of Berwick before it was regained by the Scots in 1318 are from roughly made dies of class VII. The contrast between their coarse work and the fine style of the Scottish coins of Robert Bruce which followed them illustrates the wide gulf between the skills of a local non-specialist metalworker and those of a professional foreign engraver commissioned to produce dies for the first Scottish coinage for more than twenty years. Obverse dies of class VII are of varied but uncouth appearance, with a rough trifoliate crown and straggly hair ending in three short bars each side. Except on a VII/VI mule (with the retrograde reading) there is no colon on the reverse, enabling the division of the inscription, sometimes blundered, to revert to its normal pattern (with *Vill* in the first quarter).

Class VIII

Berwick was probably the only Scottish mint in use for Robert Bruce and David II between 1318 and 1333, and some surviving mint accounts suggest that it was soon put to use, on a modest scale, for Edward III. David II's earliest coinage consisted of halfpence and farthings only, and in some accounts for the mint under English rule for the period from 1333 to 1342 only the fractions are mentioned. Since it is unusual for mint accounts to be closed in June, it could be that the forty pounds accounted between Michaelmas 1333 and June 1334 constituted all that was minted before the reduction in weight and fineness at London in 1335. There is nothing in the accounts to indicate whether any of the 161 pounds accounted for Berwick between September 1334 and October 1342 (most of it in 1334-6) was struck at the lower standard after May 1335, but one of the Berwick farthings from the Stanwix hoard contained only 82.8 per cent silver plus gold, with 15.9 per cent of copper.

The medieval arms of Berwick feature a bear (*bera* in Old English) which was adopted as the badge of the town. Edward III's coins of Berwick are distinguished by having a bear's head in one or two quarters of the reverse, in the same way that a scallop shell occurs on coins of this period of Reading. Berwick's use of a symbol in this way must, however, antedate that of Reading, which only received its dies in 1338. Blunt originally classified the pence and halfpence with one bear's head as VIIIa, placing them in 1333-5, before the halfpence and farthings with two bear's heads; but discovery that the mint accounts refer only to halfpence and farthings between 1333 and 1342 led him to accept that the coins with two bear's heads, his class VIIIb (here class VIII), must represent the coinage of that period. Those with one bear's head (Blunt VIIIa, here class IX) are thus now attributed to the coinage at reduced weight from 1344.

Halfpence of VIII, with the two bear's heads, are scarce, and the farthings rare, but both considerably less so since the discovery of the Stanwix hoard. Their obverse readings are curious, especially for fractional denominations, in that they tend to omit *Rex* but include some form of *Dei Gra* which, although normal on Scottish coins since 1280, had only hitherto been used in the English coinage in the case of Edward I's groats where there was room for a longer inscription. Pellet stops and contractive commas are found on some of these coins. The halfpennies and some of the earlier farthings are from well-made dies, but later farthings are of coarser work and often poorly struck. Even if these coins were struck to two standards, there is no obvious mark of difference, like the star on London coins, to distinguish the baser issues after May 1335. The chamberlain's account for 1336/7 shows profits of 3s. 1d., at 3d. per pound implying only £12 6s. 8d. of coinage, because the moneyer had died on 20 February. The last extant record is for £22 10s. in the period from July 1341 to October 1342.

Ireland

From the Edwardian recoinage onwards, minting took place in Ireland intermittently, in three phases during the reign of Edward I and once, very briefly, under Edward III in 1339. There was no evident continuity with the pre-1279 issues of Richard Olof. Nevertheless, the first period of activity of the Dublin mint, joined not long afterwards by Waterford, began before the end of Edward I's original recoinage in England. The surviving records of this First Phase are fragmentary, and their contents are somewhat ambiguous, since they were compiled in response to allegations of corruption against Stephen of Fulbourn, Bishop of Waterford and Treasurer of Ireland, and not as a direct record of mint activity and output. Nevertheless, they give useful information about the Dublin mint and an indication of the scale of its operations. Accounts of the wardens of the exchange from May 1279 (when the London recoinage accounts begin) to September 1281 show less than £5,000 in both Fulbourn's and the mint's account, but the bulk of the coinage followed the appointment as master early in 1281 of Alexander Normanni of Lucca. The account for March 1281 to June 1282 records some £31,400, and that for June 1282 to September 1284 £2,169. An audit of the accounts was ordered in August 1283, suggesting that the First Phase of the coinage may already have ceased by that date. Even major recoinage mints like Bristol and York were active for less than two years, and it is unlikely that the process would have taken much longer at Dublin. The only mention of Waterford's mint at this period records a payment of £1,415 to Fulbourn for bullion supplied by him between November 1281 and November 1282.

The Second Phase belongs to the 1290s. Irish coins of this phase are very rare, as would be expected from a time when the volume of coinage in England was at a low ebb. The (now lost) *Red Book of the Irish Exchequer* contained a reference to the despatch of dies to Ireland at this period, dated by the names of the officials involved to within the years 1292-5. In 1295 a mint was opened at Cork and this provides a fixed chronological point for the later coins of the Second Phase. The account in the Irish Pipe Roll from February 1295 to August 1297 records various receipts and payments by the keepers of the mint, including £26 6s. 9d. as *monetagium* for the exchange of £400 9s. 2d.; but the rarity of Cork coins suggests that the mint was not active for long. The Third Phase of the coinage, and the last in Edward I's reign, constitutes an extension of the English recoinage of 1300 to Ireland. Foreign workmen were hired for the purpose by the warden of the London mint and Alexander of Lucca was reappointed master of the Dublin mint. From 7 May to 5 June 1300 the profits of the exchange accrued to the king; eight sackfulls of pollards, weighing 626 lb., were purchased and their conversion into sterling produced £351 5s. 1d. in new money. From 16 June 1300 to 29 June 1301 the profits of the exchange were granted to the Frescobaldi, including the purchase of pollards, and a mutilated account records that 11,040 lb. of these were delivered to Alexander to be recoined. After a pyx trial in August 1302 he was acquitted of his office, but his work appears to have been completed by June 1301.

In the First Phase Dublin's output exceeded that of Waterford in the proportion of about 3:2. Whether or not a mint in his city was to the bishop's financial advantage we do not know, but the revival of the mint of Waterford, after an interval of more than eighty years, may have been due to the influence of Bishop Stephen, who had been appointed to the see in 1274 and became head of the Anglo-Irish administration in 1280. Coins of Waterford also occur in the Second Phase, but both classes of penny with the Waterford signature at that period are of unofficial style. A Waterford halfpenny, however, shares an official obverse die with a halfpenny of Cork and thus provides evidence of regular coinage at Waterford (for the last time) c. 1295.

The new coins of 1280 retain the triangular frame for the king's portrait which had been characteristic of the Irish issues in the names of John and Henry III. But the triangle, consisting of an outer beaded band with a thin line inside it, now points downwards, thus allowing more space at the top to accommodate the wider Edwardian forms of crown and hair. The inscription is the same as on contemporary English pence, but divided into three segments: *Edw R/Angl D/ns hyb*. There are usually small points between the words, abbreviation marks after *R, Angl* and *hyb*, and a contraction mark above *Dns*. Because of the limited space around the triangle, the lettering on the obverse is much smaller than that on the reverse, but although this enhances appearance and legibility it deprives us of the normal means of identifying which kinds of obverse and reverse dies belong together, and this complicates the classification of pence of the First Phase. Successive generations of students have grappled with the series, from Burns with the material from Montrave and Allen with that from the Boyton find, but although the general shape of the coinage is now established a number of questions remain unresolved. Dolley and Seaby provided an overall survey in 1968, but their arrangement has been modified in several respects as a result of more recent work by North. With the exception of Waterford pence of the Second Phase, the dies were made in London, but although many of the punches for crown, face or hair were the same as occur on contemporary English coins, some were not.

Class I

The numerous pence of the First Phase, here for convenience referred to collectively as class I, are most readily recognised by a trefoil of small pellets below the king's bust (the upper pellet often merges into the drapery and so may not be visible). In outline, North's division of class I obverses may be summarized as follows:

A   Tall crown, not from English punches; rare.
B   Two crown punches with splayed side fleurs, as used on English coins of Fox group IIIg.
C   The later of the two IIIg crowns. Cross before *Edw* (with Roman *E*).
D   A very rare type, with the later IIIg crown as in B and C, but new 'gaunt' face and sharply curved hair.

Dublin used all four of these obverse types, Waterford B and D only. Reverse dies of this phase are differentiated according to the form of the letter *S*: reverse 1, having a waisted body, with two wedges added; and reverse 2, an integral punch with central swelling, as introduced in the second half of 1280 on English dies from Fox group IIIf-g onwards. With the later S there is a third form of Dublin reverse, on which a Gothic *n* replaces Roman *N*, a feature recalling some rare obverse dies of late group III at York and Bury. Also reminiscent of late group III in the English series is a pellet-barred N which occurs (very rarely) in class IB.

Most of the Dublin obverses of class I, and nearly all of Waterford, belong to IB. North divides class IB into two sub-groups, according to their crown punches, in the same sequence as they occur on English coins of group IIIg: B1 having rather clumpy side fleurs, B2 with the side fleurs more clearly defined and more widely spread. These two crowns are often difficult to distinguish, but their identification enabled North to demonstrate that only dies with the B2 crown were supplied to Waterford, indicating that the second mint was brought into action some time after Dublin. The next largest group is IC, also with the crown of B2, but easily differentiated by having a cross instead of the usual pellet before *Edw*, and a straight-backed *E*. Pointing to the use of a scroll-tailed *R* in IC, and the fact that this class is confined to Dublin, North has suggested that IC obverse dies, despite being paired with type 3 reverses, may have been made during the period of IB before the Waterford mint came into operation. Pence of IA, with an 'Irish' crown, are quite rare, this being one of the factors that led North to suggest that class IA may belong to the period of limited output before Alexander's appointment. The crown of IA has tall fleurs, those at the side being only slightly curved outwards, and the intermediate ornaments are also unusually tall. Very few specimens of the rare class ID have been identified, but the variety is of some significance since it is also found muled with a reverse of class II, suggesting that it comes at the end of the class I series. The face and hair punches are distinctive, but in other respects the ID coins resemble some of late class IB. The face is a narrow oblong, with hollowed eyes; the hair is sharply curved outwards at the top, and the rows of curls slope upwards more acutely than on earlier punches.

Obverse lettering in class I varies considerably, but not in any very obvious sequence. As a general guide, the letter *R* with a scroll tail tends to indicate relatively early dies (IA, IB1 and IC), whereas a wedge-tailed *R* is found on few obverses of IA or IB1, but becomes normal in IB2 (and ID). On dies of IA with the wedge-tailed *R* the uprights have slightly concave sides. *S* is usually formed of two crescents and two wedges, but a swollen-centred *S* is occasionally found – in IA, IB2 and IC. Although a reasonably straightforward sequence of dies, based on letter forms and the punches for crown, hair and face, can be established for most of the English series at this period, the same cannot be said of the Irish pence of class I, and it seems likely that the periods of use of different punches for the same letter or other feature may often have overlapped.

Unfortunately the three types of Dublin reverse in class I do not provide as much indication of sequence as might have been hoped, since all three are found in combination with obverses of both IA and IB. In IA reverse 1 with the early *S* appears to be less rare than reverse 3 with the Gothic *n*, and this pattern, together with the 'Irish' crown, argues for placing IA early. On the other hand, almost all the reverse dies made for Waterford have the earlier *S*, including that used in ID at this mint. The distinctive obverse dies of IC are virtually only found with Gothic *n* reverses (the only exception being one of type 2), causing one to wonder whether they might have been produced in a separate *officina*. Apart from this almost exclusive pairing of class IC obverses with type 3 reverses at Dublin (a pattern not repeated on halfpence), the combination of different obverse and reverse varieties was apparently haphazard. All this suggests (as does a similarly confused pattern in the contemporary recoinage issues of Alexander III in Scotland) a relatively short period of minting in which dies from different batches, and with differing features, were available for use concurrently, and perhaps not always in the same sequence as that in which they had been made.

Most of the Irish halfpence and farthings, although without a trefoil below the bust, undoubtedly belong with the pence of class I. Of both the fractional denominations Waterford coins are rather less scarce than those of Dublin. The bulk of the halfpence were presumably struck alongside pence of later class IB. Some, perhaps the earlier, have no pellets as stops or before *Edw* and the obverse lettering on these, as on pence, is smaller than on the reverse. Others have pellets in the inscription and large lettering on both sides. Since both these varieties are well represented of Waterford, the halfpenny denomination (as in England) was probably not introduced until the coinage had been under way for some time. A few Dublin halfpence with a Roman *E* in *Edw* may be compared with pence of class IC (and so, like the equivalent pence, could perhaps predate some of the IB coins), but they usually have a Roman *N* on the reverse. There is little variety among the class I farthings, which have a tall trifoliate crown and bushy hair. Because of size, the inscription on the farthings is reduced to *E R Anglie*, the form introduced on English farthings during 1280.

Classes II-IV

In view of the shortage of supply of bullion to the English mints during the 1290s it is somewhat surprising that mints should have been reopened in Ireland at this period. However, although they are all very rare, two distinct classes of pence, with related halfpence, belong to this Second Phase of the Edwardian coinage in Ireland. The Dublin pence of class II (North E) are distinguished by having a small rosette on the breast, as on English pence of Fox group VII; but their lettering is more like that of Fox group VI, with the *c* and *e* each from a single punch and distinctly closed. Since the lettering on English pence post-group V is much reduced in size, the smaller fount enabled the same letter punches to be used for the first time on both sides of the Irish pence. The Irish class II crown is from the same 'antler' punch as used in groups VI and VIIa, showing the same small nick in the band beside the central fleur, as is evident on many of the English pence. The ID/II mule is an unexpected link with the coinage of the First Phase after what must have been an interval of some ten years or so, but it does argue for class II being the first issue after the revival of the Dublin mint.

Class III (North F) includes all the coins of Cork and so although not closely related to any of the English groups it may be precisely dated. Most if not all of the Cork coins were probably minted in 1295 and since Cork pence of this class, although rare, are considerably less so than those of Dublin, it is unlikely that class III was in issue at Dublin either for very long. A curious feature of the Dublin pence and some of Cork is the use of small crosses as intermediate ornaments in the crown (other Cork coins have stalked pellets there). The chief distinguishing feature of the class, however, is a small point in each corner of the triangle.

There are no farthings of the Second Phase and the halfpence are all of considerable rarity. The class II halfpenny of Dublin is a reduced version of the penny and, unlike any known example of London, where very few halfpence were minted at this period, it has a rosette on the breast. Its crown, narrow and spiky, resembles that on English farthings of the 1290s. Another variety of Dublin halfpenny (without the rosette) has a bust with features comparable to English halfpence of the 1290s and shares with the rosette coin a curved lower contour of the bust. Of class III there are halfpence of Dublin, Waterford and Cork. A pellet in each corner of the triangle, as on pence, is found on halfpence at Dublin and Cork, and some of them also share with class III pence the use of *c* for *e* in *Cdw*. At Waterford and Cork there is a further variety of halfpenny which, despite lacking extra marks, must be associated with class III since it includes an obverse die-link between the two mints and Cork features only in that class.

The existence of this Waterford-Cork die-link suggests that the mint at Waterford may have been closed when Cork's was opened. The two ports lie only some 60 miles apart on the south coast of Ireland and the transfer of minting from one to the other would have been relatively simple. No Waterford pence of this period are known from normal dies; but there are coins of curious appearance of both classes II and III. The Waterford pence of class II resemble those of Dublin quite closely, but the dies are rather crudely executed. Except that it has pellets in the corners of the triangle, the Waterford coin associated with class III bears little resemblance to the pence of Cork and Dublin, having a large head, with short hair and a tall crown. It is notable that these abnormal coins relate to two consecutive classes, and since there are no regular Waterford pennies of either class which could have served as models for imitation, there is a case for regarding them as having been produced at Waterford despite their unofficial appearance. The class III Waterford dies at least were presumably of local manufacture, and the coin itself looks to be of debased metal, perhaps hinting at irregularity in the mint which led to its closure. Dolley argued that the sole occurrence of a mint in Cork at this moment could have been related to the temporary transfer of authority, after the death of the Justiciar in April 1295, to a member of the locally powerful FitzGerald family; and that the early closure of the Cork mint might have been associated with the arrival in October 1295 of an English Justiciar, John de Wogan, anxious to conserve the rights of the crown by restricting coinage to Dublin. But the Cork account runs from February 1295; and while the opening of this mint and the fact that most of the coins of class III are from Cork, and not from Dublin, both suggest unusual circumstances, we have no means of telling whether the reasons were political, administrative or commercial.

However that may be, coins of the Third Phase of Edward I's Irish coinage (North group G; here class IV) are confined to Dublin. There is no numismatic evidence to suggest that coinage had taken place in Ireland in the late 1290s, and Alexander's reappointment in 1300, for the same purpose of converting crockards and pollards as in England, implies that the Dublin mint had probably been in abeyance for some time. Coins of class IV, which were the result of this conversion, are easily recognised from having a single pellet beneath the bust and a crown with tall central fleur. Two divisions of the class IV pennies can be distinguished by differences in the lettering. The rarer type, IVa (North G1), which has small lettering with pronounced serifs on both sides, is closer stylistically to preceding issues and so may be the earlier of the two. Class IVb pennies have larger lettering on the reverse (North G2). No mules have been noted between the two, but if they exist they should be identifiable by the obverse letter *e*, which in IVa is closed with a long curved front and in IVb is composed of a crescent and three (often coalescing) wedges.

OBVERSE LETTER *e* in IRISH GROUP IV

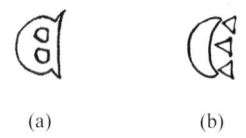

(a)   (b)

(a) Closed *e* with curved front, IVa; (b) Crescent and wedges, IVb.

The rare halfpennies of class IV usually have a pellet below the bust like the pennies, and large lettering on the reverse. The crown is taller than in class I, and has straighter sides. Late Dublin farthings also have a pellet below the bust, with a much wider and flatter crown than those of class I.

Edward III

Under Edward III the Dublin mint was briefly revived during the period of the English debased (and star-marked) fractional issues of group XVe. Plans were made for an equivalent Irish issue in 1336, in connection with arrangements for new mining activity.

Edward I – Edward III

Dies were then ordered for Irish halfpence and farthings, but the project was delayed and in June 1338 dies were again ordered, eight pairs each for halfpence and farthings, and (rather surprisingly) eight pairs also for pence. Their despatch to Dublin was authorised in March 1339, and a limited issue took place in the ensuing months. Two halfpence and one farthing attributable to this coinage have survived. The halfpence are from different dies, their obverses having the English crowns 1 and 2. The issue was presumably short-lived, and an order for the dies to be surrendered was made in November 1340, by which time the mint had probably been closed for some time. The coins differ from the Irish issues of Edward I in reading *Edwardus Rex*, and the halfpence, like their English counterparts, have stars in the inscription on both sides. Although no star is visible on the mis-shapen and poorly struck farthing, the lettering, portrait and small visible portion of the crown have affinities to the English farthings of XVe.

Imitations

Imitation of English sterlings on the Continent reached its peak during the Edwardian era, driven by the same respect for the influential model as had been the case in the Short Cross and Long Cross periods, but now with increasing focus on the potential for intrusion into the English currency itself. Edward I's new reverse type was first reproduced in Brabant, where the established armorial type of obverse, with a lion in a shield, was now combined with a single cross reverse instead of the voided cross sterling type copied in the 1270s. But straight counterfeits of the Edwardian sterling, accurately copying the type on both sides, soon appeared, and by 1283 the English government was already aware that some imitations were indistinguishable except by weight. Many of the early continental imitations, however, even if escaping notice at a superficial glance, were easily identifiable, since their inscriptions refer to their actual issuers and on the crockards and pollards the head is uncrowned. That such began in the 1280s is confirmed by the presence of two crockards in a small find at Cardiff in which the English element ends with group IVe. The main issuers were local rulers in the Low Countries, situated chiefly in the area of modern Belgium. The most prolific were the duke of Brabant and the counts of Flanders-Namur, Hainault, Luxembourg and Looz. Some can be closely dated by their authorship, such as those of Bishop William of Cambrai (1292-6). Debasement in France and the Low Countries in the late 1290s led to increased production of crockards and pollards of inferior standard; these entered the English currency in substantial numbers, thus reducing the supply of foreign silver to the English mints. In a hoard of the late 1290s from Mellendean in the Scottish borders crockards and pollards constituted a considerably higher proportion of the total (more than ten per cent.) than the coins of the Scottish kings themselves. Several attempts were made in the 1280s and 1290s to confiscate inferior foreign coin but, to judge by the contents of hoards, with only limited success until the renovation of 1300 put an end to the menace of crockards and pollards.

One of the consequences of this was that continental issuers ceased to produce coins that could be readily distinguished from Edward's, and thenceforward concentrated on minting sterlings with a crowned bust of English appearance. Some of these continued to carry the actual names of their issuers, but to make them more difficult to identify continental moneyers frequently resorted to ingenious means of disguising the names of their rulers – those of John the Blind of Luxembourg (1309-46), for example, adding an *E* before his name, and converting the *o* of *Io(h)annes* into an omega (*w*), so that the inscription would begin *Eiwa* like the English *Edwa*. Direct counterfeits with English inscriptions were, however, also produced in increasing numbers. Many of them are extremely close and deceptive copies. By 1282 Hubert Alion had left London to work for Count Gui de Dampierre at Namur and many of the other mint personnel who had been engaged for the English recoinage had also returned to continental mints. Mint workers were an international cadre, and the same will have happened after 1300.

Some of the direct copies certainly pre-date the 1300 recoinage. A trifoliate crown and the reading *Edw R* point to imitation of the earlier Edwardian issues. One imitative group, including the distinctive reading *Edw Re* (not a form found on regular English coins after group I), has occurred in the Mellendean and other pre-1300 hoards. Even the Foxes were sometimes misled by counterfeits: for instance, their inclusion of York as a mint in group IIIg was based on coins now thought to be imitations; and their chosen illustration of an imitative type of 'Durham' coin, to represent group Xb with a plain cross, caused problems in the arrangement of Bishop Bek's coinage by exaggerating the apparent number of plain cross Durham coins at this point in the series.

Many of the good direct copies seem to have been made in the 1310s, often reproducing the typical concave lettering of group X as well as the post-1300 (and mainly post-group X) reading *Edwar R*. Generally they are of the sterling silver standard, or approaching it. Their weight tends to be at the lower end of the normal range for English originals, so that their collective low weight may betray them even if individually they might escape suspicion. As is evident from Mayhew's monumental survey of the Edwardian imitations, inappropriate combination of dies, a perennial feature of imitative series, is frequently to be found. The 'Durham' Xb on the Fox plate is one of a counterfeit group that includes die-links between reverses naming London, Canterbury and Durham. Irish triangle obverses are found paired with 'London' reverses and 'Dublin' reverses with English obverses. The mint at Yves, working for Gaucher de Châtillon, Count of Porcien (1312-22), produced parallel series in his own name and in imitation of the English, and sometimes mixed the dies. Often imitations can be identified as such by these means, but ultimately it is only a thorough recognition of the detailed characteristics of the originals that enables the abnormality of counterfeits to be detected, and this has only been fully achieved for Edwardian sterlings within the last generation.

Mint Output

The accounts of the warden of the mint show amounts of bullion purchased and the actual quantities of coins issued throughout the period at London and Canterbury; only the London account for 1310/11 is missing. Amounts of bullion received by the mint were reckoned in pounds, shillings and pence, by weight. The two sets of figures normally correspond closely, although when they differ it was presumably because of short-term differences of timing. The amounts shown in the table are for coin issued, except from September 1281 to May 1285, when no entries were made for issues, and the figures for bullion purchased are given instead. From the 1290s onwards the accounts were normally made up to the end of the exchequer year at Michaelmas (29 September), denoted by M, from 30 September in the preceding year; where this is the case no day or month is given in the table (e.g. 1292/93). Mint charges were slightly higher for the fractional denominations, with the convenient consequence that separate totals are recorded at London for halfpence and farthings. The deduction for purchases of English silver were greater than for foreign silver, so that the two had to be accounted separately. This shows that during the original recoinage English silver greatly exceeded foreign, as old currency was withdrawn, but from 1281 foreign silver was the principal source (especially at Canterbury) except during the renovation of 1299/1301 when the reminting of deficient English coin from circulation again predominated. No accounts were enrolled for the regional mints of 1280-1, since they were farmed to Turnemire, but those for 1299-1302 are preserved in full.

The amount of coin struck per lb weight into halfpence and farthings sometimes varied slightly within a single accounting period, so that the total coined, in money terms, cannot be computed precisely. In such cases (marked by *) the figure given in the table is the maximum, as if all silver had been coined at the highest number of coins permitted during the period. The only account in which the range of possibilities is wide is that of farthings from May to October 1280, during which the amount was increased from 197d. to 243d. when the weight reduction and restoration of the fine silver standard took place in mid-year; in this case the outer limits of the range are £2,550 - £3,038. The other periods within which rates per pound varied were for halfpence October 1280 – April 1281, 1308/09, 1315/16, and 1328/32, and for farthings October 1280 – April 1281 and all dates from 1308/09 onwards; in all these cases the range was very small, for most purposes immaterial.

From September 1281 the number of dies made for London and Canterbury are recorded in the mint accounts, because 7s. was due for each dozen to the holder of the serjeanty of the dies (of which 2s. was the actual cost of cutting them). Between 1281 and 1324 nearly forty thousand dies were supplied to London and Canterbury, more than eleven thousand of them in the four years 1305-9. Dies were normally issued in sets of one obverse with two reverses, so that a dozen would consist of four obverses and eight reverses. By comparing the numbers of dies with amounts of coin issued we may obtain reliable figures for die output at this period. These suggest that the average product of an obverse die at the two principal mints under Edward I and Edward II was around 32,000 coins, with reverses accounting for half this amount. Variation from one period to another could be due to several factors – intensity of output (much lower after 1310), the mix of denominations, the quality of the dies or the degree of acceptable wear before they were replaced. The extra royal mints in this year received 994 dies for the issue of ten million pence, an overall average of 30,000 coins per obverse die; but surviving coins show that the obverse dies were often in poor condition, and the average varied significantly between mints – from 21,700 at Chester to 34,600 at Bristol.

A pyx trial held at Bury St. Edmunds in 1297 records that a total of 7,120 pounds of silver had been struck at the abbot's mint since 1280. The coins show that about thirty sets of dies were involved. This means an average output per obverse die of more than 60,000 coins, implying that care must have been taken to keep the abbot's dies in production for as long as possible. Surviving coins of Bury suggest that the proportion of the total output of this period represented by issues of the moneyer Robert of Hadleigh was not less than three-quarters, giving a sum of at least £5,000 minted in his name.

1279–1343

	London			Canterbury
	£ pence	£ halfpence	£ farthings	£ pence
28.4.1279 – 20.11.1279	93,847	-	-	-
20.11.1279 – 1.1.1280	14,051	-	-	-
1.1.1280 – 18.5.1280	46,939	-	5,123	
18.5.1280 – 18.10.1280	104,207	2,724	* 3,038	
1.1.1280 – 18.10.1280				35,640
18.10.1280 – M.1281	84,555	* 2,355	* 5,570	22,924
M.1281 – 21.10.1283	78,992	-	-	40,849
21.10.1283 – 20.5.1285	38,052	-	-	23,795
20.5.1285 – 15.8.1286	73,112	496	152	29,870
15.8.1286 – 15.6.1287	43,426	253	46	29,049
15.6.1287 – 3.11.1287	26,234	158	170	17,364
3.11.1287 – 3.11.1288	37,149	213	81	15,258
3.11.1288 – 15.7.1290	20,513	183	573	5,468
15.7.1290 – 15.7.1291	1,691	203	537	921
2.9.1291 – M.1292	4,253	91	-	780
1292/93	2,460	61	51	749
1293/94	5,154	-	1,225	91
1294/95	5,711	20	982	-
1295/96	3,605	284	780	-
1296/97	5,863	101	810	-
M.1297 – 14.10.1298	1,124	182	729	-
15.10.1298 – M.1299	13,203	-	253	-
1299/1300	108,165	-	192	22,619
1300/01	40,490	375	1,285	10,666
1301/02	5,518	-	1,600	3,108
1302/03	4,577	61	1,175	3,827
1303/04	15,734	51	1,458	15,501
1304/05	69,864	30	1,326	36,015
1305/06	63,758	41	1,164	32,833
1306/07	89,569	30	557	54,897
1307/08	70,754	-	830	46,451
1308/09	97,837	92	* 873	43,671
1309/10	21,927	30	* 1,575	26,273
1310/11	Missing			5,157
Oct. 1311 – M.1312	13,799	-	* 409	4,959
1312/13	7,120	20	* 297	7,022
1313/14	30,623	-	* 460	36,109

Edward I – Edward III

	London			Canterbury
	£ pence	£ halfpence	£ farthings	£ pence
1314/15	11,367	41	* 797	20,978
1315/16	449	257	* 457	2,610
1316/17	7,044	81	* 817	15,081
1317/18	13,185	134	* 228	21,751
1318/19	8,729	10	* 321	17,883
1319/20	8,577	21	* 155	16,060
1320/21	9,325	-	* 245	5,618
1321/22	1,189	-	* 142	3,811
1322/23	804	10	* 225	1,090
1323/24	1,635	-	* 123	-
1324/25	-	10	* 108	-
1325/26	-	-	* 143	-
1326/27	61	-	* 179	-
1327/28	-	-	* 153	-
1328/29	392	17	* 324	145
1329/30	61	5	* 435	-
Jan. – M.1331	-	10	* 503	638
1331/32	-	10	* 408	-
1332/33	-	-	* 668	-
1333/34	-	-	* 390	-
M.1334 – May 1335	-	-	305	-

After debasement				
May – M.1335		192	212	
1335/36		1,382	1,907	
1336/37		395	926	
1337/38		711	780	
1338/39		1,367	510	
1339/40		1,278	659	
1340/41		790	341	
1341/42		5,048	317	
1342/43		14,452	301	
M. – Dec. 1343		3,486	21	

Provincial Mints, 1300-02; pence only		£
Bristol	May – Oct. 1300	13,578
Chester	July – Nov. 1300	1,468
Exeter	June – Dec. 1300	3,918
Newcastle	June – M.1300	5,275
	1300/01	12,666
	1301/02	3,007
York and Kingston	April – Dec. 1300	17,992

Calendar 1279 – 1343

1279   Gregory de Rokesley and Orlandino de Podio appointed wardens (Jan.; first account from April). William and Peter de Turnemire master-workers (March), plus Hubert Alion (April). First dies for new coinage delivered 17 May. Keepers of dies sworn in 6 July. Exchanges primed and good old coin sent to ten cities (June); first issue of new money 4 Aug.
     Groats and round farthings authorized.
     Canterbury: Abp. John Pecham's participation authorised (June); dies ready Nov.
     Durham and Bury: dies ordered Nov.

1280   Indenture with William de Turnemire (Dec. 1279) for mints of London, Canterbury (eight furnaces), Bristol (12 furnaces) and York (12 furnaces) from 1 Jan. (Rokesley's and Podio's account ended 2 Jan.). Twopence extra (i.e. 245d.) to be coined per pound from 1 Jan. (to Feb. 1281).
     Halfpence first issued (Aug.).
     Bury: first coins of Robert of Hadleigh (26 June).
     Chester: cash sent to float exchange (Dec.).
     Lincoln: keeper of dies appointed (May/Oct.).
     Newcastle: cash sent to float exchange (Aug.).
     York: Abp. William Wickwane's two dies authorised (Aug.); Peter de Turnemire master at royal mint.
     Dublin: Alexander Normanni of Lucca master (account from March 1281).

1281   Minor royal mints closed during summer; last references to exchanges at Newcastle (May), Chester and Lincoln (July).
     Minting of halfpence and farthings suspended.

1282   Waterford mint in operation.

1283   Durham: death of Bp. Robert de Insula (June); Antony Bek elected (temporalities Sept.).
     Bury: inquiry into mint irregularities.
     Dublin: accounts audited (Aug.).

1285/6 Minting of halfpence and farthings resumed.

1286   Death of Alexander III of Scotland.

1287   Bury: Richard of Lothbury appointed master (18 Nov.).

1290   Death of Queen Margaret of Scotland; Edward I assumed suzerainty.

1291   Mint output much lower for nine years from 1290/1.

1292   Scottish crown awarded to John Balliol.

1294   Canterbury mint closed until 1299.

Edward I – Edward III

1295   Cork mint in operation.
1296   John Balliol deposed (July); English coinage commenced at Berwick.
1297   Bury pyx trial; Roger de Rede appointed moneyer (May).
1299   Statute of Stepney (15 May) prohibited import of foreign coin; pollards and crockards to be current at $\frac{1}{2}$d each from Christmas.
1300   Crockards and pollards demonetized from Easter.
          Council (March) ordered exchanges and moneyers at Kingston, Newcastle, Bristol, Exeter and (postscript) Chester; all mints except Newcastle closed by Dec.
          York: dies granted to Abp. Thomas Corbridge.
          Dublin: Alexander of Lucca reappointed master; exchange profits to king (7 May to 5 June), then granted to Frescobaldi (June 1300 – June 1301).
1301   Dublin mint probably closed.
1302   Newcastle mint closed.
          Durham temporalities seized by king (1 July).
          Dublin: Alexander of Lucca acquitted at pyx trial.
1303   Durham: Bek's temporalities restored (July).
1305   Durham: Bek's temporalities again seized.
1307   Death of Edward I (7 July); Bek's temporalities restored (4 Sept.).
1310   Lords Ordainers defy king.
1311   Durham: death of Bek (3 Mar.); Bp. Richard Kellawe appointed (temporalities May).
1314   Battle of Bannockburn; recovery of Scottish fortunes.
1315   Mint output sharply reduced (1315/16).
1316   Durham: death of Kellawe (9 Oct.); Bp. Louis de Beaumont appointed (temporalities May 1317, dies granted 1 June).
1318   Berwick regained by Scots.
1323   Canterbury mint closed (until 1328/29).
1327   Edward II deposed (20/21 Jan.); Edward III acceded 25 Jan.
1328   Bury: new die ordered (22 Jan.).
1329   Death of Robert I of Scotland.
1330   Edward III assumed personal rule (Oct.).
          Last coinage of pence at London until 1344 (1329/30).
1331   Writ for dies to York (April), repeated (July) after exchequer objection overruled.
1333   Berwick recovered from Scots (July).
          Durham: death of Bp. Beaumont (24 Sept.); Richard de Bury appointed (temporalities 7 Dec.).
1335   Debasement of halfpence and farthings, from May.
1336   Durham: new dies ordered for Bp. de Bury (Nov.).
1337   Start of the Hundred Years War: Philip IV declared Aquitaine confiscate (May), Edward III claimed French crown.
1338   Reading mint opened.
          Dublin: dies ordered (June).
1339   Dublin: despatch of dies for halfpence and farthings authorised (March).
1340   Naval victory at Sluys.
          Bury: new die supplied (16 May).
          Dublin: order for surrender of dies (Nov.).
1343   Accounts closed 15 Dec., prior to weight reduction.

1279–1343

GROATS 1279 – 1281

Fourpence: wt. (1279-80) 88.9 gr. (5.76g.)., or (1280-1) 88.2 gr. (5.71g.).

Obv. Crowned facing bust in quadrilobe; small cinquefoil each side of head; trefoil in each spandrel. *Edwardus Di Gra Rex Angl*. Rev. Long cross with foliate ends; group of three pellets in each angle. Two circles of inscription: *Dns/hibn/e Dux/Aqut, Lon/don/ia C/ivi*. Stops colons of two or three pellets. Gothic *n* except in *Dns* (where *N* is often pellet-barred). London only.

Var. a (Fox 5). Small face, short hair: drapery of two wedges; rosette below bust; crown with flat band or with added crescents between ornaments. Colon stops. Some dies have trefoils with annulet centres. *N* in *Dns* normal, pellet-barred, unbarred or reversed. Rare.

Vars. b (Fox 6) and c (Fox 3). Triple colon stops on rev. *Aqut'*.
  b Larger face and longer hair. Rosette on centre of drapery. Pearl ornaments in crown supported by crescents. Triple colon stops. VR.
  c One obv. die, as b but colon stops, crown with plain band, and curved drapery with hooked ends. Revs. same as b. ER.

Var. e (Fox 4). Crown with tall central fleur between spearheads. Large oval face. Thick curved drapery (without mark). *Aqut'*. Triple colon stops, or very rarely colons; usually none after *Angl'*. *S* waisted or rarely with swollen centre. VR; also ER b/e mule.

Vars. f (Fox 1,2) and g (Fox -). Broad face, pellet eyes; drapery of two wedges. Crown with spread side fleurs. *S* with swollen centre; *N* in *Dns* usually pellet-barred. *hbin'*.
  f Triple colon stops. Short hair; three pellets below bust. Quadrilobe of three or two lines. Also c/f and e/f mules; all ER.
  g Colon stops on obv. (not before *Di*); two annulets after *Ang*. Bifoliate crown. Trefoils in spandrels composed of annulets. ER.

Var. d (Fox 7). Pointed face; crown with tall central fleur between spearheads; rosette on curved drapery. Three-leaf trefoils in spandrels. Colon stops. *S* with swollen centre. Reversed *N* (without mark after it) in *Dns*. Slipped trefoils in cross-ends. VR.

PENCE 1279 – 1343

Wt. 1279 and Feb. 1281 onwards, 22.2 gr. (1.44g.); 1280-1, 22.0 gr. (1.43g.).

Trial type: *Ed':Rex:Angl'.Dns hyb'e* (*n* Gothic), undraped bust facing, crown with three strawberry leaves; rev. long voided cross, rose in each angle, *Edw/ardu/s Dei/Gra*. Unique.

Normal type: Crowned and draped bust facing; crown with central and two side fleurs (trifoliate to group IX, bifoliate from group X), with ornaments between. Rev. long single cross with group of three pellets in each angle.

Group I (1279). London only (*Civi/tas/Lon/don*). Crown with thick straight band.
Ia *Edw Rex Angl Dns hyb*, wedge abbreviation after *Angl* and sometimes after *hyb*; Gothic *n* on obv.; *A* with drooping top bar. Early variety of crown (ER) has bifoliate side fleurs and forked central fleur. Ia is VR as true coin, rare as Ia/c or Ic/a mule.

Edward I – Edward III

Pence

Ib *Ed Rex Anglie Dns hibn*, Roman *N* (reversed in *Anglie*), colon after *Rex*; small lettering; no drapery. One obv. die, ER.

Ic *Edw Rex Angl Dns hyb* or var. (incl. *Edw Re*), Roman *N* often reversed, small lettering, sometimes with pellet stops. Also rare mules Ic/a and Ia/c.

Id *Edw R Angl Dns hyb*, Roman *N* (normal, reversed or rarely unbarred), larger lettering. Var. has annulet on breast (rare). Also ER mules Id/c and Ic/d.

Group II (1279-80). Crown with thinner band, shaped to spearhead ornaments. *Edw R Angl Dns hyb* (until group IX). Straight-sided lettering. Abbreviation marks wedges. Roman *N* normally reversed.

IIa Large face as in Id. Central fleur of crown usually has dexter petal broken.

IIb Small, narrow face with chin resting in fork of long neck. New crown with tall fleur. Transitional coins with IIa crown and IIb face, or IIa face and IIb crown, are labelled IIab.

London: IIa, IIab (rare), IIb.
Bristol (*Vill/a Br/isto/llie*): IIab (ER), IIb.
Canterbury (*Civi/tas/Can/tor*): IIa (ER), IIb.
Durham (*Civi/tas/Dur/eme*, until group VI): IIb only, no episcopal mark.
York royal (*Civi/tas/Ebo/raci*): IIa (ER), IIb.

Group III (1280-82). Normally crescent-shaped abbreviation marks, sometimes commas. Spearheads in crown (except IIIa and b). No episcopal mark on Durham coins.

IIIa and IIIb Pearls in crown (rarely bifoliate). IIIa, drapery with hooked ends; London only. IIIb, drapery a segment of circle; mints as IIb (Bristol rare, Durham VR). Also rare mules: London IIb/III, IIIa/II, IIIb/II; Bristol IIb/III, IIIb/II; Canterbury IIb/III; Durham IIIb/II; York IIIb/II.

IIIc Band of drapery hollowed in centre. Spearheads in crown henceforward (rare var., IIIbc, has IIIc drapery but pearls in crown as IIIb). *h* normally with incurved tail.

IIId Drapery of two wedges. *h* with out-turned tail. Southern mints only (described as IIIe by Fox in *BNJ VII*).

IIIe As IIId but long, narrow face, with flatter crown. *N* sometimes pellet-barred (late). Northern mints only (described as IIId by Fox in *BNJ VII*).

IIIf Large face with prominent nose. Composite crown with spread side fleurs. Late *S* with swollen centre (always on obv. dies; coins with waisted *S* on rev. may be mules with IIId, e or g). Gothic *n* on York dies.

IIIg Wide, spread crown (three varieties); small, smiling face on most. Early (waisted) or late (swollen) *S*.

Mints of IIIc – IIIg

London: IIIbc (rare), IIIc, IIId, IIIf, IIIg.
Bristol: IIIc, IIId, IIIf, IIIg.
Bury St. Edmunds, *Robe/rtu/s de h/adl'*: IIIc (rare); *Robe/rt de/ hade/leie*: IIIc, IIId, IIIg (and ER irregular var. with Gothic *n* and *hib*).
Canterbury: IIIbc (ER), IIIc, IIId, IIIf, IIIg.
Chester (*Civi/tas/Ces/trie* or *Cest/rie*): IIIg only.
Durham (no episcopal mark): IIIc, IIIe, IIIg.
Lincoln (*Civi/tas/Lin/col'*): IIIc, IIId, IIIf, IIIg.
Newcastle (*Vill/a No/vica/stri*): IIIe only.

Pence

York royal: IIIc (VR), IIIe, IIIf (only as ER mules IIIe/f and IIIf/e).
York archiepiscopal (quatrefoil on rev. cross for Abp. William Wickwane): IIIe (some with quatrefoil on breast), IIIf/e mule (ER).

Group IV (1282 – c. 1289). Abbreviation marks large commas; e and c conspicuously open. Face usually oval.

IVa   Large initial cross. Spread crown.
   Early IVa: Face and late crowns of IIIg; short hair. Straight-sided letters with prominent serifs.
   Late IVa: New oval face; taller crown and longer hair. Letters thicker, or with concave sides; some have very large *S*; *A* often unbarred.
IVb   Oval smiling face with bushy hair. Crown with tall central fleur, and straight sinister side fleur with outer petal often damaged (as if bifoliate). Lettering usually hollow-sided.
IVc   Longer face with bushier hair. New crown with top of sinister fleur turned in, and nick in band by dexter fleur. *A* sometimes unbarred.
IVd   Pellet before *Edw* and *Civi*. Usually unbarred *A*. Nicked crown as in IVc.
IVe   Usually three pellets on breast (at London and Canterbury), and one on rev. Nicked crown at first, but most coins have new spread crown and 'ropy' hair. *A* unbarred.
London: IVa, IVb, IVc, IVd, IVe (pellet before *Lon*; rarely without pellets on breast), and rare mules IVc/d, IVd/c, IVd/e and IVe/d.
Canterbury: IVa, IVb, IVc, IVd, IVe (pellet before *tor* or *tas*; rarely without pellets on breast), and rare mules IVc/d, IVd/c, IVd/e and IVe/d.
Bury St. Edmunds, *Robe/rtu/s de h/adl'*: IVa. *Robe/rt de/ hade/leie*: IVa, IVb, IVc (*Dn hyb*, ER). *Vil/la S/Edm/udi*: IVe (no extra pellets, ER).
Durham, no episcopal mark (Bp. Robert of Holy Island, to June 1283): IVa (var. closed *e*), IVb (VR).
— , with cross moline (Bp. Antony Bek, from Sept. 1283): IVb (moline in *Civi* quarter, rare); IVb (initial crosses moline both sides, so *Civ/itas*, henceforward until IXa), IVc, IVd (no pellet on rev., so perhaps IVd/c or d/e mule, ER), IVe (composite cross moline, VR; no extra pellets, except before *tas* on one unusual rev. die only known muled with later obvs.).

Group V (c.1289-90/1). Single pellet on breast. Spread crown. Large flans, abnormally tall letters, and very large initial cross.

Va   Face of IVe, but new bushier hair. *C* with triangular serifs. London and Canterbury only.
Vb   Long, narrow face, tighter hair. Some have almond eyes. Large round-backed *C* with thinner serifs. Breast pellet occasionally omitted.
London: IVe/Va (ER), Va/IVe (VR), Va, Vb/a, Vb.
Canterbury: Va (VR; var. *Edvr*), Vb/a, Vb.
Bury St. Edmunds: Vb only (VR; *Vil/la S/Edm/udi or undi*).
Durham (Bek's cross moline both sides): Vb/IVe (ER), Vb (rare).

Group VI (early 1290s). Smaller dies and lettering; *c* and *e* closed. Crown with widely spread fleurs.

VIa   Large oval face; almond eyes. Often coarse workmanship. Initial cross normally thin and plain (VIa1); var. of fine style has cross thicker and patty (North VIa2, ER). Usually no abbreviation marks, rarely commas. London only.

Edward I – Edward III

Pence

VIb Smaller face with pellet eyes; more bust and neck. Neat initial cross patty. Crescent abbreviation marks. Double-barred *N*, barred *A* and waisted *O* on some dies.

London: VIa/Vb (ER), VIa (rare), VIb (vars. *Edwa, hyb'n*).
Canterbury: VIb/Vb mule only (ER).
Bury St. Edmunds (*Villa/Sci/Edm/udi*): VIb only (VR).
Durham (Bek's cross moline both sides): Vb/VIb (ER), VIb/'IVe' (ER), VIb (rare).

Group VII (early 1290s). Small dies and lettering; *c* and *e* closed; *N* normally double-barred; comma abbreviation marks. Usually a rose on breast at London and Canterbury. Almond eyes. Large initial cross patty.

VIIa Squarer face with short hair; crown as in group VI.
VIIb Crown with side fleurs less spread; larger, bushier hair.

London: VIIa/VIa (ER), VIIa/VIb (ER), VIIa (var. *Yb*), VIa1/VIIb (ER), VIb/VIIb (ER), VIIb. VIIa and VIIb without rose, ER.
Canterbury: VIIa (rare), VIIb (no rose, *N* not double-barred, VR).
Bury St. Edmunds: VIIa only (ER; no rose, *N* not double-barred; *Villa/Sci/Edm/udi* or *Vill/a Sci/Edm/undi*).
Durham (Bek's cross moline both sides): VIIb/'IVe' only (ER; no rose, irregular obv. die with large letters).

Group VIII (c. 1294/5-1299). No mark on breast. Crown as VIIb with tall central fleur of which sinister foil is often damaged. Letter *h* with notched back. *N* sometimes double-barred or unbarred. Crescent or comma abbreviation marks (often after *h* and/or *B* of *hyb*). London and Bury only.

VIIIa Normal *S* with slightly swollen centre.
VIIIb *S* with larger swelling and top tilted forward.
VIIIc As VIIIb but band of crown arched. London only.

London: VIIIa (var. *Edwa*), VIIIb and VIIIc.
Bury St. Edmunds (*Vila/Sci E/dmu/ndi*): VIIIa (rare), VIIIb (VR).

Group IX (1299-1300). Often with star on breast.

IXa Large flans. Tall lettering, with top-tilted *S*; *A* sometimes barred; new *h* without notch. Earlier coins (IXa1) have the crown of VIIIb, a large, plain initial cross, and often contraction marks (but not after *h*); later (IXa2) a flatter crown (crown 1 of IXb1), small initial cross patty, and contraction marks only rarely.

IXb Small flans. Shorter lettering, straight-sided; *A* unbarred; normal *S*. Contraction marks rare (early). Var. (ER) has pellet instead of star on breast. Crown either (IXb1) as IXa2, or (IXb2) with nearly straight-sided sinister fleur; but the two crowns were used in parallel and crown 1 outlasted crown 2. A more sequential subdivision of IXb may be based on the letter *N*: first (A), a barred Roman *N*; next (B), unbarred (Roman) *N*; finally (C), and most commonly, with 'pothook' uprights.

IXc As IXb but contraction marks and larger and cruder letters, with barred *A* and Roman *N* (often reversed); portrait often abnormal. None of London; true coins of Bury only; other mints only known from mules with IXb1 or X. Rare.

London: IXa1, a2; IXb1, b2; mule IXb1/X (ER).
Canterbury: IXa1, a2; IXb1, b2; also rare mules IXb1/c, IXb1/X and IXc/X.

Pence

Durham: IXa1, a2, Bek's cross moline both sides, *Civ/ita/s Dur/ene* or *itas/Dur*; IXb1, b2, cross moline or plain on obv. only, *Civi/tas/Dur/ene*; also rare (plain cross) mules IXb1/c, IXb1/X, IXc/X and X/IXc. Some local dies (ER) in IXa2 (moline) and IXb (moline or plain) have crude portraits, coarser letters (including open *e*), and wedge contraction marks.

Bury St. Edmunds: IXa2, *Vila/Sci E/dmu/ndi*, rare; IXb1, b2, *Vill*; IXc, *Ew, Vill'*, ER.

Newcastle: IXb1, b2, *Vil* or *Vill/Nov/cas/tri*; IXb1 often muled with X revs.; also rare mules IXb1/c (*Vill/Nov* or *Novi*) and IXc/X.

Mints of IXb1 and b2 only: Bristol (*Vill/Bri/sto/lie*), Exeter (*Civi/tas/Exo/nie*), Kingston-upon-Hull (*Vill/Kyn/ges/ton*, var. *Vil'*), York royal (*Civi/tas/Ebo/raci*). Mints of IXb1 only: Chester (*Civi/tas/Ces/trie*, var. *Ses*), York episcopal (with quatrefoil for Abp. Thomas Corbridge).

Group X (1300-10). Obverse readings longer than *Edw*; *hyb* often reduced to *hy, hb, h.* Bifoliate crown standard henceforward. Lettering normally concave-sided.

Primary phase (XP; Wood 'Xab'), 1300-c.1305.

P1-3. Very commonly muled with revs. of IX. *R* usually with ornate tail. Often comma after *Angl, hyb*.

P1. *Edwar R* (var. *Edwr R*, VR). 1a, trifoliate crown (VR). 1b, bifoliate crown (rare).

P2. *Edward R* (P2 and P3 constitute Fox Xa). Large letters: usually overlapping *W*. Wide bifoliate crown, with low central fleur (as P1b).

P3. *Edward R*. Smaller, neat letters; overlapping *W*; broken *S* begins (late). P3a, crown as in P1b and P2. P3b, crown with taller central fleur.

P4-6. Not muled with revs. of IX.

P4. *Edwr'R'*; often also *Angl', hyb'*. Normal or overlapping *W*; broken *S*. Rare.

P5. *Edwar R* (Fox Xb). Crown as before, or larger and wider. Lettering often large; broken *S* only on early dies. Early coins have contraction marks after all except *Dns*.

P6. *Edwa R*. Two crowns as in P5. Stub-tailed *R* and serpentine *S*. VR.

Mints of group X, Primary phase (see group IX for IX/X mules).

London: P1a (VR) and P1b (rare), mules only, with revs. of IXa or IXb; P2 (mostly mules with revs. of IXa, b or c); P3a (mostly mules with revs. of IXa or IXb), also ER var. with annulet on breast; P3b (including mules with revs. of IXb), also ER var. with pellets on breast and above shoulders; P4 (rare); P5; P6 (VR).

Canterbury: P1a and 1b (both rare); P2; P3a and P3b; P4 (rare); P5 (some with pellets in obv. inscription); P6 (VR).

Bury St. Edmunds (*Vill/Sci E/dmu/ndi*): P3a and P3b (both VR); P4 (rare); P5; P6 (VR).

Durham (*Dur/em(i)e* or *en(i)e*),
   Plain initial cross: P2/IXc (VR); P2; P3a/IXc (VR), P3a (and var. *Rex*, ER).
   Cross moline (Bek): P5 only.

Newcastle (*Vill/Nov(i)*): P1a and P1b (both VR); P2; P2/3.

Secondary phase of group X (XS; Wood 'Xcf'), c.1305 – 1310. Normal reading *Edwa R Angl Dns hyb* (very rarely *Edwar R*).

S1. Crown 1 (asymmetrical central fleur; dexter fleur angular; spearhead ornaments). Oval face, short hair. Terminal stops very rare. S1a, *Edwa(r) R Ang*, VR. S1b, *Edwa R Angl*.

S2. Crown 2 (shapely central fleur; vestigial ornaments). Large face with pointed chin; bushy hair. Often with broken *e* and *h* ('Mayfield' lettering). Some have terminal stops.

Edward I – Edward III

Pence

S3. Crown 3 (tall central fleur with high foils; dexter spearhead tilted inwards). S3a, Mayfield lettering, with broken *e* and *h*, some have terminal stops, face as in S2, or long and narrow. S3b, new lettering with broad, round-backed *e*, and *h* with out-turned tail; *o* often broken; long, narrow face, or 'classic bust' (with hollowed drapery and neck depression).

S4. Crown 4 (neat central fleur; sinister fleur with hooked foil; dexter ornament close to side fleur). Otherwise as S3b with classic bust. Rare.

S5. Crown 5 (tall central fleur; dexter ornament hooked outwards and distant from leaning side fleur). Terminal stops frequent. Often straight-sided *I*, *N*, *M* on rev. dies. S5a, large flans; tall letters; initial cross usually delicate cross patty. S5b, smaller flans; dumpy letters and initial cross.

S6. Crown 3 reused. Very small *s*. VR.

    Mints of group X, Secondary phase.

London: S1a (VR) and S1b; S2; S3a and S3b; S4 (VR); S5a and S5b; S6 (VR).
Canterbury: S1a (VR) and S1b; S2; S3a and S3b; S4 (VR); S5a and S5b; S6 (VR).
Bury St. Edmunds (*Vill/Sci E/dmu/ndi*): S1b; S2; S3a and S3b; S4 (VR); S5a and S5b (both rare); S6 (VR).
Durham (*Dur/eme*),
    Plain initial cross: S1b (VR); S2 (rare); S3a and S3b (both rare); S5a (rare).
    Cross moline (Bek; * indicates some with plain cross altered to moline): S1b; S2; S3a* and S3b*; S4 (VR); S5a* (VR) and S5b.

    Group XI (1310 - c.1314). *Edwa R*, gradually replaced by *Edwar R*. Crown with (early) malformed, or (normally) broken dexter ornament; central and sinister fleur with well-formed and out-turned side-foils (except XId). Lettering normally straight-sided; *D* often broken at base; *O* of two crescents. Stops infrequent. Thick initial cross.

XIa. Round-backed *c* and *e*. XIa1, small lettering, as in XS5b-6, with stub-tailed *R* and squat *A*. XIa2, larger lettering; *R* with scroll-tail, normal *A*. XIa3, open *c* and *e* (cf. Berwick class V), rare.

XIb. Closed *c* and *e*, with pointed backs. XIb1, lettering as XIa2-3, except for *c* and *e*; prominent eye-lids. XIb2, tall, narrow letters; *N* with hollowed uprights and no serifs. XIb3, square *N* with wide serifs; small face.

XIc. Letter *A* with right limb upright. Rare; normally muled with XIb.

XId. As XIb3, but crown 3 of group X, type S3, and initial cross of wedges (cf. XIII). Used with revs. of XIb3 or XIc; Canterbury only.

London: XIa1, a2, a3 (rare); XIb1, b2, b3; XIb/c and XIc/b (both VR).
Canterbury: XIa1, a2, a3 (rare); XIb1, b2, b3; XIc, XIb/c and XIc/b (all rare); XId (rare).
Bury St. Edmunds (*Vill/Sci E/dmu/ndi*, henceforward): XIa1 (ER), a2, a3 (rare); XIb1, b2, b3 (all rare); XIc (VR).
Durham (*Dur/eme*),
    Plain cross: XIa1 (VR).
    Cross moline (Bek, to March 1311, and vacancy March – May 1311): XIa1, a2, both sometimes with moline over plain cross.
— (*Dun/elm*): Obv. plain cross, rev. crozier (to left) at top of cross (Kellawe, from June 1311): XIa2, a3; XIb1 (ER var. has two crozier heads), b2, b3; XIc (ER). Also ER mules, Bek/Kellawe (XIa2, or a2/3) and Kellawe/Bek (XIa3/2).
See also Berwick (XIa3).

Pence

Group XII (c.1314). *Edwar R* (very rarely *Edwa R*). Small face. Crown with large central fleur. All relatively rare. See below for mints and varieties.

XIIa Thick initial cross. Crown with broad upturned side petals; ornaments pellet, trefoil or none. Small letters as in late XI.

XIIb Thin initial cross patty. Cruciform central fleur; spearhead ornaments. Larger lettering. London and Bury only (ER).

XIIc Thin cross patty. Tiny heart-shaped petals and ornaments in crown. *R* straight-sided with wide serif. London and Bury only (ER).

Group XIII (c.1314-1317). *Edwar R* (very rarely *Edwa R*). Small face. Crown with 'battle-axe' central fleur and arrow-head ornaments; the sinister fleur breaks and is sometimes patched up. Thin initial cross patty. Later coins have *e* with broken lower back. See below for mints and varieties.

Group XIV (c.1317-c.1319). *Edwar R*. Large smiling face, with narrow eyes. Crown with tall central fleur but no intermediate ornaments. Initial cross thicker than in XIII on most coins. Broken *e* on early dies. Small stops occasionally on obv.

Mints of groups XII - XIV

London: XIIa (VR; also ER mules XIIa/XIb and c); XIIb (ER); XIIc (ER); XIII; XIV (small stops on some VR coins).

Canterbury: XII (a only, rare; also ER mule XIIa/XIc); XIII; XIV.

Bury St. Edmunds: XIIa (VR); XIIb (ER); XIIc (ER); XIII (rare); XIV. Small stops (pellets or wedges) on some coins (VR) of XIII and XIV.

Durham, obv. plain cross, rev. *Dun/elm* with crozier (Bp. Kellawe, to Oct. 1316, and vacancy, Oct. 1316 – May 1317): XII (a only, VR); XIII.

— , obv. lion and one or two lis (Bp. Beaumont, from June 1317), rev. *Dun/elm*, no crozier: XIII (rare); XIV (var. with wedge or pellet stops, VR); also XIV, plain cross on obv., with revs. of XIV or XVc (both ER, 'London'/Durham mules?)

Group XV (c.1319 - 1343). Crown with lower and more shapely fleur than in XIII and XIV; stalk-like ornaments, the dexter one tilted outwards. *Edwar R*.

XVa Large smiling face as in XIV. *h* with out-turned tail; *e* with pointed back.

XVb As XVa, but new small face, and some smaller letters.

XVc Large unsmiling face, with rounder eyes. *h* with crescent tail; tall *e* with flattened back. Coins often poorly struck (especially at Bury and Durham).

XVd (Edward III, from 1328) Gothic *n* on most dies; usually stops in obv. legend. All rare. XVd1, plain initial cross. XVd2, initial cross with pellet on centre; three extra points with pellets in *tas* quarter of rev. XVd3, plain initial cross; no extra points on rev.; broken *e*.

London: XVa; XVb; XVc (also mule with Durham Beaumont obv., ER); XVd1, ER.

Canterbury: XVa; XVb; XVc; XVd1, also XVd1/c and c/d1 mules, all ER; XVd2 (includes one die with Roman *N*), also XVI/XVd2 mule, all ER.

Bury St. Edmunds: XVa (rare); XVb; XVc (some, ER, with wedge or pellet stops); XVd1, Gothic *m*, ER.

Durham, obv. lion and one or two lis (Beaumont), *Dun/elm*: XVa, one lis before lion (VR); XVb, two lis; XVc (rarely with obv. stops; also ER 'London'/Durham and Durham/London mules); also XIV (plain cross)/XVc and XVI/XVc mules (both ER).

— , obv. initial cross, rev. lozenge with small crown in centre of cross (Bp. de Bury, from Dec. 1333), *Dune/lmi* with Roman *M*, and Roman *N* or Gothic *n*: XVd3 only, VR.

Edward I – Edward III

Pence

Reading (scallop shell in *Vil* quarter): XVd3 only, *Vil/la R/(adi)/ngy*, Roman *N* on rev. Unique.

York (Archbishop Melton; quatrefoil on rev. cross), *Ebo/raci* or *Ebor/aci*: XVd2 only (ER var. has four pellets in angles of initial cross; two obv. dies have Roman *N*), rare.

HALFPENCE 1280 – 1335

Wt. 11.1 gr. (0.72g.), or slightly lower (minimum 10.8 gr., 0.70g.).

   Type as pence. Groups III - VIII, *Edw R Angl Dns hyb*; group X, varied; rev. readings as pence (except Newcastle). London only except in group III (and Berwick in Xh). W. refers to Withers.

   Group III (1280 - 1).
Earlier varieties: Side fleurs of crown turned inwards. *A* usually barred; early (waisted) *S*. Drapery a segment of circle with wedges above (IIIbc, Withers 1, spearhead ornaments in crown); or hollowed band or two wedges (IIIcd southern and IIIe northern; W.1a).
Late var. (IIIg; W.2): Spread side fleurs in crown. Large letters; usually unbarred *A*; most with late (swollen) *S*.
London: IIIbc (rare), IIIcd, IIIg, and rare mules IIIcd/g and IIIg/cd.
Bristol: IIIcd, IIIg (rare), and rare mule IIIcd/g.
Lincoln: IIIcd, rare.
Newcastle: IIIe, single pellet in each angle of cross, *No/vic/as/tri*, large letters, pellet-barred *N*, rare.
York: IIIe, some dies with larger lettering.

   Group IV (1281-c.1289). London only henceforward.
IVc (W.3) Similar to IIIg, but small letters (*A* unbarred, swollen *S*) and smaller crown. Rare.
IVe (W.4) Three pellets on breast, pellet before *Lon*. Swollen or waisted *S*. Also mules IVc/e and IVe/c; all VR.

   Group VI (early 1290s; W.6). Small head; short, bushy hair; large crown (central fleur damaged), with only vestigial petals to sinister side fleur. Neat letters; closed *c* and *e*; integral *S*; some with waisted *O*. Var. *Edwa*. No contraction marks. Rare; also ER mules, VI/IV and IV/VI.

   Group VII (early 1290s; W.5). Wider head; almond eyes. Larger letters; *N* usually double-barred; open *c* and *e*; usually composite *S*. Initial cross nearly plain. Small wedge or comma marks. Also IVe/VII, VII/VI and VI/VII mules. All rare.

   Group VIII (c. 1294-99; W.8). Tall crown with straight sides. Initial cross patty. *h* with notched back; closed *c* and *e*; plain *O*; integral *S*; *N* normally single-barred. Var. *Edwa*. Some small wedge stops. Also VIII/VI and VIII/VII mules. All rare.

   Group X, Primary (XP) (1300 +). *Edwar R Angl Dns hyb*. Concave lettering. Long, narrow face. Crown 1, trifoliate (W.9, rare); or crown 2, bifoliate (W.10, VR).

Halfpence

Group Xh (From c. 1305; same general type continues to 1335 alongside pence of XI-XV; W.11-13). *Edwardus Rex A(n)* or *Angl(i)*, rarely *Ang*. Bust as XP, with crown 1 or 2 as in XP, or tall crown 3 revived from group VIII. Lettering varied. Also ER mules with pre-X reverses. See also Berwick.

FARTHINGS 1279 – 1335

1279-80. Type A. Wt. 6.85 gr. (0.44g.), fineness 0.766
1280 onwards. Types B, C and D. Wt. 5.55 gr. (0.36g.), fineness 0.925.

Type A: As penny, but *Edwardus Rex.*
Group I, London only (*Lon/don/ien/sis*). Crown without intermediate jewels.
Ia (A1) Large face; bifoliate crown (var. has vestigial third foil to dexter fleur). Large letters; usually a colon before *Rex*; Roman *N*s often reversed. Withers 1-3. Rare; var. *Lon/dri/en/sis*, ER.
Ic (A2) Smaller face; trifoliate crown (some have extra line above or below main band). Smaller letters; usually colon before *Rex* (rarely after); *N*s sometimes reversed. W.4-6. Rare; also rare mules A1/2 and A2/1 (incl. *Londriensis*).

Group II (A3). Narrow face; large trifoliate crown with jewels, and base almost straight. Small letters, compact initial cross; no stops. W.7.
London, Londoniensis, *N* normal or reversed. Rare; also rare A2/3 mule.
Bristol, *Vila/Bri/sto/l(l)ie*. ER.
York, *Civi/tas/Ebo/raci*. VR.

Group III, early (A4). Broader face; base of crown more arched. Larger letters; initial cross less neat. W.8.
London, *Londoniensis*, *N* not reversed. Rare.
Bristol, *Vill/a Br/isto/llie* or *Vil/a Bri/sto/lie*. VR.
York, ER.

Type B: Large bust reaching nearly to edge of coin; no inner circle. Inscription *E R An/glie*.
B1. IIId (southern), IIIe (northern). Crown with straight-sided outer fleurs. W.10-12.
   IIIg. Crown with spread side-fleurs. W.13. London only.
London, *Londoniensis*, IIId, IIIg. Early transitional var. (W.9, ER) has bust high up (as A4).
Bristol, IIId, VR.
Lincoln, IIId, VR.
Newcastle, *No/vic/as/tri* (pellet-barred *N*), IIIe, ER.
York, IIIe, ER.
B2. IV (late). Small spread crown; square initial cross. Neat letters, composite *S*. W.14, 15. London only (*Civi/tas/Lon/don* henceforward), VR.
B3. V. Tall, crude crown, too wide for head. Thick, plain initial cross. Lettering irregular, integral *S*. W.18, 19. London only. Rare; also ER mules B3/1.
B4. VI-VII. Large face with pellet or almond eyes; neater tall crown; bushy hair of thick strands. Open *c* and *e*, composite *S*. W.16, 17. London only. Rare.

Edward I – Edward III

Farthings

Type C: As type B, but *E R An/gl Dn*. London only.
C1. (Cf. group VIII). Tall crown; short, wide hair. Letters on obv. concave. W.20.
C2. (Cf. VIII-IXa). Flatter crown; compact hair. Straight-sided letters; *A* and *N* usually unbarred. Plain initial cross. W.21-4.
C3. (As IXb?). Flat, splayed crown; short bushy hair. Letters with pronounced serifs, *A* and *N* unbarred. Small initial cross patty. W.25-7. Rare; also ER mule C3/Xq.

Type D (group Xq): As type A, but smaller module. *Edwardus Rex (A-Ang)*; var. (ER) has inscription beginning at 180°. Crown without intermediate ornaments. London only (apart from Berwick, Xq2). Principal varieties – Xq1 (W.28): Flat crown, with spread central lis; large oval face; concave letters; initial cross patty. *Rex (A)*. Xq2 (W.29-30): Taller crown, lis with wedge-shaped petals; smaller face usually with pellet eyes; initial cross nearly plain; lettering coarser; *N* sometimes unbarred; often *Rex A(n)*. Xq3 (W.31): Crown with unevenly shaped fleurs; spade-shaped face with pointed chin; neat letters; *N* sometimes unbarred; initial cross patty, or of four wedges (cf. groups XIII-XIV).

HALPENCE AND FARTHINGS, 1335 – 1343

Fineness 10 oz. (0.833 silver). Weights: $^1/_2$ d, 10.7 gr. (0.69g.); $^1/_4$ d, 5.3 gr. (0.34g.). Mints: London, Reading; see also Berwick, Dublin.

HALFPENCE. Star in inscriptions. *Edwardus Rex An(g)*. Usually unbarred Roman *N*s.
  XVe1. Six-pointed star after *An* (rarely *Ang*) and before mint name. Some dies (VR) have Gothic *n*. Three forms of crown (Woodhead classes 1-3).
  XVe2. Star (normally of eight-points) after *Ang* and (usually) after mint name (or sometimes before *Civi*). Tall bifoliate crown. *G* often large. Rev. pellets often conjoined.

FARTHINGS. As halfpence; rare.
  XVe1. Star after *A* (or *An* but no star) and before mint name. Low crown.
  XVe2. Star after *Ang* and after (rarely before) mint name. Tall crown. Pellets conjoined.

London: Halfpence, XVe1; e2. Farthings, XVe1, rare; XVe2, VR.
Reading, halfpence only, *Vil/la R/adi/ng(y)*, scallop shell in one quarter: XVe1, star after *Villa*, scallop in *Vil* quarter; XVe2, star after *ng*, scallop in *Vil* or *ng* quarter. All ER.

MINT OF BERWICK-UPON-TWEED
(Local dies except class V)

PENCE

Class I. Coins of fine style. *Edw R Angl Dns hyb* (Ia) or *hyd* (Ib), often with crescent (or wedge) contraction marks. Trifoliate crown. Roman *N*. *E* on obv. open Gothic, on rev. Roman. Two busts: wide-face, with bulbous nose and pellet on chin, or narrow-face, with thin pointed nose. Normally *Vill/a Be/rev/vici*.

1279–1343

Berwick

Class II. Coarse work. *Edw(a)*. Closed Gothic *e* on both sides. Some with small pellet stops.

IIa Crude trifoliate or bifoliate crown, ornamented with large pellets. Loosely made letters. Usually *Vill/a Be/rre/wyci, vici* etc. Var. *hybe*.

IIb Neater bust with bifoliate crown. *Edw* only; *r(e)w/*(or *v)/(v)ici*. Letters more solid. Loosely dotted circles. Three obv. dies.

IIc Bifoliate crown with pointed band. Large snout-like nose and mouth. Very barbarous. *Edwa R*; with or without a large pellet on neck. *r(e)w/ici* or *rev/vici*. Rare. The position of this variety in the series is uncertain.

Mules Ia/IIa, Ib/IIa (including var. *Ed R*), Ia/IIb (ER).

Class III. Fine workmanship. *Edwa*. Neat bust with usually trifoliate crown. Roman *E* on rev. Usually *Vill/a Be/rev/vici*. No mules with II.

IIIa Gothic *n* in *Dns*. Some revs. read *Wil/la B/ere/vici* or *wici*.

IIIb Roman *N* in *Dns*; *N* sometimes pellet-barred.

Class IV. As III but *V* and *W* with wide serifs. *Edwa*. Usually a pellet on breast.

IVa Gothic *n* in *Dns*. Trifoliate crown. Some (early) lack breast pellet.

IVb Gothic *n* in *Dns*. Bifoliate crown. Eyes usually pellets between two semi-circles.

IVc Roman *N* in *Dns*. Bifoliate crown. Eyes usually pellet-in-ovals, sometimes solid.

Mules IIIa/IV, IIIb/IV (rare), IVa/IIIa (VR).

Class V. London-made dies (XIa3). Crown with broken dexter ornament. *Edwa(r) R* etc. (one obv. has stop after *R*). Roman *N*s, open *e* and *c*. Colon before *Vil/la B/ere/wyci* (or *wici*). Rare; also mule V/IV (ER).

Class VI. Obv. dies of class V with bust refurbished, paired either with rev. dies of class V, or with coarse new dies (one retrograde) copied from class V (usually with colon before *Villa*) but with closed *e*.

VIa *Edwa R* (Blunt V*). Face with squinting eyes; hair and coarse v-neck punch altered. Rare.

VIb *Edwar R* (Blunt VI). Portrait altered as for VIa, but with (trifoliate) crown also renewed. VR.

Class VII. Coarse work. *Edw(a)(r) R*. Rough trifoliate crown; spread and stringy hair; v-neck. Closed *e*, or on rev. composite Roman *E* with pellet front. Roman *N*, sometimes reversed. *Vill/a Be/rev/vici*, or *riv*, or blundered. Rare; also ER VII/VI mule.

For pence with bear's head in one quarter of rev. (Blunt VIII) see 1344-51.

HALFPENCE

Class I. *Edw R Angl Dns hyb*; *N* Roman. *Angl'* on one die. Neat style as pence (with narrow or wider bust). *Vill/a Be/rev/vici*; Roman *E* on rev. ER.

Class II (position in series uncertain; an apparent V/II mule may indicate a post-1290s date for the halfpence of this class). Coarse work. *Edw R Angl Dns hyb*; *N* Roman. Thick initial cross. Thick hair, oval eyes. Loose circles. Closed Gothic *e* both sides. *Vill/a Be/rew/ici*. ER.

Edward I – Edward III

Berwick

Class III. Fine work. *Edwa*, with open Gothic *e*. Trifoliate crown. Wider hair than class I. Usually *Vill/a Be/rev/vici*; Roman *E* on rev.

IIIa   Gothic *n* in *Dns*. *hb*. Rev. var. *Vil/la B/ere/wic*. VR.

IIIb   Roman *N* in *Dns*.

Class IV. Star or pellet on breast. Roman *E* on rev. VR.

Class V. London-made dies (Xh). *Edwardus Rex An* (reversed *N*). Colon before *Vil/la B/ere/wici*; Gothic *e* henceforward. VR.

Class VIII (Blunt VIIIb). *Vil/la B/erv/ici*, bear's heads in *Vil* and *erv* quarters. *Edwardus D(ei) Gr(a)*. Some have pellet or colon stops.

For halfpence with one bear's head (Blunt VIIIa) see 1344-51.

FARTHINGS

Class I. *Edwardus Rex* or *Edwardus Angl*. Neat style as pence. *Vil(l)/a Be/rev/vici*; Roman *E* on rev. Withers described a largely illegible coin with crude portrait and pellets in the crown as a II/I mule. All ER.

Class III. Finer work. *Edwa R* etc. Bust with widely splayed crown, and wide hair. *Vill/a Be/rev/vici*, with Roman *E*. ER.

Class IV. Crude style. *Edwa R Angl Dns hyb*. Annulet eyes; with or without pellet on breast. *Vill/a Be/rev/vici*, with Roman *E*. ER.

Class V. London-made dies (Xq2). *Edwardus Rex*. Bifoliate crown. Colon before *Vil/la B/ere/wici*. ER.

Class VII (?). Coarse work. *Edwa R Angl Dn*. Loose circles. *Vil/la B/ere/wic*; Gothic *e*. ER.

Class VIII (Blunt VIIIb). *E(d)wardus Dei Gra, Edwardus:D' G(r)(a)*, or *Edwardus Ang(lie)*, etc. Some have pellet or colon stops. *Vil/la./Ber/vici, Vil/la B/erv/ici*, etc., with bear's heads in two quarters. Rare.

IRELAND

PENCE

Edward I (1272-1307) only. Obv. Crowned Edwardian bust facing in triangle. *Edw R/Angl D/ns hyb*, usually with pellet stops and contraction marks. Small lettering. Rev. as English type; larger lettering. Mints: Dublin, *Civi/tas/ Dubl/inie,* IA-D, II, III, IV; Waterford, *Civi/tas/ W* (or *V)ate/rfor'*, IB, ID, plus II and III from irregular dies; Cork, *Civi/tas/ Corc/agie*, III only.

Ireland

First Phase (1280-83). Class I. Trefoil of pellets below bust (very rarely omitted). Open *e*. Three rev. types: 1, Roman *N*, *S* with waisted body and two wedges; 2, Roman *N*, *S* with swollen centre; 3 (Dublin only), as 2 but Gothic *n*.

IA. Dublin only (revs. 1, 2, 3). Usually a pellet before *Edw*. 'Irish' crown with tall fleurs and ornaments; the side fleurs curved outwards less than in IB. *R* with scroll or wedge tail. Var. with barred *A* lacks pellet before *Edw*. VR.

IB. Dublin (revs. 1, 2, 3), Waterford (normally rev. 1; rev. 2 ER). Pellet before *Edw* (rarely omitted). Two English (IIIg) crowns with widely splayed side fleurs (B1, clumpy; B2, wider and more sharply defined). Some lack stops. Trefoil below bust very rarely omitted. *R* usually wedge-tailed; scroll tail on (usually) early dies. Var. (ER) has colon before *Civi* (Dublin, rev. 1).

IC. Dublin only (normally rev. 3; rev. 2 ER). Cross before *Edw*, with Roman *E*. Crown as IB. Scroll-tailed *R*.

ID. Dublin (rev. 3) ER; Waterford (rev. 1) VR. As IB, but long, gaunt face with hollowed eyes, and wide hair with sharp curve. Wedge-tailed *R*.

Second Phase (mid-1290s). Classes II and III. Small neat lettering on both sides. No mark before *Edw*. Closed Gothic *e* and *c*.

II (North E; c.1294). Rose on breast. Antler crown of English groups VI and VIIa. Lettering as English group VI. Dublin (VR), also ID/II mule (ER); Waterford (ER, irregular dies).

III (North F; 1295, +?). Pellet in each corner of triangle. Spread crown usually with small crosses as intermediate ornaments. Some read *Cdw*. Dublin (ER; var. reads *Angle/Ds hyb*); Cork (VR; some have pellets-on-stalks in crown); Waterford (ER, irregular dies).

Third Phase (1300-1). Single pellet below bust. Small lettering on obverse. Dublin only.

IV (North G). Crown with tall central fleur. Thin wedge after *Angl*.

IVa Lettering on reverse smaller than in IVb, with pronounced serifs. Neat closed *e* on obv. with long curved front. Rare.

IVb Larger lettering on reverse. Wider crown. Obv. *e* formed of crescent and three wedges. Var. has pellet before *Edw*.

HALFPENCE

Edward I (1272-1307). Types and mints as pence.

First Phase (1280-83). Class I. No mark below bust.

IB. Open Gothic *c* and *e*; *S* of crescents and wedges. Dublin (Roman *N* on reverse), Waterford. IB1, no pellet before *Edw*, no stops, small obv. letters. IB2, pellet before *Edw*, usually stops in inscription, larger lettering both sides.

IC. Roman *E*, with (Withers 5) or without (W.4) a pellet before it in *Edw*. Rev. as IB, or (ER) with Gothic *n* and swollen *S*. Dublin only, rare.

Second Phase (mid-1290s). Classes II and III. Smaller letters. Usually closed Gothic *c* and *e*. *S* from single punch.

II (North E; c.1294). Rose on breast, curved drapery and narrow crown. Dublin only (W.6), ER. Another Dublin obv. die (W.7), without marks, but rounded drapery,

Edward I – Edward III

Ireland

         may also be of this period.

III (North F; 1295). Wire-line hair. Some read *Cdw*. All VR.
         Dublin: pellet in each corner of triangle, pointed drapery (W.8).
         Waterford (*Wate/rfor* or *Vate/rfo*): splayed crown, rounded drapery, no extra marks (W.3) VR. One obv. is die-linked to Cork.
         Cork: as Waterford, with (W.2) or without (W.1) pellets in corners of triangle.

    Third Phase (1300-1). Dublin only.

IV (North G). Usually a pellet below bust, which has long neck (W.9). Tall crown with straight sides. Wire-line hair. Usually large lettering on rev. VR.

Edward III (1327-77). Debased issue of 1339 (as English XVe). Large oval pellet below bust. *Edw/ardu/s Rex*. Star before *Edw* and after *tas*. Dublin only, ER.

FARTHINGS

Edward I (1272-1307). Types as pence and halfpence, but *E R A/ng/lie*. Dublin, I, IV; Waterford, I only.

    First Phase (1280-2/3). Class I. Tall trifoliate crown, bushy hair, pellet eyes; triangular drapery, without neck punch. *R* with wedge tail, open *c* and *e*. Var. *E R/Ang*. Dublin (rare), Waterford.

    Third Phase (1300-1). Class IV. Pellet below bust (W.3), or occasionally omitted (W.2). Wide trifoliate crown, wire-line hair; long neck, pointed drapery. *R* with scroll tail, closed *c* and *e*. Dublin only, VR.

Edward III (1327-77). Debased isue of 1339 (as English XVe). Large pellet below bust. Unique specimen, readings apparently as halfpenny, but no stars visible due to striking.

CHAPTER IV

1344 - 1351
EDWARD III

With the exception of the debasement of the 1540s, the seven years from 1344 constituted a period of more rapid structural change than any other in the history of the English coinage. In addition to two reductions in the weight of the silver penny, they saw the beginnings of a sustained English gold coinage, which passed through three experimental stages before settling down to a lasting pattern in 1351, and which vividly illustrates the problems of meeting the needs both of the domestic economy and of international trade with a bimetallic currency.

Since the thirteenth century English merchants had become increasingly dependent upon foreign gold coins for large business transactions, to which their own currency, normally consisting only of the silver penny and its fractions, was no longer suited. And now since 1337 the king himself had become reliant on loans from Italian bankers to finance his war with France. In 1339 Parliament had suggested that foreign gold coin should be accepted as legal tender in England for payments of 40s. or more, but although this idea was not then implemented a new proposal was put forward in 1343 for England and Flanders each to produce a gold coin acceptable in both countries to the exclusion of all others. The purpose of this was to deal with the problems arising from overvaluation of the gold florin of Florence. Weighing 54 gr. and tariffed at 3s., the florin was held through the power of the Italian moneylenders at a premium of 18 per cent in relation to the French *écu* (which at 71 gr. passed for about 3s. 4d.). Since 1339 Edward had been borrowing in florins large sums which he could only repay in sterling or in wool for sterling value, and in due course it became inevitable, in the interests of English merchants as well as of himself, that England should have its own gold coinage. Because nothing had come of the suggested Anglo-Flemish monetary union, Edward soon resolved to proceed alone. In December 1343 he entered into a contract with two Florentine goldsmiths, whose names appear in English as Kirkyn and Nicholyn, as master-workers for coinage in both gold and silver. The gold was to be based on an English equivalent of the florin, known as the leopard and valued at 3s., of which a hundred (£15) were to be struck from the Tower pound, together with its double and its half. As defined in a contract of 1349, the fineness of Edward III's gold coinage was 23 ct. 3½gr. (99.5 per cent), a standard that was to remain unchanged until the sixteenth century.

The weight of the penny was not spelt out precisely. According to the indenture the new coins were to be as good as and of the weight of the sterlings current in the land, or better. Fox assumed that this meant the same standard weight as before (22.2 gr.), but a new indenture with Percival de Porche of Lucca in July 1344 stipulated that 22s. 2d. (266 pence) should be struck from a pound of silver and, since there is no discernible early group of 1344 pennies weighing above the 20.3 gr. applicable under Percival's indenture, it seems likely that this weight, or something close to it, had been in effect from the outset. Most of the earlier pence in currency at the time had been minted between 1300 and 1323, and after twenty to forty years of active circulation they were, as hoards demonstrate, generally no longer close to their full weight. The formula prescribed in the indenture of December 1343, designed to reproduce the actual rather than the original weight of pence in current use, could then very reasonably have been interpreted as meaning a reduction of about ten per cent.

Two factors ensured that the coinage of gold leopards was not successful. First, the king of England was not able, like the Italians, to enforce an artificially high valuation for

Edward III

his own gold coin, so that it was refused abroad and returned to the exchequer at home. Second, the minting charges were much too high: although £15 was struck from the pound the king took 20s. in seignorage and after the master's costs of 3s. 6d. the merchant received back only £13 16s. 6d. Furthermore, the values of the leopard series, 6s., 3s. and 1s. 6d., were inconvenient in relation to both the standard accounting units, the mark of 13s. 4d. and the pound of 20s. In June 1344 the king granted Parliament's petition that no one should be obliged to take his gold coins for sums below 20s., and in August they were demonetized.

Edward's next gold coinage was related not to the florin but to the French *écu*. Percival's indenture of July 1344 provided for a gold noble valued at 6s. 8d., half a mark or a third of a pound, with its half and quarter. £13 3s. 4d. (i.e. 39½ nobles) was to be struck from the Tower pound, thus reducing the ratio of gold to silver from 1:12 to 1:11. After deductions, a merchant would now receive back £12 15s. At 136.7 gr. the new noble weighed slightly less than twice the *écu*, but the difference was marginal. However, although more than £7,000 was minted in gold in eleven weeks from July to September 1344, the price of gold was rising and less than £10,000 was coined in the next twelve months, to September 1345. In order to encourage bullion to the mint the master's allowance for costs was reduced by 1s. 4d. in June 1345, but this had little effect and by July 1346 less than £5,000 more had been coined. In that month a further and more substantial change was therefore made. Nicholyn and Kirkyn returned to the scene, agreeing with the king to mint new nobles at 42 to the pound (£14) and giving a mint price for gold of £13 8s. 4d. after charges of 11s. 8d. Although the Florentines left soon afterwards, the terms of their contract persisted under other masters until 1351, with some increase in output in the later 1340s except during the Black Death of 1348-9. This terrible plague, which swept northern Europe and is estimated to have eliminated a third or more of the population of England within a matter of months, had far-reaching economic consequences. Labour became scarce, cereal prices rose as the land could not be properly harvested, and gold and silver undervalued by foreign standards left the country. It was only a matter of time before a further reform of the coinage, involving a revaluation of silver as well as gold, was undertaken.

Some minor adjustments had been made to the silver coinage, but by the time of the Black Death pennies had virtually ceased to be struck. From June 1345 the pound of silver was to be coined into 268 pence, giving an extra twopence per pound to those who brought in silver, and from July 1346 the figure was raised again to 270 (22s. 6d). Special rates were introduced for halfpence (23s. 3d. per pound weight, less 1s. 5d. in charges) and farthings (23s. 5d. less 1s. 7d.), with the result that from 1346 silver coinage was increasingly concentrated on the fractions.

Although orders were made in February 1348 and May 1349 for a mint to produce silver coin on the English standard at Calais, which had been held by Edward since 1347, no such coinage was to materialize until the 1360s. London was thus the only mint for English gold in the 1340s. It was also the only one to participate in the new silver coinage for the first few months. Later in 1344 other mints, Canterbury, York, Durham and Reading, were reopened or reactivated. Of the mints of group XV only Bury St. Edmunds and Dublin no longer feature, the former now closed for good, the latter until the fifteenth century. Berwick, however, did continue to function at this period, on a modest scale.

1344–1351

Classification

Lawrence began his monograph on the coinage of Edward III with the reform of 1351, and no detailed survey of the coins of 1344-51 as a whole has been published. The fullest account of the leopard coinage is that of Sir John Evans (1900) and the two series of pre-1351 nobles were treated by Potter in 1963. The basic account of the silver is that of Shirley-Fox (1928), subsequent information and discoveries being recorded in North's *Sylloge*. The arrangement of the silver described in the following pages, although based on the foregoing works, divides the series into three parts in order to demonstrate their sequence and relationship: (a), a brief, early issue of London pence from experimental dies; (b), the bulk of the pence of all mints, with most of the halfpence and farthings; and (c) late halfpence, and a few pence and one farthing from ecclesiastical mints only. It has been customary among numismatists to refer to silver coins of this period as Florin pence or halfpence, but this is misleading in two respects. First, although the earliest gold of Edward III was sometimes referred to by contemporaries as florins (*jussit rex florenos fieri* according to the author of the *Chronicon Angliae*), not surprisingly since the leopard was based on the florin, this was not the official name for the leopard or for either of the two other denominations. Second, most of the silver was not struck during the first seven months of 1344, when the leopard series was current, but subsequent to July 1344 when the gold coinage was of nobles. It is therefore convenient to revive the designation of group XVI as accorded to these coins by the Foxes when they originally planned to include it as such in their account of the Edwardian penny series. By the use of subdivisions of the group this also enables the structure of the coinage to become apparent. There is little detailed correspondence between the gold and silver, except for a chevron-barred *A* on gold from 1346 and on some silver of XVIc. But in chronological terms one may say that the silver contemporary with the first issue of gold would have been London pence of XVIa and early XVIb; with the second issue of gold, the bulk of the XVIb pence, a few early halfpence (XVIb) and farthings; and with the third issue of gold, pence of XVIb (few) and XVIc, most of the halfpence of XVIb, all the halfpence of XVIc, and most of the farthings.

Gold Coins

The designs of the three new denominations introduced in January 1344 are among the most attractive of any in the whole of English coinage. They can fairly stand comparison with the magnificent gold coins of France and Flanders at this high point in the flowering of Gothic art. The leopard is a splendid coin. It shows a crowned lion sejant with a mantle emblazoning the quartered arms of France and England flowing from its collar. On the epitaph in Westminster Abbey Edward III is described as *invictus pardus*, and the lion, known heraldically as a leopard, was already a powerful symbol of the English crown. The double-leopard was less original in design. It has a delicately rendered figure of the king, enthroned with orb and sceptre, beneath a Gothic canopy, and set against a field decorated with fleurs-de-lis. Its immediate model was Edward's sixth great seal, used from 1340, but more generally it is an English adaptation of the *écu à la chaise* of Philip VI. Reproducing the two seated lions that flank the king on the seal, the coin type to that extent fits the description in the proclamation of 'a coin of two leopards' in design as well as in value. The half-leopard, or helm, looks back to the great seal in another way. The crowned lion standing on a cap of maintenance above a helmet - almost identical in form to the helmet, cap and crest on the Black Prince's monument in Canterbury Cathedral - closely resembles the headgear worn by

Edward III

the equestrian figure of the king on the reverse of his 1340 seal. The obverse inscriptions of this series are the first on English coins to include the title of King of France which Edward had claimed, by proclamation, in 1337 at the outset of the Hundred Years' War, and which was now reflected in the quartering of the royal arms.

On all three values the reverse design consists of an elaborate decorated cross, ornamented with quatrefoils as on the French *chaise d'or* and other contemporary continental gold, and sometimes described as a 'royal' cross. On the two larger coins the cross is contained within a quadrilobe, or double tressure of four arcs, with English lions (instead of the crowns on the French model) in the spandrels. On the double the limbs of the cross terminate with foliate sprays, and a crown above; on the leopard with trefoils (and without the crowns). But a more interesting feature of the reverses is that their inscriptions consist of scriptural texts. This was a usage already established for gold and larger silver coins on the Continent, but now was the first occasion that they were adopted in the English coinage. There was no need for a mint name since at this period gold was only struck at the Tower. On the double-leopard is a quotation from Luke IV, 30, which was to become the standard legend on the largest English gold coins for more than two centuries: *Jesus Transiens Per Medium Illorum Ibat* (Jesus passing through the midst of them went His way). Various imaginative interpretations of its significance have been proffered, but it was commonly used on amulets as a protective motto and may have no particular relevance on the coin, except perhaps as a deterrent to clippers. On the coin *Jesus* is rendered as *Ihc*, representing the first three letters of the name in Greek capitals (IHC) converted, anomalously, into Gothic script. The text on the leopard is *Domine Ne in Furore Tuo Arguas Me* (O Lord, rebuke me not in thine anger; Psalm VI, 1) and on the helm *Exaltabitur in Gloria* (He shall be exalted with honour; Psalm CXII, 9). These two also were to continue long in use on English gold, until the reign of Edward IV.

Between January and July 1344, £32,000 of leopard gold was minted, equivalent to more than 200,000 coins if all in leopards. Yet only nine examples have survived, three doubles, four leopards and two helms. Many issues of medieval gold of similar or smaller size have left more survivors, but the rarity of the leopard series today also reflects its early withdrawal as the overvalued coins were returned to the Treasury and in due course reminted. All known specimens are from different pairs of dies and a much larger issue was no doubt originally in contemplation. Great care seems to have been taken in making individual dies. The lettering is elegant and the elaborate designs are meticulously rendered. Except on reverses of the double-leopard, which have double saltires as on the early nobles, the stops on all dies are annulets, as on most of the pence of 1344-5.

The noble series introduced in July 1344 to replace the leopards was to set the pattern for the English gold coinage for more than a century. While the quarter, with its shield within a tressure, echoes the type of the original French *écu* of St. Louis (1266), the noble and its half present an altogether new appearance. The king of England is here shown standing in a ship, with drawn sword and shield of arms, a design variously interpreted as emphasizing the royal embodiment of the ship of state or, more directly, the claim to naval supremacy since the defeat of the French fleet at the battle of Sluys in 1340. Although the figure of the king on the nobles is disproportionately large in relation to the ship, the composition as a whole is a powerful one, the message of which was not lost on those who handled them – "Foure things our noble sheweth to me, King, Ship and Sword and Power of the See". On the reverses the mottoes from the leopard series are retained; unlike their successors, all pre-1351 nobles omit *autem* after *Ihc*. The types also are based on the elaborate cross of the previous issue, but now with the crowns and lions more prominent and all within an eight-arc tressure.

Of Edward's second gold issue (1344-6) even less was minted than of the first. Again the survival rate was very low: only two nobles, two halves (both of recent discovery) and three quarters are known. Yet the two nobles show a number of differences. Potter's die 1 has the same style (A) of lettering as on the dies for the halves and quarters, broad and plain, with unbarred *A* and a curly-tailed *R*. Die 2 has narrower lettering (B), from a fount which was also used on the earliest noble dies of 1346, and including the chevron-barred *A* characteristic of the third gold issue generally. A very curious feature of the noble from die 2 is that instead of rigging it has three large pellets punched in above the sterncastle. Quarter-nobles of both the 1344 and the 1346 issues have a tressure of only six arcs around the shield, instead of eight as became normal from 1351 onwards, but on 1344 quarters alone the reverse tressure consists of a single band. The other principal feature differentiating the gold of 1344-6 from later types is *L* (for the London mint) in the central panel of the reverse cross, instead of the king's initial. Stops on the second and third gold issues are usually double saltires (on most noble reverse dies also both sides of the initial cross); and the spelling *Edwar*, without the final *d*, a feature of the leopard series, continues until 1351. On all pre-1351 gold *et* is represented by a reversed *Z* with a horizontal cross-bar.

Gold of the third issue (1346-51), the product of more than twice as much bullion as the previous two together, is accordingly rather less rare. Very few examples are known of the half-noble, however, and a tendency to concentration on the noble and its quarter, especially the latter, continues. Potter distinguished two main obverse types of the third issue noble: I, with the design and epigraphy very similar to those of the type 2 noble of 1344-6, and with the bowsprit shown as if it was passing behind the forecastle; and II, of coarser work, with the bowsprit projecting from within the forecastle, and with larger lettering (style C). The two types also appear to be distinguishable according to the size of flan, nobles of the large-lettered type II having a diameter of c.36mm. against c.34½mm. for type I (with its smaller letters of style B). Styles B and C lettering both include a chevron-barred *A*, which finds a parallel on pence and some halfpence of group XVIc. Reverse dies combined with type I obverses have either style B or, more usually, style C lettering, while type II nobles have the same style (C) on both sides, with the exception of one unusual reverse with a different fount (D) that includes an unbarred *A*. Although the standard weight of the noble of 1346-51 was 128.6 gr., a few specimens weigh around the 1351 figure of 120 gr. and this led Lawrence and Potter to wonder whether they could have been struck after the next weight reduction. At least in some cases, however, the lower weight is evidently due to clipping, as undoubtedly happened on subsequent occasions when the weight of the gold coinage was reduced.

As Potter perceptively observed before the heavier half-noble had appeared, a half of the third issue in the British Museum (Bredgar hoard) has neat lettering (with unbarred *A*) on the obverse, like the earliest heavier noble and the pre-1346 quarters, suggesting a mule from an old obverse die of the previous issue. True half-nobles of the lighter issue have irregular lettering, including chevron-barred *A*, sometimes accompanied by very small saltires. The much less rare quarters are more uniform. They have lettering of style B, and are readily distinguishable from those of 1344-6 both by having *e* for *L* in the central panel and by the double tressure on the reverse. On some of them the stops are single saltires.

Pence

Although the Foxes had intended to devote a section of their monograph on Edwardian sterlings to the issues of 1344-51, which they had referred to as group XVI, the death of Earle Fox left the work uncompleted. Shirley Fox, however, later published a study of this series which in most respects remains the primary point of reference. He was unable to settle certain questions relating to the coins of Durham, but the subsequent discovery of a number of die-links by Elmore Jones enabled most of these to be resolved.

Edward III

London was overwhelmingly the most productive mint of this coinage, with relatively minor contributions also from Canterbury and from the ecclesiastical mints of York, Durham and Reading. The last English coins from the semi-detached mint at Berwick also evidently belong to this period. London's output of pence was heavily concentrated in the first eighteen months: almost nine-tenths of its total of some £70,000 for the whole period was struck between January 1344 and June 1345. The last issue of London pence amounted to the insignificant sum of £53 between June 1349 and April 1350. The reason for this decline was twofold: first, the quantity of bullion coming to the mint fell sharply from 1346, and second, there was increasing concentration on the production of halfpence from such silver as was still available.

Canterbury's limited and intermittent activity was confined to the years 1344-6 and its coins are rare. Of the £2,200 of pence for which the mint accounted, £1,900 were struck between September 1344 and June 1345. No figures exist for the other mints, but comparative numbers of specimens in hoards such as Derby (1927) suggest that the output of York might have been between £5,000 and £10,000, and that of Durham towards the lower end of that range. Reading pence, being rare, perhaps represent an issue of £1,000 or less.

REVERSE MARKINGS ON PENCE OF GROUP XVI

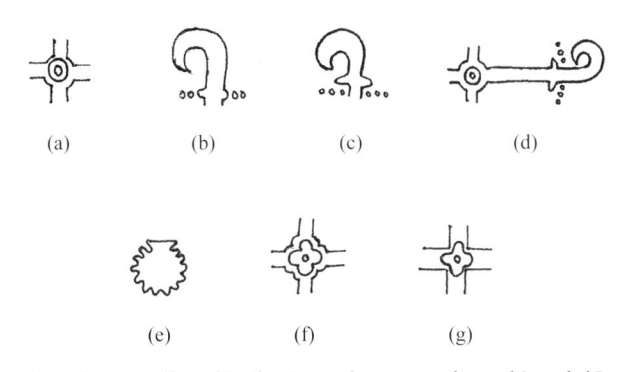

(a) Durham, pellet, d3; (b, c) Durham, croziers, d4 and d5;
(d) Durham, crozier and pellet, d6; (e) Reading, escallop, XVIb, c;
(f) York, full quatrefoil, XVIb; (g) York, recessed quatrefoil, XVIb

With the exception of a few early dies, coins of group XVI are easily separable from others of the Edwardian period by their broad, florid lettering and by their portrait which has wide, bushy hair, broad shoulders and a larger and much more detailed crown than hitherto. Fox divided the London pennies into two main series, the earlier (here XVIa) consisting of several rare varieties of unusual work, and the normal series (here XVIb) containing the bulk of the London issues and almost all those from other mints.

Of XVIa there are five obverse varieties, distinguished by abnormal forms of bust, crown, inscription and stops. These varieties, labelled A-E by Fox, constitute an early and experimental phase before the design became standardized. All pence of XVIa except variety C are very rare. A simple division of the five early varieties can be made according to whether they have thin lettering (XVIa1) or the rounder and more florid fount (XVIa2) that is characteristic of the normal pence of XVIb. The lettering of XVIa1 has hollow sides and is very narrow; it includes a reversed Roman *N* in *Dns* and usually in

Angl and *London*, and *A* and *T* with prolonged serifs. On Fox variety C the small size of the letters and the omission of stops permitted a longer form of obverse inscription, with *Edwar* and *Rex* in full. There is some variation in the style of bust on these early pence, which have a chubby face and hair less spread than on later coins of group XVI. One other obverse die (Fox B), easily recognisable by its thick, plain strands of hair, is known with the narrow lettering of XVIa1. This introduces the regular form of abbreviated obverse reading – *Edw R Angl Dns hyb*, and is notable for having pellet stops, including a colon before *hyb*. Obverse B is only known from a mule the reverse of which has normal group XVI florid lettering; but its proper pair may exist in the form of a XVIa1 reverse die, with a colon after *don*, itself known only from a mule with a XVIa2 obverse of Fox variety A. Mules between obverses of XVIa1(C) and normal reverses also exist, and it seems likely that the use of the narrow lettering of XVIa1 was confined to a very small number of dies at the outset of the new coinage.

Except for a few dies on which the lettering is slightly smaller than it was soon to become, reverses of XVIa2 are not obviously distinguishable from those of XVIb with Gothic *n*. Obverses of XVIa2, however, consisting of Fox varieties A, D and E, show a number of experimental features. The one A die, with annulet stops as in XVIb1-3, has a bust with compact hair as in XVIa1, and a low crown of plainer form somewhat resembling that on pence of earlier groups (this presumably being the reason why Fox placed it first among the 'unusuals'). On Fox D and E this is replaced by a taller and much more elaborate crown, the central fleur of which has its side foils ending in upturned hooks as on most dies of XVIb1. On the single die of variety E the stops are pellets; on those of D, annulets.

MINTS OF GROUP 1344-51

	XVIa1	XVIa2	XVIb1	XVIb2	XVIb3	XVIb4	XVIb5	XVIc
London	x	x	x	x	x	x		
Canterbury				x		x		
York						x		
Durham						x	x	x
Reading						x		x

The normal group XVI pence (apart from those of Durham) were classified by Fox into four obverse types according to their inscriptions, with particular reference to the form of the letter *N*. This letter was also the basis for defining reverse varieties at London: (a) with Gothic *n*, (b) with Roman *N* and (c) with *N* reversed. Obverses read *Edw(a) R Angl Dns hyb*; curiously, when stops are present (XVIb1-3), there is none after the abbreviation of the king's name. The first type of obverse (XVIb1), with Gothic *n* and annulet stops, begins with dies on which the crown has hook-ended petals to the central fleur as on XVIa2(D) and (E), and its position is confirmed by a XVIb1/a1 mule, and by the normal reverses paired with it, all of which have Gothic *n*. Like XVIa it is confined to London. Type 2, in which there is some variety of bust, is similar to type 1, except that it reads *Edwa* instead of the usual *Edw* and that its reverses include Roman *N* as well as Gothic. The earliest pence of Canterbury are of type 2, one being a XVIb2/XVd mule which demonstrates the relatively early position of the *Edwa* dies. Type 3, still with annulet stops, has Roman *N* on the obverse; it is confined to London and is found with all three varieties of reverse. Type 4 obverses have reversed *N* and again its London reverses are of

Edward III

all three kinds; Fox also records a fourth reverse type, with reversed *N* double-barred, but this has not subsequently been verified. The position of type 4 at the end of the main series is suggested by its being the only variety of XVIb (except at Durham) without stops.

Although it can be seen that there was a gradual progression from Gothic to Roman to reversed Roman *N* on both obverse and reverse dies, and this is of value for classification and general sequence, the issue and the use of dies with different kinds of *N* probably overlapped and did not necessarily have any significance for the mint. London pence of XVIb2-4, although all including Roman *N* reverses, are much more plentiful with Gothic *n* in *London*, despite the displacement of Gothic *n* from obverse dies after XVIb2. Also, while most coins of Canterbury are of XVIb4, their reverses all have Gothic *n*. Because the bulk of the issue of pence took place in the first eighteen months, dies were required in large quantities at that time, particularly at London. By September 1344, or very soon afterwards, obverse dies of XVIb4 must have been available, since the dies sent to Canterbury, whose accounts begin in that month, were all of b2 or b4, and Canterbury coins of XVIb2 are extremely rare. This suggests that pence could also have been minted from b4 dies at Reading, York and Durham before the end of 1344. Reading pence of XVIb4, with the scallop shell in the *Vil* quarter, are apparently all from a single obverse die; in the mint name *N* is reversed, as on the obverse. Although not abundant, the York pence of Archbishop William Zouche, who had held several senior positions under Edward III including keeper of the privy seal, are much less rare than those of Canterbury and Reading: there are two varieties of the quatrefoil on the centre of the reverse cross, one small and fully recessed within the limbs of the cross, the other larger and of more normal form. No coins were subsequently struck at York until 1353, and it seems likely that the issue of York pence of XVIb4 did not extend much beyond 1344-5.

Three sets of dies were ordered to be provided to Richard de Bury at Durham in August 1344, and a further order was made two months later. Bishop de Bury died in April 1345 and dies were ordered for his successor, Thomas Hatfield, in August. Hatfield, the king's candidate for Durham after de Bury's death, had long been active in the royal service, and continued to be so after his appointment, even assisting the Black Prince at Crécy in the following year. Building on the work of Elmore Jones, North has defined four obverse types in group XVI at Durham (D1-4) and six reverse types (d1-6, all of which have Gothic *n* in *Dun-*). The table shows the pattern of obverse and reverse combinations in this complex Durham series. The earliest penny from Durham (D1/d1) is of type b4, without episcopal marks. These XVIb4 pence read *Dunelm* (with Roman *M*) or *Dunelп* (with the second *N* Roman and reversed). Being unmarked, Fox attributed them to the vacancy after de Bury's death but, as the least rare of the Durham varieties of group XVI, it is unlikely that they belong only to a period of some four months in 1345 before Hatfield's dies were ordered, without any identifiable predecessors to represent the issues of the last eight months of de Bury's life at a time when in London the new coinage was at its most intense. More probably they, or most of them, were struck for de Bury from the dies ordered in the second half of 1344, although the lack of any special mark on them is curious. Remarkably, they include a mule from an old reverse die of group XVc which, unlike the intervening XVd, also lacked episcopal marking.

All subsequent Durham varieties are very rare. The next two obverses (D2 and D3) have no parallel at London or elsewhere and so presumably resulted from a need for new dies when they were not, or no longer, being made for other mints. Their longer reading *Edwar* led to the shortening of *Angl* to *Ang* (D3) or, on one abnormal die (D2), of *hyb* to *Yb*. The revival of Gothic *n* (and *m* in *Dunolm,* as the mint is now spelt) also suggests a different phase of die-production from that for other mints and justifies the classification of these rare *Edwar* coins as XVIb5. The D2 obverse is presumably the earlier since it

1344–1351

Durham Varieties of Group XVI

Reverses	XVc plain	XVIb4 plain (d1)	XVIb5 plain (d2)	XVIb5 pellet (d3)	XVIb5 crozier (d4)	XVIc crozier (d5)	XVIc crozier and pellet (d6)	1351 crozier and hollow
Obverses								
XVIb4, D1	m	x						
XVIb5, D2			x					
" , D3			m	x	x		m	m
XVIc, D4					m	x		
1351							m	x

m – mules and possible mules.

retains one reversed Roman *N* (in *Dns*), and the reverse paired with it (d2) still has no episcopal mark. This last unmarked reverse die is also muled with a D3 obverse, reverses with which are more usually marked, either with a pellet in the centre of the cross (d3) or with a crozier-head before *Civi* (d4, reading again *Dunelm*). It may be that, like de Bury's dies in 1344-5, Hatfield's earliest were also without episcopal marking. *Edwar* obverse dies (XVIb5) must have been introduced for Durham at about the same time as reverses with special marks (d3 and d4), but although London struck two million pence after June 1345 it is not known to have used obverse dies later than XVIb4. On that basis, one would expect obverse dies made for Hatfield in August 1345 still to have been of XVIb4.

Last in the sequence of Durham obverses is an extraordinary die (D4), reading *Edwardus Rex Ain*. With their *A*s chevron-barred, this die and its crozier-marked reverse (d5) belong to a late stage in the coinage, here designated XVIc. Reverse d5 reads *Civitas Dunolme*, but another reverse die (d6) with the chevron *A* has the remarkable inscription *Vila Dunolmie*. There is no obvious reason why on this die, as on the earliest of 1351, the traditional and correct designation of the see as a *Civitas* should have been displaced. That this was an aberration and not a reflection on the bishop or his see is clear from the fact that both the d6 and the 1351 *Vil(l)a* reverse dies incorporate the bishop's crozier and a hollow in the centre of the cross. The crozier alone occurs both on the XVIc *Dunolme* reverse (d5) and on the *Dunelm* d4 die (paired with obverses of XVIb5 and XVIc). There is also the d3 *Dunolm* reverse with pellet centre, without the crozier, suggesting that both pellet and crozier, separately or combined, were used to denote Hatfield's dies. Since it is doubtful whether any of the Durham dies of XVIb5 can have been issued as early as May 1345, when other mints were still using dies of XVIb4, the *Dunolm* reverse variety d2 may also conceivably be attributable to Hatfield, despite its lack of a distinguishing mark.

The full king's name and the omission of the Irish title on the Durham obverse of XVIc, which look forward to the form used from 1351 onwards, are paralleled on a recently discovered penny of Reading (*Rex Ang*) which, with chevron-barred *A* on both sides, may also be classified as XVIc. Since dies were only issued in very limited quantities to these ecclesiastical mints, new ones must have been needed for abbot and bishop after the minting of pence had ceased elsewhere or possibly, in the case of London, while old dies of XVIb4 were still available. The chevron *A* may point to a date in the period of the third issue of gold on which the same form of letter is found. On the Reading penny the crown is of the florid form as found in XVIb, but the Durham penny has a new and plainer crown, suggesting that it may be the later of the two.

Edward III

Halfpence and Farthings

Halfpence and farthings do not figure in the London accounts before September 1345, but from that date until May 1348 £7,300 was struck in halfpence. In the next three years, however, after the minting of pence had all but ceased, the rate of output of halfpence nearly trebled. Altogether, some fourteen million halfpence were issued, almost as many as the total number of group XVI London pence. Farthings were not minted on anywhere near so substantial a scale, and the accounts show that, like pence, they were largely displaced by halfpence from 1348. The only other mints of which fractional coins exist are Reading and Berwick. Halfpence and farthings of Reading are extremely rare, but halfpence of Berwick (no farthing is known of this mint) are no longer so rare since the discovery of the Stanwix hoard.

There is considerable diversity among the abundant London halfpence of group XVI. The basic obverse division is between an earlier series, here described as XVIb, reading *Edwardus Rex*, and later varieties, here XVIc, with *Rex An*. The finely drawn bust on most of the XVIb halfpence (b1) is a reduced version of that on the XVIb pence. Lettering is neat and there is no punctuation. Later and scarcer examples of XVIb halfpence, however, have a bust more roughly rendered, a colon or two saltires before *Rex*, and coarser lettering (b2). Reverses of XVIb vary considerably, with the pellets at first neat, later larger, often elongated and sometimes joined together.

Halfpence of XVIc are considerably less plentiful than those of XVIb. Their obverses include several varieties with a rounder bust (c1), some of which have a pellet or more rarely a saltire each side of the crown. A few have a colon before *Rex*, as in XVIb2. Again the style of lettering and the shape of the reverse pellets vary, and some reverse dies have an extra small pellet or cross added in one quarter, in counterpart to the marks by the crown. A different style of bust, with narrow face and short hair, is found on some halfpence of XVIc which Fox placed first in his description of the *Rex An* halfpence. However, since the other XVIc halfpence have a bust more akin to that in XVIb those with the new and narrower face may rather be the last of the series (XVIc2), and this is the more likely in view of the fact that on some of the XVIc2 halfpence the *A* is clearly chevron-barred.

Although one and a quarter million were struck, London farthings, extremely rare before the era of metal detectors, are still uncommon. All known specimens read *Rex* only, like XVIb halfpence, and since more than 80 per cent of them had been struck by May 1348 it is doubtful whether new dies would have been needed thereafter which might have had a longer reading like the halfpence of XVIc and the late Reading farthing. The portrait on most of the London farthings resembles that on the early halfpence, and has a low crown. They are easily distinguished from pre-1344 farthings by the bushier hair and Gothic *n*.

Reading halfpence and farthings, with the scallop shell in one quarter, are extremely rare, but they occur of both XVIb and XVIc. *N* on the reverses is still of the reversed Roman form. The XVIc farthing is a recent discovery. It has the *Rex An* inscription as well as a coarser bust than farthings of XVIb and, as with the XVIc penny, is evidence of the supply of dies to Reading for the other denominations when London was apparently no longer minting anything but halfpence.

Berwick-upon-Tweed

The last English coins of Berwick are pence and halfpence, from local dies, with a bear's head in one quarter of the reverse. Blunt described these as class VIIIa, as if pre-dating the halfpence and farthings with two bear's heads (class VIIIb). The weights of the few surviving pennies, however, argue for their attribution to the period following the reduction of 1344, and they and the corresponding halfpence are accordingly here referred to as class IX. The pennies have a rounded collar; on halfpence the drapery is more pointed. The crown on both is tall, narrow and bifoliate. Inscriptions vary. One penny has a normal English reading, *Edw R* etc., but others have *Edwradus* in full and omit *R(ex)*. Because of poor striking the readings on halfpence are difficult to decipher, but they appear to include *Edwardus Dei Gra R* and *Edwardus Anglie D* (again without *Rex*). The inclusion of *Dei Gra*, ahead of its use on the regular English coinage, is curious, but may reflect usage in Scotland, since it had occurred on Scottish coins since Alexander III.

In issuing a receipt for items taken over from his predecessor in 1353, the new chamberlain of Berwick listed eighteen dies for halfpence and farthings. Since there is no reference to penny dies, and no farthings are known of class IX, these dies may have been from the pre-1344 issues. There is no numismatic evidence to suggest that English coinage took place at Berwick after 1351.

Mint Output

Except that distinction was no longer made between English and foreign bullion purchased, the mint accounts for silver continued the pattern in use before 1344, with amounts of coin issued shown separately for pence, halfpence and farthings. There was, however, slight variation in the numbers of pence struck from the pound of silver. From January 1344 (probably) the figure was 266d., increased to 268d. in June 1345 and to 270d. in July 1346. For halfpence and farthings the respective figures were 279d. and 281d. throughout, except that the entry for halfpence from November 1346 to Michaelmas 1347 is recorded as 279d.-280d. London's accounts for silver and gold both run from 20 January 1344 to 24 June 1351. Accounts for pence issued at Canterbury occur only from 30 September 1344 to 23 June 1345 and from 30 July to 19 December 1346. In the tables M indicates Michaelmas (29/30 Sept.), and when no day or month is given (e.g. 1344/45) this means that the accounting period ran from one Michaelmas to the next.

SILVER	LONDON			CANTERBURY
	£ pence	£ halfpence	£ farthings	£ pence
20.1.1344 – 10.7.1344	23,186	-	-	-
10.7.1344 – M.1344	13,586	-	-	-
1344/45	24,757	-	-	1,902
1345/46	5,040	2,079	688	239
1346/47	1,384	c.2,909	429	106
1347/48	1,531	6,677	253	-
M.1348 – 2.6.1349	-	4,292	105	-
2.6.1349 – M.1350	53	9,661	8	-
M.1350 – 24.6.1351	-	7,833	31	-

Gold is recorded only by weight, and not by denominations issued since the weights and deductions for mintage and seignorage were all proportionate.

Edward III

GOLD. London only		
£15 per lb.:	20.1.1344 – 10.7.1344	£31,949
£13 3s. 4d. per lb.:	10.7.1344-M.1344	7,378
	1344/45	9,970
	M.1345 – 30.7.1346	4,611
£14 per lb.:	30.7.1346 – M.1346	3,714
	1346/47	36,593
	1347/48	43,299
	M.1348 – 2.6.1349	11,101
	2.6.1349 – M.1350	36,298
	M.1350 – 24.6.1351	1,490

Calendar 1344 – 1351

1343   Contract with Kirkyn and Nicholyn for new coinage including gold leopard (Dec.).

1344   New London mint accounts from 20 January; Canterbury from 30 Sept.
Contract with Percival of Lucca (July) for gold noble; silver at 266d. per pound.
Leopard gold coinage demonetized (Aug.).
Durham: three sets of dies ordered for Bp. de Bury in August and October.

1345   Master's allowance for minting gold reduced (June); silver at 268d. per pound.
Issue of halfpence and farthings resumed from September.
Durham: Richard de Bury died 14 April. Bp. Thomas Hatfield granted temporalities (June), dies ordered (August).

1346   Second contract with Kirkyn and Nicholyn, for nobles of reduced weight (July); silver at 270 pence per pound, and higher for halfpence and farthings.
English victory at Crécy (Aug.).
Last Canterbury mint accounts closed 19 Dec.

1347   Calais taken by English.

1348-9   Black Death.

1351   London mint accounts closed 24 June.

GOLD 1344-1351

1st issue, Jan. - July 1344

DOUBLE LEOPARD: wt. 108 gr. (7.0g.), 6s. Obv. King with orb and sceptre enthroned between two leopards' heads, beneath canopy, with lis in field; *Edwr D Gra Rex A/n/g/l/ s Franc Dns hib*; annulet stops. Rev. Ornamental cross, with crowns within quadrilobe, lions in spandrels; *Ihc Transiens Per Medium Illorum Ibat*; double saltire stops. ER.

1344–1351

Gold

LEOPARD: wt. 54 gr. (3.5g.), 3s. Obv. Crowned leopard sejant left, with heraldic mantle; *Edwar D Gra Rex Angl s Franc Dns hib*. Rev. as double, but trefoils instead of crowns at cross-ends; *Domine Ne in Furore Tuo Arguas Me*. Annulet stops (double on rev.). ER.

HELM: wt. 27 gr. (1.75g.), 1s. 6d. Obv. Helmet crested with lion sejant, lis in field; *Edwr R Angl s Franc D hib*. Rev. Ornamental cross fleury; *Exaltabitur in Gloria* (var. *-tar*). Annulet stops. ER.

2nd issue, July 1344 - July 1346. *L* in central panel of rev. Stops double saltires.

NOBLE: wt. 136.7 gr. (8.86g.), 6s. 8d. Obv. King in ship; *Ed/war D Gra Rex Angl s Franc Dns hyb*. Die 1: broad, plain lettering (style A); die 2: narrower lettering (style B), three large pellets above sterncastle. Rev. Floriate cross; *Ihc Transiens Per Medium Illorum Ibat*. ER.

HALF-NOBLE: wt. 68.35 gr. (4.43g.), 3s. 4d. As noble 1, same obv. reading, with plain lettering (*A* unbarred). Rev. *Domine Ne In Furore Tuo Arguas Me*. ER.

QUARTER NOBLE: wt. 34.2 gr. (2.22g.), 1s. 8d. Obv. Shield in six-arc tressure; *Edwar Rex Angl s Franc D hyb*. Rev. Floriate cross within single tressure; *Exaltabitur in Gloria*. ER.

3rd issue, July 1346 - June 1351. *e* in central panel; otherwise types as 2nd issue. *A* usually chevron-barred. Stops usually double saltires.

NOBLE: wt. 128.6 gr. (8.33g). Obv. type I, Bowsprit behind forecastle; style B letters; diameter c. 34.5 mm. II, Bowsprit through forecastle; larger letters (style C); diam. c. 36 mm. VR.

HALF NOBLE: wt. 64.3 gr. (4.17g.). No ornaments on corner points of rev. central panel. Also 2nd/3rd issue mule; all ER.

QUARTER NOBLE: wt. 32.1 gr. (2.08g.) As 2nd issue, but *Edwar R*, and double tressure on rev. Some have single saltire stops. Rare.

SILVER 1344 - 1351

PENCE. Jan. 1344 – June 1345, 266d. per lb., wt. 20.3 gr. (1.32g.). June 1345 – July 1346, 268d. per lb., wt. 20.15 gr. (1.31g.). From July 1346, 270d. per lb., wt. 20.0 gr. (1.30g.).

XVIa. Early experimental varieties with abnormal busts, crowns and inscriptions. London only. (Note: the Fox labels, A-E, are commonly used, as here, by reference to his table of varieties, but in his text vars. B and C are transposed.)
    a1. Narrow, concave-sided lettering. Normally Roman *N* reversed, rarely Gothic *n*.
    Fox C: *Edwar Rex Angl Dns hyb*, no stops. Several varieties of bust; compact hair. Also muled with later revs. All rare.
    Fox B: *Edw R Angl Dns hyb*, Gothic *n* in *Angl*, Roman *N* (not reversed) in *Dns*; pellet stops (colon before *hyb*). One obv. die, only known from mule with later rev. Rev. colon after *don*, only known from mule with XVIa2 (A) obv. Both mules ER.

Edward III

Pence

a2. Normal florid lettering with Gothic *n*. *Edw R Angl Dns hyb*.
    Fox A: Low crown; annulet stops. One die only (VR); also (ER) mule with rev. of XVIa1.
    Fox E and D: Elaborate crown, with hook-ended central fleur. Stops pellets (E, one die, ER) or annulets (D, VR).

XVIb. Main issue. Bust with bushy hair, wide shoulders and elaborate crown. *Edw(a)(r) R Angl Dns hyb*. London revs. have (a) Gothic *n*, (b) Roman *N*, (c) reversed Roman *N*. Mints: London (b1-4), Canterbury (b2, 4 only), Durham (b4, 5 only), Reading (b4 only), York episcopal (b4 only).
    b1. *Edw*, annulet stops, Gothic *n*. Crown with hooks (cf. XVIa2) or normal. London only.
    b2. *Edwa*, annulet stops, Gothic *n*.
    b3. *Edw*, annulet stops, Roman *N*. London only.
    b4. *Edw*, no stops, reversed Roman *N*.
    b5. *Edwar*, no stops, Gothic *n* and *m*. Durham only (see below: obv. vars. D2 and D3; revs. d2, d3 and d4).

XVIc. Chevron-barred *A*, Gothic *n*, *Edwardus Rex Ain* (Durham) or *Ang* (Reading).
    Durham: One obv. die (D4), no stops. Plainer crown than in XVIb. Rev. dies d5 (crozier) and d6 (crozier and pellet). All ER.
    Reading: Colon before and after *Rex*. Florid crown as in XVIb. Scallop in *Vil* quarter. ER.

Durham group XVI obverses
D1. Normal XVIb4.
D2. XVIb5. *Edwar R Angl Dns Yb; N* reversed in *Dns*. One die only.
D3. XVIb5. *Edwar R Ang Dns hyb*.
D4. XVIc. *Edwardus Rex Ain*. One die only.

Durham reverses, Gothic *n* in *Dun* throughout. *Civi/tas*, d1-5.
d1. XVIb4. *Dun/elm* or*/eln*, Roman *M* or *N* reversed. No marks.
d2. XVIb5. *Dun/olm*, Gothic *m*. No marks.
d3. XVIb5. *Dun/olm*, Gothic *m*. Pellet in centre of cross.
d4. XVIb5. *Dun/elm*, Gothic *m*. Crozier (to left) before *Civi*.
d5. XVIc. *Dun/olme*, *H* for *M*. Crozier before *Civi*.
d6. XVIc. *Vil/a Du/nol/mie*, Gothic *m*. Crozier (to left) after *Vil*; pellet in centre.

Mints of XVIb and XVIc
London: XVIb1 (rev. a; also ER mule with rev. XVIa1); b2 (revs. a; and b, rare); b3 (revs. a; and b, c, both rare); b4 (revs. a; and b, c, both rare).
Canterbury (all revs. have Gothic *n*): XVIb2/XVd2 mule (ER); XVIb2 (ER); b4 (VR).
Durham, without episcopal marks, Bp. de Bury to April 1345: D1/XVc mule (ER); D1/d1. Bury, vacancy April-Aug. 1345, or Hatfield?: D2/d2 (ER), D3/d2 (ER).
—, with episcopal marks (Bp. Thomas Hatfield, from Aug. 1345): D3/d3 (pellet in centre) and D3/d4 (crozier), both VR; D4/d4 (ER); D4/d5 (crozier), ER; D3/d6 (crozier and pellet), ER. Also ER mules with Pre-treaty dies, D3/1351 and 1351/d6.
Reading (*Vil/la R/adi/ngy*, *N* reversed; scallop shell in *Vil* quarter): XVIb4, rare; XVIc, ER.
York, with quatrefoil on centre of cross for Abp. William Zouche: XVIb4 only.

HALFPENCE. Wt. 9.7 gr. (0.63g.); 279d. per lb. London and Reading only.

XVIb *Edwardus Rex.* Some have conjoined pellets on rev.
    b1. Fine bust; no stops. London (Gothic *n*); vars. *Edwadus, Ewardus*. Reading (ER), *Vil/la R/adi/ngy*, reversed Roman *N*; scallop in *la R* quarter.
    b2. Coarser bust; colon or two saltires before *Rex*. London only.

XVIc *Edwardus Rex An* (with Gothic *n*). Some have conjoined pellets.
    c1. Round bust as XVIb (several varieties). Some have colon before *Rex*; pellets or (VR) saltires by crown; extra pellet or (rare) cross in one quarter of rev. London only.
    c2. Long narrow face with short hair and little neck. Chevron-barred *A*.
        London; Reading (ER), reversed Roman *N* on rev.; scallop in *adi* quarter.

FARTHINGS. Wt. 4.8 gr. (0.31g.); 281d. per lb. London and Reading only.

XVIb. *Edwardus Rex*, no stops; neat portrait. London, rare; Reading, as halfpenny, with scallop in *la R* quarter, ER.

XVIc. *Edwardus Rex An*, no stops; coarser portrait. Reading only, as halfpenny but scallop in *Vil* quarter; ER.

MINT OF BERWICK-UPON-TWEED

Class IX (Blunt VIIIa). Local dies. Bear's head in one quarter of rev.

PENCE. Tall bifoliate crown; pellet eyes; rounded drapery. *Edw R Angl Dns hyb* or *Edwradus.Angl D'hb*. Roman *N* forward or reversed. *Vill/a.Be/rvv/ici* or *Vil/la B/erw/ici*. ER.

HALFPENCE. *Edwardus Dei Gra R* or *Anglie D* (another appears to read – *(D)ns h*); pellet stops. *Vill/a Be/rvv/ici* or *Vil/la B/erv/ici*. Rare.

CHAPTER V

1351 - 1411
Edward III – Henry IV

With his monetary reform of 1351 Edward III took the fourth and final step towards a sustainable bimetallic currency system. By indenture dated 20 June the king appointed Henry de Brisele and John of Chichester as joint master-workers to produce a new coinage at lower weights, based on a noble of 120 gr. and a penny of 18 gr. The three gold denominations were to continue as before, but with 45 nobles struck from a pound of gold against the 42 prescribed in 1346. Instead of 270 pence, 300 were now to be minted from a pound of silver. In practice, however, most of the silver would be struck in coins of higher value. Edward I's few groats of fourpence had long since disappeared from the scene, but this denomination, now revived on a much greater scale, quickly became the cardinal component of the currency and remained so almost continuously for the next two hundred years. In addition, the halfgroat was now included in the coinage for the first time. With the weight of silver coins reduced by 10 per cent but of gold by less than 7 per cent, the ratio of gold to silver fell from 11.6:1 to 11.2:1, a more accurate reflection of market prices than the previous tariff under which gold had been somewhat overvalued. Ironically, at £15 per pound of gold the 1351 noble represented exactly the same value as the abortive leopard issue, but the key difference was that after seignorage and minting charges the merchant was now to receive £14 10s. 9d. instead of only £13 16s. 6d. in 1344. For silver he would get 23s. 10d. per pound, i.e. 25s. less 14d. of charges.

In the aftermath of the Black Death a reduction in the standard of the coinage had become inevitable. The loss of population resulted in a shortage of labour and a decline in agricultural and other output, and this in turn led to a temporary surplus of currency and increased incentive to export it to continental mints offering more competitive prices. Yet Parliament was reluctant to see a permanent debasement, and in response the king vainly promised to restore the standard when practicable. He also accepted a clause in the Statute of Purveyors of 1352 which Parliament came to interpret as restraining the crown from altering the basics of the coinage without its consent. As a result the 1351 standard was not replaced for sixty years, even though towards the end of that period the supply of bullion to the mint fell to levels inadequate to sustain the currency. In the short run, however, there was an abundance of coin. By the end of December 1353 London had minted £218,000 of silver in thirty months, only about half the amount issued in a similar period following the recoinage of 1279, but a considerable sum nonetheless. If a wholesale recoinage had been intended, as under Henry III and Edward I, it would have needed a change of type and the addition of regional mints. Nevertheless, although old coin was not demonetized, it was profitable to have it reminted if above the new weight, and large quantities of old silver, even if clipped, must have been converted. This did in due course lead to the opening of a royal mint, for silver only, at York, where nearly £26,000 was issued between July 1353 and May 1355 – the only occasion during the sixty years when a second royal mint in England was brought into operation. From 1354 the volume of bullion bought by the London mint began to decline; a further £123,000 of silver coin was struck during the three years 1354-6, but the reminting of old currency was by now a reducing factor and less than £50,000 was struck in the last four years of the 1350s.

On 31 May 1355 a new contract was entered into between the king and William Potter, which contained a number of variations from that of 1351. Since the value of bullion had risen slightly in the meantime, the prices offered by the mint were improved a little by reduction of its charges from 9s. 3d. to 6s. 8d. per pound of gold and from 14d. to 11 9/16d. for silver. Another change was the addition of fractional coins, which had been excluded previously in view of the large volume of small change from the 1330s and 1340s still in circulation.

In 1356 further contracts on similar terms were entered into with different masters in January (Hugh de Wychyngham) and November (de Brisele again), but in March 1361 a new indenture with Walter dei Bardi lowered the charges for minting gold and silver to 5s. and 10d. per pound respectively. This gave returns to the merchant of £14 15s. and 24s. 2d., and these rates continued to apply until the reign of Henry IV. Bardi's first contract lasted for only fifteen weeks, before he was displaced by another Italian, Robert de Portico (from June 1361); but in February 1363 he resumed the mastership and then held it for the next thirty years. The higher mint prices from 1361 led to a slight increase in silver output, although not for very long. In the twelve months from September 1361 output of silver rose to £14,000, but the annual rate immediately thereafter declined below £4,000, a figure only once (in 1374/5), and then marginally, exceeded in the rest of the century. In the 1370s and 1380s often less than £1,000 a year was issued. After an increase in 1389/91, the mint produced only £1,200 in total over the next five years; but there was a slight improvement in the last three years of Richard II's reign. During the first nine years (1399-1408) of Henry IV, however, the warden accounted for only £1,750 in all, despite mint charges being cut from 10d. to 8d. a pound by reducing the seignorage to the nominal figure of one penny. In the three years 1405-8 less than £200 of silver was coined, and accounting then ceased altogether until the weight was reduced in 1412.

In western Christendom generally there had been a growing shortage of silver in the later fourteenth century, as the traditional source of supply from central European mines declined. Gold, however, was being mined in Hungary and Silesia on a substantial scale, supplemented by gold that reached the Mediterranean from Africa. At first London was able to compete for supplies successfully against other European mints. In 1351, since English gold coins had only been in issue for the last seven years, and not in great quantity, there were few of them in circulation to be reminted at a lower weight. Nevertheless, from 1351 to 1360 the mint bought more than 50,000 lbs. of gold and issued nearly £800,000 worth of gold coins. Output fluctuated wildly: thus, £167,000 in the first sixteen months, but as little as £12,000 in a similar period from December 1355. The increased mint price in 1361 led to a rise in purchases for a period following Bardi's contract, but after 1362/3 only reaching £25,000 of gold coin in one of the next six years. In 1368/9 there was exceptional output of £73,000, but this was the last year of extensive gold coinage at London in the fourteenth century, as the English mint price became increasingly uncompetitive. During the twenty-two years of Richard II's reign (1377-99) £268,000 of gold was coined at London; in the nine years of the heavy coinage of Henry IV, up to 1408, only £45,000.

From the 1360s the minting of English gold coin was not confined to London. In 1347 the town of Calais had fallen to Edward III, and in 1348 the king proposed that silver coin should be minted there on the English standard. Although nothing came of this, in 1349 and 1350 authorization was given to strike coin conforming to that of France, and surviving examples show that a mint at Calais came into operation at this period. The continental staple, or trading centre, through which all exports of English wool had to pass, had long been situated at Bruges, but this arrangement came to an end in 1362 and the staple was transferred to Calais for the following season. In March 1363 de Brisele was appointed master-worker in Calais to operate what was in effect a branch of the

Edward III – Henry IV

London mint, so that foreign currency tendered for the purchase of English wool could be converted into English coin on the spot. The mastership at Calais passed to the Florentine Bardet de Malapilys in 1371; but in October 1394 an Englishman, John Wildeman, was appointed master for both London and Calais, and the joint office was perpetuated under his Italian successor, Nanfre Molakyn, from July 1395.

To start with, the new English mint at Calais coined both gold and silver. Brisele's indenture included provision for a hundred pounds weight of silver to be minted annually into farthings (a requirement not contained in any of the London indentures of the period), but no Calais halfpence or farthings of Edward III are known and few if any are likely to have been struck. Less than £4,000 of silver coin was minted at Calais, and most of the surviving coins are groats. The small sum recorded in the second of the two relevant accounts, which runs for twelve months from April 1364, suggests that minting of silver may have ceased well before April 1365. Gold, however, continued to be coined at Calais for the rest of Edward's reign and, with some interruption, throughout and beyond Richard II's, until the mint was eventually closed for want of bullion in 1403/4. In the forty years since its inauguration, the Calais mint had produced more than £570,000 of English gold coin, in total almost exactly the same as London and a measure of the importance of the wool trade at this time. Although the accounting periods of the two mints do not exactly coincide, in some years the levels of output at Calais were such as significantly to reduce the amount of gold reaching the London mint. In 1363-5, its first two years, Calais was already coining more gold, and in 1365-8 its output was some four times greater than London's. Following the resumption of hostilities with France in 1369, the staple was temporarily removed from Calais (June 1369 to August 1370) and less gold was struck at either mint in the 1370s, particularly after 1374. At Calais only £90 was coined between May 1381 and January 1384, and nothing at all for the next three years, the staple having again been moved (to Middleburg) in 1383, as a result of the French military threat to Calais. After the staple returned to Calais in 1388 minting was resumed, but from October 1397 to closure some six years later the sums coined were very small.

The decline of the manorial system and an increasingly market-based economy in the fourteenth century led to growing social tensions, culminating in the so-called Peasants' Revolt of 1381. Some of the grievances of the insurgents were financial, among them a heavy poll tax levied in 1380 and the acute shortage of small change. During Richard's reign monetary matters caused growing concern. The prevalent official view, which conflicted with the interests of the merchants, was that the prosperity of a state depended directly on the quantity of precious metals within its borders. A new impost had been placed on imports in 1379, and in 1382 Parliament asked a committee of senior figures in the City of London to review a series of currency issues, including the shortage of bullion, the clipping of gold coin, the gold:silver ratio and the import of weak coin from Scotland and Flanders. The committee's view was that control of bullion could only be achieved by control of trade: bills of exchange should be banned, and a revaluation of gold coins should be considered – solutions that Parliament was disinclined to accept. In 1391 the king ordered that half of the proceeds of imports should be spent on English goods, and this was extended to the whole of the proceeds by Henry IV in 1402. But none of these measures could succeed in compensating for a fundamental undervaluation of gold and silver by the English mint.

The removal of the staple and the eclipse of the mint at Calais in the 1380s may be directly related to what has been termed the war of the gold nobles. When the staple returned to Calais the king revived an old regulation that merchants should use only

English gold coin to pay for wool. Meanwhile Flemish mints had begun to produce copies of the noble at slightly lesser weight and fineness, attracting gold away from the English mints. England retaliated by imposing a duty on continental exports to be paid in foreign gold. This helped to revive mint activity at Calais, but English nobles were then banned from circulation in Flanders. Although on his accession Henry IV immediately revoked the duty, and the Flemish lifted their ban in 1400, the rising market price of gold made it increasingly difficult to attract bullion to the mint, and it was only a matter of time before the situation had to be recognized by an English devaluation. In February 1409 a draft contract was drawn up with a new master, Richard Garner, for the mints of London and Calais to strike gold at £16 per pound instead of £15, and silver at 28s. instead of 25s. The need for small change was recognized by providing, for the first time since before 1351, that halfpence (at 28s. 4d. per pound) and farthings (at 29s.) should be struck at slightly lower proportionate weights in order to compensate for the extra cost of minting. As in 1351, the new tariff would have again adjusted the ratio between silver and gold in favour of silver. Although the proposal seems never to have been implemented, reform could not be much longer deferred, and in 1411 a new agreement was made with Garner for a lighter coinage, implemented at Easter in the following year, with the noble reduced to 108 gr. and the penny to 15 gr.

Of the concessionary mints of the sterling period only those of the archbishop of York and the bishop of Durham survived beyond 1351. As before, their production was confined to pence. The mint at Canterbury, which had played a key role in the coinage since the twelfth century, now went into abeyance until revived by Edward IV in the 1460s, presumably because the needs of the south-east could all be met by the Tower without conceding a share of profit to the archbishop. Durham and York, however, continued to provide a useful extension to the north. Although Durham's contribution was no longer as relatively important as it had been under Edward I and II, it continued to participate actively and its coins of the 1350s are quite plentiful. Thereafter its output declined, although perhaps not proportionately more than that of the London mint itself after 1360. Durham pennies of Edward III's later years and of Richard II are scarce. No new dies were authorised for Durham during the heavy coinage of Henry IV, which is hardly surprising in view of the general shortage of silver coinage at that period. Dies were supplied less frequently to Durham than to other mints and tended to remain in use for longer (although less continuously). One result of this was that, whereas at London old dies for silver were on occasions withdrawn and replaced, the same did not necessarily occur at Durham. Thus there are Durham mules between dies from before and after 1351, and again spanning the transitions of 1361. The crozier-limbed reverse cross adopted by the long-serving Bishop Thomas Hatfield (1345-81) before 1351 continued to appear on Durham pennies throughout Edward's reign, but not on those of his successor, John Fordham (1381-8), under Richard II. Until the 1360s English (*Dur-*) and Latin (*Dun-*) forms of the mint name alternated, but *Dunolm* became the norm from the 1370s onwards.

In the case of York the arrangements operated in one respect as in the pre-1351 coinage of Edward III, namely that activation of the archbishop's mint did not require, as it had done under Edward I and II, a royal mint to be in operation at York at the same time. Indeed, when the king set up his own mint in York in July 1353 that of Archbishop Thoresby, which had only been opened two months previously, was suspended until the royal mint was closed in 1355. Thenceforward the archbishop's mint played an important role in the coinage; from the 1360s it provided most of the new supply of pence in circulation, and from the 1370s they were the largest silver coins in regular production. York pence

Edward III – Henry IV

are the only abundant coins of Edward III's last years, and from the reigns of Richard II and Henry IV (before 1411) they are only outnumbered by London halfpence. For an extended period during Richard's middle years the mint appears to have been unable to obtain dies from London, to judge by the number of York coins from crude local dies.

The proportions in which the several denominations were struck varied considerably from time to time. In gold the emphasis was normally on nobles, and to a lesser extent on quarters. Gold of the 1350s is plentiful, but the halves are the scarcest, particularly those of the first few years, continuing their relative rarity from the pre-1351 issues. In the 1360s the fractions are numerous, particularly quarter-nobles, but from Edward III's last years half-nobles are extremely rare and, unless old dies were used, quarters non-existent. From 1377 to 1408 nobles continued to account for the great bulk of the gold coinage, and the halves and quarters of the later years, when bullion supplies were failing, are of increasing rarity. Except in the period immediately following its opening in 1363, gold coins struck at the Calais mint are usually rarer than their London equivalents.

At London the groat and halfgroat accounted for most of the silver minted until the 1380s. Attempts by the crown from time to time to prescribe the relative quantities to be struck in each denomination seem generally to have been ignored in practice, because merchants preferred to use the larger coins and they were more economical for the mint to produce. Potter's indenture of 1355 laid down that a third of each £100 should be in groats, another third in halfgroats, £30 in pence and £3 6s. 8d. in halfpence. If these proportions were adhered to, there would have been twice as many halfgroats as groats. Halfgroats of the 1350s and 1360s are generally at least as common as groats, but thereafter they are increasingly scarce; under Henry IV (before 1411) the halfgroat appears for a brief period to have been the senior silver coin in issue, but circumstances were abnormal in view of the extreme shortage of bullion until the weight reduction of 1412. In the case of pence the 1355 indenture would have made this by far the most abundant coin, but the material nowhere nearly approaches the prescribed proportion and indeed the volume of sterlings of Edward I and II still in circulation would have rendered it unnecessary. The same is true of the fractions, of which few were produced until the 1360s, when the issues of Edward III's early years had largely disappeared. In 1379 the Commons petitioned for a renewed supply of halfpence and farthings, and their plea for more small change was repeated on several occasions throughout the reign of Richard II. From this point onwards halfpence were produced on a greater scale than any other denomination. Farthings also have only survived in any numbers from the later years of the fourteenth century. At this period a farthing was the price of a loaf of bread or four pints of ale, and the shortage of petty currency was a continuing concern. Record survives of an inititiative by the City fathers who commissioned a coinage of £80 of farthings (76,800 coins) to be distributed from the Guildhall on a chosen day in May 1380. With the king's approval Parliament ordained in 1402 that one third of all silver brought to the mint should be struck into halfpence and farthings (half in each), but even if this was implemented in the following year (1402/3), when 129 pounds of bullion were minted, the issue would have resulted in fewer than 40,000 of these small coins.

At many points the coinage of this period reflects the principal feature of its political history – the fluctuating progress of hostilities between England and France. Put simply, the Hundred Years' War consisted of two main phases, each beginning with a relatively short period of English success, followed by a longer period of decline and failure. In 1356, ten years after the great English victory at Crécy, French forces were defeated at Poitiers, in northern Aquitaine, and their king, John the Good, was taken prisoner by the Black Prince. After four years in captivity the French king agreed to pay a large ransom in 1360 and, under the Treaty of Brétigny, he conceded to Edward III sovereignty of the duchy of Aquitaine, the county of Ponthieu and the town of Calais. In return Edward gave up all claim to the throne of France and to the northern Plantaganet dominions of Normandy, Maine and Anjou. But in due course the nobility of Aquitaine rebelled against its English sovereign and war began again in 1369. Things did not go well now for the English. In 1372 their superiority at sea was challenged by a Franco-Castilian naval victory off La Rochelle. On land, by the time that a two year truce was agreed at Bruges in 1375, they retained control in the south-west only of a strip of coastal territory around Bordeaux and Bayonne, and in the north only of the town of Calais and its march.

After a long illness the Black Prince died in 1376, a year before his father, so that when Edward III died he was succeeded in 1377 by his grandson Richard at the age of ten. The stage was thus set for a long period in which Edward's descendants competed for the English crown. Richard himself was a complex character: cultured and determined, but in his adult years extravagant and wilful. In the early years of his minority the powerful position of his uncle John of Gaunt, Duke of Lancaster and now the eldest surviving son of Edward III, aroused resentment and unrest in a number of quarters, notably in London. Following the Peasants' Revolt the friends with whom Richard had surrounded himself as he sought to assume personal rule became increasingly critical of Gaunt, who in 1386 left the country to claim the crown of Castile, in the right of his second wife, the Spanish princess Constanza. Richard's friends were in their turn bitterly resented by other nobles, including another of his uncles, Thomas, Duke of Gloucester. Led by Gloucester, with the Earl of Arundel and Gaunt's son, the young Henry Bolingbroke, the Lords Appellant (so called because they appealed to Parliament to impeach Richard's favourites) came to power in 1387 after defeating a royal force at Radcot Bridge in Oxfordshire. Following this Richard's leading courtiers were convicted of high treason in the 'Merciless Parliament' of 1388.

In 1389 Richard succeeded in reestablishing his own rule and concluded a truce with France, initially for three years, which was hoped to pave the way to lasting peace. After the death of his first queen in 1394, Richard married in 1396 the infant daughter of Charles VI, Isabella of France, and the formal alliance then made between the two kingdoms was cemented by a twenty-eight year truce. Richard now felt strong enough to round on his enemies of 1387-8: Gloucester and Arundel were charged with treason in the Parliament of 1397, and in the following year Henry Bolingbroke was exiled for ten years. When John of Gaunt died in February 1399 the king declared his possessions forfeit to the crown. However, in the despotic act that thus disinherited Bolingbroke, Richard had over-reached himself. He was in Ireland in June 1399 when Henry crossed from France to claim his inheritance, and on his return to England via Wales the king found himself deserted. Taken prisoner by his cousin, Richard was forced to abdicate in September; and early in the following year he died in captivity in Pontefract Castle, most probably murdered on Henry's orders. Henry IV's own subsequent reign (1399-1413) was not much less troubled than Richard's had been, marred in its earlier years by rebellion and continued dynastic struggle, and latterly by the king's failing health and the quarrels of his sons.

Whereas frequent devaluation on the Continent led to the introduction of a wide variety of new types, many of them of great beauty (especially in France and Flanders), the fiercely defended stability of the English coinage left the basic designs unchanged for many generations, except in relatively minor detail. On nobles and halves there is some variation, particularly in the earlier stages, in the number of ropes in the rigging fore and aft and in the disposition of lions and lis on the ship's side. From the last years

Edward III – Henry IV

of Edward III to 1412 the forecastle and sterncastle have battlemented tops instead of the usual large pellets. The most prominent innovation, however, was the addition of a long pennant, fluttering astern of the sword, which, except on some of the earlier coins of Calais, was used to distinguish the nobles and half-nobles of that mint. On reverses the only variety occurs in the central panel. Early (pre-pennant) Calais nobles and halves are differentiated from those of London by having the mint initial instead of the king's in the panel. Quarters of the 1350s still often have *e* in the panel, but thereafter the initial was usually replaced by a little ornament, generally a lis or pellet, more suited to the limited central space on the smallest gold coin. In the early Treaty coinage some experimental designs, involving a cross potent and annulets, were used on quarter-nobles but they are rather ugly and were soon discontinued. In the case of quarters struck at Calais there is often no evident means of distinguishing them from London's.

While the design of the small silver continued unchanged after 1351 there was no recent English precedent for the groat and none at all for the halfgroat. Edward I's groat had set the pattern for larger silver of having two concentric circles of inscription on the reverse, but Edward III introduced a motto in the outer one instead of a continuation of the royal titles from the obverse. *Posui Deum Adiutorem Meum* (I have made God my helper – cf. Psalm LIV, 4) was to remain in use on larger silver coins for more than two hundred years. An early experiment to replace the group of three pellets in each angle of the cross with a crown, reminiscent of the type already used on Edward III's base sterlings for Aquitaine, was quickly abandoned, perhaps in order to avoid any implication of reduced fineness. As already established on pence, the long cross on the reverse had plain patty ends, and not the elaborate floral form used by Edward I. On the obverse a large crowned head within a tressure of nine arcs, pointed with trefoils, was preferred to the sterling-sized head in a quadrilobe of 1279. The design of Edward III's groat, replicated in miniature on the halfgroat, was not in fact a complete innovation. Between 1337 and 1345 a monetary alliance between Luxemburg, Namur and Liège had produced a common type of *demi-gros* on which a crowned head, based on that of the English sterling, had already been surrounded by a fleured tressure, and coupled with a double-inscription reverse (although the cross extended only through the inner ring).

Two hoards buried towards 1360, from Beaumont (Cumbria) and Durham (1930), contained substantial representation of the coinage of the 1350s. Although few other finds of silver coins buried in the second half of the fourteenth century are on record, there are enough surviving coins from the 1350s and 1360s in good condition to suggest that more hoards from this period are likely to have been discovered long ago. Much of the material, however, especially from the 1370s onwards, comes from hoards buried after the weight reduction of 1412, and is often clipped to the lower weight as well as being worn from decades of active circulation. The 1897 find at Balcombe, Sussex, contained twelve gold nobles together with more than seven hundred silver coins, mostly of Edward III and Richard II, but hoards confined to gold are of more frequent occurrence. For example, 200 gold coins of Edward III were found at East Raynham, Norfolk, in 1910, and 131, ending with Richard II, at Bredgar, Kent, in 1940. Gold was obviously a more convenient medium for hoarding and seems quickly to have replaced silver as a store of wealth. The East Raynham nobles, for example, would have been the monetary equivalent of 16,000 pence, and so greater in value than almost all the silver hoards of the pre-gold era. Foreign gold coins, unconverted into English, also played some part in the monetary stock at this period, although the hoards in which Flemish nobles have been present are few.

Scottish coins are also sometimes found in English hoards, although far less so than had been the case in the sterling period. In 1355 Edward III issued a proclamation against the latest Scottish pence on the grounds of their deficient weight. Up to this time Scottish coins had more or less matched the English standard and circulated freely in England. David II remained in custody at the English court until 1357, but a few months after his release he initiated a reform of the Scottish coinage, including groats and halfgroats designed as equivalent to the English, and Edward accepted that the two should again be interchangeable. But a weight reduction in 1367 and another under Robert III (1390-1406) led to further restriction on the currency of Scottish coins, and by the end of the century they were only to pass in England for half their nominal value. Ironically, however, the groats of Robert III, whose reign coincided with a period of extreme shortage of bullion for English coinage, are very common; but the need for an upward valuation of silver, as had been advocated by the Chancellor, Michael de la Pole, in 1385, was still not recognised in England. In the second half of the fourteenth century many other European countries reacted to the scarcity of silver by reducing the weight or the fineness of their coinage, and debasement of the silver was widely adopted particularly for minor coins which would otherwise have been too small. Alloy was first added to Scottish pence and halfpence in the 1390s, but it did not prevent them from finding their way into English currency, as evidenced by the find from Skipton Bridge, Yorkshire, or the fifteenth century hoard from Attenborough in Northamptonshire. When the Commons petitioned Henry IV in 1402 for more small change they referred to people of necessity using Scottish coins and 'Galley halfpennies', the latter being petty currency (principally Venetian *soldini*) brought by sea from Italy, despite the repeated efforts of the authorities to exclude them.

Classification

During the 1360s, while the Peace of Brétigny remained in force, Edward dropped the French title from his great seal and his coins, which thus refer only to England, Ireland and Aquitaine. On those of the 1350s, prior to the treaty, and of the period from 1369, after it was broken, the claim to France is regularly recorded (when the inscription is long enough) and Lawrence conveniently labelled these three phases of the light coinage of Edward III, by reference to Brétigny, as Pre-Treaty, Treaty and Post-Treaty. The Pre-Treaty series includes the heavy output of the recoinage and constitutes by far the greatest proportion of the coinage of 1351-77. Although the Treaty issues of the 1360s are much less abundant than those of the Pre-Treaty period, they substantially outnumber the Post-Treaty coinages, as the mint increasingly struggled to obtain supplies of bullion. Lawrence's fundamental study contains extensive lists of varieties of all denominations, and a general discussion of the characteristics of the coins of each of the main periods. But he did not always provide a satisfactory subdivision within the periods, and it was left to Potter to produce a more detailed analysis. Potter's two important papers on the gold and silver of this reign provide not only considerable refinement of Lawrence's scheme but also modification of it in certain respects.

English coins of the second half of the fourteenth century are more austere in appearance than those of the fifteenth, reflecting the plainer idiom of high Gothic. Until the 1390s, the letters are bold and clean, with straight-sided uprights, and now generally made from single punches. Roman *N* (often reversed, or consisting simply of two *I*s without a bar) outscores the Gothic form. Stops are mostly annulets in the 1350s and 1360s, saltires almost invariably thereafter. For a mass-produced coinage the dies are generally well made, and when dies were not readily available from London for the bishops' mints the deficiencies of local workmanship are very obvious.

The reign of Edward III saw the introduction of small symbols or heraldic devices into the design of some coins, hitherto virtually confined to the marks of particular issuers or mints, such as the cross moline of Bishop Bek at Durham, or the bear's head at Berwick. The earliest was a crown instead of a cross at the head of the inscription, on a group of dies of the mid-1350s, but later various additional marks were incorporated into the type. These take the form of annulets, crescents, crosses, fleurs, escallops, lions and suchlike, which are sometimes found on or behind the rudder on nobles and halves, above the shield on quarter-nobles, and on the king's breast on silver. They are not at this period generally found in the inscriptions, but in the fifteenth century they were to come into regular use as mintmarks, stops and ornaments in the field. Much speculative ingenuity has been applied to explanations of their meaning. In the mint indenture of June 1361 there occurs for the first time a requirement that the master should place a mark on all coins produced under his authority so that they could be recognized thereafter. Since this indenture also contains reference to the trial of the pyx, a sample test of weight and fineness that was meant to be held quarterly, Lawrence argued that it might be possible to identify privy-marks (including minor characteristics such as broken letter punches as well as the more obvious symbols) which had been used to differentiate the coins minted in successive quarterly periods. This theory was to have a profound and misleading effect on the approach of other scholars to the classification of late medieval English coins, since the indenture itself makes no connection between the trial of the pyx and the master's privy mark, and subsequent study has shown that the two were unrelated. Symbols, broken letters, punctuation and so on are nevertheless of value in arranging the coins in sequence, and connecting those of different denominations, even though the significance of particular marks may remain obscure.

The arrangement of the coins of Richard II and Henry IV is much less straightforward than that of Edward III's. Since modern techniques of classification were developed no student has attempted a comprehensive study of the coins of either reign. The essential problem is that there is no consistent relationship between different denominations, and particularly so between the metals. This has led to disconnected studies of gold and silver, and the devisal of separate classifications. For Richard II Potter has dealt thoroughly with the larger silver and Purvey with the pence and fractions. However, Webb Ware's detailed work on Richard's gold remains unpublished, although his arrangement is adopted in the Schneider *Sylloge*. Henry IV's heavy gold coinage was listed and classified by Blunt, with Potter again covering the silver. For the purposes of the present work the coinage of Richard II has been divided into two periods, the first including issues of the earlier part of the reign (to c.1390) during which the lettering is straight-sided in the manner of Edward III's, and the second the issues of the 1390s when indented lettering was introduced. Within these periods there are considerable problems in co-ordinating varieties of different denominations, since their production was often uneven. For example, in the early 1390s there was quite an extensive coinage of gold and halfpence, but very few halfgroats. The picture is further complicated by differential practice in the use of the French title. After the truce of 1389 the French claim was dropped from dies for nobles and half-nobles, and perhaps for halfgroats, but not for groats. When, presumably following the king's French marriage in 1396, halfgroat dies were again produced late in the reign with the English title only, this form was not adopted on the gold; and although groat dies without the French title are known to have been made at this stage (since they were brought out of storage to be altered for use by Henry IV in 1412), they do not appear to have been used in Richard's own reign. The study of Henry IV's heavy coinage is further complicated by its rarity. Although a progression of varieties can be worked out for the gold, so little silver was struck at London that very few dies were needed (except for halfpence) and no comparable sequence can be defined.

The Pre-Treaty Period, 1351-61

Lawrence divided the Pre-Treaty issues into seven series or groups, labelled A-G, according to differences in lettering and the form of the initial mark. Although series was his preferred term, this perhaps reflects his concept of an orderly system of privy-marking, since it carries with it some implication of regularity and thoroughness that the material does not in fact exhibit. Furthermore, the sub-groups within group G could not sensibly be called sub-series. For these reasons the term group has here been used. Lawrence's main divisions remain valid, although the groups themselves are patchy and inconsistent in content. Thus, the only true coins of group A are pennies; some groups are represented for some denominations in gold only by obverse dies (half-nobles of B and C), or only by reverses (nobles and halves of A, quarter-nobles of C and nobles of D); groups D and F are common for silver but very rare for gold; and so on. Dies were withdrawn when they needed replacement and not because they had become obsolete for some administrative reason. What we see, therefore, is a normal die-chain for each denomination, with extensive muling at points of transition from one group to the next, but also a number of cases where the groups involved are not adjacent. Because of the greater longevity of obverse dies, the reverse die of a mule between groups is usually later than the obverse, but in some cases the converse is true, while in others the existence of mules both ways must indicate a period during which the dies of two groups were in concurrent use (the A/C and C/A mule pennies are a case in point). Typical of the normal mules between consecutive groups are D/E and F/G groats and halves, all of which are reasonably common. Mules with the obverse later than the reverse are generally much rarer: E/D and G/F London groats, for example (although at York, which received a few batches of dies rather than gradual replenishment, E/D groats are commoner than true coins of group D). The longer-range mules, such as C/E and E/G, tend to be very rare in any denomination.

The principal defining characteristics of the seven Pre-Treaty groups are summarized in the next table. Four of them, C, D, E and G, are very large, and in silver all of them except group A contain numerous minor varieties of inscription or other features, as recorded in Lawrence's lists. In a later study Potter investigated the internal structure of the main groups in more detail, basing his conclusions largely on epigraphical changes and the evidence of dies involved in muling. Group A, consisting of dies of only three denominations, represents a moment of transition from the pre-1351 coinage; group B is a short and experimental phase of the new coinage proper, before it settled down into an established pattern with group C; and group F, which belongs to the middle of the Pre-Treaty period and effectively separates the recoinage issues from the long group G, is remarkable for having a crown as the initial mark instead of the usual cross. Until group F variation of detail within the groups was largely incidental, the result of replacement of worn or broken punches, but with group G the position altered. Small marks of differentiation, undoubtedly intentional, were introduced into the design, providing a basis for subdivision of the group into consecutive varieties. On the London silver of group G an annulet or saltire is usually found within one of the groups of pellets on the reverse. Since this mark could occur in any of the four quarters, and in some sub-groups did so, Lawrence believed that it was a privy-mark designed to distinguish dies used in each of four pyx periods in the mint's accounting year; but even if the theory of quarterly privy-marking were valid, neither the pattern of die-links nor the tendency of the mark to be most frequently in the first quarter earlier in group G, and in the fourth quarter later, would be consistent with it.

London Pre-Treaty Groups and Mules

	Noble	Half-Noble	Quarter-Noble	Groat	Half-Groat	Penny	Half-Penny	Farthing
A	R	R				X		
A/C						m		
B	X	O	X	X	X			
B/A	m	m						
B/C	m			m	m	m		
B/D				m				
B/E			m					
B/G			m					
C	X	O	R	X	X	X		
C/A		m				m		
C/B				m	m			
C/D	m				m	m		
C/E	m	m				m		
D	R			X	X	X		
D/C				m				
D/E				m	m			
E	X	X	R	X	X	X	X	X
E/D				m	m			
E/F	m			m	m	m		
E/G	m			m	m	m	m	
F	X			X	X	X	O	
F/C						m		
F/E	m			m	m	m		
F/G	m			m	m	m	m	
G	X	X	X	X	X	X	R	X
G/E	m		m					m
G/F	m			m				

X – true coins; m – mules; O – obverse only; R – reverse only.

A reasonably close chronology for successive groups can be established on the basis of the mint accounts in relation to surviving coins, and of the activity of the royal mint opened at York for the recoinage. Groups A and B belong to a brief period immediately following the appointment of the new masters in June 1351. Silver coins of group C

Characteristics of Pre-Treaty Groups

Group	Initial Mark	Lettering	Approximate Dates
A	Neat cross patty	Large. Gothic *n*.	Summer 1351
B	Square cross	Small, composite. Open *c* and *e*, Roman *M* and *N*. Wedge-tailed *R*.	Summer 1351
C	Square cross	As B, but closed *c* and *e* and rounded *m*.	Late 1351 – c. end 1352
D	Square cross (breaking)	Integral letters. *R* with curled tail. Often *c* for *e*.	1353, to summer
E	Plain cross of four triangles	*R* often with forked tail. *c* and *e* often broken at lower front	1353-5
F	Crown	*c* and *e* unbroken or broken at top.	1356
G	Thick cross patty with concave ends	Some with *c* and *e* sliced at top (Gb-c) or at bottom (Gd). Later, *e* with bar protruding (Gg) or open (Gh).	Late 1356 – early 1361

are so much more plentiful than those of group B that dies with group C lettering must have become available at most within two or three months. Group D was in issue in the second quarter of 1353 when Archbishop Thoresby received his first dies, and a few dies of this group were among those ordered for the royal mint at York in July 1353. Most of group D would fall within the mint account from November 1352 to May 1353, when output of silver coin remained very high but little gold was minted, consistently with the abundance of group D silver and the rarity of its gold. This would place the end of group C, the silver of which is about twice as numerous as that of group D, toward the end of 1352. Some dies of group E went in the first batch for York royal, and there must have been some overlap, at least in their availability, of D and E dies in the summer of 1353. London groats and gold of group E are very common, in line with large totals of both minted from 1353 to 1355. The rarity of nobles of group F, of which the silver is quite plentiful, accords with the sharp decline in gold coined during 1356. Group G might thus run from late 1356 to the end of the Pre-Treaty period, the quantities of surviving coin reflecting the increased minting of gold from 1357, and steady but lower issues of silver from that date, as recorded in the accounts. Consistent with this dating is the revival of the archbishop's mint at York in February 1357 with pence of early group G. The treaty drafted at Brétigny during the summer of 1360 was agreed by the two kings at Calais in October, but not ratified by Parliament until January 1361; and the new coinage without the French title, which replaced the Pre-Treaty series, was probably the result of the indenture of 5 March 1361 with Walter dei Bardi.

Edward III – Henry IV

INITIAL MARKS OF THE PRE-TREATY PERIOD

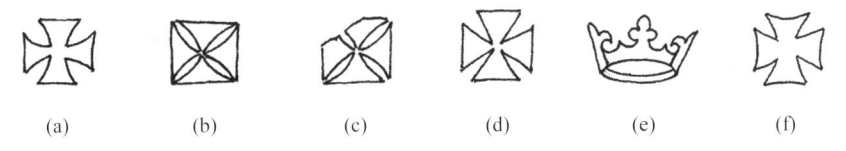

(a) Cross patty, group A; (b) Square cross, groups B-D; (c) Square cross broken, group D; (d) Group E cross; (e) Crown, group F; (f) Group G cross.

With the possible exception of group F, with its crown mintmark, the main groups as now defined are only of relevance to modern students and did not in their time relate to particular accounting periods or masterships. Potter argued that the crown of group F could have been the mark of his namesake, William Potter of Ipswich, who was master from May 1355 to January 1356, but other evidence suggests that this group is more likely to belong to 1356, in which case the crown may perhaps have been used under Potter's successor, Hugh de Wychyngham, whose mastership from January to October 1356 covered a period of appropriately high silver and low gold output. The first occurrence of halfpence, in group E, could then be seen as a consequence of the new authority to coin this denomination included in Potter's indenture of May 1355.

The intensive reminting of old coin involved an average of more than £6,000 of silver a month at London from June 1351 to September 1354. That the bulk of the recoinage had by then been achieved is illustrated by the figures for York which show greatly reduced activity in its last few months. Gold output was more irregular: there was no large stock of old native gold coin for reminting. An early burst during the first year of the recoinage (1351/2) and a further peak in 1353/4 were each followed by decline, but from 1357, while silver coinage was much lower, the minting of gold again increased strongly, perhaps reflecting the benefits of recent military success in France.

Almost half the gold coin minted between 1351 and 1411 was produced during the 1350s. For much of the Pre-Treaty period the noble was virtually the only denomination struck in gold. Until the late 1350s (group G) the junior gold is very rare. So few dies were made for half- and quarter-nobles that mules across several groups are not infrequent – the obverse die of the B/G quarter-noble must have been at least five years old. As nobles and halves have no initial mark on their obverse, their classification depends largely on their lettering which was from the same punches as used for groats.

In silver, the Pre-Treaty figure of £389,000 constituted an overwhelming majority (more than 85 per cent.) of the total recorded in the London accounts during the period of the 72 gr. groat, and two-thirds of this occurred during the first three years of the recoinage as large quantities of old silver coin were reminted. Hoards show that groats and halfgroats of the 1350s retained a material presence in the currency well into the fifteenth century. The groat was the mainstay of the coinage throughout, although very large quantities of halfgroats were struck during the recoinage (especially group C). In the later 1350s halfgroats were coined on a much reduced scale. Many pre-1351 pennies remained in circulation and that lessened the need for new coins of this denomination. After the recoinage, such new pence as were produced came more from Durham and York than from London. The archbishop's mint at York now began to assume a much greater role in the coinage than in the earlier Edwardian period. Whereas under Edward I the archbishop had only been allowed to have his own coinage when a royal mint was in operation in the city, the position was now diametrically reversed: henceforward he could only have his mint when the king did not, and Thoresby's coinage was therefore interrupted when the royal mint was opened for recoinage in 1353.

Larger coins gave scope for longer inscriptions. Nobles, half-nobles and groats have the king's name (without its Latin ending) followed by *Dei Gratia* and his titles as King of England and France and Lord of Ireland, all much abbreviated. Quarter-nobles usually omit *Dei Gratia* but often retain the Irish title, while halfgroats omit both but read *Edwardus* in full. Pennies also have *Edwardus* but only include the English title, plus sometimes a redundant &. Misspellings are uncommon (e.g. *Edwad, Eward, Edvard*, etc.), but the strange form *Lomdom*, which is found on a considerable number of dies from group D to early group G, may not be accidental, although if not its significance is obscure. Equally curious are certain broken letters (usually *c* and *e*) which occur in groups E to G, although the idea that these were deliberately mutilated, as some have supposed, rather than merely damaged, remains speculative. When the corner of a letter has been sliced away, it may be that this was done to tidy up a punch which had become defective in that area.

An undoubtedly intentional form of marking takes the form of a small lis placed by one of the lions on the reverse of gold coins of the Pre-Treaty and early Treaty periods. The lis is very occasionally omitted on nobles, more often on halves. Although sometimes found on a quarter-noble, it does not normally occur on this denomination – there is scarcely space for it. For more than forty years after 1361 it is absent, but under Henry IV the practice was revived (although with different symbols) and continued intermittently during the next two reigns. The occurrence of these marks on several occasions over nearly a hundred years shows that they cannot have been used to designate separate issues. More probably they relate to some system of checking or authorizing the issue of dies for the mint's most valuable products, although why they were used at some periods but not at others is a mystery.

Group A

The first of the new dies for the 1351 recoinage were for denominations already in issue before the reduction in weight, and so did not involve groats or halfgroats, which needed a new design. The lettering of group A, which is large and bold, includes Gothic *n* and is similar in general appearance to that on the preceding heavier coinage, although with the *A* now unbarred and *h* with an elegant curled tail. The initial cross is neat patty. In gold group A is represented only by a few reverse dies for nobles and half-nobles, in silver by pence of London and Durham. All are rare. The noble dies are only found paired with obverses of group B, the half-noble dies with obverses of groups B and C. After these no further reverse dies for half-nobles were made before group E. As on the pre-1351 gold, stops are double saltires and the nobles omit the word *Autem*. Little care seems to have been taken with either denomination to insert the *e* in the central panel in an upright position.

London pennies of the recoinage are easily identifiable since those of group A, and of later groups up to E, have an annulet within each group of pellets on the reverse. London pennies of true group A are perhaps rarer than mules with group C. London obverses have double annulet stops; the reverses have either the same, or double saltires, or none, and some of them have a small annulet, presumably a mark of identification, above the *T* or *A* of *tas*. At Durham old dies of group XVI remained available and are muled both ways with the new dies of group A. Even though the weight of the penny was only reduced by ten per cent, there is a perceptible difference in size between the pre-1351 dies and those of the new coinage. Like the last of the Durham reverses of group XVI (d6), the group A dies have a crozier at 90° and a central hollow on the cross (although without a pellet in it), and they also perpetuate the anomalous use of *Villa* instead of *Civitas*. They do, however, introduce new features of group A in the form of double saltire stops on both sides, and annulets between the groups of pellets as at London. An English form of the mint-name (*Durrem*) is now found for the first time since the death of Bishop Bek forty years earlier.

Dies of group A can only have been produced for a very short time, perhaps even days, before the new lettering of group B was introduced. An explanation for the almost immediate replacement of a serviceable set of letter punches could be that the group A fount was too large to be used on reverses of the new groat and halfgroat, with their two circles of inscription, or indeed for the smaller obverse dies of the lighter noble, without restricting the space available for its complex design.

Groups B and C

The characteristic initial cross of groups B and C (continued, often in a damaged state, into group D) is formed of four concave-sided wedges which meet at the corners, giving the impression of a square with four narrow indented ovals meeting at the centre. When worn this mark often looks like a solid square. Except in the inner circle of the reverse on groats, where they are larger, the letters of groups B and C are small and neat, and usually of composite form, made up from two or more punches, the *R*, for instance, consisting of an upright, a crescent and a wedge. A shapely and integral *S*, however, is introduced in group C. Dies of group B have the letters *e* and *c* open and a square Roman *M*, those of group C a rounded *m* with closed *e* and *c* (except in *Civitas*). *N* in both groups is of the Roman form, but usually reversely barred. A new symbol for *&*, in the form of a barred 7, was now introduced and remained in use throughout the Pre-Treaty period. Stops are normally single annulets. Coins of group B are generally rare, those of group C very common. Group B dies are very carefully made, but there is some deterioration in the workmanship of groats and halfgroats as group C progresses.

Nobles of group B are scarce, and mules with reverses of A or C more so. Group C nobles, however, are plentiful as true coins, but although C obverses are also found in combination with reverses of groups B, D and E the first two of these three mules are very rare. In the case of half-nobles no true coins of B or C exist, the rare coins from obverse dies of these two groups having reverses of group A. Of the quarter-nobles there are true coins of group B, but no new obverses were then made until group G, and there are B/G mules as well as B/C and B/E. All these quarter-noble mules are of great rarity. Nobles and halves of these two groups have three ropes fore and aft, but there is some diversity in the ornaments on the ship's side, with four or more lis and three lions alternating and the lis often in pairs. Gold of this period usually shows four whole lis in the first quarter of the royal arms, and three in the fourth, but there are often also small inverted crescents at the edges representing the inner foils of truncated fleurs.

There is considerable variety in the inscriptions on gold of group B, constituting a gradual transition from earlier forms to the normal readings of the Pre-Treaty period. The smaller lettering on group B and C nobles allowed a fuller obverse reading, beginning *E/dward Dei Gra* instead of the previous *Ed/war D Gra*, although a few early group B dies still have *Ed/* above the bowsprit as before. On halves, however, the pre-1351 form *Edwar D Gra* continued in group B (once with the old *Ed/* break), but this was changed to *E/dwar Dei G* in group C. Whereas group A noble reverses had read *Ihc* and *Transiens*, as pre-1351, from group B onwards the spelling *Tranciens* is normal, while in group B *Ihc* is usually replaced by *Ihe(s)*, or in group C sometimes by *Ihes(u)*. Like earlier nobles, one of group B omits *Autem*; this left space for *Am* (for *Amen*) to be added at the end. From group B onwards, the last letter or two of *Medium, Illorum* and *Ibat* are frequently dropped; during group C *Per* gives way to *P* and this continues in later groups. One group B quarter-noble die reads *Edwar R Angl*, as pre-1351, but others have *Edwar D G Rex*, and sometimes omit the Irish title; an abbreviation of *Amen* occurs on some of the reverses.

Groats and halves of group B are quite rare; but there are also several B/C mules (and even a few C/B groats), indicating that a substantial number of C reverses must have been issued while B obverses were still available. An experimental early groat of group B has crowns instead of pellets in the quarters of the reverse cross, and on another there are traces of crowns underneath the groups of pellets. A few early groat dies of group B have pellet stops or none, but otherwise annulets were invariable in this group. Most B groats read *Edwar D Gra*, but *Edward* is then found and, on some B/C mules, *Gra* is shortened to *G*. Reverses of group B groats and halfgroats have the inscription variously distributed between the four segments; the groats always have *Meum* in full, but from group C onwards it is reduced to *Meu*. Another feature of B groats is that the top two cusps of the tressure are fleured above the crown, a practice which was discontinued in the course of group C. Halfgroats, however, show a less consistent pattern, with the top cusps usually fleured, but sometimes not, in both the groups. Extensive minor varieties of reading are found in the abundant group C silver. The letter *A* often has a small hook at the bottom of its right limb. Groats read *Dei G, Di G* or *D G*, probably in that order.

Halfgroats of group C are by a long way the commonest of this denomination from the fourteenth century. In the second Reigate find there were twice as many halves as groats of group C. The silver coins of group C are far more numerous compared with those of group B than is the case with gold, and new (group C) dies for silver must have been needed much sooner than for nobles.

No penny dies were made with the open *c* and *e* of group B; those of group A must have sufficed for the time being. When pence reappear in group C, there are mules both ways with group A at London, mostly with the earlier reverse. Bishop Hatfield's dies, which no longer have annulets between the pellets, now again read *Civitas* (with his crozier, but without indentation in the centre of the cross) and the mint name reverts to a Latin form (*Dunelmie*). Although on groats and halfgroats the mint name precedes *Civitas* until group E, and sometimes beyond, the position of the crozier before *Civitas* implies that this was taken as the start of the inscription on Durham pence from group C onwards, as it had been in the sterling period.

LETTER FORMS IN PRE-TREATY GROUPS

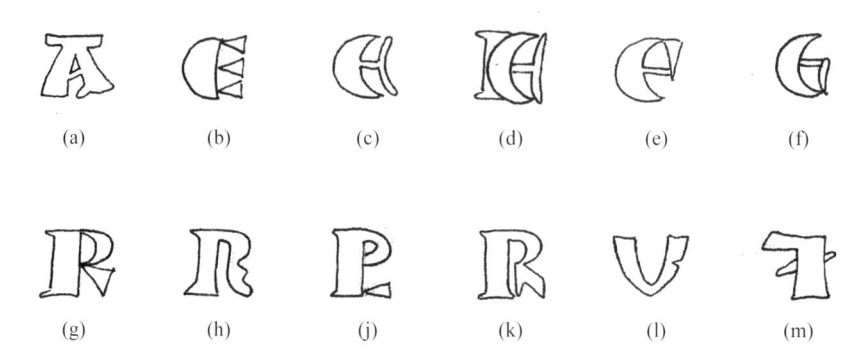

(a) Hooked *A*, group C; (b) Open *e*, group B; (c) Closed *e*, group C;
(d) Squared *E*, groups D-E; (e) Letter *e* defective at foot, group E; (f) Broken *e* of group F;
(g) Wedge-tailed *R*, groups B-C; (h) *R* with curled tail, groups D-E;
(j) New *R* with horizontal wedge, group E; (k) *R* with forked tail, group E;
(l) Nicked *V*, group E; (m) Symbol for &, groups B-G.

Group D

Group D differs from groups B and C principally in the lettering, which is heavier and plainer, with thick uprights, small serifs and a new *R* with a curled tail replacing the wedge-tailed letter of B and C. Like other letters, this *R* was now put in from a single punch. During group D the punch for the square cross patty began to break at one corner, and then down the side. Lawrence relied upon the broken initial cross to define his series D, but this is not really satisfactory, partly because the damage was gradual, but also because the broken cross occurs far more frequently on reverses than on obverses. Furthermore, *pace* Lawrence, there are some dies with the new lettering of group D on which the cross is still intact, and it therefore makes more sense, as Potter suggested, to define the boundary between groups C and D on the basis of the change of letter fount. In this respect, therefore, Lawrence's 'series' D and group D as here defined do not fully coincide. Earlier dies of group D have *N* reversely barred, as in groups B and C, but this soon gave way to an unbarred *N* consisting simply of two uprights. Other epigraphic features are the frequent use of *c* for *e,* and a straight-backed *E* (not a clean letter, but a compromise between the Roman and Gothic forms) found in the king's name on some London and York halfgroats and Durham pence. Since the new integral letters of group D were slightly smaller than the composite letters of group C, there was sometimes space at the end of the obverse inscription: on groats this might be filled up by putting annulets between the letters of *hyb*, while on pence the & symbol was often, rather anomalously, added on its own after *Angli*, almost as if it had the meaning of *etcetera*. The use of *M* (Roman) for one or both *N*s in *London* occurs on several dies, and another oddity, on one groat die, is an inverted *F* in *Franc* (both these features recur in later groups). More generally, the dies of group D are often of rather less careful workmanship than their predecessors.

London silver of group D is abundant, although less so than group C. Groats and halfgroats are frequently muled with group E, groats only with the later reverse, halfgroats both ways. An exceptional groat combines a D reverse with an obverse of group B, but the only groat mules with the previous group have the earlier reverse (D/C); one of these rare coins is from the only recorded D obverse die with fleurs on the cusps above the crown. The only other D/C mule noted is a Durham penny, the more normal forward combination (C/D) being found at London of both pence and halfgroats. From group D to group G there are some Durham coins with irregular busts, but since the dies in question seem to have normal lettering their crude busts may have been the result of local refurbishment.

Groats, halfgroats and pence from the York royal mint between July 1353 and May 1355 are of groups D and E, the latter being much the more plentiful. There are also abundant E/D groat mules and a few E/D halfgroats. The rare York groat of group D is easily recognisable from the omission of the *G* of *D G*. Of the 33 reverse dies for York groats in the Record Office, seven were of group D, nineteen of group E and seven indecipherable: some of the first batch of eighteen of these dies supplied in July 1353 would therefore seem to have been of group E. In May 1353 the new archbishop, John Thoresby, had had his order for dies and there are a few York pennies of group D with a quatrefoil on the reverse the dies for which were presumably delivered to Thoresby before his mint was suspended for the royal coinage in July. Although Thoresby's surviving pence of this group are generally in poor condition, the broken state of the square cross is clear, as is appropriate for an issue near the end of the currency of group D.

Very few new dies for gold were evidently needed at this period. Group D is represented only by two noble reverses muled with obverses of group C; both of these C obverse dies survived further, to be paired later also with reverses of group E.

Group E

The defining feature of this large group is a new and slightly smaller initial cross, consisting of four triangular wedges with straight sides merged to join at the centre. Some characteristic new letters also appear. The *R* of group D was soon replaced, first by an *R* with the tail horizontal, at the foot, like a *P* with a wedge below it, then (and mostly) with a thin vertical line inside the tail, which thus has a forked appearance. Some early coins have a reverse-barred *N*, but it is more usually unbarred. On many groats there is a cut near the middle of the outer side of the right stroke of the letter *V*. The use of *c* for *e*, as in group D, is still sometimes found. The squared *E* and inverted *F* noted under group D also again occur, on some early groats and pennies of London (the inverted *F* also on a few early nobles). Later in the group the letters *c* and *e* are commonly found weak or broken away at the lower front.

Nobles of this group are very common but half-nobles, whether as true coins or as C/E mules, are extremely rare and quarters exist only as mules with obverse dies of B or G. Nobles occur muled with obverses of groups C and F or, very rarely, with later reverses (E/F and E/G). There is a gradual deterioration of workmanship in the obverse design of the nobles, which show a reduction from four quatrefoils to three on the sterncastle; and then a distortion of the shape of the ship, with the sterncastle tilted inwards and the forecastle extended upwards so that it sometimes excludes the forward rigging and the bowsprit. Stops on nobles are at first annulets, later sometimes saltires (these occurring much more rarely on reverses than on obverses); on halves, saltires; and on quarters, annulets. No half-noble reverse dies had been made since group A, and group E reverses read *Rurore* for *Furore* and *Arouas* for *Arguas,* presumably copying the curious letter *F*, with a front stroke like an *R*, and the almost circular *G*, like an *O*, that occur on group A dies, as well as their Gothic *n*. The mis-spellings *Ghloria* or *Gahlori* on the quarters are less obviously explicable.

On the silver the stops are always annulets. Sometimes they occur in curious places – between the *R* and *D* of *Edward* or the *F* and *R* of *Franc*. The mint name still normally comes first (under *Posui Deum*), but on a few groats *Civitas* precedes it for the first time. Groats of group E are very common. At London D/E groats and halfgroats are also plentiful but E/D mules, although common for York groats, are rare of both denominations. Two very odd London obverse groat dies, one at least of which is coupled with orthodox group E reverses, have a large head set low down and fleurs on the cusps above the crown; they are presumably unofficial, and perhaps point to irregular activity by moneyers with access to mint equipment. Some London groats have a lis instead of a fleur either on the breast alone, or on the other cusps as well. Another has a tressure of eight arcs only. One variety of York halfgroat also has a lis on the breast, another has ten arcs to the tressure. Overall, York halfgroats are plentiful. Various odd spellings are found on the silver of group E. *Edvard* occurs on several groat dies and halfgroats usually omit the *N* of *Fra(n)ci*. *Tas* is sometimes represented by *tao, tor,* or *tos.* As in group D, *N* in *London* may be replaced by an *M*.

London pennies of group E are scarcer than the larger silver. Some still have an annulet within each group of pellets on the reverse, but later in the group these were dropped. The only London mule with an earlier die has an obverse of group C. York and Durham pennies often have *&,* or occasionally four annulets in quatrefoil, after *Angli*. One York die reads *Edward* instead of the normal *Edwardus*, creating space for *Fra* to be added. London and Durham dies are muled both ways with group F, but York royal was closed during the currency of this group and its accounts end in May 1355. Thoresby's coinage was not, however, resumed until 1357, in group G.

Rare halfpence and farthings, identifiable by their lettering, were produced at London in this group, after an interval since the 1340s. Gothic *n* in *London* and on the obverse of the halfpenny probably reflects pre-1351 models. For the first time in the Pre-Treaty period, provision for the halfpenny was included in the indenture of May 1355. The word used is *maille*, normally meaning a half-denomination, but it could also refer more generally to a fractional coin (e.g. the French *maille tierce*, one third of the *gros*), and may therefore have been understood as authority for minting farthings as well.

Group F

This group is remarkable for its very distinctive mintmark, a crown instead of the usual cross. Apart from the two brief preludial groups A and B, the silver coins of group F are much scarcer than those of the rest of the Pre-Treaty groups, and it cannot have lasted for as much as a year. The use of the crown was such a prominent departure from the norm that it is natural to associate it with some administrative development at the mint; and this lends some credence to the idea that, although the dies made for the bishop of Durham also carried this mark, group F at London could represent the coinage of the mastership of Hugh de Wychingham for nine months in 1356. There is little gold of group F and this would fit with the much reduced output recorded for that period. Although there are quite a number of group F noble dies, several are only recorded on mules with group G, suggesting that the lower volume of gold coinage in 1356 was unexpected.

No half or quarter nobles of group F are known, neither true coins nor mules, and the nobles are very rare, particularly when muled either way with E or G. Obverse stops are saltires (sometimes also before *E/dward*), on the reverse annulets. Noble obverses, lacking the crown mark, can be separated from the later obverses of group E with saltire stops by the new lettering of group F. The *R* of group F has a curled tail with a flat bottom. The letters *e* and *c*, now rounded at the top and more elegant, are no longer broken at the bottom, but are either unbroken or with a break at the top. Obverses of group F nobles can be distinguished from those of early group G by the letter *X* which in group F, as before, is compact, with pointed feet, but which was replaced by a more splayed punch in group G.

On the silver, which is not rare, the stops are always annulets. Muled London groats with the reverse later than the obverse (E/F and F/G) are also quite plentiful, but those with the obverse later (F/E and G/F) are very rare. Halfgroats, notable for having lis instead of trefoils on the cusps, are not rare either as true coins or as F/G mules, but mules either way with group E are rare. A few groat and halfgroat dies still read *London Civitas*, but *Civitas London* is now more usual. London pennies, like the latest of group E, lack the annulets within the four groups of pellets, but F/G mules may be identified by an annulet in one quarter. There are pence of London and Durham muled both ways with group E, but except for E/F mules of Durham they are very rare. The London mules with group E were identified by Lawrence on the basis of the forms of the letter *c* on the reverse. The Durham mules are readily recognised by the change from *Dunelmie* in group E to an English spelling again (*Durene*) in group F. On some Durham obverses the bust is again of unusual appearance. Early London pennies have the same style of bust as in groups D and E, but a new and larger head was introduced during the course of this group. A unique halfpenny with the crown mark has a small annulet outside the pellets in one quarter, as found on some early dies of the next group, and so should be classified as an F/G mule.

Group G

This long and complicated group is well represented in all denominations from the noble to the penny, and comprises the varied issues of the later 1350s. The coins are most simply distinguished from those with a cross initial mark prior to group F by the shape of the cross, which in group G is patty with the outer ends concave, unlike the square cross of the early groups and thicker than the straight-ended cross patty of group E. Another convenient means of identification is the annulet within one of the groups of pellets on the reverse that occurs on many of the silver coins of group G. As in previous groups, the stops in the earlier stages of group G are annulets, but these gave way in due course to saltires, sooner on the gold than on the silver. Some early coins have Roman *N*s (barred either way), but the unbarred form is otherwise normal throughout. On the basis of the groats, Lawrence defined eight sub-groups, Ga to Gh, and allocated (in some cases speculatively) most of the gold and smaller silver to one or other of these, using letter forms or other small details where the main distinguishing features of the groats were not replicated. Muling between sub-groups is very frequent, and quite a number of sub-groups for different denominations are known only from muled obverses or reverses. Although collectively the coins are common, certain denominations of particular sub-groups are either rare or non-existent.

The main features of the eight sub-groups of the groats are summarized in simplified form in the table. Ga has an annulet below the bust, Gg and Gh a small cross on the

PRE-TREATY GROUP G GROATS: DISTINGUISHING FEATURES OF SUB-GROUPS

	LETTERING	OBVERSE	REVERSE	STOPS
Ga	Barred *N* on obv. and often on rev.	Annulet below bust. Top cusps fleured.	Annulet in one quarter.	Annulets
Gb	Unbarred *N*. *c* and *e* often sliced at top.	No breastmark. Top cusps unfleured.	Annulet in one quarter.	Annulets, very small on late dies
Gc	As Gb.	No obv. dies for groats.	Saltire in one quarter.	Saltires
Gd	*c* and *e* often broken at bottom.	Top cusps unfleured.	*ta.s.* Annulet in *tas* or *don* quarter.	Annulets
Ge	As Gf; no broken letters.	Point above crown. Top cusps fleured.	*t.a.s.* Annulet in *don* quarter.	Annulets
Gf	No broken letters.	Top cusps fleured.	*t.a.s.* Annulet in *don* quarter.	Annulets
Gg	*e* with central bar protruding.	Small cross or lis on breast. Top cusps fleured or not.	*t.a.s.* Annulet in *don* quarter.	Saltires
Gh	Open *e*.	Small cross or lis on breast. Top cusps fleured or not.	*t.a.s.* Annulet in *don* quarter.	Saltires

Edward III – Henry IV

breast. There is a point above the crown in Ge. The cusps above the crown are fleured in Ga, Ge and Gf, and sometimes in Gg and Gh. There is an annulet (occasionally omitted) in one quarter of the reverse in all sub-groups except Gc, which has a saltire quartermark instead. Saltire stops replace annulets in Gc and Gg-h. Before Gd there is no stop in the syllable *tas*, in Gd one pellet (*ta.s*) and in Ge to Gh two (*t.a.s*). This feature thus divides group G into an earlier (pre-pellet) phase, comprising Ga to Gc, and the pellet-marked phase covering the remainder of the group. In the pre-pellet phase the annulet (or saltire) is most often in the *Civi* quarter, from Gd onwards normally under *don*.

Groats of Ga and Gb are very common. Obverses of Gb differ from those of Ga not only in omitting the annulet below the bust, but also in having *N* unbarred and the top cusps unfleured. Conversely, two early Ga dies without annulet are not to be confused with Gb in view of their barred *N* and top fleurs. Rare mules between Ga and Gb can sometimes be identified by characteristics of reverse lettering: thus a sliced *e* indicates a reverse of Gb, while certain Ga reverses have letters with very pronounced serifs, especially in the inner legend. Early reverses of Ga, including all those muled with obverses of groups E and F, have the annulet in the *Civi* quarter. The annulet is occasionally placed outside the group of pellets or, very rarely, omitted altogether. It may vary in size, and one reverse (on an E/G mule) even has a small annulet under *Civi* and a large one under *don*. Early obverse dies of Ga have a correct Roman *N*, but this soon gave way to *N* reversed, and that in turn was replaced by the unbarred *N* at the start of Gb. The *N* in *London* also began with the barred form, correct and then reversed, but unbarred *N* was introduced on reverses well before the end of Ga. On reverse dies with barred *N* the annulet is always in the *Civi* quarter, but with the unbarred *N* it occurs in all four.

On groats of Gb the *N* is always unbarred, but the annulet stops and the letters *c* and *e* provide some evidence for sequence. In the later stages of Gb the normal annulets, with large central hole (as in Ga), were replaced by a smaller version, with thick ring and tiny hole, and soon after this the letters *c* and *e* are found with the upper left part sliced off. One Gb die has true fleurs-de-lis instead of trefoils on the cusps, but there are few other oddities in this sub-group, which saw the last occurrences both of the *Lomdom* reading and of *Lon* positioned under *Posui*. The latest groats of the pre-pellet phase have the annulets on the reverse replaced by saltires. Lawrence classified them as Gc (a sub-group represented by nobles, half-nobles and pence, with saltire stops both sides) but since their obverses, with annulet stops, are indistinguishable from Gb, and in many cases from the same dies, they ought properly to be classed as Gb/c mules, as Lawrence himself designated the equivalent annulet/saltire halfgroats. There is also a very rare mule with annulet below the bust (Ga/c). As in late Gb, the sliced *c* and *e* occur on many Gc dies. On reverses the annulet (Gb) and saltire (Gc) are found in each of the four quarters, or very rarely omitted.

VARIETIES OF LETTER *e* IN GROUP G

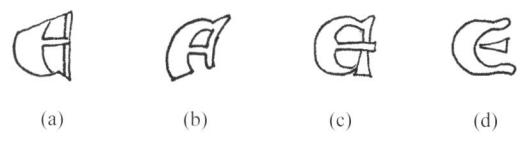

(a)   (b)   (c)   (d)

(a) Sliced *e* of group Gb-c; (b) Broken *e* of group Gd; (c) *e* with protruding bar, group Gg; (d) Open *e* of group Gh.

Groats of the scarcer pellet-marked phase begin with Gd, defined by their *ta.s* reverse. Annulets (of normal size) are restored as stops and as the quartermark which is now found only under *ta.s* or (more usually) *don*. True Gd groats are quite rare but Gd obverses, easily distinguished from the next two sub-groups by their unfleured top cusps, are more often found muled with later reverses. The letters *c* and *e*, rather broader than before, now often show a different form of damage from that seen in Gb and Gc, having the bottom broken away.

Henceforward London-made dies for groats and some other silver have the two pellets in *t.a.s*. Groats of Ge and Gf, which both have the top cusps fleured again, differ only in that the scarce Ge (for which there is no direct parallel in other denominations) has a small point above the central fleur of the crown. Both have the normal-sized annulet stops, and the quartermark is now under *don* for the rest of group G. Ge is in effect only a minor variety of Gf, placed earlier by Lawrence on the pattern of muling. On groats of Gg and Gh, which have a small cross (or lis) on the breast, saltires reappear as stops (but not for the quartermark). Dies of these two sub-groups differ in the punches for the letter *e* which in Gg often has the cross-bar protruding through the upright and in Gh is wide open at the front, a distinction conveniently applicable to reverses and to other denominations. Groats of Gg are rare, but there is also a number of mules with earlier sub-groups and with Gh. Of Gh itself only one true groat was known to Lawrence and Potter, and the variety remains extremely rare. The scarcity of these late varieties is consistent with the dwindling sums of silver coined in 1360/1.

Halfgroats of the pre-pellet phase generally reflect the pattern of the groats, but the pellet-marked phase is represented only by rare *t.a.s* reverses of Gf. Muling is frequent, but always with the reverse die the later. Like the groats, Ga and Gb halves have annulets as quartermark and stops, Ga with the annulet also below the bust. The only common halves of group G are those of Ga; there are also E/Ga and F/Ga mules, of which the latter are quite plentiful. On these mules the annulet (if present) is almost always in the *Civi* quarter, and sometimes outside the pellets. On later Ga reverses, as on groats, the annulet may occur in any of the four quarters. On the rare Gb halves the characteristic sliced *c* and *e* are often found, and these letters enable a Ga/b mule to be identified. No halfgroat obverse dies of group G were made after Gb, but reverses of Gc, with saltire stops, and of Gf with *t.a.s*, were used with obverses of both Ga and Gb. In Gb the annulet has been noted only in the *tas* and *don* quarters, but some dies omit it altogether, and there is no quartermark on any of the Gc or Gf halfgroat reverses.

London pence follow a course in some respects similar to the halfgroats – Ga common, later varieties progressively rarer. One early Ga die (reading *Angl*) started life without an annulet on the breast, but this was soon added. Most of the reverses paired with it also lack a quartermark. Another early penny die has an extra pellet outside the group in the *Civi* quarter, but most Ga reverses have the normal annulet quartermark, usually under *Civi*. Gb pence, without the annulet on breast, sometimes also lack a quartermark but when present the annulet is under *Civi*. The reverse of an F/Gb mule, without quartermark, is identifiable by the characteristic sliced *c* which occurs on some penny dies of Gb, as on other denominations. The same *c* also appears on some dies of Gc, the saltire quartermark and stops of which facilitate the recognition of mules. The only London pence of the pellet-marked phase of group G are in the form of rare mules Gc/f and Gf/g, the *t.a.s* reverse of the latter having a saltire before *Lon* to indicate Gg. As with halfgroats, the quartermark was discontinued on the later pence of both London and Durham.

Group G is only represented for halfpence by the reverse of the F/G mule, which has a tiny annulet beside the pellets under *Lon*. The farthing, however, exists as a true coin of group G, with an annulet within the pellets in one quarter. The *N* on group G farthing dies is Roman, and this assists in the identification of mules both ways with group E.

Bishop Hatfield's Durham pence of group G have a crozier before *Civi*, and from Ga to Gg they read *Dureme*. Ga and Gb have annulet stops, Ga with an annulet on the breast and sometimes in the *Civi* quarter, Gb without either. A variety of Ga with unbarred *N* instead of *m* in *Durene* may be a Ga/F mule. Others have a portrait of rougher work, like the irregular busts at Durham in the previous three groups. Gc, with saltire stops, includes a reverse with saltire also under *tas*, the only occurrence of this quartermark outside London. There follows a group of coins, apparently intermediate between the pre-pellet and pellet-marked phases, with annulet stops but no points in *tas*. One with the *e* broken at the bottom relates to Gd. On another, a pellet before *Dur* could perhaps be the equivalent of the point in *ta.s* at London and York. There is, however, no parallel elsewhere to a Durham variety with a large annulet on each shoulder. Thereafter, a normal sequence is resumed, Gf and Gg having points in *t.a.s*, respectively with annulet and saltire stops and their different forms of the letter *e*. A small trefoil on the breast on some pence of Gg echoes the breastmark on London groats and York pence of this sub-group. There must have been a continuing need for new Durham dies at the end of the period, since the Gh pence of this mint, with open *e* and the spelling *Durelmie*, are the least rare silver coins of this sub-group, and there is another even later variety (here Gj) which Lawrence illustrated but could not classify. This remarkable coin, without parallel elsewhere, reads *Rex Anglie Dn*, as if consciously avoiding the French title disclaimed in 1360. Its place in the series is confirmed by a mule combining the distinctive Gj reverse (with crozier before *tas*) with an obverse of the Treaty A coinage that followed in 1361.

The reopening of Archbishop Thoresby's mint, after his coinage had been interrupted by the establishment of the royal mint at York in 1353-5, followed an indenture made on 18 February 1357. Although listed by Lawrence as Ga, the first variety, without annulet on breast, has the small annulet stops associated with Gb. There is no quartermark on the reverse of this or any of the other York coins of the group. The only other York die of the pre-pellet phase is an obverse with saltire stops which, being muled with a *ta.s* reverse, is probably to be classified as Gc. York pence of Gd, with annulet stops again, usually also have an annulet on the breast as well as the point in *ta.s*. From about this time (when non-London varieties were also being produced at Durham) there are York pence from local dies, of coarse work and with unusual busts, the characteristics of which do not associate them with any particular London sub-group. The official sequence was then resumed with pellet-marked *t.a.s* dies of Gf (annulet stops) and Gg (saltire stops and breastmark), many of which have a small cross instead of the usual pellet in the centre of the quatrefoil. A large pellet in this position was, however, restored with Gh which, unlike its Durham counterpart, retains the points in *t.a.s*.

Although the extensive gold of group G does not closely relate in all respects to the silver, lettering, stops and other features enable most of the dies to be associated with corresponding sub-groups of the groats. The design on the nobles and halves is often stiffly rendered, as in group E. Only the nobles provide a full run of varieties, and the principal characteristics of the sub-groups are summarized in the following table. Lawrence's arrangement is not entirely satisfactory, in particular because it fails to draw a clear distinction between Ga, Gb and Gc. Several of the refinements suggested by Potter have therefore been adopted here. In contrast to the silver, pre-pellet gold is considerably scarcer than that of the pellet-marked phase.

True Ga nobles, with annulet stops and an annulet before *E/dward* matching the

1351–1411

Pre-Treaty Group G Nobles: Distinguishing Features of Sub-Groups

	Obverse			Reverse		
	Lettering	Before *Edw*	Stops	Stops	Central *e*	Marks by Lis
Ga	Unbroken	Annulet	Annulets	Annulets	Large	None
Gb	*c* and *e* unbroken or top-sliced	Nothing	Annulets	Annulets	Small	None
Gc	As Gb	Saltire	Saltires	Saltires	Small	None
Gd	*c* and *e* broken at bottom	Nothing	Annulets	Saltires	Small	One pellet or annulet
	"	Annulet or saltire	Saltires	Saltires	Small	"
Ge	Unbroken	Saltire	Saltires	Saltires	Small	Two pellets
Gf	Unbroken	Nothing	Saltires	Saltires	Small	Two pellets
Gg	*e* with protruding bar	Nothing or saltire	Saltires	Saltires	Large	Two pellets
Gh	Open *e*	Saltire or none	Saltires	No rev. dies		

annulet breastmark on the silver, are rare. They have a large *e* in the central panel of the reverse. Ga obverses are more frequently paired with later reverses, on which the central *e* is smaller. A similar obverse without the annulet before *Edward* is classed as Gb, the natural reverses of which are identified by the small central *e* in combination with annulet stops. Gc, last of the pre-pellet nobles, introduces saltire stops on both sides and usually has a saltire also before *Edward*. In Gb and Gc the letters *e* and *c* are either unbroken as in Ga or have a slice across the top as found on groats of these two sub-groups. Gd nobles are characterised by having a single pellet or annulet by the top lis on the reverse, analogous to the single stop in *ta.s* on silver. In one case a Gc die was converted to Gd by the addition of an annulet. Obverses of Gd nobles are identifiable by their *e* and *c* which, as on the silver, are now usually broken at the bottom. Except for one variety of Gd with annulet stops and no mark before *Edward*, the nobles did not, like the silver, now revert to annulet stops after Gc, but continued with saltires for the remainder of group G. After Gd the letters *e* and *c* are again unbroken, with two pellets by the lis on the reverse being equivalent to the two stops in *t.a.s* on silver from Ge onwards. Arguably, a saltire before *Edward* on one or two noble obverses, with the new lettering, and otherwise as Gf, could be seen (as by Potter) as a counterpart to the pellet above the crown on groats of Ge; but this is somewhat speculative. Gf would thus consist of the other coins with small central *e* on the reverse, but without the saltire. Dies of sub-groups Gg and Gh are distinguished by their characteristic forms of the letter *e*, Gg with the protruding central bar, and the rare Gh (obverses only) with the open *e*. Gg reverses, occasionally lacking the two pellets, now have a larger central *e* again. Interchanges of dies between the sub-groups of G nobles are frequent. Earlier varieties are also occasionally muled with the two preceding groups (E/G, G/E, F/G and G/F), while one Gf obverse (in a worn condition) and a Gg reverse survived for use in combination with dies of Treaty A.

Although much less rare than those of earlier groups, neither the half-nobles nor the quarter-nobles of group G are common. In the rarer (pre-pellet) phase there are two half-noble obverses with annulet stops, one with an annulet before *Edward* (Ga), the other without (Gb); and one with saltire stops (Gc). The Gc reverse has the typical sliced letters of this sub-group, and a pellet instead of the *e* in the central panel; it also lacks the usual small lis in the upper right quarter. All the pre-pellet half-noble G reverses, like the group E die, retain the Gothic *n* and curious spellings derived from the group A prototype. In the pellet-marked phase there are two pellets by the top lis on the reverse, as on the cognate nobles. Stops are saltires and the reverse inscription is normal, with *N* Roman and reversed. As on the nobles, the three forms of the letter *e* define the half-noble dies of Gf, Gg and Gh. Reverses of Gg and Gh have small trefoils instead of the usual fleurs in the spandrels, and they generally omit the small extra lis by the lion. On one of Gh the two pellets flank the upper right crown instead of the top lis. Again, there is much muling between sub-groups. Although both obverse and reverse dies of Gg half-nobles are known, they feature only on mules with Gf or Gh, and no true Gg half-noble has yet been found. Gh, on the other hand, is less rare of this denomination than of other gold or London silver; the output of gold remained high in the last six months of the period.

Quarter-nobles are also mostly mules. The first obverse die of group G, and the only one to have annulet stops, was described by Lawrence as of Ga; but since it has no annulet before *Edward*, it is more logically labelled Gb. It is paired with reverses of group E and of Gd. No obverse attributable to Gd is known, but the reverses have saltire stops and a single annulet by the top lis or the adjacent lion, together with a pellet in the central panel and the spelling *Gahlori* in the manner of the previous latest quarter-noble reverses of group E. Of group Gf there are several dies for quarters: the reverses have two pellets by the top lis, and now revert to normal, with *e* in the panel and *Gloria*. Both Gd and Gf reverses are muled with an obverse of group B. The last quarter-noble dies of group G are reverses of Gg, known only from Gf/g mules. Although, like some of the Gg nobles, they lack pellets by the lis, the typical protruding *e* places them securely. The only unmuled quarters in the group are those of Gf: all the mules are of considerable rarity.

The Treaty Period, 1361-69

By omitting the French title, English coins of the 1360s explicitly record the suspension of hostilities between the two kingdoms during that period – although the quartering of the French arms (a more noticeable feature than the inscription) was retained throughout on Edward's gold. Renunciation of the French crown had not been one of the formal terms of the Peace of Brétigny, but formed part of subsequent negotiations between the kings, along with agreement on a substantial ransom. A new great seal without the French title was brought into use in October 1360, but the change was probably not implemented on the coinage until after the treaty had been ratified by Parliament three months later. Under Charles V, who succeeded John II in 1364, French interests were pursued more vigorously. In May 1369, responding to unrest in Aquitaine, Charles declared war and in June Edward retaliated by resuming the French title.

Two series of coins, very unequal in scale, belong to this period. Lawrence described the earlier series as the Transitional Treaty coinage and the second and much larger one as the Treaty coinage proper. Brooke's use of Treaty A and Treaty B is, however, to be preferred, not least because it lends itself more conveniently to subdivision. Introduction of each of these new series seems likely to have been associated with the appointment of a new master, Treaty A because of its prominent new annulet privy-mark, and Treaty B because of its obvious discontinuity from Treaty A and the significant administrative break that this must represent. Except at Durham, which as usual was a law unto itself, there are no mules between Treaty A and B in either gold or silver, virtually the only such occasion in the whole groat period until the Tudors. Durham had also produced the only coin that can be attributed specifically to the winter of 1360/1, the Gj penny which relates to the close of the Pre-Treaty series in numismatic detail, but in its inscription to the Treaty period.

Lawrence suggested that the Treaty A coinage belonged to the six-month accounting period from March to September 1361, following the appointment of Walter dei Bardi as master in the March. Brooke, on the other hand, identified the Treaty A group as the work of Robert de Porche between June 1361, when he was appointed master, and his replacement by dei Bardi in February 1363. The Brooke chronology, which has unfortunately taken root in the literature of the subject, is untenable on a number of counts. In the first place, there is a run of London coins of the Treaty B group which on numismatic grounds clearly precede the coinage of Calais; the Treaty B coinage at London must therefore have begun well before the opening of that mint in February 1363. The bullion figures tell a similar story, although they must be treated with caution, since there is a gap in the accounts for silver in 1365/7. The very large amounts of gold struck in 1361-2 may have included the reminting of French crowns received from the royal ransom. More than sixty per cent of both gold and silver recorded at London in the whole Treaty period from 1361 to 1369 had been minted by February 1363, but instead of Treaty A coins being materially more plentiful than those of Treaty B, the opposite is the case, with Treaty B accounting for a large majority of the coins in both metals. These objections to Brooke's dating were recognised by Potter, who proposed that Treaty A should be attributed to dei Bardi's first short tenure in March to June 1361, and the start of Treaty B to de Porche from June onwards. Until new hoard evidence becomes available it is difficult to measure accurately the relative proportions of coins of Treaty A and B, but the period March-June 1361 accounted for 18 per cent of the gold and 5 per cent of the silver recorded between 1361 and 1369, and these figures do not seem incompatible with the ratios of surviving material. Potter's attribution of Treaty A to dei Bardi, on the basis of the mint accounts, has the added advantage of enabling its annulet privy-marks to be seen as a response to the new condition in the indenture of March 1361 requiring the master to mark his coinage in a recognisable way.

Within the remainder of the period to 1369 there is no break equivalent to that between Treaty A and B, but Potter's suggestion that the reintroduction of annulet privy-marks in the later part of Treaty B could represent the return of dei Bardi in February 1363 is worthy of consideration. This coincides with the opening, under the former London master Henry de Brisele, of the mint at Calais, whose groats and halfgroats exhibit an annulet on the breast like a contemporary variety at London. At Calais silver was struck only between February 1363 and April 1365, although it may have ceased before 1365 since only £390 is recorded after April 1364. Gold, however, continued to be struck at Calais until the end of the reign and beyond. At London there was a decline in the volume of both gold and silver coinage during the first half of the 1360s. No silver at all is recorded for two years from September 1365, but the minting of gold continued uninterrupted and there is no obvious hiatus in the silver series at this time. It is legitimate to wonder whether silver coinage was in fact suspended for this period, since in each of the three years before and after the gap the amount coined never fell below £1,400, and there is no other occasion in the late middle ages when minting was discontinued at London for more than a few months except when supplies of bullion or foreign coin for exchange had dried up.

Treaty A Group (1361)
The earliest coins to reflect the Treaty of Brétigny in their legends are also distinguishable from the Pre-Treaty issues in many other respects. Workmanship tends to be careless, and style poor, and there are several curious mis-spellings on the gold. Whole words are sometimes omitted. Although in general aspect the coins have some resemblance to those of late group G, with saltire stops, the obverse inscriptions are extensively reorganized, the Gothic *n* is used more often than the Roman, and annulets or pellets are now added prominently to the design. In the king's titles France is replaced by Aquitaine, and Ireland is generally now spelt *hib*, with *I*, not *Y*. Although there are nobles muled with Pre-Treaty G, there are no such links in the London silver. Dies for the new coins appear to be the product of different engravers, working to a new specification, such as might follow a change of mastership.

Gold coins of Treaty A may be divided into two classes, the first (A1) with neat lettering of uniform size and including various experimental inscriptions, the second (A2) with more consistent readings that contain certain unusually large letters – *F, h, I, N* (Roman only) and *P*. All A1 gold is rare. So are A2 nobles, but A2 halves and quarters are relatively plentiful. Of the four A1 noble obverse dies, two describe Edward as king of England and Aquitaine. The die-sinkers must at first have been unclear as to how to set out the new titles, but the other two A1 dies, and all of A2, have the correct form, king of England and lord of Ireland and Aquitaine. The first two A1 reverses (with *Per* in full) omit *Transiens*; the other three mis-spell it, *Transievs*, and reduce *Per* to *P* and *Illorum* to *Illorr*. Most nobles (and halves) of Treaty A continue to have the small lis by a lion on the reverse, but a new feature of their design, not seen since nobles of the early Pre-Treaty period, is the vertical division of the planking on the ship's side, which occurs on all dies except the first A1 noble obverse (a die only known as a mule with a reverse of Pre-Treaty group Gg). On reverses, instead of trefoils at the corners of the central panel there are now annulets or, later (in A2), sometimes pellets. The unrealistically high forecastle of the late Pre-Treaty nobles and halves continues.

The first A1 obverse of the half-nobles is the only one to include the Irish and Aquitanian titles, having created space by reducing the king's name to *E/d*. The others, with the king's name fuller, have only *D*, or nothing, after *Ang(l)*. One A1 reverse has the correct reading, *Domine Ne In Furore* etc., but the others omit the negative, making the sense a curse rather than an imprecation. The *Ne* is also omitted on all the A2 half-noble reverses, several of which have the error reading *Arguts*. Halves of A2, now with a standard form of the English and Irish titles, have large *h* and *I* on the obverse, large *F* and *I* on the reverse. As on nobles, later halves of A2 have pellets instead of annulets at the corners of the central compartment. On one reverse, *c* for *e* in the centre must be a die-sinker's error since the English mint at Calais was not yet open.

On quarter-nobles there are usually annulets or trefoils on the cusps of the tressure, and in the spandrels trefoils or pellets. The A1 quarters have Roman *N* in *Angl(ie)*, but Gothic *n* on the reverse. In A2, the *N* is variable, and the one consistent large letter is the *I*. The central design on the reverse of Treaty A quarter-nobles also varies. An early A1 reverse has *e* in the panel, like the larger gold; but most subsequent reverses have a bold cross potent, instead of the central compartment, with annulets or pellets at the corners, this being the only material departure from the normal type on any of the gold coinage between 1351 and 1411.

Treaty A silver coins are considerably rarer than the gold, as the much smaller quantity of silver than of gold purchased by the mint during 1361 would indicate they should be. Lawrence recorded only fourteen London obverse dies in all —five each for groats and pennies, three for halfgroats and one for halfpence. Groats and halves are unmistakable, with annulets instead of fleurs at the two cusps beside the crown. The equivalent mark on pennies and halfpennies is an annulet or pellet at the two upper corners of the initial cross. There are no experimental inscriptions on silver as on A1 gold, and since many of the dies exhibit large letters *h, I* and *P* they were presumably produced at the same time as dies for the A2 gold. On silver the *n* is always Gothic, except in *London* on the groats which, unlike all other groats until after 1411, have letters of the same size in both circles of reverse inscription. The titles are England, Ireland and Aquitaine on the groats, the first two only on halfgroats and pence.

Pence omit *Rex*, although putting *Anglie* in full. On halfgroats and pence the crown is composite, a large central fleur being put in from the same punch as the lis on the reverse of the gold, presumably because an old crown punch had broken. Pence of York and Durham closely follow the London pattern, even to the extent of the curious omission of *Rex*. Those of York have Thorseby's quatrefoil on the reverse, with a pellet in the centre. Hatfield's pence read *Dorelme*, but there are also mules with the 'Pre-Treaty' Gj reverse (*Dureme*) and with an obverse of Treaty B.

Bardi's contract provided for each pound of gold to be coined into fifteen nobles, forty-five half-nobles and thirty quarter-nobles; and a quarter of all silver minted to be in groats, a third each in halfgroats and pence, and a twelfth in halfpence. Although these proportions would not have been exactly followed, the rarity of Treaty A nobles and groats and the relative abundance of the half- and quarter-nobles are broadly in accordance with them.

Treaty B Group (1361-69)

Coins of the Treaty B group differ from those of Treaty A not only in details of design and inscription, but also in their more elegant appearance. The lettering is broad, well-made and in high relief, and the workmanship is now generally of a high standard. Except in the inner circle on the reverse of groats and halves, where Roman *N* (usually reversed or unbarred) was used in *London Civitas* (in larger letters and in that order again), the *n* of Treaty B is almost always Gothic. The initial cross is of slender patty form with prominent ends – almost a cross potent. A curule *X* is found on almost all the gold but *X* on silver is put in from the initial cross punch placed saltirewise. & is now a reversed *Z*. Except on a few early pence, the spelling of *hyb* with a *Y* was now resumed. Saltire stops, usually doubled, occur throughout on the gold and on the reverse of the larger silver, but on groat obverses only on the earliest varieties. Groats and halves again have fleurs on all the cusps.

Edward III – Henry IV

INITIAL CROSSES AND LETTERS OF THE TREATY PERIOD

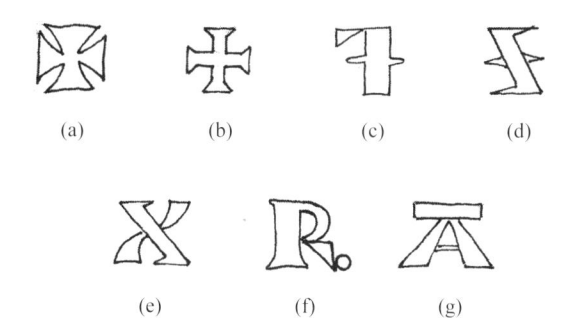

(a) Initial cross of Treaty A; (b) Initial cross of Treaty B (also used diagonally for *X*); (c) Symbol for &, Treaty A; (d) Symbol for &, Treaty B (with or without cross-bar); (e) Curule *X*, Treaty B gold; (f) Ball-tailed *R*, Treaty B2g; (g) Barred *A*, Treaty B2.

In both gold and silver the Treaty B coinage divides itself into two broad groups. The first of these (B1) has no mark before the king's name, and the letter *A* is unbarred. On the second (B2) there is often an annulet before *Edward*, coupled with a barred *A* in the last position on the reverse. This arrangement is, however, complicated by the existence of several coins that lack either or both of these privy-marks but which on other grounds are attributable to the B2 period. As usual, the groats offer the fullest series for classification but except in respect of the main division, between B1 and B2, other denominations only correspond with the groats in part. The obverse of the typical Treaty B groat (Lawrence varieties f to k) has bold double annulet stops, and the reverse double saltires; but before this standard stopping was adopted come several scarce early varieties of group B1 (labelled a to e by Lawrence) on which the obverse stops are either double saltires or single annulets, and those on the reverse are sometimes single saltires. The last groats of group B1 have the standard stopping (var. f), and these were followed, before the adoption of the regular B2 privy-marks, by others (var. g) on which there is an annulet added on the breast. Lawrence described four subsequent varieties, one of which, with a long face and coarser lettering (h), is now recognised as a contemporary forgery. The other three Lawrence varieties either have no annulet before *Edward* but a barred *A* in *Adiutore* (i) or, with the annulet, *A* either unbarred (j) or barred (k). As Potter observed, this arrangement of the later Treaty groats is somewhat confused, and other evidence is of value in establishing a sequence – notably the form of the bust, certain variations in the last segment of the reverse inscription, and the dies involved in mules with Post-Treaty reverses.

Potter defined three main types of Treaty B groat on the basis of the portrait: 1, a young-looking bust, with natural eyes and a thinnish, smiling face; 2, an older bust, rather squat, with small round eyes in an oval face; and 3, also with a severe expression and round eyes, but with a tapering chin, a thick line of drapery between the shoulders, and a new crown with thick, squared petals instead of the slender, curving form found with busts 1 and 2. This new crown is clearly the last in the Treaty series since it continues after 1369 and into the reign of Richard II. Bust 1 is found on all the early groats with double saltire (vars. a, b) or single annulet (vars. c, d) stops on the obverse; or with single saltires on the reverse (vars. d, e); and on the first of those with double annulets/double saltires (var. f). Apart from the stopping, the most noteworthy variant with bust 1 is an odd die of variety c on which there is a reversed Roman *N* in *Angl* and both *Dei* and *Dns* are reduced to *D*. Bust 2, which is the most plentiful, spans the transition from B1 to B2. Like the latest groats with bust 1, the first with bust 2 are of variety f, with standard stopping and no extra marks. A few of these have the curule *X* proper to the dies for gold. As shown by an f/g mule, next come the rare groats (var. g) with an annulet instead of a fleur on the breast, and a pellet at the tail of the *R* on the reverse. Since variety g accounts for all known groats of Calais, these dies were presumably made at the beginning of 1363. They are probably to be regarded as constituting the start of the second group of the Treaty B coinage, since an annulet introduced prominently into the design was clearly a deliberate mark, and the position of variety g at the head of B2 is confirmed by its use of a new letter *Q* (with the tail consisting of a pellet, instead of a dash as in B1), which occurs on subsequent groats. London groats of variety g are very rare, suggesting that the subsequent introduction of the annulet before *Edward* and of the barred *A* will have taken place during the first half of 1363. With the second bust, groats of B2 are commoner than those of B1, and they almost always have the new privy-marks on both sides (var. k). Dies with the new markings seem to have been carefully paired at this stage, since mules with no annulet and barred *A* (i), or with annulet and unbarred *A* (j), are extremely rare with bust 2.

CROWNS ON TREATY B GROATS

(a)   (b)

(a) Crown of Treaty B, busts 1 and 2; (b) Crown of Treaty B, bust 3, and Post-Treaty.

Groats of the last phase of the Treaty period, with bust 3, are more complicated and Lawrence's scheme of varieties does not work properly here. Whereas the annulet before *e* was placed at the top or by the middle of the letter with bust 2, on bust 3 groats it is found at the top, middle or bottom, or (most commonly) not at all. Bust 3 groats are rare, but they include reverses with three distinct forms of reading in the last segment of the outer inscription – *em Meu(m)*, *(e)um Meu(m)*, and *m Meu(m)*. The first of these is simply a continuation of the normal ending on Treaty groats, the last is that found on early Post-Treaty groats, and the ungrammatical *(e)um* dies seem therefore to be intermediate. Annulets occur on a few of the obverse dies used with each ending (or with Post-Treaty reverses), but barred *A* only with the first of them. Towards the close of the B2 period, therefore, there is no consistency in the presence or omission of the annulet on groats, while the barred *A* was discontinued before the end. A curule *X* occurs on one late die, which is also muled with a Post-Treaty reverse.

Treaty B halfgroats are also abundant, but they offer much less variation than the groats. There is no early series with varied stops, and a single bust is used throughout. Many of the reverse dies omit the *D* of *Adiutore*. B1 is represented by halfgroats equivalent to the groats of variety f, with no extra marks. Variety g, with annulet on breast and the pellet-tailed *R*, is very rare of London, but there is a die-link with Calais which only struck this type. The substantive issue of B2 halves follows the groats of variety k in having the annulet before *Edwardus* in the upper or middle position; the companion reverses show two versions of the barred *A* in *Adiutore*, one abnormally large. The last group of halfgroats, with the annulet in any of the three positions as on groats with bust 3, reverts to an unbarred *A*, with the consequence that these coins (var. j) have sometimes been described as B2/1 mules. Apart from the parallel occurrence of unbarred *A* on many groats with bust 3, the late position of these halfgroats is also supported by the equivalent use of variant reverse endings from *ore Me* to *m Meu*, including *eu Meu*. Mostly the Treaty B halfgroats read *London Civitas*, like the groats, but several of these late reverse dies have *Civitas* first. Obverse stops on Treaty B halves are normally double annulets, as on groats, but the last halfgroat obverse die without the French title, known only from mules with later reverses, looks forward to the Post-Treaty period also in having double saltire stops.

On London pence of this period *R* for *Rex*, after its omission in Treaty A, is restored to the inscription but, most unusually, it is placed after *Angl*. Of B1 there are pence with a saltire after *Lon* or *don* (recalling the saltire on early nobles), but no other marks, and on a few of the earliest the old Treaty A spelling *hib* still appears. Most of the later London pence have a pellet before *Edward*, a barred *A* in *tas* and an annulet after *don*, but some dies lack the pellet or the annulet. The rare Calais pence have a pellet after *Villa*, as on groats and halves of this mint, but they lack the annulet breastmark of the larger silver.

The most plentiful Treaty B pence are those of Archbishop Thoresby at York, marked by the usual quatrefoil on the reverse (although this sometimes takes the form of a small incuse cross). Most omit the Irish title. The usual inscription is *Edwardus Rex Angli*, with reversed Roman *N* and pellet stops. Some with this reading have a voided quatrefoil (also on the breast) or an annulet before *Edwardus*, but the characteristic barred *A* of the B2 group is not found on York pence. There is some variation in the bust, including one of local work. A much rarer York reading is *Dei G Rex An*, with Gothic *n* and single annulet stops, and these coins have an extra point with the pellets in two reverse quarters. Most of the York pence are thus from dies made specially for this mint, outside the normal London production; but there are also a few with the London obverse reading, sometimes with a pellet before *Edward*.

Bishop Hatfield's Durham pence, which are not rare, show the normal York obverse reading, but with annulet stops and sometimes a Gothic *n*. Their reverses normally read *Dureme* (followed by a crozier to left or right), but there are also rare mules with Treaty A reverses reading *Dorelme*, and a strange variety without crozier reading *Dunelmis*; since there is nothing to suggest that Hatfield's temporalities were suspended at this time, the omission of the crozier, coupled with an abnormal spelling, probably indicates no more than the work of someone other than the regular engraver. A pellet before *Dur* on another variety is reminiscent of the stop after *Villa* at Calais. Neither a mark before *Edwardus* nor a barred *A* in *tas* occurs at Durham.

Halfpence of the Treaty B period, though not particularly common, are the only material issue of this denomination in the post-1351 coinage of Edward III. The earliest (B1), without a mark before *Edw* or a barred *A*, have colon stops on the obverse, and a small pellet after or within the *n* of *don*. Later halfpence (B2) have single annulet stops, and a wedge or pellet before *Edw*, usually with an annulet after *don* and a barred *A* in *tas*. Although the Calais indenture mentions halfpennies, none are known of that mint. Farthings, also of London only, are very rare. Like the halfpence they have a characteristic neat bust, with hair gathered tightly by the face. Lettering is very small, with Roman *N*, and a cross patty *X* sometimes visible.

Gold of the Treaty B period is of fine style, and the nobles and halves are among the best of all post-1351 issues. Two letters of *Ed/ward* are placed before the bowsprit and *Aq/t* is divided by the sail. Lions on the ship's side face forward, and the lis appear in pairs. The standard arrangement of the rigging is three ropes aft and two forward. On the reverse there is no longer a small lis added by a lion, and the central panel now has neat trefoils (with hollowed petals) at its corners. Stops are double saltires throughout, except by &. Although *n* is always Gothic, as on silver, the characteristic *X* patty is only found on a few early quarter-nobles and the normal form on gold is a curule *X*. Calais nobles and halves have *c* for *e* in the central panel, and some obverse dies have a pennant from the sterncastle, which was to become a standard feature on Calais gold subsequently. B1 nobles have all *A*s unbarred and, except for a few of Calais, a saltire before *Ed/ward*. In B2 there is an annulet before *Ed/ward* (or above the fold of the sail) on London nobles, and (normally) a quatrefoil at Calais. London B2 nobles have barred *A* in *Ibat*, and sometimes in *Gra* and *Aqt*, but the barred *A* is not found at Calais except on one variety, without quatrefoil but with an annulet after *Ed*, which has barred *A* in *Gra*, *Aqt* and *Ibat*. London nobles all have a single saltire each side of &, but Calais dies of B1 have single trefoils there. Half-nobles of both mints have similar features to the nobles. The barred second *A* in *Arguas* on the reverse, however, although invariable on B2 halves of London, is not found on Calais dies. Rare B2/1 mules are found in the London nobles, but the only half-noble mule noted is from a Calais B1 obverse and a London B2 reverse, with central *e*, presumably sent in error. The existence of B1 gold of Calais suggests that dies for gold were prepared for this mint slightly earlier than those for silver, which are not known without the annulet that associates them with the start of B2. A few B2 London nobles and Calais halves have a small crescent on the forecastle, and these are presumably late because the same mark is found on some early coins of the Post-Treaty period.

After the unsuccessful experiments with design in Treaty A, the quarter-nobles now revert to the traditional reverse type, with a small ornament – lis, annulet or quatrefoil – in the centre of the panel. Those with the lis constitute a full series and have been provisionally attributed to London. Early B1 dies, with *A* unbarred and without mark before *Edward*, have *X* patty as on silver, but this was later replaced by the curule *X* as used on the larger gold. B2 lis-marked quarters have an annulet before *Edward* and (except on B2/1 mules) a barred *A* in *Gloria*. Quarter-nobles of B1 and B2 with an annulet or quatrefoil in the reverse panel are much rarer than those with the lis. Since a quatrefoil is found on B2 nobles and halves of Calais, but not on London gold, quarters with this mark, which have a cross or crescent above the shield, may also belong to Calais, despite its occurrence also on some pence of London and York. Some quarters with an annulet on the reverse, but a circled cross above the shield, also probably belong to Calais, since their unbarred *A* in *Gloria*, even when the obverse is of B2, matches the unbarred *A*s in *Ibat* and *Arguas* on B2 nobles and half-nobles of Calais.

Edward III, Post-Treaty Period, 1369-77

In June 1369, within days of the abrogation of the Treaty, Edward's French title was restored on the great seal, and the same alteration was made on coin dies probably not long afterwards. Collectively, Post-Treaty coins are not unduly rare, but they are much scarcer than the Pre-Treaty and Treaty series. The amount of gold bullion passing through both royal mints, and of silver through London, during the last eight years of Edward III's reign was in each case less than half that of the 1360s. From 1373 to the end of the reign gold coinage was on a reducing trend at both London and Calais. In 1369/70 silver output remained at a similar level to that of the last two years of the Treaty period, but thereafter it fell sharply, except for a revival during the twenty-two months from September 1374 to July 1376 which accounted for nearly two-thirds of the Post-Treaty silver total. Although various points of correspondence can be noted between gold and silver, and between different silver denominations, there is no consistency in this and separate schemes of classification for the silver, as proposed by Potter, are therefore necessary.

Apart from some early nobles, which except for the added French title retain the characteristics of Treaty B2, the Post-Treaty series exhibits a new style of lettering, taller and narrower than before and easily recognised from a number of typical letters. The initial cross is thick and patty. The &, no longer a reversed *Z* (except, curiously, on Calais half-nobles), somewhat resembles the Pre-Treaty barred *7*, but with a long downstroke at the left side. *L*, with a very pronounced upper serif, is almost a rectangle. As in the Treaty series, a Gothic *n* is normal other than in *London*, where (except occasionally on pennies) it is Roman and most frequently reversed, with a contraction mark above the last letter. A few early dies have a chevron-barred *A*. The gold has a new saltire *X*, but on silver, apart from a few early York pennies, the *X* now usually has a curule shape, with a characteristic crooked left foot, and this punch is found on most coins of the First Period of Richard II. Ireland is now spelt *hib*, and *Dei* contracts to *Di*. *Civi* returns to its position under *Posui*, and remains there henceforward. As before, stops are mostly saltires, although pellets or occasionally annulets occur on some early silver. One or more saltires, or on some halfgroats and pence pellets, are regularly found in the inner inscription, frequently before *Civi* and *Lon*. Extra small points in the design are a characteristic feature of many Post-Treaty dies of all denominations.

LETTER FORMS ETC. OF THE POST-TREATY PERIOD

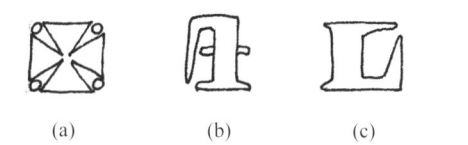

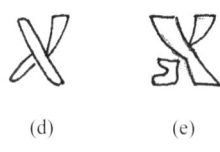

(a) (b) (c) (d) (e)

(a) Initial cross, early Post-Treaty (later without pellets); (b) Post-Treaty &;
(c) Rectangular *L*, Post-Treaty; (d) Plain asymmetrical *X*, Post-Treaty gold;
(e) *X* with crooked left foot, Post-Treaty silver (and early Richard II).

Nearly all of the gold of the Post-Treaty period was struck into nobles. Half-nobles are extremely rare and no quarters with Post-Treaty features have been found. However, since Treaty quarter-nobles of group B2 are so plentiful, some of the numerous Treaty dies could have remained in use beyond the summer of 1369; their inscription did not extend beyond *Rex Angl*, and no revision may have been felt necessary (most of the quarter-nobles of Richard II also have only the English title). The earliest nobles with the restored French title (class 1) are of a transitional nature, indistinguishable from those of Treaty B2 except for the addition of *Fra*. Thus, they continue such features as the pellet-topped castles, 3-2 ropes in the rigging, an annulet before *Ed/ward*, the spelling *hyb*, and often barred *A* in *Aqt* and *Ibat*. As before, some of the dies also have a small crescent in the forecastle (when the crescent is missing, so is the bowsprit). Calais nobles of class 1, much rarer than those of London, may be identified by having *c* in the centre of the reverse, since their obverses lack the Calais pennant, and some are from an obverse die that had already been used at London. Because their reverses do not differ from their predecessors, the class 1 nobles have sometimes been described as Post-Treaty/Treaty mules, but their lettering on both sides is homogeneous, in the Treaty B style, and they merely constitute a brief extension of the preceding series, confined to this one denomination, after the rupture of the treaty.

The regular nobles (class 2) have the same lettering as other denominations of the Post-Treaty period. They are scarce, but considerably more abundant than those of class 1. Since Calais obverses now show the pennant, there was no longer need to have the mint initial instead of *e* in the centre of the reverse. Class 2 nobles differ in many respects from those of class 1, besides the lettering. The pellet ornamentation of the castles was now replaced by battlements, and there is only a single rope to the forecastle. On London dies there is usually an annulet before the inscription (sometimes above the sail), on Calais dies a quatrefoil. *hib* is normal although some London nobles still have *hyb*. The central *e* on the reverse has a small point (or at London sometimes a cross) before it. There are also on some reverse dies small points at the sides or base of the lis, and some Calais obverses have one or two pellets beside the shield. At both mints there are a few muled nobles with class 2 obverses but reverses from dies of the earlier style (class 1 or Treaty B2). It is not obvious why the old lettering was discontinued, when the punches generally appear to have remained serviceable, but it is notable that whereas class 1 nobles read *Fra* those of class 2 have *Franc*, and reasons of space could therefore perhaps have contributed to the decision to introduce narrower letters.

The only London half-noble of this period is a mule, from a Treaty B2 obverse die, with annulet before *Edward*, and a reverse with Post-Treaty lettering. This reverse die has a small point beside the central *e*, after the manner of the class 2 nobles. A similar reverse is found on rare early half-nobles of Richard II that are struck from Edward III dies, but with *Edw* altered to *Ric*, which show that obverse dies for Post-Treaty half-nobles were indeed made, whether or not any were actually used in Edward's reign. In having 3-1 ropes they replicate the pattern of the class 2 nobles, as do the Calais half-nobles of this period which, although extremely rare, do exist both as true coins and as mules with Treaty B or Richard II reverses. These Calais halves follow the class 2 Calais nobles in designating their mint by means of a pennant and not a central *c*, and also in having a quatrefoil before the inscription.

Although Treaty/Post-Treaty mules in silver are rare, there are enough of each denomination to suggest that the earliest dies with the new lettering were reverses, and that no attempt was made to withdraw serviceable Treaty obverses immediately because of the change of titles. All new groat and halfgroat reverse dies muled with Treaty obverses have minor abnormalities of legend or stopping – such as omission of the initial cross or an absence of stopping in the inner circle. The true Post-Treaty groats begin with three obverse dies having four small points at the corners of the initial cross and a row of annulets across the breast, generally taken to represent the top of a coat of mail. Two of these dies (type 1a) include all four titles, England, France, Ireland and Aquitaine, but the last of these was then dropped, as subsidiary to the second, allowing less drastic abbreviation (type 1b). Type 1 reverse dies usually have *Meum* in full, and on a few of the earliest (also on mules with Treaty obverses) pellets or annulets occur in the outer legend instead of or in addition to saltires. On the next groats (type 2) the inscription is less abbreviated, with the English and French titles (*Francie* or *Franc*) only – Ireland does not reappear on English silver coins until the sixteenth century. The last segment on the reverse of type 2 groats normally reads *em Meu*, those with *Meum* in full probably being 2/1 mules. Type 2a has a point above the central fleur of the crown and two beside the breast fleur. The more plentiful groats of type 2b have two points beside the central fleur only. Lastly (type 3) there is a group of groats without the extra points. On groats of types 2 and 3 chainmail of pellets is sometimes visible.

Halfgroats, which carry only the English and French titles, often have pellets in the inner legend instead of saltires – one of the abnormal early reverses muled with a Treaty obverse has both a pellet and a saltire, although pellets and saltires are never mixed on normal reverses. What is presumably the first of the new halfgroat obverse dies (Potter's type 1) is exceptional in more than one respect: it is the only halfgroat die of this reign to include *Di Gra* or to show pellet-mail on the bust, and it has the face from a very large punch with unusually wide nose and mouth that was also used on a London penny. It must however be doubtful whether this single die should be regarded as equivalent to the type 1 groats since, despite its exceptional inscription, it lacks points by the initial cross and in having mail of pellets rather than annulets and a point each side of the central fleur of the crown it has features relating to groats of type 2. The next halfgroats (type 2) are from two dies without *Di Gra* but still with points by the crown, followed by others (type 3) without the points. Type 2 halfgroats and some of type 3 have the same large head as type 1, but for others of type 3 a more normal sized punch was used. Finally, there are two dies (type 4) with a small neat head and more neck, as found on the earlier halves of Richard II. These type 4 dies are found paired not only with normal reverses with Post-Treaty lettering, but also with reverse dies from around the end of the reign of Richard II, when they must have been brought back into use after an interval of some twenty years or more.

Post-Treaty pence are difficult to classify because, although there is considerable variation in bust, inscription and ornamentation, their sequence is not always clear. The picture is not assisted by the fact that pence of York and Durham are usually in very poor condition. No points are found by the central fleur of the crown, such as occur on groats and halves, but some London and York reverses have an extra small point in each angle of the cross, or in one or two quarters. Obverse stops are usually double or single saltires, and at London and York there is often a saltire in the reverse inscription. At all three mints *Civi* is sometimes preceded by an initial cross. Two London dies (type 1) shorten the king's name to *Edward*, allowing room for the French title; one of these has very short hair and an annulet on the breast. Their reverses have no extra points, but one has a cross before *Civi*. The rest of the London pence read *Rex Anglie*. One (type 2a) has the very large head as on halfgroats, and a cross on the breast. Then there are pence with a more normal large head (type 2b) and an annulet or nothing on the breast. Others, and by analogy with the halfgroats probably the last, have a small head and a voided quatrefoil on the breast (type 3).

York pence are the commonest coins of the Post-Treaty period and exhibit greater variety than those of London. Some obverses reading *Edward* include the French title, and one has *Di Gra Rex Ang*, but the normal form is *Edwardus Rex Anglie* as at London. Some early dies have pellet or annulet colon stops. One has four points around the initial cross, as on type 1 groats, and several an annulet, cross or lis on the breast. Archbishop Thoresby died in 1373, after an episcopate that had seen his mint play an increasingly active part in the provision of the national currency. At the end of the York Post-Treaty series may be placed rare coins with a small bust and these, at least, are probably to be attributed to Thoresby's aristocratic successor, Alexander Neville, who received his temporalities in June 1374.

At Durham Bishop Hatfield's coinage continues, with his crozier after *Dunolm*. All the Durham pence read *Edwardus*, even though one die (with an annulet colon after *Rex*) reads *Angl & Fr*. Several dies have an annulet or a lis on the breast and, as at the other mints, both a larger and a smaller bust are found.

No halfpence of the Post-Treaty period have been identified, but there are a few farthings, probably late since they have a tiny head with little if any neck, as on those of Richard II.

Richard II (1377-99) – Structure

For the numismatist Richard's reign is perhaps the most difficult period in the late middle ages. Although various symbols were used to mark individual groups of dies (especially for the gold), and corresponding features sometimes occur between denominations, there is no consistency in this and for much of the time the mint does not seem to have been following any systematic approach to the marking of dies. Variation in obverse readings is also greater than in most other reigns. The situation is complicated by the fact that the gold, the large silver and the small silver have been treated separately by three different students, each with his own classification. Although each scheme is based on division into four types, not only do these often not coincide (see table) but they are not always internally consistent. For example, type II has radically different meanings for nobles (Webb Ware), groats (Potter) and York pence (Purvey), while Potter calls the last groats of the reign type IV but the related halfgroats type IIIb. Furthermore, several denominations – notably half- and quarter-nobles and the larger silver – were not struck continuously (or, at least, not in such numbers as to have required the regular production of new dies), so that consistency of correspondence between them is not to be expected. Resolution of these problems must await a full study of the coinage of this reign, and for the time being we have little option but to use the existing labels, despite their inherent inconsistencies. Nevertheless, there are two fundamental signposts to the structure of the coinage, the lettering and the royal titles, that enable the material to be allocated between two main periods.

Simplified Summary of Richard II Classification

	First Period, 1377-c.1390 Straight-sided lettering		Second Period, c.1390-1399 Indented lettering	
	Edwardian	Regular (A)	'Fishtail' (B)	Mixed (C)
Gold (after Webb Ware)				
Nobles	Ia	Ib#	II* III	IV
Half-nobles	Ia	Ib	II* III	IV
Quarter-nobles	Ia	Ib	III	IV
Larger Silver (after Potter)				
Groats	I	II	III	IV
Halfgroats		II#	IIIa	'IIIb' (here IV*)
Smaller Silver (after Purvey)				
London pence		I		IV
York pence	(I)	II, ? and local#	III	IV
Durham pence		X		
London halfpence	'Early' (here I)	'Intermediate' (here II)	III#	IV

* without French title (larger coins); # with or without French title

In the First Period, before the 1390s, the letter-fount was plain and straight-ended, with the uprights straight-sided, or nearly so, and the serifs flat, in the general manner of Edward III's coinage post-1351; but in the later part of the reign a new style was adopted, with indented serifs and concave uprights, which was to set the general epigraphic

Edward III – Henry IV

pattern for the fifteenth century. This later style has often been described as 'fishtail' but, as Potter observed, that is not always strictly accurate since fishes' tails are usually pointed while the serifs of the new letters often have rounded ends. Potter's figures for the numbers of dies and surviving examples of groats and halfgroats suggest that about thirty per cent of the larger silver of the reign has indented lettering of styles B and C (types III and IV), and Purvey has proposed a similar proportion for the London halfpence. When correlated with the mint accounts, these figures would point to the introduction of indented lettering around 1390. On nobles, which for twenty years past had used the four titles, this coincides with the dropping of the French title, probably to be seen as a consequence of the three-year truce agreed in 1389. Each of the two main letter groups can be further subdivided: the first begins with a brief Edwardian style, merely a continuation of that in use at the end of the previous reign, followed by a new style (A) of generally similar character but from different punches including, notably, a simpler *&*. 'Fishtail' lettering is more variable, especially on the gold, but, while most of the coins with indented letters may be grouped together (style B), there is also a mixed and dumpier version (style C), incorporating some old punches (e.g. *e, m* and R1) and some very small letters (particularly the *A*), that is found on a few coins near the end of the reign. Several late dies of the Second Period (although not for groats) show a dumpy *I* which develops a fracture across the bottom right corner. Coins with style C lettering (type IV) are considerably rarer than those with style B (type III for silver, II-III for gold), and it is unlikely that they predate the last year or two of the reign. (North and others have referred to styles A, B and C as types I, II and III, but in view of the confusion already existing in the numeration of the coin types themselves, it seems better to use letters than numbers for this purpose.)

One of the main reasons for the lack of regular correspondence between Richard's gold and silver lies in their different patterns of output. As Potter observed, silver coinage during the king's minority averaged over £1,000 per annum, but with the assumption of power by the Lords Appellant in 1388-9 it fell sharply, before recovering when the king regained conrol. Nearly £17,500, or four fifths of Richard's silver, had been struck in the fourteen years to September 1391. The next five years accounted for £1,200 in total, but between 1396 and 1399 silver output returned towards the levels of the earliest years of the reign. At London gold was struck more consistently throughout, although at a slightly higher average annual rate during the 1390s than before. Most of the silver coins therefore belong to what may be termed the First Period (to c. 1390), while in the Second Period London's gold is commoner than its silver.

Gold of the First Period is divided by Webb Ware into types Ia and Ib, the former with the Edwardian fount, the latter with the new style A lettering. The equivalent division adopted by Potter for the groats is into types I and II. However, the replacement of individual Edwardian letter punches was a gradual process, and any such division is therefore to an extent arbitrary, according to which letters are chosen for the definition. Further and separate systems have been used by Purvey for pence and halfpence. For halfpence, the most abundant denomination at London, Purvey has used the terms 'Early' and 'Intermediate', for which I and II may conveniently be substituted since, in broad terms, they represent roughly equivalent proportions of the First Period halfpence to those for Potter's types I and II of the groats. For the York pence, however, Purvey's types I and II are constituted differently from any other silver, with type I much more extensive than type II.

The main 'fishtail' phase, in the Second Period, is represented in the nobles and halves by Webb Ware's types II and III, the former without the French title, the latter with it restored. Groats of Potter's type III are rare, halfgroats very rare, neither denomination being known with style B lettering but without the French title, like type II nobles. Purvey's arrangement of the smaller silver now approximates to Potter's scheme for groats, both ending with a type IV with style C lettering, as does Webb Ware's classification of the gold. The last halfgroats of the reign, and possibly two late groat dies (which are not known to have been used before being altered for Henry IV's light coinage), are without the French title, but whether this may reflect political considerations (after Richard's French marriage in 1396) is less clear than in the case of the type II nobles. As a general rule, omissions from the inscriptions on smaller coins (including quarter-nobles) give an unreliable message because of the constraints of space.

Richard II, First Period (1377 – c.1390)

Groats of this period were divided by Potter into type I, with the Edwardian reversed *F* for &, and type II, with a reversed *Z*. The type I groats are rare, with only four obverse dies noted, but those of type II are the most numerous of Richard's groats, accounting for around half of all those known of the reign. Generally they follow the style of late groats of Edward III, with the same smallish oval face, round eyes, a broad nose, and the hair close to the cheeks (falling a little lower on the dexter side). As before, the lettering is plain and straight-sided, with reversed Roman *N*s in *London* and a bar above the second of them. While the Post-Treaty *X*, with its crooked left limb, occurs on most coins throughout the First Period, only one of the four type I groat obverse dies has the Edwardian letter fount throughout, including its narrow, hunch-backed and short-legged *R* (R1), although this letter form occurs on several reverses. This obverse, presumably the earliest, is also notable for including, exceptionally, a vestige of the Irish title (*Francie D*). R1 was followed by two new and wider punches (useful for identification on the lower denominations), one (R2) more angular, with its tail bent back towards the upright, the other (R3) with the tail trailing. For reverses Potter chose the letter *m* as the determining feature of his two types – a very small *m* for type I and a thicker form, with very narrow hollows, for type II; on this basis there are several I/II but very few II/I mules. On reverse dies of type I the letters in the outer inscription vary in size, while in the inner ring they are tall, like those of the Post-Treaty series, although several of the punches are new. One die has been noted with a saltire before *Lon*, but otherwise there are no stops in the inner circle, and in this respect also reverses of the new reign differ from late groats of Edward III which normally have two or even three saltires there. In type II the lettering of the outer legend is more regular in size, and that in the inner circle has long, pointed serifs; two of the dies have *tas* instead of *Civi* under *Posui*.

LETTERING OF RICHARD II, FIRST PERIOD

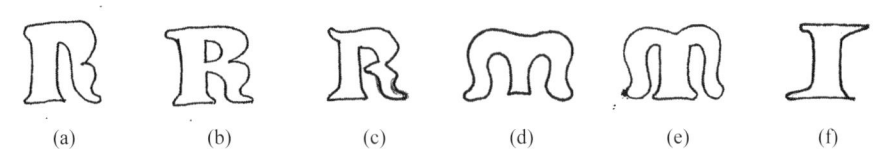

(a) Narrow Edwardian *R*, type I (Potter's R1); (b) Broad and angular new *R* of type I (R2);
c) *R* of type II with trailing tail (R3); (d) Small *M* of type I; (e) Larger *M*, type II;
(f) & of type II.

Most of Richard's halfgroats also belong to the First Period, and they show the same letter punches as the groats. Of the six obverse dies involved, three read *Di Gra Rex Anglie*, and three include the French title, with consequent abbreviation. In the latter case the *&* is of the new form, and since all six obverse dies use R3 Potter ascribed them to his type II. Their reverses, however, include a few with R2 or the Edwardian R1, and these were described by Potter as of his type I.

Small points above the crown, either one above the central fleur or with two more above the intermediate ornaments also, occur on two early groat dies (of type I and early type II) and on three of the halfgroat dies (one with and two without the French title), recalling the small points about the crown and breast-fleur on some Post-Treaty groats and halves of Edward III. This must raise some question as to whether, as proposed by Webb Ware, the *Rex Anglie* halfgroat dies were made at the end of the First Period in response to political developments, as with the nobles. Halfgroat reverses of Potter's type I are found with one of the *Rex Anglie* dies as well as with two ending *Fr*, but there are no II/III halfgroat mules such as occur among the groats; this pattern also perhaps points to a relatively early position for all the halfgroat dies with style A lettering.

A few type II groat obverse dies survived to be used with reverses of type III, with the new indented lettering of style B. One of them (with two saltires after *Franc*) was first used, unblemished, on a late type II groat, but on II/III mules it exhibits severe pitting to the left of the bust, as if it had been put aside for a period during which it rusted. If this indicates an interval between the minting of groats of types II and III, it could explain why there are no groats without the French title to match the nobles and halves of Webb Ware's type II: silver coinage in the early 1390s was so limited that no new groat dies may have been needed at that stage.

Pence of Richard II's First Period are known of the same three mints as of late Edward III. Those of London are again rare. There is usually a saltire before *Civi* on pence of this period, although on one York reverse variety it occurs after *aci* instead. The normal reading is *Ricardus Rex Anglie* but one or two London dies include the French title. Except for having a Gothic *n* on the reverse, the scarce Durham pence are generally similar to those of London. They have a small lis on the breast, as also sometimes found at London. Thomas Hatfield died in 1381 and if any coinage was produced for him under Richard II it would have been from old dies of Edward III. His successor was John Fordham (1382-8), who had been secretary to the Black Prince and Privy Seal to Richard. A writ to the exchequer of February 1384 provided for receipt of Hatfield's old dies and for delivery of the customary allocation of three sets to the new bishop. This was the only supply of dies to Durham authorised during Richard's reign. One of the two obverse dies employed is found in a rusty condition on some specimens, suggesting that it may have been used only occasionally, over a period. Fordham returned to Ely, in his native Cambridgeshire, in 1388, and was followed at Durham by Walter Skirlaw. Over the years Skirlaw had been in and out of favour at court, but was much engaged in royal service from 1376. If any Durham coins were minted during his episcopate they would have been struck from Fordham's dies. The disused mint buildings in Durham were leased out in 1394, but the general shortage of bullion after the 1380s may have led to closure of the mint some years earlier. Coinage at Durham was to remain in abeyance until after the weight reduction of 1412.

The minting of pence at York was on a much larger scale. Purvey divided the York obverse dies of London style into two types, by reference to minute details of lettering. There is almost always a small lis or cross on the breast in his type I, but not in type II. All have the English title only. On a late variety of type I there is a small pellet above each shoulder. This feature, together with a cross on the breast, was to be reproduced on a long series of locally made dies, of coarse workmanship. Presumably there were difficulties in obtaining dies from London for an extended period since at least a dozen local York obverse dies have been noted and many of them must have been kept in use almost to destruction, to judge by the defective impressions on some of their products. Also, there are several separate varieties identifiable by variations in the obverse inscription, mostly with regard to the spelling of *Anglie*, which assumes some odd forms such as *Angie* or *Angilie*, but including also one or two dies with the French title, and two reading *Angl Dns Eb* with a phonetic attempt at the Irish ending. Purvey suggested that the position in the series of the local dies, muled not only extensively with London-made dies of his types I and II but also occasionally with type III (which belongs to the Second Period), was between his types II and III. Archibald, however, having studied the extensive material from the Attenborough hoard, has preferred to place them immediately after the late type I dies with pellets on the shoulders which they were copying, and thus before type II. The pattern of muling, more with type I than with type III, would be consistent with this. Either way, the number of these local dies and their heavy usage seem to indicate sustained output from the northern mint in the 1380s, as in the 1370s, regardless of increasing difficulty in attracting bullion to the Tower. Most of the York coins of the First Period were presumably struck for Archbishop Alexander Neville, until this high-handed and disputatious prelate was eventually removed by translation to the nominal see of St. Andrews in 1388. There is, however, no means of distinguishing between his coins and those of his successor Thomas Arundel who, although at times a critic of Richard, was to help negotiate the king's French marriage in 1396.

Halfpence of the First Period are abundant, a response to the repeated pleas to Parliament to remedy the shortage of small change. They have a neat bust, with the hair close to the face, from the same punch as used for nobles of type I. The earliest varieties (I) have a cross (or lis?) or annulet on the breast (reflecting the ornamentation of nobles of the period), double saltire stops, and reversed Roman *N*s in *London*, with a contraction bar as on the larger silver. A mule from a reverse die of Treaty period type, with barred *A*, Gothic *n* and an annulet after *don*, perhaps indicates that halfpence continued to be struck, from old dies of the 1360s, during the Post-Treaty period. Type I halfpence are rare, but those without a breastmark that followed (type II – Purvey's 'Intermediate' type) are the commonest coins of Richard's reign. Except for a few early coins with normal Roman *N*s in *London*, a Gothic *n* was now adopted on type II halfpence and continued in use for the rest of the reign and beyond. Some variety was however introduced in the stopping, which may consist of saltires or pellets, doubly or singly, or wedge-and-saltires (of which the wedges probably represent contraction marks). On late obverses of type II halfpence the Post-Treaty crooked *X* was replaced by a new form, as found on the earliest of the fishtail nobles. Obverse dies of both types I and II were to be reused after many years with reverses of type IV at the end of the reign.

Most of Richard's farthings were also struck during the earlier part of the reign. Although rare, they are less so than any other post-1351 farthings. The portrait is often shown with some neck and bust, and the face is small, with a pointed chin, as on half-nobles of type Ib. Like the late farthings of Edward III, Richard's have colon stops. A variety has groups of four pellets instead of three in the quarters of the reverse, sometimes described as rosettes.

London struck gold throughout this period, although substantially more in the later part of it than in the earlier. Calais, however, minted only a few hundred gold coins between May 1381 and January 1384, and none at all for the next three years, this presumably explaining the increase in gold available to London at that time. Nobles of this period, although a little less plentiful than those of the 1390s, are not uncommon, but the halves are rare, especially those of Calais. Having lapsed in the Post-Treaty period, quarter-nobles were now revived. They carry no evident marks of differentiation between the mints, but since there are so few halves of Calais it is likely that most if not all of the quarters also were struck at London.

Webb Ware's type I covers all Richard's gold with plain lettering, Ia consisting of the rare coins with late Edwardian lettering and Ib the much more extensive series from the new letter punches of style A. This division roughly approximates to that between Potter's types I and II for the silver, but the correspondence is not exact. Nobles of type I, like the Post-Treaty nobles of Edward III, include all four titles, England and France, Ireland and Aquitaine, and the halves (unlike their predecessors) mostly do so as well, although inevitably with severe abbreviation.

The Ia phase was brief. The two London obverse dies for nobles closely reproduce the Post-Treaty type, with the same lettering (and symbol for &), and details of the design (such as 3-1 ropes) unchanged except that there is a small lis instead of an annulet above the sail. No new obverse dies for Ia nobles are known at Calais, but three old Edwardian dies were used with *R*-marked reverses, and in addition to these mules, one of the three Calais Post-Treaty dies involved is also found with *Edw* altered to *Ric*. At London two half-noble obverses were also altered similarly, to be used with either *e* or *R* (over *e*) reverses. One of these two obverse dies has no mast or ornaments on the ship's side, suggesting that it may have been an unfinished Edwardian die brought into use early in the new reign, no London Post-Treaty half-nobles being known from obverse dies of that period. Of Calais also there is no new Ia half-noble obverse, although as with the early nobles of this mint there is an (unaltered) Edwardian obverse muled with a reverse of Richard.

Of type Ib there are nobles and halves of both mints. Those of Calais are much the rarer, reflecting the virtual inactivity of this mint for nearly six years from 1381. London Ib nobles have an annulet above the sail, and those of Calais a quatrefoil, in both cases like late nobles of Edward III. Earlier Ib reverses still have the trefoils at the corners of the central panel composed of three solid pellets, as in the Post-Treaty series, but the outer pellet is broken on later Ib dies (and often in IIa). The very rare Calais Ib halves have the same quatrefoil as on the nobles, but London halves have a saltire above the sail and this also occurs on an abnormal late Ib noble die which, exceptionally, has two ropes to the prow. The last Calais noble of Ib also has 3-2 rigging but is the more remarkable, in that it drops the French title and so anticipates the defining characteristic of the following type.

Quarter-nobles of the First Period begin with a very rare type (Ia) having the king's initial in the central panel, a feature quickly dropped on this occasion as it had been when last essayed (in 1361), because the letter was too large for the limited space available on the smallest gold coin. In the less rare type Ib the *R* was replaced by a small lis. One of the new reverse dies has four small points at the corners of the initial cross, as had occurred on a few late coins of Edward III, and the same is also to be seen on one noble die of type Ib. Quarters of Richard's reign normally include the English title only, but one obverse die of Ib, with a trefoil above the shield, is also notable for reading *Rex Angl & F*. If any quarter-nobles were struck at Calais during Richard's reign, the trefoil and French title on this die might have been intended for differentiation, but this is speculative.

Richard II, Second Period (c. 1390 – 1399)

As in the 1370s and 1380s, a large majority of the gold available in the 1390s was minted into nobles. Those with style B lettering, divided by Webb Ware into two types according to whether they (II) omit or (III) include the French title, are of considerable variety, and the lettering itself is far from uniform. The first nobles with indented lettering (IIa) are from coarsely made dies. Unusually, those of Calais, without special marks, are considerably more plentiful than those of London, which often have a saltire above the sail. This position was reversed at the next stage, in which the IIb nobles with a trefoil of pellets over the sail, and described as being of robust style, are plentiful of London but very rare of Calais. Still without the French title there are, finally, rare nobles of both mints, without particular marks, but characterized by what Webb Ware has described as a porcine face, with a broad, snout-like nose (IIc). One IIc obverse die was first used at London and then, with an added pennant, sent to Calais. Reverses of type II begin with the trefoils at the central panel from the broken punch with solid pellets, as in type Ib, but this was replaced by a trefoil composed of three annulets, followed in IIc by a new solid trefoil punch with a central hole. Another useful reverse feature for purposes of classification is the crown, which in IIa, and into IIb, often appears with a break in the upper band, by the left fleur.

FRACTURED PUNCHES ON GOLD OF RICHARD II, SECOND PERIOD

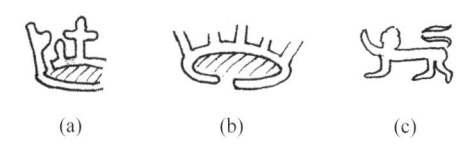

(a) Crown with upper band broken by left fleur, type II nobles;
(b) Crown with brokenlower band, type III nobles; (c) Leopard's tail broken, type III nobles.

The earliest nobles with the French title resumed (IIIa), common of both mints, also lack special marks. Again one London die went to Calais with added pennant. On reverses the trefoils consist of three annulets again, but their dies are often distinguishable from IIb by a break in the lower band of the crown (which permits the identification of IIc/IIIa mules). Later nobles of type III are rare. IIIb, otherwise similar to IIIa, has small marks on the rudder, a lis at London and a lion at Calais. In IIIc the marks are by the shield, a trefoil between shield and prow at London, but two separate pellets, above and below the right of the shield, at Calais. At each mint two IIIb dies were converted by having the new marks of IIIc added. Throughout type III a broken leopard punch was used, showing increasing damage to the tail.

Richard's last nobles (IV), of London only and very rare, resemble the first heavy nobles of Henry IV. Most of these are marked by new symbols on the rudder, first an escallop shell (IVa), then a crescent (IVb). One of the former has the escallop added to a IIIc die. There is also a remarkable die (IVa1) on which the escallop occurs not as a ruddermark but as a stop before and after *Gra*. The shell was a badge of pilgrimage in the middle ages, but why it should suddenly have appeared on the coinage at this point is mysterious – the more so since the use of pictorial symbols within the inscription is a most exceptional occurrence before the reign of Henry VI. There are no nobles or halves with either an escallop or a crescent on the rudder from Calais, where very little gold was minted in Richard's last two years.

Half-nobles of the Second Period are all rare, particularly those of Calais. The halves of type II, without the French title, are of London only, and very rare. One has a roundel with incuse saltire above the sail; another has annulet stops on the reverse, their only occurrence noted on any coin of this reign. With the French title restored (and many variations in the abbreviated readings), there are halves of both mints. Those without extra marks correspond to the IIIa nobles. Of IIIb there is a London half with a lion on the rudder, a mark found on nobles only at Calais. The last Calais half-noble of the reign has a saltire to the left of the rudder because of which it has provisionally been taken to be equivalent to nobles of IIIc without ruddermarks but with symbols added in the field. At London the last half has a small crescent on the rudder, like the IVb nobles.

The rare quarter-nobles of the Second Period are easily recognised, not only by their lettering but also in having a pellet within the central panel instead of an *R* or lis. As before there is no apparent indication of the mint, and it is doubtful whether any belong to Calais. Because of the shorter inscription on the smallest gold coin, readings without the French title occur at several periods, and no quarters can therefore be associated with the nobles of type II on that basis. The first quarter-noble with indented lettering is a mule from an old and rusty obverse die of type Ib. Two varieties with trefoils, above the shield or in the spandrels, are associated with type IIIc, because of the trefoil that occurs on IIIc nobles. The die with trefoils in the spandrels is found with the mixed lettering of style C on the reverse (presumably a IIIc/IV mule), which supports the late position of the trefoil-marked dies within type III. The IIIc obverses both include the French title, but it does not feature on another quarter (tentatively classified as IIIa because it has no special mark), which has the first letters of the inscription apparently overpunched; for this reason it was once regarded as being from an altered die of Edward III, but the indented lettering precludes this and the original reading remains a mystery. There is, however, no ambiguity about the final Richard quarter-noble which has an escallop above the shield like the ruddermark on IVa nobles.

FEATURES OF LATE COINS OF RICHARD II

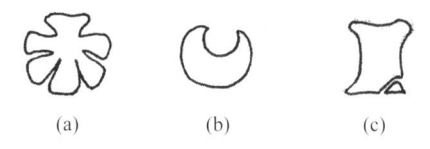

(a)   (b)   (c)

(a) Escallop, York III and late Richard gold; (b) Crescent, late gold;
(c) Cracked *I* punch, later 1390s.

Later groats of Richard II are rare; few if any would have been struck during the first half of the 1390s, which may be why there are no Richard groats without the French title. A distinguishing feature of reverses of silver coins of types III and IV is the close grouping of the pellets in the quarters of the cross, which tend to coalesce into a trefoil. Potter counted seven obverse dies of type III groats, with the waisted uprights and concave serifs of style B lettering. The first of these (IIIa), which is also muled with reverses of types I and II, is of a transitional character. It retains the traditional style of bust and crown, and the spellings *Di* and *Franc* from type II. Other oddities are a tenth fleur on the tressure and part of an extra arc (to the left of the crown), and a composite letter *F* made from a punched upright and engraved strokes. Later groat dies (IIIb) read *Dei* and have a new form of bust with the hair on one (the dexter) or both sides set at an angle and leaving a gap between hair and cheek. This wider setting of the curls is a notable feature of much of Henry IV's silver coinage as well as of Richard's later issues. One of the IIIb groat obverses (*Franci*) with the new bust still has the old crown, with short intermediate ornaments, but others have a new crown all the elements of which are taller. The reversed *N*s in London are often double-barred on type III reverses, and the contraction mark over the second one is now dropped.

The last groats in Richard's name (type IV), from two obverse dies distinguished by a crescent on the breast, are extremely rare. Although in some other respects they have affinities with type III, there are no mules with earlier types and the dies include some new and thicker letter forms; the very small *A* and *T* are distinctive. Walters thought that these crescent coins might have constituted the missing heavy groats of Henry IV, of whom the crescent was a personal emblem; but it also appears on some late Richard nobles, and there is no obvious reason why Henry's own name should at some stage have been used on new dies for every other denomination of silver and gold but not for groats. There are also, however, two groat obverse dies, very similar in style to Richard's type IV but lacking the French title; although they read *henric* and carry distinguishing marks of Henry IV's light coinage (pellet and annulet), there are signs that the king's name may have been altered, in which case these dies could have been made late in Richard's reign but not brought into use until 1412.

Halfgroats of the last decade of the fourteenth century are of great rarity and unusual interest. In addition to those in Richard's name there are some in Edward III's, from old Post-Treaty obverse dies coupled with reverses not earlier than the 1390s. Only one Richard obverse die is recorded with style B lettering. It includes the French title, and its lettering is as on the type IIIa groat, with the composite *F*. It was used with a type II reverse as well as with new reverse dies of its own period. The last two obverse dies of Richard II, although also described by Potter as of his type III, are in fact entirely different from this one, in bust, crown, tressure and lettering, as well as being without the French title, and like their related reverses they are better classed as type IV. The face is broader in the cheeks, the crown is lower (from two different punches, one abnormally wide) and the tressure flatter. Lettering is mixed, but dumpier than before (style C), with the crack in the *I* punch well developed. Although these late halfgroats do not, as has sometimes been imagined, have a crescent on the breast, they are in other respects stylistically similar to the groats of type IV.

Halfgroat reverse dies of late Richard II are also of two main types. The earlier (Potter's 'IIIa') has letters from the same elegant punches in the outer inscription as the single type IIIa obverse die, with neat but slightly larger letters in the inner circle. The later type of reverse (Potter's 'IIIb', but here type IV) has mixed lettering with a number of the same heavier letters as on the last two obverse dies, and including a characteristic (reversed) *N* in *London* with thick, concave uprights and prominent hollowed serifs. Reverse dies of both these types are found combined with the one Richard type III obverse and with the two Post-Treaty obverse dies of Edward III (reading *Frac* and *Franc*) which were brought back into use at this period (both of these having already been paired with normal late Edward reverses in the 1370s); and one of the type III reverses involved provides a die-link between the Richard type III obverse and the *Frac* Edwardian obverse. The type IV halfgroat obverses have only been found with cognate reverses; one of these reverses, however, has unbarred *N*, a die also used with a Henry IV obverse, and perhaps indicating a Richard/Henry mule. Taken on its own, therefore, the evidence of reverse die usage would suggest that the sequence of the respective obverse dies of this period could be Richard type III (with reverses of types II, III and IV), Edward III revived (with III and IV reverses) and lastly Richard type IV (with reverses of type IV, and perhaps also of Henry). However, the circumstances in which Edwardian dies were reused at this time are obscure, and, as discussed below, it is easier to think of reasons why this highly exceptional step should have been taken just after rather than during the reign of Richard II.

London pence of the Second Period are also of considerable rarity. The only ones attributable to the end of Richard's reign are of type IV, with style C lettering. Only two obverse dies are recorded. Like the last Richard halfgroats, these both lack the French title, although this is less significant on the smaller coins. Their normal reverses differ from their predecessors in having Gothic *n* and the pellets grouped as trefoils. Dies of these type IV Richard pennies are muled both ways with Henry IV's. No London penny of Richard's type III is known, but one reverse die combined with a Henry obverse might be regarded as a representative of that type since it has indented lettering with reversed Roman *N*s. Of York, however, there are pence of both types III and IV. Although they are less rare than those of London, the number of dies involved was not great even though they were as usual more heavily used. Of type III, with style B lettering, there are three York obverse dies, all with the French title. The face is abnormally large, reminiscent of that on some late halfgroats and pence of Edward III, with shortish hair close to the head and a much flatter crown than before. Type III reverse dies, with tightly grouped pellets, are notable for having an escallop after *Ebor*, the mark that occurs on Richard's type IVa gold. One type III York obverse die, with a bad die-flaw across the head below the crown, has been found paired with a reverse of type II, and there are also mules both ways between type III and local dies. It is noteworthy that in the case of all these (very rare) mules their dies were in a worn or damaged condition, raising the possibility that they might have been produced at a later time from old dies that had been laid aside. The last York pence in Richard's name, of type IV, share the characteristic splayed hair and style C lettering of other contemporary coins. They are very rare. Two of the three obverse dies involved have the English title only.

Like the larger silver, halfpence and farthings of the Second Period are considerably scarcer than those of the First. Halfpence are found with both the indented (B) and the dumpy (C) lettering, corresponding respectively to types III and IV of other denominations. Purvey estimated that those of type III constituted around twenty per cent, and of type IV around ten per cent, of all halfpence of the reign. The portrait on the type III halfpence has a lower crown and longer neck than in type II. There is often a central hollow in the contour of the bust and a thin line around its lower edge. A few dies of type III read *Rex Angl F*, possibly echoing the resumption of the French title on type III nobles; halfpence and nobles were the denominations in most plentiful production during the later 1390s. In type IV the hair is set wider, with a tiny inner curl; the face is U-shaped, the chin is broader, and the shoulders narrower. There are two sizes of head, corresponding with the punches used for nobles and half-nobles respectively. Reverses of type IV were muled with a number of obverse dies of types I and II, and one type IV obverse was paired with a reverse of type II; but Purvey noted only one occurrence of a II/III mule. There may have been some extra call for halfpence at the end of the reign, involving the revival of any available old dies.

Farthings like those of the First Period may have continued to be produced in the 1390s. However, one very rare type which undoubtedly belongs to the Second Period has a larger head than before, with a wide jowl, from the same punch as was used for Richard's last half-noble.

Henry IV, Heavy Coinage, 1399-1411

The London bullion accounts of the reign of Henry IV run from 15 October 1399, shortly after Richard had been deposed and Henry was proclaimed king. They show entries for some £45,000 of gold and only £1,750 of silver up to Michaelmas 1408, with no record thereafter until the year 1411/12 when coinage was resumed on a much increased scale following the weight reduction at Easter 1412. The first year's output of Henry's heavy coinage was the largest annual figure for both metals, and almost half the total bullion had passed through the London mint in the first three years, to September 1402.

In only one of the six succeeding years up to 1408 did the output of gold reach £5,000. The silver figures also follow a declining trend, although on an even smaller scale, only once reaching £100 in any year after 1403/4, and concluding with the derisory sum of £8 in 1407/8. At this point, despite the traditional reluctance to recognise the increasing relative value of the precious metals by reducing the weight of the coinage, and in face of the Statute of Purveyors, the king must have felt nevertheless that circumstances could no longer be resisted. For there exists a draft indenture between the crown and Richard Garner, appointed in February 1409 as master worker at the mints of London and Calais and keeper of the exchange in London, under which forty-eight gold nobles were to be struck to the pound instead of forty-five and 28s. of the larger silver instead of 25s. This would have reduced the weight of the noble from 120 gr. to 112½ gr. and of the penny from 18 gr. to just over 16 gr., against the 108 gr. and 15 gr. eventually adopted in 1412. There are no mint accounts between 1409 and 1412, and this prompted Blunt to wonder whether their absence was deliberate, to conceal an experimental debasement. However, the suggested weight reduction if implemented would presumably have resulted in a measurable increase in output, as indeed occurred following the slightly larger reduction of 1412, and there is no numismatic evidence to indicate that this happened. Although in theory it should be possible to identify coins struck on the 1409 scale by their weight, only the higher denominations are heavy enough for such a change to be reliably detected; but no nobles on an intermediate weight standard have been found, and there are no groats at all of this period. Since the draft indenture seems never to have been enrolled, the lack of accounts for the relevant years may mean no more than that the mint remained closed through want of bullion.

All denominations of the heavy coinage of Henry IV are rare, partly because of the limited output of new coin but also, probably, because the weight reduction of 1412 provided an incentive to have recent gold coins melted for reminting. Although a recent find from the coast of Holland has added to the small number of heavy nobles, their survival rate remains low. Least rare of the coins of this period are halfpence and York pence, both continuing the relatively prominent roles they had played in the previous reign. London struck little silver larger than halfpence – the groat of the heavy coinage is lacking altogether, while the heavy halfgroat and penny of this reign are two of the classic rarities of the late medieval English series. As the bullion figures suggest they might be, heavy London gold coins are less rare than silver apart from halfpence, although quarter-nobles are very rare and halves more so. Calais struck only about one-third as much gold as London, and its coins are correspondingly fewer.

FRENCH ARMS IN FIRST QUARTER ON HENRY IV GOLD

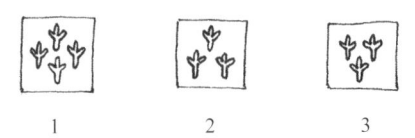

1, Four fleurs-de-lis; 2, One lis above, two below; 3, Two lis above, one below.

With the material so sparse and probably incomplete, it is difficult to define the structure of the coinage, but in addition to the mint accounts the gold supplies two important pointers. The first, as usual, is epigraphy. Many of the dies for silver still exhibit the coarser lettering of the later 1390s (style C). Relatively early in Henry's reign, however, since it occurs on virtually all his heavy gold coins, a new style of lettering (D) was introduced, not unlike some of the 'fishtail' founts of the 1390s, but finer and more elegant. In style D the *G* is at first round and curled, *&* is unbarred and the top-bar of *T* is shaped (D1). At the end of the London noble series some new forms of style D are found, notably *G* with a more pointed base, *&* with a central cross-bar, *T* with the top-bar straight and thin, and the feet of letters such as *A* more indented (D2). The other significant feature for sequence is heraldic – the form of the French arms in the first quarter of the shield. Although the ancient royal arms of France, a field *semée de fleurs-de-lis*, had been replaced on French coinage under Charles VI, since the 1380s, by three lis only (supposedly an allusion to the Holy Trinity), this change was not reflected in the quartering of the arms on English coins until the reign of Henry IV. His earliest gold still has the arms of France ancient (type 1), with four whole lis in the first quarter. The new three-lis arms then occur in two forms, first with one lis above and two below (type 2), and then in their final shape, with two lis above and one below (type 3).

Based on these three types of arms, the extant varieties of gold are as shown in the table (using Blunt's original numeration of the nobles according to their ruddermarks).

HENRY IV HEAVY COINAGE GOLD: TYPES OF FRENCH ARMS

	Arms 1	Arms 2	Arms 3
LONDON			
Nobles	Ia	Ib	II, III
Half-nobles	x	x	
Quarter-nobles	x		x
CALAIS			
Nobles	I, IIa	IIb, III	
Half-nobles		x	
Quarter-nobles		x	

London nobles usually have a small crescent on the rudder, like the last nobles of Richard II. Those with the intermediate arms (Blunt Ib) are rarer than those with the four lis (B.Ia). Late in the series (and probably after the closure of Calais in 1403/4) come the nobles of type 3, with new letter forms, the inner tressure on the reverse corded rather than beaded, and a small lis or saltire by the lion in one quarter. These extremely rare coins are found with four different varieties of obverse: as mules with type 1 or 2; with a new obverse (B.II), still with the earlier form of fine lettering (D1) but with a lis instead of a crescent on the rudder and with annulet stops (type 3a); and with an obverse die (type 3b), having new lettering as on the reverse, and a pellet on the rudder (B.III). This 3b die is the only obverse known in Henry's heavy gold coinage with the same late lettering (D2) as on obverses of his halfgroats and London pence. The 3a die was subsequently used in the light coinage with an annulet added on the ship's side. Another old obverse die was also amended in this way: it is of particular interest in that the lettering is late (with barred *&*) but the arms are of type 2, a combination not recorded for any extant heavy noble.

Most of the Calais gold was struck in 1399-1401, and its accounts were finally closed in March 1404, after recording only £300 in the last twelve months. Calais nobles are only found with the early and intermediate forms of the French arms. On the former a small coronet is placed vertically behind the rudder (B.I), or on it horizontally (B.IIa). With type 2 arms the ruddermark is either the horizontal coronet again (B.IIb) or a small star (B.III), both of the highest rarity.

Half-nobles of both mints are exceptionally rare. Those of London follow the nobles of types 1 and 2, with a crescent on the rudder. The only variety recorded of Calais (type 2) has no ruddermark, but the coronet occurs on the reverse, instead of an initial cross.

Quarter-nobles are found with all three types of arms. The normal reverse type has a pellet in the central panel, as on the later quarters of Richard II. Those of type 2, all from the same pair of dies, are with reverse mintmark coronet as on the Calais half-noble, and as such are the only quarters of any reign that can be attributed to Calais with full confidence. With a crescent above the shield, other heavy quarters may equally surely be attributed to London. Those with type 1 arms are from an obverse die curiously reading *henricus* in full but omitting *Rex*. The second crescent-marked obverse (type 3) is paired with two reverses: one with a central pellet (perhaps a 3/1 mule); the other with a lis (as also found in the light coinage). One other quarter-noble with a lis in the reverse panel probably belongs to the heavy coinage. It carries no special marks, although most unusually its stops are trefoils composed of three large pellets (as on the cusps); unfortunately it is so heavily clipped that its letter forms are unclear, but its combination of type 1 French arms with what appears to be thicker lettering than on any other heavy gold coin of Henry IV suggests an early point in the reign.

Dies for the heavy silver coinage exhibit either coarser lettering in the late Ricardian style C or the finer fount of style D as used for Henry's gold. In the former category come the York pence, most halfpence, all the reverse dies for halfgroats and most of the reverses for London pence. (There is also one London penny obverse die with dumpy letters, but this is only known from a later coin on which the symbols of the light coinage have been added.) With style D lettering are a few halfpence, the obverses of halfgroats and London pence, and one penny reverse. It could be that a new and more elegant fount was introduced for gold early in the new reign, while coarser lettering remained in use for a while on silver; but, if so, it would have been a most unusual situation, and the relationship between different denominations at this period remains puzzling.

It is strange that no heavy groats of Henry IV appear to have been struck, since the minting of larger coins was more profitable and at most periods halfgroats were less extensively produced. Only two obverse dies each, however, are found on halfgroats and London pence. They all have the finer lettering of the new reign and a small star on the breast. On the basis of the mint accounts, one would expect these dies to have been made during the period 1399-1404, after which silver coinage declined to insignificance. Certain features of Richard II's coinage, such as the wide hair, flat tressure (although with larger fleurs on the cusps) and trefoil-pellets, continued on Henry's silver. However, all four of the new halfgroat and penny obverse dies have the pointed *G* of style D2, as on the type 3b London noble, and the halfgroat dies also have the distinctive cross-barred &. On the face of it, therefore, this would place them at a point corresponding to a relatively late date in the gold coinage (after the last dies made for Calais). However that may be, it is curious that no new reverse dies for halfgroats with style D letters appear to have been made during Henry's heavy coinage to match their obverses. The halfgroat reverses involved are similar to reverses of Richard's type IV, with irregular style C lettering, although *N* in *London* is unbarred on Henry's halfgroats (except that on one of the dies the second *N* appears to consist of a *D* with a heavy upright punched over its right side). Technically, therefore, all Henry's heavy halfgroats seem to be mules with the reverses earlier than their obverses. Although these reverse dies, with unbarred *N*, are commonly regarded as belonging to the coinage of Henry IV, they do tend to show signs of age; and since one is also found with a type IV Richard obverse, it is not inconceivable that it, and perhaps others, could have been made during the previous reign.

Edward III – Henry IV

In the case of the London pence, most of the surviving examples are undoubtedly mules between the reigns. Both obverse dies include the French title again. One of them has a small head on a tall neck; the other, with a larger head, has three small, faint points above the crown, like some dies for silver of the 1370s and 1380s. Three types of reverse are found on Henry's heavy London pence: (i) with the waisted lettering and reversed Roman *N* of style B (type III) of Richard II; (ii) with the dumpier style C lettering of Richard's type IV; and (iii) with new Henrican lettering and an extra small point in two quarters. The penny with reverse type iii is the only silver coin larger than a halfpenny to have been struck from both dies with style D lettering. Those with reverses of types i and ii are Henry/Richard mules, one of the latter being from the same reverse die as a true coin of Richard II. There is also, more surprisingly, one case of the converse mule, a penny in the Fitzwilliam Museum from a Richard type IV obverse (with the name mutilated) combined with the same type iii reverse die as is found with its own Henry IV obverse.

The only denomination in Henry's heavy coinage that includes true coins with both style C and style D lettering in sequence is the halfpenny. In general appearance the former halfpence (class 1) are similar to those of the 1390s, with some variety of bust. Often the head is small, on a tall neck, with tight hair (like Richard's type III); or the face may be more U-shaped, with wider hair and a small pellet as an inner curl beside each cheek (as on Richard's type IV). Sometimes also there is a fine line below the bust. The later halfpence (class 2), which are rarer, have a distinctive tall bust with hunched shoulders. They have sometimes been attributed to the light coinage, because others of them have annulets added beside the neck. However, there are no light London silver coins (above the farthing); attributable to the beginning of the new coinage but without its distinguishing fieldmarks, and these unmarked halfpence are more logically regarded as late products of the heavy coinage. In the Attenborough hoard there was a halfpenny from a normal Henry class 2 reverse die combined with an aged and rusty Richard obverse.

One of the two Henry IV farthings in the 1868 Highbury find was attributed to the heavy coinage on the grounds of general similarity to late farthings of the previous reign and a lack of features linking it to the light coinage. One or two other specimens have subsequently emerged. They have a large head, with little or no neck, somewhat as on Richard's last type, but the crown is slightly larger.

Two new obverse and three reverse dies for pennies were provided in May 1400 for the archbishop of York, who had returned his old dies to the exchequer in February. The style C lettering is small and coarse, and the omission of *D G* allowed room for longer forms of the French title – *Franc* and *Francie*. Both dies were heavily used, but presumably not beyond the execution of Archbishop Richard Scrope after he had aligned himself with the northern rebellion of 1405. By the time his successor, Henry Bowet, received his temporalities at the end of 1407 coinage had virtually ceased at London and Bowet's earliest coins belong to the light coinage from 1412 onwards, which also saw the revival of minting at Durham, after a much longer interval.

To summarize, all the halfgroats and most of the London pence are from old reverse dies; both the penny and the halfpenny undoubtedly occur also as Richard/Henry mules; and one halfgroat may also be a Richard/Henry mule if all halfgroat reverse dies with unbarred *N* were made under Henry IV. Only one conclusion can be drawn from this extensive muling between the reigns. Clearly, a number of Richard's dies, including obverses, must have remained in use for Henry IV. As long ago as 1905 Walters had suggested that a Richard (type IV) halfgroat had been defaced by means of a line impressed through the king's name, a suggestion received with some scepticism until in 1936 Blunt noticed similar mutilation of the letters *Ric* on the Fitzwilliam mule penny. More recently a comparable defacement has been observed on a late Richard noble. In each case the mutilation appears to have been made to the coin, not to the die, and the mule penny shows that it must have been done in the reign of Henry IV. Whether it was applied systematically to all or most of the coins struck from obverses that survived from the previous reign we cannot tell, but it seems a cumbersome process and might perhaps have been confined to individual groups of coins such, for example, as those used by the royal household. One can only speculate about this but the defacement does corroborate the message of the mules that the London mint continued to use old dies for some time after the accession of Henry IV. It is against this background that the reuse of two halfgroat obverse dies of Edward III deserves reconsideration. Although the evidence of reverse die pairing might point to an earlier date, Blunt argued that old Edwardian dies could have been found more acceptable at the beginning of Henry IV's reign than those in the name of the cousin whom he had deposed, and this would offer a plausible context for their revival. It would also help toward the resolution of another conundrum – the apparent lack of early Henry IV obverse dies for London silver, other than halfpence, to match the relatively high output recorded early in the new reign. While some of this seems to have been from dies of Richard II, and a considerable part of it may have been in Henry's halfpence, a situation in which (for whatever reason) new dies for larger silver were for a time not being produced would provide suitable circumstances for the revival of old ones, particularly if they avoided Richard's name.

Mint Accounts

London accounts are complete for the whole period, save for a (perhaps improbable) nil entry for silver alone in 1365-7 and for both metals in the period 1408-11, just before the recoinage. There are also accounts for silver in the short periods of activity at York in 1353-5 and at Calais in 1363-5. Apart from a temporary closure in 1384-7, accounts for Calais gold run from 1363 to 1404, when the mint finally closed for lack of bullion. With few exceptions, London accounts from 1357 onwards were made up to Michaelmas, to coincide with the exchequer year, with interim accounts also to February, March, April or June in 1357-63, but for whole years thereafter. Accounting dates at Calais were much more irregular, although often set at twelvemonth intervals. Where accounts run from one Michaelmas (M) to the next, no day or month is indicated (e.g., 1357/58).

LONDON	£ gold	£ silver	YORK	£ silver
24.6.1351-24.6.1352	144,490	70,962		
24.6.1352-6.5.1353	28,322	79,286		
7.5.1353-M.1354	172,233	114,063	14.7.1353-24.12.1354	23,452
M.1354-31.5.1355	52,093	23,605	25.12.1354-29.5.1355	2,365
31.5.1355-24.12.1355	32,658	24,689		
24.12.1355-6.11.1356	8,278	28,330		
6.11.1356-M.1357	77,243	18,138		
1357/58	112,167	12,315		
1358/59	97,988	10,423		
1359/60	62,909	6,143		
M.1360-5.3.1361	48,341	1,128		

Edward III – Henry IV

London	£ gold	£ silver		
5.3.1361-M.1361	159,528	4,892		
1361/62	131,141	14,164	Calais	£ silver
1362/63	37,746	3,148	20.2.1363-10.4.1364	3,348
1363/64	20,487	2,839	10.4.1364-13.4.1365	487
1364/65	15,657	1,485		£ gold
1365/66	16,519	0	20.2.1363-10.4.1364	52,930
1366/67	11,116	0	10.4.1364-13.4.1365	10,247
1367/68	25,203	2,194	13.4.1365-13.4.1366	95,806
1368/69	72,715	1,535	13.4.1366-20.3.1368	113,960
1369/70	22,205	1,945	20.3.1368-26.10.70	61,023
1370/71	15,446	801	26.10.1370-16.10.1371	15,463
1371/72	21,826	174		
1372/73	14,597	453	16.10.1371-4.11.1373	70,086
1373/74	9,642	466	4.11.1373-4.11.1374	10,982
M.1374-24.9.1375	10,414	4,168	4.11.1374-4.11.1375	3,122
24.9.1375-24.7.1376	5,645	2,915		
24.7.1376-20.9.1377	4,101	225	4.11.1375-15.5.1381	29,769
20.9.1377-M.1384	34,163	8,849	15.5.1381-7.1.1384	90
1384/87	34,373	3,272		
19.1.1388-M.1389	27,370	354	17.1.1387-17.1.1390	32,537
1389/90	24,409	2,243		
1390/91	23,034	2,736		
M.1391-9.12.1392	25,427	410	17.1.1390-17.1.1393	6,618
9.12.1392-M.1393	13,036	222	17.1.1393-17.1.1394	22,184
1393/95	27,106	368	17.1.1394-17.10.1395	19,680
1395/96	8,058	212		
1396/98	34,351	1,469	17.10.1395-18.10.1397	10,564
M.1398-15.10.1399	16,636	1,432	18.10.1397-25.8.1399	363
15.10.1399-M.1400	12,623	565	25.8.1399-M.1401	12,745
1400/01	4,794	187		
1401/02	4,576	107	M.1401-30.3.1403	2,597
1402/03	4,486	162		
1403/04	4,716	451	30.3.1403-30.3.1404	301
1404/05	3,324	87		
1405/06	5,413	101		
1406/07	2,989	80		
1407/08	2,176	8		

Calendar 1351 – 1411

1351   Indenture for new coinage with Henry de Brisele and John of Chichester (20 June).

1352   Statute of Purveyors supposedly restricting the crown's freedom to alter coinage.
       York: Death of Abp. William Zouche (July); Abp. John Thoresby translated from Worcester (temporalities 8 Feb. 1353).

1353   Indenture with Henry de Brisele alone, terms as 1351 (28 March).
       York: First dies ordered for Abp. Thoresby (2 May). Dies ordered for royal mint (July); mint account runs from 14 July.

1355   Proclamation against light Scottish pence.
       York royal mint account closed (29 May).
       Indenture with William Potter (31 May); mint charges reduced, first post-1351 authority for fractions (*mailles*).

1356   Indentures with Hugh de Wychyngham (27 Jan.) and Henry de Brisele (1 Nov.)
       English victory at Poitiers; King John II of France captured (Sept.).

1357   King David II of Scotland released against ransom (Oct.).
       York: Indenture for reopened mint of Abp. Thoresby (18 Feb.).

1358   New Scottish coinage on English standard, to be interchangeable.

1360   Peace of Brétigny (near Chartres) confirmed at Calais (24 Oct.); French ransom agreed.

1361   Treaty of Brétigny/Calais ratified by Parliament (Jan.).
       Indentures with Walter dei Bardi (5 March; gold charges reduced) and Robert de Porche (20 June; privy mark first stipulated).

1363   Indentures for the Tower mint with Walter dei Bardi (11 Feb.) and for Calais with Henry de Brisele (1 March; 100 lb. of silver to be coined annually in farthings).
       Calais took over staple from Bruges; mint accounts commence (20 Feb.).

1365   Calais silver coinage accounts cease (13 April).
       No account for silver coinage at London (30 Sept. 1365 – 29 Sept. 1367).

1367   Devaluation in Scotland; currency of new Scottish money prohibited.

1369   War renewed. French title resumed (11 June). Staple removed from Calais (June).

1370   Calais staple resumed (Aug.).

1372   Indenture for Calais with Bardet de Malepilys (20 May).
       French naval victory off La Rochelle.

1373   Exchange rate between Scottish and English money set at 4:3.
       York: Death of Abp. Thoresby (6 Nov.); Alexander Neville elected (temporalities 6 June 1374).

1375   Truce of Bruges restricts English territory in France to Calais, Bordeaux and Bayonne.

1376   Death of Edward the Black Prince (8 June).

1377   Death of Edward III (21 June); Richard II acceded (22 June). John of Gaunt regent.

1379   First petition of the Commons for minting of halfpence and farthings. Bullion to be lodged at mint in respect of exports.

1380   Farthings distributed at Guildhall (May).

1381   Peasants' Revolt faced down by king.
       Durham: Death of Bp. Hatfield (8 May); John Fordham elected (temporalities 23 Oct.).

Edward III – Henry IV

1382   Board of enquiry into currency.
1383   Richard II married to Anne of Bohemia (Jan.).
       Staple removed from Calais to Middleburg.
1384   Durham: new dies authorised (Feb.).
       Calais mint account closed for three years from Jan. 1384.
1385   Michael de la Pole, Chancellor, recommended increase in value of currency.
1386   John of Gaunt left England.
1387   Lords Appellant assumed power.
       Calais mint resumed gold coinage (Jan.).
1388   York: Abp. Neville translated to St. Andrews (30 April); Thomas Arundel translated from Ely (temporalities 14 Sept.).
       Durham: Bp. Fordham translated to Ely (3 April); Walter Skirlaw translated from Bath and Wells (temporalities 13 Sept.).
1389   Richard II regained control; three year truce with France.
1393   Devaluation of Scottish coinage.
1394   Death of Queen Anne (June).
       Indenture for Tower and Calais mints with John Wildeman (9 Oct.).
       Durham: disused mint buildings leased out.
1395   Indenture for Tower and Calais mints with Nanfre Molakyn (9 July).
1396   Richard married to Isabella of France (Oct.).
       York: Abp. Arundel translated to Canterbury (25 Sept.); Robert Waldby translated from Chichester (temporalities 6 March 1397).
1397   York: Abp. Waldby died (between 29 Dec. 1397 and 6 Jan. 1398).
1398   Henry of Bolingbroke banished.
       York: Richard le Scrope translated from Lichfield (temporalities 23 June).
1399   Death of John of Gaunt (Feb.); his property forfeited.
       Richard II taken captive (19 Aug.), ceased to reign (29 Sept.); Bolingbroke acceded as Henry IV (30 Sept.); first new mint account from 15 Oct.
1400   York: old dies returned to exchequer (Feb.); new dies delivered (May).
1402   Indenture for Tower and Calais mints with Walter Merewe (1 July).
       Parliament ordered one sixth of silver bullion to be minted into halfpence and one sixth into farthings.
1404   Calais mint accounts closed (March) until 1422.
1405   York: Abp. Scrope executed (8 June) after northern rebellion.
1406   Durham: Death of Bp. Skirlaw (24 March); Thomas Langley appointed (temporalities 9 Aug.).
1407   York: Abp. Henry Bowet translated from Bath (temporalities 1 Dec.).
1408   No London mint accounts from Sept. 1408 to Nov. 1411.
1409   Richard Garner appointed master; draft indenture for Tower and Calais mints, reducing weights of gold and silver coins.
1411   Parliament (Nov.) approved reduction of weights from Easter 1412.

1351–1411

WEIGHTS 1351 – 1411

Gold £15 per lb. weight

Noble	6s. 8d.	45 per lb.	120 gr. (7.78g.)
Half-noble	3s. 4d.	90 " "	60 gr. (3.89g.)
Quarter-noble	1s. 8d.	180 " "	30 gr. (1.94g.)

Silver £1 5s. per lb. weight

Groat	4d.	75 per lb.	72 gr. (4.67g.)
Halfgroat	2d.	150 " "	36 gr. (2.33g.)
Penny	1d.	300 " "	18 gr. (1.17g.)
Halfpenny	½d.	600 " "	9 gr. (0.58g.)
Farthing	¼d.	1,200 " "	4.5 gr. (0.29g.)

NOBLES 1351 - 1411

Type generally as before but normally king's initial in central panel of rev., *e* (Edward III), *R* (Richard II) or *h* (Henry IV).

EDWARD III, PRE-TREATY PERIOD, 1351-61. London only. Titles normally *E/dward Dei Gra Rex Angl & Franc D hyb*; & as 7 with bar. Rev. normally *Ihc Autem Tranciens P(er) Mediu(m) Illoru(m) Iba(t)*. Small lis in one (usually first) quarter by lion (very rarely omitted).

A. Rev. only (muled with B obverses). *Autem* omitted; *Per* in full; *Transiens*. Double saltire stops. Large lettering, generally as 1346, with Gothic *m* and *n*; but *A* unbarred. Central *e* often reversed. Var. has saltires by lis at cross-ends.

B. Square initial cross. Double or single annulet stops (or none on obv.). Open *c* and *e*; Roman *M* and *N* (usually reversed); *A* barred or unbarred. Usually *Ihe(s)* for *Ihc*; *Tranciens* henceforward; *Per* in full. One early rev. die omits *Autem* and ends *Illorem Ibat Am*. Vars. *Ed/wa(r)d, hib, hybe*. Rare; also B/A mule (VR).

C. Square initial cross. Single annulet stops (or none on obv.). Closed *c* and *e* (earlier revs. have open *e* in centre); Gothic *m*; Roman *N* reversed; *R* with wedge tail. Early dies have *Ihes(u), Per*; later *Ihc, P*. Also B/C mule (VR).

D. Rev. only (muled with C obverses, ER). Square initial cross, defective. New lettering with integral *R*. *P* for *Per* (henceforward).

E. Plain initial cross patty. Stops annulets at first, later saltires. *N* usually unbarred. *c* and *e* often broken at bottom. Vars. *hib, hy* or omitted; inverted *F* in *Franc*. Workmanship deteriorates. Later dies have three quatrefoils instead of four on castles, and forecastle extended upwards. Also C/E mule (rare).

F. Mm. crown. Stops obv. saltires, rev. annulets. New lettering, with *c* and *e* unbroken or broken at top. *N* unbarred. VR; also E/F and F/E mules (ER).

G. Initial cross patty, with concave ends. *R* usually has long curved leg. Bowsprit sometimes omitted. Three, four or five lis in French arms. Lis on ship: Ga-c, single or paired by central lion, outer usually omitted; Gd-f, usually single lis, inner and outer. Also mules E/G, G/E, F/G and G/F, all VR or ER. For extensive muling of varieties within G, see below.

Pre-pellet phase (Ga-c).

Ga. Annulet before *E/*. Annulet stops. *c* and *e* unbroken or broken at top. Large central *e* on rev.

Gb. As Ga but no annulet before *E/* and smaller central *e* on rev. Var. omits *P*.

Edward III – Henry IV

Nobles

Gc. Saltire stops both sides. Usually a saltire before *E/*. Small central *e* on rev. Pellet-marked phase (Gd-h).
Gd. Single pellet (or annulet) by top lis on rev. (also one Gc die with annulet added). Obv. stops annulets, with nothing before *E/*; or saltires, with annulet or saltire before *E/*. Rev. stops saltires; small *e* in centre. *c* and *e* often broken at bottom.
Gf. Two pellets by top lis on rev. Saltire stops. No broken letters. Small *e* in centre of rev. One die with saltire before *E/* is perhaps Ge.
Gg. Saltire stops. Obv. as Gf, but *e* with protruding bar. Large *e* in centre of rev. Pellets by top lis sometimes omitted. Var. *Ybat*.
Gh. Obv. only (muled with revs. of Gf or Gg). As Gg but open *e*. VR.
Group G mules: E/Gc, F/Gb, F/Gg, Ga/E, Ga/F, all VR or ER. Ga/b, Ga/c, Ga/d, Ga/f; Gb/c, Gb/d, Gb/f; Gc/d, Gc/f; Gd/f; Gf/g, Gf/Treaty A; Gg/d, Gg/f; Gh/f, Gh/g; several of these mules are rare.

EDWARD III, TREATY A PERIOD, 1361. London only. No French title. & is barred 7. Saltire stops. Lis and lions varied. Usually vertical lines on planking of ship's side. Only *E/* before bowsprit. High forecastle. Annulets or pellets at corners of central panel on rev. Small lis by lion in one quarter. Coarse work. All rare.

A1 Experimental obv. inscriptions. Four dies: *E/dward(us) Dei Gra Rex Anglie & Aquta Dns;* or *D E;* or *Angl Dens hyb;* or *Dns hib & A*. Roman *N* or Gothic *n* on obv. Ropes 3 aft; 1, 2 or 3 forward. Rev. readings vary: two early dies (with trefoils instead of fleurs in spandrels) read *Per* and omit *Transiens*; others read *Transievs*, *P* and *Illorr*. Gothic *n*. Annulets at corners of panel. VR; also ER mules with Pre-Treaty obv. (Gf) or rev. (Gg).
A2 *E/dward Dei Gra Rex Angl Dns hib(n) & Acq*. Large letters *h, I* and *P; N* Roman (large; obv. only) or Gothic. Rev. annulets or (later) pellets at corners of panel; *Transiens* or *-ciens*, *Per* or *P, Illorr*. Rare; also ER mules Gf/A2 and A1/2.

EDWARD III, TREATY B PERIOD, 1361-9. London, Calais (*c* for *e* in centre of rev.; without or with pennant from stern). No French title: *Ed/ward Dei Gra Rex Angl Dns hyb & Aq/t*; & is reversed Z. Ropes 3-2 (or 3-1). Double saltire stops. Gothic *n*, curule *X*. Rev. large trefoils at corners of panel, no small lis by lion. *Transiens; Per* again in full. Fine work.

B1 Unbarred *A* in *Aqt* and *Ibat*.
London: Saltire before *Ed* (above or below sail).
Calais: Trefoils by &. Saltire or no mark before *Ed*. Without or with pennant. Rare.
B2 London: Annulet before *Ed*. Barred *A* in *Ibat* and sometimes in *Gra* and *Aqt*. Late var. (VR) has crescent on forecastle. Also rare mules B2/1.
Calais: Saltires by &. With or without pennant. Quatrefoil before *Ed,* unbarred *A;* or annulet after *Ed,* barred *A* in *Gra, Aqt* and *Ibat.* All VR.

EDWARD III, POST-TREATY PERIOD, 1369-77. London, Calais. French title resumed. Saltire stops.
1. Lettering as Treaty B2; usually barred *A* in *Aqt* and *Ibat*. *Ed/ward Dei G(ra) Rex Ang(l) & Fra Dns hyb & A(q)t*; annulet before *Ed*. Pellet-topped castles. With or without crescent on forecastle, and bowsprit. Ropes usually 3-2.
London: Var. ropes 2-2, 2-1. Rare.
Calais: No pennant, *c* for *e* in centre of rev. Var. *Tranciens*. VR.
2. New tall lettering. & is reversed *F* with long front. *Edw/ard Di Gra Rex Angl & Franc Dns hyb & Aq-Aquit*. Castles now with battlements. Ropes 3-1. Small point with *e* in centre of rev. (both mints). Sometimes pellet(s) by lis on rev.
London: Usually annulet over sail, or before *Edw*. Sometimes cross instead of point by central *e*. Vars. *Edw/ardus*; annulet on top right cusp. Also ER mule 2/1.

1351–1411

Nobles

Calais: Quatrefoil over sail; pennant. *hib.* Sometimes pellet(s) by or below shield.

RICHARD II, FIRST PERIOD (type I), 1377-c.1390. London, Calais (with pennant). Straight-sided lettering (style A). French title included. Ropes normally 3-1. Saltire stops. *R* in centre of rev.; trefoils of solid pellets at corners of centre panel. *A* in *Ibat* often chevron-barred.

Ia. *Ric/ard Di Gra Rex Angl & Franc Dns hib & Aq.* Lettering as late Edward III; reversed *F* for *&*.
London: Small lis over sail. VR.
Calais: No new obv. dies; *Ric* over *Edw* only (ER). Rev. dies mostly muled with unaltered Edward III obvs. (VR).

Ib. New lettering, with reversed *Z* for *&*. Usually *D* for *Di; D* for *Dns*. Top pellet of trefoils by rev. panel breaks.
London: Annulet over sail, or saltire on last die (which has 3-2 ropes). Early var. has points in angles of initial cross.
Calais: Quatrefoil over sail. Last die (ropes 3-2) omits French title. All rare.

RICHARD II, SECOND PERIOD (types II-IV), c. 1390 - 1399. London, all types; Calais (with pennant), types II and III only. Indented lettering (types II, III; style B), or mixed (type IV; style C). Ropes normally 3-1. Saltire stops.

Type II. No French title; *Ric/ard Dei Gra*. Style B lettering. Trefoils on rev. solid (broken), then composed of annulets; finally, solid with central hole.

IIa. Somewhat crude style. *hib, Aqt.* Some have upper band of rev. crown punch broken.
London: Usually saltire over sail. Var. ropes 3-2.
Calais: No mark over sail.

IIb. Neat dies; 'robust' style. *hib, Aqt.* Trefoil over sail (both mints).
London: Also ER IIb/a mule (broken rev. crown).
Calais: Rare.

IIc. Porcine face. No marks. *hyb; Aq(ui)t.* On rev. solid trefoils with central hole.
London: Also IIc/b mule (with annulet-trefoils). All VR.
Calais: One London obv. has pennant added. All rare.

Type III. French title resumed. Style B lettering. Annulet-trefoils again on rev. Leopard punch on rev. has tail broken behind head.

IIIa. Fine style. No marks. *Ric/ard Di Gra* (or *D G*). Many rev. dies have crown with nicked lower band.
London: Also ER IIc/IIIa mule.
Calais: One obv. has annulet-trefoil above sail. Another (from London) has pennant added. Also ER IIc/IIIa mule.

IIIb. As IIIa, but marks on rudder and usually *Rica/rd*.
London: Small lis on rudder. Rare.
Calais: Lion on rudder. VR.

IIIc. As IIIa, but marks by shield, *D(e)i, G(ra)* and *F(ranc)*.
London: Trefoil (slipped or plain) by shield. Two new dies and two of IIIb with trefoil added. Rare.
Calais: Pellet above and below shield. Two new dies and two of IIIb with pellets added. Rare.

Type IV. Style C lettering. London only.

IVa. With escallop mark.
IVa1. *Di Gra Rex Angl & Franc Dns hyb & Aqt*, with saltire stops except for escallop after *Di* and *Gra.* ER.

Edward III – Henry IV

Nobles

	IVa2. Escallop on rudder; slipped trefoil by shield. *Dei G(ra), F(ranc), Dns*. One new die and one of IIIc with escallop added. VR.
IVb.	Crescent on rudder. *D(e)i, D(ns)*. VR.

HENRY IV, HEAVY COINAGE, 1399-1411. London (types 1-3), Calais (with pennant; types 1, 2 only). *hen/ric D(e)i Gra Rex Angl & Franc D(ns) hi(b) & Aq(i)(t)*. & is reversed Z. Fine lettering (style D). Ropes normally 3-1. *h* in centre of rev. panel; annulet-trefoils at corners; initial cross patty. Stops normally double saltires.

1.	Arms of France ancient in first quarter of shield (four whole lis). Earlier (D1) lettering (curled *G*, *T* with shaped top bar, unbarred *&*).
	London: Crescent on rudder (Blunt Ia). VR.
	Calais: Vertical coronet behind rudder, no mast (B.I); or horizontal coronet on rudder (B.IIa). ER.
2.	New French arms with three lis, one above two. D1 lettering.
	London: Crescent on rudder (B.Ib). Vars. have ropes 4-1; or initial cross pierced or omitted. ER.
	Calais: Horizontal coronet (B.IIb) or star (B. III, *he/nric*) on rudder. ER.
3.	New French arms with two lis above one. London only. Rev. lis or saltire by lion in one quarter; inner tressure corded. Later (D2) lettering (except on obv. of 3a), with pointed *G*, *T* with plain top; barred *&*. Also mules with obv. of type 1 or 2. All ER.
3a	One obv. die with lis on rudder, D1 lettering (as types 1 and 2), stops broken annulets (B.II; this die reused in light coinage with annulet added on ship's side).
3b	D2 lettering. One obv. die, with pellet on rudder, *henr/ic* (B.III).

HALF-NOBLES 1351 - 1411

Type generally as before but normally king's initial in central panel of rev., *e* (Edward III), *R* (Richard II) or *h* (Henry IV).

EDWARD III, PRE-TREATY PERIOD, 1351-61. London only. Titles normally *E/dwar D(ei) G(ra) Rex Angl & Fra(nc) (D) (hyb)*; & as 7 with bar. Rev. normally *Domine Ne In Furore Tuo Arguas Me*. Usually a small lis by lion in one quarter, or in one spandrel. None of group D or F.

A.	Rev. dies only, muled with obv. of B or C. Stops double saltires. Large lettering; Gothic *m* and *n*; *A* unbarred. Central *e* upright, inverted or tilted.
B.	Obv. dies only of (rare) B/A mules. Annulet stops. Open *c* and *e*; Roman *N* reversed. *D Gra, Fra*. Early var. has *Ed* before bowsprit.
C.	Obv. dies only, muled with rev. of A (VR) or E (ER). Annulet stops. *Dei G, Franc_D*. Closed *c* and *e*; Roman *N* reversed. Ropes 3-3.
E.	Initial cross patty. Saltire stops (obv. single, rev. double). One obv. die, ropes 3-1, unbarred *N*. Rev. Gothic *n*. *Rurore, Arouas*. Sometimes *c* for *e* in *Nc*. Also C/E mule; all ER.
G.	Initial cross patty, with concave ends. Bowsprit sometimes omitted. Frequent muling between sub-groups (see below).
	Pre-pellet phase (Ga-c). Roman *N* unbarred on obv., Gothic *n* on rev. *Rurore, Arouas*. All VR.
Ga.	Annulet stops and annulet before *E/*. Ropes 3-2. *e* in centre of rev.

1351–1411

Half-Nobles

Gb. As Ga but no annulet before *E/* and ropes 3-3.

Gc. Saltire stops. Ropes 2-0. Pellet instead of *e* in centre of rev.

Pellet-marked phase (Gf-h). Two pellets by top lis on rev. Roman *N* (sometimes reversed) both sides. Saltire stops. *Furore, Arguas.*

Gf. Fleurs in spandrels. Normal *e* in centre of rev.

Gg. Trefoils in spandrels. *e* with protruding bar. Mules (rare) with Gf or Gh only.

Gh. Trefoils in spandrels. Open *e*. Var. has two pellets by crown instead of lis.

Group G mules: Ga/f; Gb/c; Gb/f; Gc/b; Gf/g; Gg/h; Gh/g. Several of these are rare.

EDWARD III, TREATY A PERIOD, 1361. London only. No French title. & is barred 7. Saltire stops. Usually vertical lines on planking of ship's side. Ropes 2 or 3 each side. Only *E/* before bowsprit (sometimes omitted). Annulets or pellets at corners of central panel on rev. Usually small lis by lion in one quarter. Coarse work.

A1 Experimental obv. inscriptions. Five dies (two with annulet above crown), *E/d Dei Gra Rex Angl Dns hib & Acq*, or *E/dwardu(s)* (or *-di*) *Dei G Rex Angl D* or *E/dward Dei Gra Rex Ang*. Rev. *Ne* usually omitted; sometimes Roman *N*. Annulets at corners of panel. Rare.

A2 *E/dward Dei G Rex Angl D h(i)b*. Large letters *F, h* and *I*. Gothic *n*. *Ne* always omitted; often *Arguts*. Annulets (earlier) or pellets (later) at corners of panel. Var. has *c* in central panel (ER). Also mules A1/2 (VR) and A2/1 (ER).

EDWARD III, TREATY B PERIOD, 1361-9. London, Calais (*c* for *e* in centre of rev.; some have pennant from stern). No French title. & is reversed Z. Double saltire stops. *Ed/ward Dei G Rex Angl D hyb & Aq/t*. Ropes 3-2. Gothic *n*; curule *X*. Trefoils at corners of rev. panel, no small lis by lion. Fine work.

B1 Unbarred A.

London: Saltire above fold of sail or before *Ed*. Var. *hib*.

Calais: Trefoils by &. Sometimes saltire above sail. With or without pennant. VR.

B2 London: Annulet above sail or before *Ed*. Second *A* in *Arguas* always barred.

Calais: Saltires by &. Quatrefoil before *Ed*. *A* unbarred. Pennant from stern. One die has crescent on forecastle. Also Calais (B1)/London (B2) mule (*e* in centre). All VR.

EDWARD III, POST-TREATY PERIOD, 1369-77. London, Calais. French title resumed. New lettering but still reversed Z for &. Saltire stops. No crenellations on castles.

London: Rev. only, muled with Treaty B obv. *e* and pellet in centre of rev. ER. (See under Richard II for London obv. dies of this group with altered name).

Calais: Pennant from stern. *Edw/ard* (or *Ed/ward*) *Di Gra Rex Angl & Franc (D)*. Quatrefoil before inscription. Ropes 3-1. *e* in centre of rev. Also mule with Treaty B rev. All ER.

RICHARD II, FIRST PERIOD (type I), 1377-c.1390. London, Calais (with pennant). Straight-sided lettering (style A); Gothic *n*. French title included. Saltire stops. Ropes 3-1. Trefoils of solid pellets at corners of rev. panel.

Ia. As Edward III, Post-Treaty. & is reversed *F*. Obv. Edward III dies with *Edw* altered to *Ric*.

London: Rev. new, or *R* over *e*. Also Ia/Edward mule. All ER.

Calais: Rev. only, muled with Edward obv. ER.

Ib. New lettering; & is reversed Z. *Ricard D(i) G Rex Angl & Franc D h* or *& F D hib & Aq*.

London: Usually annulet or saltire over sail. Rare.

Calais: Voided quatrefoil over sail. ER.

Edward III – Henry IV

Half-Nobles

RICHARD II, SECOND PERIOD (types II-IV), c. 1390 - 1399. London, all types; Calais (with pennant), III only. Indented lettering (types II, III; style B), or mixed (type IV, style C).

Type II. No French title. Style B lettering. London only. *Dei G* or *D Gra*. One has incuse saltire above sail. Rev. saltire or annulet stops. VR.

Type III. French title resumed. Style B lettering. Annulet-trefoils on rev.

IIIa. No extra marks. Varied obv. readings. London rare, Calais ER.

IIIb. Lion on rudder. London only. ER.

IIIc. Saltire behind rudder. Calais only. ER.

Type IV. London only. Style C lettering. Crescent on rudder (IVb). ER.

HENRY IV, HEAVY COINAGE, 1399-1411. London (rev. initial cross patty; types 1-2), Calais (with pennant; type 2 only). *hen/ric Di G(ra) Rex Angl & Fr(a)n(c) D h(i) (&) A(qt)*, & is reversed Z. *h* in centre of rev. panel, annulet-trefoils at corners. Saltire stops. Fine lettering (style D1) as on nobles of types 1 and 2.

1. Arms of France ancient in first quarter of shield (four whole lis). London only. Crescent on rudder, ropes 3-1 (equivalent to Ia nobles); *Frn*. ER.

2. New French arms with three lis, one above two. Ropes 2-1.
    London: Crescent on rudder (equivalent to Ib nobles); *Franc*. ER.
    Calais: No mark on rudder; rev. mm. coronet. ER.

QUARTER-NOBLES 1351 - 1411

Type generally as before but obverse tressure now always of eight arcs; also varied reverse designs in Treaty A issue, 1361. In centre of reverse king's initial, *e* (Edward III) or *R* (Richard II), or lis, annulet, quatrefoil, pellet or cross.

EDWARD III, PRE-TREATY PERIOD, 1351-61. London only. Titles normally *Edwar (D G) R(ex) Angl & Fran(c) (D hyb)*; & is barred 7. *A* unbarred.
Rev. *Exaltabitur in Gloria*; usually *e* in centre. None of group A, D or F.

B. Square initial cross. Annulet stops (often double on rev.). Open *c* and *e*; *N* reversed. Pellet below shield. Closed *e* in centre of rev. Early obv. reads *Edwar R, hyber*; others *D G Rex*. Some early rev. dies have abbreviation of *Amen* after *Gloria*. Rare.

C. Rev. only, muled with B obv., ER. Square initial cross. Closed *e*; hooked *A*; *N* reversed. *e* in centre. Single annulet stops.

E. Rev. only, muled with obvs. of B or G (both ER). Initial cross patty. Pellet in centre of rev. *N* unbarred. Annulet stops. Two dies, *Ghloria* and *Gahlori*.

G. Initial cross patty, with concave ends. *Edwar R (D G* omitted). *e* in centre of rev. Roman *N*, normally unbarred. True coin Gf only; all others mules.
   Pre-pellet phase (Gb only).

Gb. Obv. only (one die), muled with revs. of E and Gd (both VR). Annulet stops. Barred *N*. No annulet before *Edwar*.
   Pellet-marked phase (Gd-g). Saltire stops.

Gd. Revs. only, muled with obvs. of B (ER) or Ga (VR). Single annulet by top lis or lion. *Gahlori*. Pellet in central panel of rev.

Gf. Two pellets by top lis on rev. Normal *e. Gloria*. Small *e* in central panel. Also ER mule B/Gf.

Gg. Revs. only, muled with Gf obv. (VR). *e* with protruding bar. *Gloria*. Large *e* in central panel. No pellets by top lis. Var. *Exatabitur*.

1351–1411

Quarter-Nobles

EDWARD III, TREATY A PERIOD, 1361. London only. No French title. & is barred 7. Saltire stops. Pellets, annulets or trefoils on cusps. Annulets or pellets around centre of rev.

A1   *Edwr R Anglie & Dnus hv* (one die), pellets on cusps; or *Edwar Dei Grac Rex Angl D* (two dies), trefoils or annulets on cusps. Trefoils in spandrels both sides. Roman *N* on obv., Gothic *n* on rev. In centre of rev. *e* or pellet in panel with pellets at corners, or cross potent with annulets in angles. VR.

A2   Mixed lettering, large *I. Edwar Dei Gra(c) Rex Angl (D)*, Gothic *n*. Annulets or trefoils on cusps; pellets (omitted on one die) in obv. spandrels; trefoils or pellets in rev. spandrels. Rev. Gothic *n* or large Roman *N*. Vars. *Glora, Glria*. In centre, pellet in panel with annulets at corners (one die) or cross potent with annulets or large pellets. One rev. die has lis above second lion. Also VR mules A1/2 and A2/1.

EDWARD III, TREATY B PERIOD, 1361-9. London, Calais. No French title: normally *Edward Dei Gra Rex Angl*. Gothic *n*. Curule *X* unless stated. Saltire stops. Neat trefoils on obv. cusps. Nothing in spandrels. Small panel with neat trefoils at corners in centre of rev., containing lis, annulet or quatrefoil.

London (?), with lis in centre of rev.: B1. No mark before *Edward. A* unbarred. *X* patty or curule. B2. Annulet before *Edward.* Barred *A* in *Gloria*, barred or unbarred *A* on obv. Also rare mule B2/1.

Calais (?), with annulet (rare), or quatrefoil (VR), in centre of rev., unbarred *A* in *Gloria*: B1. No mark before *Edward.* Nothing, cross (with quatrefoil on rev.) or cross in circle above shield. B2. Pellet before *Edward*, cross in circle above shield; or annulet before *Edward*, barred *A* in *Angl*, crescent above shield (with quatrefoil on rev.).

EDWARD III, POST-TREATY PERIOD, 1369-77. No quarter-nobles recorded.

RICHARD II, FIRST PERIOD (type I), 1377 – c.1390. London (? and Calais; mint not indicated). Style A lettering. Saltire stops. Solid trefoils by rev. panel.

Ia.   *Ricard Dei Gra Rex Angl. R* in centre of rev. VR.

Ib.   New lettering. *D(e)i Gra Rex Ang(l)*, or (with small lis above shield) *D Gra Rex Angl & F.* Lis in centre of rev. Var. has four pellets by initial cross. Rare.

RICHARD II, SECOND PERIOD (types III, IV), c. 1390-1399. Mint not indicated. Indented lettering. Pellet in central panel of rev.

IIIa.   *Ricard Dei Gra Rex Angl, Ric* apparently overpunched. Also Ib/IIIa mule. All VR.

IIIc.   Trefoil of annulets above shield, *Di G Rex Angl & Franc*; or trefoils in spandrels, *Di Gra Rex Angl & F* (muled with IV rev.) All VR.

IVa.   Escallop over shield. *Dei Gra Rex Angl*. Also mule with IIIc obv. (trefoils in spandrels) has rev. with style C lettering. All ER.

HENRY IV, HEAVY COINAGE, 1399-1411. London (types 1, 3), Calais (rev. mm. coronet; type 2 only). Normally saltire stops.

1.   Arms of France ancient in first quarter of shield (four whole lis). London only.

1a.   *henric Dei Gra Rex Angl*, trefoil stops. No mark above shield. Lis in centre of rev. *Gloriah.* ER.

1b.   Crescent over shield, *henricus Di Gra Angl & Fran (Rex* omitted). Pellet in centre of rev. VR.

2.   New French arms with three lis, one above two.
     Calais only: one pair of dies, *henric Di Gra Rex Angl & Fra*, nothing above shield. Mm. obv. none, rev. coronet. Pellet in centre of rev. ER.

Edward III – Henry IV

Quarter-Nobles

3. New French arms with three lis, two above one.
London only: one obv. die, *henric Di Gra Rex Angl Fr*, crescent over shield. Initial cross patty. Lis in centre of rev.; var. with pellet in centre may be 3/1 mule. ER.

GROATS 1351 - 1411

Normal type: obv. crowned facing bust within a double tressure of (usually) nine arcs, the cusps ornamented with trefoils or small fleurs (omitted on two arches above crown, unless stated); rev. long cross patty, a group of three pellets in each angle, within two rings of inscription, *Posui Deum Adiutorem Meum* in outer circle, mint name in inner circle. Initial mark both sides.

EDWARD III, PRE-TREATY PERIOD, 1351-61. Titles normally *Edward D G Rex Angl & Franc D hyb*; & as 7 with bar. Usually *Posui/Deum A/diutor/em Meu.* London (B-G), York (D, E only). Mint name precedes *Civitas* in B-D, usually in E, rarely thereafter.

B. Square initial cross patty. Open *c* and *e*, Roman *M*. *N* reversed or unbarred. Stops pellets (VR and early) or annulets. Top cusps fleured. Often *Edwar* and *Gra*; some have *Di, hybe(r)*. Rev. *Lon/don/Civi/tas*; *Meum* in full. Var. (ER) has crowns instead of pellets in angles of cross. All rare.

C. As B, but Gothic *m*, closed *c* (except in *Civi*) and *e*. Wedge-tailed *R;* Roman *N* reversed; *S* from single punch; some have *A* with hooked limb. *D, Di* or *Dei*. Annulet stops. Top cusps often still fleured. *Meu* henceforward. Also rare B/C and ER C/B mules.

D. Square initial cross patty often damaged. Plain lettering, very small serifs; integral *R* with curled tail; *N* in *London* barred (early) or (usually) unbarred; closed *c* in *Civi*; sometimes *c* for *e*. Stops annulets or (VR) none.
London: Some with *M* for *N;* var. has inverted *F*. Also mules B/D (ER) and D/C (rare; one die has top cusps fleured).
York (*Ebo/raci/Civi/tas*): Reads *D Rex*, rare (E/D mules more usual).

E. Plain initial cross patty. Annulet stops (occasionally within words). *N* reversed, or often unbarred; *c* and *e* sometimes broken at bottom. Rev. stops rarely omitted.
London: Some early dies have squared *E,* or inverted *F*. Some with *M* for *N* in *London*. Small fleurs on breast or on all cusps (except at top) sometimes replaced by lis. Var. (ER) has tressure of eight arcs. Two irregular dies have tall crown and top cusps fleured. Also D/E and (ER) E/D mules.
York: Also E/D mules.

F. Mm. crown. Annulet stops. Roman *N* reversed, or more commonly unbarred; *c, e* and *D* sometimes broken. *Civi* now usually below *Posui*. Also E/F and VR F/E mules.

G. New initial cross patty, with concave ends. Stops usually annulets (except Gc, g, h, saltires). Annulet (Gc, saltire) within group of pellets in one quarter, occasionally omitted. *N* usually unbarred; *c* and *e* sometimes broken. Fleurs normally trefoil-shaped.

  Pre-pellet phase (Ga-Gc). No pellets in *tas*.

Ga. Top cusps fleured. Annulet below bust except on two early dies. Often *hy* or *h* for *hyb*. *N* barred (usually reversed) or unbarred (on rev. only, later). Rarely *Lomdom*. Annulet on earlier reverses in *Civi* quarter (sometimes outside pellets), later in any quarter (or none). Some revs. have lettering with prominent serifs.

1351–1411

Groats

Gb. As Ga but no annulet below (taller) bust, and top cusps unfleured; on one die fleurs are true fleurs-de-lis. *N* always unbarred; *c* and *e* often (later) sliced at top left. Annulet stops, very small on late dies. Annulet in any quarter (or none). Last occurrence (rare) of *Lon* under *Posui*. Var. *Ib* for *hyb*.

Gc. Reverses only (Gb/c mules). Saltire stops. Saltire within pellets in any quarter (or none). *c* and *e* often sliced.

Pellet-marked phase (Gd-Gh). Pellet(s) in *tas*.

Gd. Annulet stops. Top cusps unfleured. One pellet in *ta.s*. Annulet in *tas* or *don* quarter (or none). Broad *c* and *e*, often broken at bottom. Rare.

Ge. As Gf but small pellet above central fleur of crown.

Gf. Annulet stops. All cusps fleured. Two pellets in *t.a.s*. Larger and thinner *c* and *e* (unbroken). Annulet in *don* quarter.

Gg. Saltire stops. Small cross (or lis) on breast. Often with bust badly centred or fleurs misplaced. With or without fleurs on top cusps. Annulet in *don* quarter. Pellets in *t.a.s*. *e* often with protruding bar. Rare.

Gh. As Gg but open *e*. Shoulder fleurs sometimes missing. ER (but less rare as Gh/Gg mule).

Group G mules: E/G (VR), F/G, Ga/F (ER). Ga/b, Ga/c; Gb/a, Gb/c (Lawrence 'Gc'), Gb/d, Gb/f, Gb/g; Gd/c, Gd/f, Gd/g; Ge/d, Ge/g; Gf/d, Gf/g; Gg/f; Gh/g; all rare or VR except Gb/c.

EDWARD III, TREATY A PERIOD, 1361. No French title: *Edwar Dei G Rex Angl Dns hib(n) & Ac(q)*; & is 7 with bar. Annulet on cusp each side of crown; top cusps fleured or not. Saltire stops. Obv. Gothic *n*, rev. Roman *N* reversed. Some large letters (*h*, *I* and *P*). London only (*Civi/tas/Lon/don*, letters of same size as outer circle). VR.

EDWARD III, TREATY B PERIOD, 1361-9. No French title: *Edward Dei G Rex Angl Dns hyb & Aq(t)*; & is reversed Z). Top cusps fleured. Usually cross patty *X*; Gothic *n* on obv. Stops obv. saltires or annulets, rev. saltires. Lawrence varieties a-k. Three busts: 1. Smiling face with natural eyes; fleurs in crown have curved side foils. 2. Broader, oval face with round eyes; crown as with bust 1. 3. Narrow face with tapering chin, round eyes; thick line of drapery; crown with short, thick foils. London, normally *London Civitas* (with Roman *N*, reversed or unbarred), all varieties. Calais, *Vil/la.C/ale/sie*, B2(g) only.

B1. No mark before *Edward*; unbarred *A* in *Adiutore*. London only. Lawrence varieties a-f. Bust 1 (a-f) or 2 (f only).
   (a) Double saltire stops both sides.
   (b) Stops double/single saltires. Rare.
   (c) Stops single annulets/double saltires. Var. (ER) has *D* for *Dei* and *Dns*, and reversed *N* in *Angl*.
   (d) Stops single annulets/single saltires. Rare.
   (e) Stops double annulets/single saltires. VR.
   (f) Stops double annulets/double saltires. Bust 1 or 2. Rare var. (bust 2) has curule *X*.

B2. Stops double annulets/double saltires throughout. Bust 2 or 3. London only, except (g).
   With bust 2:
   (g) As B1(f) but annulet on breast and pellet-tailed *R* on rev. Calais (stop after *Villa.*), rare; London VR, also ER mule B1(f)/B2(g).
   (k) Annulet before *Edward* and barred *A* in *Adiutore*; annulet or barred *A* very rarely omitted (vars. i, j).

Edward III – Henry IV

Groats

With bust 3 (all rare): with or often without annulet before *Edward*; late var. (with annulet) has curule *X*. Rev. endings vary from *em Meu(m)* to *(e)um Meum* and then *m Meu(m)*; barred *A* only with first form. Equivalent Lawrence varieties: (k) annulet/barred *A* (ER); (i) no annulet/barred *A*; (j) annulet/unbarred *A*; (f) no annulet/unbarred *A*.

EDWARD III, POST-TREATY PERIOD, 1369-77. French title resumed. *Di* for *Dei*. & is barred 7 with long front. Saltire stops, usually double on obv., single in rev. inner inscription. Obv. Gothic *n*, rev. Roman *N* (usually reversed, occasionally unbarred). *Civi* under *Posui*. Normally contractive bar above *N* in *don*. London only.

1. Four or three titles. Four pellets around obv. initial cross. Row of annulets (mail) across breast. Rev. ending normally *m Meum*. A few early rev. dies (with type 1a obv., or muled with Treaty B2 obv.) have pellet or annulet stops. All VR.
1a. *Edward Di G Rex Angl & F Dns hib & A(q)* - two dies.
1b. Ends *Franc D hib* - one die.
2. Two titles: *Edward Di Gra Rex Angl & Franc(ie)*. Plain initial cross. Pellets by fleur(s). Chainmail of pellets sometimes evident. Rev. ending normally *em Meu*. Also VR 2/1 and 1/2 mules.
2a. Pellet above central fleur of crown and each side of breast fleur. VR.
2b. Pellet each side of central fleur of crown. Rare.
3. As type 2, but no pellets by fleurs. *Franc(ie)*. With (VR) or without pellet mail on breast. All rare.

RICHARD II, FIRST PERIOD (types I, II), 1377-c.1390. London only. Style A lettering (straight-sided). French title included: *Ricard Di Gra Rex Angl & Franc(ie)*. Saltire stops. Gothic *n* on obv., Roman *N* reversed in *London* (usually with contraction mark above second *N*).

I. Bust as Edward III, Post-Treaty. Four obv. dies. & is reversed *F* with long front. Letter *R* Edwardian (R1) or wide and angular (R2). First obv. reads *Francie D*; another (*Francie*) has pellet above crown. Rev. small *m*. One die has saltire before *Lon*, otherwise no stops in inner circle. VR.
II. New (more regular) letters: & is reversed *Z*; larger *m*; Roman *N*s in *London* forward or reversed; *R* with trailing tail (R3). One die (early) has three pellets above crown. Last die (with two saltires after *Franc*) mostly used (with rust mark to left of bust) with revs. of type III. Revs. usually end *Meu* with contraction mark above *u*; *tas* is occasionally below *Posui*. Also mules I/II (rare) and II/I (VR).

RICHARD II, SECOND PERIOD (types III, IV), c. 1390-1399. London only. Lettering style B (indented; type III) and C (mixed; type IV). Saltire stops. Inscription as before (French title included). Gothic *n* on obv.

III. Waisted lettering with rounded concave serifs (style B). Reversed *N* on rev. (often double-barred), without contraction mark. Revs. normally end *Meu'*; pellets close or coalescing. Also rare mules IIIa/I, IIIa/II, IIIb/II, II/III.
IIIa. Bust as type II. *Di, Franc*. Improvised letter *F*. One die (VR).
IIIb. New bust with wide hair, usually with new crown (tall side fleurs). *Dei, Franci(e)*. Rare.
IV. Crescent on breast. *Di, Francie*. Mixed lettering (style C), waisted but thicker than B, with very small *A* and *T* in rev. outer legend. *N* on rev. unbarred or reversed. Tall crown with indentations on band; thick hair, less widely splayed than in III. Rev. pellets joined as trefoils. ER.

HENRY IV, HEAVY COINAGE, 1399-1411. No groats extant; probably none struck.

HALFGROATS 1351 - 1411

Type as groats. Tressure of nine arcs with top arches unfleured, unless stated.

EDWARD III, PRE-TREATY PERIOD, 1351-61. Titles normally *Edwardus Rex Angl(i) & Fra(n)c(i); &* as 7 with bar; no Irish title. Rev. usually *Pos/ui Deu/Adiut/orem*. Annulet stops (occasionally omitted), except where stated. London (B-G), York (D, E only). Mint name precedes *Civitas* in B-E, sometimes in F, rarely in G.

B. Square initial cross patty. Open *c* and *e*, Roman *M*. Roman *N* usually reversely barred. *Angl;* but *Angli* on some B/C mules. Some have top arches fleured. Rev. varied outer readings include *A/diuto/re Me*. Rare.

C. As B, but Gothic *m*, closed *c* and *e*. Reversed *N*. Wedge-tailed *R*. Some have *A* with hooked limb. Usually *Angli* henceforward. Top arches fleured or unfleured. Also B/C and C/B mules, both VR.

D. Square initial cross patty often damaged. Roman *N*, or reversed, or unbarred. Integral *R*. Often *c* for *e*.
    London: Var. has squared *E* in *Edwardus*. Also rare C/D mule.
    York: Var. has squared *E*.

E. Plain initial cross patty. *N* unbarred; *F* sometimes inverted.
    London: Also D/E and (VR) E/D mules.
    York: One var. has ten arc tressure, another has lis on breast (both VR). Also ER mule E/D.

F. As E but mm. crown and small lis (not fleurs) on cusps. *c, D* and *e* sometimes broken. Also mules E/F (rare) and F/E (ER).

G. New initial cross patty, with concave ends. Usually an annulet in one quarter. *N* reversed or (mostly) unbarred. Normal trefoil fleurs on cusps. *London* now normally follows *Civitas*. Some variation in rev. outer legend.

Ga. Annulet below bust, and in one quarter of rev. Top arches sometimes fleured.

Gb. No annulet below bust. Annulet in *tas* or *don* quarter, or none. Top arches not fleured; side fleurs sometimes also omitted. *c* and *e* sometimes sliced. Rare.

Gc. Reverses only (VR). Saltire stops. No quartermark. *c* and *e* sliced.

Gf. Reverses only (rare). Points in *t.a.s.* No quartermark.

Group G mules: E/Ga (VR), F/Ga; Ga/b (VR), Ga/c (VR), Ga/f (rare); Gb/c (VR), Gb/f (rare).

EDWARD III, TREATY A PERIOD, 1361. No French title: *Edward Rex Anglie Dns hib*. Annulet on cusp each side of crown. Saltire stops. Gothic *n*. Composite crown with central fleur added. London only (*Civi/tas/Lon/don*), VR.

EDWARD III, TREATY B PERIOD, 1361-9. No French title: *Edwardus Rex Angl Dns hyb*. Stops normally obv. double annulets, rev. saltires. All cusps fleured. Cross patty *X*; Gothic *n* on obv. *D* of *Adiutore* often omitted. Rev. ending *re Meu* except in B2(j). London (normally *Lon/don/Civi/tas,* with Roman *N* reversed or unbarred), all varieties. Calais (*Vil/la.C/ale/sie*), B2(g) only.

B1 No mark before *Edwardus*; unbarred *A* in *Adiutore*. Lawrence variety f. Var. omits breast fleur.

B2 (g) As B1 but annulet on breast and pellet-tailed *R* on rev. Calais (stop after *Villa.)* and London, both VR. London-Calais obv. die-link noted.

    (k) Annulet before *Edwardus*; barred *A* in *Adiutore*. Large or small fleurs on cusps. Also ER mule B1/B2(k).

Edward III – Henry IV

Halfgroats

(j) Annulet before *Edwardus*; unbarred *A*. Rev. endings varied – *ore Me, m Meu, e Meu* or *eu Meu*. Some read *Civitas London*. One late obv. die (only used for mules with Post-Treaty revs.) has double saltire stops. All VR.

EDWARD III, POST-TREATY PERIOD, 1369-77. French title resumed. & is barred *7* with long front. Normally double saltire stops with single saltire(s) or pellet(s) in rev. inner inscription. Obv. Gothic *n*, rev. Roman *N* reversed (or rarely unbarred). Rev. ending usually *em Meu*. London only. *Civi* under *Posui*. Normally contractive bar above *N* in *don*. All scarce or rare; also rare Treaty/Post-Treaty mules.

1. *Edward Di Gra Rex Angl & Fr*; one die. Very large head. A point each side of central fleur of crown. Row of pellets on sinister breast. VR.
2. *Edwardus Rex Angl & Franc*. Very large head. Point each side of central fleur. VR.
3. *Edward(us) Rex Angl & Franc(ie)*. Head very large or intermediate size. No points by fleur. Rare.
4. *Edwardus Rex Angl & Fra(n)c*. Small head. Two obv. dies, both also used with late Richard II rev. dies. VR.

RICHARD II, FIRST PERIOD (types I, II), 1377-c.1390. London only. Style A lettering (straight-sided). With and without French title. Saltire stops. Gothic *n* on obv., Roman *N* reversed in *London* (usually with contraction mark above second *N*). All scarce or rare.

I. Rev. dies only, used with type II obverses. Letter *R* Edwardian (R1) or wide and angular (R2). VR.
II. Small head as on last coins of Edward III. New letter *R* with trailing tail (R3); & is reversed *Z*. Rev. dies usually without stops in inner legend, and ending *em Meu* (with contraction mark above *u*); vars. have *re Meu* (with saltire instead of initial cross), or saltire(s) before *Civi*. No mules with type III reverses.
  (i) With French title: *Ricard D(i) G Rex Ang(l) & Fr(anc)*. One die (*Fr*) has three points above crown.
  (ii) Without French title: *Di Gra Rex Anglie*. Two dies have points (one or three) above crown.

RICHARD II, SECOND PERIOD, c. 1390-1399. London only. Lettering style B (indented; type III) and C (mixed; type IV). Saltire stops. Gothic *n* on obv., Roman *N* in *London*.

III. One obv. die only (IIIa), with bust as type II, but new (style B) letters, with composite *F*. With French title: *D G Rex Angl & Fra*. Rev. dies end *em Meu*; pellets close or joined. Also mules III/II, and Edward III/type III. All ER.
IV. Two obv. dies (Potter 'IIIb'): mixed, irregular lettering with dumpy uprights (style C). Bust with oval face and low crown (very wide on one die). Without French title: *Dei Gra Rex Angl(ie)*. Rev. var. *m Meu*. *N* on rev. usually barred (one with unbarred *N* die-links with Henry IV). Pellets close or joined. Also mules with type III or Edward III obverses. All ER.

Edward III obv. dies reused: two type 4 Post-Treaty dies (with small bust), reading *Frac* and *Franc*, are each found also with rev. dies of both types III and IV of Richard II. ER.

HENRY IV, HEAVY COINAGE, 1399-1411. London only. *henric Di Gra Rex Angl & F*; & with cross-bar. New, shaped lettering (D2) on obv. with waisted uprights and pointed base to *G*. Two obv. dies, with tall narrow bust; small star on breast; large fleurs on cusps. Revs. have dumpy lettering (style C), similar to Richard type IV but with unbarred *N*, and may be old dies. ER.

1351–1411

PENNIES 1351 - 1411

Normal type: obv. crowned facing bust; rev. long cross patty with group of three pellets in each angle. Initial mark on obv. only. King's name often has Latin ending (*-us*).

EDWARD III, PRE-TREATY PERIOD, 1351-61. Titles normally *Edwardus Rex Angli (&); &* as *7* with bar. London (A, C-G); York royal (D, E); York, Archbishop Thoresby (D, G); Durham, Bishop Hatfield (A, C-G). London pence have annulet between each group of pellets in groups A-D and most of E; also Durham in A only.

A.   Initial cross patty. Large letters with Gothic *m* and *n*, *A* unbarred. *Anglie*.
       London: Stops double annulets or (rarely, and only after *tas*) double saltires. Some dies have annulet above *T* or *A* of *tas*. Rare.
       Durham: *Vil/la/Dur/rem*. Crozier (to right) before *la*; hollow in centre of cross; annulet within each group of pellets. Double saltire stops both sides. VR; also ER mules both ways with pre-1351 dies, XVI(D3)/A and A/XVI (d6).

C.   Square initial cross patty. Roman *N* reversed; *A* often with hooked limb; wedge-tailed *R*. Annulet stops, or none.
       London: *Angli*. Also rare C/A, and VR A/C mules.
       Durham: *Civi/tas/Dune/lmie*, or *Dun/elmi*; Gothic *m*. No annulets within pellets (henceforward). Crozier before *Civi*. *Angli(e)*. Var. has trefoil of pellets on breast.

D.   Square initial cross patty often damaged. Roman *N*, or reversed, or (mostly) unbarred; sometimes *c* for *e*; integral *R*. *Angli (&)*. Annulet stops or none.
       London: Also C/D mule.
       Durham: Crozier before *Civi/tas/Dune/lmie*. Some with squared *E* in *Edwardus*. Others have crude bust. Var. *Ewardus*. Also ER D/C mule.
       York, Abp. Thoresby (May - July 1353): Quatrefoil on rev. cross. VR.
       York royal (from July 1353): No quatrefoil.

E.   Plain initial cross patty. *N* usually unbarred; *c*, *D* and *e* often broken. Annulet stops. Var. with four annulets after *Angli* (Durham, York).
       London: Earlier reverses with annulets between pellets, later without. Vars. squared *E*; inverted *F*; *Edwardws*; *tos*. Also C/E mule, ER.
       Durham: Crozier before *Civi/tas Dune/lmie*. Some with irregular bust.
       York royal: ER var. reads *Edward Rex Angl & Fra*.

F.   Mm. crown. Annulet stops or none. *N* usually unbarred.
       London: No annulets within rev. pellets; coins with annulet in one quarter of rev. are F/G mules. Also F/C, F/E and E/F mules (all ER).
       Durham: *Angli* (or *-gil*) &. Crozier before *Civi/tas/Dur/ene*. Some with crude bust. Also rare E/F and VR F/E mules.

G.   New initial cross patty with concave ends. *N* usually unbarred. London, Durham and York listed separately.

    Group G pence of London

Ga.   Annulet stops. Annulet under bust (omitted at first on one early die, *Angl*), and within pellets in one quarter (*Civi*, *Lon* or *don*), except on some early coins. Early var. without annulet on rev. has extra point in *Civi* quarter. Var. *Lomdom*. Also mules E/Ga (ER) and F/Ga (rare).

Gb.   Annulet stops. No annulet below bust; *Angl &* or *Angli*. With or without annulet in *Civi* quarter. Some have sliced *c*. Also mules F/Gb (rare) and Gb/Ga (annulet in *Lon* quarter, ER).

Edward III – Henry IV

Pence

Gc. Saltire stops; *Angli*. Saltire in *Civi* or *tas* quarter, or none (Gc/b mule?). Also rare mules Gc/a and Gb(no stops)/Gc.

Gf. Annulet stops. Pellets in *t.a.s,* but no quartermark. Not found as true coin, only as VR Gc/f and Gf/g mules.

Gg. Rev. only (Gf/g mule, VR), pellets in *t.a.s,* but no quartermark. Saltire before *Lon*.

Group G pence of Durham, Bishop Hatfield

Ga-Gh all have crozier before *Civi;* Ga-Gg normally read *Dur/eme*, with Gothic *m*.

Ga. Annulet on breast and sometimes in *Civi* quarter. Annulet stops on obv. and often on rev. Some have irregular bust. Vars. *Dur/ene* with unbarred *N*, *Der/eme*. Rare; also ER mules E/Ga and Ga/F.

Gb. No annulet on breast or in rev. quarter. Annulet stops (usually obv. only). Rare.

Gc. Saltire stops. Some with saltire in *tas* quarter. *c* and *e* sometimes sliced. Var. *Dor/eme*. Rare.

Intermediate varieties. Annulet stops. No mark in rev. quarters or pellets within *tas*.

(i) *e* broken at bottom (Lawrence 'Gd'). Rare.

(ii) Normal *e* (Lawrence 'G*'). Pellet before *Dur*. Rare.

(iii) Annulet on each shoulder (Lawrence 'G**'). Rare.

Gf. Annulet stops. Pellets in *t.a.s*. Rare. Also F/Gf and Intermed. (iii)/Gf mule, both ER.

Gg. Saltire stops. *e* with protruding bar. Pellets in *t.a.s*. Var. has trefoil on breast. Rare.

Gh. Saltire stops. *Dure/lmie*. Open *e*. No pellets in *tas*. Rare; also mules Gd/h (ER), Gg/h (VR) and Gh/g (VR).

Gj. *Edwardus Rex Anglie Dn* (Roman *N* unbarred); annulet stops. Crozier to right before *tas; Dur/ene*. VR; also ER mule Treaty A/Gj.

Group G pence of York, Abp. Thoresby (quatrefoil on rev. cross; no quartermarks)

Gb (Lawrence Ga). Small annulet stops. No breastmark. *Angli*. Small pellet in centre of quatrefoil. Neat work. Rare.

Gc. Obv. *Edwadus* with saltire stops, with Gd rev., may be Gc/d mule. ER.

Gd. Large annulet stops. Usually annulet on breast. *Angli &*. Usually a pellet in *ta.s*. Large pellet in rev. quatrefoil.

G local. Coarse work. Unusual busts. Pellet stops. Small quatrefoil on rev.

Gf. Annulet stops. Pellets in *t.a.s*. Cross or pellet in quatrefoil.

Gg. Saltire stops. Saltire on breast. Pellets in *t.a.s*. Cross in quatrefoil. Rare.

Gh. Saltire stops. Open *e*. Pellets in *t.a.s*. Pellet in quatrefoil. True coin and Gg/h mule, both ER.

EDWARD III, TREATY A PERIOD, 1361. No French title: *Edwar(d) Anglie Dns hib*. Gothic *n*. Annulet or pellet at upper corners of initial cross (often not visible). Saltire stops (obv.). Composite crown with central fleur added.

London: *Edwar*. VR.

Durham, Bishop Hatfield: *Edwar, Dore/lme*, crozier to right before *Civi*. VR; also ER mule with 'Pre-Treaty' rev. (Gj).

York, Archbishop Thoresby: *Edward;* pellet in quatrefoil on rev. VR.

EDWARD III, TREATY B PERIOD, 1361-9. No French title: royal mints (London and Calais), *Edward Angl R Dns hyb*, with Gothic *n* and obv. stops double annulets. York and Durham listed separately.

B1. No mark before *Edward*. *A* in *tas* unbarred. London only. (a) *hib* (VR), saltire after *Lon* (ER) or *don*. (b) *hyb*, saltire after *don*. (c) *hyb*, annulet after *don*.

Calais type (equivalent to groats and halfgroats of B2g), nothing before *Edward, Vil/la.C/ale/sie*, VR.

Pence

B2.   Pellet before *Edward*; barred *A* in *tas*. London only. With or without annulet after *don*. Also VR mule B1c/B2.

Treaty B pence of York, quatrefoil on rev. cross for Abp. Thoresby

(a)   *Edwardus Dei G Rex An*, *X* patty, Gothic *n*. Obv. stops single annulets. Extra point outside pellets under *Civi* and *aci*. VR.

(b)   *Edwardus Rex Angli*, *X* patty, Roman *N* reversed. Pellet stops on obv. Some with annulet or quatrefoil before *Edwardus*, and quatrefoil on breast. Varied busts.

(c)   *Edward Angl R Dns hyb* (as at London); Gothic *n*, double annulet stops. One has pellet before *Edward* and annulets in rev. legend. VR.

Treaty B pence of Durham, Bishop Hatfield

Crozier to left before *Civi; Dur/eme*. *Edwardus Rex Angli*, *X* patty, Gothic *n* or reversed Roman *N*. Stops annulets or pellets. One has stop before *Dur*. Var. (VR) reads *Dune/lmis* without crozier. Also (VR) mule Treaty B/A (*Dore/lme*).

EDWARD III, POST-TREATY PERIOD, 1369-77. French title resumed (earlier dies only). *&* is barred *7* with long front. Gothic *n* and normally double or single saltire stops on obv. Some rev. dies (all mints) have initial cross; many (London and York) have saltire (or rarely a pellet) before *Civi* or elsewhere in rev. inscription. Several London and York dies have tiny extra points in angles of rev. cross, or extra points in one or two quarters.

London: Roman *N* on rev. normal, reversed (often with bar over *N* in *don*), or unbarred. Also rare mules with Treaty obverses.

    1.   With French title: *Edward R Angl & Franc* (pellet on breast) or *Rex Angl & Fr*. Large head. VR.

    2.   *Edwardus Rex Anglie*. (a) Very large head; saltire on breast. VR. (b) Large head; annulet or nothing on breast. Occasionally Gothic *n* on rev. Rare.

    3.   As 2, but small head, and quatrefoil on breast. Rare.

York (*Ebo/raci* or *Ebor/aci*): Quatrefoil on rev. cross for Archbishops Thoresby (to 1373) and Neville (from 1374); also vacancy 1373-4. *Edward(us) Rex Angl & Franc, Fr D* or *F(r);* or *Di Gra Rex Ang*; or *Edwardus Rex Anglie (et)*. Early var. (VR) has four points by obv. initial cross. Obv. stops normally saltires, rarely annulets or pellets. Larger or smaller head. Lis, cross, annulet or nothing on breast.

Durham (*Dun/olm*, Gothic *n*), Bishop Hatfield: Crozier to left after *olm*. *Edwardus Rex Angl & Fr* or *Rex Anglie*. Larger or smaller head. Annulet, lis or nothing on breast. Var. has two annulets after *Rex*. Rare; also ER mule with Treaty B obv.

RICHARD II, FIRST PERIOD, 1377-c.1390. London, Durham, York. Style A lettering (straight-sided). Gothic *n* on obv. Saltire stops.

London (Purvey type I): Reversed Roman *N* in *London*; saltire before *Civi*. *Ricardus Rex Anglie* or *Ricard Rex Angl & Fra(n)c* (*&* is reversed *Z*). With or without small lis on breast. VR.

Durham: Bishop John Fordham, from 1384; no episcopal mark. Two obv. dies, small lis on breast; *Ricardus Rex Anglie*. Rev. with or without saltire before *Civi*; *Dun/olm* (Gothic *n* and *m*). Rare.

York: Quatrefoil on rev. for Abp. Alexander Neville, to 1388; Thomas Arundel from 1388. London-made dies: *Ricardus Rex Anglie*. Usually a saltire before *Civi*. Type I, lis or cross on breast; some late dies have a small point above each shoulder (one reads *Anglie &); Ebo/raci* or *Ebor/aci*. II, no mark on breast; some have line below bust; *Ebo/raci*.

Edward III – Henry IV

Pence

Local dies (between types I and II?): Crude style. Pellets on shoulders and cross on breast. *Ricardus Rex Ang(l)(i)e, Angil(i)e* or *Ang(i)(l) Fr(an)*, or *Ricard Rex Angl Dns Eb*. Many with saltire or pellet in rev. inscription. *Ebo/raci* (*e* sometimes reversed). Also rare mules I/local, local/II.

RICHARD II, SECOND PERIOD, c. 1390-1399. London, York. Lettering styles B (type III) and C (type IV). Saltire stops.

London:
- III. Rev. only, style B lettering, Roman *N* reversed. Muled with Henry IV obv. ER.
- IV. *Ricard Rex Anglie*; one has quatrefoil at end. Gothic *n* and fractured *I* both sides, style C lettering. Rev. pellets joined as trefoils. Also muled both ways with Henry IV. All ER.

York: Quatrefoil on rev., for Abps. Arundel to 1396, Robert Waldby 1396-7 and Richard le Scrope from 1397. London-made dies.
- III. Style B lettering. *Ricard Rex Angl & Fran*. Large face with close hair and flat crown. Rev. pellets close or joined; pellet in centre of quatrefoil. *Ebor/aci*. Escallop after *tas*; sometimes two saltires after *aci*. Rare; also VR mules III/II, III/local and local/III.
- IV. Style C lettering. Wide hair. *Ricard Rex Anglie F* or *Ricardus Rex Angl & F*. Rev. pellets joined as trefoils. *Ebo/raci*, sometimes with double saltire after *tas*. VR.

HENRY IV, HEAVY COINAGE, 1399-1411. London, York. Gothic *n*. Saltire stops.

London: Star on breast. One of the two obv. dies has three very small points above crown. New larger lettering (D2, with pointed *G*), *henric D G Rex Angl F*. Rev. extra points beside pellets in two quarters (also muled with Richard II obv.); or mules with Richard II rev. dies with lettering style B (III; Roman *N* reversed) or style C (IV; Gothic *n*). All ER.

York: Quatrefoil on rev. for Abp. Scrope (d.1405). Two obv. dies. Large head, with wide hair. Style C lettering. *henric Rex Angl & Franc(ie); &* is reversed *z*. Rev. close pellets; *Ebo/raci*. Rare.

HALFPENCE 1351 - 1411

Type as pennies. London only.

EDWARD III, PRE-TREATY PERIOD, 1351-61.
- E. *Edwardus Rex An*. Initial cross patty. Annulet stops or none. Gothic *n* both sides; curule *X*. Fork-tailed *R*. VR.
- F. *Edvardus Rex*. Mm. crown. Obv. only, muled with rev. of G. ER.
- G. Rev. only, of F/G mule, with an annulet outside the pellets in *Lon* quarter.

EDWARD III, TREATY A PERIOD, 1361. *Edwardus Rex An*, Gothic *n*, no stops. Pellets at upper corners of initial cross. Drapery on bust. Tall letter *I* in *Civi*. VR.

EDWARD III, TREATY B PERIOD, 1361-9. Cross patty *X*; Gothic *n*. *Edwardus Rex An*. Rare.
- B1. Nothing before *Edwardus*. Colon stops on obv.; pellet after, or in *n* of, *don*. *A* in *tas* unbarred. Var. has wedge before *Edwardus*.
- B2. Annulet stops on obv. Usually a pellet before *Edwardus*. Annulet after *don* and *A* in *tas* barred on most dies. Also VR mule B1/2.

EDWARD III, POST-TREATY PERIOD, 1369-77. None identified; perhaps B2 dies remained in limited use.

RICHARD II, FIRST PERIOD, 1377-c.1390. Straight-sided lettering (style A).

1351–1411

Halfpence

I. Cross or annulet (VR) on breast (Purvey 'Early'; Withers 1A and 1B). *Ricard Rex Angl* (Gothic *n*), double saltire stops. Roman *N* (usually reversed) on rev., with contraction mark over second *N*. Some with saltire before *Civi*. Rare. Also ER mule I/Edward III Treaty B2.

II. As I, but no mark on breast (Purvey 'Intermediate'; W.1). Stops double or single saltires or colons. *Ang(l)*. Rev. Gothic *n*. Also VR mules I/II and II/I.

RICHARD II, SECOND PERIOD, c. 1390-1399. Gothic *n*.

III. Waisted lettering with 'fishtail' serifs (style B). Face with slightly pointed chin. Bust often with indented chest, with thin line below; tight hair (W. 4, 5). *Ricard Rex Angl – Anglie* or *Angl F.* Saltire stops. Var. has extra pellet under *t* of *tas*. Rare; also VR mule II/III.

IV Dumpy lettering (style C), with *I* often fractured. Larger or smaller bust, with narrow shoulders; face with broad chin; hair wider, usually with small inner curl (W. 2, 3). *Angl-Anglie*. Saltire stops. Rare; also VR mules I/IV, II/IV and IV/II.

HENRY IV, HEAVY COINAGE, 1399-1411. Saltire stops. Gothic *n*.

1. Thick lettering (style C). *henric Rex Angl(ie)*. Busts vary; usually rounded chin; hair often shows small inner curl; sloping shoulders. Rare.

2. Fine lettering (style D2). *Angl*. Bust with hunched shoulders; narrow face; neatly stranded hair. VR; also ER mule with Richard II obv.

FARTHINGS 1351 - 1411

Type as pennies and halfpennies. London only.

EDWARD III, PRE-TREATY PERIOD, 1351-61.

E. *Edwardus Rex,* Gothic *n*. Stops annulets, pellets or none. VR.

G. *Edwardus Rex An*. Unbarred Roman *N*. Annulet stops. Annulet within pellets in one quarter. Also E/G and G/E mules. All VR.

EDWARD III, TREATY B PERIOD, 1361-9. *Edwardus Rex*, cross potent *X* on some. Pellet stop or none. Roman *N* (barred or unbarred) on rev. VR.

EDWARD III, POST-TREATY PERIOD, 1369-77. Small head without neck. *Edward Rex Angl*, colon stops (but not at end), Gothic *n* or Roman *N*. ER.

RICHARD II, FIRST PERIOD, 1377-c.1390. Small head with little or no neck. *Ricard(us) Rex Angl(ie)*. Gothic *n*. Stops pellets or saltires. Rare. Var (ER) has groups of four small pellets ('rosettes'), instead of three, in quarters of cross.

RICHARD II, SECOND PERIOD, c.1390 - 1399. As before, but long face with broad jowl. *Angl*. Saltire stops, and saltire instead of initial cross. ER.

HENRY IV, HEAVY COINAGE, 1399-1411. *henric Rex Angl*. Initial cross pommy. Long face as late Richard II. Pellet stops (?). Gothic *n*. ER.

CHAPTER VI

1412 - 1464
HENRY IV – EDWARD IV

For more than a century after the death of Edward III the succession to the English crown was periodically disputed between his descendants. The rules of succession were fluid, and uncertain in detail. In particular, there was doubt as to whether the royal succession could be transmitted through the female line. No question arose in the case of Richard II, eldest son of the Black Prince who was eldest son of Edward III; but Richard was childless when he was deposed in 1399. Though it was inevitable in the circumstances that Henry IV should have succeeded, it was not clear which branch of the royal family had the best right in blood to do so. The Lancastrians, represented by the three Henries who occupied the throne from 1399 to 1461, could base their claim on their descent from Edward III in unbroken male line through John of Gaunt, his third son, and owed their name to the Duchy of Lancaster which came to Gaunt through his first wife; while the Yorkists, who in due course displaced them, were descended from the fourth son, Edmund, Duke of York, but also, through the female line, from the second son, Lionel, Duke of Clarence, and so the senior line if transmission through a female was accepted. The struggle between adherents of the red rose of Lancaster and the white rose of York was to dominate the scene for much of the second half of the fifteenth century. After Henry IV, however, renewed hostilities between rival claimants did not break out until the 1450s, by which time the Hundred Years' War with France had, from the English perspective, drawn to an inglorious close.

With the infirmity of Henry IV's last years, his ambitious eldest son became increasingly involved in public affairs and in March 1413 succeeded as King Henry V. Although in his first two years he had faced conspiracies against his rule, by 1415 he was already laying claim to the former Angevin territories in France and, after negotiations were broken off in June, he resolved to take advantage of the internal quarrels in France between the Armagnac and Burgundian factions, and to invade. His first campaign culminated in the battle of Agincourt in October, which proved to be a victory as significant as those of Crécy and Poitiers in the Edwardian phase of the war. Three years later, after further campaigning and sieges, Henry achieved another decisive advance when Rouen fell in January 1419. Soon afterwards the murder of Duke John of Burgundy led to defection of the Burgundian faction from the French to the English cause. By the Treaty of Troyes in May 1420 Henry was recognised as heir to the French throne and was married to Princess Katherine, daughter of the ailing King Charles VI, in the following month. But Henry died at the end of August 1422, two months before Charles, and it was his infant son, only nine months old, who as Henry VI of England succeeded to the kingdom of France in October 1422. Although the Dauphin also styled himself King of France after his father's death, there was little substance to the claim until he was crowned Charles VII at Rheims in 1429.

In contrast to his warlike father, Henry VI grew up a studious and pious man, unsuited to the responsibilities and rivalries of late medieval government. He was declared of age shortly before his sixteenth birthday in 1437, but by this date the tide of war on the Continent had already turned in favour of the French. In 1435 the alliance between England and Burgundy came to an end, and the French regained Paris in 1436. A truce was negotiated in 1445 under which marriage was arranged between Henry and Margaret of Anjou, niece of the French queen; and at the end of the year the English ceded Maine, an old Angevin territory, to the French. Four years later the truce was broken, but further defeat followed and by 1453 England had lost all her territory in France apart from Calais. Until the birth of Henry's son Edward in 1453 the heir to the throne had been his cousin Richard Duke of York. When Henry suffered a period of insanity in 1453-4 York was appointed Protector of the Realm; but after the king's recovery influence was regained by the Duke of Somerset, another descendant of John of Gaunt, whom York had sought to hold responsible for the English defeat in France. The ensuing quarrel between York and Somerset now culminated in the first engagement of what came to be known as the Wars of the Roses, when Somerset was defeated and killed at the battle of St. Albans in 1455, and the king was taken prisoner. Four years later Queen Margaret attempted to overthrow the Yorkists, but after another Yorkist victory at Northampton in 1460 the king was forced to recognise York as his heir ahead of his own son Edward. Although York himself fell at the battle of Wakefield in December 1460, his son Edward, proclaimed king as Edward IV on 4 March 1461, established his rule by routing the Lancastrian forces at Towton in Yorkshire shortly afterwards. He was then to hold the throne for the next twenty-two years, apart from a few months in the winter of 1470-1 when the Lancastrian party achieved a brief, and fatal, restoration of Henry VI. Historians in consequence often speak of the years 1461-70 as Edward's first reign, and of the years 1471-83, following his decisive victories over the Lancastrians at the battles of Barnet and Tewkesbury, as his second reign.

The impact on the English coinage of historical events in the first half of the fifteenth century is less immediately obvious than in the second half of the fourteenth. Whereas Edward III and Richard II had dropped the French title during periods of treaty or truce, no such change was made under the Lancastrians. Henry V continued to be styled *Rex Anglie et Francie* even after he had been officially designated heir to the French throne (and titled *Heres Franciae* on many of the coins struck for him in France); and although the land was lost, his successors were not to abandon the claim for nearly four hundred years. The course of the French war was, however, a major influence on the availability of bullion to the English mints. While there was a reasonable supply to London after the weight reduction of 1412, it was not until the Burgundian alliance opened up trade with the duke's territories in Brabant, Flanders and northern France after 1420 that wool exports began to bring huge quantities of silver to Calais. Conversely, not long after Burgundy's change of allegiance in 1435 the English mint at Calais went into terminal decline.

After the difficulties encountered by Richard II in contemplating a reduction in the weights of the coins, the crown had been understandably circumspect when, late in the reign of Henry IV, reconsideration of the matter became urgent. One of the reasons why Garner's draft indenture of 1409 does not appear to have been implemented may have been that the reductions it proposed did not go far enough. Without Parliamentary support, however, it was arguable that it would have contravened Edward III's Statute of Purveyors, and when in November 1411 the issue was revisited Parliament decreed a larger reduction, to take effect from Easter 1412; but this was to be on an experimental basis only for two years, after which it should cease if it had not proved satisfactory. Once the new coinage was underway it must quickly have been evident that the reduction of the weight of the noble from 120 gr. to 108 gr. and of the penny from 18 gr. to 15 gr. was a necessary, if at first only partially effective, means of reviving supplies of gold and silver to the mint. No indenture of 1412 with Garner is extant, but the terms of the new coinage, which had applied from the outset, are set out at the start of the next reign in the contract of April 1413 with Lewys John. This provided for fifty nobles (£16 13s. 4d.) per pound of gold and 360 pence (30s.) per pound of silver. After seignorage and minting costs of 5s. 10d. for gold and 1s. for silver, the mint would be offering prices of £16 7s. 6d. and £1 9s. per pound respectively, against £14 15s. and £1 3s. 6d. in the old heavy coinage (or £15 13s. 4d. and £1 6s. 10d. as would have applied under the draft proposals of 1409). In July 1421 these terms were amended to reduce the master's allowance by 10d. on gold and 2d. on silver, thus increasing the mint price per pound by equivalent amounts. But when a new contract was drawn up in February 1422 with Bartholomew Goldbeter the charges for silver were restored to 12d. per pound although for gold they were to remain at the 1421 figure of 5s. These rates were repeated in a further contract with Goldbeter dated 16 February 1423 which differed from that of the previous year only in including responsibility for royal mints at York and Bristol in addition to London and Calais. The 1423 provisions were perpetuated in subsequent indentures with new masters in September 1431 (William Russe) and July 1434 (John Paddesley), but in Robert Manfeld's indentures of December 1445 and December 1451 (repeated for Sir Richard Tunstall in April 1459) the charges were raised to 5s. 10d. for gold and 1s. 2d. for silver, and York and Bristol are no longer mentioned. Edward IV's contract of May 1461 with Thomas Montgomery is not extant but is likely to have provided for the existing arrangements to continue. These were eventually replaced in August 1464 by a new structure involving a 25 per cent. revaluation of the gold coin and a reduction in the weight of the penny from 15 gr. to 12 gr. which resulted in an equivalent rerating of silver.

The increased value of silver from Easter 1412 was perhaps enough to discourage active export, but most of the older silver coin in circulation was already clipped down to somewhere near the new weight and there does not therefore seem to have been sufficient incentive to cause much of it to be brought in for reminting. The first accounts run from November 1411, four months before the new values became effective, and some silver may be expected to have been struck before April 1412. But by the following November less than £3,000 had been accounted, and although in the next five years there were issues of £33,500 the total amount of silver minted during these first six or seven years was only a small fraction of that coined in an equivalent period after the reduction of 1351. In the next four and a half years (from September 1417 to March 1422) output declined to less than £9,000 in total, and when volumes increased dramatically from 1422 onwards most of the production took place in Calais. With gold, on the other hand, the situation was different. More than £600,000 was minted at London between 1411/12 and September 1417, with a further £190,000 from 1417 to March 1422. These sums for gold are much more in line with the output of the 1350s, and it is clear that the tariff for English gold was now internationally competitive again. Even after the Calais mint had been reopened the bulk of the gold, unlike the silver, continued to come to London. The Parliament of May 1421, noting that much of the gold in currency was not of lawful weight or alloy, provided that holders of deficient coin should be pardoned if they sent it to the mint for recoining by the following Christmas, after which only good coin was to be acceptable – an arrangement that was to be cited in a petition from the northern counties for a mint at York.

Although Parliamentary authority to coin money in York and Bristol was given in November 1422, and this was reflected in Goldbeter's indenture of February 1423, no mint at Bristol was to materialize at this period and the task of reopening a royal mint in York Castle appears to have taken many months. Accounts for coinage at York run for twelve months from August 1423, amounting to the significant sum of £42,300 in gold coin but less than £500 in silver. More than half of this coinage took place from August to October 1423. The northern counties petitioned the Parliament of October 1423 for the return of the master and his workmen who by that time were said to have been to York, carried out their work and then gone away. Minting was in due course resumed on a small scale between March and August 1424. York in these years thus became the only extra royal mint in England to contribute to the coinage between 1412 and 1464, although in 1425 a master was appointed to the mint in Dublin and silver pence were briefly struck there for Henry VI.

With the cessation of hostilities in France from 1420 and the consequent revival of the wool trade the staple successfully petitioned Parliament in 1421 to reopen the mint in Calais on the ground that the Treasurer was refusing payment except in English nobles. During the period of inactivity since 1402/3 new masters of the Tower mint had continued to be appointed to Calais also, but the reopening nevertheless took some time to achieve. Dies for gold and silver were delivered in May 1422 and the first coins issued in July. Comparison of the bullion minted at London and Calais from 1422 throws up some interesting contrasts. From 1422 to 1431 Calais produced £102,000 of gold, less than one fifth of London's output. At each mint more than 60 per cent. of these totals had been produced in the first two years or so, after which the rate of output steadily declined. At Calais the volume of gold coinage fell from a monthly average of over £3,000 in 1422-4 to below £800 a month in 1424-7; only £6,000 in total was struck in 1428-31, the last accounting period in which any Calais gold is recorded. London meanwhile maintained a much higher volume, still averaging more than £3,000 a month in 1424-7 and £1,500 a month in 1427-31.

In silver the relative position of the two mints was reversed. London coined only £28,000 from the start of Goldbeter's first contract in 1422 to 1431, more than a third of it in the first eighteen months. Calais, on the other hand, was concentrating on gold at that stage, and although in its first nine years its coinage of silver was in total around nine times that of London, only £10,800 was minted in the first eighteen months and it was not until 1424 when its output of gold began to decline that there was a huge increase in its silver coinage. From February 1424 to September 1432 Calais coined a total of £275,000 at an average rate of nearly £2,700 a month. The account for eleven months in 1431/2 shows £39,000 of silver minted at Calais, a figure to be compared with only £3,500 at London in two years from September 1431. The relative supremacy of Calais in silver was therefore even more marked at the start of the 1430s than in the later 1420s. In the four years from 1432 to 1436 nearly £100,000 was coined, although at a declining rate. The Foreign Roll records that 1,770 lbs. of silver (£2,655) was coined at Calais in seven weeks in February and March 1436 but that in the previous eleven months no coin had been minted on account of the war with the Duke of Burgundy. The last surviving Calais account, for £585, belongs to 1439/40 but it is not clear to how long a period this relates. By this date the weakened English position in France had greatly reduced the activity of the Calais staple. Possibly the mint may have continued to function occasionally on a small scale for a little longer, but the absence of Calais silver coins from the second half of Henry VI's reign is consistent with the mint having closed finally at about this date or not long afterwards.

The end of gold coinage at Calais did not result in a compensating increase at London. The market price of gold and its ratio to silver were strengthening, and the amount of it reaching the mint correspondingly declined. During the 1430s London minted gold at an annual rate of between £5,000 and £10,000, but rarely reached £5,000 a year in the 1440s or 1450s. In total the figures were £71,000 from 1431 to 1441, and £41,000 from 1441 to 1452, but only £15,000 from 1452 to 1460. The situation with silver was very different. In the 1430s and 1440s output remained relatively low. Apart from a special issue of

Henry IV – Edward IV

£3,000 in halfpence separately accounted in 1446/7, only £23,000 in silver coin was struck in eighteen years from September 1431 to October 1449, nearly half of it in the thirty months from Michaelmas 1438. But in the last eleven years of Henry VI London issued £74,000, considerably more than it had done in the whole of the reign before that time. Following the change of government, there are no accounts for the years 1460-2, but those for 1462-4 show nearly £5,000 of gold and £18,000 of silver, the former in particular at an annual rate above those achieved in the later 1450s.

As they had done since Edward III, the northern episcopal mints continued to make an essential contribution to the supply of pence in the Lancastrian period. York remained by far the more prolific of the two, but hoards suggest that at several points in the series the pence of Durham also outnumbered those from London. Senior bishops in the fifteenth century played an increasingly prominent role in political and diplomatic affairs. Henry IV's appointments to York and Durham were both active Lancastrian supporters: Henry Bowet at York, who had joined the Lancastrian party in the 1390s, was a confidential agent of the king, while Thomas Langley at Durham, who twice served as Chancellor, had been a protégé of John of Gaunt. When Langley was appointed to Durham in 1406 coinage in England had virtually ceased and he evidently had to wait until 1412, when he chose as his moneyer one of the Mulekyn family from Florence, before receiving his first set of dies. Langley died in November 1437 and Robert Neville, member of an increasingly powerful family, was then translated to the see from Salisbury, his temporalities being confirmed in April 1438. After Neville's death in July 1457, there was again little delay in appointing a successor, Laurence Booth, Chancellor to Queen Margaret and Keeper of the Privy Seal, who obtained his temporalities in October. Although after the battle of Towton Booth attended Edward's first parliament, he seems not to have retained the new king's favour since his rights were seized in December 1462 and not restored until April 1464. Durham coins of Henry VI are not very plentiful, and minting was only occasional at this period.

At York Archbishop Bowet also obtained his first dies soon after the weight reduction of 1412, and his pence of Henry V are the most abundant coins of that reign. Bowet died in October 1423, but a permanent successor, John Kemp, who had been Chancellor of Normandy under Henry V and was soon to serve as Chancellor of England, was not appointed until 1425 and only received his temporalities in April 1426. Kemp then held the see until he was promoted to Canterbury in July 1452. Some of his coins of the 1430s lack the archbishop's traditional quatrefoil on the reverse cross, but there is no historical evidence to suggest that his minting rights may have been suspended. Kemp was succeeded by William Booth, Laurence's elder brother, whose rights were granted in September 1452, and who remained in office until his death twelve years later. Kemp's and Booth's coins are common but, like some of Bowet's, many of them were struck from local dies which often depart from the London norm and so present problems of dating. It is, however, apparent from the surviving material that the output of the archbishop's mint from the 1430s was, if not continuous, at least more frequent and sustained than that of Durham.

In July 1463, after a lapse of more than a century, minting rights were confirmed to the Archbishop of Canterbury, now Thomas Bourchier, the king's second cousin. These were extended to include halfgroats, never previously allowed to an ecclesiastical mint, and halfpence, as well as pence; but no Canterbury coins attributable to the heavy coinage are known, and it appears that the mint was not opened until after the weight reduction of the following year.

English coins of the first half of the fifteenth century retained the basic designs established under Edward III. A few minor variations occur in details of the nobles and halves, and there are occasional departures from the normal nine-arc tressure on groats and halfgroats. But, apart from reduced size, there are several features which combine to give coins of the Lancastrian period a less austere appearance than that of their predecessors. First, there is a marked change of style. The hollow-sided uprights and less angular lettering introduced in the 1390s developed into a more ornate form. Roman *N*s survived into the light coinage of Henry IV only briefly on some of the earliest dies, after which the Gothic *n* became universal, and the larger fount previously used in the inner circle of the reverse on groats was discontinued for lack of space on the smaller flans. On silver the face and crown are generally larger, the hair fuller and more defined, usually with horizontal tufts of hair protruding below the crown. The whole portrait thus occupies more of the smaller available space within its tressured frame. At the same time there are often added symbols in the field or on the breast or neck, so that the composition is more crowded. The same is true of the inscriptions, with new and more elaborate versions of the initial cross and the addition of various ornaments between the words instead of the annulets or saltires which had been almost invariable up to the 1420s. The use of different symbols as stops to distinguish the dies of one issue from another had been adopted in Scotland under Robert III in the 1390s, but although this practice was not introduced into the English coinage until around 1430 it was then taken up in earnest, with a profusion of mascles, rosettes, cones, leaves, trefoils and stars, usually in addition to saltires but sometimes entirely displacing them. Shortly before the death of Henry V, the traditional cross at the head of the inscription was replaced on the reverse of gold coins by a lis; but by the end of the period the cross had disappeared from silver as well. Edward IV introduced a Yorkist rose instead and so began a new pattern whereby variations on the device chosen for this mintmark were to assume a central function in defining successive issues up to the seventeenth century.

Edward III's hierarchy of denominations in both gold and silver remained unchanged until 1464, although by that date only the largest values, the noble and groat, were in regular production. The gold noble continued to enjoy an often embarrassing degree of popularity abroad, leading to an outflow of coin and imitation in the Low Countries. English nobles of the 1420s were minted on a vast scale, but from the 1430s the rising price of gold led to a rapid decline in output. The later gold coins are of considerable rarity, the fractions particularly so. No half- or quarter-noble of Henry VI is known later than the 1430s, and although there is a heavy quarter of Edward IV no half-noble of this reign has yet been found. The proportions laid down for coinage at Calais in 1422 were, from each Tower pound of gold, eight ounces to be minted in nobles ($33^{1/3}$), three ounces in half-nobles (25) and one ounce in quarters ($16^{2/3}$). In practice, nobles are so much more abundant than halves throughout the period that it is difficult to believe that they were actually struck in these proportions. Part of the function of the half-noble was performed by the French *salut* which from 1423 was minted to an identical standard. Quarter-nobles are likely to have been rather more plentiful than hoards suggest, providing as they did a useful value intermediate between groats and nobles.

The groat remained the mainstay of the silver coinage, minted extensively throughout, but in huge quantities at Calais in the 1420s and early 1430s. Halfgroats were also produced in great abundance at that period, but after the 1430s the denomination seems to have gone out of favour, perhaps because there were by then enough in circulation. The Calais conditions of 1422 provided that equal quantities of groats (4 oz.) and halves (2 oz.) should be struck from the pound of silver, but surviving coins do not suggest that anything like the stipulated proportions were struck in pence (3 oz.), halfpence (2 oz.) or

Henry IV – Edward IV

farthings (1 oz.). Halfpence were minted in quantity under Henry V and into the 1430s, but in a sign of growing shortage the Parliament of 1445 ordered that halfpence and farthings should be struck at 33s. instead of 30s. to the Tower pound, thus reducing their weight by nine per cent. This regulation was to run for a maximum of two years from April 1446, and because the mint charges were higher than normal there is a separate entry for the coinage of 1,872 lbs. of silver into halfpence in the accounts for 1446/7. It is not stated that farthings were included in this figure but, even without the slight reduction involved, farthings had since 1412 weighed less than four grains and were now so small as to be impracticable for normal use. Although they are known of most issues, they are generally very rare and the lack of variety among those of the later years of Henry VI suggests that the mint was increasingly reluctant to produce them.

The huge scale of minting in the early years of Henry VI required a very large number of dies. This was particularly true of the mass-produced Calais silver coinage, for which thousands of dies were supplied between 1425 and 1431. Even in this period of exceptional activity the standard of die-cutting remained quite high, although not surprisingly there are occasional errors, such as altered stops or misplaced letters (with the error often corrected). There are also some oddities of spelling: for example, *Excultabitur* on some quarter-nobles of Henry V or (a more obviously phonetic form) *Sivi* for *Civi* on some groats and halfpence of Henry VI.

Finds from this period have been relatively few, although some of them were large. Unfortunately little is known of the hoard found at Highbury, in north London, in 1868, which is reputed to have contained some 7,000 coins ending with Henry V. These included many pence and fractions, not normally prominent in hoards, but also base Venetian *soldini*, the notorious 'galley halfpence' which according to the records were still reaching London in considerable numbers at this time. Another hoard ending with coins of Henry V, found at Attenborough, Nottinghamshire, in 1966, is also important for its long runs of the lower denominations. A silver find of c. 1450, made at Holwell, Leicestershire, in 1864, was notable for the fact that more than two hundred out of around seven hundred coins were pence of York, a high proportion even for a northern hoard. As before, gold was often hoarded separately from silver, and finds of up to a hundred gold coins buried in the 1420s and 1430s have been made at Horsted Keynes in Sussex (1929), at Borth, Cardiganshire (1930) and at Pulham, Dorset (1983). Naturally, most of their contents were nobles, but out of the one hundred coins from Pulham two were half-nobles and three were quarters. The largest gold hoard, completed just before Edward IV's reform of 1464-5, comes from Fishpool, Nottinghamshire (1966). It included greater variety than usual - among its 1,237 coins 223 were foreign: salutes and crowns from France, nobles, riders and lions from the Burgundian Netherlands, and demies and crowns from Scotland. The 104 half-nobles and 22 quarters perhaps offer a more representative view of the role of English fractional gold than the more selective earlier hoards. Unusually, two hoards buried in the 1450s from Reigate in Surrey (1972 and 1990) combined gold and silver - three gold out of 985 coins in Reigate I but 136 gold out of 6,703 coins in Reigate II. The Reigate hoards are a prime source of coins of Henry VI, but both included some very old silver, extending back to 1280 in Reigate II. Although buried a little after 1464, two other hoards have provided important runs of pre-1464 silver: Wyre Piddle, Worcestershire (1967) and Stamford (1866). No full record was made of the Stamford hoard, but it contained over 3,000 coins and was the source of many of the groats of Henry VI and of the heavy coinage of Edward IV in public and private collections today.

Imitations of Lancastrian silver coins are rare, but Wyre Piddle contained seven forgeries of which two were of groats and one of a penny of Henry VI; and there were two plated forgeries of gold nobles in Fishpool. The noble remained popular on the Continent during the fifteenth and sixteenth centuries, not confined to identifiable Burgundian issues, but including extensive deceptive copies of English coins of the 1420s, which can only be distinguished by minor variations of inscription or design. Such imitations are not found alongside the originals in hoards of the fifteenth century, and it seems that they were produced more than a century and a half later at mints in the Netherlands, along with copies of ryals of Edward IV and Elizabeth, about the time that an English army under the Earl of Leicester was sent to assist the Low Countries in their struggle against Spain in the 1580s.

Classification 1412 – 1422 (Henry IV-V)

The first ten years after the weight reduction of 1412 constitute for the numismatist one of the more awkward periods of the later middle ages. Although many of the coins bear additional symbols they often do not correspond from gold to silver, from one denomination to another or, in the case of pence, from mint to mint. Furthermore, except in the earliest phase, there are no symbols in the obverse field on groats which, as the largest silver coins, generally provide the most complete series in any coinage for the purpose of classification. Confusion has been increased by differences of view about the allocation of varieties between the reigns of Henry IV and Henry V, with the result that no consensus has been achieved for the designation of successive classes. In his detailed study of 1930, Brooke divided the coinage of 'Henry V' into nine classes, of which his classes I-III are in fact more likely to belong to Henry IV. This classification, largely dependent on the fracture and replacement of individual letter punches, was a serious attempt to provide a scheme that could be applied to all denominations, regardless of the differing symbols upon them. However, despite its technical value in demonstrating details of sequence, Brooke's 1930 arrangement has proved difficult to use in practice, partly because of its intricacy, but also because it can only confidently be applied to unworn and well-struck specimens. Brooke himself appreciated the problem, and only two years later, in *English Coins*, he put forward a simplified scheme, consisting of seven classes (A-G), based more on symbols than on letter forms. Again, coins of the earliest classes should more probably be attributed to Henry IV, so that Henry V's definitive coinage begins with class C, when a cinquefoil (commonly described in numismatic literature as a 'mullet') was introduced into the design of all denominations from the noble to the penny. Subsequent studies of the coinage of 1412-22 by Potter and Harris have included adaptations of both of Brooke's arrangements, which can be of value to specialists but are less well suited to general use as a result of their complexity. As with his work on earlier series, Potter concentrated mainly on the groats and halves, while more attention has been paid to the pence and halfpence by Harris.

Prior to Brooke, students such as Walters and Lawrence had attributed all the pre-cinquefoil varieties of the light coinage to Henry IV, regarding the cinquefoil as an indicator of the new reign, and this was also Potter's view. Brooke's study was founded on the assumption that what he chose to regard as privy-marks would have been changed quarterly for the purpose of the pyx trials. This led him to conclude from the first series of light nobles that these were ample to account for the four quarters of the year from April 1412 to March 1413, as a slipped trefoil occurs severally in each of the four quarters of the reverse cross. This arrangement then took with it the accompanying silver, leaving the coins of both metals that comprised his classes A and B to be allocated to Henry

V. Such a division, however, ill accords with the mint accounts. Precise calculations cannot be made, because the accounts do not specify how much of the totals of gold and silver purchased by the mint in the ten months from November 1412 fell within the last four months of Henry IV's reign, and how much within the first six of Henry V's. A similar question arises in 1422 in respect of the last six months of Henry V. But of the gold bullion recorded between November 1411 and March 1422 it may be estimated that nearly a quarter had probably been purchased before the death of Henry IV, and of the silver around one tenth. On the basis of Brooke's arrangement, the Henry IV light gold in the Fishpool hoard amounted to about twelve per cent of the total for 1411-22 and the Henry IV light silver coins in the Reigate II hoard to less than six per cent, in each case significantly less than one would expect if Brooke's regnal division were valid. Although survival rates do vary, these percentages are improbably low. Adding in the coins of classes A and B would bring them up to around eighteen per cent for gold and nine per cent for the silver, considerably closer to what the mint accounts imply. In the present work the earliest issues at reduced weight (i.e. all those allocated by Brooke to Henry IV) have been designated the Primary series of Henry IV's light coinage, or class P, and classes A and (most of) B, the Secondary series, in order to retain Brooke's now familiar labels but without his regnal attribution. When dies of any of these three classes have had a cinquefoil added, this is indicated by an asterisk (e.g. class P*). Die-interchanges between class P and class A or B being relatively frequent, many such coins have since 1930 been listed as Henry V/Henry IV mules, as they would have been under Brooke's arrangement, but few if any of them actually merit that description.

Walters and Potter considered that the introduction of the cinquefoil, from the end of class B onwards, had been specifically designed to distinguish the coinage of Henry V from that of his father. While this may have been the practical effect, there is no other case in English coinage, before the introduction of numerals in the sixteenth century, where it could be argued that the succession of a new king with the same name was recognised by a mark of differentiation on his coins; but such marks were, as required by indenture, sometimes used to indicate the coinage of a new master, and this would provide a natural explanation of the position in 1413. Henry IV died on 20 March and a new contract for the coinage was concluded with Lewys John on 14 April. At about this time all dies in current use appear to have been recalled and reissued with the addition of a cinquefoil. It is not always clear, especially on worn coins, whether a mark has actually been added to existing dies, but there are sufficient undoubted examples of classes P*, A* and B* to show that the cinquefoil was systematically applied to a range of dies originally issued at various points during the early stages of the light coinage, and this must have been related to some administrative or accounting purpose. It is difficult to imagine any circumstance more likely to have given rise to such a need than a change of mastership, and this would therefore help to substantiate the view that all coins of classes P, A and B without the cinquefoil should be attributed to John's predecessor, Garner, and so to the reign of Henry IV. In this connection it may be noted that John's mastership continued until February 1422, six months before the death of Henry V, and that the cinquefoil continued to appear on the bust or in the field on the majority of the coins generally agreed to belong to this reign (classes C to F), although not on the very latest (classes G and H).

In the early months of the new coinage, presumably to help identify the lighter coins, an annulet and a pellet were added to the design, although these had been discontinued before class B. With class C, however, the use of marks was revived. The symbols found in the field on coins of classes C to F of Henry V are the annulet (broken or whole), the 'mullet' or cinquefoil, the pellet and the trefoil. In broad terms, class C in Brooke's revised arrangement is identified by broken annulets, class D by whole annulets, class E by pellets and class F by trefoils, but because of their erratic occurrence many entries, such as halfgroats of D and E, or Durham pence of E and F, are missing from the scheme. The only one of these symbols found on groats of Henry V is the so-called mullet. This is in fact quite unlike the heraldic device of that name, which represents a spur and is accordingly depicted with a hollowed centre and pointed limbs, like a pierced star. On the coins this mark is never pierced and usually has more of a floral appearance, with blunt or rounded ends in the manner of a cinquefoil. Its first occurrence on new dies comes at about the juncture of classes B and C, and its use thereafter was widespread on both gold and silver before class G. The annulet also occurs extensively on coins of classes C to F (except the groats). To start with the annulet is broken, but new punches with the annulet whole were in due course introduced. Harris has suggested that the earlier annulet punch may have been produced by folding a lamina round a pin, so that the circle was not continuous, and a gap gradually developed giving rise to the 'broken' annulet. However that may be, there seems to have been some overlap in the use of different punches – indeed, some nobles and halfpence appear to show both sorts of annulet on the same coin. Also, it is sometimes difficult to be sure whether the annulet is broken or not; the result would differ according to how hard or evenly the punch was struck into the die, or how cleanly the coin itself was struck. Ghosting of the reverse cross often affected the definition of annulets on pence and halfpence, and with repeated use of dies the annulet could sometimes look more like a solid pellet. In the case of pence, because there is no absolute division into an earlier series with broken annulets (i.e. class C) and a later one (class D) with whole annulets, it is necessary to use a new classification into types based on other features such as the bust, the beaded circles and the module.

The last group wholly attributable to Henry V is class G, the London dies of which lack the cinquefoil and all other extra marks. Brooke suggested that this change might be connected with Goldbeter's replacement of John as master in February 1422. Brooke and Whitton, however, were unaware that the mint accounts of Calais, which struck all but the earliest varieties of the Annulet coinage, ran from July 1422, and consequently regarded the Annulet series as belonging entirely to Henry VI. Now it is recognised that the Annulet coinage began a few months before the death of Henry V, Woodhead has proposed that this, rather than class G, should be associated with Goldbeter's appointment. Since class G was not extensive, either interpretation is possible, and the question remains unresolved. Meanwhile, it is convenient to have a shorthand means of referring to such early Annulet coins as may have been struck before the end of August 1422, and the term class H is accordingly used here for these last issues of Henry V.

Henry IV, Light Coinage (1412-13)

The first year of the new coinage saw wide variations in the style and detail of the coins. Inactivity at the mint in preceding years meant that there was a shortage of available skilled staff at every level. In September 1412 the warden was ordered to recruit moneyers and die-sinkers. Several engravers must have been involved in the early stages, their work differing greatly in quality. At first many of the dies were of the same module as those used in the heavy coinage, but the weight reduction meant flans of lesser diameter and a consequent need for smaller dies. However, dies too large for the coins (especially for pence) continued to be produced for some time into the reign of Henry V, often causing problems for detailed classification when only the bottom of the letters can be seen. With the exception of a few coins struck from altered dies of earlier

Henry IV – Edward IV

date, the first coins at the reduced weight, those of the Primary phase (class P), are easily recognisable not only by symbols of the light coinage added to the design, but also by their lettering and initial cross. As on the last dies made for gold of the heavy coinage, the letters are elegant and waisted, & is represented by a barred upright, and the cross is formed of four wedges with concave sides. On silver the initial cross is smaller and plainer; and the pellets in the quarters of the reverse are still tightly grouped, as they had been since the later years of Richard II. *N* in *London* is Roman on groats and pence. London silver coins of class P (above the halfpenny) have an annulet and pellet by the crown: first, and briefly, with the annulet to the right; then, more usually, to the left. The annulet, which also occurs on the ship's side on most of the nobles and halves, beside the shield or on the tressure of the quarter-nobles, by the bust on halfpence and on the breast of the pence of York, was clearly intended to be an identifying mark of the new light money, since it was added to certain old dies for both nobles and groats when put to use at the start of the recoinage. Another characteristic mark of class P is the slipped trefoil, already found on very late dies for heavy nobles, but primarily associated with the first phase of the light coinage, in which it is found as a breastmark on much of the silver. On the larger gold it is placed on the ship's side and by one of the lions on the reverse; on the quarter-noble, by the shield. It also occurs in one or both inscriptions on groats and occasionally on other denominations.

INITIAL CROSSES AND SYMBOLS ON THE LIGHT COINAGE OF HENRY IV

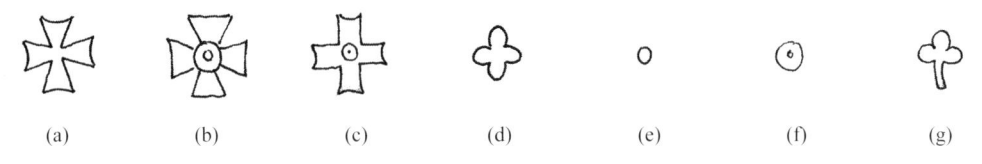

(a)   (b)   (c)   (d)   (e)   (f)   (g)

(a) Initial cross of class P gold; (b) Cross of class A; (c) Cross of class B;
(d) Quatrefoil, classes P-B; (e) and (f) Pellet and annulet, classes P and A;
(g) Slipped trefoil, class P.

Potter divided the obverses of the Primary groats, all marked with annulet, pellet and slipped trefoil, into three types. The first of these consists of four dies on which the annulet is placed to the right of the crown and the pellet to the left. On the second and third types the fieldmarks are reversed, annulet to left and pellet to right. The type I groats lack the French title, and are the only ones from the fifteenth century to do so. Two of the four known obverse dies of type I are in the style of late Richard II, with a wide face and thick lettering, and their inscriptions look as if they may have been altered from *Ricard* to *henric* (Ia). On the other two (Ib) the name does not seem to have been altered, but there are again features reminiscent of the 1390s (such as the crown punch), although the hair and face are thinner and the chin more pointed. Perhaps the two Ia dies were originally made at about the same time as the late Richard halfgroats (type IV) without the French title and, for some obscure reason, never used in that reign, but brought out many years later and then validated for use in Henry's light coinage. If so, one could argue that the Ib dies might have been made near the start of Henry's reign, but again not used until 1412 when the appropriate symbols were added. Potter considered that some of the reverse dies used with the type I obverses also exhibit different, and presumably earlier, epigraphical characteristics than are found on normal reverse dies of the Primary phase.

Only one obverse die each marked with pellet/annulet (as opposed to annulet/pellet) is known for the halfgroat and the penny. The type I halfgroat die and its accompanying reverses have Henry IV lettering and were clearly new dies made for the light coinage, this halfgroat obverse and the two for groats of type Ib being the only undoubtedly new dies with the pellet on the left. The bust on the first light halfgroat has a slipped trefoil on the breast, but is otherwise similar to that on the heavy halfgroats. Gothic *n* on the reverses also distinguishes the light halfgroats of Henry IV from their heavy equivalents; one of the type I reverses, curiously, has *Lon* under *Posui*, not seen thus since the 1360s. The unique type I penny does not have Henry IV lettering, and is possibly, like the groats, from an altered obverse die, with the name recut and the light coinage symbols added. Its reverse die, unique for a London penny of class P in having Gothic *n*, was very rusty, consistently with its having been left unused for many years.

Of the seven other obverse dies recorded for groats of the Primary phase Potter placed first (his type II) two of them reading *Dei Gra*, with even numbers of arcs in the tressure (eight and ten), the other five dies, with *Di* and nine arcs, constituting his type III. The face is thin, the hair straggly, and the die-sinking progressively more careless, with crown, bust, hair or tressure arcs sometimes misplaced. The type III groats are the least rare of the Primary series, but their obverse dies are more often found muled with Secondary dies (P/A and P/B) than with their true reverses. Indeed, there are, unusually, not many more groat reverse dies with Primary lettering than there are obverses, but they show some variety in the arrangement and stopping of the inscription. All read *Adiutorem* in full (as Richard's groats had done), although with different breaks – *A/diutor/em*, *A/diutore/m,* or *Ad/iutorem/,* and sometimes with two saltires after the *d*. Very occasionally one of the *n*s in *London* is of the Gothic form, but the *N* on the reverse of true class P groats is otherwise always Roman (usually reversed, but occasionally unbarred). These groats, and the cognate pence, are the only such coins of the fifteenth century to use the Roman *N*.

The halfgroat of later class P, with annulet/pellet by the crown, is a smaller version of the groat. One of the two obverse dies (II) has ten arcs in the tressure, the other (III) nine. Like those of the pellet/annulet halfgroats, the reverses all have Gothic *n* in *London,* but *m* of *Adiutorem* is now dropped on some late dies. The London pence have larger lettering as on the groats, including Roman *N*. Potter divided them into two types according to the bust: type II, with long face and hair (and exceptionally including a die with *Di Gra*), and type III, with the head smaller and the hair shorter. The halfgroats and London pence of later class P are of considerable rarity. Obverses of both are also found muled with later reverses, although less intensively than in the case of the groats, and the PIII* die only after a cinquefoil had been punched over the pellet.

Pence of Henry IV's light coinage from the episcopal mints are rare, and belong to the Primary series. They do not carry the annulet and pellet by the crown of the London silver. At Durham Langley's first coins have a bust with wide hair and a long neck, much like that on a late London penny of the heavy coinage. The trefoils of coalesced pellets on the reverse, and Gothic *n* in *Dunolm,* also lead one to wonder whether these dies may have been prepared during the heavy period but not delivered until the weight reduction had restored the viability of the bishop's mint. There is a slipped trefoil on the breast, as on London pence of class P; but the reading *henricus* in full is not matched on any other penny of Henry IV, and could indicate that these dies were made at a time when other dies were not in regular production. Archbishop Bowet of York returned old dies (presumably Scrope's) to the exchequer on 5 October 1412, and two new obverses with four reverses were ready for delivery within a fortnight. These have normal class P lettering, which must therefore still have been in use six months after the launch of the new coinage at Easter. They also display a liberal use of annulets – on the breast, as obverse stops and (double) before *Civi* and *Ebo*.

CLASSES AND MULES OF HENRY IV, LIGHT COINAGE

	P	P/A	P/B	A	A/P	A/B	B	B/P	B/A
Nobles	x	m	m	x	m		x	m	
Half-nobles	x							m	
Quarter-nobles	x			x				m	
Groats	x	m	m	x	m	m	x	m	m
Halfgroats	x		m	x		m	x		
Pennies	x			x					
Halfpennies	x			x			x		

x – true coins; m – mules

The silver coins of class A are entirely different in appearance from those of class P, and from anything that follows. The common defining characteristic of the class is the lettering, which has been described as 'stunted'. The letters are short and broad. They are also very neat, unlike those of the immediately previous and succeeding classes. Notable letters are *P* with its foot extending far to the right, *O* and Gothic *n* with wide central hollows, and *m* with the sides exaggeratedly curved. Most dies also show an unusual form of initial cross patty, very small and consisting of four broad wedges and a point within a hollow centre (sometimes referred to as a sunk annulet). Stops are saltires, often double. All denominations of class A are very rare.

There are two obverse dies for class A groats, with a highly unusual portrait, often described as the 'emaciated bust'. The face is large, set low on the shoulders, with little neck; the mouth, with prominent lips, turns down at the corners. Opinions have differed about the appropriateness of the term emaciated but, as Potter observed, the hollowed outline around the nose and mouth does convey a gaunt appearance. With the reduction in the diameter of the light groats there was no longer so much room for large letters in the inner inscription: from class A onwards the inner letter fount is the same as the outer. Also, while a few rare early Secondary groat reverses still include the *m* of *Adiutorem*, the normal reading henceforward is *A/diutor/e'*. There is no equivalent to the emaciated bust on halfgroats, but two dies have the class A lettering and initial cross, combined with a taller and thinner portrait more like that in class B. Pennies (of London only) are found both with a smaller version of the groat's emaciated bust (Aa) and with a taller bust as on the halfgroats (Ab). Both types include *Di Gra* in the obverse legend, a novelty on this denomination. The pennies and one of the halfgroat dies have an annulet and pellet by the crown, as in class P, and one of the penny dies with the taller bust is also found with a cinquefoil punched over the pellet (Ab*).

Groat dies of class A are more often paired with those of class P or B than with each other. There is also an A/B mule halfgroat. The period of production of dies with class A lettering must have been extremely short and their usage not much longer. Although they entered the general stock of dies, the interchange of A groat dies with both adjacent classes, the direct mules between classes P and B (in gold as well as silver) that miss out class A, and the absence of any groat or halfgroat die of class A with cinquefoil added, all indicate that the class A die-sinker made only a minimal contribution to the recoinage. The sudden arrival and disappearance of his elegant and unusual fount, coupled with a highly distinctive bust, could suggest the work of an expert foreign engraver whose services and some of whose tools were not available for long, although the punches for the crown on class A groats and the large fleurs on the cusps continued in use into class B.

The stunted lettering of class A was soon displaced by the larger fount of taller and relatively less broad letters, by which class B is principally defined. The initial cross, larger than that of class A, is plain, or slightly patty, with indented ends; a hollowed centre, enclosing a pellet, is sometimes visible. The groats are also readily identifiable by the bust, which has a small face and a long neck with a goitrous swelling. This portrait lacks the hollows around the mouth and nose of class A, but the eyes are outlined with a hollow between the eyelids and the brows. There is some slight variety in the rendering of the face, but the overall aspect is consistently severe. The mouth is small and thin, and turns down at the sinister corner, contributing to a sour expression that has given rise to the term 'scowling bust'. Since Brooke only coins of true class P have generally been regarded as representing the light coinage of the reign of Henry IV, while class B seemed to constitute just one element of the more extensive coinage of Henry V. Partly for this reason, and partly because of the number of conspicuous individual varieties among the groats of class P, they have been more sought for collections than those of class B; but groats of class B are also of considerable rarity, as their very slight representation in hoards bears out.

LETTER FORMS IN THE SECONDARY PHASE OF HENRY IV'S LIGHT COINAGE

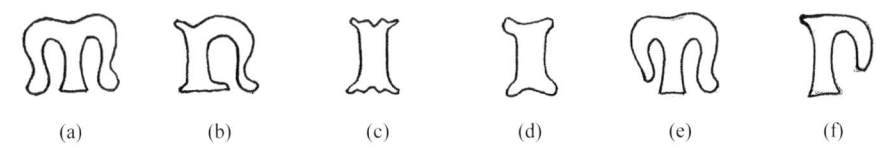

(a) Letter *M* of class A; (b) Letter *n* of class A; (c) Palmate *I* of early class B;
(d) Knobbed *I* of later class B; (e) Letter *M* without left foot, class B; (f) Defective *n*, class B.

The class B groats begin with three obverse dies (B1) that have the same large fleurs on the cusps as in class A; on the first two of them, as on the groats of class A, the cusps above the crown are fleured and there is a quatrefoil after *henric*. These three dies (and their equivalent reverses) also have in common a distinctive letter *I* with the ends ornamented in palmate form (Brooke's I1a). Early reverse dies of class B, perhaps those made to pair with obverses of B1, have *m* with the left limb wanting an outturned foot. In B2 the cusp fleurs are slightly smaller and the *I*, again tall, has curved serifs that end in small knobs (I2). Among other various class B letter forms, found on groats and other denominations, are a tall Gothic *n* (Potter's N2), which loses the end of its tail (N2a) from the last die of B1 onwards, and large *c, e* and *I* later in the class. Of the six groat obverse dies of class B2a, with the letters I2 and N2a, two are known only without a cinquefoil added, two both without and with a cinquefoil on the sinister shoulder, and the other two only with it. The final groat obverse die of class B has a small star-like cinquefoil instead of a breast fleur (B2b).

Halfgroats of class B are very rare. They have a tressure of ten or eleven arcs (with the top cusps either fleured or not). Although the portrait does not exactly match the 'scowling' bust of the groats it may be distinguished from that on halfgroats from class C onwards by still having a low crown like that of class A. One die has a cinquefoil on the breast. Because of the larger lettering of class B, some halfgroat reverses have the initial cross omitted and abbreviation of *Deum* and *Meum* to *Deu* and *Me*. The reverse pellets are still often tightly grouped, or coalescing. No penny obverse die that can be associated with class B has been found without a cinquefoil.

Fractions of Henry IV's light coinage are all very rare and difficult to classify because often on halfpence only part of the letters is on the flan, while as usual the tiny punches for the farthing do not match those on dies for larger silver. Weights of individual specimens of the smallest coins are an unreliable guide, but a farthing with a long face (and no neck or shoulders) has a slipped trefoil after *Rex* and so must belong to the light coinage (class P), while Withers associates the broader face and taller crown on another variety with the punch used on some nobles of classes B and C.

Primary halfpence include varieties with annulets by the neck (Pa) or by the hair or crown (Pb). The former have the same bust and lettering as class 2 heavy halfpence, and some may be from old dies amended. One of the dies for Pb halfpence, which have a smaller portrait with little bust, has been noted both before and after a cinquefoil was punched over the annulet to the right (this is the only occurrence of the cinquefoil on a halfpenny). Although Primary halfpence, like halfgroats, have Gothic *n* on the reverse, one die has the first *N* in *London* Roman and the second Gothic (like a late PIII groat). Also with annulets by the crown, halfpence with the lettering of class A are either otherwise similar to those of class Pb, or have what resembles a miniature version of the emaciated bust. With class B letters (including the *n* with defective right leg) there are rare halfpence, with or without annulets, some with single saltires after *tas* and *don*, as on a few groats of class B1; the portrait is tall, with a small head, long neck and full shaped bust. Because of the lack of annulets (or other marks in the field) on some of these B halfpence, they have sometimes been attributed to class G of Henry V, but their lettering and other features (including propeller pellets) clearly place them much earlier.

Gold of Henry IV's light coinage consists mainly of nobles. Although none are common, those of class P are the most plentiful. A few early Primary nobles still have crenellated castles (Pbi), as do coins from two late heavy obverse dies (with arms of types 2 and 3) to which an annulet has been added on the ship's side (Pa). On most dies, however, the forecastle and sterncastle are topped with pellets (Pbii). Reverse dies of class P nobles (and halves) are easily recognised by virtue of having a small point before the *h* in the central panel of the reverse, perhaps a counterpart to the pellet by the crown on silver. The lettering is of the elegant style found on the last heavy nobles. Various other features of the late heavy coinage also continue – a slipped trefoil in one quarter of the reverse and on the ship's side (usually accompanied by an annulet on the new dies), 3-1 rigging, more than one letter of the king's name before the bowsprit, and the spelling *hib*. The Secondary nobles, however, have 3-2 rigging, *hyb*, and a small quatrefoil, or occasionally a slipped trefoil, above the sail and by the lion in the *Autem* quarter. They also have *h* only before the bowsprit (this was to become standard for the rest of the Lancastrian era), and they omit the title of Lord of Aquitaine which had been included on all earlier nobles since the 1360s, but was now dropped for good. Nobles with the stunted lettering of class A are found both as true coins and as mules both ways with class P dies, but all are extremely rare. Class B nobles, with the new tall lettering (often including the defective *n* of this class, and a large and sinuous *S*), are less rare, and are also occasionally found muled with class P dies. On reverse dies of class B the beaded circle and the inner tressure are less tightly dotted than before. Three of the obverse dies are found with a cinquefoil added by the king's wrist (B*), two of them also known in their unaltered state.

The light half-nobles of Henry IV are of great rarity. Those of class P follow the nobles in having the castles first crenellated (Pi) and then pellet-topped (Pii), an annulet and a trefoil on the ship's side, rigging with only one rope to the bow, and a trefoil by one lion on the reverse. No half-noble with class A features has been found, and class B is represented only by two obverse dies, which replicate the 3-2 rigging and *h/enric* of the corresponding nobles. The earlier of these dies, without extra marks, is paired with a class P reverse. The other, only known with a reverse of class C (i.e. with a new, undamaged *n*), has a broken annulet on the ship's side and a quatrefoil before *h/enric*.

Although less so than the halves, the light quarter-nobles of Henry IV are nevertheless very rare. Primary quarters have slipped trefoils each side of the shield, with or without small annulets below. The extremely rare class A quarter-noble, with the characteristic initial cross and stunted lettering, also has annulets below the trefoils by the shield. The trefoils on the cusps of this coin consist of larger pellets than the cusp trefoils of class P; and it has stars instead of trefoils at the corners of the reverse panel. Of class B there are two obverse varieties, both with slipped trefoils beside the shield: one (a) has trefoils on the tressure, the other (b) annulets. The former (also muled with a class P reverse) has annulets below the slipped trefoils by the shield, as in class A. The Bb die is known both before and after the addition of a cinquefoil.

Henry V (1413 – 1422)

The coinage of Henry V is, for all but the last six and a half months of the reign, the product of Lewys John's mastership, during which the cinquefoil featured on a majority of the dies. The post-cinquefoil coda includes the unmarked class G and the beginning of the Annulet issues which were to continue under Henry VI for all or most of the remainder of the 1420s. At the outset, in 1413, there was a brief transitional phase when some, perhaps all, of the obverse dies in use were from the previous reign, amended by addition of the cinquefoil. Such altered dies have been noted of all denominations except the half-noble and farthing, and of all three classes of the light coinage of Henry IV. In the classification they are indicated by the addition of an asterisk: thus, class P* (groat, halfgroat, penny and halfpenny), class A* (penny) and class B* (noble, quarter-noble, groat and penny). In at least one case, that of the groat of class B2b, a new class B die was made with the cinquefoil breastmark as part of the original design, this mark being placed on the cusp where there would previously have been a fleur. A few other obverse dies of class B may also have been made, or at least first brought into use, after the change of master; but where class B dies are only known with the cinquefoil added (as, for example, one of the class B2* noble dies), it is of course possible that they had already been used in the pre-cinquefoil phase but that specimens to demonstrate this have not yet come to light. Most of the old, amended dies of earlier classes probably did not remain in use for very long and the new features of class C must have been introduced almost immediately. Thus begins the definitive coinage of Henry V, inaugurating for several years under John a period of standardised design (although with an array of added symbols), to replace the stylistic miscellany of the first year of the recoinage under Garner. As a result of the weight reduction there was a shrinkage in the size of dies and coins. In the middle years of Henry V this was often exaggerated, especially in the case of nobles and groats, by the use of thicker flans, reducing their diameter still further. Coins of this middle period are also easily recognised by their beaded circles, consisting of large teeth, less closely knit than usual.

The added cinquefoil on old dies of Henry IV throws an interesting light on what dies were still in use at the end of that reign. Gold was struck in some quantity in the first year of the new coinage, and this probably explains why no class P obverse dies for gold may have survived to be amended and only one early reverse die (on the B*/P noble) remained available. The absence of any half-noble with added cinquefoil merely reflects the great rarity of the half at this period. In silver some class P dies lasted longer and all denominations except the tiny farthing are found with the cinquefoil; the groat and penny have more recent reverses but the halfgroat and halfpenny were still paired with reverses of class P. Obverse dies of class A, however, were few, and only the penny has been found with a cinquefoil over the pellet by the crown. Groats and halves of class B* with added cinquefoil are to have been expected, since the B2b groat shows that the cinquefoil arrived just before the use of class B punches ceased. On the other hand, it is odd that there are no class B pence without a cinquefoil, although this could be due to non-survival. One of the very rare B* London pennies follows the class A pence in reading *Di Gra*. The B penny dies have a distinctive U-shaped face, with annulet and cinquefoil by the crown (which is from the same punch as that used for class A pence). Their reverses have a larger circle than in class P, similar to that used with the Ab* obverse. Because of its low crown, with cinquefoil and annulet (in that order, as on subsequent pence) beside it, a rare type of York penny from local dies may also belong to the late class B period, soon after the cinquefoil was introduced.

In silver the replacement of class B by class C is clearly defined by changes in the portrait: in the bust on groats, and in the crown on halfgroats and pence. On all but the earliest dies of class C there is also a new, unbroken *n* replacing the fractured *n* of late class B. The new groat bust, which continued in use beyond the end of the reign, is less severe in aspect than its predecessors. Potter has described it as the 'frowning' bust, but this is not entirely apt; smiling or youthful, as sometimes used, would better convey the less gloomy impression that it gives. It would be reading too much into the picture to see the new bust as a conscious reference to the accession of a younger king (who in fact wore his hair short); but the contrast between the variety of busts in the early stages of the light coinage, under Henry IV, and the uniformity of the new reign at least implies the use of improved techniques in die-making after a change of master. The mouth is now short and straight, with a thick lower lip and the upper lip touching the nose. The eyelids merge into the brow and a deep recess each side by the bridge of the nose runs upwards into the forehead. Short tufts of hair emerging almost horizontally below the sides of the crown are now more prominent than in classes A and B, and were to become a regular and characteristic feature of the portrait on groats throughout the fifteenth century.

The lack of fieldmarks on groats means that none of them can be associated with classes D, E and F on the same basis as other denominations. There is, however, one late obverse die (without the *c* in *Franie*), the epigraphy of which corresponds with that on other denominations of class F. The key letters are *n* with the top left corner cut away and *P* without its lower left corner, and these also occur on a few late groats attributable to class G. Otherwise, the main series of Henry V's groats falls to be described under class C. Earlier coins (Ca) have a narrow *D* with the back peaked only on the outside, but on the bulk of them (Cb) there is a broader *D* with peaks inside and out. Ca lettering also includes a tall *I* (Potter's I3), as in late class B, replaced in Cb by an *I* with a shorter shaft (Potter's I4). From class C onwards there is usually a quatrefoil after *Posui*, and Ca groats normally have one after *henric* as well. The initial cross in Ca has a pellet in the centre, followed early in Cb by a simple pierced cross, although on worn or weakly struck specimens both versions tend to look like plain crosses, with the central hollow not visible. The same sequence of crosses is found on other denominations. From class B onwards, to the end of the reign and beyond, groats typically have double saltires after *tas* and *don*, as also do some of the smaller silver.

CINQUEFOIL AND LETTERS OF HENRY V'S COINAGE

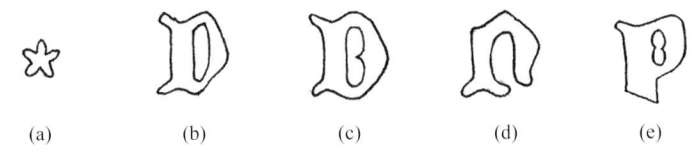

(a)   (b)   (c)   (d)   (e)

(a) Cinquefoil, *passim;* (b) Narrow *D,* class Ca groats and halves; (c) Broader *D,* class Cb; (d) Sliced *n,* classes F and G; (e) Sliced *P,* classes F and G.

Halfgroats, considerably scarcer than the groats, are much more variable in appearance. They differ conspicuously from those of earlier groups in having a new and much taller crown, with five circular hollows along the band. On class C halfgroats, usually with a cinquefoil on the breast, the only fieldmark is a broken annulet to the left of the crown (occasionally placed instead of a fleur on the adjacent cusp). They fall into the same subdivisions as the groats, identifiable by letters like the *D* and *I* and the initial cross, but also by the bust. In Ca the neck is tall, with central swelling, and the shoulders arched; Cb has a shorter neck and the shoulders are flatter. The cinquefoil is missing on more halfgroats than groats of class C, but it is doubtful whether any such unmarked halfgroat dies could be early enough for the absence of the cinquefoil to indicate that it was not introduced until after the arrival of the tall crown. On reverses there is extensive variation in the outer inscription, and the pellets point towards the centre of each group of three, often seeming to join in the shape of a propeller. An unexpected curiosity is a mule between an obverse of Ca and a reverse of Richard II more than thirty years old. While there seem to be no halfgroats with a whole annulet (alone) by the crown, such as could be described as class D, an unbroken annulet does occur on one late die, but together with a trefoil (to the right) that places it with class F.

Although Brooke's simplified classification for Henry V pennies looks straightforward, it is by no means easy to arrange the coins of classes C to F in a satisfactory sequence. York pence of this period are by far the most plentiful, and many of them are from locally made dies. Pence of London and Durham are quite scarce. Those of the episcopal mints, often badly struck, are generally found in poor condition, making detailed identification difficult. Class C was described by Brooke as having a 'mullet' (i.e. cinquefoil) to the left of the crown and a broken annulet to right; class D similarly, but with the annulet unbroken; class E, with an added pellet; class F with cinquefoil and trefoil; and class G with no marks in the field. There are, however, other features of the coins which cut across this arrangement, and which can only be accommodated within a different classification. For this purpose the coins are grouped into three main types, defined chiefly by reference to module, bust and inscription. This classification only works adequately for the pence of London, Durham and York from London-made dies; those from local dies at York are often a law unto themselves. Type 1 consists of early pence on large flans. The diameter of the neatly dotted circles within the legends is about 12.5 cm., and this provided space for a large bust. Although the portraits vary, they all show a measure of neck and shoulders, the outline of which is often rounded. The size of the dies also gave room for extended obverse readings. Type 2 is marked by a reduction in the size of dies and flans. The circles are smaller (11.5 cm. diameter, or less), composed more loosely and of larger teeth. This meant more abbreviated readings and less room for the portrait, of which the head is set low down at the expense of all but a trace of neck and shoulders. The crown punch used in both types (perhaps the same as on halfgroats) is tall,

Henry IV – Edward IV

with prominent hollows on the band. Most of the coins of type 1 have the broken annulet of Brooke's class C, but the whole annulet of class D is also found. Type 2 includes coins of classes C, D, E and F. There is no absolute dividing line between types 1 and 2, but the change to type 3 is clearcut. Type 3 is equivalent to Brooke's class G at London, with a distinctive new bust, and fieldmarks only on coins of the episcopal mints. In order to indicate both type and class, both may be used together – thus 1(C), 2(D) etc.

On early London pence of type 1 (C and D) the normal inscription is *henric Rex Angl & Fran(c)* but the reading with *henricus* in full and no French title, more commonly used at York and Durham, is also found occasionally at London. There are double saltires after *tas* and *don*, and some reverse dies still have the tightly grouped 'propeller' pellets. An old die of class P* survived into this period, and was first employed at London with a class B reverse before being sent to Durham. In type 2 there are again London pence with both forms of annulet (C and D); the latest London pence of type 2 are, however, the scarce coins with a trefoil instead of the annulet (F). With the smaller format the French title shrinks to *F*, although *Di Gra* was restored before the end of 2(F), and retained in type 3(G), at London only. Some type 2 reverses have a quatrefoil after *tas*, others annulet stops or none.

Type 1 Durham pence occur of both classes C and D. Obverse readings vary, but the earliest is *henricus Rex Anglie*, followed by a quatrefoil. A quatrefoil is also found after *tas* and *olm* on all Durham coins of type 1. The delivery of the old Henry IV die of class P* to Durham at the end of its life may or may not be related to the fact that no type 2 dies appear to have been made for the bishop's mint. There are records of modest coinage at Durham in 1416/17 and 1418/19, but it is quite possible that for a few years no new dies were supplied to this mint, which at several periods used its existing ones to exhaustion. The last of Langley's coins under Henry V (like Bowet's at York) present something of a puzzle. In style of bust and general aspect they belong to type 3, equivalent to the unmarked class G at London; but they carry the extra symbols of class D, cinquefoil and whole annulet, by the crown (as one would expect to find on Durham pence of type 2 if they existed), and an annulet within the pellets under *Civi*, anticipating the style of marking reverse dies of the Annulet coinage that followed. Despite their extra marks, and the fact that they read *henricus Rex Anglie* as in the Annulet coinage, these late Durham pence may provisionally be connected with the period of class G by virtue of showing the type 3 bust. At any rate, they could hardly be much later, since the Durham mint building was out on lease by Michaelmas 1423, and Langley's coinage was not resumed for several years.

The York series for Archbishop Bowet is very plentiful. Many of the coins, of all varieties except 2(E), are from locally made dies (occasionally muled with London-made dies). They often do not correspond closely to the London model, the cinquefoil sometimes looks more like a rosette, and there is considerable variation in their obverse readings. In 1415 the York mint-master, John Esyngwald, was accused of having had dies made in the city, but after reference to the archbishop, who was perhaps made aware of the precedent under Richard II, he remained in office and further local dies were undoubtedly used at York in the years that followed. The London-made dies at York generally follow the pattern of the London series, beginning with type 1 (C and D), with fuller readings, followed by type 2 with more abbreviation. The 2(E) penny has a presumably intentional pellet above the cinquefoil; but why this sole representative of the pellet-marked class E among the silver of Henry V above the halfpenny should come from the archbishop's mint is mysterious. In type 2 there are also York coins of class F, with a trefoil either above the cinquefoil or, as at London, instead of the annulet. The next York pence (type

3) have an annulet below *Civi*, as at Durham. Although normally described as of class G, these coins read *henricus Rex Anglie* (again as at Durham), and they also have marks by the crown, but at this mint the cinquefoil and trefoil of class F. Finally, there are similar coins, from local dies, with a cinquefoil and lis by the crown, a combination not found at other mints. Archbishop Bowet died in October 1423, but Esyngwald was authorised to coin during the vacancy and it seems possible that the plentiful cinquefoil/lis pence, or some of them, could belong to this period. However, if so, this would constitute a unique case in the post-1351 coinage of both royal and episcopal mints at York producing pence concurrently.

Halfpence of Henry V are abundant, indeed the commonest coins of the reign after the pence of York. The halfpenny is the only denomination of classes C to F with fieldmarks on which the cinquefoil (due to size) does not feature. Instead, it has two annulets by the crown (classes C and D) or an annulet and a trefoil, either way round (class F). On some coins, described as class D, one of the annulets (usually the right) is broken but the other whole. Class E may be represented by a very rare variety with whole annulets, and a pellet to left above the crown. Rare farthings, without marks, are attributable to this period by virtue of their loosely beaded circles; they have a pointed chin and a very thin neck.

Gold of Henry V is relatively common, although the half-nobles are all rare. The mint accounts show considerably more gold minted between 1413 and 1417 than in the later years of the reign. Except for class G, there is normally, as before, a quatrefoil above the sail; and the nobles continue to show a quatrefoil by the lion in the first quarter of the reverse, although on the halves an annulet is used instead. The cinquefoil is placed by the king's wrist on nobles, as on the altered dies of class B*, but on halves it was put above the shield where there was more space. The commonest nobles are those of class C, which have a broken annulet on the ship's side. Early class C dies may be distinguished from those of class B* by the *n*, from the new, unbroken punch, and a slightly smaller *S*. As with groats, the class C nobles show two forms of the letter *D*, narrow in Ca, broader in Cb. The rare nobles of class D are similar to those of class Cb, but have an unbroken annulet above the wrist as well as the cinquefoil below it, and a small trefoil between shield and prow. As on late groats of Henry V, reverse dies of class D (and later classes up to the earliest Annulet issue) have the letter *P* (Brooke's P9) with the bottom left corner of the upright sliced off, and this can assist in the identification of mules, such as D/C (with sliced/normal *P*). Class E nobles, still with cinquefoil, annulet and trefoil as in class D, are distinguished by having a pellet at the sword-point and in the *Ibat* quarter. The annulet by the wrist is whole, but that on the ship's side is still occasionally broken. On early class E dies the rigging is still 3-2, but one rope was soon dropped at each end, and the resultant 2-1 arrangement became standard for the rest of the Lancastrian era. Class F nobles lack the pellets of class E, but they have a trefoil in the *Ibat* quarter and sometimes another instead of the annulet on the ship's side. True class F nobles are extremely rare, but E/F, F/G, G/F and F/Annulet mules also occur.

Henry V half-nobles have no mark by the sword-arm; the cinquefoil above the shield is invariable in classes C and F. There are no obverses attributable to class D or E, nor reverses of class F, but dies of these three classes are found as mules (F/D and F/E). The annulets on the ship's side and by the lion in the *Domine* quarter are broken in class C, but unbroken on the reverses of classes D and E (the latter matching the E nobles in having a pellet by the lion in the fourth quarter). There is no annulet on the ship's side in class F, but sometimes a trefoil between shield and prow. The ropes are usually 3-2 in class C, but follow the pattern of the nobles in adopting 2-1 from class F onwards.

Quarter-nobles of Henry V, until class F, have annulets on the cusps of the tressure. Unlike those of Henry IV (but in common with the pennies of Henry V) quarter-nobles of classes C to F drop *Di Gra*, allowing a longer form of the French title. Most have a broken annulet to the left of the shield and a cinquefoil to the right (class C), but a whole annulet is occasionally found (class D). There are no pellet-marked dies attributable to class E, but a trefoil to the left of the shield instead of an annulet indicates class F. Unusual readings in class F include *Frac* or *Fran* instead of *Franc*, and *Excultabitur* (by which a D/F mule may be recognized), meaning, whether intentionally or not, 'he shall be worshipped' rather than the usual 'exalted'.

Late in the reign of Henry V, after class F, there was a sudden change (class G). This involved the removal of extra marks in the field on London coins, the disappearance of the cinquefoil from the bust on groats and halves, and the introduction of new portraits on halfgroats, pence and halfpence. The letter *n* sliced at the top left is commonly found on coins of this class. Mules with class F and with the annulet-marked coinage that followed put the position of class G beyond doubt, and the scarcity of the unmarked coins points to an issue of short duration. The plain initial cross with hollow centre continues in use in class G, but the beading of the circles is now again neat and tight. Gold coins have a small cinquefoil, or star, after the first word of each inscription, followed by annulets between all the other words. With class G the customary quatrefoil above the sail on Henry V nobles disappears, although it is still found on the halves. The quarters retain the traditional lis above the shield, but there are no ornaments on the cusps of the tressure. As on London pence, *D(e)i Gra* is now resumed on quarter-nobles, to the exclusion of the French title. Noble dies of class G are found muled both ways with class F, and there are G/Annulet mules of all three denominations in gold.

Stops on the silver of class G are saltires, as before. Halfgroats and London pence have a fine new bust with hollowed neck and armpits, a contrast with that on their less tidy predecessors. Halfgroat reverses still have the quatrefoil after *Posui*, as in preceding classes. Of five halfgroat obverse dies noted by Brooke, four have an *I* with elaborate serifs, and this distinguishes them from the earliest obverse dies of the Annulet group, on which the *I* is plain, with concave sides and serifs. The distinction is, however, simpler in the case of pence, since the obverse readings differ, with *Di Gra* included in class G. Brooke also described halfpenny dies of class G, but only in the form of G/Annulet or Annulet/G mules. Here the obverses are differentiated by the bust which on Annulet halfpence has the bottom outlined with a line of drapery. No new bust was introduced on groats until well into the Annulet series, but Potter identified a few late Henry V groats with neatly beaded circles and the characteristic sliced *n* of this period, but without a cinquefoil on the bust, and these may reasonably be associated with class G.

As noted above, the new class G penny bust is also found on coins of Durham and York which do, however, differ from class G at London in a number of respects – their obverse inscription, the marks by the crown and the annulet in the *Civi* quarter. It may be that these episcopal dies were not all made simultaneously with the London class G dies, but it is doubtful whether the new type 3 bust would have been used for Durham and York before London, in spite of the pre-G markings that occur at those two mints.

The only coins of the Annulet group which can be attributed with reasonable confidence to Henry V (class H) are a few rare early varieties that occur of London but not of Calais. Some further varieties, known of both mints, must also have been struck in Henry V's reign, between the opening of Calais in July and the king's death at the end of August, but there is no means of judging accurately where a numismatic division between the reigns should fall. Candidates for class H may be sought for silver among the early Annulet varieties with the same initial cross as in class G (and earlier). Pre-Calais Annulet groats of group Ia may be distinguished by the letter *n*, with the arch high and pointed, and either sliced at top left as in class G or with a small tang added at the fractured corner (this *n* was soon replaced by punches more rounded at the top). Early halfgroats of Ia, with eleven arcs to the tressure and reading *Angl & Fr*, sometimes have *Me*, rather than *M*, at the end of the reverse inscription, as in class G, and again this variety is confined to London. Some at least of the Ia pence and halfpence, with the early initial cross, must also belong to the class H period. In the case of gold the subdivision of the Annulet coinage is based on different features, since the initial cross is replaced by a lis. The earliest nobles and half-nobles, of London only, have the same arrangement (A) of the ornaments on the ship's side as in class G (lion, lis, lis, lion, lis), and these evidently belong to the phase before dies were sent to Calais in May 1422. The same is true of quarter-nobles with a small lis as mintmark. Thereafter, however, as with the silver, there is no means of telling which coins of the immediately succeeding varieties were struck after the revival of Calais but before the end of August 1422.

Woodhead's view that Goldbeter's coinage under the indenture of February 1422 began with the Annulet type would mean that class G belonged to the winter of 1421/2, while Brooke's association of the change of mastership with the dropping of symbols in the field after class F would place class G between the Goldbeter indenture and the start of the Annulet coinage shortly afterwards. The prominent marking of the Annulet coins might be taken as representing a new system of control with the advent of a new master. It might, on the other hand, have been introduced when the reopening of Calais mint was imminent, related to a decision to differentiate between London and Calais obverse dies for silver as well as gold, annulets by the bust at Calais being a counterpart to the traditional pennant on Calais nobles. Indeed, retention of the unusual class G stopping formula on reverse dies for gold of the Annulet coinage could be taken to imply continuity under the same regime, since the contrast between classes F and G is at least as marked as that between class G and the Annulet series. The choice between these two interpretations does not however involve a difference of more than a few months, or perhaps even weeks.

Classification and Chronology, 1422 – 1464

Being decorated with a succession of different marks or symbols, coins of the first reign of Henry VI and of the heavy coinage of Edward IV lend themselves more readily to systematic arrangement than those of Henry IV or Henry V. Whitton's admirable monograph on Henry VI records detailed readings and die-varieties for all denominations and the text (apart from a number of chronological questions caused by the theory of quarterly privy marks) provides a convincing analysis of the material and commentary on its structure. A subsequent survey of the groats by Potter is, however, valuable for drawing a clearer distinction between the norm and aberrations from it, and for demonstrating that the number of observed varieties in different classes is not on its own a valid basis for estimating duration of issue, without having regard to relative numbers of surviving specimens. In *English Coins* Brooke had defined eleven broad classes or groups of Henry VI's coinage and these, with his numeration, were adopted by Whitton, together with extensive subdivision. Although the familiar names of these issues have a certain charm, for some purposes they are cumbersome and the numerals more convenient, especially for example when dealing with mules.

Henry IV – Edward IV

Suggested Group Dates, 1422-1464

Group and Label		Suggested Dates
I	Annulet	1422 – late 1420s
II	Rosette-Mascle	⎫ End of 1420s and
III	Pinecone-Mascle	⎬ first half of 1430s
IV	Leaf-Mascle	⎭
V	Leaf-Trefoil	later 1430s
VI	Trefoil	⎫ early
VII	Trefoil-Pellet	⎭ 1440s
VIII	Leaf-Pellet	mid 1440s – c. 1455
IX	Unmarked	⎫ c. 1455
X	Cross-Pellet	⎭ - 1460
XI, I	Lis-Pellet	1461 (Henry and Edward)
II-IV	Edward IV, mm. rose	1462-4

While convenient for reference, the Brooke-Whitton groups for Henry VI do not represent divisions of the coinage of anything like equivalent importance. Although most of them may be regarded as substantive issues, the frequency of muling, sometimes between non-adjacent groups involving one die that was quite old (e.g. Leaf-Trefoil/ Annulet or Pinecone/Trefoil), shows that such 'issues' were not self-contained tranches of coinage in the sense that old dies were withdrawn when those with new marks were supplied. Once issued, dies might be used as long as they were serviceable, regardless of any privy-marks then in current use. At the episcopal mints old dies were not regularly replaced, or were sometimes supplemented by local dies perpetuating an earlier model. In the pages that follow the eleven groups of Henry VI and the first four types of Edward IV (as defined by Blunt and Whitton) are discussed in five sections, corresponding to the principal phases of the coinage, each characterised by a different mark: Annulet, Mascle, Trefoil, Pellet and Rose. First comes the Annulet group I, covering most of the 1420s. Annulet silver, like that of several later groups, is conveniently subdivided by Whitton according to variations in the form of initial cross, but the use of a lis mintmark instead of a cross on the gold of Henry VI precludes a parallel classification of that kind between silver and gold throughout the reign. Although within this and later groups the different crosses can be placed in a likely progression, there seems to have been some flexibility in their use, often probably with an overlap between two forms and with variation between different denominations. There are sometimes also clear differences in the pattern of die supply to London and Calais, dies being ordered when needed, so that significant varieties or sub-groups (e.g. Id, the 'Annulet-Trefoil' type at Calais) may be represented at only one of the mints.

The Mascled phase, most of which belongs to the first half of the 1430s while silver coinage was still concentrated at Calais, consists of three groups in which mascles were accompanied successively by rosettes (II), pinecones (III) and large leaves (IV). In the Trefoiled phase, during which Calais makes its final appearance, there are also leaves, but now much smaller. Before the trefoils disappeared, pellets were added so that group VII, combining pellets and trefoils, but consisting only of London groats, is transitional between the Trefoiled and Pelleted phases. The last phase of Henry's heavy coinage has pellets in combination successively with leaves (VIII), saltires (X) and lis (XI). Type IX, however, is anomalous, represented only by one obverse die each for groats and halfgroats to which for some reason no distinguishing marks were added. Of the last of the Pelleted groups there are of Henry VI only some rare groats, but the Lis-Pellet type was continued with a range of denominations under Edward IV. However, the lis was essentially a Lancastrian symbol, introduced at the end of Henry V's reign and alluding to the conquest of France – on the *salut d'or* and the billon *blanc* struck at Henry VI's French mints the type shows a fleur-de-lis and a lion together, representing the now twin realms of France and England. With the arrival of Edward IV in 1461, it was not therefore long before the lis was displaced by a Yorkist rose.

Although the first reign of Henry VI spanned a period of nearly forty years there are few fixed points available within it for constructing a numismatic chronology. The royal mint at York was in operation during the twelve months from August 1423. Calais had reopened at the end of July 1422 and remained active for around twenty years, but its accounts in the 1430s are fragmentary and the date of its closure, c. 1440 or soon thereafter, is not precisely known. There were new appointments as archbishop of York in 1425 (Kemp) and 1452 (William Booth) and as bishop of Durham in 1438 (Neville) and 1457 (Laurence Booth); but their value for dating the coinage is limited since exercise of their minting rights was intermittent and many of the York coins are from local dies. Correlation between the observed volume of successive issues and the totals of bullion coined is as usual an important indicator, but for this reign it is complicated by the fact that the accounting periods are often long and irregular and those of London and Calais do not match. The difficulties thus caused confront us at the outset.

The Annulet coinage of group I was on a very large scale in gold at London and in silver at Calais. As noted in the previous section, early London Annulet coins of some denominations are identifiable as preceding the first issues of Calais, and are thus attributable to the spring of 1422 (Henry V, class H). The next varieties, represented at Calais but prior to those found also of York, may be dated to 1422/3, followed first by the York types and then by the post-York varieties of London and Calais. Thereafter the picture is less clear. The revival of the archbishop's mint at York in the Rosette-Mascle issue was related by Brooke to Kemp's appointment in 1425, but the pence in question come late in group II and cannot be dated so early; there must therefore have been an interval before Kemp received his first dies. Very little gold was struck at Calais during the years 1428/31, the last period for which there is a relevant account. Noting that the London mint accounts for 1425 to April 1427 record payment for dies for both gold and silver coinage at Calais, but that subsequent payments, in the accounts ending March 1430 and Michaelmas 1431, were for silver coinage dies only, Whitton believed that Rosette-Mascle coins must have been current by the spring of 1427, since the last known dies for Calais gold come at the beginning of group II. Woodhead has, however, pointed out that the Calais silver of successive issues in the two Reigate hoards and the London gold in the Fishpool hoard, when measured against the respective mint accounts, would imply a transition from Annulet to Rosette nearer to 1430 than 1427 although the London silver in Reigate II points to the earlier date. In the Fishpool hoard there were 55 Calais nobles of group I and three of group II, i.e. only some 5 per cent of the total were of the Rosette period. The Calais accounts record £102,000 of gold coinage between 1422 and 1431, of which the last period, May 1428 – August 1431, contributed £6,000, or 6 per cent. On these (admittedly small) figures, the group II Calais gold looks as if it might roughly equate with the amount coined in 1428–31, perhaps implying a starting date for group II a year or two before 1430.

Gold coinage at London fell away from 1433/4 onwards, to a few hundred pounds weight annually. The last London nobles that are not extremely rare are those of group III, and it therefore seems probable that the Mascled phase came to an end c. 1435. The decline of the Calais mint after group IV (the last in which Calais groats are not very rare) may then be seen to reflect the economic consequences of the Treaty of Arras between Philip of Burgundy and the French in 1435. This would allow the Trefoiled phase to occupy the late 1430s and early 1440s. The first Durham pence with the mark of Bishop Neville, appointed in 1438, are of group V, while the last groats of Calais, being of early group VI, would accord with closure of the mint in or soon after 1440. The commonest halfpence of the second half of the reign are probably those of the Leaf-Pellet issue, so that the separately accounted special minting of fractions in 1446-7 may have consisted largely, or solely, of group VIII. This extensive group also includes the first London-made dies sent to York since group III, perhaps occasioned by the appointment of a new archbishop in 1452. Group VIII may have continued into the middle 1450s since it is more plentiful than group X, the only other major group pre-1461. This would be consistent with the Durham evidence. The first coins of Laurence Booth who took the see in 1457 are of group X, from Neville dies altered by having the initial *B* punched over the saltire to the right of the bust. Since there are no group X coins of Neville himself, such dies were presumably made not long before his death, implying that group X must have been current by c. 1456.

The Lis-Pellet type had barely begun when Henry was deposed in March 1461, and its continuation under Edward IV (type I) may not have lasted even to the end of the year. Edward's two principal personal symbols, the sun and the rose, were incorporated in his new great seal in December 1461 and about the same time, we may suppose, the rose would have replaced the Lancastrian fleur-de-lis on the coinage. Of the three types of Edward's heavy coinage with mintmark rose type IV is the rarest and type III the commonest. Mint accounts for 1460-2 are missing, but on the assumption of reasonably consistent output in 1461-4, types II and III could each represent about a year's output, in 1462 and 1463, the latter perhaps extending into 1464, with the rare type IV curtailed by the recoinage in the following September.

Henry VI, Annulet Group (I)

Huge quantities of gold were minted at London in the first two years of Henry VI, and of silver at Calais, with the result that London nobles and Calais groats of the Annulet series are each the commonest medieval coins of their kind. Conversely, London silver and Calais gold are quite scarce. In the later 1420s supplies of bullion to both mints declined, and the later Annulet varieties of all denominations are relatively rare. All five values in silver were struck at all three royal mints, but those of York's short period of activity in 1423/4 are all very rare – the farthing only recently discovered. Even rarer are the pence produced at Dublin in 1426, the only occasion between the 1330s and the 1540s when coins of the same weight and fineness as the English were struck in Ireland. Some of the York episcopal pence could constitute an extension of the late coinage of Henry V into the Annulet period, but the ecclesiastical mints do not appear to have been active in the later 1420s.

With rare exceptions silver coins of the Annulet group have an annulet within the groups of pellets in two quarters of the reverse. A late variety (Id) has an annulet in only one quarter, and on a few earlier Calais groat and halfgroat reverse dies the annulets are omitted altogether, seemingly by accident. This is the first occasion on which obverse dies for silver coinage at royal mints were systematically identified according to the mint for which they were destined. Thus Calais dies have annulets beside the bust and York dies fleurs-de-lis similarly, while those of London are unmarked. Occasionally a die went to the wrong mint – so we find a Calais penny without obverse annulets or 'London' groats with them. In the latter case the same reverse die is paired with more than one Calais obverse, showing that a London reverse must have been included by mistake in a batch for Calais.

On the groat to the halfpenny there is a sequence of initial crosses according to which the bulk of the Annulet silver may be divided into three main sub-groups. First (Ia) there is a brief continuation of the plain pierced cross as used in the later coinage of Henry V (Walters cross I). Next (Ib) is a shaped cross (Walters cross II) with a larger central hole; this cross comes in two forms, one with rounded concave angles, the other (described by Whitton as a 'wheel' cross) consisting of four wedges issuing from a large annulet. The third sub-group (Ic) has a plain cross with slightly indented ends. Finally, with the same plain cross as in Ic, there is a rare type, confined to Calais and known as Annulet-Trefoil (Id), which has a trefoil added to the left of the crown, a trefoil instead of an annulet after *Posui* on groats and halfgroats, and an annulet in the third quarter only. Groats and pence are known as true coins of Id, but halfgroats only as mules. Silver coinage at London was at a low ebb in the late 1420s and these Annulet-Trefoil coins presumably belong to a time when new dies were not needed there.

INITIAL CROSSES OF HENRY VI GROUP I

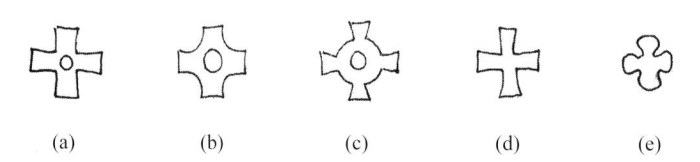

(a) Henry V-style pierced cross, Ia; (b) and (c) Shaped pierced crosses, Ib; (d) Plain cross, Id; (e) Cross pommy, farthings only.

Whitton worked out a sequence in some detail for the groats. Ia, with the old initial cross, is rare and includes the earliest London Annulet coins before minting at Calais began, as well as the issues of the last few weeks of Henry V's reign when both mints were operating. Ia groats read *Anglie* in full, and the breast cusp is fleured as in earlier classes. These two features continued for a while with the second cross, and this variety (Ib1) must still have been current in the summer of 1423 since it accounts for all the groats of York which received its dies in the July. Thereafter the breast fleur was dropped (Ib2), and in due course *Anglie* was reduced to *Angl* (Ib3). During Ib3 a new face punch was introduced, with high arched eyebrows that give it a rather startled look. The plain cross of Ic occurs on halfgroats to halfpence but curiously not on groats except on the reverse of the rare Annulet-Trefoil type.

Throughout group I the stops on silver are still saltires, as they had been for the past fifty years, but this was to be the last group before much greater variety was introduced. On obverses the saltires are used singly, but on reverses of groats (and often of halfgroats and pence) they are doubled, as under Henry V. The only exceptions are the annulet (or in Id, the trefoil) after *Posui*, and an annulet after *Eboraci* on the larger coins of York.

On groats and nobles Whitton noted the use of various conspicuous letter punches which can be useful for more detailed classification. Ia groats still have the sliced *P* in *Posui*, and this letter also occurs in *Per* on early (pre-York) nobles. An *R* with the top left corner sliced is first found on a few Calais groats of late Ib1 (post-York), and continues at Calais and London through Ib2 and into Ib3. In Ib3 there is an *e* with a nick in its back on the last groat dies with sliced *R* and on a few others. On nobles the sliced *R* appeared soon after the change to the last of three types of fleurs, again followed by the nicked *e*. There was then a phase without defective letters, before a new *A* with the top bar tapered at the left end was introduced on groats late in Ib3, continuing through Id and much of group II, and over a similar period on nobles.

DISTINCTIVE LETTERS IN GROUP I OF HENRY VI

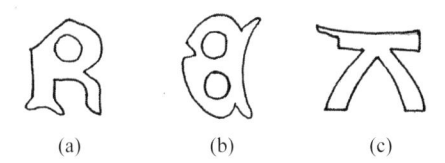

(a)   (b)   (c)

(a) Sliced *R*, Ib1-3; (b) Nicked *e*, Ib3; (c) Tapered *A*, Ib3-II.

The series of Annulet halfgroats begins (Ia) with coins that, except for the annulets in two reverse quarters, closely resemble those of class G. They have the same very neat bust, with the face tapering towards the chin, and a tressure of eleven arcs. They mostly read *Angl* (as in G) – *Anglie* is occasionally found in Ib as well as Ia and does not have the same significance for sequence as it does in the case of groats. Early halfgroats with the second cross initial mark, including those of York, still have an eleven arc tressure (Ib1). With Ib2 the tressure was reduced to nine (thicker) arcs and when this was combined with a more rounded face and fuller hair the appearance became more crowded. Reverses of Ia and Ib have no initial cross. The reading on the earliest variety of Ia ends *re Me*, as in class G, but *ore M* is otherwise normal in Ia and Ib. The plain cross of Ic, however, was accompanied by a smaller letter fount which allowed room both for an initial cross before *Posui* and for *Meum* in full. Ic halfgroats of London are considerably scarcer than those of Calais, belonging as they do to the late 1420s when less silver was reaching the mint. No true Id halfgroat has been noted, but dies for both sides are represented by mules with Ic and II.

The junior Annulet silver is unremarkable. The three crosses appear in sequence on pence and halfpence of London and Calais and, as with the larger coins, York's short appearance occurs in Ib. As with halfgroats, the pence begin with a continuation of the tapered head of class G, but this was later replaced by a U-shaped face, coupled with longer hair and a new crown with a taller central fleur. The penny is the lowest denomination represented in the Annulet-Trefoil type of Calais. The reading without *Di Gra* separates early London obverses of Ia from those of class G, but the division is less clear in the case of halfpence. Brooke's description of obverses with a 'Henry V' bust as of class G and of those with the bust outlined as of the Annulet group may seem logical, but since it results in the absence of any true halfpence of class G, it must be open to question. At least, it is further evidence of the intimate relationship between class G and early Ia, and so perhaps an argument in favour of their both being attributable to Goldbeter. The tiny farthings have no annulets between the pellets, but those of Calais (with one exception) and York are unmistakable by virtue of the annulets and lis by the bust. Their initial cross is pommy and this enables the unmarked London farthings of this issue to be identified. What seems to be the earliest Calais farthing, with a Henry V-style bust, is without annulets by the neck, but (unlike any other farthings of this period) has annulets as obverse stops instead.

The only known coins of the Dublin issue of 1426 are pennies, with Henry's title as Lord of Ireland, and a star beside the bust. Annulets at the end of each inscription and a plain initial cross link them with the period of Ic at London.

In style and much of their detail Annulet gold coins constitute a continuation of Henry V class G, and mules with class G obverses are found of all three denominations (there is also an F/Annulet noble). On nobles and halves there is an annulet by the king's wrist, where the cinquefoil had been before class G, and another on the reverse, in place of the fleur in the spandrel below *Ihc*. Except in the reverse legend, there is no annulet on the quarter-nobles, but the combination of the mintmark lis and the characteristic stopping places them securely within group I. They are further differentiated from class G in having trefoils on the cusps of the tressure. Reverses of Annulet gold have the same stops as on the gold of class G – a cinquefoil after the first word and then annulets – but the obverses differ in having a lis instead of a cinquefoil after *henric*, and trefoils instead of annulets thereafter. On nobles *Medium* regains its final *m*, but *Autem* is reduced to *Aut*, both adjustments that were to endure.

At first the London nobles and halves have the same arrangement (A) of ornaments on the ship's side as in class G: lion, lis, lis, lion, lis. Since there are no comparable coins of Calais, these rare IA London coins may be attributed to the period before the despatch of dies to Calais in May 1422, and so fall within the definition of class H of Henry V. Although the purpose of it is obscure, two altered noble dies show that a deliberate but very short-lived change in the Irish title was made at this time: one of the G/Annulet mules has the *y* of *hyb* altered to an *i*, and the earliest IA nobles also read *hib*; but the converse alteration then occurs, from *hib* to *hyb*, and the latter reading then became standard throughout group I. The G/Annulet mule quarter-noble has a small lis as reverse mintmark, and if all the rare annulet quarters with the small lis on both sides are correctly attributed to London they would also qualify as belonging to class H.

Ornaments on the ship were soon altered to three lis and two lions alternately (B) and this remained the normal pattern for the rest of the reign of Henry VI. The only other arrangement in the Annulet series (C) is a Calais variant of B with three lions and two lis. Three forms of fleur in the spandrels on IB nobles were identified by Brooke, and these are useful as an indicator of sequence:
1. Large fleur with the two side foils long and plain;
2. A small fleur consisting of three neat foils of equal size, with pointed tips; and
3. Large, with long, curled side foils.

No. 1 fleurs, which occur on all IA nobles and the earliest of IB, probably did not outlast 1422. Unless a second batch of dies for gold was sent to York, no. 2 fleurs seem to have been replaced by no. 3 during the summer of 1423, since both forms are found on the rare nobles attributed to York – these have a large lis above the sterncastle, matching the lis by the bust on silver coins of this mint. The first Calais nobles, with no. 1 fleurs, have the mint initial instead of the king's in the centre of the reverse, but those with nos. 2 and 3 have the usual *h*. Some London IB reverses with no. 2 fleurs have a control mark by the lion in the first quarter, as used intermittently in earlier reigns; normally this is a small trefoil, but once a large pellet.

Henry IV – Edward IV

FLEURS IN THE SPANDRELS OF HENRY VI ANNULET NOBLES

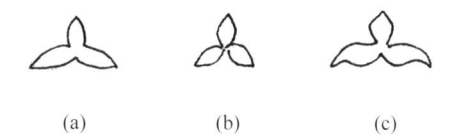

(a)   (b)   (c)

(a) Large fleur 1 with two plain side-foils; (b) Small fleur 2;
(c) Large fleur 3 with curled side-foils.

Half-nobles are much scarcer and less varied than the nobles, although they follow a similar general pattern. The London IA half-noble is extremely rare. Some of the IB London halves have a trefoil by the lion, as on nobles. Other variants include occasional omission of the annulet by the wrist or in the reverse spandrel. Calais reverses follow the nobles in having first *c*, then *h* in the central panel. Calais and York obverses differ from London's not only in the pennant and lis, but also in having a trefoil each side of &.

As in earlier reigns there is some difficulty in establishing which quarter-nobles were struck at Calais, and in this case there is the added complication of the third mint, at York. Conveniently for mint attribution, there are three main types of Annulet quarters. The most plentiful has a single lis above the shield; the second has three lis about the shield (one above and one each side); and the third has two lis above it. Walters assigned the three-lis quarters to York, as if the two lis beside the shield matched the two lis by the bust on the York silver. Whitton, however, noted that the three-lis quarters were not the rarest type, and suggested that they were of Calais, which struck more than twice as much gold as York in the Annulet period. The rarer two-lis type, all evidently from a single obverse die, would then belong to York. On this basis the two lis beside the shield on the three-lis type could be seen as reflecting the two annulets by the bust on Calais silver; and when a different formula was needed a year later for the York quarters, the two lis were both placed above the shield. This arrangement leaves the suitably common single-lis quarters to London, an attribution confirmed by the existence of rare varieties with a trefoil or pellet below the shield, analogous to the London Annulet nobles and half-nobles with those marks by a lion on the reverse. Most of the single-lis quarters have the same large lis initial mark on both sides as do the three-lis and two-lis types, but a few have a much smaller lis. Noting that there were varieties having an annulet instead of a cinquefoil, or a cinquefoil over an annulet, after *Exaltabitur* in both the large and the small lis types, Whitton assumed them to be parallel series from different mints. As the large lis coins were much the commoner he thought these should be attributed to London and the small lis coins perhaps to Calais. To the latter idea there is, however, a serious objection. Because the G/Annulet mule has a small lis mintmark on the reverse, and Calais was not operating either during class G of Henry V or at the beginning of the Annulet series, the mule is most likely to have been struck at London. If so, the two sizes of lis initial mark would have significance for sequence rather than mint, London beginning the Annulet series with the smaller lis but soon changing to the larger mark (which is from the same punch as used on the senior gold) at or before the time when dies were also needed for Calais. In support of this, all the small lis obverses read *Dei*, the normal form in class G, whereas with the exception of one die of the three-lis type all obverses with the larger lis mark read *Di*, as in post-Annulet groups.

Henry VI, Rosette, Pinecone and Leaf-Mascle Groups (II-IV)

After the Annulet issue, a new method was introduced for marking the dies of different series, based on the use of various symbols in the legends. This was the first occasion on which such a system had been used in England. Clearly, it represents a significant change of mint-practice from earlier English coinage of the groat era in that, whereas the periods between words had previously with few exceptions been marked, if at all, by simple stops (normally annulets or saltires), from this group onwards for the rest of the reign of Henry VI a wide variety of symbols was introduced into the inscriptions, and they seem often to have been placed in different positions as if to designate particular dies or batches of dies.

The one symbol common to each of the next three groups was the mascle, in company successively with rosettes (II), pinecones (III) and leaves (IV). Group II underwent an early trial period during which rosettes only were used as stops on gold, although on silver saltire stops were at first retained throughout on obverse dies, with the rosettes only on reverses (after *Posui* and the mint name). These early varieties are mostly without mascles altogether, although a few experimental dies for Calais groats and halfgroats were made with mascles added in the spandrels by the hair. Thereafter on gold one mascle instead of a rosette was usually introduced on each die, and in a few early cases a rosette-only die had a mascle overpunched on one of the rosettes. On silver also a mascle was added on each side, with saltires sometimes retained for the other obverse stops until eventually replaced by rosettes. The mascle on groats of group II in its earliest version is very small, followed by a medium and then a larger form.

In group III pinecones were substituted for rosettes, with the system otherwise virtually unchanged. Whitton identified nine or ten different punches for the cones, differing in shape, stalk, cross-hatching or tilt. The cones always have rounded upper ends and this provides a useful distinction between them and the leaves found in the next group. In group IV, unlike the Leaf-Trefoil series (group V), the leaf is delicately shaped, like a rose-leaf, with a pointed tip, and pronounced midrib and stalk. Being larger than the rosettes and cones, the leaf could not easily be accommodated between the words and was often therefore placed across a beaded circle. When unworn the leaf sometimes has a transparent appearance, blending unobtrusively into the design. On nobles and halves it was set low in the waves and on silver below the bust on groats and halfgroats or on the breast of the smaller coins.

SYMBOLS IN HENRY VI GROUPS II – V

(a) (b) (c) (d) (e)

(a) Rosette, group II; (b) Pinecone (several slight variants), group III; (c) Large leaf, group IV; (d) Small leaf, group V (and later); (e) Mascle, groups II-IV.

The mascle phase of the coinage covers a period during which the Calais mint ceased to produce gold coin altogether after the earliest stages of group II, and London's output continued the decline that had begun in the later part of group I. In silver the supremacy of Calais reached its peak in group II; the differential then narrowed in group III although it

Henry IV – Edward IV

did not disappear until after group IV. The halfgroat played a reducing role, with London concentrating chiefly on groats and halfpence, while York met most of the need for pence after the revival of the ecclesiastical mints. While oddities of spelling continue to occur, the workmanship of group II remains good, although it begins to deteriorate in group III, perhaps reflecting the frequent changes of officials in the mints in the 1430s, a period of military reverses in France and unsettled government at home.

All London nobles of these three groups are rare, III the least so. Half-nobles are, as usual, the rarest of the gold, group III represented only by a II/III mule and group IV unknown to Whitton, but subsequently found in the Fishpool and Reigate II hoards. Quarter-nobles are also of considerable and increasing rarity as supplies of bullion dwindled in the 1430s. The last dies for gold to reach Calais were probably delivered at the start of group II, since the only dies for both sides of the half-noble and for obverses of nobles are without mascles, and one of the noble reverses has the mascle after *Per* over a rosette. The only quarter-noble without mascles has rosettes each side of the shield, which Whitton not unreasonably saw as analogous to the lis by the shield on the presumed Calais quarters of group I. However, a die-link between the unmascled reverse of this coin and another quarter, without rosettes by the shield, casts doubt on the Calais attribution. That some quarters without rosettes by the shield were struck at London is evident from the existence of a II/III mule, because there is no Calais gold of group III. The only natural way in which a Calais attribution for the coin with rosettes by the shield could be sustained, would be to make the (not impossible) assumption that Calais dies were returned to London when its gold coinage ceased.

With the advent of group II conventional forms of stopping disappeared completely from the dies for gold. At first the stops are rosettes only, later rosettes and mascles. London dies of group II without mascles are known for both sides of the noble but for the obverse only of the half-noble. As noted for Calais, some originally unmascled London dies were also amended by punching a mascle over a rosette. On the earliest mascled obverse dies of group II the mascle is placed after *Gra*, but it was soon moved to after *Rex*, where it remained in groups III and IV. Mascles usually occur on group II reverses after *Per* on nobles, before *In* and *Me*, or *Tuo*, on halves, and after *In* on quarters. In groups III and IV the pattern is similar, but with occasional variation. Since pinecones are larger than rosettes, saltires reappear by & in group III, for reasons of space; and in group IV there are saltires at the other periods also, because of the size of the leaf punch. In group II alone nobles and halves have a lis by the king's wrist. The practice of placing a small mark by a lion on reverse dies, which had been normal up to class F of Henry V, absent in class G, and only spasmodic in group I, was restored to regularity in group II and survived into group III, but the lis (as it was at this period) is lacking from a few late pinecone dies and was never thereafter revived. There is little variation in obverse readings throughout the mascle phase, except in the Irish title on nobles. This was normally *hyb* in group II, but *hib* on II/III mules and at the start and finish of group III, with even *hiyb* on several dies in the middle of that group. Early in group II *Transiens* gives way to *Tranciens*, which then frequently loses a letter (*A, I* or the second *n*) in group III.

For silver, the most useful broad indicator of sequence within the groups is, as in the Annulet series, the form of the obverse initial cross. On the reverse of groats and halfgroats there is always a cross before *Posui*, of the plain form, and, although generally lacking on the lower denominations, the same cross is also found, exceptionally, on the reverse of a few Calais pence of group III. In group II the earliest coins (IIa) have the same obverse cross as on the latest varieties of group I: the shaped pierced cross on groats, and a plain cross on all the others. These were followed by two forms of floriate cross: the first with the ends splayed and trifurcate, in the form described heraldically as a cross patonce (group IIb);

the other, a more conventional cross fleury with lis-shaped ends (group IIc). The same two forms are also found in group III, suggesting that they may to some extent have been in use together. But in both groups the cross patonce tends to appear on earlier dies than the cross fleury. The cross fleury occurs extensively on the smaller silver of group II but is rare on Calais groats and unknown on those of London. In group III the cross patonce made its last appearance and the cross fleury then became the standard form, continuing (except in group IV) to be so until the end of the reign. That the form of cross was still used as a deliberate distinguishing feature is suggested by the occurrence of two different ones on groats of group IV: first a voided cross, which when worn may look like a broad, plain cross (group IVa); and then a normal plain cross (group IVb) – its only occurrence on the obverse of groats of this reign. After group IIa the lesser denominations follow the arrangement of the groats except that in group III pence with a cross patonce are lacking, and in the case of halfgroats and halfpence of group IV the voided cross (which is rather large) does not occur.

INITIAL CROSSES ON GROUPS II – IV OF HENRY VI

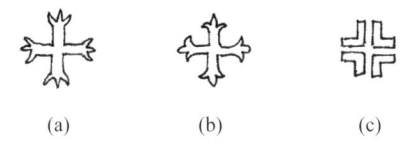

(a) (b) (c)

(a) Cross patonce, groups II-III; (b) Cross fleury, groups II-III (and later);
(c) Voided cross, group IVa.

As to the symbols, the normal arrangement on groat and halfgroat reverses of groups II-IV is a mascle in the middle of the inner reverse legend (before *Lon* or *la*) and the rosette, cone or leaf at the end (after *don* or *sie*). The leaf on group IV groats was often placed on the circle below *Meum*. The practice of putting the current mark after *Posui*, begun with the annulet or trefoil of group I, was retained with the rosette and pinecone in groups II and III, but discontinued with the leaf of group IV except on the odd early die. As on gold, most groats and halves of these groups have an obverse mascle after *Rex*, but early dies of group II either have no mascle, or one after *Gra*, or even on a rare variety of Calais groat, after *henric*. On pre-mascle group II obverse dies the stops are at first saltires, then rosettes, or mixed. In addition to the appropriate symbols, saltires continued to feature on reverse dies throughout these groups, but for much of group II they are absent on obverses, returning (as on gold) in group III only beside the &, before resuming regular appearance in group IV.

The Reigate II numbers (with mules included under the later group) give a clear idea of the continued dominance of Calais over London for silver output in the mascle period. Indeed, in group II the Calais advantage, at nearly 20:1, was double what it had been in group I. In group III it fell to around 6:1. The scarce group IV was to be the last in which Calais retained its superiority.

GROATS AND HALFGROATS OF GROUPS II – IV IN THE REIGATE II HOARD

| | GROATS ||| HALFGROATS |||
	II	III	IV	II	III	IV
CALAIS	812	566	31	120	58	3
LONDON	43	93	2	5	13	1

Henry IV – Edward IV

Calais groats are by far the commonest coins of group II, and there are many minor varieties of reading. At this mint there is a clear difference between obverses of group I and early group II, the transition being marked by removal of the annulets beside the bust; at the same time a new & was introduced, without a central bar, and the barred & thus enables London mules to be identified. At Calais Ib/II mules are relatively common, but the only groat mule between the Annulet-Trefoil and Rosette types has the later obverse. The series of true group II Calais groats begins with varieties on which neither rosette nor mascle has yet been introduced into the obverse inscription, and the stops are still saltires. Reverses paired with these early obverses are often without a mascle. The earliest mascled variety of obverse is probably that with two very small mascles inserted in the spandrels beside the bust (IIa2). For the rest of the group the obverse mascle is in the inscription, moving forwards until it settled in the space after *Rex*. On groats the initial cross fleury can only have been introduced near the end of group II, since those of IIc are rare of Calais and absent at London. All the London groats from group II reverses but unmarked (i.e. pre-mascle) obverses have the barred & of group I and seem therefore technically to be Ib/II mules, even though they are the commonest London variety of group II groat and accounted for more than half the London rosette groats in the Reigate II hoard. There are no comparable London groats with the unbarred & (IIa1), and the absence of other varieties found at Calais at this period (Id and IIa2) points to a period when the existing stock of Ib obverse dies remained adequate for London's reduced output. True group II groats of London are all quite scarce.

Groats of groups III and IV are of much less variety than those of group II, each group again being subdivided according to the obverse initial cross. The Calais pinecone groat with cross fleury (IIIb) is rare, and there is no IVb (plain cross) groat of London. Calais groats of group III are less plentiful than those of groups I and II, but still very common, while group IV is the last in which they are not actually rare. London's groat production improved both absolutely and relatively in group III, but only a single pair of London dies seems to have been made for Leaf-Mascle groats. The one group IV London reverse appears to read *Don/don* or *non/don*, because *don* was originally put in the third segment and then an *L* punched over the *D* to correct it. Perhaps this die was discarded on account of the error, since true group IV London groats are very rare, but there are also mules with reverses of III or V (the latter rare but not especially so).

Halfgroats of these three mascled groups broadly follow the pattern of the groats, although they are much less abundant. Occasional longer forms of the French title are found (*Franc* or *Fran*) or shorter forms of the English (*Ang, Anl*), but variant inscriptions are much fewer than on the groats. In group II the earliest coins have a plain initial cross (IIa), as on the later halves of group I. On pre-mascle Calais dies the mint is abbreviated to *Calis*, as in group I, but the full name is found once the mascle was added before *la*. All London halfgroats of group II are of some rarity. In group II the cross fleury occurs more often on halfgroats than on groats, and in group III also, unlike the groats, the equivalent halves usually have the initial cross fleury (IIIb), the cross patonce of IIIa not being found at all at Calais. The voided cross does not feature on halfgroats of group IV, in which few dies were made for this denomination. Calais halves of group IV are very rare, and no true Leaf-Mascle halfgroat is known of London, although both obverse and reverse are found in combination with dies of later groups.

All London pence of these groups are quite rare, but except for group IV those of Calais are reasonably common. York and Durham reappear in groups II and III. As on the larger silver, the obverse mascle is usually placed after *Rex* (except on London pence of group IV) and the rosette or pinecone before it. On reverses the appropriate symbol is placed after the mint name of London or Calais, as on the larger silver. From the two royal mints there are pence of IIa without rosette or mascle on the obverse. Whitton described the London coins of this kind as Annulet/Rosette mules, but since true IIa pence certainly exist of Calais (in addition to Ic/II and Id/II mules) it is not obvious why their London equivalents should not be classified in the same way. Except for the plain cross in IIa and the absence of any cross patonce dies in group III (at any mint), the pence of these groups reproduce the pattern of obverse initial crosses on the groats. A few early group II reverse dies for Calais and London pence have no mascle in the inscription; as with the halfgroats, on such coins of Calais the mint name is still *Calis*, as in group I, but this was extended to *Calisie* when a mascle was added. One of the letters of *henricus* is sometimes omitted on Calais dies of groups II and III. Group III pence of London and Calais usually retain the full reading *Anglie;* but others and all of group IV have *Angl*, which is the only form on the group III pence of York and Durham.

Langley's last coins at Durham are of groups IIa and IIIb, the mint revived after an interval from its closure in 1422/3. It is not mentioned in the receiver's account for 1428/9, and may therefore not have been reopened until c. 1430. The IIa pence, with mascles after *Rex* and *Duno/lmi*, have no rosette, but a star to the left of the crown; those of IIIb, which may have provided the profit recorded in 1434/5, have no marks in the field. A curious parallel between the dies for Durham and York in group II is to be noted in the reverse readings, *Duno/lmi* sometimes having *O* punched over another letter (*L*?), giving the appearance of a *D*, while the York signature often reads *Ebd/raci* (although without evident overpunching).

The York coins of Archbishop Kemp (1425-52), of groups IIc and IIIb, are much the most plentiful pence of any mint in the mascle period. Many are from local dies. The initial cross fleury in group II may indicate that coinage at York was not resumed until slightly later than at Durham (with the plain cross only). Group II York pence, which have the traditional quatrefoil in the centre of the reverse (containing a large pellet), go through three phases: first (A) with crosses by the hair; next (B), and least commonly, with saltires by the hair; and finally (C) with stars by the crown. A variant of II(C) has a star instead of a rosette before *Rex*. The rare early group III pence of York are similar to those of II(C), with stars by the crown (A). They were followed (B) by varieties with a star or rosette on the breast but without fieldmarks or a quatrefoil on the reverse. The lack of quatrefoil is curious, in that this normally indicates products of the king's mint at York; but on earlier occasions (in 1353 and 1422) when unquatrefoiled pence were struck, they were accompanied by other denominations appropriate to a royal mint, including groats and halfgroats, which are absent in this case. Since there is no record of a rift between the crown and archbishop in the 1430s, which might have led to the suspension of his temporalities, the omission of the quatrefoil at this period was presumably, if not accidental, at least without its usual significance. The absence of any York pence after group III until group VIII does not necessarily mean that the mint was inactive for the remainder of Kemp's episcopacy, but could be explained by the abundance of coins of group III from local dies, with repeated copying of earlier models as appears to have happened under Richard II.

Halfpence of groups II and III are plentiful, in particular those of London which at this period tended to leave the production of pence largely to York and to concentrate on the halves instead. As a result, the halfpenny is the only silver denomination of groups II-IV of which London coins are common enough to outnumber those of Calais by a considerable margin. There are, however, many varieties at both these mints, mostly as a result of the different positioning, or omission, of rosettes, cones and mascles. At Calais Ic/II mules are self-evident, but Whitton's classification of comparable London halfpence without a mascle on the obverse is based (somewhat arbitrarily) upon the presence (Ic) or absence (IIa) of a contraction mark after *Angl*. Most coins read *henric Rex Angl*, but *henricus* is also found in group III, *henricu* once at London in group IV, or at Calais *henic* in IIa and IIb. Since the only London halfpenny with the initial cross patonce attributed to group II by Whitton (with two mascles as stops) reads *henricus*, Withers has suggested that it is more likely to belong to group III. The usual spelling in group II is *Calis*, but *Calisie* first appeared on halfpence in IIa and became the norm in group III, invariable thereafter. A similar sequence of initial crosses appears on halfpence to that on halfgroats, the rare halfpence of group IV thus all having a plain cross. In view of this some very rare group III London halfpence with a plain cross are here provisionally labelled IIIc.

Farthings of these groups are all very rare. Although not always visible, the appropriate symbols occur in the legends in groups II and III. No Calais farthing later than group III is recorded, but group IV is represented by a London coin with a leaf on the breast.

MULES INVOLVING GROUPS I – IV OF HENRY VI, LONDON (L) AND CALAIS (C)

	NOBLE	HALF-NOBLE	QUARTER NOBLE	GROAT	HALF-GROAT	PENNY	HALF-PENNY
I/II			L	L,C	L,C	C	L,C
I/III							C
II/I	C			C			C
II/III	L	L	L	L,C	L,C	L,C	L,C
II/IV							L
III/I				C	C		C
III/II			L	L,C	L	L,C	C
III/IV				C			C
III/V				C			
IV/III				L		L	C
IV/V				L	C	L	
IV/VI	L						
IV/VIII					L		
V/I		L					
V/III				L,C			
V/IV				C	L		C
VI/IV				C			

Whitton knew of no mules in gold between the Annulet and Rosette issues, but the Reigate II hoard contained a I/II quarter and the Fishpool hoard a Calais II/I noble. In groups II-IV also there is much less muling in gold than in silver. II/III mules occur of all three denominations, but they are all extremely rare, as is the only III/II mule, a quarter-noble. Die-interchanges between groups are considerably more numerous in silver, particularly at Calais. Except for a Calais II/III halfgroat, the four main denominations are found as I/II and II/III mules of both mints (assuming that Whitton is correct in his identification of Ic/II pence of London), the groats in each case being relatively common. Mules with earlier reverses are as usual much less frequent. The III/II combination exists in three silver denominations at each mint, but all are rare. More noteworthy is the survival of annulet dies, especially reverses, into the pinecone period at Calais, since II/I are so much rarer than III/I mules. The I/III mule is only found as a halfpenny, but III/I mules occur as groats, halfgroats and halfpence, the groats being not particularly rare. Pinecone/Leaf Mascle mules in the form of III/IV Calais groats are also reasonably plentiful, but are unknown at London, while the extremely rare converse mules (IV/III) are unknown of Calais except for halfpence. None of the mules involving group III or IV in combination with Trefoil dies (V-VI) are common, but the only two such interchanges at Calais, the III/V and V/III groats, are among the least rare of them.

Henry VI, Trefoiled Groups (V-VII)

Brooke and Whitton used the labels 'Leaf-Trefoil' (V), 'Trefoil' (VI) and 'Trefoil-Pellet' (VII) for three related groups in which trefoils feature prominently (but not invariably). These terms are, however, somewhat confusing, since silver coins in all three groups have a leaf on the breast, while some 'Leaf-Trefoil' coins have no trefoil. Obverses of group VI, in which Calais participated for the last time, are clearly defined, by trefoils each side of the neck on silver and by a trefoil in the design on gold. Leaves and trefoils occur extensively in the legends on coins of group V (hence 'Leaf-Trefoil'), but only trefoils and saltires in groups VI and VII. Only group V is represented by coins of all denominations; and group VII consists of groats alone. Gold of this period is again extremely rare. The only plentiful coins are the groats and halfpence of London. Calais groats are not particularly rare, but the last English coins from the French mint are otherwise extremely rare, no more than the odd specimen or two being known of the halfgroat, penny and halfpenny of group VI.

Whitton's division of the obverses of London groats of group V into Va and Vb and of group VI into VIa, VIb and VIc represents the sequence of main varieties, although other subdivisions might have been made according to which features were given priority. Their defining characteristics are set out in the table; all except Vb have a small leaf on the breast cusp instead of a fleur.

CHARACTERISTICS OF HENRY VI GROAT OBVERSES, GROUPS V – VII

GROUP	FEATURES	OBVERSE STOPS	LONDON	CALAIS
V	Usually trefoil or leaves or both in inscription.			
Va	Leaf on breast cusp.	Saltires only, or with trefoil, or with leaves or with both.	X	X
Vb	Breast cusp plain.	Three leaves and a trefoil.	X	
VI	Leaf on breast; no leaf in inscription.			
VIa	Trefoils by neck.	Saltires plus trefoil(s) but no leaf.	X	X
VIb	Trefoils by neck; fleurs in spandrels.	Saltire stops only.	X	
VIc	Trefoils on shoulder cusps.	Trefoil after *Rex*, otherwise saltires.	X	
VII	Trefoils by neck, leaf on breast, pellets by crown.	Ditto	X	

Henry IV – Edward IV

London groats of group V are more plentiful than those of group VI, while of Calais, conversely, there is only one obverse of V, but several of VI. The obverse initial cross is fleury throughout on groat obverses of both mints. The single Calais die of Va, having the usual leaf on the breast, but no leaf or trefoil in the inscription, is found muled with the two preceding groups; it probably comes very early in group V since although a version of this obverse variety, with all saltire stops, also exists at London, it seems quickly to have been replaced by London obverses with a trefoil, or leaves, or both. The late London Va formation, with leaves after the first three words and then a trefoil after *Rex*, which accords with the group V noble, continues on groats into Vb where it is the only form.

In VIa and VIc, but not in VIb, there are trefoils in the obverse inscription on all varieties of groat. The earliest VIa London coins have trefoils after the first three words, but on most of the VIa groats of both mints there is only one or two, after *Di, Gra, Rex* or *Fran(c)*. All the Calais obverses of VIa have fleurs on the shoulder cusps, but they are only found at London at the beginning of the sub-group, indicating that the last groat dies for Calais were made very early in group VI (a conclusion supported by the epigraphical evidence). Apart from permutation of the stops there is little variety in the obverse inscriptions on groats of VIa, confined to the length of the French title and, rather curiously, *Ang* for *Angl* on all the Calais dies. In VIb, the dies of which are easily recognised by tiny fleurs in the spandrels, and VIc, in which the trefoils by the neck are not in the field but attached to the shoulder cusps, there is even less variety of reading. There are fleurs on the shoulder cusps on only a few early dies of VIb, reading *Franc*, but *Fran* without the shoulder fleurs is the normal style. Of VIc, with the shoulder trefoils, there is only one die reading *Fran*, with a trefoil after *Di*, but otherwise the inscription does not vary at all, having no stop or mark after *henric* or *Di*, a trefoil after *Rex* and the consistent mis-spelling *Frane*. In VII, with the trefoils again beside the neck but pellets now added by the crown, the reading is standardized once more, retaining the trefoil after *Rex*, and with the absence or presence of saltires after *henric* the only variation.

While the groat obverses of these three groups thus follow a relatively simple pattern, with a clear sequence of varieties, the situation with regard to their reverses is anything but straightforward. Varieties of reverse exist in bewildering confusion, without consistency as to the form of the initial cross, the inclusion of trefoils or leaves, or the occurrence of other stops. Although Whitton concluded that in some cases particular configurations of reverse featured at more than one stage in the process, he observed that certain letters provided a clue to the identification of earlier or later dies and chose the letters *A* and *m* to illustrate the point. Using obverses for reference, he showed that an old form of *A*, with an almost rectangular top-bar, which had been introduced before the end of group II, remained in use throughout group V and into the beginning of group VIa (including all the VIa dies of Calais). This letter (A1) was then replaced by another (A2) with the bar pointed at the bottom left end, and almost simultaneously the old *m*, with the central shank defective at the bottom right corner (M1), gave way to an undamaged M2. Reverse dies of the same period as group V obverses must therefore show A1 and M1, while any with A2 and M2 cannot be earlier than VIa. Technically this enables some mules between groups V and VI to be identified, but the general pool of dies in use at this time was so varied that such mules are not of comparable significance to the more overtly heterogeneous mules of earlier groups, and Whitton very reasonably did not therefore separate them in his lists.

LETTER FORMS IN HENRY VI GROUPS IV – VI

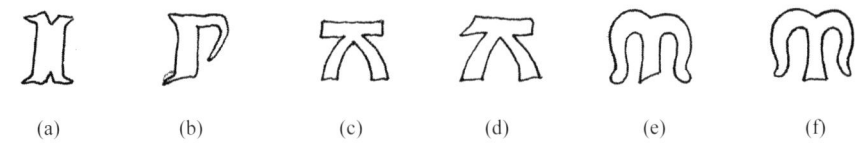

(a) (b) (c) (d) (e) (f)

(a) Indented *I*, groups IV-V; (b) Broken *n*, halfpence groups V-VI;
(c) Normal *A* (A1), groups II-VIa; (d) *A* with pointed bar (A2), group VIa and later;
(e) *M* with defective centre limb (M1), group III-VIa;
(f) Undamaged *M* (M2), group VIa and later.

Although the numbering is not intended to imply an absolute sequence, reverse dies of groups V-VII may be divided into three broad categories: (i) with a cross fleury before *Posui*, as on the obverses; (ii) with a plain cross; and (iii) without a cross at all. There is also great variation in the use of stops and symbols on reverse dies, and in marked contrast to obverses, presumably not least in part for purposes of differentiation. On London reverses the cross fleury is rare, but it is invariable at Calais; if this became a deliberate difference, it could explain why one reverse die with the cross fleury has had *Sivit(as)* (a variant London form in this group) altered to *Calis(ie)*. London cross fleury dies (type i), with or without a trefoil, have A1 and M1, and are attributable to group Va, although they also occur (as mules) with obverses of IV, VIa and VIb. Plain cross dies (type ii), without trefoil or leaf, or commonly with a leaf before *Lon* and a trefoil after *don* (and sometimes even with a latter-day mascle before *tas*), are the normal reverses in group V; but a few without an initial cross (type iii) are also found with obverses of both Va and Vb. Plain cross London reverses remain the norm in VIa, partly displaced in VIb and VIc by dies of type iii normally without a leaf or trefoil. In VIb, VIc and VII the use of single instead of double saltires (notably before *don*) becomes more frequent, along with finer workmanship, and an increasing proportion of such reverse dies have an extra pellet in two quarters (type iv). These type iv dies presumably belong to the Pellet-marked phase of the coinage (group VII onwards). Other (rare) reverses, with large pellet stops in *Adiutor.e* or after *Posui*, also seem to be foreshadowing the Pelleted phase.

DENOMINATIONS OF HENRY VI GROUPS V – VII

	V	VI	VII
Nobles	L	L	
Half-nobles	L		
Quarter-nobles	L		
Groats	L,C	L,C	L
Halfgroats	L,C(r)	L(r),C(o)	
Pence	L,C,D		
Halfpence	L,C	L	
Farthings	L		

L – London; C – Calais; D – Durham. (o) – obverse only; (r) reverse only.

Henry IV – Edward IV

Halfgroats of this period are much scarcer than the groats, with proportionately fewer varieties of reading and ornamentation. They are virtually confined to London coins of group V. No London obverse is known of VI, and no Calais obverse of V or reverse of VI. The London halves of Va, which are rare, have a leaf on the breast and after the first three words of the inscription, but no leaf on the reverse and no trefoil on either side. The initial cross on both sides is plain, as it had been on halfgroats of group IV. Va obverses are found either muled with IV, or with unmarked reverses. The less rare halves of Vb have a cross fleury on the obverse and often a trefoil after *Rex*. On reverses there is a trefoil after *don*, with or without a leaf before *Lon*. Vb halfgroat obverses either (i) have leaves in the inscription as in Va, but (like Vb groats) usually not on the breast, or (ii) the converse. Rare variants have tressures of eight arcs (Va) or seven (Vbii), instead of the usual nine. While no true Calais halfgroat of group V is known, the reverse die of a mule (with obverse of group IV), which lacks mascle, leaf or trefoil, corresponds to the London reverses of Va and is probably to be so classified. In group VI also Calais is only represented by a mule with group IV. This has trefoils by the neck (the only known halfgroat to do so), a leaf on the breast, and a trefoil after *Gra*. London's occurrence in group VI, however, depends upon a single reverse die with a trefoil after *Deum*, as found on rare groats of VIbi.

No penny of any mint is known of group VI. Those of group V (London, Calais and Durham), all of which are rare, have a leaf on the breast. Like the halfgroats, the London pence of group V begin (Va) with a plain obverse initial cross, as in IV. There is no trefoil in the legends, but a leaf before *Rex* and sometimes also after *Angli*. Whitton regarded such coins as V/IV mules, by virtue of an *I* with serrated serifs on the reverse, as used in group IV; but the Calais pence of Va (extremely rare, and unknown to Whitton) have trefoils in both legends coupled with the serrated *I*, which must therefore have continued in use into group V. The reading on these last recorded pence of Calais is unusual for this denomination in shortening the king's name so as to include the French title – *henric Rex Angl & F*, with a trefoil before *Rex*. Pence of Vb, with the obverse initial cross fleury, are known of London and Durham. Those of London have a trefoil after *Rex* and *don*, and usually a leaf before *Lon*, as on the larger silver; exceptionally, they also have a (plain) cross before *Civi*. The first Durham coins since group III show no trefoil, but a leaf after *Rex*. On the centre of the reverse cross are two interlinked rings, from the armorial bearings of Bishop Robert Neville, who received his temporalities in April 1438. These coins therefore probably contributed to the above average profit of the mint in 1438/9, at the start of the new episcopate.

London halfpence of group V are relatively plentiful, more so than group VI. Except for a rare variety of VI with cross fleury, they all have a plain initial cross. Mostly they have a leaf on the breast, but this is occasionally omitted in V. There is often a leaf (V only) or trefoil in the obverse (but not reverse) inscription, but some of each group have only saltires. Halfpence of group VI, with conspicuous trefoils by the neck, are unmistakable, but reverse dies of the two groups, and obverses of V on which a leaf or trefoil is absent or unclear, may be recognised by the punch for the letter *n* which has a broken tail. Like some groats of Va, halfpence of group V sometimes read *Sivi*. When found with a VI obverse this spelling probably indicates a VI/V mule, while a reverse with extra pellets under *tas* and *don* suggests VI/VIII. Of Calais there is an obverse of group V, with a trefoil before *Rex*; this is found on one V/IV mule, but with its correct reverse, having a trefoil after *Villa*, only on a piedfort. No Calais farthing is known of either group, and the London farthings are very rare.

The very low output of gold at this period is illustrated by the fact that, among only four obverse dies for nobles, there are three distinct types, thus presumably made at intervals. One of them relates to group V silver, the other two to group VI. The single type each of the half and quarter corresponds to the earliest of the nobles. There is also a IV/VI mule noble and, more remarkably, a V/I half-noble. All three denominations of group V are without extra marks, but have leaves after the first three words of their inscriptions, followed by a trefoil, as on some group V groats. The true group V half-noble was unknown before the Reigate II hoard. The noble obverse dies attributable to group VI have saltire stops, with either (VIa) a trefoil on the sword pommel (and a leaf by the shield), or (VIb) the trefoil below the shield. Up to VIa the ornaments of the ship's side on the noble had, since early group I, been of variety B, with three lis and two lions alternating; but the two VIb dies have variety C, with three lions and two lis, which had only occurred previously on a rare Calais variety of group I. The group V noble reverse is the last to read *Tranciens*, as in preceding groups (since II), *Transiens* returning in group VI, accompanied by the strange form *Auto* for *Autem*.

The Pelleted Groups of Henry VI (VIII-XI) and Edward IV (Type I)

The last phase of Henry VI's heavy silver coinage contains three main groups in which extra pellets by the crown and in two quarters of the reverse, as already introduced on the Trefoil-Pellet groats of the transitional group VII, are the common feature. The pellets are accompanied successively by a leaf (VIII), a saltire cross (X) and a lis (XI) on the breast or neck. Except on a few early coins of group X there are no marks by the bust on the silver of these groups. Type IX is used to refer to the obverses of very rare groats and halves that are without either pellets or breastmark. Henry's Lis-Pellet group, represented only by groats, had not been introduced long before he was deposed, but it was continued, with the full range of silver, under Edward IV. Gold of the Pelleted phase is of great rarity and virtually confined to nobles. London groats and halfpence are again plentiful, but except for pence of York the other denominations are all rare. Apart from the absence of Calais, the pattern was thus very similar to that of the preceding Trefoiled series. That there are more surviving coins of the Leaf-Pellet (VIII) than of the Cross-Pellet (X) or Lis-Pellet (XI) groups mainly reflects its longer duration.

COINS OF THE PELLETED PHASE OF HENRY VI (VII – XI) AND EDWARD IV (I)

	VII	VIII	IX	X	XI	I
Nobles		L		L		L
Quarter-nobles						r
Groats	L	L	L	L	L	L
Halfgroats		L	L	L		L
Pennies		LDY		LDY		L
Halfpennies		L		L		L
Farthings		L		L		L

L – LONDON (r – reverse only); D – DURHAM; Y – YORK

The small extra pellets in two opposite quarters of the reverse of silver coins (except Durham pence) are almost invariable. Those added inside the circle, above the three large pellets, are easily observed, but in a considerable number of cases, more frequent in the later stages of the period, they are placed on the line of the beaded circle where they are sometimes very difficult to see. Occasionally one of the extra pellets is on the circle and one inside it. Reverse dies without pellets added are very few and probably accidental. On reverses there is usually no initial cross or other mintmark. The obverse cross on late groats and pence of Henry VI is fleury throughout, but on a few coins of Edward it is plain. The plain cross also occurs on some halfgroats and halfpence, and on farthings. Stops are generally saltires, although they are increasingly few and on later dies, particularly reverses, they are often absent. One group VIII noble has annulet stops, but there is no parallel to this on silver. Various symbols used in earlier groups sometimes recur in the legends: trefoils early in group VIII, a leaf and, more extensively, the mullet and mascle in group X.

A characteristic of most groats of groups VIII-XI is the tendency of the bust to be placed as high up within the tressure as possible, with the crown fitted tightly under the top arcs and arched shoulders clear of the lower arcs. In summary, the classification of their obverses is as follows:

VIII   Leaf-Pellet. Leaf on breast or neck. Pellets by crown.
    VIIIa   Leaf on breast. *Angl*.
    VIIIb   Leaf on breast. *Angli*.
    VIIIc   Leaf on neck.
    VIIId   As VIIIc, but pellets by crown and by hair. One die only.
IX   Unmarked – nothing on breast, no pellets by crown. One die only.
X   Cross-Pellet. Saltire(s) by or on neck. Pellets by crown.
    Xa   Saltires beside neck; leaf on breast. One die only.
    Xb   Saltire on neck. No mascles in obv. inscription.
    Xc   Saltire on neck. Mascle(s) in obv. inscription.
XI   Lis-Pellet. Lis on neck. Pellets by crown. (Also Edward IV, type I)

The plentiful Leaf-Pellet groats have been divided into three main sub-groups, VIIIa, VIIIb (the scarcest) and VIIIc. The leaf on breast which had figured in the Trefoiled phase remained in place in VIIIa and VIIIb (sometimes at the expense of the fleur), and although it was moved onto the neck in VIIIc, it returned briefly to the breast in Xa. Since groats of group VII read *Angl*, and those of VIIIc *Angli*, Whitton separated VIIIa and VIIIb on the basis of these spellings. VIIIa groats often read *Francie* and some of VIIIc *Franci*, rather than the more usual *Franc*, but there is otherwise little material variation in the obverse readings throughout the group. Unexpected revivals in the obverse inscription are a trefoil after *Angli* on a few groats of VIIIb and a leaf after *Franc* once in VIIIc. A variant of VIIIc has two pairs of pellets, by the crown and by the hair, but although known to Whitton from a single coin he gave it the separate label VIIId in view of certain possibly related items – the obverses of some rare York pence of the same group, and reverse dies (for a group VIII halfpenny and a type IX groat) with an extra pellet in all four quarters.

The earliest and rarest of the main varieties of Cross-Pellet groats is constituted by the single die of Xa with a saltire each side of the neck, an arrangement only matched among the smaller silver on halfpence and some pence of York. With a leaf still on the breast, this Xa die represents the moment of transition from group VIII to group X. The substantive series of Cross-Pellet groats has no leaf, but a saltire placed upon the neck. Those without a mascle but usually with a mullet or two in the obverse inscription are described as Xb. The mullet is sometimes described as a star, but on clear specimens a very small central piercing is visible. Since some of the rare groats of group XI, with a lis instead of a saltire on the king's neck, have a mascle after *henric*, those of group X with (one, two or three) mascles are presumably the latest of the Cross-Pellet series (Xc).

1412–1464

LETTERS AND SYMBOLS IN LATE GROUPS OF HENRY VI

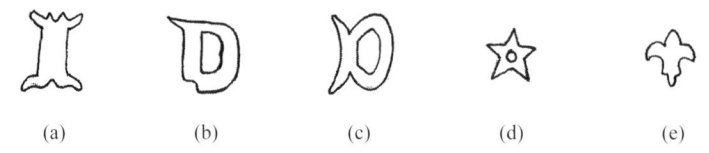

(a)   (b)   (c)   (d)   (e)

(a) Elaborate *I*, group VIII onwards; (b) Broken *D*, group VIII-X;
(c) Concave fronted *D*, group Xc-XI; (d) Mullet, group X; (e) Lis, group XI.

Groat reverse dies of the Pelleted groups are less varied than those of the Trefoiled phase, largely because during group VIII the saltire stops mostly disappear. Dies with no stops, rare before group VIII, soon became the norm. Some reverses of group Xb and Xc have a mullet after *Posui*, and these are occasionally muled with obverses of group VIII. With the exception of a possible IX/VIII mule groat with a plain initial cross on the reverse, marks before *Posui* do not reappear until the Lis-Pellet issue, when a plain cross or lis is sometimes found. In the course of group VIII, on the evidence of obverses, the punch for the letter *D* developed a break at the bottom left corner (Whitton's D2), and during Xc, it was replaced by a new one with concave front (D3). On this basis, Xb groats with D3 on the reverse should be Xb/c mules.

Halfgroats are rare of group VIII, and increasingly so thereafter. Whitton described the only Leaf-Pellet obverse with initial cross fleury as VIIIa, and the remainder, with a plain cross, as VIIIb. However, since the VIIIb/V mule (which omits the leaf on breast) has a plain cross and reads *Angl* as in group V, the VIIIa die, reading *Angli* as on some halfgroats of VIIIb and on those of IX and X, is not necessarily the earliest of the Leaf-Pellet group. The very rare Cross-Pellet halves, having mullets after *henric* and before *Meum*, correspond to the groats of Xb.

The late groats and halfgroats of Henry VI without breastmark or pellets by the crown, from one obverse die of each denomination, were separately classed by Brooke and Whitton as the 'Unmarked Issue', or type IX, thus placing it between the Leaf-Pellet and Cross-Pellet issues. That these unmarked dies do belong at about this point is indicated by the readings: the groat has *Angl* for *Angli*, a form otherwise only found on groats at this period in Xb; and the halfgroat has the copula after, instead of before, the French title, an oddity of composition also only found on groats of Xb. In the Reigate II hoard the latest groats were four of type IX and one of the very rare Xa, further indication that the unmarked die belongs close to the start of the Cross-Pellet issue. There is also a IX/X mule halfgroat. Reverses coupled with the unmarked groat obverse include the normal kind, with extra pellets in two quarters, the unique die with four extra pellets, and another unusual die, with a plain cross before *Posui* and saltires in the outer legend, which the lettering (D2) suggests might be attributed to group VIII, rather than to group XI in which reverse initial marks only otherwise occur. However, why two unmarked obverse dies should have been made at this time, and without matching unmarked reverses, is a mystery. Possibly they were the work of a locum engraver – the bust on the groat is set lower down, and the face broader, than on most groat dies of the period, while the crown on the IX halfgroat is not from the regular punch of groups VIII and X, and its initial cross fleury is not found in the Pelleted groups after VIIIa.

Obverses of pence of groups VIII and X, of London, Durham and York, have pellets by the crown, the intial cross fleury, and normally read *henric Rex Angli* (instead of *henricus Rex Angl* previously). Those of group VIII usually have a leaf on the breast (occasionally omitted at York), as sometimes do the York coins of group X, on which the saltires are beside the neck as on Xa groats and halfpence. At London and Durham there is a rare variety of VIII with a trefoil after *henric*, and the London pence of X have a mullet or mascle(s) or both in the obverse legend. Except for these special symbols, stops are saltires (but usually none on the reverse). An idiosyncracy found at all three mints in group VIII, and in group X at York, is the addition on some dies of a mid-word saltire, after the *n* of *henric* or more rarely of *Angli*. Another oddity is the use of an *I* with elaborate serifs on a number of coins of group VIII onwards, evidently a deliberate feature since on some London pence this *I* and a plain *I* were used together in *Anglii*. Notable rare variants are the York pence of group VIII with pellets beside the hair as well as by the crown, in the manner of the VIIId groat, and a London penny of group X with the full spelling *henricus*. The York coins of both groups are usually attributed to Archbishop William Booth, who received his temporalities in September 1452; although the currency of group VIII began before that date, the provision of new London-made dies may reasonably be associated with the new archbishop, after Kemp's apparently extended use of local dies based on group III. At Durham both groups show Neville's interlinked rings on the centre of the reverse cross, as in group V. However, although the coins of VIII, which must have generated the profit accounted in 1453/4, are undoubtedly attributable to Neville, who died in July 1457, those of X, which presumably provided the output recorded in the accounts for 1458/9 and 1459/60, have a saltire and *B* beside the bust, suggesting that Cross-Pellet dies had been made for Neville but before use their obverses were altered to show the initial of his successor Laurence Booth. The reverses of some of these coins of Booth, still with Neville's rings, show the groups of pellets joined by stalks, but the significance of these is unclear. Another puzzle is why a Neville obverse die of group VIII should apparently have survived into the reign of Edward IV then to be paired with three local dies with the mint name *Dunolin*.

Halfpence and farthings of group X are much rarer than those of group VIII. The halfpence of group VIII are abundant enough to be associated with the separately accounted issue of some one and a half million at reduced weight in 1446-8. Both groups read *Angli*, as on late halfpence of group VI. They also correspond to the contemporary larger silver in normally having pellets by the crown and, on most reverse dies, added in two quarters, or in one case (VIIIa) in all four. Obverses with the initial cross fleury (VIIIa and Xa) and with a plain cross (VIIIb and Xb) feature in both series, VIIIa and Xa including dies with a saltire after *n* of *henric* as on pence. The leaf on breast of group VIII is retained in Xa, as on groats and York pence, because saltires were first put beside the bust, but in Xb the leaf is replaced by a saltire on the neck. Some rare Xb halfpence have a mullet after *henric* as on larger silver. Farthings of VIII and X, both with a plain initial cross, are miniature versions of the halfpence of VIIIb and Xb; the variant *henrc* is found among both.

The only known gold coins of the Pelleted period under Henry VI are nobles (all of great rarity), although there is a quarter of Edward IV from a Lis-Pellet reverse die, raising the possibility that fractions might have been struck in negligible quantities during the 1450s also. There are two obverse varieties of the Leaf-Pellet noble, and one of the Cross-Pellet type. Whitton knew only of one of the former, the other two appearing at Fishpool. Most of the reverse dies seem to have a pellet by the central *h* on the reverse, which is sometimes supine or inverted. Whitton's variety of group VIII noble has a pellet each side of *h* in *h/enric*, which is followed by a trefoil as on some early VIII pence; there are an annulet, lis and leaf in a row by the bottom left of the shield, and a pellet at the inner end of the spar above the crown. The other variety of VIII has a pellet at each end of the spar and only a leaf to left of the shield; there is a gap between the king's waist and the gunwale, the outline of the shield is thin and the prow is indicated by two straight lines – all features which it shares with the group X noble, and which point to it being the later of the two types of group VIII. The last of Henry's nobles belong unmistakably to the Cross-Pellet issue, with saltires by the shield and above the sail, and mascles in both inscriptions.

Group XI must have been introduced very shortly before the Yorkist victory of March 1461, because the only known Lis-Pellet coins in Henry's name are groats, and they are very much rarer than the equivalent groats of Edward IV (type I). The use of a mark before *Posui*, absent on virtually all dies since VIb, was resumed, though not consistently, on Lis-Pellet groats in the form of a plain cross, a small lis or occasionally (under Edward IV) a saltire. Early Edwardian groats (Ia) still sometimes have a cross fleury, but this was often replaced by a plain cross, with the lis either (Ib) still on the king's neck, or on the breast cusp (Ic), some of these last omitting the pellets by the crown (Id). Two Ib dies have a mascle in the obverse inscription (after *Franc*). Lettering suggests that Ia and Ib may have been concurrent.

All the lesser silver of type I is of great rarity, the halfpenny perhaps the least so, although it is still the rarest type of this denomination in the heavy coinage of Edward IV. On halfgroats the lis is always on the breast cusp, and varieties exist with both cross fleury (Ia) and plain cross (Ib) as for groats. On the penny, halfpenny and farthing the lis is on the neck (once omitted on a farthing) and the initial cross (obverse only) is always plain. The type I pence of London have a mascle after *Rex*, and by shortening the king's name made room for the French title which had not been used on pence under Henry VI. The fractions read *Edward Rex Ang* (halfpence) or *Angli* (farthings), without stops.

On the earliest (Lis-Pellet) gold nobles of Edward IV there are again pellets by the crown, with the defining lis below the shield. These coins, from two obverse dies, differ markedly from the late nobles of Henry VI in having the king's name more prominently shown, across the top of the coin and unbroken by the design; they also omit a rudder, and the rigging is doubled to four ropes and two. The reverse dies, two of which have the spelling *Transens*, retain the Henrican mintmark lis. One appears to have *e* over *h* in the central panel, but the others have a pellet by the initial as on late nobles of Henry VI. Before the Fishpool find, which contained thirty-two examples, Edward's Lis-Pellet nobles were extremely rare, but they are still very seldom seen on the market since most of those from Fishpool were retained by the British Museum. This hoard also contained the Edward quarter-noble, the first recorded of this reign and the only known quarter after group V of Henry VI. Its obverse is later (type II), but lettering, the mintmark lis, a mascle after *Gloria* and a pellet in the central panel associate the reverse unambiguously with type I.

Edward IV, Heavy Coinage, Types II-IV, with Mintmark Rose

Following the relatively short extension of the Lis-Pellet group into the new reign, all the remaining coins of Edward's heavy coinage, up to 1464, have the rose as mintmark (on both sides of groats and halfgroats), the three main types defined by Blunt and Whitton being distinguished by other symbols in the inscriptions or the field. The extra pellets in two quarters of the reverse that had been normal on silver in the later groups of Henry VI no longer appear, and the mintmark lis on gold was now replaced by the

Henry IV – Edward IV

rose. There are three forms of rose, all with five petals: first, large with indented petals; second, small with plain petals; and third, with detached petals around a central pellet. The first form occurs on the obverses of type II groats, the second on reverses of groats and obverses of nobles of type II, and the third on coins of types III and IV. Stops are normally saltires, although pellets occur on a few groats, pence and halfpence, and trefoils on the type III noble and a rare variety of groat. Characteristic features are quatrefoils by the neck in types II and III (occasionally saltires in III), a crescent on or below the bust on the larger silver of type II, an eye in one inscription on many of the coins of type III and on some of type IV, and annulets by the bust in type IV. As in the later coinage of Henry VI, most of the silver was minted into groats and halfpence. Halfgroats, London pence and farthings are all very rare, and the number of known dies for gold is in single figures.

ROSE PUNCHES AND EYE ON HEAVY COINAGE OF EDWARD IV

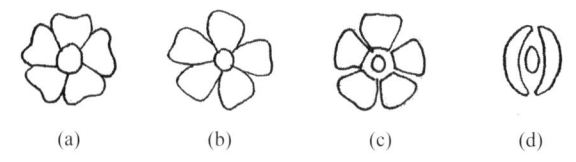

(a) Well-shaped rose with indented petals and hollow centre; (b) Smaller, more angular rose; (c) Rose with central pellet and detached petals; (d) Eye, types III-IV.

Blunt and Whitton divided the rose-marked groats and halfgroats of the heavy coinage into three types, based largely on the marks by the bust – the quatrefoils of types II and III, the annulets of type IV; and the ornament on the breast – crescent (II), trefoil (III) or fleur (IV). Since there are no breastmarks on the junior silver, the division between types II and III by obverses is less clearcut; but it is facilitated by the fact that, on the evidence of groats, the eye in the reverse inscription was not introduced until just after the start of type III. Groats of type III are more plentiful and varied than type II, but all denominations of type IV, terminated by the recoinage of 1464, are considerably rarer than those of II and III. The three types occupied a period of only around three years, and there is the usual muling between consecutive types: I/II (groat), II/I (penny), II/III (groat and halfgroat), III/II (halfgroat and penny), and III/IV and IV/III (groat). A few groat dies of types III and IV continued in use after the reduction in weight from 60 gr. to 48 gr., but they were too large for the lighter coins and were soon replaced.

The crescent-marked groats of type II have saltires on the reverse only in the outer legend. Variants of this type have an annnulet or pellet by the obverse mintmark, or in one case a second rose. In type III the crescent is replaced on the breast cusp by a trefoil of small pellets, quite distinct from the large fleurs on the other cusps; and on reverses of these groats saltires were introduced into the inner legend, along with an eye (except on rare early dies) between *tas* and *Lon*, or occasionally after *Lon*. Rare variants of type III include an early obverse with pellet and annulet beside the rose, echoing the use of these marks in type II, and a late die, without eye or stops in the inner legend, which has trefoils in the outer one, an exceptional use of trefoil stops on silver so early in the reign. The annulet-marked heavy groats of type IV are very rare – more so perhaps than light coins from the same dies. Although the eye (after *tas*) is retained in type IV, these late coins otherwise dispense altogether with stopping on the reverse.

Halfgroats, which follow the general scheme of the groats, are of some variety, but all very rare. One die of type II has the crescent well below the bust, another (without quatrefoils by the bust), appears to have a crescent on the neck. Reverses are, usually, without stops, and one also lacks the mintmark rose. Type III halves have the eye after *tas*, and one of their obverses also follows type III groats in having a trefoil of small pellets on the breast. There is no breastmark in type IV, where the eye is again found on one reverse variety.

Heavy London pence with mintmark rose are also all of great rarity. They are without breastmark but, as on the larger silver, those of types II and III have quatrefoils by the bust, and of type IV annulets. Reverses of type III have an eye between *tas* and *Lon*. Mules (II/I and III/II) confirm the sequence. On the single obverse die of type II, which has pellet stops, *Angl* is still followed by &, but the French title itself was dropped after its brief revival in type I. However, *Di Gra* is introduced instead, its first appearance on pence since class G of Henry V, but the start of its regular use henceforward.

The rare York pence of Archbishop William Booth correspond to the London coins of type III, although usually without an eye on the reverse. Similar coins without the archbishop's quatrefoil in the centre of the reverse cross have been attributed to the *Sede Vacante* between Booth's death in September 1464 and confirmation of the temporalities of his successor George Neville in the following June. If this attribution is correct such coins should all belong to the light coinage, but their weight does not always suggest so and it is possible that the lack of a quatrefoil is without significance, as for example in group III of Henry VI, and possibly in some later cases under Edward IV.

Early Durham pence of Edward IV, from local dies and often poorly struck, are not rare. They are of very coarse style, omitting *Di Gra* and with the mint name spelt *Dun* or *Don/oli(n)*, the *in* being a disarticulated *m*. The letter *e* is often reversed, and the stops vary from saltires or pellets to quatrefoils or stars. The initial mark is usually a cross. Few of these coins weigh more than 12 gr. (and then only slightly). Some of the lighter examples could perhaps belong to a period following the reduction of 1464 – although there are other Durham coins, from London-made dies with Booth's initial and mintmark rose, which accord with type V and can therefore be dated to 1464/5. The *Dunolin* series includes some coins, presumably early, with pellets by the crown, but earlier reverses have no extra marks. Three such reverses are found muled with an old group VIII obverse of Henry VI, although probably not struck until after the change of king, since there are no comparable local obverse dies in Henry's name. Later reverses have a rose on the centre of the cross, some of them also an extra pellet in one quarter as on light groats of type V. Although Laurence Booth had attended Edward IV's first parliament in 1461, he had enjoyed preferment under the previous regime and his loyalties may have appeared suspect at the time of a Lancastrian incursion into Northumbria late in 1462; at any rate, his temporalities were suspended from the end of 1462 until April 1464, shortly before the introduction of the light coinage, but there is no obvious interruption to the coin series.

Halfpence with quatrefoils or saltires by the bust, more numerous than those without (III), are classed as type II because some of them have pellet stops as on pence of that type; but Blunt and Whitton recognised that this implied many more halfpence of type II than of type III, in contrast to the greater abundance of the groats of type III, and a case could therefore equally well be made for attributing the unstopped coins to type III. Otherwise the type III halfpence are quite rare, especially a variety with an eye after *tas*. The halfpence of type IV, like the groats, are considerably rarer than those of the two preceding types. Halfpence usually read *Di Gra Rex*, or similarly, but *Rex Anglie* is also found on some of types III and IV. Of the extremely rare farthings of this period one is attributed to type II by virtue of its saltires by the bust; another, without them, to type III.

There are three die-pairs of rose-marked nobles, classifiable as II/I, II and III, of which the Fishpool hoard contained eight, two and twenty specimens respectively (only the II/I mule was previously known). On all of them the king's name reverts to its traditional (and less satisfactory) position, starting by the forecastle; but it is now (for the first and only time on the obverse in the noble series) preceded by the mintmark. Four ropes are retained aft, but there is now only one forward. The type II obverse of the mule, however, preserves one curious feature of type I in the form of its missing rudder. Both type II obverses have a quatrefoil by the wrist, the type III a saltire (as by the bust on some halfpence of type III). The characteristic eye of type III is placed after the obverse mintmark rose, and its trefoil stops can be matched on a late variety of type III groat. Reverses of types II and III have the ungrammatical *Ibatur*, and on the former there are two small roses instead of fleurs in the upper spandrels. The only rose-marked fractional die is the obverse of the II/I quarter-noble, unusual for its tressure of ten tight arcs. No gold is known with the annulets of type IV.

Mint Accounts, 1411 – 1464

Gold was minted at £16 13s. 4d. (i.e. 50 nobles) to the pound; silver at £1 10s. (360d.), except for the special issue of fractions in 1446-7 at £1 13s. per pound.

London accounts are complete throughout, apart from 1460-2 (following the change of government). Although many London accounts run in step with the Exchequer year, from one Michaelmas (M) to the next (indicated in the tables by dates with the years alone, e.g. 1424/25), some begin or end at Easter (March or April), or in June or December, and their length varies from a few weeks to several years. Detailed accounts survive for the activity of York in 1423-4, showing 1,499 lbs. of gold bought in August to October 1423 and 1,039 lbs. in May to August 1424. The Calais accounts for gold run from 1422 to 1431, by which time gold coinage had ceased there. Calais silver accounts are continuous until 1436 but thereafter there is only one item recorded c. 1440.

The London account for 1425-7 records payment to Goldbeter's graver, Gilbert Brandeburgh, for 2,713 dies for gold and silver coinage at Calais. Subsequent payments, in the accounts for 1428-30 and 1430-1, relate to 1,405 and 2,187 dies respectively for Calais silver only.

Durham records include some references to profits accounted to the bishop by his mintmasters in individual years, but they are incomplete. Except in a period (of uncertain length) following the recoinage of 1412, when the profits have been estimated to imply the minting of around 500 lbs. of silver, the profits were meagre. Estimates of output in 1416/7, 1418/9 and c. 1421 total around £600 of coin. For 1438/9 the figure is £235, but in other years under Henry VI (1434/5, 1453/4, 1458/9 and 1459/60) the sums are much lower, ranging from £36 to £115. There are no entries from the 1440s.

1412–1464

LONDON	£ gold	£ silver	YORK AND CALAIS	£ gold	£ silver
29.11.1411-29.11.1412	149,876	2,912			
29.11.1412-M.1413	138,829	5,464			
1413/17	313,515	28,069			
M.1417-31.3.1419	47,760	3,158	YORK		
31.3.1419-M.1420	43,325	2,221	12.8.1423-14.8.1424	42,310	
M.1420-31.3.1422	98,476	3,326	30.9.1423-7.8.1424		496
			CALAIS		
30.3.1422-M.1424	329,115	10,386	30.7.1422-30.1.1424	60,612	10,771
1424/25	57,767	2,419	24.2.1424-24.12.1427	35,590	
M.1425-20.4.1427	51,306	4,054	25.2.1424-31.1.1428		101,618
20.4.1427-M.1427	12,704	898	20.2.1428-3.8.1431		134,491
1427/28	28,198	1,746	20.5.1428-2.8.1431	6,018	
M.1428-31.3.1430	25,481	4,342			
31.3.1430-M.1431	21,683	4,222	31.10.1431-M.1432		39,274
1431/33	19,056	3,493	1432/33		41,025
1433/34	10,582	855	1433/34		27,136
M.1434-24.6.1435	5,000	785	1434/35		19,793
24.6.1435-M.1436	8,427	546	1435/36		9,718
1436/37	5,663	820			
1437/38	5,252	2,216			
M.1438-18.12.1439	9,094	6,433			
18.12.1439-16.4.1441	8,423	4,127	c.1440		585
16.4.1441-M.1443	11,522	794			
1443/44	4,062	234			
1444/45	2,700	311			
M.1445-13.12.1445	628	63			
13.12.1445-24.6.1447	3,944	980			
" " halfpence		3,088			
24.6.1447-24.6.1448	1,465	133			
24.6.1448-11.10.1449	3,414	1,052			
11.10.1449-M.1450	5,951	6,953			
M.1450-9.4.1452	6,918	16,184			
9.4.1452-1.4.1453	4,367	6,135			
1.4.1453-21.4.1454	2,064	5,408			
21.4.1454-28.3.1456	2,492	8,205			
28.3.1456-M.1457	2,137	9,993			
1457/58	1,414	5,491			
1458/59	324	4,655			
1459/60	1,887	10,564			
1460-62	No accounts				
15.9.1462-1.9.1464	4,891	17,828			

Henry IV – Edward IV

Calendar 1412 – 1464

1412 London mint accounts resumed (29 Nov. 1411).
 New coinage operative from Easter (3 April) – Richard Garner master: gold at £16 13s. 4d. per lb., silver at 30s. per lb.
1413 Death of Henry IV (20 Mar.); succeeded by Henry V.
 Indenture with Lewys John on existing terms (14 April).
1415 English victory at Agincourt (Oct.).
 York: master John Esyngwald accused of causing dies to be made in the city.
1419 Fall of Rouen (Jan.).
1420 Treaty of Troyes (May); Burgundian alliance facilitated English wool exports.
 Henry V married Princess Katherine of France (2 June).
1421 1413 indenture amended to reduce charges (26 July).
1422 Indenture (13 Feb.) for London and Calais mints with Bartholemew Goldbeter; first dies issued to Calais, 16 May (accounts from July).
 Death of Henry V (31 Aug./1 Sept.); succeeded by Henry VI. Death of Charles VI of France, also succeeded by Henry VI (Oct.).
1423 Contract with Goldbeter extended to include mints at York and Bristol (16 Feb.).
 York: royal mint accounts run from Aug. (gold), Sept. (silver). Death of Abp. Henry Bowet (20 Oct.); Esyngwald authorised to coin during *sede vacante* (6 Nov.).
 Durham: mint building leased out (by Michaelmas).
1424 York royal mint closed (Aug.).
1425 Indenture for coinage at Dublin.
1426 York: temporalities granted to Abp. John Kemp (22 April).
1431 Indenture with William Rus for mints at London, Calais, York and Bristol (8 Sept.).
1432 Indenture with John Paddesley for same four mints (10 July).
1435 Treaty of Arras; Anglo-Burgundian alliance ended.
1436 French regained Paris.
1437 Henry VI declared of age (12 Nov.).
 Durham: death of Bishop Thomas Langley (20 Nov.).
1438 Durham: Bishop Robert Neville appointed (temporalities 8 April).
c.1440 Calais: Latest extant mint account.
1445 Anglo-French truce, Henry VI married Margaret of Anjou.
 Indenture with Robert Manfeld for mints at London and Calais (13 Dec.).
1446 Parliament ordered halfpence and farthings at 33s. per lb. (for two years from 8 April).
1451 Manfeld contract renewed (18 Dec.).
1452 York: Abp. Kemp translated to Canterbury (21 July); William Booth appointed (temporalities 6 Sept.).
1453 Richard, Duke of York, Protector of the Realm during king's insanity (1453-4). All English territory in France lost except Calais.
1454 Duke of Somerset regained influence.
1455 Duke of York briefly recovered control after victory at St. Albans, king taken prisoner, Somerset killed.
1457 Durham: death of Bp. Neville (9 July); Laurence Booth appointed (temporalities 18 Oct.).
1459 Indenture with Sir Richard Tunstall for London and Calais (11 April).

1460 First contract for Irish coinage at reduced weight.
       Lancastrians defeated at Northampton (July).
       Henry VI recognised Duke of York as heir to throne (Oct.).
       Duke of York killed at battle of Wakefield (Dec.).
1461 Henry VI deposed (4 March); succeeded by Edward IV; Yorkist victory at Towton (29 March).
       Indenture with Thomas Montgomery at the Tower (23 May).
1462 Durham: Bp. L. Booth's temporalities seized (Dec.).
1463 Canterbury: Abp. Thomas Bourchier granted dies for halfgroat, penny and halfpenny (10 July).
1464 Durham: Bp. L. Booth's temporalities restored (April).
       Indenture with William, Lord Hastings (13 Aug.); noble revalued to 8s. 4d., weights of silver coins reduced by 20 per cent.
       York: death of Abp. W. Booth (12 Sept.).

WEIGHTS, 1412 – 1464

Gold £16 13s. 4d. per lb. weight

Noble	6s. 8d.	50	per lb.	108 gr. (7.0 g.)
Half-noble	3s. 4d.	100	" "	54 gr. (3.5 g.)
Quarter-noble	1s. 8d.	200	" "	27 gr. (1.75 g.)

Silver £1 10s. per lb. weight (except fractions in 1446/7)

Groat	4d.	90	per lb.	60 gr. (3.89 g.)
Halfgroat	2d.	180	" "	30 gr. (1.94 g.)
Penny	1d.	360	" "	15 gr. (0.97 g.)
Halfpenny (normally)	½d.	720	" "	7.5 gr. (0.49 g.)
Farthing (normally)	¼d.	1440	" "	3.75 gr. (0.24 g.)
1446/7 £1 13s. per lb. weight				
Halfpenny	½d.	792	per lb.	6.82 gr. (0.44 g.)
Farthing	¼d.	1584	" "	3.41 gr. (0.22 g.)

NOBLES 1412 - 1464

Type as before. King's initial in central panel of rev., *h* (Henry IV, V and VI) or *e* (Edward IV). Normal rev. inscription *Ihc Aut(em) Transiens Per Mediu(m) Illoru(m) Ibat*.

HENRY IV, LIGHT COINAGE, 1412-3. London only. Saltire stops. *Autem*.
   Primary series – class P. Titles normally *hen/ric Di Gra Rex Angl & Franc Dns hib & Aq*. *&* is barred *I*.
Pa.   Heavy coinage obv. dies (type 2 or 3 arms), with annulet added on ship's side. Rev. old heavy dies, or new (Pb). ER.
Pb.   New dies. Elegant lettering and initial cross patty, with concave sides. Saltire or nothing on rudder. Slipped trefoil, usually plus annulet, on ship's side. Ropes 3-1. Castles (i) crenellated (ER), or (ii) pellet-topped. Usually *hen/ric* (rarely *henr/* or *he/*), *hib*, and *Frac*. Rev. slipped trefoil by lion in one quarter, and on one die after *Ibat*. Usually a point before central *h*. Rare.

Henry IV – Edward IV

Nobles

Secondary series – classes A and B. *h/enric, hyb*. Aquitaine title omitted henceforward. New *&* (as barred *S*). Ropes 3-2.

A. Short, wide ('stunted') lettering. Initial cross patty (as in class P) or with sunk annulet centre. *Franc*. Nothing on rudder. Small quatrefoil above sail and by lion in *Autem* quarter. Also muled both ways with Pb. All ER.

B. Taller lettering. Initial cross patty with sunk annulet centre, or rarely plain. Annulet or nothing on rudder. Quatrefoil or slipped trefoil above sail and by lion in *Autem* quarter. Less tightly dotted circle and inner tressure on rev. Also muled both ways with Pb. All VR. For B* dies with cinquefoil see under Henry V.

HENRY V, 1413-22. London only (B* - G). Saltire stops (except on G). Usually a small quatrefoil above sail. *h/enric Di Gra Rex Angl & Franc Dns hyb*. Quatrefoil by lion's head in *Autem* quarter.

B* Three dies of class B have a cinquefoil added by wrist. VR; also B*/P mule (ER).

C. Cinquefoil by sword arm. Pierced initial cross, with or without pellet in centre. Annulet on rudder (early only), or broken annulet on ship's side. Ropes 3-2. Var. *hib*. Ca, narrower *D*; Cb, wide *D* with back peaked inside and outside.

D. Cinquefoil and annulet by sword arm. Pierced cross (no pellet) henceforward. Trefoil by shield. Broken annulet on ship's side. Ropes 3-2. Letter *P* sliced at bottom left (until earliest varieties of Annulet coinage). Also D/C mule; all VR.

E. Cinquefoil and unbroken annulet by wrist. Trefoil by shield. Annulet (broken or not) on ship's side. Pellet at sword point, and at tail of lion in *Ibat* quarter. Ropes 3-2, later 2-1. Also E/D mule; all rare.

F. Cinquefoil (and usually annulet) by sword arm. Annulet or trefoil on ship's side. Trefoil by shield and by tail of lion in *Ibat* quarter. No pellet at sword point or on rev. Ropes 2-1 (henceforward). Also E/F mules; all ER.

G. No extra symbols in field or on ship's side; no quatrefoil above sail. Ornaments (A) on ship, lion, lis, lis, lion, lis. Stops cinquefoil after *h/enric* and *Ihc*; otherwise annulets. Also mules G/F and F/G; all VR.

H. Annulet nobles with ornaments A (London only) and some other early varieties of the Annulet group (London and Calais) were struck under Henry V; see below.

HENRY VI, 1422-61. London (I-VI, VIII, X), Calais (with pennant at stern; I, II only), York (I only). *h/enric Di Gra Rex Angl & Franc Dns hyb*. Ropes 2-1. Mm. lis. Rev. *Aut* for *Autem* (except VIb).

I. Annulet issue (begun under Henry V). Annulet by wrist and in top right spandrel on rev. Stops, obv. lis after *h/enric*, then trefoils; rev. cinquefoil after *Ihc*, then annulets. Ornaments on ship's side: IA (London only), lion, 2 lis, lion, lis; IB, lis, lion, lis, lion, lis. Fleurs in spandrels: 1, large, with long plain side foils; 2, three small, neat foils of equal size; 3, large, with long, curled side foils.

London: IA, *hib* or *hyb*. Fleurs no. 1. Also mules F/Annulet and G/Annulet; all VR. IB, *hyb*. Fleurs nos. 1, 2 and 3. Rare vars. have trefoil or pellet by lion on rev. (with fleurs no. 2); or trefoil instead of lis after *h/enric*; *Ibmt*.

Calais: IB. Fleurs 1-3. Earliest vars. (VR) have *c* for *h* in centre of rev. (and fleurs no. 1). IC (VR) has variant ornaments, lion, lis, lion, lis, lion.

York: IB. Lis over sterncastle. Fleurs 2 or 3. VR.

II. Rosette and Rosette-Mascle issue. Lis by wrist and by lion in *Ihc Aut* quarter. Stops rosettes (*passim* on earliest dies), later with mascles after *Gra* (or *Rex*) and *Per*.

Nobles

London: *Transiens* on early dies, then *–ciens*. One obv. (muled with III rev.) reads *hib*. All rare.

Calais (the last Calais noble): All obv. stops rosettes; mascle after *Per* (once over a rosette) VR; also ER II/I mule.

III. Pinecone-Mascle issue. London only henceforward. Mascle after *Rex* and (normally) *Per*; saltires by &; other stops cones. Nothing by wrist. Usually lis by lion in first quarter. *hib, hyb* or *hiyb*. *Tranciens*, often omitting one or two letters. Var. *Mecium*. One rev. has central *h* inverted. Rare; also ER mule II/III.

IV. Leaf-Mascle issue. Leaf in waves below ship. Mascle after *Rex* and *Per*, other stops saltires. *Tranciens*. No lis by lion on rev. (henceforward). ER.

V. 'Leaf-Trefoil' group. One obv. die; no extra marks; ornaments B (three lis, two lions). Trefoils after *Rex* and *Per* (also once after *Medium*); other stops leaves, with saltires by &. *Tranciens*. ER.

VI. 'Trefoil' group. Obv. saltire stops. VIa, Trefoil as sword pommel; leaf below shield; ornaments B. VIb, Trefoil below shield to left; ornaments C (three lions, two lis). *Ds hib*. Rev. *Auto, Transiens, Illo*. Stops saltires, with trefoils after *Auto* and *Per* (and once a pellet before *Per*). Also IV/VI mule; all ER.

VIII. Leaf-Pellet issue. Leaf to left of shield. Ornaments B. Pellet by *h* in central panel. *Transiens*. Rev. stops saltires (sparsely).
- (i) Annulet, lis and leaf to left of shield. Pellet at inner end of spar. Pellet each side of *h* in *henric*. *hy*. Obv. stops annulets, with trefoil before *Di* and saltires by &. Var. omits pellet by central *h*. ER.
- (ii) Leaf only by shield. Pellet at each end of spar above crown. Saltire and pellet above sail. *hy/b*. Saltire before *e* of *h/enric*, otherwise no obv. stops. VR.

X. Cross-Pellet issue. Saltire to left of shield and above sail. *Dns Y*, with mascle before *s*. Mascles after *Aut* and *Illoru*; pellet by central *h*. ER.

EDWARD IV, HEAVY COINAGE (1461-4). London.

I. Lis-Pellet issue. Lis below shield. King's name across top of coin – *Edward/D(i)/Gra Rex Angl & Fran(c) Dns h(y)b*. One or two pellet(s) by crown. Ropes 4-2; no rudder. Rev. mm. lis. *e* and pellet in central panel (or *e* over *h*). *Trans(i)ens*. VR.

II,III. Mm. rose. Ropes 4-1. King's name starts by forecastle. *e* (without pellet) in central panel. *Ibatur*.

II. Quatrefoil by wrist. *E/dward Di Gra Rex Angl & Franc Dns hyb*. Small rose mm. on obv., large on rev. Saltire stops. Rev. small roses in two upper spandrels; *Illou*. Also mule II (no rudder)/I (*Transens, Iloru*). All ER.

III. Saltire by wrist. Obv. reading as II, but *Edward* all below forecastle, and *hib*. Large rose mm. both sides, followed on obv. by eye. Trefoil stops. VR.

HALF-NOBLES 1412 - 1464

Type as before. King's initial *h* in central panel of rev. (Henry IV, V and VI). No half-noble is known of Edward IV.

HENRY IV, LIGHT COINAGE, 1412-3. London only. Saltire stops.
Primary series – class P.

P. Elegant lettering and initial cross patty, with concave sides. *henric Di Gra Rex Angl & Frac D h Aq*. Annulet and trefoil on ship's side. Slipped trefoil by lion

Henry IV – Edward IV

Half-Nobles

in one quarter of rev. Point before central *h*. Castles (i) crenellated (ropes 2-1), or (ii) pellet-topped (ropes 3-1 or 2-1). ER.

Secondary series – class B (no half-noble of class A is recorded).

B. Obverses only, muled with class P or C rev. Tall lettering. Ropes 3-2. *h/enric*; *Fra D hy(b)*. B/P mule has no extra marks. B/C mule has broken annulet on ship's side and quatrefoil before *h/enric*. Both ER.

HENRY V, 1413-22. London only. *h/enric Di Gra Rex Angl & Fr D hyb*, or var. Saltire stops. Cinquefoil above shield. No mark by sword arm.

C. Broken annulet on ship's side. Ropes 3-2 or 3-1. Pierced initial cross with pellet in centre. Broken annulet by lion's head in *Domine* quarter. Var. omits *D* before *hyb*. Rare; also ER B/C mule.

D. Rev. only, muled with F obv. Pierced initial cross. Unbroken annulet by lion's head. VR.

E. Rev. only, muled with F obv. Pierced cross. Pellet in *Arguas* quarter, annulet in *Domine* quarter of rev. Vars. have no trefoils in spandrels, or omit initial cross. Rare.

F. No annulet on ship's side. Sometimes a trefoil between shield and forecastle, or quatrefoil above sail. Obv. only, muled with D or E rev. Ropes 2-1 (henceforward). *F D*, or *Dn* or *Ds, hy*. Rare.

G. Unmarked issue. Quatrefoil above sail, but no symbols in field. Ornaments (A) on ship, lion, lis, lis, lion, lis. Ropes 2-1. Pierced initial cross. Cinquefoil after *h/enric* and (sometimes) *Domine*, saltires by &, otherwise annulet stops. *Fr*. VR.

H. Annulet half-nobles with ornaments A (London only) and some other early varieties of the Annulet group (London and Calais) were struck under Henry V; see below.

HENRY VI, 1422-61. London (I-V), Calais (with pennant at stern; I, II only), York (I only). *h/enric Di Gra Rex Angl & Franc*. Ropes 2-1. Mm. lis.

I. Annulet issue (begun under Henry V). Annulet by wrist and in top right spandrel on rev. Stops, obv. lis after *h/enric*, then trefoils; rev. cinquefoil after *Domine*, then annulets. Ornaments on ship's side: IA (London only), lion, 2 lis, lion, lis; IB, lis, lion, lis, lion, lis.

London: IA, *Fran*, ER (Henry V, class H); also ER mule G/Annulet. IB, no trefoils by &; rare var. has trefoil by lion in *Domine* quarter; annulets by wrist or in spandrel occasionally omitted.

Calais: IB. Trefoils by &. Earliest var. (ER) has *c* for *h* in centre of rev.

York: IB. Lis over sterncastle. Trefoils by &. VR.

II. Rosette and Rosette-Mascle issue. Usually lis by wrist. Lis by lion in *Domine* quarter. Stops rosettes without (early) or with mascles.

London: Obv. stops all rosettes (*Frnc*; ER), or with mascle before or after *Rex*, and one or two mascles on rev. Vars. ropes 2-0; or lis by wrist omitted. All VR.

Calais (the last Calais half-noble): Stops all rosettes both sides. ER.

III. Pinecone-Mascle issue. London only henceforward. Rev. only (II/III mule). Mascle after *Tuo*, other rev. stops cones. No lis by lion on rev. ER.

IV. Leaf-Mascle issue. Leaf on obv. by shield and in waves below ship; on rev. to left of upper cross-end. Mascles after *Rex* and *Furore*, other stops saltires. ER.

V. 'Leaf-Trefoil' group. Leaves after first three words on obv., then trefoils; rev. leaves after *Domine* and *In*; *Tuo* omitted. Also V/I mule; all ER.

No half-nobles are known of groups VI-XI of Henry VI, or of the heavy coinage of Edward IV.

QUARTER-NOBLES 1412 - 1464

Type as before; lis in central panel of rev. (except Edward IV, a pellet). Normally eight arc tressure on obv.

HENRY IV, LIGHT COINAGE, 1412-3. London only. Lis above shield. Saltire stops.
Primary series – class P.
P.   Elegant initial cross and lettering. *D(e)(i) Gra Rex Ang(l).* Slipped trefoils, or trefoils over annulets, by shield. Small trefoils on cusps. Var. has slipped trefoil after *Gloria*. VR.
Secondary series – classes A and B. *Di Gra Rex Ang(l) & F.*
A.   Short, wide ('stunted') lettering. Initial cross patty with sunk annulet. Slipped trefoils (at middle) and annulets (below) beside shield. Trefoils of large pellets on cusps. Stars at corners of central panel on rev. ER.
B.   Tall lettering; pierced initial cross with pellet centre. Trefoils at corners of central panel (henceforward).
   Ba Trefoils on cusps; quatrefoil over annulet each side of shield. Also Ba/P mule. All VR.
   Bb Annulets on cusps; quatrefoil each side of shield. ER. For Bb* see Henry V.

HENRY V, 1413-22. London only. *henric Rex Angl & Franc* (C – F). Saltire stops. Lis above shield. Trefoils at corners of rev. panel. Annulets on cusps (C-F).
Bb* Cinquefoil added at bottom right of shield. ER.
C.   Broken annulet to left, cinquefoil to right of shield.
D.   As C but unbroken annulet. Rare.
F.   Trefoil to left, cinquefoil to right of shield. *Frac* or *Fran*. Var. *Excultabitur*. Rare; also D/F mule (VR).
G.   Lis above shield, but no other symbols in field. No ornaments on cusps. *D(e)i Gra Rex Angl*. Star after *henric* and *Exaltabitur*; other stops annulets. VR.
H.   Annulet quarter-nobles with one lis above shield, and small lis mintmark (London only), also muled with G obv., and probably some other early varieties of the Annulet group were struck under Henry V; see below.

HENRY VI, 1422-61. London (I-V), Calais (I and ? II), York (I only). *henric Di Gra Rex Angl*. Mm. lis. Lis above shield.
I.   Annulet issue (begun under Henry V). Trefoils on cusps. Stops, obv. lis after *henric*, then trefoils; rev. cinquefoil after *Exaltabitur*, annulet after *in*.
   London: One lis above shield. IA (Henry V), Small lis mm. *Dei*. Vars. have annulet, or cinquefoil over annulet, after *Exaltabitur*. Also G/Annulet mule; all VR. IB, Large lis mm. *Di*; once *Angli*. Some obv. dies have trefoil or pellet below shield. Rare vars. have annulet, or cinquefoil over annulet, after *Exaltabitur*.
   Calais: One lis above and one each side of shield. IB. Large lis mm. Once *Dei*, normally *Di*. Vars. have annulet, or trefoil over lis, after *Di*. All rare.
   York: Two lis above shield. IB. Large lis mm. *Di*. One obv. die only. VR.
II. Rosette and Rosette-Mascle issue. Rosette stops without (early) or with mascles.
   London: Mascle before or after *Rex*; rev. no mascle, or one after *In*. Var. omits lis above shield. VR; also ER I/II mule.
   Calais or London: Lis above and rosette each side of shield. No mascles. ER.

Henry IV – Edward IV

Quarter-Nobles

III. Pinecone-Mascle issue. London only henceforward. Mascle after *Rex* and before or after *In*, other stops cones. Also II/III (no lis above shield) and III/II mules; all ER.
IV. Leaf-Mascle issue. Mascle after *Rex* and before *In*, other stops saltires. *Ang.* Leaf below *R* of *Glori*. ER.
V. 'Leaf-Trefoil' group. Trefoils after *Rex* and *In*, other stops leaves (two after *Exaltabitur*). ER.

No quarter-nobles are known of groups VI-XI of Henry VI.

EDWARD IV, HEAVY COINAGE (1461-4). London. Unique type II/I mule only.
I. Rev. die only, mm. lis. Pellet in central panel. *Exaltbitur*; saltires after *In;* colon and mascle after *Gloria*.
II. Obv. die only, mm. rose. *Edward Di Gra Rex Ang & Fr*, saltire stops. Tressure of ten arcs, with small trefoils on six lower cusps; no lis above shield.

GROATS 1412 - 1464

Type as before. Normally a nine arc tressure. Gothic *n* (except on rev. of Henry IV, class P).

HENRY IV, LIGHT COINAGE, 1412-3. London only. Saltire stops.
    Primary series – class P. Annulet and pellet by crown; slipped trefoil on breast and often in legend. Initial cross patty. Roman *N* (reversed) in *London* (lettering larger in inner circle). *Adiutorem* in full; and usually *Meum*.
PI. Pellet to left and annulet to right of crown. French title omitted. *henric Dei Gra Rex Anglie*. Thick lettering. Also mules with revs. of PII or PIII. All ER.
    PIa. Two dies with *henric* altered from *Ricard* (?), with pellet and annulet added. Wide face and hair.
    PIb. Two dies with Henry's name unaltered. Thinner face and hair.
PII. New, waisted lettering; smaller, elegant initial cross. Annulet to left, pellet to right of crown. Wide hair. *Dei Gra Rex Angl & Franc*, & is barred *I*. Two dies, with eight (low crown) and ten arcs to tressure. ER.
PIII. As II but nine arcs, and *Di, Anglie*. Five dies; one reads *Francie*. Extensively muled with Secondary rev. dies (P/A and P/B). ER vars. have Gothic *n* in *Lon* or *don*. One obv. die found both without and with cinquefoil on breast (see Henry V). All VR.
    Secondary series – classes A and B. No marks by crown. *Di Gra Rex Anglie & Franc*; & is barred *S*. Gothic *n* in *London* (lettering same size in inner circle as in outer, now and henceforward). Normally *A/duitor/e*, and double saltires after *tas* and *don*.
A. Short, wide ('stunted') lettering. Two obv. dies only, with 'emaciated bust'; large fleurs on all cusps. Small initial cross, usually broad and patty with sunk annulet. One or two saltires after *Di*. Quatrefoil after *henric* and *Posui*. Some early revs. read *A/duitore/m*. Also muled both ways with PIII or B dies; all VR.
B. Taller and narrower lettering; tail of tall *n* often broken. Larger initial cross, plain or slightly patty, with incuse annulet or hollow centre. 'Scowling bust', with turned down mouth, and long neck with central swelling. Usually a quatrefoil after *henric*; sometimes quatrefoil or saltire after *Posui*. Also mules A/B, and both ways with PIII; all VR.
B1. Large fleurs on cusps (as in A). Letter *I* with palmate serifs. All VR.
    B1a. Two dies, with top arches fleured and quatrefoil after *henric*.
    B1b. One die, with top arches unfleured, and no quatrefoil.

1412–1464

Groats

B2. Smaller fleurs on cusps (top unfleured). Later dies have large *c, e* and *I*. Rare.

B2a. Breast cusp fleured. Some obv. dies have cinquefoil added (see B2a*, Henry V).

B2b has star on breast (see Henry V).

HENRY V, 1413-22. London only (B* - G). Saltire stops.

PIII*/B and B2a* – one old PIII* and four B2a* dies of Henry IV have cinquefoil added on shoulder or breast. All VR.

B2b. Star on breast cusp instead of fleur. *Fran.* VR.

Henry V definitive issues. New bust with narrow mouth and thick lips. *henric Di Gra Rex Anglie & Franc; &* is barred *S*. Quatrefoil after *Posui*; usually double saltires after *tas* and *don*.

C. Often loosely dotted circles. Usually a cinquefoil on sinister shoulder. Sometimes struck on small flans.

Ca. Initial cross with pellet centre. Usually quatrefoil after *henric*. Narrow letter *D*, with back peaked outside only. Var. *Angl*. Also rare B/C mules.

Cb. Pierced initial cross, without pellet. No quatrefoil after *henric*. Wider *D*, back peaked both sides. Vars. *henrc* and *France; Londos*.

F. One obv. die, as Cb but *Angl & Franie*, letter *n* sliced at top left, and *P* sliced at left foot; and finely toothed circles. VR.

G. No cinquefoil on bust. Neat circles. Pierced cross. *Anglie & Franc*. Letters *n* and *P* as in class F; squashed *h*. Quatrefoil after *Posui*. VR.

H. Some early varieties of the Annulet group (London and Calais) were struck under Henry V (see below).

HENRY VI, 1422-61. London (I-XI), Calais (I-VI only), York (I only). *henric Di Gra Rex Angl & Franc.* Mm. cross. Nine arc tressure, with top cusps unfleured.

I. Annulet issue (begun under Henry V). Barred *S* for *&*. Annulet after *Posui* (except Id), otherwise saltire stops (usually double saltires after each word in mint name). Annulet between pellets in first and third quarters of rev. (Id, third quarter only).

Ia. (Some = Henry V, class H.) Plain pierced initial cross as under Henry V. *Anglie*. Fleur on breast.

Ib. Shaped pierced initial cross.

Ib1. *Anglie*. Fleur on breast.

Ib2. *Anglie*. No fleur on breast. Usually broken *R*.

Ib3. *Angl*. No fleur. Some have broken *R*. Old Henry V portrait, or new face with arched brows.

Ic. Plain initial cross – not recorded for obv. of groats.

Id. Annulet-Trefoil issue, Calais only. Trefoil to left of crown. *Angl*; no fleur. Trefoil instead of annulet after *Posui*. Annulet in *Cali* quarter only. Obv. initial cross as Ib, rev. plain.

London (no marks by bust): Ia, VR; Ib1, Ib2 and Ib3.

Calais (annulets by bust; *Vil/la/Cali/sie*): Ia, VR; Ib1/Ia, ER; Ib1, Ib2 and Ib3 (VR Ib1 and Ib2 Calais/'London' mules were struck at Calais); rare Ib vars. omit annulets in rev. quarters; Id, rare; Ib3/Id, VR.

York (two lis by neck; *Civi/tas/Ebo/raci*, followed by annulet): Ib1 only, VR.

II. Rosette-Mascle issue. Rosette after *Posui*, and normally mascle in obv. legend. Usually mascle before *Lon* and *la*, rosette after *don* and *sie*. Other stops rosettes

Henry IV – Edward IV

Groats

or saltires. *&* is unbarred *S*. Rev. initial cross plain. IIa, pierced initial cross on obv. IIb, obv. initial cross patonce. IIc (Calais only), obv. initial cross fleury.

London: IIa. Coins with obv. stops saltires throughout (without rosette or mascle)have barred *&* and so are probably not IIa1 but Ib/II mules. IIa3, Mascle in obv. legend, after *Gra* (other obv. stops rosettes and saltires), or after *Rex* (other obv. stops rosettes). Rare.

IIb. Mascle after *Rex*; other obv. stops rosettes. Rare.

Calais: IIa1, No mascle on obv., with stops saltires or rosettes or mixed. IIa2, Mascle in two side spandrels, with obv. saltire stops (early, rare). IIa3, Mascle in obv. legend, after *henric* (saltire stops; *D* of *Frand* is *c* reversed), or after *Gra* (other stops rosettes, saltires), or after *Rex* (other stops rosettes). Earliest revs. have no mascle. Also mules Ib/II, and IIa/I (ER). IIb. Mascle after *Gra* (rare) or *Rex*; other obv. stops rosettes. Also ER mule IIb/Id. IIc. Mascle after *Rex*; other obv. stops rosettes. Rare.

III. Pinecone-Mascle issue. Mascle after *Rex*, saltires by *&*, other obv. stops cones. Rev. cone after *Posui*, mascle before *Lon* and *la*, cone after *don* and *sie*; other rev. stops saltires. Rev. initial cross plain. IIIa, obv. initial cross patonce. IIIb, obv. cross fleury.

London: IIIa; IIIb. Vars. *tai* (IIIa); *tos* (IIIa and b); rev. initial cross omitted (IIIb). Also mules IIIa/II (ER) and II/III.

Calais: IIIa; IIIb (rare). Var. (IIIa) omits cone after *Posui*. Also mules IIIa/I, IIIa/II (rare) and IIb/III.

IV. Leaf-Mascle issue. Leaf in spandrel below bust and on circle below *Meum*. Usually no mark after *Posui*. Mascle after *Rex* and before *Lon* and *la*; other stops saltires. Rev. initial cross plain. Obv. initial cross: IVa, voided; IVb, plain.

London: IVa only. One pair of dies. *D* under *L* of *Lon*, preceded by mascle. VR; also mules IVa/III (ER) and IVa/V (rare).

Calais: IVa, IVb. Vars. leaf after *Posui* (IVa); *Fran* (IVb). Also rare IIIb/IV mule.

Groups V, VI and VII. Trefoiled groups ('Leaf-Trefoil', 'Trefoil' and 'Trefoil-Pellet'). London (V, VI and VII), Calais (Va and VIa only).

Obverses V-VII: Initial cross fleury throughout.

Va. Leaf on breast. Saltire stops, usually with trefoil and/or leaves.

Vb. No leaf on breast. Stops three leaves, then trefoil after *Rex*; saltires by *&*. London only.

VI. All vars. have small leaf on breast cusp; trefoils by neck or shoulders; no leaves in inscription.

VIa. Trefoils by neck. Stops saltires, with one, two or three trefoils (three-trefoil dies have fleurs on shoulder cusps).

VIb. Trefoils by neck; small fleurs in spandrels. Saltire stops only. *Franc* (with fleurs on shoulder cusps) or *Fran*. London only.

VIc. Trefoils on shoulder cusps. Saltire stops, with trefoil after *Rex (Frane)*, or once after *Di (Fran)*. London only.

VII. Leaf on breast, fleurs on shoulder cusps, trefoils by neck, pellets by crown. London only.

Reverses V-VII: London (i-iv), Calais (i only).

(i) Initial cross fleury. No leaf in legend. Saltire stops, without, or with trefoil(s) (after *Deum, Meum*, or *tas* at London; or at Calais, before *Meum*, before or after *la* or *sie*). London var. *Sivi*.

(ii) Plain initial cross. Saltire stops (rarely none); without trefoil or leaf; or with trefoil(s) after *Meum, Lon* or *don*; or often with leaf before *Lon* and trefoil after *don* (and sometimes a mascle before *tas*).

1412–1464

Groats

(iii) No cross before *Posui*. No leaf; rarely a trefoil after *Lon* or before *don*; otherwise saltire stops (rarely none). Late vars. have pellet in *Adiutor.e*, or colon after *Posui*.

(iv) No cross before *Posui*; extra pellets in *tas* and *don* or *Civi* and *Lon* quarters (VII, or mules with later Pelleted groups).

London. Va: with revs. i, ii (mostly) and iii (rare). Vb: revs. ii, and iii (rare). VIa: revs. i (rare), ii (mostly) and iii (VR). VIb: revs. i (rare), ii (rare), iii and iv. VIc: revs. iii and iv. VII: revs. iii and iv. Also rare mules IV/i, IV/ii and Va/III.

Calais. Va: rev. i only (VR); var. *Cali* (over *Civi*)/*sie*/*Vil*/*la*. VIa: rev. i only (rare). Also mules III/i (VR); and V/III and V/IV (both ER).

Groups VIII, X and XI. Pelleted groups (Leaf-Pellet, Cross-Pellet and Lis-Pellet). London only. Pellets each side of crown, and added in two quarters of rev. (either above the group of three larger pellets, or on line of dotted circle). Obv. initial cross fleury. *henric Di Gra Rex Angl(i) & Franc(ie)*. Shoulders often raised above tressure. Stops usually saltires when present. Normally no cross or mark before *Posui*. *A*/*diutor*/*e Meum*.

VIII. Leaf-Pellet issue. Leaf on breast or neck. Pellets by crown and added on rev. Often no stop after *Di*. Sometimes no stops on rev.

VIIIa. Leaf on breast. *Angl*. (i) *Francie*, with or without fleur on breast cusp below leaf. (ii) *Franc*; breast cusp unfleured.

VIIIb. Leaf on breast. With or without fleur on breast cusp. *Angli & Franc*. (i) Trefoil after *Angli*. Rare. (ii) No trefoil. Vars. *henic I Di Gra; Frac*.

VIIIc. Leaf on neck; fleur on breast. *Angli & Franc(i)*. Vars. have leaf or *c* after *Franc*. One obv. die (ER) with two pellets by crown and two also by hair labelled VIIId by Whitton. Rev. extra pellets occasionally omitted. Var. *Divi* (i.e. *c* reversed). Coins with mullet after *Posui* are VIIIc/X mules.

IX. Unmarked type. One obv. die only (VR) with no pellets by crown, no leaf or fleur on breast. Bust set low. Abbreviation mark, but no stop, after *Di* and *Gra*. *Angl & Franc*. Normal revs. with two added pellets (one has plain cross before *Posui*), or ER var. with four.

X. Cross-Pellet issue. Saltire(s) by or on neck. Pellets by crown; and added on rev. (very rarely omitted). Often no stops on rev.

Xa. Saltire each side of neck. Leaf and fleur on breast. *Angli & Franc*. Saltire stops on obv., rev. none. One obv. die only, VR.

Xb. Saltire on neck. Breast cusp usually fleured. *&* omitted or after *Franc*. Often a mullet after *Posui*. (i) No mullet in obv. legend; two saltires after *Angli* or no obv. stops; rare. (ii) One or two mullets in obv. legend, after *henric, Franc (&)*; no other obv. stops; *Angl(i)*, var. *Anli*.

Xc. Saltire on neck; fleur on breast. Mascle(s) in obv. legend. *Angli & Franc*. Often a mullet after *Posui*. (i) Three mascles, after *henric, Gra, Franc*; pellet after *Angli*; no other obv. stops; rare. (ii) As (i) but no mascle after *Franc;* var. has pellets by hair instead of crown. (iii) Mascle after *henric* only; no other obv. stops; *&* omitted.

XI. Lis-Pellet issue (continued under Edward IV). Lis on neck; breast cusp fleured. Pellets by crown, and normally added on rev. *Rex Angli Franc*. With or without mascle after *henric*. Nothing, plain cross or lis before *Posui*. VR.

EDWARD IV, HEAVY COINAGE (1461-4). London only. Types I-IV. *Edward Di Gra Rex Angl & Fran(c)*.

I. Lis-Pellet issue. Lis on neck or breast. Plain initial cross on obv. (except Ia). Pellets by crown; and added in two quarters of rev. Stops saltires or none. Rev. mm. lis, or plain cross, or none. All rare.

Henry IV – Edward IV

Groats

Ia.   Obv. initial cross fleury. Lis on neck; breast cusp fleured.

Ib.   Plain initial cross on obv. Lis on neck. Breast cusp with or without fleur. Var. with mascle after *Franc* reads *Dei* and *Angli*.

Ic.   Plain cross on obv. Lis on breast cusp. *Angl(i)*. Var. (Id) lacks pellets by crown.

Types II, III and IV. Mm. rose (both sides). London only. No pellets by crown or added on rev. Saltire stops or none.

II.   Quatrefoils by bust; crescent on breast cusp. *Fra-Franc*. Var. *Grac*. Occasionally an annulet, pellet or second rose (ER) by obv. mm. Rev. stops only in outer legend. Also rare mules I/II.

III. Quatrefoils by bust and small trefoil on breast cusp (either or both rarely omitted). *Fran-Francie*. Var. *Ang*. Rev. saltire stops in both legends, and usually an eye after *tas* or before or after *Lon*. Vars. pellet and annulet by obv. mm.; trefoil stops on rev. (outer legend only) and no eye. Also rare II/III mules.

IV.   Annulets by bust; with or without fleur on breast cusp. New & with cross-bar. Var. *Angli*. Obv. stops saltires or none, rev. none; eye after *tas*. Rare; also VR mules III/IV and IV/III.

Note: Some dies of types III and IV remained in use after the weight reduction of August 1464 (see type V in next chapter).

HALFGROATS 1412 - 1464

Type as before. Normally nine arc tressure. No fleurs on cusps above crown or on breast unless stated. Gothic *n* throughout.

HENRY IV, LIGHT COINAGE, 1412-3. London only. Saltire stops.

Primary series – class P. Annulet and pellet by crown. Slipped trefoil on breast. *henric D(e)i Gra Rex Angl & F*. Earlier rev. dies read *Adiutorem* in full (variously distributed between the quarters of the cross).

PI.   One (new) obv. die: pellet to left of crown, annulet to right; nine arcs; *Dei*. Var. has *Lon* under *Posui*. ER.

PII. Annulet to left of crown, pellet to right. Tressure of ten arcs. *Di*. ER.

PIII. As PII, but nine arcs. One rev. has saltire instead of initial cross, and slipped trefoil after *don*. VR. See Henry V for added cinquefoil.

Secondary series - classes A and B.

A.   Short, wide ('stunted') lettering. Small initial cross patty with sunk annulet (obv. only). Tall bust with narrow face. Top cusps unfleured. *henric Di Gra Rex Angl & F*. One of the two obv. dies has annulet and pellet by crown. *A/ diuto/re Me(u)*. ER.

B.   Taller lettering. Larger initial cross, plain patty with hollowed centre (usually omitted on rev.). Tall bust, with low crown (as in A). Tressure of ten or eleven arcs (top fleured or unfleured). Also mules with earlier obverses, PIII/B or A/B; all ER. See Henry V for added cinquefoil.

HENRY V, 1413-22. London only. Saltire stops.

PIII* and B* - Henry IV obverses, with cinquefoil added on shoulder (PIII*) or breast (B*). ER.

1412–1464

Halfgroats

C. New tall crown, with five circular hollows on band. *Di Gra Rex Angl(ie) & F*. Broken annulet to left of crown (occasionally omitted). Usually cinquefoil on breast; rarely on sinister shoulder or omitted. Top cusps sometimes fleured. Loosely dotted circles. Rev. readings vary. Quatrefoil after *Posui*, but usually no initial cross on rev. Often saltire after *tas, don*. 'Propeller' pellets.

Ca. Tall neck with central swelling; arched shoulders. Initial cross with pellet centre. Narrow *D*, peaked outside. Tressure of eleven or twelve arcs. Rare; also muled (ER) with Richard II (type II) rev.

Cb. Shorter neck and flatter shoulders. Usually pierced initial cross. Wider *D*, with back peaked both sides. Vars. have broken annulet both sides of crown or neither.

F. As Cb but whole annulet to left of crown, trefoil to right. One obv. die, with eleven arcs (top cusps unfleured). Rare.

G. No extra marks. Pierced initial cross (obv. only). New bust with hollowed neck and armpits. Tressure of eleven arcs. Circular, separated pellets on rev. Quatrefoil after *Posui* continues. Rare.

H. Earliest varieties of the Annulet group (London and Calais) were struck under Henry V.

HENRY VI, 1422-61. London (I-VI, VIII-X), Calais (I-VI only), York (I only). *henric Di Gra Rex Angl & F-Franc*. Mm. cross. Usually nine arc tressure, with top cusps unfleured.

I. Annulet issue (begun under Henry V). Barred *S* for *&*. Annulet after *Posui* (except Id), otherwise saltire stops (usually double saltires after each word in mint name). Annulet between pellets in first and third quarters of rev. (Id, third quarter only).

Ia. (Some = Henry V, class H). Pierced initial cross (obv. only) as under Henry V. *Angl* or *Anglie, F* or *Fr*. Eleven arc tressure; neat bust with short hair. Rev. ends *Me* (VR) or *M*.

Ib. Rounded pierced initial cross, on obv. only.
    Ib1. Eleven arc tressure. *Angl, F* or *Fr*.
    Ib2. Nine arc tressure; fuller hair. *Angl* or *Anglie, F* or *Fr*.

Ic. Plain initial cross, on both sides. Smaller letters. Nine arc tressure (henceforward). *Angl, F* or *Fr*. Rev. ends *Meum* (henceforward).

Id. Annulet-Trefoil issue, Calais only. Plain initial cross both sides. *Angl & F*. Trefoil to left of crown and after *Posui*. Annulet between pellets in *Cal* quarter only. Not found as true coins, but obv. and rev. known separately from mules.

  London (no marks by bust; double or single saltires after *tas* and *don*, or none): Ia, rare; Ib1 (rare), Ib2; Ic (rare), also VR Ic/b mules.

  Calais (annulets by bust; *Vil/la/Cal/is'*): Ia, rare; Ib1 (rare), Ib2; Ic (annulets in rev. quarters rarely omitted), and VR Ic/b mules; Id – rare mules only, Ic/d, Id/c and Id/II.

  York (two lis by neck; *Civi/tas/Ebo/raci*, followed by annulet): Ib1 only, ER.

II. Rosette-Mascle issue. Rosettes after *Posui* and mint-name. Mascle in inner legend (second segment) except on earliest dies. Unbarred *&*. *Angl & F*. Rev. initial cross plain. IIa, obv. initial cross plain. IIb, cross patonce. IIc, cross fleury.

  London: IIa. Obv. stops saltires throughout (those with barred *&* are Ic/II mules). Early revs. lack mascle. Var. *Fran*. Rare.

  IIb and IIc. Mascle after *Rex*; other obv. stops rosettes. Both rare.

Henry IV – Edward IV

Halfgroats

Calais: IIa. Early obv. dies (including rare var. with mascles in two side spandrels) have saltire stops throughout. Later obvs. have mascle after *Gra* or *Rex* and other stops rosettes (or saltires by *&*). Var. *Ang*. Rev. *Cal/is* (early; no mascle), or normally *Cali/sie* (with mascle before *la*). Also Ic/II and Id/II mules.

IIb. Obv. rosette stops, with mascle after *Gra* or *Rex*.

IIc. Obv. rosette stops, usually with mascle after *Rex*. Var. *Anl*.

III. Pinecone-Mascle issue. Mascle after *Rex*, saltires by *&*, other obv. stops cones. Usually *Angl & F*. Rev. initial cross plain, mascle in inner legend, cone after mint name and usually after *Posui*; other rev. stops saltires. IIIa, obv. initial cross patonce, London only. IIIb, obv. cross fleury.

London: IIIa; IIIb (var. *Franc*); both rare. Also VR mules IIIb/II and IIc/III.

Calais (*Cali/sie* henceforward): IIIb only; vars. *Re, Ang, Anl, Fran*. Cone after *Posui* sometimes omitted. Also mules IIIb/I (VR) and II/III (ER).

IV. Leaf-Mascle issue. Leaf in spandrel below bust and usually on circle below *Meum*. Plain initial cross only. Stops mostly saltires. No mark after *Posui*.

London: True coin not recorded; only known from mules with later groups (IV/VIII and Va/IV). Obv. mascle before *Anl; Fran*. Rev. no mascle.

Calais: Without or with mascle after *Rex*; mascle before *la*. VR.

V. 'Leaf-Trefoil' group. No trefoils by neck. Rev. initial cross plain. *A/diutor/e Meum* (as before).

Va. Obv. initial cross plain. Leaf on breast. Tressure of eight (ER) or nine arcs. *henric Di Gra Rex Angl & F*; leaves after first three words. No leaf on rev. or trefoil on either side. True coins, London only, rare; also VR mule Va/IV. Calais, rev. only, on VR IV/Va mule.

Vb. Obv. initial cross fleury. Often a trefoil after *Rex*. *F* or *Fr*. Usually trefoil after *don*; often leaf before *Lon*. London only. (i) Usually no leaf on breast, but leaves after *henric, Di* and *Gra*. (ii) Leaf on breast but not in obv. inscription. Tressure of nine, or seven (VR), arcs.

VI. 'Trefoil' group. London, rev. only (Vb/VI mule; VR): no initial cross; trefoil after *Deum; Adiut/ore M*. Calais, obv. only (VI/IV mule; ER): trefoils by neck; small leaf on breast; plain initial cross; trefoil after *Gra; Anl, Fra*.

Groups VIII-X. Pelleted groups (plus IX unmarked). London only. Pellets each side of crown, and added in two quarters of rev. (above group of large pellets, or on dotted circle). No initial cross on rev.

VIII. Leaf-Pellet issue. Leaf on breast. Pellets by crown and added on rev. Saltire stops, often omitted on rev.

VIIIa. Initial cross fleury. *Angli & Fran*. One obv. die only, VR.

VIIIb. Plain initial cross. *Angl & F* (var. omits pellets by crown) or *Angli & Fran(c)*. No stops on rev. Rare; also VR mules IV/VIII, VIIIb (omits breast leaf)/Vb and Vb/VIII.

IX. Unmarked type. One obv. die only (ER), with initial cross fleury. No breastmark, pellets by crown, or obv. stops. *Angli Franc &*. Extra pellets in two quarters; saltire before *Meum*.

Xb. Cross-Pellet issue. Saltire on neck, pellets by crown and added on rev. Plain initial cross. Mullet after *henric* and before *Meum*; no other stops. *Angli Franc*. VR; also ER mule IX/X.

XI. Lis-Pellet issue. No Henry halfgroat known; see below, Edward IV, type I.

EDWARD IV, HEAVY COINAGE (1461-4). London only. Types I-IV. *Edward Di Gra Rex Angl & Fra-Franc*.

1412–1464

Halfgroats

I. Lis-Pellet issue. Lis on breast cusp. Pellets by crown; and added in two quarters of rev. Saltire stops (or on rev. none). Initial cross (obv. only): Ia, fleury (*Fran*); Ib, plain (*Fra*). Both ER.

Types II-IV. Mm. rose (usually on both sides). No pellets by crown or added on rev. Saltire stops or none.

II. Quatrefoils by bust; crescent below bust. *Franc*. No eye on rev. ER.
III. Quatrefoils by bust; fleur or trefoil, or nothing, on or below breast. *Fran(c)*. Eye after *tas*. Also III/II (var. omits quatrefoils, breastmark and rev. mm. rose) and II/III mules; all ER.
IV. Annulets by bust; no breastmark. *Fra(n)*. Colon, saltires, eye or nothing after *tas*. ER.

PENNIES 1412 - 1464

Type as before. Gothic *n* (except on rev. of Henry IV, class PII-III). No initial cross on rev. unless stated.

HENRY IV, LIGHT COINAGE, 1412-3. Usually saltire stops.
    Primary series – class P. London, Durham, York.
London: Annulet and pellet by crown; slipped trefoil on breast.
PI. Pellet to left of crown, filled annulet to right. Rounded lettering, *henric Rex Anglie* (altered die of Richard II?). Gothic *n* both sides. Pellets coalesced. ER.
PII. Annulet to left, pellet to right of crown. Large bust with long face. *Rex Anglie* or *Di Gra Rex Angl*. Roman *N* on rev. (unbarred or reversed). ER.
PIII. Annulet and pellet as PII. Small bust, short hair. *Rex Anglie*. Slipped trefoil before *Civi* or after *tas*; reversed Roman *N* on rev. Also PII/III mule; all ER. See Henry V for two dies with cinquefoil, muled with later rev.
Durham (Bishop Langley): no marks by crown, slipped trefoil on breast; *henricus Rex Anglie*; tall bust. *Civi/tas/Dun/olm'* (with Gothic *n*), saltire or pellet stops, or none; pellets tightly grouped. VR.
York, pellet in quatrefoil on reverse cross (Archbishop Bowet): *henric Rex Anglie*. Annulet on breast and after *henric*. No marks by crown. *Civi/tas/Ebo/raci*; double annulets usually before each word. Tight pellets. Rare.
    Secondary series – class A (London) only. No pence of class B without cinquefoil are recorded.
A. Short, wide ('stunted') lettering. Initial cross patty with sunk annulet. Annulet to left, pellet to right of crown. Large ('emaciated') bust without neck (Aa), or taller bust with neck (Ab). *henric Di Gra Rex Ang(l)*. Annulet before *Lon*. Pellets tightly grouped. ER. See Henry V for Ab* die with cinquefoil.

HENRY V, 1413-22. London, Durham (Bp. Langley), York (quatrefoil on rev. cross for Abp. Bowet); plus Calais, class H only.
B*. Tall lettering. Initial cross with hollowed centre. Annulet and cinquefoil by crown. Large inner circles.
    London: U-shaped face; crown as class A. Annulet to left, cinquefoil to right. *Rex Angl & Franc* or *Di Gra Rex Ang & F*. Also mules PIII*/B and Ab*/B; all VR.
    York: Cinquefoil (left) and annulet by low crown; local dies. VR.
Classes of Henry V pence as defined by Brooke (1932):

Henry IV – Edward IV

Pennies

- C. Cinquefoil (left) and broken annulet (right) by crown. London, Durham, York.
- D. Cinquefoil and whole annulet by crown or hair. London, Durham, York.
- E. As D, but with pellet above cinquefoil. York only.
- F. Cinquefoil and trefoil by crown. London, York.
- G. New portrait. No marks in field at London.

Classification by types of bust etc. is as follows:

1. Large bust, with clear neck and (often rounded) shoulders. Tall crown with prominent hollows on band. Neatly dotted circles of c.12.5 cm. diameter. Fuller obv. readings. Includes classes C (mostly) and D.
2. Smaller dies, with loosely toothed circles of c. 11.5 cm. or less. Head set low, with little neck or shoulders; crown as in type 1. French title usually reduced to *F*. Includes classes C to F; none of Durham.
3. Fine bust, with hollowed neck and armpits. Neat circles resumed. Includes classes D (Durham), F (York) and G (London).

London: Type 1 (C and D). *henric Rex Angl & Fran(c)* or (rarely) *henricus Rex Anglie*. Double saltires after *tas* and *don*. Some have propeller pellets.

Type 2 (C and D). *Rex Angl(ie) & F*. Quatrefoil after *tas* and saltires after *don*, or annulets at both.

Type 2 (F). Cinquefoil (left) and trefoil (right) by crown. *Rex Angl(ie) & F* or (rarely) *Di Gra Rex Angl & F*. No stops on rev.

Type 3 (G). *Di Gra Rex Angl*. Rare.

Durham (*Dun/olm*): Type 1 (C and D). *henricus Rex Anglie*, followed by quatrefoil; or *henric Rex Angl & Fran* (without quatrefoil). Quatrefoil after *tas* and *olm*. Also ER mule with P* obv. die previously used at London.

3 (D). *henricus Rex Anglie*. Annulet in pellets below *Civi*; saltires after *tas* and *olm*. Rare.

York: There is much variation among the York coins from local dies and they often do not conform to the norm for London-made dies as recorded here.

Type 1 (C and D). *henric(us) Rex Angl-Anglie & Fra*. Often a quatrefoil or saltire after *tas*. London or local dies.

Type 2 (C and D). *Anglie & F*. Some have double annulets after *tas*. London or local dies.

Type 2 (E). As 2(D), but pellet added. *Ebo/rac*. London dies only. Rare.

Type 2 (F). *Anglie & F*. (a) Trefoil above cinquefoil to left of crown, annulet to right; or (b) cinquefoil left and trefoil right. London or local dies.

Type 3 (F). Cinquefoil and trefoil as type 2(F)(b). *henricus Rex Anglie*. Mostly local dies. Usually annulet within pellets below *Civi*.

For local dies with cinquefoil to left and lis to right of crown, see under Henry VI.

- H. Some early varieties of the Annulet issue (London and Calais) were struck under Henry V.

HENRY VI, 1422-61. ROYAL MINTS: London (I-V, VIII, X), Calais (I-V), York (I only); plus Dublin (I only, 1426). See separate listing for episcopal mints. *henricus Rex Anglie*. Mm. cross (normally on obv. only).

- I. Annulet issue (begun by Henry V). Annulet between pellets in first and third quarters of rev. (Id, third quarter only). Saltire stops.
- Ia (Some = Henry V, class H). Pierced initial cross as under Henry V.
- Ib. Rounded pierced cross.

1412–1464

Pennies

Ic. Plain initial cross.

Id. Annulet-Trefoil issue, Calais only. Trefoil to left of crown. Annulet in *Cal* quarter only.

London (no marks by bust; double or single saltires after *tas* and *don*, or none): Ia, rare; Ib; Ic.

Calais (annulets by bust; *Vil/la/Cal/is'*, with double saltire stops): Ia, rare; Ib; Ic (ER var. without annulets on obv., London die); Id, and mules Ic/d, Id/c, all VR.

York (lis by bust; *Civi/tas/Ebo/raci*, followed by annulet): Ib only, ER.

Dublin, star to right of bust; *henricus Dns hibnie*; mm. plain cross (Ic). Rev. *Civi/tas/Dubl/inie*. Annulet after *hibnie* and *Civi*, but no annulets between pellets. ER.

II. Rosette-Mascle issue. Usually rosette before and mascle after *Rex*, otherwise double saltire stops on obv. *Anglie*. IIa, Obv. initial cross plain. IIb, Cross patonce (Calais only). IIc, Cross fleury.

London: IIa (regarded by Whitton as Ic/II mules) and IIc, both VR. Usually mascle before *Lon* and rosette after *don*.

Calais (*Cal/is* early; normally *Cali/sie*): IIa, IIb and IIc. Usually mascle before *la* (except on *Calis* dies) and rosette after mint name. IIa, early obv. var. has double saltire stops only; also VR mules Ic/II and Id/II. IIb, vars. omit *I*, *n* or *V* from *henricus*. IIc, var. omits rev. rosette.

See also Durham and York.

III. Pinecone-Mascle issue. Pinecone before and mascle after *Rex*. Obv. initial cross fleury only. *Anglie*, later *Angl*.

London: Mascle before *Lon* and cone after *don*, or no marks. Also VR mules IIc/III and III/II.

Calais (*Cali/sie* henceforward): Mascle before *la*, cone after *sie*. Var. *henrcus*. Some have (plain) initial cross on rev. Also VR mules IIc/III and III/II.

See also Durham and York.

IV. Leaf-Mascle issue. Leaf on breast; mascle in obv. legend. *Angl. I* with serrated serifs. IVa, Initial cross voided (London only). IVb, Plain initial cross.

London: Mascle before *Rex;* rev. no leaf or mascle. IVa, ER; IVb, rare; IVb/III (plain *I* on rev.), ER.

Calais: IVb only. Mascle after *Rex* and before *la;* leaf below *sie*. Rare.

V. 'Leaf-Trefoil' group. Leaf on breast. Leaf or trefoil in obv. legend (other stops saltires). London, Calais (Va only).

Va. Plain initial cross (obv. only).

London: *henricus Rex Angli*, with leaf before *Rex*, and leaf or not after *Angli*. No symbols on rev. VR.

Calais: *henric* trefoil *Rex Angl & F*. Trefoil after *la*. ER.

Vb. London sole royal mint (see also Durham). Obv. initial cross fleury, rev. plain. *henricus Rex* trefoil *Angl'*. Trefoil after *don*, and usually leaf before *Lon*. Rare; also VR mules IVb/Vb and Vb/Va.

Groups VIII and X. Pelleted groups (Leaf-Pellet and Cross-Pellet). London sole royal mint; see also Durham and York. Pellets each side of crown, and added in two quarters of rev. (either above group of larger pellets, or on line of dotted circle). Obv. initial cross fleury. *henric Rex Angl(i)*.

VIII. Leaf on breast. (i) Trefoil after *henric*, saltire before *Angl*. VR. (ii) No trefoil. Saltire stops (rarely on rev.). *Angli* or *Anglii*. Some have saltire after the *n* of *henric* or *Angli*. Vars. omit pellets by crown, or extra pellets on rev. Rare.

Henry IV – Edward IV

Pennies

X. Saltire on neck. Mullet and/or mascle(s) in obv. legend. *henric(us)*. VR.

HENRY VI, 1422-61. ECCLESIASTICAL MINTS: Durham (II, III, V, VIII, X) and York (I, II, III, VIII, X).

DURHAM, for bishops Langley, Neville and L. Booth.
   Bishop Thomas Langley (1406-37)
IIa. Rosette-Mascle issue. Langley's star to left of crown. Initial cross plain. *Duno/lmi* (or *'Dund'* with *O* over *L*). No rosettes; mascles after *Rex* and *lmi. Anglie*. Rare.
IIIb. Pinecone-Mascle issue. Initial cross fleury. Cone after *henricus*, mascles after *Rex* and *lmi*. No marks in field. *Angl*.
   Bishop Robert Neville (1438-57). Two interlinked rings on centre of reverse cross. Obv. initial cross fleury throughout; none on rev.
Vb. 'Leaf-Trefoil' issue. Leaf on breast. *henricus Rex* leaf *Angli*. No marks in rev. legend; *Dun/olm*. Rare.
VIII. Leaf-Pellet issue. Leaf on breast, pellets by crown. Saltire stops. *Angli. Dun/olm* or *elm*. (i) Trefoil after *henric*. VR. (ii) No trefoil; saltire after *hen*. Rare; also VR mules with (local) rev. *Dun/olin* (see Edward IV).
   Bishop Laurence Booth (1457-76)
X. Cross-Pellet issue. Pellets by crown. Saltire and *B* by neck (saltire occasionally omitted). Saltire stops (and after *n* of *henric*). *Angli*. Interlinked rings on centre of rev. (as for Neville); some with groups of three pellets linked by stalks. *Dun/olm*. Rare.

YORK (normally pellet in quatrefoil in centre of rev.), for archbishops Bowet, Kemp and W. Booth.
   Archbishop Henry Bowet (1407-23)
I. Annulet issue. As Henry V, type 3, with annulet within pellets below *Civi*, but with cinquefoil to left of crown and lis to right. Local dies. Possibly continued after Bowet's death.
   Archbishop John Kemp (1425-52)
II. Rosette-Mascle issue. Initial cross fleury henceforward. *henricus Rex Anglie*. Mascle after *Rex* and usually before *tas*. Many from local dies. A, Crosses by hair, no rosettes; *Ebd/raci*. B, Saltires by hair, no rosettes; *Ebo*, or *Ebd* (B/A mule?). C, Stars by crown; rosette or star before *Rex;* mascle, with or without rosette, or neither, on rev.
III. Pinecone-Mascle issue. Mascle(s), cone, or no marks in rev. inscription. Cone before and mascle after *Rex. Angl*. Mostly from local dies. A, Stars by crown; quatrefoil on rev.; rare. B, No marks by crown; no quatrefoil on rev.; star or rosette on breast.
   Archbishop William Booth (1452-64)
VIII. Leaf-Pellet issue. Leaf on breast. Pellets by crown, and usually added in one or two quarters of rev. *henric Rex Angli*. Saltire stops (and sometimes after *n* of *henric* or *Angli*).
VIIIa. Two pellets by crown only. Leaf on breast occasionally omitted. Vars. read *Anglie* or *Anglii* (sometimes with leaf between *II*).
VIIIb. Two pellets by crown and two by hair (cf. VIIId groat). VR.
X. Cross-Pellet issue. With or without leaf on breast. Saltires by neck. Pellets by crown and added in two quarters of rev. Saltire stops (and sometimes after *n* of *henric*). Rare.

Pennies

Edward IV, Heavy Coinage (1461-4).
London:
Ib. Lis-Pellet issue. Lis on neck. Pellets by crown, and added in two quarters of rev. *Edwar'*, or *Edwad', Rex* mascle *Angl' & Fra*. Plain initial cross (obv. only). ER.
Types II-IV. Mm. rose (obv. only). No breastmark. *Edward Di Gra Rex Angl*. No pellets by crown or added on rev.
II. Quatrefoils by bust. *Angl &*. Pellet stops on obv. Also II/I mule; all ER.
III. Quatrefoils by bust. Saltire stops on obv. Eye after *tas* or before *Lon*. Also III/II mule; all ER.
IV. Annulets by bust. Saltire before *Di*. ER.
Durham: Bp. Laurence Booth (suspended 1462-4). From local dies, and often of light weight. Plain initial cross. *Edward Rex Ang-Anglie*; *e* often reversed; var. *Edwar Di Rex*. Some have pellets by crown. Stops saltires, pellets or, more rarely, quatrefoils or stars. Rev. *Dun* or *Don/ol-olin*, sometimes followed by trefoil or quatrefoil; (i) no extra marks, (ii) rose on centre of cross, (iii) rose on cross and extra pellet in one quarter. Also VR mules with revs. of Booth type (i) and an obverse die of Neville (Henry VI, group VIII).
York: Abp. William Booth (d. Sept. 1464).
III. Mm. rose. Quatrefoils by bust. *Edward Di Gra Rex Angl*. Saltire stops or none. Var. has eye after *tas*. (a) Quatrefoil on rev. for Booth. VR. (b) No rev. quatrefoil (possibly *sede vacante* 1464/5?). ER.

HALFPENCE 1412 - 1464

Type as before. Gothic *n*. No initial cross on rev.

Henry IV, Light Coinage 1412-3. London only. Mostly saltire stops on obv. *henric Rex Angl*.
  Primary series – class P. Elegant lettering (as late heavy coinage D2). Neat circles.
Pa. Tall bust, with hunched shoulders (as heavy coinage class 2). Annulets by neck. VR.
Pb. Smaller bust with little body. Annulets by hair or crown. Var. has Roman *N* in *Lon;* another has pellet stops. VR.
  Secondary series - classes A and B.
A. Stunted letters. Annulets by crown. Bust low set or taller. Initial cross patty with sunk annulet centre. VR.
B. Taller lettering; *n* with broken tail on some. Annulets by crown, or none. Initial cross pierced with pellet centre. Tall neat bust, with shaped body. Propeller pellets. Rare.

Henry V, 1413-22. London only. *henric Rex Angl*. Pierced initial cross. Saltire stops on obv. and sometimes on rev. Loosely dotted circles.
Pb*. Henry IV obv. die with cinquefoil over annulet to right of crown. ER.
C. Broken annulets (or nicked pellets) by crown, hair or (rarely) neck.
D. As C, but one or both annulets unbroken.
E. Whole annulets by crown, and pellet above crown to left. Var. *Anglie F*. VR.
F. Annulet to left, trefoil to right of hair, or *vice versa*.

Henry IV – Edward IV

Halfpence

G. No marks by bust (which lacks line across bottom). Only recorded from so-called G/Annulet or Annulet/G mules. Rare.

HENRY VI, 1422-61. London (I-VI, VIII, X), Calais (I-V), York (I only). *henric Rex Angl* (rarely *Ang, Angli*). Mm. cross (obv. only).

I. Annulet issue (begun under Henry V). Annulet between pellets in first and third quarters of rev. Saltire stops (single or double). Contraction marks after *henric* and *Angl*. Ia (some = Henry V, class H). Pierced initial cross as under Henry V. Line below bust. Ib, Rounded pierced cross. Ic, Plain initial cross.

London (no marks by bust; no saltires on rev.): Ia, includes F/Annulet (ER), Annulet/G and G/Annulet mules, all rare; Ib; Ic.

Calais (annulets by bust; *Vil/la/Cal/is'*, with double saltire stops): Ia, rare; Ib, rare; Ic.

York (two lis by bust; *Civi/tas/Ebo/raci*, no rev. stops): Ib only, ER.

II. Rosette-Mascle issue. Usually rosettes and mascles in legends, other obv. stops saltires. IIa, Plain initial cross. IIb, Cross patonce (Calais only). IIc, Cross fleury.

London: IIa, *henric*; mascle before or after *Rex*, or none; rosette before *Rex* and after *don*, or none; early coins have no rosette or mascle (those with *henric'* may be Ic/II mules). IIc, *henric*; normally rosette before *Rex*, and sometimes before or after *Lon*, after *don*, or none; mascle normally after *Rex*, and sometimes before *tas* or *Lon*, or none; var. *henrc*.

Calais: Normally rosette before, mascle after *Rex* (ER var. without either may be London/Calais mule). IIa, *Cal/is* or (rarely) *Cali/sie*; rosette after mint name, or (rarely) before *la*; mascle before *la* or (rarely) *Vil*, or after mint name; vars. *henic, Ang*; also mule Ic/II. IIb, *Cal/is*; mascle before *la*, rosette after *is*; var. *henic*; rare. IIc, *Cal/is;* var. lacks rosette before *Rex*; also VR mule IIc/I.

III. Pinecone-Mascle issue. Usually cone and mascle in obv. legend, and sometimes either or both on rev.

London: IIIa, initial cross patonce; *henricus*; var. has mascles before and after *Rex*; sometimes mascle before *Lon*, cone after *don*; rare, also VR mule IIc/III. IIIb, initial cross fleury; *henric(us)* (var. *Rx*); sometimes mascle before *tas* or *Lon* and cone after *don*. IIIc, plain initial cross, *henric*; VR.

Calais (*Cal/is* or *Cali/sie*): IIIb only, initial cross fleury; *henric(us)*; mascle before *la* and cone after mint name; also rare mules II/III and VR mules Ic/III, III/I and III/II.

IV. Leaf-Mascle issue. Leaf on breast and on rev. inner circle. Plain initial cross. *henric Rex Angl(i)*. Obv. stops saltires with or without mascle.

London: Mascle before or after *Rex*, or none. Leaf below *s* of *tas* or *n* of *Lon*. Var. *henricu*. VR; also ER mule II (no leaf on breast)/IV.

Calais (*Cali/sie*): No mascle on obv., but on rev. before *la*. Leaf under *sie*. VR; also ER mules both ways with III.

V. 'Leaf-Trefoil' group. Plain initial cross (obv. only). Letter *n* with broken tail. Saltire stops.

London: Leaf on breast (occasionally omitted). Often leaf or trefoil after *henric* or *Angl*. Vars. *heric; Re; Angli*. No marks on rev. Some read *Sivi*.

Calais (*Cal/isie*): Leaf on breast. Trefoil after *henric* and *Villa*. Piedfort of true coin, and V/IV mule, both ER. Last type of this mint.

1412–1464

Halfpence

VI. 'Trefoil' group. London only (henceforward). Leaf on breast and trefoils by neck. Saltire stops, with trefoil after *Rex* or *Angl*, or none (*Angli*). Initial cross plain; or (VR) fleury (with *henrc*). Rev. vars. *Sivi* (VI/V) or with extra pellets under *tas* and *don* (VI/VIII) may be mules. All rare.

VIII. Leaf-Pellet issue. Leaf on breast. Pellets by crown, and extra pellets added in two quarters of rev. (sometimes omitted). *henric Rex Angli*. Saltire stops or none.

VIIIa. Initial cross fleury. Often a saltire after *n* of *henric*. Some have Roman *N* in *Angli*. Var. has pellets added in all four quarters.

VIIIb. Plain initial cross. VR.

X. Cross-Pellet issue. Usually pellets by crown; extra pellets in two quarters of rev. (sometimes omitted). *Angli*. Saltire stops or none. All rare.

Xa. Initial cross fleury. Saltire each side of neck. Leaf on breast; VR var. omits pellets by crown. Some have saltire after *hen*.

Xb. Plain initial cross. Saltire on neck. No leaf on breast. Some have mullet after *henric*.

EDWARD IV, HEAVY COINAGE (1461-4). London only.

I. Lis-Pellet issue. Lis on neck. Pellets by crown, and usually added in two quarters of rev. Plain initial cross. *Edward Rex A(n)g*; no stops. VR.

Types II-IV. Obv. mm. rose. No pellets by crown or added on rev.

II. Quatrefoils or saltires by bust. *Edward Di Gra(c) Re(x)(A)*. Stops pellets, saltires or none. Var. (VR) has eye after *tas*.

III. No marks by bust. *Rex Angli(e)* or *Di Gra Rex*. No stops. Rare.

IV. Annulets by bust. *Rex Angli(e)* or *Di Gra Rex*. No stops, or rarely pellets or saltires. Rare.

FARTHINGS 1412 - 1464

Type as before. Gothic *n*. No initial cross on rev.

HENRY IV, LIGHT COINAGE, 1412-3. London only. All ER. Class P: Long face, no bust. *henric Rex Angl;* slipped trefoil after *Rex*. *I* for *n* (or *N*?) on rev. (*Loi/doi*). Class B (?): Broader face and taller crown (cf. some B and C nobles); *Angli*.

HENRY V, 1413-22. London only. Small pointed face with thin neck. *henric Rex Angl-Anglie*. Stops saltires, or rarely pellets. Loosely beaded or corded circles. No special marks. VR.

HENRY VI, 1422-61. London (I-VI, VIII, X), Calais (*Villa Calis;* I-III only), York (I only). *henric Rex Angl(i)*. Mm. cross (obv. only).

I. Annulet issue (begun under Henry V). Mm. cross pommy. No annulet between rev. pellets. Normally saltire stops, rarely pellets.

   London: No marks by bust; *Angl(i)*; no stops on rev. Neat dotted circles. ER.

   Calais: Early type – No annulets by (Henry V style) bust; annulet stops on obv.; colons after *la* and *is*; ER. Normal type – Annulets by (fuller) bust; *Angl;* stops after each word on rev. VR.

   York: Two lis by bust; *Angl; Civi/tas/Ebo/raci*, no rev. stops. ER.

Henry IV – Edward IV

Farthings

II. Rosette-Mascle issue.
   London: Initial cross fleury or pommy (?). Rosette and mascle by *Rex;* rosette over *n* of *don* on one die. ER.
   Calais: Initial cross pommy. Rosette and mascle by *Rex* (or none), and on rev. VR.
III. Pinecone-Mascle issue. Cone and mascle by *Rex*.
   London: Plain initial cross. With or without cone on rev. Var. *tor* for *tas*. VR.
   Calais: Initial cross pommy. Mascle and cone on rev. ER. Last known type of Calais.
IV. Leaf-Mascle issue. London only henceforward. Plain initial cross. Leaf on breast (and after *Civi*?). ER.
V. 'Leaf-Trefoil' group. Plain initial cross. Trefoil before *Rex*. Leaf on breast (or omitted?). No marks on rev. Var. *tos*. VR.
VI. 'Trefoil' group. Leaf on breast and trefoils by neck. ER.
VIII. Leaf-Pellet issue. Leaf on breast. Pellets by crown, and usually added on circle in two rev. quarters. Plain initial cross. *henric Rex Angli* (var. *henrc*). Stops saltires or none. Rare.
X Cross-Pellet issue. As VIII but saltire instead of leaf; and pellets by crown sometimes omitted. VR.

EDWARD IV, HEAVY COINAGE (1461-4). London only.
I. Lis-Pellet issue. With or without lis on neck. Pellets by crown; with or without pellets added in two quarters of rev. *Edward R(ex) Angli*; no stops. ER.
II. Mintmark rose. Saltires by bust. No extra pellets. *Edward Di Gra Rex( )*. ER.
III. As II but no marks by bust. *Di Gra Rex (A)*. VR; also ER mule (omitting *Rex*) with type I rev. (extra pellets).

CHAPTER VII

1464 - 1526
Edward IV – Henry VIII

The later years of the fifteenth century and the first quarter of the sixteenth saw profound changes – political, economic and cultural – all of which were in some degree reflected in the English coinage of the period. By the 1520s England, like its continental neighbours, had largely completed the transition from the medieval to the early modern world. While the main concern of the crown in the 1460s had been with the internal struggle for power, within two generations Edward IV's Tudor grandson Henry VIII was to inherit a stronger and richer realm, and could aspire to exercise once again the kind of influence in European affairs that the Plantagenet kings, and his great ancestor Henry V, had once enjoyed.

Such an outcome could hardly have been predicted in the middle of the Wars of the Roses. By 1464 Richard Neville, Earl of Warwick, had crushed Lancastrian resistance in the north and Edward's tenure of the throne appeared more secure. But Edward's clandestine marriage in May 1464 to Elizabeth Wodeville, whose family was insufficiently illustrious to be acceptable to the senior nobility, and the subsequent elevation of members of her family to prominent positions, contributed to a breakdown of relations with Warwick who in due course defected to the Lancastrian cause. In September 1470 Warwick arrived from France, Edward fled to Burgundy, and Henry VI was released from the Tower to regain a nominal crown. But in March 1471 Edward returned, with his brother Richard of Gloucester; Warwick was killed at the battle of Barnet in April; and in May the defiant Queen Margaret with the remnants of Lancastrian support was defeated at Tewkesbury, where her son, Prince Edward the last undoubtedly legitimate male heir of the House of Lancaster, fell in the field. With the murder of Henry VI shortly afterwards Edward was left in undisputed possession of the kingdom. In 1469 an economic agreement had been proposed with Charles the Bold, Duke of Burgundy, who had married Edward's sister in 1468; and in 1475 they arranged a joint invasion of France. Edward was, however, disappointed by Burgundy's contribution and Louis XI managed to buy him off with a payment of 75,000 crowns and an annuity of 50,000 crowns thereafter. This agreement was repudiated by Louis in 1482, but Edward died suddenly in April 1483 before he could retaliate. His second reign had been one of greater security for his own position, and increasing prosperity for his kingdom.

The premature death of Edward IV set off a train of events whereby, within three years, England passed from a seemingly well established Yorkist dynasty into the control of another king of Lancastrian descent. Edward's elder son was only twelve years old when his father died. Richard of Gloucester moved quickly to advance his position, confining the new king Edward V and his younger brother Richard Duke of York to the Tower, arresting the Wodevilles, and having himself declared Protector early in May. Gloucester was ruthless with anyone who stood in his way. Lord Hastings, Edward IV's Lord Chamberlain and probably the most influential and independent councillor of his later years, was arrested and summarily executed, without trial, on 13 June. Gloucester's supporters then argued that his brother's marriage had been invalid on the ground that at the time of Edward's wedding to Elizabeth Wodeville he was already precontracted to marry Lady Eleanor Butler, and that their children should therefore be regarded as illegitimate. On 26 June Richard claimed the throne for himself, and before long his nephews were said to have been murdered in the Tower. Thus began a troubled reign of twenty-six months during which Richard was never able to gain general acceptance as legitimate ruler.

Edward IV – Henry VIII

The death of Richard III on the battlefield of Bosworth in August 1485, defeated by the supporters of Henry Tudor, ended the rule of the House of York, although Yorkist support continued in Ireland and the north, and Henry VII, as he now was, had to deal with insurrection, conspiracies and impostors for several years. Henry's father was the son of Henry V's widow Katherine of Valois; but his claim to the throne came through his mother Margaret Beaufort, grand-daughter of John Beaufort, who was the eldest of the sons of John of Gaunt, by his mistress Catherine Swinford, and so half-brother to Henry IV. By marriage to Edward IV's eldest daughter Elizabeth in 1486, Henry VII at last united the Red Rose with the White, a union symbolised by the double rose of the Tudors. One of the ways in which Henry sought to strengthen the position of the crown was to reduce its dependence upon parliamentary taxes by efficient exploitation of other sources of income. In the 1470s Edward IV had encouraged trade, which as well as bringing greater general prosperity produced more receipts from customs for the crown. This policy Henry continued, preferring to conclude commercial treaties than to pursue a foreign policy based on costly war. His only military venture overseas was an expedition in 1492 when he successfully laid siege to Boulogne, resulting in the Peace of Etaples and a large indemnity from the French king. Edward had also enlarged the crown's income from its landed estates by better management, entrusting their supervision to expert administrators among the men of his household, and so largely freeing this revenue from the cumbersome control of the Exchequer. Adopting and building upon his predecessor's policy here, and assisted by his Chancellor Archbishop Morton, Henry energetically exploited all the available sources of royal revenue, enforcing fees, fines, benevolences and other dues with relentless efficiency. By these means the austere Henry VII amassed a fortune greater than that bequeathed by any previous English king to his successor.

When Henry VII died in 1509, his son's claim to the throne, through both the Lancastrian and the Yorkist lines, was undisputed. Henry VIII, who succeeded shortly before his eighteenth birthday, had more lavish tastes and, for the time being, the resources to indulge them. Determined not to be outshone by the rulers of Europe he quickly involved himself in their affairs. In June 1509 he married Katherine of Aragon, widow of his elder brother Arthur, thus becoming son-in-law to Ferdinand of Spain, whose grandson, the future Charles V, was heir not only to the Spanish kingdoms but also to the vast Hapsburg inheritance of his other grandfather, the Emperor Maximilian. Anxious for glory, and encouraged by Ferdinand to enter into alliance against France, Henry mounted a campaign in 1513 which culminated in the capture of Tournai, while the Scots, faithful to their French alliance, suffered a devastating defeat at Flodden and the death of their king James IV. In 1502 James had married Henry's sister Margaret, whose Tudor blood was, by the twist of fortune, to see their great-grandson, another Scottish king James, onto the throne of England a century later.

From 1515 English foreign policy was led by Cardinal Wolsey, formerly royal chaplain to Henry VII and now Lord Chancellor and Archbishop of York. Disappointed by the lack of support from Ferdinand and Maximilian, Henry VIII was ready to agree to Wolsey's plan to turn France into an ally. But after a few years the old ambition to recover former English territories in France resurfaced, and Henry embarked on further campaigns, with little success. Money was needed, but Parliament was reluctant. Taxes imposed in 1523 had to be withdrawn in 1524, and Henry's financial position began to pose serious constraint on his ambitions. Gold and silver, increasingly needed for economic expansion, were fetching higher prices at continental mints, and it was not long before reform of the coinage had once again to figure among the remedies. In 1526 Wolsey was given authority to align the values of English coins with those from the

Continent, which he did by uprating existing English gold coins, introducing new ones and reducing the weights of the silver.

The second half of the fifteenth century and the early years of the sixteenth brought major changes in the coinages of western Christendom. Newly discovered silver mines in the Tyrol, and later in Saxony and Bohemia, added greatly to the amount of coin in circulation, while gold from Guinea was increasingly diverted from Italy by Portuguese maritime adventurers. Both these factors contributed to the introduction of larger silver coins, at first in Italy but soon also northwards, providing a new vehicle for realistic personal portraiture in the Classical tradition as had been developed by the medallists of the Italian Renaissance. These changes gradually spread through northern Europe, although they reached England relatively slowly. Not until 1504 did Henry VII become the first English king to commission a true portrait for his coinage, ahead of Louis XII in France, but long after James III of Scotland, a ruler of artistic tastes whose coin portraits are among the earliest and were already in circulation before Henry's accession.

After more than a century of sameness in the structure and appearance of the English coinage, the fifty years following Edward IV's monetary reform of 1464/5 were to see the addition of new and larger denominations as well as fundamental changes in design. Little more than three years after he had first replaced Henry VI on the throne, and evidently as soon as he felt that his hold upon it was reasonably secure, Edward had introduced the largest single adjustment that had ever yet been made to the valuation of the English currency. By increasing the amount of money coined from a pound of silver from 30s. to 37s. 6d. in 1464 he reduced the weight of the penny from 15 gr. to 12 gr., and while the weight of the noble remained unchanged its value was increased to 8s. 4d., raising the product of a pound of gold from £16 13s. 4d. to £20 16s. 8d. By these means the face value of both metals was raised by 25 per cent, leaving the ratio of gold to silver at 11.1:1, the same as it had been since 1412. The indenture of August 1464 with Lord Hastings, as master of the mint, provided for deductions of 50s. per pound for gold and 4s. 6d. per pound for silver, for minting charges and seignorage, giving mint prices of £18 6s. 8d. instead of £16 7s. 6d. for gold and 33s. instead of 28s. 10d. for silver. Since the 1450s there had been a moderate but steady flow of silver to the Tower mint at the old price, and the revised tariff, as well as attracting new silver, provided a powerful incentive for the recoinage of old groats of 60 gr., most of which still weighed more than enough to yield a good profit even after the substantial increase in seignorage. As on previous occasions of recoinage, extra royal mints were commissioned to assist.

Because the gold:silver ratio was to remain unchanged, the 8s. 4d. noble had no more chance of success than its 6s. 8d. predecessor, and it soon became apparent that a further move was needed if gold as well as silver was to be attracted to the mint. The chosen course, set out in a new indenture of March 1465, was to increase the face value of a pound of coined gold to £22 10s., but to raise the mint price by substantially more, from £18 6s. 8d. to £21 9s. 2d. The cost to the king was a reduction in his profit from 47s. 8d. to 18s. 6d. a pound, but since the previous tariff had brought no bullion to the mint the loss was purely theoretical. In order to implement this new structure the weight of the noble, now restored to its traditional value of 6s. 8d., was reduced from 112 gr. to 80 gr. (and its design changed), and a 'new noble', at the pre-1412 weight of 120 gr. but now valued at 10s., was added, together with its half and quarter.

There followed the usual pattern after a recoinage of progressive increases in the mint prices for bullion, by the lowering of charges, in order to maintain a supply of gold and silver to be coined. From Michaelmas 1466 mint charges on silver were reduced to 3s. 2d. per lb and a year later to 2s. 8d., giving a mint price of 34s. 10d., 1s. 10d. higher than

Edward IV – Henry VIII

at the outset. From October 1470, under Henry VI, the price was raised to 35s. 6d., again at the expense of the king's profit, and from Edward's return in 1471 the total charges were reduced to 1s. 6d. with 1s. for mintage and only 6d. for the king. This tariff, with silver now priced by the mint at 36s. per lb., remained unchanged until 1492 when Henry VII, not renowned for needless generosity, raised the price to 36s. 6d. by reducing the master's charge to 10d. and his own to 2d. Apart from a temporary reduction in the weight of halfgroats early in the 1490s, no further amendment was then made for thirty years. From June 1522 until October 1523 the amount of coin to be struck from a pound of silver was temporarily increased from 37s. 6d. to 39s. 6d. (reducing the weight of the penny to 11.39gr.) and since all of the increase was to be passed on to the merchant this had the effect of raising the mint price to 38s. 6d. Comparable reductions in charges and increased mint prices applied to gold, although without the experiment of 1522/3. The price was raised to £21 15s. 6d. per lb. in 1467, to £21 19s. 6d. in 1470 and to £22 2s. 6d. in 1471, by progressive erosion of the seignorage from 18s. 6d. in 1465 to 5s. in 1471. Mintage remained at 2s. 6d. per lb. until 1492 when it was cut to 1s. 10d., and with seignorage down to 8d. the mint price was raised by 5s. to £22 7s. 6d., where it remained until 1526.

These tariffs are recorded in the mint accounts as well as in the periodic indentures between king and master-worker. Hastings, who held this office from 1464/5, was reappointed, with revised charges, in 1469. No indenture is extant for Henry VI's restoration but when Edward returned in 1471 his coinage was entrusted to Sir Richard Tunstall, a Lancastrian supporter who had been appointed to run the mint for Henry VI in 1459 and had resumed the responsibility in 1470/1. Less than a year later, however, Hastings was recalled, and again reappointed in 1477. In February 1483 Edward IV's last mint indenture was made, with Bartholomew Reed, and although in July Richard III replaced him with his loyalist Robert Brackenbury, Reed was reappointed by Henry VII, jointly with Sir Giles Daubeney, in 1485, and again in 1492 with John Shaw. Henry VII's last indenture was made in November 1505 with Robert Fenrother and William Reed, and Henry VIII's first with his friend William Blount, chamberlain to Katherine of Aragon, in August 1509 (extended to cover Tournai in March 1514). All these indentures include the traditional provisions for a pyx trial and privy mark.

The Tower indenture of March 1465 had provided that the mix of coins should be set with regard to the convenience of the public, but this clause was dropped in later indentures and in practice the convenience of the moneyers was, as usual, one of the most influential considerations. Thus the natural emphasis in silver was on groats, as the largest denomination, with halfpence next, by necessity, since these were still authorised only at royal mints. Pence continued to be provided chiefly by York and Durham. Few halfgroats had been struck since the 1430s, but when the mint at Canterbury was revived in the 1460s it immediately concentrated on this denomination and did so again in Edward's second reign. Henceforward it provided a high proportion of the halfgroats in circulation. In 1523 Parliament laid down the proportions in which silver was to be coined at London - 50 per cent in groats, 20 per cent each in halfgroats and pence, and the remaining 10 per cent in halfpence and farthings in the ratio of two to one. At the same time a new type was prescribed for the farthing which, weighing only 3 grains since 1464, had become so small that it was as awkward to use as it must have been to produce. So few of them have survived that they can hardly have been minted in any quantity.

In the first two years of coinage from 1464 at the new tariff 55,000 lbs. of silver passed through the Tower mint, producing £104,000 in coin, or nearly five times the amount struck in the previous two years. The increase in production of gold coin, however, was much more dramatic - from less than 300 lbs. in 1462-4 to more than 12,000 lbs. (£279,000) in 1464-6. When accounts resume in 1468 minting charges had been reduced but the totals for 1468-70 are in the case of both gold and silver only about one third of those for 1464-6 and it may be assumed that the missing accounts for the intervening period would have shown a declining trend after a successful recoinage. Figures for 1471-5, after Edward's return, when mint charges had again been lowered, show rates of output similar to those of the late 1460s, averaging around 140 lbs. of gold per month and more than 700 lbs. of silver. If this level had been sustained through Henry's restoration his London coinage would have amounted to about £20,000 in gold and approaching £10,000 in silver.

During the remainder of Edward's second reign the amount of bullion coined at London diminished further, to averages of 80 lbs. of gold per month in 1477-83 and 150 lbs. of silver. The abundance of halfgroats struck at Canterbury may go some way to explaining the falling off in London's silver coinage in the last few years of Edward IV. The small totals recorded separately for May - June 1483 have caused endless debate among numismatists about what coins may be attributed to the reign of Edward V (chillingly referred to in one of Richard III's early accounts as the time of Edward the Bastard). Thereafter there was something of a revival in the silver coinage between July 1483 and September 1484, reflecting Richard's need for money to consolidate a precarious position.

For the first four years of Henry VII silver coinage continued at a level comparable to that of the last ten Yorkist years, but less gold was coined. For the next five years (1489-94), for some unexplained reason, the warden was excused from rendering accounts in the normal way. Within this unaccounted period, halfgroats were for a time struck substantially below the standard weight at the king's mints of London and York. The reason for this is evident from the recently published text of a proclamation issued during the winter of 1492/3, soon after the return of the king's army from his expedition to Boulogne in the autumn of 1492. The lightweight coins, which became known as 'dandyprats' (a colloquial term that sometimes had a meaning of three-halfpence in the sixteenth century), had been issued with the intention of passing them off on unsuspecting Frenchmen, but many who received them were soldiers and victuallers of the English army. The king therefore ordered that they should cease to be legal tender in January 1493, but should be taken to the Tower mint by 2 February to be exchanged for coins of full weight and value. In 1491 the king had sought a 'benevolence' from his subjects to enable him to pursue his interests on the Continent; the plate and bullion then collected went to the mint where it was coined into £17,393 worth of twopenny pieces, a total of more than two million of these light halfgroats. Exchequer records show that during the accounting year to Michaelmas 1493 John Shaw received £5,275 by way of reimbursement for costs of their redemption at face value. The term 'good pence of twopence' in a proclamation of 1505 was an acknowledgement that not all of the king's halfgroats could meet that description.

Because of the absence of mint accounts for five years from 1489 there is particular interest in the figures recorded from 1494 onwards. Over the next ten years gold coinage gradually returned towards levels that had prevailed in the later years of Edward IV, but silver increased more sharply, especially from 1497/8. A peak was reached in 1504/5 when 24,000 lbs. of silver (£45,000) was minted, covering the period when coinage with the new profile type was fully launched. Annual totals then gradually declined again, but in 1507/8, the last full year of Henry VII, silver coinage still amounted to 12,800 lbs., higher than any figure recorded for Edward IV after 1466. In gold there had been a slower but more sustained increase. Averaging less than 1,000 lbs. annually until 1500, output rose steadily thereafter, reaching an annual average of more than 4,000 lbs. in the last four years of the reign. Although not matching the levels of output achieved at the end of the reign of Henry VII, gold continued to reach the mint in quantity until 1518/9, after which it began to tail off.

Silver, on the other hand, fell away sharply under Henry VIII. From 1514/15 onwards silver coinage was at a very low ebb, and the mint often idle in this department. The accounts for 1517/18 show no silver bought in five out of the twelve months and, although activity picked up in the summer of 1519, there are nil entries month after month from April to November 1520. The experimental weight reduction in 1522-3 resulted in £29,400 of silver coin, but in the absence of accounts from 1523 to 1526 it must be doubted whether much silver was minted in the last three years before the recoinage.

The new gold coins of 1465 had required new designs to distinguish them from the old noble series that had changed little in appearance since the 1340s. For the 'new noble' of 10s., known as the rose-noble, or later as the ryal, the old noble type was embellished with exuberant Yorkist symbolism: on the obverse a large rose was added on the side of the ship and a banner with a large Gothic *e* at the stern, while the old royal cross on the reverse was replaced by a large sun, with a rose on the centre and four of the rays, at the points of the compass, ending in crowns. The ryal design was used for the half-ryal and for the reverse of the quarter, the obverse of which retained the shield from the quarter-noble, but surrounded it with *e* and rose and sun, and reduced the arcs of tressure to four. The three reverse mottoes were unchanged from those on the old noble and its fractions. Ryals and halves from the provincial mints are identified by an initial letter in the waves but, as with many of the old quarter-nobles, the quarter-ryals lack any indication of their mint. Although of the same weight as Edward III's rather austere nobles, Edward IV's ryals tend to be struck from slightly larger dies, the broader but thinner flans giving scope to display a more flamboyant design. Virtually all the gold coined during the second half of the 1460s was minted into ryals and their fractions; but the design was manifestly unsuitable for Henry's restoration in 1470/1 and it was abruptly discontinued. The ryal and its parts continued to figure in mint indentures up to the first coinage of Henry VIII, but apart from a very small issue of ryals of Tudor style made early in the reign of Henry VII, and an even smaller one under Henry VIII, the minting of these denominations was not repeated.

The 6s. 8d. noble was to be called an angel, after its new design: this shows the archangel Michael spearing a dragon - a more balanced and fluid composition that contrasts with the stiffness of the traditional noble. The ship was transferred to the reverse, with a shield of arms and a cross replacing the figure of the king. The new mottoes adopted for the angel and its half (known as the angelet) referred to the Holy Cross in the centre of the design – *Per Crucem Tuam Salva Nos Christe Redemptor* (Save us through Thy cross, O Christ our Redeemer) and *O Crux Ave Spes Unica* (Hail, O Cross, our only hope). As to the design itself, this was the first purely religious type in the English coinage of the later middle ages. Very few angels were struck during Edward's first reign, but from the return of Henry VI in 1470 they displaced the ryal series and remained the principal embodiment of English gold coinage for the next fifty years. Although its essential type remained unaltered throughout, the appearance of the angel was brought up-to-date in the early 1490s. The original Gothic St. Michael, with large wings and spiky feathers, was replaced by a realistic figure in armour more in keeping with the humanistic idiom of the age. This new form was to remain more or less unchanged throughout the Tudor period and beyond. The change of style, which coincided with the start of the escallop mintmark and the introduction of mannered lettering, was associated by Potter with the appointment at Michaelmas 1494 of Alexander of Bruchsal to the office of engraver, but other evidence now suggests that it must have taken place earlier.

For more than two decades after 1464 the general appearance of the silver coinage, with its impersonal facing bust and medieval crown, was very little altered. Groats of Edward IV's first reign normally have quatrefoils, or later trefoils, in the field but from 1470 marks are only occasionally found by the bust, except for a short period under Henry VII in the late 1480s. Henry VII's reign was, however, to be a period of almost continuous evolution in design. His earliest silver coins are simply an extension of the Yorkist series, but within two or three years two arches, meeting in a point below a central orb and cross, were added to the old open crown or circlet, the first significant typological innovation since Edward III. An arched crown had become a symbol of empire, and its adoption by Henry VII on his coins may be seen as a small but conscious step in the development of the Tudor concept of sovereignty. Shortly after its introduction other innovations were considered. On an experimental groat type (c. 1488), known only from a single reverse die, a portcullis replaces the traditional groups of pellets in the centre. The portcullis, which was to become a prominent Tudor symbol, was the badge of the Beaufort family, thus emphasising the new king's royal descent and conveniently open to interpretation as a punning reference to his ('two-door') dynasty. Not long afterwards more radical options were considered. In March 1489 the warden of the mint was instructed to produce new punches, with an image in the likeness of a king and with the royal arms upon a cross. One of the consequences of this order was a unique groat with an enthroned figure of the king and on the reverse a shield displacing the inner circle of inscription as well as the central pellets. For some reason this type, although a handsome design, was rejected for the groat, but adopted for the penny instead. Despite the difficulty of compressing such an intricate composition into a small space, it was to remain the standard type for the penny for more than fifty years, even after its weight and size had been reduced in 1526. Many other developments did however take place in the appearance of the groat during the 1490s. Jewels were added to the arches of the crown, face and hair were more realistically treated, some elaborate fleuring was used on the cusps of the tressure and a sequence of decorative terminals replaced the old, plain cross-ends.

The two most important dates relating to the coinage of Henry VII are 1489, in which the pound coin was first authorised, and 1504, when the new design with an authentic profile portrait was introduced on the silver coinage and a groat of twelve pence, or shilling, made its first appearance. Since Edward IV's first reign the gold coinage had reverted to the half- and quarter-mark in the form of angel and angelet. Although the ryal of ten shillings had been briefly revived early in the reign of Henry VII, it was in October 1489 that the most significant step was taken towards a pound-based system, with a commission to the master for the minting of a new gold sovereign of twenty shillings. There are five different types of Henry VII's sovereign and the denomination seems to have been coined periodically through the reign on a limited scale, even if perhaps an original provision that two were to be struck from every pound of gold may not always have been carried out. Henry's shilling, however, one twentieth of the sovereign, as the groat had been one twentieth of the noble, put in only a very limited appearance. All known varieties belong to the early and experimental phase of the profile coinage and it seems quickly to have been discontinued. Neither sovereign nor shilling has been found in hoards of this period, and the new system only began to mount a sustained challenge to nobles and groats from the 1540s.

Henry VII's sovereigns are among the most magnificent coins ever produced in

Edward IV – Henry VIII

England. Large gold coins had been introduced in several European states during the later years of the fifteenth century, but the immediate inspiration for the English sovereign seems to have been the *réal d'or* of Maximilian, King of the Romans, which, as regent for his son Philip the Handsome, he had had struck in the Netherlands in 1487. Like Maximilian's, Henry's coin portrayed the ruler, with orb and sceptre, seated on a Gothic throne, with a shield of arms on the reverse. On the sovereign the shield is set upon a Tudor rose which, in its later versions, takes on a more prominent aspect as the shield reduced in size.

At the Parliament held in the first three months of 1504 an Act was passed *Pro Reformatione Pecuniarum*, to deal with the problem of clipping. As often ordained in the past, coins that were cracked or only slightly worn would continue in use; but in order to ensure that clipped coin should not remain current, a new measure was introduced requiring groats and halfgroats to "have a sercle about the utter part thereof". Translated into numismatic language, this meant that the new coins were to have a dotted border outside the inscription, a feature which appears on the last of the facing-head coins (the later groats with mintmark greyhound's head and those with cross-crosslet). In a proclamation dated 5 July 1504 the necessary guidance was spelled out. Coins minted before the Act could be regarded as unclipped if three of the cross-ends and most of the obverse inscription were intact. Those minted after the Act should not be current unless they had the full print on both sides. In the case of Burgundian double patards, which had been made legal tender by Edward IV in 1469, the inscription had to be complete on one side or the other. On 3 July, two days before the proclamation, the master had received a mandate to take on extra workmen at the Tower, and on 12 July the king delivered to him £1,000 in coin for reminting. Clearly, the Act *Pro Reformatione* anticipated a substantial recoinage of clipped money, and the record bullion figures for the twelve months from Michaelmas 1504 show that this must indeed have happened. In April 1505 a further proclamation announced that an extra exchange was being established at Leaden Hall in the City of London where clipped coin could be surrendered in return for halfgroats – their use for this purpose having the effect of preventing anyone from claiming that they had received deficient groats from the exchange.

The chronicler Robert Fabyan, a London alderman who died in 1513, refers to the introduction of "grotes and shyllynges with half faces" as if these had been authorised by the Act of 1504 against clipping. Although the Act itself does not mention the change of design Fabyan's reference suggests that coins with the profile portrait first appeared not long afterwards as the numismatic evidence indicates. The earliest of them were struck alongside facing bust groats with the dotted 'sercle', but the profile type must soon have displaced the old design since the facing bust groats with mintmark cross-crosslet are too scarce to account for the large sums of silver minted from 1504/5 onwards. Confirmation of this may be seen in the issue of halfgroats at the Leaden Hall exchange, since this denomination, revived with the profile type, had not been minted at the Tower since the early 1490s. The reverse design on the new profile groats and halfgroats was a shield of arms over a long cross, as had been used on pence since 1489. This comprehensive change of type was no doubt seen as a simpler means of identifying new unclipped coins than the addition of an outer dotted border (although that feature was not discontinued).

The recoinage of 1464 had involved the commissioning of additional mints which came into operation, after the usual interval, in 1465, and all of which were to strike gold as well as silver. The principal contributors were the royal mints at York and Bristol, which both remained active until shortly after the restoration of Edward IV. The accounts for York were closed in September 1471 and those for Bristol in July of the following year.

1464–1526

The only available figures for these two mints, for 1469/70 and 1471/2, show output by that time at levels too modest to justify retaining their establishments. In fact, it is remarkable that they had remained open so long – on no other occasion after the twelfth century had recoinage mints lasted for more than two or three years. The Patent Rolls contain orders dated July 1465 in respect of mints at Bristol, Coventry and Norwich, but when rates of seignorage were reduced in September 1465 the order related only to London, York and Bristol. From this it may be supposed that Coventry, here making its only appearance in the English coinage, and Norwich, where coins had not been struck since the reign of Henry III, had by then already ceased minting. The scarcity of coins of these two mints accords with a period of activity of perhaps no more than a few weeks. Numismatic evidence indicates that the royal mint at York did not commence operations until slightly later than the others, consistent with its absence from the July orders but inclusion in September. The royal mint at York was revived briefly by Richard III, when only groats were struck there, and again by Henry VII c.1492 when it produced considerable quantities of (light) halfgroats. Calais continued to be included in the appointment of successive mintmasters at the Tower, but its mint was never reopened and the only English coinage that took place in France after Henry VI was the small issue of silver at Tournai in 1514.

In Ireland no coinage on the English standard was produced during this period, although there were extensive issues of lighter weight (many of them of English type) under Edward IV, Richard III and Henry VII, for which mints at Drogheda, Galway, Limerick, Trim and Waterford supported Dublin at one time or another. Concern about the circulation of Irish pence was a recurrent theme in the 1490s, and this appears to have been one of the factors which in February 1499 gave rise to a meeting of the Council, attended by the masters Reed and Shaw, at which it was resolved that the minting of pence should be terminated. Because relatively few pence had been struck at London, the principal effect of this was to close the episcopal mints and to transfer their workload to the Tower – a situation reflected in letters of 31 December 1500 under privy seal which refer to the need to compensate Alexander of Bruchsal for his extra labour since the king had restrained the mints of Canterbury, York and Durham. The increased output of the Tower mint from 1504, following introduction of the profile type, seems likely to have involved the reminting of much earlier coin; but because this was not a recoinage in the proper sense no additional royal mints were commissioned, although the two archiepiscopal establishments were soon contributing an abundant supply of the new halfgroats.

From the end of the twelfth century to the first half of the fourteenth Canterbury had been the second mint in the kingdom. Its return to minting after more than a century may have been a product of Edward IV's wish to secure the allegiance of his second cousin Thomas Bourchier. The king's grant to Archbishop Bourchier in 1463 included the right to coin halfgroats and halfpence, the first occasion on which an ecclesiastical mint had been permitted to issue coins of higher value than the penny. No heavy coins of Canterbury are known, and the mint did not apparently commence operation until after the weight reduction of 1464. The earliest Canterbury coins are prominently adorned with the archbishop's symbols, including the Bourchier knot from his coat of arms. Bourchier died in 1486, only seven months after the accession of Henry VII, and there are no Canterbury coins of his after the Edwardian period, but the appointment of the Lancastrian loyalist John Morton to the see late in 1486 was soon followed by a revival of coinage at Canterbury, with the same emphasis on halfgroats as there had been under Edward IV. The earliest coins of this mint under Henry VII show Morton's initial on the centre of the reverse cross, and the mintmark tun is a reference to his name. No

Edward IV – Henry VIII

Canterbury coins can be associated with the episcopate of Henry Deane (1501-3), which fell during the period of restraint of the provincial mints. But of Archbishop William Warham (1503-32) there are extensive issues of profile halfgroats from 1504 onwards, as well as a few pence and halfpence of Henry VIII's first coinage.

After the weight reduction of 1464 the northern episcopal mints continued to provide most of the pence in circulation. Indeed, under Edward IV their relative contribution was even greater than before. York pence are by far the commonest coins of the reign, those of Durham less so, but still numerous. The lack of Durham coins of Henry VI's restoration in 1470/1 could have been due to the shortness of the reign rather than to any political objections, since Bishop Laurence Booth (1457-76) had been Keeper of the Privy Seal to Henry before 1461, although animosity between Booth and Warwick might have been a factor. In the 1470s Booth and his successor William Dudley (1476-83) were licensed to coin halfpence also; this was the only occasion on which Durham minted other than pence, but it must have done so on a very limited scale because survivors are of great rarity. From 1483 onwards the two mints remained prolific, although in the 1490s London increased its production of pence, and in due course, after the constraint of 1499, replaced them. When the archbishop of York's mint was revived for Thomas Savage (1501-7) no more pence were struck but instead, for the first time, it was authorised (like Canterbury) to coin halfgroats and halfpence, of which the former are plentiful. After the adoption of the profile type the series of York halfgroats continued in abundance up to 1526 and beyond. Pence, however, were not to be minted again at York for more than thirty years, between 1499 and the time of Archbishop Lee after 1531, although there are a few York halfpence of Henry VIII's first coinage to represent what must have been a very small and perhaps occasional issue of this denomination. Durham, on the other hand, resumed the production of pence early in the reign of Henry VIII for Thomas Ruthall (1509-23) and outperformed London and Canterbury in this respect into the 1530s. The indenture by which the mint was resuscitated in 1510 provided for the minting of the equivalent of an extra twelve pence from a (Tower) pound of silver, but the reason for this curious departure from normal practice remains obscure.

The use of a bishop's initial on pence of Durham, first found late in Henry VI's first reign in the form of *B* by the bust for Laurence Booth, was continued, and extended, under the Yorkists and Tudors, providing much useful numismatic data. Sometimes the personal initial was combined with *D* for *Dunelmensis (D S* for John Shirwood or *R D* for Richard Fox). A similar practice was adopted at York, although with greater prominence for St. Peter's key (or keys) instead of the initial of the see. When the sovereign type was adopted for pence and the profile bust on halfgroats, the keys were placed below the shield on the reverse because there was no longer space by the bust. Under Henry VIII the initials were placed above or beside the shield, for the same reason. The first occurrence of initials for both Christian name and surname together was *X B* for Christopher Bainbridge (1508-14) at York, *X* representing the Greek letter for *Ch*. Personal initials were used more sparingly at Canterbury, the first being *m* for Morton (1486-1500), on the centre of the cross, followed under Henry VIII by *W A* by the shield for William Warham, this being the only use of the title *Archiepiscopus*.

Although there have been more hoards from the Yorkist and early Tudor periods than from the first half of the fifteenth century, most of them were found more than a hundred years ago and records of them are inadequate. Two exceptions are the hoards of 221 gold coins from Park Street, near St. Albans (1886), buried c. 1520, and of 433 silver coins from Clay Coton, Northamptonshire (1865), buried c. 1505, which were described in sufficient detail to enable their contents to be correlated with modern classification. More recent finds of silver have come from Wyre Piddle, Worcestershire (1964), 219 coins buried c. 1466, Ryther, Yorkshire (1992), 817 coins to c. 1487, and Hartford, Huntingdonshire (1964), 1,108 coins buried late in the reign of Henry VII. As previously, gold and silver were hoarded separately, for different purposes. Despite frequent references to foreign gold coins in contemporary records, there were none in the Park Street hoard (which ran from Edward IV ryals to angels of Henry VIII), and they may normally have been reminted. The only foreign silver coins to feature in English hoards in any quantity are the double-patards of the Burgundian Netherlands, which had been legal tender since 1469. Their highest concentration was in a find at Hounslow, Middlesex (1861), from the late 1490s, which included 86 (23 per cent), while the 83 in the Hartford hoard amounted to less than 8 per cent. Portuguese half-reals (*chinfraos*) or Venetian *soldini* are also sometimes present, but otherwise the non-English content of silver hoards rarely goes beyond a few coins from Scotland and Ireland.

Forgery does not seem to have been a major problem for hoarders, and after the Stamford and Wyre hoards of the 1460s there is an absence of the slightly dished coins that indicate public vigilance against plated groats. A general shortage of petty currency, however, vividly described in several of the Paston letters, made it more difficult to exclude inferior coins from Scotland and Ireland despite the government's efforts to discourage them. In 1499 and again in 1505 it was ordered that Scottish 'spurred' pennies (with mullets instead of pellets on the reverse) were only to pass as halfpence, while repeated proclamations in the 1490s unsuccessfully attempted to prohibit the use of Irish coin altogether. Many of the Irish pence of Edward IV have a York-style quatrefoil on the reverse, and this also occurs on coins (with a silver content of only c. 80 per cent) from a hoard of late fifteenth-century counterfeit pennies which was found on the Thames foreshore at Queenhithe in 1980, and had perhaps been hurriedly abandoned for fear of detection. Another City find, of 153 forged Scottish placks all from a single obverse die, recovered from a cesspit near London Bridge in 1955, also suggests that counterfeit coin may often have been brought to London by sea from the Low Countries. Small change was always in short supply, and the lead (or pewter) tokens which Erasmus noted in early sixteenth-century England offered only a local solution.

Edward IV Light Coinage – Classification and Chronology

Blunt and Whitton's classic work on Edward IV's coinage divides the London groats of reduced weight into eighteen 'types', based on their mintmarks (which in some types are not the same on obverse and reverse). Seven of the types (V-XI) belong to the first reign and the remaining eleven (XII-XXII) to the years 1471-83. Type XXII, which was in issue when Edward IV died, continued for a few months thereafter, during the nominal reign of Edward V and even, it seems, for a short period under Richard III. These eighteen types are of uneven status since, for example, types IX and XI appear to be little more than reverse varieties of type X, and some of the cross types (XVI-XX) are too rare to have constituted substantive issues. Transferring this arrangement of types to other mints and denominations is at best a complicated and imprecise exercise. Although the coins of the short-lived recoinage mints, Coventry and Norwich, all conform to the London mintmarks, those of the two other royal mints subsequently diverged, York after type VI and Bristol after type VIII. Groats of the first reign are easily recognisable by having quatrefoils, or latterly trefoils, by the bust, whereas with rare exceptions those of the second reign have no marks in the field. Generally, there is much less variation in the

Edward IV – Henry VIII

inscriptions than there had been in the first reign of Henry VI.

Ryals and halves are usually without a mintmark on the obverse, while pence and halfpence as usual lack a reverse mintmark. This creates problems where the groat mintmarks on the two sides are not the same. In such cases the appropriate type may have to be determined by reference to letter forms, stops or ornaments. Although the ryals almost invariably have trefoil stops, light silver coins of the first reign begin with saltires, adding trefoils in type VII, which gradually replace the saltires. A more useful indicator on ryals is the form of fleurs in the spandrels, which normally accord with those on the cusps on groats: large, shapely fleurs until late type VII, then small trefoils. In the second reign larger trefoils were introduced on groats during type XV and large fleurs again during type XVIII.

FLEURS ON RYALS AND GROATS OF EDWARD IV

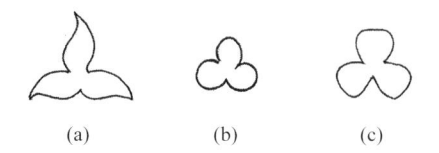

(a)   (b)   (c)

(a) Large fleurs, V – late VII; (b) Small trefoils, late VII – XV;
(c) Large trefoils, XV – XVIII.

Many of the coins of the three ecclesiastical mints cannot be allocated satisfactorily to an individual 'type' in the Blunt and Whitton scheme, and they have therefore been listed here according to separate notations. In the case of York pence the picture is confused by local dies early in Neville's coinage (1465) and by the frequent occurrence of a rose mintmark in the second reign. Most of the Canterbury halfgroats of the second reign also have mintmark rose and although Blunt and Whitton tentatively ascribed type numbers to successive varieties there is little evidence to connect them with particular London types. At Durham local dies were used from 1473, and the coins of this mint then form an independent series which equally cannot be related to the London structure.

The return of Henry VI in 1470-1 provides a central fixed point in the chronology of Edward IV's coinage. Brooke attributed coins with mintmark short cross fitchy (type XII) to Edward's first reign, but die-links and lettering demonstrate that it is a post-Henry type, an arrangement which has the satisfactory consequence of enabling the replacement of the ryal by the angel to be seen as a political result of the Lancastrian restoration. The absence of mint accounts for 1466-8 makes it difficult to judge when mintmark crown (type VII) may have replaced sun (type VI), but in view of the abundance of types VII and VIII the change probably occurred not later than 1466. Blunt and Whitton suggested that mintmark long cross fitchy (types X-XI) could have been introduced following the indenture of March 1469, and it indeed seems unlikely to have been before this.

1464–1526

Mintmarks of Edward IV, 1464 - 70

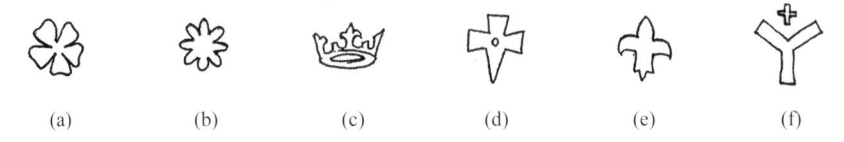

(a) Rose, V, IX; (b) Sun, VI, etc.; (c) Crown, VII – VIII; (d) Long cross fitchy, X – XI; (e) Lis, York; (f) Pall, Canterbury.

Type XII is a rare issue representing a brief continuation from Henry VI in 1471. The next three types, with mintmark annulet (XIII-XV), may be dated 1471-3, with XIV (small annulet) being the last type at Bristol which closed during July 1472. On the evidence of a type XV London-made die (with mintmark pellet-in-annulet) supplied to Durham, this type should have been in issue before July 1473, when Booth was licensed to have his dies made locally.

Blunt and Whitton allocated type XV and the subsequent types with cross mintmarks (XVI-XX) to the remainder of the 1470s, believing that mintmark cinquefoil (XXI) did not begin until 1480. However, the numbers of surviving angels of the different types (and of their respective representation in the Park Street hoard), suggest that cinquefoil angels constituted about half the output of gold in the second reign, which would mean that this mintmark must have been in issue for considerably longer than the three years from 1480 to 1483. Measuring these figures against the amounts of gold minted from 1471 to 1482, Webb Ware has argued that mintmark cinquefoil must have been introduced not later than 1476. Equivalent calculations can be made for silver, using the numbers of groats of different types in the Clay Coton and Hartford hoards, with a similar result. Furthermore, an untraced variety of York penny of Neville (d. 1476) with mintmark cross-and-pellet (XVIII) need not be questioned, if the cross marks can all be dated before c. 1476. Confirmation of the earlier commencement of the cinquefoil coinage may also be had from the oldest surviving gold trial plate in the Royal Mint, made in the seventeenth year of Edward IV (1477), which carries the impression of the reverse of a cinquefoil angel; and the trial of the pyx held on 1 December 1475 (the only such recorded trial in the second reign), which covered the Tower output from 1471 to November 1475, could accordingly be seen as an exercise to take stock before the introduction of type XXI. Edward's last type, with mintmark sun-and-rose (XXII), is sufficiently rare for its issue to have begun close to the end of the reign, and the lack of groat mules between XXI and XXII supports its association with Reed's indenture of February 1483.

A simplified summary of the groupings adopted for Edward's coinage according to the types and mintmarks of the groats is set out in the table.

Edward IV – Henry VIII

TYPES AND MINTMARKS OF EDWARD IV LIGHT GROATS OF PRINCIPAL MINTS

Type	Mintmarks London	Bristol	York		Suggested Dates
V	Rose	Rose			1464/5
VI	Sun	Sun	Sun		1465/6
VII	Crown	Crown	Lis/crown, or Lis		1466- c. 1469
VIII	Crown/Sun	Crown/Sun	Sun or Lis		
IX	Rose (rev. only)				
X	Long Cross Fitchy/ Sun	Sun	Lis/Sun		1469/70
XI	Long Cross Fitchy		Lis		
Henry VI	Various Crosses, or Lis	Crosses, Trefoil or Rose	Lis		1470/1
XII	Short Cross Fitchy	Rose	Lis		1471
XIII	Large Annulet/Trefoil				
XIV	Small Annulet	Small Annulet, or Sun			1471-3
XV	Pellet-in-Annulet				
XVI	Cross, or Cross and Four Pellets				
XVII	Pierced Cross				
XVIII	Cross and Pellet				1473-5
XX	Pierced Cross with Pellet Centre				
XIX	Pierced Cross				
XXI	Cinquefoil				1476-82
XXII	Sun-and-Rose				1483

Edward IV, Early Light Coinage (Types V and VI), 1464-6

In the first phase of the light silver coinage the mintmark rose (type V) continued in use from the heavy coinage, but it was replaced by the sun (type VI) in the summer of 1465. Only in these two types did all the other royal mints use the same marks as London. The London mint accounts run from September 1464, the month after the indenture to reduce the weights, and show high output over the following two years as old silver in currency was brought in for reminting. Rose-marked London groats at 48 gr. are accordingly very plentiful.

The new gold coinage ordered in March 1465 also begins with rose-marked coins, although they were only produced for a few months at most before the change of mintmark and are far from common. Some separation between the production of dies for gold and silver at this stage is suggested by the fact that the former normally have trefoil stops, the latter saltires, although a few cases of the converse do occur. The new mints at Bristol, Coventry and Norwich commissioned in July 1465 all received a few dies with mintmark rose, but not the royal mint at York which was added shortly afterwards. The larger coins of the provincial mints have the initial letter of the mint name on the obverse – in the waves below the ship on ryals and halves, and on the breast of groats. On Bristol silver the mint name is very variously spelt – *Brestoll* or *Bristoll, Brestow, Bristow* or *Bristov*. Silver coins of the two lesser mints, at Coventry and Norwich, which were very soon closed, are scarce, and their gold is rare.

Muling between types V and VI is frequent, and there must have been a short period in the summer of 1465 when dies with both mintmarks were available together. At the point of transition there are also some dies for provincial gold with a rose before the sun. On the evidence of York pence attributed to the vacancy of 1464/5, the sun mark would have been brought into use, at the latest, by June 1465 when Archbishop Neville obtained his temporalities.

ROYAL MINTS OF THE EARLY LIGHT COINAGE OF EDWARD IV

	V	V/VI	VI/V	VI	VII
Ryal	L(+N?)	L	L	LBCNY	LBY
Half-ryal	N(+L,B?)			LBCY	LBY
Quarter-ryal		L(+?)	L(+?)	L(+?)	L(+?)
Angel	L				L
Groat	L	L	LBCN	LBCNY	LBY
Halfgroat	L	B	L	BCNY	LBY
Penny	L			L	LB
Halfpenny	LB			LNY	LBY

L – London, B – Bristol, C – Coventry, N – Norwich, Y – York

London's long-standing emphasis on groats and halfpence continued, together with the leading role of York and Durham in producing the bulk of the pence in circulation. The addition of Canterbury, however, brought a revival of the halfgroat, now that the archbishop was given the right to coin the three main denominations below the groat. The complex coinages of the episcopal mints are discussed in a separate section hereafter, but they all made an important contribution to the provision of the junior silver during the recoinage and after.

The earliest light groats were struck from dies prepared for the heavy coinage, which proved to be too large for the new, smaller flans. These rare coins can usually be distinguished from clipped heavy groats by being slightly thinner and having less regular edges. New dies of reduced module were soon available, however, at first closely reproducing the design of the last heavy coins (including usually the eye after *tas*), but then with some modification. Sometimes new and smaller reverse dies were combined with old, larger obverses. The lower denominations are very rare and this transitional process can therefore be seen in full only on the groats. Heavy dies, with the inner circles measuring approximately 21 mm on the obverse and 20 mm on the reverse, have either quatrefoils or annulets by the bust, and so belong to types III and IV of the heavy series. Old dies of these two types may well have been brought into use more or less simultaneously, since copies of both of them were made, at first with the old lettering, but soon with a new, smaller fount more suited to the reduced size of the circles on the reverse. Although most of the light groats from heavy dies are of the annulet type (being the one current at the time of the weight reduction), Blunt and Whitton suggested that this type (which they described as Va whether from old or new dies) may soon have been discarded in order to avoid confusion with the Calais annulet groats of the 1420s which still made up a considerable proportion of the old currency in mid-century. However that may be, the quatrefoil type was to become the standard form for the rest of the recoinage period. The early light quatrefoil groats, equivalent to the Va annulet groats, are described as Vb, in which the new dies can readily be distinguished from the few old heavy ones that were still available, not only by their size and their usually smaller lettering, but also in having a large fleur on the breast instead of the neat trefoil of type III.

After this period of die trials, which cannot have lasted for more than a few weeks, groats of the quatrefoil type settled down to their final smaller module, with the inner circles measuring about 18½ mm on both sides. The first phase in this form (Vc) continues the later lettering of Va and Vb and their carelessly made crown, with open foils at the side of the central fleur; but the eye no longer appears on the reverse, and instead there is an extra point within the group of pellets in one quarter. The dies of Vc are neatly made, with either large fleurs or small trefoils on the cusps, and a fleur, trefoil, rose or nothing on the breast. Vc reverses are also occasionally found muled with obverses of either Va or Vb.

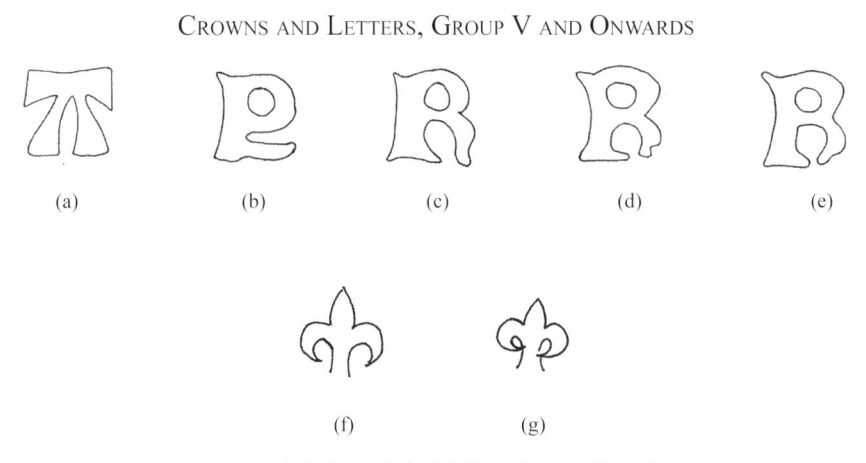

CROWNS AND LETTERS, GROUP V AND ONWARDS

(a) (b) (c) (d) (e)

(f) (g)

(a) Bow-legged *A*, from Vd; (b) *P* with long foot, from Vd;
(c) Blunt and Whitton's R3 with out-turned tail, Vd-VI; (d) BW's R4 with notched tail, VII-VIII,
(e) B-like R5, VIII onwards; (f) Central fleur of crown, Vc; (g) Squat fleur, Vd.

The final rose-marked phase (Vd) is represented by London groats which show a new fount of letters and a crown with a squat, pointed central fleur with small circular side foils. Large fleurs are now always found on the obverse tressure including, except for a few early dies, the breast cusp. The new 'rugged' lettering has concave uprights: conspicuous letters are *P* with a long foot and a bow-legged *A*. Near the end of type V the point within one group of pellets mostly disappears, although it is occasionally found on early London reverses of type VI. London groats of Vd are more plentiful than those of Va-c, and constituted the bulk of the silver coinage during the early months at the reduced weight.

London groats with the sun mintmark of type VI are also very common. Mostly they continue to show large fleurs on the cusps, and quatrefoils by the bust. There are comparable coins of all the four provincial mints, plentiful of Bristol and York, scarce of the short-lived mints of Coventry and Norwich. Having opened slightly later than the others, York received no rose-marked dies; but Bristol, Coventry and Norwich were each sent late Vd reverses (without the extra point) among their first batch of groat dies, along with new sun-marked obverses of type VI. One Coventry groat (VI) is recorded with an incongruous *B* on the breast, and there seems to have been some confusion in the distribution of dies at the start of the recoinage, because there is also a York groat from an altered London obverse of type VI with its *e* over a fleur, while a rare variety of London Vd/VI mule shows the breast fleur punched over an *e*. Most curiously of all there is a VI/Vd groat with a London signature, from a York obverse die (easily identifiable for omitting *x* of *Rex);* this obverse is also known paired with a York reverse, so it is likely that it was the London reverse and not the York obverse that had been wrongly delivered. The V/VI mule with fleur over *e* is the only clear evidence of rose-marked groat obverse dies having been made for any of the new mints, but a small group of imitative groats, based on first reign types but betrayed by abnormalities of design or spelling (e.g. *Francus),* includes examples with mintmark rose both sides purporting to come from Coventry and Norwich. Although saltires were the normal stops on silver of types V and VI there are trefoils on the reverse of one London Vb/c mule and in the outer legend on some Bristol groats of type VI; and a lis (as on the obverse of some ryals) is sometimes found in the inner legend on type VI groats of London and Bristol.

The smaller silver of the royal mints is rare. On the lower denominations, because of reduced space, the quatrefoils by the bust are sometimes replaced by saltires or 'mill-rinds' (the heraldic term for a cross with round-ended limbs which can appear disarticulated, as if not put in by a single punch); or, on halfpence of type VI, by trefoils. A few light London halfgroats (Va) are known with annulets from heavy coinage dies of type IV, and from new dies there is a halfgroat with quatrefoils by the bust (Vd), without a rose on the reverse but with an extra point in the *Civi* quarter, as on groats of Vc and Vd (a similar reverse is also muled with an obverse of type VI). Curiously, although there are no groats from type V obverses except at London, there are a few Bristol V/VI halfgroats, the only certain case of larger provincial silver with obverse mintmark rose. Bristol is also the least rare royal mint for halfgroats of type VI, reverse dies of which sometimes lack a mintmark. London is represented for halfgroats in this type only by extremely rare VI/V mules, York, Coventry and Norwich by coins of true type VI, the last two of great rarity.

A worn London penny, weighing 11.6 gr., from a heavy coinage obverse die with annulets by the neck, probably belongs after the weight reduction and was so listed by Blunt and Whitton; its reverse die has the diameter of the beaded circle smaller than is found on heavy pence, and this could be a parallel to the early light groats from old heavy obverse dies combined with reverses of reduced module. One London penny from new

Edward IV – Henry VIII

dies, with the obverse mintmark not visible, has an angular rose-like mark partly covered by the *C* of *Civi*, and so could perhaps be a representative of type V. Otherwise, the only undoubted early light penny from a royal mint is of London, type VI. It is possible that penny dies were also provided to provincial mints during types V and VI, but little used. Halfpence are known of London (V and VI), Bristol (V), Norwich (VI) and York (VI), but not yet of Coventry. London halfpence, with saltires, crosses or trefoils by the bust, are the least rare denomination below the groat. However, these of type V with mintmark rose and saltires by the bust cannot reliably be separated from similar halfpence of the heavy coinage, since the difference in weight and diameter of the circles is so slight on the lowest denominations. A few halfpence of type VI have an extra pellet in one quarter within the group of three, as on some of the early larger silver of this type. No undoubted light farthing is known earlier than mintmark crown, although as with halfpence any farthings with mintmark rose would be difficult to distinguish from their heavy predecessors.

   No change was made in the gold coinage until after the indenture of March 1465, by which time the light silver coinage had been under way for more than six months. Blunt and Whitton suggested that the latest pair of noble dies was contemporary with the early light groats but, as noted in the previous chapter, details of its lettering have been associated by Archibald with the heavy halfgroats of type III. However, if nobles of the old type had continued to be struck after the reduction of the weight of the silver coins in September 1464, they might well have been from this pair of dies. From March 1465 until the return of Henry VI in 1470 English gold coinage consisted almost entirely of the new rose noble and its fractions. Very few angels of Edward IV's first reign are extant and they can only have been struck on rare occasions. Three of the four known varieties have the mintmark rose of type V (on the reverse only). These coins, like the only other first reign angels (of type VII), are struck on larger and thinner flans than later angels and this accounts for a number of differences in design. On first reign angels the figure of St. Michael is contained wholly within the inner circle, except for the cross at the upper end of his lance, which serves to divide the beginning and end of the inscription at 330°. On the reverse there is a sun above the cross, and a large rose and sun beside it instead of the later *e* with smaller rose. In type V the rose is to the left of the cross and the sun to the right. What is probably the first of the obverse dies has a toothed dragon with a second head at its tail. Except for one of the reverses, which uses the letter fount of groats of Vd, the dies of these type V angels show the same small lettering as on early light halfgroats, but incorporating the long-footed *P* from the groats. They were probably struck soon after the new gold coins were authorised in March 1465, and the 6s. 8d. denomination then virtually discontinued as superfluous once ryals of 10s. with their halves and quarters were in circulation.

   All gold of the ryal series with mintmark rose is rare, because the sun displaced it soon after the new gold coinage was authorised, and before dies were generally available for the regional mints. The only gold coins of type V that occur in any number are the London ryals and they are not common. All the halves and quarters with either rose or sun are of considerable rarity. The new ryals, heavier than their immediate noble predecessors, are struck on broad flans like the angels. Elements of the obverse design break the inscription not only, as on the old nobles, by the sail and the forecastle or bowsprit, but also by the banner at the stern. There are large fleurs in the spandrels of the reverse tressure, as on early light groats. A few ryals of types V and VI follow the numismatically convenient precedent, set by the last of the pre-1464 nobles, of having the mintmark on both sides of the coin, but the obverse mark, which had sometimes been placed above and sometimes below the sail, was soon dropped, causing some ambiguities of classification in these and later types. London ryals of type VI are much commoner than those of type V and include varieties with lis or quatrefoil in the obverse inscription, with trefoil stops within the word *(h)ib*, and with the curiously aspirated reverse ending *hibat*, an error repeated at Bristol and presumably resulting from the graver's familiarity with the Irish title. From type VI (until type VIII) several very odd spellings of *Transiens* are found (e.g. *Tranniens, Trasiens, Tranansiens*, etc.) which hardly look accidental. In addition to the latent mules revealed by die-linking, some mules with later reverses can be identified by their letter *R*, which in type VI normally has a slightly outturned tail (R3). Type VI ryals occur of all four new mints, those of Bristol being the least rare. As at London, some have quatrefoils in the obverse legend. The sole record of a provincial ryal with mintmark rose is of a coin of Norwich unverified for more than a century; but its existence is credible, since the only known half-ryal of any mint with mintmark rose is also of Norwich. There is no type VI half recorded for Norwich, as there is for the other three new mints, and it may therefore be that dies for Norwich gold were made slightly before those for the other mints, and a second pair of dies was never needed at Norwich for this denomination. On many of the half-ryals, of this and later types, the lettering is small, from the halfgroat fount. It is possible that some very rare early half-ryals of London and Bristol without mintmark on either side also belong to the period of type V, rather than of type VI as Blunt and Whitton provisionally classified them. Provincial half-ryals have a mintmark on the reverse only, and some of them a rose before the sun; only those of type VI at London have the sun on the obverse also.

Early quarter-ryals are all rare, those with mintmark rose being represented only by V/VI and VI/V mules. An early experimental obverse type, similar to that of the old quarter-nobles, retained the shield within an eight-arc tressure, but now with a rose above it; this is known only from the VI/V mule, although there is also a forgery with mintmark rose both sides perhaps copied from a lost original. The normal type has a tressure of only four arcs, a 'quadrilobe', following a fashion adopted also in France, the Low Countries and elsewhere at this period. The larger arcs allowed room for a rose and sun beside the shield, as well as an *e* above and lis below. The type V die has a pellet each side of the *e*, and its inscription starts at the bottom. As well as the usual trefoil stops, type VI reverse dies are also found with roses or saltires. As with many of the quarter nobles, there is no indication whether any of the known quarter-ryals were struck outside London unless, by analogy with ryals and halves, a rose before the obverse sun on one die points to a provincial mint.

Edward IV, First Reign, Types VII-XI

Without mint accounts for 1466/8 it is not possible to estimate when the intensive phase of the recoinage came to an end. But it may well have extended beyond the sun-marked type VI, since coins of the next two types are very plentiful. Although Coventry and Norwich had soon closed, Bristol and York continued to provide active support for London for the rest of the 1460s, and the abundance of Canterbury halfgroats of the period shows that at least for a time considerable amounts of silver were received for conversion by the archbishop's mint. Most of the coins of the later 1460s from the episcopal mints are from London-made dies, and they frequently use the London mintmarks.

The type structure for the period based on the London groats is not always easily applicable to other mints and denominations. Most of the coins of the second half of the 1460s from London and Bristol have a crown as mintmark on the obverse, although

Edward IV – Henry VIII

latterly this was replaced at London by cross fitchy (types X-XI). London groats with obverse mintmark crown were divided by Blunt and Whitton into three types, according to whether the reverse mark is a crown also (VII), or a sun (VIII), or a rose (IX); those with obverse cross fitchy have either a rose (supposedly 'X/IX' mules), a sun (X) or another cross fitchy (XI) on the reverse. Groats of Bristol follow the London pattern of marks only until type VIII, the last type of this mint in the first reign (X) having a sun both sides. York, however, generally used non-London marks after type VI: usually a lis, sometimes a sun, but a crown (unaltered) only on some early reverses of type VII. Other features, such as the fleurs on the tressure, the ornaments by the bust, the stops, and some letter punches, are useful in the identification of mules and in establishing the nearest equivalent London type for groats of York and Bristol when their mintmarks diverge. Most London groats of type VII have the same large fleurs on the cusps as had been used in earlier types, while most of type VIII have very small trefoils. In types VII and VIII, as in earlier types, there are quatrefoils by the bust, followed by trefoils, and finally nothing, in type X. Trefoil stops, rare on silver in type VII, become more frequent in type VIII, gradually replacing the earlier saltires. The most useful letter is *R*, which on most dies of types VII and VIII has a notched tail (BW's R4) but was then replaced by a *B*-like form (R5) in later types (the only occurrence of R5 on type VIII groats is on a few late dies of York).

Types VII – XI of Edward IV at Royal Mints
(according to Blunt and Whitton)

	VII	VIII	IX	X	XI
Ryal	LBY	LBY		LBY	
Half-ryal	LBY	L(B)Y	LY	L	
Quarter-ryal	L(+Y?)	L			L
Angel	L				
Groat	LBY	LBY	L	LBY	LY
Halfgroat	LBY	LBY		LY	
Penny	LB	LB		L	
Halfpenny	LBY	LBY		L	
Farthing		L		L	

L – London; B – Bristol, (B) mule only; Y – York

London groats of type VII are the commonest of the first reign and those of type VIII are also plentiful; type X is scarce, while types IX and XI are both very rare but exist only as reverse varieties. London obverses of type VIII differ from those of type VII in having a neat quatrefoil instead of a fleur on the breast. Although trefoils replaced fleurs late in type VII and were normal in type VIII, a few early dies of type VIII have the old fleurs, so there was evidently an overlap in the use of the two forms of ornament, but probably over only a very short period. However, *B* and *e* instead of the quatrefoil on the breast at Bristol and York mean that the division between the types at these mints has to rely upon the cusp ornaments alone. The new trefoils are so small that from type VIII onwards they are often found on the top cusps above the crown which, almost without exception, had been bare since Henry IV. Variants of type VII at London include the use of a Bristol obverse die, missing quatrefoils or cusp fleurs, omission of the reverse crown mintmark, or its placement after *Posui*, and the odd spelling *Meua* for *Meum* (which also occurs in some later types). York groats of type VII all have obverse mintmark lis, with a crown or lis on the reverse; a reverse with lis punched over crown suggests that the lis/crown groats are the earlier. With the small cusp trefoils of type VIII the mintmark on both sides at York is either a sun (reflecting the reverse mark at the other mints) or a lis. Presumably sun is the earlier here since it is found overpunched by lis on a few reverse dies. Strangely, there are also obverse dies with lis over crown, perhaps a corrected die-sinker's error or the conversion of dies made for type VII that were never used, as no York groats are known with obverse mintmark crown unaltered.

A remarkable early London variety of type VIIIa groat has a sun before the obverse crown mintmark; and a later double mark is to be found in the form of rose and crown. Because of the rose, Blunt and Whitton described this latter obverse as type IX, but it is not found with a rose-marked IX reverse and since it uses R4 it may belong to the period of type VIIIb. Groat reverses of type IX, on some of which the curious reading *Londoo* occurs, do not appear to have any matching obverse dies. Indeed, no crown-marked groat obverse die found with a rose-marked reverse uses R5, as IX reverses do, and there is no obvious distinction to be made between normal London obverses of VIIIb and the supposed obverses of type IX. The first appearance of R5 on the obverse of London groats comes with type Xa, and since there are X/IX 'mules' with R5 on both sides it may be wondered whether the rose-marked groat reverses might rather constitute a rare early variety of type X (also found muled with VIII obverses), and one soon discarded in favour of a revival of the sun. Type X groats continue the practice of different mintmarks on each side, now a long cross fitchy (LCF) on the obverse and a sun on the reverse, although shortly before the end of the first reign the mintmark LCF is found on a few reverse dies as well (XI). There is more than one punch for the cross, which is dagger-shaped (with the point often protruding through the dotted circle) and may have a pierced centre. London groats of types X and XI usually have trefoils by the bust (Xa and XIa), but some dies of each have no marks in the field (Xb and XIb), setting a pattern which was to endure, with few exceptions, until the reign of Henry VII. In practice, however, types X and the much rarer XI are really a single type with varieties of reverse, because their obverses are indistinguishable and some of the dies are found combined with both sun and LCF reverses. No dies of this period without trefoils by the bust occur at Bristol or York. Bristol has mintmark sun both sides, York lis/sun (Xa) or lis both sides (XIa). At both mints Xa/VIII mules are identifiable by the letter R4 on their reverses.

The only plentiful halfgroats of this period are those of Canterbury (described in the separate section on episcopal mints). Halfgroats from the royal mints, all scarce or rare, generally follow the pattern of the groat mintmarks, although less completely; the least rare are the London coins of type VII, but they are not common. On the cusps there are small trefoils throughout, and some dies have the arches ornamented above the crown. Quatrefoils by the bust occur in types VII and VIII, but not invariably: sometimes there are saltires or trefoils instead. Saltire stops gradually give way to trefoils, or to none. A few early London halfgroats of the rare type VIII have a quatrefoil on the breast like the

Edward IV – Henry VIII

groats of that type, but otherwise the breast cusp has a trefoil or nothing. Bristol halves are rare of both types VII and VIII, especially the latter, which has no marks by the bust; none has been attributed to the period of types X-XI. A variety with trefoils by the bust has been described as an VIII/VII mule, although as trefoils occur on some London halves of type VII presumably a comparable coin of Bristol could also be so classified. All York halves are also rare. Again there is no straightforward distinction between types VII and VIII, or indeed type X, all of which have mintmark lis. One very rare variety with an *e* on the breast (the only halfgroat of the first reign with a mint letter), and with the reverse mintmark lis placed after *Posui*, is classed as BW type VIII, on the ground that a comparable reverse is muled with an obverse having trefoils by the bust and accordingly labelled type X (although the type X attribution is itself somewhat speculative in view of the occurrence of trefoils in earlier types at other mints). London halfgroats with LCF are rare. All have reverse mintmark sun, and like the groats of type X they are found both with (Xa) and without trefoils (Xb) by the bust. One of Xa (which omits &) is from the same reverse die as a coin of type VIII.

London pence and halfpence of types VII and VIII are more abundant than the halfgroats, but of type X (not recorded for the other mints) they are very rare. Both denominations of Bristol and the halfpence of York are all of considerable rarity. No pence were struck at the king's mint in York in the 1460s, but those of the archbishop are very common. London pence and halfpence of type VII are the commonest of the first reign. Small silver of the royal mints, without reverse mintmark, was mostly assigned by Blunt and Whitton to type VII if there are quatrefoils or saltires by the bust, and to the scarcer type VIII if trefoils. However, there are London pence from more than one die with a trefoil to the left and a quatrefoil to the right ('VII'), while a rare variety with a quatrefoil on the breast, as on groats and some halfgroats of type VIII, is understandably classed as VIII despite having quatrefoils by the bust. Another anomaly is that London halfpence with trefoils by the bust are described as VII unless they have trefoil stops (VIII). A London farthing with trefoils could be described under either type, since there was little room for ornaments larger than trefoils on so small a coin. The only post-VIII minor coins, with (a) or without (b) trefoils by the bust, are London pence, halfpence and a farthing with the LCF of type X. Because of the continuing lis mintmark, if any York halfpence belong to the period of type X they have not been so identified.

The gold coins may be arranged approximately in correspondence with the groats, but since the lettering of types VII and VIII is the same there is no absolute boundary between the two. For ryal reverses Blunt and Whitton took the change from large fleurs to trefoils in the spandrels of the tressure as the division between VII and VIII, and this must be largely correct although the groats suggest perhaps not precisely so. For the halves this criterion does not work, since they have trefoils in their (smaller) spandrels throughout. The quarters, having a mintmark on both sides, present less of a problem as regards type, but there is no apparent means of determining whether any of them were struck at Bristol as was the case with the larger gold. All gold of Bristol is rare. Type VII is the commonest of the reign for all the London gold, and York halves of this type are also plentiful. Gold of type VIII is scarce, and with the rose mark (described as type IX) there are only in gold some very rare halves of London and York. Cross fitchy ryals are scarce, as the minting of gold tailed off toward the end of the 1460s, and the late halves and quarters much rarer. Throughout the series trefoils remain the normal stops on gold, although saltires are found occasionally on London ryals of type VIII, on London and York halves of type VII, and on quarters of both types. As in type VI there is sometimes a quatrefoil in the inscription on ryals and halves, and some early dies of type VII show small lis in the obverse legend, again as in the previous type. On quarters there is great variety, with saltires, lis and roses often instead of, or mixed with, trefoils, especially on the reverse. Like some groats of types VIII-X, several dies of the half-ryals have lettering from the smaller (halfgroat-sized) fount.

The common ryals of type VII are straightforward. Those of London and Bristol, with mintmark crown on the reverse, often have an inverted comma below the contraction mark after *Aut*. York ryals, like the silver, now have the lis mark, although an early transitional die has the sun of type VI beside it. Because they normally have no obverse mintmark, muled ryals and half-ryals are often difficult to detect. Sometimes muling can only be identified from the pattern of die-linking, as for example with a Bristol VII/VIII ryal, the obverse die of which was mostly used for true coins of type VII. More remarkably, two unrosed obverses of type V reappear with reverses of type VII, and one of them even with a reverse of type VIII. Obverse dies of ryals and halves (except those with small lettering) may be associated with type VII rather than type VI if they have R4 with its indented tail. Ryals with trefoils in the spandrels (type VIII) generally have the same reverse mintmarks as in type VII. There are, however, two important exceptions in type VIII at London: one has mintmark sun instead of crown, the other has a sun punched over the crown. The latter variety may have been intended not as an alteration, so much as a combined mark, since it is found on all three denominations at London, as well as on half-ryals of York. The London ryal involved is of further interest in that its obverse is struck from an old die of type VI with a pellet added below the shield, this being a feature of several normal dies of type VIII. Some reverse dies of type VIII and later have trefoils on the cusps of the tressure, as well as in the spandrels. Obverse variants include the omission of all ornaments on the ship's side or of the fleurs-de-lis that flank the lions. Among the London ryals of type X is a variety with small letters, and *Dei* in full, as on some groats of this type. During type X there was some modification of the design, with the normal five-line ship giving way to a four-liner, and finally with the after rigging reduced from three ropes to two. An untraced York ryal with mintmark sun both sides, and small trefoils in the spandrels, has been tentatively attributed to this period; but the only late Bristol ryal is a mule with the sun on the reverse only, its obverse being of type VIII as shown by the letter R4. The same criterion also identifies some VIII/X mules of London.

Half-ryals are generally the scarcest denomination. The least rare are those of type VII, in which London and Bristol have mintmark crown, and York a lis. If with mintmark crown alone, London half-ryals can only be classified as type VIII if they have a pellet above or below the shield, like some type VIII ryals, or a lis in the waves, a feature of unknown significance, but presumably late since it occurs in type IX and there is also a reverse die-link with a normal coin of type VIII (support, incidentally, for the view that the lis-marked halves should not be attributed to York as once they were). Other mintmarks indicating type VIII or the transition between VII and VIII are, however, found: sun and crown at London and Bristol, sun over crown at London and York, and at London the combination of sun on the obverse with the normal reverse crown. To type IX are attributed very rare halves with a rose mintmark, but combined with the letter R4: these are London coins with rose/crown (another exceptional case of an obverse mintmark), which have a lis in the waves and sometimes also a pellet above the shield, as in type VIII; and York coins with a rose beside the lis on the reverse. The only half-ryals with mintmark LCF are of London, and extremely rare; one has pellets instead of trefoils in the spandrels.

By virtue of having an obverse mintmark quarter-ryals should be easier to classify than the larger gold, but against this is the lack of a mint initial for Bristol or York. There

Edward IV – Henry VIII

is considerable variety of detail throughout. The rose and sun beside the shield may be placed either way about. In the spandrels there are usually trefoils, but sometimes nothing or, in the case of one early variety of type VII, pellets (with pellets also by the *e* above the shield). London quarters have mintmark crown for type VII; in type VIII they show either sun over crown both sides, or sun on the obverse with crown or sun and crown on the reverse; and the series ends with the LCF of type XI. Quarters attributable to York have first lis/crown, like some early York groats of type VII, and then lis both sides.

The reverse of the only known first reign angel later than type V has the crown mintmark of type VII. It differs in a number of details from the earlier coins, notably in having a much smaller sun by the cross, and to its left.

Henry VI, Second Reign (1470-1) and Edward IV, type XII

Although the principal type of mintmark at London before, during and after the short reappearance of Henry VI was some kind of cross, and there is continuity between his coinage and the earliest of Edward IV's second reign that followed, there had been a complete break when Edward was replaced in October 1470. Except possibly at York there are no mules between Edward's types X-XI and Henry's coinage, and the new government must have hastened to have Edwardian dies withdrawn and replaced by new ones in Henry's name. Otherwise (and apart from greater variation in the form of the mintmark) the silver coinage was very little affected. In gold, however, the transformation brought about by the change of dynasty was fundamental.

CROSS INITIAL MARKS OF HENRY VI, 1470 - 1

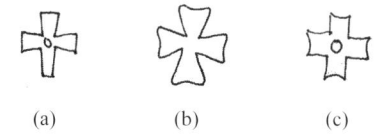

(a)   (b)   (c)

(a) Short cross fitchy; (b) Cross patty; (c) Restoration cross.

No fewer than four distinct mintmarks were used on groats during the six months of the Restoration. The two main London marks were an elegant broad-ended cross patty (CP) and a plain pierced cross with straight limbs and indented ends known as the Restoration Cross (RC). Two other (much rarer) marks are also found on London groat reverses, lis and cross fitchy, the latter a shorter version of the LCF mark used in Edward's types X-XI. This short cross fitchy (SCF), which has a rather blunt foot, was to be the defining London mark of type XII at the beginning of Edward's second reign. Although differing in appearance from LCF, the SCF may well not have been conceived as a separate mark, and indeed to what extent the use of three varieties of cross during the Restoration was deliberate for purposes of differentiation is unclear. Allen showed that CP and the commoner RC were in use concurrently on groat obverses and that each of these crosses (in one case the same CP die) was combined with all four of the reverse marks, lis, SCF, CP and RC, possibly in that order in the light of XII/RC and XIV/RC mules. York continued to use its now customary lis, although a rare variety has the Yorkist mintmark sun on the reverse, incongruously for Henry VI and so presumably a Henry/type X mule from an old Edwardian die. Bristol, however, used two of the

London marks, RC and SCF, plus a trefoil and a rose; RC and trefoil occur on both sides, SCF and rose on reverses only. Rose was to be the Bristol mark on groats of type XII, trefoil the reverse mark on London groats of type XIII. There was no break in the die-chain with the return of Edward IV, and reverse die-links between Henry and Edward groats are found at all three mints. Some Henry groats of Bristol are from a batch of dies with the spelling *Willa* corrected to *Villa* by having two saltires punched over the first *V* of the *W*, and when such reverse dies (even those not known with Henry obverses) are found with type XII obverses they are to be regarded as Edward/Henry mules. One of the Edward York groats of type XII, die-linked to Henry VI, has on its reverse a plain form of the letter *I*, introduced in type VIII, which Allen had noted as being found only on earlier Henry VI dies; during the Restoration it was displaced by an *I* with wider and serrated ends which had first been seen in type XI and was to continue into types XII and XIII. No coins of the York royal mint, which was closed by September 1471, are known after type XII until the reign of Richard III.

NOTABLE LETTERS OF EDWARD IV, SECOND REIGN

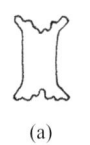

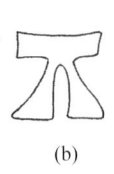

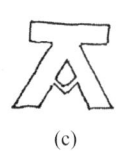

(a) Serrated *I*, X – XIII and Henry VI; (b) BW's flat-footed A4, XIV;
(c) Chevron-barred *A*, from XVI; (d) Pot-hook *A*, XVIII – XXI;
(e) Letter *R* of new fount (BW R6), XVIIIb – XXII.

Several dies for both gold and silver of Henry VI have the spelling *henricu*. Groats, especially of London, are quite plentiful, although those of York and, more particularly, of Bristol are scarce. Stops on groats of Henry (and type XII) are generally saltires or trefoils, occasionally a lis or, as on gold, a pellet; or sometimes none. As before, the top arcs on groats and halves may be plain or trefoiled. Where stops occur on the smaller silver, they are usually trefoils. All the smaller Henry silver is rare: halfgroats of Bristol have not yet been found, while of York (where pence were still struck only for the archbishop) the halfpenny is missing. All the silver of type XII, except for London groats, is also rare: there are groats and halves of all three mints, pence of London and Bristol, but halfpence of London only.

Few halfgroats were struck at this period. The London coins of Henry and the unique example of Edward's type XII have the obverse mintmarks respectively RC and SCF, some of the former with the mark also on the reverse. York halfgroats have mintmark lis both sides, this mark on Henry's coins being larger than in Edward's first reign, evidently from the groat punch. The same larger lis occurs on the reverse of the type XII York halfgroat, suggesting the use of a Restoration die. The extremely rare York halfgroats of Henry have *e* on the breast, as only exceptionally (type VIII) on this denomination hitherto. Bristol's type XII halfgroat, also with the mint initial, has obverse mintmark rose, as on other denominations, but on the reverse is the SCF, the only occurrence of this mark on any type XII groat or halfgroat outside London, although it had appeared on a few Bristol groats of the Restoration.

Pence and halfpence lack a reverse mintmark, as usual. The inclusion of *D(e)i Gra* on

Edward IV – Henry VIII

London halfpence of Henry's second reign is a simple means of distinguishing them from those of his first. Because the small silver of the Restoration is so rare the occurrence of one or other form of cross on known pence or halfpence of London and Bristol is likely to be due less to design than to chance of survival. One of the very few obverse dies used for Henry VI pence at London has Archbishop Neville's *G* and key by the bust: as more than one London reverse was paired with it, the Neville die can never have been sent to York (the only ecclesiastical mint where coins were struck during the Restoration). In type XII the pence of the northern bishops follow London's mintmark SCF, to which Bristol's rose is the only exception. No farthing has yet been noted after type X, before the Restoration, until the reign of Richard III.

The return of Henry VI brought an abrupt end to the ryal series of the second half of the 1460s. Edward's ryal, flaunting his initial and the Yorkist rose and sun, was not readily adaptable to a Lancastrian idiom, and we may suppose that this was at least as instrumental as the relative convenience of value in the decision to revive the 6s.8d. angel-noble which had been struck only in insignificant quantities from 1465. On the reverse the symbolic sun at the masthead was replaced by a realistic nautical 'crow's-nest', and beside the cross the sun and rose gave way to *h* with the traditional Lancastrian lis, but in other respects the design of Henry's angel was generally similar to Edward's. It was, however, struck on a smaller but thicker flan, resulting in the saint's head breaking the inscription at the top. There is often a small cross or trefoil within the nimbus. This type, with a Gothic St. Michael in spiky feathers, was to continue virtually unchanged into the reign of Henry VII, apart from the initial and symbol by the shield, which in Edward's second reign were *e* and rose.

Henry's London angels are not rare, considering their brief period of issue, but there are very few of Edward's type XII. Gold of this period normally has trefoil stops, sometimes saltires, while a few Restoration angels and type XII halves have pellet stops on the reverse. Two Henry obverse dies, evidently experimental, have lettering from the groat fount, but the smaller size of angel dies from 1470 soon led to the use of the halfgroat punches. Where possible, for various elements of the design, such as the prow and poop of the ship, early Restoration angels also use the same punches as Edward's half-ryals. A few of Henry's London angels have the RC mintmark on the obverse (either side of the saint's head) but otherwise the Restoration gold does not have an obverse mintmark. In type XII, however, both angels and angelets, only known of London and very rare, have the SCF on the obverse, without a mark on the reverse. The reverse mark on Restoration gold, sometimes omitted on angels, is normally to the right of the masthead, the RC being more frequently found than the cross patty in this metal. Bristol angels, with *B* in the waves, are of great rarity and only a single angelet of this mint is known. There are none with *e* for York in the waves, but a few angels and halves with reverse mintmark lis (to left) have sometimes been attributed to this mint. Some support for this idea may come from the fact that a small group of two obverse and three reverse dies, to which the lis-marked angel reverse belongs, is not die-linked into the main London series. However, since the lis occurs on the reverse of some London groats, a York attribution for the lis-marked gold must be regarded with caution. The type XII (and XIV) angels, and many of Henry's, have the spelling *Cruse* for *Cruce*. Another (converse) phonetic confusion is *Spece* for *Spes* on the Bristol half; a similar die is found without the *B* and so presumably of London. On type XII angelets the inscriptions are switched between obverse and reverse resulting, in the case of mules with obverses of type XIV, in coins that have the king's name and titles on both sides.

Henry VI's second reign provides a valuable insight into the structure of late medieval coinage in a self-contained period as short as six months. The result is somewhat perplexing, since there appears to be no tidy pattern in the use of dies with different mintmarks or other features, such as would suit numismatic theories about privy-marking or sequence. Yet care seems to have been taken in the marking of dies, perhaps for the purpose of identifying particular dies themselves rather than the coins struck from them. Allen and Webb Ware have shown that dies for angels and groats of the Restoration were produced in batches, with common features such as the contractions used for *Crucem* and *Redemptor*. With the groats there is a clear distinction between obverse dies (with both mintmarks) without trefoils on the cusps above the crown, which read *henric*, and those with trefoiled cusps which normally read *henricu*. Individual dies for gold, however, also seem to have been deliberately varied in minor detail for purposes of identification – no two angel obverse dies, and almost no reverses, have inscriptions identical in both spelling and punctuation.

HENRY VI RESTORED, AND EDWARD IV TYPES XII – XV, AT ROYAL MINTS

	HENRY VI RESTORED	EDWARD IV			
		XII	XIII	XIV	XV
Angel	LB(+Y?)	L		LB	L
Angelet	LB	L		L	
Groat	LBY	LBY	L	LB	L
Halfgroat	LY	LBY	L	L	L
Penny	LB	LB		L	L
Halfpenny	LB	L		L	L

L – London; B – Bristol; Y – York.

Edward IV, Annulet Series, Types XIII - XV

Type XII, the brief extension of cross-marked dies into Edward's second reign, was followed by a series of coins with annulet mintmarks. Blunt and Whitton divided the London coins into three types: XIII, consisting only of London groats and halves, with a large annulet obverse mintmark; XIV (the most abundant of the three), with a smaller annulet; and XV, with an annulet enclosing a pellet. Although there are mules within this series, as well as between type XII and types XIII and XIV, apart from one angel there are no mules between unaltered annulet dies and dies of the second cross-marked group that followed, suggesting that the change of mintmark between types XV and XVI coincided with an administrative break that caused the first interruption in the die-chain since the return of Henry VI. The royal mint at York had already ceased operations, but of type XIV there are a few groats and angels of Bristol, the last coins of this mint before its closure (until the debasement of Henry VIII) in July 1472.

Edward IV – Henry VIII

London Mintmarks of Edward IV, Annulet Series

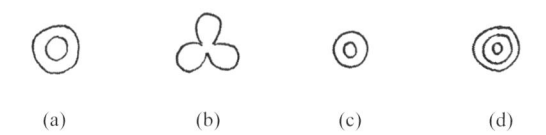

(a) Large annulet, XIII obv.; (b) Trefoil, XIII rev.; (c) Small annulet, XIV;
(d) Pellet-in-annulet, XV.

The groats and halfgroats of type XIII are differentiated from type XIV not only by the size of the annulet mintmark, but also in having small annulet stops on the obverse and, in a revival of the practice often adopted in the first reign, a different mark on the reverse, a large trefoil on groats and a rose on halves. On the reverse of type XIII groats and on some of type XIV the stops are trefoils, but saltires were introduced on both silver and gold in type XIV and continued to be used for the rest of the reign. On halfgroats the ornaments on the tressure (excluding the cusps above the crown) were small trefoils throughout the group, but on the groats (which sometimes have the top cusps fleured) the small trefoils were replaced by larger ones early in type XV. Other changes in type XV were *Dei* for *Di* on all denominations except a few early groats, and the addition (XVb) of roses beside the bust on groats shortly after the introduction of the larger trefoils.

Groats of type XIII are rare and the fact that London dies of type XIV as well as of type XIII are muled with type XII (and even once with a Restoration reverse) emphasises the shortness of the period in use of type XIII dies. Type XIV London groats are much the most plentiful of the annulet series, those of type XV being rare, especially the earlier variety without roses by the bust (XVa). Bristol groats, which include mules with type XII obverses, are all rare. Their mintmark is either an annulet as at London or a sun, dies with the latter mark being distinguishable from sun-marked dies of the first reign by the absence of marks by the bust and by a new letter *A* with broad, flat feet, introduced in type XIV. The sun may be the later of the two marks since sun obverses have saltire stops instead of trefoils.

No Bristol halfgroats are known later than type XII. As with the groats, type XIV is the least scarce of the London halfgroats, those of type XIII being very rare, of type XV even more so. On halfgroats of types XIII and XV the reverse mintmark is a rose, small and neat on the former, large on the latter. Although halves of type XIV normally have the annulet mark on the reverse also, it is omitted on some; a coin with a large annulet on the obverse and no mark on the reverse could thus perhaps be a XIII/XIV mule. The London pence and halfpence of types XIV and XV are rare, especially the type XV pence. Some of the episcopal pence of this period have mintmarks found on London coins – the annulet at York and trefoil, rose and pellet-in-annulet at Durham.

Angels are known of types XIV and XV, halves of XIV only. The common type XIV angels have the annulet mintmark usually on both sides, to left or right of the head on the obverse; it is occasionally omitted on the reverse. One reverse die has the annulet possibly over a cross although no such unaltered die of type XII is known. Bristol angels, extremely rare, have no reverse mark, and on one obverse die the annulet appears to be struck over a trefoil. They read *Dei* for *Di*, as do several of the London angels, this spelling being introduced earlier on angels than on the silver. Stops on type XIV angels are usually trefoils, but as on the silver saltires begin to appear in this type, and are standard from type XV onwards. Angel dies of types XIV and XV are muled both ways. Type XIV was the last in which there is a cross or a trefoil in the nimbus. In type XV *Crucem* and *Xpe* replace *Crusem* and *Xpc*, and *Redempt* becomes the standard reading. Some reverse dies of type XV appear to have the rose beside the cross punched over a sun.

The rare angelets of type XIV, now with the king's titles correctly on the obverse, follow the example of quarter-ryals of the first reign in introducing roses into the reverse inscription, a feature that was to continue until type XXI. Although no angelet is known of type XV, dies appear to have been prepared since, as with all the silver denominations, coins of type XVI are found with the mintmark cross punched over an annulet (the central pellet not, of course, visible).

Edward IV, Second Cross Series, Types XVI - XX

After the annulet-marked types there was a reversion to the cross which, in various forms, served as the initial mark on a series of varieties defined by Blunt and Whitton as types XVI-XX. Whether these varieties really constitute distinct 'types' in any more meaningful sense than, say, the different crosses on the Restoration coinage of Henry VI, is open to question, especially since there is very heavy muling between them and only two of the types (XVI and XVIIIb) are known for all denominations. In contrast to the abundance of die-interchanges between types within the series, however, there is only one such link (an angel with a type XV obverse) with the preceding annulet series and very few with the cinquefoil type (XXI) that followed. Indeed, a deliberate break between the annulet and cross series, while many dies of type XV remained fresh, is indicated by the fact that there are examples of type XVI, of every denomination except the angel, on which a cross has been punched into the die, on one or both sides, over the pellet-in-annulet of type XV, giving the appearance of a four-spoked wheel. The other coins described under type XVI, including all the angels and most of the groats, have either (rarely) the same plain cross but without the annulet beneath it, or (much more frequently) a cross with a pellet in each angle. The definition of the remaining types is based on the groats. Type XVII, of which angels and halfpence are also known, has mintmark pierced cross without adjacent pellets, type XVIII a pierced cross with a single pellet in one quarter. The last two types have a pierced cross, respectively with a small central pellet (type XX) and without any pellet (type XIX), there being in addition to groats of these types only some rare halfpence (XIX) and a few dies for gold that are known solely from mules. The groats and angels of type XIX can be readily distinguished from those of type XVII with similar mintmark by their lettering and other detailed features.

CROSS AND CINQUEFOIL INITIAL MARKS IN EDWARD IV TYPES XVI – XXI

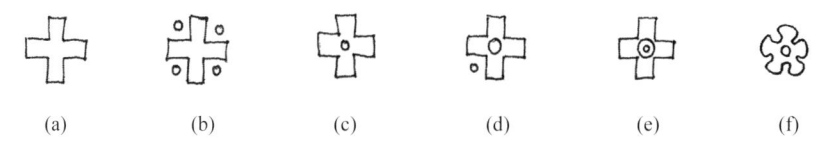

(a) Plain cross, XVIa; (b) Cross with four pellets, XVIb; (c) Pierced cross, XVII and XIX; (d) Cross with one pellet, XVIII; (e) Pierced cross with central pellet, XX; (f) Cinquefoil, XXI.

Edward IV – Henry VIII

The groats of these cross types fall into two phases. Those of types XVI, XVII and XVIIIa, which constitute the first phase, follow type XV in having large trefoils on the cusps of the tressure (usually on all, but occasionally omitted above the crown in types XVII and XVIIIa). On type XVIIIa the pellet is always in the upper left angle of the initial cross, but on type XVIIIb, in which the pellet is in one of the lower angles, a number of more significant changes were also made. In the second phase, consisting of types XVIIIb, XIX and XX, large fleurs replaced the trefoils on the cusps, new lettering was introduced and roses and suns were often added on the reverse in conjunction with the saltire stops that occur throughout the second cross series. During type XVIIIb there also appears to have been a general replacement of groat dies of the earlier phase, since dies of types XVII and XVIIIa do not interchange with dies later than, nor dies of types XIX and XX with dies earlier than, XVIIIb.

Edward IV, Types XVI – XX, Groats and Mules

Obv.	Rev. XVIa	XVIb	XVII	XVIIIa	XVIIIb	XX	XIX
XVIa	x						
XVIb	m	x	m				
XVII		m	x	m	m		
XVIIIa			m	x	m		
XVIIIb			m	m	x	m	m
XX					m	x	m
XIX					m	m	x

x – true coin; m – mule

With type XVI a new feature appears that was to continue on most groats almost to the end of the reign, namely a chevron-barred A in *Angl* and *tas*. In type XVI the plain initial cross seems likely to have preceded the cross with four pellets, since plain cross over annulet is the only mark found on angelets, halfgroats and pence, while groat dies muled with type XVII always have the cross and four pellets. For convenience the coins with the plain cross, usually over the annulet, may therefore be designated XVIa, those with the cross and four pellets XVIb. Plain cross alone is only certainly found on groats, on one side or both; such coins are of some rarity. Although there was no problem with amending their reverses, there are no XVIa groats from altered obverse dies of type XV, presumably because of the roses by the bust in XVb. Groats of type XVIb are scarce, but the least so of the silver coins of types XVI-XVIIIa. The rare smaller silver of this phase consists of halfgroats of type XVIa only and pence and halfpence of types XVI and XVII. All read *Dei*, like the groats, and some halfgroat and halfpenny dies are without stops. The halfgroats of this phase have small trefoils on the tressure, as in types XII-XV, but now on all the cusps. As usual, the pence and halfpence are normally without an initial cross on the reverse, an exception being a penny of type XVII. Pence of type XVI read *Angle*, like those of type XV, and one obverse die is recorded from pennies struck both before and after the cross of type XVIa was punched over the pellet-in-annulet. Halfpence are the only silver coins of type XVI apart from groats to include new dies of type XVIb as well as those of type XV converted to type XVIa.

Gold of the first phase consists of angels of all three types, but angelets of type XVI only. All read *Dei* like the silver. As in type XV, stops are now generally saltires although some XVI angels have a large trefoil between two saltires at the end of the obverse and on the rare halves (which read *Angle* like the XV-XVI pence) there is a rose in the reverse inscription, as first found in type XIV. The angelet of type XVIa, with cross over annulet on both sides, shows that dies were made for type XV even if perhaps never used before the alteration (as also seems to have been the case with the reverse of halfgroats). The obverse of the XV/XVI angel, probably left unaltered due to an oversight, not only gave rise to the sole example of a mule between these two types but also resulted in the angel being the only denomination in either metal unrepresented in type XVIa. All the true type XVI angels were struck from new dies with the cross and four pellets of XVIb. They are also found muled both ways with the rare type XVII and with reverses of types XVIIIa and b.

Of the three component types of the second phase, type XVIIIb is common and includes all denominations, while types XIX and XX are much scarcer and more limited. The seemingly minor adjustment of the initial mark in type XVIII, from having a pellet in the upper left quarter (a) to a pellet in one of the lower quarters (b), was accompanied or quickly followed by more fundamental changes, in lettering and ornamentation. On groats of type XVIIIb the new fount has carefully drawn and well proportioned letters (reducing *Dei* to *Di)*.

At first the old B-like *R* (R5) was used, but this was soon replaced by an *R* with an outward-turning tail (R6). The copula now has a transverse bar, and two ornamental letters, *A* and *V* with 'pot-hook' ends, occur irregularly on the obverse and in the outer legend on the reverse (surviving occasionally up to type XXI). The roses and suns that often appear on the reverse are also usually in the outer legend. Perhaps the most obvious new feature of the type XVIIIb groats, however, is the large fleurs on the tressure, which were to continue for the rest of the reign and beyond. Because of their size these are omitted above the crown and there is usually no fleur on the breast. Groats of type XVIIIb are the next commonest of the second reign after those with the mintmark cinquefoil of type XXI. All obverse and reverse combinations of initial cross are found, that with the pellet in the lower right quarter on the obverse and in the lower left on the reverse being the most usual. The revival of the pierced initial cross in type XIX was accompanied by the addition of a pellet each side of the bust and in one or two quarters of the reverse. When worn the pierced initial cross with central pellet of type XX is easily confused with the pierced cross of type XIX, but the rare groats of type XX have no other extra pellets and they are also notable for lacking the usual saltire stops on the obverse. Reverse dies with roses (but no suns) occur in both these types, in type XX always after *Deum*. Since the only groat mule between one of the cross types and the cinquefoil mark that follows is of types XXI/XIX, there are grounds for thinking that type XIX may come after type XX. Another pointer in this direction is that an extra pellet on the reverse occurs both on groats of type XIX and on some of type XXI, but not on those of type XX.

No London halfgroats or pence have been found of types XIX or XX, but those of type XVIIIb are not unduly rare. The saltire stops are usually omitted. The halfgroats follow the groats in having *Di* for *Dei* and larger trefoils (occasionally over the crown, but not on the breast). One obverse die known only from an XVIIIb/XVI mule still has the old lettering (including A5 with sloping feet), but on all other dies a new fount is used (with the flat-footed A6). There are no barred *A* or 'pot-hook' letters on the halfgroats, but this fount is otherwise similar to that on the groats, and was also used for the gold of type XVIIIb onwards. Halfpence of type XIX have pellets by the bust like the groats (but not also on the reverse). The cross mintmarks were mostly not used on pence of York and Durham, although the two mints were undoubtedly active at this period. Canterbury, however, and with it the main supply of halfgroats, may still have been in abeyance.

Edward IV – Henry VIII

Gold of the second phase consists mostly of angels and halves of type XVIIIb. Types XX and XIX are represented only by mules. Type XVIIIb angels still normally read *Dei* rather than *Di*, although *Di* occurs on the rare half, once with a rose after it. On angelet reverses of this type there is sometimes a sun as well as a rose in the legend, as on groats. The only type XX die is an angelet obverse, first muled with an XVIIIb reverse and later converted for use in type XXI by having a cinquefoil punched over the initial cross. An angel obverse and reverse of type XIX (not found together in combination but respectively muled with an XVIIIb reverse and a XXI obverse) are identifiable by the combination of the initial pierced cross and the new lettering with A6.

London coins of Edward IV, Types XVI –XXI

	XVI	XVII	XVIII	XIX	XX	XXI
Angel	x	x	x	m		x
Angelet	x		x		m	x
Groat	x	x	x	x	x	x
Halfgroat	x		x			x
Penny	x	x	x			x
Halfpenny	x	x	x	x		x

m – mules only

Edward IV, Type XXI, Mintmark Cinquefoil

Type XXI, the last substantial issue of Edward's reign, bears the mintmark cinquefoil. Dies of the preceding types with cross mintmarks were withdrawn and, in contrast to the heavy die-interchanges between the various cross types, there is a nearly complete absence of mules between the cross and cinquefoil marks. In silver there is a single cinquefoil/cross groat (XXI/XIX) and in gold a few angels from an old reverse die, also of type XIX. The only case of mintmark alteration at this point, of the kind found so extensively at the previous break in the die-chain (between types XV and XVI), is the last angelet obverse die of the cross series which had the pierced cross of type XX, still partly visible, overpunched with a cinquefoil. The normal form of the mintmark is the stylized heraldic cinquefoil, with five angular knobs linked to a central ring with a hollowed centre. On the reverses of a few groats (some of which also have a point within the pellets in one quarter, as in type XIX, and so may be early), there is a pellet before the cinquefoil. A pellet before the mark also occurs on two angel obverses which are certainly late, so there is no obvious connection between the pellet-marked groats and angels. The only variant of the cinquefoil mark itself is a cluster of five petals, more like a loosely rendered rose, found on some rare angels, groats and halfgroats.

Cinquefoil groats are the commonest of the second reign, and immediately recognisable by having a neat rose on the breast. Stops on the groats are saltires, with often roses in the reverse inscription, as before, and also now occasionally on the obverse. Groats continue to have the chevron-barred *A* in *Angl* and *tas*, and on a few dies in all relevant words. The occasional pot-hook *A* and *V* occur for the last time in this type. As since type XVIIIb, there are large fleurs on the cusps, sometimes also above the crown. Only *Di*, as in the second phase of the cross series, is found on groats, but *Dei* is revived on some halfgroats, pence and halfpence. The London halfgroats, which although scarce are less rare than any of the cross-marked types, differ from their predecessors in having smaller trefoils on the cusps (all except the breast). Apart from saltires on a few halfgroat reverses, the smaller silver is without stops. Cinquefoil pence and halfpence are the only reasonably plentiful examples of these denominations from London in the second reign, but there are still no farthings. A feature often visible on halfpence of the second reign is a small nick in the lower outline of the bust, below the sinister shoulder, presumably from a developing flaw in the punch; by type XXI this is usually quite clear.

As in the first reign, most of the halfgroats of this period came from Canterbury; and pence continued to be supplied mainly by York and Durham. The cinquefoil occurs on some of the York pence of Archbishop Laurence Booth (who died in May 1480), and on the reverse of a few Canterbury halfgroats. Otherwise the usual mintmark on the later episcopal coins of the second reign is a rose.

Cinquefoil angels, from more than thirty obverse dies, are much the commonest of the reign and constitute almost half of all those noted of types XII-XXI. They (and the much rarer angelets) differ from previous types in having the ship drawn with five lines of planking instead of four. Some have a small horizontal leopard immediately below the forecastle. The angels continue to read *Dei*; and this is now revived on some of the halves, which have roses in the reverse legend as in earlier types, and include the variety from the altered obverse die of type XX. Mid-way through type XXI there were changes in the letter fount used for angels and halfgroats, the small *G* and *L* being replaced by larger versions and the old (broken) *R* by an undamaged punch. The last few angel dies are identifiable by a new punch for the dragon's head with a broken loop for the ear, and these include the two dies with a pellet by the cinquefoil. That the old die of type XIX used on mule angels was brought into use towards the end of the cinquefoil period is shown by the late lettering on all the type XXI obverses combined with it and by the new dragon's head punch on most of them.

Ecclesiastical Issues of Edward IV's Light Coinage

The reign of Edward IV saw many important changes in the contribution made by the episcopal mints to the English currency. Most significant was the restoration to the archbishop of Canterbury of minting rights after a lapse of more than a century since the sterling period. Since these included halfgroats and halfpence as well as pence, the resumption of minting at Canterbury, in one of the most commercially active areas of the country, made an immediate impact. Hoards show that under Edward IV and Henry VII it provided a large majority of all the halfgroats in circulation. York continued to produce most of the country's supply of pence, abetted now by considerably increased output from Durham.

Coins of these three mints require separate treatment because at many points they do not correspond closely to those of London or the other royal mints, and often the same typological framework will not work. Sometimes they carry the London mintmarks, but the rose is frequently used on coins of the episcopal mints that cannot possibly be of the same period as London type V or IX. Added to this are problems arising from the use on several occasions of locally made dies at the northern mints. Furthermore, most of the pence of York and Durham, even when not worn from long circulation, are poorly struck, often on rather small flans, so that fully legible examples of some varieties are virtually non-existent. On the other hand, there is valuable additional evidence at York and Durham from the inclusion for the first time of the personal initials of successive prelates. As in earlier periods, it has generally been assumed that coins lacking ecclesiastical marks on one or both sides were struck when a bishop's temporalities were not being exercised, either because they had been suspended as a result of a quarrel with the crown or when the see was vacant between appointments. But while such may often have been the case, it is clear that this formula was not always scrupulously followed (as witness, for example, the unquatrefoiled York pence of the previous reign), and numismatists have thereby sometimes been led astray.

Canterbury, 1464-1483

It is no surprise that the revival, and extension, of rights of coinage for the archbishop of Canterbury in favour of Thomas Bourchier should have had such material consequences for the structure of the coinage. For reasons of economy and convenience, medieval mints tended to concentrate their output on the largest denominations permitted. Just as London (and other royal mints when operating) had for some time produced relatively few pence, being content for the most part to leave those to York and Durham where the higher values were not authorised, so did the addition of a new episcopal mint with authority to coin halfgroats have a similar effect on the minting of this denomination at the royal mints. The new Canterbury coinage also involved innovation in appearance. Canterbury coins of the sterling period, the profits of which had been shared between king and archbishop, had carried no episcopal marking, but Bourchier's incorporated two features from his personal arms, a knot and a spur, one on each side of the coin, as well as using the archiepiscopal *pallium* for the mintmark. Bourchier's knot is placed prominently on the obverse, below the bust, and the spur curves to the left from the inner circle to join the pellets in one quarter of the reverse. The *pallium*, or pall, is shown as a Y-shaped mark, often with a small cross in the fork as in the archbishop's arms. In the later stages of the first reign all the archbishop's armorial charges were dropped from the coinage and the pall was replaced by the London mintmark crown. The removal of Bourchier's marks led Brooke to propose that the mint was at this point transferred from the archbishop to the king. There are, however, powerful arguments against such an interpretation. All the verified royal mints of Edward IV have left their mark in the mint accounts or other public records of the time. Furthermore, the preferred denomination at every royal mint from 1351 until Henry VIII was the groat, and there could have been no case for denying this to Canterbury if it had been under royal control. Whatever the reason for removing the archbishop's symbols – were they just too boldly displayed for the king's taste? – there is no evidence to support the theory that this marked the end of his coinage.

Nearly all the output from Canterbury in the second half of the 1460s therefore consisted of halfgroats and Blunt and Whitton attempted to construct a typology relating them to types V-IX in the London series. However, although London and York halfgroats of types V and VI have large fleurs on the cusps, followed by small trefoils from type VII onwards, Canterbury halfgroats with large fleurs were all classed as type Va, with small trefoils from Vb onwards. Under this scheme BW types V, VI and early VII are all with obverse mintmark pall, with pall, rose, sun or none on the reverse; of these, types V and VI have Bourchier's knot and spur, type VII lacking one or the other of them. Type VII then continues with mintmark crown and without episcopal marks, representing the commencement of the so-called 'royal' series. From types V to VII marks beside the bust, when present, are quatrefoils, saltires or 'wedges', trefoils in this position indicating types VIII (mintmark crown) and IX (mintmark rose). Until the trefoils in type VIII, there is little consistency in the choice of ornaments beside the bust. VIa is defined as having saltires by the bust, and VIb either quatrefoils or four irregular shaped pellets, or 'wedges', two by the hair and two by the bust (in one case quatrefoils were punched over the two lower wedges); but there is no regularity in the mintmarks on reverse dies coupled with these varieties, and more than half of the individual varieties listed by Blunt and Whitton for types VI and VII (pall) are described technically as mules. The true structure of this extensive and complex coinage will only become evident when a full die-study is undertaken, but in the meantime it is convenient to list the varieties in broad groups without attempting to define what are the regular pairings and which might be regarded as mules.

Group A (BW Va) includes all the halfgroats with large fleurs, which should be the earliest, although whether the reverse mintmark rose found in this group relates to the rose of type V at royal mints is an open question. Group B, with small trefoils on the cusps, contains all the other coins with obverse mintmark pall plus the knot and spur (BW Vb-VIb), whether the reverse mintmark is pall (Ba), none (Bb), rose (Bc) or sun (Bd). In group C (BW VII) are those coins still with the pall on the obverse, but without one or both of the other marks. All halfgroats of this last group known to Blunt and Whitton omitted either the knot (Cb) or the spur (Ca), but not both, and so were listed as mules; but the die-combination with neither of Bourchier's personal marks is also now recorded (Cc). This shows that on halfgroats (as on pence) Bourchier's marks were dropped shortly before pall was replaced by crown as mintmark (group D). At this point the series becomes simpler, Canterbury coins of groups D, E and F following the London sequence of marks, crown (VII), crown/sun (VIII) and rose (IX). The position of the rose appears to be confirmed by a IX/VIII mule, but since the rose of type IX at London is so rare this could merely be one of the periodic cases of rose being used at an episcopal mint regardless of what was happening elsewhere.

Canterbury pence and halfpence of the first reign are all very rare. They have the same sequence of the main mintmarks, pall and crown, as the halfgroats, but no post-crown small silver is known with mintmark rose. However, what is presumably the earliest variety of penny (type 1) does have the rose and may belong to the period of London type V. It has a pall to the left of the bust and Bourchier's knot in the field to the right, an awkward arrangement that seems soon to have been abandoned. On the next pence (type 2) the pall becomes the mintmark and the knot and spur are also as in groups A and B of the halfgroats. These are followed by pence and halfpence (type 3) still with mintmark pall, but without

Bourchier's personal marks, equivalent to halfgroats of group C; and then (type 4) with mintmark crown, as on halfgroats of group D. Halfpence (type 5) but not pence are known with mintmark crown and trefoils by the bust, and so classed as type VIII (alongside the halfgroats of group E).

There are no Canterbury coins of Henry VI's second reign, but it is possible that the mint had ceased activity before 1470. It was not to resume until well into Edward IV's second reign of which its coins, in common with most of those of the royal mints, are easily recognised by the lack of marks beside the bust. As before, there are halfgroats, pence and halfpence, the first very common, the last two of considerable rarity. Two obverse mintmarks are found on each denomination, long cross fitchy and rose, constituting respectively groups G and H for halfgroats and types 6 and 7 for pence and halfpence. Obverses with LCF have no breastmark, but with rose, except for one very rare variety of penny, all have a *C* in this position. Only the halfgroats have a reverse mintmark, a cinquefoil with the LCF, and rose with rose. Blunt and Whitton took the LCF/

cinquefoil halfgroats as representing the cinquefoil-marked type XXI, and associated, very speculatively as they acknowledged, the three main varieties of rose halfgroat with types XVIII-XX. However, the rare LCF/cinquefoil halfgroats have coarser lettering (e.g. the *O* and *R*), unlike that on late London coins of Edward IV, whereas the finer fount of the rose halfgroats, which includes an *R* with an increasingly weak and defective tail, can be matched on London dies as late as those of the boar's head Edward halfgroat of 1483. Now that a longer duration is postulated for mintmark cinquefoil, the LCF coins of all denominations could be placed relatively early in the cinquefoil period, followed by those with rose. On the basis of mules, and of deterioration of the letter *R*, the order of the three varieties of group H halfgroats with mintmark rose may have been as follows:

Ha   Trefoils on cusps, but not over crown; no mark on centre of reverse cross (BW type 'XIX'). Unbroken *R*.
Hb   All cusps trefoiled; *C* on centre of cross (BW type 'XVIIIb'). *R* weakening.
Hc   No trefoils on cusps; small rose on centre of cross (BW type 'XX'). *R* often broken.

York, 1464-1483

York pence of Edward IV attributed to periods of *sede vacante* may be sought among coins that lack either episcopal markings by the bust or the quatrefoil on the centre of the reverse cross (none of the latter were products of the royal mint, which left the supply of pennies to the archbishop). Archbishop William Booth died in September 1464, a month after the lighter coinage was ordered, and the earliest light coins of this mint should therefore belong to the vacancy of the see that followed. Like Booth's heavy pence, the very rare York pence of this period have quatrefoils by the bust, but they lack the quatrefoil on the reverse (type 1). Their mintmarks, rose and sun, follow the first two London marks after the weight reduction (types V and VI). Booth's successor was George Neville, brother of the Earl of Warwick to whom Edward largely owed his throne. Neville had acted as the king's receiver for the see since Booth's death, but although he was elected archbishop in March his temporalities were not confirmed until June 1465 (which thus provides a *terminus ante quem* for the introduction of mintmark sun, as used during the vacancy).

The remainder of the York pence of Edward's first reign all have the quatrefoil on the reverse and many of them show Neville's initial *G* with the key of St. Peter beside the bust. According to Blunt and Whitton the earliest of these (type 2) are common coins struck from crude local dies, with mintmark rose or cross, on which *Gra* or *Dei Gra* is omitted. There are, however, two reasons for wondering whether this is correct. First, since mintmark rose tends to occur at random in the episcopal coinages of Edward IV, its appearance here is not necessarily to be related to its use at royal mints at the start of the light coinage. Second, local dies normally copy a recent official model: the latest *sede vacante* pence have mintmark sun (1b), not rose (1a), and such a striking innovation as the *G* and key (the latter never having been used before on a York coin of this era) is not the sort of initiative that might have been expected from a local engraver. In the absence of direct evidence, the traditional arrangement has been maintained here, but it needs to be regarded with some reservation.

All the other York pence of the first reign (types 3-5) are from London-made dies. With *G* and key they have the London type VI mintmark sun at first (3a), followed by a large lis (3b) in the same way as happened with type VII in the York royal coinage. During the period of the lis mark (which largely corresponds with crown at London) one

York penny obverse has no marks by the bust (perhaps matching some type VII London groats) but others replace the *G* and key by quatrefoils (3c), or later by trefoils (4), the latter being described as of type VIII. Late in the first reign the *G* and key return, at first (5a) with a smaller lis mintmark, or, as in type X, more rarely a long cross fitchy (5b).

York was the only one of the three episcopal mints at which coins were struck under Henry VI in 1470-1, perhaps in recognition of the part played by Warwick in his restoration. These rare pence of Henry's second reign revert to mintmark lis (6), but are otherwise similar to the last of Neville's previous coins in Edward's name; some have the characteristic Restoration reading *henricu*. In April 1471 Neville obtained Edward's pardon for having held his see through Henry's brief reinstatement, although he was kept at the Tower until June. In April 1472, however, he was arrested for communicating with the king's opponents, and was imprisoned again for three years, during which time the revenues of the see reverted to the crown. Although released in the summer of 1475, he died a year later, in June 1476. York pence of the first five years of Edward's second reign, which are of considerable variety, may thus be divided between the three phases, before, during and after Neville's suspension. His coins of 1471-2 at the start of Edward's second reign, which continue the *G* and key and reverse quatrefoil, now have mintmark short cross fitchy (7b), as at London in type XII, and include an old 3c die of type VII, with quatrefoils by the bust, on which a cross fitchy has been punched over the mintmark lis (7a). Pence attributable to Neville's long suspension in 1472-5 are relatively scarce. One die of type 7b with *G* and key was reused with an unquatrefoiled reverse (8). Although there are also rare coins (probably 9a/8 mules) combining an obverse with mintmark annulet and an unquatrefoiled reverse, most of the coins of the suspension period do have the quatrefoil but remove the *G* and key from the obverse. These either have the London mintmarks of types XIV and XVI, annulet (9a) and cross-over-annulet (9b), both very rare, or a rose (9c). This last mark was also used on the latest coins of the suspension period, with an *e* and rose beside the bust (10); although *e* and rose are the marks by the cross on Edward's second reign angels, in this case, by analogy with Durham, the *e* might represent the mint initial, not the king's. With Neville's reinstatement in 1475 the mintmark rose continues, briefly at first with *G* and rose by the bust (11), and then reverting to *G* and key (12a), a rare variety of which has the mintmark rose over annulet. Finally, there is record of a type of Neville penny with the mintmark cross-and-pellet (12b). The existence of coins of this description was questioned by Blunt and Whitton on the basis that (on their chronology) type XVIII was dated too late to have been produced in Neville's time; but if a longer period is to be allowed for mintmark cinquefoil (XXI) than they supposed, the cross-and-pellet mark could well have been in use before his death in June 1476.

Most of the York pence of the remainder of Edward's reign have mintmark rose again. Laurence Booth, who as bishop of Durham had been appointed custodian of the see for the king during the vacancy caused by Neville's death, received the temporalities for himself as archbishop less than four months later, at the beginning of October 1476, and held the see until his own death in May 1480. A very rare type (13) without marks by the bust, but a rose on the breast, has been tentatively associated with the months of vacancy between Neville and Booth; but whether the rose breastmark is related to that on the cinquefoil groats must be doubtful. However, on the coins of Booth himself, which are marked by *B* and key (14), the cinquefoil mintmark of type XXI does feature occasionally (14b) instead of a rose (14a), further support for the view that the cinquefoil mark was already current in the later 1470s. Booth's death created a vacancy between May and September 1480 when Thomas Rotherham, chaplain to the queen, lawyer and diplomat, who had been Chancellor to Edward IV and was to hold the see for the next twenty years, was translated from Lincoln. To these months of vacancy are attributed rare coins with the old Booth obverse type, with *B* and key, but combined with an unquatrefoiled reverse (15). Apart from replacing the initial of Booth's surname with *T* for his own Christian name, most of Rotherham's coins (16), with the quatrefoil restored (except on a 16/15 mule), are similar, although there are a few with a star on the breast and others with a star to the right of the crown also.

Durham, 1464-1483

Laurence Booth held the see of Durham from 1457 until June 1476, when he was appointed to York. He had obtained restoration of his temporalities in April 1464, and after the weight reduction of August 1464 he received official dies with his initial on both sides. Almost all the Durham dies of the period 1464-70 were London-made and carry London mintmarks. Type 1, with mintmark rose (V), has the initials of the bishop and his see by the bust (*B D*) and a *B* (in this type only) also on the reverse cross. A rare variety of this type has a crude bust of local work. In type 2, with mintmark sun (VI), there is a quatrefoil to the left of the bust, and the *B* moves to the right. The mint name in type 2 is *Dunolm* but otherwise it is always *Der(r)am* from 1464 until the local preparation of dies was resumed in 1473. There are, however, rare mules from type 2 obverses combined with earlier reverses of type 1 or of local work. Types 3 and 4 have the mintmark crown of London types VII and VIII, those of type 3 with a combination of *B* or *D* or quatrefoils by the bust, those of type 4 with trefoils or lis.

Despite Booth's past Lancastrian associations no coins of his, comparable to those of Neville at York, are known of Henry VI. For the two years after Edward's coinage was resumed in 1471 Durham received numerous dies from London, but in June 1473 Booth was licensed to have his own dies made, these to include (for the first time ever at either of the northern episcopal mints) dies for halfpence as well as pence. Two months later a York goldsmith, William Omoryghe, was commissioned to make twelve obverse and twenty-four reverse dies for Durham pennies, and four and eight respectively for halfpence. More penny dies were ordered in 1474, suggesting a substantial output at this period, although evidently not without some problems since in 1475 Booth was exonerated for the issue of coins of deficient weight and alloy after declaring that it had happened without his knowledge. Booth's successor as bishop of Durham was William Dudley, Dean of Windsor, who received his temporalities in October 1476 and held the see until his death in November 1483. Further dies, including some for halfpence, were commissioned from Omoryghe by Dudley in 1476.

The first of the London-made dies of 1471-3 have no additional marks on either side (type 5), although there is no historical evidence to suggest that this could have been due to delay in the confirmation of his temporalities after Edward IV's return. These unmarked coins show either (5a) a short cross fitchy, the London mintmark of type XII, or a trefoil (5b) as found on the reverse of type XIII groats. One of the SCF dies supplied, easily identifiable in having the *e* of the king's name punched over the mintmark, had already been used at London, perhaps pointing to a desire to revive coinage at Durham as soon as possible after the removal of Henry VI. The unmarked type 5 was soon followed by coins with *B* and trefoil by the bust and a *D* on the centre of the cross (type 6). These are found with three mintmarks, at first (6a) a trefoil as in 5b, then a pellet-in-annulet (6b) as on London type XV (but apparently overmarked with a cross, as for XVIa), and perhaps lastly (since it continues into type 7), a rose (6c). Most of the coins of this period with mintmark rose, however, have small lis by the bust and this type (7) appears to have been the last of the reign from London-made dies.

The remaining Durham coinage of Edward IV (including halfpence) is from local dies, the reverses having *D* in the centre and reading *Dunolmie*. Most of the types of penny are very common. On the evidence of mules with London-made reverse dies of type 6 or 7 reading *Deram*, the first (a) of the five main local types has *B* to the left of the crown, a *V* on the breast, often saltires by the bust, and a mintmark described as a pansy rather than a rose, because it has five long, slender petals. There are then three types (b, c and d) with a normal form of rose as mintmark: these have no *B* or *D* by the bust and their attribution to Booth or Dudley, or to the short vacancy between June and October 1476, must be conjectural. Finally (e) there are coins with *D* and *V* by the bust and mintmark cinquefoil. Reverses of type a and most of type b have a small *v* by the pellets in the *Civi* quarter, and most of the reverses of all types have a small extra point within the group of pellets in all or one of the quarters. Type b has two small crosses above the crown, the rare type c is without extra marks on the obverse, and type d has a *V* to the right of the bust.

The arrangement of these five types of penny presents some problems. Type a with *B* and type e with *D* can be allocated to Booth and Dudley respectively, the latter appropriately having the London mintmark of type XXI. Blunt and Whitton attributed the unmarked type c to the *sede vacante* of 1476, partly because the type is suitably rare for a four month period, but this is speculative. Dudley's share of the ten years from 1473 to 1483 was more than twice as long as Booth's and on this count it would not be unreasonable to regard type d as Dudley's, whether or not the *V* is to be seen as the initial of his Christian name. Why type a of Booth should have a *V* on the breast is obscure. The meaning of the small *v* on the reverse in types a and b is also enigmatic; perhaps it is simply the mark of William Omoryghe, although there is no precedent or parallel in English medieval coinage for an engraver thus displaying his own initial.

Durham halfpence of this period are of great rarity. They have the old reading *Deram*, not *Dunolmie* like the pence which would have been too long for their limited space. Some have lis or crosses by the neck, one of them having *B* for Booth to the left of the crown as on pence of type a. Another variety has *V* by the neck, like the type d pence which may belong to Dudley's episcopacy.

Edward IV-V, Type XXII (1483), and Richard III (1483-5)

The mintmark of type XXII, the last issue in the name of Edward IV, is (as heraldically described) a sun and rose dimidiated (SR), that is, a combination of a halved sun to the left and a halved rose to the right. It thus combines the two favourite emblems of the king, but in a few cases this was altered to a boar's head (BH), the personal device of his brother Richard III. There is more than one version of each of these two marks and, as established by Winstanley and Webb Ware, over the period of two and a half years from early 1483 to Richard's death in 1485 they alternated in the following sequence:

SR1 Edward IV, type XXII, and as extended under Edward V; plus Richard III, type I.
BH1 Late Edward dies (type XXII), with BH1 over SR1; plus early dies of Richard also with BH1 over SR1 (type IIa).
BH2 Richard, type IIb, with boar's head as the original mark.
SR2 Richard, type IIIa.
SR3 Richard, type IIIb (groats only) – this mintmark briefly continued by Henry VII.

Edward IV – Henry VIII

MINTMARKS, 1483 -5

(a) (b) (c) (d) (e)

(a) Sun-and-rose, SR1, Edward IV type XXII – Richard III type I;
(b) Boar's head, BH1, Edward XXII (BH) and Richard III, type IIa; (c) BH2, Richard type IIb;
(d) and (e) SR2 and SR3, Richard type III.

The sun half of SR1 consists of six short and stumpy rays, and the whole mark is neater and narrower than the later versions. Later SR1 dies usually have a pellet in the centre of the mark, lacking on earlier dies. SR2, also with a large central pellet, has six longer rays, giving a wider shape to the whole mark. The rare SR3 has four short rays, presenting a more serrated appearance. Of the boar's head there are two main divisions, although there is some variation in detail since the mark often seems not to have been put in from a single punch. BH1 is small and crude, with an unbroken lower line from the back of the head to the point of the chin. BH2 is larger and more stylized, with a prominent upward tusk, and the outline broken by a curl at the back of the lower jaw. The pattern of use of these marks was similar on both gold and silver. The earliest angel and groat dies of Richard III have SR1 in continuation from the previous reigns. BH1 then replaced SR1, usually by overpunching, at first on obverse dies only, but later also very occasionally on the reverse of groats (but not of angels). BH2 follows BH1, to be succeeded in its turn by SR2. The final mark on Richard groats, SR3, is not found on angels of this reign, but does occur on a few early angels as well as groats of Henry VII. This sequence of marks is based partly on extensive muling between them, but is corroborated by changes in certain letter punches, *I* and *V* on angels and *L* and *M* on groats. When (as often) the SR mark is not both clearly struck and unworn, the two six-rayed forms can be differentiated by the lettering of their dies. SR1 is found only with I1 and V1 on angels and with L1 and M1 on groats; SR2 with I2 and V2, L2 and M2. Although on the largest denominations there are three main mintmark phases, SR, BH and SR again, the angelet and penny of Richard III are only known with the boar's head. Halfgroats and halfpence are found with both BH and SR but none of the SR dies belongs to the pre-BH phase with SR1.

ROYAL MINTS OF EDWARD IV – V (TYPE XXII) AND RICHARD III

KING'S NAME TYPE MINTMARK	Edw. XXII SR1	Rd. I SR1	Edw. XXII (BH) BH1	Rd. II BH1,2	Rd. III SR2,3
Angel	L	L	L	L	L
Angelet	L			L	
Groat	L	L	L	L	LY
Halfgroat			L	L	L
Penny	L		L	L	
Halfpenny	L		L	L	L
Farthing					L

L – London; Y – York

The coinage of the year 1483 and the question of what coins may be attributable to the two and a half months of the young king Edward V have been the subject of numismatic argument hardly less lively than the historical debate about events in the months that followed the death of Edward IV on 9 April. Eleven weeks later, on 26 June, his son Edward was deposed by Richard of Gloucester, who had had himself appointed Protector in early May. In the mint accounts for 1483 the figures are divided into unusual periods: February to April; May and June; and July to September. These dates represent, respectively, the period from the indenture with Bartholomew Reed of 12 February to the death of Edward IV, the brief coinage of Edward V (the Memoranda Roll explains that this took place without indenture but by mandate of the Lord Treasurer), and the beginning of the reign of Richard III, whose indenture with Robert Brackenbury was made on 20 July. The amounts of bullion coined were as follows:

1483	GOLD		SILVER	
Feb. – April	141 lbs. 8 oz.	£3,188	573 lbs. 6 oz.	£1,074
May, June	49 lbs.10 oz.	£1,121	434 lbs. 3 oz.	£814
July – Sept.	178 lbs.	£4,005	2182 lbs.	£4,091

Until Blunt pointed out that the Edwardian coins of type XXII, with mintmark sun-and-rose, were too plentiful, and from too many dies, to represent the exiguous amounts of bullion minted in May-June 1483, they had for many years been attributed to Edward V. Blunt and Whitton therefore suggested that the introduction of the SR mark should be associated with Reed's indenture of February 1483, two months before the death of Edward IV. As at the beginning of type XXI, so at the end of it there is a shortage of mules with the adjacent type, and Reed's indenture, close to the end of Edward IV's reign, offers an explanation for the administrative discontinuity that this represents. To Edward V Blunt attributed only coins from such obverse dies as had BH punched over SR, regarding this as a move by Richard to mark his appointment as Protector. Subsequently it was argued that the relative numbers of dies and surviving examples of Edward groats with SR and BH indicated some continuation of the unaltered SR under Edward V, while most recently Webb Ware has suggested, on the basis of die-links among the angels and groats, that SR dies were not altered to BH until after Richard's accession. For the whole period from February 1483 until the death of Richard III the structure of the coinage is evident only from the angels and the groats, the lesser denominations having been struck too sparingly to constitute a representative series.

The implications of Webb Ware's thesis are far-reaching. Since the boar's head overmarking applies to the earliest coins in Richard's name with mintmark sun-and-rose, as well as to those of Edward, he associates this with the advent of Brackenbury, Richard's nominee, as master. This is indeed the most obvious occasion on which such overmarking might have been thought appropriate (analagously to the cinquefoil added to dies in current use on Lewys John's appointment in 1413). If so, it would imply that minting had continued during the weeks between Richard's usurpation on 26 June and 20 July when Brackenbury received his indenture (as it had done in May and June on the authority of the Treasurer), such minting represented by an extension of the Edwardian type XXII accompanied by the type I angels and groats in Richard's name with mintmark SR1. If, on the other hand, minting had been suspended until Brackenbury's appointment, the overmarking could not have taken place until a little while later. Either way, the Edward SR coinage must have extended not only through the reign of Edward V, but even beyond it. Because the gold coins carry the king's name or initial on each side, they provide invaluable evidence of die-linkage between the reigns. Thus, the existence of muled angels involving unaltered Edwardian dies in combination with dies carrying Richard's name or initial proves that some Edward SR dies remained in use after Richard's accession. This gives the resultant scheme for the coinage of the year 1483:

Edward IV, Feb. – April	Type XXII, mintmark SR1.
Edward V, May – June	Type XXII continued.
Richard III, July (+?)	Edwardian type XXII continued (unaltered), plus new dies for angels and groats, mm. SR1, in Richard's name (type I)
Richard III, thereafter	Edward and early Richard SR1 dies overmarked with BH1, followed by new Richard dies with BH2.

Although much sought after because of their historical associations, groats of type XXII are not very rare, and the longer period allocated to the type under the new arrangement is therefore convenient. As many as sixteen obverse dies have been noted, and within this total several small batches of three or four dies can be identified. Thus, eight dies have a pellet below the bust, four of them reading *Edward* and four *Edvard*; others, without the pellet, have either a chevron-barred *A*, as in preceding types of Edward IV, or, with the usual unbarred *A*, omit the fleur on the breast like the earliest groats of Richard III which they closely resemble in all but the king's name. Four of these type XXII dies, from three different batches, subsequently had a boar's head punched over the sun-and-rose, and groats from these altered dies – referred to here as XXII (BH) – are very rare. Lettering on the Edward groats of type XXII is similar to that in type XXI, but with new *L*, *R* and unbarred *A*. A more deliberate break with type XXI is the removal of the rose from the breast and from the reverse inscription (on angelets as well as groats). There is little variety in the reverses of type XXII groats, apart from different forms of the letter *e* and a barred or unbarred *A* in *Civitas* and *Adiutore*. Reverse dies of groats with BH1 on the obverse, in the names of both Edward and Richard, usually have a distinctive thick cross. Although several reverse dies (including one reading *Posu/i*) are found both with Edward SR obverses of type XXII and with SR obverses of Richard's type I, none of them is known to have been used with any of the four Edward dies with SR overpunched by BH. Of the reverses used for XXII (BH) groats, however, none is combined with an unaltered Richard type I obverse, but some occur on Richard groats of type IIa (with mintmark BH1). The pattern of die-linking among the groats thus indicates that the amendment of Edwardian dies to produce XXII (BH) took place after the first use of SR dies in Richard's name, three of which were also to be overmarked in the same way. This remarkable conclusion is confirmed by a reverse die-link in the gold: one angel die, with a flaw after *Redempt*, was used both for a coin of Richard type I and for a mule with an Edwardian XXII (BH) obverse, and the flaw is more developed on the latter.

The rare angels of Edward's type XXII have SR1 on both sides. One batch of four obverses reads *Dei*, as in type XXI, and another group of three has *Di*, as on the earliest angels of Richard III. Two of the dies subsequently had BH1 punched over SR1, and both of these read *Di*. That this is the later reading is also evident from the fact that a third (and unaltered) die with *Di* is recorded both with an Edwardian reverse and with another on which *e* has been amended to *R* (as was the case with a few Edwardian angel reverses early in the new reign). As the second batch, the *Di Gra* type XXII angels can therefore be seen as possible candidates for the May-June issues under Edward V, if any new dies were needed during that period. Some, however, could have been struck after Richard III's accession, before the mintmark was altered to BH. Type I Richard angels, from a single obverse die with SR1 unaltered, are extremely rare, unlike the corresponding groats. Important mules occurring at about this point demonstrate that at least one obverse and one reverse angel die of type XXII remained in use unaltered for a time under Richard III. One of these is the angel noted above from an Edwardian type XXII obverse (perhaps left unaltered by accident) coupled with a type XXII reverse on which *R* has been punched over *e*. There is another similar, except that the Edwardian obverse has BH1 over SR1; and a third has a Richard BH1 obverse with an unaltered Edwardian reverse. All these serve to corroborate the inference from the groats, that the boar's head overmarking did not take place immediately at the start of Richard's coinage, and that some unaltered Edwardian dies were in service together with new Richard dies early in Richard's reign (even, in the case of the reverse of the third angel mule, after the overmarking of obverses).

The small BH1 mark, used primarily if not entirely to amend existing dies, was presumably designed to identify coinage under the mastership of Brackenbury for some administrative purpose. There is a groat with BH1 on both sides, but it is extremely rare to find this mark on the reverse. One or two groat and angel dies have a transitional form of the mintmark, smaller than the regular BH2 although with its broken jaw line; but the large BH2 seems to have been quickly brought into use for new dies. Nearly three times as much silver was coined in the twelve months from Michaelmas 1483 as in the last eleven months of Richard's reign, and nearly twice as much gold, implying that BH2 may have been replaced by SR2 before the summer of 1484 since for groats at least SR2 is substantially the commoner mark. Confirming the sequence of marks, there are, in both angels and groats, BH1/BH2 mules and interchanges both ways between BH2 and SR2. There is also an abnormal reverse angel die, reading *Crusem* (as in type XIV of Edward IV) and with the initial *R* apparently punched over a rose; this die began life with mintmark BH2 but seems later to have had the SR2 mark impressed over it.

The BH2 angels (type IIb) are from only three obverse dies, but their survival rate per die is higher than that of SR2 angel dies which although still serviceable would have been withdrawn immediately upon the arrival of Henry Tudor. Among the several BH2 reverses is a batch of four with the leopard below the forecastle inverted and the full word *Tuam*. On type III angels, with SR2, there are some noticeable changes. There is a new and larger *I*, with serrated ends (I2), and a *V* with bowed sides (V2), while a taller St. Michael, instead of looking down at the dragon, now faces outwards. Late SR2 dies, on which the letter *e* is broken at the top, read *Ricad* and, in the case of reverses, have a cross with a shorter horizontal limb than previously (a punch which continued in use under Henry VII).

LETTER FORMS IN RICHARD III'S COINAGE

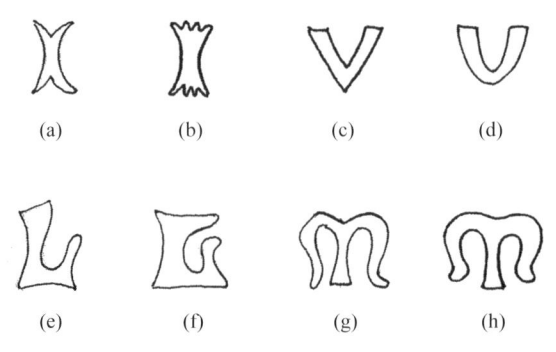

(a) Winstanley's I1, angels mms. SR1 – BH2; (b) I2, angels mm. SR2;
(c) V1, angels mms. SR1 – BH2; (d) V2, angels mm. SR2; (e) L1, groats mms. SR1 – BH2;
(f) L2, groats mms. BH2 – SR3; (g) M1, groats mms. SR1 – BH2;
(h) M2, groats mms. BH2 – SR3.

Edward IV – Henry VIII

Type IIb groats, with BH2, can be placed in sequence according to epigraphic changes. They begin with L1, a thin and lop-sided letter, and a normal *m* (M1), followed by the more elaborate L2 and, subsequently, by M2 with an extended tongue. As with the type III angels, there are innovations in the groats with mintmark SR2. There is a new crown with taller ornaments and smaller piercings, and a pellet is sometimes found in the spandrel below the bust, as in type XXII. The revival in type III of a mint at York, the centre of Richard's support in the north, supplies a rare example of the opening of a second royal mint in England other than for the purposes of recoinage. Since the mid-1470s the Tower mint accounts had recorded that there was no coinage elsewhere, but this note ceases after 1483/4, pointing to a date for the small York issue within the period of the account for 1484/5, when Richard was in the north. The York groats, from only three obverse dies, carry no mintmark on the reverse, and the same variety is also found at London, where it is likewise very rare. Near the end of Richard's coinage there are a few groat dies with the third and last main version of the sun-and-rose mark. Winstanley observed that on one of the obverse dies with SR3 the portrait, with fuller cheeks, resembled that on some of the early groats of Henry VII.

All the lesser denominations of this period are rare, and their survival may be incomplete. Of the last Edwardian angelets, of type XXII, only two specimens have been found, from the same pair of dies. They differ from earlier types of Edward IV not only in the SR mintmark, but also in reading *Ang*, instead of *Angl*, and in lacking a rose in the reverse legend. Unlike the type XXII angels, they revert to a four-line ship. No Edward angelet is known with the boar's head mintmark; but with this mark there are extremely rare examples from two obverse dies in Richard's name, their reverses having either an angel-sized rose by the cross or a more suitable smaller one. The half-angel must have been struck very sparingly in this period, and (as with London pence) no new dies may have been needed during the currency of mintmark SR2.

Though not as rare as the angelet, the half-denomination of Richard III in silver is still of considerable rarity. There is a solitary Edwardian halfgroat of type XXII (BH), but none is yet known with unamended mintmark SR1 in either Edward's or Richard's name. The Edward half has small trefoils on the cusps, as in type XXI, and reads *Angl Fra*, without the copula. Richard halfgroats are from two obverses with mintmark boar's head and three with sun-and-rose. As before, they share their letter fount with the angels. The BH halves have thin lettering (with the plain I1) and a small head, and their reverses lack a mintmark, in all these respects as on the coin of type XXII (BH). The obverse dies with mintmark SR2 have a larger head, one of them with a pellet below the bust as on some type III groats; they and their matching reverses (including a mintmark) use new and heavier letters, such as *I* (I2) and *R*, while the reverses of SR2 halves without mintmark have the earlier lettering so that these coins are probably III/II mules (rather than halfgroat equivalents to the York-type groats).

One of them, from the same reverse die as the Edwardian halfgroat, is thus a Richard/Edward (III/XXII) mule. There are no Canterbury halves (or any other coins of the archbishop) from Richard's reign. The last of the Edwardian Canterbury halfgroats have the same lettering as on the XXII (BH) and Richard type II halves, including the characteristic *R* with defective tail. It is quite possible that their dies continued in use beyond the death of Edward IV. Thomas Bourchier had pledged his honour to the queen dowager for the security of her second son, to allow him to join Edward V in the Tower; but relations between Bourchier and Richard III, to whom he had not originally been opposed, deteriorated. The absence in Richard's name of any Canterbury coinage, so abundant under both Edward IV and Henry VII, may be a reflection of this.

London pence are all extremely rare. In Edward's name they exist of type XXII both in its original and in its amended version. The cross-end punch on their reverses is damaged on the right side. The only recorded London penny in the name of Richard III, with the same damaged cross-ends, has mintmark BH2. Halfpence, although very uncommon, are the least rare of the lesser London silver. They are easily recognised by their 'propeller' pellets. The type XXII dies, reading *Dei* or *Di*, and using the same letter fount as the late Edwardian angels and halfgroats, accordingly show the broken-tailed *R* of this period; and the nicked bust is now prominent. There are no halfpence in Richard's name with mintmark SR1, but the striking of this denomination continued after June 1483, since type XXII halfpence are now known with SR altered to the boar's head. Of Richard's own halfpence those with mintmark boar's head, with a distinctive long, gaunt face, are rarer than those with SR2 and new lettering, on which the head is small and rounder. Farthings of this reign (the first since the 1460s) are also now known, with mintmark SR2.

The flow of ill-struck and often illegible pence from the northern episcopal mints continued unabated. Thomas Rotherham of York was arrested by Richard in June 1483, but soon released. His coins from Richard's reign are similar to his issues under Edward IV, with a *T* and key by the bust, although the *T* is smaller and the key more upright under Richard. Three obverse dies have the boar's head mintmark, one (omitting the *T* and key) has SR2, and another has either a sun-and-rose or possibly a plain rose which could place it as the earliest mark, in continuity from the last York pence of Edward IV. No pence of Bishop Dudley of Durham are known of Richard III, but this is unsurprising since he died in November 1483. His successor, the learned John Shirwood, although consecrated in May 1484, was not confirmed in his temporalities until August 1485, six days before the battle of Bosworth; but his petition to the king in December 1484 for three obverse and nine reverse dies had been accepted and his coins of this reign are not particularly rare. They carry the bishop's initial *S* on the breast; only two of the obverse dies appear to have been used, both with mintmark lis. On the reverse there is a *D* on the centre of the cross, as on Dudley's coins of Edward IV, and the mint signature is *Dirham*.

Henry VII - Structure and Classification

In view of its complexity, it is no wonder that the coinage of Henry VII was not among the reigns of the groat period to be subjected to early systematic study. In a previous generation Carlyon-Britton had produced two important papers on the earliest and late issues (including the critical discovery that the first profile groats were produced alongside the last of those with the facing bust), but the numismatically eventful 1490s remained a forbidding challenge until tackled by Potter and Winstanley. While its technical details are not always easy to follow, their monograph of 1962-4 constitutes a remarkable feat of numismatic analysis, clarified and enhanced by Metcalf's *Sylloge* of the coins of Henry VII in the Ashmolean Museum (incorporating the Winstanley collection). Although Winstanley alone signed the section on the pence and fractions and Potter that on chronology, the bulk of the text, though written by Potter, was in substance a joint work. Their arrangement divides the material into five types (with subdivision), based on the groats which constitute the only continuous series through the reign in the silver coinage and display a sequence of design changes, mintmarks, lettering and other features. Unfortunately, however, several other denominations often do not follow the mintmarks or type structure of the groats. The same type framework cannot therefore

Edward IV – Henry VIII

be applied precisely to much of the smaller silver and the term 'group' (with the same numeration) is used here to indicate a looser or more approximate relationship.

The groats exhibit progressive development of the portrait, notably in the crown and hair, and of the form of the cross-ends on the reverse. Type I continues the impersonal facing portrait from previous reigns; types II, III and IV are defined according to successive varieties of the arched crown and more realistic hair; and type V covers the new design with profile bust and shield of arms from 1504/5. The table shows the types of the groats with their relevant mintmarks, cross-ends and styles of lettering. The gradual development and replacement of these features enables a detailed sequence to be worked out for the groats that to some extent is reflected, even if not fully reproduced, on other denominations.

Principal Features of Henry VII Groats

Group	Design	Mintmark	Lettering	Cross-ends	Stops
I	Open crown	IA, Composite	A	1	Saltires
		IB, Lis, Cross Fitchy, Rose	A	1	Saltires, trefoils
II	Crown with two plain arches	1, No mark	A	1	Trefoils, saltires
		2, Cinquefoil	A	1, 2	Trefoils
IIIA	Two jewelled arches	Cinquefoil	B	3	Rosettes
IIIB	do., inward curls	Escallop	B, C, D, E	3, 4	Rosettes, trefoils
		Pansy	E	4, 5	Rosettes
IIIC	Outer arch only jewelled, realistic hair	Pansy	E	5, 6, 7	Rosettes, saltires
		LHC	E	7	Saltires
		LIR	E	7	Saltires
		Anchor	E	7, 8	Saltires
		GH1	E	8	Saltires
		GH2	F	9	Saltires
IVA	Single bar, 4 jewels	GH2	F	9	Saltires
IVB	Single bar, 6 jewels	GH2	G	9, 10	Saltires
IIIC		Cross-crosslet	G	10	Saltires
IVA		Cross-crosslet	G	10	Saltires
IVB		Cross-crosslet	G	10	Saltires
V	Profile portrait	Cross-crosslet	G	11	Saltires
		Pheon	G	11	Saltires

After the introduction of the arched crown in type II the traditional plain cross-end (no. 1) was slightly modified (no. 2), but with the advent of the jewelled crown groats of type III there was a sudden change of style, involving new and more elaborate founts of lettering (B, C, D and E), a sequence of 'antler'-style terminals (nos. 3, 4 and 5), and the frequent use of rosette stops. Thereafter there was a reversion to less extravagant forms of cross-end, and saltire stops were resumed for the rest of the reign. In the course of type IIIC, during the currency of mintmark greyhound's head, a broader and plainer letter fount (F) was used for a short period, before a narrower and more graceful style (G) became established at the end of type III for the rest of the reign. Within their basic format, there is a degree of variety in the size and form of letters in both styles E and G. A notable feature of Henry VII's coinage is the occurrence of broken letters, the product of intricate, ornamental punches that fractured more readily than their plainer predecessors, and thus offer valuable evidence of sequence.

CROSS-ENDS ON GROATS OF HENRY VII

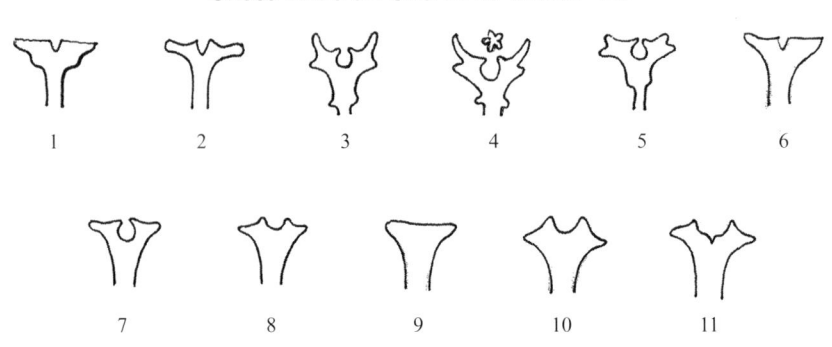

There are various problems with the smaller silver coins, on which cross-ends are less elaborate than many of those on groats. Separate notation is therefore needed for some of them. On halfgroats and pence the cross-ends progress from no. 1 or 2 to a pierced form similar to no. 7 on groats, since the intermediate groat forms would have been too large on the smaller coins. London halfgroats were not issued continuously, and those of types I, III and V that compare readily with the groats are all rare. Scarce London and York (royal) halfgroats of the 1490s (notable for their deficient weight) belong to the general period of early group III, but mostly with different mintmarks and without clear relationship to the groats. The most abundant facing bust halfgroats are those of Canterbury, also of the group III period, and of York (episcopal), which are later, but neither of these series relates directly to the groats. The Canterbury halves of group III, being without Morton's initial on the reverse cross, have often been described as issues of the king and archbishop jointly, but there is no more evidence for this than for the supposed royal coinage at Canterbury under Edward IV.

The sovereign pence are equally difficult to classify, since those of the middle of the reign (which are the commonest) normally lack a mintmark and do not closely follow the lettering or cross-ends of the groats. Neither Winstanley's arrangement of these, nor Allen's more recent classification, provides a numeration of varieties by which they can be readily connected to other denominations, and the type associations of these coins can therefore only be approximate.

The one type of ryal and the first two types of sovereign have the early epigraphy (A) associated with groups I and II, but the three later types of sovereign, not carrying mintmarks found on groats or angels, used special founts of lettering less clearly related to that of other denominations. Although angels do mostly follow the mintmarks of the groats, and can be grouped in accordance with them, the principal revision of their design, replacing the angular medieval version of St. Michael with a more naturalistic figure, remained unchanged when the profile groats were introduced, so there is no clear division between those related respectively to groups IV and V.

The introduction of the profile groats in 1504 is one of the few secure points in the chronology of the reign. For the preceding period of almost twenty years there is little to rely upon. Potter, like others before, assumed that the sovereign with mintmark cross fitchy was the direct result of the commission of October 1489 and provided a date for the cross fitchy groats struck mid-way through type I. However, comparison of the relative numbers of groats of Richard III and of Henry VII type I with the mint accounts shows that the whole of type I must have been complete before 1489, and this brings forward all subsequent types. Potter believed that mintmark escallop did not begin until 1494, nor pansy until 1496; but Archibald's discovery, that letter punches used for a medalet dated 1494 were the same as on some pansy groats of type IIIC, again indicates that the Potter dating is too late. Type IIIC pansy must have been underway well before the end of 1494, and earlier dates are therefore needed for the no mark and cinquefoil groats of types II and IIIA and the escallop groats of type IIIB. One of the consequences of this is to allow the sovereign with mintmark cinquefoil to occupy a position closer to the original order for the new gold coin in 1489. In the table revised dates are suggested for the main types and marks. These dates receive some support from the relative numbers of groats and angels in hoards when measured against mint output, although the lack of accounts for 1489-94 adds to the uncertainty inherent in calculations of this kind.

Chronology of Henry VII's London Mintmarks

Mintmark (& Type)	Potter Dates	Now Suggested
Various (I)	1485-91	1485-87/8
No mark, cinquefoil (II, III)	1491-4	End of 1480s
Escallop (III)	1494-6	From c. 1490/1
Pansy (IIIB, C)	1496-9	From c. 1492/3.
Leopard's head crowned (IIIC) } Lis issuant from rose (IIIC) }	1499-1500	Mid-1490s
Anchor (IIIC)	1500-2	Later 1490s - c. 1502
Greyhound's head (IIIC - IV)	1502-4	c. 1502 – 1504
Cross-crosslet (IIIC - V)	1504-5	1504-5
Pheon (V)	Late 1505-1509	1505-9

Henry VII, Group I

For two or three years Henry left the coinage in the same format and appearance as that of his Yorkist predecessors, except for his name and initial and the mintmark. Groats with the old open crown continued to be produced until 1487 or 1488. They divide conveniently into two phases: A, with composite mintmarks and no marks in the obverse field; and B, with single mintmarks and crosses or saltires by the neck. The composite marks are: (i) halved sun-and-rose, with four rays, the same mark as SR3 on the last of Richard III's groats; (ii) halved lis-and-rose (LR); and (iii) a lis superimposed over the left side of a rose or sun-and-rose. The SR mark was soon displaced on groats by marks incorporating the lis. The LR mark is neat and clear, but it is not found on the gold and seems soon to have been replaced by the later and less elegant marks consisting of a lis with a rose or SR below (these two are sometimes difficult to distinguish). Since die-combinations suggest that all three main marks of type IA were in use together, it is not obvious that the marks with lis superimposed (iii) represent an intended differentiation from the LR mark and may be no more than makeshift substitutes for it. The lis varies in size and shape, partly defacing the rose or SR, with their petals or rays in differing positions above and to the right. It is probably fanciful to see specific historical allusion in these marks – the lis-and-rose dimidiated as a celebration of the marriage of Henry Tudor to Elizabeth of York in January 1486, or the lis on sun-and-rose as a reference to victory over the Yorkists and the claims of the impostor Lambert Simnel in 1487. But the prominence given to the lis, last used in the Restoration of 1470-1 as a Lancastrian emblem to replace the Yorkist sun, undoubtedly represented a general political message, with the lis-and-rose a calculated answer to the sun-and-rose of the rival dynasty.

MINTMARKS OF HENRY VII GROUP I

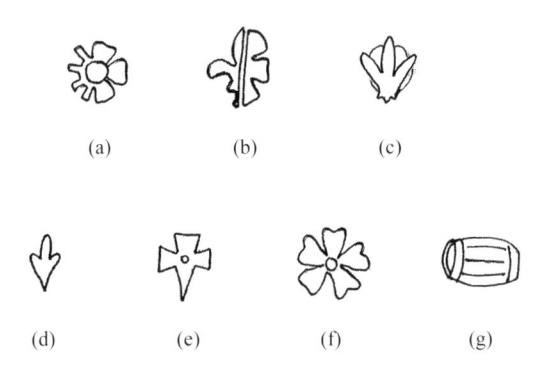

(a)   (b)   (c)

(d)   (e)   (f)   (g)

(a) Sun-and-rose 3, Richard III and Henry type IA; (b) Halved lis-and-rose, IA;
(c) Lis on rose or sun-and-rose, IA; (d) Small lis, IB; (e) Cross fitchy, IB; (f) Rose, IB;
(g) Tun, Canterbury.

On Henry VII groats the SR mark is found only on two reverse dies, both paired with LR obverses, but perhaps originally prepared for Richard's coinage. Obverse dies with the LR mark were more frequently used with reverses having other marks, LR reverses being rare (and only found with LR obverses). The lis-on-rose mark comes in at least four forms, all obverses with one of them having a rose on the breast. Most of the other obverses with lis-on-rose lack a fleur on the breast, whereas all three with lis-on-SR have it. Probably these varieties are merely to be seen as evidence of dies being produced in batches. Dies with different marks, or with differing versions of the same mark, are so frequently and multifariously paired in this series that no attempt seems to have been made to produce groats with the same mark on each side such as might define successive issues. Both lis-on-rose and lis-on-SR were probably in use at the end of the period of IA dies since mules are found both between obverses with lis-on-rose and IB reverses (without mintmark), and between a lis-on-SR reverse and a IB obverse with mintmark rose.

Angels of type IA are very rare, angelets more so. No angels are known with the halved lis-and-rose, but sun-and-rose occurs not only on reverse dies, as with the groats, but also on three new obverse dies with Henry's name, demonstrating that the use of the SR mark in the new reign cannot be explained entirely by the use of old dies of Richard. The only angelets of type I, however, are from two obverse dies with *Ricard* apparently altered to *henric* and with mintmark SR (their reverses have a lis over the SR mark). If an extension of sun-and-rose on angels took the place of the halved lis-and-rose on groats, the two metals came together again with the lis-on-rose which occurs on angels on both obverse and reverse dies (on which a four-line ship reappears). But although lis-on-SR also figures on angels it is not found on reverses and both the obverse dies noted with this mark have Richard's name altered, as on the angelets. Yet these two dies were not necessarily among the earliest used for Henry. Angels with the three obverse marks, SR, lis-on-rose and lis-on-SR are all found both with SR and lis-on-rose reverses, but only lis-on-SR is recorded with a later reverse having no mark. Type IB angels are extremely rare, being represented only by a few specimens with obverse mintmark rose and features comparable to IB groats in their trefoil and pellet stops, and in lacking a mintmark on the reverse. The rose obverses are also notable for introducing the Irish title on angels.

While the IB angels are far rarer than those of IA, IB groats are the commoner of the two. Unless gold coinage was on an extremely small scale for a period, which the mint accounts do not imply, gold dies of IA must have remained in use during part of the issue of the IB groats. These are found with three mintmarks, (i) lis, (ii) cross fitchy and (iii) rose. With the lis there is one groat obverse die, with cross fitchy three, and with the rose many. Groats of IB are immediately recognizable in having quatrefoils beside the neck. *A* is usually barred and, with the exception of the lis die, they have a fleur on the breast cusp. The lis and cross fitchy groats constitute a transitional phase at the beginning of type IB, and both have distinctive readings: *henrcus Di* on the lis die, *henricus Dei* on the cross fitchies (instead of the usual *henric Di*). The longer reading on the former may have been the reason for the use of the lis, a tiny mark suitable to be squeezed in between the *c* of *Franc* and the king's name; on the cross fitchy dies the space problem was resolved by shortening *Franc* to *Fr* or *Fra*. The lis obverse has pellet stops, cross fitchy dies saltires with once a pellet after *Rex*. Reverse dies used with the lis obverse and some of those found with cross fitchy obverses have no initial mark but a lis elsewhere in the reverse inscription. Otherwise reverse stops are quatrefoils/saltires until the later dies used with cross fitchy, on which trefoils are introduced. Reverses of cross fitchy groats without a lis, and especially those with trefoil stops, are indistinguishable from the normal reverses of rose-marked groats.

The rose-marked groats constitute most of the issues of IB. That they began almost immediately after the end of IA, despite the occurrence of the four dies with lis and cross fitchy, is suggested by the mules with the lis-on-rose mark on the reverse. The rose is found on a few reverses but, between the end of IA and the introduction of the cinquefoil mark in type IIB, groat reverse dies are otherwise without a mintmark. Normally the rose is well-shaped, with a central pellet, as above the shield on angels; but some early dies have smaller and less well formed versions of the mark. Most of the rose dies have the quatrefoils by the neck disposed as saltires, but a few early ones still have them upright as on the lis and cross fitchy obverses. Stops on the rose groats are trefoils, but one late obverse (possibly the last) has small stars instead. No rose groat is known with stars on the reverse, but three star-stopped reverse dies are recorded with obverses of type II, and these may originally have been supplied with the star-stopped rose obverse: in which case, the type II coins involved should perhaps be regarded as IIA/IB mules.

Smaller silver with the open crown of type I is all rare. Very few halfgroats or pence of London are known. The halfgroats conform to the groats of IA in the mintmark lis-on-rose (although on the obverse only), and in their saltire stops and absence of marks by the neck; one is muled with an old reverse of Richard III. The IA halves have a broad-chinned head within a plain tressure of nine flat arcs, of entirely different appearance to the later halfgroats (type IIIC) on which a flat open crown breaks the tressure. London pence exist of both IA, with mintmark lis-on-rose and no stops or marks by the neck, and of IB with crosses by the neck and trefoil stops. Comparable halfpence are a little less rare. Those of IA have been noted with the mintmark either halved lis-and-rose or lis-on-rose, and those of IB with cross fitchy and rose.

Coins of the ecclesiastical mints are generally more plentiful than those of London.

After IA Canterbury seems to have taken over responsibility for halfgroats from London, since they begin with IB coins from Tower-made dies for Archbishop John Morton, appointed late in 1486, and have his canting mark, a tun, on the obverse and his initial *m* on the centre of the reverse cross. The *m* is also found on Canterbury pence and halfpence of IB, with crosses by the neck, both very rare. In May 1486 four obverse and eight reverse dies for pence were prepared for the Archbishop of York, and replacements were provided in July 1487. The earlier batch (IA) may be identified with Rotherham's first coins of the new reign (four of which were the latest coins in the Ryther hoard), with *T* and a trefoil by the neck and mintmark lis-on-SR (one of these apparently having *henric* over *Ricard*). They have the traditional quatrefoil in the centre of the reverse cross, and an extra point in two quarters, but his IB pence, presumably from the 1487 dies, with *T* and a cross by the neck, have the royal initial *h* instead of the quatrefoil. Durham pence of Shirwood, still with *S* on the breast and *D* on the reverse cross, are placed to IB by Winstanley presumably on the ground that there is a trefoil after *De* of *Deram*; but this is a loose arrangement of three pellets, unlike the neat trefoil stops on groats and other coins of IB, and since there are no marks by the bust it seems more likely that Shirwood's pence continued, without much interruption, from the previous reign, as a Henry/Richard mule implies. When (as often) the inscriptions are unclear, the early Durham pence of the new reign can be identified by differences in their portrait and crown, and by the *D* on the cross, which is now in a supine position.

London Mintmarks of Henry VII Groups I and II

	Halved Sun/ Rose	Halved Lis/Rose	Lis on Sun/ Rose	Lis on Rose	Lis	Cross Fitchy	Rose	None	Cinque- foil
Sovereign						x			x
Ryal						x			
Angel	x		x	x			x	x	x
Angelet	x		x						
Groat	x	x	x	x	x	x	x	x	x
Halfgroat				x					
Penny				x				x	x
Halfpenny		x				x	x	x	x

Henry VII, Group II

Although notable for a number of important changes, the second group of the reign continues certain characteristics of the first – the old epigraphy of style A, the traditional design of the angel, and unornamented cross-ends on the silver. At first there was no mintmark (IIA); most of the London coins, however, have an heraldic cinquefoil (IIB) like that on type XXI of Edward IV. The most significant of the innovations were the introduction of the gold sovereign, the revival of the ryal with an updated and Tudorised design, the adoption of an arched crown, some typological experiment in the groats, and a completely new design for the penny.

With the ending of the immobilized open crown portrait on silver after type I, the English coinage thus entered upon a period of rapid change. In the early stages of the

Edward IV – Henry VIII

process the groat itself was relatively little altered. Two plain arches, surmounted by a cross on a small globe, were added to the crown, breaking the tressure at the top. Since the cross intrudes into the inscription, it seems at first to have been regarded as taking the place of an initial mark. These no-mark groats were, however, soon followed by the issue with the cinquefoil mark. Two exceptional types of groat were produced during the course of group II. The earlier of these has the pellets and the centre of the reverse cross replaced by a portcullis, a device which was to become a frequent Tudor symbol on the coinage. On the other is a full-length figure of the king enthroned, coupled with an armorial reverse, which although rejected as a type for the groat had nevertheless been adopted for the penny. The king in majesty could, however, be much more appropriately displayed on the new gold sovereign. There were in addition a number of lesser changes of note, such as the use on some of the angels of the *Ihc Autem* inscription, the introduction on groats of complex patterns of stopping in the inner reverse inscription, which were to become an important feature of later issues, and the first hesitant departure from the plain form of medieval cross-end that had been in use on reverse dies for silver since 1279.

MINTMARKS OF HENRY VII GROUP II

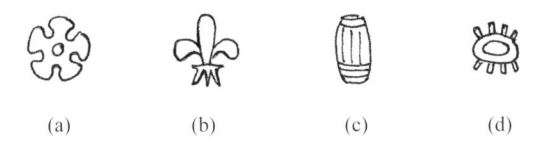

(a)   (b)   (c)   (d)

(a) Cinquefoil, IIB; (b) Large lis, portcullis groat; (c) Tun, Canterbury; (d) Eye, Canterbury.

Of the regular groats of type II, considerably more than half have the mintmark cinquefoil. The scarce groats without mintmark do however constitute a distinct phase in the coinage during which several minor modifications of design occurred. As on the later rose groats of type IB the stops in type IIA are normally trefoils, and there are now small trefoils instead of fleurs on the tressure. The first form of arched crown is wide, with a gap between the base and the fleured band above it (crown 1). This crown is accompanied by one short strand of hair protruding below it at the sides, instead of three as normal previously. A different crown, which appears on the rest of the IIA groats and on all those of IIB, is narrower and taller, with the fleured band close to the base (and three short strands of hair again below). This was labelled crown 2 by Potter and Winstanley, reflecting the sequence of usage within type II, although it is in fact from the same punch as the open crown of type I, with arches added. IIA obverses with crown 2 and two of those with crown 1 have a trefoil or trefoils disposed in various positions by the cross at the top, evidently as part of some system of marking the dies. All five obverse dies with crown 1 have saltires by the neck, as do about half of the more numerous dies of IIA with crown 2; later IIA dies (and all of IIB) are without them. The rare early reverses with star stops may, as suggested above in connection with the late star-marked obverse of IB, have been made to pair with it; they are the only dies in the type IIA grouping with stops in the inner inscription and are found exclusively with crown 1 obverses. Reverse dies with trefoil stops, in the outer inscription only, are found with both crowns, as are the less frequent reverses with saltire stops or none. Finally, there is a reverse die with a trefoil after *Posui* and a pellet before *Meum*, paired with a crown 2 obverse reading *henrc*; the extremely rare coins of this variety may be IIA/IIB mules. The reverse die with the portcullis type is notable for two other features: the large lis mintmark, and a new form of cross-end (no. 2), with cleft shank and shaped feet, which was to be adopted on regular groats during type IIB. Two normal obverse dies of IIA (crown 2) are combined with the portcullis reverse, one with and one without saltires by the neck; the former die is known also from several groats with the ordinary reverse type.

With the cinquefoil mark (IIB) further changes of design occur. On the cusps large fleurs resume their place, instead of the trefoils of IIA. Crown 2 of type IIA continues, but now again with one strand of hair below the sides. Some early IIB groats have no mintmark on the reverse, and these may include IIB/IIA mules. Such unmarked reverses are without stops, except for the die with trefoil after *Posui* and pellet before *Meum* already known with a IIA obverse. This latter variety may, however, belong to IIB since a IIB obverse combined with it has a pellet by the cinquefoil mintmark, suggesting the possibility of an intentional pair. At first the IIB groats have the old plain cross-end (no. 1), but this was soon replaced by the more shapely no. 2. At about the same time the plain cross above the crown gave way to a cross with a tapering stem and indented patty ends, and a sinuous reversed *S* was introduced for *et*. Other indicators of sequence within IIB are the letter *A* on the obverse (unbarred earlier, barred later), the cusp fleurs and the stops. Earlier dies have six fleurs (three each side, without one on the breast); then there is a rare variety with four; and finally, and most frequently, there are again six fleurs (or seven, with one added on the breast), combined with reverses on which the *n* has a broken tail and trefoil stops are added in different combinations (evidently varied deliberately) in the inner circle of inscription. Although lettering of pre-Tudor style (A) continued throughout groups I and II, one freakish late cinquefoil die has *henric* in the new mannered style (B) of early type III, as if by way of experiment, with the rest of the inscription from the old fount.

FEATURES OF TYPE II GROATS OF HENRY VII

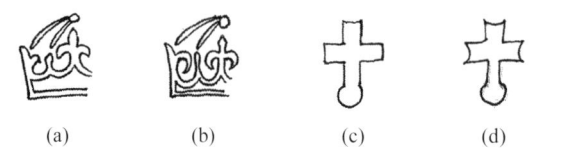

(a)   (b)   (c)   (d)   (e)

(a) Crown 1, IIA; (b) Crown 2, IIA-B; (c) Cross above crown IIA and early IIB;
(d) Cross above crown, later IIB; (e) New & in IIB.

The unique sovereign type groat with mintmark cinquefoil relates in its details to the four-fleur variety of the normal IIB series. The enthroned figure of the king on this coin is a small scale version of that on the unique cinquefoil sovereign. Although no other mint struck groats for Henry VII, it was decided, despite the restricted space, to include *London* below the king's feet, the mint name having been removed from the reverse by the new design of the royal shield of arms surrounded only by the old *Posui* outer inscription.

Halfgroats of type II are of Canterbury alone, still with Morton's initial on the reverse, but with crosses by the neck and no initial mark on the obverse, like the IIA groats. Of two varieties, both rare, the earlier (IIa), also found muled both ways with I, has pellet stops on the obverse, a tun after *Gra* and an eye after *Posui*. The second (IIb), muled with both I and IIa, has trefoil stops on the obverse, and a tun before *Posui* but not on the obverse.

Like the portcullis groat, the replacement on pence of the traditional type, unchanged in essentials since Edward I, by a miniature figure of the king enthroned, and accompanied (as on the sovereign type groat) by the royal arms on the reverse, may be seen as a consequence of the instruction to the warden in March 1489 to produce new designs for the coinage. In view of its intricacy, it is strange that the sovereign type should have been adopted for the third denomination in silver when it was only used on the largest gold coin and was abandoned for the groat after a momentary experiment. With the exception of the Canterbury coins of group III, it was to appear on all pence of the next fifty years, until the debasement of Henry VIII. There are no pennies with the old facing head and a plain arched crown corresponding to the groats of type II, as there had been of each of the three mints with the open crown of type I, and there are reasons for believing that the advent of the new penny type fell within the period of the IIA groats. The earliest sovereign pence have the plain cross-ends that were replaced on groats during the currency of type IIB, while their arched crown places them after type I. The first type, without pillars to the throne, is lacking of Durham and therefore seems likely to belong before the indenture of September 1489 between Bishop Shirwood and George Strayll. If the lack of a mintmark on the earliest sovereign pence reflects the usage of the IIA groats, their introduction could be dated, in all probability, to the spring or summer of 1489.

All the sovereign pence of this period have style A lettering. The first pillarless type (Ai), with plain cross-ends, is represented by only a single specimen of London, and by some scarce coins of the archbishop of York which attest their origin not only by the mint signature but also by the addition of two keys below the shield. The immediate addition of keys at York when the penny type was changed lends support to the view that the traditional quatrefoil on the centre of the cross of the old type had been seen as the handle of a key. On the London penny the sceptre is in the king's right hand, topped by a small fleur-de-lis, and the orb in his left, but on the York type the positions of sceptre and orb are reversed, an experimental arrangement that was not repeated on subsequent coins of this or either of the other mints. The next type of London pence (Bi), with a single pillar added to the throne on the dexter side, has cleft cross-ends as introduced on later IIB groats, and appropriately carries the cinquefoil mintmark. These coins also have small arches indicated on the front of the throne, beside the king's legs (Allen type 2). The mintmark and the arches were then dropped on the last coins with cleft cross-ends (Bii). At York there is no mintmark on the arched throne type, but the sequence is otherwise as at London. In types Bi and Bii the pillar is topped by a trefoil, and the sceptre-head is either a trefoil or a lis. The Durham pence of Shirwood have his initials, *D S*, by the shield, and the upper limb of the cross terminates in a crozier-head. The earliest of them (Aii), which are rare, presumably followed soon upon the Strayll indenture, and are transitional between the London and York coins of types Ai and Bi in that they lack stops and pillars but have cleft cross-ends together with a trefoil or trefoils in the positions later occupied by pillars. Shirwood's later pence, with one pillar and the arched throne (Bi), have a crozier leaning against the king's shoulder (with its head in place of an obverse initial mark).

A few halfpence have a double-arched crown in conjunction with style A letters. The London coins conform neatly to the division of the groats, those without mintmark (IIA) having crosses by the neck and plain cross-ends, those with mintmark cinquefoil having no marks in the obverse field, and cleft cross-ends, as in IIB. Canterbury halfpence belonging to the IIA period show an obverse mintmark that seems to be a tun; they have Morton's initial on the reverse cross, although a mule with a London reverse has also been noted.

Angels of group II are the last of the series in medieval style. They are of similar rarity to angels of type I, those of IIB with mintmark cinquefoil being rarer than the no-mark coins of IIA, unless IIB/III mules, with reverse mintmark escallop, are taken into account. No angelets are known of this period. Type II angels have trefoil stops, and although they have no mintmark on the reverse the dies can be divided between IIA and IIB by their inscriptions and by the size of the rose by the cross, which is unusually small on IIA reverses. IIA dies have either the normal angel motto or *Ihc Autem* as on the old nobles and ryals, whereas on IIB dies only *Per Cruc* (so spelt) is found. The Irish title, introduced on IB angels, reduces to *Dns* in IIA, and disappears in IIB, leaving the inscription to end incongruously with &. On some late dies the ship is more deeply U-shaped, in this respect foreshadowing the form on angels in the new style of group III.

The rarity of type II angels may be due in part to the minting of ryals and sovereigns. Two types of sovereign (Grierson types A and B) and the only type of Henry VII ryal all have the old lettering of style A. With the king in each case wearing an arched crown, these sovereigns and the ryal evidently belong to the period of group II, and this fits conveniently with other evidence. On the unique sovereign of type A the reverse mintmark is a cinquefoil, on those of type B and the ryals it is a cross fitchy. Although several specimens are known of both the ryals and the type B sovereigns, only one pair of dies was involved in each case.

In general appearance the obverse of Henry VII's ryal follows the format of Edward IV's, although there are a number of differences in detail. The ship has no yard-arm, sail or mast (this presumably thought to have been hidden behind the king); the forecastle and sterncastle are shown in two, not three, dimensions; and they are decorated with small roses instead of quatrefoils, although there is no longer a rose on the ship's side. The king's crown, with two plain arches, looks very much like that on IIA groats, with the cross above breaking into the inscription. The stops are trefoils as on groats of types IB and II. Instead of a coat of mail, Henry wears a waisted breastplate and armour in Renaissance style, and carries an elegantly shaped shield with concave sides. A second banner is added forward, with the initial *h,* while the ensign aft has a griffin-like Welsh dragon for the Tudor king. The reverse, however, is something of a surprise, with the arms not of England but of France on the centre of a large double rose: the whole perhaps intended to be seen as the French lilies imposed on the English rose as if in an escutcheon of pretence. The punch for the fleurs-de-lis in the French shield is the same as that used for the mintmark before *Posui* on the portcullis groats. This punch was presumably made for the ryal die, and not for the groat (for which it is too large), so the ryal itself should be dated before the last phase of the IIA groats, c. 1488.

The cinquefoil sovereign (A), known only from a somewhat worn specimen, is a splendid coin. The figure of the king enthroned, with sceptre and orb, stands out from a plain background. On the reverse there is a large and elaborate imperial crown above the shield of arms, with the Tudor rose behind. These designs are closer than those of any other Henry sovereign to Maximilian's *réal d'or* of 1487. The type A sovereign has trefoil stops and features of lettering, such as the barred *A* and the reversed *S* for &, which although from separate and larger punches associate it with cinquefoil groats around the middle of type IIB.

Why the issue of this superb piece was so quickly discontinued we can only guess. At this time of experimental innovation in coin design type A was perhaps only part of a series of trial or pattern types. The type A and B sovereigns could thus represent competing designs by different artists, produced at about the same time. Type B, with mintmark cross fitchy, has its style A lettering from the normal groat punches of the time. The king's head

Edward IV – Henry VIII

is rather large for the body and the design does not stand out clearly from a background diapered with fleurs-de-lis. On the type B reverse there is no crown above the shield, neither the shield nor the rose has lines of hatching, and the whole is set within a tressure adorned with tiny leopards and lis. A curiosity of the inscription suggests the possible influence of type A, on which the Irish title appears as *Dns Ibarne* (a long form without parallel in English medieval coinage): type B, with *Gracia* and *Anglie* in full, reads *Dns Ibar* but the *ne* is transferred to the reverse, so ending with the nonsensical *Ibatne*.

Many writers have assumed that the cross fitchy on the type B sovereign associated it (and the ryal) with the cross fitchy groats of IB; but these groats cannot be dated later than 1487, two years before the commission for the sovereign. The cross fitchy mark suggests that the type B sovereign may be by the same hand as the ryal, but it does not necessarily imply that they were exactly contemporary – there are minor differences between the two (*Transciens* on the sovereign, and quatrefoil stops instead of trefoils), in addition to the shields on the reverse. A better case can be made for regarding the cinquefoil sovereign as being related to groats with the same mintmark; on the basis of the earlier chronology that now seems required, this coin may be seen as an early response to the commission of October 1489, and the unique sovereign type groat, also with mintmark cinquefoil, as a related experiment. While the design of the type B sovereign has much in common with later types, type A is in many respects so exceptional that, on typological grounds also, it seems a strong candidate for the distinction of heading the English sovereign series.

Henry VII, Group IIIA and IIIB

A sudden change now took place in the depiction of St. Michael and the dragon on the angels, while the gradual evolution of the groat design continued. Before the end of the cinquefoil groats jewels were added to both arches of the crown, a new fount of lettering (style B) was brought in, and a much more elaborate terminal replaced the plainer form of cross-end used for the bulk of the cinquefoil groats. These late cinquefoil coins (type IIIA) were soon succeeded by the extensive series of groats with as mintmark an escallop shell, on which the portrait shows another stage in its development, with new and more realistic hair (type IIIB). During the escallop issue three further styles of lettering (C, D and E) and another cross-end (no. 4) were introduced, as well as a wide range of ornaments on the cusps of the tressure. The last groats with the two jewelled arches of type IIIB have the mintmark pansy (a floral cinquefoil), and are much like the latest escallop coins, although a fifth type of cross-end was adopted shortly before the change to type IIIC (with only the outer arch jewelled), to which most pansy groats belong.

MINTMARKS IN HENRY VII EARLY GROUP III

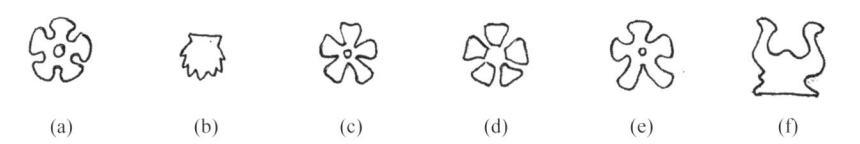

(a) Cinquefoil, IIIA; (b) Escallop, IIIBi; (c) Pansy 1, IIIBii and IIICi; (d) Pansy 2, angels IIICi; (e) Pansy 3, IIICi; (f) Dragon, sovereign type C.

Groats of type IIIA, all with mintmark cinquefoil, are rare. Three obverse dies have been noted, and there are mules both ways with types IIB and IIIB. The obverses show a bust with a slightly narrower face but otherwise similar, apart from the crown, to that of types I and II, with the hair still curling outwards at the lower ends. The new ornate cross-end (no. 3) has a swelling at the neck and tall antler-like ends enclosing a circular hollow. Simultaneously with the adoption of the new forms of crown, face and cross-end, the old style A lettering with its concave-sided uprights gave way to style B, a new plain form with straight uprights and with two highly distinctive letters, the open 'Greek' *E*, like a 3 reversed, and a Roman *M* of a characteristic Renaissance form with the legs sloping outwards. This style B lettering is accompanied by rosette stops.

ORNAMENTS ON CUSPS OF ESCALLOP GROATS

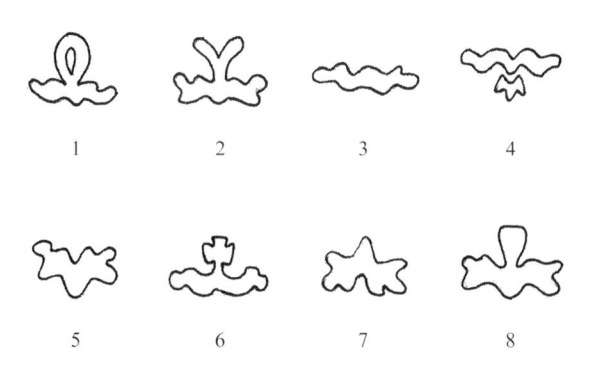

While early groats of type IIIB continue the style B lettering, cross-end no. 3 and rosette stops of IIIA, the new escallop mintmark was accompanied by a more compact and less stylized arrangement of the hair, with the ends curled inwards. One very early die, paired with a type IIB reverse and obviously experimental, has the hair brushed horizontally, an ornate crown with a large cross in place of the central lis, and the cusps unfleured. Other rare varieties include an early obverse with rosettes in the spandrels and a late reverse with double annulet stops and a star before *Civi*. Normal escallop groats exhibit a wide variety of ornaments on the cusps. Potter and Winstanley identified eight of them, of which nos. 1, 2 and 8 are elaborate fleurs but the others are of strange shapes: three of them are extremely rare, no. 3 simply a wavy line and nos. 4 and 5 apparently inversions of the same punches as nos. 6 and 7. Whether these various forms represent a deliberate system for marking dies or merely a further aspect of typological experiment it is not possible to say. But some intentional differentiation certainly applied during the currency of the escallop mark, for the rosette stops on earlier groats gave way in the middle of the period to trefoils, and later in turn to rosettes again; and during this last phase, with the rosettes resumed, their disposition was varied in the same 'coded' manner as had been done on late groats of type IIB.

Soon after the start of type IIIB the lettering was changed again. Style C, with deeply notched serifs, is more ornate than style B, although it retains the Roman *M* of style B and at first also the Greek *E*. Another fount, style D, with more rounded forms soon followed, of which *L* with a sinuous front and the curvy *V* are notable. Groats of the earlier rosette-stop phase have lettering of styles B, C and D, and those with trefoil stops have style D only. But the resumption of rosette stops was accompanied by yet another new letter fount, style E, which with some variation had a much longer period of use, surviving until after the introduction of the greyhound's head mintmark late in type IIIC. Lettering E reverts to a notched style not dissimilar to lettering C, but with a Gothic *m*, the *L* with two notches in the bottom and notches even in the arms of the *V*. Broken letter punches often occur in style E. Two other reverse features should be noted. Reverses with the neat lettering of styles B, C and D read *Deum A/diutor/e Meum* (the three *M*s all being Roman); those with style E letters, which are rather larger, required one to be dropped from each of the three segments, thus *Deu' A/diuto/e' Meu*, while on obverses the ending is usually shortened to *Fra*. Just before the end of the escallop mark, cross-end 3 was replaced by no. 4, similar in shape but wider and with a small rosette inserted within its horns.

EPIGRAPHIC STYLES ON GROATS OF HENRY VII TYPES IIIA AND B

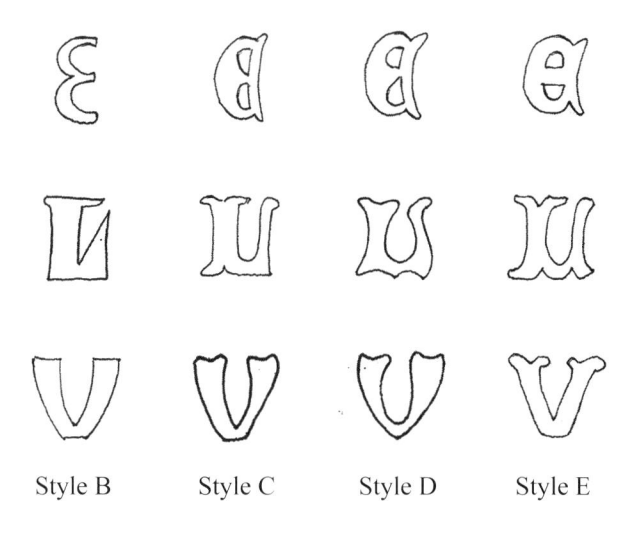

Style B	Style C	Style D	Style E

The last groats of type IIIB, with mintmark pansy, are scarce. In their rosette stops and lettering of style E (with some broken letters) these coins are a continuation from the escallop series, with which they are muled both ways. Some early dies have a pellet beneath the right arm of the cross above the crown, but otherwise there are no special marks. The only significant innovation during the IIIB pansy phase was another cross-end, no. 5, a less elaborate and more compact form than nos. 3 and 4, but still with three-pointed horns enclosing a circular hollow.

The smaller silver of this group does not correspond closely with the groats, but lettering, stops and sometimes the mintmark establish the connection. There are halfgroats of London, York (royal) and Canterbury (Morton), sovereign type pence of London and the episcopal mints at York and Durham, pence of Canterbury with a facing bust, and halfpence of London and Canterbury.

No halfgroats appear to have been struck at London between IA and III, the earliest coins of which, from a single obverse die, have mintmark escallop on both sides. Although this type has been labelled IIIA, with the escallop mark and lettering D these rare halves belong alongside early IIIB groats. They have a crown with two arches, the outer one jewelled, and the cusp ornaments are apparently tiny rosettes, like those in the spandrels on an early escallop groat. Following these escallop coins the groat mintmark was dropped on halves in favour of a lis, and a lozenge enclosing a pellet was added in the centre of the reverse cross. The lozenge type seems to have been designed to identify issues of reduced weight, since these halves usually fall significantly (up to 30 per cent or more) below the standard of 24 gr. With earlier dating now proposed for the escallop groats, with which they have epigraphical affinities, there is no chronological difficulty in identifying the lozenge halfgroats with the dandyprats of the Boulogne episode in 1492. They come from the royal mint of York as well as London, although of neither mint are they common. The earlier variety, IIIB(a), has trefoil stops and lettering D, as on groats of the middle escallop period, while type IIIB(b) has rosette stops and lettering E as on late escallop and early pansy groats. York halves frequently have reverses with later features than their obverses.

Canterbury halves of group III, of fuller weight and usually with Morton's tun (but now without his initial on the reverse), are very plentiful and somewhat more complicated. Potter and Winstanley divided them into four classes, of which A and B correlate to IIIB groats, C and D to those of IIIC. They all have a bust with a crown of two arches, of which only the outer one is usually jewelled, and new more realistic hair as on groats of type IIIB. In the rare class A the mintmark is a lis, as at London and York, sometimes with a tun also on the obverse. Although the obverse dies, with trefoil stops and lettering D, have earlier characteristics than the reverses, on which the lettering is of style E and the stops are rosettes, they were presumably made at about the same time. Both obverses and reverses in class B have rosette stops and style E letters; the obverse mintmark is now always a tun (occasionally with a lis beside it), but reverse dies have a lis, tun or nothing.

Sovereign type pence attributable to the period of early group III are of London and York – Durham's absence suggesting that the types concerned may have fallen between Shirwood's last issues, under the three-year contract from 1489, and January 1495 when Richard Fox's coinage was commissioned. As in type B, they have a single pillar on the dexter side, the other being implicitly obscured by the king's arm and the orb he holds. First there are rare coins (Ci), like type Bii except that the form of cross-ends resembles no. 7, with a hollow between two shaped feet; but no. 7 was not introduced on groats until the end of the pansy mark in type IIIC, and it therefore seems that the pierced form on these pennies, on which there would have been no room for the elaborate shapes of nos. 3, 4 and 5, was nevertheless the equivalent of them on a small scale. A pierced cross-end is not likely to have been adopted on penny dies before it was used on groats, so the Ci pence of London and York, although still with style A lettering, probably belong to the period of early group III, before letter punches in a more ornate style were made for this denomination. The next type (Cii), muled both ways with Ci at London, has new lettering and rosette stops, associating it with the period of the escallop groats. At London the mintmark is a lis but as usual there is none at York.

Some rare Canterbury coins of this period are the only pence of the reign to show a facing bust with an arched crown. They have the mintmark tun, rosette stops, style E lettering and cross-end 7, and probably belong to the same period as the Canterbury halfgroats of class IIIB. Following the example of halfgroats and pence, Canterbury halfpence now no longer have Morton's initial on the reverse cross. Like those of London, they have a broad single arch to the crown, which sometimes disappears into the beaded circle. The cross-ends are pierced, except on a few coins with the old cleft form, which may be III/II mules. Stops vary, but include the characteristic rosettes of the time.

Gold of this period consists of angels with mintmarks escallop and pansy, angelets with pansy, and the third type of sovereign, with mintmark dragon. There are no cinquefoil angels with lettering B, as on the groats of type IIIA, but the escallop angels of IIIB, less rare than angels of type II, are found with styles B, C and E. All have rosette stops. The three styles of lettering are matched by three varieties of type. The two obverse dies of variety (a), the first of the new design with humanistic saint, have a neat St. Michael in armour with feathers shown protruding downwards from the bottom edge of a short breastplate, as he spears a thin dragon with a cockerel-like head. The spearhead on one of the dies of variety (a) is a cross potent, as it was to become on all angels from type IIIC onwards. The old form of 'hammer cross' (or cross-crosslet) spearhead was, however, restored for the remaining angels of type IIIB. Reverses of IIIB angels also show some modification of design – the broad U-shaped ship (as already seen on the last dies of type II) now has saltire hatching on the castles, and the base of the shield is more rounded. On obverse dies of variety (b) St. Michael's figure is broader, feathers protrude sideways from a longer breastplate, his wings are larger, his right knee is bent, and there is a rosette each side of the nimbus. Except for a lack of these rosettes, and for new lettering of style E, obverses of variety (c) are similar to those of (b). Dies of varieties (a) and (b), by virtue of their B and C lettering, must have been made quite early in the escallop period. The style E lettering of variety (c) angels is of the small size as used on Canterbury halfgroats and demonstrates their association with silver of late type IIIB. No angel dies are known of the middle escallop phase with lettering D and trefoil stops, but the relatively small issues of gold did not require the continuous provision of new dies as for silver. This also explains the more frequent combination of old and new dies for gold. Thus cinquefoil angel obverses of type IIB are muled not with reverses of escallop IIIB(a) but with IIIB(b) and (c). There is also extensive muling between (a), (b) and (c) within IIIB, and a mule between escallop (c) and a pansy reverse. The last IIIB angels, with mintmark pansy, are similar to those of escallop (c), except that the stops are not always rosettes but sometimes saltires or none. They have the same cross-crosslet spearhead and the small lettering of style E, whereas the pansy angels of IIIC have the cross-potent spearhead and larger E lettering. No pansy (or subsequent) angels are known with the *Ihc Autem* legend, which alternates with *Per Crucem* in early IIIB, but then seems to have been dropped. Pansy angelets are rare, those with rosette stops belonging to the IIIB period.

A new pair of sovereign dies was produced in this period (type C). There is no direct correspondence of detail with the silver or angels of early group III, unless the neat star stops are related to the early escallop groat reverse with a small star before *Civi*. The letters are from a large fount not used elsewhere on the coinage; but in its plain uprights, open *E*, *L* with a short wedged front and Roman *M*, it bears some resemblance to style B, which would point to the end of the cinquefoil or start of the escallop period. The figure of the king is smaller, better proportioned and more finely executed than in type B. The hair, as on the silver of type III, is no longer of the conventional medieval form. In late Perpendicular Gothic style, the throne is much more ornate, with highly decorated back and pillars, the latter surmounted by the Tudor royal beasts, a greyhound sejant and a dragon (as used for the mintmark). Although fleurs-de-lis still feature in the background they are fewer and no longer sit in a lattice frame. On the reverse the shield and rose are a little smaller, with more emphasis on the surrounding tressure. All in all this is a magnificent if ostentatious coin, a self-confident assertion of Tudor royal authority.

Henry VII, Group IIIC, Mintmarks Pansy – Anchor

Most of the groats with mintmark pansy show a new form of crown, still with two arches, but now with only the outer one jewelled. Along with this, the hair was depicted with less stiff and more realistic curls, and the face was refined, with pupils added to the eyes, and a generally more pleasant expression. At the same time a new and larger fount of lettering (style E2) was introduced. This type, classified as IIIC, continued throughout the remainder of the currency of the pansy mark and the next three mintmarks, leopard's head crowned (LHC), lis-issuant-from-rose (LIR) and anchor. Some of the last facing bust groats, with mintmarks greyhound's head and cross-crosslet, also have the characteristics of type IIIC but during the currency of those marks a number of substantial changes were introduced, including the profile portrait, and they are therefore discussed separately hereafter. The smaller silver does not correspond closely to the groats, generally having different mintmarks, while the gold, although it uses the same marks as the groats, does not include coins with the leopard's head. The reason why there are no LHC angels is perhaps that this mark, originally the standard hallmark for silver, but having been replaced in this capacity by a lion passant, was by now used as the townmark for London silver and so may have been deemed inappropriate for use on gold coins. The mark itself did not prove very satisfactory, since the fine details of the face were only visible if very clearly struck and were vulnerable to wear. The next mark, with the top of a lis sprouting from the lower half of a rose, is a variation on the combined lis and rose marks used at the start of the reign to symbolize the Tudor fusion of Lancaster and York, but like LHC it did not last long. It was succeeded by the much longer-running anchor mark, something of a departure from the usual heraldic devices, but whether intended as a general reference to English maritime power, or with some particular allusion, we do not know.

LONDON MINTMARKS OF HENRY VII, ESCALLOP TO ANCHOR (GROUP III)

	ESCALLOP	LIS	PANSY	LHC	LIR	ANCHOR
Angel	x		x		x	x
Angelet			x			x
Groat	x		x	x	x	x
Halfgroat	x	x				
Penny		x	x			
Halfpenny		x	x			

LHC – Leopard's head crowned; LIR – Lis-issuant-from-rose

A silver medallic jetton, once regarded as a groat produced for the pretender Perkin Warbeck in the Low Countries, is in fact struck from dies made with letter punches used for English groats of the IIIC pansy period; it carries the date in Arabic numerals 1494 (old style) and thus provides a secure point, between 25 March 1494 and 24 March 1495, within the pansy phase of the coinage (could it perhaps be connected with the arrival of Alexander of Bruchsal at Michaelmas that year ?). Two forms of mintmark pansy are found on groats. Pansy 1, the earlier and commoner version, is the same as that used in type IIIB and has five petals of similar shape and size, with a small hollow in the centre. An intermediate form on angels (pansy 2) is not found on groats. On the late form, pansy 3, the two lower petals are longer than the others and curve towards the centre. Cross-end 5 occurs on earlier reverses, to be followed in succession by two new forms: no. 6,

Edward IV – Henry VIII

a much plainer terminal, with shaped feet, not unlike no. 2 but thicker; and no. 7, which also has plain feet rather than antlers, but enclosing a circular hollow as on nos. 3 and 5. Curiously, the rare pansy IIIB/C mule groats all have late reverses with the pierced cross-end 7. The stops are sometimes still rosettes, but more often saltires, or occasionally none; saltires now became the normal stops for the rest of the reign and beyond. The new E2 lettering generally resembles E1 as on late groats of type IIIB, but it is a little larger and more elaborate, the curved sides of *C, D* and *O* having interior peaks, and the uprights of several letters adorned with wavy serifs. The letter *R* is less narrow (R5) than the form on IIIB pansy groats (R4), and a new *M* (M5) with out-turned feet replaces the plain form of the old E1 alphabet. Broken letter punches are again frequent. Towards the end of the pansy series the spelling *Ang* gave way to *Agl*, which became standard henceforward, on other denominations also. The *Agl* pansy groats are generally rather larger than their predecessors, with flans of c. 26-7mm diameter as opposed to c. 24-5mm earlier, perhaps reflecting an early but unrecorded attempt to discourage clipping, as is known to have been made in 1504. This larger module, associated with cross-end 7, continues throughout the rare LHC and LIR marks, and into the early anchor period. The LHC and LIR groats also resemble the pansy 3 coins in having saltire stops and *Agl*, although broken letters are not found on LIR dies. While muling between different mintmarks otherwise tends to be unusual in this reign, mules among these large diameter groats between pansy 3, LHC, LIR and early anchor are relatively plentiful, and in the case of LHC and LIR dies they are not significantly rarer than the true coins with those marks.

NOTABLE LETTERS IN GROUP III OF HENRY VII

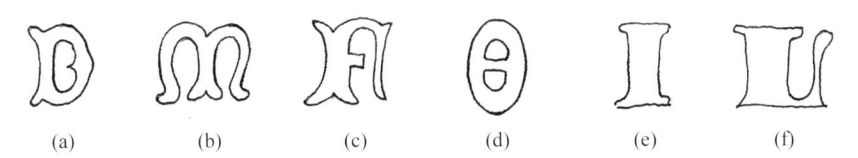

(a)   (b)   (c)   (d)   (e)   (f)

(a) Letter *D* of style E, with interior peak, IIIB; (b) *M* with out-turned feet, IIIB (M5);
(c) Broken *F*, Canterbury halfgroats, IIIB-C; (d) Theta-like *O*, Canterbury halfgroats, IIID;
(e) and (f) Thick, plain letters *I* and *L* of style F, IIICv-IVA.

The earliest of the abundant groats with mintmark anchor are a continuation of those with the preceding marks, with cross-end no. 7 and the larger flan, and lettering of style E2. On these coins the anchor is always inverted. Very soon, however, the module was slightly reduced and a new cross-end, without a circular hollow (no. 8), was made to fit the smaller dies. A yet more ornate version of style E lettering was also introduced (E3), with longer serifs and double notches, but the elaborate punches were apt to suffer damage and broken letters reappear. The appearance of the coins was further spoiled by careless workmanship, both in the placing of the letters and in their selection, which gave rise to overpunching to correct mistakes. On these new and smaller groats, which comprise the bulk of the anchor series, the anchor is either upright or inverted, without any obvious pattern. Late in the anchor period, as evidenced by mules with the greyhound mark, some groat dies again have the plainer lettering of style E2, either combined with a smaller anchor mark having a short shank and always inverted, or without any mintmark on the obverse.

Angels of this period with mintmark pansy revert to the cross potent spearhead as found in early type IIIB, and they are further differentiated from the pansy angels of IIIB by having lettering of the slightly larger style E2. They show both pansy 1 and pansy 3, as on groats, but also the intermediate pansy 2 consisting of five separate petals not tidily joined at the centre. As on silver, stops are sometimes rosettes, but more usually saltires, occasionally none. Since there is no gold with the LHC mintmark, angels with the pansy 3 mark are muled both ways with the rare mintmark LIR. But there is also an anchor/pansy mule, further pointing to the shortness of the interval between those two marks. Anchor angels, which are reasonably plentiful, have the mintmark upright, inverted or horizontal (conveniently, in view of the narrower band for the legend than on groats). As with groats, there is also a late variety with no obverse mintmark, represented by a die reading *Anglie* in full. The spearhead is either a cross potent, as on the pansy and LIR angels; or of a cross pommy form, with a large pellet on each of the three arms; or the cross-crosslet revived. Although most of the anchor groats have the elaborate new E3 lettering, the angels with this mark retain the style E2, more appropriate in size, which was used throughout, except for a single die, with pansy 3 and two saltires beside it, which has small and irregular lettering not noticed on other coins of the period.

The half-angel denomination in IIIC, with saltire stops, is very rare and occurs only with the pansy and anchor marks. IIIC pansy reverses were mostly used with an anchor obverse, but no anchor-marked reverse is known. These anchor/pansy mules suggest that no angelet dies were made with mintmark LIR.

If any sovereigns were struck during this period they were presumably still from the dies of type C with mintmark dragon, from which at least sixteen specimens have been noted.

As in the earlier part of group III, the smaller silver does not relate closely to the groats. Light halfgroats of the London and York royal mints, with the lozenge-centred reverse cross, follow those of type IIIB in their mintmark lis, but are of markedly different appearance in having a large open crown which breaks the tressure at the top. Earlier coins, IIIC(a), confined to London, have rosettes in the outer inscription only, later ones (b) in both inscriptions. The less scarce halves of type IIIC(b) are from slightly smaller dies, with reduced lettering, and their reverses are often found muled with earlier obverses, of IIIB at York and of IIIC(a) at London.

Morton's Canterbury halfgroats are unchanged in basic type. Two groups, IIIC and IIID, with lettering of the E2 style, belong to this period. Most have the mintmark tun both sides, but exceptionally one obverse die of IIIC has the pansy 1 mark beside the tun. Normally there are no stops on these Canterbury halves, but a few obverse dies of IIIC have rosettes or saltires. In IIIC, which is very common, the letters *F* and *P* are broken, and the cross-end with pointed horns has a swelling at the neck. In IIID the cross-end is flatter, with a smaller piercing, and no neck-swelling (as no. 7 on late pansy to early anchor groats); there are no broken letters, and the *O* has interior peaks which meet to form a central bar as in a Greek theta. In another link with the pansy groats, *Agl* replaces *Angl* during IIIC.

Sovereign type pence of the pansy-anchor period (Ciii) are more plentiful of York and Durham than of London, although they ceased altogether with the restraint of the episcopal mints in 1499. As before, reverses have pierced cross-ends. Winstanley's division into type II with a single pillar and type III with two pillars is not an absolute indicator of sequence, although single-pillar dies predominate in the earlier stages and the number of twin-pillar dies increases later. While the lettering is not identical with that on larger coins, it reflects the generally more ornamented style of this period. *Agl* (or *Ag*, or *Al*) replaces *Ang* on some of the later dies. There is now greater variety in the ornaments topping the sceptre and pillars. Following Lawrence, Allen has argued that these ornaments were changed to mark successive batches of dies – possibly in the sequence lis, saltires, crosses, rosettes and broken lis. After lis ornaments, London issues virtually ceased, although there are a few coins with crosses. Generally there is no mintmark, but an exceptional London reverse die is known with a pansy before *Civi*. Rotherham's York pence, with the keys below the shield, include some with saltires on the seat of the throne. Bishop Richard Fox's Durham coinage, following the indenture of January 1495, differs from that of his predecessor not only in respect of his initials (*D R* or *R D*) but also in dropping the crozier and substituting a mitre above the shield. One late Fox reverse was still available years later to be paired with an obverse issued to his successor Thomas Ruthall at the beginning of the reign of Henry VIII.

There is little to distinguish the later from the earlier halfpence of group III. There is usually no mintmark, occasionally a lis. Very exceptionally, one London coin has mintmark pansy, but this is the only groat mark to appear on a halfpenny between cinquefoil and pheon. Farthings with forked cross-ends, all of considerable rarity, are normally without features that enable them to be placed at all confidently in relation to larger denominations; but one perhaps shows an anchor mintmark.

Henry VII, Transition to Profile Portrait Types (IIIC – V)

The final stage in the series of Henry VII's groats with the facing bust was a period of experiment and innovation. Alongside the normal groats of the traditional type a small issue was made of groats, halfgroats and shillings with the head in profile. There is a subtlety in the execution of the likeness that captures both the strength and the refinement of the subject; and the composition is the more effective for being set against a plain field without the tressure that had surrounded the head on the larger silver for the previous century and a half. Like many of the early portrait types of northern Europe these coins show the bust in low relief. Although the groat was still struck on a thin flan, in the medieval manner, the short-lived shilling was thicker and would have been suitable for a more sculpted portrait like those of the Italian medallists. Indeed, we may wonder whether it was not the decision to produce a larger silver coin that actually prompted the introduction of portraiture at this moment. Nevertheless, Henry VII's new coins retained the traditional Gothic lettering, which was to survive on English coinage longer than elsewhere – the Renaissance combination of personal portraiture captioned in Roman script was not fully established in England until the 1550s. However, to emphasize the personal identity of the king, in contrast to the stylized royal head of the middle ages, the numeral *VII* (or on a few early dies, *Septim*) was added after Henry's name. Carlyon-Britton, who first demonstrated the overlap between the facing and profile head groats, used the term tentative issue to describe the early varieties of profile groat (VA), and this conveniently indicates their experimental nature. But the new type must quickly have gained acceptance, since the facing head was soon discontinued and profile groats were thereafter struck in large numbers. The shilling, however, cannot have been found a sufficiently useful denomination at this stage since, like Edward I's groat, it also disappeared after only a limited issue, not to be revived for forty years.

Silver coinage with the facing bust thus continued after 1500, but not for long. The last of the facing-head groats of Henry VII, with the mintmarks greyhound's head and cross-crosslet, exhibit further changes in the form of the crown which, very curiously, show the same progression on obverse dies with each of the two marks. Yet the evidence of mules, and of epigraphy and cross-ends, shows clearly that the two marks were used in sequence and not in parallel. The earliest form is a continuation of type IIIC, having the crown with two arches and jewels on the outer arch, as already found with mintmarks pansy to anchor. This was followed by a new type, IV, in which the crown has a wide single arch ornamented either (IVA) with small saltires ('crockets'), or (IVB) with short uprights. Groats with both mintmarks are plentiful, but type IV is rare with the greyhound's head as is type IIIC with the cross-crosslet.

MINTMARKS OF HENRY VII IN LATE GROUP III AND GROUP IV

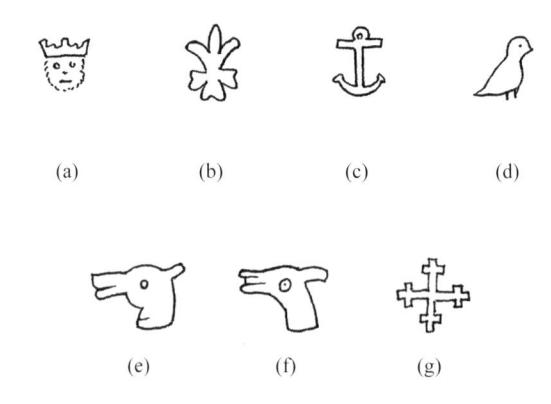

(a)   (b)   (c)   (d)

(e)   (f)   (g)

(a) Leopard's head crowned (LHC), IIICii; (b) Lis-issuant-from-rose (LIR), IIICiii;
(c) Anchor (or inverted), IIICiv; (d) Martlet, York; (e) Greyhound's head (GH1), IIICv(a);
(f) Greyhound's head (GH2), IIICv(b)-IVB; (g) Cross-crosslet, IIICvi-IVB.

Much debate has been had about the numismatic implications of the Act of early 1504 against clipping and of the consequent Proclamation of 5 July. The Act, which provided that all coins thenceforward should have the beaded outer circle intact, was implemented near the close of the greyhound's head issue, when the rare groats of type IVB with this mark (like all the subsequent facing-bust groats, with mintmark cross-crosslet) were struck on slightly larger flans to accommodate the outer circle. On this basis cross-crosslet must have succeeded greyhound's head in the first half, or perhaps the first quarter, of 1504. The Proclamation provided that groats coined before the Act were to be regarded as unclipped if they showed three ends of the cross and most of the inscription on the other side; and that groats coined since the Act should not be current unless they had a full impression on both sides. Burgundian double-patards (without a long cross in their design) should be current if they had the inscription complete on one side or the other. Alongside the text are woodcut illustrations of three coins: a greyhound's head type IV groat showing all four cross-ends; a double-patard with the obverse inscription intact; and a cross-crosslet type IV groat with only three cross-ends visible. Grierson has pointed out that the groat used to illustrate an acceptable pre-Act coin has the cross-crosslet mintmark, while the post-Act coin has the greyhound's head, implying that cross-crosslet preceded greyhound's head. There is no difficulty in placing the last of the greyhound's head groats between the Act and the Proclamation, but a groat with the cross-crosslet mintmark should not have been regarded as a coin struck before the Act. The weight of numismatic evidence points strongly to the sequence anchor-greyhound's head-cross-crosslet, and it must be that the cross-crosslet woodcut is incorrect as a representation of a pre-Act coin. There is no reference in the text to the mintmarks, although it is possible that the cross-crosslet was introduced in order to make post-Act coins more readily recognisable. In fact, the illustrations are not taken from actual coins, as betrayed by a number of points of detail: a late greyhound's head groat should not read *Anglie* in full; a cross-crosslet reverse should not show a Roman *E* or *M*; and neither should have chevron-barred *A*s, or *Meum* in full.

In type IIIC two punches were used for the greyhound's head. The earlier (GH1) is a large head with a thick neck, but the eye and ears are small. The second version of the mark (GH2) is neater, with a larger eye but smaller head and neck, and longer ears extending backwards and often downwards. With GH1 the reverse cross-end is the unadorned no. 8, as on the later anchor groats of reduced module, but the lettering reverts to that of the earlier anchor groats. The stops are saltires, as are now normal for the remainder of the reign, but on many GH1 dies and some with GH2 the saltires are damaged, with one or more arms broken. One odd pair of GH1 dies has the reading *henic* and a saltire before the reverse mintmark. With the introduction of GH2 the lettering and cross-end were both changed. The new terminal (no. 9) is of a very plain form, and accompanied by a plainer and smaller fount of letters (style F), with thick uprights and less prominent serifs. There are mules both ways between GH1 and GH2, but there are also coins from GH2 obverse dies of type IIIC combined with reverse dies with mintmark rose. Their plain cross-ends and fount F lettering place the rose dies in the period of the GH2 mark, probably near the start of it since there are more IIIC GH1/rose than IVA GH2/rose mules. The punch for the rose mintmark is the same as that above the shield on the reverse of angels.

The rare GH2 groats of type IVA, which continue the style F lettering and cross-end no. 9 from type IIIC, are notable for the ornaments on the cusps of the tressure. On three of four dies of the type an elaborate trefoil punch, with the petals indented, was used instead of the normal (broader and flatter) fleur, apparently identical with the strawberry-leaf which appears in the crown on shillings and on the earliest groats with the profile portrait. Another link with the shillings is the odd reverse reading *A/diuto/eu* on some GH2 groats of type IVA. The last stage of the GH2 groats (IVB) is distinguished not only by the modification of the crown, now with the arch shown in double outline and ornamented with three short uprights instead of three saltires each side of the central globe and cross, but also by a new style of lettering (G). This is thinner and more graceful in shape than style F, but it is often marred by damaged punches, such as *E, F* and *R* which broke at the top. These rare coins of type IVB usually still have the plain cross-end no. 9, but on a few reverses there is a new one (no. 10) with splayed, concave feet. However, the type IVB groats with GH2 are chiefly of interest in being the first to be struck on slightly larger flans with a complete beaded outer edge, compliant with the Act of January 1504.

It is strange to find that a few of the earliest groat dies with mintmark cross-crosslet reverted to the double-arched crown of type IIIC, but their position is not in doubt since not only are the greyhound's head reverses, with which they are found muled, of late type IVB, but they continue, as do all the crosslet facing-head groats, with cross-end no. 10 and lettering of style G from the last of the GH groats, together with the fuller flan and beaded edge. One curious IIIC die reads *henrikic*, the *K* a broken *R*, following a whole one, which Potter saw as indicating that the broken letter fulfilled some intended function. The more abundant cross-crosslet groats with the single arched crown of type IV show remarkable variation in the spelling or abbreviation of *Anglie* and *Aglie*, as if in accordance with some deliberate pattern in the manufacture of the dies. *Fra, Fr* and *F, diuto* and *diutor*, and the use of double as well as single saltire stops may also have been designed for some purpose of die-coding. Most of the type IVA crosslet groats have the arch of the crown shown as a single bar, decorated with two small saltires on each side; but rare varieties occur with the bar in double outline, once with six saltires, instead of four. Again as in the greyhound's head series, the last form of crown (IVB) has uprights instead of saltires on a single arch in double outline. The introduction on cross-crosslet groats of type IV of a new *F* punch, with a long downstroke at the front, can be matched on a few early cross-crosslet groats with the profile bust, again pointing to parallel issue of the two series.

SPECIAL LETTER FORMS ON HENRY VII LATE GROUPS

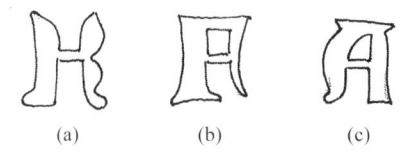

(a)   (b)   (c)

(a) Broken *R*, style G, late IIIC; (b) Long-fronted *F*, style G, IV and some early profile groats; (c) Shaped and barred *A*, halfgroats, IVc (York) and early V.

Although all the shillings and the pre-crosslet tentative profile groats are rare, there is considerable variety of detail among them, as so often at a period of experiment. In outline, there are three main types of tentative groat, the first two of which are paralleled in the shillings. Type 1 consists of early dies without a numeral. In type 2 a numeral is added, at first *Septim'*, but soon as *VII*. The sequence of obverse mintmarks on groats of types 1 and 2 is small lis (1a), none (1b and 2a), large lis (2b) and greyhound's head (2c). On shillings also the small lis (1) is followed by the larger lis (2), but dies for this denomination ceased to be made before the mintmarks of the regular (facing-bust) series were adopted for the profile groats. Type 3, confined to groats, is an extension of type 2, but with mintmark cross-crosslet.

On tentative groats the base of the crown consists of two bands, and there are six ornaments on the arch, as against three bands and four ornaments on the regular profile issues (VB) that followed. Particularly on the early varieties, the portrait on tentative groats (and on shillings) is usually more finely drawn than on the regular profile series, and the hair is more tightly curled at the bottom. Groats of type 1 have hair-line inner circles, within the beaded border, an attractive way of encircling the new portrait in the absence of a tressure. The first two dies (1a) have the small lis as obverse mintmark and special lettering, both features of the earliest shilling dies. The next two (1b) have no mintmark, but the same delicate lettering of early style G as on type 2 shillings. Without a numeral, their fuller readings also mark out these four dies as early – two read *henricus*, three *Dei* and three *Anglie*, forms which never appear in types 2 or 3. On groats of tentative type 2 the six saltires on the crown are replaced by uprights. Only the earliest 2a die reads *Septim;* with one exception in 2b, all the rest have the numeral *VII*. The *Septim* die alone in type 2 still has the hair-line circles, which were then discarded no doubt to save effort but at the expense of appearance. Two other obverse dies of type 2a have small pellets over the uprights on the arch of the crown. Most of the reverse dies used with tentative

Edward IV – Henry VIII

obverses of types 1 and 2a still have cross-end no. 10, as on the cross-crosslet facing-head groats, but in 2b and 3 this was superseded by a new form (no. 11) which has the outer side of the feet rounded, with a small spike protruding. The same mintmarks (or none) occur on reverse dies of tentative groats as on obverses, although they were extensively interchanged and mules are thus frequent. In one case a shilling reverse die was used for a type 2b groat. Type 2c profile groats, with mintmark greyhound's head (GH2), are of great rarity both as lis/GH mules and (especially) as true coins.

The type 3 tentative groats, with mintmark cross-crosslet, although rare, are much less so than those of types 1 and 2 and are of more settled design. They do, however, continue to show the same variation as before in the readings *Angli*, *Agli* and *Agl* in both the main sub-divisions, 3a with six uprights on the crown and 3b with six crockets. The most remarkable dies of this period are two obverses (described as 3c, although not obviously the latest) which have a fleured tressure before and behind the bust, but are otherwise similar to 3b. One of the two has no numeral, almost as if an unfinished die prepared for the facing-bust type had been completed with the new profile portrait. The combination of tressure and profile, however, makes a crowded and unsatisfactory design, and the experiment, if such it was meant to be, was quickly abandoned. Possibly the issue of type 3 tentative groats may have extended beyond the period of the last facing-bust groats with the cross-crosslet mintmark.

In all main features of their design, and in many of their details, the shillings are very similar to the earlier tentative profile groats, although their reverse dies differ in having a small ornament within the cross-ends. Most of the extra weight of the shilling was achieved by thickness, and only a little by greater diameter, so that the reuse of a shilling reverse die with a groat obverse was not too awkward. Probably the dies for the first shillings were prepared at about the same as those for the first profile groats, since two pairs for each were made with a special set of letter punches not traced on any other coins. The first two shilling obverse dies (type 1) also have wire-line inner circles and the same small lis mintmark as on the earliest profile groats, although their reverses do not have the wire-line circles. The first pair of shilling dies (1a, known from more than a dozen specimens, mostly in fine condition and no doubt put aside for their novelty) is easily recognized by the large beading of the outer circles, and by the reading *henricus* in full, as on two of the type 1 profile groats. Both pairs of type 1 shilling dies are also distinctive in having no numeral on the obverse (permitting *Anglie* in full) and a small lis in the cross-ends (the same lis as used in the royal arms and for the mintmark), whereas type 2 dies read (a) *henric Septim* or (b) *henric VII* (with *Angl*), and the ornaments in the (less florid) cross-ends are slipped trefoils. Although three obverse dies each are known of types 2a and 2b, all are extremely rare and fewer type 2 shillings in all are known than those from the two obverse dies of type 1. The portrait on types 1 and 2a is of very fine work, as on the early profile groats, but the dies of type 2b are less carefully made.

There is nothing to suggest that the issue of light lozenge-marked halfgroats at London and the royal mint of York continued until the late stages of the IIIC period. The end of the long series of Canterbury halves had come before Morton's death in September 1500, perhaps in some way related to the restraint of February 1499. Rather surprisingly, therefore, the only halfgroats attributable to the early 1500s are from the archiepiscopal mint at York, which had never previously been permitted to strike anything other than pennies. Rotherham's successor, Thomas Savage, a trusted courtier of Henry VII, received his temporalities in April 1501 and although there is no documentary record of authorisation to revive the archbishop's mint at this time, or to coin other denominations, the extensive issues of facing-bust halfgroats, from London-made dies, with mintmark martlet and marked (as Rotherham's pence had been) with the keys of York, must belong to the earlier years of Savage's tenure. For convenience, these York halfgroats are described as type IV, although they are only partly synchronous with the type IV groats, and indeed must have begun before the end of IIIC. York halfgroats of the first (IVa) of the four principal varieties have lettering of the ornate style E and their broken saltire stops connect them with greyhound's head groats of late IIIC. They have a key each side of the bust, with a double-arched crown, and are remarkable for being the only facing-bust halfgroats, in a period of more than a hundred and fifty years, without a tressure around the portrait. A more minor oddity is that some of their reverses have *Eboraci* before *Civitas*. These IVa halves are quite plentiful, as are those of IVb with which they are extensively muled. In type IVb the tressure is restored (with, unusually, small saltires on the cusps), creating rather a crowded appearance because of the keys and the large crown; the lettering is of style F, similar to that on groats with mintmark GH2. The other two types, IVc and IVd, show style G lettering, a smaller version of that on the last of the greyhound's head groats and on all the facing-bust groats with mintmark cross-crosslet. The rare type IVc, with a shaped and barred *A* of the general style found on early profile halves, is notable for omitting the keys by the bust, and it has in the past, accordingly, sometimes been attributed to the vacancy following Savage's death in September 1507; such a date, with the profile type by then well established, is much too late, but there is no obvious explanation (other than accident) for the missing keys in the middle of an uncontroversial episcopate. Type IVd, much more plentiful, has the keys restored, and a new (unpierced) cross-end with pointed feet (no. 10). The degree of muling between the four types of these York halfgroats suggests intensive minting over a few years at most, between the summer of 1501 and late 1504 or early 1505, when the coinage of profile halves was actively taken up at London and Canterbury as well as at York. Also attributable to Savage is a rare type of York halfpenny, with a key below a tiny bust. This again was a denomination not hitherto allowed to the archbishop.

Only one variety of London halfgroat of the tentative period has been identified (VA). It is the sole profile halfgroat without a numeral, corresponding to the shillings and groats of type 1. This is confirmed by the mintmark (obverse, none; small lis on the reverse), and by the heavy beading of the outer borders in the manner of the earliest pair of shilling dies. As the minting of halfgroats at the Tower had been in abeyance for some years, the fact that only a single pair of dies of this kind is known suggests that they were made more as an essay for the new type, than to initiate a new series of London halfgroats at this very early stage.

The decision of Council in February 1499 to ban the minting of pennies had put an end to the output of York and Durham for a time, and this presumably explains why there are no York pence for Savage despite reactivation of the mint for production of halfgroats and halfpence. London, however, resumed the minting of pence during the greyhound's head period, although at first the pence themselves did not carry a mintmark. They are easily distinguished from earlier sovereign type pence in having the (lis-topped) pillars shown in double outline. Stops are saltires, sometimes broken as on GH groats. Lettering is either large and ornate (cf. style E) or small and plainer (cf. style F). In due course a new larger fount was introduced, accompanied by a cross-crosslet mintmark, but this type, or most of it, probably belongs to the period after the end of the facing bust groats.

London halfpence of this period may be distinguished by having the same small bust, with a single-arched crown, as on the York coin of Archbishop Savage. If farthings were still being struck at this time, they should probably be sought among those with saltire stops and forked cross-end (as no. 10).

Edward IV – Henry VIII

Angels with either greyhound's head or cross-crosslet are not particularly rare. It is not possible to draw a clear dividing line between those with mintmark cross-crosslet struck during the period of the last facing-bust groats and those of the subsequent period of the regular profile groats of VB. On angel dies with the GH1 mark the lettering is either of style E (usual on obverses) or of the same small fount as used for Savage's York halfgroats (usual on reverses). GH2 dies have style F letters and saltire or rosette stops. The sequence of cross-crosslet angel dies is difficult to establish, since different letter punches were not used consistently. But obverse dies with rosettes or saltires by the halo, as found also on angels with mintmark pheon, are likely to be later and these probably belong to the VB period of the regular profile groats. Cross-crosslet angels without marks by the halo usually have the spear-end as a cross potent, although two dies have a crosslet spear-end and some of the reverses found with these two have rosette instead of saltire stops.

Angelets are again of considerable rarity. The first variety constitutes the sole occurrence of the greyhound's head on this denomination. GH1 is found on one reverse die only, coupled with two obverse dies without mintmark. The next variety, from a single pair of dies and also extremely rare, has the mintmark rose on both sides, echoing the rose mark on reverses of some early GH2 groats. Finally, there are coins from the same rose obverse die, but paired with two reverse dies with mintmark cross-crosslet.

One of these angelet reverse dies with the cross-crosslet has a small rosette at the end of the inscription, flanked by four crosses, in a manner very similar to the rosette between four saltires after *Ibat* on the fourth type of gold sovereign (D), and suggesting that they belong to the same general period. The reverse of type D otherwise differs little, except in the lettering and stops, from the reverse of type C, with which it shares the mintmark dragon. The obverse, however, with mintmark lis, has a smaller and neater figure of the king, on a wider throne with two front pillars each side and a highly decorated and elaborate back. This breaks through the inscription to the edge of the coin, requiring some abbreviation of the king's titles. The stops are now saltires, as on contemporary groats; and the special lettering, which has affinities with style G, is fully Gothic except for the Roman *M*, and includes an unusual *A*, unbarred in the middle and with a bar at the top only to the left. This alphabet is less severe than that of type C and in keeping with the more delicate, if less imposing, design of the new type. The type D coins, all from a single pair of dies, are the least rare of Henry VII's sovereigns.

Last Issues of Henry VII and the First Coinage of Henry VIII

After fifteen years of novelty and change in the middle of the reign, the coinage settled into a more stable pattern for the last four years of Henry VII and the first seventeen of Henry VIII. During this long period the profile portrait of Henry VII remained unchanged on groats and halfgroats, despite its obvious unsuitability when coupled with the title of the son who had not reached his eighteenth birthday at his father's death in April 1509. Henry VIII's own portrait was not to appear until a new coinage was prepared in 1526. Soon after the introduction of the profile type the archbishops' mints were reinstated, largely for the production of halfgroats, and in 1510 Durham resumed its minting of pence. The only additional royal mint that features during this period was a short-lived establishment at Tournai after it fell to the English in 1513. The change of reverse type on groats and halves and the consequent loss of their inner inscription had not mattered while they were only struck at London, but was less satisfactory when Canterbury and York were revived in the last years of Henry VII, and in due course this led to the replacement of the *Posui* legend by their mint names. The 1520s saw a momentary reappearance of the ryal and, in 1523, a more serious attempt, accompanied by a change of type, to revive the minting of farthings. Otherwise, the only significant development was the experimental reduction in the weight of the silver coinage in 1522-3, foreshadowing the definitive revaluation of 1526, and causing a sharp increase in the amount of silver minted.

The regular profile groats of Henry VII and those of Henry VIII's first coinage show relatively little variety. As on other coins of this period, their stops are saltires or crosses. Lettering remains Gothic throughout, and the spelling *Agl* is now standard. *henric* and *VII* or *VIII* are both followed by the query-shaped contraction mark as used in manuscripts to denote *-us* (thus showing that *VII'* and *VIII'* were read as *Septim'* and *Octav'*). Although profile groats of Henry VII of the tentative type (VA) with mintmark cross-crosslet may have outlasted the issue with the facing bust, the change of crown, from two bands to three and from six ornaments on the arch to four, constitutes a conveniently identifiable point by which the profile had become the sole and established type (VB). At first the mintmark cross-crosslet continued in its simple form, but towards the end of its currency it was qualified by the addition of pellets or saltires beside the cross-crosslet or the cross above the crown, the most usual version being in the form of a colon before the mintmark. Cross-crosslet was succeeded as mintmark by a downward pointing pheon (heraldically, the head of a dart or javelin), possibly, to judge by the relative number of surviving coins, as early as the end of 1505. If so, this would allow the pheon mark to be associated with the appointment of new masters, Robert Fenrother and William Reed, in November 1505, which involved a month's break in the mint accounts. That the groats with qualified cross-crosslet mintmark come at the end of the crosslet series is indicated by the fact that most pheon/cross-crosslet mules have the colon by the reverse mark. But cross-crosslet obverse dies both with and without the colon have been found with the mintmark overstamped by pheon; these, as well as a plain cross-crosslet/pheon mule, show that unqualified cross-crosslet dies were also still available when the pheon mark was introduced. The groats with pheon over cross-crosslet constitute a departure from normal practice under Henry VII, in whose coinage altered mintmarks are otherwise unknown. They are, however, less of a surprise than some other rare transitional coins at the juncture of the two marks, which have a cross-crosslet in the normal position of the mintmark at the start of the inscription and a pheon at the end, or occasionally *vice versa*. Dies with these double marks are known for both obverses and reverses (more usually the latter). No groat has apparently yet been recorded from both dies double-marked, but such dies were paired with single-mark dies with either cross-crosslet (usually with a colon) or pheon. Although a few very rare groats from dies with two consecutive mintmarks are found under Edward IV, the purpose of this double-marking is equally difficult to explain in either reign.

MINTMARKS ON HENRY VII GROATS, 1509-26

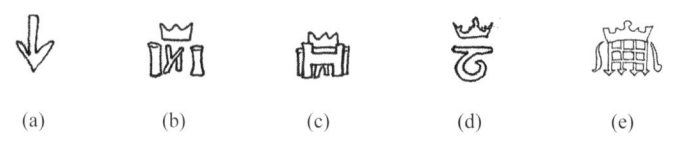

(a)   (b)   (c)   (d)   (e)

(a) Pheon (also late Henry VII); (b) Castle; (c) *H* and Castle, gold only; (d) Crowned *t*, Tournai; (e) Portcullis (or without chains).

Edward IV – Henry VIII

Rare early groats of Henry VIII also have mintmark pheon. However, it cannot have lasted long in the new reign since the extra digit of the numeral has been squeezed in as if added to dies prepared for Henry VII. The two remaining mintmarks of the first coinage were the castle and the portcullis. The castle has been interpreted, very plausibly, as the tower of Castile, a compliment to Katherine of Aragon and Castile, whom Henry married a few weeks after becoming king. The Beaufort portcullis, by now well established as a symbol of the Tudor dynasty, is surmounted by a small open crown and usually has curved chains attached at the sides (although these are sometimes omitted, particularly on reverse dies of groats, and more often on the lesser denominations). On some obverse dies a pellet is found by the castle or portcullis, or before *Gra* on portcullis groats. Also, the castle may be flanked by saltires. These extra marks are reminiscent of those on late cross-crosslet groats of Henry VII. Groats with the pheon and castle, and a few early ones with the portcullis, have the numeral *viij*; but most portcullis groats have either the same form without dots above the digits, or *viii* (with or without the dots). In contrast to the previous reign, there are no mules between mintmarks on London silver of Henry VIII's first coinage.

LONDON MINTMARKS OF LATE HENRY VII AND HENRY VIII FIRST COINAGE

	GREYHOUND'S HEAD	ROSE	LIS	CROSS-CROSSLET	PHEON	CASTLE	CROWNED PORTCULLIS
Sovereign				x	x		x
Ryal							x
Angel	x			x	x	x	x
Angelet	r	x		r	x	x	x
Shilling			x				
Groat	x	r	x	x	x	x	x
Halfgroat			x		x		x
Penny				x	x	x	x
Halfpenny			x		x	x	x

r – reverse only

In May 1512 and June 1513 Henry VIII organized an army to invade France, in a revival of the English claim to the French throne. The second of these expeditions achieved some success, culminating in the capture of the city of Tournai after a short siege in September 1513. Henry held Tournai for five years, before entering into a treaty with France in 1518 by which he ceded the city to the French in return for a payment of 600,000 francs to be paid over twelve years. Some extremely rare groats of French type with a crowned shield on the obverse were struck in his name, reading (in Roman letters) *Civitas Tornacensis 1513*; but their design was not suited for currency in England and, under indenture of March 1514 specifying only groats and halves, they were quickly succeeded by coins of English type. The latter, with Gothic lettering, are very similar to the normal English coins of the period, and their appearance shows that the dies were made at the Tower. They differ only in having as mintmark a Gothic *t* surmounted by a small arched crown, and in their inscriptions. Their obverses have the French title before the English, and unlike London dies they lack a numeral, perhaps because Henry VIII was the first and only English king to have minted there. The reverses read *Civitas Tornacen* (a rare case

409

of an adjectival mint name in the English series) instead of the *Posui* legend. Groats of this English type are rare, the comparable halfgroat extremely so. Some very rare London portcullis groats have a small trefoil in the forks of the cross-ends, and these trefoil dies are sometimes paired with obverses on which the portcullis has been punched into the die over a *t*. Such obverse dies must originally have been prepared for use at Tournai, and perhaps also the reverses marked with trefoils to differentiate them from London dies.

The dies with portcullis over *t* provide a useful clue to the dating of the mintmarks. They have the early form of numeral (*viij*), and include dies with the fullest (and rare) reading of the French title, *Fra*; so they probably come near the beginning of the portcullis series. These dies were presumably never sent to Tournai, perhaps because it was decided to spell out Henry's French claim by putting that title first and by advertising the French mint name on the reverse. At any rate, there are good grounds for thinking that in late 1513, or soon after, the current London mark was portcullis, and that it was then still in its early stages. Although this would mean a currency period of twelve years or more for the mintmark, coins of all denominations with the portcullis are considerably more plentiful than those with the castle. Since the weight reduction of 1522-3 amounted to less than 2½ gr. per groat, the lighter coins struck during these years are not obviously identifiable.

Smaller silver of this period is all relatively scarce from London, the production of the lower values being again provided largely by the ecclesiastical mints. Like the groats, halfgroats henceforward carry the king's numeral. The regular London profile halves of Henry VII have mintmark lis or pheon. The earliest have a shaped and barred *A* (and some of them an apostrophe contraction mark in place of the *n* in the king's name), but most dies with mintmark lis and all with pheon have a plain, unbarred *A*. That the lis on these halfgroats was the equivalent of the cross-crosslet on groats is demonstrated by late lis dies having a colon before the lis, exactly like the colon before the cross-crosslet. The introduction of the pheon (muled both ways with :lis) represents a reversion, for the first time since the escallop halfgroats of early type III, to the use of the same mark as on groats. This practice, which had been normal before the 1490s, was now again to be followed for the remainder of the groat period. The minting of halfgroats at London, however, appears soon to have been suspended for a few years. None of the London profile halfgroats of Henry VII have the pierced cross-end (no. 11), as found on the last halves of the reign from Canterbury and York, which explains why pheon halves are rare when groats with this mark are so common. Suspension of the issue of halfgroats from London probably occurred some time before 1509; it evidently continued for a few years into the new reign, no halves of Henry VIII being known with mintmark castle. Those with mintmark portcullis often have the mark on the obverse only or, if also on the reverse, without its chains.

In the later years of Henry VII the coinage of pennies was confined to London. Those with mintmark cross-crosslet may have been struck both during the period of the last of the facing bust groats with that mark (IV-VA) and after the profile had become established (VB). Pence with mintmark pheon do all, of course, belong to the latter phase. Since pennies of this period do not carry a regnal numeral, it is possible that some with the pheon could belong to the short extension of this mark, as on groats and angels, into the next reign. Mintmarks castle and portcullis are then found in the first coinage of Henry VIII, the former much the rarer. Like the pence, halfpence of this group have no numeral but can be divided between the Henries by virtue of their mintmarks. London coins of Henry VII have mintmarks lis and pheon. The former, which is rare, matches the lis used at the same time on London halfgroats as the equivalent of cross-crosslet. The castle and portcullis both occur on halfpence of Henry VIII, castle again the scarcer.

Farthings of the old type, sparingly coined after the first half of the fifteenth century, had been easily confused with small halfpence. So Parliament's decision to revive the denomination in 1523 involved a change of design. A portcullis replaced the king's bust on the obverse and a rose on the centre of the reverse cross displaced the pellets. It was stipulated that one thirtieth of all bullion coined should be in farthings, but the coins are so rare that it must be doubtful whether this provision was adhered to.

Angels of this period occur in considerable numbers. Although there is no definitive means of separating the cross-crosslet angels related respectively to the groats of types IV and VB, those that must belong to the later stages of the crosslet mark exhibit various features associating them with the pheon angels or with the regular profile groats. Since pheon angels have one or more saltires by the halo, a number of cross-crosslet dies which also have saltires (one to four) or in one case three rosettes, by the halo presumably come late in the currency of the mark. All have the cross-crosslet spear-head, and many of them also have the query-shaped contraction mark after *henric* that is invariable on pheon angels and VB groats, although only occasional on VA groats. Some have two pellets above or beside the mintmark, as on late cross-crosslet groats. Also as in the groat series, there are dies combining the cross-crosslet and pheon marks; one of the obverse dies of this kind is paired with reverses with each mark singly, and another with a reverse with a cross-crosslet and two pellets. The obverse dies with two mintmarks all read *Aglie*, as do most of the cross-crosslet angels with marks by the halo (others of which read *Angl* or *Agl*). All three spellings are found abundantly on pheon angels of Henry VII, which are very common.

Unlike his father's, Henry VIII's angels carry a numeral, and this demonstrates that new dies for this denomination must have been made with the pheon mark in the new reign. But pheon angels of Henry VIII are rare, and they were followed in turn by those with the castle and portcullis which are both very plentiful. On castle and portcullis dies a pellet or saltire is sometimes found by the mintmark. A notable variant of the castle mintmark has side towers joined by a horizontal bar to resemble a capital *H*, thus combining the king's initial with the Spanish emblem of his bride. Apart from the occasional omission of elements of the reverse design (*h*, rose or rudder), there is little variety among the angels of this coinage except for the form of the numeral. On those with mintmark pheon it is *viij* divided by pellets; on castle angels, the same or without the dots or pellets; and on portcullis angels, *viii*, sometimes undotted.

Angelets are known with all four mintmarks of this period, cross-crosslet, pheon, castle and portcullis, although all those with cross-crosslet are from the older obverse die with mintmark rose. Some of these coins could have been struck during the later (VB) part of the currency of the cross-crosslet after the end of the facing bust groats. Pheon angelets, also very rare, have this mintmark on both sides; they might have continued into Henry VIII's reign, since some of his other angelets, with mintmarks castle and portcullis, also lack a numeral. Henry VIII's angelets are rather less rare than his father's. In addition to varieties equivalent to the contemporary angels, including the castle-with-*H* mintmark, they include a portcullis/rose mule from a very old reverse die of Henry VII with rosette stops, the only occurrence of muling between mintmarks in the London coinage of 1509-26. Some portcullis dies have oddities of spelling.

The last sovereign obverse die of Henry VII, with mintmark lis, shows a slightly larger figure of the king, but on a narrower throne with decorated pillars (type E). The field is plain, but the design is flanked by a tressure of small fleurs broken at the top by the throne and at the bottom by a portcullis with its chains extending sideways. The two reverse dies, one with mintmark cross-crosslet, the other with pheon, have a design similar to types C and D but without lis or lions on the petals. Coins with both mintmarks are very rare, but each includes one or two specimens from the same dies struck at double weight. These were probably presentation pieces rather than the result of an attempt to introduce a double sovereign into currency. The next obverse die for the sovereign, still without a numeral, but carrying Henry VIII's mintmark portcullis, is similar to type E of Henry VII, but the three portcullis reverses paired with it differ from type E in having the rose again ornamented with lions and lis, and saltires added in the spandrels. These first coinage sovereigns of Henry VIII are extremely rare, but their obverse die, surviving a number of alterations and repairs, resumed occasional output after 1526 with different mintmarks.

Henry VIII's first mint indenture includes a (traditional) reference to the ryal (or half-sovereign) as well as half- and quarter-ryals. The fractions are not known, and the authenticity of a coin in the British Museum purporting to be a ryal of this period has often been held in doubt. One reason for this is that the king is wearing an open crown, an anachronism perhaps copied from its prototype. The design on both sides is based on the ryal of Edward IV, but reading *henric VIII*, with *h* on the pennant, a portcullis instead of a rose on the ship's side, and mintmark portcullis on the reverse. Lettering and other details are put in from punches used for portcullis angels. That ryals featured in a post-1526 pyx trial in company with George nobles suggests that they may have been produced towards the end of the portcullis period.

Ecclesiastical Mints from c. 1505

Unlike those of London, the extensive and continuous series of halfgroats from Canterbury and York are full of variety, and not without some ambiguities of arrangement. Loss of the mint name at the moment when it would have been most useful to numismatists has led to considerable debate about the correct allocation of some of the earlier profile halfgroats (without London mintmarks) between the two archbishops. Under Henry VII, and briefly at first under Henry VIII, the marks at both mints were martlet and rose (sometimes in combination), but with rare exceptions those of York may be identified by the keys below the shield, with keyless types left to Canterbury. Most of the coins of Henry VIII, however, have different mintmarks: Latin cross (*alias* cross fitchy), lis and pomegranate at Canterbury, star, pansy, escallop and cross voided at York. The significance (if any) of most of these marks is not known, but pomegranate, the device of Granada, is an allusion to Henry's Spanish queen and was also to feature a generation later on the coinage of her daughter, Mary. Mint attribution is assisted, from quite early in Henry VIII's reign, by the addition of initials of the archbishops or, at York, a cardinal's hat; and not long afterwards the position was made explicit by replacing the traditional *Posui* legend with *Civitas Cantor* and *Civitas Eboraci*. The archbishop of Canterbury throughout was William Warham, appointed Chancellor and translated from London in 1504. At York Christopher Bainbridge was translated from Durham in September 1508 to replace Archbishop Savage who had died twelve months earlier. Bainbridge had served as Master of the Rolls under Henry VII in 1504-7. In 1511 he was given command of the Papal army in Italy, and elected a cardinal; but he died at Rome in July 1514, reputedly poisoned by one of his own chaplains. He was immediately succeeded by Thomas Wolsey who became a cardinal the following year.

The progress of the halfgroat series at the two archiepiscopal mints, while not identical, was similar in a number of respects and, in the case of Henry VII, can be summarised in a common classification as follows:

Va   Mm. martlet. Cross-ends 10. Ornate *A*, *he'ric*.
Vb   Mm. martlet. Cross-ends 10. Plain *A* and *henric* henceforward.
Vc   Mm. rose. Normally cross-ends 11.
Vd   Mms. martlet and rose. Cross-ends 11 henceforward.

The first of the Canterbury profile halfgroats (Va) have mintmark martlet and the ornate

Edward IV – Henry VIII

barred *A* on both sides. These rare coins also have the *he'ric* reading as on early London halves. The same obverse type is also found at York, but only in the shape of a mule with a later reverse. The much more abundant Vb, with plain unbarred *A*, reverts to the normal reading *henric*, and these two features continue for the rest of the series. As well as the York Va/b mule, there are mules both ways between Va and Vb at Canterbury. Both these types have cross-end 10, with two thick feet, but from the common type Vc onwards, with brief exception, the cleft and pointed cross-end 11 is used instead. The exceptions consist of a very rare Canterbury Vb/c mule and a coin with the normal mintmark rose of Vc both sides. The latter has no keys below the shield, but shares an obverse die with a York Vc/b mule. The omission of keys on the reverse of this coin may have been accidental (or the result of sending a Canterbury die to York in error), but its position in the series would not, as it happens, be incompatible with a date falling within the vacancy of the see, between the death of Savage in September 1507 and the grant of temporalities to Bainbridge in December 1508, during which Thomas Pygott had authority to mint halfgroats and halfpence. The rose of Vc is normally small like that beside the cross on angelets, but on a few obverse dies of both mints the angel-sized punch is used. The Vd halves, rare at both mints, still have obverse mintmark rose at York, but now with a martlet on the reverse; at Canterbury the marks are transposed, martlet/rose. The martlet was to be the mintmark of the earliest main issue of halfgroats at both Canterbury and York under Henry VIII, and there is a York rose/martlet mule between the reigns, with Bainbridge's initials on the reverse.

Halfgroats of Henry VIII's first coinage from Canterbury and York do not run quite so closely parallel a course as those of Henry VII, but the two series do share certain common developments. First (Ia), without initials, they have the old mintmarks rose (Canterbury) and martlet (York). Next (Ib), with Warham's and Bainbridge's initials added for the first time, they both use mintmark martlet. On the last of the type I (*Posui*) halves, still with initials at Canterbury but with keys and a cardinal's hat at York, different mintmarks were adopted (Ic). Finally, with a sequence of further new marks, there are the more extensive issues with each mint name (type II).

CANTERBURY MINTMARKS, 1509 - 1526

(a)   (b)   (c)   (d)   (e)

(a) Rose; (b) Martlet; (c) Latin cross; (d) Lis; (e) Pomegranate.

The earliest of Henry VIII's Canterbury halfgroats (Ia) is a very rare variety with mintmark rose both sides – the only coin of the new reign from this mint without Warham's initials on the reverse, and so possibly from an old die of Henry VII. This was followed (Ib) by the revival of mintmark martlet, with *W A* (*Willelmus Archiepiscopus*) added above the shield; reverse dies of this type sometimes have martlet over rose, again suggesting the use of dies from the previous reign, but now suitably amended. The next stage (Ic) saw the initials moved to beside the shield (where they were to remain), the first departure in the series from martlet or rose as mintmark, and the last occurrence of the *Posui* legend. The new mark has often been called a cross fitchy, but as Whitton observed it does not have the pointed lower limb characteristic of a cross fitchy and would accordingly be better described as a Latin cross. Of the two mintmarks used on Canterbury halfgroats of type II a Latin cross/lis mule indicates lis to be the earlier; the last of Warham's halves of 1509-26, and the only ones that are not rare, are those with mintmark pomegranate.

At York also the first halfgroats of the new reign (Ia) are without initials. They retain the traditional keys below the shield and the mintmark, on both sides, is the familiar martlet, as on the last reverse dies from this mint under Henry VII. One of the obverses used was a die from the previous reign, with the numeral altered and martlet punched over rose. Another Henry VII die is found (unaltered) in combination with a reverse of the next type (Ib), on which *X B* for Christopher Bainbridge were added by the shield (probably at about the same time as Warham's initials appeared at Canterbury), but the keys were dropped. Still with the *Posui* legend there was finally a new type (Ic), with mintmark radiant star (or heraldically, estoile, with six wavy rays), which has the keys restored and now for the first time a cardinal's hat below them. Type Ic is without initials, and could theoretically have been a late issue of Bainbridge, after his election as cardinal (even though he was abroad at the time); but if so there would be no variation to indicate a change of prelate thereafter, until Wolsey's initials *T W* were included near the end of the series. The removal of Bainbridge's initials in favour of the hat seems more likely to have been an innovation of Wolsey's, particularly if his attachment to this symbol on his subsequent coinage is any indicator. Shortly after the hat was introduced the mint name was adopted on the reverse, and on the earliest *Eboraci* halfgroats the mintmark is still the estoile. This was followed by a succession of marks – plain star, pansy, escallop and voided cross. The star is simply a straight-sided version of the estoile and was probably not intended to be distinct from it. During the currency of plain star two pellets were added beside the cardinal's hat, where they remained until the end of mintmark escallop. The last of the marks on York halves was the voided cross, at first without initials, but soon with *T W* by the shield. All the voided cross halves are rare.

YORK MINTMARKS, 1509 – 1526

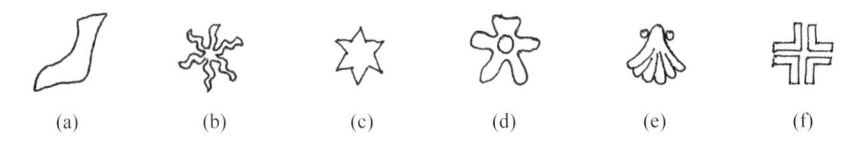

(a) Martlet; (b) Estoile; (c) Star; (d) Pansy; (e) Escallop; (f) Voided cross.

Of the ecclesiastical mints York did not, for some unexplained reason, resume the minting of pence between 1499 and the 1530s; an indenture with the archbishop's master in May 1523 refers only to halfgroats and halfpence. But there are pence of Archbishop Warham at Canterbury in the first coinage of Henry VIII, the earliest of which, of great rarity, has mintmark martlet with *W A* above the shield, like the Ib halfgroat of this mint; pence with initials beside the shield and mintmark pomegranate, corresponding to the IIb *Cantor* halfgroats, are somewhat less rare. Halfpence were struck for both archbishops, reproducing mintmarks used on halfgroats: Latin cross and pomegranate at Canterbury, where Warham's initials *W A* are placed beside the bust; star, escallop and cross at York, where St. Peter's key is placed below the bust, as it had been in Archbishop Savage's time. All these archiepiscopal halfpence are of considerable rarity, and other mintmarks perhaps await discovery.

The Durham mint, dormant since 1499, also reappears early in the new reign, for Bishop Thomas Ruthall who held the see from June 1509 and, as a close associate of Wolsey, was appointed to the Privy Seal in 1516. In September 1510 Ruthall had concluded an unusual indenture under which the master was to pay ten pounds per annum for the privilege of coining pence at 41s. (492d.) per Troy pound for a period of seven years. The mint was reopened two months later. At the Tower the rate was 37s. 6d. (450d.) from the pound of 5400 grains, and the equivalent from the Troy pound of 5760 grains would have been 480d., or 40s. If the figure in the indenture is correct, and was implemented, the bishop's mint would have produced an extra 12d., resulting in a weight of 11.7gr. to the penny, instead of 12 gr., a difference too small to be verifiable from surviving coins; but it must be wondered whether the bishop's mint would have been allowed to coin at a lower standard than the king's, and the figure of 41s. perhaps arose from a misunderstanding as to how the coinage charges of 1s. per pound should be accounted. Rent was paid for the mint from 1510 to 1515, but thereafter it seems to have been closed for the remainder of Ruthall's episcopacy except perhaps for a brief revival in 1519/20 when unpaid rent is recorded. Ruthall died in February 1523. His pence have the initials *T D* (for *Thomas Dunelmensis*) on the reverse, although there is also a mule with a reverse from an old die of his predecessor. Most of Ruthall's coins have mintmark lis; at first the initials are above the shield, as on the first variety at Canterbury, thereafter beside it, rarely above the line of the cross, normally below it. His last variety has the mintmark estoile, as on York halfgroats. Durham dies for Wolsey were authorised in March 1523 and delivered not later than 11 April, the ascendant cardinal having been granted the temporalities of the bishopric of Durham *in commendam* in April 1523, in addition to his archiepiscopacy at York. The mint was soon closed (until 1527), and Wolsey's Durham pence of the first coinage are extremely rare. They carry a mintmark described as a spur rowel (eight spokes with a hollow centre), with his cardinal's hat below the shield and his initials beside it. In order to differentiate him from the Thomas whom he succeeded, the initial of his surname was used in this case – *D W* for *Dunelmensis Wolsey*.

DURHAM MINTMARKS, 1510 – 1526

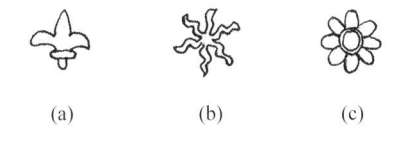

(a)   (b)   (c)

(a) Lis; (b) Estoile; (c) 'Spur rowel'.

Mint Accounts

Gold was minted at £22 10s. to the pound throughout; silver at £1 17s. 6d. (450d.), except for the period between 1 June 1522 and 26 October 1523 when it was increased to £1 19s. 6d. (474d.), causing a sharp increase in output.

Mint accounts for the Tower exist for most of the period, but all that are known for the other royal mints are two accounts each for Bristol and York under Edward IV, relating to the periods immediately before and after the readeption of Henry VI, and one for Tournai in 1514. Except in the case of a change of king or mintmaster, requiring a new indenture, the accounts normally ran from one Michaelmas (M) to the next. The first gap at London is for the years 1466-8, when output was probably reducing after the main effort of the

1464–1526

	£ Gold (£22 10s. per lb.)	£ Silver (£1 17s. 6d. per lb.)
LONDON		
1.9.1464 – M.1466	278,774	103,751
M.1466 – 25.10.1468	Accounts missing	
26.10.1468 – M.1469	46,001	15,276
1469/70	51,512	15,122
M.1470 – 13.4.71	Accounts missing	
1.5.1471 – M.1471	19,807	9,748
1471/72	48,444	20,102
1472/73	37,778	13,455
1473/74	34,607	11,245
1474/75	29,591	13,474
M.1475 – 5.5.1476	10,166	3,606
6.5.1476 – M.1477	40,551	7,896
1477/78	25,224	3,924
M.1478 – 14.9.1479	23,567	5,098
14.9.1479 – M.1480	31,222	3,656
1480/81	17,865	1,828
1481/82	17,280	3,208
M.1482 – 25.12.1482	2,184	26
Feb. – April 1483	3,188	1,074
May – June 1483	1,121	814
July – M.1483	4,005	4,091
1483/84	16,539	13,326
M.1484 – 22.8.1485	8,741	4,641
7.10.1485 – M.1486		7,693
2.11.1485 – M.1486	10,624	
1486/87	7,763	3,563
1487/88	9,082	4,971
1488/89	5,361	5,108
1489/94	No accounts made	
1494/95	23,764	9,227
1495/96	13,192	4,330
1496/97	17,211	8,458
1497/98	19,534	14,449
1498/99	22,096	25,057
1499/1500	18,133	19,856
1500/01	24,964	20,664

Edward IV – Henry VIII

	£ Gold (£22 10s. per lb.)	£ Silver (£1 17s. 6d. per lb.)
LONDON		
1501/02	29,570	18,658
1502/03	28,622	14,575
1503/04	36,282	25,896
1504/05	47,523	45,148
1505/06	95,553	38,514
1506/07	85,608	30,302
1507/08	122,692	23,987
1508/09	119,251	9,240
1509/10	69,153	3,190
1510/11	50,488	1,149
1511/12	26,926	10,382
1512/13	73,147	13,562
1513/14	31,940	958
1514/15	41,988	1,024
1515/16	53,529	180
1516/17	Accounts missing	
1517/18	45,894	1,000
1518/19	54,930	14,233
1519/20	36,279	64
1520/21	27,078	1,856
M.1521 – 5.1522		3,887
1521/22	14,687	
		at £1 19s. 6d. per lb.
1.6.1522 – M.1522		10,904
1522/23	9,141	18,496
M.1523 – 1526	Accounts missing	
		at £1 17s. 6d. per lb.
BRISTOL		
1469/70	3,201	1,952
14.4.1471 – 23.7.1472	2,638	1,693
YORK		
1469/70	1,980	2,460
14.4.1471 – 9.1471	1,229	454
TOURNAI		
1514		4,464

recoinage. No accounts survive for the seven months of the Lancastrian restoration, presumably because there was no continuity of administration upon Edward IV's return. The next interruption in the series occurred in 1489-94 when the warden's duty to submit annual accounts was suspended. During the first coinage of Henry VIII accounts are missing for 1516/17 and from 1523 until the recoinage of 1526. We do not therefore know whether the pattern of very low mintage of silver was resumed after the end of the weight reduction of 1522/3.

Calendar 1464 - 1526

1464   Indenture (13 Aug.) with Lord Hastings: gold noble (wt. 108 gr. as before) revalued to 8s. 4d. (£20 16s. 8d. per lb.); silver groat 48 gr. (37s. 6d. per lb.); charges, gold 50s., silver 4s. 6d. per lb.
York: Abp. William Booth d. 12 Sept.; George Neville granted custody of temporalities (16 Sept.).

1465   Indenture (6 March) with Lord Hastings: gold (£22 10s. per lb.) ryal, 120 gr., 10s., angel, 80 gr., 6s. 8d., charges 20s. 10d. per lb.; silver unchanged.
York: George Neville appointed archbishop (temporalities 17 June).
Mints of Bristol, Coventry and Norwich commissioned (6 July).
Seignorage reduced at London, York and Bristol (Privy Seal, 16 Sept.); Coventry and Norwich presumably closed.

1467   Mint charges reduced - see 1469.

1469   Indenture (2 March) with Lord Hastings: charges per lb. 14s. 6d. for gold, 2s. 8d. for silver (with effect from 29 Sept. 1467).
Proposed monetary convention with Burgundy; double patards to be current in England.

1470   Henry VI restored 3 Oct., Edward IV to Netherlands.

1471   Indenture (6 March) with Sir Richard Tunstall: denominations as before, but excluding ryal; charges per lb. gold 10s. 6d., silver 2s. (effective from 23 Oct. 1470).
Henry VI deposed 11 April, Edward IV restored.
Last account for York royal mint closed (Sept.)

1472   Indenture (23 Feb.) with Lord Hastings: denominations again include ryal; charges per lb. (effective from 14 April 1471) gold 7s. 6d., silver 1s. 6d.
York: Abp. Neville arrested (25 April).
Last account for Bristol mint closed (23 July).

1473   Durham: Bp Laurence Booth licensed to make own dies and to coin halfpence (21 July); dies commissioned, 4 Aug.

1475   Trial of the pyx (Dec.) covering coin minted from 1471 to Nov. 1475.
York: Abp. Neville released.

1476   York: Abp. Neville d. 8 June; King's Receiver, 28 June; Bp. Laurence Booth translated from Durham (temporalities 1 Oct.).
Durham: Bp. William Dudley appointed (temporalities 14 Oct.).

1477   Indenture (3 Feb.) with Lord Hastings, terms as 1472.
Durham: Dies ordered by Bp. Dudley.

1480   York: Abp. Booth d. 19 May; Thomas Rotherham appointed (temporalities 9 Sept.).

1483   Indenture (12 Feb.) with Bartholomew Reed, terms as since 1472.
Edward IV d. 9 April; Edward V acceded. Richard, Duke of Gloucester, Protector (May). Edward V deposed, 25 June; Richard III acceded, 26 June.
Hastings executed (13 June). Indenture (20 July) with Robert Brackenbury, terms as since 1472.
Durham: Bp. William Dudley d. 29 Nov.

Edward IV – Henry VIII

1484   Durham: Bp. John Shirwood appointed (March 1484; temporalities 16 Aug. 1485, but exercised previously).

1485   Richard III d. 22 Aug. at Battle of Bosworth; Henry VII acceded.
Indenture (4 Nov.) with Sir Giles Daubeney and Bartholomew Reed: terms as since 1472.

1486   Henry VII m. Princess Elizabeth of York (18 Jan.).
Canterbury: Abp. Thomas Bourchier d. 30 March; John Morton appointed (Oct.; temporalities 6 Dec.).
Dies supplied to York (May).

1487   New dies supplied to York (July).

1489   Mandate to warden to make punches with new designs (28 March).
Warden excused from making accounts (Michaelmas 1489-94).
Durham: Indenture with George Strayll to coin pence, three years from 29 Sept. 1489.
Indenture (28 Oct.) with Daubeney and Reed to coin gold sovereign.

1491   First prohibition of circulation of Irish coins (repeated several times later).

1492   Expedition to France (Oct. - Nov.) and siege of Boulogne; Peace of Etaples.
Lightweight halfgroats (dandyprats) issued.
Indenture (20 Nov.) with John Shaw and Bartholomew Reed, terms as since 1472 but reduced charges: gold, 2s. 6d. per lb.; silver, 1s.

1494   Durham: Bp. Shirwood d. 14 Jan.; Richard Fox appointed (July; temporalities 8 Dec.).
London mint accounts resumed from Michaelmas.
Alexander of Bruchsal appointed engraver (September).

1495   Durham: Indenture with William Richardson (20 Jan.), and new dies supplied.

1499   Decision of Council (11 Feb.) to suspend minting of pennies (involving closure of mints at York and Durham).
'Farthings of gold' (quarter-ryals ?) delivered to king (30 June).

1500   York: Abp. Rotherham d. 29 May.
Canterbury: Abp. Morton d. 15/16 Sept.
Extra work at Tower mint following restraint of ecclesiastical mints (Privy Seal, 31 Dec.).

1501   York: Abp. Thomas Savage appointed (Jan; temporalities 29 April).
Canterbury: Abp. Henry Deane appointed (May; temporalities Aug.).
Durham: Bp. Richard Fox translated to Winchester (*ante* 20 Aug.).

1502   Durham: Bp. William Sever appointed (June; temporalities 15 Oct.).

1503   Canterbury: Abp. Deane d. 15/17 Feb. William Warham appointed (Nov.; temporalities 24 Jan. 1504).

1504   Act of Parliament (Jan. - March) *Pro Reformatione Pecuniarum*.
Proclamation (5 July) re clipped groats (further workmen to be recruited, 3 July; king sold £1000 of old money to mint, 12 July).

1505   Durham: Death of Bp. Sever.
Proclamation re exchange of clipped groats for good halfgroats at Leaden Hall (27 April).
Indenture (22 Nov.) with Robert Fenrother and William Rede (as 1492).

1507   Durham: Bp. Christopher Bainbridge appointed (Aug.; temporalities 17 Nov.).
York: Abp. Savage d. 2 Sept. Thomas Pygott to keep archbishop's mint during vacancy (halfgroats and halfpence only).

1508   York: Christopher Bainbridge translated from Durham (Sept.; temporalities 12 Dec.).

1464–1526

1509   Henry VII d. 21 April; Henry VIII acceded 22 April, m. Katherine of Aragon 11 June.
        Durham: Bp. Thomas Ruthall appointed (June; temporalities 3 July).
        Indenture (6 Aug.) with William Blount (as 1505).
1510   Durham: Indenture (20 Sept.) for seven years with Roger Richardson for pence at 41s. per lb. Troy (bishop to receive £10 per annum from master). Mint reopened in November.
1513   Henry VIII in France (June - Oct.); Tournai captured (Sept.). James IV of Scotland killed at Flodden (Sept.).
1514   Tournai: Indenture (7 March) for groats and halfgroats as at Tower mint.
        York: Abp. Bainbridge d. 14 July; Thomas Wolsey appointed (temporalities 5 Aug.).
1521   Pope Leo X created Henry VIII *Fidei Defensor*.
1522   Weights of silver coin reduced (31 May); £29,400 in light coin struck between 1 June 1522 and 26 Oct. 1523.
1523   Parliament prescribed proportions of silver denominations to be minted, and new design for farthing.
        Durham: Bp. Ruthall d. 4 Feb.; Thomas Wolsey appointed *in commendam* (Feb.; temporalities 30 April); his first dies received by 11 April.
        York: Indenture (1 May) for halfgroats and halfpence as at Tower (abp. to receive £5 per annum from master).
        Tower mint accounts missing from Michaelmas 1523.
1526   Commission to Cardinal Wolsey to align English coin with continental; existing English gold coins enhanced in value; new gold coins introduced; weight of silver coins reduced.

WEIGHTS 1464 - 1526

Gold: 23 ct. 3½gr. fine (½gr. alloy) - 99.5 per cent. £22 10s. per lb.

Sovereign (20s.)	240gr.	15.55g.
Ryal (10s.)	120	7.78
Half-ryal (5s.)	60	3.89
Quarter-ryal (2s. 6d.)	30	1.94
Angel (6s. 8d.)	80	5.18
Angelet (3s. 4d.)	40	2.59

Silver: 11oz. 2 dwt. fine (18 dwt. alloy) - 92.5 per cent. 37s. 6d. per lb. Tower

Shilling (12d.)	144gr.	9.33g.
Groat (4d.)	48	3.11
Halfgroat (2d.)	24	1.56
Penny	12	0.78
Halfpenny	6	0.39
Farthing	3	0.19

Exceptions (silver only)
Tower and York royal mints, 1492: Halfgroat c. 16gr. (1.04g.), or even less.
Durham, from 1510 (41s. per lb. troy): Penny 11.71gr. (0.76g.).
Tower, 1522-3 (39s. 6d. per lb. Tower): Groat 45.57gr. (2.96g.); halfgroat 22.78gr. (1.48g.).

Edward IV – Henry VIII

SOVEREIGNS 1489 - 1526

Obv. King enthroned, robed, crowned and holding orb and sceptre. Rev. Shield of royal arms in centre of double Tudor rose.

HENRY VII, types A-E (1489-1509).

A. Mm. cinquefoil both sides. Lettering style A, large format. Trefoil stops. Obv. field plain. Crown with two arches, the outer jewelled. *henric Di Gra Rex Angl & Franc Dns Ibarne*. Rev. Large shield with broad elaborate crown above; no ornamental border around the rose; shield and rose hatched. *Ihs Aute Trancies Per Mediu Illoru Ibat*. Unique.

B. Mm. obv. none, rev. cross fitchy. Lettering style A (small). Obv. field diapered with lis in lattice framework. Crown with two arches, the outer jewelled. *henricus Di Gracia Rex Anglie et Franc Dns Ibar*, saltire stops. Rev. Smaller shield, uncrowned; tressure of ten arcs around rose, adorned with tiny lions, lis and trefoils. *Ihc Autem Transciens Per Medium Illorum Ibatne*, trefoil stops. ER.

C. Mm. dragon both sides. Large lettering from special fount, with tall, plain uprights (cf. style B), open rounded *E* and Roman *M* and *N*. Star stops. Ornate throne with decorated back, and pillars topped by greyhound and dragon. Lis in field. Crown with single jewelled arch. *henricus Dei Gracia Rex Anglie et Francie Dns Ibar*. Rev. As type B, but smaller shield, and rose within more prominent tressure. *Ihesus Autem Transiens Per Medium Illorum Ibat*. VR.

D. Mm. obv. small lis, rev. dragon. Tall, narrow Gothic lettering (cf. style G), with Roman *M*; the *A* with second limb upright and barred only at top left. Saltire stops. Tall throne, with wide seat, and elaborate back extending to top edge of coin. Lis in field. Crown with single jewelled arch. *henricus Dei Gra Rex Angl et Fran Dns hibn*. Rev. similar to type C; small rose between four saltires after *Ibat*. Rare.

E. Lettering similar to type D; saltire stops. Obv. mm. lis (one obv. die). King in tall crown (with four crockets on arch), on simpler throne, with chained portcullis below (breaking inscription), within border of small fleurs; field plain. *henricus Dei Gracia Rex/Anglie et Franc Dns hib*. Rev. reading and (general) design as types C and D, but tressure of small floral sprays, without lis or lions.
   (i) Rev. mm. cross-crosslet. VR.
   (ii) Rev. mm. pheon. ER.
   'Double-sovereigns' (of double weight, on thicker flans of similar diameter) are known from the same dies as both (i) and (ii).

HENRY VIII, first coinage (1509-26). Mm. crowned portcullis. One obv. die, type and reading as type E of Henry VII. Rev. as types C and D, but *Tranc-* or *Transiens*. ER.

RYALS 1465 - 1526

FIRST PERIOD, 1465-70. EDWARD IV, first reign only, types V-X. King in ship, with sword and shield; rose on ship's side between lis, lion and lion, lis; banner with *e* at stern. Coins of Bristol (*B*), Coventry (*C*), Norwich (*n*) and York (*e*) have mint initial in waves below rose. *Ed/ward Di Gra Rex Angl & Franc/Dns Ib*. Rev., within a tressure of eight arcs, a small rose on centre of a sun, of which four rays constitute a cross with floreate terminals, with four crowned lions in between. *Ihc Aut Transiens Per Medium Illoru(m) Ibat*. Stops usually trefoils. London (V-VIII, X), Bristol (VI-VIII, X), Coventry (VI), Norwich (V, VI), York (VI-VIII, X).

Ryals

V.   Mm. rose. Large fleurs in spandrels of tressure.
       London: Mm. both sides (one obv. die only, *D/ns*, ER), or on rev. only. Rare.
       Norwich: Mm. on rev. only. ER (unverified).

VI.   Mm. sun on rev. only (except at London). Large fleurs. Usually letter R3 (with slightly outturned tail).
       London: Mm. both sides (above or below sail on obv.) or rev. only. Some with lis or quatrefoil in obv. inscription, and trefoils within *(h)ib*. Vars. *E/d*; *Tranniens*; *hibat*. Also rare mules V/VI (mm. rose/sun) and VI/V (no obv. mm., but quatrefoil or lis in obv. inscription). Some latent V/VI and VI/V mules without obv. mm. may also be identified by die-links.
       Bristol: Vars. *Frnc*, *hibat*; *P* for *Per* and rose before *Ibat*; trefoils before *b* of *(h)ibat*. Rare.
       Coventry: Vars. quatrefoil after *Frnc*; *P* for *Per* and rose before *Ibat*. VR.
       Norwich: Var. quatrefoil after *Frnc*. VR.
       York: Saltire stops on obv. VR.

VII.   Large fleurs in spandrels. Mintmark on rev. only. Trefoil stops. Letter R4 (with notched tail) distinguishes obv. dies from VI.
       London: Mm. crown. Vars. lis in obv. inscription; *Frncie*, *Fran/c*; quatrefoil before *Dns* or after *Ibat*; two crescents after *Aut*; *Transien*, *Transies*, *Trasiens*, *Tranansiens*, *Illoum*. Also VR mules V/VII and VI/VII. (N.b. these are the ryals most commonly imitated in Flanders, often reading *Fran* and *Ihd*.)
       Bristol: Mm. crown. Vars. quatrefoil after *Franc*; two crescents after *Aut*; fleurs omitted. ER.
       York: Mm. lis, or (ER, early) sun and lis (BW 'VIB'). With or without quatrefoil in obv. inscription. Var. *Transienns*. Rare.

VIII.   As VII but small trefoils in spandrels. Mintmark on rev. only. Trefoil stops. Letter R4.
       London: Mm. crown (BW VIIIA); sun over crown, an old die of VI with pellet added below shield (ER; BW VIIIB); or sun (BW – ; obv. has reversed *e* for *D*; ER). Some have quatrefoil in one inscription. Vars. pellet below shield; *Fra/nc*; saltires after *Ib (Illorm)* or before *Per*; *Transies*, *Traniens*. ER var. with mm. sun both sides may be X/VIII mule. Also VR mules V/VIII, VI/VIII, VII/VIII and VIII/VII (pellet below shield).
       Bristol: Mm. crown. Var. has trefoils on cusps, but no ornaments on ship. VR; also ER mule VII/VIII (with same obv. die as true coins of VII).
       York: Mm. lis. With or without quatrefoil in obv. inscription. Vars. *Fran* (with pellet below shield); trefoils on some cusps. VR.

X.   Small trefoils in spandrels. *B*-like letter R5. Trefoil stops. *E/* or *Ed/*.
       London: Mm. long cross fitchy on rev. only. Late obverses have ship of four lines instead of five; and on latest rigging is 2-1 instead of 3-1. Vars. *Dei* (small letters on obv.); *Fra/nc*; no lis on ship's side; *Medum*. Rare; also ER mule VIII/X.
       Bristol: Mm. sun. Rev. die only, mule VIII (no ornaments on ship)/X. ER.
       York: Mm. sun both sides. No lis on ship. Trefoils on cusps. ER (unconfirmed).

Second Period, early Henry VII only (c. 1488). One pair of dies; ER. Lettering style A; trefoil stops. Obv. King in ship (no mast, yardam or sail visible), in armour; crown with two plain arches; shield of royal arms with concave sides; *h* on forward banner, dragon on after banner; small rosettes on forecastle and sterncastle. *hen/ri/c Di Gra Rex*

Edward IV – Henry VIII

Ryals

Angl & Franc Dns Ibar. Rev. Shield of French arms on double rose. Mm. (rev. only) long cross fitchy. *Ihc Autem Transiens Per Mediu Illoru Ibat*.

THIRD PERIOD, HENRY VIII, first coinage (1509-26). Type as Edward IV, but *h* for *e* on banner and portcullis instead of rose on ship's side. *he/nric VIII Di Gra Rex Angl & Franc/Dns Ib*. Mm. (rev. only) crowned portcullis with chains. *Ihc Aut Transiens Per Medium Illorum Ibat*. Saltire stops. Unique.

HALF-RYALS 1465 - 1470

EDWARD IV, FIRST REIGN only, types V-X, 1465-70. Types as ryals. *Ed/ward Di Gra Rex Angl & /Franc*. Ornaments on ship usually lis, lion (rose) lion, lis. Coins of Bristol (*B*), Coventry (*C*), Norwich (*n*) and York (*e*) have mint initial in waves below rose. *Domine Ne In Furore Tuo Arguas Me*. Small trefoils in spandrels. Stops usually trefoils. Some dies have small lettering. London (V-X), Bristol (V-VIII) Coventry (VI), Norwich (V), York (VI-IX).

V.   Mm. rose or none.
    London: No mm., *Frnc*, small letters on obv. (type V or VI?). ER.
    Bristol: No mm. (type V or VI?). ER.
    Norwich: Mm. rose (rev. only). Two lions but no lis on ship's side. ER.

VI.   Mm. sun.
    London: Mm. sun both sides (below sail on obv.). *E/d*. Saltire stops on obv. VR.
    Bristol: Mm. on rev. only. Var. *Argus*, with rose after *Me*. VR.
    Coventry: Mm. on rev. only. One obv. die only. Var. *Argus*, with rose after *Me* and trefoils in three spandrels only. ER.
    York: Mm. on rev. only. Vars. *Argus*, once with rose after *Me; Fr/anc Dns*. VR.

VII.   Mm. crown (or lis at York) on rev. only.
    London: Mm. crown. Vars. *E/d*, *Dei* and *Fanc*; *Fran*, *Fr/anc*; *Argus, Argas*; quatrefoil in inscription; saltire stops on obv. (with no trefoils in rev. spandrels).
    Bristol: Mm. crown. Vars. lis or quatrefoil in inscriptions; *Argus*. VR.
    York: Mm. lis. Vars. *Dei*; lis in obv. inscription; saltire stops on obv.; *Argus*, *Argua*; quatrefoil after *Me*; one or all trefoils in spandrels omitted.

VIII.   Generally as VII, but usually with a combination of mms. sun and crown. Some have small letters (as on halfgroats).
    London: Mm. on rev. only except C.
        A. Mm. crown. Lis in waves or pellet above shield. Rare.
        B. Mm. sun over crown. Quatrefoil after &. Var. *Argas*. VR.
        C. Mm. obv. sun, rev. crown. Pellet below shield. *F/ranc*. VR.
        D. Mm. sun and crown. Lis in waves. VR.
    Bristol: Rev. die only of mule VII (with three lis in obv. inscription)/VIIID, mm. sun and crown, *Argus*. ER.
    York: Mm. sun over crown (rev. only), cf. London VIIIB. ER.

IX.   Mm. includes rose.
    London: Mm. obv. rose, rev. crown. Lis in waves. Vars. pellet above shield; *F/ranc* or *Fr/anc*; quatrefoil after inscription. VR.
    York: Mm. rose and lis (rev. only). Vars. pellet above shield; *Dei*; saltire stops on obv. (VII/IX mule). All ER.

Half-ryals

X. Mm. long cross fitchy on rev. London only. Stops obv. trefoils, rev. trefoils or saltires. Var. pellets instead of trefoils in spandrels. ER.

QUARTER-RYALS 1465 – 1470

EDWARD IV, FIRST REIGN only, types V-VIII, and XI, 1465-70. Normal obv. type: shield within quadrilobe (except VIA), with *e* above, lis below. *Edward Di Gra Rex Angl (&) (Fr)*. Rev. type as ryal. *Exaltabitur in Gloria*. Mm. on both sides. Different mints are not indicated.

V. Mm. rose. Obv. Quadrilobe; pellets beside *e*; rose to left, sun to right of shield; trefoils in spandrels. Trefoil stops. Inscription starts at bottom. Obv. die found only as V/VI mule; rev. die (trefoil stops) only found as VI/V mule; both ER.

VI. Mm. sun both sides.
    A. Rose above shield, within eight arc tressure; obv. stops saltires. No marks in spandrels. *Angl & F*. Obv. die found only as (ER) VI/V mule.
    B. Quadrilobe; rose/sun by shield; trefoils in spandrels. Stops obv. trefoils, rev. trefoils, saltires or (V/VI mule only) roses. Vars. rose after *Angl* or *Gloria; Exatabitur*. VR.

VII. Mm. crown or lis.
    (a) Mm. crown both sides. Rose/sun or sun/rose by shield. Early var. (ER) has pellets by *e* and in spandrels, and *Agl*; otherwise trefoils or nothing in spandrels. Stops obv. trefoils, saltires (rare), lis or none; rev. trefoils, roses, lis or mixed. Vars. *Exaltabitutur, Exaltabittur; Glor(i), Goria*; quatrefoil before rev. mm.
    (b) Mm. obv. lis, rev. crown (York?). Rose/sun by shield; trefoils or nothing in spandrels. Stops obv. saltires or trefoils, rev. trefoils. *Exaltabitutur in Glor(i)*. ER.
    (c) Mm. lis both sides (York?). Rose/sun by shield. Trefoils in spandrels and as stops. Quatrefoil or rose before rev. mm. ER.

VIII. Mms. sun and crown.
    (a) Mm. sun over crown both sides (altered dies of type VII). Rose/sun by shield. Nothing in spandrels. Stops obv. trefoils, rev. lis. ER.
    (b) Mm. obv. sun, rev. crown. One obv. die, sun/rose by shield, trefoils in spandrels, *Fra*. Stops obv. trefoils, rev. roses, with or without lis or trefoils. Var. *Exatabitur*. Rare.
    (c) Mm. obv. sun, rev. crown and sun. Same obv. die as VIIIb. Trefoil stops both sides. ER.

XI. Mm. long cross fitchy both sides. Rose/sun or sun/rose by shield; trefoils in spandrels. Stops obv. saltires (without lis below shield) or trefoils (*Edwrd*), rev. trefoils with or without roses. ER.

ANGELS 1465 - 1526

FIRST PERIOD, 1465-1470. EDWARD IV, FIRST REIGN only, types V and VII. Obv. St. Michael spearing dragon, to right; cross at lance-head breaks inscription. Rev. Ship with cross as mast; ropes 3-1; sun and rose beside cross, rays of sun above, shield of royal

Edward IV – Henry VIII

Angels

arms below. *Per Cruce(m) Tua(m) Salva Nos Xpiste* (or *Xpc*) *Rede(m)ptor*. Thin coins on broad flans. Presumed to be of London only.

V. Mm. rose (rev. only). Rose to left, sun to right of cross. *Edward Di Gra Rex Angl & Franc Dns hiber(ni)* or *Ib*. *Cruce Tua*. Small trefoil in field each side above ropes.
   1. *Xpiste Redeptor*. Each variety unique.
      1a. Toothed dragon with second head at tail. Trefoil stops. *hiber*.
      1b. Normal dragon. Obv. saltire stops, rev. trefoils. *hiberni*.
   2. *Xpc' Redemptor*. Trefoil stops. *Dns Ib*. Sun by cross very large. ER.
VII. Mm. crown (rev. only). Small sun to left, rose to right of cross. No trefoils above ropes. *Dns Ib*. *Crucem, Tuam* in full; *Xpc Redemptor*. Stops obv. saltires, rev. trefoils. ER.

SECOND PERIOD, 1470 – c. 1490. Henry VI restored, 1470-1 (*h* and lis by cross); Edward IV, second reign, 1471-83 and Edward V, 1483 (*e* and rose by cross); Richard III, 1483-5 (*R* and rose by cross); early Henry VII, from 1485 (*h* and rose by cross). Thicker coins on smaller flans than in First Period. Type similar, but: saint's head and nimbus break inscription; crow's nest instead of sun above cross on rev.; ropes normally 2-1.

HENRY VI, SECOND REIGN (1470-1). *h* and lis by cross.

London: Obv. mm. restoration cross (RC) (to left or right of head), or more usually none. *henric(u)(s) D(e)i Gra Rex Angl & Franc(ie)*, stops trefoils (var. saltires). Some have cross or trefoil in nimbus. Rev. Many variations in spelling and breaks in inscriptions. Stops trefoils, pellets or mixed. Mm. cross patty (right of ship; *Cruse*), RC (to right or left of ship; *Cruse*) or none (usually *Cruce*, var. *Crucse*). Also (mint uncertain, York ?), mm. lis (to left); *Cruc, No*. ER.

Bristol: *B* in waves. Mm. RC (rev. only; to right) or none. Two obv. dies; one reads *Franc Dns*. Stops obv. trefoils, rev. trefoils with or without pellets. *Cruse* or *Cruce*. Vars. lis by cross omitted; trefoils in rev. field. ER.

EDWARD IV, SECOND REIGN (1471-83). *e* and rose by cross. *Edward D(e)i Gra Rex Angl & Franc*. *Xpe* or *Xpc*. Types (London) XII-XXII, except XIII and XX; Bristol, XIV only.

XII. Mm. short cross fitchy (obv. only; to right). London only. Cross in nimbus. Stops obv. trefoils, rev. none. *Di*; *Cruse, Rede'tor*. VR.

Types XIV-XV. Annulet series.

XIV. Mm. small annulet. Trefoil stops. *Cruse*.
   London. Mm. on both sides or on obv. only, to left or right of head. Cross, trefoil or nothing in nimbus. *Di* or *Dei*; *Franc(ie)*. Usually *Redetor*, but varied. Vars. no bowsprit; lis after *Franc*; saltire stops on rev.; *Crwse, Cr(u)se(m)*.
   Bristol: *B* in waves. Mm. on obv. only, to right. *Dei*. Trefoil in nimbus. ER. Last type of this mint.

XV. Mm. pellet-in-annulet both sides. London only. Saltire stops. *Dei; Crucem; Redempt*. No ornament in nimbus. Some rev. dies have rose over sun to right of cross. Rare; also rare mules XIV/XV and (ER) XV/XIV (no mm.; no stops, *Crusem, Rede'tor*).

Types XVI-XIX. Second cross series. London only henceforward. Mm. cross (various forms) both sides, to right of head on obv. Ship of four lines. No ornament in nimbus. Saltire stops. Normally *Dei, Crucem, Redempt*.

Angels

XVIb. Mm. cross with pellet in each angle. No stops on rev. Vars. large trefoil between saltires after *Franc; Redemt*. Rare; usually muled with later revs. Also ER mule XV/XVI.

XVII. Mm. first pierced cross; letter A5. Rare; also VR mule XVI/XVII.

XVIII. Mm. pierced cross with pellet in one angle.

XVIIIa Pellet in upper left angle of cross. Also mule XVI/XVIIIa; all rare.

XVIIIb Pellet in lower left or right angle of cross. Vars. *Di; Cruce*; pellet after *Crucem*. Also rare mules XVI/XVIIIb, XVIIIb/XVII, XVIIIa/b.

XIX. Mm. second pierced cross; new lettering (with A6). *Cruce*. Only recorded from VR mules XIX/XVIIIb and XXI/XIX.

XXI. Mm. cinquefoil (last dies have added pellet). Ship of five lines. Saltire stops. *Crucem, Redempt* (vars. *Redemp, Redemt*). Small *G* and *L* replaced by larger in mid-type. Some rev. dies have small leopard below forecastle. Stops sometimes omitted on rev. Also VR mules XXI/XIX.

EDWARD IV-V (1483).

XXII. Mm. sun-and-rose dimidiated (SR1) both sides. *Edward D(e)i Gra Rex Angl & Franc. Dei*, then *Di. e* and rose by cross. Saltire stops, omitted on some rev. dies. Many rev. dies have small leopard below forecastle. Five-line ship. VR; also ER mule with *R* over *e* on rev.

RICHARD III, 1483-5. *Ricard Di Gra Rex Angl & Franc* (types I-III). Saltire stops. *R* and rose by cross. Usually small leopard below forecastle. Five-line ship.

XXII(BH). Obv. dies (in Edward's name) of XXII (*Di*), with mm. boar's head (BH1) over SR1. Rev. as XXII, with *e* and rose. Also mule with *R* over *e* on rev. All ER.

I. Mm. SR1 both sides (one obv. die only). Edwardian lettering, with I1 (serifs with single notch) and V1 (straight-sided). Rev. new dies with *R* and rose, or old dies with *R* over *e* (see above for XXII/I mule). ER.

II. Mm. boar's head (BH).

IIa. Obv. as I, but mm. BH1 over SR1. Rev. mm. SR1. ER; also unique mule IIa/XXII (unaltered *e* and rose).

IIb. Mm. BH2 both sides. Vars. *R* over rose (?) by cross (*Crusem*) – die later altered from BH2 to SR2?; *Tuam* (with leopard on prow inverted). All rare; also ER mules IIa/IIb.

III. Mm. SR2 both sides. Taller St. Michael, with head facing. New lettering with I2 (serrated) and bow-sided V2. Earlier obvs. read *Ricard*; later *Ricad*. Vars. leopard omitted; *Rededmt*. Late revs. have narrower cross. All rare; also VR mules both ways with IIb.

HENRY VII, types I-II (1485 – c. 1490). Gothic St. Michael. *h* and rose by mast. Ship of five or four lines. *Xpc*.

IA. Compound mint-marks (both sides). No Irish title - *henric Di Gra Rex Angl s Franc*. No cross in nimbus. Ropes 2-1. Saltire stops.

(i) mm. halved sun-and-rose (SR3). Two rev. dies apparently have *h* over *R*. *Cruse(m), Tua(m), Red(e)(mpt)*. Small shield. VR.

(iii) mm. lis-on-rose, or (obv. only; two dies with *Ricard* altered to *henric*) lis-on-SR. No stops on rev. *Cruce(m), Tua, Redem* or *Redet*. Large shield; four-line ship. VR; also ER mules IAiii/i and i/iii, and IAiii (lis-on-SR)/no mm.

IB. Mm. rose on obv. only (above nimbus). With Irish title - *Rex Angl s Franc Dns I/b*. Short angel. Ropes 3-1. *Cru/sem Tuam, Redmtor*. Stops obv. trefoils, rev. pellets (but double saltires before *Per* in place of mm.). ER.

Edward IV – Henry VIII

Angels

II. No mm. on rev. Ropes 2-1. Trefoil stops.
IIA. No mm. (but a saltire before *henric*). *Rex Angl s Franc Dns/ (I).* Small rose by mast. *Per Cruc(e),* or *Cruse, Tua(m) Salva Nos Xpc Redetor* or *Ihc Aute(m)* etc. *(Ibat* omitted). VR; also ER mules with obverses of type I.
IIB. Obv. mm. cinquefoil. *Rex Angl s Franc s.* Rose of normal size. *Per Cruc* reading only; *Tua, Xpc Redetor.* VR; also ER mules (distinguished by size of rose) IIA/B and IIB/A.

THIRD PERIOD, from early 1490s (Henry VII – VIII). New figure of St. Michael in armour. Legend *Per Crucem,* or (early IIIB only) *Ihc Autem*. Ropes 2-1.

HENRY VII, groups III - V.
IIIB. *Rex Angl(ie) z Fr-Franci. Xpe.* Mannered letter styles.
    (i) Mm. escallop both sides. Rosette stops. Rev. spellings very variable. (a) Lettering style B. Thin St. Michael, with small wings, and hips towards dragon. Spearhead cross-crosslet or cross potent. *Per Crucem* or (c/a mule only) *Ihc Aut.* ER. (b) Lettering style C. St. Michael with larger wings, and hips away from dragon. Spearhead cross-crosslet. Rosette each side of nimbus. *Ihc Aut* or *Per Cruce(m)*. All rare; also ER mule with IIB obv. (c) Lettering style E (small). As (b) but without rosettes by nimbus. *Per Cruce* only. Also mules with IIB obv.; and, within IIIB, c/a, c/b and b/c. All VR.
    (ii) Mm. pansy both sides. Lettering style E (small), with some broken letters (*e, F, n*). Type as escallop (c). Spearhead cross-crosslet. Stops rosettes, or (rarely) saltires or none. *Per Cruce* legend only. Also mule escallop (c)/pansy. All VR.
IIIC. Lettering style E (larger). *Fr-Franc. Per Cruc(e)* legend only henceforward; usually *Xpe; Re-Redem.*
    (i) Mm. pansy, in three forms: 1, with joined symmetrical petals; 2, with petals not joined; 3, with longer lower petals (late, VR). Spearhead cross potent. Broken *n* continues. *Angl.* Stops saltires, or sometimes rosettes or none. *Xpc* or *Xpe.* Also ER mule IIIBii/IIICi.
    (iii) Mm. lis-issuant-from-rose. Spearhead cross potent. *Angl z Frr.* Stops saltires. VR; also ER mules both ways with mm. pansy (IIICi).
    (iv) Mm. anchor (inverted, upright or horizontal). *Angl* or *Agl(i).* Late var. omits obv. mm. and reads *Anglie.* Spearhead cross pommy, cross potent or cross-crosslet. Stops saltires. Also ER mule anchor/pansy (IIICi).
Groups IV-V. *F-Fra; Cruc(e), Tua, Xp(e), R-Rede.*
IV. (i) Mm. greyhound's head both sides (GH). *Agl(ie).* Spearhead cross-crosslet. (a) Mm. GH1 (large head, small ears). Lettering style E (normal on obv.) or small fount (on most revs). Saltire stops. Vars. *henri*; *Red* omitted. Rare; also ER mules both ways with anchor. (b) Mm. GH2 (small head, long ears). Lettering style F. Stops saltires or rosettes. Var. *Dei.* Rare; also ER mules both ways with GH1.
    (ii) Mm. cross-crosslet. No marks by nimbus. Lettering style G. *Angli(e)* or *Agli(e).* Spearhead cross potent or cross-crosslet. Saltire stops. Also ER mule GH2/cross-crosslet.
V. Spearhead cross-crosslet. Lettering style G. *Angl* or *Agl(ie).* Crook-shaped contraction marks except on some dies of i(a). *Cruce, Tua, Xpe, R-Rede.*

1464–1526

Angels

(i) Mm. cross-crosslet both sides. Stops saltires or rosettes. (a) Plain mm. cross-crosslet (the normal form). Saltires (one to four) or rosettes (three) by nimbus. *Aglie*, or rarely *A(n)gl*. (b) Mm. cross-crosslet with two pellets above, or (ER) beside. As a, with saltires by nimbus. Rare; also VR mules a/b. (c) Mm. cross-crosslet before and pheon (upwards) after inscription. Saltire(s) by nimbus. Also mules c/a and c/b; all VR.

(ii) Mm. pheon (downwards) both sides (omitted on one rev. die). No numeral. *Agl(ie)* or *Angl*. Saltire stops. Saltire(s) (one to four) by nimbus. Also VR mules with rev. of Vi(c).

HENRY VIII, first coinage, 1509-1526 Type as before. *henric viij* or *viii* (with or without dots above or between digits) *Di Gra Rex Agl Z F-Fra*. Spearhead cross-crosslet. Mm. both sides. Saltire stops. Crook-shaped contraction marks on obv. *Cruce, Tua, Xpe, Red-Redet.*

(i) Mm. pheon (downwards). *viij*. VR.

(ii) Mm. castle, four forms (extensively muled): (a) unadorned; (b) with pellet before castle; (c) castle between saltires; (d) *H* (Roman) over castle. *viij* or *viii*. Var. omits *h* and rose.

(iii) Mm. crowned portcullis, three forms (also muled): (a) unadorned; (b) with saltire before; (c) without chains. *viii*, with or without dots above, no dots between. Vars. rudder or rose omitted.

ANGELETS 1465 - 1526

FIRST PERIOD (1465-70). Although authorised in 1465, no specimen of the half-angel (angelet) is known of Edward IV's first reign. The earliest are of Henry VI.

SECOND PERIOD, 1470 – early 1490s. Henry VI restored 1470-1 (*h* and lis by cross); Edward IV, second reign, 1471-83, and Edward V, 1483 (*e* and rose); Richard III, 1483-5 (*R* and rose); early Henry VII, 1485 – c. 1490 (*h* and rose). Type as angel. Rev. *O Crux Ave Spes Unica*. London only, except Henry VI.

HENRY VI, SECOND REIGN (1470-1), *h* and lis by cross or shield. Mm. on rev. only.
London: Mm. lis (to left of ship), cross patty (to right) or restoration cross (to right). *he(n)ric(u) D(e)i Gra Rex Angl & Fr(a)*. Stops obv. trefoils, rev. trefoils or saltires. Var. *Spece*. ER.
Bristol: *B* in waves. Mm. restoration cross (to right). *henricu Di Gra Rex Ang & F*. Stops obv. trefoils, rev. saltires. *Spece*. Unique.

EDWARD IV, SECOND REIGN (1471-83), *e* and rose by cross. London only.
XII. Mm. short cross fitchy (obv. only). *O Crux* etc. on obv.; *Edward Di Gra Rex Angl & Fr(a)* on rev. Stops trefoils or (rev.) pellets. Some have cross in nimbus. VR.
XIV. Mm. small annulet both sides. Obv. *Edward Di Gra Rex Angl*. Some have cross in nimbus. Rev. *O Crux* etc. Stops trefoils or saltires, and roses (rev. only). Also mules XIV/XII (with titles on both sides). All VR.
Types XVI-XX. Second cross series. Mm. cross (various forms) both sides, to right of head on obv. Plain nimbus henceforward. Rose in rev. inscription. Saltire stops.

Edward IV – Henry VIII

Angelets

XVIa. Mm. cross over annulet both sides. *Dei Gra Rex Angle.* ER.

XVIIIb. Mm. pierced cross with pellet in lower right angle (obv.) and lower left angle (rev.). *Di, Angl.* Vars. rose after *Di*; sun after *Unica*. VR.

XX. Obv. only (XX/XVIIIb mule). Mm. pierced cross with central pellet. *Di.* ER.

XXI. Mm. cinquefoil both sides (also altered obv. die of XX, with mm. cinquefoil over pierced cross, ER). *Di* or *Dei*. Saltire stops, with two roses added in rev. legend. Five-line ship. Rare.

EDWARD IV-V (1483).

XXII. Mm. sun-and-rose dimidiated (SR1) both sides. *Edward Di Gra Rex Ang.* Saltire stops (no rose in rev. legend). Four-line ship. *e* and rose by rev. cross. ER.

RICHARD III, 1483-5. *Ricard Di Gra Rex Angl.*

II. Mm. boar's head (BH1). Five-line ship. *R* and rose by rev. cross. ER.

HENRY VII, type I only (from 1485).

IA. Mm. halved sun-and-rose (SR3) on obv.; rev. lis-on-SR. *henric* (altered from *Ricard) Di Gra Rex Angl.* Saltire stops. *h* (over *R*?) and rose by mast. ER.

THIRD PERIOD, from early 1490s. New figure of St. Michael in armour.
HENRY VII, groups III-V. Mannered letter styles.

IIIB. Mm. pansy. Rosette stops. *Rex Angli.* VR.

IIIC (i) Mm. pansy. Saltire stops. *Agl z F*. Also mules both ways with IIIB. All ER.

(iv) Mm. anchor (inverted). Obv. only, as ER mule with pansy rev. Saltire stops. *Agl.*

IV. (i) Mm. obv. none, rev. greyhound's head (GH1) to left of mast (one rev. die only). *henric Di Gra Rex Agl z*. Rosette by nimbus. No stops on obv., rev. saltires. ER.

(ii) Mm. rose both sides. *Rex Ag.* Rosette stops. ER.

V. (i) Mm. cross-crosslet, two rev. dies only, muled with the rose obv. die of IVii. Saltire stops; one die has rosette between four saltires after *Unica*. VR.

(ii) Mm. pheon both sides. *Rex Agl z.* No numeral. Saltire stops. Var. has crook contraction mark after *henric*. VR.

HENRY VIII, first coinage, 1509-1526. Saltire stops. *henric viij*, or *viii*, or without numeral, *Di Gra Rex A(g)l (Z)*. Usually crook contraction mark after *henric*.

(i) Mm. pheon. No angelet is known with numeral, but since it is omitted on some of those with the other two mms. of this coinage it is possible that some of type Vii above, e.g. var. with crook mark, could belong to the new reign.

(ii) Mm. castle, three forms: (a) unadorned; (b) with pellet before castle (obv. only); (d) *H* (Roman) over castle. With or without numeral *viij*. Rare.

(iii) Mm. crowned portcullis both sides (usually with chains). With or without numeral *viii* (dies without numeral have comma not crook after *henric*). Vars. *henrc*; *Unn(i)ca*. Rare; also ER mule portcullis/rose (Henry VII, type IVii).

1464–1526

SHILLINGS, 1504

Henry VII only (cf. tentative profile groats, type VA). Obv. Portrait in profile to right; crown with single broad arch, decorated with six saltires. Rev. Shield of royal arms over long forked cross. *Posui/Deu A/diuto(r)/e(u) Meu(m)*. Saltire stops.

1. Mm. small lis. Special lettering; no numeral. Hair-line inner circle on obv. Two pairs of dies. Rev. Florid forked cross-ends enclosing small lis.
   - (a) *henricus Di Gra Rex Anglie Z Fr. A/diuto/e.* Outer borders of heavy beading. VR.
   - (b) *henric, Fran. A/diuto/eu.* More finely toothed borders. ER.
2. Mm. large lis. Lettering style G. With numeral; *Angl Z Fr(a).* Hair-line inner circles both sides. Cross-ends no. 11, enclosing slipped trefoils.
   - (a) *henric Septim.* Three obv. dies. *A/diutor/e Meum.* ER.
   - (b) *henric V.I.I.* or *VII.* One obv. has small uprights instead of saltires on crown. *A/diuto(r)/e.* One rev. die also muled with type 1b obv., and another used for type VA (2b) groat. All ER.

GROATS 1464 - 1526

First Period, 1464 - late 1480s, Edward IV to early Henry VII: Traditional type; stylized facing bust with open crown; nine arc tressure with top cusps usually unfleured. Rev. cross and pellets as previously; *Posui/Deum A/diutor/e Meum.*

Edward IV, First Reign, light coinage (1464-70). *Edward Di Gra Rex Angl &_Fran(c).* London (V-XI), Bristol (VI/V-VIII, X), Coventry (VI/V, VI), Norwich (VI/V, VI), York (VI-VIII, X, XI). Mint initial, *B, C, n, e,* on breast at regional mints.

V. Mm. rose both sides. Normally fleurs on cusps (to type VII), except above crown; breast fleur sometimes omitted. (i) Early coins from dies of heavy coinage, types III and IV, with diameter of circles 21mm (obv.), 20mm. (rev.). (ii) Normal issues from new, smaller dies.

Va. Annulets by bust. Eye after *tas*. Saltire stops or none. London only.
   (i) Heavy coinage dies (type IV). Rare.
   (ii) New dies, copying type IV, but usually smaller lettering; circles 19.5/19mm. Vars. *Franci*; one rev. (with larger letters) lacks rose, and has eye after *don* not *tas*. Rare; also VR Vai/ii mules.

Vb. Quatrefoils by bust. Eye after *tas* (rarely omitted). Large fleurs on cusps, except above crown. Saltire stops. London only.
   (i) Heavy coinage dies (type III), with small trefoil instead of fleur on breast. Var. *Posu*. VR.
   (ii) New dies, copying type III, but usually smaller lettering; circles 19.5/19mm. Large fleur on breast. Vars. *Gracia*; quatrefoil after *Franc* but none by bust. Rare; also VR Vbi/ii mules.

Vc. Quatrefoils by bust. Small, neat dies (circles 18.5mm). London only. (i) Fleurs or (ii) small trefoils on side cusps. Fleur, trefoil, rose or nothing on breast. Central fleur of crown tall, with open side foils. No eye after *tas*; extra point within pellets in one rev. quarter. Saltire stops. Also mules with earlier obv., Vaii/c (ER) and Vbii/c (rare; exceptionally with trefoil stops on one rev.).

Vd. Quatrefoils by bust. New 'rugged' lettering, with incurved uprights, bow-legged *A* and *P* with elongated serif. Large fleurs on cusps (omitted on breast on rare

Edward IV – Henry VIII

Groats

earliest dies). Usually new crown with small central fleur tilted to left, and circular side foils. Saltire stops (rarely omitted on rev.). No eye after *tas*.

London: Extra point in one quarter of rev.; omitted on (VR) latest dies. Vars.: *Eward* and *Francie*; *Ang*; *Posu*. Also rare mules Vcii/d.

Provincial mints - rev. dies only (VI/Vd mules); no extra point on rev.

    Bristol: *Vil/la B/res/toll*, or *B/res/tow* or *B/ris/tow*.
    Coventry: *Civi/tas/Cove'/tre*. Rare.
    Norwich: *Civi/tas/Nor/wic'*. Rare.

VI. Mm. sun both sides. Quatrefoils by bust. Large fleurs on side cusps.

London: Saltire stops (or none on rev.). Fleur or nothing on breast. Sometimes a lis after *tas*. Vars. *Edvard* (no quatrefoils by bust); *Re* for *Rex*; no fleurs on cusps; *Posu*; extra point in one quarter (cf Vd). Also rare mules Vd/VI (vars.: fleur over *e* on breast; *Frnc*) and VI/Vd (ER var., with *x* omitted, has *e* on breast, York obv. die - ? struck at York).

Bristol: *B* on breast (once omitted). *Bres-*, or *Bris-*, *toll*, *Bristow*. Stops obv. saltires; rev. saltires, trefoils or mixed. Some dies omit quatrefoils by bust. Vars.: fleurs above crown; fleur omitted to right of crown; lis before *Vil*. Also rare VI/Vd mules.

Coventry: *C* on breast. *Cove'* (or *Cov'e*)/*tre*. Saltire stops. Vars.: *Fran*; *B* instead of *C* on breast. Also rare VI/Vd mules.

Norwich: *n* on breast. *Nor/wic* or *vic*. Saltire stops. Var.: *Dem*. Also rare VI/Vd mules.

York: *e* on breast (var. has *e* over fleur). *Civi/tas/Ebo/raci*. Saltire stops. See above for York/London VI/Vd mule.

VII. London and Bristol, mm. crown both sides; York, mm. lis/crown or lis both sides. Large fleurs or small trefoils on cusps. Quatrefoils by bust.

London: Mm. crown. Breast cusp fleured. Also rare mules VI/VII and VII/VI.

VIIa   Fleurs on cusps. Stops usually saltires, or none; var. stops, lis on obv. or after *Deum*, or trefoils on rev. Other vars. omit all fleurs, or breast fleur, or quatrefoils.

VIIb   Trefoils on cusps. Saltire stops. Var. has rev. crown after *Posui*. Rare.

Bristol (*B/res* or *ris/toll* or *tow*): Mm. crown. Also rare mules VI/VII and VIIa/VI.

VIIa   Fleurs on cusps. Obv. stops saltires, rarely pellets; rev. saltires or none. Vars. *B* over *e* on breast; lis after *Deum*; *Meu*; *Wil/la*.

VIIb   Trefoils on cusps. Rev. stops saltires, trefoils or mixed. Rare; also rare mules VIIa/b.

York: VIIa Mm. lis/crown. Fleurs on cusps. Saltire stops.

VIIb   As (a) but mm. lis both sides (var. lis over crown on rev.). Var. *e* over fleur on breast.

VIIc   Mm. lis both sides. Small trefoils on cusps. Stops obv. saltires, rev. trefoils, saltires, mixed or none. Rare; also rare mules VIIb/c and VIIc/a.

VIII. Quatrefoils by bust. Fleurs or trefoils on cusps. Normally letter R4.

London: Mm. crown/sun. Quatrefoil on breast cusp. Also rare mules VIIa/VIII, VIIb/VIII.

VIIIa   Fleurs on cusps (but not over crown). Saltire stops. Obv. mm. sun and crown (ER) or crown alone. Also mule VIIIa/VII. All VR.

VIIIb   Trefoils on cusps (sometimes also above crown), rarely omitted. Stops saltires, rarely trefoils, or none. Vars. *Ang; Angli; Francie* or *Francis*. Obv. die with rose before crown (ER) was described by BW as type IX, but has R4 and is only recorded with rev. of VIII.

Groats

Bristol (*B/ris/tow*): Mm. crown/sun. Trefoils on cusps. Stops saltires, trefoils, mixed or none. Rare; also VR mule VIIa/VIII.

York: VIIIa Mm. sun both sides. Trefoils on cusps. Saltire stops or on rev. none. Also rare mules VIIa/VIIIa (var. *Ebo/rac*).

VIIIb Mm. lis both sides (sometimes over obv. crown or rev. sun). Trefoils on cusps (sometimes over crown). Stops saltires, trefoils or none. Vars. no *e* on breast; *Edwad*. Also rare mule VIIIb/a.

IX. Mm. rose, a London reverse type only. Stops saltires or trefoils. R5. Some read *Lon/doo* (with *tas/L* over *Lon/d*). Combined with obv. dies of VIIIb (var. has small letters on obv., and *Franci*) or X (also including small letter variety). All VR.

Types X and XI. Small trefoils on cusps (sometimes also over crown). *B*-like *R* (R5). (a) Trefoils by bust. (b) No marks by bust.

London: X, mm. long cross fitchy/sun. Stops saltires, trefoils, mixed or none.

Xa. Trefoils by bust. With or without trefoils on breast and above crown. Vars. quatrefoils or saltires instead of trefoils by bust (ER); pellets in upper angles of cross fitchy; *Dei; Franci(e); Frran; Civitaa*. Some have small letters. Also Xa/IX (*Lon/doo*), VR.

Xb. As Xa but no trefoils by bust. Trefoils normally on all cusps.

XI. Mm. long cross fitchy both sides; XIa and XIb as Xa and Xb except for rev. mm. VR.

Bristol: Xa only. Mm. sun both sides. Stops trefoils or none. Rare; also VR Xa/VIII mule (R4 on rev.).

York: Xa, mm. lis/sun. Stops obv. trefoils, rev. saltires or none. Also VR mule Xa/VIII (R4 on rev.).

XIa, mm. lis both sides. Stops obv. saltires or trefoils, rev. saltires or none. Vars. *e* over trefoil on breast; rev. mm. lis over long cross fitchy. Rare.

HENRY VI, SECOND REIGN (1470-1). *henric(u) Di Gra Rex Angl & Franc*. Saltire or trefoil stops or (rev.) none. Small trefoils on cusps (present or absent above crown).

London: Mm. obv. cross patty or restoration cross (RC); rev. lis, short cross fitchy (SCF), RC or cross patty. Vars. (mm. RC) *Gracia*; lis or pellet after *Deum*.

Bristol: *B* on breast. Mm. obv. trefoil or RC; rev. rose, trefoil, SCF or RC. Var. *henricus, Ang*. Some rev. dies read *Wil/la* with two saltires over first arm of *W*. Rare.

York: *e* on breast. Mm. lis both sides. Var. small lis after *Franc*. Also ER mule Henry VI/Edward, type Xa (mm. sun).

EDWARD IV, FIRST REIGN (1471-83), types XII-XXII. *Edward D(e)i Gra Rex Angl & Franc*. No marks by bust, except XVb and XIX. London (XII-XXII), Bristol (*Bristow, B* on breast; XII, XIV), York (*e* on breast; XII only).

XII. Letter *I* with wide, serrated ends (I2); plain, narrower *I* (I1) indicates rev. dies of Henry VI. *Di*.

London: Mm. SCF both sides. Trefoils usually omitted above crown. Stops trefoils, saltires or (rev.) none. Var. *Ang*. Rare: also ER mules XII/Henry VI (mm. RC; also, with rev. mm. SCF, some dies already used for Henry).

Bristol: Mm. rose both sides. No trefoils above crown. Stops obv. trefoils, rev. saltires. Rare; also VR mules XII (mm. rose)/Henry VI (*Wil/la* with two saltires).

York: Mm. lis both sides. No trefoils above crown. Stops obv. trefoils, rev. saltires or none. Last type of this mint. Rare; also VR mules XII/Henry VI (narrow *I*).

Edward IV – Henry VIII

Groats

Types XIII – XV. Annulet series.

XIII. Mm. obv. large annulet, rev. trefoil. London only. Small trefoils on cusps (but rarely over crown). *Di.* Stops obv. annulets (var. saltire after *Angl)*, rev. trefoils or none. Also mules both ways with XII. All VR.

XIV. *Di.*

    London: Mm. small annulet both sides or (VR) obv. only. Small trefoils on cusps (but rarely over crown). Stops obv. trefoils, saltires or mixed, rev. trefoils, saltires or none. Vars. *Edwrd, Edvard; Fran; Meua.* Also VR mules XIV/Henry VI (RC) and both ways with XII and XIII.

    Bristol: Mm. small annulet both sides (rarely omitted on rev.). Trefoil stops. Small trefoils on all cusps. Rare; also ER mules XII/XIV (mm. rose/annulet; or no rev. mm. but saltire before *Posui)*.

    Mm. obv. sun, rev. small annulet (or sun both sides?, unverified). Stops saltires or none. Trefoils on cusps except over crown. Var. *B* over trefoil on breast. Rare. XIV is the last type of this mint.

XV. Mm. pellet-in-annulet both sides. London only henceforward. Stops saltires or (rev.) none.

XVa. No roses by bust. Small (rarely, late, large) trefoils on all cusps. Last type with Vd crown. *Di,* then *Dei.* Var. *Franc &.* VR.

XVb. Roses by bust. Large trefoils on all cusps. New taller and more upright crown. *Dei.* Rare; also VR mule XIV/XV (shares rev. die with XVb).

Types XVI – XX. Second cross series. London only. Mm. cross (various forms), both sides. Usually saltire stops. Phase 1 (XVI-XVIIIa): Large trefoils on all cusps, and *Dei.* Phase 2 (XVIIIb-XX): Large fleurs (not on breast or above crown), and *Di;* often roses in rev. outer legend.

XVI. Mm. cross, (a) plain, (b) with four pellets. Stops crosses (saltires) or (rev.) none. Chevron-barred *A* in *Angl* and often in *tas* (and in subsequent types).

XVIa. Mm. plain cross, sometimes over pellet-in-annulet (XV dies altered). VR.

XVIb. Mm. cross with pellet in each angle. Also rare mules XVIb/a.

XVII. Mm. first pierced cross (no marks by bust). Saltire stops. Var. lacks trefoils above crown. Also VR mules both ways with XVIb.

XVIII. Mm. pierced cross with pellet in one angle. Saltire stops.

XVIIIa. Pellet in upper left angle of cross. Last type with XVb crown, trefoils on cusps (rarely omitted above crown), *Dei,* unbarred *&* and *B*-like R5. Also mules both ways with XVII. All VR.

XVIIIb. Pellet in lower left or right angle of cross (all four combinations known; obv. right, rev. left, the commonest). Large fleurs replace trefoils on cusps, omitted above crown and on breast. New crown with prominent hollows below ornaments. *Di.* New lettering, including barred *&,* and occasional pot-hook *A* and *V.* Saltire stops, normally with roses and/or suns in rev. outer inscription. Vars. *Edvard;* fleur on breast; no rev. mm. (early die, roses after *Posui* and *don).* Also rare mules both ways with XVII and XVIIIa.

XX. Mm. pierced cross with central pellet. Large fleurs on cusps, *Di.* No stops on obv., saltires on rev. Rose after *Deum;* pot-hook *V* in *Deum, Meum.* No extra pellets on rev. Also mules both ways with XVIIIb. All VR.

XIX. Mm. second pierced cross. Pellets by bust. Large fleurs on cusps, *Di.* Saltire stops, with rose(s) on rev. Usually extra pellet(s) in one or two quarters of rev. Occasional pot-hook *V.* Also mules both ways with XVIIIb and XX. All VR.

Groats

XXI. Mm. cinquefoil (sometimes with pellet added before rev. mm. and in *don* quarter). Rose on breast. Large fleurs on cusps (rarely above crown). *Di*. Saltire stops. Occasional pot-hook *A* or *V*; or chevron-barred *A*. Often rose(s) in rev. inscription, rarely in obv. Also ER mule XXI/XIX.

EDWARD IV-V (1483). London only.

XXII. Mm. sun-and-rose dimidiated (SR1) both sides (usually with empty centre). *Edward_Di Gra Rex Angl & Franc*. With fleur on breast and pellet below (*Edward* or *Edvard*); or without pellet (*A* barred); or without fleur or pellet (*A* unbarred). Saltire stops. Thin cross on rev. Vars. *Edwrd*, *Posu/i*. Rare.

RICHARD III (1483-5). *Ricard Di Gra Rex Angl & Franc* (types I-III). Saltire stops. London only, except also York in IIIa.

XXII (BH). Obv. dies of XXII in Edward's name, with mm. boar's head (BH1) over SR1. London only. Rev. dies as XXII, or more usually with thick cross and mm. with prominent central pellet. VR.

I. Mm. SR1 both sides (usually with empty centre). London only. Edwardian lettering with L1 and M1. Thin cross on rev. Var. *Dei*. Rare.

II. Mm. boar's head (BH). London only.

IIa. Obv. dies of I with mm. BH1 over SR1; rev. dies with mm. SR1, or BH (ER). All rare.

IIb. Mm. BH2 both sides. Letters L1 and M1; then L2 and M1; finally, L2 and M2. Also ER mules IIa/b and IIb/a.

III. Mm. sun-and-rose. Letters L2 and M2. New crown with smaller piercings in band, and longer spikes.

IIIa. Mm. SR2.
London: Mm. normally on both sides; very rarely on obv. only. With (rare) or without pellet below bust. Some dies omit fleur on cusp to left of crown.
Also ER mules both ways with BH2 (IIIa/IIb and IIb/IIIa).
York: Mm. on obv. only. VR.

IIIb. Mm. SR3 (sun with only four rays). London only. Also IIIa/b mule. All VR.

HENRY VII, type I (1485-87/8). Open crown. London only. Lettering style A. Normally *henric Di Gra Rex Angl & Franc*; & is barred *S*. *A* unbarred or barred. Plain cross-ends (no. 1).

IA. Compound mint-marks (both sides). No marks by bust. Saltire stops (not in inner circle on rev.).
  (i)   rev. dies only (VR), with mm. halved sun-and-rose (SR3), combined with obv. dies of ii.
  (ii) mm. halved lis-and-rose (LR). No fleur on breast. VR; also VR mules ii/i and ii/iii.
  (iii) mm. lis-on-rose or lis-on-SR. Rose, fleur or nothing on breast. Rare; also VR mules with revs. of IB (no mm.; lis in inscription).

IB. Single mint-marks. Quatrefoils, crosses or saltires by bust. Stops varied (often in both rev. inscriptions). Obverse dies with all three marks are sometimes found with revs. of IAiii.
  (i)   mm. small lis (obv. only; one die). *henrcus, Franc*. No fleur on breast. Obv. pellet stops, rev. quatrefoils with lis after *don*. ER.

Edward IV – Henry VIII

Groats

(ii) mm. cross fitchy (obv. only; three dies). *henricus Dei, Fr(a)*. Fleur on breast. Obv. stops saltires (one with pellet after *Rex*); rev. saltires or trefoils, with lis after *Lon* or *Posui* and *Adiutore* on (VR) early dies. Rare.

(iii) mm. rose, usually on obv. only, very rarely on rev. *henric Di, Franc*. Fleur on breast. Crosses by bust usually in saltire position. Obv. stops trefoils (once stars, *Francie*), rev. saltires or trefoils. Also ER mule IBiii/ii (rev. with lis).

SECOND PERIOD, c. 1488 - 1504 (Henry VII): Traditional type modified, with arched crown breaking tressure, and other gradual changes to portrait. Rev. cross soon has forked or ornamental ends (causing abbreviation to *Deu*, *Meu*). London only. Exceptional types (enthroned figure/shield on cross; and rev. variety with portcullis on centre of cross) occur in the period of type II.

II. Crown with two plain arches, surmounted by cross on globe breaking tressure; eight arcs, or six (with or without part of two more, upper). Lettering A. Normally *henric Di Gra Rex Angl & Franc.*

IIA. No mintmark. Saltires by neck except on late dies. Small trefoils on cusps. & is barred *S*. Crown no. 1 (broad; rare) or no. 2 (taller and narrower). Plain cross-ends (no. 1). Stops obv. trefoils, rev. (outer circle only) normally trefoils, saltires or none. Early rev. var. (VR) has stars after *Posui, Deum* and *tas* (IIA/IB mule?). Vars. *henrc; Ang; Franci*; pellet before *Meum* (ER; probably IIA/B mule).
Exceptional rev. type (ER): portcullis in centre of rev., mm. large lis; cleft cross-ends.

IIB. Mm. heraldic cinquefoil, both sides or obv. only. No marks by neck. Crown no. 2. Fleurs on cusps (first, on six; then on four, rare; lastly on six or seven). Reversed *S* for & replaces barred *S* on later dies. Early revs. (rare) have cross-end no. 1; soon replaced by no. 2 (with cleft shank and arched feet). Trefoil stops; or, on rare earliest revs., none. Later obvs. have barred *A*. Coded stopping introduced in inner circle on late rev. dies. Vars. *henric* (only) in style B letters; *Agl*; pellet by cinquefoil and before *Meum* (early; VR).
Exceptional type (unique): mm. cinquefoil both sides. Obv. king enthroned, *London* beneath; *Fra*. Rev. royal arms over long cross, *Posui* etc., no inner inscription, cross-end no. 2. Trefoil stops.

Types IIIA and IIIB. Crown with two jewelled arches, breaking tressure of six arcs. *Angl z Fra-Franc.*

IIIA. Mm. cinquefoil only. Hair as earlier (curled outwards at bottom). Lettering B (plain, with Greek *E* and Roman *M*). Fleurs on six or (usually) all seven cusps of six-arc tressure. Stops rosettes (doubled in rev. inner circle). Cross-end no. 3 (with antler ends, enclosing a circular hollow). Rare; also VR mules both ways with IIB.

IIIB. New compact hair, curled inwards.

(i) Mm. escallop. Lettering style B, C, D or E. Stops rosettes or trefoils. Cross-ends no. 3, or 4 (enclosing rosette). Several varieties of ornament on cusps. Late revs. read *Deu A/diuto/e Meu*. ER vars. - early obv. with no fleurs, cross in crown, horizontal hair (IIIB/IIB mule); another with rosettes in spandrels; late rev. with annulet stops and star before *Civi*. Also VR mules both ways with IIB and IIIA.

(ii) Mm. pansy. Lettering style E (early, with plain Gothic *M* and narrow *R*). Stops rosettes. Cross-ends no. 4, or 5 (antler horns curved outwards). Rare; also VR mules escallop/pansy.

1464–1526

Groats

IIIC. Crown with two arches, only the outer one jewelled. Tressure of six arcs, broken by crown. Broad fleurs on cusps. New portrait with realistic hair. Lettering style E. *henric Di Gra Rex Ang*, or *Agl, Z F-Fra*. Stops on rev. usually coded, occasionally omitted. *Posui/Deu A/diuto/e Meu* or similar.

 (i) Mm. pansy (1, with symmetrical petals; 3, larger, with longer 'legs', late and rare). Later coins have larger flans (26/27 mm. diameter). *Ang* (normally), or *Agl* (late). Often some broken letters. *m* has notched central limb and out-turned feet at sides. Stops rosettes or saltires. Cross-ends no. 5, 6 or 7. Vars. *hennric*; *Dei*; fleurs omitted. Also VR mules both ways with IIIB (rev. type defined by letter *m*).

 (ii) Mm. leopard's head crowned (LHC). *Agl(i)*. Some have broken C and D. Saltire stops. Cross-ends no. 7. Rare; also VR mules both ways with pansy.

 (iii) Mm. lis-issuant-from-rose (LIR). *Agl*. No broken letters. Saltire stops (var. none). Cross-ends no. 7. Rare; also VR mules both ways with LHC.

 (iv) Mm. anchor (upright or inverted; some late obv. dies omit mm.). *Agl*. Lettering more ornamental (E3), or plainer later (E2); some broken letters. Saltire stops. Cross-ends no. 7 (early, rare) or 8 (flans again reduced). Also rare mules both ways with LIR.

Facing bust groats with mintmarks greyhound's head and cross-crosslet. Saltire stops throughout. Type IIIC as before; *A/diuto(r)/e Meu*; coded stops. Type IV, similar but crown with one wide arch consisting (normally) of a single (IVA) or double line (IVB) with ornaments.

 Mm. greyhound's head (GH).

IIICv. Saltire stops, whole or defective (with one or three limbs broken). Broad fleurs on cusps. *Agl; A/diuto/e*. Several different punches for *n* in *Lon/don*.

 (a) Mm. GH1 (large head, thick neck, small ears) both sides. Lettering style E. Cross-ends no. 8. Vars. *henic* (with saltire before rev. mm.); no obv. stops. Also VR mules with obvs. of IIICiv (mm. anchor or none).

 (b) Mm. GH2 (small head and neck, long ears) both sides, or GH2/rose (rare). Plain lettering, style F (or G, only on ER mule with IV rev.). Plain cross-ends no. 9. Also VR mules b/a and a/b (rev. mm. GH2 or rose).

IVAi. Crown with one single-line arch ornamented with four small saltires. Mm. GH2 both sides. Fleurs on cusps usually 'strawberry leaves'. *Angl* or *Agli*. Lettering F. Cross-ends no. 9. Some read *A/diuto/eu Meu*. VR; also ER mules with revs. of IIICva (mm. GH1) or IIICvb (mm. GH2 or rose).

IVBi. Crown with one double-line arch ornamented with six small uprights. *Angl* or *Agli(e)*. Mm. GH2 both sides. Broad fleurs on cusps. Lettering G. *A/diutor/e Meu*. Cross-ends no. 9 or (rare) 10. Slightly larger flans; full outer beaded edge. Rare; also ER mules both ways with IIICvb.

 Mm. cross-crosslet. Lettering style G (with some broken letters), broad fleurs on cusps, and cross-ends no. 10 throughout. *Angl-Anglie,* or *Agl-Aglie; F-Fra*.

IIICvi. Crown with two arches, the outer jewelled. Vars. *henrikic, henkic*. Rare; also ER mule with mm. GH2 (IVB) rev.

IVAii. Crown with one single-line arch ornamented with four saltires (ER vars. double-lined arch with four or six saltires).

IVBii. Crown with one double-line arch ornamented with six uprights.

Edward IV – Henry VIII

Groats

THIRD PERIOD, 1504-1526, Henry VII-VIII: Realistic portrait in profile to right. Rev. shield with royal arms over forked cross; single circle of inscription. Stops saltires or crosses.

Type VA, 'Tentative Profile' series of Henry VII, struck alongside greyhound's head and cross-crosslet groats with facing head. Profile bust without tressure (except 3c); the base of the crown consists of a double band. Hair ends in tight curls. Titles varied. *Posui/Deu(m) A/diutor/e Meu(m)*. No mint name; London only.

1. No numeral. Six saltires on arch of crown. Hair-line inner circles. *henric(us) D(e)i Gra Rex Angli(e) z Fr(a)*. Rev. mm. small or large lis. *Deum, Meum* in full. Cross-ends no. 10 or 11.
    (a) Obv. mm. small lis. Special lettering (cf. type 1 shillings). ER.
    (b) No obv. mm. Lettering G. VR.

2. With numeral. Six uprights on arch of crown. Lettering G (coarse). *Di; Angl or Agl(i)*.
    (a) No obv. mm.; rev. large lis, saltire or none. Earliest pair of dies (ER) has hair-line circles and *henric Septim*. Normally *henric VII*. Cross-ends no. 10 or 11. VR; also ER mules both ways with 1b.
    (b) Mm. large lis both sides. *henric VII*. Cross-ends no. 11. VR; also ER mules 2b/2a (no rev. mm., cross-ends 10) and 2b/shilling die type 2.
    (c) Mm. GH2 both sides. *henric VII, Agl* only. Cross-ends no. 11. Also mules 2b/2c (numeral omitted on one obv. die). All ER.

3. Mm. cross-crosslet both sides. *henric VII; Angl, Agl(i)*. Cross-ends no. 11. All rare. (a) Six uprights on arch of crown; (b) six saltires on arch; (c) as (b) but tressure around head (ER).

HENRY VII, type VB. London only. Regular Profile bust, no tressure. Base of crown consists of three bands; four saltires on arch of crown. Hair ends in looser curls than in VA. *henric VII Di Gra Rex Agl Z F-Fra;* query-shaped contraction marks after *henric* and *VII*. Rev. shield over long cross. *Posui/Deu A/diutor/e Meu*.

(i) Mm. cross-crosslet.
    (a) Plain mm. cross-crosslet (the normal form).
    (b) Mm. cross-crosslet with colon beside (usually before) it. Vars. have (instead) pellet(s) or saltire(s) above or to left of cross above crown. Rare; also VR mules both ways with a.
    (c) Mm. cross-crosslet and pheon (at beginning and end of inscriptions respectively, or *vice versa*). Also ER mules a/c, b/c and c/b. All ER.

(ii) Mm. pheon (occasionally over cross-crosslet, a or b, ER). Also ER mules with crosslet obv. (a) or rev. (b or c).

HENRY VIII, first coinage (1509-1526). London, Tournai. Types as VB above, with portrait of Henry VII. Stops single or double, crosses or saltires.
London: *henric VIII Di Gra Rex Agl Z F-Fra;* query-shaped contraction marks after *henric* and *VIII*. *Posui/Deu A/diutor/e Meu*. Normally no marks in forks of rev. cross.
    (i) Mm. pheon. Numeral *viij*. VR.
    (ii) Mm. castle. Numeral *viij*. Many have pellet or two saltires by obv. mm.
    (iii) Mm. crowned portcullis (sometimes without chains, especially on rev.). Some have pellet before obv. mm. (rare) or before *Gra*. Numeral *viij* (early, rare) or without dots above, or *viii* (with or without dots). VR vars. have obv. mm. over crowned *t*, with normal rev. or with trefoils in forks of cross.
Tournai: Mm. crowned (Gothic) *t. henric Di Gra Rex Franc Z Agli(e);* without numeral. *Civi/tas/ Torn/acens*. Rare.

1464–1526

HALFGROATS 1464 - 1526

First Period, 1464 - late 1480s. Traditional type, with open crown, normally tressure of nine arcs with top cusps unfleured. Rev. cross and pellets as previously. *Posui/Deum A/diutor/e Meum.*

Edward IV, First Reign, light coinage (1464-70). *Edward Di Gra Rex Angl & F-Franc.*
    Royal Mints: London (V-VIII, X), Bristol (V/VI-VIII), Coventry (VI), Norwich (VI), York (VI-VIII). Normally no initial letter on breast at provincial mints.

V.   Mm. rose.
Va.   Annulets by bust. Mm. rose both sides. Light coins from type IV dies of heavy coinage. Large fleurs on side cusps. No stops. London only. ER.
Vd.   New, smaller dies. Saltire stops.
    London: Mm. rose on obv. only. Quatrefoils by bust; large fleurs on cusps. Extra point in *Civi* quarter. VR.
    Bristol: Obv. only (V/VI mules, with or without rev. mm.; ER). Saltires by bust; small trefoils on cusps.
VI.   Mm. sun, usually both sides. Saltire stops.
    London: Obv. only (VI/V mules). Quatrefoils by bust; large fleurs on cusps. ER.
    Bristol: Saltires by bust; trefoils on side cusps. *Vil/la B/res/* or *B/ris/tow*, or (without mm. or stops on rev.) *B/res/toll*. Rare; also ER V/VI mules.
    Coventry: Crosses by bust; trefoils on side cusps. *Civi/tas/Cov'e/tre*. ER.
    Norwich: Saltires by bust; trefoils on side cusps. *Civi/tas/Nor/vic'*. ER.
    York: Quatrefoils by bust; fleurs on cusps (including breast). *Fra. Civi/tas/Ebo/raci*. VR.
VII.   Quatrefoils, saltires or trefoils by bust. Small trefoils on cusps, sometimes also above crown.
    London: Mm. crown both sides. Saltire stops or none. All rare.
    VIIa   Quatrefoils by bust. Usually trefoil on breast. Var. rev. stops trefoils.
    VIIb   Saltires by bust. No trefoil on breast.
    VIIc   Trefoils by bust. No trefoil on breast. Vars. saltire and trefoil by bust; fleur after *Posui*. Also VIIa/c mule.
    Bristol (*B/ris/tow* or */tol(l)*): Mm. crown both sides, or obv. only. Saltires, crosses or quatrefoils by bust. Stops saltires, trefoils or none. Rare.
    York: Mm. lis both sides. Saltires or quatrefoils by bust. Stops saltires, trefoils or none. Rare.
VIII. London and Bristol, mm. crown/sun; York, mm. lis. Small trefoils on cusps (not above crown).
    London: Mm. crown/sun.
    VIIIa   Quatrefoils by bust and on breast. No stops. Rare; also VR mule VIIIa/VII.
    VIIIb   Saltires by bust, trefoil on breast. Stops saltires or none.
    VIIIc   Trefoils by bust and on breast. Stops trefoils or none.
    Bristol (*B/ris/tol*): Mm. crown/sun. No marks by bust. Trefoil on breast. Stops obv. trefoils, rev. none. Also mule VIII/VII; all VR.
    York: Mm. lis both sides (on rev. after *Posui* or under *P*). *e* on breast. Quatrefoils by bust. Stops obv. saltires, rev. trefoils. Also mule VII/VIII; all VR.
X.   With (Xa) or without (Xb) trefoils by bust. Stops trefoils or none.

Edward IV – Henry VIII

Halfgroats

    London: Mm. long cross fitchy/sun. Small trefoils usually on all cusps, but sometimes omitted on breast and over crown. Xa and Xb both rare; also ER mule Xa/VIII (same rev. die as VIIIc coin, with double-punched *o* in *don*).

    York: Mm. lis both sides. Trefoils on all cusps except breast. Xa (only) and X/VIII mule (lis after *Posui*); both ER.

HENRY VI, SECOND REIGN (1470-1). *henric(u) Di Gra Rex Angl & Fr(a)*. Stops obv. trefoils, rev. none.

London: Mm. restoration cross both sides or obv. only. *henric(u)*. With or without trefoils on cusps above crown. VR.

York: Mm. lis (large) both sides. *e* on breast; trefoils on all other cusps. *henricu*. ER.

EDWARD IV, SECOND REIGN (1471-83), ROYAL MINTS. *Edward Di Gra Rex Angl & Fr-Fran*. No marks by bust. Types (London) XII-XXI except XVII, XIX, XX; Bristol and York, XII only.

XII.   London: Mm. short cross fitchy (obv. only). No stops. ER.

    Bristol (*B/ris/tow*): Mm. rose/short cross fitchy. *B* on breast. Obv. stops trefoils, rev. none. ER.

    York: Mm. lis both sides (rev. lis larger than pre-1470, a Restoration die?). Trefoil on breast. No stops. ER.

Types XIII-XV. Annulet series. London only henceforward. Small trefoils on cusps (not above crown).

XIII.   Mm. obv. large annulet, rev. small rose, or none (mule?). Stops obv. annulets, rev. none. VR.

XIV.   Mm. small annulet both sides, or (VR) obv. only. Stops obv. saltires, rev. none. Rare; also ER mules both ways with XIV.

XV.   Mm. obv. pellet-in-annulet, rev. large rose. Stops none or (rev.) saltires. *Dei*. ER.

Types XVI and XVIII. Second cross series. London only.

XVIa.   Mm. cross over pellet-in-annulet (XV dies altered) both sides, or obv. only. Small trefoils on all cusps. *Dei*. No stops on obv.; rev. none or (on dies without mm.) saltires. Rare.

XVIIIb.   Mm. pierced cross with pellet in one lower quarter. Larger trefoils on cusps (not on breast or, usually, above crown). *Di*. New, neater lettering introduced during type. Stops saltires (obv. only) or none. Var. trefoils above crown. Rare; also VR mules both ways with XVI.

XXI.   Mm. cinquefoil both sides (sometimes small size). Small trefoils again on cusps (not on breast). *Di* or *Dei*. Stops saltires (rev. only) or none. Rare.

No Edward halfgroat with unaltered mm. sun-and-rose dimidiated (type XXII) is known.

CANTERBURY MINT, 1464-83. Archbishop Thomas Bourchier, 1454-86. *Civi/tas/Can/tor*.

Edward IV, First Reign, light coinage, 1464-70. Groups A-F. *Edward Di Gra Rex Angl & F-Franc*.

Group A (BW type Va). Large fleurs on cusps. Bourchier's knot below bust. Spur in one quarter of rev. Stops saltires or none.

    Mm. obv. pall; rev. pall, rose (some have quatrefoils by bust) or none.

Group B. As A, but small trefoils on cusps. Knot, spur and stops as in A. Var. *tas* under *Posui*.

    Ba.   Mm. pall both sides: quatrefoils or none by bust (BW Vb); wedges by bust (BW VIb/Vb).

Halfgroats

- Bb. Mm. pall obv. only: no marks by bust (BW Vb); quatrefoils (or quatrefoils over wedges) by bust (BW VIb/VIa); saltires by bust (BW VIa; var. *An*).
- Bc. Mm. obv. pall, rev. rose: quatrefoils by bust (BW Vb); wedges by bust (BW VIb/Vb).
- Bd. Mm. obv. pall, rev. sun (BW VIb): wedges or quatrefoils by bust.

Group C. Obv. mm. pall. Knot, spur or both omitted.
- Ca. With knot but no spur: no rev. mm.; wedges or quatrefoils (var. *Edard*) or nothing by bust (BW Va/VII or VIb/VII).
- Cb. With spur but no knot: quatrefoils or nothing by bust; rev. mm. pall (BW VII/VIb)or none (BW VII/VIa).
- Cc. With neither knot nor spur: no rev. mm.; quatrefoils by bust (BW –). Rare.

Group D (BW VII 'royal'). Mm. crown both sides, or obv. only. Quatrefoils, mill-rinds or saltires by bust. Trefoils on top cusps.

Group E (BW VIII). Trefoils by bust. With or without trefoils above crown. Obv. mm. crown, rev. sun or none. Also VR 'mule' (BW VIII/VII) with mm. crown both sides.

Group F (BW IX). Trefoils by bust. Mm. rose both sides. Rare; also ER mule mm. rose/sun (BW IX/VIII).

Edward IV, Second Reign, Groups G, H, 1471-83. No marks by bust.

Group G (BW XXI). Mm. obv. long cross fitchy, rev. cinquefoil. Cusps plain. *Dei*. Rare.

Group H. Mm. rose both sides. *C* on breast. Fine lettering. Ha. Cusps trefoiled except over crown; no stops on obv.; no mark on centre of rev. cross (BW 'XIX'). Hb. All cusps trefoiled; *C* on centre of cross; saltire stops (BW 'XVIIIb'). Hc. No trefoils on cusps; no stops on obv.; rose in centre of cross (BW 'XX'). Also mules Ha/b and Hc/b.

RICHARD III, 1483-5. London only. Mm. sun-and-rose dimidiated or boar's head. No stops. Propeller pellets.

- XXII (BH). Obv. die of XXII in Edward's name, with mm. boar's head (BH1) over sun-and-rose (SR1); no mm. on rev. *Edward Di Gra Rex Angl Fra*. No stops. Trefoils on all cusps except breast. Unique.
- IIb. Mm. boar's head 2 (obv. only). *Ricard Di Gra Rex Angl & Fra*. Small head. Two obv. dies, ER.
- IIIa. Mm. sun-and-rose 2, both sides or obv. only. Larger head. New heavier lettering. *Fr*. Three obv. dies, of which one has pellet below bust. Coins without rev. mm. are probably mules with preceding types. All VR.

HENRY VII, type I, 1485-87/8. Open crown. London, Canterbury. *Posui/Deum A/diutor/ e Meum*. Lettering style A. Plain cross-ends (no. 1).
- IA. London only. Mm. lis-on-rose (obv. only). Tressure of nine arcs, cusps unfleured. No marks by bust. *henric Dei Gra Rex Angl & F*, saltire stops. VR; also unique mule with rev. of Richard III (mm. SR2).
- IB. Canterbury only. Mm. tun (obv. only). Tressure of seven arcs, trefoils on cusps (not over crown). Crosses by bust. *Di, Fr(a)*. Trefoil stops, or (rev.) none. *m* (Abp. Morton, from 1486) on centre of cross. *Civi/tas/Can/tor*. Rare.

SECOND PERIOD, c.1488 – 1504, HENRY VII, types II-IV: London (III only), York royal (III only), Canterbury (II, III), York episcopal (IV only). Traditional type modified, with arched crown breaking tressure, and other gradual changes to portrait. Rev. cross soon has forked or ornamental ends (causing abbreviation to *Deu, Meu*).

Edward IV – Henry VIII

Halfgroats

II. Canterbury only (Abp. Morton). Crown with two plain arches, breaking tressure. Trefoils on cusps. No initial mark on obv. Crosses by bust. *Di, Fra. m* on centre of cross. *Posui* etc. as before. All rare.

IIa Tun after *Gra*, and eye after *Posui*. Obv. stops pellets; saltire after *Deum*. Also VR mules both ways with IB.

IIb Mm. tun before *Posui*, but none on obv. Obv. stops trefoils. Also VR mules I/IIb, IIa/b and IIb/a.

III. London and York royal.

IIIA (cf. groats of early IIIB), London only. Mm. escallop both sides (on obv. above cross of crown). Tressure of six arcs, broken by crown with two arches, the outer jewelled. *henric Di Gra Rex Angl z Fr*. Rosettes on cusps. Lettering style D. Trefoil stops. Pierced cross-ends; no lozenge in centre of cross. *Deum, Meum*. One obv. die, VR.

IIIB and IIIC, London and York royal. Coins of deficient weight ('dandyprats'). Mm. lis both sides. Cusps plain. Lozenge enclosing pellet in centre of rev. cross. Pierced cross-ends. *Fr-Fran*.

IIIB. Crown and tressure as IIIA.
(a) Lettering D. Trefoil stops. Often lis on breast. *Deum, Meum*. London, rare. York, obv. dies only (muled with IIIC revs.), rare.
(b) Lettering E. Rosette stops. *Deu, Meu*. London, rare. York, var. has *tas* under *Posui;* rare, more usually muled with IIIC revs.

IIIC. Broad open crown, breaking tressure of six arcs. Rosette stops. Some broken letters.
London: (a) Lettering style E. Rosette stops on rev. in outer legend only. Usually *Deu, Meu.* Var. (ER) has unbroken (nine arc) tressure. Also ER mule IIIC(a)/IIIB(a). (b) Smaller dies and letters (often *Deum, Meum*). Rosettes in both rev. legends (coded in inner). Also rare IIICa/b and b/a mules.
York royal: (b) only. Small letters. With or without rosettes in inner rev. legend. Also many mules with obv. dies of IIIB(a) and (b).

IIIA-D, Canterbury, Abp. Morton. Tressure broken by crown with two arches, of which the outer alone is normally jewelled. No *m* in centre of rev. Pierced cross-ends; on IIIA-C the horns are pointed, and there is a swelling at the neck.

IIIA (cf. groats of type IIIB). Mm. obv. lis, or tun and lis; rev. lis. Obv. lettering D, trefoil stops. *Angl*. Rev. lettering E, rosette stops. Rare; also ER mules with *m* on rev. (IIa and IIb).

IIIB. Mm. obv. tun (above or beside cross), rarely tun and lis; rev. lis, tun or nothing. Stops rosettes or (rev.) none. Lettering E (sometimes broken).

IIIC. Mm. tun both sides or (obv., ER) tun and pansy. Lettering E, with broken letters. No stops, or rarely saltires or (obv. only) rosettes. Late dies read *Agl(i)*.

IIID. Mm. tun. Lettering E (without broken letters); *O* with central bar. No stops. *Agl*. Cross-ends flatter, with very small piercing, and no swelling.

HENRY VII, type IV, YORK (episcopal mint) only. Mm. martlet both sides. Keys (except on IVc) beside bust for Archbishop Thomas Savage (1501-7). No facing bust halfgroats of London or Canterbury at this period. Crown with two arches, the outer jewelled. Tressure of six arcs (except IVa), usually with saltires on cusps. *henric Di Gra Rex Agl Z F(r)*. Saltire stops (except IVa), often coded on rev. *Posui/Deu A/diuto/e Meu. Civi/tas/Ebo/raci*.

441

1464–1526

Halfgroats

IVa   Keys; no tressure. Ornate lettering (E). 'Special' trefoil stops (truncated saltires). Pierced cross-ends. Some read *Ebo/raci/Civi/tas*.

IVb   With keys and tressure. Thick lettering (F). Saltire stops henceforward. Pierced cross-ends. Also muled both ways with IVa.

IVc   No keys; tressure. Lettering G; ornate barred *A*. Pierced cross-ends. Rare; also VR mules both ways with IVb.

IVd   With keys and tressure. Lettering G; plain unbarred *A*. Unpierced cross-ends (no. 10). Also VR mules both ways with IVb and IVc.

THIRD PERIOD, 1504 - 1526 (Henry VII-VIII): Realistic portrait in profile to right, without tressure. Rev. shield over forked cross; single circle of inscription (*Posui* etc. at London, and on earlier issues of Canterbury and York; later coins have *Civitas Cantor* or *Eboraci*). Saltire stops.

HENRY VII, type V. *Posui/Deu A/diuto(r)/e Meu*.

Tentative issue, cf. Profile groats VA. London only. Mm. obv. none, rev. lis. *henric Di Gra Rex Angli Z Fr*, without numeral. Bold-toothed outer circles. Cross-ends no. 10. ER.

Regular issue, cf. Profile groats VB. *henric VII Di Gra Rex Ag(l) (Z)*. London, Canterbury, York. Normally *A/diuto/e*, sometimes *or/e*.

    London: Mms. (both sides) lis, pheon. All have cross-ends no. 10.
1. Mm. lis. Ornate barred *A*. Earliest var. reads *he'ric*. VR.
2. Mm. lis. Plain unbarred *A* (henceforward). Vars. have pellets or saltire above cross of crown. Also VR mules 1/2.
3. Mm. :lis. Rare; also mules 1/3 (ER) and 2/3 (rare).
4. Mm. pheon. Also mules both ways with 3; all rare.

    Canterbury (Archbishop Warham): Mms. martlet, rose. No marks in rev. field.

Va.   Mm. martlet both sides. *he'ric*. Ornate barred *A*. Cross-ends no. 10. Var. *A/diutor/eu*. VR.

Vb.   As Va but *henric* and plain unbarred *A* (both henceforward). Also VR mules both ways with Va.

Vc.   Mm. rose. (i) Cross-ends no. 10 (only on VR Vb/c mule with obv. mm. martlet). (ii) Cross-ends no. 11. Mm. rose both sides (some have large rose on obv., rare).

Vd.   Mm. obv. martlet, rev. rose. Cross-ends no. 11. Rare.

    York (Archbishop Savage to Sept. 1507; *sede vacante*, 1507-8): Mms. martlet, rose. Keys below shield.

Va.   Mm. martlet – obv. die only with ornate barred *A* and *he'ric*, muled with rev. of Vb. ER.

Vb.   Mm. martlet both sides. *henric* and plain unbarred *A* (both henceforward). Cross-ends no. 10. Some read *Al*.

Vc.   Mm. rose both sides (some have large rose on obv., rare). Normally cross-ends no. 11, but ER var. has cross-ends 10 and omits keys. Also rare mules Vc/b.

Vd.   Mm. obv. rose, rev. martlet. Cross-ends no. 11. Rare. This type is also muled with Henry VIII rev. of Abp. Bainbridge (ER).

Edward IV – Henry VIII

Halfgroats

HENRY VIII, first coinage, 1509-1526. London, Canterbury, York; Tournai. Types as before, with portrait of Henry VII. *henric viii Di Gra Rex A(g)l (Z)(Fr)* (except Tournai).
- London: Mm. crowned portcullis, both sides or obv. only (on rev. usually without chains). *viij* or *viii* (without dots). *Posui/Deu A/diuto/e Meu*. Rare.
- Canterbury (Abp. Warham): Type I, *Posui* etc.; type II, *Civi/tas/Can/tor*.
  - Ia. Mm. rose both sides. No initials on rev. (Henry VII die?). ER.
  - Ib. Mm. martlet (sometimes over rose on rev.). *W A* above shield (some from altered dies of Henry VII ?). Rare.
  - Ic. Mm. Latin cross (sometimes called cross fitchy). *W A* beside shield. VR.
  - IIa. Mm. lis. *W A* beside shield. Also mule Ic/IIa; all VR.
  - IIb. Mm. pomegranate. *W A* beside shield.
- York (Abps. Christopher Bainbridge, from 1508, d. 1514, types Ia and Ib; and Thomas Wolsey, from 1514, types Ic and II): Type I, *Posui* etc.; type II, *Civi/tas/Ebo/raci*.
  - Ia. Mm. martlet (sometimes over rose on obv.; altered die of Henry VII). Keys below shield. No initials. Rare.
  - Ib. Mm. martlet. No keys. *X B* beside shield. Rare; also ER mule Henry VII, Vd/Ib.
  - Ic. Mm. estoile (radiant star). *Posui* etc. Keys below shield; cardinal's hat beneath. No initials. VR.
  - II. *Eboraci*. All have keys below shield and hat beneath (sometimes with two pellets beside). No initials on IIa-IIe.
    - (a) Mm. estoile.
    - (b) Mm. plain star.
    - (c) Mm. pansy.
    - (d) Mm. escallop. ER var. has escallop over pansy.
    - (e) Mm. voided cross. No initials. Rare; also ER mule IIe/d.
    - (f) Mm. voided cross. *T W* beside shield. Rare.
- Tournai: Mm. crowned *t*. *henric Di Gra Rex Fra Z Agl*; rev. *Civi/tas/Torn/acen*. ER.

PENCE 1464 - 1526

FIRST PERIOD, 1464 - late 1480s. Traditional type: facing bust with open crown; rev. cross and pellets. Mm. on obv. only unless otherwise stated.

EDWARD IV, FIRST REIGN, light coinage (1464-70). *Edward Di Gra Rex An-Angl*. ROYAL MINTS: London (V-VIII, X), Bristol (VII, VIII).
- Va. Mm. rose. London only. Same obv. die as heavy coinage, type IV, with annulets by neck. Rev. die of reduced module. ER.
- VI. Mm. sun. London only. Quatrefoils by bust. *Edwrd*. No stops. ER.
- Types VII and VIII. Mm. crown. No stops on obv. London and Bristol.
  - London:
    - VII. Quatrefoils (var. trefoil and quatrefoil) or saltires by bust.
    - VIII. 1, Quatrefoils by bust and on breast. 2, Trefoils by bust. Both rare.
  - Bristol (all VR):
    - VII. Quatrefoils, crosses or saltires by bust. *Vil/la B/ris/tow*.
    - VIII. Trefoil to right of bust. *B/ris/toll*. Var. with trefoil before *s* of *tas*, and with quatrefoils by bust may be VII/VIII mule.

443

Pence

Type X. Mm. long cross fitchy. London only. Normally no stops. Xa, trefoils by bust; vars. *Edwar*; trefoil after *Rex*. Xb, no marks by bust. All VR.

HENRY VI, SECOND REIGN (1470-1).
London: 1, Mm. restoration cross, *henricu Di Gra Rex Angl,* VR. 2, Mm. cross patty, *henric, Ang,* VR. 3, Mm. lis, *G* and key by bust, *henricu* (York/London mule), ER.
Bristol: Mm. short cross fitchy. ER.

EDWARD IV, SECOND REIGN (1471-83), ROYAL MINTS. Types (London) XII-XVIII, XXI-II; Bristol, XII only. *Edward D(e)i Gra Rex An-Angle.* No marks by bust. Normally no mm. on rev.
XII.   *Di.* All ER.
       London: Mm. short cross fitchy. *Angl.*
       Bristol: Mm. rose, *Ang'.*
Types XIV-XV. Annulet series. London only. No stops.
XIV.   Mm. small annulet. *Di.* Rare.
XV.   Mm. pellet-in-annulet. *Dei, Angle.* ER.
Types XVI-XVIII. Second cross series. London only. Normally no stops.
XVIa. Mm. cross over pellet-in-annulet (XV obv. die altered). *Dei, Angle.* ER.
XVII. Mm. pierced cross obv. only, or both sides. *Dei, Angl.* VR; also ER mule XVI/XVII.
XVIIIb.Mm. pierced cross with pellet in one lower quarter (obv. only). New letter fount. *Di* or *Dei. Angl.* Var. has saltires after *Angl'*. Rare; also ER mule XVIIIb/XVII (with rev. mm.).
XXI.   Mm. cinquefoil. *Di* or *Dei, Ang(l).* London only. Rare.

EDWARD IV-V (1483)
XXII. Mm. halved sun-and-rose. *Dei, Ang.* London only. Rev. cross-end punch broken. ER.

RICHARD III, 1483-5. London.
XXII (BH). Obv. of XXII in Edward's name, with mm. boar's head (BH1) over halved sun-and-rose. ER.
IIb.   Mm. boar's head (BH2). *Ricard Di Gra Rex Angl.* Unique.

CANTERBURY MINT, 1464-83. *Edward Di Gra Rex An-Angl. Civi/tas/Can/tor.*
   Archbishop Thomas Bourchier, 1454-86.
Edward IV, First Reign, light coinage, 1464-70. Types 1-4 (type 5 known of halfpenny only).
1.   (V?; BW –). Mm. rose (?). Pall to left of neck, Bourchier's knot to right. Spur in *tor* quarter. ER.
2.   (BW type VI). Mm. pall. Knot on breast and breaking inscription after *Di.* Quatrefoils, saltires or nothing by bust. Spur in one quarter of rev. Saltire stops or none. Rare.
3.   (VIIa). Mm. pall. No knot or spur. Crosses by bust. Also 3/2 mules (with spur; quatrefoils or saltires by bust; BW VII/VI). All VR.
4.   (VIIb). Mm. crown. Quatrefoils by bust. ER.
Edward IV, Second Reign, 1471-83. Types 6-7. No marks by bust or added on rev.
6.   Mm. long cross fitchy (BW XXI). No mark on breast. *Dei.* ER.
7.   Mm. rose (BW XIX). 7a, nothing on breast. 7b, *C* on breast. Both VR.

Edward IV – Henry VIII

Pence

YORK MINT, 1464-85. *Civi/tas/Ebo/raci*; quatrefoil on rev. except nos. 1, 8 and 15. London-made dies, except no. 2.

Edward IV, First Reign, light coinage, 1464-70. Types 1-5. *Edward Di Gra Rex Angl* or similar.

Sede Vacante, Sept. 1464-June 1465.
1. Quatrefoils by bust. No quatrefoil on rev.
    1a (BW V). Mm. rose. VR.
    1b (BW VI). Mm. sun. VR.

Archbishop George Neville, 1465-76 (suspended 1472-5).
2. Local dies. *G* and key by bust. *An-Anglie*.
    2a. Mm. rose. *Gra* or *Dei Gra* omitted. Some with saltire stops.
    2b. Mm. cross. *Dei Gra* omitted.
3. London-made dies (henceforward). Some with saltire stops.
    3a (BW VI). Mm. sun. *G* and key by bust.
    3b (BW VII). Mm. large lis. *G* and key.
    3c (BW VII). Mm. large lis. Quatrefoils by bust (once omitted). Rare.
4. (BW VIII). Mm. large lis. Trefoils by bust. Rare.
5. (BW X). *G* and key by bust.
    5a. Mm. small lis.
    5b. Mm. long cross fitchy. Rare.

Henry VI restored, 1470-1. *he(n)ric(u) Di Gra Rex Ang(l)*.
6. Mm. large lis. *G* and key. Trefoil stops. VR.

Edward IV, Second Reign, 1471-83. Types 7-16. *Edward D(e)i Gra Rex Ang(l)* or similar.
7. (BW XII). Mm. short cross fitchy. Quatrefoil on rev.
    7a. Mm. cross fitchy over lis (old die of type VII, no. 3c, with quatrefoils by bust). ER.
    7b. Mm. cross fitchy. *G* and key by bust.

Abp. Neville suspended, 1472-5.
8. (BW 'XIV', *recte* XII). Mm. short cross fitchy; *G* and key; 7b die reused. No quatrefoil on rev. ER.
9. No marks by bust. Quatrefoil on rev. resumed.
    9a (BW XIV). Mm. small annulet. Also 9a/8 mule with unquatrefoiled rev. All VR.
    9b (BW XVI). Mm. cross over annulet. VR.
    9c (BW 'XVI'). Mm. rose.
10. (BW 'XVI'). *e* and rose by bust. Mm. rose.

Abp. Neville restored, 1475-6.
11. (BW 'XVI'). *G* and rose by bust. Mm. rose. VR.
12. (BW 'XVI'). *G* and key by bust.
    12a. Mm. rose, or (ER) rose over annulet.
    12b. Mm. cross and pellet (i.e. BW XVIII). ER (unverified).

Sede Vacante, June – Oct. 1476.
13. Mm. rose. No marks by bust. Rose on breast. Quatrefoil on rev. VR.

Archbishop Laurence Booth, 1476-80.
14. *B* and key by bust. Quatrefoil on rev.
    14a. Mm. rose. *Di* or *Dei*.
    14b (BW XXI). Mm. cinquefoil. VR.

Sede Vacante, May – Sept. 1480.
15. *B* and key by bust, but rev. unquatrefoiled. Mm. rose. VR.

Pence

Archbishop Thomas Rotherham, Sept. 1480-1500.
16. (BW XXI). *T* and key by bust; quatrefoil on rev. Mm. rose. *Di* or *Dei*. Rare vars. have star on breast, with or without star to right of crown. Also ER mule 16/15.

Richard III, 1483-5. Quatrefoil on rev. for Rotherham. *Ricard Di Gra Rex Ang*.
II. Mm. boar's head. Small *T* and upright key by bust. Rare.
III. Mm. sun-and-rose (or once perhaps a rose?). Small *T* and key, or no marks, by bust. VR.

DURHAM MINT, 1464-85.

Edward IV, First Reign, light coinage, 1464-70. Types 1-4. *Edward Di Gra Rex Ang(l)*. Normally London-made dies.

Bishop Laurence Booth, 1457-76.
1. (BW V). Mm. rose. *B D* by bust. *B* on centre of rev. cross. *Civi/tas/De(r)/(r)am*. Some have saltire stops. Also rarely with crude local bust.
2. (BW VI). Mm. sun. Quatrefoil and *B* by bust. Usually saltire stops. *Dun/olm*. No *B* on rev. Rarely with crude local bust. Also VR mules with earlier revs. (2/local, heavy type; and 2/1).
3. (BW VII). Mm. crown. *De(r)/(r)am*. Often trefoils in rev. legend.
   3a. *B* and quatrefoil by bust. VR.
   3b. *D* and quatrefoil by bust. Rare.
   3c. Two quatrefoils by bust.
4. (BW VIII). Mm. crown. *De(r)/(r)am*. Sometimes trefoils or quatrefoil in rev. legend.
   4a. Trefoils by bust. Rare.
   4b. Lis by bust.

Edward IV, Second Reign, 1471-83. Types 5-7 (Booth continued; London-made dies, 1471-3) and local a-e (1473-83). *Di* or *Dei*.
5. No marks by bust. *De/ram*, with trefoils before and/or after *De*. No *D* on centre of cross.
   5a (BW XII). Mm. short cross fitchy. One obv. die (with *e* over mm.) was previously used at London. All VR.
   5b (BW XIII). Mm. trefoil.
6. *B* and trefoil by bust. *D* on centre of rev. cross. Saltire stops. *Der/am* or *De/ram*.
   6a (BW XIII). Mm. trefoil. *Di*.
   6b (BW XV, or XVIa). Mm. (cross over?) pellet-in-annulet. *Dei*. Rare.
   6c (BW XIV). Mm. rose. *Dei*.
7. Mm. rose. Two small lis by bust. *D* in centre of rev. *De(r)/ram*, with or without trefoil.

Local dies (for remainder of Edward IV's reign), types a-e. *Edward D(e)i Gra Rex An-Angl*. Normally saltire stops; occasional pellets in a and b. *D* in centre of rev. *Duno/lmie*. Most have an extra point in one, or all four, quarter(s).
(a) *B* (Booth) to left of crown, *V* on breast. Mm. pansy-like rose. Nothing or saltires by bust. *v* in *Civi* quarter. Also rare mules local a/6 or 7 (*Deram*).

Booth (1473-6), or Dudley (1476-83), types b, c and d.
(b) Mm. rose. No initials on obv. Crosses over crown. Sometimes a saltire on the breast. Often a *v* in *Civi* quarter.
(c) Mm. rose. As (b) but no crosses over crown. Rare.
(d) Mm. rose. *V* to right of bust (Dudley?). Rare.

Edward IV – Henry VIII

Pence

Bishop William Dudley, 1476-83.
(e) Mm. cinquefoil (BW XXI). *D V* by bust. *D* in centre of rev. occasionally omitted.

Bishop John Shirwood (from 1484), under Richard III (1483-5).
Mm. lis. *S* on breast. No marks by bust. *Ricard Di Gra Rex Ang*. Reversed *D* on centre of cross. *Dir/ham*. Rare.

HENRY VII, type I (1485-c.1489). Traditional bust, with open crown. *henric D(e)i Gra Rex An-Angl*.
- London: IA. No marks by bust. Mm. lis-on-rose. *Rex Ag* or *Angl*. No stops. VR. IB (Winstanley 'II'). Crosses by bust. No mm. but small cross before *henric*. Taller crown. Trefoil stops. VR.
- Canterbury: IB only. Mm. tun (Abp. Morton, from 1486). Saltires by bust. Low crown. Trefoil stops. *m* in centre of rev. ER.
- York, Abp. Thomas Rotherham: IA. Mm. lis on sun-and-rose (?). *T* and trefoil by bust. Often a saltire on breast. Low crown. No stops. One has *henric* over *Ricard*. Quatrefoil on rev. cross. Extra pellet in two quarters. Rare. IB. Mm. rose (?). *T* and cross by bust. Taller crown. Trefoil stops. *h* in centre of rev. VR.
- Durham: IA only (W. 'IB'). Mm. cross. *S* (for Bp. Shirwood) on breast. No marks by bust. No stops on obv. *De* trefoil/*ram*. Supine *D* on centre of rev. cross. Rare; also ER mule Henry VII/Richard III.

SECOND PERIOD, c.1489 – 1526 (Henry VII-VIII). Except at Canterbury in group III of Henry VII, all pence are now of the 'sovereign' type: Obv. king enthroned, with arched crown; sceptre in his right hand, orb in left; *henric Di Gra Rex A-Ang*. Rev. shield over long forked cross. London (Henry VII and VIII); York (Henry VII only; *Ebor/aci* or *Ebo/raci*; keys below shield for Abp. Thomas Rotherham, 1480-1500); Durham (Henry VII, *Dir/ham*, with initials of Bp. John Shirwood, 1484-94, or Bp. Richard Fox, 1494-1501, by shield; Henry VIII, *Dur/ram*, with initials of Bp. Thomas Ruthall, 1509-23, or Bp. Thomas Wolsey, from 1523); Canterbury (Henry VIII only; with initials of Abp. William Warham by shield).

Facing bust type; Henry VII, group III.
Canterbury (Archbishop Morton): Mm. tun both sides, or obv. only. Portrait as groats of type IIIC, crown with two arches, the outer jewelled. *henric Di Gra Rex An(g)*. Rosette stops. Lettering E. No *m* on rev. Pierced cross-ends. *Civi/tas/Can/tor*. Rare.

Sovereign type (henceforward).
Types A and B, period of Henry VII, group II.
A. Plain throne without pillars. Lis-headed sceptre. No mintmark. Lettering A. London (Ai), York (Ai), Durham (Aii).
- Ai Plain cross-ends (Winstanley I; Allen1i).
- London: No stops. ER.
- York: Sceptre in king's left hand. Pellet stops. Keys below shield (throughout York series). *Ebor/aci*.
- Aii Cleft cross-ends (W. – ; Allen 1ii).
- Durham: Trefoil(s) in lieu of pillar(s). Annulet before *henric* on one die. No stops. Upper limb of rev. cross terminates in crozier-head. *D S* (Shirwood) by shield. VR.

1464–1526

Pence

B. Throne with one pillar (to dexter), topped by trefoil. Lis or trefoil on sceptre. Cleft cross-ends. Lettering A. Some have trefoil stops.
   Bi 'Arches' in side panels of throne (Allen 2).
   London: Obv. mm. cinquefoil (W.IIa). Rare.
   York: No mm. Some have open crown, with trefoil above. *Ebor/* or *Ebo/*.
   Durham: Head of crozier (by sinister shoulder) occupies position of mm. Crozier head above shield, as in Aii. *D S* by shield.
   Bii Unarched throne (W.IIb; Allen 3i). No mintmark.
   London: Trefoil as sceptre-head. Rare.
   York: Lis sceptre-head. No stops. *Ebo/raci*.

C. Period of Henry VII, group III; Allen type 3. One or two pillars. Varied ornaments on pillar(s) and sceptre. Pierced cross-ends.
   Ci. Single pillar, to dexter. Lettering A. No mintmark. As Bii except for cross-ends. London, York; both rare.
   Cii. Usually single pillar. Still *Rex A-Ang*. Mannered lettering. Rosette stops.
   London: Mm. lis. Trefoil-topped pillar and sceptre. Also VR mules both ways with Ci.
   York: No mm. Lis or trefoils on pillar and sceptre.
   Ciii. Usually two pillars. Lettering similar to style E. Some late dies read *Agl, Ag* or *Al*.
   London: No mm., or (ER) mm. pansy on rev. No stops, or saltires. Lis-topped sceptre. Pillars topped by trefoils, lis, or (VR) crosses.
   York: No mm. No stops; or broken rosettes. Lis or trefoil sceptre-head. Pillars topped by lis, saltires, crosses or rosettes. Some (with cross ornaments) have saltires on panels of throne.
   Durham (Bp. Richard Fox, from Jan. 1495): No mm. or crozier. Lis or (VR) cross sceptre-head. Pillars topped by lis, trefoils, saltires, crosses or rosettes. Mitre above shield. *D R* (large) or *R D* (large, then small) by shield.

Group IV. London only. Two double-pillars; lis on pillars and sceptre. Saltire stops (sometimes broken). *Rex A, An, Ag, Al* etc. No mm. (Winstanley IVa). Pierced cross-ends. Lettering similar to (large) style E, or smaller (cf. style F), or rarely muled large/small.

Group V. Type as previous. London only. Lettering style G.
   (i) Mm. cross-crosslet (W.IVb), both sides or one side only (var. has cross-crosslet as *X* of *Rex*). Rare.
   (ii) Mm. pheon, both sides or one side only. Rare.

HENRY VIII, first coinage, 1509-26. *henric Di Gra Rex A(g)l (z)*, no numeral. Two double-lined pillars; lis on pillars and sceptre. Saltire stops. Pierced cross-ends. London, Canterbury, Durham.
   London: Mm. castle (obv. only), VR.
      Mm. crowned portcullis (obv. only), rare.
   Canterbury: initials *W A* on rev. for Archbishop William Warham.
      Mm. martlet (both sides), initials above shield. ER.
      Mm. pomegranate (obv. only), initials beside shield. VR.
   Durham (*Dur/ram*): initials *T D* for Bishop Thomas Ruthall, 1509-23, or *D W* for Thomas Wolsey, from 1523, above or beside shield. Mm. both sides.
      Mm. lis. (i) *T D* above shield. Also ER mule with Fox (*R D*) rev. of Henry VII (Ciii).
               (ii) *T D* beside shield, above (rare) or below line of cross.

Edward IV – Henry VIII

Pence

Mm. estoile (radiant star). *T D* beside shield, below line. VR.

Mm. spur rowel. *D W* beside shield, above line; cardinal's hat below. ER; also ER mule with second coinage rev. (mm. trefoil, *T W*)

HALFPENCE 1464 – 1526

FIRST PERIOD, 1464 - late 1480s. Traditional type with open crown; reverse cross and pellets (with cross-ends patty). Mm. on obv. only.

EDWARD IV, FIRST REIGN, light coinage (1464-70), types V-VIII and X. *Edward Di Gra Rex (A-Angl)*. ROYAL MINTS – London (V-VIII, X), Bristol (VII, VIII), Norwich (V, VI), York (VI-VIII).

V.   Mm. rose.
     London: Not always distinguishable from heavy coinage. Saltires by bust. Some have saltire or trefoil stops. Rare.
     Bristol (*B/ris/tow)*: Crosses by bust. ER.

VI.   Mm. sun.
     London: Saltires or trefoils by bust. No stops, or saltire(s) at end. Some have extra pellet in *tas* or *don* quarter. Var. *Edwad*. Rare.
     Norwich (*Nor/wic* or *vic*): Quatrefoils by bust. Var. *Eward*. ER.
     York: Saltires by bust. *Eward*. ER.

Types VII and VIII. London and Bristol, mm. crown; York, mm. lis.
     London: VII, Saltires, crosses or trefoils by bust; no stops, or rarely saltires; var. *Edwd*. VIII, Trefoils by bust and after *Rex;* VR.
     Bristol (*B/ris/tov* or *tow*): No stops. All VR. VII, Saltires or mill-rinds by bust. VIII, Trefoils by bust; var. *Edvard*.
     York: Mm. lis. VII, Saltires by bust; *Ebo/rac;* ER. VIII, Trefoils by bust; *raci;* vars. *Angl*; trefoil after *Rex;* all VR.

X.   Mm. long cross fitchy. London only. Xa, trefoils by bust, rare. Xb, no marks by bust, VR.

HENRY VI, SECOND REIGN (1470-1), ROYAL MINTS. *henricu D(e)i Gra Rex*.
London: Mm. short cross fitchy or Restoration cross. VR.
Bristol (*B/ris/tov*): Mm. cross (uncertain form). ER.

EDWARD IV, SECOND REIGN (1471-83). *Di* or *Dei Gra Rex (A)*. London sole royal mint: types XII, XIV-XIX, XXI-II. No marks by bust, except XIX. Bottom edge of bust has nick often visible on sinister side.

XII.   Mm. short cross fitchy. *Di*. VR.

Types XIV-XV. Annulet series.
XIV.   Mm. small annulet. *Di*. Vars. *Edwrd;* trefoil after *Rex; Di G Rex An*. Rare.
XV.   Mm. pellet-in-annulet. *Di* or *Dei*. VR.

Types XVI-XIX. Second cross series.
XVIa. Mm. cross over annulet (XV die altered). *Dei*. ER.
XVIb. Mm. cross with four pellets. *Dei*. VR.
XVII.   Mm. first pierced cross. No marks by bust. *Dei*. Var. saltire after *Rex*. Rare.
XVIII. Mm. pierced cross with pellet in one lower angle (XVIIIb). *Di* or *Dei*.
XIX.   Mm. second pierced cross. Pellets by bust. *Dei*. VR.
XXI.   Mm. cinquefoil. *Di* or *Dei*.

1464–1526

Halfpence

CANTERBURY MINT, 1464-83. *Edward Di Gra Rex. Civi/tas/Can/tor*.
Archbishop Thomas Bourchier, 1454-86.
Edward IV, First Reign, light coinage, 1464-70. Types 3-5 (cf. types of pence). With marks by bust.
3 (VIIa). Mm. pall. With or without trefoils by bust and as stops. No knot or spur. ER.
4 (VIIb). Mm. crown. Saltires or mill-rinds by bust. VR.
5 (VIII). Mm. crown. Trefoils by bust. VR.

Edward IV, Second Reign, 1471-83. Types 6-7. No marks by bust.
6. Mm. long cross fitchy (BW XXI). No marks on breast or on rev. *Di*. ER.
7. Mm. rose. *Dei*. *C* on breast. 7a, no *C* in centre of rev. (BW XIX). 7b, *C* in centre of rev. (BW XVIIIb). Both ER.

DURHAM MINT, 1473-83. Local dies (cf. pence of types a – e). Mm. rose. *D* in centre of rev. cross (rarely omitted). *De/ram*.
(a) Lis, crosses or no marks by neck. With or without *B* (for Bp. Laurence Booth, to 1476) to left of crown. *Edw*(or *v*)*ard Dei Gra Rex*. VR.
(d) *V* to left of neck. (? Bp. William Dudley, from 1476). VR.

EDWARD IV-V (1483), London.
XXII. Mm. halved sun-and-rose. *Edward Dei* or *Di Gra Rex*. Bust nicked at bottom on sinister side. VR.
RICHARD III, 1483-5. London only.
XXII (BH). Obv. of XXII in Edward's name, with mm. boar's head over halved sun-and-rose. ER.
II. Mm. boar's head. Gaunt bust, with long face. *Ricard Di Gra Rex*. ER.
III. Mm. sun-and-rose (SR2). Face smaller and rounder. VR.

HENRY VII, type I (1485 – c. 1488). London, Canterbury (Archbishop Morton). Open crown. *henric D(e)i Gra Rex*. Cross-ends no. 1. Lettering style A.
    London: IA. Mm. halved lis-and-rose. No marks by neck. No stops. Pellets joined. Rare. IB. Mm. cross fitchy (ER) or rose (rare). Usually crosses or trefoils by neck. Trefoil stops if any.
    Canterbury: IB only. Saltires by neck. *Rex An*. Mm. tun. *m* on centre of rev. cross. VR.

SECOND PERIOD, c. 1488 – 1526 (Henry VII-VIII). Traditional type modified, with arched crown. Cross-ends plain (briefly), then forked or ornamental. Mm. on obv. only, or none.
Groups II, III (Henry VII). London, Canterbury (Morton). *henric Di Gra Rex (An)*.
II. Tall crown with two plain arches. Lettering A.
IIa. Crosses or saltires by neck. Plain cross-ends.
    London: No mm. Stops trefoils or none. Rare.
    Canterbury: Mm. tun. *m* on centre of rev. cross. Var. has single arch (as in III). All VR; also ER Canterbury/London mule.
IIb. No marks by bust. London only. Mm. cinquefoil or none. Trefoil or saltire stops, or none. Cleft cross-ends. Rare; also VR IIb/a mule.
III. Lower crown with single arch. More elaborate lettering. Cross-ends cleft (III/II mules?), or pierced.

Edward IV – Henry VIII

Halfpence

London: Usually no mm.; exceptionally lis or pansy. Stops trefoils, none or rosettes (some broken).

Canterbury (Morton, but no *m* on rev.): Mm. none or lis. Stops saltires, rosettes or none. All VR.

Late Henry VII, groups IV-V. London, York (Archbishop Savage). *henric Di Gra Rex A(n)* or *A(g)l*. Very small bust. Saltire stops, if any. Pierced cross-ends.

London: IV. No mm. V. (i) Mm. lis, rare. (ii) Mm. pheon, rare.

York (Abp. Savage): IV. Mm. martlet or none. Key below bust, to left or right. VR.

HENRY VIII, first coinage (1509-26). London, Canterbury, York. Small bust with arched crown. *henric Di Gra Rex A(g)(l)(z)* – no numeral. Pierced cross-ends.

London: Mm. castle. VR.

Mm. portcullis (without chains).

Canterbury (Abp. Warham, *W A* by bust): Mm. Latin cross (alias cross fitchy) on rev., and ? on obv. ER.

Mm. pomegranate. Var. (mule?) appears to have cross before *Civi*. VR.

York (Abp. Wolsey): Key below bust. Mms. star, escallop. Both ER.

FARTHINGS 1464 - 1526
London only

FIRST PERIOD, 1464 - late 1480s. Traditional type with open crown; reverse cross and pellets (with cross-ends patty). Mm. on obv. only.

EDWARD IV, FIRST REIGN, light coinage (1464-70), types VIII and X. *Edward Di Gra Rex*.
 VIII. Mm. crown. Trefoils by neck. ER.
 Xa. Mm. long cross fitchy. Trefoils by neck. *Rex A*. ER.

Henry VI restored (1470-1) and Edward IV, second reign (1471-83): not recorded.

RICHARD III, 1483-5.
 III. Mm. sun-and-rose (SR2). ER.

Henry VII, type I (late 1480s): not recorded.

SECOND PERIOD, 1490s (and beyond?). Type as before, but single-arched crown and forked cross-ends. Diameter of circles 6 mm.

Henry VII, group III (?). *henric Di Gra Rex (A)*. No mm., or uncertain (anchor?). ER.

THIRD PERIOD, 1523 – 6. New types.

Henry VIII, first coinage. Mm. portcullis (obv. only). *henric Di Gra Rex*. Obv. portcullis in centre. Rev. Rose over centre of long forked cross. Saltire stops. *Civi/tas/Lon/don*. VR.

CHAPTER VIII

1526 - 1544
HENRY VIII

The second quarter of the sixteenth century was a period of continuing change throughout Europe, in politics and the economy, as well as in religion and culture. The power of the papacy and the loose structure of medieval Christendom were confronted by the new climate of the Renaissance, with its revival in art, letters and scholarship, and by the aspirations of emergent nation states. The doctrine of the Catholic church came under challenge from theologians such as Erasmus and its structure from Luther and the reformers. Princes vied with each other by diplomatic as much as by military means, while the expansion of commerce was aided by fresh sources of precious metals from the New World that kept the mints of Europe continuously busy. That the full impact of these forces was felt earliest and most powerfully in England was largely due to the personality of its king and the circumstances of his reign. Extravagant, despotic and ruthless, Henry VIII nevertheless, with his assault on clerical privilege and property, remained generally popular for many years, while the combination of a potent will, a passion for efficiency, and an elastic conscience enabled him to impose major changes on the governance and administration of his realm despite the difficulties inherent in transition from the medieval to the modern world. Fortunately, many of Henry's aspirations for himself and his dynasty coincided with his ambition for his kingdom – the enhancement of national prestige, the unification of the realm, the centralisation of government, and the elevation of royal authority at the expense of the church and of the remaining feudal franchises. Unfortunately, however, his reluctance to constrain expenditure resulted in periodic phases of great financial need, one of the eventual consequences of which was the collapse of a once highly respected currency.

The dramatic sequence of events that unfolded in the late 1520s and the 1530s was triggered by the king's exasperation at Queen Katherine's failure to provide him with a surviving male heir to perpetuate the House of Tudor. From 1527 Henry's attention was increasingly focused on the idea of annulment of his marriage, on the ground that he had married his deceased brother's wife within the church's prohibited degrees of affinity; but Wolsey's lack of success in obtaining Rome's approval, coupled with his conduct as Papal Legate, and the overmighty position he had built in power and wealth, led in 1529 to his disgrace, involving surrender of the Great Seal and most of his worldly riches, including the great palace of Hampton Court. His successor was the layman Sir Thomas More, as Henry sought progressively to replace the power of the church with secular authority. The breach with Rome was a gradual one, culminating in the Act of Supremacy in 1534, which ended papal jurisdiction and recognised the king as Supreme Head of the Church in England. More's refusal to take the oath of acknowledgement led to his own execution in 1535, and to the rise of Thomas Cromwell, author of the Act. Cromwell was appointed Vicar-General and as such proceeded to accelerate the dissolution of the monasteries and the sequestration of their wealth. Meanwhile Thomas Cranmer, succeeding Warham as archbishop of Canterbury, had in May 1533 declared the king's marriage to Katherine invalid, and shortly afterwards he publicly crowned Anne Boleyn whom Henry had already secretly married. Having borne him a daughter, the future Queen Elizabeth, in September 1533, Anne also failed to produce a Tudor prince, and alleged infidelity resulted in her own downfall and execution in May 1536. Henry's marital adventures are of particular relevance to numismatists, since his gold crowns and some base groats struck for Ireland carried both his own initials and those of some of his wives.

Henry VIII

Henry's third queen was Jane Seymour, whom he married in the same month as Anne's removal, but who was to die only days after she had fulfilled Henry's hopes by giving birth to a son in October 1537. With the Tudor succession now apparently secure, Henry no longer felt impelled to undertake another immediate marriage. Cromwell, however, was anxious to promote an alliance with the Lutheran princes of northern Germany but his plan to marry the king to Anne of Cleves misfired disastrously since Henry found her actively unattractive; married in January 1540, Anne was divorced in July, and Cromwell paid for the episode with his head. Henry's next wife, the young and flighty Katherine Howard, was queen only from July 1540 to February 1542, when she was beheaded for misbehaviour. Finally, in 1543, the king married the respectable widow Katherine Parr who outlived him.

One of Henry's broader objectives was to build a single realm within the British Isles. To this end he extended Parliamentary representation to Wales, Cheshire and Berwick (and even to Calais) and brought the lordship of Ireland within his kingdom. By Act of the Irish Parliament Henry became King of Ireland and Supreme Head of the Irish Church. His new title, already proclaimed in Ireland in the summer of 1541, was announced in England on 23 January 1542, but officials were not to be impeached for omitting to use it until after the end of April. In view of its importance in the king's eyes, the amendment of his titles on the coinage, the most widely promulgated medium of the government's official message, may then have been made without delay.

The span of Henry VIII's second coinage, from 1526 to 1544, was a time of change as rapid in financial matters as it was in political affairs. In 1526 Cardinal Wolsey had been given authority to reform the coinage in order to meet the problems of a rising silver price and of competition from continental gold coins. The following period saw not only a reduction in the weight of existing denominations in both metals, but the introduction of five new kinds of gold coin, three of which were soon superseded. It also saw the first steps in the debasement of the fineness of the coins which was to reach catastrophic proportions in the 1540s. Alongside these structural changes there were far-reaching developments in the production of the coinage and in the appearance of the coins. A realistic personal portrait of the king appeared for the first time, new designs and inscriptions were introduced, experiments were made in the use of the Roman alphabet and in due course the ecclesiastical coinages at Canterbury, York and Durham came to an end.

The first stage of the reform, in August 1526, involved revaluation of existing gold coins by ten per cent, the introduction of a new coin called the 'Crown of the Rose' and a reduction in the weight of the groat from 48 to 42 2/3 gr.. The crown, in following the weight and 23 ct. fineness of the French *écu*, was the first English gold coin to fall below the traditional standard of 23 ct. 3½ gr. for fine gold. But it held no competitive advantage against the *écu* and its currency value at 4s. 6d. was inconvenient. After consideration by a specially appointed committee a revised scheme was put in place by Wolsey in November 1526. This incorporated a new coin of standard gold called the George noble, further uprated the currency values of sovereigns and angels and replaced the 4s. 6d. crown with a 'Crown of the Double Rose'. The new crown was heavier than its forerunner but reduced in fineness to 22 ct., and current at 5s., thus resulting in a slightly higher mint price for gold. The arrangements put in place in November 1526 were repeated in an indenture of April 1533. By this time standard gold coins had been largely displaced by crowns, partly because of the more competitive rating of crown gold, but also because of the inconvenient valuations of the old coins after the latest rerating – the sovereign at 22s. 6d. and the angel at 7s. 6d. Another factor was that 22 ct. gold, more durable than standard gold, was more suitable for coins destined for active circulation, as was now increasingly the case. Although the George noble was an attempt to restore a coin with the traditional value of 6s. 8d., in the sixteenth century the mark of 13s. 4d. was gradually displaced by the pound as the principal unit of account, and the George noble failed to provide serious competition for the 5s. crown.

The financial harvest from suppression of the monasteries came from two sources: first, between 1536 and 1540, from seizure of their plate and jewels; and second, in the 1540s especially, from the disposal of lead from their rooves and the rent and sale of lands. Yet despite the scale of these appropriations the king again found himself in need of additional revenue. Previous recoinages had since the fourteenth century been undertaken to recognise the rising value of the precious metals on the international market, but for Henry VIII a reduction in the standard of the coinage was to be a deliberate move to create profit for the crown by deceiving the public, as the amount of alloy in the currency was progressively increased. This process, initiated formally in 1544, is described in the next chapter, but a surreptitious step towards it had been taken in 1542 while the terms of the 1533 indenture were still in operation. An indenture of May 1542 authorised reductions in the fineness and the weights of both gold and silver coin, as well as the addition of a shilling. While coinage continued at the old standard, parallel mint accounts show that debased coin was also struck under the new contract. Initially the bullion for this was supplied by the king from his own resources. Although the new coin would have enabled the mint to offer a higher price to attract bullion on the market, its issue would soon have resulted in the debasement being detected. The base coin was therefore kept in store until the changes could be made public. At first, between July and November 1542, there was steady production of the new coin in both metals until government sources dried up. Thereafter a little gold was struck in February and March 1543, and some silver in March-April 1543 and February-March 1544. By this time, however, it had become clear that a clandestine debasement could not work since volume would only be achieved when the matter was openly acknowledged. No base coins have been identified as belonging specifically to this period. It has sometimes been suggested that they would have been melted down, but there would have been little point in this if their weight and fineness were the same, or almost the same, as those of the early issues of the debasement proper, in 1544-5. If they were also of the same type, it is more likely that the base coins of 1542-4 would simply have been taken out of store when the new coinage was promulgated in 1544.

The designs of the coinage of 1526-1544 marked a further break with the medieval past. Henry was thirty-five years old in 1526 and his first personal coin portrait shows him well past his youth. Although he was to grow a beard the following year, his face on the groats remained unbearded until the debasement coinage of 1544. The new coins of 1526 are prominently adorned with Tudor roses: as key elements of the design of the two crowns, on the mast of the George noble and as the mintmark on the early gold and London silver. Henry seems to have seen the rose as a symbol not just of his dynasty but of himself personally, as reflected in accompanying inscriptions. The crowns and small silver have legends based on the motto *Rutilans Rosa Sine Spina* (The dazzling rose without a thorn), in conjunction with the king's own name or initial. Roman lettering, directly reflecting the French model, was adopted for the crown of the rose, and although most of the other coins still have the old Gothic forms, the Roman letter punches were also used for some early dies of groats, half-groats and the half-noble. Thereafter only Roman *M* or *N* are occasionally found, on crowns and smaller silver, until the Roman fount was eventually adopted more generally in the later 1540s. Another sign of change

Henry VIII

is the increasing use of a numeral after the king's name; adopted by Henry VII on groats and halves, and by Henry VIII in his first coinage on angels also, it was now extended to crowns, although not to the noble, nor yet to the small silver. In a further development, where space was needed, *8* sometimes replaced *VIII*, as on the crown of the rose, the half-crown and late groats from 1542 on which the Irish title was inserted. Finally, there are cases at this period of the king's name being switched to the reverse, as was to happen more conspicuously under Edward VI. Thus the George noble, adapted from the types of the angel, has saint and motto on the obverse, ship and titles on the reverse, as once before, on early angelets of Edward IV. More curiously, while the king's titles are placed around the shield on the obverse of the crowns of the double rose, his name itself appears before the *Rutilans* motto with the rose on the reverse.

Fine Gold

Although some £20,000 was minted in gold coins of traditional fineness between 1526 and 1544, the coinage of crown gold in the same period was perhaps (allowing for some missing accounts) around twenty times as great. As survivors of limited output, and as candidates for reminting during the debasement, all the fine gold coins – sovereigns, angels, nobles and their halves – are understandably rare. No ryal of the second coinage has yet been found, but its existence is attested by inclusion in a pyx trial in company with nobles and angels. Sovereigns did not reappear until the mid-1530s, and in the early stages of the new coinage most of the fine gold minted was presumably in George nobles which, with their halves, are the only fine gold coins known with the inaugural mintmark rose.

MINTMARKS ON FINE GOLD, 1526-1544

	ROSE	LIS	SUNBURST	LIS	ARROW
Noble	x				
Half-noble	x	r			
Angel	(x)	x?	x		
Angelet	(x)	x?			
Ryal	(x)				
Sovereign			x	x	r

r – reverse only; (x) – not known, but presumably struck;
x? – lis-marked coins may be of this period.

With saint and dragon on the obverse and the familiar ship on the reverse, the George noble reflects the influence of the design of the angel, whose previous slot as the half-mark coin it had now come to occupy. In full armour, with his cross on the breastplate, a mounted St. George is shown attacking a dragon beneath his horse. Despite the difficulty of portraying a more elaborate composition than the standing figure on the angel, and on a slightly smaller scale, the noble is an impressive coin. There are two distinct types, the first of which, although illustrated in an Antwerp merchants' handbook of 1580, has only lately been represented by an actual specimen. On this the saint is brandishing a sword behind his head, reminiscent of the type of the gold riders of the Low Countries familiar since the fifteenth century. The reverses of both types of the noble differ from that of angels in having a rose instead of a shield above the hull of the ship. On the first type, however, there are also two extra mast-crosses, flanking the central cross and at a lower level, in an allusion to Calvary. With all Roman letters on the obverse and some on the reverse, this is undoubtedly the earlier of the two types. For some reason – perhaps the inclusion of the two thieves' crosses – the first type must have been found inappropriate and was quickly replaced. The second type, with Gothic lettering throughout, retains the central rose on the reverse, but otherwise reverts more closely towards the design of the angel, with a single cruciform mast, and the royal initials *h K* beneath its arms, where angels have *h* and rose. At the same time the obverse type was improved by giving St. George a spear, as St. Michael had on angels (he could scarcely have reached the dragon with his sword). The motto on nobles is taken from a fourth-century hymn by Prudentius (another line of which had already provided the legend for Scottish copper pennies of James III): *Tali Dicata Signo Mens Fluctuare Nequit* – Consecrated by such a sign the mind cannot waver. This inscription is placed on the obverse, with reference to the cross on St. George's breast, but since there was also a (more prominent) cross on the reverse, it could equally have been used on the upper die, as in the case of the cross legends on angels and angelets. On the first type the infinitive is *fluctuare*, on the second in the deponent form *fluctuari*. The legend is spelt out in full on the first type, but with some shortening on the second; *Signo* is usually contracted to *Sig*, followed by a very small *o*, as in contemporary manuscripts. Although rare today, the noble is known from several dies, with slight variation in the king's titles on the reverse. Oddly, the regnal numeral is lacking; since long forms of *hibernie* figure on the noble, this could easily have been abbreviated as on other denominations if space was wanted, so it may be that the new coin, not issued by his predecessors, was felt of itself to be sufficiently identified with its originator.

Only three half-nobles are known. They follow the second type of noble in their design and (although more contracted) their inscriptions. For many years the denomination was recorded only from a single specimen, with mintmark rose both sides and predominantly Roman letters placing it near the start of the new coinage. Recently two others have come to light, both with some Gothic letters on the reverse. Although all known George nobles have mintmark rose only, one of the two new halves has mintmark lis on the reverse, indicating a more extended period of issue for the noble series than has sometimes been assumed.

All angels and halves of the second coinage are very rare, their issue largely displaced by the less fine, but more convenient and more profitable 5s. crown. No rose-marked angel is known, although there is an accomplished continental copy of one in the British Museum. The presence of angels and nobles in the pyx trial of June 1527 shows that both were struck in the first year of the new coinage, but despite their slight overlap the issue of nobles and angels must have been largely consecutive. Little fine gold appears to have been coined in the 1530s, once crown gold had become established, which would account for the shortage of angels of this period. With the exception of one angel with sunburst, all known second coinage angels and angelets (these from a single pair of dies) have mintmark lis. Whitton noted one angel with the lis on the obverse apparently punched over another mark; he suggested that this might be lis over sunburst (by analogy with sovereigns), but the space looks too narrow for so wide a mark as sunburst and lis over rose seems a more likely possibility. The much less rare angels of the early debasement period also have mintmark lis, but they can be easily distinguished by their Arabic *8* and the Irish title.

Sovereigns, originally provided by the commission of 1489, were included in a regular mint contract for the first time in the indenture with Rowlett and Bowes of

Henry VIII

April 1533. Second coinage sovereigns occur with mintmarks sunburst, lis and (on the reverse) arrow. The sequence of these marks is demonstrated by die-combinations and recut marks. Only two obverse dies were involved, and one of these was the portcullis die from the first coinage which underwent three stages of alteration. The earliest of the post-1526 sovereigns has a sunburst on each side punched over the portcullis without entirely obliterating it. The same pair of pre-1526 dies was then again amended by the impression of a lis over the sunburst, with some minor adjustment to adjacent letters. Very few sovereigns are known from the old portcullis dies in this third state, but the same obverse is also found with a new reverse die on which the lis is the original mark. At this point the old obverse die appears to have been withdrawn for more fundamental treatment, and a new die with mintmark lis brought into use. This second obverse die, paired with two lis and one arrow reverse, shows some minor variations of design, in the king's crown, in having three saltires added below the portcullis, fleurs instead of pellets below the chains, and the reading *Frane* (later corrected) for *Franc*. Finally, the first obverse die was restored to service after a thorough refurbishment involving replacement of much of the inscription, recutting of the fretted decoration of the back of the throne, and alterations to the king's face and crown and the fleured border. In this fourth state the die is found coupled with two lis and two arrow reverse dies, including all those used with the second obverse. The later of the arrow reverse dies has a single tressure, instead of a double one, and lacks the small lions and lis within it. The lis/arrow coins are the least rare of Henry VIII's sovereigns of this coinage.

Like the sunburst angel the sunburst sovereign is unique. The revival of this great coin, designed for presentation rather than currency, after a lapse of many years and with a rare and abnormal mintmark, naturally invites speculation as to its circumstance and purpose. Potter suggested that the choice as mintmark of the sun breaking from the clouds may have been designed to convey happiness after tribulation on some special occasion, such as celebration of the birth of Henry's long-awaited son on 12 October 1537 (or conceivably in anticipation of it). The first dated entry for the minting of fine gold in the incomplete mint accounts is in the year 1536/7, and although fine gold had undoubtedly been struck earlier in the coinage it is tempting to associate the 31 lbs. then recorded with the sunburst sovereign and angel, even though this would imply slight slippage in the Michaelmas accounting date, if the issue of these coins was indeed related to the royal birth. Some more mundane explanation for the sunburst gold must therefore remain a possibility.

Crown Gold

Henry's first essay at a gold coin below the ancient standard of fineness was not a success. The crown of the rose, of 23 ct. gold and valued at 4s. 6d., is known from three specimens only. Its types were closely based on the French crown the obverse of which, with a crowned shield of arms, had given this coin and its imitators the names of *écu*, *scutum* or crown since the fourteenth century. Roman lettering (except for *h*, usually Gothic), as already for some years standard elsewhere in northern Europe, contributes to the generally foreign appearance of Henry's first crown. The reverse shows the fleured cross of the French model adapted by a large rose imposed upon its centre, and with an English lion and a crowned *h* in alternate angles. One form of the reverse inscription begins with *Dns hib*, in continuation of the king's titles from the obverse, followed by the *Rutilans Rosa* formula; the other (followed on later crowns) repeats the king's name before *Rutilans*, so emphasising the identification of the rose with his personal image. The neat appearance of Henry's new crown, and of those that followed, is enhanced by their having a fine wireline circle within the beaded ring.

The successor to Henry's first crown was a little heavier but, with its fineness lower at 22 ct., it was to pass for the round sum of 5s. Its reverse type, instead of the cruciform design of its predecessor, was a full blown rose with a double layer of petals, with a crown above and crowned *h* and *K* beside it. Rather oddly, Henry's name (now with his numeral *VIII*) was left on the reverse with the *Rutilans* legend. To save space, the contracted form *Sie Spia* occurs before the end of the rose mark, and is standard thereafter – another example of the tendency for *n* to be dropped, which on coins dates back to Henry VII, with *A(n)gl* and *he(n)ric*. The king's titles, separated from his name, are disposed on the obverse around the shield. There have long been differences of view about which sides of the crowns of the double rose should be referred to as obverse and reverse, with implications for which was the lower and which the upper die. Kenyon described the rose side of the crowns, but the shield side of the halfcrowns, as the obverse on the ground that these were the sides that carried the king's name. Since the design of both denominations is the same, this arrangement was clearly unworkable and subsequent writers such as Brooke and Whitton described the rose side of both denominations as the obverse. However, a stronger case can be made for the opposite view. Of the five main items for consideration, only one (the crown of the double rose in Henry's name) has the king's name on the rose side; all the other four – the crown of the rose, at the head of the series; the halfcrown in Henry's name; and the crown and halfcrown in Edward's name – have both name and titles on the shield side. So, even taking the name as the decisive factor (which in the Renaissance period it often was not), the argument favours the shield side as the obverse, as it had been for two centuries in the case of the foreign gold coins that the English crown was designed to challenge. This is accordingly the arrangement adopted here.

Some of the early crowns of the double rose with mintmark rose include Roman letters in their inscriptions, like the groats. The only other mintmarks recorded on crowns of 1526-42 are the lis and arrow, comparable but extremely rare coins with mintmark pheon all having the Irish royal title and so belonging to the period 1542-4. With the first change of mintmark, to the lis, crowned initials were added to the obverse also, providing an immediate differentiation from the superseded crown of the (single) rose. The last of the Roman letters, *N*, still sometimes occurs with mintmark lis. Mintmark arrow replaced lis before the end of the king's marriage to Katherine in May 1533, since the first arrow crowns still have *h K* by the designs. Also with mintmark arrow are coins with *h A*, *h I* and *h R*. Those with *h A* refer to Henry's second marriage, to Anne Boleyn, from May 1533 to May 1536; and those with *h I* to his third, to Jane Seymour, from May 1536 to October 1537. The *h R* crowns mostly belong to Henry's wifeless years from 1537 to 1540 but, since there are no late crowns with *h A* for Anne of Cleves or *h K* for his last two Katherines, *h R* was presumably left unchanged on English coins during his later marriages; however, the series of base Irish groats had not begun until after the end of his first marriage and those with *h K* may therefore be attributable to Katherine Howard. It must be doubtful how much notice had been taken of the correct initials on the crowns, because there are extensive interchanges between dies with different initials (although not between *h A* and *h I*), some of Katherine's surviving beyond the demise of her successor. The combinations are shown in the following table.

Henry VIII

ROYAL INITIALS ON CROWNS OF THE DOUBLE ROSE

Obv. (shield)	*h K*	*h A*	*h I*	*h R*
Rev. (rose)				
h K	x	m	m	
h A	m	x		m
h I			x	m
h R	m		m	x

m = mule

The halfcrowns follow closely the design and arrangement of the crowns of the double rose, although without the small crowns above the initials. Because of the reduced space, the king's name was dropped from the reverse, and combined with abbreviated titles on the obverse (including *8* for *VIII*). None of the halfcrowns of this period are common. Like the crowns, those with mintmark rose have no initials on the obverse, and some (probably the earliest, to judge by their Roman letters) have none on either side; others have *h K* on the reverse. Halfcrowns with mintmark lis, and *h K* on both sides, include a lis/rose mule with the lis on the obverse over rose. With mintmark arrow there are halfcrowns with either *h K* (one with obverse arrow over lis) or *h I* on both sides, but none with *h A*. The only halfcrowns with *h R* are those with mintmark pheon and the Irish title.

Tower Mint Silver Coins

The reduction of the weights of the silver coinage in 1526 led to a very large increase in bullion brought to the mint, and groats of the new coinage are extremely plentiful. They bear the mintmarks rose, lis, arrow, sunburst and pheon, but the sequence of these marks has been a matter of dispute because of the use of the lis at more than one point in the series. On the earliest groats, with mintmark rose, there are abundant signs of the typological experiment so frequently found with a new coinage. Of three main versions of Henry's portrait the first (i) shows him with short hair and a heavy jowl; the second (ii) with a pointed chin and an unbroken line from brow to nose (the 'Greek profile'); and the third (iii), which became standard throughout the rest of this extensive coinage, with hair longer and more swept back, less drapery, a slighter jowl and a (shorter) Roman nose. The crown on all busts also marks a break with the past, consisting now of a central cross patty between two fleurs-de-lis, instead of three ornamental leaves. Groats with busts i and ii are rare, but rose groats with bust iii are common. The first groats with bust i are from dies very carefully made. In the forks of the reverse cross they have a floral ornament, instead of a saltire as soon became the norm. Much of the lettering – notably *A, C, E* and *N* - is from a handsome Roman fount which, despite its neatness and clarity, was not used for very long. It gradually gave way to an alphabet of the old style, the last Roman letter to survive being the plain *D*, also used reversed as a closed Gothic *C*. The combination of Henry's portrait in contemporary style with a medieval circumscription gives the groats of this coinage a somewhat anomalous appearance. With bust i and sometimes with bust ii the longer forms *Di, Gra* and *Rex*, rather than the normal *D G R*, are found. Thereafter the main variation of obverse reading is in the French title, ranging from *Fra* to *France* (never *Francie*), although the form *heric* is occasionally found on a late rose or early lis die. The stops on all denominations of this coinage are saltires throughout, as they had been since the last years of Henry VII.

MINTMARKS ON TOWER COINS 1526 – 1544

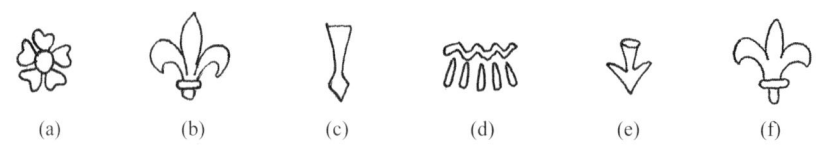

(a) Rose; (b) Lis A and B; (c) Arrow; (d) Sunburst; (e) Pheon; (f) Lis C.

Late rose groats are muled both ways with mintmark lis, and share with early lis groats a brief revival of the spelling *Adiutoe* (as often found in the previous reign) as well as a distinctive form of the letter *m* with the outside of the right limb chipped. Lis groats are extremely common, but mules with pheon and details of lettering show that some of them belong to the period after mintmarks arrow and sunburst. Those attributable to the period between rose and arrow (lis A) may be distinguished by having one of two forms of the letter *F*, both with an open front and a nearly flat top (Potter's F2 and F3). Because of weakness in striking the *F* may not always be clear, so that F2 could be confused with the later F4; but groats of lis A with F2 can also be identified by the chipped *m* and the form of the letter *A*, which has a flat bar on early second coinage groats but a peaked top later.

Arrow groats are also very abundant. Whitton had believed that this mark on groats came relatively late in the series, but epigraphical details enabled Potter to locate it after lis A. Some of the earliest groat dies with mintmark arrow show it more like an arrow-head with distinct barbs, and this form has been noted punched over lis. There are also rare mules both ways between lis A and arrow. The more usual form of the arrow mark is pointed, but splayed at the feathered end, and thus looking rather like the bolt of a crossbow. Some of the arrow groats extend the English title to *Aglie*. Sunburst groats, although not rare, are nevertheless much scarcer than the preceding marks. The possibility that sunburst had some special function is suggested not only by the revival of the sovereign (contrasting with an absence of crowns) but also by the lack, unique in this coinage, of any mules in silver with other marks. A few sunburst groats have the open F3, but most show a new, heavier punch, with a short, thick closing bar sloping inwards and an undulating top (F4); Potter argued persuasively that when this letter occurs on lis groats it demonstrates that they belong to a second period (lis B) of the use of this mark, post-sunburst, a sequence that now finds corroboration from the halfpence. The letter *e* may also be indicative: from sunburst (if not earlier) the central bar is often so weakly struck as to give the appearance of a *c*. Further confirmation of Potter's sequence is found in the form of mules both ways between lis and pheon, which show F4. There is also a reverse die of that period without mintmark which has been noted with both lis and pheon obverses. Pheon groats are rare, and the currency of lis B is likely to have extended to 1540 or beyond.

Henry VIII

LETTER FORMS ON GROATS OF HENRY VIII'S SECOND COINAGE

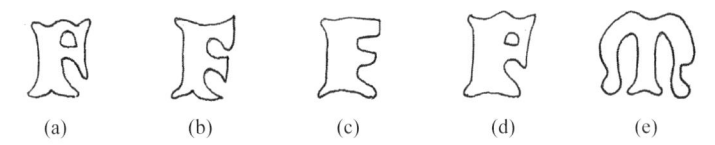

(a)   (b)   (c)   (d)   (e)

(a) F1, mm. rose; (b) F2, mm. rose and lis A; (c) F3, mm. lis A, arrow and sunburst;
(d) F4, mm. sunburst to pheon; (e) Chipped *M,* mm. rose and lis A.

Late groats with the profile portrait, post-dating the proclamation of Henry's Irish title in January 1542, read *Agl Fra z hib Rex*, with *8* for *VIII* to accommodate the longer style. These rare coins normally have mintmark pheon on both sides, or obverse pheon, reverse lis. Even rarer are examples with lis both sides, or lis/pheon, pointing to a third period with mintmark lis, beginning just before the end of the profile bust coinage (lis C), but continuing on early base groats with the facing bust. This late lis is more compact than that used in the lis A and B periods; its side foils are less curled, and the horizontal band is wider. Whitton remarked that the appearance of the *hib Rex* profile groats differed from that of their predecessors, since they seemed to have been made from puncheons and flans prepared for the third coinage, while Potter referred to them as being of obviously baser metal – the implication being that these groats were representatives of the first debased coinage, authorised by the covert indenture of May 1542. Under this, however, not only was the fineness lowered, but the amount to be coined per pound was increased from 45s. to 48s., reducing the weight of a groat from 42 2/3 gr. to 40 gr.; and as *hib Rex* profile groats generally weigh measurably above 40 gr., they do not meet the terms of this indenture. Brooke may therefore have been correct in associating these coins with the last issues at the 1526 standard recorded in the mint accounts up to March 1544.

There is less variety among the smaller London silver of the second coinage. Halfgroats have mintmarks (on both sides, or obverse only) rose, lis, arrow and sunburst, but are not known with pheon except on extremely rare coins with the Irish title as on groats. In another echo of the groats, *Di* is found early in mintmark rose, but apart from the shortening of *Fra* there is no other variation in the obverse legend. *Adiutoe* is invariable on reverses. There are no experimental busts on rose halfgroats, but some Roman letters occur on a few early dies. These do not include a Roman *M*, but curiously this letter does occur on a few coins with later marks. Reverses with mintmark rose lack saltires in the forks of the cross except when Roman letters are included. Otherwise there is little obvious consistency throughout the series in the inclusion or absence of a mintmark on reverse dies, or of saltires in the forks. As with groats, rose and lis halfgroats are both common, the latter more so. These two marks are muled both ways. Some of the lis/rose mules have the obverse lis over a rose; and lis reverses altered to arrow are also known. Arrow halfgroats are scarce, those with sunburst extremely rare, no mules being known with either of these marks. Whether any late lis halfgroats were produced in parallel with the lis B groats is not clear, but the absence of pheon halves except with *hib Rex* suggests that relatively few halfgroats were being struck at London anyway in the last years of the second coinage.

Although retaining the types of the first coinage, pence and halfpence of the second coinage may nevertheless be readily distinguished, even when their mintmarks are unclear, by their strange inscriptions. Their obverses read *h D G Rosa Sine Spina* (often with the *n*s omitted), instead of having the king's name and titles. London halfpence also differ from their predecessors in replacing the customary pierced cross-ends with a cross patty. On earlier halfpence of the second coinage the hair is put in from the same neat and narrow punches as had been used before 1526. Later the hair is wider, and spiky or serrated. Some halfpence with both mintmarks lis and arrow have the new and wider hair. As it is unlikely that punches for the two styles would have been in parallel use for an extended period, the readiest explanation of this pattern is that the old hair punches were replaced during the currency of mintmark arrow, and that the coins with new hair and mintmark lis should be attributed to the revival of this mark (lis B) in the period after arrow and sunburst, in the later 1530s, as in the case of lis B groats. On the (pre-arrow) lis A halfpence, as they should thus be called, the mintmark is usually large, but a much smaller mark occurs on some, and on all of the lis B coins. Confirmation that the change of hair occurred in the mid-1530s is to be seen in the halfpence of the archbishops: all those of Wolsey (d. 1530) and Warham (d. 1532) have the tight and narrow hair, while those of Lee and some of Cranmer's have the later style. Lettering on halfpence of this coinage is always Gothic except for a Roman *N* which occurs on a number of coins from lis to sunburst. None of the London pence of the second coinage are common. The Tower mint seems to have concentrated on groats and halves at the outset, since pence and halfpence with mintmark rose are much rarer than those with lis or arrow. Both denominations are extremely rare with sunburst. A late variety of halfpenny, known only from a few specimens on which the mintmark is not clear, has an annulet on the centre of the reverse cross, as on early Tower halfpence of the debasement period.

Farthings of this coinage, although of several varieties, are all extremely rare. One type (B), with a rose on the reverse cross, follows the 1523 design, while another (A) has no rose on the reverse but a single large pellet in each angle of the cross. Both types have the inscriptions *Rutilans Rosa* and *Deo Gracias*. Since type B had been introduced before 1526 while type A was later to be used during the debasement, it could have been expected that, within the second coinage, type B would have preceded type A. However, it is the pellet type that is known with mintmark rose (as well as with lis and sunburst) while the rose type has only been found at London with mintmark arrow and at Canterbury from dies delivered in 1534, suggesting that there may have been a (perhaps temporary) reversion to the 1523 type in the 1530s. More specimens are needed before a reliable pattern can be established.

No single scheme of London mintmarks will fit the various species of gold as well as silver in this coinage. The groat sequence – rose, lis A, arrow, sunburst, lis B, pheon, lis C – may, in the absence of evidence to the contrary, be taken as relevant to the lesser London silver, although lis B has not been differentiated for halfgroats or pence, while pheon (pre-*hib Rex*) and lis C are each represented only by groats. Correspondence of lettering between London and York groats suggests that lis A began before Wolsey's death in 1530, and since lis groats are so common it may reasonably be assumed that lis A accounted for a significant part of the very large output of Tower silver in the years 1527-30. In the earlier stages of the coinage the mintmarks on crowns followed those on silver, placing the introduction of arrow before Katherine of Aragon's removal in May 1533, in which case arrow could perhaps have been the mintmark adopted following the appointment in early April, as one of the new masters, of Martin Bowes who was to use this mark during the debasement (a sheaf of arrows being the crest to his coat of arms). Whether or not the sunburst sovereign and angel are representatives of the fine gold coinage recorded in 1536/7, c. 1537 would be a suitable approximate date for this mintmark, having regard to known mint output and numbers of surviving silver coins, on the assumption that many of the lis groats belong to the lis B period. Although the return

Henry VIII

of lis after sunburst on silver is matched on sovereigns, the last sovereigns of the second coinage have reverse mintmark arrow and in this respect are following not the silver but the crown gold, on which arrow remained in use until silver and crown gold finally came together in 1542 with mintmark pheon and the Irish title. In view of the relative rarity of pre-*hib Rex* groats with mintmark pheon, the introduction of this mark can hardly be dated before 1541.

Ecclesiastical Mints

Canterbury, York and Durham continued to make an indispensable contribution to the currency. In February 1529 Wolsey had resigned from the see of Durham and his death in November 1530 created a vacancy at York also. At Durham he had been succeeded in February 1530 by the eminent lawyer Cuthbert Tunstall, who as bishop of London had kept the Privy Seal in the 1520s, while the new archbishop of York, from December 1531, was the theologian Edward Lee. For some years a reluctant Warham had come under increasing pressure from Henry and Wolsey to hasten an end to the marriage with Katherine, and when the aged archbishop died in August 1532 he was replaced at Canterbury with the more compliant Thomas Cranmer, whose temporalities were confirmed in April 1533. Thus, within a space of less than five years each of the three ecclesiastical mints was operating for a new incumbent, and each of these was to be the last to exercise the long-standing privilege of coinage attaching to his see. Collectively, coins of all the mints are plentiful, although pence are only common of Durham, which was restricted to this denomination, while much of the coinage for the archbishops was in halfgroats. Whitton argued that the episcopal coinages may have ceased in November 1534 following the passing of Cromwell's Act of Supremacy. But while this was undoubtedly an important step in the curtailment of ecclesiastical privileges it is not evident that their mints were an immediate casualty. Certainly they had ceased to function before the debasement; and there are no *hib Rex* halfgroats of Cranmer or Lee attributable to the years 1542-4. But there is evidence to suggest that all three mints had remained active for most of the second coinage. A pyx trial was held at Canterbury in December 1537. In April 1536 the archbishop of York commanded the master of his mint not to deal in monastic plate fraudulently converted to private use, and silver from the shrine of St. Wilfrid at Ripon was sold to him in 1541-2. At Durham the mintmaster paid annual rent as late as 1540/41. Since the activity of episcopal mints tended to be intermittent, it is possible that their closure was due to no more than a shortage of bullion at the time. When Canterbury and York were revived in 1545 it was of course as royal mints – it would have been against the crown's whole purpose for large profits to accrue to the bishops from the debasement.

In general features the episcopal coins, from dies made at the Tower, follow the London pattern closely, although a mint name continues to figure on the larger silver instead of the London *Posui* legend, and there is some variation in the reverse cross-ends on pence and halfpence. Some early halfgroats read *Di G*, as at London, and at Canterbury Roman letters are in evidence also. With rare and often probably accidental exceptions, the initials of the bishop are placed by the shield (or beside the bust on halfpence), as in the preceding coinage, together with the cardinal's hat below for Wolsey at York and Durham; but York coins no longer carry keys beneath the shield – perhaps simply the consequence of less space on smaller dies. At York Wolsey and Lee each used the initial of his surname, and so probably did Cranmer at Canterbury, although his *T C* might theoretically have been a reference to his see (*Cantuariensis*), in the same way as had long been the case with *D* at Durham. Wolsey, however, having used *D W* in the first coinage, to distinguish himself from the *T D* of his Durham predecessor Thomas Ruthall, now in the second coinage dropped the customary *D* and aligned his initials at Durham with the personal *T W* that he had already been using before 1526 at York.

CANTERBURY MINTMARKS OF HENRY VII'S SECOND COINAGE

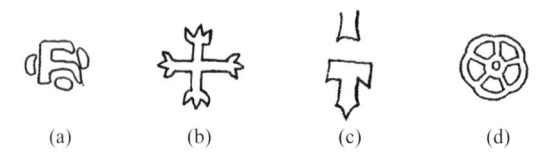

(a) (b) (c) (d)

(a) Warham's uncertain mark; (b) Cross patonce, Warham; (c) *T,* Warham; (d) Catherine wheel, Cranmer.

Halfgroats are the only common coins of Canterbury, where the regular mintmarks on Warham's coinage were an uncertain composite mark, a cross patonce and then a *T*. The first of these has been variously interpreted as a worn cross patonce, a rose or a pomegranate. Epigraphical details, however, show that the cross is later than the uncertain mark and is therefore ruled out. Although when worn this enigmatic mark might resemble a pomegranate, Warham's last pre-1526 mark, or a rose, neither of these explanations is convincing, since when unworn it shows a nearly rectangular outline (like an *h* with a low hump and a long top bar) imposed on an irregular, perhaps floral, design. An early and extremely rare variety of Canterbury halfgroat has mintmark rose on the reverse, reflecting the London mintmark of the time, but perhaps no more than a die-sinker's error. Some halfgroats with Warham's mark omit his initials *W A*, but since these include coins with Roman letters (less rare, incidentally, than on London halfgroats) they are far too early to be attributed to the *sede vacante* after his death, and this may be simply an oversight on a batch of early dies produced in a hurry. The reading *Civitor Cantor* on one halfgroat also suggests careless haste, although the same mis-spelling occurs, less understandably, on a York halfgroat of Wolsey. Successive forms of the letter *L* and halfgroats with cross patonce/*T* (perhaps too plentiful to be regarded as mules in the normal sense) make it clear that mintmark *T* followed cross patonce and was the last of Warham's mintmarks. Possibly it stands for William Tyllsworth, if already connected with the coinage, since he was appointed master of Cranmer's mint in January 1534 and was later to use his initial as mintmark when working the Canterbury mint for the king from 1545. There are two versions of the *T* on halfgroats: the more ornamental one has a pointed tongue issuing downwards from its foot, which in the plainer version is indented. Although Tyllsworth's indenture of January 1534 refers only to the usual three denominations, from halfgroat to halfpenny, the February warrant for the supply of dies to the archbishop's mint also included the farthing, the only occasion on which an episcopal mint was empowered to strike the smallest denomination. That the Canterbury farthing dies were delivered and used has been shown by the recent appearance of a specimen of the rose type (B), as used at London with the contemporary mintmark arrow. For reasons unexplained (it could hardly have been a cynical reference to his part in removing the queen), Cranmer's sole mintmark was the Catherine wheel, which appears not only on the regular denominations

Henry VIII

but also on the tiny farthing. Although mintmarks are usually found on both sides of the archbishop's halfgroats, they are sometimes omitted on halfgroat reverses and occur only on obverses of the smaller coins. Pence of Canterbury are known with Warham's mark, cross patonce, *T* and wheel, but all are of considerable rarity. Unlike those of London in this coinage, which have pierced cross-ends, Warham's pence (but not Cranmer's) have open forks. Warham's halfpence are also very rare, Cranmer's less so. Usually they have a cross patty on the reverse, but one with mintmark *T* has pierced cross-ends and was regarded by Whitton as a mule with a pre-1526 reverse despite the interval of time.

York Mintmarks of Henry VIII's Second Coinage

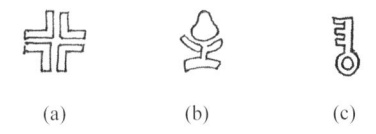

(a) Voided cross, Wolsey; (b) Acorn, Wolsey; (c) Key, Lee.

The York coinage is chiefly remarkable for the famous Wolsey groat, the only instance of this coin being struck at an archiepiscopal mint. It has sometimes been implied that one of the charges of treason made against Wolsey in 1529 was that he had usurped the king's prerogative by issuing so large a coin, but the actual indictment related to the placing of his cardinal's hat under the king's arms on groats – or, as Shakespeare put it:

> That, out of mere ambition you have caused
> Your holy hat to be stamp on the King's coin.
> *Henry VIII*, Act III, sc. 2.

Wolsey's death, on his way to London in the following year to answer his charges, preempted a response from the architect of the 1526 recoinage which could have thrown interesting light on coinage policy and the role of the ecclesiastical mints. The Wolsey groats have either the mintmark cross voided, in continuation from the first coinage, or an acorn, and there are mules both ways between the two. The attribution of some voided cross groats without *T W* to the vacancy following Wolsey's death will not work, either on grounds of the sequence of marks or in view of the retention of the offending hat. Most of Wolsey's voided cross groats, like most of London with mintmark rose, have the letter F1, while the rare Acorn groats all have F2 as on London coins of the late rose and early lis A periods. Wolsey's halfgroats have only the voided cross, although this mark is sometimes varied by the addition of a pellet in one angle. All Wolsey's halfpence of this coinage are very rare. So few of them are known that more clear specimens are needed to establish the stages of the series. With a key still below the bust, as pre-1526, there are examples both with and without *T W* beside it, the mintmark when visible being the voided cross. An acorn halfpenny, however, with initials, is without a key, matching the absence of keys on the reverse of York halfgroats of this coinage.

Dies with the initials *E L* for Archbishop Lee were authorized in April 1532. The mintmark on his coins is an upright key. His halfgroats are common, but pence and halfpence much rarer. Halfgroats with mintmark key, but no hat or initials, have usually been attributed to the vacancy of 1530-1; although this seems chronologically possible, the supposed use of Lee's mintmark in advance of his appointment does cause one to wonder whether the omission of initials was any more intentional in this case than in others of the period. Furthermore, in 1532 the mintmaster, George Gale, admitted to the production only of halfpence after Wolsey's fall in 1529, which implies that he did not mint halfgroats in 1530-1, if he was being truthful. Lee's initials are occasionally shown in reverse order on halfgroats and halfpence, presumably by accident rather than with a different meaning such as *Lee Eboracensis*. The *E* is Roman on halfgroats, on pence and halfpence Gothic for reasons of space.

DURHAM MINTMARKS OF HENRY VIII'S SECOND COINAGE

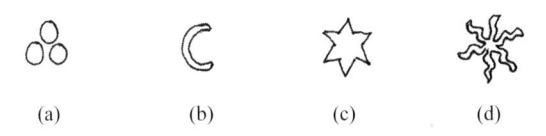

(a)   (b)   (c)   (d)

(a) Trefoil, Wolsey; (b) Crescent, Wolsey; (c) and
(d) Plain star and Estoile, Wolsey and Tunstall.

The reappearance of the York penny under Archbishop Lee, after an interval of more than thirty years since the restraint of 1499, is no more readily explicable than its previous extended absence. In the meantime, however, the pence-only mint of Durham may have gained from the lack of competition at York, since Durham pence of Henry VIII are very common. Even though the mint operated for Wolsey from November 1527, when it was reopened, only until his resignation in February 1529, his pence of the second coinage, with *T W* and his hat on the reverse, are found with three different mintmarks, trefoil, crescent and star. Their sequence is shown by trefoil mules with spur rowel (from an obverse die of the first coinage) and with crescent, and by the retention of the star, sometimes as an estoile but otherwise unchanged, on all later coins of this mint. Those without initials or hat are attributable to the vacancy in 1529, followed by a much more abundant series for Tunstall (*C D*) belonging to the occasions when the mint was operational in 1530-34 and 1537-41 – a long period for a single mintmark.

Mint Accounts

From 1526 the accounts were based on the Troy pound of 5760 grains instead of the traditional 5400 grain Tower pound. When the weight of the silver coins was reduced by minting 45s. (540d.) from the Troy pound, this was equivalent to 42s. 2¼d. (506.25d.) from a Tower pound compared with 37s. 6d. (450d.) between 1464 and 1526.

Because of the differences in their fineness, there are separate accounts for fine gold (at the ancient standard of 23 ct. 3½ gr.), used for sovereigns, George nobles and angels (and their halves), and for the 22 ct. gold used for crowns and halfcrowns of the double rose. Challis gives a total figure for fine gold minted between 1526 and 1544, but three surviving individual entries amount only to 91 lbs. out of the 746 lbs. that this represents. No account is extant for the minting of 23 ct. gold into crowns of the rose in the second half of 1526. Most of the entries for gold follow the usual pattern of accounting periods

Henry VIII

from one Michaelmas to the next (shown as 1526/7, etc.), but the dates for silver are more erratic. Both involve a break at March 1533 related to the appointment of Rowlett and Bowes as masters. No accounts have been found for either metal for 1534/6, and there are three other gaps in the record for gold and one for silver. Separate figures are recorded for gold and silver struck experimentally at reduced weights and fineness between July 1542 and March 1544 under the secret indenture of May 1542.

Incomplete data exist for pyx trials during the period. Silver, fine gold and crown gold are all recorded as having been tried on 4 June 1527; silver and crown gold on 30 October 1534 and 16 June 1540; and silver alone on 21 November 1527, 20 May 1530 and 1 March 1533. There was another trial on 8 May 1537 of which the details are not known, and an undated (early) document records that ryals, nobles, half-nobles, angels and angelets were then tried together.

FINE GOLD (23 ct. 3½ gr.) £27 per lb. Troy			
1536/7	£849	M.1543-31.3.1544	£851
1540/1	779	Total 1526-44	20,157
CROWN GOLD (22 ct.) £25 2s. 6d. per lb. Troy			
1526/7	£122,036	1536/7	£25,403
1527/8	30,930	M.1537-31.5.1540	78,218
1528/9	13,396	1.6.1540-M.1540	No accounts
1529/30	9,911	1540/1	10,869
1530/1	8,046	1541/2	No accounts
M.1531-28.2.1533	No accounts	1542/3	6,922
1.3.1533-30.10.1534	27,311	M.1543-31.3.44	4,566
1.11.1534-M.1536	No accounts		
SILVER at 45s. per lb. Troy			
22.10.1526-4.6.1527	£30,832	M.1537-30.4.1538	£13,012
4.6.1527-20.5.1530	213,200	22.4.1538-21.4.1542	155,635
20.5.1530-1.3.1533	90,911	21.4.1542-M.1542	No accounts
1.3.1533-20.10.1534	46,053	1542/3	5,800
1.11.1534-M.1536	No accounts	M.1543-31.3.1544	5,418
1536/7	42,519		

Base coinage, 1542-4 Gold (23 ct., £28 16s. per lb.) Silver (9 oz. 2 dwt.?, 48s. per lb.)
1.7.1542-31.3.1544 £15,595 £52,927

Calendar 1526 – 1544

1526 Commission to Cardinal Thomas Wolsey (24 July) to align English coinage with continental: from 22 Aug., currency value of existing gold denominations uprated by 10 per cent; Crown of the Rose (23 ct.; 4s. 6d.) introduced. From 5 Nov., further enhancement of fine gold coins, to 12½ per cent (sovereign, 22s. 6d.; angel, 7s. 6d.); introduction of George noble (fine gold, 6s. 8d.) and Crown of the Double Rose (22 ct., 5s.); weight of silver coins reduced by 11 per cent.

1527 Durham: mint reopened (Nov.).

1529 Durham: Wolsey translated to Winchester from Durham (8 Feb.); followed by indictment in Oct.
1530 Durham: Cuthbert Tunstall appointed (temporalities 25 March); mint indenture 4 July.
York: death of Wolsey (29 Nov.).
1531 York: Edward Lee appointed (temporalities 3 Dec.).
1532 Canterbury: Abp. Warham d. (22 Aug.).
York: dies authorized for Abp. Lee (12 April).
1533 Indenture (6 April) with Ralph Rowlett and Martin Bowes for continuation of existing coinage.
King's marriage to Katherine of Aragon annulled (23 May); marriage to Anne Boleyn (25 Jan.), declared valid 28 May; birth of Princess Elizabeth (7 Sept.).
Canterbury: Thomas Cranmer appointed to see (temporalities 19 April).
1534 Thomas Cromwell appointed Secretary to Henry VIII; Act of Supremacy (Nov.), Henry recognised as Supreme Head of the Church in England.
Canterbury: Warrant (Feb.) for archbishop's dies includes farthing.
1536 Commission (6 March) to Tower mint to coin silver c. 10 oz. fine for Ireland.
King's marriage to Anne Boleyn invalid (17 May; execution 19 May); marriage to Jane Seymour (30 May).
1537 Prince Edward (VI) b. 12 Oct.; Queen Jane d. 24 Oct.
1540 King's marriage to Anne of Cleves (6 Jan.), annulled (9 July); marriage to Katherine Howard (8 July).
Commission (13 July) to Tower mint to coin Irish groats at 9 oz. 2 dwt. fine.
1541 Durham: final closure of mint.
1542 Henry proclaimed King of Ireland (23 Jan.).
Queen Katherine Howard executed (13 Feb.).
Secret indenture (16 May) with Bowes and Rowlett for gold at 23 ct. and silver at 9 oz. 2 dwt. (?), and at reduced weights.
1543 King's marriage to Katherine Parr (12 July).
1544 Existing mint organisation terminated (31 March).
Commission (13 May) to Tower mint to reduce Irish groats to 8 oz. fine.
Indenture (28 May) for English coin similar to May 1542, with new mint organisation.

WEIGHTS AND FINENESS, 1526 – 1544

REGULAR COINAGE.
Fine Gold: 23 ct. 3½ gr. fine; £27 per lb. Troy (5760 gr.)

Sovereign (22s. 6d.)	240 gr.		15.55 g.
Ryal (11s. 3d.; not known)	120		7.78
Angel (7s. 6d.)	80		5.18
Angelet (3s. 9d.)	40		2.59
George noble (6s. 8d.)	71	1/9	4.61
Half-noble (3s. 4d.)	35	5/9	2.30

Crown Gold: (i) Aug. – Nov. 1526, 23 ct.
Crown of the Rose (4s. 6d.) – intended to be equivalent to the French *écu* which had a nominal weight of c. 53 gr. (3.43 g.)
(ii) From Nov. 1526, 22 ct.; £25 2s. 6d. per lb. Troy

Crown of the Double Rose (5s.)	57	21/67 gr.	3.71 g.
Halfcrown (2s. 6d.)	28	44/67	1.86

Henry VIII

Silver: 11 oz. 2 dwt. fine; 45s. per lb. Troy
    Groat (4d.)   42   2/3 gr.   2.76 g.
    Halfgroat (2d.)   21   1/3   1.38
    Penny   10   2/3   0.69
    Halfpenny   5   1/3   0.35
    Farthing   2   2/3   0.17

PROVISIONAL BASE COINAGE, May 1542 – March 1544
Gold: 23 ct.; £28 16s. per lb.
    Sovereign (20s.)   200 gr.   12.96 g.
    Angel (8s.)   80   5.18
    Ryal, half-angel and quarter-angel *pro rata*
Silver: 9 oz. 2 dwt. (?); 48s. per lb.
    Teston (12d.)   120 gr.   7.78 g.
    Groat (4d.)   40   2.59
    Penny   10   0.65
    Halfgroat, halfpenny and farthing *pro rata*

SOVEREIGNS 1526 - 1544

Value (of earlier sovereigns) Aug. 1526, 22s.; from Oct. 1526, 22s. 6d.
Types as pre-1526: Obv. King on Gothic throne, portcullis at feet; *henricus Dei Gracia Rex/Anglie et Franc Dns hib*. Rev. Shield on large Tudor rose, within double tressure enclosing lions and lis (except on one arrow die); *Ihesus Autem Transiens Per Medium Illorum Ibat*. Gothic letters except *M*; saltire stops.
Mm. sunburst over portcullis both sides (altered dies of first coinage). Saltires in spandrels. ER.
Mm. lis: lis over sunburst (same dies as before), or new dies (*Frane*). Saltires in spandrels. ER.
Mm. arrow, rev. only, combined with both lis obverses. No saltires in spandrels. The later of the two revs. has single tressure, without lions or lis. VR.

No ryal, or half-sovereign, of this coinage is extant; but the coin features in an early pyx trial.

ANGELS AND ANGELETS 1526 - 1544

ANGEL. Value 7s. 6d.
Types as pre-1526: Obv. St. Michael spearing dragon; *henric VIII D G R Agl z F-France*. Rev. Shield on mast of ship, *h* and rose beside; *Per Cruce Tua Salva Nos Xpe Rede*. Saltire stops; Gothic letters.
Mm. rose. Not known, but pyx record and contemporary imitation indicate that it existed.
Mm. lis. One obv. has lis over another mark (rose?). All VR.
Mm. sunburst. ER.

ANGELET. Value 3s. 9d.
Types as angel; *Agl z Fr. O Crux Ave Spes Unica*. Saltire stops; Gothic letters.
Mm. lis. One pair of dies. ER.

1526–1544

GEORGE NOBLES AND HALF-NOBLES FROM 1526

NOBLE. Value 6s. 8d.
1. Obv. St. George (with his cross on breastplate) mounted, to right, with sword behind head; prostrate dragon beneath. *Tali Dicata Signo Mens Fluctuare Nequit*, Roman letters. Rev. Rose over ship, with three cruciform masts; no royal initials. *henric D G R Agl z Franc Dns hybernie*, mixed Roman and Gothic letters. Mm. rose both sides. Saltire stops. Unique.
2. As type 1, but saint attacking dragon with lance; *Fluctuari*, and some abbreviation (*Dica, Mes, Neqt*, etc.). Rev. Rose over ship, *h K* above, single cruciform mast. *henric D(i) G R Agl(ie) z Fra-Franc Dns hiber-hibernie*. Mm. rose both sides. Gothic letters. VR.

HALF-NOBLE. Value 3s. 4d.
Type as George noble 2: obv. St. George, rev. ship. Inscriptions more abbreviated. Saltire stops. ER.
Obv. mm. rose. Roman letters, *Fluctuari Neqt*. Rev. (a) mm. rose; Roman letters except *h; hybe*. (b) mm. rose; Gothic letters except first *N; hi*. (c) mm. lis; mixed letters; *hib*. Revs. a and b share an obv. die.

CROWNS 1526 - 1544

1. Crown of the Rose (Aug. 1526): value 4s. 6d.
Obv. Crowned shield. *henric 8 Dei Gra Rex Agl z Frac*. Rev. Cross fleury with rose on centre; lion and crowned *h* in alternate angles. *Dns hib*, or *henric, Rutilans Rosa Sine Spina*. Mm. rose both sides. Wireline inner circles. Roman letters (but *h* mostly Gothic). Saltire stops. ER.
2. Crown of the Double Rose (from Nov. 1526): value 5s.
Obv. Crowned shield, usually between crowned initials. *Dei G R Aglie France Dns hibernie* or abbrev. (except pheon). Rev. Crowned double rose between crowned initials. *henric VIII Rutilans Rosa Sine Spina* or abbrev. (often *Sie Spia*). Usually Gothic letters. Saltire stops.
Mm. rose. *h K* (large letters) on rev. only. Earlier dies have mixed Roman and Gothic letters.
Mm. lis (rare obv. var. has lis over rose). *h K* (smaller) both sides. Var. with Roman *N*. Also ER lis/rose mule.
Mm. arrow. Crowned initials on both sides. Gothic letters throughout.
1. *h K* (1533). One rev. has arrow over lis. All rare.
2. *h A* (1533-6). Rare; also VR mules both ways with *h K*.
3. *h I* (1536-7). Also VR mule *h I/h K*.
4. *h R* (from 1537). Rare; also mules (all VR or ER) *h K/h R, h R/h A, h R/ h I* and *h I/h R*.
Mm. pheon (1542-4), with Irish royal title. *h R* both sides. As before, but *Dei G Aglie Franc z hiberei* (or *–ie*) *Rex*. ER.

470

Henry VIII

HALFCROWNS 1526 - 1544

Halfcrown of the Double Rose: value 2s. 6d.

Obv. Crowned shield, usually between initials. *henric 8 Di Gra Rex Agl z France* or abbrev. (except pheon). Rev. Crowned double rose, usually between initials. *Rutilans Rosa Sine Spi(n)a*. Saltire stops. Letters usually Gothic.

Mm. rose. No initials on either side (VR); or *h K* on rev. only. Some with mixed Roman and Gothic letters.

Mm. lis (over rose on one obv. die). *h K* both sides. Var. has Roman *N*. Rare; also VR mule lis (over rose)/rose.

Mm. arrow. Initials both sides. All letters Gothic.
1. *h K* (1533). One obv. has arrow over lis. VR.
3. *h I* (1536-7). Some have dots beside waist of I. Rare.
h A and *h R* not recorded.

Mm. pheon (1542-4), with Irish royal title. *h R* both sides. *henric 8 D G Agl F z hib Rex*. ER.

LONDON GROATS AND HALFGROATS, 1526 - 1544

GROATS

1. With English and French titles only (1526-Jan. 1542).
Obv. Profile portrait of Henry VIII to right. Three busts (i and ii, mm. rose only): (i) Heavy jowl, short hair, full drapery (Laker bust A), VR; (ii) Greek profile, pointed chin (Laker B and C), rare; (iii) Roman nose, longer hair (Laker D). Normally *henric VIII D G R Agl z Fra-France*. Rev. Shield over long cross, saltires in forks. *Posui/Deu A/diuto(r)/e Meu*. Stops saltires.

Mm. rose. Bust i, VR; ii, rare; normally bust iii. Vars. with busts i and ii: *Di, Gra, Rex*; half-rose in cross-ends (VR); some with Roman *A, C, D, E, N*. Vars. (late) with bust iii: *Adiutoe*; *heric*.

Mm. lis A (sometimes omitted on rev.). Bust iii only (henceforward). Letter *F* open-fronted (F2, F3); right limb of *m* often chipped. Early vars.: *Adiutoe*; *heric*. Also mules rose/lis (rare) and lis/rose.

Mm. arrow, either barbed (early, rare; sometimes over lis), or (normally) pointed. Some read *Aglie*. Also rare mules arrow/lis A and lis A/arrow.

Mm. sunburst. No mules. Letter F3 (VR) or F4 (with heavy front and wavy top).

Mm. lis B. Letter F4. One rev. die omitting mm. also found with obv. mm. pheon.

Mm. pheon. Also mules pheon/lis B and lis B/pheon. All rare.

2. With Irish royal title (1542-4). Type as before but *henric 8 D G Agl Fra z hib Rex*
Mm. pheon. VR.
Mm. lis C. ER; also mules lis C/pheon (ER), pheon/lis C (VR).

HALFGROATS

1. With English and French titles only (1526-41).
Obv. Profile portrait of Henry VIII to right. *henric VIII D G R Agl z F-Fra*. Rev. Shield over long cross, sometimes with saltires in forks. *Posui* legend; always *Adiutoe*. Usually Gothic letters. Saltire stops. Mm. both sides or obv. only.

Mm. rose. Early dies (VR) include Roman letters; also var. *Di*.

Mm. lis. Some have Roman *M*. Also rare mules lis (sometimes over rose)/rose and rose/lis.

1526–1544

London halfgroats

Mm. arrow, sometimes over lis. Some have Roman *M*.
Mm. sunburst (obv. only). Roman *M*. ER.
2. With Irish royal title (1542-4). Type as before but *henric 8 D G Agl Fra z hib Rex*. Mm. pheon both sides. ER.

LONDON SMALL SILVER 1526 - 1544

PENCE
Obv. Sovereign type; *h D G Rosa Si(n)e Spi(n)a*. Mm. usually on obv. only. Rev. Shield on long cross with pierced ends. *Civitas London*. Gothic letters. Saltire stops.
Mm. rose. Rare.
Mm. lis. ER var. has mm. on rev. also.
Mm. arrow.
Mm. sunburst. ER.

HALFPENCE
Obv. Facing bust with single-arched crown; *h D G Rosa Si(n)e Spi(n)a*. Mm. on obv. only. Rev. Long cross patty and pellets. *Civitas London*. Some Roman *N*s, otherwise Gothic letters. Saltire stops.
Mm. rose. Narrow hair. Gothic *n* on rev. VR.
Mm. lis A (mm. often large). Narrow hair. *N* Roman or Gothic.
Mm. arrow. Hair narrow or wider. *N* Roman or Gothic.
Mm. sunburst. Wider hair. Roman *N*. ER.
Mm. lis B (small). Wider hair.
Late type (ER), with wide hair, mm. uncertain, has annulet on centre of rev. cross.

FARTHINGS
Obv. Portullis; *Rutilans Rosa*. Rev. *Deo/Gra/ci/as*. A: Long cross patty with single pellet in each angle. B: Rose on long cross patty. Gothic letters. Saltire stops.
Mm. rose, rev. A. Mm. lis, rev. A. Mm. arrow, rev. B. Mm. sunburst, rev. A. All ER.

CANTERBURY FROM 1526

Archbishops: 1. William Warham (d. Aug. 1532), *W A* by shield or bust; mintmarks, Warham's uncertain mark, cross patonce and *T*.
2. Thomas Cranmer (from April 1533), *T C* by shield or bust; mintmark Catherine wheel.
Types as London, except as stated. *Civitas Cantor*; normally Gothic letters; saltire stops.

HALFGROATS
1. Warham. *W A* by shield.
Mm. Warham's mark both sides or obv. only; or with rev. mm. rose (ER). Vars.: *Di*; some Roman letters; saltires in forks; or *W A* omitted.
Mm. cross patonce both sides.
Mm. *T*, ornamental or plain. Also cross patonce/*T*.

Henry VIII

Canterbury

2.   Cranmer. *T C* by shield.
Mm. Catherine wheel, both sides or obv. only.

PENCE
1.   Warham. *W A* by shield. All have cross-ends with open forks. Mm. on obv. only.
Mm. Warham's mark. ER.
Mm. cross patonce. VR.
Mm. *T*. ER.
2.   Cranmer. *T C* by shield.
Mm. Catherine wheel (obv. only). Pierced cross-ends. Var. has *T D* (i.e. reversed *C*) by shield. All VR.

HALFPENCE
1.   Warham. *W A* by bust. All have narrow hair.
Mm. Warham's mark. Rev. long cross patty. ER.
Mm. cross patonce. Rev. long cross patty. ER.
Mm. *T*. Rev. pierced cross-ends (mule with pre-1526 rev.?). ER.
2.   Cranmer. *T C* by bust. Narrow or wider hair.
Mm. Catherine wheel. Rev. long cross patty. Rare.

FARTHING
Cranmer. Rose on centre of long cross on rev. (as London type B). Mm. Catherine wheel. ER.

YORK FROM 1526

Archbishops: 1.   Thomas Wolsey (d. Nov. 1530), *T W* by shield or bust, cardinal's hat below shield; mintmarks, voided cross and acorn.
              2.   Edward Lee (dies from April 1532), *E L* or *L E* by shield or bust; mintmark key.
Types as London, except as stated. *Civitas Eboraci*; Gothic letters; saltire stops.

GROATS
Wolsey only. *T W* by shield, hat below. Usually saltires in forks of cross-ends.
Mm. voided cross. Var. (VR) omits *T W*; early var. reads *Di*.
Mm. acorn. Also mules both ways with voided cross. All rare.

HALFGROATS
Mm. on both sides.
1.   Wolsey. *T W* by shield, hat below.
Mm. voided cross (sometimes with pellet in one quarter). Var. *Civitor*.
2.   Lee. *E L* (or *L E*) by shield; no hat.
Mm. key. Rare var. omits initials.

PENCE
Lee only. *e L* by shield. Mm. key (obv. only). Pierced cross-ends. ER.

1526–1544

York

HALFPENCE
1. Wolsey. Narrow hair.
Mm. voided cross. With or without *T W* by bust; key below. ER.
Mm. acorn. *T W* by bust. No key. ER.
2. Lee.
Mm. key. *e L* or *L e* by bust. Wider hair. Rare.

DURHAM PENCE FROM 1526

Bishops: 1.   Thomas Wolsey (to Feb. 1529), *T W* and cardinal's hat on rev.; mintmarks, trefoil, crescent and star (or estoile).
           2.   Cuthbert Tunstall (from July 1530), *C D* by shield; mintmark star.

Sovereign type as London, except as stated. *Civitas Durram;* Gothic letters; saltire stops.

1.   Wolsey. *T W* by shield, hat below.
Mm. trefoil, both sides or obv. only. Cross-ends with open forks, or more rarely pierced. Also ER mule with pre-1526 obv. (mm. spur rowel).
Mm. crescent (obv. only), at various angles. Open forks or pierced cross-ends. Also rare mule crescent/trefoil.
Mm. star (plain) both sides or obv. only. Pierced cross-ends. Also ER mule star/trefoil.
Sede vacante (issue of c. Feb. – c. Aug. 1529).
Mm. star or estoile, obv. only. Without initials or hat. Pierced cross-ends. Rare.
2.   Tunstall. *C D* by shield.
Mm. star both sides; or star or estoile on obv. only. Pierced cross-ends, sometimes with saltires within. Gothic or Roman *M*.

CHAPTER IX

1544 - 1551
Debasement, Henry VIII – Edward VI

Although in his last years Henry VIII's health was poor, neither his strength of will nor his unorthodox attitude to government deserted him. The last of the major initiatives of his reign was a ruthless exploitation of the coinage in pursuit of easy income for the crown. When Henry died on 28 January 1547 the debasement that he had launched was in full swing, and it was left to his successors to grapple with the problems that it had created. Edward VI (1547-53) was only nine years old when he succeeded his father and, although he took a precocious interest in public affairs, the administration of the realm was in the hands of the Council of Regency that Henry had named shortly before he died. The king's maternal uncle, Edward Seymour, was declared Protector and soon created Duke of Somerset. Well-meaning but maladroit in the face of political and religious unrest, Somerset was displaced in 1549 by the tougher and more ambitious Earl of Warwick. But it was to be two more years before the government was in a position to commission a new coinage of fine gold and silver in October 1551.

The combination of Henry's financial needs with a general rise in the value of the precious metals in Europe had led inevitably to further reconsideration of the coinage. Notwithstanding formidable levels of taxation, and despite the remarkable wealth that flowed from the dissolution of the monasteries and the disposal of their assets, the crown could not fund war on two fronts, against both France and Scotland. Additional revenue was essential and this was to come from plundering the coinage. Experiments with debasement had been made in Ireland in the 1530s and the temptation to adopt a similar course in England was not long resisted. The secret indenture of May 1542 with the master-workers at the Tower had provided for the minting of both gold and silver at reduced fineness, and the silver also of lower weight. Gold was to be struck at 23 carats, instead of 23 ct. 3½ gr., and although the weight of the angel remained at 80 gr. its value was raised from 7s. 6d. to 8s. Provision was made for the addition of a quarter-angel (now with the convenient value of 2s.) and for the revival of the sovereign, half-sovereign and shilling (or 'teston'). The sovereign was now to be rated again at 20s., instead of 22s. 6d., but its weight was more than correspondingly reduced, from 240 to 200 gr. The amount of gold coin to be struck from a pound of less fine metal was thus now raised from £27 to £28 16s. The situation regarding the silver is less clear, because of the ambiguous wording of the 1542 indenture: the pound of coined silver was to hold ten ounces of sterling silver and two ounces of alloy, that is, two ounces of alloy more in the pound than previously. This has sometimes been taken to indicate a fineness of 10 oz., but 10 oz. of sterling silver (92.5 per cent. fine) mixed with 2 oz. of alloy would give a standard of 9 oz. 5 dwt., while 2 oz. more of alloy than in the previous standard of 11 oz. 2 dwt. would mean 9 oz. 2 dwt. for the new silver money. Between July 1542 and March 1544 £52,900 of silver coin was minted at this standard, some of it presumably in testons, together with £15,600 of 23 ct. gold. But coinage of both metals at the 1526 standards had not ceased: so we also find entries in the accounts between September 1542 and March 1544 for £11,200 of 11 oz. 2 dwt. silver, for £850 of fine gold and £11,500 of crown gold. The baser coin was not issued to the public, but stored in the Jewel Tower at the Palace of Westminster until the new coinage could be openly announced. Because the mint could not otherwise attract bullion, the need for this had become pressing by 1544, and the debasement was formally proclaimed on 16 May, with the fineness of the silver now set explicitly at 9 oz. 'out of the fire'.

The higher prices that could now be offered by the mint brought in large amounts of bullion and old coin, and between June 1544 and March 1545 £149,000 of base silver was minted and £166,000 of 23 ct. gold. But with campaigns against the French and Scots to be financed Henry's need for more profit was becoming desperate, and in March 1545 the coinage of both metals was further debased, gold to 22 ct. and silver to only 50 per cent. fine (6 oz.), a level at and below which base silver is commonly described as billon. In order to accelerate the recoinage, mints at York and Canterbury were reopened for the king in May and June respectively, a new mint was established in Southwark from July, and a separate operation under Thomas Knight was added at the Tower. In the twelve months to March 1546 the combined output of all the mints was £440,000 of 6 oz. silver, while coinage of 22 ct. gold, confined to Southwark and the two establishments in the Tower, amounted to £372,000.

Despite these substantial issues and the considerable profits that they yielded, the crown needed even more, and in April 1546 a further reduction in the standards of gold and silver was authorized, the former to 20 ct. (the lowest in the English gold coinage since the seventh century), and the latter to one third silver (4 oz.). Output continued at a vigorous pace, particularly of silver, and another mint was added at Bristol. Accounts relating to the year to March 1547, two months after the death of the old king, show totals of £263,000 coined in 20 ct. gold and £454,000 in 4 oz. silver. In June 1547 an impractical plan by Somerset to produce gold coin at 23 ct. fine and silver at 10½ oz. was rapidly aborted. Although the Council of the young king was anxious to restore the standard of the coinage, circumstances did not yet allow it and the existing pattern continued unchanged until 1549. In order to maintain supplies of bullion to the mints, buying prices of gold and silver were gradually raised, reducing the rate of profit but encouraging further heavy output. Although the volume of gold coinage declined during the period, that of silver increased as a result of the withdrawal and reminting of testons. Most of these had been struck before March 1546, at 9 oz. or 6 oz. fine, and their conversion into smaller coins of 4 oz. silver produced large extra revenue. In April 1548 it was announced that testons would cease to be legal tender after the following December, but few came in at first and although some were reminted into smaller silver during 1548 at Southwark and York their currency was later extended to May 1549, and finally to July, by which time all the mints had participated in the conversion on a significant scale.

In March 1548 the Dublin mint was revived, and in the following December a new mint was added in the Strand, "at Duresme Place in the suburbes of London". Both of these were indented to mint silver coin according to the 4 oz. standard of 1546; but Durham Place was soon to be authorized to coin gold also, and to participate, along with all the other English mints except York, in a new coinage of shillings. The first issue of these shillings, produced only in February 1549, was struck at twice the fineness (8 oz.) of the smaller silver but at half the weight, 8 oz. fine instead of 4 oz. and 96s. instead of 48s. to the pound. But because of the small size of these finer shillings a new format was adopted in April 1549 whereby the fineness was reduced to 6 oz. but the weight proportionately increased (72s. to the pound). More than £700,000 of 6 oz. shillings was struck at the Tower and Southwark, much of it in 1549 from the reminting of testons. But these mints produced very little of the smaller silver, which was now left mainly to York, Canterbury and Bristol. Canterbury also struck £74,000 of 6 oz. shillings, but Bristol only £3,000 and York none. There are no accounts of the debasement period for any of these last three mints beyond 1549, nor for Durham Place where shillings and smaller silver had been struck in limited amounts throughout the year. The mint at York, however, was to participate in the new fine coinage of 1551, being the only debasement mint, apart from the Tower itself, to do so.

The revival of the shilling early in 1549 was accompanied by a change in the pattern of the gold coinage. Instead of 20 ct. gold at £30 to the pound, the 22 ct. standard of 1545/6 was restored but at a lower weight (£34 to the pound), and gold on this basis was issued from the Tower and Southwark in 1549 and 1550, with a very small contribution from Durham Place in 1549. Finally, a completely different set of gold coins was commissioned at the end of 1550, from Southwark only, consisting of a sovereign of 24s. and an angel of 8s. and their halves, to be struck at £28 16s. to the pound (as in 1544/5) but at the ancient fine gold standard of 23 ct. 3½ gr. Such fine coins were undervalued at these rates and all or most of the £2,800 worth that was minted pursuant to this commission during the first half of 1551 was probably for the king's own use.

The last and worst of the billon coins of the debasement period have, however, survived in reasonable abundance. On 14 April 1551 the Tower and Southwark mints were commissioned to mint shillings at only 3 oz. fine: between April and July sums of £80,700 were issued from Tower I and £92,200 from Southwark, with an unrecorded contribution from Tower II. Ostensibly the reason for this final spasm of debasement was to raise funds to clear debt and prepare for restoration of a true silver coinage, but the pressing financial needs of the crown were as ever a contributory factor. At the same time plans were made to decry the base silver by 25 per cent., the shilling to ninepence and the groat to threepence, but although the new values were proclaimed on 30 April the government made the extraordinary decision that they should only be effective from 31 August. Not surprisingly, this led to rumours of a further reduction in values, as indeed duly transpired when the teston was decried to 6d. on 16 August.

In September 1551 Warwick's administration was actively engaged in planning for a new coinage of fine silver, and on 5 October a fresh commission was issued providing for silver at 11 oz. 1 dwt. fine, to be accompanied by fine gold at £36 per pound and crown gold at £33 per pound. Although the mint began to produce the new coin from October 1551, relatively little bullion was available as the public were reluctant to take the heavy loss involved in exchanging their billon coins for fine silver. More than half of the £42,000 of new silver coin struck by March 1552 had come from bullion supplied by the High Treasurer. Yet even now the issue of base coin was not entirely abandoned. In December 1551 the York mint, which was also engaged in the fine silver coinage, was instructed to convert old coin into pence and halfpence at 4 oz. fine, and this also happened at the Tower, which was to continue to produce small change of 4 oz. silver throughout the reign of Mary (1553-8). Not until 1561 was the base coin of the 1540s and 1550s eventually demonetized. As a preliminary to this, in September 1560 Edwardian 6 oz. shillings were cried down by 25 per cent, from the sixpence at which they had been current since 1551, to 4½d., and the 3 oz. shillings to 2¼d. To establish their new values the 6 oz. shillings were to be countermarked with a portcullis before the king's face, and the 3 oz. shillings with a greyhound behind the head; but few countermarked shillings have survived because they were called in during 1561 for reminting into fine Elizabethan coin.

Although new mints were not operational before the early summer of 1545, the senior responsibilities for the coinage had been reformed in May 1544 in a way suggesting that a large expansion of minting and minting capacity, and its profit potential, were already in preparation. Sir Edmund Pekham, cofferer to the king, was appointed High Treasurer. Sir Martin Bowes, a senior mint official since the 1520s and master-worker since 1533, and Stephen Vaughan were designated Under-Treasurers for the Tower mint. Each of the new mints was to have its own Under-Treasurer, an office that emphasizes the importance of the royal revenue more directly than the old title of master-worker. The other Under-Treasurers, appointed in 1545, were Thomas Knight at the second establishment within the Tower, Sir John York, translated to Southwark from his post as assay-master at the Tower, and William Tyllsworth and George Gale, previously master-workers to the archbishops, at Canterbury and York. In due course William Sharington was appointed at Bristol (April 1546), Thomas Agard at Dublin (February 1548), and John Bowes at Durham Place (December 1548). Several of these Under-Treasurers have left an identifiable mark on the coinage in the form of initials or heraldic devices on the dies used to strike coin for which they were accountable: for example, *K* for Knight, *WS* for Sharington, a swan for Martin Bowes and an ostrich head for Pekham. The use of a bow as mintmark at Durham Place is also obviously a reference to its Under-Treasurer's name, but evidence is lacking to determine whether the inclusion of three bows, as well as a swan, in Sir Martin's arms should be taken as indication of a family connection between the two of them.

Throughout the debasement period Tower I remained the senior establishment. Its output was almost always on a larger scale than that of any other mint, accounting for more than £1m. of silver coin from 1544 to 1551 and £3/4m. of gold. The Tower supplied all the dies used at Southwark, Canterbury and York, and a few to Bristol and Dublin where separate engravers were employed for much of the time. Only Durham Place had an independent engraver throughout. Not surprisingly at a time of such frantic minting some mistakes were made in the delivery of dies, resulting for example in mules between dies with Tower and Southwark mintmarks. But care was generally taken to ensure that dies carried the appropriate marks, as evidenced by alterations such as *K* over arrow, *E* over arrow and various others. Instead of a mint name as elsewhere, reverse dies at both the Tower mints, from teston to halfgroat, used the old *Posui Deum* motto, as had been the case when there were no other active mints.

The mint established in 1545 across the Thames was situated in a grand building originally called Suffolk House (after the Duke who had it built) but renamed Southwark Place when it had come into the king's hands. Although Southwark was not technically part of London, the signature on its coins was *Civitas London*, and its mint was in practice an extension of the Tower. The identity of the mint is confirmed by the use of *S* and *Y* (for John York) as mintmarks on many of its coins. After the Tower, Southwark was by far the most important mint of the debasement. It produced £788,000 in silver (£152,000 of it from the reminting of testons), and was the only mint, apart from the Tower, either to coin a material amount of gold (£393,000), or to remain active until the end of the debasement in 1551. After the closure of the mint, York returned to Tower I where he replaced Bowes as Under-Treasurer on 29 September 1551 for the fine coinage then about to be initiated. On the earliest of the new coins his initial *Y* appears as mintmark.

Apart from their evolution from the episcopal establishments of earlier times, the mints of Canterbury, now in the former Christchurch priory, and York, at first in the castle and after 1546 in St. Leonard's hospital, had a number of features in common during the debasement. Their periods of operation approximately coincided. York opened in May 1545, Canterbury in June; York's last account of the debasement closed in October 1549, Canterbury's in the December. Neither mint struck gold, drawing their precious metal as they did from ecclesiastical rather than mercantile sources. Both were confined to groats until November 1545, struck from dies with Roman or mixed lettering. Reverse dies of each were marked with a spur from the shield to the inner circle. Yet there were differences. Canterbury struck no groats for a period in 1545-8 but participated in the named coinage of Edward VI in 1547 as well as in the shilling issues of 1549. York struck no shillings in 1549, and none of the earlier coins in Edward's name; but although the total output of Canterbury was greater, York coined more new money from testons, starting in June 1548, than did Canterbury from January 1549.

Debasement, Henry VIII – Edward VI

In order to assist the opening of the mint in Bristol castle in May 1546 an initial batch of dies was sent from the Tower. The complement of its officials was almost as large as Southwark's, and included its own engraver, one Giles Evenet, whose dies are immediately recognizable by their elaborate Gothic lettering and the profusion of ornaments in the inscriptions. Evenet's dies included some for portrait pence of Edward VI, which are somewhat less rare than those of other mints and may have had a more extended issue. As the focus of England's western trade, Bristol was well situated as an economic centre. It had also, incidentally, become a bishopric in 1542, with the result that its mint name in this coinage is now *Civitas Bristolie* for the first and only time. Outside the London area Bristol alone was authorized to coin gold, and minted all denominations of silver from the teston downwards. Up to September 1547 gold coinage, all at the 20 ct. standard, amounted only to £12,500. Under Sharington £57,000 of English 4 oz. silver coin was issued to the same date, but his accounts also include a coinage of nearly £9,000 of 3 oz. coin for Ireland in the summer of 1546, which can be identified among the harp-type Irish groats of Henry VIII by their typical Evenet lettering and ornaments. Accounts thereafter for 1547-8 were destroyed by Sharington in order to cover his tracks. At the end of 1548 he was dismissed for malpractice, and replaced by Sir Thomas Chamberlain. Arrested on charges of corruption, Sharington was convicted of having coined testons without warrant, of having issued coin that was too light in weight, and of having falsified his books of account. An accomplice of the Protector's treacherous brother, Thomas Seymour, he made a full confession which may have saved his life; but he was perhaps not alone among Under-Treasurers in having tried to cheat the crown - the accounts of Martin Bowes, Knight and Tyllsworth were all found to be unsatisfactory in various ways. No gold coins were struck under Chamberlain from January to October 1549, but his output of silver amounted to £50,000, the majority of it from the reminting of testons. Only £3,000 of this is identifiable as having been struck into 6 oz. shillings, the rest being converted into smaller silver.

The decision to set up a further mint at the end of 1548 at Durham Place (also sometimes known as Durham House, and formerly the London residence of the bishops) may have had something to do with the fact that its Under-Treasurer, John Bowes, was an associate of Protector Somerset. Of the new mints in the London area this alone was to have its own engraver, which suggests the anticipation of heavier output than actually transpired, since it was so near the Tower that secure transport of dies can hardly have been a problem. The first commission for this mint, dated 2 December 1548, was for coinage of the old 4 oz. silver groats and their parts; the second, on 29 January 1549, included four denominations of gold, from sovereign to half-crown, as well as the proposed new shillings and sixpences. None of the silver from this mint is common, and although three distinct type varieties are known of the half-sovereign (the only extant gold coin from this mint), all are extremely rare. Net profits accounted by John Bowes were only £9,100, and total output has been estimated as below £100,000, much less than that of any other of the debasement mints in England. Coins of Durham Place are recognizable not only by the mintmark bow, but also by the use on many of them of different inscriptions from those at other mints. The small silver has no mint name, but instead the legend *Redde Cuique Quod Suum Est* (Render to each his own), an echo of the famous passage in St. Matthew's gospel (ch. 22), 'Render unto Caesar . . .'. This was interpreted by Symonds as a possible allusion to the conversion of old Henry VIII testons into Henry groats while the mints were also producing new shillings with the name and portrait of Edward VI.

The opening of the mint in Dublin castle in 1548 was designed to obtain the profits available from reminting the Irish currency into 4 oz. silver. The indenture with Agard dated 10 February was similar to those for other mints made in the same month, and differed from the arrangements of 1547 in reducing coinage charges from 28s. per pound to 26s.

8d. Because of the preparations needed, minting at Dublin did not start for a month or two, and seems at first to have been confined to the larger coins, since in September Agard sent to the Lord-Deputy specimens of the first pence and halfpence. A letter to Somerset dated 22 November 1548 indicates that only £5,000 had by then been struck, and during 1549 the mint became inactive through lack of bullion. Agard died in the summer of 1549, and the total profits returned by him amounted to only £6,600, of which £2,368 in the form of arrears was accounted by his son in 1550. In June 1550 the Privy Council resolved to reopen the mint to coin foreign bullion; Pirry was promoted from comptroller to Under-Treasurer with an indenture from August; and minting was resumed in October. Pirry accounted for profits of £900 for 1550 and £11,500 for 1551. By the time that the mint was revived again in June 1552, the English shillings of Edward VI had been decried by 50 per cent., and the commission to Pirry refers to 1,500 lbs. Troy of fine silver to be minted (at 36s. to the pound instead of 72s.) into money "called pieces of sixpence". Pirry was dead before December 1552, when the surviving officers of the mint were ordered to produce a further issue of £8,000.

As is often the case at times of monetary upheaval, the debasement period produced a variety of experiments and innovations in design. The range of portraits, less formal than that of Henry VII and the 1526 profile of Henry VIII, exemplify the widening artistic horizons of the time. The facing and three-quarter busts of Henry VIII belong to the age of Holbein, while the attractive representations of the young Edward VI embody new departures such as the half-length figure, the bust in armour and an uncrowned head. Tudor symbolism remains pervasive, with the large rose on the testons particularly prominent. New mottoes were added in 1549, along with transposition of the legends whereby the king's name and titles were placed on the reverse. 1549 also saw the belated introduction of dates (in Roman numerals) on the English coinage, long after they had become common elsewhere. During the 1540s many of the medieval aspects of the coinage began to disappear. Among the most notable developments were the addition of supporters to the royal arms on sovereigns and halves, a more modern style of rendering the king's throne, and an oval-shaped shield with garniture on Edward's shillings and gold. The introduction of clean Roman lettering was one of the more obvious changes, although there was to be a brief reversion to the Gothic alphabet with the restoration of the coinage in 1551.

At the same time, however, the physical appearance of the currency degenerated. Base silver coins, blanched in acid to improve their surface on issue, soon became discoloured and blotchy in use. Wear on the parts of the design of testons and groats in highest relief revealed their inner content. Parson Brock, comptroller at the Tower and Southwark between 1544 and 1548, was chided not only for presiding over the debasement as a priest, but also for having given his sovereign a red and copper nose. A couplet of the time runs thus:

    These testons looke redde; how like you the same?
    Tis a tooken of grace: they blush for shame.

As the debasement progressed, the production of dies and striking of the coins deteriorated under pressure of work, and by the end of the 1540s the currency was in a disreputable condition. It was also in a chaotic muddle. Taking into account changes in fineness, weight and face value, literally dozens of different kinds of coin were produced between 1544 and 1551. In addition to this there were reductions in the valuations of existing silver, halving them in two steps in 1551. Although goldsmiths and merchants were quick to determine changes affecting the currency, the public at large must have been in a state of utter confusion, unable to conduct money transactions with any confidence or certainty. In 1545, after the second stage of the English debasement, even the Scots, the deficiencies of whose coinage had been the cause of frequent complaint by the English since the fourteenth century, at last turned tables and forbad the currency in their own realm of "the new Inglis grote … with the braid face". However, disastrous as the process was for the users of base coin, the policy of debasement proved to be an outstanding contributor to the government's coffers – "our holy anchor", in the phrase of Thomas Wriothesley, one of Henry's secretaries of state. Challis has calculated that the profits for the whole period exceeded £1¼ million. Yet the surprising fact is that prices did not in the short run feel a fuller impact from such inflationary debasement.

Arrangement and Classification

Coins of the debasement were struck on such an enormous scale that they present peculiar, sometimes intractable, problems of arrangement. Although produced within a span of only seven years they are more diverse, in terms of weight, fineness and general design, than the coinages of many much longer periods, while in numismatic detail they are so varied as to make description and record a complex task. Indeed, there is so much variety in busts, mintmarks, ornaments, lettering and stops, and in muling between them, that it is impracticable, particularly in the case of groats, to attempt to list all the permutations in which such features occur. Moreover, there were times when coins in the names of both Henry VIII and Edward VI were minted simultaneously, most notably in 1549-51 when the regular suite of denominations from the half-sovereign downwards in Henry's name continued to be produced alongside Edward shillings and portrait gold on separate standards of weight and fineness.

The final section of Whitton's monograph on the coinage of Henry VIII also covers the posthumous series struck in his name from 1547 to 1551 and the rare autonomous issues of Edward VI in 1547, which are closely related to their posthumous equivalents. Whitton's work on the debasement period, a brilliant study of an exceedingly complicated series, was the last that failing health allowed him to undertake. Simultaneously Carlyon-Britton was working on the base silver coinages post-Henry VIII and his article on the subject, though often overlooked, remains of use. Whitton's work has required little addition or amendment, but there are valuable contributions by Jacob on testons and by Chown on the groats of Bristol. The Edwardian gold and silver coinages from 1549 to 1551 were covered by Potter, and the shillings have since been authoritatively reviewed by Bispham.

A central difficulty in the classification of the material is that there is no generally applicable succession of types or classes of the kind found in most of the late medieval English series, because although there are several common features between denominations and mints, many of them are not systematic or consistent. Furthermore, it is doubtful whether there are any reliable means of determining which coins fall on one side or the other of the boundaries between issues of different fineness. Symonds had described the issues of 1542-4, 1544-5, 1545-6 and 1546-7 respectively as the Third, Fourth, Fifth and Sixth Coinages of Henry VIII, and such in an official sense they were. Possibly the ready identification of coins of differing standard was sometimes purposely avoided in the interests of deceiving the public. But in the absence of numismatic means of separating them, the debased issues of Henry VIII are commonly described collectively as the Third Period of his coinage. On the basis of testons Jacob suggested that the introduction of the pellet-in-annulet mark could have been intended to indicate the 1545 reduction to 6 oz. fineness on Tower dies; and that a similar explanation might apply to an annulet on the inner circle in respect of the further reduction in standard in 1546. This annulet occurs at the Tower on a few specimens of most denominations from half-sovereigns to halfpence, late in the currency of trefoil stops and on groats at about the point of transition between busts 2 and 3. Such marks, known as *points secrets*, had long been used in France and elsewhere (most recently on coins of Henry's nephew James V from 1539) for various purposes of mint identification or control, but any interpretation of their function during the debasement must remain speculative.

For the earlier years of the debasement period the most useful framework for chronology is provided by the stops. Six broad classes can be defined, applicable, more or less, to all denominations and to all mints in receipt of Tower-made dies. In the case of groats the evidence of stops can be supplemented by other features, of which the succession of bust types is the most important. The normal combinations are set out hereunder, with suggested dates.

STOPS USED IN THE DEBASEMENT PERIOD

Class	Dates	Stops	Groat busts
i	1544-5	Saltires	1
ii	1545-6	Trefoils and/or defective saltires	2, 3
iii	1546 (from c. April)	Sleeves	3, 4
iv	1547-8	Mascles or lozenges	4, 5
v	Late 1547	Pierced crosses with saltires	5
vi	From 1548	Small squares or round pellets	5, 6

Saltire stops, as in earlier coinages back to Henry VII, remained in regular use throughout the period up to May 1544 and for some time beyond, probably into early 1545. But by the time the new mints were operating in the summer of 1545, saltires had mostly given way to trefoils. Often it appears that the trefoils are no more than defective saltires, and sometimes they can be seen to be from a damaged punch still recognizable as a saltire. Not long before the opening of the Bristol mint in May 1546 a new form of stop was introduced, described by Brooke as hooks but by Carlyon-Britton as sleeves (because of their resemblance to the curved and bent device known as the *manche* in heraldry). Early Tower-made dies sent to Bristol included some with trefoil stops and some with sleeves. It is quite possible that there was some overlap in the manufacture or issue of dies with trefoil and with sleeve stops, which may have had no more significance than indicating the need to replace old punches or the work of a die-sinker with a different set of tools.

STOPS ON BASE COINS IN NAME OF HENRY VIII

(i) Quatrefoils; (ii) Trefoils/fractured quatrefoils; (iii) Sleeves; (iv) Lozenges; (v) Pierced crosses; (vi) Pellets, square or round.

Early in 1547, about the time of Henry VIII's unexpected death in January or soon afterwards, a number of changes occurred. In rapid succession, a new portrait (bust 4) was adopted on groats, sleeve stops gave way to lozenges, Gothic lettering was replaced

Debasement, Henry VIII – Edward VI

by Roman, and coins with Edward's own name and portrait made a transitory appearance. On half-sovereigns, although Henry's name was generally retained, the face is clearly Edward's and this provides confirmation that the introduction of Roman letters and lozenge stops, which applies to other denominations, may be dated to the beginning of the new reign. Coins in Edward's name were struck at Tower I, Southwark and Canterbury, and it seems likely that a wish to accompany the new king's portrait with a clear inscription, in the Renaissance manner, may have prompted the adoption of Roman script at this point. The lozenge stops found on these Edwardian coins occur also on the gold and billon in Henry's name which continued to be struck at the same time. It is not clear whether, at the mints which used the new Edward type, this interrupted the old king's type or the two proceeded in parallel. But this early coinage in Edward's name is rare and cannot in any case have lasted long. It is not difficult to see that there could have been advantages in continuing to produce a posthumous coinage with Henry's face and name, shielding Edward from association with the unpopular debasement and making it less obvious that all the new coin was of only 4 oz. silver. As late as February 1550 he was commissioning the Southwark mint to recoin testons not into shillings of his own type, but into smaller coins "with the hole face and inscripcion of our most deare late Father".

The stops used in 1547 and described as lozenges are in fact, in their early stages, voided (i.e. hollow) lozenges and so could be described as mascles. When worn or struck from a deteriorating punch they may have a more solid appearance, like a normal lozenge. But they should not be confused with the smaller 'square pellets' or diamonds which occur on many later coins. Square or round stops (both described as pellets), with the occasional addition of saltires, were introduced in 1548 and then used for the rest of the posthumous coinage. But before pellets, and with or after lozenges, come stops of a curious form described by Brooke as pierced crosses and by Carlyon-Britton as incurved mascles (often accompanied by saltires). These occur at mints which received their dies from the Tower, but not on all denominations, and it seems likely that they were not in use for long. Their occurrence on groats with mintmark *K*, but not with grapple, would place their introduction before the end of 1547, since Thomas Knight died early in 1548 and his final account closed in the previous December; but the evidence of Canterbury groats suggests that both lozenges and pierced crosses may still have been in use for a few months into 1548. A peculiarity of obverse dies with pierced crosses is a monogram of *ET* instead of *z* for *&,* a feature that also occurs on some Durham Place shillings of 1549. With the pellet period from 1548 onwards the stops cease to be of chronological value, but although this is a disadvantage with regard to the posthumous Henry coinage, which continued until 1551, the majority of the silver from 1549 was minted into dated Edwardian shillings.

Tower I Mintmarks, 1544-51

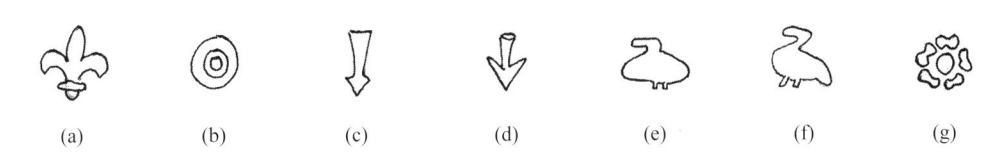

(a) Lis, mainly silver classes i-iv; (b) Pellet-in-annulet, mainly gold classes ii-iii; (c) Arrow, classes iv-vi; (d) Pheon, 1549; (e) and (f) Swan I and II, 1549-50; (g) Rose, 1551 (Tower I?).

1544–1551

Except on the shillings, mintmarks are of less value for sequence than one might have hoped since at some mints they were not used, or only occasionally, while at others they were infrequently changed and sometimes omitted. In the case of gold coins and the Edwardian shillings, however, which carry no place names, they are the principal means of distinguishing between the products of different mints. On all the larger Tower silver in Henry's name the traditional *Posui* legend was retained. At the Tower under Henry VIII (and for a moment afterwards) the mark on silver was a lis, on gold the lis only rarely but more usually a pellet-in-annulet. Although a second mint had been operating in the Tower since 1545, it is not until early in 1547 that the Tower coinage divides into two streams, for both gold and silver, one with mintmark arrow, for Sir Martin Bowes, representing the primary mint, the other with a succession of different marks for the output of Tower II. Since Bowes remained in office throughout the period, the arrow continued in use at Tower I until the end of the posthumous series. The secondary sequence begins with *K* for Knight in 1547, with lozenge stops and then pierced crosses, replaced by grapple in 1548, with pellet stops. Grapple is not known to have been a personal mark of Knight's successor Stephen Vaughan, but it undoubtedly identifies some or all of his coinage; a possible interpretation of this very unusual mark is as a 'sea-moor', referring to the Protector Edward Seymour, Duke of Somerset, of whom Vaughan is known to have been an associate. Dated shillings show that grapple was still in use during 1549, followed by martlet with the date 1550, a pattern that could reflect Vaughan's death late in 1549 and his succession by Sir Nicholas Throckmorton in January 1550. Bispham has suggested that martlet was Throckmorton's sign, being the heraldic mark of cadency for a fourth son (which he was). In the posthumous series with Henry's name the martlet is shown in profile to the right, but on the Edwardian gold and shillings it is left-facing. There can, however, be little doubt of their equivalence, since both follow grapple in a similar sequence. Posthumous half-sovereigns and groats are also known with a small plain lis as mintmark, which Whitton, perhaps correctly, regarded as the last of the secondary marks even though the lis groats are known with bust 5 but not bust 6 and mules involving lis dies would not be incompatible with an earlier position in the series for this mark.

The only other mint of the base coinages in Henry's name to use a succession of mintmarks was Southwark. The marks were *S*, Gothic *e* and Roman *E*, in that order. With minor exceptions, *S* and *e* were used under Henry VIII, *E* posthumously. *S* for Southwark presents no problem; but *e* and *E* have defied convincing explanation – could this initial have been meant to signify *Eboracum* as Latin for the name of Under-Treasurer York, whose *Y* is found on Southwark shillings?

Southwark Mintmarks, 1544-51

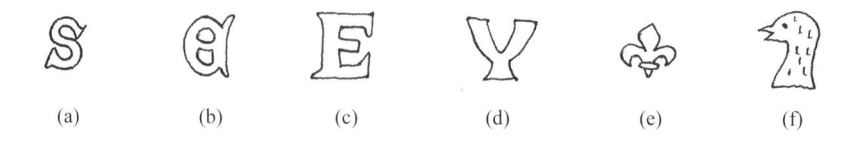

(a)   (b)   (c)   (d)   (e)   (f)

(a) *S,* class ii; (b) *e,* class ii; (c) *E,* classes iv-vi; (d) *Y,* 1549-50; (e) Lis, 1551 (Southwark?); (f) Ostrich head, gold 1551.

With the introduction of dates on Edwardian shillings in 1549 there are fewer problems of arrangement. Mintmarks serve to identify the different mints. Also, mules between marks can demonstrate sequence. The principal difficulty in describing the phases of the earlier coinage of Edward's reign relates to the overlap of different issues. As with the base coinages of Henry VIII, Symonds numbered them by reference to successive indentures, regardless of whether the coins struck in response to them could be separately identified, or which king's name appeared on them. Thus his First Coinage (April 1547) and Second Coinage (February 1548) both included gold at 20 ct. and silver at 4 oz., and the 1548 indenture constitutes an administrative but not a numismatic division. His Third (January 1549), Fourth (April 1549) and Fifth (December 1550) Coinages were chiefly related to the issue of Edward shillings at three different standards, although the January 1549 indenture also provided for gold coins at reduced weights but improved fineness.

At its simplest, the coinage of the first four and a half years after the death of Henry VIII may be divided into two phases. During the first ('pre-shilling') phase, in 1547 and 1548, all the coinage was at the same standard as had pertained under Henry since April 1546. Sovereign and teston, the two largest, were soon discontinued, but otherwise the denominations were unchanged, with the emphasis on half-sovereigns, crowns and groats and halves. With the exception of the very limited issue of gold and billon coins with Edward's name (and the substitution of his face for his father's on Henry half-sovereigns) the types were broadly unchanged. Most of the issues of this pre-shilling phase were therefore no more than a posthumous continuation of the last coinage of Henry VIII. The second, or shilling, phase ran from February 1549 to July 1551. Most of the silver was minted into Edwardian shillings, but alongside them the lesser values continued to be struck in 4 oz. silver according to the posthumous formula. The weights of the gold coins were reduced, but their fineness was raised from 20 to 22 ct. Like the shillings, the new gold coins carried the name and portrait of the young king, although the minting of 20 ct. gold in Henry's name did not cease entirely during the shilling phase. There was also a small and wholly exceptional issue of fine gold at Southwark in the first half of 1551. As new shillings gradually displaced the posthumous issues, the coinage of the new reign at last began to take on more of an identity of its own. After the short-lived experiment in 1547 with gold and billon in Edward's name the idea of reform and a silver coinage of restored fineness had never been far from consideration, but practical problems and financial necessity repeatedly deferred its implementation. With the reform of October 1551 this step was at last achieved, but it was to be another ten years before the base money was finally swept away.

Henry Gold and First Coins in Edward's Name

Base gold coins in Henry's name were struck at three standards, 23 ct. in 1544/5, 22 ct. in 1545/6 and 20 ct. from April 1546 onwards. These three standards roughly relate to the three divisions of the base coinage of Henry's lifetime as defined by changes in the punctuation – class i, saltires; ii, fractured saltires or trefoils; and iii, sleeves. Sovereigns and halves at 23 ct., with angels and their fractions, were only struck at the principal Tower mint, between June 1544 and March 1545. Crowns and halfcrowns replaced the angel series when the fineness was lowered to 22 ct. in April 1545. The new establishment, Tower II (the products of which are not separately distinguishable before 1547), began to contribute in July 1545, followed by Southwark in the September. A few Tower-made dies for sovereigns, half-sovereigns and crowns were sent to Bristol, where the mint opened in May 1546, and although all such dies for Bristol gold had trefoil stops, some of those for billon had sleeves, so that class iii must have begun, at the latest, soon after the introduction of 20 ct. gold. Some late class ii dies, of the Tower only, for half-sovereigns, crowns and halfcrowns, have the annulet on the inner circle that may refer to the reduction to 20 ct. fineness in April 1546.

The minting of Henry sovereigns probably ceased in 1547. There are no mint accounts for 20 ct. gold beyond 1548 but there are Henry half-sovereigns, crowns and halfcrowns with mintmarks grapple and martlet which indicate that these denominations continued to be struck during the shilling phase of the posthumous period, despite the introduction of 22 ct. Edwardian portrait gold early in 1549.

The following table shows the mints at which Henry VIII and posthumous Henry gold was struck (from Tower-made dies) of each of the six Henry classes and also, for illustration, of the rare Edwardian issue of 1547 which is closely linked to Henry class iv.

MINTS AND CLASSES OF HENRY VIII AND POSTHUMOUS GOLD

Class	i (saltires)	ii (trefoils)	iii (sleeves)	Edw. VI (lozenges)	iv (lozenges)	v (pierced crosses)	vi (pellets)
Sovereign	T	TSB	TS		TB		
Half-sovereign	T	TSB	TS	TS	TSt	TS	St
Angel (+ ½ and ¼)	T						
Crown		TSB	T	T	TSt		TSt
Halfcrown		TS	T	T	TSt	T	TSt

Mints: T – Tower I; S – Southwark; t – Tower II; B – Bristol (Tower-made dies only)

Sovereigns and Half-Sovereigns of Henry's Type

None of the sovereigns of the debasement period are common, although they are less rare than earlier issues of this denomination. Most of them were struck at the Tower or at Southwark during Henry's lifetime, although there are also a few of Bristol. The lettering is normally Gothic, but there is a very rare type with Roman letters, from the Tower and Bristol, which belongs to the early posthumous period. Half-sovereigns in Henry's name are relatively plentiful, and while minting of the sovereign was concentrated in the earlier stages of the debasement, the half gradually assumed the position of the largest coin in normal production, which it was to occupy throughout the posthumous period.

Sovereigns or half-sovereigns in Edward's name were struck in three spells during the debasement: first (halves only), in 1547 as part of the limited issue of Edwardian gold and billon produced very early in the new reign; second, in 1549-50, alongside the portrait shillings; and third (sovereigns only), as part of a small special issue of gold at Southwark in 1551. The last two of these are discussed in separate sections later, but consideration of the first is included here because of the close affinity between the early Edwardian half-sovereigns and their posthumous Henry counterparts.

As can be seen from the next table, the Henry sovereigns were struck at two sizes, two weights and three standards of fineness: first, large (I) and small (IIa), at 200 gr. and 23 ct. gold; then (IIb1), from March 1545, at 192 gr. and 22 ct.; and finally (IIb2), from April 1546, at the same weight but at only 20 ct. The type I sovereigns, which are extremely

Debasement, Henry VIII – Edward VI

Henry VIII Sovereigns of the Debasement

Type	Date	Weight	Fineness	Module	Stops	London obv. dies	Southwark obv. dies
I	1544	200 gr.	23 ct.	large	saltires	A	
IIa	1544/5	200	23	small	trefoils	B	
IIb1	1545/6	192	22	small	trefoils	B, D	E
IIb2	1546	192	20	small	sleeves	C	F

rare and have no parallel among the halves, are of large module (diameter c. 42 mm.) and imposing appearance. Like the pre-1542 sovereigns they have tall Gothic letters (apart from a Roman *M*) and saltire stops. Except that a rose replaces the portcullis below the king's feet and his head is older, large and bearded, the design on the one obverse die of type I (Whitton A) is generally similar to that of the second coinage, and is perhaps the work of the same engraver. On the reverse the traditional shield-on-rose type now gave way to a blazon of the royal arms, a crowned shield held aloft by lion and dragon supporters, with a monogram of *HR* in a panel below. The reduced module of type II (diameter c. 38 mm.), adopted in advance of the reduction in weight, required some modification, most obviously the omission of the tressure around the design and a smaller (and more successful) portrait. The throne, now with the sides of its back curving outwards at the top, is smaller and less elaborate, and there are small bird-like figures on top of the pillars instead of the earlier candlesticks. Apart from a reduction in size, the reverse type remained unchanged. As in type I, the mintmark on type IIa is a lis, but smaller in size, and the stops are now trefoils. The IIa sovereigns, like those of type I, were struck only at the Tower, and their introduction must be dated before the lowering of weight and fineness in March 1545. The single IIa obverse die (B), however, continued in use after this reduction, to judge by the weights of some surviving specimens. Of the two other obverse dies used for the lighter Tower sovereigns of type IIb, the earlier (D) has trefoil stops, with mintmark pellet-in-annulet, and the later (C) sleeve stops, with mintmark lis. These dies, and the reverses used with them (all with mintmark lis), have rather coarser Gothic lettering, with one or two intrusive Roman letters (*R* and sometimes *E*). Sovereigns from die D with pellet-in-annulet are extremely rare, whereas on the halves this is the normal Tower mintmark while the lis is the rarity.

Sovereigns at 22 ct. (IIb1) were struck between March 1545 and March 1546; if any were produced in the first six months of this period, they could only have come from die B or D at the Tower, because the June 1545 indenture for Southwark did not include gold, the commission for which was only given in September. The sleeve stops on Tower die C point to a date after the second reduction of fineness in April 1546. Southwark sovereigns are known with lettering and stops corresponding to both Tower dies D and C. The earlier of the two IIb Southwark obverse dies (E) and its two reverses have mintmark *S*, with trefoil stops, and lettering like that of Tower die D; while the second obverse (F) and one reverse with mintmark (Gothic) *e* have sleeve stops and lettering like Tower die C. These two *e* dies are not known paired together, but only as mules with mintmark *S*. On the Southwark reverses with mintmark *S* there is no letter below the shield, but the *e* reverse has *e* also between the shield and the *HR* panel.

Two types of Henry sovereign, both extremely rare, were struck at Bristol, with Sharington's *WS* monogram as mintmark. The first shows the same workmanship, lettering (except for a Gothic *m*) and trefoil stops as the Tower and Southwark IIb2 sovereigns from obverse dies D and E, indicating that those types may belong late in the 22 ct. issue as dies were not sent to Bristol before the spring of 1546. The later type of Bristol sovereign has Roman letters and rosette stops. These stops can be matched on some of the profile gold in Edward's name, and other details (such as the small lis in the royal arms which lacks a band round the stem) also suggest that the second Bristol type belongs to the posthumous period. Brooke noted the similarity of these Roman-lettered Bristol sovereigns to others, also with rosette stops, on which the mintmark lis has two stamens beside the central foil (described by Whitton and others as 'lis with feelers'), and wondered whether they might also have been struck at Bristol. However, it does not seem likely that Bristol, where all other dies carried the monogram of either Sharington or Chamberlain, would have used the lis mintmark otherwise peculiar to the Tower, even though this was an unusual version of the mark (it occurs most prominently in this form on the medieval gold florin of Florence). Whitton is therefore probably correct in placing the sovereigns with Roman letters and the Florentine lis, despite their stops, as an early Tower issue of the new reign. This is the only type of Tower sovereign attributable to the posthumous period, and no equivalent Southwark coin is known.

The half-sovereign (or ryal) had been little favoured in the Tudor period hitherto, but those of the debasement period in Henry's name are among the commoner English gold coins of the sixteenth century, the ten-shilling value being presumably found more manageable in production and more convenient in general currency than the pound. The design was basically the same as that of the sovereign, except that Henry's portrait was removed in 1547; there are some other minor variances, such as the occasional omission of the sceptre, and the figures on the pillars become more obviously angels, with arms and legs as well as wings. The pattern of issue was also in some ways comparable to that of the sovereigns. The earliest types were produced at the Tower only, before other mints were opened; there were then parallel series from the Tower and Southwark; and the only other mint for the denomination was Bristol, on a very small scale. But in some other respects, and not only in the volume of issue, there are important differences from the sovereigns. The starting point of the half-sovereign series was later (there is no equivalent of the type I large-module sovereign, of pre-1542 style) and their issue continued at a vigorous pace into the reign of Edward VI, when the sovereigns faded. But the most interesting feature of the half-sovereigns is that, with the accession of the young king, the obverse design was modified to include his own face and figure even though the inscription, except on a few early dies, remained that of his father. While some of the earliest half-sovereigns of Henry VIII are well-made and presentable, under the pressure of high volume and hasty production workmanship declined and later examples are often weakly struck.

The first Tower halves, which correspond to the small module but full weight sovereigns of type IIa, are the only ones to have the lis mintmark, and are extremely rare. They have small Roman letters (including the *H* with ornamental bar that is found on painted panels and in woodcarving at this period), with the reading *et* in full, and very small saltires as stops. Very similar to these, but at the lower weight (96 gr.), are the earliest of the IIb halves, with the pellet-in-annulet mintmark (smaller and neater than on later varieties). Some of these coins still have *et*, but this was soon replaced by *z* for *&*. The next Tower variety still has the small Roman alphabet, but now with trefoil stops, and this may date from September 1545 or after, since it is matched by equivalent coins from Southwark with mintmark *S*. There then follows a sequence of varieties from the Tower and Southwark, with successive changes of lettering and stops. Large Roman letters

Debasement, Henry VIII – Edward VI

replace the small early fount, occasionally with the inclusion of a few Gothic letters, still with trefoil stops or with defective saltires of normal size. Next there was a phase with Gothic letters, first with trefoil stops and then with sleeves. Soon after the introduction of the Gothic fount the *e* replaced *S* as the mintmark at Southwark. Earlier half-sovereigns with mintmark *S* (like the *S* sovereigns) had nothing between the shield and panel on the reverse, these perhaps corresponding to groats with *S* in the cross-ends; later ones, with *e* added below the shield, would then be the counterpart of groats with *S* and *e* in the cross-ends. All the halves with mintmark *e* have the same letter below the shield, again as on sovereigns. The last of them has Roman letters with lozenge stops and so probably post-dates Edward's accession, even though still with Henry's portrait.

Parallel issues of half-sovereigns from the Tower and Southwark continued into the new reign, now with Edward's youthful portrait, his father's name in Roman letters and a reshaped throne with plainer back. The Tower coins are henceforward divisible by their mintmarks into separate streams representing the output of the two establishments. At the main mint in the Tower mintmark pellet-in-annulet was replaced by arrow (for Martin Bowes) which continued through the posthumous period with the usual sequence of stops. A similar series from Southwark has mintmark *E* throughout, this mark not introduced on half-sovereigns until after Henry's death although appearing earlier on crowns. The output of Tower II is identifiable by the succession of secondary marks beginning with *K* for Thomas Knight, found only with lozenge stops, followed by grapple and martlet, with saltire and then pellet stops, and finally lis with pellets only. The rare 20 ct. half-sovereigns (from Tower I and Southwark) with Edward's own name and lozenge stops had come early in his reign, like his autonomous crowns. At both mints the Edwardian obverses shared *HR* reverse dies with half-sovereign obverses in Henry's name, all the coins in Edward's name being therefore technically Edward/Henry mules. Evidently no reverse dies were made with *ER* in the panel to pair with the Edward obverses, an indication of the very tentative nature of the Edwardian type.

Posthumous halves with pierced cross stops from Tower I and Southwark read *Angl* (unusually, with *n*); and the longer form *Dei Gra* for *D G* is often found at Southwark, with lozenge stops, and at Tower II with mintmarks *K*, grapple and martlet. A curious feature of the posthumous half-sovereigns is the irregular usage of the mintmarks. Sometimes they are found as initial marks in the inscription on both sides, sometimes on one side, sometimes on neither; but *K*, grapple and *E* (rarely *e*) also usually occur below the reverse shield, even if there is none at the head of the inscription. Mules and altered marks are not uncommon. In the Tower series mintmark arrow mules both ways with pellet-in-annulet from Henry's reign and with the later Tower II mintmark lis. There are no mules with the actual initial mark *K*, but one obverse coupled with a grapple reverse has the same lozenge stops as *K*-marked dies, and a reverse with no initial mark but *K* below the shield is muled with a mintmark *E* obverse of Southwark. Although grapple is not muled, one reverse die has this mark over *K* in both places. Martlet is muled only with a lis reverse. At Southwark, under Henry, there had been mules both ways between *S* and *e*, while several dies with mintmark *S* had this altered to pellet-in-annulet for the Tower. In the posthumous period reverse dies were also converted the opposite way, for use at Southwark, with *E* over arrow, and one of these is muled with an old *e* obverse. There is even an (*E*)/*S* mule combining an old pre-*e* reverse with a new obverse which, although without mark, has the inscription and stops of the early *E* period.

As with the sovereigns, the issue of half-sovereigns from Bristol was very small. The single pair of London-made dies, with Gothic letters, trefoil stops and Sharington's monogram, are of rather coarse work. They correspond to the 1546 sovereigns from this mint.

Angels and Fractions

Since the coinage of 23ct. gold ceased in March 1545 the 8s. angels of the debasement period must belong before that date (and consequently, before any of the additional mints were opened). They could perhaps extend back into the period of the secret indenture in 1542-4, although 23ct. gold was mainly struck between June 1544 and March 1545. Chamberlain is recorded as having found 43lb. of angels in silver at Bristol after he replaced the nefarious Sharington in 1549, but there is no evidence to suggest that angels were ever produced legitimately at Bristol after 1472.

In addition to the angel and its half, the quarter-angel was now added for the first time. The fractions are rarer than the angels. The mintmark on all three denominations is the lis, but the *hib Rex* title distinguishes the angels and halves from those of the second coinage. Angels often have an annulet, or 'gun-hole', on the ship's side, and another behind the saint's head. Stops are usually saltires or trefoils, but half-angels have annulets on the reverse and a die of the second coinage which survived into this period was reused both with its original saltire stops and with the saltires overpunched with annulets. An annulet (or rarely three) is also found on the side of the ship on half-angels, but not on the quarters. On some quarter-angels the slightly stiff armoured figure of St. Michael that had been standard on angels since the 1490s was replaced by a more animated St. Michael, in a tunic and with elbow raised, but the new design was never adopted for the two higher values where it might have been seen to better advantage. The quarter does not have its own motto, since the royal titles, in a more extended form than on the larger coins, are continued on the reverse.

Crowns and Halfcrowns of Henry's Type

The issue of crowns and halves during the debasement period followed a pattern broadly similar to that of the half-sovereigns, although the series is more fragmentary. In the absence of crowns related to the earliest (heavy) sovereigns and half-sovereigns of types I and IIa, Brooke and Whitton assumed that the minting of crowns and halfcrowns was not resumed until weight and fineness were reduced in April 1545. Although the reduction in weight was small, from 50 gr. to 48 gr. for the crown, surviving specimens do appear to conform to the lower standard. As to fineness, there is no obvious boundary between the coins struck at 22 ct. in 1545-6 and those of 20 ct. from April 1546, although as with other denominations an annulet on the inner circle on some rare Tower coins may be an indicator of the reduction. The series of 20 ct. crowns and halfcrowns of the double rose, like that of the posthumous Henry half-sovereigns, was largely displaced after 1548 by the Edwardian portrait gold coins of the same values, which were struck at the revived standard of 22 ct. during the shilling phase from February 1549 onwards. Late posthumous crowns and halves are consequently rare.

As in the second coinage, the normal disposition of the legends is that the king's name is placed before the *Rosa* motto on the rose side (reverse) of the crowns, with the royal titles around the shield, while on halfcrowns the name precedes the titles on the shield side (obverse); but there are a number of departures from this pattern on individual dies. Nearly all base crowns of Henry's reign omit the word *Rutilans* (it was restored on the Roman-lettered dies from 1547), but with one exception all the halves, both of Henry's reign and Edward's, include it since the placing of the king's name on the obverse of these allowed more room for the motto on the reverse. Throughout the series there are many variations in the spelling and shortening of the words *Sine Spina*. One form, *Spine*, repeats the ending of *Sine* by assimilation, but *Spinis* may be an intentional plural since the arrow halfcrown die involved is of the literate kind with pierced-cross stops. On crowns there was development in the design of the crown above shield and rose. Instead of three ornamental leaves, as in the second coinage, the crown now has a central leaf between two lis and this continues into Edward's reign, when the leaf was replaced by a cross patty on a number of dies. All the posthumous coins have Roman letters, except that the initial in the field is sometimes still a Gothic *h*, especially on halves where limited space was a consideration.

At the head of the Tower series are rare crowns of good style, with Gothic letters (except for *H* in the field) and trefoil stops, on which the mintmark pellet-in-annulet is small and neat. These are the only pre-1547 base crowns to include on the reverse any part of the word *Rutilans* which, being preceded by the king's name, must have been felt to cause undue abbreviation. Their early date is indicated by the fact that comparable crowns are lacking at Southwark where gold was not struck until September 1545. Except for the omission of *Rutilans*, other Tower crowns of Henry's lifetime are similar, but of coarser work and with a larger mintmark. None of them has Roman letters in the inscriptions. A remarkable variant (matched also on a halfcrown) has the royal titles on both sides, without the king's name on either. Stops are normally trefoils or defective saltires, less commonly sleeves. Tower halfcrowns of Henry VIII are much scarcer than the crowns. They follow a pattern similar to, but less complete than, the crowns, beginning with dies of fine style. Unlike crowns, however, they sometimes include Roman letters in the legends, although Gothic are normal. The late Henry type with sleeve stops is only known in the form of a reverse die muled with an earlier (trefoil-stopped) obverse.

Still with mintmark pellet-in-annulet are halfcrown dies with Roman letters and lozenge stops, thus showing that pellet-in-annulet was not replaced until just into the new reign. One of these is also muled with an arrow obverse on which the *h* by the shield has been altered to *E*. Otherwise, the rare Tower crowns and halves from 1547 have the same mintmarks, with the exception of lis, as the half-sovereigns: at Tower I, arrow; and at Tower II, *K*, grapple and martlet. The mintmark is often placed on one side only. Both denominations are also known from Tower I with Edward's own name, *E R* in the field, and mintmark arrow, but they are extremely rare. Mules with the preceding mintmark, pellet-in-annulet, include a crown combining an old Gothic-lettered Henry obverse with a new *E R* reverse, on which no king's name appears at all. One extraordinary arrow halfcrown with lozenge stops has the *Rutilans* motto on both sides, preceded on the obverse by *H D G*. The early coins with mintmark arrow, to which those in Edward's name belong, have the pre-1547 form of crown, with lis-leaf-lis; but this was soon replaced by lis-cross patty-lis (although the lis are omitted on the reverse of one abnormal halfcrown with the arrow inverted which, like comparable groats, has saltire stops and *ET* in monogram for *et*). Coins from Tower I all have mintmark arrow, usually with lozenge stops, but later and rarely with saltires (halfcrown only) or pellets, while at Tower II those with mintmark *K* have lozenge stops and those with grapple and martlet pellets. Coins with *K* and grapple are extremely rare. Those with martlet represent an extension of the 20 ct. posthumous issues into the shilling phase of the coinage. On martlet crowns the ornaments revert to lis-leaf-lis.

The Southwark crowns and halves of Henry's lifetime, all of which are rare, normally have the same Gothic letters and trefoil stops as early Tower coins. There are none with sleeves. The mintmarks are, as on the larger gold, *S* and *e*, with the addition on crowns of the capital Roman *E*, the only occurrence of this noted on gold before 1547. Mintmark *S* is extremely rare, but it includes the only Southwark dies of this period with Roman letters, a crown obverse muled with an *E* reverse, and one pair of halfcrown dies.

Mintmark *e*, with Gothic letters only, usually occurs on both sides, but sometimes on the reverse alone. It is the least rare of the Southwark marks of Henry's reign. Exceptionally, the *e* halfcrown dies have Henry's name on the reverse, omitting *Rutilans*, with just his titles around the shield. Mintmark *E* at this period occurs only on crown reverse dies muled with *S* or *e* obverses. Southwark crowns and halves from 1547 onwards, all with mintmark *E*, are even rarer. There are none from this mint in Edward's name. The earlier variety of posthumous Henry crown, still with the mintmark on the reverse only, has lozenge stops; the later, with small, square pellet stops and *E* on both sides, has the obverse and reverse legends transposed. Halfcrowns also are found with the two kinds of stops, although the pellets here are round.

At Bristol the earliest crowns were struck from London-made dies, with coarse Gothic lettering and trefoil stops, like those of similar date (1546) from the Tower and Southwark. These coins, which have Sharington's monogram on the obverse only, are very rare, but the dies are muled both ways with those of the following, much more abundant, issue from Bristol-made dies. The crown dies of Bristol style, on which the *WS* mark sometimes appears also on the reverse, exhibit an elaborate variety of stops – pellets, annulets, saltires, trefoils, quatrefoils, lis and roses. *Rutilans* is always omitted. Features found on a few early dies are a plain (barred) *A* and the numeral *VIII*, each soon replaced, by the shaped Bristol *A* and an Arabic *8* (which sometimes left room for *henricus* in full). Like those for larger Bristol silver, some dies for crowns (but not for halves) have a small pellet below the shield and rose. There are no crowns or halves with Chamberlain's *TC* monogram, and their production had evidently ceased before he took over the mint; although accounts survive for silver coinage at Bristol in 1549 there are none for gold. Halfcrowns of Bristol are much rarer than the crowns. None are known with London lettering, and all have a smaller version of Evenet's elaborate fount; stops are pellets and saltires. On Bristol halfcrowns the *WS* monogram, like some Tower mintmarks, was placed only on the reverse die. Unlike the crowns, which have lis-leaf-lis in the crown, the halves have the lis-cross-lis that first occurs at the Tower in the posthumous period. But the issue of halfcrowns may have been very limited, since they show little variety and there are no clues to later work such as the shaped *A* on crowns.

Henry Silver and First Coins in Edward's Name

Silver (or rather, billon) in Henry's name continued to be struck after his death until 1551, despite the introduction of Edwardian shillings in 1549. Mint accounts record 4 oz. posthumous silver being coined up to October 1549 at York, to December 1549 at Canterbury, to January 1550 at Tower I, and to March 1551 at Southwark. There are no accounts for 4 oz. silver at Tower II after 1547, but mintmarks indicate that this mint also continued to produce it. At the Tower and at Southwark the mintmarks were the same as on the posthumous gold.

The base silver of Henry's lifetime was, like the gold, minted at three standards, although the reductions were much more drastic: to 9 oz. in 1544/5, 6 oz. in 1545/6 and 4 oz. from 1546 onwards. Again as with the gold, these three standards approximately coincide with classes i, ii and iii according to their punctuation. In the billon series at the Tower an annulet on the inner circle, possibly associated with the further debasement of standard in April 1546, occurs on a few Tower testons, groats, pence and halfpence of late class ii. Tower-made dies sent to Bristol about the same time include some for groats and pence of class iii as well as for testons, groats and halfgroats of class ii, an indication that trefoil stops gave way to sleeves in the spring of 1546.

The only mint of the 9 oz. issue was Tower I, from June 1544 to March 1545. York, Canterbury and Southwark were added in 1545, following the reduction to 6 oz. silver, and Bristol in May 1546, shortly after the final reduction to 4 oz. fineness in April. York and Canterbury, opened respectively in May and June 1545, were to coin groats, and groats alone, until November. When the restriction to groats at Canterbury expired, this mint seems to have discontinued striking groats altogether for an extended period, since none are known with sleeve stops, groats were omitted from the first indenture to Canterbury under Edward VI in April 1547, and the groat was not recommissioned until February 1548.

In the following table are set out the mints at which Henry VIII and posthumous Henry silver was struck (from Tower-made dies) of each of the six classes and also, for illustration, of the rare issue of 1547 in Edward's name which is closely linked to the posthumous Henry coins of class iv.

MINTS AND CLASSES OF HENRY VIII AND POSTHUMOUS SILVER

Class	i (saltires)	ii (trefoils)	iii (sleeves)	Edw. VI (lozenges)	iv (lozenges)	v (pierced crosses)	vi (pellets)
Teston	T	TSB	TS		T		
Groat	T	TSCYB	TSYB	TS	TStCY	TStCY	TStCY
Halfgroat	T	TSCYB	TC	TSC	TStCY	S	StCY
Penny	T	TSCY	TSCYB	TS	TStCYB		StCY
Halfpenny		TCY		T	CY	C	TCY

Mints: T – Tower I; S – Southwark; t – Tower II; C – Canterbury; Y – York;
B – Bristol (Tower-made dies only)

Testons

The need for rapid reminting of the fine silver currency into debased coin was no doubt one factor in the revival of the shilling, in the indenture of 1542, after a long interval since Henry VII's unsuccessful experiment at the beginning of the century. The new coin was broader and thinner than its predecessor. Now called a teston (or in modern works commonly testoon), it was to play a material part in the earlier years of the debasement. The name is taken from Italian *testoni*, the larger silver coins, notable for their realistic portrait heads (*teste*) of Renaissance rulers, which had appeared from the 1470s onwards. Although the testons are rarely well struck, particularly in the later issues, the facing head on the obverse is a powerful portrayal of the old king, although the crowned rose on the reverse, an enlargement of the design on the gold crown, is less well suited to increased size. Like the gold, the teston was only struck at the Tower, Southwark and Bristol; and as with the sovereign in gold, nearly all of the issue of this largest of the silver coins took place during Henry's lifetime. Considerable numbers of testons, most of them of 9oz. or 6oz. silver, were melted down from 1548 to be recoined into groats at 4oz., so that their scarcity today is not indicative of the volume in which they were originally produced.

Earlier testons (group A), confined to the Tower, have the Roman numeral *VIII* and *Di Gra*, both reflecting the extra space on the larger flan; and on the reverse, as if intentionally to lengthen the reading, *Adiutorem* becomes *Adiutorium* or even stranger forms such as *Adiutoerium*. On the later and commoner group of Tower testons (group B) the obverse inscription begins *henric 8 D G*, and their reverses almost always read *Adiutorium*. Lettering is chiefly Gothic throughout, although (as on sovereigns) Roman *M, E* and *R* often occur, and at the end of the series (group C) there is one posthumous variety with the full Roman alphabet. As on other denominations, stops are at first (group A) saltires or broken saltires, then in group B usually broken saltires or trefoils, followed by sleeves, and finally lozenges in group C. Southwark testons are of group B only.

Further indications of sequence are to be found in mintmarks and in the form of individual letters. In group A the Tower mintmark is a lis, but on the last obverse dies of the group a pellet-in-annulet was added after *Rex;* in at least one case it was inserted on a die that was originally without it, suggesting to Jacob that it could have been a mark intended to identify the introduction of the 6 oz. standard in 1545. On some reverses, in order to fill space, a second lis was placed after *Meum*. The pellet-in-annulet became the standard mintmark in group B until the advent of sleeve stops, when the lis reappears on one or two obverse dies, although the few group C dies revert to pellet-in-annulet. Roman *M* is invariable in group A, but was replaced by Gothic *m* early in group B. Conversely, the *e* of group A is usually Gothic, but after developing damage at the top this punch gave way to a Roman *E* late in group A, and for much of group B, until a second Gothic *e* was introduced shortly before the stops were changed to sleeves. Another varied letter is *A*. One early and very carefully made pair of dies (notable for the reading *heric*) has the bar across the top in the usual manner, but otherwise throughout group A, and well into group B, the *A* is capped only to the left, as on early sovereigns.

Three principal varieties of bust were used on testons of the Tower and Southwark. Bust 1, with wide open eyes, has prominent locks of hair protruding beneath the sides of the crown. On bust 2 the hair is more closely cropped and the eyes appear half closed. The third bust, which tends to be in low relief, has a lop-sided look; the hair is again sparse, and the bags under the eyes are pronounced. There are no jewels on the lower band of the crown of bust 3, and instead of crockets the ornaments on the arch are usually large pellets, as on Edward groats and on some of the posthumous Henry groats with bust 4. Bust 1 is overwhelmingly the most abundant, being used on all the coins of group A, and on most of group B at both mints. Bust 2 is very rare and is confined to coins of group B with saltire or fractured saltire stops. Bust 3 too is rare, especially at Southwark, and occurs in group B only with sleeve stops, but it is also found on the single known obverse die of group C.

Southwark testons, which are uncommon, had a less extended period of issue than those of the Tower. Their production presumably began in early group B at 6 oz. fineness when the mint was opened in June 1545. As on the gold, the normal mintmarks on Southwark testons are *S*, then *e*, and frequently muled. Early dies with *S* have Roman letters, like some of the first groats of this mint, but otherwise the lettering is mainly Gothic with a few individual Roman letters, as at the Tower. On Southwark obverses the busts and stops follow a similar pattern to those of group B in the Tower series, with sleeves replacing fractured saltires during the currency of mintmark *e*. There are no stops as such on the reverse of Southwark testons because, with *Civitas London* being so short an inscription for such large coins, the surplus space was filled with groups of three large floral ornaments. A single reverse die has mintmark Roman *E* (perhaps over *e*), but this is not necessarily an indication that testons may have continued to be struck at Southwark under Edward VI since *E* was also used on a few crowns that probably belong to the end of Henry's reign.

There is no means of distinguishing Sharington's illicitly minted testons from his earlier products. As in the case of the lesser denominations, a few London-made teston dies were provided when the Bristol mint was opened in April 1546; these have trefoil stops and confirm that sleeves had not yet replaced trefoils at the Tower by that date, and that bust 1 was still in use for testons. On Bristol-made dies Evenet's portrait is based on Tower bust 1, with a thick fur collar, and they show his normal decorative lettering and ornamentation. There is usually an elaborate leaf instead of a cross in the centre of the crown above the rose, and a small point below it, like that below the shield on Bristol groats. In production for only a little over a year, all testons of this mint are rare, particularly those from London dies.

The main variation in the reverse design lies in the outer petals of the rose, and in the size and shape of the crown. At first the petals were put in by a neat punch with a central swelling on the inside and a slightly concave outer edge, and dies with this form show one of the five petals horizontally below the crown. Before the end of group A a wider petal punch was employed, which continued throughout group B, with the petals normally disposed so that two of them meet below the middle of the crown. These new petals have a nick in the central swelling on the inside, and their external contour is not indented, with the result that the whole rose has a more circular outline. In group A the crown above the rose is large and wide, but in group B it is usually from smaller punches, one of which shows the far side of the lower band, making a complete hoop.

The earliest of the Tower testons have the same alphabet and saltire stops as the first base sovereigns (type I, of large module), while the broken saltires, or trefoils, associate the next issue with the type IIa sovereigns of reduced size. Both these kinds of group A testons would thus belong to the 9 oz. fine coinage up to March 1545. The last of the *henric VIII* testons, the rare variety with a small pellet-in-annulet after the inscription, may be related to the earliest issue of 22 ct. gold crowns, and would in that case be of silver only 6 oz. fine. The *henric 8* testons would then run from c. April 1545 onwards, with Southwark soon joining in and the changes to sleeve stops and 4 oz. silver coming about a year later. An annulet on the inner circle on a few late trefoil-stopped group B Tower dies, and a pellet-in-annulet on one reverse with sleeve stops, could thus fall at about the time of the second reduction in fineness, and may have been connected with it. The last testons must be those of group C with lozenge stops and mintmark pellet-in-annulet, which were known to Jacob from only three specimens. One of these is a lozenge/sleeve mule, with Gothic letters; the other two are converse mules, with the lozenge stops on their reverse dies, one of which has Roman letters. It is not clear how long testons continued in production after Henry's death, but the extreme rarity of the posthumous group C suggests that, despite their inclusion in Edward's first indentures in April 1547, they must soon have come to an end. When in 1549 Sharington confessed that he had coined testons at Bristol to a great sum from May to July 1547, in defiance of the prohibition against their striking, he may have been referring to an instruction of which other record has been lost but which applied to all the mints involved.

Groats

As it had been throughout the late middle ages, the groat remained the key denomination for most of the debasement period, until the introduction of the portrait shillings of Edward VI in 1549, although even then the minting of groats did not cease. It is therefore the groat coinage, and particularly that from the Tower, that is the most useful for establishing the sequence of stops, mintmarks and other features. In the varied form of the bust groats also exhibit an important component which, although not for the most part relevant to the other silver denominations, does assist in the process of arranging and dating other details of design. Taking all these elements together, and noting which of them occur on groats from mints other than the Tower, it is possible to construct an approximate chronology by reference to the dates of operation of the mints concerned.

Apart from the busts, the main features for consideration are the stops, lettering, cross-ends and mintmarks. Stops follow the normal sequence - saltires, trefoils and sleeves under Henry VIII, lozenges, pierced crosses and pellets from 1547. It has often been inferred that the base coins can be allocated between the two reigns in another simple way: those with Gothic lettering to Henry, those with Roman to Edward. But this is not absolutely true in respect of any denomination, and among the groats there are exceptions both ways. Although the division largely holds good for Tower groats, many of the early groats of the three mints opened in 1545 have Roman letters, while Gothic letters probably continued briefly into 1547 and recur exceptionally on a few much later groat dies at the Tower and at York. There are, however, certain reverse features indicative of an approximate division between the reigns. In Henry's lifetime the Tower and Southwark mints each had an individual pattern of ornaments in the forks of the reverse cross (with no marks there on groats of the other mints that used centrally made dies), and the limbs of the cross are plain except for their terminals. Posthumous groats of all mints have a knop on the cross-arms, just inside the inner circle; and in the forks, at first (1547-8) a crescent (more correctly, perhaps, a broken annulet), and later, with the advent of pellet stops, a half-rose for the remainder of the series from 1548.

ORNAMENTS IN CROSS-ENDS OF BASE GROATS

(a)   (b)   (c)   (d)

(a) Annulet, Tower classes i, ii; (b) Pellet-in-annulet, Tower, classes ii-iv;
(c) Crescent, Tower and other mints, classes iv-v; (d) Half-rose, Tower and other mints, class vi.

Of the six separate bust types defined by Whitton, Laker has shown that all except nos. 3 and 4 include a fair amount of variation. Bust 1 has a large head, nearly facing, with a drooping moustache, set above a fur-collared mantle. Bust 2 is narrower, and turned further to the spectator's right, thus showing the (king's) right ear and a wedge of neck behind the beard, but very little of the lock of hair on the other side. Busts 3 and 4, the former quite scarce, the latter more so, are entirely different. Instead of a cloak, the king wears a plainer garment with the collar folded down. The head is turned three-quarters to the right, without a lock of hair protruding on either side, and the eyes often appear half-closed. The head of bust 3 is small, that of bust 4 much larger and without shoulders. Bust 5 is quite similar to bust 1 (perhaps intentionally so), and Evans did not distinguish between them; the head is, however, generally bigger, the nose larger and more prominent, and the fur collar curves up further beside the cheeks. A variant of bust 5 has a small rose clasp on the mantle. Bust 6 is three-quarter facing, without a cloak, and superficially resembles bust 3; but the head is smaller, with more open eyes, and the

Debasement, Henry VIII – Edward VI

drapery more finely drawn. Stops and other features should always enable busts 5 and 6 to be distinguished from nos. 1 and 3 without difficulty. Mintmarks and stops indicate that there was often some parallelism or overlap between the busts, notably 2 with 1, 3 with 2 and 6 with 5. Bust 2 was used at the three new mints opened in May-June 1545, at Canterbury and York sometimes with a rosette clasp, and it certainly continued into 1546, being found among the rare London dies sent to Bristol when that mint was opened in April 1546. Bust 3, also represented at Bristol, is unlikely to have been in use much before that date. Busts 3 and 4 are both lacking at Canterbury, belonging as they do within the groatless period at this mint between late 1545 and early 1548. Bust 4 covers the transition from Gothic to Roman lettering as well as that from sleeves to lozenge stops, and since the lozenge-stopped bust 4 groats share several common features with the early portrait groats of Edward VI, the use of this bust probably fell within the first half of 1547. The bust more usually found with lozenge stops, however, is no. 5 which, in view of the rarity of bust 4, must have appeared long before the end of that year. Later, presumably in 1548, it was joined but evidently not replaced by bust 6, which was already current when the mint at Durham Place was opened in December 1548. In terms of the debasement, all or most of the groats of 9oz. fine silver (up to March 1545) would have bust 1, those of 6oz. silver (April 1545 to March 1546) bust 1 or 2, and those of 4oz. silver (from April 1546 onwards) substantially busts 3 to 6.

Groats of both establishments at the Tower carry the *Posui* legend instead of a mint name. Those of Henry's lifetime have mintmark lis on both sides, replaced at or about the beginning of Edward's reign by mintmark arrow at Tower I and at Tower II by the same series of secondary marks as on other denominations, *K*, grapple, martlet and lis. As Whitton recognised, busts, stops, cross-end ornaments and mules all indicate that arrow and the secondary marks ran in parallel. Ornaments in the forks of the cross-ends on Tower groats with bust 1 were small annulets followed, during the currency of bust 2 and trefoil stops, by a larger annulet enclosing a pellet. Soon after the change of reign (with bust 4 and lozenge stops) the pellet-in-annulet was replaced by the crescent which in turn gave way during the period of bust 5 and pellet stops to the half-rose. An extremely rare variety of early Tower groat (perhaps one of those struck under the secret indenture of 1542) has saltires in the cross-ends, the standard ornament in the second coinage. The reverse is similar to reverses of the last of the profile groats, but whether this variety should be regarded as a mule is an open question. Possibly the introduction of annulets in the forks of the cross occurred marginally later than the adoption of the facing bust, since there is also a coin on which saltires have been overpunched with annulets. With saltire stops and annulets in the forks, the regular groats with bust 1 occur only of the Tower mint, belonging to the first year of acknowledged debasement, of silver 9 oz. fine, before the standard was reduced to 6 oz. fine and additional mints were brought into operation in the second quarter of 1545. There is some variety in the clasp that fastens the cloak of bust 1, often represented by a round brooch with two pendant ties, sometimes by a trefoil of small pellets. Most bust 1 groats have a larger lis mintmark than was used subsequently. Before bust 1 was discontinued, the punch for the saltire stops began to break, so that the stops described as trefoils which are normal with bust 2 are often defective saltires.

On the evidence of the dies sent to Bristol, when the last reduction in fineness took place in April 1546 groat dies with bust 2 and trefoil stops and with bust 3 and sleeve stops were both available; and the occurrence of an annulet on the inner circle with each of these busts thus seems to fall at about the time when the move to 4 oz. silver was made, lending support to Jacob's idea that this mark was designed to indicate the reduction in fineness. With bust 2 there is an obverse die on which the small lis mintmark is punched over a large circular mark, as if pellet-in-annulet had been in contemplation as an obverse mintmark for groats (equivalent to the mark on some of the Tower gold and testons) before it was decided to use it in the reverse cross-ends instead. The last definitive type of Tower groat of Henry's reign has sleeve stops, introduced during the period of bust 3, but exceptionally sleeves have also been noted with a fur-collared bust, another indication of overlap in the use of successive styles of portrait. One bust 3 Tower groat has an abnormal reverse with Roman *E*. With sleeve stops there was a change in the abbreviation mark after *henric;* previously this had been a query-shaped mark as found in manuscripts to indicate *–us,* but thereafter a normal apostrophe was used.

The earliest Tower groats with bust 4, with sleeve stops, are the last of the series to retain Gothic letters and the pellet-in-annulet in the reverse cross-ends. Within the relatively short currency of this bust all these features were altered in rapid succession: to lozenge stops, Roman letters and new cross-ends with crescents in the forks, and mintmark arrow or *K* instead of the hitherto invariable lis. In all these respects the later bust 4 groats coincide with the portrait groats of Edward VI. How soon after the death of Henry VIII in January this new coinage for the young king was prepared we do not know; but it could well have been related to the first indentures of Edward's reign which were made on 5 April 1547. If the portrait coinage was both the reason and the occasion for the adoption of the more legible Roman alphabet this was nevertheless replicated, with other associated features, on the contemporaneous issues that continued with Henry's face and name. Minor embellishments suggest that unusual care was taken with the designs of the Edwardian type: for example, the cross-ends are more ornate, and large pellets decorate the canopy of the crown (as on late testons). A very rare Tower variety of Edward groat has the French spelling *Edoard* (more usually found on Canterbury halfgroats); at this very moment a French engraver, Antony Levens, was working at the mint. The greatest curiosity, however, of this early Edwardian issue is a mule combining a normal groat reverse of the time, with mintmark arrow, and a pattern obverse die (for a shilling, or groat?) with Edward's portrait, the *Timor* legend, and the date 1547 in mixed Roman and Arabic figures (*MDXL7*).

When precisely bust 4 was introduced cannot be determined with any certainty. There would have been no special reason to produce a new Henry bust just because of the old king's death, but bust 3 had not proved very satisfactory – the punch was in low relief and not well defined – and at some point in the winter of 1546/7 its replacement would probably have been needed in the normal course. Although an occasional groat die at the Tower and Southwark combines Gothic lettering with lozenges (as do the earliest lozenge-stopped Canterbury halfgroats and pence), the change of alphabet and stops was virtually simultaneous. If the Edwardian type was introduced in April 1547, there would remain a period of nine weeks between the death of Henry VIII and the end of the account on 31 March during which the mint presumably continued on the old format. To these weeks, and therefore to the start of the posthumous period, should probably be attributed the very rare early coins with bust 4, sleeves and Gothic letters, and perhaps even some of the last groats with bust 3. The Edward portrait coinage itself is too rare to have lasted long, and bust 4 with Roman letters likewise. The latter was soon replaced by the long-serving bust 5, at first still with lozenge stops, then with pierced crosses and saltires, and finally with pellets.

Debasement, Henry VIII – Edward VI

Tower II Mintmarks, 1547-51

(a) *K* (Knight), class iv; (b) *6,* gold, 1549; (c) Grapple, 1549; (d) Crowned leopard's head, 1550; (e) Martlet right, posthumous; (f) Martlet left, Edward VI, 1550; (g) Small lis (without band), class vi.

Mintmark arrow of Tower I is found with all three forms of stop, but bust 6 with this mark is lacking. On one groat with pierced crosses the arrow is inverted, as on a gold halfcrown. Mintmark *K*, the earliest of the Tower II series, is found with both busts 4 and 5, usually on one side only – more often on the reverse, where it is also found struck over arrow. A *K*/arrow mule has also been noted. Mintmark grapple is found only on reverse dies, martlet and lis often so. Dies with these three marks all have half-roses in the forks. Stops are usually pellets, square or round; saltires are also found on some martlet coins, and grapple or martlet reverses may be without stops. Grapple and martlet obverses both show bust 5 or 6 but lis bust 5 only; if mintmark lis is correctly placed last in the Tower II sequence, the absence of any lis groats with bust 6 would suggest that bust 5 remained in use alongside bust 6 until the end of the posthumous series. In an exceptional revival, two obverse dies combined with grapple reverses have a form of (Roman-influenced) Gothic alphabet, as if looking forward to its full restoration on the fine silver coinage of 1551; one of them even includes the numeral *VIII*. Mintmark lis, small, spare, and lacking a band round the stem, is found in several mule combinations: arrow/lis, *K*/lis, lis/grapple and lis/martlet. In the posthumous series generally, there is extensive muling of dies with different stops and mintmarks. A few of the Tower coins without mintmark on either side may also be the result of muling.

Within a few months of the order in March 1545 to reduce the fineness from 9 oz. to 6 oz. silver, the three new mints at Canterbury, York and Southwark had begun to mint groats. By commission to the Under-Treasurers of Canterbury and York dated 27 March those two mints were authorised to strike four denominations only, from the halfgroat to the farthing, but this was soon countermanded (28 May) when they were instructed to coin only groats until 1 November following, to the exclusion of the lower values. In the case of York this instruction was in October extended until Easter 1546. Unlike the Tower series, groats of all three of these mints struck during Henry's lifetime include coins with both Roman and Gothic lettering, or a mixture of the two, but apparently starting with Roman only. These early Roman-lettered groats have trefoil or defective saltire stops. Some of them at Canterbury and York read *Di Gra* instead of the usual *D G.* The bust is no. 2, although certain versions have sometimes, as by Whitton, been described as varieties of bust 1, allocation of variants of the first two busts between them being in some cases a matter of taste. Groats of Henry's reign of these three mints have no initial mark on either side. At Canterbury and York the forks of the reverse cross are empty. At Southwark the earlier groats have an *S* in each fork, later ones an *e* in the upper and lower and an *S* in the side forks. Most of those with *S* only were probably struck at 6 oz., and those with *e* and *S* combined may all post-date the reduction to 4 oz. in April 1546.

Bust 3 with trefoil stops is extremely rare at Southwark, where sleeves were soon adopted with this bust and retained, very briefly, with bust 4. The late Southwark groats of Henry's reign generally have Gothic letters, the reversion to Roman coming, as elsewhere, along with lozenge stops. Southwark was the only mint beside Tower I to strike portrait groats of Edward VI, all very rare and including one exceptional coin with S in the side forks of the cross (matched on the reverse of a posthumous sleeve/lozenge mule that still retains the plain forked cross-ends). Otherwise, the Southwark Edward groats have crescents in ornate cross-ends and, as at the Tower, are the exact counterparts of posthumous groats with bust 4 in Henry's name. These last introduce a Roman *E* as mintmark which, although occasionally omitted, normally occurs on reverse dies for the rest of the series. For the remainder of the posthumous period the busts, stops and ornaments in the forks at Southwark follow the same pattern as at the Tower. There are also various mules involving Tower dies with mintmarks *K* or lis, and some altered reverse dies with *E* over arrow or lis.

At York also the later groats of Henry's reign show Gothic lettering. The last groats with open forks and a spur on the reverse are those with Roman letters and lozenge stops, some of which have a small lis initial mark on one side or other, the only certain occurrence of a mintmark in this position on any of the base York coins in Henry's name. There are the usual mules between late Gothic-lettered dies and the posthumous Roman-lettered type with lozenge stops. The sequence of subsequent varieties at York generally coincides with that of the southern mints, although a most unusual item is a bust 6 die with Gothic letters.

There are no Edward portrait groats from either York or Canterbury, the first because it did not strike this type in any denomination, the second because it had ceased to coin groats from November 1545 and was not authorised to mint them again until 1548. The Canterbury series then only reappears with bust 5, lozenge or pierced cross stops, and crescents in the forks. Unless Canterbury had resumed the minting of groats before the commission of February 1548, these features must have continued into 1548, suggesting a period when both lozenge stops and pierced crosses were in use together. Thenceforward Canterbury followed the same sequence of features as at other mints. One groat with bust 5 and pellet stops has the *TE* monogram for *et*, otherwise found only in conjunction with pierced crosses. Another late obverse variety (bust 6) has a small mintmark rose, the only case of a mintmark on Canterbury groats.

MINTMARKS OF CANTERBURY, BRISTOL AND DURHAM PLACE, 1545-49

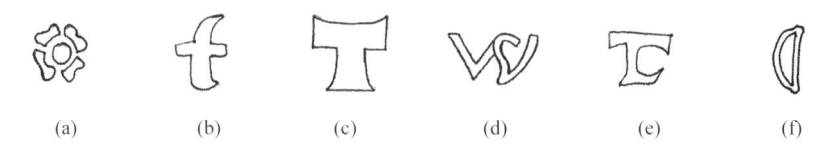

(a) Rose, Canterbury class vi; (b) and (c) *t,* and *T,* Canterbury, Tyllsworth, 1549;
(d) *WS* monogram, Bristol, Sharington, 1546-8; (e) *TC* monogram, Bristol, Chamberlain, 1549;
(f) Bow, Durham Place, Bowes, 1548-9.

That the last two mints to be commissioned in England, at Bristol and at Durham Place, were provided with their own die-sinkers suggests that the workload on the engravers at the Tower, who were already servicing five existing establishments, had reached its limit. Evenet at Bristol was skilful and innovative, creating a florid Gothic alphabet and a range of decorative symbols with which to adorn his dies. Unlike the Tower engravers he does not omit the *n* of *Angl*. Also, perhaps as a personal mark, he placed two small pellets on most of his dies, one below the shield, to the left, the other on the inner circle at about 150°. As with other denominations, a few London-made groat dies were sent to inaugurate the Bristol mint in April 1546, providing a valuable dated context for the evidently overlapping use of two types of bust (2 and 3) and stops (trefoils and sleeves). All Bristol groats from London-made dies are very rare, and they were soon muled with, and displaced by, Evenet's own dies. Sharington's *WS* monogram and Chamberlain's *TC* occur only on reverses, although one London-made obverse appears to have *WS* overpunched by the *h* of *henric*. Chown's analysis has shown that reverses of the groats with the *WS* mintmark can be divided into three types with successively (1) small annulets, (2) trefoils and (3) lis as ornaments within the forks of the cross-ends. That type 1 belongs at the head of the series is shown both by mules with London-made dies, and by the detailed features of the coins. Thus there are no extra symbols on obverses of type 1 groats, and the type begins (1a) with dies having a rose after *Civitas* but no mark before *Bristolie* such as occurs on all subsequent types (starting with a quatrefoil there in types 1b and 2). On obverses of the trefoil-marked type 2 there is often a symbol after *Rex*, a cross, rose or trefoil, and sometimes a cross or lis within the inscription. Type 3, which has small neatly shaped lis both in the forks and before *Bris*, saw a change of bust. Types 1, 2 and early 3 had shown a bust (1), similar to the early fur-collared Tower busts, with an arched band to the crown, below which there is a tuft of hair protruding on each side. On later groats of type 3 the crown has a nearly flat band, and there is no hair visible on the sinister side (bust 2). The final type (4), on which bust 2 continues, reverts to trefoils in the forks, and Chamberlain's *TC* monogram replaces Sharington's. It might have been expected that types 2 and 4, both with trefoils in the forks, would have been consecutive, and not separated by the lis-marked type 3; but the fact that the only Sharington groats with bust 2 are of type 3 makes that improbable. Based on relative numbers of surviving coins Chown has estimated that the series of Bristol groats struck during Henry's lifetime would not have extended much, if at all, beyond type 1.

Groats of Durham Place, with mintmark bow (on both sides) for John Bowes and the *Redde Cuique* legend, are relatively rare. They were struck from dies made independently of the Tower, but following its lead in a number of respects. Thus the portrait is modelled on bust 6, obverse stops are square pellets and there are crescents in the forks on some reverses. Others have a floral spike, within a more elaborate cross-end, perhaps echoing the replacement elsewhere of the crescent by a half-rose. Crescents are not found with bust 6 on Tower-made dies, so the engraver seems to have been borrowing features eclectically from coins of other mints. Reverse stops are saltires alone, not otherwise found on groats of this period.

Halfgroats

Halfgroats were struck in much smaller quantities than groats, except at Canterbury and perhaps at York. This is shown not only by the fact that at other mints they are much scarcer than groats, but also by their relative lack of variety. Almost all of them have a single type of bust, with fur-collared mantle, resembling bust no. 1 on groats. The only other form is a three-quarter bust like no. 6 which occurs on a few late coins of York and Dublin. However, despite the lack of evidence from bust types that is available for groats, the arrangement of the halfgroats can be based on the usual sequence of stops, and on the legends – for example, in the Roman-lettered posthumous series *Agl Fra* is reduced progressively to *A F*. Portrait halfgroats of Edward VI were struck at the same two mints as Edward groats, Tower I and Southwark, but also at Canterbury where no groats were being minted at this period. The Gallic spelling *Edoard* is found at Canterbury and Southwark.

None of the halfgroats with the *Posui* legend of the Tower mints are common. Those of Henry's reign are distinctly rare. They mostly have Gothic letters, and mintmark lis like the groats, with saltire or trefoil stops, and usually an annulet in the forks. The last variety of the reign, with sleeve stops, is extremely rare; it lacks both a mintmark and ornaments in the forks. Of the Roman-lettered *Posui* halfgroats from 1547, all of which are rare, most have the mintmark arrow of Tower I. These include the rare coins in Edward's name, some of which unexpectedly have the Southwark reading *Civitas London*; one can only guess whether these are Tower coins with the wrong inscription or Southwark coins with the wrong mintmark. Of the Tower II marks, generally confined to the reverse, only the first two, *K* and grapple, have been found on halfgroats. But there are also very rare arrow/*K* and arrow/grapple mules, as well as a Tower I/Southwark mule with arrow/*E*, again pointing to confusion in the destination of individual dies. Except for the grapple coins, with pellets, all *Posui* halfgroats with Roman letters have lozenge stops.

Southwark produced even fewer halfgroats in Henry's reign than the Tower, and they are extremely rare; under Edward, however, Southwark's output was more extensive. As with the groats, Southwark halfgroats begin with *S* in the forks (with mixed lettering), followed by *e* and *S* (with Gothic letters). Southwark halfgroats in Edward's name are very rare and, as noted above, may include a coin with mintmark arrow. From 1547 the full sequence of stops, lozenges, pierced crosses and pellets, is found on coins both with mintmark *E* and (like one late groat) without mintmark, suggesting that the halfgroats without mark may have been issued alongside those with *E* rather than at the end of the series as Whitton thought. Southwark is the only mint of which halfgroats with pierced cross stops are known.

Canterbury and York, the commonest mints for halfgroats of the debasement period as they had been in earlier coinages, continue to exhibit similarities. Those of Canterbury are the most plentiful, and for a long period were the highest denomination struck there, while the issue of groats was suspended. Generally, the halfgroats of these two mints have no initial mark on either side, and open forks, but the earliest have pierced cross-ends. These early coins have either Gothic or mixed letters, saltire or trefoil stops and, as on groats, a spur from the top of the shield (York) or a spur or a pellet below the shield (Canterbury). At Canterbury, with mainly Gothic letters, there are also late coins of Henry VIII with sleeve stops, and others with lozenges which, despite their Gothic lettering, may (like some equivalent pence of this mint) fall in the new reign. The portrait halfgroats from Canterbury are perhaps the least rare of all the early issue in Edward's name. They include some odd variants of the mint name (*Canton, Castor*). Most of the York halfgroats of the new reign and all of Canterbury retained the old Henry bust, now with Roman letters, and lozenge or pellet stops. The size of the letters varies, and some of Canterbury with pellet stops and small, neat lettering have Tyllsworth's initial *t* as mintmark on one side or the other. At York the late bust, like no. 6 on groats, is sometimes found. That York and Dublin were the only two mints with Tower-made dies to use this bust on halfgroats may have been a consequence of other mints concentrating from 1549 on either shillings or groats.

Bristol halfgroats, like groats, have the monogram mintmark of Sharington or

Chamberlain on the reverse only. Early London dies have trefoil stops, but on Evenet's dies, which have pellets below the shield and on the inner circle as on groats, the stops are mainly pellets or saltires, with an occasional cross, lis or trefoil. Halfgroats are not known with annulets in the forks, but the other groat ornaments, trefoils and lis, occur, together with quatrefoils. Chamberlain's halfgroats are scarce.

The reverse legend on halfgroats of Durham Place, which are extremely rare, is the same as on groats, but more abbreviated. They usually have small annulets in the cross-ends and a normal halfgroat fur-collared bust as at other mints, but one is a smaller version of the groat, with the bust copied from no. 6, the *ET* in monogram, and crescents in the forks.

Small Silver

Although concentration on the larger coins suited both the convenience of the moneyers and the rapid generation of profit for the king, the lower values were probably minted on a considerable scale in the first few years, since some of the pence and halfpence are not rare today. As in the second coinage, these two normally read *h D G Rosa Sine Spina* (with abbreviation or varied spelling, particularly of *Spina*). On the reverse is the mint name, except at Durham Place. The *Posui* legend was not used on coins below the halfgroat, and smaller silver reading *Civitas London* without mintmark could be either from the Tower or from Southwark. With Edward's portrait there are pence of Tower I (mintmark arrow), Southwark (mintmark *E*) and Bristol, and halfpence of 'London' and Bristol. The Edwardian halfpence are extremely rare, the pennies less so. Otherwise the halfpence and most of the pence have a facing bust, like a miniature of that on the testons, or in the case of some late pence of 'London', Canterbury, York and Dublin a three-quarter bust like no. 6 on groats or the late halfgroat bust. Reverse types, the shield on pence and the cross and pellets on halfpence, are the same as before.

Rare early Tower pence of Henry with mintmark lis (including the variety with annulet on the inner circle) have pierced cross-ends, as do the even rarer early pence of Southwark with mintmark *S* or *e*. There is also a Southwark penny, with mintmark *e* on the obverse, with sleeve stops and the open forks which are invariable henceforward. Posthumous pence have mintmarks (on one side only) arrow at Tower I, *K* and grapple at Tower II, and *E* at Southwark. 'London' pence without mintmark of Henry's reign, with open forks and sometimes with Roman or mixed letters, have trefoil or sleeve stops, and those of the posthumous period have the usual features: Roman letters, at first large, later small; lozenge or pellet stops (no pence with pierced crosses have been noted of any mint); and sometimes the late three-quarter bust. It is not clear whether the great rarity of pence with Southwark mintmarks is due to the very limited output of Southwark pence altogether, or merely that most of them did not carry a mintmark.

At Canterbury and York also the rare early pennies have pierced cross-ends. Like the larger denominations of these mints they have a spur between shield and inner circle. Stops are saltires or trefoils, and lettering is Gothic except in the case of some coins of York on which it is mixed. Later issues under Henry lack the spur and are also identified by their open forks and sleeve stops. Still with Gothic letters, but with lozenge stops, are a few pence of Canterbury, but in the posthumous period lozenge stops, or the later pellets, are otherwise combined with Roman letters except for an occasional Gothic *h*. Instead of open forks, some of the Canterbury pence with lozenge stops have the cross-ends patty, as more frequently on halfpence. A smaller Roman fount was introduced along with the pellet stops, as at the Tower, and some of the pence of both mints with these features also have the late three-quarter bust.

The penny of Durham Place is extremely rare. Its facing bust may suggest that the three-quarter bust had not yet been adopted on pence elsewhere. It has pellet stops, but differs from pence of other mints in reading *H 8 D G*, and in having ornamental cross-ends and a heavily abbreviated version of the *Redde Cuique* inscription.

At first Bristol pence conform to the pattern of other coins of this mint in the early use of London-made dies (with sleeve stops on the obverse), followed by Bristol dies with the usual variety of stops. These last have forks either open, as on the London dies, or with trefoils; and their obverses read *he 8 D G*. They have a distinctive portrait, the head smaller, the bust larger, than at other mints, and the diameters of their dies and flans are greater. However, there are also later dies with a normal bust, Roman letters and lozenge stops (in one case muled with an Evenet obverse), this being the only case noted of London-made dies at Bristol in the posthumous silver series. At this mint Edward's portrait is only found on pence and halfpence. The pence are less rare than Edward pence of the Tower and Southwark.

Except that none has been found of Durham Place, and that those of Southwark are not separately identifiable, halfpence in Henry's name were struck at the same mints as pence, and are of relatively little variety. Cross-ends are often patty rather than with open forks, especially on earlier issues. Those of 'London' include rare coins of Henry VIII with Gothic letters, mintmark lis and a pellet-in-annulet in the centre of the reverse, which must be of the Tower; Roman-lettered posthumous coins without mintmark could, however, include some from Southwark, and the same might also be true of extremely rare halfpence in Edward's name, which are otherwise known only of Bristol.

Canterbury and York halfpence are scarce. Under Henry the letters are mainly Gothic, but sometimes mixed; posthumously, Roman or mixed. Stops at these two mints include the normal sequence, except for sleeves, although halfpence with pierced crosses are only recorded of Canterbury. Bristol halfpence do not include any from London dies; they have a double leaf in the forks of the cross. As on pence, the Henry portrait on Bristol halfpence has less head and more body than at other mints. These coins are very rare, but less so than the Bristol halfpenny with Edward's portrait.

One farthing of Henry's debasement is known. The reverse type, a single pellet in each quarter of a cross, reproduces that of the majority of the second coinage farthings, together with the *Deo Gracias* legend. The obverse, however, has a five-petalled rose instead of a portcullis.

Edward Sovereigns and Fractions, 1549 – 1550

As well as introducing the shillings of Edward VI the proclamation of 24 January 1549 ordered four gold coins at the improved standard of 22 ct. fineness: the sovereign, half-sovereign or 'Edward Royal', quarter-sovereign and half-quarter-sovereign (i.e. half-crown). Although their fineness was ten per cent better than the preceding gold, the weights were reduced by slightly more, by minting £34 instead of £30 from the pound of gold. The mints of this coinage were both establishments at the Tower, Southwark and Durham Place, the last of these with its own engraver pursuing his individual course. Tower I, where the account ran to October 1550, was as usual the most productive mint, followed by Southwark where the account was closed two months later.

Like most of the lesser gold of this coinage, and the shillings, the sovereigns have small square pellet stops. The inscriptions are in clean Roman letters – their only occurrence on sovereigns in Edward's name. The design of the sovereign was similar to that of the earlier sovereigns and half sovereigns of the debasement period, although the king now wears doublet and hose and holds a sword instead of a sceptre. Also, there is no rose below his feet, as on earlier sovereigns, because of the reduced size of the design necessitated by the lower weight and smaller module. Two dies each are known with the Tower I mintmark arrow and with the Southwark mintmark *Y*. These sovereigns are very rare and their issue probably did not last long; the dies however have wireline inner circles, which suggests that they may not have been made until the period of the second issue shillings from April 1549.

On the obverse of the lower values is a right-facing profile portrait of the king, coupled with an oval shield with garniture on the reverse. A crown above the shield on gold serves as a deliberate differentiation between half-sovereigns and shillings. The half- and quarter-sovereigns have *E R* beside the shield, but the initials are omitted on the half-quarters because of their small size. The earliest examples (type 1) of all three denominations show the king bare-headed in a manner similar to the portrait on a set of patterns, made near the beginning of the reign, for half-sovereign, crown and half-crown which have an elegant rose on the reverse. The portrait was, however, soon brought more into line with that on the shillings by the addition of a crown (type 2). The type 1 coins are from dies with beaded circles and transposed inscriptions as on the 8 oz. shillings struck in February 1549. Again as with the early shillings, the type 1 gold is of good style, with well-made lettering, but workmanship thereafter deteriorated. In type 2 the inscriptions are disposed in the normal way and wireline circles also show their correspondence with the 6 oz. shillings struck from April 1549 onwards. The only exception to these distinctions between the two types is that the earliest half-quarters of type 2 still have dotted circles. The bust on the gold is armoured, but otherwise the design of the type 2 gold closely resembles that of the shillings (except for the crown on the reverse).

The mintmarks also are related to those on the shillings, although without some of the later shilling marks. On quarters and half-quarters the mintmark often appears on the obverse only. Tower gold exhibits a separate series of marks for each of the two mints, like the shillings. Arrow is the only Tower I mark in type 1, but in the course of type 2 it was replaced by swan (the punch is that designated swan I on shillings), and there are mules between the two marks. No mark indicative of Tower II is found on first issue shillings, but very rare half- and quarter-sovereigns of type 1 with an arabic *6* (tilted forward, like a Greek *sigma*) probably represent this mint in gold. In type 2, however, well-known Tower II marks appear - grapple and martlet, the latter only known on halves. All the gold of this coinage attributable to Tower II is of considerable rarity, in accordance with its very small output. Southwark is represented by mintmark *Y*, and to judge by relative rarity the output of this mint diminished sharply during 1549 since although *Y* occurs on both types of the three fractional denominations, the only *Y*-marked coins that are not particularly rare are the type 1 halves.

The earliest Tower obverse dies for half-sovereigns (1a) have the *Timor* legend with the date *MDXLIX*, exactly as on first issue shillings. But a separate motto was soon adopted for halves (1b), and used on the smaller gold throughout: *Scutum Fidei Proteget Eum* (The shield of faith shall protect him). This being slightly longer than the *Timor* motto, there was now no space for a date, although on type 2 halves there was often enough room for rosettes between the words instead of the small square stops that are otherwise normal. Late Tower halves with mintmarks swan and martlet show decoration of the breastplate (2b), but those of type 2a, with arrow and grapple, like all coins of the lower values, still have plain armour as in type 1. There are also *Y* halves of types 2a and 2b from Southwark, but the latter is extremely rare.

MINTMARKS OF EDWARD VI SOVEREIGNS AND FRACTIONS 1549-50

MINTS	20s	10s		5s		2s. 6d.	
TYPES		1	2	1	2	1	2
TOWER I							
Arrow	x	a,b	a	x	x	x	a,b
Swan			b		x		b*
TOWER II							
6		b		x			
Grapple			a		x		a
Martlet			b				
SOUTHWARK							
Y	x	b	a,b	x	x	x	b
DURHAM PLACE							
Bow		x	x				

* – mule swan/arrow only

From Durham Place, although commissioned in January 1549 to coin all four values in gold, the only extant examples are half-sovereigns. There are three types with mintmark bow, all extremely rare and each represented by a single obverse die. Although they are of similar basic design to the Tower and Southwark coins, there are material differences. The first of them must be the unique coin dated *MDXLVIII*, often for that reason regarded as a pattern, but more probably constituting an exceptional use of old style dating. This coin has the *Scutum* legend on the obverse (die 1) with an uncrowned portrait, but the bust almost half-length with a high collar, showing the upper arms and chest, and the head accordingly much smaller than on Tower coins. A second unique coin (die 3) has a similar tall bust, but crowned, and the *Scutum* legend (without date) on the reverse, reflecting changes on the Tower halves. But another type (die 2), more akin to Tower type 1 in its normal uncrowned bust, transposed inscriptions and beaded circles, has a legend differing (as with the silver of this mint) from that on Tower dies: *Lucerna Pedibus Meis Verbum Est* (The word is a lantern unto my feet; Psalm 119, 105). While the obverse portrait of die 3 is based on die 1, and the *Lucerna* type sits uneasily between two with *Scutum*, the changes from uncrowned to crowned bust, from transposed to normal inscriptions and from a beaded to a wireline circle suggest that this numbering of the dies may represent their actual sequence of manufacture. Dies 2 and 3, however, must have been in concurrent use, since mules with the obverse from die 3 and the reverse of the *Lucerna* type (thus having the king's name on both sides) are no rarer than true *Lucerna* coins. Stops on the Durham Place gold dies are neat crosses with concave sides, as on some of the shilling dies of this mint.

Southwark Edward Gold, 1551

Between January and June 1551 the Southwark accounts record the minting of 96 lbs. of fine gold, pursuant to a commission of the previous December addressed to Sir Edmund Pekham, High Treasurer, Sir John York, Under-Treasurer, and other officers of the Southwark mint. That this was an exceptional issue is suggested by the naming of Pekham himself, other commissions of the period being addressed to the respective Under-Treasurers. The coins ordered were a sovereign of 24s., a ryal of 12s., and an angel of 8s. and its half, to be struck at £28 16s. per lb., giving the weight of a sovereign as 240 gr. No provision for silver was included. Fitting the terms of this commission is a series of very rare and handsome gold coins of traditional types with Edward's name. Their mintmark, an ostrich's head with thick neck and prominent beak, is a canting reference to the name of the Pekham family, one branch of which is known to have used an ostrich as its crest.

In addition to authorised denominations there are double-weight sovereigns of this coinage, adding support to the view that this was a special order designed to provide pieces for the king's personal use or for presentation on his progress (as 50 lb. of gold struck in 1552 was stated to be). The return to a full-sized 240 gr. sovereign, at the ancient standard with only half a grain of alloy, was accompanied by a revival of the design (and Gothic alphabet) of the pre-debasement coins of Henry VIII, the king in full robes with a portcullis beneath his feet, and on the reverse a small shield in the centre of a large Tudor rose. Gothic inscriptions may also have been designed to recall a more orderly monetary era, a deliberate break from the Roman lettering associated with coins of the worst phase of the debasement.

The angel and half-angel with ostrich head are the only such coins in Edward's name, or indeed of his reign – with one exception, namely that one of the pairs of angel dies was altered by having the ostrich head overpunched with a tun for use in the subsequent coinage at the Tower after the Southwark mint was closed. The Pekham half-angel exhibits some unexpected features. The stops are pellets not saltires; the reverse carries the *Per Crucem* legend of the angel instead of the traditional *O Crux Ave*; and although the *e* above the shield is large and Gothic, the inscriptions on both sides (except for *c*) are from a fount of small Roman letters.

No gold ryal of the Pekham series is known. Mention should however be made of a related item with the ostrich head mintmark. Two strikings in silver are known from dies evidently prepared at the same time as those for the Pekham gold, and it may be wondered whether this type could have been a pattern for the design of the ryal. The obverse has a mounted figure of the king, brandishing an almost horizontal sword above his head, and closely resembling that on the reverse of Edward's great seal; on the reverse of the pattern is a crowned shield between the royal initials, with the *Timor Domini* legend and the date *MDLI*. This type was sometimes described by early writers as the 'horseman shilling'. The obverse has no precedent in the Tudor coinage, as those of Pekham's known gold coins do – its unfamiliarity being perhaps a reason why the design was not adopted.

Edward Shillings 1549 – 1551

Three issues of shillings with Edward's name and portrait were made in two and a half years from 1549 to 1551, at different combinations of weight and fineness:
1. February 1549. 8 oz. fine, 60 gr.
2. April 1549 – 1550/1. 6 oz. fine, 80 gr.
3. April – July 1551 (and in 1552 at Dublin). 3 oz. fine, 80 gr.

Although weighing only 50 per cent more, the 8 oz. shillings were current at three times the value of the 4 oz. groats that were still being minted. Preaching in St. Paul's before the king, Hugh Latimer had caused royal offence when he spoke of "a pretty little shilling", that he had "put it away almost for an old grote". Not surprisingly, the 8 oz. shillings proved unacceptable to the general public and almost immediately had to be replaced by the second issue, with the fineness reduced but the weight increased, so as to maintain the same silver content but in a larger coin. The commission of 24 January 1549 had included provision also for half-shillings, but none are known and presumably none were struck since they would have caused even greater confusion with groats and halfgroats in circulation. The final stage of the debasement was reached in 1551 when the fineness was halved to 3 oz.: in the words of the king's *Journal*, authorisation was given "to make 20,000 pound weight for necessity somewhat baser to get gains 160,000 £ clear by which the debt of the realm might be paid, the country defended from any sudden attempt, and the coin amended". The amendment of the coin eventually took place in October 1551 although a last episode of the old order occurred at Dublin in the following year. Unless the 3 oz. coins were used to meet the government's own liabilities, it is difficult to see how the mints would have been able to put them into circulation once it had been announced in April 1551 that they would be derated to ninepence in August.

Edward's shillings are notable for being the first English coins to carry dates. This was, however, only a qualified step into the modern world since they are shown in the Roman form rather than in the arabic numerals that had already been widely adopted elsewhere in Europe. Thus 1549 was often expressed on the coins as M:D:XL.IX, with stopping between what would have been the four separate digits of an arabic date. Being first struck in February it might have been expected that the earliest shillings would have been dated 1548 in the old style, according to which the legal year began on Lady Day (25 March); but although the new style, with the year beginning on 1 January, was not formally adopted until 1752, the coins (excepting the one Durham Place half-sovereign dated 1548) demonstrate its common usage two hundred years earlier. While the use of dates is of assistance in ordering the material, it must not be assumed, in this series as in any other, that care was always taken to ensure that they were accurate.

Six English mints were engaged in the production of base shillings. Tower I and Southwark participated in all three issues, but Tower II only certainly in the second and third. Canterbury, which had not previously been commissioned to mint coins larger than the groat, features in the first and second issues, although it appears to have been closed at the end of 1549. Durham Place, where output ceased in October, produced both 8 oz. and 6 oz. shillings, but Bristol struck only 6 oz. shillings, on a very small scale, in May and June 1549. Since these two mints had their own engravers their dies mostly do not correspond closely to those of the other mints.

None of the shillings carries a mint name, and their attribution thus rests upon the mintmarks which, in the first and second issues, mostly accord with those on other denominations. There is very extensive muling between successive marks, especially at Tower I, which is convenient for purposes of attribution and sequence. At first the mark for Sir Martin Bowes at Tower I was the arrow, as already used on his earlier coinages since 1547, but during 1549 it was followed by pheon and then by swan. The pheon, which does not occur on any other denomination at this period, is extremely rare and, as a barbed arrow-head, is probably to be regarded as just a variant of arrow rather than as a separate mark. As Carlyon-Britton observed, swan is found in two forms: swan I, a squat bird with very little neck, was replaced, soon after the date on reverse dies was advanced to 1550, by swan II which has a long curved neck and a downturned tail that looks almost like a third stumpy leg. No shillings of the first issue are known with mintmark 6, as found on the early portrait gold attributed to Tower II, but this mint is represented in the second issue by its usual later marks, grapple (1549) and martlet (1550). Additionally, there is an extremely rare third mark, known only on shillings and attributable to this mint by virtue of a mule with martlet: previously described as a pelt, this mark has more recently been identified as a crowned leopard's head (as once used very briefly on groats of Henry VII). At Southwark the mark used throughout the first and second issues was York's initial *Y*, although an *E* before the *Y* on one obverse die of the first issue is an unexpected echo of the mintmark on the posthumous Henry coinage from this mint. With the third issue the use of personal marks was discontinued. So, on the 3 oz. shillings of 1551, in an apparently deliberate departure from previous practice, and facilitating identification of the coins of this wretched final issue, the principal royal emblems of the period, rose, lion and lis, were employed instead.

Debasement, Henry VIII – Edward VI

MINTMARKS, BUSTS AND DATES ON EDWARD VI BASE SHILLINGS

MINT AND MINTMARK	BUST	8 oz. 1	2	6 oz. 3	4	5	6	3 oz. 6
TOWER I								
Arrow		IX	IX	IX	IX	IX		
Pheon						IX		
Swan I						IX,L		
Swan II						IX,L		
Rose								L,LI
TOWER II								
None?		IX?						
Grapple				IX	IX			
Leopard's head					L			
Martlet						L	L	
Lion								L,LI
SOUTHWARK								
Y		IX		IX	IX	IX,L	L	
Lis								LI
CANTERBURY								
Rose		IX						
t, T				IX	IX	IX		
BRISTOL								
TC				IX				
DUBLIN								
Harp								LII

IX – 1549; L – 1550; LI – 1551; LII – 1552

The three lesser mints used the same mintmarks on shillings as on their 4 oz. silver. At Canterbury the mark on 8 oz. shillings was a rose, as on some of its posthumous groats, and on 6 oz. shillings, as on halfgroats, the initial *t* (or rarely *T*) of William Tyllsworth. The extremely rare shillings of Bristol carry the usual *TC* monogram for Chamberlain who had taken over in January 1549. All the shillings struck at Durham Place under John Bowes have the bow as mintmark.

The basic types of the shillings were common to all mints – a crowned right-facing bust of the king in elaborate vestment, and an oval shield with garniture and *E R* beside it. Their design was thus broadly similar to that of the contemporary 22 ct. gold, although on the gold the king is shown in armour (and bare-headed on the earliest issue) and there is always a crown above the shield. A coinage of Edward portrait shillings had been in contemplation since the beginning of the reign, as evidenced by patterns dated 1547 and 1548 which, despite some detailed variation in type and inscription (notably the omission of *D G*), generally foreshadowed the design actually adopted in 1549. The shillings were also to retain the motto that had been used on the patterns (but not otherwise previously) – *Timor Domini Fons Vitae* (The fear of the Lord is a fountain of life; Proverbs 14, v.27). On the 8 oz. shillings, as on one of the 1547 patterns, the *Timor* legend is placed on the obverse and the king's name and titles around the shield, but on the baser issues that followed the inscriptions occupy their normal positions. While their transposition on the first issue shillings may have been intended as an additional means of differentiating 60 gr. shillings from 40 gr. groats, the conjuncture of a motto with the king's portrait makes a sharper contrast than in the case of precedents, such as George nobles and crowns, which have the royal titles on the reverse but do not portray the king himself.

Another feature peculiar to the first issue shillings and the type 1 gold is their beaded circles, as had been normal in earlier coinages. On later shillings and type 2 gold the circles are linear (wireline). Almost all the first issue shillings from Tower-made dies show the same bust (no. 1), in which the head is rather larger than on shillings of the second and third issues. The only exception to this is the very rare bust 2, with an even larger head and the crown tilted further back than on bust 1. Bust 2 obverse dies have no mintmark, but their reverses show the mintmark arrow of Tower I. All 8 oz. shillings are quite rare, as one would expect of an issue confined to the one month of February 1549. The arrow shillings of Tower I are rarer than the *Y* shillings of Southwark, in accordance with their relative output as shown in the mint accounts. A few 8 oz. shillings lack a mintmark on either side, and their obverse dies are notable for reading *Vite*, the normal form on 6 oz. and 3 oz. shillings, instead of *Vitae* as on all other coins of the first issue. One of them has traces of a mintmark on the reverse which looks like a *TC* monogram, perhaps deliberately erased on a die never delivered to Bristol (Chamberlain's account has no entry for 8 oz. shillings). Potter thought the *Vite* 8 oz. shillings might have been struck at York but, although dies were prepared for 6 oz. shillings with a York mintmark, they were then altered for use at other mints, and there is no evidence for the actual coinage of shillings of any issue at York. More plausibly, Bispham has suggested that the *Vite* 8 oz. shillings were products of Tower II (where gold was struck during the period of the first issue, if the coins with mintmark *6* are correctly attributed); but perhaps Canterbury should also be considered as a possible claimant for them in view of an unexplained discrepancy between the great rarity of 8 oz. shillings with mintmark rose and the not inconsiderable output recorded in the Canterbury mint accounts for February 1549.

One of the few Tower shillings with bust 2 weighs 71 gr. which may indicate that it was struck after the weight increase of April 1549 from an old die of the first issue. Otherwise, all the 6 oz. shillings (except some from Durham Place) were struck from new and slightly larger dies with the king's titles on the obverse and *Timor* on the reverse, in the normal manner, and with wireline circles inside the inscriptions. A new and plainer letter fount was introduced, and the general workmanship both in die-sinking and striking was less careful, as is often the case at a time of heavy output. Four further busts are found on Tower-made dies of the second issue (nos. 3-6). The last of these is extremely rare with second issue mintmarks, but was to be the only bust used on the 3oz. shillings of the third issue. Busts 3, 4 and 5 were used on 1549 shillings of the Tower mints, Southwark and Canterbury, and bust 3 also on a Tower-made die sent to Bristol. Bust 5 was used extensively for the later dies of 1549 and on all the 6 oz. shillings dated 1550, except for the very few late coins with bust 6. Differences between the bust types are more easily observed than described, but the following pointers may help to identify them. Bust 3 has a hollow below the shoulder, so that the lower contour of the bust is indented at this point. The rare bust 4 is similar but without the hollow; its front outline is flatter and extends further forward than that of bust 5. On bust 5 the lapels and collar are larger and more intricately decorated, and the chin is more pointed. The neck and collar of bust 6 are very narrow, and this bust is also distinguishable by having large and well-shaped fleurs-de-lis beside the central cross of the crown.

Only one mintmark is found at each mint in the early phase of the second issue, with busts 3 and 4, although Tyllsworth's initial at Canterbury occurs in both lower and upper case. Shillings of this period with Tower I's arrow and Southwark's *Y* are abundant, those

Debasement, Henry VIII – Edward VI

with the grapple of Tower II and the *t* or *T* at Canterbury much less so. At some stage plans were made to supply shilling dies to York, to match the addition of this denomination at Canterbury and extend the parallelism between these two mints. Such plans must, however, have been quickly countermanded, because rare coins are found of the five other mints with their respective mintmarks punched over *G*, the initial of the York Under-Treasurer Gale. These amended dies are sometimes paired with each other, sometimes with normal unaltered dies of the appropriate mint. All the altered obverse dies show bust 3, suggesting that this was the first bust to be used in the second issue. Bristol shillings have rosettes in the inscriptions, in the usual Evenet manner, but one obverse die at least appears to be of Tower workmanship, with bust 3, and the *TC* monogram apparently over an erased *G*.

Tower II and Canterbury coins with bust 5 dated 1549 are recent discoveries, but neither is a surprise: the Canterbury account runs to December 1549, while Tower II remained in operation (on a limited scale) until 1551, and the variety among the 1549 bust 5 shillings of Tower I suggests that this bust was brought into use well before the first date change. Bust 5 shillings dated 1550 were only struck at the two Tower mints and Southwark, those of Tower II being again very rare. In addition there are 1550 shillings of Tower II and Southwark with the thin-necked bust 6, but so few that this bust must have been introduced very near the end of the second issue. As the Tower II coins with bust 6 have mintmark martlet it seems likely that martlet rather than leopard's head (known only with bust 5) may have been the last mark on 6 oz. shillings at this mint.

Occasional variants of the design in the second issue may be noted. On some shillings of Tower II and Southwark there is a larger and coarser shield, filling most of the reverse field, and on others the *E R* is omitted. A further link between these two mints is a Southwark reverse with mintmark *Y* over grapple. The only other altered marks noted in this issue, apart from those punched over *G* on withdrawn York dies, link Tower I and Southwark – swan over *Y* (1549) and *Y* over swan (1550).

The third and basest issue of Edward shillings was commissioned at the Tower mints and Southwark in April 1551. Accounts for Southwark (£93,000) and Tower I (£81,000) run from April to July; subtracting these figures from a total output from the English mints recorded in 1556 of £217,000 in 3 oz. silver leaves a sum of approximately £43,000 attributable to Tower II, for which no separate account is extant. When the 3 oz. shillings were decried to 2¼d. in September 1560 they were said to bear one of four mintmarks, harp (for Dublin), lis, rose and lion. Shillings with mintmark lis both sides are only known with the date 1551 (*MDLI*), but there are very rare mules lis/*Y* (1550) and *Y*/lis (1551) which link the lis to Southwark. These mules can be seen as the result of using old *Y* dies, but there are also a few dies dated 1550 with mintmark lion or rose over lion (but never with rose as the original mark). It seems more likely that the date on these rare coins was incorrect than that the new mintmarks had been introduced on late 6 oz. shillings, to no obvious purpose, before the 3 oz. issue was authorised. With the correct date of 1551 there are Tower coins with mintmarks rose and lion, of which Bispham has attributed the former, as the commoner, to Tower I and the lion to Tower II. The lion itself is a meagre beast, lacking forelegs and put in from the punch used in the royal arms. The existence of a 1551 shilling with mintmark lion on the obverse, but rose over lion on the reverse, is further illustration of the confusion in the supply and marking of dies inherent in periods of hectic mint activity. All the shillings of the third issue have bust 6 which can assist in identifying 3 oz. shillings when, as not infrequently with such poorly struck base coins, both date and mintmark are unclear.

Durham Place shillings stand apart from those of other mints in several ways, most obviously in the bust and legends. Although the changes in the disposition of the inscriptions and from beaded to linear circles, which separate the 8 oz. and 6 oz. shillings of other mints, were reflected at Durham Place, the division between the two is not absolute at this mint and most of the dies from the first issue remained in use in the second. There are two styles of bust. On dies made for the first issue the neat portrait (bust 1) is unlike anything found at the Tower although, with its open collar and high-arched crown, it bears a close resemblance to a pattern dated 1547, both perhaps based on a portrait of Edward by the Dutch artist Guillim Scrots, who had been invited to the English Court by Henry VIII in 1545/6. Bust 2 occurs only on new obverse dies cut for the second issue; in general aspect, but not in detail, it resembles the Tower busts of 1549. All the bust 1 dies have the motto on the obverse, one of them copying the *Timor* legend with *MDXLIX* from Tower-made dies but the others using a quotation from Psalm 132, v. 18: *Inimicos Eius Induam Confusione* (As for his enemies I shall clothe them with shame). Since the *Inimicos* legend (which was retained in the second issue) is longer, these dies do not carry a date. One pair of dies with bust 2 still has the inscriptions transposed, the only case of this at any mint on new dies of the second issue; but on other and less rare 6 oz. shillings the king's name and titles accompany his portrait, bringing Durham Place into line with the practice at other mints. Stops on Durham Place shillings are small crosses.

The lack of a clear division by dies between the first and second issue at Durham Place means that shillings of the two standards with bust 1 can only be separated by weight (or metal). Bust 1 dies and their accompanying reverses mostly have beaded circles as at other mints in the first issue, and those with bust 2 wireline circles, but there are exceptions to this both ways (a bust 1 obverse with wireline, and an *Inimicos* reverse with beaded circle), and even a first issue reverse with a linear inside a beaded circle. A peculiarity of several Durham Place dies is the use of an *ET* monogram like that on some Tower-made dies of 1547/8 with pierced crosses (or 'incurved mascles') as stops, perhaps indicating the work of the same engraver, since on some Durham Place shillings the cross stops have concave sides. In view of the resemblance of the busts he might even have been the engraver of the 1547 pattern (which incidentally provides the earliest use of wireline circles at this period). Frosting of the inner caul of the crown or of the garniture of the shield reveals a die-sinker ready to experiment. Although Durham Place shillings are all rare, the considerable variety in their dies suggests that a larger issue may have been in contemplation. Unfortunately, John Bowes seems not to have accounted for the work of his mint in the normal way. Its closure after less than a year may have been mainly the result of a shortage of silver, although the relative frequency of striking cracks in the flans suggests that technical issues were also a problem at this mint.

Dublin

A mint at Dublin, where coinage had not taken place since the fifteenth century, was formally constituted in February 1547, shortly after the death of Henry VIII who had approved it. Although there were costs of transportation when coins for Ireland were minted in London or Bristol, the extra expense incurred in running a small and less than fully efficient outpost would outweigh them unless volume was high. Between March 1548, when the mint finally became operational, and early 1553 when it closed, total output at Dublin may not have reached £100,000. The first Under-Treasurer was Thomas Agard who had been a servant of Thomas Cromwell in the 1530s and had extensive experience of the administration of Ireland. Agard died in August 1549, or thereabouts. He was succeeded in office by the comptroller, Martin Pirry, under whom coinage was resumed in August 1550, when minting was authorised until Michaelmas 1551. After another interval Pirry was reappointed in June 1552 to mint 3 oz. coins (decried to sixpence in August 1551), but he died soon afterwards, probably in November, so that a new order was needed on 27 December to provide for further coinage of £8,000. Exactly whether or when this was executed is not recorded, but the mint was probably closed early in 1553.

DUBLIN MINTMARKS 1548-52

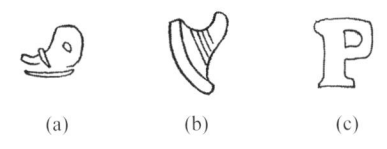

(a)   (b)   (c)

(a) Boar's head, Agard, 1548-9; (b) Harp; (c) *P,* Pirry, 1550-2.

Agard's mandate was to coin at 4 oz. fine silver the same denominations as in England, from the groat to the halfpenny, except that English coins in Ireland had a face value 50 per cent higher, so that groats and halfgroats were to pass for sixpence and threepence. Agard's groats and halfgroats have as mintmark a left-facing boar's head, his personal badge, and are from dies engraved locally by Henry Coldwell, a London goldsmith. According to Laker's analysis of the Dublin groats, the earliest of them have a large portrait, with a head loosely resembling that of the English bust no. 5, but without a fur collar, and in that respect more like the English busts nos. 3 and 4. The boar's head local reverse dies used with the large head obverses have a long floral spike or trefoil in the cross-ends. A later form of Irish reverse, still with mintmark boar's head, has rosettes in the inscription; the accompanying obverses show a much smaller bust, possibly based rather crudely on bust no. 6, and as mintmark a small harp. Coldwell had ceased to cut dies by March 1549, and it may be that no more local dies were made at Dublin thereafter. Official English dies with busts 5 and 6 (without mintmark) were then sent to Dublin at some point. Bust 5 is found paired both with an Irish boar's head reverse, and with a Tower-made die, with half-roses in the cross-ends, on which the mintmark appears to be harp over boar's head. Reverses used with the English bust 6 dies also have the half-roses, together with mintmark harp or *P*; but there is also a mule with an Irish rosette-stopped late boar's head die. The boar's head groats are scarcer than the English types, and this is in accord with the evidence of the output figures, which indicate that less than a quarter of the 4 oz. fine Dublin coinage was struck in the first phase, 1548-9, under Agard or in the months after his death. That the profits of the mint for 1550-1 were more than three times those of 1548-9 suggests that not only the dies with Pirry's initial but also the harp-marked dies which fall between boar's head and *P* should be attributed to the second phase of the mint's activity.

The lower values are much scarcer than the groats. Halfgroats follow a similar pattern of busts and mintmarks to the groats. However the local bust as well as the earlier English bust is fur-collared; these are followed by the late three-quarter facing halfgroat bust as at York. As on posthumous coins of the English mints, pence have either the facing or the three-quarter bust. The Dublin halfpenny, with facing bust, is a considerable rarity.

Pirry's issue of 3 oz. sixpenny 'shillings' in 1552, including its possible brief extension after his death, cannot have been very large. They are struck from dies using the bust 6 and shield punches from the Tower, but with mintmark harp and a very small fount including several Gothic letters. These coins clearly circulated in England, since some were countermarked in 1560 with the greyhound behind the head. There are also various brassy counterfeits, both struck and cast, of the 1552 Dublin shilling, with the harp mintmark, some bearing the date *MDXLIX* instead of *MDLII*; and others, struck in coppery metal from dies of official-looking workmanship dated *MDLII*, but with *Y* as the obverse mintmark.

Mint Accounts, 1544 – 1551

Accounts for this period are complex because of the frequent changes of fineness and weight, each category being accounted separately. Most of the accounts for the whole period are extant for Tower I, which participated in every phase and category of the coinage save for the small special issue of fine gold (at Southwark) in 1551; and for Southwark, next in importance, from its opening in July 1545. There are, however, no accounts for 20 ct. gold after 1548 although the numismatic evidence suggests that production (at the Tower and Southwark) continued into 1549-50.

There are full accounts for the silver-only mints at Canterbury and York from 1545 to 1549, but those for other mints are incomplete. Tower II accounts run from 1545 but are missing for billon after 1547. Bristol accounts are lacking between October 1547 and Chamberlain's appointment in January 1549, because Sharington had destroyed them. There are no actual accounts for Durham Place or Dublin (although some other figures are recorded). Separate accounts (marked T) were kept for the reminting of testons from 1548. In summary, the various issues and the mints involved for which accounts are extant were as follows:

23 ct. gold	£28 16s. per lb.	June 1544-March 1545	Tower I only.
22 ct.	£30 per lb.	April 1545-March 1546	Tower I; Tower II (from July); Southwark (from September).
20 ct.	£30 per lb.	April 1546-Dec. 1548	Tower I; Tower II; Southwark; Bristol (to Sept. 1547).
22 ct.	£34 per lb.	Jan. 1549-end 1550	Tower I (to Oct. 1550); Tower II (1549 only); Southwark.
23 ct. 3½ gr.	£28 16s. per lb.	Jan.-June 1551	Southwark only.
9 oz. fine silver	48s. per lb.	June 1544-March 1545	Tower I only.
6 oz. fine	48s. per lb.	April 1545-March 1546	Tower I; Tower II (from July); Southwark (from July); Canterbury (from June); York (from May).
4 oz. fine	48s. per lb.	April 1546-March 1551	Tower I (to Jan. 1550); Tower II (to Dec. 1547); Southwark; Canterbury (to Dec. 1549); York (to Oct. 1549); Bristol (to Oct. 1549).
8 oz. shillings	96s. per lb.	Feb. 1549	Tower I; Southwark; Canterbury.
6 oz. shillings	72s. per lb.	April 1549-March 1551	Tower I (to Oct. 1550); Southwark; Canterbury (April-Dec. 1549); Bristol (May-June 1549).
3 oz. shillings	72s. per lb.	April-July 1551	Tower I; Southwark.

Debasement, Henry VIII – Edward VI

In addition to the accounts themselves, some further evidence as to approximate volumes is available indirectly from the results of two commissions of enquiry set up in 1547 and 1550 which were principally concerned with the profits from the mints. These show revenues of some £97,000 accounted to the High Treasurer additional to those contained in the returns of the Under-Treasurers. The largest amounts within this total were in respect of the profits of Tower II post-1547, £37,000 from Vaughan and £38,000 from Throckmorton, suggesting output in excess of £300,000. Also included in Pekham's accounts were the profits of Durham Place from John Bowes (£9,000), and further sums from Sharington at Bristol and Agard at Dublin. The main figures from Dublin for 1548 (Agard) and 1549-50 (Pirry) had been reported to Sir William Brabazon, Receiver-General for Ireland. On the basis of all the sources Challis has estimated that Dublin's output would have been approximately £14,000 in 1548/9, £48,000 in 1550/1 and £32,000 in 1552/3.

Tower I, 1544-1551

Gold		Silver	
23 ct. £28 16s. per lb.		9 oz. 48s. per lb.	
1.6.44-31.3.45	£165,931	1.6.44-31.3.45	£149,287
22 ct. £30 per lb.		6 oz. 48s. per lb.	
1.4.45-31.12.45	£142,485	1.4.45-31.3.46	£176,155
1.1.46-31.3.46	63,600	4 oz. 48s. per lb.	
20 ct. £30 per lb.		1.4.46-31.3.47	£122,042
1.4.46-30.9.46	£82,620	1.4.47-30.9.48	155,237
1.10.46-31.12.46	24,960	1.1.49-31.1.50(T)	37,344
1.5.47-31.12.48	239,520	8 oz. shillings 96s. per lb.	
22 ct. £34 per lb.		1.2.49-28.2.49(T)	£9,355
1.2.49-31.10.50	£48,246	6 oz. shillings 72s. per lb.	
		1.4.49-30.4.49	£3,477
		1.5.49-30.9.49(T)	78,678
		1.10.49-31.10.50	244,792
		3 oz. shillings 72s. per lb.	
		1.4.51-31.7.51	£80,749

Tower II, 1545-1551

Gold		Silver	
22 ct. £30 per lb.		6 oz. 48s. per lb.	
1.7.45-[31.3.46]	£69,326	1.7.45-[31.3.46]	£66,172
20 ct. £30 per lb.		4 oz. 48s. per lb.	
[1.4.46]-31.3.47	£37,470	[1.4.46]-31.3.47	£73,754
1.4.47-31.12.47	18,765	1.4.47-31.12.47	19,406
1.1.48-31.12.48	21,767		
22 ct. £34 per lb.			
From early 1549	£5,678		

SOUTHWARK, 1545-1551

Gold		Silver	
22 ct. £30 per lb.		6 oz. 48s. per lb.	
15.9.45-31.3.46	£96,767	1.7.45-31.3.46	£98,047
20 ct. £30 per lb.		4 oz. 48s. per lb.	
1.4.46-28.2.47	£111,700	1.4.46-31.3.47	£105,386
1.5.47-31.12.48	153,285	1.5.47-30.9.48	96,895
22 ct. £34 per lb.		1.4.48-31.7.49(T)	46,998
1.1.49-31.12.50	£28,594	1.10.48-31.1.49	27,981
23 ct. 3½gr. £28 16s. per lb.		1.5.50-31.3.51(T)	4,798
1.1.51-30.6.51	£2,777	8 oz. shillings 96s. per lb.	
		1.2.49-28.2.49(T)	£24,430
		6 oz. shillings 72s. per lb.	
		1.4.49-30.9.49(T)	£76,167
		1.10.49-31.3.50	38,669
		1.4.50-30.9.50	63,720
		1.10.50-31.3.51	115,340
		3 oz. shillings 72s. per lb.	
		1.4.51-31.7.51	£92,209

BRISTOL, 1546-1549

Gold		Silver	
20 ct. £30 per lb.		4 oz. 48s. per lb.	
1.5.46-31.3.47	£6,415	1.5.46-31.3.47	£40,399
1.7.47-30.9.47	6,130	1.4.47-30.9.47	16,411
		1.10.47-31.12.48	No accounts
		1.1.49-31.10.49	£14,349
		1.1.49-31.10.49(T)	32,584
		6 oz. shillings 72s. per lb.	
		1.5.49-30.6.49(T)	£1,938
		1.5.49-30.6.49	1,101

Debasement, Henry VIII – Edward VI

CANTERBURY, 1545-1549		YORK, 1545-1549	
Silver only		*Silver only*	
6 oz. 48s. per lb.		6 oz. 48s. per lb.	
1.6.45-30.4.46	£51,141	1.5.45-31.3.46	£48,696
4 oz. 48s. per lb.		4 oz. 48s. per lb.	
1.5.46-31.3.47	£43,066	1.4.46-31.3.47	£68,966
1.4.47-30.9.47	13,651	1.5.47-31.10.49	45,456
1.10.47-31.3.49	84,656	1.6.48-31.8.49(T)	90,182
1.1.49-31.12.49(T)	40,329		
1.4.49-31.12.49	9,596		
8 oz shillings 96s. per lb.			
1.2.49-28.2.49	£9,024		
do (T)	7,392		
6 oz. shillings 72s. per lb.			
1.5.49-31.8.49(T)	£30,654		
1.7.49-31.12.49	43,326		

Calendar 1544 – 1551

1544   End of coinage under 1533 indenture (31 March).
       Debasement announced 16 May (mint accounts from 1 June): gold at 23 ct., silver 9 oz. fine. Administration of coinage reformed.

1545   Fineness reduced to 22 ct. gold and 6 oz. fine silver (March). Recoinage mints opened at York (May) under George Gale, Canterbury (June) under William Tyllsworth and Southwark (July) under Sir John York, and new operation at the Tower under Thomas Knight (July). Canterbury and York restricted to groats until 1 Nov., extended (20 Oct.) to Easter 1546 at York. Southwark authorised to coin gold (Sept).

1546   Further reductions in fineness, to 20 ct. gold and 4 oz. silver (1 April).
       Bristol mint opened under William Sharington (May); also struck 3 oz. Irish harp groats (Aug. – Sept.).

1547   Death of Henry VIII (28 Jan.); accession of Edward VI. Edward Seymour designated Protector and created Duke of Somerset (deprived of power, Oct. 1549).
       New reign indentures (5 April); groats excluded at Canterbury.
       Tower II: last account of T. Knight deceased, ended Dec.; succeeded by Stephen Vaughan.
       Abortive plan for fine coinage of 23 ct. gold and 10½ oz. silver (June).

1548   Minting charges for billon reduced from 28s. per pound to 26s. 8d. (Feb.).
       Testons to be converted into 4 oz. silver (from Feb.); announcement (April) of their demonetization in Dec.
       Dublin: mint authorised (10 Feb.) under Thomas Agard; coinage from groat to halfpenny from March.
       Canterbury: resumed authority for minting of groats (16 Feb.).
       Durham Place: new mint under John Bowes authorised (2 Dec.), to coin 4 oz. silver; plus gold and 8 oz. shillings (29 Jan. 1549).

1549 Bristol: Sharington (removed Dec. 1548) charged with irregularities, and replaced by Thomas Chamberlain (Jan.); mint closed (Oct.).
Weight of gold coins reduced, but fineness increased to 22 ct. (24 Jan.); 8 oz. shillings and halves commissioned.
Edwardian shillings first issued (Feb.), 8 oz. fine, wt. 60 gr.; second issue (from April), 6 oz. fine, 80 gr.
Currency of testons extended to May, and finally to July.
Dublin: death of Agard (Aug. ?).
Mints at Durham Place (Oct.), York (Oct.) and Canterbury (Dec.) closed.
Tower II: death of Vaughan (late 1549); succeeded by Nicholas Throckmorton (Jan. 1550).
1550 Dublin mint reopened under Martin Pirry (August); minting resumed from October.
Commission (18 Dec.) to Sir Edmund Pekham and officials of Southwark mint to coin fine gold sovereign (24s.), ryal (12s.), angel (8s.) and half (4s.) at £28 16s. per lb.
1551 Tower and Southwark commissioned to mint shillings 3 oz. fine (14 April).
Proclamation (30 April) to decry base silver by 25 per cent with effect from 31 Aug.; testons further decried to 6d. (16 Aug.).
Debasement ended and Southwark mint closed, July.
New coinage of fine gold and fine silver commissioned (5 Oct.).
1552 Silver at 3 oz. authorised at Dublin (June).

WEIGHTS AND FINENESS, 1544 – 1551

GOLD

June 1544-March 1545 – 23 ct. fine; £28 16s. per lb. Troy (5760 gr.)
Sovereign (20s.)	200 gr.	12.96 g.
Half-sovereign (10s.)	100	6.48
Angel (8s.)	80	5.18
Half-angel (4s.)	40	2.59
Quarter-angel (2s.)	20	1.30

April 1545-March 1546 – 22 ct. fine, and from April 1546 – 20 ct.; all at £30 per lb.
Sovereign (20s.)	192 gr.	12.44 g.
Half-sovereign (10s.)	96	6.22
Crown (5s.)	48	3.11
Halfcrown (2s. 6d.)	24	1.56

From February 1549 – 22 ct. fine; £34 per lb.
Sovereign (20s.)	169 7/17 gr.	10.98 g.
Half-sovereign (10s.)	84 12/17	5.49
Quarter-sovereign (5s.)	42 6/17	2.74
Half-quarter (2s. 6d.)	21 3/17	1.37

January-June 1551 (Southwark only) – 23 ct. 3½ gr. fine; £28 16s. per lb.
Sovereign (24s.)	240 gr.	15.55 g.
Ryal, not known (12s.)	120	7.78
Angel (8s.)	80	5.18
Half-angel (4s.)	40	2.59

Debasement, Henry VIII – Edward VI

SILVER
June 1544-March 1545	9 oz.fine	48s. per lb.
April 1545-March 1546	6 oz.	48s. "
April 1546-1551	4 oz.	48s. "
Teston (12d.)	120 gr.	7.78 g.
Groat (4d.)	40	2.59
Halfgroat (2d.)	20	1.30
Penny	10	0.65
Halfpenny	5	0.32
Farthing	2½	0.16
Shillings, February 1549	8 oz.	96s. per lb.
April 1549-March 1551	6 oz.	72s. "
April-July 1551	3 oz.	72s. "
8 oz. fine	60 gr.	3.89 g.
6 oz. and 3 oz. fine	80	5.18

SOVEREIGNS OF 20s. 1544 – 1547

Weight 200 gr., fineness 23 ct., 1544-5 (types I and IIa); 192 gr., 22 ct., 1545-6 (IIb1); 192 gr., 20 ct., from April 1546 (IIb2 and Posthumous).

Mints: Tower, Southwark, Bristol.

HENRY VIII: Mostly Gothic letters. Obv. King with old, bearded head, enthroned; rose below feet. Rev. Crowned shield with lion and dragon supporters; *HR* monogram in panel below.

I. Large module (diameter c. 42 mm.); 200 gr.. Tower only, 1544. Mm. large lis. Gothic letters except Roman *M*; saltire stops. Straight-sided throne; candlestick on each pillar; tressure around. *henric 8 Di Gra Anglie/Francie et hib'e Rex.* Rev. *Ihesus Autem Tranciens Per Medium Illoru(m) Ibat.* One obv. die only (Whitton A); ER.

IIa. Smaller module (diameter c. 38 mm.); 200 gr. Tower only, 1544-5. Mm. small lis. Gothic letters except *M*; stops trefoils. Obv. as I, but no tressure, smaller portrait, curved throne, bird-like figures on pillars; *Angl Francie z hibern Rex.* Rev. *Ihs, Trnsiens.* One obv. die (B, also used at reduced weight); ER.

IIb. Small module; 192 gr., (1) 22 ct. (2) 20 ct. Types as IIa. *Agl, hiber(n).* Coarser Gothic lettering, with a few Roman (*E, M, R*) on some dies. *Trans-* or *Tranciens*.
    TOWER: (ii) Trefoil stops. Mm. lis both sides (obv. die B continued in use), VR. Mm. obv. pellet-in-annulet (die D)/rev. lis, ER.
    (iii) Sleeve stops. Mm. lis (die C). Also (iii)/(ii) mules. All VR.
    SOUTHWARK: (ii) Trefoil stops. Mm. *S* (obv. die E). No letter below shield. Also muled both ways with (iii). All VR.
    (iii) Sleeve stops. Mm. *e*, with *e* also below shield. Only known from ER mules with (ii), *S/e* and *e* (die F)/*S*.
    BRISTOL (IIb2 only): London-made dies, with (ii) trefoil stops. Mm. *WS* monogram (obv. only). *Franci.* ER.

HENRY POSTHUMOUS: Small module, 192 gr. Tower, Bristol. As II but Roman letters and rosette stops.

1544–1551

Sovereigns

TOWER: Mm. Florentine lis. One obv. die, *Henric 8 D Gra Agl Franc z Hiber Rex*. Rev. *Aute, Tranciens, Mediu, Illoru*. ER.

BRISTOL: Mm. *WS* monogram both sides. As Tower, but *Dei* in full, *Fran, Hib*; and *Autem, Transiens, Medium, Illor*. ER.

HALF-SOVEREIGNS (KING ENTHRONED) 1544 – 1551

Weight 100 gr., fineness 23 ct., 1544-5 (type IIa); 96 gr., 22 ct. (IIb1); 96 gr., 20 ct. (IIb2, and post-Henry VIII).

Mints: Tower I and II, Southwark, Bristol.

HENRY VIII: Obv. King with old, bearded head, holding orb and (occasionally omitted) sceptre, on throne with curved sides and diapered back, bird-like figures on pillars, rose below feet. Rev. Crowned shield with lion and dragon supporters; *HR* monogram in panel below. Inscriptions in Roman (usually), Gothic or mixed letters, with much variation, but based on *Henric 8 D G Agl Francie z Hib Rex* and *Ihs Autem Transiens Per Medium Illorum Ibat*.

EDWARD VI: *Edward 6 D G Ag Fran z Hib Rex*, in large Roman letters. Youthful portrait on throne with plain, rounded back. Angels on pillars. *HR* monogram in panel. Stops (iv) lozenges.

HENRY POSTHUMOUS: Type as Edward's, with youthful portrait (except once at Southwark), but *Henric 8 D G* etc., Roman letters.

TOWER, HENRY VIII:

IIa. 100 gr. Mm. lis. Stops (i) small saltires. Small Roman letters, with ornamental *H*. *Di Gra, et Hiber*. ER.

IIb. 96 gr. Mm. pellet-in-annulet. Stops: (i) small saltires; small Roman letters; *et* (rare) or *z*. Stops (ii) trefoils or defective saltires; letters small or large Roman, Gothic (some with mm. punched over *S*), or mixed; always *z* for &; some (rare) have annulet on inner circle. Stops (iii) sleeves, Gothic letters, rare.

TOWER, EDWARD VI: Mm. arrow. Rev. *HR* monogram in panel. VR.

TOWER I, HENRY POSTHUMOUS:

Mm. arrow. Stops (iv) lozenges; obv. mm. sometimes omitted; no mark below shield; also rare mules both ways with pellet-in-annulet (iii). Stops (v) pierced crosses or saltires; *Angl, ET* monogram; also rare arrow/lis mule.

TOWER II, POSTHUMOUS:

Mm. *K* (rev. only; or no i.m., but *K* below shield). Stops (iv) lozenges. *Dei Gra*. Also mules (*K*)/grapple and *E/K*. All rare.

Mm. grapple (both sides, or either; or none, but grapple below shield). Stops (vi) pellets, but saltires on a rev. die with grapple over i.m. *K* and below shield. *Dei Gra*. Rare.

Mm. martlet (both sides as i.m., but not below shield). Stops (vi) pellets, or (rev.) saltires. *Dei Gra* or *D G*. Var. *His* for *Ihs*. Also martlet/lis mule. All rare.

Mm. lis (both sides as i.m., but not below shield). Stops (vi) pellets only. *D G*. Also mules both ways with arrow, and martlet/lis. All rare.

SOUTHWARK, HENRY VIII: IIb only. 96 gr.

Mm. *S*. Stops (ii) trefoils or saltires. Letters small or large Roman, Gothic or mixed. With or without *e* below shield. Also muled both ways with mm. *e*. All rare.

Mm. *e*, with *e* also below shield. Stops: (ii) trefoils; Gothic letters; also *e/S* mule. Stops (iii) sleeves; Gothic letters; also muled with obv. mm. *S*, or rev. (iv) *E* over arrow.

Debasement, Henry VIII – Edward VI

Half-Sovereigns

SOUTHWARK, EDWARD VI: Mm. *E* (over arrow on obv., and sometimes on rev.). Rev. *HR* monogram in panel. Below shield *E* (sometimes broken or reversed), *e* or nothing. VR.

SOUTHWARK, HENRY POSTHUMOUS:

Mm. *e* on obv. Portrait of Henry VIII, but with Roman letters and lozenge stops; mule only, with rev. Gothic letters and sleeve stops. ER.

Mm. *E* (both sides, or rev. only; sometimes over arrow). Portrait of Edward VI. *E* (sometimes broken or reversed), or *e*, or nothing below shield. Stops (iv) lozenges; rarely with *Dei Gra*; also rare mules *e* (iii)/*E*, -/*S* and *E*/- (with *K* below shield). Stops (v) pierced crosses with saltires; *Angl, ET* monogram; rare. Stops (vi) pellets, rare.

BRISTOL, HENRY VIII, Tower-made dies only: Mm. *WS* monogram (obv. only). Gothic letters; *Aut, Medi, Illor*. Stops (ii) trefoils. VR.

ANGELS AND FRACTIONS, 1544-1545

Weight of angel 80 gr. Fineness 23 ct.

TOWER mint under HENRY VIII, only. Obv. St. Michael spearing dragon (as before); rev. shield on ship, cross above, *h* and rose beside. Mm. lis. Gothic letters.

ANGEL (8s.): Usually an annulet by saint's head and on ship's side. *henric 8 D G Agl Fra z hib Rex; Per Cruce Tua Salva Nos Xpe Rede*. Stops saltires or trefoils.

HALF-ANGEL (4s.): Usually one or three annulets on ship's side. *he(n)ric 8 D G* etc.; *O Crux Ave Spes Unica*. Stops obv. saltires, rev. annulets. Also muled with 2nd coinage rev. (unaltered, or with annulets punched over saltire stops). All rare.

QUARTER-ANGEL (2s.): *henricus VIII D(e)i Gra Agl(ie)/Francie et hibernie Rex*. Some with Roman *N*. Stops saltires or trefoils. Angel armoured as before; or in tunic, with elbow raised. Rare.

CROWNS 1545 – 1551

Weight 48 gr. (from April 1545). Fineness, 1545-6, 22 ct.; 1546-8, 20 ct.

Mints: Tower I and II, Southwark, Bristol.

HENRY VIII: Normally Gothic letters. Obv. Crowned shield (crown with central leaf between two lis); crowned *h R* beside. *Dei Gra Agl(i) Fra(nc) z hib Rex* or similar. Rev. Crowned rose, crowned *h R* beside. *henric 8 Rosa Sine Spina (Spine,* etc.), usually abbreviated; *Rutilans* normally omitted.

EDWARD VI: Crowned *E R* in field both sides. Roman letters. Crown lis-leaf-lis. Obv. *Edward 6 D G Ag Fr z Hib Rex*. Rev. *Rutilans Rosa Sine Spine*. Tower I only.

HENRY POSTHUMOUS: Roman letters. Normally *Dei Gra* etc. on obv. and *Henric 8 Rutilans Rosa Sine Spina*, or abbreviated, on rev. Crown lis-leaf-lis or lis-cross-lis.

TOWER, HENRY VIII: Mm. pellet-in-annulet. Gothic letters.

(ii) Trefoil stops.
    (a) Neat work. Small mm. *henric 8 Rutila Rosa Sine Spi. Di Gra Agli.* Roman *H* by shield; Roman or Gothic by rose. VR.
    (b) Larger mm. Usually coarser work. Gothic *h* in field. *Rutilans* omitted. One has *et* for *z*. Some (rare) with annulet on inner circle. Var. (ER) has *Dei Gra* etc. on both sides.

1544–1551

Crowns

(iii)   Sleeve stops. *Rutilans* omitted. Rare.

Tower I, Edward VI: Mm. arrow. Lozenge stops. Also mule with Henry obv. (iii), mm. pellet-in-annulet. All ER.

Tower I, Henry Posthumous: Mm. arrow (on one or both sides).

(iv)   Lozenge stops. Rare.

(vi)   Pellet stops. VR. Also var. with transposed legends and numeral omitted – obv. *Henric D G Rutilans* etc., rev. *Dei Gra* etc.; this obv. die also muled with normal (iv) rev.; both ER.

Tower II, Posthumous:

Mm. *K* (obv. only). Lozenge stops (iv). Crown lis-cross-lis. VR.

Mm. grapple. Pellet stops (vi). *D G*. Crown lis-cross-lis. ER.

Mm. martlet. Pellet stops (vi). Crown lis-leaf-lis. VR.

Southwark, Henry VIII: Stops (ii) trefoils. *Rutilans* omitted.

Mm. *S*. One obv. (muled with *E* rev.) has Roman letters and saltire stops. All VR.

Mm. *e* (both sides or rev. only). Rare.

Mm. *E*, only known (pre-1547) on revs. muled with *S* or *e* obv. All VR.

Southwark, Posthumous: Mm. *E*.

(iv)   Lozenge stops. Mm. on rev. only. Rev. *Henric 8 Rutila* etc. ER.

(vi)   Pellet stops. Mm. both sides. Crown lis-cross-lis. Transposed legends, obv. *Henric 8 Rutilans* etc., rev. *Dei Gra* etc. VR.

Bristol, Henry VIII and Posthumous: All have mm. *WS* monogram, Gothic letters and omit *Rutilans*.

London-made dies: Mm. on obv. only. Stops (ii) trefoils. *Aglie*. Also mules with Evenet type. All VR.

Bristol dies: Evenet letters. Mm. usually on obv. only. Crown lis-leaf-lis. Some with pellet below shield and rose. Stops pellets, plus annulets, saltires, trefoils, crosses, lis or roses. Obv. *D(ei) G(ra) Angl(ie) Fra(nc) z hib Rex*; rev. *henric(us) (VIII or) 8 Rosa Sine Spine (-na)*. Var. has *R h* by shield.

HALFCROWNS 1545 – 1551

Weight 24gr. Fineness, 1545-6, 22 ct.; 1546-8, 20 ct.

Mints: Tower I and II, Southwark, Bristol.

Henry VIII: Normally Gothic letters. Obv. Crowned shield between *h R*; *henric 8 D G Agl Fr z hib Rex* or similar. Rev. Crowned rose between *h R*; abbreviation of *Rutilans Rosa Sine Spina*.

Edward VI: *E R* in field both sides. Roman letters. *Edward 6 D G Ag Fr z Hi Rex*. Tower I only.

Henry Posthumous: Types and legends as pre-1547. Roman letters. *H* or *h* in field.

Tower, Henry VIII: Mm. pellet-in-annulet (both sides or rev. only).

(ii)   Stops trefoils or broken saltires. Usually Gothic letters, but sometimes Roman or mixed. Some with annulet on inner circles. Rare; ER var. has *Dei Gra* etc. on both sides, and *H R* by shield.

(iii)   Stops sleeves. Rev. only, muled with (ii) obv. ER.

Tower I, Edward VI: Mm. arrow. Lozenge stops. ER. For *Henric 8* obv. die with *E* over *h* by shield see mule next below.

Tower I, Henry Posthumous:

Mm. pellet-in-annulet. Lozenge stops. Also mule with obv. mm. arrow (and *E* over *h*). All ER.

Debasement, Henry VIII – Edward VI

Halfcrowns

Mm. arrow (both sides or obv. only).
- (iv) Lozenge stops. Rare; ER var. has obv. *H D G Rutilans Rosa Sine Sp*, with *Rutilans* etc. also on rev.
- (v) Saltire stops. Mm. inverted. *ET* monogram for *z*. *Spinis*. Also muled with normal arrow rev. (iv). All VR.
- (vi) Pellet stops. Rare.

TOWER II, POSTHUMOUS:

Mm. *K* (rev. only). Lozenge stops (iv). Rare.

Mm. grapple (rev. only). Square pellet stops (vi). VR.

Mm. martlet (both sides). Pellet stops (vi). Rare.

SOUTHWARK, HENRY VIII: Stops (ii) trefoils.

Mm. *S* (both sides). Some with Roman letters. VR.

Mm. *e* (both sides). Obv. *Dei Gra Agl Fra z hib Rex*; rev. *henric 8 Rosa Sine Spin (Rutilans* omitted). VR.

SOUTHWARK, POSTHUMOUS: Mm. *E* (either side or both). Stops (iv) lozenges, or (vi) pellets. All VR.

BRISTOL, HENRY VIII and POSTHUMOUS: Evenet's local dies only. Crown lis-cross-lis. Mm. *WS* monogram on rev. only. *h R* in fields. *Ang*. Stops obv. pellets, rev. saltires. ER.

EDWARD SOVEREIGNS AND FRACTIONS 1549-1550

Fineness 22 ct. Mints: Tower I, Tower II, Southwark, Durham Place.

All in name of EDWARD VI, with Roman letters.

SOVEREIGN (20s., 169 7/17 gr.). Tower I and Southwark only. All VR. Stops square pellets. Obv. King enthroned, in doublet and hose, with sword and orb. *Edward VI D(ei) G(ra) Agl Fran et Hib Rex*. Rev. Crowned arms with lion and dragon supporters; *E R* in panel below. *Ihs Autem Transiens Per Medium Illor(u) Ibat*. Tower I, mm. arrow. Southwark, mm. *Y*; one has rose after *Rex*.

HALF-SOVEREIGN, or 'Edward Royal' (10s., 84 12/17 gr.), Tower and Southwark. Obv. Profile bust right in armour, without (1) or with (2) crown. Rev. Oval garnished shield with crown above and *E R* beside.

1. Uncrowned bust. Motto on obv. Dotted inner circles.
   - (a) Obv. *Timor Domini Fons Vite MDXLIX*; rev. *Edward VI D G Agl Fra z Hib Rex*. Square pellet stops both sides.
   - (b) Obv. *Scutum Fidei Proteget Eum*, no date, rosette stops; rev. *Edward etc*. Stops obv. rosettes, rev. pellets.
2. Crowned bust, with (a) plain or (b) decorated breastplate. Name and titles on obv., *Scutum* etc. on rev. Undated. Wireline inner circles. Stops normally obv. pellets, rev. rosettes.

Tower I, mm. arrow: 1a, ER; 1b, rare; 2a. Mm. swan: 2b, rare (ER rev. var. has pellet stops); also 2b, swan/arrow mule, VR.

Tower II, mm. *6*: 1b, ER. Mm. grapple: 2a, obv. var. has rosette stops, all VR. Mm. martlet (to left): 2b, VR.

Southwark, mm. *Y*: 1b; 2a, VR; 2b, ER.

QUARTER-SOVEREIGN, or Crown (5s., 42 6/17 gr.). Tower and Southwark only. Types as half-sovereign. Mm. often on obv. only. Pellet stops.

1. Obv. Uncrowned bust, *Scutum* etc. Rev. *Edward* etc. Dotted circles.

1544–1551

Edward Sovereigns and fractions

2.   Obv. Crowned bust, *Edward* etc. Rev. *Scutum* etc. Wireline circles.

Tower I, mm. arrow: 1, VR; 2 (var. omits *E R)*, rare. Mm. swan: 2, ER.
Tower II, mm. 6: 1, ER. Mm. grapple: 2, VR.
Southwark, mm. *Y:* 1, 2, both VR.

HALF-QUARTER-SOVEREIGN, or Halfcrown (2s. 6d., 21 3/17 gr.). Tower and Southwark only. Types as half and quarter, but no initials beside shield. *Edward VI D G Ag(l) Fr z H(i) R(ex)*. Pellet stops. Mm. often on obv. only.

1.   Obv. Uncrowned bust, *Scutum* etc. Rev. *Edward* etc. Dotted circles.
2.   Crowned bust.
    (a) Obv. *Scutum* etc., rev. *Edward* etc. Dotted circles.
    (b) Obv. *Edward* etc., rev. *Scutum* etc. Wireline circles.

Tower I, mm. arrow: 1, 2a, 2b, all VR. Mm. arrow/swan: 2b, ER.
Tower II, mm. grapple: 2a, ER.
Southwark, mm. *Y:* 1, 2b, both VR.

DURHAM PLACE, HALF-SOVEREIGN. Mm. bow. Stops incurved saltires.

1.   Obv. Uncrowned half-length figure in armour; *Scutum* legend with date *MDXLVIII*. Rev. *Edward VI* etc. Dotted circles. Unique.
2.   Obv. Normal uncrowned bust; *Lucerna Pedibus Meis Verbum Est*. Rev. *Edward VI* etc. Dotted circles. Undated. ER.
3.   Obv. Crowned half-length bust in armour; *Edward VI* etc. Wireline circle on obv. Rev. *Scutum* etc. . Undated. Also 3/2 mules with *Edward VI* etc. on both sides. All ER.

SOUTHWARK GOLD 1551

Fineness 23 ct. 3½ gr. All in name of EDWARD VI, with mm. ostrich's head.

SOVEREIGN (24s., 240 gr.). Obv. King enthroned, with sceptre and orb, within tressure; portcullis below. *Edward VI D G Anglie/Francie Z hibernie Rex*. Rev. Small shield in centre of double rose. *Ihesu Autem Transiens Per Medium Illorum Ibat*. Gothic letters (except *M*). Double saltire stops. ER; also ER strikings at double weight.

RYAL (12s., 120 gr.). Not known.

ANGEL (8s., 80 gr.). Traditional type, as Henry VIII. Double saltire stops. Gothic letters. *Edward VI D G Agl Fr(a) Z hib Rex; Per Cruce Tua Salva Nos Xpe Red*; *e* and rose above shield. VR.

HALF-ANGEL (4s., 40 gr.). Type as angel, but Roman letters and pellet stops. *Edward VI D G A F Z Hi Rex; Per Cru* (with Gothic *c*) *Tua Salva Nos Xpe; e* (Gothic) and rose above shield. ER.

TESTONS 1544-1547

Value 12d. (one shilling). Wt. 120 gr. Fineness: 1544-5, 9 oz.; 1545-6, 6 oz.; from April 1546, 4 oz.

Mints: Tower, Southwark, Bristol.

HENRY VIII (and POSTHUMOUS, ER). Obv. Large facing bust. Bust 1, prominent sidelocks and wide open eyes. Bust 2, close-cropped hair, less open eyes. Bust 3, sparse hair, bags under eyes, no jewels on band of crown but upper ornaments usually large pellets instead of crockets. Rev. Crowned rose. Normally Gothic letters, but often Roman *M, E, R*. Extensive muling between varieties.

Debasement, Henry VIII – Edward VI

Testons

TOWER: *Posui Deum Adiutorium Meum* or similar.
A. *henric VIII Di Gra Agl Fra z hib Rex.* Bust 1 only. Stops (i) saltires, then (ii) broken saltires or trefoils. Roman *M; A* usually capped to left only (ER var. *heric*, with full top-barred *A*); Gothic *e* replaced by Roman *E* late in group. Rev. wide crown above rose; late dies have nick on inside of outer petals. Mm. lis both sides, often duplicated on rev.; late var. (VR) has also pellet-in-annulet after *Rex*. Some revs. read *Adiutoreum* or *-oerium*.
B. *henric 8 D G Agl* etc. Stops (ii) fractured saltires or trefoils (with bust 1 or rarely 2), or (iii) sleeves (bust 3 only, VR). Roman *M* (early only), then *m*; Roman E (earlier), replaced later by Gothic *e*; *A* at first capped to left only, later with full top bar. Mm. usually pellet-in-annulet, but lis with pellet-in-annulet at end on earliest dies, or rarely lis only (on obvs. with sleeve stops). Crown above rose normally narrower than in group A, sometimes showing full hoop at bottom. Some dies (VR) have annulet or pellet-in-annulet on inner circle.
C (Posthumous). As B, but (iv) lozenge stops. Mules only, B/C or C/B (bust 3 on C obv. die). Gothic letters, or Roman on one C rev. All ER.
SOUTHWARK: *Civitas London*, with groups of florets but no stops on rev. Group B (Henry VIII) only, as at Tower.
Mm. *S.* Some (early) with mainly Roman letters. Stops (ii) broken saltires or trefoils. Bust 1, or (VR) 2.
Mm. *e* (one rev. var. has Roman *E*). Stops usually (ii) broken saltires or trefoils, with bust 1; also muled both ways with mm. *S.* Later (iii) sleeve stops (VR), with bust 1 or 3.
BRISTOL: *Civitas Bristol(l)i(e).* Gothic letters. *henric 8 D G* etc. Mm. *WS* monogram (rev. only).
London dies: Trefoil stops (ii); bust 1. Also London/Evenet mule. All ER.
Bristol dies: Evenet lettering; stops pellets, plus roses, lis, crosses, trefoils etc. Pellet below rose on rev. Rare.

GROATS 1544 - 1551

Fineness: 1544-5, 9 oz.; 1545-6, 6 oz.; from April 1546, 4 oz.
Mints: Tower I and II (*Posui* etc.), Canterbury (*Civitas Cantor*), York (*Civitas Eboraci*), Southwark (*Civitas London*), Bristol (*Civitas Bristolie*), Durham Place (*Redde Cuique* etc.), Dublin (*Civitas Dublinie*).
HENRY VIII: Gothic letters unless otherwise stated. Obv. Crowned, bearded bust nearly facing or 3/4 to viewer's right. *henric 8 D G Agl Fra z hib Rex.* Rev. Shield over long cross, often with ornaments in forks. Motto or mint name.
EDWARD VI: Portrait bust right. Roman letters, lozenge stops. *Edward 6 D G* etc. Ornate cross-ends with crescents in forks. Tower I and Southwark only.
HENRY POSTHUMOUS: Type as Henry VIII, but Roman letters unless stated, and knop on cross-arms.
  Bust types, Henry VIII (1-3) and Posthumous (4-6).
1. Large head, nearly facing; drooping moustache; fur-collared cloak. 1544-5.
2. Similar, but head narrower and turned further to viewer's right; wedge of neck behind beard; little hair visible to sinister; some at Canterbury and York have rosette clasp on mantle. 1545-6.
3. Head three-quarters to right; no hair protruding below crown; turned-down collar, without fur. 1546.

Groats

4. Similar to 3, but much larger head, without shoulders. Early 1547.
5. Nearly facing head (cf. nos. 1 and 2), but larger and with more prominent nose; some have rosette clasp. From 1547.
6. Three-quarters to right, without fur collar; as no. 3, but smaller head with eyes more open. From 1548.

TOWER, HENRY VIII: Mm. lis both sides. *Posui Deu Adiutore Meu.*
(i) Saltire stops. Bust 1. Usually large mm. lis. Saltire (ER) or annulet (rarely over saltire) in forks.
(ii) Trefoil or defective saltire stops. Smaller mm. lis.
   1. Annulet in forks. Bust 2.
   2. Pellet-in-annulet in forks. Bust 2, or 3 (rare). Some have annulet on inner circle. Var. (bust 2) has lis mm. over pellet-in-annulet, ER; var. (bust 3) has Roman *E* on rev.
(iii) Sleeve stops. Pellet-in-annulet in forks. Bust 2 (ER), 3 (normally; var. omits rev. mm.) or 4 (VR). Also muled both ways with (iv), lozenge stops.

TOWER, EDWARD VI: Mm. arrow. *Posui* etc. Var. *Edoard.* Rare. A unique piece combines a reverse of this issue and a pattern obverse die with Edward's portrait, the *Timor* legend and the date *MDXL7*.

TOWER I, HENRY POSTHUMOUS: *Posui* etc.
Mm. lis. (iv) Lozenge stops. Bust 4. Gothic or Roman letters, or muled. Pellet-in-annulet in forks. Rare; also VR mules both ways with (iii), or with Southwark (iii) rev. (*e* and *S* in forks).
Mm. arrow. (iv) Lozenge stops. Bust 4 (rare), or 5. Crescent in forks.
   (v) Stops pierced crosses with saltires. Bust 5. Crescent in forks. *ET* monogram for &. Arrow may be inverted (VR).
   (vi) Pellet stops. Bust 5. Rose in forks. Also mules with (v), including one (vi) obv. die without mm. All VR.

TOWER II, POSTHUMOUS: mms. *K*, grapple, martlet (to right), lis or none.
Mm. *K* (both sides or either; rev. mm. sometimes over arrow). (iv) Lozenge stops. Bust 4 (rare) or 5. Crescent in forks. Also rare mules with rev. mm. arrow, and with rev. of (vi) with rose in forks but no mm. (v) Stops pierced crosses with saltires. Bust 5. Crescent in forks. *ET* monogram.
Mm. grapple (rev. only). (vi) Pellet stops (or rev. none). Bust 5 or 6. Rose in forks. Obv. vars. (ER), bust 6, have Gothic letters, one including *VIII*.
Mm. martlet (both sides, or rev. only); martlet has long neck which is broken off on later dies. (vi) Pellet stops, rarely saltires (or rev. none). Bust 5 or 6. Rose in forks.
Mm. lis (both sides, or rev. only), all rare. (vi) Pellet stops. Bust 5 only. Rose in forks. Also VR mules with obv. mm. arrow (iv) or *K* (iv), and with rev. mm. grapple or martlet.
No. obv. mm., bust 5, mules: (iv)/(vi), no rev. mm.; (vi)/(iv), no rev. mm.; (vi)/(v) mm. arrow. All rare.

SOUTHWARK, HENRY VIII: *Civitas London.* Normally no mm. Letters Roman, mixed or Gothic.
(ii) Trefoil and/or defective saltire stops. Bust 2, or (rare) 3. In forks: 1, *S*; 2, *S* in side forks, *e* in upper and lower.
(iii) Sleeve stops (rarely rev. none). *S* and *e* in forks. Bust 3 or 4. Also rare mules (ii) bust 3/(iii), and both ways with (iv) mm. lis.

SOUTHWARK, EDWARD VI: Mm. *E.* Var. has *S* in side forks. All VR.

Debasement, Henry VIII – Edward VI

Groats

SOUTHWARK, HENRY POSTHUMOUS:

Mm. lis (ER mules only). Lozenge stops (iv). Obv. Roman letters, bust 4, mm. lis (Tower die), muled with Southwark (iii) rev.; or Southwark rev. with mm. lis, lozenge stops, Gothic letters and open forks muled with (iii) obv. (bust 4; no mm.).

Mm. *E* on rev. only. (iv) Lozenge stops. Bust 4 (VR) or 5. Earliest dies have Gothic letters. Crescent in forks. Early rev. var. (iii/iv mule) has *S* and *e* in forks. Also mm. *E* over arrow (ER). Muled both ways with (iii); also with obv. mm. *K*.

(v) Stops pierced crosses with saltires. Bust 5. *ET* monogram. Crescent in forks.

(vi) Pellet stops. Bust 5 or 6. Rose in forks. Vars. (ER) have no mm., or *E* over lis. Also rare (v)/(vi) mules.

CANTERBURY, HENRY VIII: No mm. Bust 2. Spur from below shield to inner circle. Stops (ii) trefoils only. Open forks. (a) Roman or mixed letters; some with *Di Gra*. Spur from left or right. (b) Gothic letters. Spur always on right. Often muled with obv. of (a).

CANTERBURY, POSTHUMOUS: Usually no mm.

(iv) Lozenge stops. Bust 5. Crescent in forks.

(v) Stops pierced crosses with saltires, or rev. none. Bust 5. *ET* monogram. Crescents in forks. Also rare mule (iv)/(v).

(vi) Pellet stops. Rose in forks. Bust 5 or 6. Var. (bust 5) has *ET* monogram (ER). Some with bust 6 have mm. rose on obv.

YORK, HENRY VIII: No mm. Spur from top of shield to inner circle.

(ii) Trefoil or defective saltire stops. (a) Roman or mixed letters; some with *Di Gra*. Bust 2. Spur from top right of shield. (b) Gothic letters. Bust 2, or 3 (rare). Spur from right or left of shield. Often muled with obv. of (a).

(iii) Sleeve stops. Bust 3, or 4 (VR). Spur from right or left. Also rare mule (ii)/(iii).

YORK, POSTHUMOUS: Mm. lis or none. Spur in (iv)(a) only.

(iv) Lozenge stops. Roman letters. (a) Mm. lis (VR) or none. Bust 4. Spur at top left. Empty forks. All rare; also VR mules with (iii) obv. (bust 4), and with revs. of (ii)(b) and (iii). (b) No mm. Bust 5. No spur (henceforward). Crescent in forks.

(v) Stops pierced crosses with saltires, or rev. none. No mm. Bust 5. *ET* monogram. Crescent in forks.

(vi) Pellet stops. Normally no mm. (but ER obv. var. with Gothic letters may have mm.). Bust 5 or 6. Rose in forks. Also VR mules (iv)/(vi) and (vi)/(v).

BRISTOL, HENRY VIII and POSTHUMOUS. *Civi/tas/Bris/tolie.*

Gothic lettering throughout; local dies with ornate alphabet and symbols, except for a few early coins from London-made dies. Mm. (rev. only) *WS* monogram for William Sharington (April 1546-Dec. 1548) or *TC* monogram for Thomas Chamberlain (Jan.-Oct. 1549).

London-made dies (Henry VIII): Nothing in forks of cross. (ii) Trefoil stops. Bust 2. (iii) Sleeve stops. Bust 3. All VR.

Bristol dies, Evenet lettering: All have a rose after *Civitas*. Type 1, Henry VIII, possibly plus some of type 2; remainder posthumous. Two Evenet busts. Much minor variation in symbols, but main reverse types are as follows:

1. Annulets in forks. Mm. *WS*. No extra marks on obv. Bust 1 (tufts of hair both sides, below curved band of crown).

    1a. No mark before *Bristolie;* colon after it. Also VR mules both ways with London dies.

    1b. Quatrefoil before *Bris*.

Groats

2. Trefoils in forks. Mm. *WS*. Quatrefoil before *Bris*. Bust 1. Some obvs. have rose, cross or trefoil after *Rex*, or cross or lis after *Ang* or *hib*.
3. Lis in forks. Mm. *WS*. Lis before *Bris*.
   3a. Bust 1. Rose after *Rex*. Also mules both ways with type 2.
   3b. Bust 2 (no hair on sinister side; crown band nearly straight). Rose, quatrefoil or nothing after *Rex*.
4. Trefoils in forks. Mm. *TC*. Quatrefoil (or rarely trefoil or lis) before *Bris*. Bust 2. Nothing or quatrefoil after *Rex*.

DURHAM PLACE, all Posthumous, Dec. 1548 – Oct. 1549. Mm. bow both sides. Bust 6. Stops, obv. pellets, rev. saltires; also sometimes saltires by obv. mm. Rev. Crescent or floral spike in forks. *Redde Cuiq(ue) Q(uod) Suum Est*. Rare.

DUBLIN (*Civi/tas/Dub/linie*, or *Dubl/inie*), all Posthumous, March 1548 – 1551. Sixpence Irish.

Local dies: 1. Large local bust (cf. English bust 5, but without fur collar). Obv. mm. usually none, rarely boar's head or harp; rev. mm. boar's head. Long floral spike or trefoil in cross-ends. Rare.
2. Small bust (cf. English bust 6). Mm. obv. harp, rev. boar's head. Rosettes in rev. inscription. VR.

English dies: 3. Obv. Bust 5; no obv. mm. Rev. (a) local die, mm. boar's head; (b) English, with mm. harp over boar's head.
4. Obv. Bust 6; no mm. on obv. Rev. (a) local die, mm. boar's head; (b) English die, mm. harp; (c) English die, mm. *P*.

HALFGROATS 1544 – 1551

Fineness: 1544-5, 9 oz.; 1545-6, 6 oz.; from April 1546, 4 oz.

Mints: Tower I and II (*Posui* etc.), Southwark (*Civitas London*), Canterbury (*Civitas Cantor*), York (*Civitas Eboraci*), Bristol (*Civitas Bristolie*), Durham Place (*Redd'* etc.), Dublin (*Civitas Dublinie*).

HENRY VIII: Gothic letters unless otherwise stated. Obv. Crowned, bearded bust in fur-collared cloak, three-quarters to right (cf. groat bust 1). *henric 8 D G Agl Fra z hib Rex*, or abbreviated. Rev. Shield over long cross, usually with ornaments in forks or pierced cross-ends. Motto or mint name.

EDWARD VI: Portrait bust right. *Edward* (or *Edoard*) *6 D G* etc. Roman letters, lozenge stops. Open forks. Tower, Southwark and Canterbury only.

HENRY POSTHUMOUS: As pre-1547; mostly bust 1, but also (on late coins of York, Dublin and Durham Place) bust 6 as on groats, small head three-quarters to right without fur collar. Obv. reading progressively abbreviated to *D G A F*. Roman letters unless stated. Open forks.

TOWER, HENRY VIII: *Posui Deu Adiutoe Meu*.
1. Mm. lis both sides. Annulet in forks. Stops (i) saltires or (ii) trefoils. Both VR.
2. No mm. Nothing in forks. Stops (iii) sleeves. ER.

TOWER I, EDWARD VI: Mm. arrow. *Edward*. Var. reading *Civitas London* but mm. arrow both sides may be of Southwark. All ER.

TOWER I, HENRY POSTHUMOUS: *Posui* etc. Bust 1 only.

Mm. arrow (both sides, or rev. only). Stops (iv) lozenges. Rare; also VR mules with revs. Tower II, mm. *K* or grapple, or Southwark, mm. *E*.

Debasement, Henry VIII – Edward VI

Halfgroats

TOWER II, POSTHUMOUS: Mms. *K* and grapple. Bust 1 only.
Mm. *K* (rev. only). Stops (iv) lozenges. Also as mule with obv. mm. arrow. All VR.
Mm. grapple (usually rev. only). Stops (vi) pellets. Rare; also VR mule with obv. mm. arrow.
SOUTHWARK, HENRY VIII: No mm. Stops (ii) trefoils. All ER.
1.   *S* in forks. Mixed Gothic and Roman letters.
2.   *e* in upper and lower, *S* in side forks. Gothic letters.
SOUTHWARK, EDWARD VI: Mm. *E*. *Edward* or *Edoard*. Var. with mm. arrow, see Tower. All ER.
SOUTHWARK, HENRY POSTHUMOUS: Mm. *E* (both sides, or rev. only), or none. Bust 1 only. Stops (iv) lozenges (also ER mule mm. arrow/*E*); (v) pierced crosses, *ET* monogram, rare; or (vi) pellets.
CANTERBURY, HENRY VIII: No mm.
(ii) Stops trefoils or saltires. Pierced cross-ends. (a) Spur from bottom left of shield or pellet below to right. Gothic letters. (b) No spur or pellet. Gothic or mixed letters.
(iii) Stops sleeves. Open forks. Gothic letters. Rare.
CANTERBURY, EDWARD VI: No mm. *Edoard* or *Edward*. Vars. *Canton, Castor*. Rare.
CANTERBURY, POSTHUMOUS: Bust 1 only. Stops (iv) lozenges, no mm., Gothic or mixed letters, rare; or (vi) pellets, no mm., or rarely *t* on one side, Roman letters.
YORK, HENRY VIII: No mm. Stops (ii) trefoils or saltires. Gothic or mixed letters. Pierced cross-ends or (later) open forks. Spur from top left or right of shield. Rare.
YORK, POSTHUMOUS: No mm. All rare. Stops (iv) lozenges, large Roman letters, bust 1; or (vi) pellets, smaller Roman letters, bust 1 or 6.
BRISTOL, HENRY VIII and POSTHUMOUS: Mm. (on rev. only) monogram of Sharington (*WS*) from April 1546 to end of 1548, or Chamberlain (*TC*) Jan.- Oct. 1549. Gothic letters.
Mm. *WS*. (a) London dies (Henry VIII). Stops (ii) trefoils; trefoils in forks. Also muled with Bristol dies. All ER.
(b) Bristol dies, Evenet lettering (Henry VIII and Posthumous). *Ang*. Quatrefoils, trefoils, lis or nothing in forks. Stops pellets with quatrefoils, crosses, lis or trefoils. Usually pellet below shield.
Mm. *TC*. Bristol dies, Evenet lettering (Posthumous). Trefoils or nothing in forks. Stops pellets (obv. only), with quatrefoils or trefoils. Usually pellet below shield. Rare.
DURHAM PLACE, POSTHUMOUS (Dec. 1548 – Oct. 1549): Mm. bow (rev. only). *Redd Cuiq Qd Suum Est*. Bust 1, stops saltires or none, annulet in forks. Bust 6, stops pellets (obv.) and saltires (rev.), crescent in forks, *ET* monogram. All ER.
DUBLIN, POSTHUMOUS (1548 – 51): Threepence Irish.
Local dies: Earlier bust. Mm. obv. none, or rarely harp; rev. usually boar's head. Trident cross-ends. Var. (VR) has rosettes in rev. inscription.
English dies: Open forks. Earlier bust, mm. none/harp, rare. Late bust, mm. none/harp or none/*P*.

PENCE 1544 – 1551

Fineness: 1544-5, 9 oz.; 1545-6, 6 oz.; from April 1546, 4 oz.
Mints: Tower I and II (*Civitas London*), Southwark (*Civitas London*), Canterbury (*Civitas Cantor*), York (*Civitas Eboraci,* or *–rac*), Bristol (*Civitas Bristolie*), Durham Place (*Red* etc.), Dublin (*Civitas Dublinie*).
HENRY VIII: Letters Gothic, Roman or mixed. Obv. Crowned, bearded bust facing, in fur-collared cloak. *h D G Rosa Sine Spina (-ne, -nis,* etc.), usually abbreviated. Rev. Shield over long cross with pierced ends or open forks. Mint name.

1544–1551

Pence

EDWARD VI (Tower and Southwark; see below for Bristol): Portrait bust right. *E D G Rosa* etc. Roman letters. Stops (iv) lozenges. Open forks.

HENRY POSTHUMOUS: Facing bust as pre-1547 unless stated; or three-quarter bust (as no. 6 on groats) without fur collar. Open forks. Normally Roman letters.

TOWER, HENRY VIII:
1. Mm. lis both sides or obv. only. Gothic or mixed letters. Pierced cross-ends. Stops (i) saltires, (ii) trefoils, or rev. none. Var. has annulet on inner circles. All rare.
2. No mm. (Tower or Southwark ?). Gothic, mixed or Roman letters. Stops (ii) trefoils, (iii) sleeves, or none. Normally open forks. Var. *Londen*.

TOWER I, EDWARD VI: Mm. Arrow. VR.

TOWER, HENRY POSTHUMOUS: Mms. arrow (Tower I); *K*, grapple (Tower II). Roman letters.

Mm. arrow (obv. or rev.). Some have Gothic *h*. Stops (iv) lozenges. VR.

Mm. *K* (rev. only). Stops (iv) lozenges. Large Roman letters. VR.

Mm. grapple (obv. or rev.). Stops (vi) pellets. Smaller Roman letters, VR.

No mm. (Tower or Southwark ?). Stops (iv) lozenges: facing bust, large Roman letters. Stops (vi) pellets: facing or three-quarter bust, large or small Roman letters.

SOUTHWARK, HENRY VIII:

Mm. *S* (obv. only). Mixed letters. Pierced cross-ends. Stops (ii) trefoils. ER.

Mm. *e* (obv. or rev.). Gothic or mixed letters. Stops (ii) trefoils (pierced cross-ends), or (iii) sleeves (open forks). All ER.

SOUTHWARK, EDWARD VI: Mm. *E* on rev. ER.

SOUTHWARK, HENRY POSTHUMOUS: Mm. *E* on rev. Stops (iv) lozenges, or (vi) pellets. VR.

CANTERBURY, HENRY VIII: No mm. Gothic letters. Stops (ii) saltires or trefoils (pierced cross-ends; some, earlier, with spur below shield; var. *Cantas*), or (iii) sleeves (open forks; no spur; var. Roman *N* on rev.). All rare.

CANTERBURY, POSTHUMOUS: No mm. Rev. cross patty, or open forks. Stops (iv) lozenges (facing bust; Gothic or large Roman letters; var. Gothic *h*; one has *Cantor* over *London)*, or (vi) pellets (facing or three-quarter bust; small Roman letters).

YORK, HENRY VIII: No mm. Gothic or mixed letters. Stops (ii) trefoils or saltires (pierced cross-ends; some with spur from top of shield), or (iii) sleeves (open forks; no spur), or none.

YORK, POSTHUMOUS: No mm. Open forks. Stops (iv) lozenges (facing bust; large Roman letters), or (vi) pellets (facing or, VR, three-quarter bust; small Roman letters), or none.

BRISTOL, HENRY VIII and POSTHUMOUS: No mm. Facing bust.

London-made dies: Stops (iii) sleeves on obv. only (Henry VIII), Gothic letters but Roman *N*, VR; or (iv) lozenges (Posthumous), Roman letters, also muled with Evenet obv., all ER.

Bristol dies with Evenet Gothic lettering: Facing bust with small head and more body than at other mints. *he 8 D G Rosa Sine Spina* or var. Stops pellets or saltires, with trefoils, quatrefoils or crosses. Trefoils or nothing in forks.

BRISTOL, EDWARD VI: Portrait bust right. Evenet lettering. *E(d) 6 D G* etc. Stops pellets or saltires, with trefoil or quatrefoil. Trefoils or nothing in forks. Rare.

DURHAM PLACE, POSTHUMOUS (1548-9): Mm. bow on rev. Facing bust. Roman letters. *H 8 D G Rosa* etc. Square pellet stops. Rev. *Red Cuiq Q Su Est*. Ornamental cross ends. ER.

DUBLIN, POSTHUMOUS (1548-51): Three-halfpence Irish. No mm. Pellet stops. Earlier (facing) bust with fur collar (VR), or three-quarter bust (rare).

Debasement, Henry VIII – Edward VI

HALFPENCE 1544 – 1551

Fineness: 1544-5, 9 oz.; 1545-6, 6 oz.; from April 1546, 4 oz.

Mints: Tower (and Southwark?) (*Civitas London*), Canterbury (*Civitas Cantor*), York (*Civitas Eboraci*, or *–rac*), Bristol (*Civitas Bristoli*), Dublin (*Civitas Dublinie*).

HENRY VIII: Obv. Crowned bust facing, in fur-collared cloak. *h D G Rosa Sine Spina*, abbreviated. Rev. Cross and pellets; cross-ends usually patty. Mint name.

EDWARD VI: Portrait bust right.

HENRY POSTHUMOUS: Type as pre-1547, but usually Roman letters. No mm. Cross-ends patty, or open forks.

LONDON, HENRY VIII: Mm. lis or none. Gothic letters. Stops (ii) trefoils. Pellet-in-annulet in centre of rev. cross. Vars. *Londen;* annulet on inner circles. Rare.

LONDON, EDWARD VI: No mm.? Roman letters. *E (6) D G* etc. Stops (iv) lozenges. ER.

LONDON, POSTHUMOUS: Stops (vi) pellets.

CANTERBURY, HENRY VIII: No mm. Gothic or mixed letters. Stops (ii) trefoils or saltires, or none. Var. *h 8 D G* etc. Rare.

CANTERBURY, POSTHUMOUS: Stops (iv) lozenges, (v) pierced crosses or saltires, or (vi) pellets; or none. Var. *H 8 D G* etc. All rare.

YORK, HENRY VIII: No mm. Mixed letters. Stops (ii) trefoils. Rare.

YORK, POSTHUMOUS: Roman or mixed letters. Stops (iv) lozenges, or (vi) pellets.

BRISTOL: Evenet dies, with Gothic lettering. Double leaf in reverse forks.

HENRY VIII (and Posthumous?): *h D G Rosa Sine Spin( )*. Old head facing. No mm. (?). ER.

EDWARD VI: *E (6) D G* etc. Pellet or saltire stops, one with trefoil after *Rosa*. ER.

DUBLIN (Posthumous only): Three-farthings Irish. Facing Tower-style bust. VR.

FARTHINGS FROM 1544

TOWER mint only, HENRY VIII. Gothic letters. Obv. Five-petalled rose. *h D G Rutil (...)*. Trefoil stops. Rev. Large pellet in each quarter of long cross patty. *Deo/Gr/aci/as*. ER.

SHILLINGS 1549 - 1551

Value at issue 12d.; from August 1551, 6d.; reduced from October 1560 to 4½d. (6 oz. coins) with portcullis stamped before the face, or to 2¼d. (3 oz. coins) with greyhound behind the head.

First issue: Feb. 1549 only, 8 oz. fine, wt. 60 gr.. Second issue: 1549 (April) - 1550/1, 6 oz. fine, wt. 80 gr. Third issue: April - July 1551 (plus Dublin, 1552), 3 oz. fine, wt. 80 gr.
Mints: Tower (I and II, 1549-51), Southwark (1549-51), Canterbury (1549),
Durham Place (Feb. - Oct. 1549), Bristol (May - June 1549); plus Dublin (1552).

Obv. Crowned bust, clothed, to right. Rev. Oval garnished shield, *E R* beside. Small square or diamond stops on Tower-made dies. Roman letters. Six bust types (excepting Durham Place):

1. Medium head, fine style. 8 oz. only.
2. Large head, with crown tilted back. 8 oz. (? plus 6 oz.).
3. Small head (henceforward); bust indented below shoulder. 6 oz. only.
4. Similar to 3, but no indentation. 6 oz. only.
5. Larger lapels and collar, pointed chin. 6 oz. only.
6. Very narrow neck and collar. 6 oz. and 3 oz.

1544–1551

Shillings

First Issue: 8 oz. fine, 60 gr. 1549 only. Beaded circles; inscriptions transposed. Obv. *Timor Domini Fons Vitae MDXLIX.* Rev. *Edward VI D G Agl Fra z Hib Rex.*

Tower I. Bust 1, mm. arrow, rare. Bust 2, mm. arrow on rev. only, ER.

Southwark. Bust 1, mm. *Y*, rare. Var. (ER) has mm. *EY* on obv.

Canterbury. Bust 1, mm. rose (on rev. only). VR.

Uncertain mint. Bust 1, no mm. *Vite.* Rare.

Second Issue: 6 oz. fine, 80 gr. 1549 (*MDXLIX*) and 1550 (*MDL*). Wireline circles. Obv. *Edward VI* etc.; rev. *Timor* etc. with date; *Vite.* Some (VR) of Tower II and Southwark, 1549, have large shield on rev.

Tower I. Mm. arrow: Bust 3, 1549 (mm. rarely over *G*); bust 4, 1549, VR; bust 5, 1549.

Mm. pheon (ER): Bust 5, 1549; also VR mules pheon/arrow and arrow/pheon.

Mm. swan: Bust 5, 1549 (swan I; ER var. has swan over *Y*); also rare mules swan/arrow, swan/pheon and pheon/swan. Bust 5, 1550 (swan I and pheon/swan I mule, both VR; swan II, and VR mules II/I and I/II).

Tower II. Mm. grapple: Bust 3, 1549 (mm. rarely over *G*); bust 4, 1549, VR (var. omits *E R*); bust 5, 1549, ER.

Mm. crowned leopard's head: Bust 5, 1550. ER.

Mm. martlet (to left): Bust 5, 1550, VR; also ER mule martlet/leopard's head. Bust 6, 1550, ER.

Southwark. Mm. *Y*: Bust 3, 1549 (mm. rarely over *G,* or on rev., ER, over grapple); bust 4, 1549, VR; bust 5, 1549; bust 5, 1550 (ER var. has *Y* over swan); bust 6, 1550, ER (var. omits *E R*).

Canterbury. Mm. *t* (or *T*, VR), 1549 only: Bust 3; bust 4, VR; bust 5, ER.

Bristol. Mm. *TC* monogram, 1549 only: London obv. die, bust 3, has *TC* over *G;* Evenet dies have rosettes in inscriptions. All ER.

Third Issue: 3 oz. fine, 80 gr. 1550 (*MDL* – incorrect date?) - 1551 (*MDLI*), plus Dublin 1552 (*MDLII*). Types as Second Issue; bust 6 only. Royal emblems as mintmarks.

Tower I (?). Mm. rose: 1550 (mm. rose over lion), VR; 1551.

Tower II (?). Mm. lion: 1550, ER; 1551, rare, also ER mule mm. lion/rose over lion.

Southwark. Mm. lis: 1551, rare; also VR mules lis/*Y* 1550 and *Y*/lis 1551.

Dublin. Mm. harp, 1552. Mixed Roman and Gothic letters. VR (n.b. base metal counterfeits exist, including dies with *MDXLIX* or obv. mm. *Y).*

Durham Place. Mm. bow. Cross stops.

First Issue, 8 oz., 60 gr.

Obv. Bust 1 (tall crown, projecting collar). (i) *Timor* etc. with date *MDXLIX* (1549). Beaded circles both sides. ER. (ii) *Inimicos Eius Induam Confusione* (no date). Beaded or wireline circles. VR. Revs. of both types read *Edward VI D G Angl Fr et Hib Rex (ET* monogram for *et*); beaded circles (once with additional wireline inside).

Second Issue, 6 oz., 80 gr.

(i) Coins from obv. dies of first issue, with bust 1, distinguished by higher weight; revs. also from first issue dies, or new dies with smaller letters reading *Fra Hiber(ni) Rex.* VR.

(ii) New dies. Wireline circles. Obv. bust 2 (similar to Tower busts, but point of collar protrudes below chin). *Inimicos* etc. Rev. *Edward VI* etc. ER.

(iii) As (ii) but obv. *Edward VI* etc., wireline circles; rev. *Inimicos* etc., circles beaded or wireline. All rare.

EPILOGUE

The first half of the sixteenth century had seen the English coinage pass through a period of gradual but accelerating change, from its medieval traditions to the culture of the early modern world. Yet although in many respects the reform of 1551 represents a watershed between old and new, not every aspect of the ancient order abruptly disappeared.

In structure the silver coinage of 1551 differed fundamentally from what had gone before. The crown of five shillings, with its half (2s. 6d.), and the shilling with its fractions, set a pattern that was to endure until the twentieth century. But this new structure took time to become established. After the death of Edward VI in 1553 the crown and halfcrown went into abeyance for almost fifty years, and it was not until the seventeenth century that England had a regular issue of large silver coins, matching the continental thalers and their parts that had spread outwards through Europe from the mining areas of Saxony and Bohemia since 1500. Under Edward's sister Mary (1553-8) the silver coinage reverted briefly to groats and halfgroats alone until her marriage to Philip of Spain in 1554, when the minting of shillings and sixpences was resumed. During the long reign of Elizabeth (1558-1603) the two sets of values ran awkwardly in parallel, with groat, halfgroat, penny and halfpenny produced intermittently alongside shilling, sixpence, threepence, threehalfpence and threefarthings. The groat itself lasted only until 1561, and was not struck at the Tower under James I (1603-25) or Charles I (1625-49), although it reappeared during the Civil War of the 1640s at several emergency mints in parts of the country where older tradition survived. The halfgroat, however, continued uninterrupted, and from Charles II (1660-85) onwards all four denominations from groat to penny were produced for small change. During the eighteenth century, with the increasing use of copper for the lowest values, these minor silver coins came to be minted primarily for the sovereign's distribution of Maundy money, but the groat had a final revival as a current coin as late as the 1830s and 1840s. The traditional fractions of the pound eventually disappeared when it was decimalized in 1971.

In the second half of the sixteenth century the most obvious descendant of medieval coinage was the angel, preserving for a time not only the half-mark denomination that had been the mainstay of English gold coinage for two hundred years, but also retaining the essentials of its medieval design. Although angels continued to be minted until the Civil War, after Elizabeth they ceased to be part of normal currency and were largely used in the royal ceremony of touching for the King's Evil, the disease known medically as scrofula, which kings of France were traditionally believed to have the power to cure. Most surviving angels of James I and Charles I therefore have a large piercing so that they could be suspended by a ribbon. After Charles I pierced angels were no longer used for this purpose, being replaced by small medalets (which nevertheless still carried the angel type). Henry VII's sovereign and ryal, inaugurated in the late fifteenth century, also had descendants in the later Tudor coinage, but their designs were not so much reproductions as adaptations of the originals.

One of the more surprising features of the new coins of 1551 was a reversion to the Gothic alphabet, perhaps an intentional evocation of older values after the Roman-lettered coins of the debasement at its worst. The Gothic script was maintained by Mary before her marriage, and even briefly revived on Elizabeth's first gold ryal in the 1580s. But by then it was no more than a conscious archaism. More enduring were the content and language of inscriptions. Mottoes with a religious flavour were not replaced until Charles II. Their place was taken by more extended royal titles, and until 1801 these continued to include the historic claim to the kingdom of France which had featured on all larger English coins since Edward III. Longest surviving of all medieval habits, however, has been use of the Latin language, retained elsewhere on the coins of western Christendom until the nineteenth or twentieth century, but still in use on those of the United Kingdom to-day.

Physical changes in the coinage have concerned content and manufacture. Medieval standards of fineness, restored in 1551, lasted until the twentieth century, when the fineness of the silver coinage was reduced to 50 per cent in 1919/20 as a result of a steep rise in the price of silver after the First World War, and to zero after the Second World War when it was replaced by cupro-nickel in 1947. For more than three hundred years all British coins have been made by machinery, although, in the face of resistance to the new technology from mint personnel, the medieval hammered method, and with it the use of broader and thinner flans for values from the shilling downwards, had survived until 1662, in the reign of Charles II. Old hammered coins, however, remained current until 1696, when they were withdrawn and reminted. In a revival of medieval practice, regional mints were set up at Bristol, Chester, Exeter, Norwich and York, and a similar exercise was conducted at Edinburgh following the Act of Union between England and Scotland in 1707. After 1551 the York mint was retained, but only for two more years, and thenceforward English coins were normally struck at the Tower of London, or latterly on Tower Hill, until the mint, no longer needing to be situated in a business centre, was removed to Llantrisant, near Cardiff, in the 1970s. Apart from 1696 and 1707 there were few exceptions to this concentration. Under Charles I a mint was established at Aberystwyth to coin silver from the mines in west Wales; during the Civil War temporary mints were set up in various places under Royalist control to pay the troops and meet other costs of the war; and in the early stages of the Industrial Revolution the manufacture of copper coins was for a few years transferred to Matthew Boulton's factory in Birmingham. Otherwise, the new coinage of 1551 brought about a lasting centralization of minting, in which echoes of the medieval past became fewer and fainter as time passed.

BIBLIOGRAPHY

Principal Works

Brooke, G.C., *English Coins from the Seventh Century to the Present Day*, 3rd edn., 1950. Overtaken in parts, but excellent (if very condensed) survey.
Challis, C.E. (ed.), *A New History of the Royal Mint, Cambridge, 1992.* Essential work of reference, with summaries of mint output and indentures.
Feavearyear, A., *The Pound Sterling: A History of English Money*, 2nd. edn. (revised by E.V. Morgan), Oxford, 1963. An economist's account.
Hawkins, E., *The Silver Coins of England*, 3rd. edn. (revised by R.L. Kenyon), 1887. Dated, but contains much information.
Kenyon, R.L., *The Gold Coins of England, 1884.* Similar in scope to Hawkins.
North, J.J., *English Hammered Coinage*, vol. 1 (to 1272), 3rd. edn., 1994, and 2 (from 1272), 3rd. edn., 1991. Very reliable catalogue of main types and varieties.
Oman, C., *The Coinage of England*, 1931. An historian's perspective.
Ruding, R., *Annals of the Coinage of Great Britain*, 3rd. edn., 1840. Still valuable.
Spink, *Standard Catalogue of Coins of England and the United Kingdom,* annually. Convenient listing, with market prices.
Sutherland, C.H.V., *English Coinage 600-1900*, 1973. Mostly derivative, but with aesthetic insight.
Woodhead, P., *English Gold Coins and their Imitations* (Schneider collection, part 1), *SCBI* 47, 1996. Excellent detailed catalogue, with comprehensive introduction.

Periodicals etc.

AgHR	*Agricultural History Review,* 1953 - .
BAR	*British Archaeological Reports,* 1974 - .
BNJ	*British Numismatic Journal*, 1904 - .
CMB	Seaby's *Coin & Medal Bulletin,* 1945 - 1991
EcHR	*Economic History Review,* 1927 - .
EHR	*English Historical Review,* 1886 - .
NC	*Numismatic Chronicle,* 1838 - .
NCirc	Spink's *Numismatic Circular,* 1892 - .
SCBI	*Sylloge of Coins of the British Isles,* 1958 - .

General

Allen, M.R., 'The weight standard of the English coinage 1158-1279', *NC* 2005, pp. 227-33.
— , 'The proportions of the denominations in English mint outputs, 1351-1485', *BNJ* 77 (2007), pp. 190-209.
Archibald, M., 'Early medieval coinage (1066-1279)', *BNJ* 73 (2003), pp. 76-88. Review article.
— , 'English medieval coins as dating evidence', in *Coins and the Archaeologist,* edd. J. Casey and R. Rees (*BAR* 4), 1974, pp. 234-71.

Buck, I.R., *Medieval English Groats*, 2000.
Grierson, P., *Coins of Medieval Europe,* 1993. Authoritative.
Johnson, C., ed., *The De Moneta of Nicholas Oresme and English Mint Documents* (13th and 14th cents.), 1956.
Lockett: *Sale Catalogue of the R.C. Lockett Collection*, Glendining, parts I (6-9 June, 1955), IV (11-17 Oct. 1956), VII (4-6 Nov. 1958), X (26-7 April 1960) and XIII (17 Oct. 1961). The most important twentieth-century collection of English coins.
Lyon, S., 'Silver weight and minted weight in England c. 1000-1320, with a discussion of Domesday terminology, Edwardian farthings and the origin of English Troy', *BNJ* 76 (2006), pp. 227-41.
Seaby, H.A. (ed.), *Notes on English Silver Coins 1066-1648*, 1948.
Stewart, I., 'English numismatics – progress and prospects', *BNJ* 58 (1988), pp. 110-22.
Stewartby, Lord, 'Lawrence and his successors', *BNJ* 73 (2003), pp. 98-106.
Woodhead, P., 'Late medieval coinage (1279-1485)', BNJ 73 (2003), pp. 89-97. Review article.

Mints and Mint Accounts

Allen, D.F., 'Dies in the Public Record Office, 1938', *BNJ* XXIII (1938-40), pp. 31-50.
Allen, M.R., 'Ecclesiastical mints in thirteenth-century England', *Thirteenth Century England VIII* (ed. M. Prestwich *et al.,* Woodbridge, 2001), pp. 113-22.
— , 'Ecclesiastical mints in fifteenth-century England', *NC* 2000, pp. 249-59.
— , 'The Archbishop of York's mint after the Norman Conquest', *Northern History*, XLI, 1, March 2004, pp. 25-38.
— , 'The Archbishop of York's mint in the 1330s', *NC* 2001, pp. 295-301.
— , 'Medieval English die-output', *BNJ* 74 (2004), pp. 39-49. Includes revised figures for Edwardian mint output, 1280-1351.
— , *The Durham Mint*, 2003. Excellent historical account (includes appendices on documents, hoards, etc.)
Blunt, C.E., 'Ecclesiastical coinage in England. Part II: After the Norman Conquest', *NC* 1961, pp. i-xxi.
— , 'Privy-marking and the Trial of the Pyx', *Studies in Numismatic Method Presented to Philip Grierson*, ed. C.N.L. Brooke *et al.*, Cambridge, 1983, pp. 225-30.
Blunt, C.E. and Brand, J.D., 'Mint output of Henry III', *BNJ* XXXIX (1970), pp. 61-5.
Caine, C., *The Archiepiscopal Coins of York*, York, 1908.
Cook, B., 'The royal household and the mint (1279-1399)', *NC* 1989, pp. 121-33.
— , 'Coining dies in late medieval England with a catalogue of the British Museum Collection', *NC* 2000, pp. 219-47.
Cooper, D.R., *The Art and Craft of Coinmaking*, 1988.
Craig, J., *The Mint*, 1953.
Crump, C.G., and Johnson, C., 'Tables of bullion coined under Edward I, II and III', *NC* 1913, pp. 200-45.
Eaglen, R.J., *The Abbey and Mint of Bury St. Edmunds to 1279*, 2006.
Reddaway, T.F., 'The king's mint and exchange in London 1343-1543', *EHR* 1967, pp. 1-23.
Sellwood, D., 'Medieval minting techniques', *BNJ* 31 (1962), pp. 57-65.

Stewart, B.H.I.H., 'Medieval die-output: two calculations for English mints in the fourteenth century', *NC* 1963, pp. 97-106; and 'Second thoughts on medieval die-output', *NC* 1964, pp. 293-303.

Stokes, E., 'Tables of bullion coined from 1377-1550', *NC* 1929, pp. 27-69 (see Stewartby, *NC* 2002, p. 373 for London 1399-1402).

Stride, H.G., *The Royal Mint*, serialised in *CMB*, 1954-60.

Woodhead, P., 'Calais and its mint: Part II', *Coinage in the Low Countries (880-1500)*, ed. N.J. Mayhew (*BAR Int.* 54, Oxford, 1979), pp. 185-202.

HOARDS AND CURRENCY

Allen, M.R., 'English coin hoards, 1158-1544', *BNJ* 72 (2002), pp. 24-84. Chronological listing.

— , 'The volume of the English currency, 1158-1470', *EcHR* 2001, pp. 595-611.

— , 'The interpretation of single-finds of English coins, 1279-1544', *BNJ* 75 (2005), pp. 50-62.

Brown, I.D., and Dolley, M., *A Bibliography of Coin Hoards of Great Britain and Ireland 1500-1967*, 1971; 'First Addendum', *NCirc* 1973, pp. 147-51.

Cook, B.J., 'The bezant in Angevin England', *NC* 1999, pp. 255-75.

— , 'Foreign coins in medieval England', *Local Coins, Foreign Coins: Italy and Europe 11th-15th Centuries*, ed. L. Travaini, Milan, 1999, pp. 231-84.

Mate, M., 'The role of gold coinage in the English economy, 1338-1400', *EcHR* 1978, pp. 126-41.

Mayhew, N.J., 'Numismatic evidence and falling prices in the fourteenth century', *EcHR* 1974, pp. 1-15.

— , 'Money and prices in England from Henry II to Edward III', *AgHR* 1987, pp. 121-32.

Metcalf, D.M., 'Some finds of medieval coins from Scotland and the north of England', *BNJ* XXX (1960-1), pp. 88-123.

Munro, J.H.A., *Wool, Cloth and Gold: The Struggle for Bullion in Anglo-Burgundian Trade, 1340-1478*, Brussels, 1973.

Spufford, P., 'Continental coins in late medieval England', *BNJ* XXXII (1963), pp. 127-39.

— , *Money and its Use in Medieval Europe*, Cambridge, 1988. Important.

Thompson, J.D.A., *Inventory of British Coin Hoards, A.D. 600-1500*, 1956. Unreliable but fundamental.

Whitton, C.A., 'Some aspects of English currency in the later Middle Ages', *BNJ* XXIV (1941-4), pp. 36-46.

Wood, D. (ed.), *Medieval Money Matters*, Oxford, 2004. Five essays on the money economy of medieval England.

SHORT CROSS AND LONG CROSS PERIODS, 1180 – 1278

Allen, D.F., *Catalogue of English Coins in the British Museum: The Cross-and-Crosslets (Tealby) Type of Henry II,* 1951. Discusses 1180 recoinage.

Allen, M.R., 'The Carlisle and Durham mints in the Short Cross period', *BNJ* XLIX (1979), pp. 42-55.

— , 'A revised arrangement of Short Cross class III and other notes on the Short Cross classification', *SCBI* 48 (1997), pp. 59-61.
— , 'Documentary evidence for the output, profits and expenditure of the Bury St. Edmunds mint', *BNJ* 69 (1999), pp. 210-3.
— , 'The provision and use of dies for Short Cross class V' *BNJ* 59 (1989), pp. 46-76.
— , 'Short Cross class Va: mules and mysteries', *NCirc* 1991, pp. 337-8.
— , 'The chronology of Short Cross class Ia', *BNJ* 63 (1993), pp. 53-58.
— , 'Mint output in the English recoinage of 1247-1250', *BNJ* 69 (1999), pp. 207-10; and 'Salaries of mint and exchange officials in the Long Cross recoinage of 1247 – 1250', *BNJ* 75 (2005), pp. 173-5.
— , 'The chronology, mints and moneyers of the English coinage, 1180-1247', *SCBI* 56 (J.P. Mass), 2001, pp. 1-12.
— , 'The quantity of money in England 1180-1247', *BNJ* 75 (2005), pp. 44-9.
— , 'Hoards and the circulation of the Short Cross coinage', *SCBI* 56 (Mass, 2001), pp. 112-30.
Allen, M.R., and Dawson, A., 'The Short Cross moneyers of Shrewsbury', *BNJ* 62 (1992), p. 193.
Archibald, M.M., and Cook, B.J., *English Medieval Coin Hoards: I. Cross and Crosslets, Short Cross and Long Cross Hoards*, 2001.
Besly, E., 'Short Cross and other medieval coins from Llanfaes, Anglesey', *BNJ* 65 (1995), pp. 46-82.
Brand, J.D., 'Some Short Cross questions', *BNJ* XXXIII (1964), pp. 57-69.
— , 'The Short Cross coins of Rhuddlan', *BNJ* XXXIV (1965), pp. 90-97.
— , *The English Coinage 1180-1247: Money, Mints and Exchanges,* 1994. Valuable historical survey.
— , 'The Shrewsbury mint, 1249-50', *Mints, Dies and Currency*, ed. R.A.G. Carson, 1971, pp. 129-50.
Brand, J.D., and Elmore Jones, F., 'The Emergency Mint of Wilton in 1180', *BNJ* XXXV (1966), pp. 116-9.
Brooke, G.C., 'Chronology in the Short-Cross period', *NC* 1910, pp. 291-324.
Carpenter, D., 'Gold and gold coins in England in the mid-thirteenth century', *NC* 1987, pp. 106-13.
Churchill, R., *Mints & Moneyers During the Reign of Henry III,* in the press.
Churchill, R., and Thomas, B., *The Brussels Hoard of 1908,* in the press.
Davis, R.L., 'Class II coins of the Long Cross coinage 1247-1248', *BNJ* XLVII (1977), pp. 138-41.
— , *British Museum* (1975) and *Royal Mint* (1977) *Henry III and Edward I Long Cross Coinage*, privately produced catalogues.
Dolley, R.H.M., 'A note on the chronology of some published and unpublished 'Short Cross' finds from the British Isles', *BNJ* XXIX (1958-9), pp. 297-321.
Jones, F. Elmore, 'The last Short Cross issue of Henry III (class 8)', *BNJ* XXV (1945-8), pp. 286-90.
Evans, J., 'The Short Cross question', *NC* 1865, pp. 255-95.
— , 'The first gold coins of England', *NC* 1900, pp. 218-51.
Fox, H.B.E., and Fox, J.S., 'Numismatic history of the reigns of Edward I, II and III', part 2, *BNJ* VII (1910), pp. 91-142. Covers late Long Cross issues.
Lawrence, L.A., 'The Short-Cross coinage, 1180-1247', *BNJ* XI (1915), pp. 59-100. Basic study.
— , 'The Long-Cross coinage of Henry III and Edward I', *BNJ* IX (1912), pp. 145-79;

X (1913), pp. 69-93; and XI (1915), pp. 101-19. Standard account.
Longstaffe, W.H.D., 'Northern evidence on the Short-Cross question', *NC* 1863, pp. 162-88.
Mass, J.P., 'Of dies, design changes and square lettering in the opening phase of the Short Cross coinage', *BNJ* 63 (1993), pp. 20-52.
— , *The J.P. Mass Collection of English Short Cross Coins, 1180-1247* (*SCBI* 56, 2001). Catalogue of major collection, with comprehensive introduction.
North, J.J., 'A re-examination of classes 7 and 8 of the Short Cross coinage', *BNJ* 58 (1988), pp. 25-39.
— , 'Some imitations and forgeries of the English and Irish Long Cross pence of Henry III', *BNJ* 65 (1995), pp. 83-119.
Seaby, W.A., 'The 1969 Colchester hoard: II. The Anglo-Irish portion', *BNJ* XLIV (1974), pp. 43-8.
Smith, S. (ed.), *The Great Roll of the Pipe for the Seventh Year of King John Michaelmas 1205,* Pipe Roll Soc., 1941. Contains detailed discussion of 1205 recoinage.
Stewart, I., 'King John's recoinage and the conference of moneyers in 1208', *BNJ* 59 (1989), pp. 39-45 (*recte* 1207, *BNJ* 65, p. 223).
— , 'English coinage in the later years of John and the minority of Henry III' *BNJ* XLIX (1979), pp. 26-41 and 51 (1981), pp. 91-106.
Stewartby, Lord, 'English Short Cross coins from the Eccles hoard', *NC* 1993, pp. 137-52.
— , 'German imitations of English Short Cross sterlings', *NC* 1995, pp. 209-60.
— , 'Robert Vi', *BNJ* 75 (2005), pp. 172-3.
Tibbo, G.K., *The Organisation of the Currency from 1180 to 1250,* University of Reading MA thesis, 1954.
Wells, W.C., 'Notes on the Long Cross coinage of Henry III, 1247-1250', *BNJ* XXII (1934-7), pp. 79-107.
Wren, C.R., *The Short-Cross Coinage 1180-1247* and *The Voided Long-Cross Coinage 1247-1279,* Herne Bay, 1992 and 1993. Introductory.
Yvon, J., 'Esterlins à la croix courte dans les trésors français de la fin du 12e et de la première moitié du 13e siècle', *BNJ* XXXIX (1970), pp. 24-60.

EDWARDIAN STERLING PERIOD, 1279 – 1351

Allen, D.F., 'The Boyton hoard', *NC* 1936, pp. 115-55.
Allen, M.R., 'The groats of Edward I', *BNJ* 74 (2004), pp. 28-38.
— , 'The volume and composition of the English silver currency, 1279-1351', *BNJ* 70 (2000), pp. 38-44.
Allen, M.R. and Vosper, M.R., 'An Edward III class 15d penny of Reading', *BNJ* 69 (1999), pp. 214-5.
Archibald, M.M., 'The Mayfield (Sussex) 1968 hoard of English pence and French gros, c.1307', *Mints, Dies and Currency*, ed. R.A.G. Carson, 1971, pp. 151-60.
Beardwood, A., 'The royal mints and exchanges', in *The English Government at Work 1327–1336,* edd. J.F. Willard, W.A. Morris, and W.H. Durham (Cambridge, Mass., 1950), pp. 35-66.
Blunt, C.E., 'The mint of Berwick-on-Tweed under Edward I, II and III', *NC* 1931, pp. 28-52.
Burns, E., *The Coinage of Scotland* (Edinburgh, 1887), I, pp. 186-220 (addenda on Edwardian sterlings from Montrave hoard).

Eagleton, C., and Kelleher, R., '1343 and all that: previously unnoticed documents relating to England's new gold and silver coins', *BNJ* 76 (2006), pp. 340-4.
Evans, J., 'The first gold coins of England', *NC* 1900, pp. 218-51.
Fox, H.B.E. and J.S., 'Numismatic History of the Reigns of Edward I, II and III' *BNJ* VI (1909), pp. 197-212; VII (1910), pp. 91-142; VIII (1911), pp. 137-48; IX (1912), pp. 181-206; X (1913), pp. 95-123 (also 'The pennies of Edward I, II and III', *NC* 1917, pp. 279-97). Classic study.
Greenhalgh, D.I., 'The Fox class VII pence of Edward I', *BNJ* 59 (1989), pp. 77-83.
Jones, F. Elmore, 'Edwardus Rex Ain: de Bury or Hatfield?', *BNJ* XXIX (1959), pp. 326-33; and postscript, *BNJ* XXX (1961), pp. 363-5.
Mate, M., 'A mint of trouble, 1279 to 1307', *Speculum* 44 (1969), pp. 201-12.
— , 'Coin dies under Edward I and II', *NC* 1969, pp. 207-18.
— , 'Monetary policies in England, 1272-1307', *BNJ* XLI (1972), pp. 34-79.
Mayhew, N.J., ed., *Edwardian Monetary Affairs (1279-1344)* (*BAR* 36; Oxford, 1977).
— , *Sterling Imitations of Edwardian type,* 1983.
— , 'Imitative sterlings in the Aberdeen and Montraive hoards', *NC* 1976, pp. 85-97.
North, J.J., *The Coinages of Edward I and II,* 1968. Introductory.
— , *Edwardian English Silver Coins 1279-1351* (*SCBI* 39, 1989); for addenda see *BNJ* 62 (1992) pp. 97-101. Fundamental catalogue with comprehensive introduction.
— , 'Irregular dies of the Durham mint c.1300', *BNJ* 54 (1984), pp. 74-80.
Potter, W.J.W., 'The gold coinages of Edward III', part I, *NC* 1963, pp. 107-28.
Purvey, F., 'The XVd Durham pennies of Edward III', *BNJ* XXIX (1959), pp. 322-5.
Shirley-Fox, J., 'The pennies and halfpennies of 1344-51', *NC* 1928, pp. 16-46.
Stewart, I., 'Bishop Bek and the Durham coins of Edward I and II', *BNJ* 54 (1984), pp. 81-5.
Stewartby, Lord, 'An Edward III Berwick farthing of reduced fineness', *NC* 2004, pp. 245-8.
Tatler, G.L.V. and Stewart, B.H.I.H., 'Edwardian sterlings in the Montrave hoard', *BNJ* XXXI (1962), pp. 80-7.
Tatler, G.L.V., 'The Bury coinage of Edward I with the name of Robert de Hadeleie', *BNJ* 68 (1998), pp. 64-76.
Withers, P., and B., *The Farthings and Halfpennies of Edward I and II*, Llanfyllin, 2001.
— , *The Galata Guide to the Pennies of Edward I and II and the Coins of the Mint of Berwick-upon-Tweed,* Llanfyllin, 2006.
Wood, C.J., 'Preliminary results of a die-analysis of approximately one hundred early Edward I pence of the mint of Berwick-on-Tweed', *BNJ* XLVII (1977), pp. 141-4.
— , 'The classification of class 10', *SCBI* 39 (J.J. North), pp. 42-53.
Woodhead, P., 'The early coinages of Edward III (1327-43)', *SCBI* 39 (J.J. North), pp. 54-78.

LATER EDWARD III AND RICHARD II, 1351 – 1399

Allen, M.R., 'Two fourteenth-century mint indentures and related documentary evidence' (York 1357, Durham 1367), *BNJ* 70 (2000), pp. 61-6.
Doubleday: Mitchell, P., Sale Catalogue of the G.V. Doubleday collection of coins of Edward III, Glendining, 7-8 June 1972.
Harris, E.J., 'The halfpence and farthings of Richard II', *NCirc* Dec. 1987, p. 325.
Lawrence, L.A., *The coinage of Edward III from 1351,* 1937, reprinted from *NC* 1926, 1929, 1932 and 1933, with additions; addenda by Whitton, *NC* 1944, pp. 116-8. Standard work.

Potter, W.J.W., 'The silver coinage of Edward III from 1351', *NC* 1960, pp. 137-81 and 1962, pp. 203-24.

— , 'The gold coinages of Edward III', *NC* 1963, pp. 107-28, and 1964, pp. 305-18.

— , 'The silver coinages of Richard II, Henry IV and Henry V', part I, *BNJ* XXIX (1958-9), pp. 334-52.

Purvey, F., 'The pence, half-pence and farthings of Richard II of the mints of London, York and Durham', *BNJ* XXXI (1962), pp. 88-108.

Stewartby, Lord, and Woodhead, P., 'Edward III Pre-Treaty Farthings', *NCirc* 2001, p. 233.

Stewartby, Lord, and Webb Ware, T.G., 'Some late Richard nobles', *BNJ* 77 (2007), pp. 281-2.

Walters, F.A., 'The coinage of Richard II', *NC* 1904, pp. 326-52.

Webb Ware, T.G., 'Richard II – A neglected reign', address to British Numismatic Society, 28 Jan. 1992 (the classification described for gold is used by Woodhead in the Schneider *Sylloge*). Copies deposited in British, Ashmolean and Fitzwilliam Museums.

Withers, P. and B., *The Halfpennies and Farthings of Edward III and Richard II*, Llanfyllin, 2002.

HOUSE OF LANCASTER: HENRY IV – HENRY VI, 1399 - 1461

Allen, M., 'Documentary evidence for the Henry VI annulet coinage of York', *BNJ* 65 (1995), pp. 120-34.

Archibald, M.M., 'Fishpool, Blidworth (Notts) 1966 hoard', *NC* 1967, pp. 133-46.

Blunt, C.E., 'The heavy gold coinage of Henry IV', *BNJ* XXIV (1941-4), pp. 22-7; and 'Unrecorded heavy nobles of Henry IV and some remarks on that issue', *BNJ* XXXVI (1967), pp. 106-13.

— , 'Some new light on the heavy silver coinage of Henry IV, 1399-1412', *Trans. International Numismatic Congress*, 1936, pp. 360-5.

Brooke, G.C., 'Privy marks in the reign of Henry V', *NC* 1930, pp. 44-87.

Buck: *Sale Catalogue of the Ivan Buck Collection,* Spink, 30 November 2005. Strong for Henry VI.

Harris, E.J., 'Silver coinage in the Henry V period', parts 1-5, *CMB* 1990, pp. 44-5, 134-6, 196-7, 235-7 and 267-71; parts 6 and 7, *Classical Numismatic Review* 1991, 3, pp. 7-8 and 1992, 1, p.3.

— , 'Die pairing on the transitional coins of Henry IV and Henry V', *BNJ* 67 (1997), pp. 20-9.

— , 'Halfgroats in the Henry IV - Henry V period', *BNJ* 68 (1998), pp. 147-8 (plus corrigenda, *BNJ* 69, p. 219).

— , 'Dies for the heavy and light pence, 1399-1422', *BNJ* 69 (1999), pp. 215-9.

Harris, E.J., & Laidlaw, S., 'A photographic record of halfpence of the Henry IV-V period', *BNJ* 70 (2000), pp. 146-7.

Lessen, M., 'York annulet silver coins of Henry VI', *BNJ* 63 (1993), pp. 59-64.

Potter, W.J.W., 'The silver coinages of Richard II, Henry IV and Henry V, parts II and III', *BNJ* XXX (1960), pp. 124-50.

— , 'The heavy groats of Henry VI', *BNJ* XXXIII (1957), pp. 299-311.

Stewartby, Lord, 'Calais quarter-nobles of Henry VI', *BNJ* 69 (1999), pp. 220-1.

— , 'Halfgroats of the middle period of Henry VI', *BNJ* 76 (2006), pp. 344-5.

Walters, F.A., 'The coinage of Henry IV', *NC* 1905, pp. 247-306.
— , 'The coinage of Henry V', *NC* 1906, pp. 172-220.
— , 'The silver coinage of the reign of Henry VI', *NC* 1902, pp. 224-266.
— , 'The gold coinage of the reign of Henry VI', *NC* 1903, pp. 286-310.
— , 'The Stamford find and supplementary notes on the coinage of Henry VI', *NC* 1911, pp. 153-75.
Whitton, C.A., 'The heavy coinage of Henry VI', *BNJ* XXIII (1938-41), pp. 59-90, 206-67, 399-439, with addenda, *BNJ* XXIV (1941-4), pp. 118-9. Standard work.
Withers, P. and B., *The Halfpennies and Farthings of Henry IV-VI,* Llanfyllin, 2003; and 'The halfpence and farthings of Henry VI: a reassessment', *BNJ* 74 (2004), pp. 50-67.

HOUSE OF YORK: EDWARD IV – RICHARD III, 1461 – 1485

Allen, D.F., 'The coinage of Henry VI restored: notes on the London mint', *NC* 1937, pp. 28-59.
Archibald, M.M., 'The Wyre Piddle (Worcs.) 1967 hoard of fifteenth-century silver coins', *NC* 1970, pp. 133-62.
Blunt, C.E., 'The coinage of Edward V, with some remarks on the later issues of Edward IV', *BNJ* XXII (1934-7), pp. 213-24.
Blunt, C.E. and Whitton, C.A., 'The coinages of Edward IV and Henry VI (restored)', *BNJ* XXV (1945-8), pp. 4-59, 130-82 and 291-339. Classic study.
Brooke, G.C., 'The mints of Canterbury and York in the reigns of Edward IV and Henry VII', *BNJ* XXI (1931-3), pp. 73-87.
Carlyon-Britton, R., 'The sequence of mintmarks preceding, during and succeeding the restoration of Henry VI', *BNJ* VII (1923-4), pp. 125-32.
Delmé-Radcliffe, M., 'Some notes on Edward IV', *BNJ* XLI (1972), pp. 180-1.
— : *Sale Catalogue of the Collection of Hammered Silver Coins Formed by Mrs. M. Delmé-Radcliffe*, Glendining, 17 April 1985. Strong for Edward IV.
Holmes, N., and Walker, D.A., 'A Henry VI/Edward IV mule penny from the Leith hoard', *BNJ* 58 (1988), pp. 84-9.
Lessen, M., 'The groats of Edward V', *BNJ* 53 (1983), pp. 180-3.
Mayhew, N.J., 'The monetary background to the Yorkist recoinage of 1464-1471', *BNJ* XLIV (1974), pp. 62-73.
Potter, W.J.W., 'The light groats of Edward IV', *CMB* 1956, pp. 2-9, 93-7 and 140-4.
Stewart, I., 'The dies of Edward V's silver coins', *BNJ* L (1980), pp. 133-5.
Stewartby, Lord, 'Edward boar's head halfpence', *BNJ* 74 (2004), pp. 183-4.
— , 'The date of Edward IV's mintmark cinquefoil', *BNJ* 79 (2009).
Symonds, H., 'Mint accounts and documents of Edward IV', *NC* 1926, pp. 99-112.
Walters, F.A., 'The coinage of the reign of Edward IV', *NC* 1909, pp. 132-219; 1910, pp. 117-45; and 1914, pp. 330-77.
Webb Ware, T.G., 'Dies and designs: the English gold coinage 1465-1485', *BNJ* 55 (1985), pp. 95-133.
— , 'The coinage of Richard III', read to British Numismatic Society, 23 June 1987. Copies deposited in British, Ashmolean and Fitzwilliam Museums.
Whitton, C.A., 'Die links between Edward IV, Edward V and Richard III', *BNJ* XXIV (1941-4), pp. 175-8.
Winstanley, E.J., 'The angels and groats of Richard III', *BNJ* XXIV (1941-4), pp. 179-89.
Withers, P. and B., *The Halfpennies and Farthings of Edward IV to Henry VII*, Llanfyllin, 2004.

The Tudor Period, 1485 - 1551

Allen, M., 'The classification of Henry VII sovereign pence', *BNJ* 66 (1996), pp. 127-30.
Archibald, M., 'The so-called Perkin Warbeck groat and the dating of the coinage of Henry VII', handout to audience at International Numismatic Congress, London, 1986.
Bispham, J., 'The base silver shillings of Edward VI', *BNJ* 55 (1985), pp. 134-43.
Brooke, G.C., 'The English and Irish coinages of 1542-1544', *NC* 1923, pp. 260-9.
Carlyon-Britton, R., 'The first silver coinage of Edward VI', *NCirc.* 1949, coll. 327-40; continued as 'The English debased silver coinage of Edward VI', *NCirc.* 1950, coll. 663-68, 63-6, 127-32, 187-90, 247-8 and 309-14.
— , 'On some early silver coins of Henry VII', *BNJ* XXIV (1941-4), pp. 28-35.
— , 'The last coinage of Henry VII', *BNJ* XVIII (1925-6), pp. 1-62.
Cavill, P.R., 'The debased coinage of 1492', *BNJ* 77 (2007), pp. 283-5.
Challis, C.E., *The Tudor Coinage*, Manchester, 1978. Important.
— , *Currency and the Economy in Tudor and Early Stuart England,* 1989.
— , 'Currency and economy in mid-Tudor England', *EcHR* 1972, pp. 313-22.
— , 'Mint officials and moneyers of the Tudor period', *BNJ* XLV (1975), pp. 51-76.
— , 'Southwark mint 1545-1551', *BNJ* XXXIII (1964), pp. 135-40.
— , 'Tower II, 1545-1552', *BNJ* XXXVII (1968), pp. 93-7.
— , 'The debasement of the coinage, 1542-1551', *EcHR* 1967, pp. 441-66.
— , 'Thomas Wolsey and the experimental weight reduction of 1522-3', *BNJ* 68 (1998), pp. 150-1.
— , 'The ecclesiastical mints of the early Tudor period: their organisation and possible date of closure', *Northern History*, X (1975), pp. 88-101.
— , 'The conversion of testoons: a restatement', *BNJ* L (1980), pp. 67-80.
Chown, J., 'The Bristol Mint under Henry VIII and Edward VI', *NCirc.* 1975, pp. 273-4.
Cook, B.J., 'Tudor coinage', *BNJ* 73 (2003), pp. 107-15. Review article.
Evans, J., 'Debased coinage bearing the name of Henry VIII', *NC* 1886, pp. 114-60.
Gould, J.D., *The Great Debasement*, Oxford, 1970.
Grierson, P., 'The origins of the English sovereign and the symbolism of the closed crown', *BNJ* XXXIII (1964), pp. 118-34.
— , 'Notes on early Tudor coinage', *BNJ* XLI (1972), pp. 80-94.
Jacob, K.A., 'Testoons in the name of Henry VIII', *NCirc.* 1975, pp. 283-6 and 334-6, and 1983, p. 268.
Kent, J.P.C., 'The ryal of Henry VIII', *BNJ* XXXII (1963), pp. 161-2.
— , 'A new type of George noble of Henry VIII', *Collectanea Historica, Essays in Memory of Stuart Rigold* (Maidstone, 1981), pp. 231-4.
Laker, A.J., *The Portrait Groats of Henry VIII*, 1978.
Lawrence, L.A., 'On the coins of Henry VII', *NC* 1918, pp. 205-261.
Metcalf, D.M., *Coins of Henry VII* (*SCBI* 23, Ashmolean Museum), 1976. Rich collection, expertly catalogued.
Morrieson, H.W., 'The silver coins of Edward VI', *BNJ* XII (1916), pp. 137-80.
Potter, W.J.W., 'Henry VIII – the sequence of marks in the second coinage', *BNJ* XXVIII (1955-7), pp. 560-7.
— , 'The coinage of Edward VI in his own name. Part I: Second period, January 1549 to October 1551', *BNJ* XXXI (1962), pp. 125-37.
Potter, W.J.W. and Winstanley, E.J., 'The coinage of Henry VII', *BNJ* XXX (1960-1), pp. 262-301, XXXI (1962), pp. 109-24 and XXXII (1963), pp. 140-60. Standard work.

Schneider, H., 'A note on Mr. Whitton's paper 'The coinages of Henry VIII and Edward VI in Henry's name' to which are added certain addenda and corrigenda', *BNJ* XXVII (1952-4), pp. 195-203.
Shuttlewood: *Sale Catalogue of the R.A. Shuttlewood Collection of Tudor Silver Coins,* Spink, 15 March 2001. Important.
Stewart, I., 'Problems of the early coinage of Henry VII', *NC* 1974, pp. 125-47.
— , 'Trefoil-marked portcullis groats of Henry VIII', *BNJ* 56 (1986), pp. 189-90.
Stewartby, Lord, 'Henry VII farthing with mintmark', *BNJ* 78 (2008).
Symonds, H., 'The Bristol mint of Henry VIII and Edward VI', *NC* 1911, pp. 331-50.
— , 'Edward VI and Durham House', *NC* 1914, pp. 138-55.
— , 'The documentary evidence for the English royal coinages of Henry VII and Henry VIII', *BNJ* X (1913), pp. 127-71 and XI (1914), p. 167.
— , 'The English coinages of Edward VI', *BNJ* XI (1915), pp. 123-67.
Symons, D., 'An unpublished hoard of the Great Debasement' (Forest of Dean; other hoards also discussed), *BNJ* 60 (1990), pp. 80-6.
Whitton, C.A., 'The coinages of Henry VIII and Edward VI in Henry's name', *BNJ* XXVI (1949-51), pp. 56-89, 171-212 and 290-332. Classic study.
— , 'Some trial pieces of Edward VI, struck in 1547', *NCirc.* 1950, coll. 69-70.
Withers, P. and B., *Small Silver Henry VIII – The Commonwealth*, Llanfyllin, 2004.

IRELAND

Challis, C.E., 'The Tudor coinage for Ireland', *BNJ* XL (1971), pp. 97-119.
Dolley, R.H.M., 'The Irish mints of Edward I in the light of the coin-hoards from Ireland and Great Britain', *Proc. Royal Irish Academy* 66 (C3), 1968, pp. 235-97.
— , *Medieval Anglo-Irish Coins* (1972).
Dolley, M., and Seaby, W.A., *Anglo-Irish Coins: John – Edward III (SCBI* 10, Ulster Museum, Belfast), 1968.
— , 'The anomalous Long-Cross coins in the Anglo-Irish portion of the Brussels hoard', *Mints, Dies and Currency*, ed. R.A.G. Carson, 1971, pp. 291-317.
Dolley, M., and O'Sullivan, W., 'The chronology of the first Anglo-Irish coinage' *North Munster Studies,* Limerick, 1967, pp. 437-78.
Dowle, A., and Finn, P., *The Guide Book to the Coinage of Ireland,* 1969.
Dykes, D.W., 'King John's Irish coinage revisited', paper read to Royal Numismatic Society, 23 March 2004.
— , 'The Irish Coinage of Henry III', *BNJ* XXXII (1963), pp. 99-116.
— , 'The Coinage of Richard Olof' (Edward I, Dublin), *BNJ* XXXIII (1964), pp. 73-9.
Laker, A.J., *The Portrait Groats of Henry VIII,* 1978.
Mayhew, N.J., 'Irregularities in the Irish Mint accounts 1279-1284', *Later Medieval Mints* (edd. N.J. Mayhew and P. Spufford, *BAR Int.* 389, 1988), pp. 87-96.
North, J.J., 'The early Irish pence of Edward I reclassified', *BNJ* 61 (1991), pp. 23-30.
— , 'The Anglo-Irish halfpence, farthings and post-1290 pence of Edward I and III', *BNJ* 67 (1997), pp. 11-19.
Symonds, H., 'The Irish coinages of Henry VIII and Edward VI', *NC* 1915, pp. 192-229.
Withers, P. and B., *Irish Small Silver, John – Edward VI*, Llanfyllin, 2004.

Bibliography

Select List of Hoards

Moor Monkton (1984)	Yorks.	c. 1185	Archibald and Cook no. 5
Wainfleet (1990)	Lincs.	c. 1195	" no. 8
Bainton (1982 and 1998)	Yorks.	c. 1200 (+?)	" no. 10
Sudbourne (1879)	Suffolk	c. 1210	BNJ XXIX (1958-9), pp. 307-11
Eccles (1864)	Lancs.	1230	NC 1993, pp. 137-51
Colchester (1902)	Essex	c. 1237	NC 1903, pp. 111-76
Montpellier (1934)	Provence	c. 1240	BNJ XLVII (1977), pp. 77-91
Leconfield (2000)	Yorks.	c. 1245	NC 2001, p. 354
Gisors (1970)	Normandy	c. 1245	BNJ XL (1971), pp. 22-43
Ribe (1911 and 1958)	Denmark	c. 1245	Nordisk Num. Ark 1971, pp. 38-59
Colchester (1969)	Essex	1256 and 1270s	Archibald and Cook no. 20
Brussels (1908)		c. 1264	BNJ XXIX (1958-9), p. 91
Hornchurch (1938)	Essex	early 1260s	BNJ XXIII (1938-41), pp. 274-9
Palmer's Green (1911)	London	mid-1260s	NC 1912, pp. 70-97
Slype (1913)	Flanders	late 1260s	NC 1914, pp. 256-9
Steppingley (1912)	Beds.	late 1260s	NC 1914, pp. 60-76
Coventry (1958)	Warwicks.	c. 1270	NC 1958, pp. 109-22
Greywell (1988 and 1993)	Hants.	1270s	Archibald and Cook no. 19
Broughton (1964)	Hants.	c. 1290	BNJ XXXV (1966), pp. 120-7
Skegby (1967)	Notts.	c. 1290	BNJ XL (1971), pp. 44-56
Dover (1955)	Kent	c. 1295	BNJ XXVIII (1955-7), pp. 147-68
Mayfield (1968)	Sussex	c. 1307	Mints, Dies and Currency, ed. Carson, pp. 151-9
Middridge (1974)	Durham	c. 1311	BNJ 59 (1989), pp. 84-90
Whittonstall (1958)	Northumb.	c. 1311	Arch. Ael. 41 (1963), pp. 65-83
Boyton (1935)	Wilts.	c. 1321	NC 1936, pp. 115-55
Renfrew (1963)	Renfrewsh.	c. 1321	BNJ XXXV (1966), pp. 128-47
Ednam (1995)	Roxburghsh.	c. 1322	BNJ 66 (1996), pp. 33-59
Bootham (1953)	York	later 1320s	BNJ XXVII (1952-4), pp. 281-93
Knaresborough (1805)	Yorks.	later 1320s	BNJ XXXII (1963), pp. 117-26
Blackhills	Kirkcudbrsh.	1330s	NC 1990, pp. 179-204
Aberdeen (1886, 1983)		1330s	BNJ XLV (1975), pp. 33-50 and 58 (1988), pp. 40-68

Select List of Hoards

Loch Doon (1966)	Kirkcudbrsh.	1330s	BNJ XXXVIII (1969), pp. 31-49
Aberdeen (1984)		c. 1345(+)	BNJ 58 (1988), pp. 40-68
Derby (1927)		c. 1350	NC 1928, pp. 47-60
Stanwix (1986-7)	Cumbld.	c. 1352	SCBI North, pp. 54-78; NC 1998, pp. 301-2
Cambridge (2000)		c. 1355	BNJ 75 (2005), pp. 63-90
Durham (1930)		c. 1360	NC 1931, pp. 201-28
Montrave (1877)	Fife	c. 1363	BNJ XXXI (1962), pp. 80-7
Coventry (1967)	Warwicks.	c. 1365	BNJ XLIII (1973), pp. 60-6
East Raynham (1910)	Norfolk	1370s	NC 1911, pp. 291-330
Aberdour (1978)	Fife	c. 1375	BNJ 58 (1988), pp. 69-83
Balcombe (1897)	Sussex	1380s	NC 1898, pp. 8-72
Bredgar (1940)	Kent	1380s	NC 1947, pp. 160-70
Pinchbeck (1985-7)	Lincs.	1380s	NC 1991, pp. 183-97
Skipton (1949 and 1997)	Yorks.	1400s	NC 1949, pp. 253-7
Highbury (1868)	London	late 1410s	NC 1871, pp. 97-125
Attenborough (1966)	Notts.	c. 1420	BNJ XXXVIII (1969), pp. 50-83
Hampshire (1905)		c. 1435	NC 1908, pp. 311-8
Pulham (1983)	Dorset	late 1430s	Christie sale 28.5.85
Horsted Keynes (1929)	Sussex	c. 1440	NC 1929, pp. 285-95
Reigate (1972 and 1990)	Surrey	c. 1455	BNJ XLVIII (1978), pp. 80-97
Fishpool (1966)	Notts.	c. 1464	NC 1967, pp. 133-46
Wyre Piddle (1967)	Worcs.	c. 1467	NC 1970, pp. 133-62
Ryther (1992)	Yorks.	c. 1487	BNJ 65 (1995), pp. 135-50
Clay Coton (pre 1864)	Northants.	c. 1490	NC 1866, pp. 136-51
Hounslow (1861)	London	late 1490s	*NC* 1861, pp. 140-3
Bury St. Edmunds (1861)	Suffolk	c. 1505	*NC* 1862, pp. 148-51
Hartford (1964)	Hunts.	c. 1510	*NC* 1974, pp. 144-7
Park Street (1886)	Herts.	pre-1526	*NC* 1886, pp. 173-203
Maidstone (1952)	Kent	c. 1535/40	*BNJ* XXVII (1952-4), pp. 58-65
Cranworth (1996)	Norfolk	c. 1545	*NC* 1998, pp. 301-2
Little Wymondley (1973)	Herts.	c. 1547	*BNJ* 60 (1990), pp. 85-6
Forest of Dean (pre-1987)	Glos.	c. 1549	*BNJ* 60 (1990), pp. 80-2
Deal (2000)	Kent	c. 1549	*NC* 2001, p. 357.

INDEX

This index consists largely of personal names. It is inevitably selective. Events are summarized in the Calendar section of each chapter. For coins, see the Synopsis of chapters I – IX on pages ii – vi. Hoards are listed in the Bibliography, pages 547-9.

Act of Supremacy (1534), 452.
Adam of Bentley, London moneyer, 54.
Agard, Thomas, Dublin Under-Treasurer, 478, 512.
Agincourt, battle, 269.
Aimer Fitz Philippi, London moneyer, 27.
Alain FitzAlan, Carlisle moneyer, 27, 40.
Alexander III of Scotland (1249-86), 112.
Alexander of Bruchsal, graver, 344, 398.
Alexander Normanni, master in Ireland, 158.
Alion, Hubert, master, 110, 164.
Allen, M. R., 21, 384, 401.
Ambrose the Clerk, Canterbury moneyer, 94.
Angel (-noble) introduced, 343.
Aquitaine, 116, 204, 224, 283.
Aragon, Queen Katherine of, 339, 452, 458.
Archibald, M., 78, 238, 355, 385.
Arnold, Canterbury mint official, 48.
Arras, Treaty, 293.
Arundel, Thomas, Abp. York, 238.
Augustale, gold coin of Frederick II, 76, 100.

Bainbridge, Christopher, Abp. York, 412.
Balliol, John, king of Scots (1292 – 6), 112.
Bardi, Walter dei, master, 200, 224.
Barons' War, 48.
Base halfpence and farthings, 151.
Beaufort, Margaret, 339.
Beaumont, Louis de, Bp. Durham, 114.
Bek, Antony, Bp. Durham, 4, 114, 130.
Berwick mint, 153, 193.
Bimetallism, 3, 184, 199, 453.
Bispham, J., 481.
Black Death, 185, 199.
Black Prince, 204.
Blount, William, master, 341.
Blunt, C. E., 10, 11, 153, 207, 348.
Boleyn, Queen Anne, 452.
Boniface, Abp. Canterbury, 95.
Booth, Laurence, Bp. Durham, 273, 293, 314, 347, 370. Abp. York, 375.
Booth, William, Abp. York, 273, 314, 373.
Bosworth, battle, 339.

Boulogne, siege, 339.
Bourchier, Thomas. Abp. Canterbury, 273, 346, 371.
Bouvines, battle, 18.
Bowes, John, Under-Treasurer, Durham Place, 478.
Bowes, Martin, Under-Treasurer, 462, 484. 484.
Bowet, Henry, Abp. York, 247, 273, 280, 287.
Brackenbury, Robert, master, 341, 378.
Brand, J. D., 21.
Brétigny, Treaty, 204, 223.
Brisele, Henry de, master, 199, 224.
Bristol mint, chs. II, III, VII, IX.
Brock, Parson, Comptroller, 480.
Brooke, G. C., 10, 224, 276, 349, 461.
Bruce, Robert, king of Scots (1306 – 29), 153.
Burgh, Hubert de, 18.
Burgundian double-patards, 345, 402.
Burgundy, Duke of, 262, 272, 338.
Burns, E., 10, 113.
Bury, Richard de, Bp. Durham. 114, 191.
Bury St. Edmunds Abbey, mint, chs. I, II, III.

Calais mint, chs. V, VI.
Canterbury mint, chs. I, II, III, IV, VII, VIII, IX.
Carlisle mint, chs. I, II.
Carlyon-Britton, R. 401, 481.
Carreghova mine, 35.
Challis, C., 481, 515.
Chamberlain, Thomas, Under-Treasurer, Bristol. 479.
Charles V of France, 224.
Charles VI of France, 245, 269.
Chester Mint, ch. III.
Chichester, John of, master, 199.
Chichester mint, ch. I.
Chown, J., 501.
Churchill, R. and Thomas, R., ch. II passim.
Cleves, Queen Anne of, 453.
Clipping, 2, 65, 72, 112, 345, 402.
Coldwell, Henry, graver, 513.
Corbridge, Thomas, Abp. York, 129.

547

Index

Cork mint, 158.
Cornwall, Richard of., 72, 97.
Coventry mint, ch. VII.
Cranmer, Thomas, Abp. Canterbury, 452.
Crockards, 112, 129, 163.
Cromwell, Thomas, 452, 512.
Crown of the Rose, 453.
Crown of the Double Rose, 453.
Countermarks (portcullis, greyhound), 477.

Dafydd ap Llywelyn, 57.
Dafydd ap Owain, 58.
Dandyprats, 342, 384, 396.
Dated coins, 508.
Daubeny, Giles, master, 341.
David II of Scotland (1329 – 71), 206.
David of Enfield, London moneyer, 85, 93, 98.
Davis, R. 79, 81.
Debasement, 454, ch. IX.
Dolley, R. H. M., 162.
Dublin mint, chs. I, II, III, and 296.
Dudley, William, Bp. Durham, 347, 375.
Durham mint, chs. I – VIII.
Durham Place mint, 476.

Eaglen, R., 52.
Ebrard Bradex, York moneyer, 27, 34.
Ecu (French gold crown), 184, 453.
Edmund, abbot Bury, 92.
Edrich of Worcester, moneyer, 27.
Edward I (1272-1307), chs. II, III.
Edward II (1307-27), ch. III.
Edward III (1327-77), chs. III, IV, V.
Edward IV (1461-83), chs. VI, VII.
Edward V (1483), ch. VII.
Edward VI (1547-53), ch. IX.
Eleanor of Provence, Queen to Henry III, 72.
Elias of Worcester, London moneyer, 53.
Elizabeth of York, 339, 386.
Eudo Chic, Canterbury moneyer (?=Iun), 53.
Evans, Sir John, 21, 186.
Evenet, Giles, engraver Bristol, 479.
Everham, battle, 72.
Exeter mint, chs. I, II, III.

Fabyan, Robert, alderman, 345.
Farthings, of Henry III, 53; reintroduced, III; heavy, 148.

Fenrother, Robert, munster, 341.
Fineness, 8, ch. IX.
FitzRobert, Simon, Bp. Chichester, 17.
Florin, 76.
Fordham, John, Bp. Durham, 202, 237.
Fox brothers, 10, 113, 188.
Fox, Richard, Bp. Durham, 401.
Frederick II, emperor, 63, 72.
French title, 187, 207, 230, 239, 410.
Fulke, London moneyer, 34.

Gale, George, Under-Treasurer York, 466, 478.
Galley halfpence, 206.
Garner, Richard, master, 202, 270.
Gaucher de Chatillon, Porcien, 164.
Gaunt, John of, 204.
Geoffrey FitzWalter, Northampton moneyer, 35.
Geoffrey Joismiri, London moneyer, 27.
George noble, 453.
Gerard FitzLefwine, York moneyer, 27.
Gilbert Bonnington, Canterbury moneyer, 81.
Gittoes, G. P., 21.
Gloucester mint, ch. II.
Goldbeter, Bartholomew, master, 271.
Gold pennies, Henry III, 76, 99.
Gothic design, 186.
Gregory de Rokesley, warden, 110.
Grey, John de, Bp. Norwich, Justiciar in Ireland, 18, 60, 65.
Grey, Walter de, Abp. York, 18.
Grierson, P., 392, 402.
Groat introduced, 109, 115.
Grosso, Venice, 76.
Gros Tournois, 76.
Gui de Dampierre, Namur, 164.

Hadleie, Robert de, Bury moneyer, 115, 121, 125.
Halfgroat introduced, 199.
Halfpenny of Henry III, 53; revived, 109, 111.
Harris, E., 276.
Hastings, Lord, master, 340.
Hatfield, Thomas de, Bp. Durham, 191, 202, 221.
Helm (gold half-leopard), 186.
Henry II (1158-89), ch. I.
Henry III (1216-72), chs. I, II.
Henry IV (1399-1413), chs. V, VI.

Henry V (1413-22), ch. VI.
Henry VI (1422-61 and 1470-1), chs. VI, VII.
Henry VII (1485-1509), ch. VII.
Henry VIII (1509-47), chs. VII, VIII, IX.
Henry Anglicus, London moneyer, 27.
Henry Frowik, London moneyer, 82.
Henry Pineferding, London moneyer, 27.
Hereford mint, ch. II.
Hoards, 545-6.
Howard, Queen Katherine, 453.
Hugh FitzLefwine, York moneyer, 27.
Hundred Years' War, 109, 187.

Ilchester mint, ch. II.
Ilger the Goldsmith, London moneyer, 53.
Imitations, 60, 97, 107, 158, 181, 296, 512.
Immobilization of design, 21.
Indentures, 8.
Ingots, 76, 96.
Insula, Richard de, abbot Bury, 19.
Ioan Chic, Canterbury moneyer, 54, 81.
Ioan FitzRobert, Canterbury moneyer, 54.
Ipswich mint, ch. I.
Ireland, 60, 97, 107, 158, 181, 296, 512.
Irish title, 453.
Isabella, Queen to Edward II, 108, 114.

Jacob, K., 481.
John (1199-1216), ch. I.
John de Burnedisse, Bury moneyer, 94.
John Digge, Canterbury moneyer, 95.
John Hardel, London moneyer, 90.
John Lewys, master, 10, 270, 277, 284.
John Terri, Canterbury moneyer, 85, 88.
Jones, F. Elmore, 21, 55, 188.

Kellawe, Richard, Bp. Durham, 114.
Kemp, John, Abp. York, 273, 292, 302.
Key of St. Peter, York, 373, 414.
Kilwardby, Robert, Abp. Canterbury, 95.
King's Lynn mint, ch. I.
Kingston-upon-Hull mint, ch. III.
Kirkham, Walter, Bp. Durham, 90.
Kirkyn, Giorgio, master, 184.
Knight, Thomas, Under-Treasurer, Tower II, 484.

Laker, A. J., 496.
Langley, Thomas, Bp. Durham, 273, 287, 302.

Langton, Stephen, Abp. Canterbury, 18.
Lawrence, L. A., 10, 21, 78.
Ledulf the Teuton, London moneyer, 54.
Lee, Edward, Abp. York, 347, 463.
Leopard (English gold florin), 184.
Levens, Antony, engraver, 498.
Lewes, battle, 72.
Lichfield mint, ch. I.
Limerick mint, ch. I.
Lincoln mint, chs. I, II, III.
Llywelyn ap Iorwerth, 57.
Local dies, 5, 130, 221, 238, 273, 287, 375.
London (Tower) mint, passim.
Long Cross moneyers, 82, 85-7, 91.
Longstaffe, W. H. D., 21.
Lords Appellant, 204.
Louis IX of France (1226-70), 76.
Louis, Prince of France, 18.

Magna Carta, 18.
Malapilys, Bardet de, master, 201.
Manfeld, Robert, master, 271.
Margaret of Anjou, Queen to Henry VI, 269, 338.
Marsh, Richard, Bp. Durham, 19.
Marshall, William, Earl of Pembroke, 18.
Mass, J. P., 21 and ch. I passim.
Maximilian, king of Romans, 345.
Meinir the Rich, Canterbury moneyer, 29.
Melton, William, Abp. York, 143.
Metcalf, D. M., 382.
Molakyn, Nanfre, master, 201.
Montfort, Simon de, 72.
More, Sir Thomas, 452.
Morton, John, Abp. Canterbury, 346.

Neville, Alexander, Abp. York, 238.
Neville, George, Abp. York, 314, 373.
Neville, Richard, Earl of Warwick, 338.
Neville, Robert, Bp. Durham, 273.
Newcastle mint, chs. II, III.
Nicholas de Hadlo, Canterbury moneyer, 90.
Nicholas of St. Albans, London and Canterbury moneyer, 20, 54, 73, 90.
Nicholyn, Lotto, master, 184.
Noble (gold half-mark), 6.
Nonant, Hugh de, Bp. Coventry, 16.
North, J. J., 21, 49, 99, 113.
Northampton mint, chs. I, II.

Northwold, Hugh, abbot of Bury, 19. 41.
Norwich mint, chs. I, II, VII.

Omoryghe, William, graver, Durham, 375.
Orlandino di Podio, Warden, 110.
Osber, Wilton and Winchester moneyer, 28.
Osmund Polre, Canterbury moneyer, 53.
Otto IV, Emperor, 18, 63.
Oxford, Council of, (1180), 14, 65; (1247) 72.
Oxford mint, chs. I, II.

Papal interdict, 18.
Parr, Queen Katherine, 453.
Peasants' Revolt, 201.
Pekham, Sir Edmund, High Treasurer, 477, 506.
Percival de Porche, master, 184.
Perkin Warbeck, supposed coins of, 398.
Peter Melekin, London moneyer, 27.
Philip IV of France (1285-1314), 6, 76, 108.
Philip Aimery of Tours, London moneyer, 14, 27.
Philip de Cambio, London moneyer, 94, 96.
Philip of Poitou, Bp. Durham, 18, 35.
Pirry, Martin, Under-Treasurer, Dublin, 480, 512.
Plantagenet, Geoffrey, Abp. York, 18.
Points secrets, 482.
Pole, Michael de la, Chancellor, 206.
Pollards, 112, 129, 163.
Portcullis, Tudor badge, 344, 389.
Portraiture, 340, 401, 480.
Potter, William, master, 199, 211.
Potter, W. J. W., 186, 234, 276, 382, 481.
Prikehurt, Alexander and John, Ipswich mint farmers (and ? moneyers), 41.
Privy sign (or mark), 10, 207.
Puiset, Hugh du, Bp. Durham, 18, 35.
Purvey, F. 234.
Purveyors, Statute of, 199, 270.
Pygott, Thomas, master, York., 413.
Pyx trial, 8, 165, 207, 412, 463.

Radulf le Frowik, London moneyer, 53.
Randulf le Blund, Bury moneyer, 89, 93.
Reading, abbot's mint, 118, 152.
Recoinage, renovation, 2, 14, 17, 73, 109.
Reed, Bartholomew, master, 341, 378.
Reed, William, master, 341.

Reginald of Canterbury, London moneyer, 75.
Reginald FitzHenry, Bury moneyer, 93.
Restoration of Henry VI, 270, 338, 361.
Rhuddlan mint, 57.
Richard I (1189-99), ch. I.
Richard II (1377-99), ch. V.
Richard III (1483-5), ch. VII.
Richard Abel, engraver, 56.
Richard Bonaventure, London moneyer, 85, 98.
Richard Fusor, Winchester mint farmer, 32.
Richard of Ilchester, Bp. Winchester, 14.
Richard of Lothbury, Bury moneyer, 125.
Richard de Neketon, London moneyer, 54.
Richard Olof, master, Dublin, 97.
Richard le Specer, Canterbury moneyer, 94.
Richard, Duke of York, 270.
Robert III of Scotland (1390-1406), 206, 274.
Robert of Bedford, moneyer(?), 61.
Robert of Holy Island, Bp. Durham, 114.
Robert de Portico, master, 200.
Robert Vi, Canterbury moneyer, 55.
Rochester mint, ch. I.
Roger le Assaur, Canterbury moneyer, 95.
Roger of Haverhull, master, Dublin, 97.
Roger of Rochester, Canterbury moneyer, 52.
Roman letters, 1, 454.
Rotherham, Thomas, Abp. York, 374, 382.
Ruthall, Thomas, Bp. Durham, 347, 414.
Ryal (or rose-noble), 343.

Salut (French equivalent of half-noble), 274.
Samson, abbot of Bury, 17, 19.
Sandwich exchange, 18.
Savage, Thomas, Abp. York, 347, 412.
Scrots, Guillim, painter, 512.
Scrope, Richard le, Abp. York, 247.
Seignorage, 9.
Seymour, Queen Jane, 453.
Seymour, Edward, Duke of Somerset, 475.
Sharington, William, Under-Treasurer, Bristol, 478.
Shaw, John, master, 341.
Shilling introduced, 344, 401.
Shirwood, John, Bp. Durham, 382.
Shrewsbury mint, chs. I, II.
Short Cross moneyers, 25-7, 30-1, 42-3, 45, 50-1, 56.
Simon, abbot of Bury, 93.
Simon Chic, Canterbury moneyer, 54.

Skirlaw, Walter, Bp. Durham, 237.
Sluys, battle, 108, 187.
Snoweshill, Richard, York warden, 143.
Southwark mint, ch. IX.
Sovereign authorized (1489), 344.
Sovereign type groat, 389.
Sovereign type pence, 391.
Stephen of Fulburn, Ireland Treasurer, 97, 158.
Sterling, 1.
Stichill, Robert, Bp. Durham, 94, 97.
Strayll, George, Durham master, 391.
Sunburst, exceptional mintmark, 457.
Symonds, H., 481, 485.

Tailor, William, Canterbury moneyer, 54.
Terricus le Chaungeor, London moneyer, 53.
Teston (shilling) introduced, 475.
Thomas of Weseham, London moneyer, 93.
Thoresby, John, Abp. York, 202, 221.
Throckmorton, Nicholas, Under-Treasurer (Tower II), 484, 515.
Toht, William, Chichester mint farmer, 41.
Tomas, son of Alan, Carlisle moneyer, 40.
Tomas de Valentina, Canterbury moneyer, 48, 54.
Tournai mint, 339, 409.
Towton, battle, 270.
Troyes, treaty, 269.
Tudor, Margaret, 339.
Tunstall, Cuthbert, Bp. Durham, 463.
Tunstall, Richard, master, 271, 341.
Turkil de Bredegate, York moneyer, 27.
Turnemire, William and Peter, masters, 110, 115, 119, 122.
Tyllsworth, William, Canterbury Under-Treasurer, 464, 478.

Vaughan, Stephen, Under-Treasurer, 477, 484.

Wallingford mint, ch. II.
Walter of Brussels, London moneyer, 90.
Walter, crusader, Canterbury moneyer, 53.
Walter, Hubert, Justiciar, 15.
Walter the Linendraper (Oxford), 27.
Walters, F., 247.
Wardens, 109.
Warham, William, Abp. Canterbury, 347, 412.
Waterford mint, chs. I, III.
Webb Ware, T., 11, 234, 350, 376.
Whitton, C. A., 10, 11, 290, 348, 463, 481.
Wildeman, John, master, 201.
William the Lion of Scotland (1165-1214), 20.
William Cokyn, Canterbury moneyer, 85.
William FitzSirici, York moneyer, 27.
William of Gloucester, goldsmith, 74, 90.
William Wace, Bp. Waterford, 61.
William, Winchester moneyer and farmer, 32.
Wilton mint, chs. I, II.
Winchester mint, chs. I, II.
Winstanley, E. J., 376, 382.
Wolsey, Thomas, Abp. York, 339, 412, 452; Bp. Durham, 415.
Woodhead, P., 278, 292.
Worcester mint, ch. I.
Wriothesley, Thomas, Secretary of State, 481.
Wychyngham, Hugh de, master, 200, 211.

York mint, all chapters.
York, Sir John, Under-Treasurer, Tower, Southwark, 478.

Zouche, William, Abp. York, 191.

KEY TO PLATES

I: 1180 – 1247

Short Cross type in name of Henry II (1154-89), but also struck under Richard I (1189-99), John (1199-1216) and Henry III (1216-72). All *silver pennies* except for 43 and 44.

Plate 1

1	Class	Ia, early (Ia1, Northampton, Raul)
2	"	" , middle (Ia4/3, London, Iefrei)
3	"	" , late (Ia5, London, Fil Aimer)
4	"	Ib1 (London, Henri)
5	"	Ib2 (Winchester, Adam)
6	"	Ic (London, Raul)
7	Class	IIi (Lincoln, Lefwine)
8	"	IIii (Worcester, Osbern)
9	Class	IIIa (Winchester, Willelm)
10	"	IIIb (London, Ricard)
11	Class	IVa (London, Stivene; colons on rev., Brand IVa*)
12	"	IVb (London, Fulke)
13	"	IVc (York, Nicole)
14	Class	Va1 (London, Henri)
15	"	Va2 (Canterbury, Coldwine)
16	"	Vb1 (London, Fulke)
17	"	Vb2 (Norwich, Gifrei)
18	"	Vb3 (Chichester, Pieres)
19	"	Vc (London, Adam)
20	Class	VIa1 (London, Walter)
21	"	VIa2 (London, Rauf)
22	"	VIb1 (London, Ilger)
23	"	VIb2 (London, Abel)
24	Class	VIc1 (London, Ilger)

Plate 2

25	"	VIx (Canterbury, Roger)
26	"	VIc2 (London, Abel)
27	"	VIc3 (Canterbury, Henri)
28	"	VId (London, Abel)
29	Class	VIIa1 (Durham, Pieres)
30	"	VIIa2 (Canterbury, Ioan)
31	"	VIIa3 early (London, Ilger; North VIIaC)
32	"	VIIa3 late (Canterbury, Salemun; North VIIaD)
33	"	VIIb1 (Canterbury, Iun)
34	"	VIIb2 (Canterbury, Simun)
35	"	VIIb3 (London, Ledulf)
36	"	VIIb4 (Canterbury, Ioan F R)
37	"	VIIc1 (London, Nichole)

38	"	VIIc2 (Canterbury, Nichole)
39	"	VIIc3 (Canterbury, Nichole)
40	Class	VIIIa (London, Nichole)
41	"	VIIIb (London, Nichole)
42	"	VIIIc (London, Nichole)
43	Halfpenny, class VIIa (London, Raulf)	
44	Farthing, " (London, Terri)	
45	Rhuddlan, Halli (i)	
46	" , Tomas (ii)	
47	" , Simond (iii)	
48	" , Henricus (v)	
49	Ireland, King John (Dublin, Wilelm P)	

II: 1247 – 1278

Long Cross type in name of Henry III (1216-72), but continued under Edward I (1272-1307) until 1278. *Silver pennies* except for 50.

Plate 3

50	Gold penny (20d.) of Henry III (London, Willem)	
51	Silver, class Ia (London)	
52	Class Ib (London)	
53	Class Ib/II (Canterbury, Willem)	
54	Class IIa (London, Nicole)	
55	"	IIb1 (Canterbury, Nicole)
56	"	IIb2 (Exeter, Philip)
57	Class IIIa1 (Northampton, Tomas)	
58	"	IIIa2 (Oxford, Henri)
59	"	IIIab1 (Carlisle, Willem)
60	"	IIIab2 (Gloucester, Ricard)
61	"	IIIb (Shrewsbury, Loren)
62	"	IIIbc (Bristol, Roger)
63	"	IIIc1 (Lincoln, Willem)
64	"	IIIc2 (Canterbury, Willem)
65	"	IIId (London, Henri)
66	Class IV (London, Davi; IVa)	
67	Class Va early (with X2, Va2; London, Davi)	
68	" Va later (with X4, Va3; Durham, Ricard)	
69	" Vb (London, Ricard; Vb2)	
70	" Vc1 (Canterbury, Willem)	
71	" Vc2 (Bury, Randulf)	
72	" Vc3 (Canterbury, Walter)	

Plate 4

73	Class Vd (Canterbury, Willeme; Vd2)	
74	" Ve (London, David)	
75	" Vf (London, Ricard)	
76	" Vg (Canterbury, Ambroci)	

77	"	Vh (Canterbury, Ricard)
78	"	Vi (Bury, Ions)
79	"	VI (Bury, Ion)
80	"	VII (London, Phelip)
81	Ireland, class V (Dublin, Ricard)	
82	" , class VII (Dublin, Ricard)	

III: 1279 – 1343

All in name of Edward I (1272-1307), Edward II (1307-27) or Edward III (1327-77).

Plate 4

83	Edward I groat (var. a)
84	" , experimental type penny
	Pennies, regular type
85	Group Ia (London)
86	" Ib (London)
87	" Ic (London)
88	" Id (London)
89	" Id (with annulet on breast)
90	Group IIa (Canterbury)
91	" IIb (Bristol)
92	Group IIIa (London)
93	" IIIb (London)
94	" IIIc (Canterbury)
95	" IIId (London)
96	" IIIe (York)

Plate 5

97	Group IIIf (London)
98	" IIIg (Chester)
99	" III (Bury, local dies, Robert de Hadeleie)
100	Group IVa (early; London)
101	" IVa (late; Canterbury)
102	" IVb (Durham)
103	" IVc (Canterbury)
104	" IVd (London)
105	" IVe (London)
106	Group Va (London)
107	" Vb (Bury)
108	Group VIa (London)
109	" VIb (London)
110	Group VIIa (Canterbury)
111	" VIIb (London)
112	Group VIIIa (Bury)
113	" VIIIb (London)
114	" VIIIc (London)
115	Group IXa (Durham)

116   "   IXb (Kingston)
117   "   IXc (Bury)
118   Group X, Primary phase, type P1 (Canterbury)
119   "   ,   "   ,   " P2 (London; rev. of IXb)
120   "   ,   "   ,   " P3 (Durham, P3a)

Plate 6
121   Group X, Primary phase, type P4 (London)
122   "   ,   "   ,   " P5 (Canterbury)
123   "   ,   "   ,   " P6 (Canterbury)
124   Group X, Secondary phase, type S1 (Canterbury)
125   "   ,   "   ,   " S2 (London)
126   "   ,   "   ,   " S3a (London)
127   "   ,   "   ,   " S3b (London)
128   "   ,   "   ,   " S4 (Bury)
129   "   ,   "   ,   " S5 (Bury)
130   "   ,   "   ,   " S6 (Canterbury; rev. of XI)
131   Group XIa (Bury, XIa2)
132   "   XIb (Durham, XIb2)
133   "   XIc (Canterbury)
134   "   XId (Canterbury; rev. of XIc)
135   Group XII (London)
136   Group XIII (Canterbury)
137   Group XIV (Canterbury)
138   Group XVa (Bury)
139   "   XVb (London)
140   "   XVc (Durham)
141   Group XVd1 (London)
142   "   XVd2 (York)
143   "   XVd3 (Durham)
144   "   XVd3 (Reading, with scallop shell)

Plate 7
      Halfpence 1280-1335
145   Group IIIce (London)
146   "   IIIe (Newcastle)
147   "   IIIg (Bristol)
148   Group IVc (London; rev. of IIIg)
149   "   IVe (London)
150   Group VI   (London)
151   Group VII (London)
152   Group VIII (London)
153   Group XP (London; crown 2)
154   "   Xh (London)
      Farthings 1279-1335
155   Type A1 (London)
156   "   A2 (London)

157	"	A3 (London)
158	"	A4 (London)
159	Type	B1 (Newcastle)
160	"	B2 (London)
161	"	B3 (London)
162	"	B4 (London)
163	Type	C1 (London)
164	"	C2 (London)
165	"	C3 (London)
166	Type	D (Xq1, London)
167	"	D (Xq2, London)
168	"	D (Xq3, London)

Base issues of 1335-43

169	Halfpenny, group XVe1 (London)
170	", " XVe2 (Reading)
171	Farthing, group XVe1 (London)
172	", " XVe2 (London)

Mint of Berwick-upon-Tweed

173	Halfpenny, Edward I, class I
174	", ", " II
175	", ", " III (IIIa)
176	", ", " IV
177	", Edward II, class V
178	", Edward III, class VIII (Blunt VIIIb)

Plate 8

Berwick Mint (contd.)

179	Penny, Edward I, class I
180	", ", " IIa
181	", ", " IIb
182	", ", " IIc
183	", ", " III
184	", ", " IV
185	", Edward II, class V
186	", ", " VI (rev. retrograde)
187	", ", " VII
188	Farthing, Edward I, class I
189	", ", " III (IIIb)
190	", Edward II, class V
191	", uncertain class (II or VII)
192	", Edward III, class VIII (Blunt VIIIb)

Ireland

193	Penny, class IA (Dublin)
194	", " IB (Dublin)
195	", " IC (Dublin)
196	", " ID (Waterford)
197	", class II (Dublin)

198 " , class III (Cork)
199 " , class IV (Dublin)
200 Halfpenny, class   IB (Waterford)
201 " , " IC (Dublin)
202 " , class II (Dublin)
203 " , class III (Dublin)
204 Halfpenny, class IV (Dublin)
205 " , group XVe (Dublin)
206 Farthing, class I (Waterford)
207 " , " IV (Dublin)
208 " , group XVe (Dublin)

IV: 1344 – 1351

All in name of Edward III (1327-77).

Plate 9

Gold (London only)
209 First issue (1344), double-leopard (6s.)
210 " " " , leopard (3s.)
211 " " " , helm (1s. 6d.)
212 Second issue (1344-6), noble (6s. 8d.)
213 " " " , half-noble (3s. 4d.)
214 " " " , quarter-noble (1s. 8d.)
215 Third issue (1346-51), noble (Potter Ib)
216 " " " , half-noble (Ib)
217 " " " , quarter-noble

Plate 10

Silver
218 Penny, group   XVIa1 (London; type C)
219 " , " XVIa2 (London; type E)
220 " , " XVIb1 (London)
221 " , " XVIb2 (Canterbury)
222 " , " XVIb3 (London; rev. b)
223 " , " XVIb4 (York)
224 " , " XVIb5 (Durham; D3/d3)
225 " , " XVIc (Durham; D4/d5)
226 " , " XVIc (Reading)
227 Halfpenny, group XVIb1 (London)
228 " , " XVIb2 (London)
229 " , " XVIc1 (London)
230 " , " XVIc2 (London)
231 Farthing, group XVIb (London)
232 " , " XVIc (Reading)
233 Berwick penny, class IX (Blunt VIIIa)
234 " halfpenny, class IX (Blunt VIIIa)

V: 1351 – 1411

In names of Edward III (1327-77), Richard II (1377-99) and Henry IV (1399-1413). All of London mint unless otherwise stated.

Plate 10
Gold – Nobles
235 Edward III, Pre-Treaty (group B/A)
236   "   , Treaty A (A2)
237   "   , Treaty B (Calais; B1)

Plate 11
238 Edward III, Post-Treaty (class 1)
239 Richard II, type I (Ia)
240   "   ,   " II (IIb)
241   "   ,   " III (IIIa)
242   "   ,   " IV (IVb)
243 Henry IV, heavy coinage (Calais; type 1)
Half-nobles
244 Edward III, Pre-Treaty (C/E)
245   "   , Treaty A (A1)
246   "   , Treaty B (B2)
247   "   , Post-Treaty (Calais)

Plate 12
248 Richard II, First Period (Calais; Ib)
249   "   , Second Period (IIIb)
250 Henry IV, heavy coinage (type 1)
Quarter-nobles
251 Edward III, Pre-Treaty (Gf)
252   "   , Treaty A (A2)
253   "   ,   " B (Calais ?; B1)
254 Richard II, First Period (Ib)
255   «   , Second Period (IVa)
256 Henry IV, heavy coinage (type 1b)
Silver – Groats
257 Edward III, Pre-Treaty, group B
258   "   ,   "   ,   " C
259   "   ,   "   ,   " D (York)
260   "   ,   "   ,   " E
261   "   ,   "   ,   " F

Plate 13
262 Edward III, Pre-Treaty, group G (Gb)
263 Edward III, Treaty A
264   "   , Treaty B1 (B1c; bust 1)
265   "   ,   " B2 (B2g; bust 2; Calais)

559

266	", ,	" B2 (bust 3)
267	", ,	Post-Treaty, type 1 (1a)
268	", ,	" , " 2 (2a)
269	", ,	" , " 3
270	Richard II,	type I
271	", ,	" II
272	", ,	" III
273	", ,	" IV

Plate 14
Halfgroats
274	Edward III,	Pre-Treaty (group C)
275	", ,	Treaty A
276	", ,	Treaty B (B1)
277	", ,	Post-Treaty (type 1)
278	Richard II,	First Period (II)
279	", ,	Second Period (IV)
280	Edward III/Richard II mule	
281	Henry IV, heavy coinage	

Halfpence
282	Edward III,	Pre-Treaty (E)
283	", ,	Treaty A
284	", ,	Treaty B (B2)
285	Richard II,	First Period (I)
286	", ,	Second Period (III)
287	Henry IV, heavy coinage, type 1	
288	", ,	" , type 2

Farthings
289	Edward III,	Pre-Treaty (G/E)
290	", ,	Treaty B
291	", ,	Post-Treaty
292	Richard II,	First Period
293	", ,	Second Period
294	Henry IV, heavy coinage	

Pennies
295	Edward III,	Pre-Treaty (Gc/Gg)
296	", ,	" (Durham, Gj)
297	", ,	Treaty A

Plate 15
298	Edward III,	Treaty B (B2)
299	", ,	Post-Treaty (2a)
300	", ,	" (Durham, Bp. Hatfield)
301	Richard II,	First Period, London
302	", ,	York, local dies
303	", ,	type III (York)
304	", ,	type IV (London)

305   Henry IV, heavy coinage, York
306   "   ,   "   London

VI: 1412 – 1464

In names of Henry IV (1399-1413), Henry V (1413-22), Henry VI (1422-61) and Edward IV (1461-83). All of London mint unless otherwise stated.

Plate 15
    Gold – Nobles
307   Henry IV, light coinage, Primary series (class Pb)
308   "   ,   "   , Secondary series (class B)
309   Henry V, with cinquefoil (class C)
310   "   , without symbols (class G)

Plate 16
311   Henry VI,   Annulet series (group I; Calais)
312   "   ,   Mascled phase (group III)
313   "   ,   Trefoiled phase (group VI)
314   "   ,   Pelleted phase (group X)
315   Edward IV, heavy coinage, type I
316   "   ,   "   , Rose group (type II)
    Half-nobles
317   Henry IV, light coinage (class P)
318   Henry V, with cinquefoil (class C)
319   "   , Annulet series (class H)
320   Henry VI,   "   (group I; York)

Plate 17
321   Henry VI, Mascled phase (group II)
322   "   , Trefoiled phase (group V)
    Quarter-nobles
323   Henry IV, light coinage, Primary (class P)
324   "   ,   "   , Secondary (class A)
325   Henry V, with cinquefoil (class F)
326   "   , without symbols by shield (class G)
327   Henry VI, Annulet series (group I)
328   "   , Mascled phase (group IV)
329   "   , Trefoiled phase (group V)
330   Edward IV, heavy coinage (type II/I)
    Silver – Groats
331   Henry IV, light coinage, altered Richard dies (PI)
332   "   , Primary series, new dies (PIII)
333   "   , Secondary series, class A
334   "   ,   "   ,   "   B1

561

Plate 18
335 Henry IV, Secondary series, class B2a
336 Henry V, class B2a*
337 " , " B2b
338 " , " Ca
339 " , " Cb
340 " , " F
341 " , " G
342 " , Annulet series, class H
343 Henry VI, " (Ib)
344 " , " (Ib; York)
345 " , Annulet-trefoil (Id; Calais)

Plate 19
346 Henry VI, Mascled phase, group II (Calais)
347 " , " , " III (Calais)
348 " , " , " IV (Calais)
349 " , Trefoiled phase, group V
350 " , " , " VI
351 " , " , " VII
352 " , Pelleted phase, group VIII
353 " , " , group IX (unmarked)
354 " , " , " X
355 " , " , " XI

Plate 20
356 Edward IV, heavy coinage, type I
357 " , Rose group, type II
358 " , " , " III
359 " , " , " IV

Halfgroats

360 Henry IV, light coinage, Primary series (class P)
361 " , Secondary series, class A
362 " , " , class B
363 Henry V, class Ca
364 " , " Cb
365 " , " F
366 " , " G
367 Henry VI, Annulet series (Ic, Calais)
368 " , Mascled phase (IIIc, Calais)
369 " , Trefoiled phase (V)
370 " , Pelleted phase (VIII)
371 " , " , group IX (unmarked)
372 Edward IV, heavy coinage, type I
373 " , Rose group (III)

562

Plate 21

   Pennies from royal mints
374 Henry IV, light coinage, Primary (class P)
375   " , Secondary (class A)
376 Henry V, class B*
377 " , type 1
378 " ,   " 2
379 " ,   " 3
380 Henry VI, Annulet series (Ic)
381 " , " (Dublin)
382 " , Mascled phase (II; Calais)
383 " , Trefoiled phase (V; Calais)
384 " , Pelleted phase (X)
385 Edward IV, heavy coinage, type I
386 "   , Rose group (IV)
  Pennies of Durham
387 Henry IV, light coinage, Bp. Langley
388 Henry V, type 1, "
389 " , " 3, "
390 Henry VI, group II, Bp. Langley
391 " , " III, "
392 " , " V, Bp. Neville
393 " , " VIII, "
394 " , " X, Bp. Booth
395 Henry VI/Edward IV mule (obv. type VIII)
396 Edward IV, heavy coinage, Bp. Booth

Plate 22

   Pennies of York
397 Henry IV, light coinage, Abp. Bowet
398 Henry V, type 1 (C), "
399 " , " 2 (F), "
400 " , " 3 (F), "
401 Henry VI, group I,   "
402 " , group II, Abp. Kemp
403 " , group IIIB, "
404 " , group VIII, Abp. Booth
405 Edward IV, type III,   "
   Halfpence
406 Henry IV, light coinage, class P
407 " , " , " B
408 Henry V, class C
409 " , later (F)
410 Henry VI, Annulet series (I: Calais)
411 " , Mascled phase (IV)
412 " , Trefoiled phase (VI)
413 " , Pelleted phase (X)
414 Edward IV, type I

563

415   "   , Rose group (type II)
          Farthings
416   Henry IV, light coinage
417   Henry V
418   Henry VI, Annulet series (I)
419   "   , Mascled phase (II; Calais)
420   Henry VI , Trefoiled phase (V)
421   "   , Pelleted phase (VIII)
422   Edward IV, type I
423   "   , Rose group (type II)

VII: 1464 – 1526

In names of Edward IV (1461-70 and 1471-83), Henry VI (1470-1), Edward V (1483), Richard III (1483-5), Henry VII (1485-1509) and Henry VIII (1509-47). All of London mint unless otherwise stated.

Plate 23
     Gold
424   Edward IV, first reign, ryal (rev. mm. rose)
425   "   ,   "   , half-ryal (York: rev. mm. sun)
426   "   ,   "   , quarter-ryal (mm. crown)
427   "   ,   "   , angel (rev. mm. rose)
428   Henry VII, sovereign, type A (mm. cinquefoil)
429   "   , ryal (rev. mm. long cross fitchy)
430   "   , sovereign, type B (rev. mm. long cross fitchy)

Plate 24
431   Henry VII, sovereign, type C (mm. dragon)
432   "   ,   "   , type D (mm. lis/dragon)
433   "   ,   "   , type E (mm. lis/cross-crosslet)
434   Henry VIII, first coinage, ryal (mm. portcullis)
435   "   ,   "   , sovereign (mm. portcullis)

Plate 25
     Angels
436   Henry VI, restored (mm. Restoration cross)
437   Edward IV, second reign (XVIIIb; mm. cross and pellet)
438   Richard III (IIb/III; mm. BH2/SR2)
439   Henry VII, old style (II; mm. cinquefoil)
440   "   , new style with mannered lettering (IIIB; mm. scallop)
441   "   , late (V; mm. cross-crosslet and pheon)
442   Henry VIII, first coinage (mm. H and castle)
          Angelets
443   Henry VI restored (rev. mm. cross patty)
444   Edward IV, second reign (XIV; mm. annulet)
445   Richard III (II; mm. boar's head)

446   Henry VII, old style (I; mm. SR3/lis-on-SR)
447   "   , new style with mannered lettering (IIIC/B; mm. pansy)
448   "   , late (IV/V; mm. rose/cross-crosslet)
449   Henry VIII, first coinage (mm. portcullis)

Plate 26
        Silver – Shilling
450   Henry VII, shilling (Ia; mm. small lis)
        Groats
451   Edward IV, first reign, type Va (heavy coinage dies, Vai)
452   "   , type Vb (dies heavy/light, Vbi/ii)
453   "   , type Vc (mm. rose)
454   "   , " Vd (mm. rose)
455   "   , " VI (Coventry; mm. sun)
456   "   , " VII (Bristol; mm. crown)
457   "   , " VIII (VIIIb; mm. crown/sun)
458   "   , " IX (Xa/IX; rev. mm. rose)
459   "   , " X (Xb; mm. long cross fitchy/sun)
460   "   , " XI (XIa; York; mm. lis)
461   Henry VI restored (Bristol; mm. Restoration cross/trefoil)
462   Edward IV, second reign, type XII (mm. short cross fitchy)
463   "   , Annulet series, type XIII (mm. large annulet/trefoil)

Plate 27
464   Edward IV, second reign, Annulet series, type XIV (mm. small annulet)
465   "   , Annulet series, type XV (XVb; mm. pellet-in-annulet)
466   "   , Second cross series, type XVI (XVIb/a; mm. cross and 4 pellets/
                                                              plain cross)
467   "   ,   "   , type XVII (mm. first pierced cross)
468   "   ,   "   , type XVIII (XVIIIa; mm. cross with pellet)
469   "   , Second cross series, type XX (mm. pierced cross with central pellet)
470   "   ,   "   , type XIX (mm. second pierced cross)
471   "   , Cinquefoil type, XXI
472   Edward IV-V, type XXII, mm. halved sun-and-rose
473   Richard III, in name of Edward, type XXII (BH), mm. boar's head over SR
474   "   , type I, mm. sun-and-rose (SR1)
475   "   , " II, mm. boar's head (BH2)
476   "   , " III, mm. sun-and-rose (SR2)
477   Henry VII, group I (IAii; mm. halved lis-and-rose)

Plate 28
478   Henry VII, group II (IIB; mm. cinquefoil)
479   "   , " II, portcullis type
480   "   , " II, sovereign type
481   "   , " IIIA (mm. cinquefoil, lettering B)
482   "   , " IIIB (mm. escallop; lettering D; IIIBi)
483   "   , " IIIC (mm. leopard's head; lettering E; IIICii)

565

484   "   , "   IIIC late (mm. greyhound's head, GH1; lettering E; IIICva)
485   "   , "   IVA (mm. GH2/rose; lettering F; IVAi/IIIC)
486   "   , "   IVB (mm. cross-crosslet; lettering G; IVBii)
487   "   , profile type, VA (mm. lis; var. 2b)
488   "   ,   "   , VB (mm. cross-crosslet)
489 Henry VIII, first coinage (mm. castle)
490   "   , Tournai (mm. crowned t)

Plate 29
    Halfgroats
491 Edward IV, first reign, recoinage type (Vd; mm. rose)
492   "   ,   "   , later (VIII; York; mm. lis)
493   "   ,   "   , Canterbury (group B; mm. pall)
494 Henry VI restored (mm. Restoration cross)
495 Edward IV, second reign, Annulet series, type XIV (mm. annulet)
496   "   , Cross series, type XVIa (mm. cross over pellet-in-annulet)
497   "   , Cross series, later, type XVIIIb (mm. cross and pellet)
498   "   , Cinquefoil type, XXI
499   "   , second reign, Canterbury (group Hb; mm. rose)
500 Richard III (III; mm. SR2)
501 Henry VII, open crown (IA; mm. lis-on-rose)
502   "   , arched crown, II (Canterbury)
503   "   ,   "   , IIIA (mm. escallop)
504   "   ,   "   , IIIB (York, mm. lis)
505   "   ,   "   , IIIC (London, mm. lis))
506   "   ,   "   , IIID (Canterbury, mm. tun)

Plate 30
507 Henry VII, arched crown, IV (York; IVb)
508   "   , profile, VA
509   "   ,   "   , VB
510   "   ,   "   , Canterbury (Va, mm. martlet)
511   "   ,   "   , York (Vd, mm. rose/martlet)
512 Henry VIII, first coinage (mm. portcullis)
513   "   ,   "   Canterbury (Ib; *Posui;* mm. martlet)
514   "   ,   "   York (IIb; *Eboraci;* mm. star)
    Halfpence
515 Edward IV, first reign, London (VII; mm. crown)
516 Henry VI restored (mm. cross)
517 Edward IV, second reign, London (mm. pierced cross; XVII)
518   "   ,   "   , Canterbury (type 7; mm. rose)
519   "   ,   "   , Durham (Bp. Booth?)
520 Edward IV-V, type XXII (mm. sun-and-rose)
521 Richard III (III; mm. sun-and-rose)
522 Henry VII, open crown (IB)
523   "   , double-arched crown (IIb)
524   "   , single-arched crown (III)

525   "   , group IV (York; key below bust for Abp. Savage)
526   "   ,   "   V (London; mm. pheon)
527 Henry VIII, first coinage, London (mm. portcullis)
528   "   ,   "   , Canterbury (*W A* by bust for Abp. Warham)

            Farthings

529 Edward IV, first reign (Xa; mm. long cross fitchy)
530 Richard III (III; mm. sun-and-rose)
531 Henry VII, group III (mm. anchor?)
532 Henry VIII, first coinage, new type (obv. mm. portcullis)

Plate 31
            Pennies – traditional type
533 Edward IV, first reign, London (Xa; mm. long cross fitchy)
534   "   ,   "   , Canterbury (mm. pall; type 2)
535   "   ,   "   , York (mm. large lis; *G* and key for Abp. Neville)
536   "   ,   "   , Durham (mm. rose; *B D* by bust for Bp. Booth)
537 Henry VI restored, London
538   "   , York, (mm. large lis; *G* and key for Abp. Neville)
539 Edward IV, second reign, London (XVII; mm. pierced cross)
540   "   ,   "   , Canterbury (type 6; mm. long cross fitchy)
541   "   ,   "   , York (type 10; mm. rose; *e* and rose by bust)
542   "   ,   "   , York (type 14: mm. rose; *B* and key for Abp. Booth)
543   "   ,   "   , York (type 16: *T* and key for Abp. Rotherham)
544   "   ,   "   , Durham (type 6; *B* and trefoil for Bp. Booth)
545   "   ,   "   , Durham (local type e; *D V* for Bp. William Dudley)
546 Richard III, London (II; mm. boar's head)
547   "   , York (II; mm. boar's head; *T* and key for Abp. Rotherham)
548   "   , Durham (mm. lis; *S* on breast for Bp. Shirwood)
549 Henry VII, London (IB)
550   "   , York (I; *T* and trefoil for Abp. Rotherham)
551   "   , Durham (IA; *S* on breast for Bp. Shirwood)
552   "   , group III, Canterbury (mm. tun for Abp. Morton)
            Pennies – sovereign type
553 Henry VII, type Ai (York)
554   "   ,   "   Bi (Durham; *D S* by shield for Bp. Shirwood)
555   "   ,   "   Cii, London (mm. lis)
556   "   ,   "   Ciii (Durham, *D R* by shield for Bp. Richard Fox)
557   "   , London, late (gp. Vii; mm. pheon)
558 Henry VIII, first coinage, London (mm. portcullis)
559   "   , Canterbury (mm. martlet; *W A* by shield for Abp. William Warham)
560   "   , Durham (mm. lis: *T D* above shield for Bp. Thomas Ruthall)
561   "   ,   "   (mm. spur rowel; *D W* by shield for Thomas Wolsey)

VIII: 1526 – 1544
The Second Coinage of Henry VIII (1509-47).

Plate 32

    Gold – all of London mint
- 562 Sovereign (mm. lis over sunburst/arrow)
- 563 Angelet (mm. lis)
- 564 Angel (mm. sunburst)
- 565 George noble, type 1
- 566   "   , " 2
- 567 Half-noble (mm. rose/lis)
- 568 Crown of the Rose
- 569 Crown of the Double Rose (mm. arrow; *h K* in field)
- 570   "   "   "   " with Irish title (mm. pheon; *h R* in field)
- 571 Halfcrown (mm. arrow; *h I* in field)

    Silver – Groats
- 572 London, bust i, mm. rose only
- 573   " , bust ii, "   "   "

Plate 33
- 574 London, bust iii (mm. lis B/pheon)
- 575 London, bust iii, with Irish title (mm. lis C)
- 576 York, bust iii, *T W* by shield and hat below, for Abp. Thomas Wolsey (mm. acorn)

    Halfgroats
- 577 London (mm. lis/rose)
- 578 London, with Irish title, mm. pheon only
- 579 Canterbury, *W A* by shield for Abp. William Warham (mm. uncertain mark)
- 580 Canterbury, *T C* by shield for Abp. Thomas Cranmer (mm. Catherine wheel)
- 581 York, *T W* by shield and hat below for Abp. Wolsey (mm. voided cross)
- 582 York, *E L* by shield for Abp. Edward Lee (mm. key)

    Pennies
- 583 London (mm. rose)
- 584 Canterbury, *W A* by shield for Abp. Warham (mm. uncertain mark)
- 585 Canterbury, *T C* by shield for Abp. Cranmer (mm. Catherine wheel)
- 586 York, *e L* by shield for Abp. Lee (mm. key)
- 587 Durham, *T W* by shield and hat below for Bp. Wolsey (mm. trefoil)
- 588 Durham, no initials or hat, *sede vacante* (mm. star)
- 589 Durham, *C D* by shield for Bp. Cuthbert Tunstall (mm. star)

    Halfpence
- 590 London, narrow hair (mm. lis A)
- 591 London, wider hair (mm. arrow)
- 592 Canterbury, *W A* by bust for Abp. Warham (mm. cross patonce)
- 593 Canterbury, *T C* by bust for Abp. Cranmer (mm. wheel)
- 594 York, *T W* by bust for Abp. Wolsey (mm. acorn)
- 595 York, *e L* by bust for Abp. Lee (mm. key)

    Farthings
- 596 London, type A (mm. lis)
- 597 London, " B (mm. arrow)
- 598 Canterbury, type B (mm. wheel)

IX: 1544 – 1551
The debasement period under Henry VIII (1509-47) and Edward VI (1547-53).

Plate 34
Gold
599 Sovereign, Henry VIII, type I, (Tower mint; mm. large lis)
600 Half-sovereign, Henry VIII, type IIa (Tower; mm. lis)
601 Sovereign, Henry VIII, type IIa (Tower; mm. small lis)
602   " ,   "   , type IIb (Southwark; mm. *S*)
603 Half-sovereign, Henry VIII, type IIb (Southwark; mm. *S*)
604 Sovereign, Henry posthumous, Roman letters (Tower; mm. Florentine lis)

Plate 35
605 Half-sovereign, Henry VIII, Bristol (mm. *WS* monogram)
606   "   , Edward VI, *HR* monogram on rev. (Tower; mm. arrow)
607   "   , Henry posthumous, but with Edward portrait (Southwark; mm. *E*)
608 Angel,   Henry VIII, Tower mint, mm. lis only
609 Half-angel,   "   ,   "   ,   "
610 Quarter-angel   "   ,   "   ,   "
611 Halfcrown, Henry VIII (Southwark; mm. *e)*
612   "   , Edward VI (Tower; mm. arrow)
613   "   , Henry posthumous (Tower II; mm. martlet)
614 Crown, Henry VIII, Tower, mm. pellet-in-annulet
615   "   , Edward VI, Tower, mm. arrow
616   "   , Henry posthumous (Tower II; mm. *K)*
617   "   , Henry VIII or posthumous, Bristol (mm. *WS)*

Plate 36
618 Sovereign, Edward VI (Southwark; mm. *Y)*
619 Half-sovereign, Edward VI, type 1a (Tower; mm. arrow)
620   "   ,   "   , type 1b (Tower II; mm. *6)*
621   "   ,   "   , type 2b (Tower; mm. swan)
622   "   ,   "   , Durham Place (type 3)
623 Half-quarter-sovereign, Edward VI, type 1 (Tower; mm. arrow)
624   "   ,   "   , type 2b (Tower II; mm. grapple)
625 Quarter-sovereign, Edward VI, type 1 (Tower; mm. arrow)
626   "   ,   "   , type 2 (Southwark; mm. *Y)*

Plate 37
627 Edward VI, 1551, Southwark, sovereign (mm. ostrich head)
628   "   , " ,   "   , angel (mm. ostrich head)
629   "   , " ,   "   , half-angel (mm. ostrich head)

Silver – Testons
630 Henry VIII, group A, bust 1 (Tower; mm. lis)
631   "   , group B, bust 2 (Southwark; mm. *S)*

632   "   , Bristol (mm. *WS* monogram; local dies)
633   Henry posthumous, group C (C/B mule), bust 3 (Tower; mm. pellet-in-annulet)

Plate 38
      Groats
634   Henry VIII, bust 1 (Tower; mm. lis)
635   "   , bust 2 (Southwark; no mm.)
636   "   , bust 3 (York; no mm.; bad striking cracks)
637   Henry VIII or posthumous, bust 4 (Tower; mm. arrow)
638   Edward VI (Tower; mm. arrow)
639   Henry posthumous, bust 5, stops (v) pierced crosses (Tower II; mm. *K)*
640   "   "   , bust 6, stops (vi) pellets (Canterbury; mm. rose)
641   Henry/posthumous, Bristol (mm. *WS)*
642   Henry posthumous, Durham Place (mm. bow)
643   "   "   , Dublin (local dies)
      Halfgroats
644   Henry VIII (Tower; mm. lis)
645   Edward VI (Canterbury)
646   Henry posthumous, bust 1 (Tower II; mm. grapple)
647   "   "   , bust 6 (York)

Plate 39
648   Henry posthumous, Bristol (mm. *TC* monogram)
649   "   "   , Dublin (local dies)
      Pennies
650   Henry VIII (Tower; mm. lis)
651   Edward VI (Tower; mm. arrow)
652   Henry posthumous, late bust (London)
653   Henry/posthumous, Bristol, facing bust
654   Edward VI, Bristol, profile type
      Fractions
655   Halfpenny, Henry VIII (London)
656   "   , Edward VI, profile type (Tower)
657   "   , Henry posthumous
658   Farthing, Henry VIII (Tower)
      Shillings of Edward VI
659   First issue (Feb. 1549), bust 1 (Canterbury; mm. rose)
660   "   "   , bust 2 (Tower I; mm. arrow)
661   Second issue (1549-50), bust 3 (Canterbury; mm. *t)*
662   "   "   , bust 4 (Southwark; mm. *Y)*
663   "   "   , bust 5 (Southwark; mm. *Y)*
664   Third issue (1551), bust 6 (Tower I?; mm. rose)
665   "   (1552), bust 6 (Dublin; mm. harp)
666   Durham Place (first issue, first bust).

KEY TO PLATES

Location of coins illustrated

Fitzwilliam Museum, Cambridge: 43, 83, 85-99, 101-3, 105-17, 120-2, 124, 127, 131-45, 147, 149, 154-5, 158-61, 170, 174-5, 177, 179-81, 183-5, 188, 192, 201, 206, 218, 220, 222, 224-5, 227-8, 234, 258-9, 261-2, 264-6, 270-2, 274, 276, 278, 283-4, 286-8, 290-1, 294-6, 298, 305, 339, 343, 345-7, 350-8, 361-5, 367-9, 373, 377, 379-82, 384, 386, 390, 393, 395-6, 400, 402-3, 407-10, 413-5, 418, 422, 450, 453-9, 461-2, 464-7, 469, 471-8, 487-94, 497, 499, 500, 512, 515, 521, 533-5, 537, 539-40, 547-50, 552, 572-3, 576, 582-3, 587-9, 593, 600, 630, 635, 637-9, 643-5, 647, 649, 652-4, 659-61, 663-4, 666.

British Museum: 84, 186-7, 189, 191, 209-12, 233, 267, 273, 314, 322, 330-2, 334, 342, 344, 360, 370-2, 374, 378, 392, 399, 404, 416, 419-21, 428, 430, 434, 468, 479, 526, 528-9, 542, 544, 564-5, 570, 611, 622, 631-2, 634, 641-2, 648, 650-1.

Private collection: 40, 49, 52-81, 100, 104, 118-9, 123, 125-6, 128-30, 146, 148, 150-3, 156-7, 162-9, 171-3, 176, 178, 182, 190, 193-200, 202-4, 207, 219, 221, 223, 226, 229-31, 257, 260, 268-9, 275, 277, 279-82, 285, 289, 292, 297, 299, 300, 302-4, 306, 333, 335-8, 340-1, 348-9, 359, 366, 375-6, 383, 385, 387-9, 391, 394, 397-8, 401, 405-6, 411-2, 417, 423, 451-2, 460, 463, 470, 482-6, 495-6, 498, 502-11, 513-4, 516-7, 519-20, 522-5, 527, 530-1, 536, 538, 541, 543, 545, 551, 553, 555-61, 574-5, 577, 579-81, 584, 586, 590-2, 595, 636, 640, 646, 655, 657.

Schneider family: All gold coins except 209-12, 314, 322, 330, 428, 430, 434, 564-5, 600, 611, 622, 629.

Other sources: Ashmolean Museum, Oxford, 629; Hunterian Museum, Glasgow, 480; J. Bispham, 662; G. Gittoes, 1-39, 41-2, 44-8; P. Woodhead, 263; R.C. Lockett Collection (Glendining sale, 11. Oct. 1956), 546; R.J. Shuttlewood collection (Spink sale 151, 15 March 2001), 481, 501, 578, 585, 594, 597-8, 633, 656, and 232 (*BNJ* 65, 1995, p. 224).

Spink *Standard Catalogue*: 51, 82, 205, 208, 233, 293, 381, 420, 518, 526, 532, 554, 596, 658; *do., Scotland, Ireland*: 82, 205, 208, 381, 665.

PLATE 1

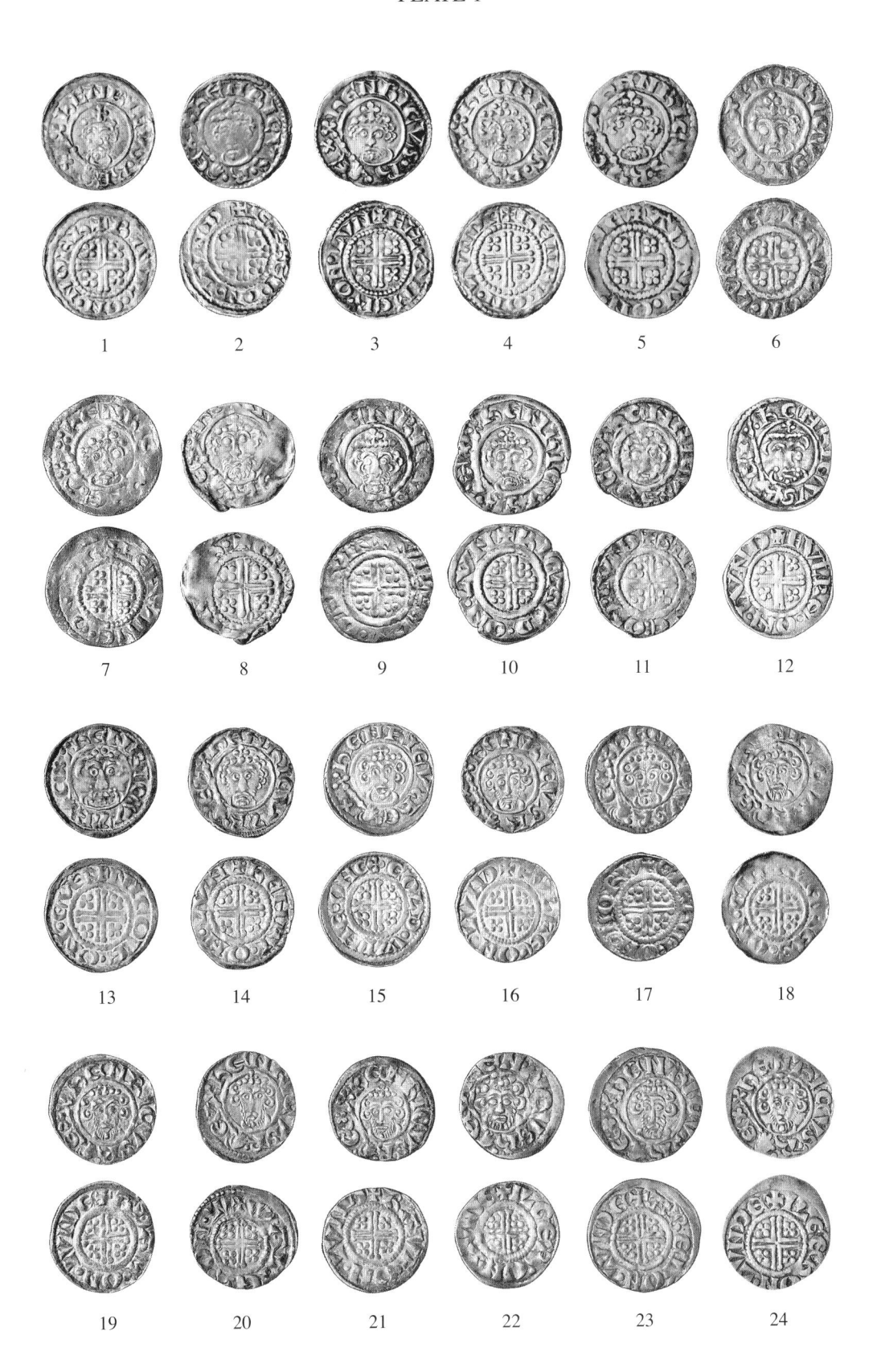

1 2 3 4 5 6

7 8 9 10 11 12

13 14 15 16 17 18

19 20 21 22 23 24

1180–1247 (1)

PLATE 2

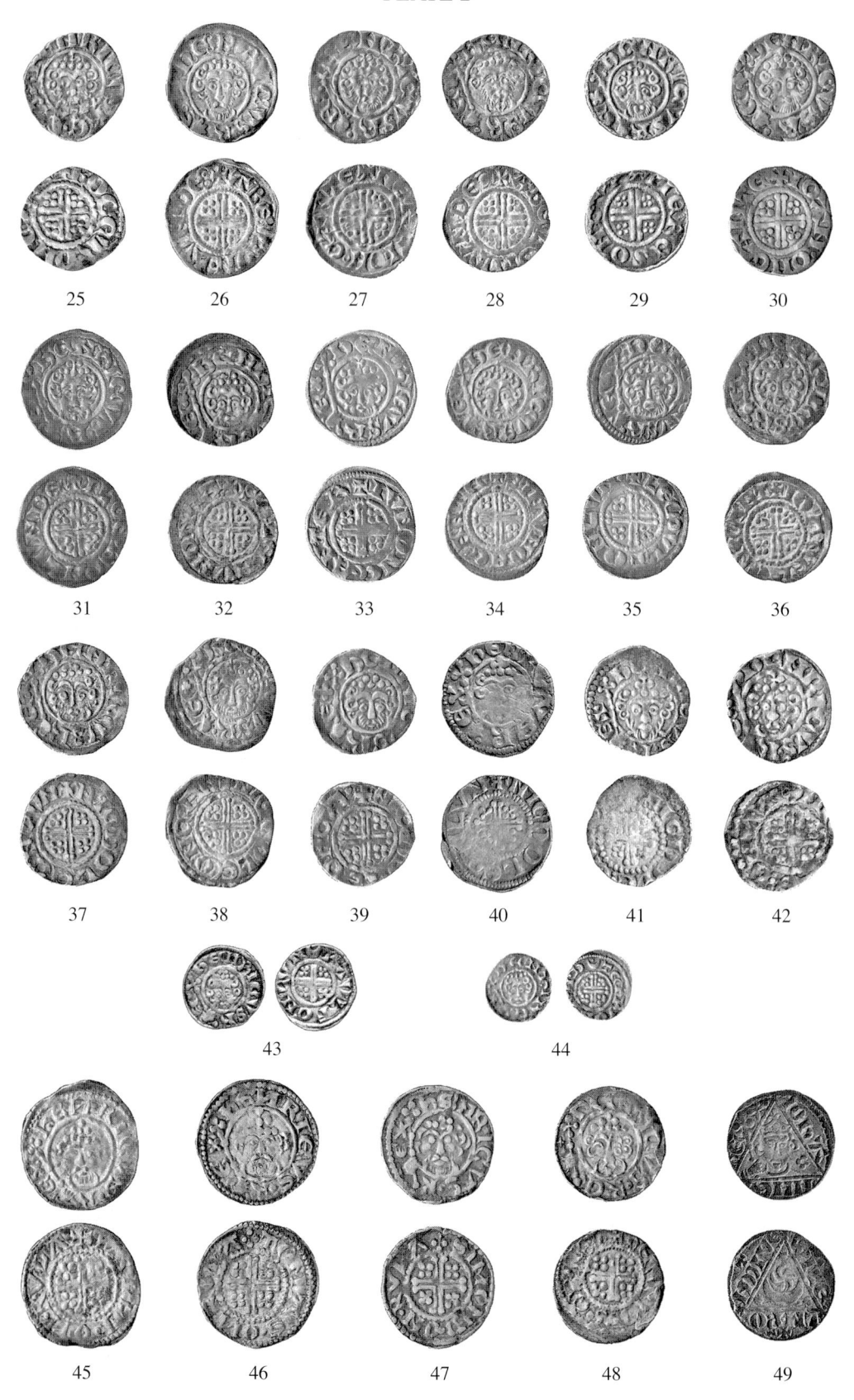

25 26 27 28 29 30

31 32 33 34 35 36

37 38 39 40 41 42

43 44

45 46 47 48 49

1180–1247 (2)

PLATE 3

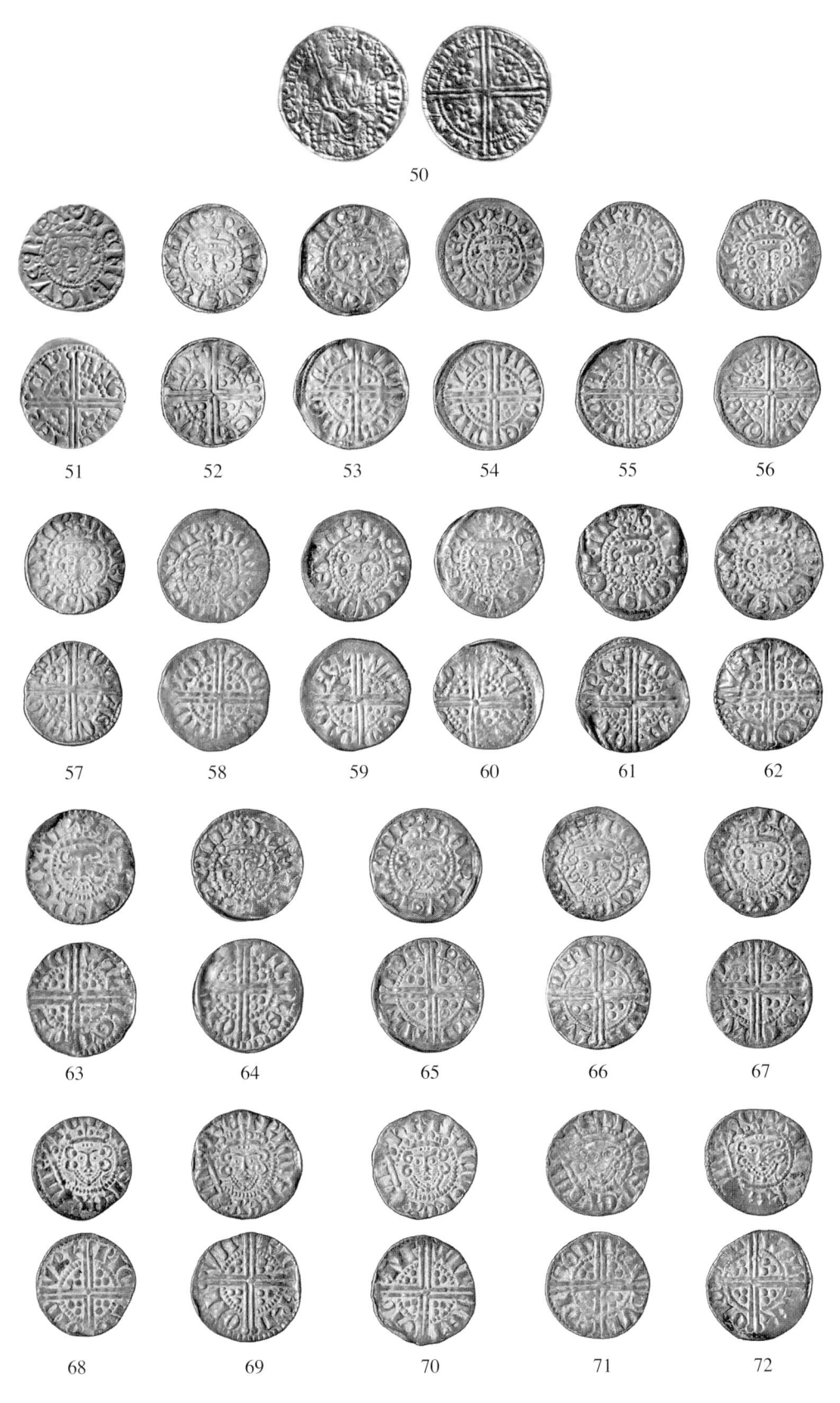

1247–1278 (1)

PLATE 4

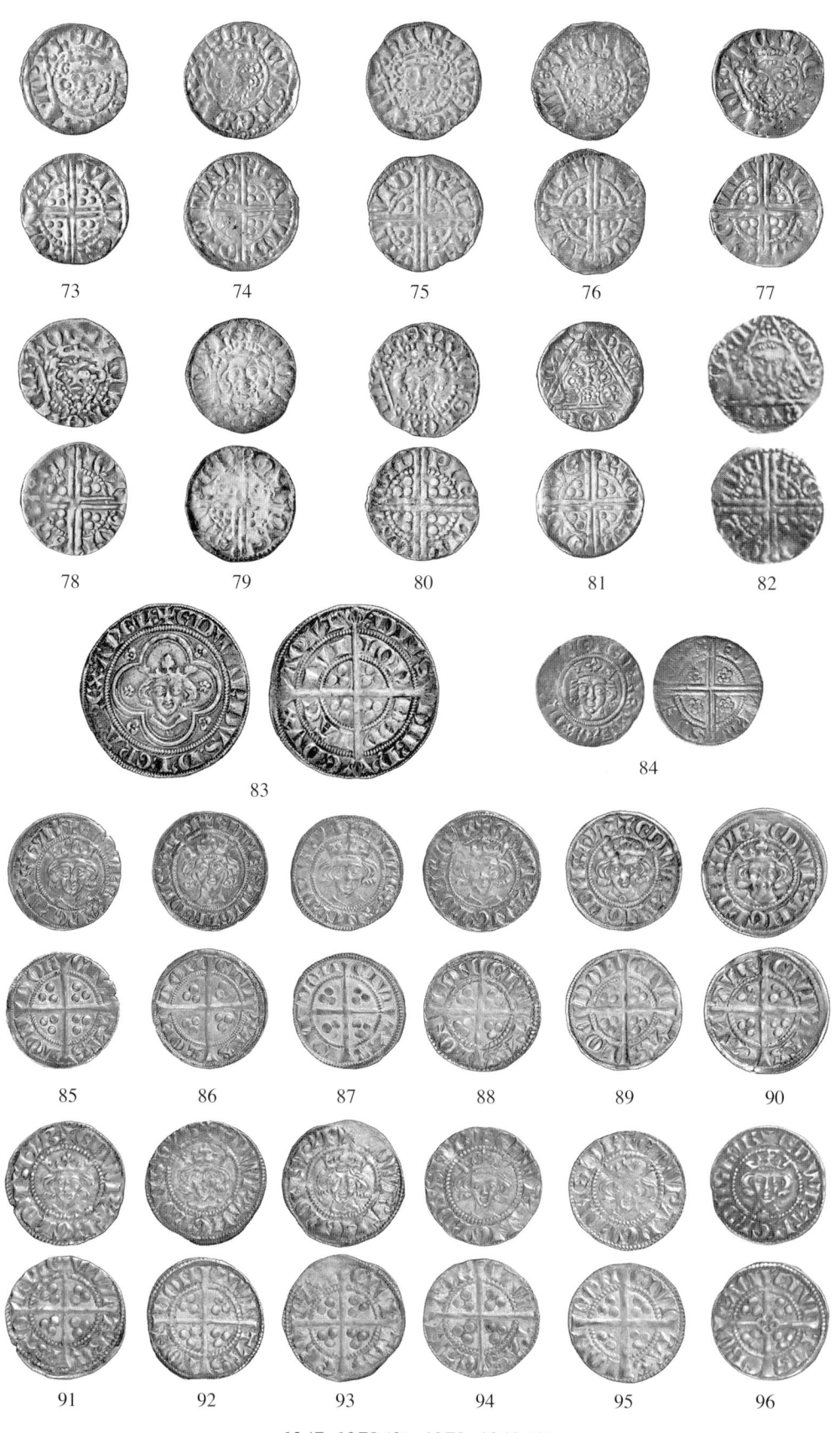

73 74 75 76 77

78 79 80 81 82

83 84

85 86 87 88 89 90

91 92 93 94 95 96

1247–1278 (2); 1279–1343 (1)

PLATE 5

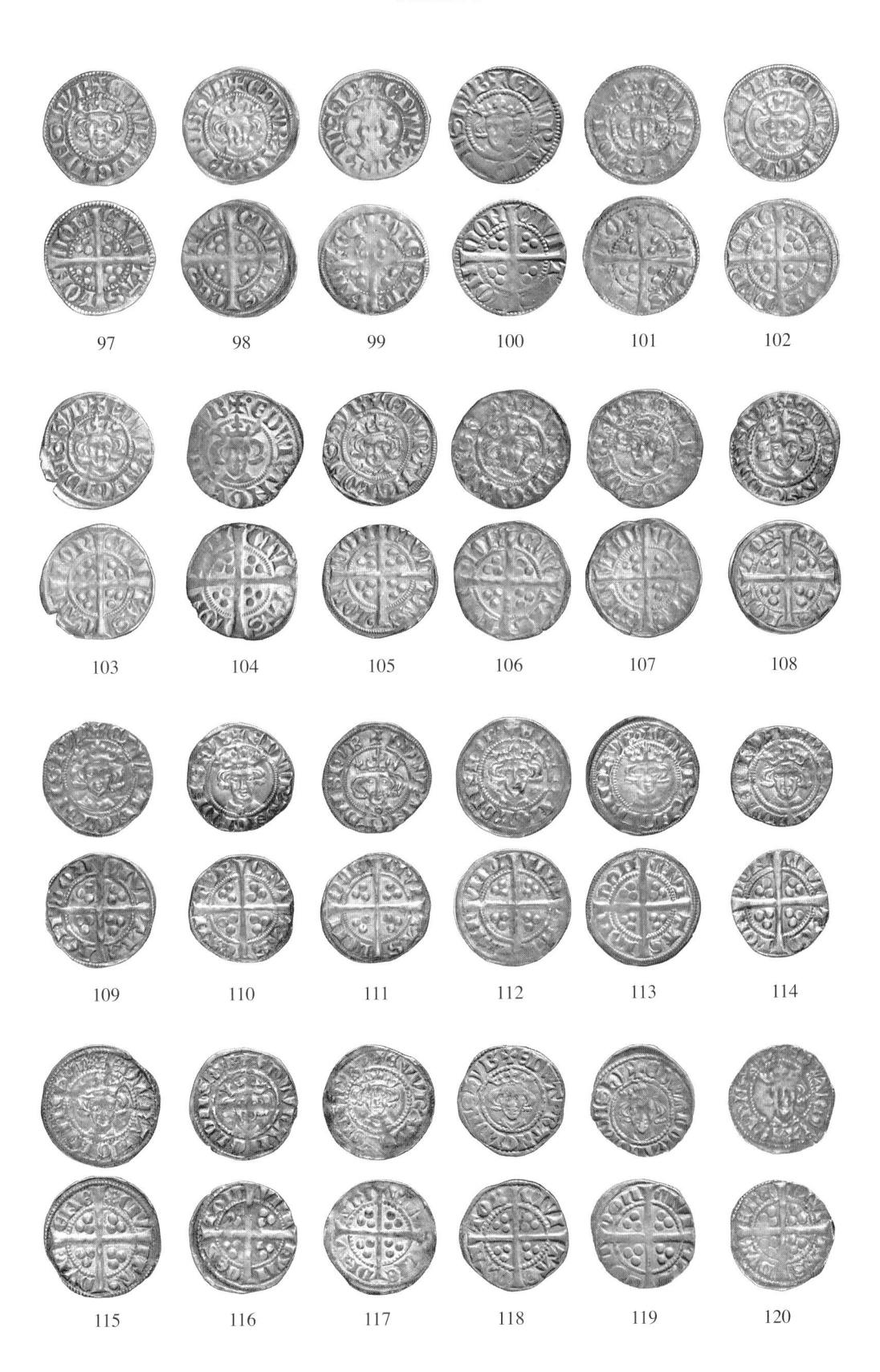

97 98 99 100 101 102

103 104 105 106 107 108

109 110 111 112 113 114

115 116 117 118 119 120

1279–1343 (2)

PLATE 6

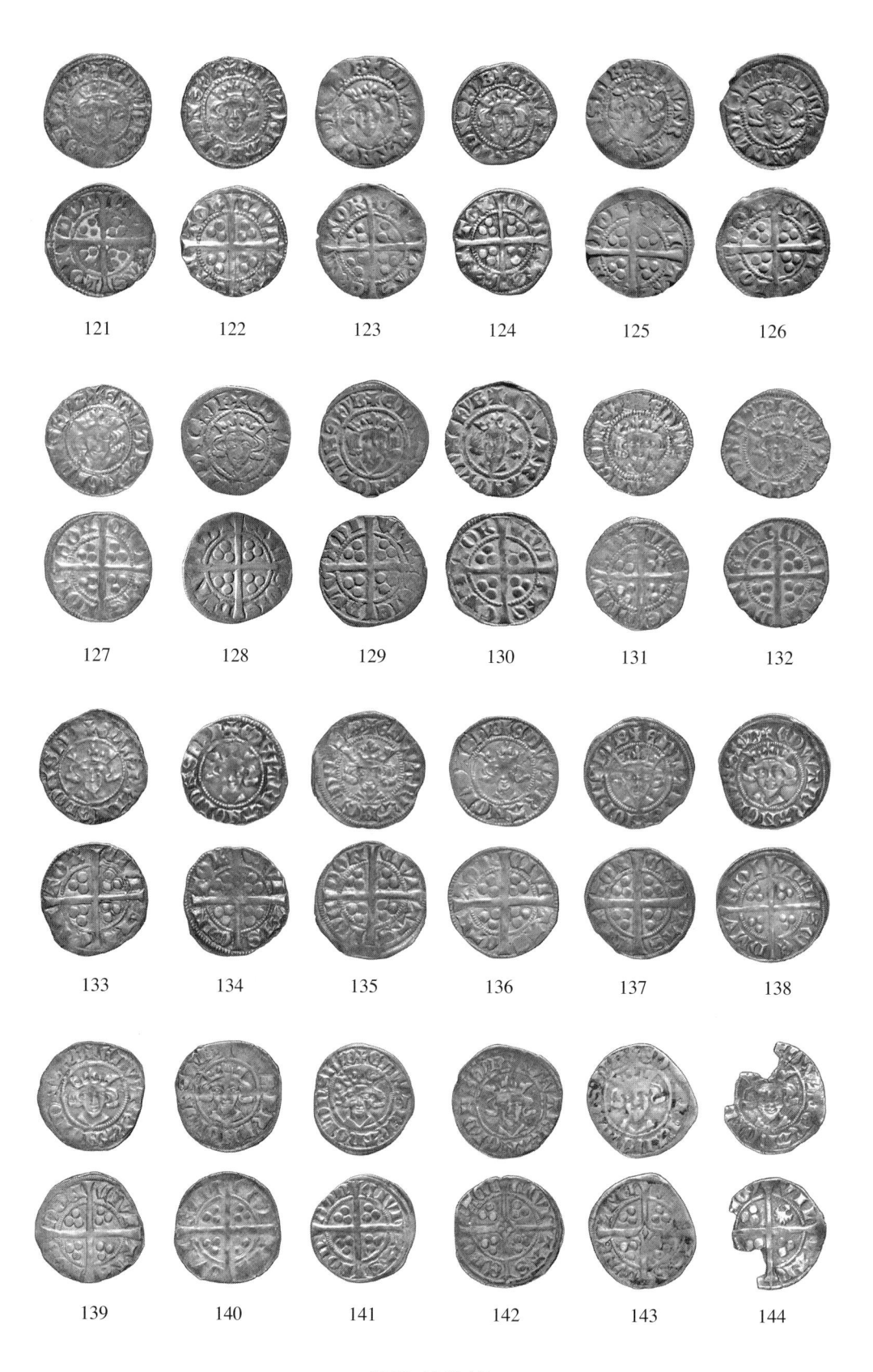

121 122 123 124 125 126

127 128 129 130 131 132

133 134 135 136 137 138

139 140 141 142 143 144

1279–1343 (3)

PLATE 7

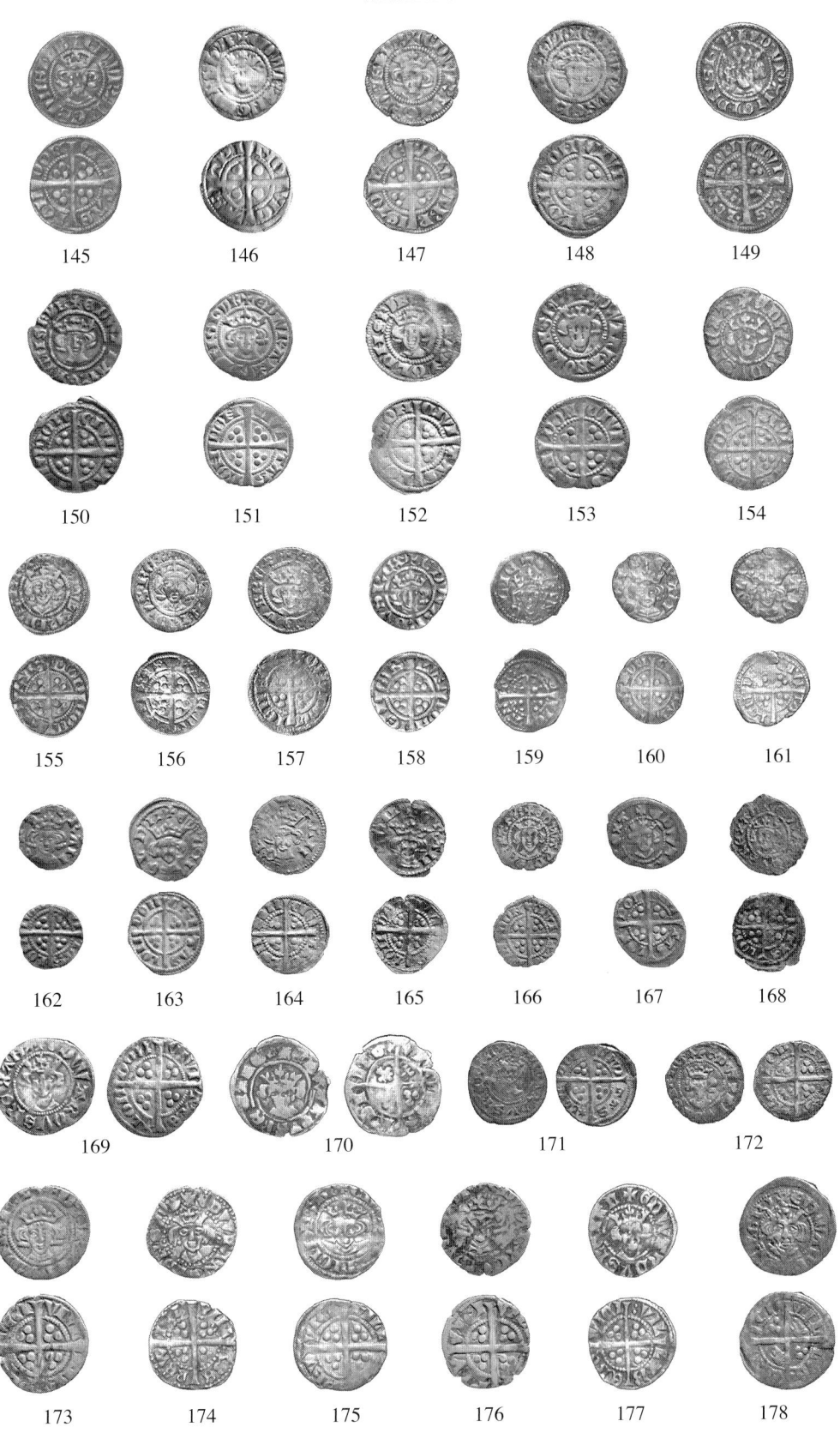

1279–1343 (4)

PLATE 8

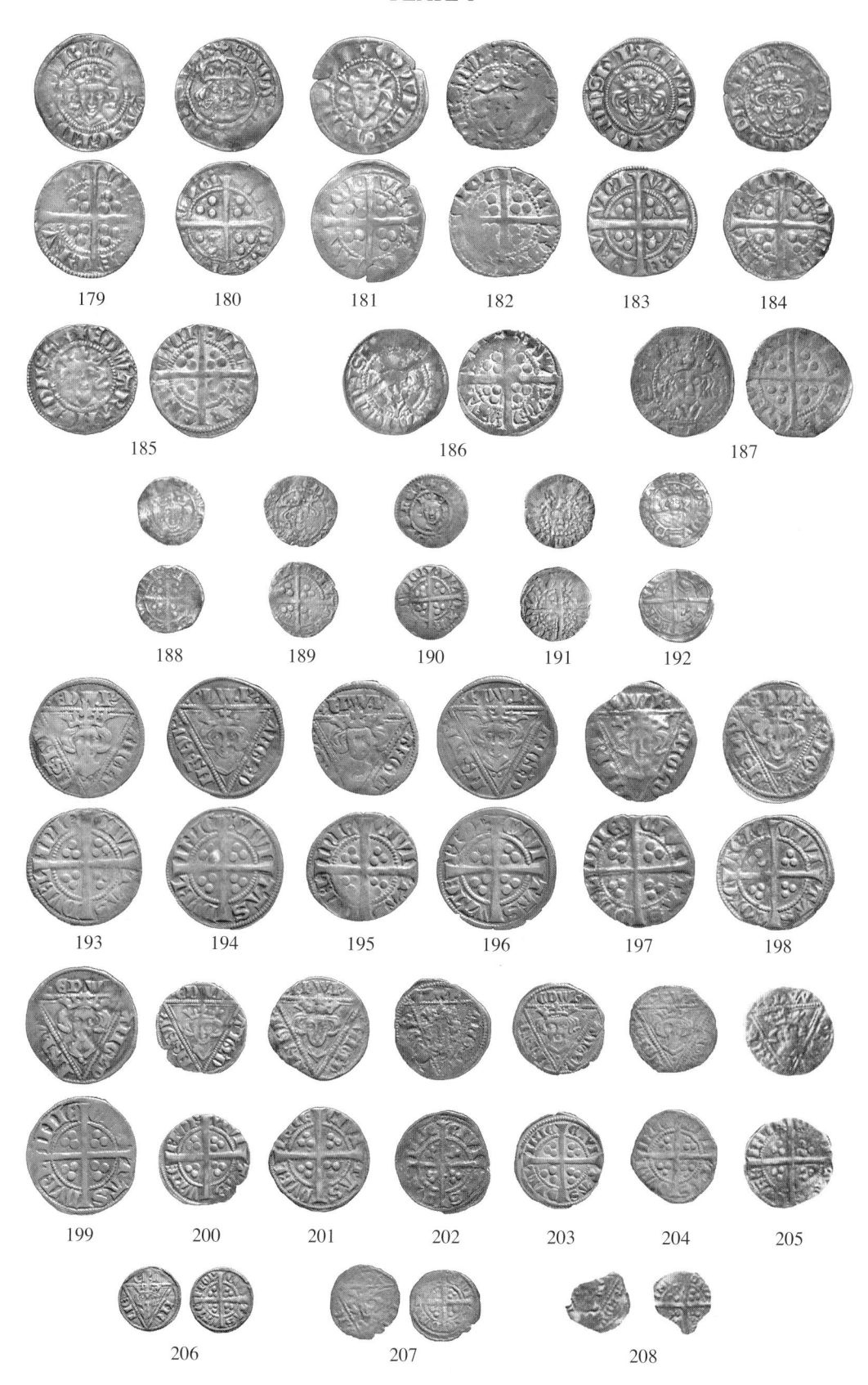

179 180 181 182 183 184

185 186 187

188 189 190 191 192

193 194 195 196 197 198

199 200 201 202 203 204 205

206 207 208

1279–1343 (5)

PLATE 9

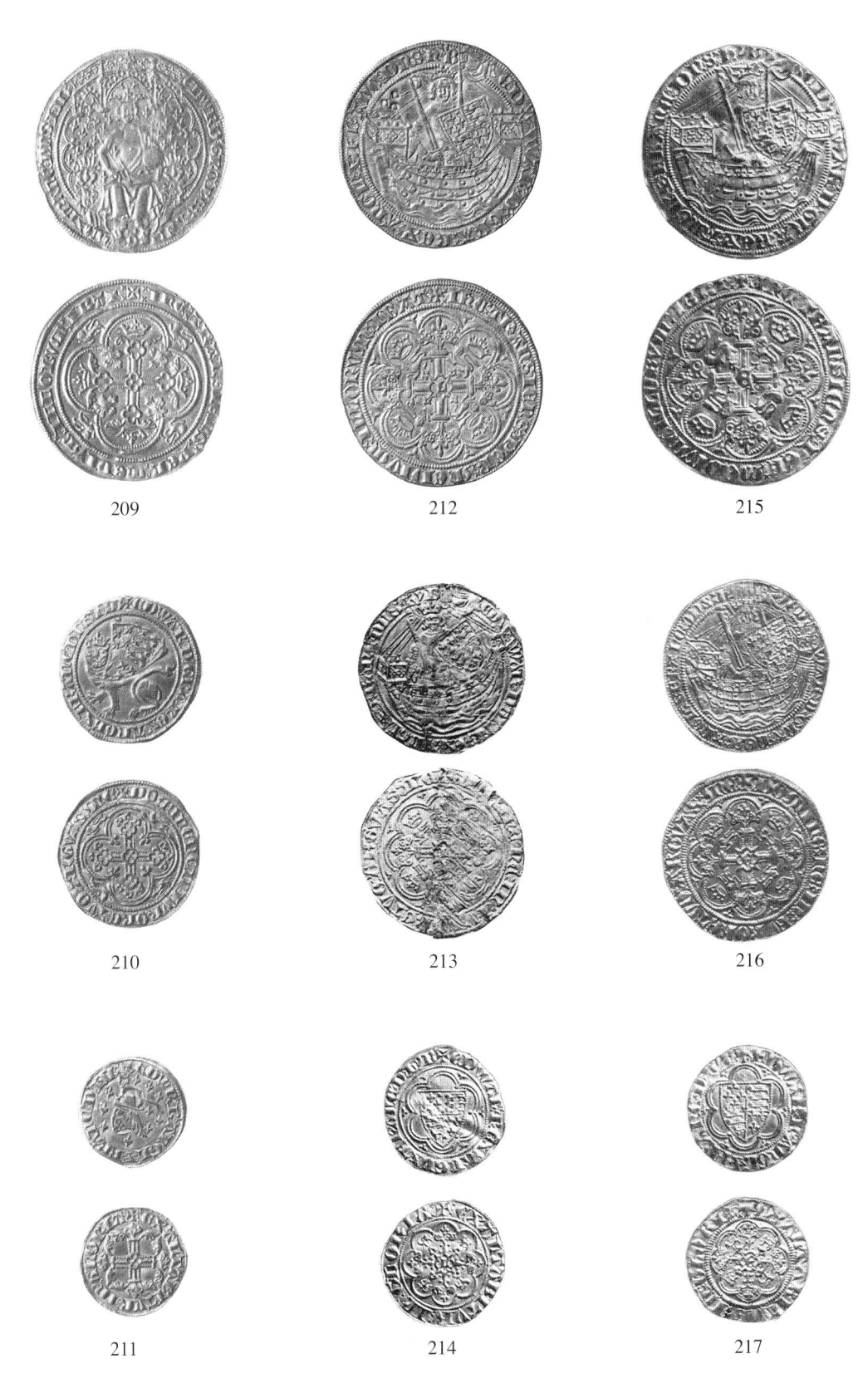

209 212 215

210 213 216

211 214 217

1344–1351 (1)

PLATE 10

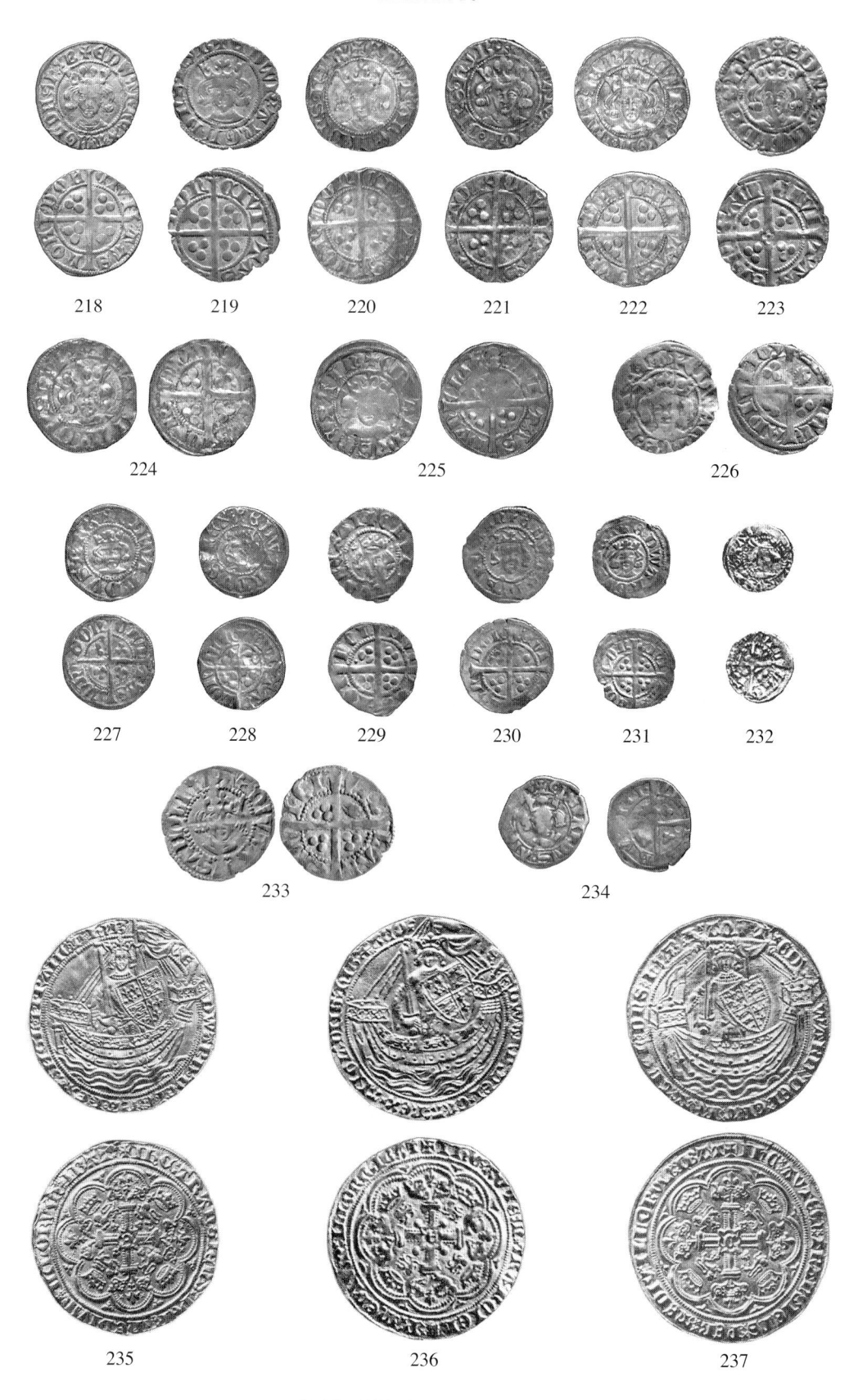

218   219   220   221   222   223

224   225   226

227   228   229   230   231   232

233   234

235   236   237

1344–1351 (2); 1351–1411 (1)

PLATE 11

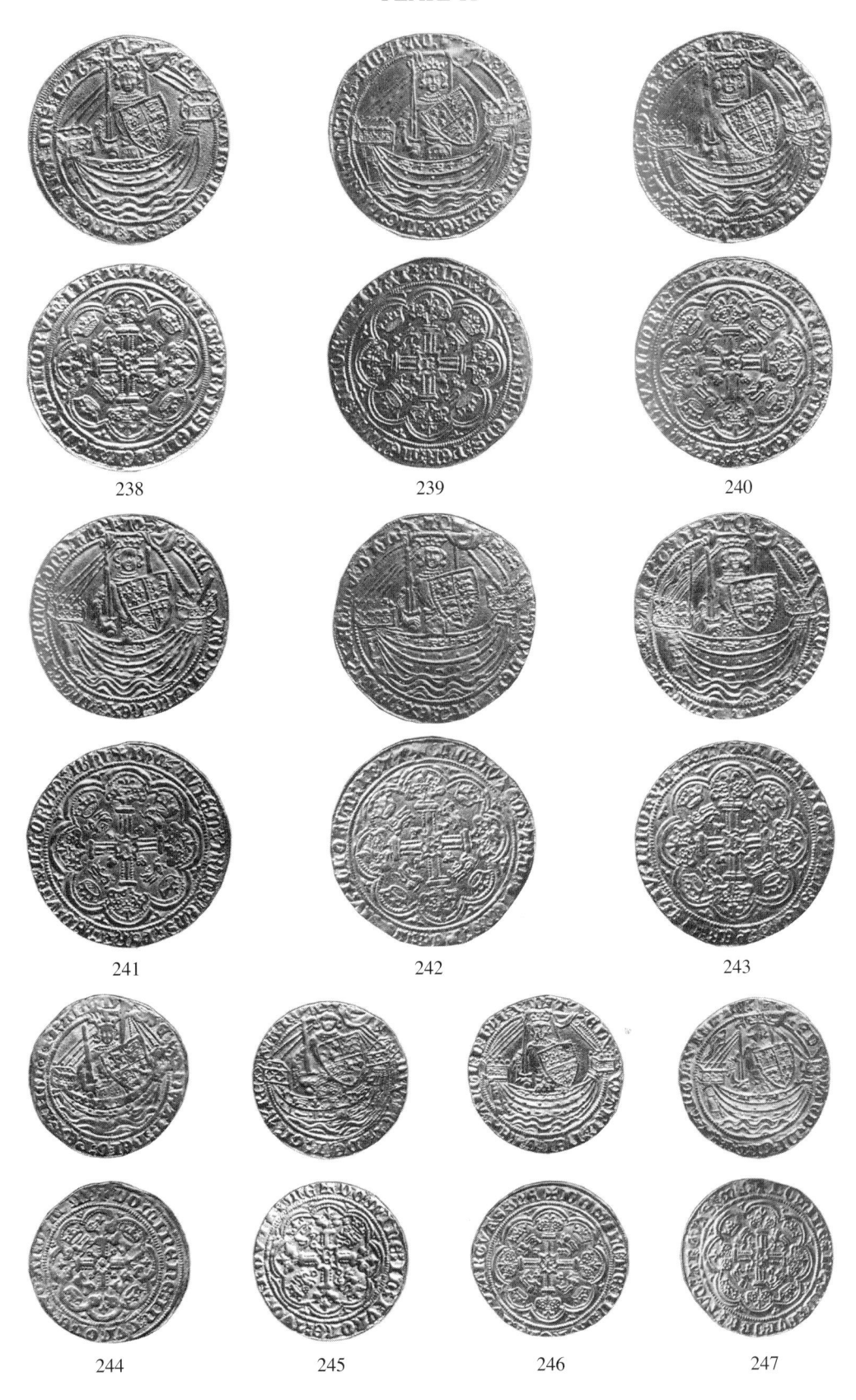

238 239 240

241 242 243

244 245 246 247

1351–1411 (2)

PLATE 12

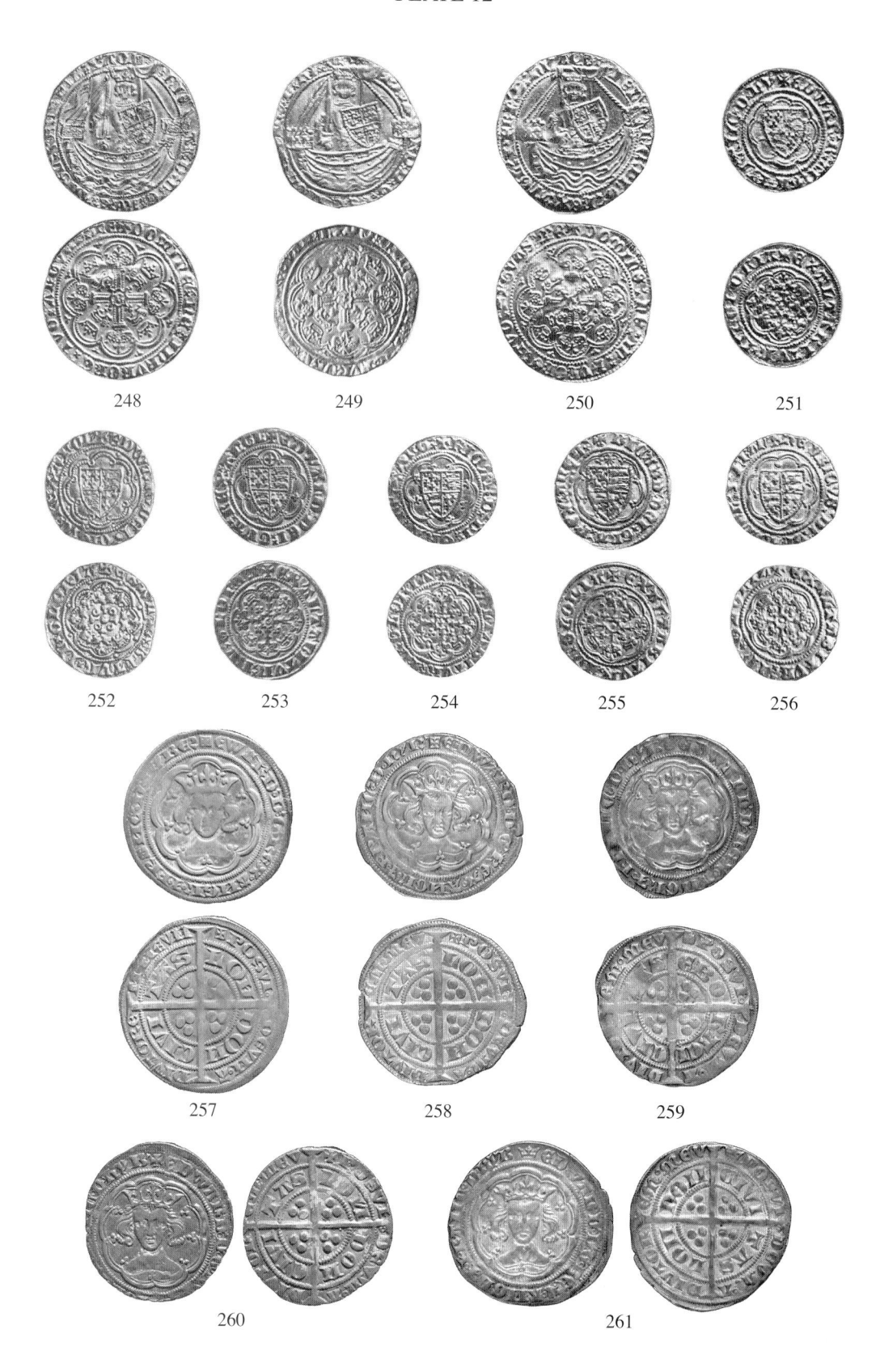

248   249   250   251

252   253   254   255   256

257   258   259

260   261

1351–1411 (3)

PLATE 13

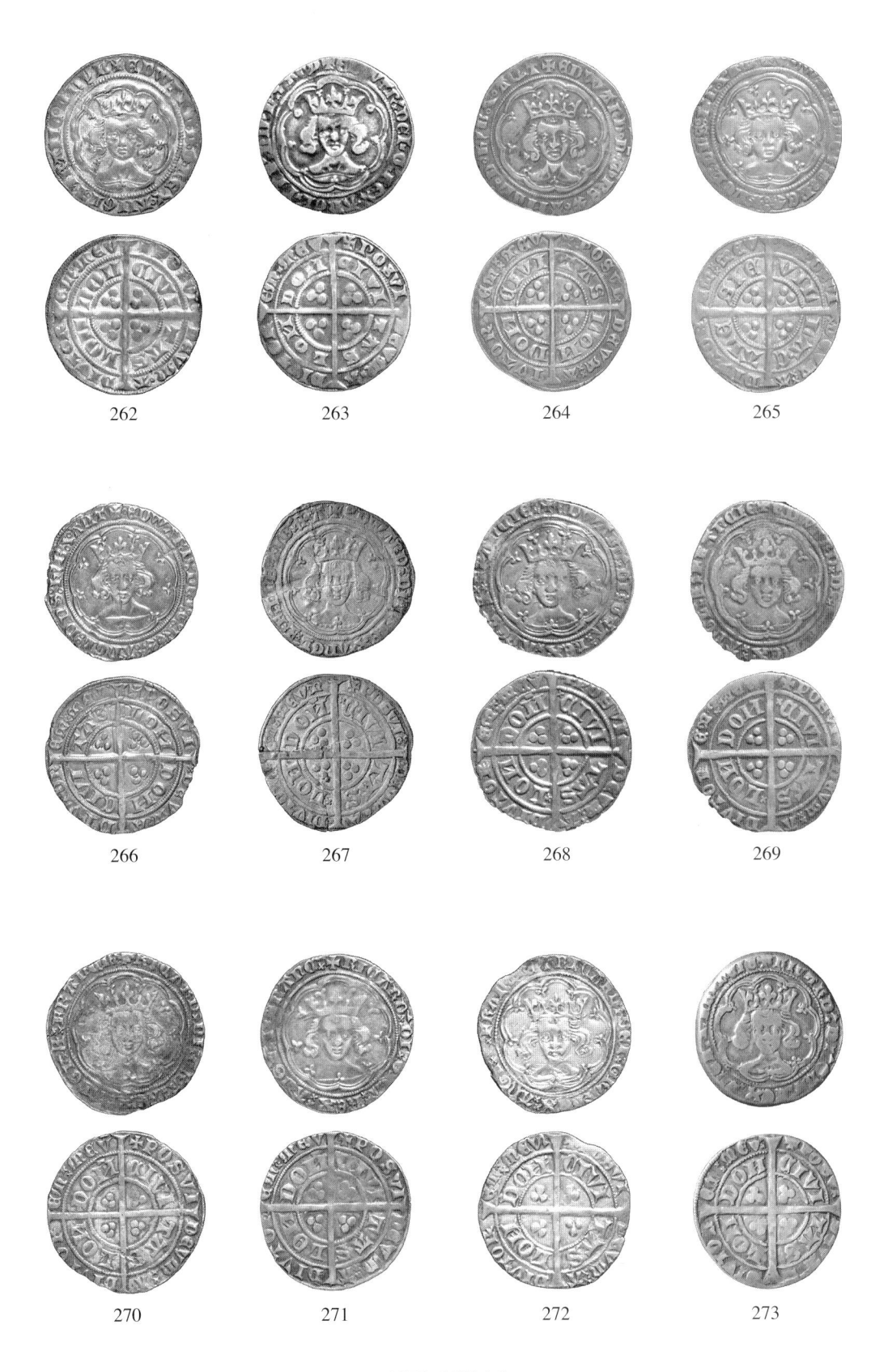

262   263   264   265

266   267   268   269

270   271   272   273

1351–1411 (4)

PLATE 14

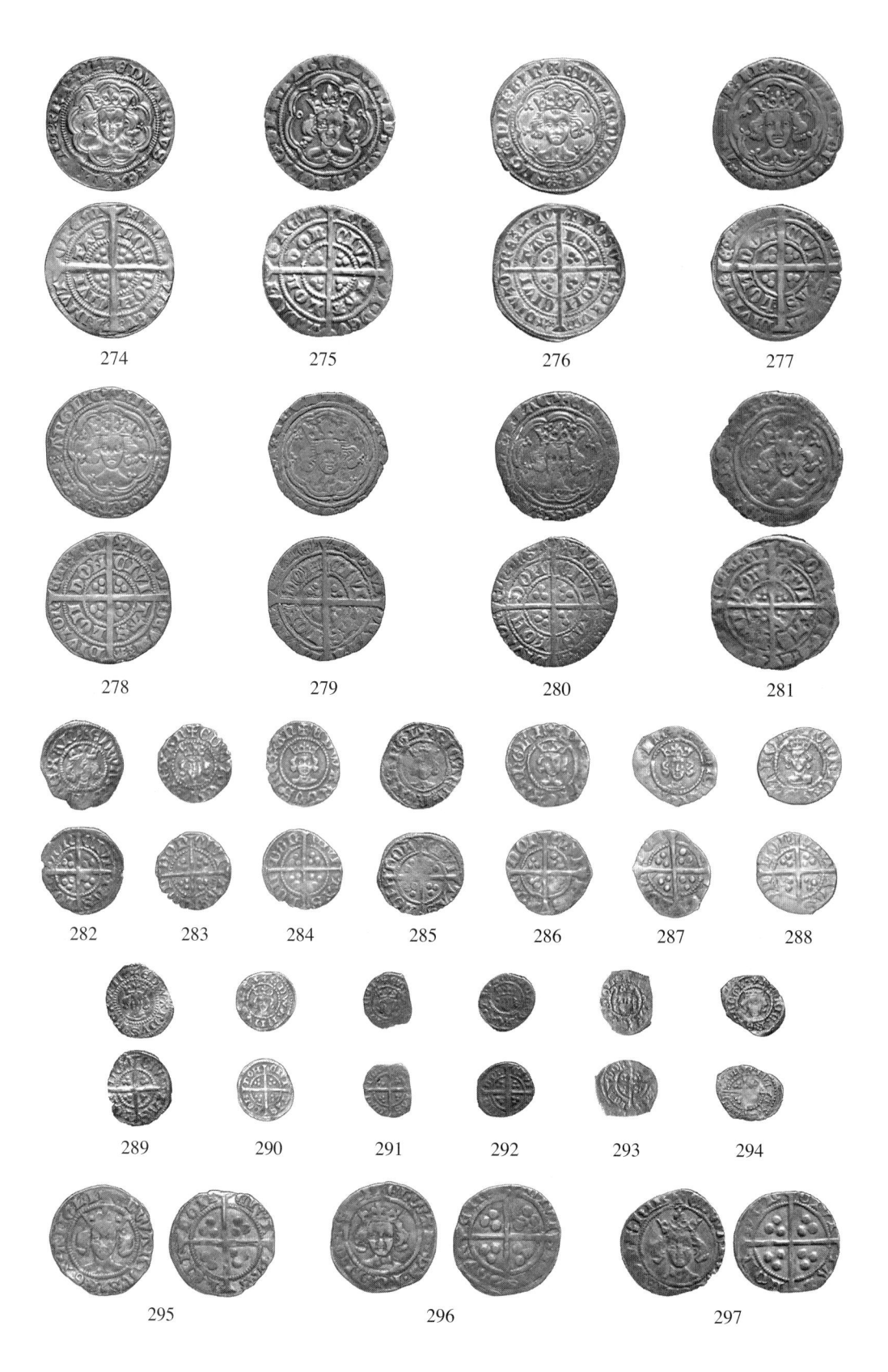

274 275 276 277

278 279 280 281

282 283 284 285 286 287 288

289 290 291 292 293 294

295 296 297

1351–1411 (5)

PLATE 15

298 299 300 301 302

303 304 305 306

307 308 309

310

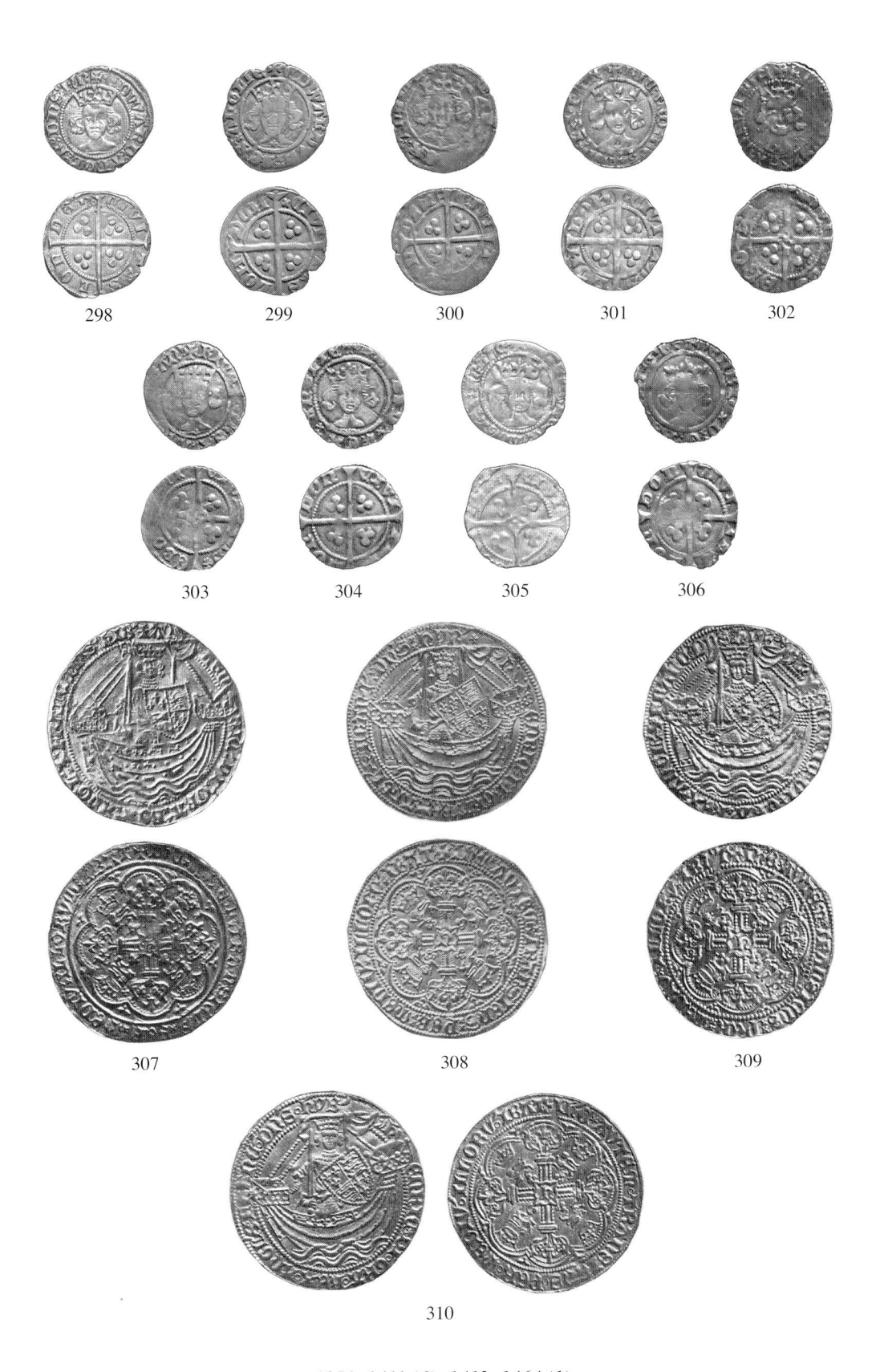

1351–1411 (6); 1412–1464 (1)

PLATE 16

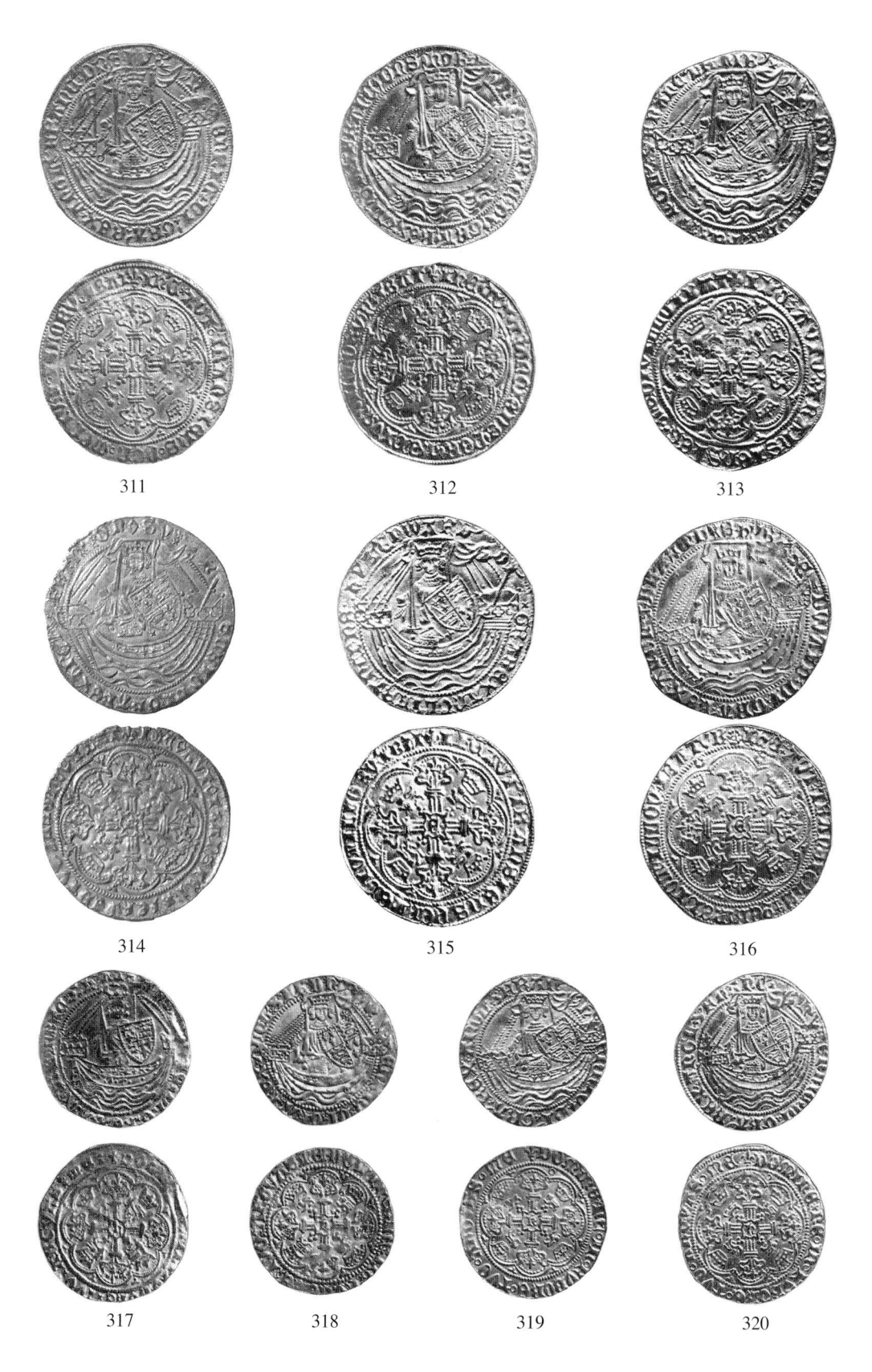

311 312 313

314 315 316

317 318 319 320

1412–1464 (2)

PLATE 17

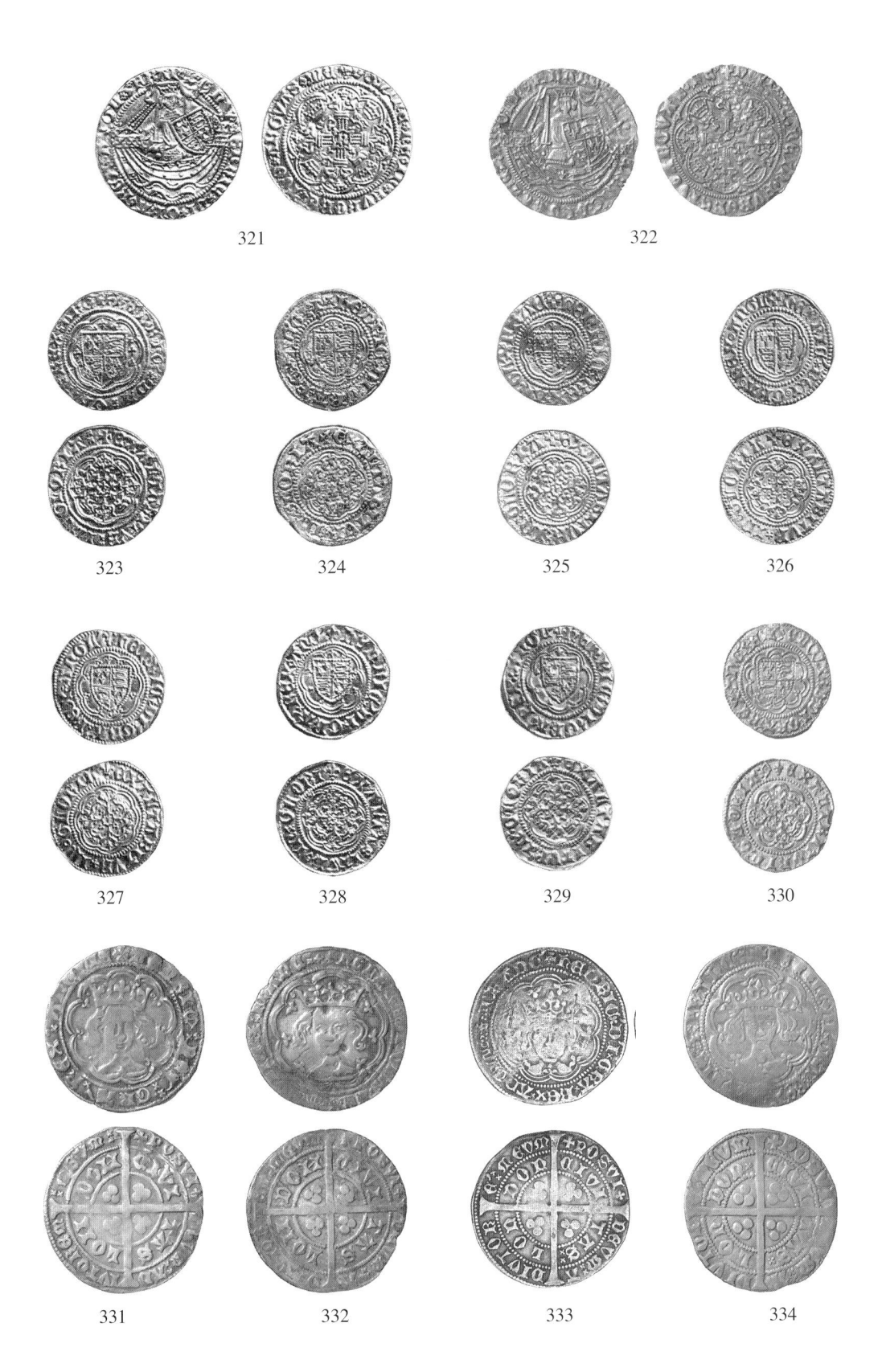

321   322

323   324   325   326

327   328   329   330

331   332   333   334

1412–1464 (3)

PLATE 18

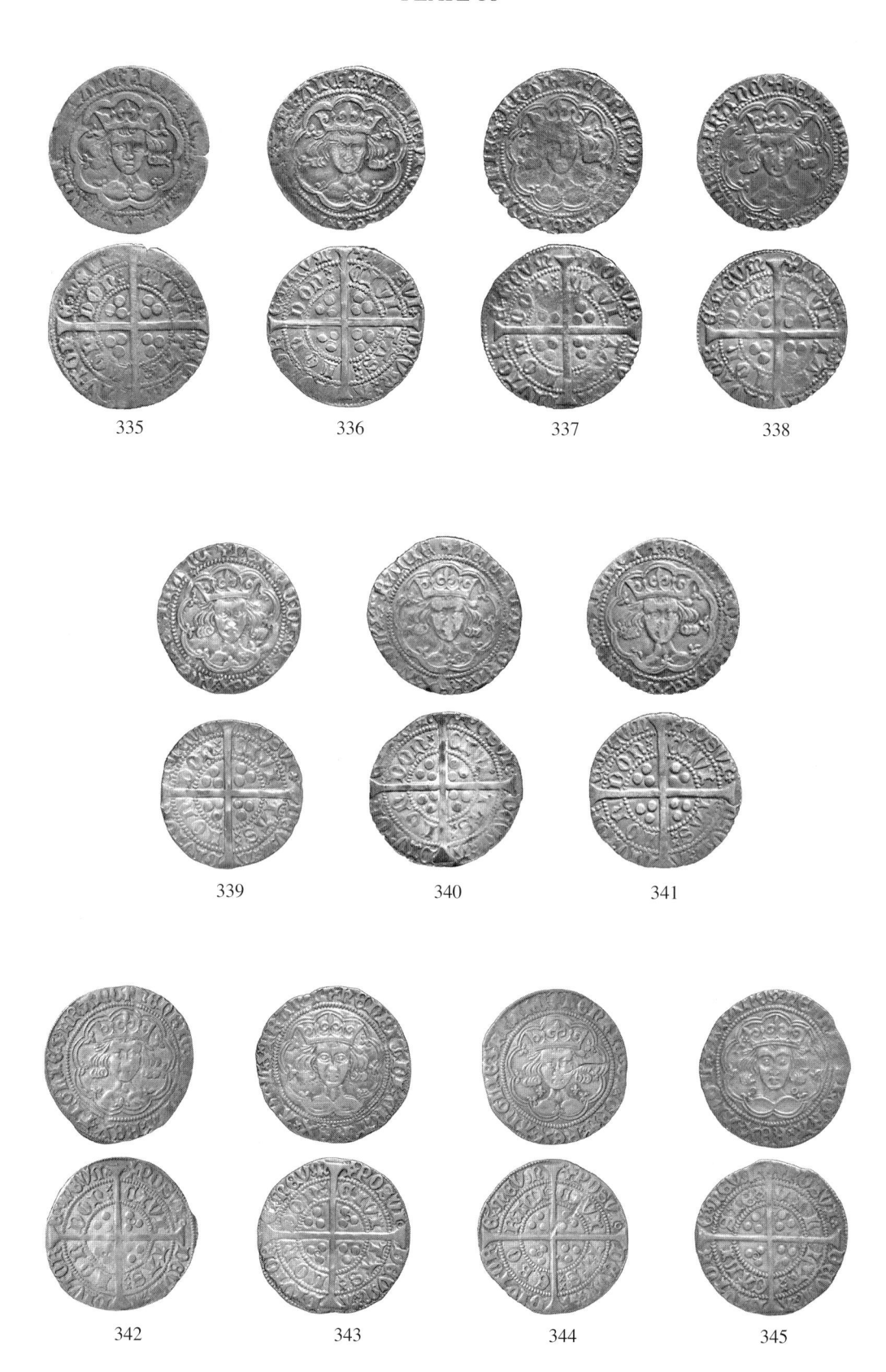

335   336   337   338

339   340   341

342   343   344   345

1412–1464 (4)

PLATE 19

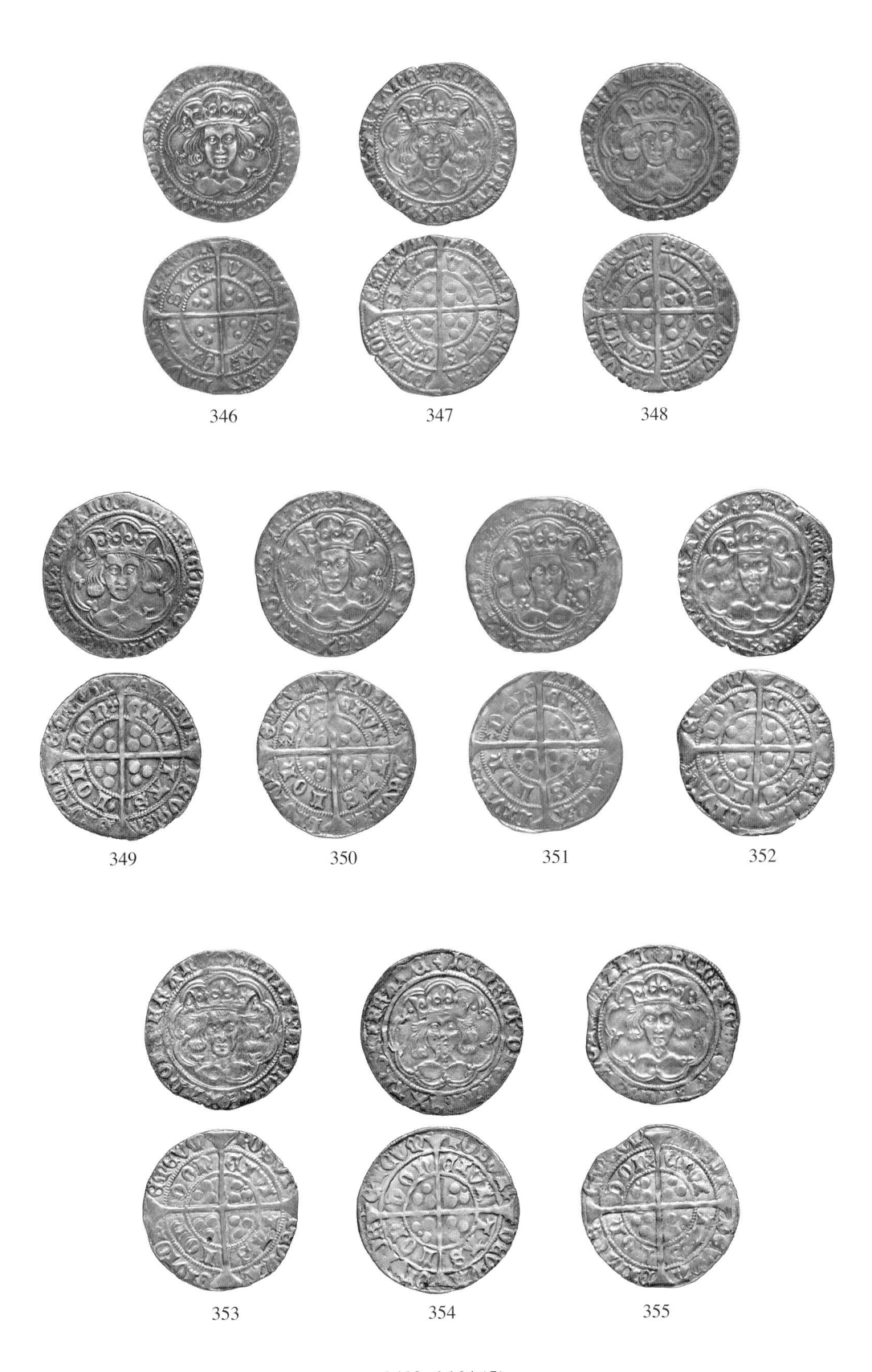

346 347 348

349 350 351 352

353 354 355

1412–1464 (5)

PLATE 20

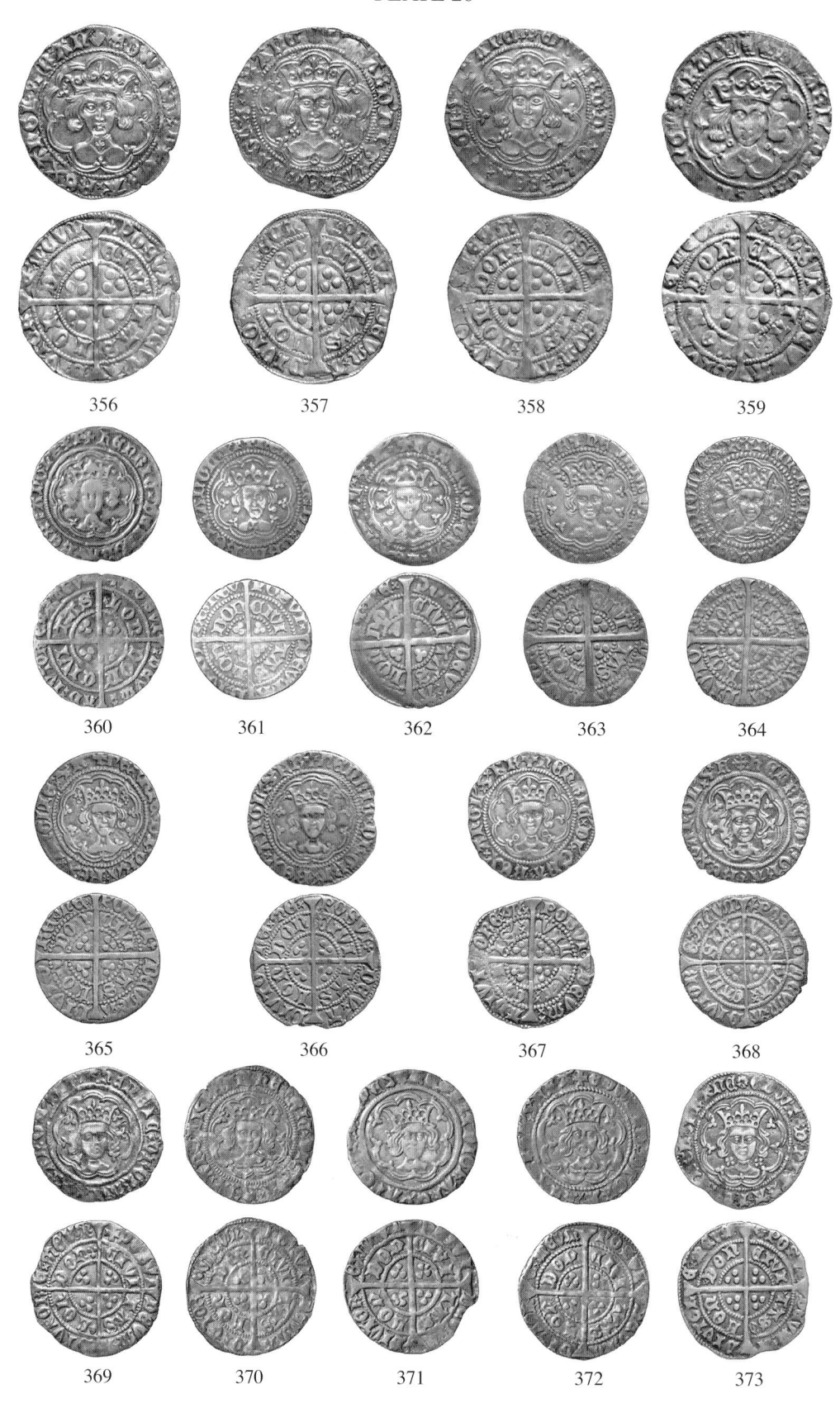

356 357 358 359

360 361 362 363 364

365 366 367 368

369 370 371 372 373

1412–1464 (6)

PLATE 21

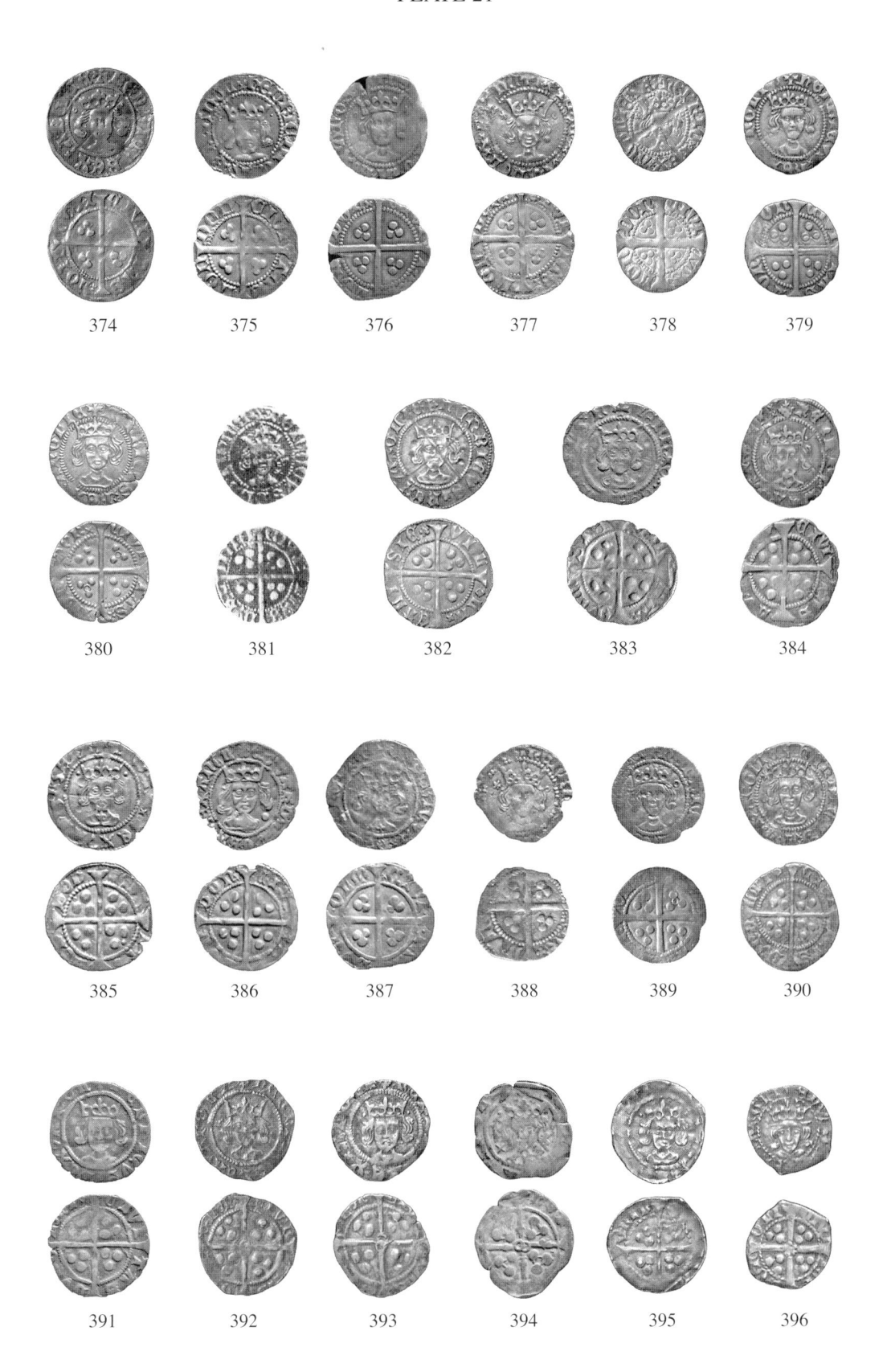

374 375 376 377 378 379

380 381 382 383 384

385 386 387 388 389 390

391 392 393 394 395 396

1412–1464 (7)

PLATE 22

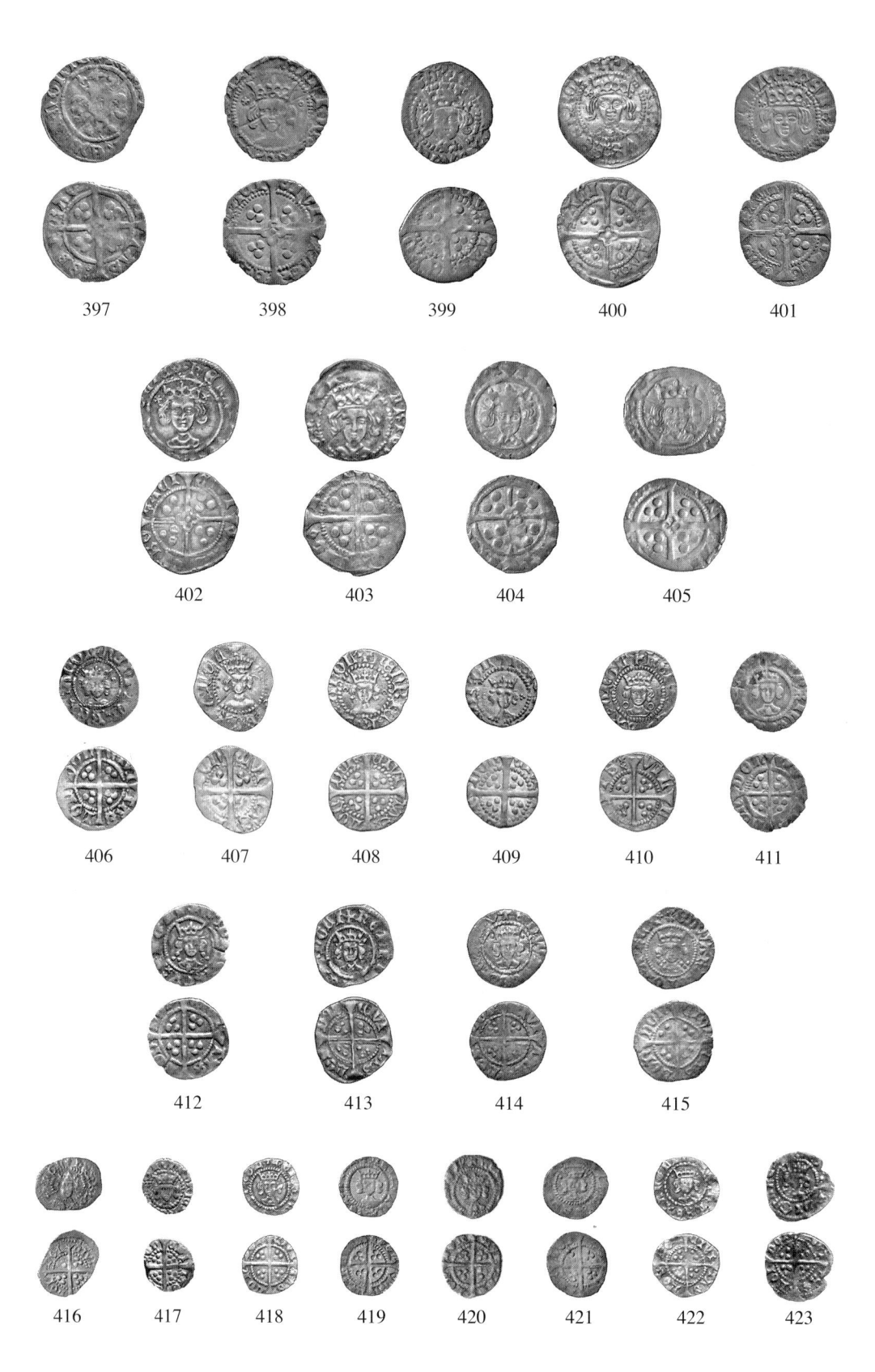

397   398   399   400   401

402   403   404   405

406   407   408   409   410   411

412   413   414   415

416   417   418   419   420   421   422   423

1412–1464 (8)

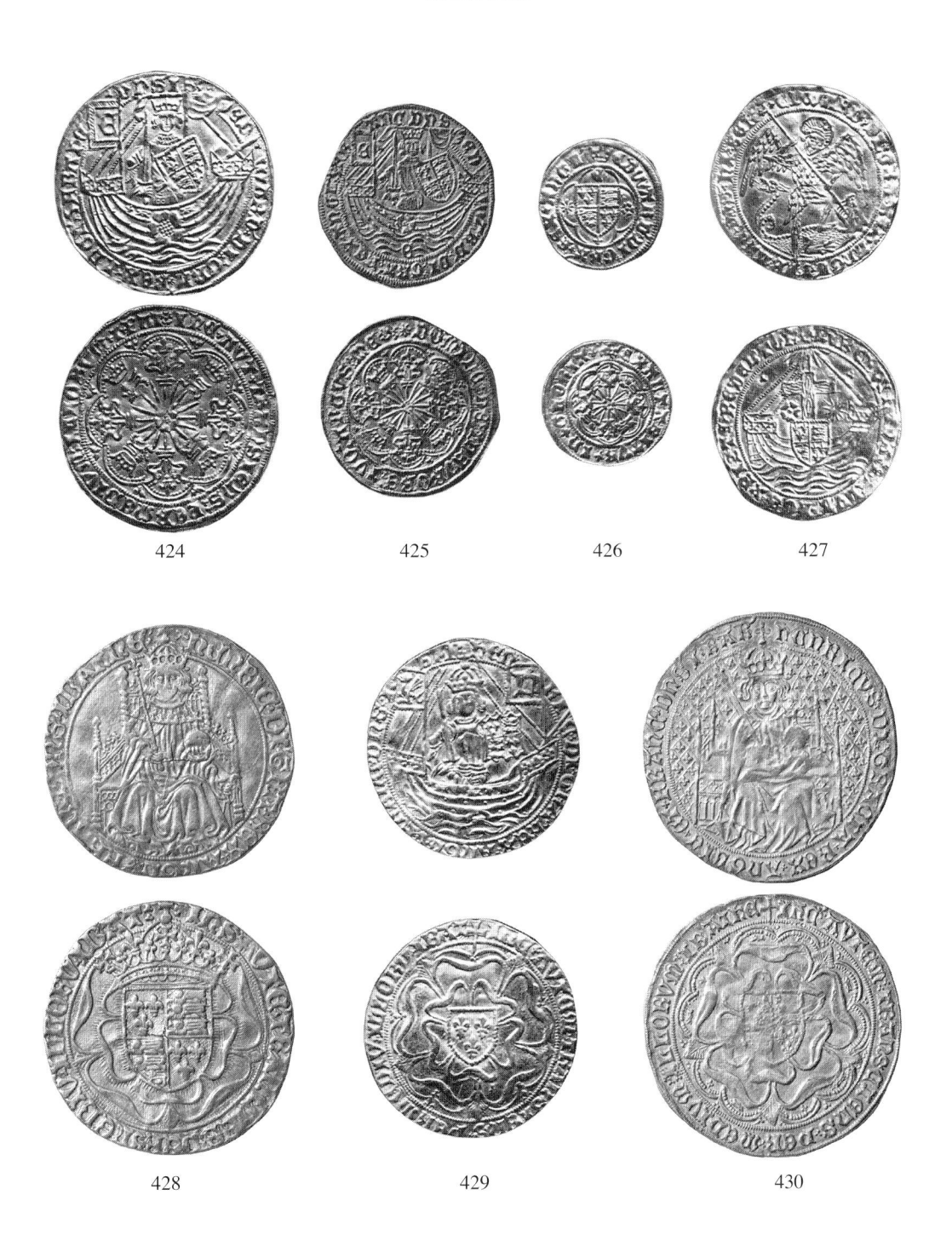

PLATE 23

424   425   426   427

428   429   430

1464–1526 (1)

PLATE 24

431 432

433 434 435

1464–1526 (2)

PLATE 25

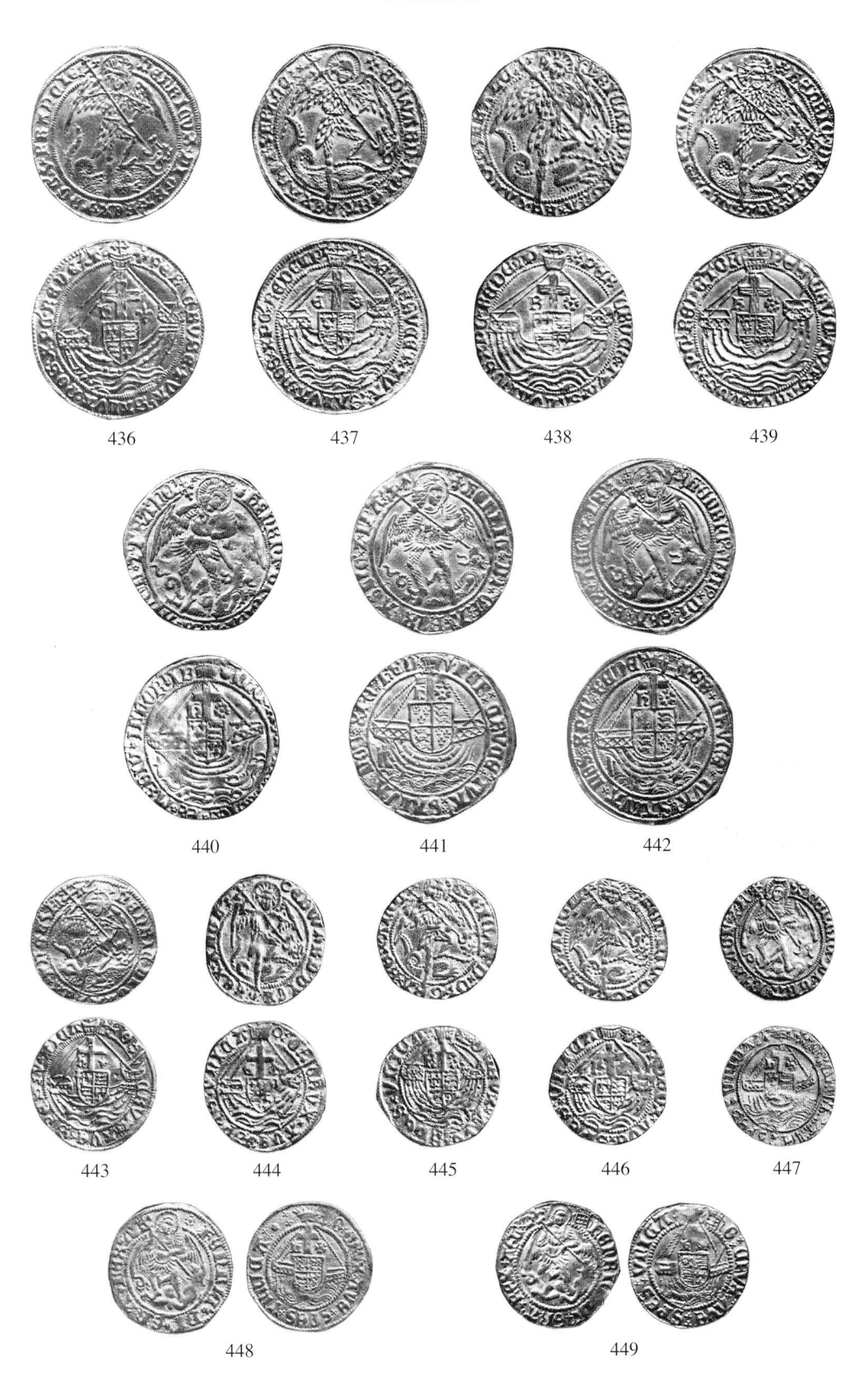

436   437   438   439

440   441   442

443   444   445   446   447

448   449

1464–1526 (3)

PLATE 26

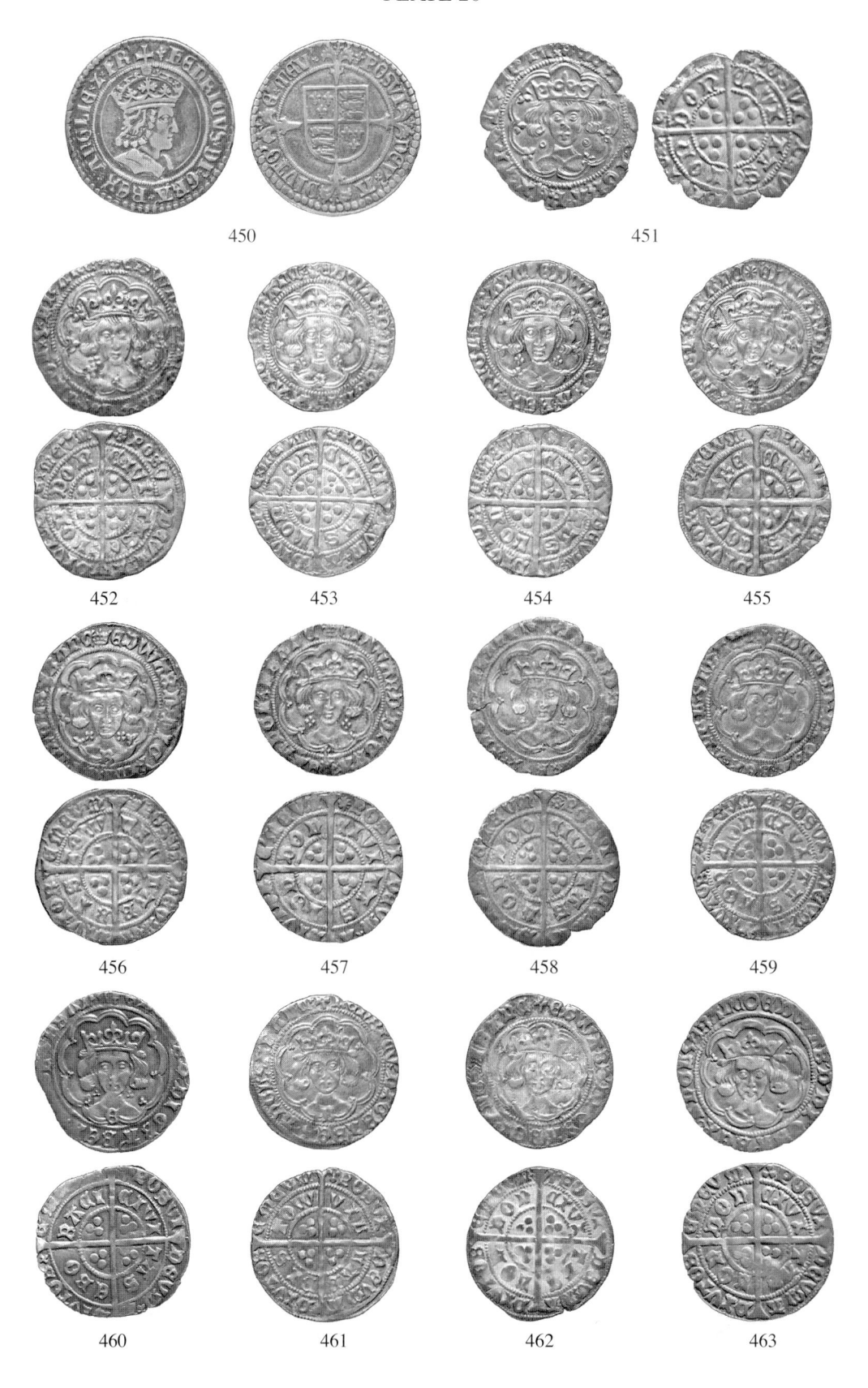

450 451

452 453 454 455

456 457 458 459

460 461 462 463

1464–1526 (4)

PLATE 27

464 465 466 467

468 469 470 471

472 473 474 475

476 477

1464–1526 (5)

PLATE 28

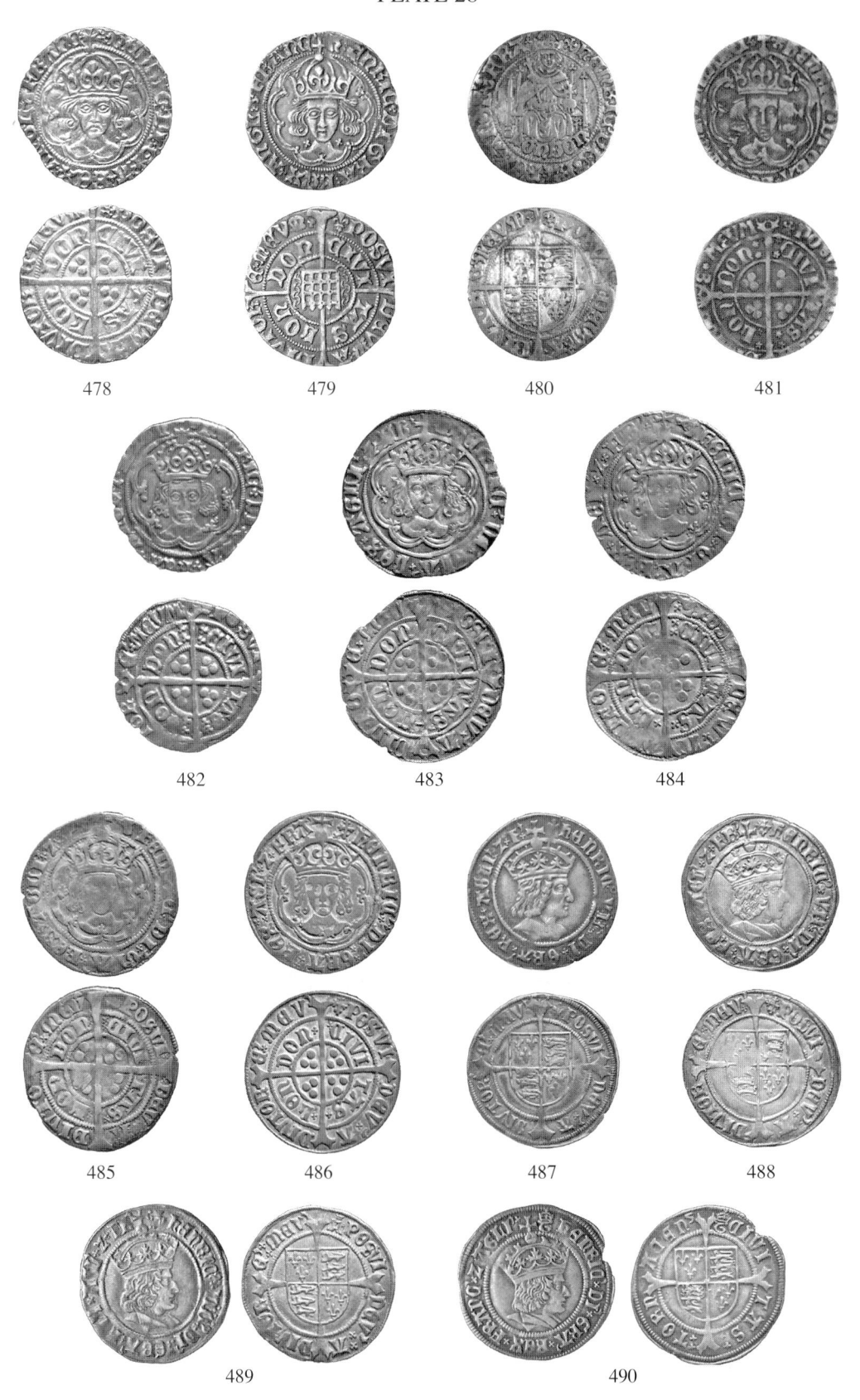

478 479 480 481

482 483 484

485 486 487 488

489 490

1464–1526 (6)

PLATE 29

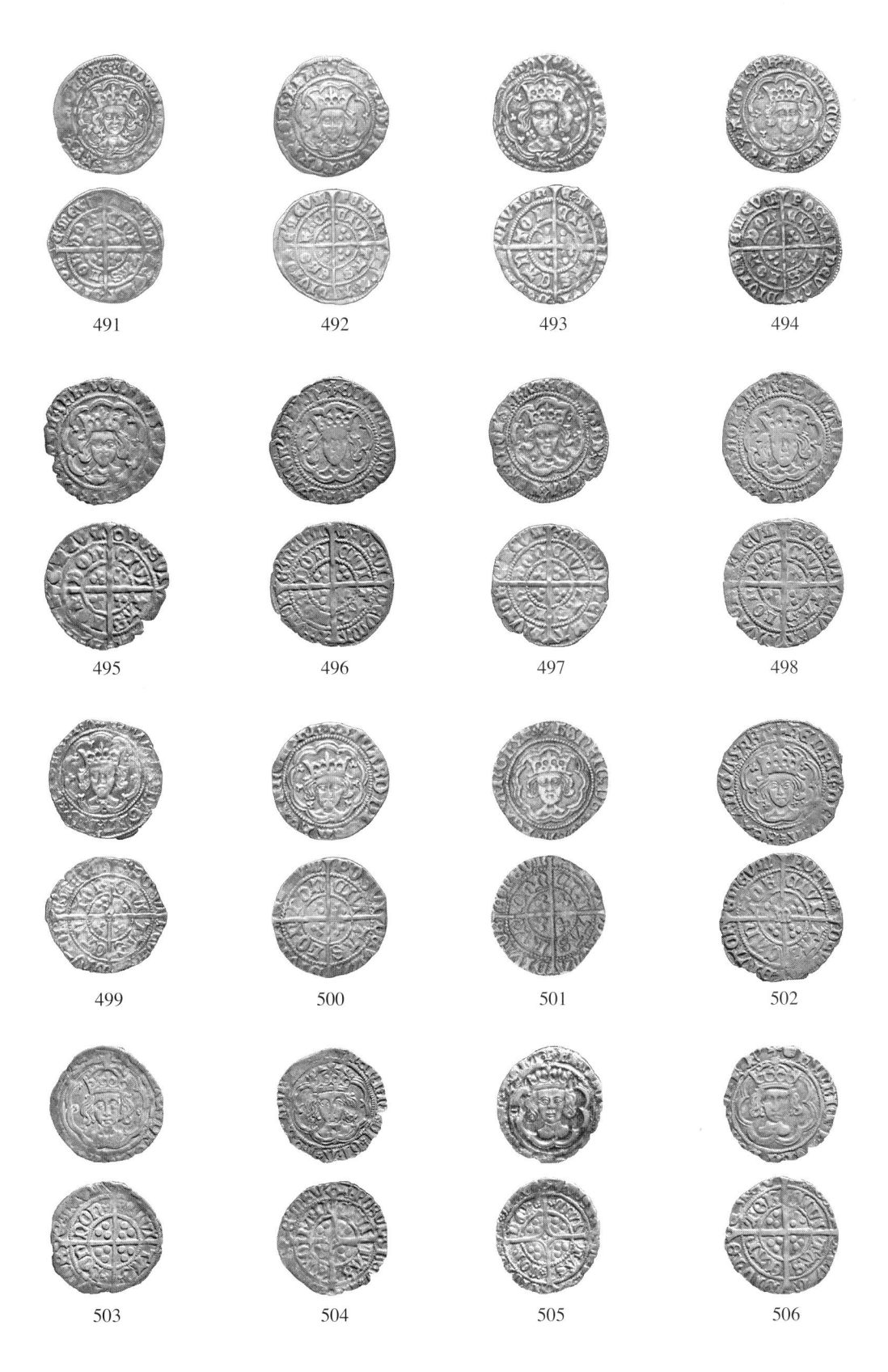

491	492	493	494
495	496	497	498
499	500	501	502
503	504	505	506

1464–1526 (7)

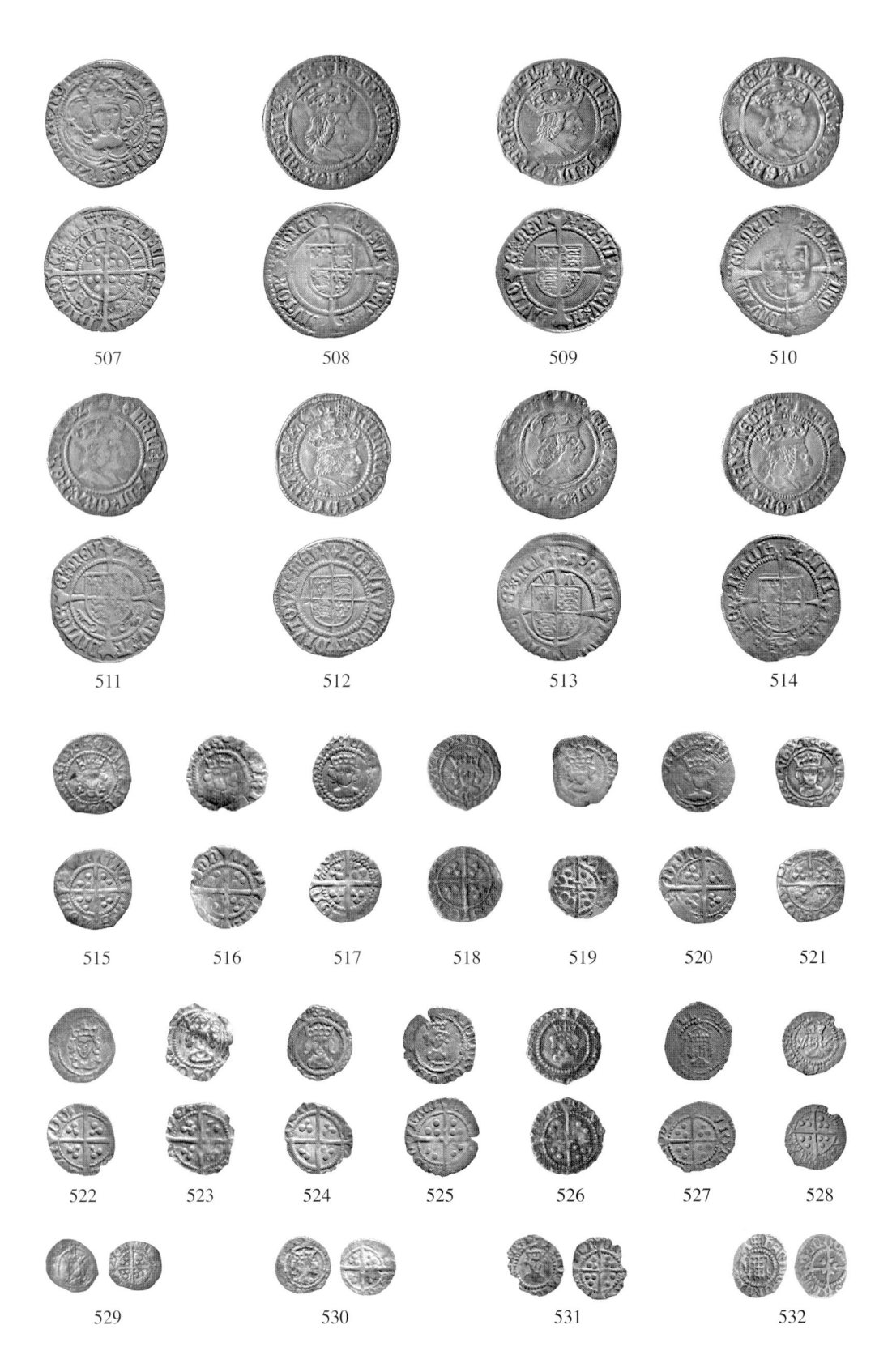

PLATE 30

507 508 509 510

511 512 513 514

515 516 517 518 519 520 521

522 523 524 525 526 527 528

529 530 531 532

1464–1526 (8)

PLATE 31

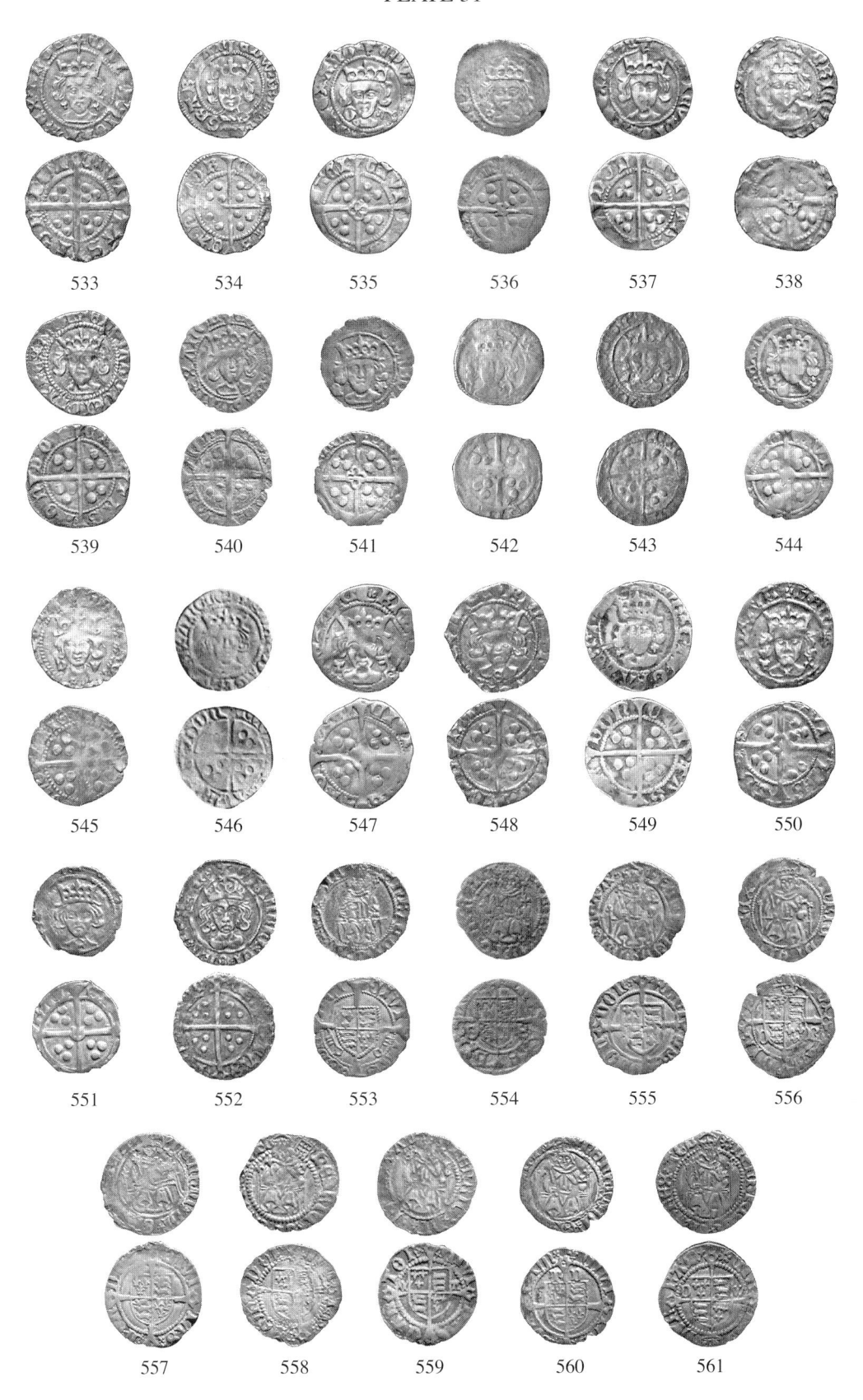

533 534 535 536 537 538

539 540 541 542 543 544

545 546 547 548 549 550

551 552 553 554 555 556

557 558 559 560 561

1464–1526 (9)

PLATE 32

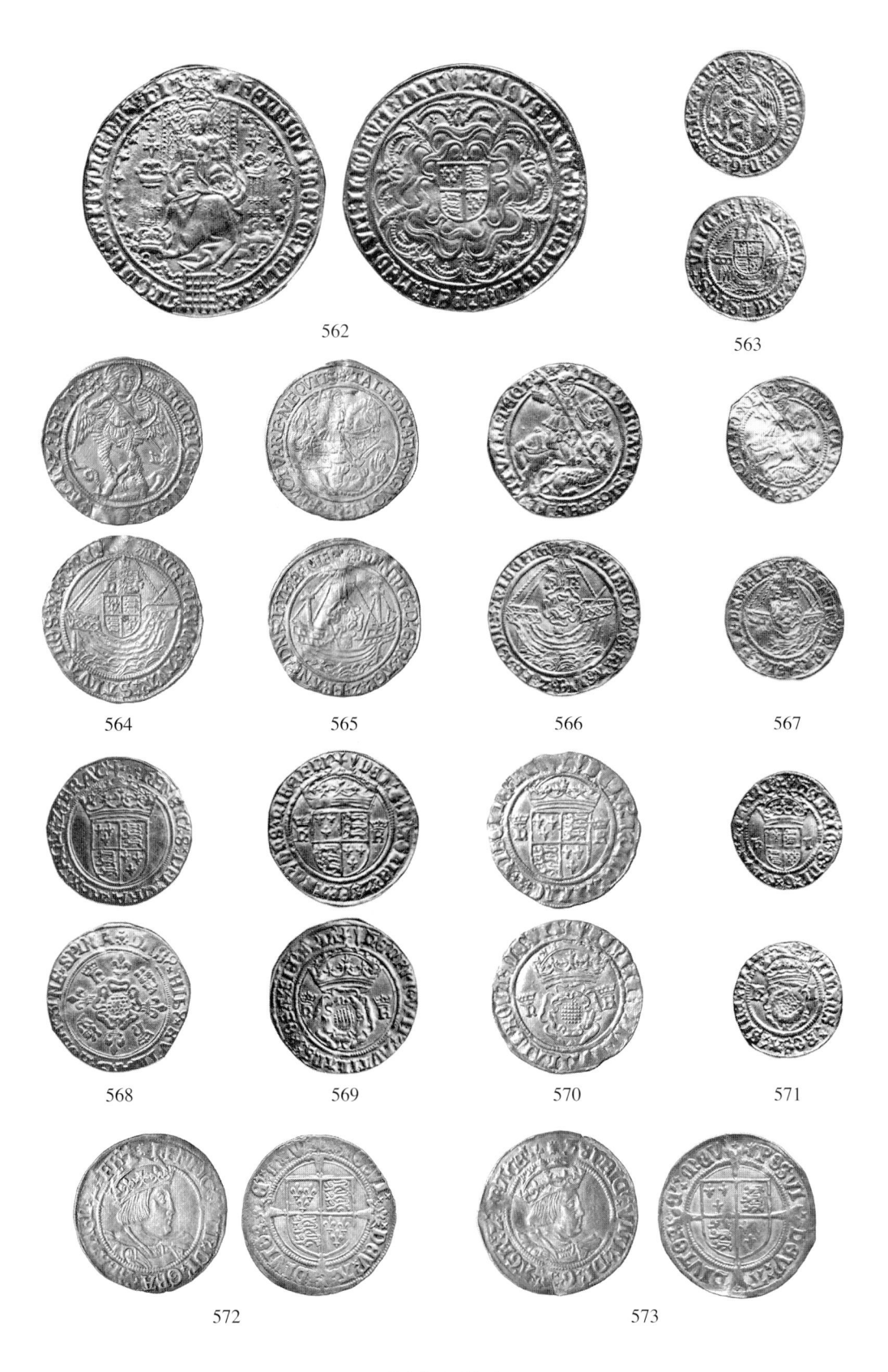

562   563

564   565   566   567

568   569   570   571

572   573

1526–1544 (1)

PLATE 33

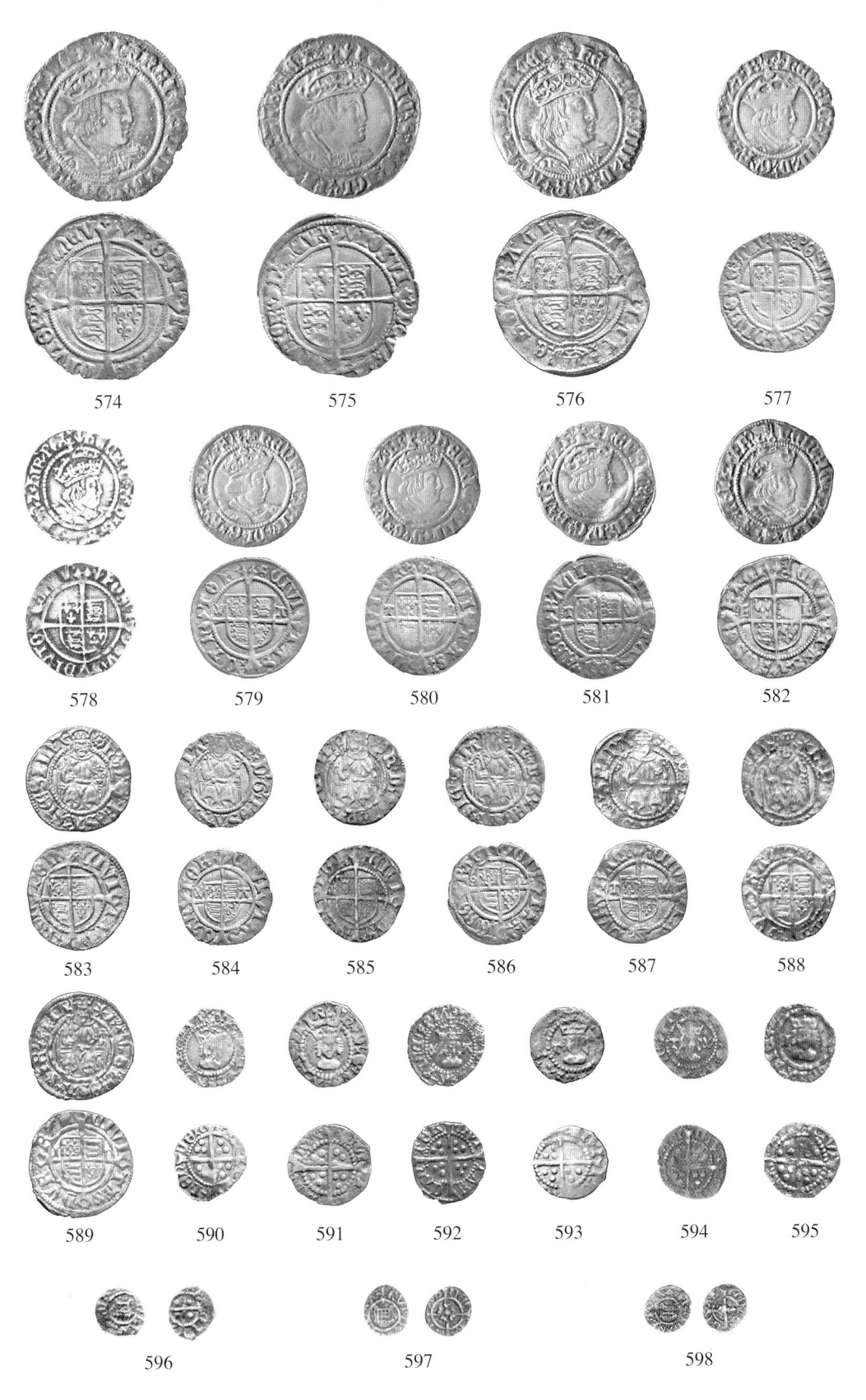

574   575   576   577

578   579   580   581   582

583   584   585   586   587   588

589   590   591   592   593   594   595

596   597   598

1464–1526 (9)

PLATE 34

599

600

601

602

603

604

1544–1551 (1)

PLATE 35

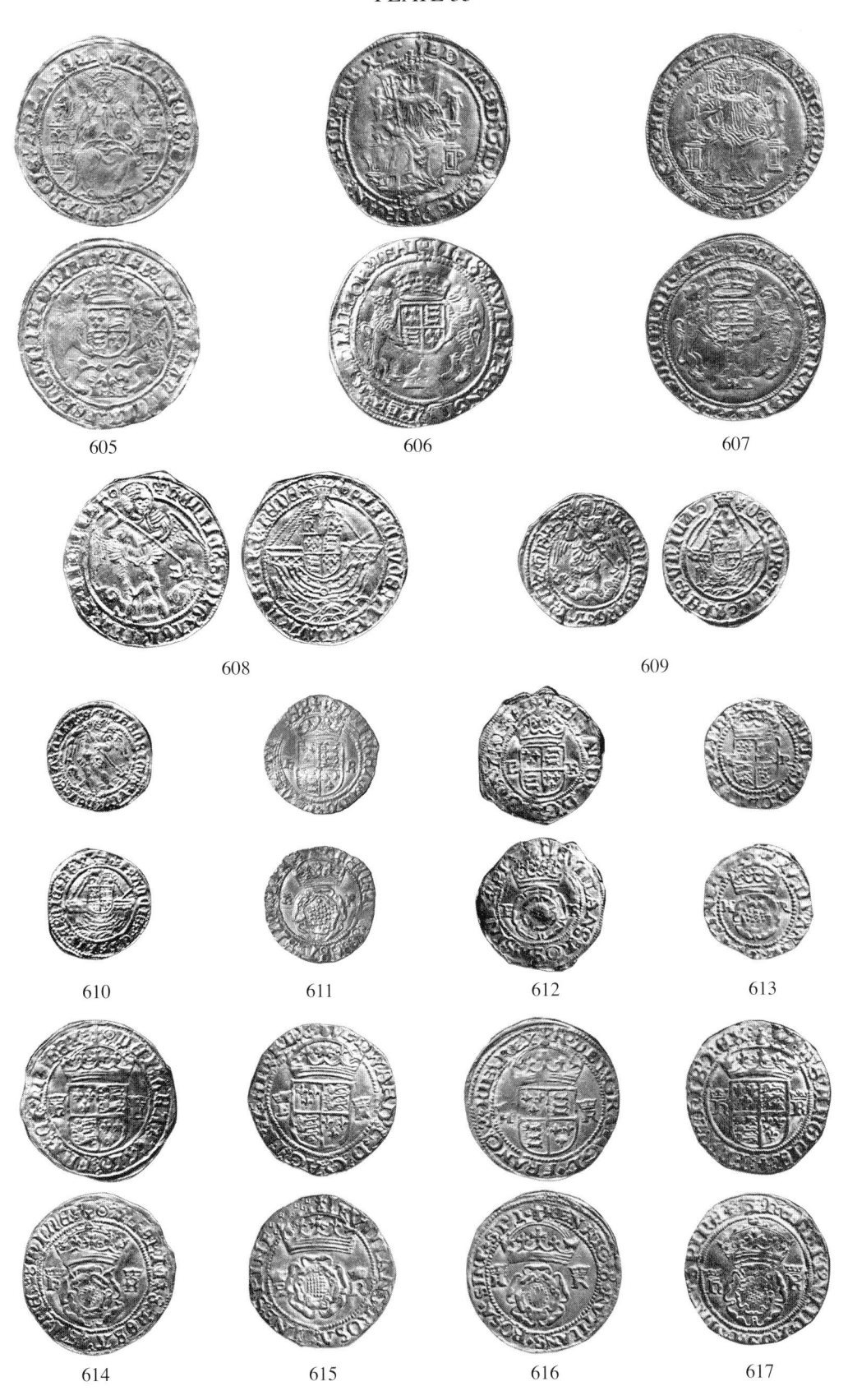

605

606

607

608

609

610

611

612

613

614

615

616

617

1544–1551 (2)

PLATE 36

618 619 620

621 622 623

624

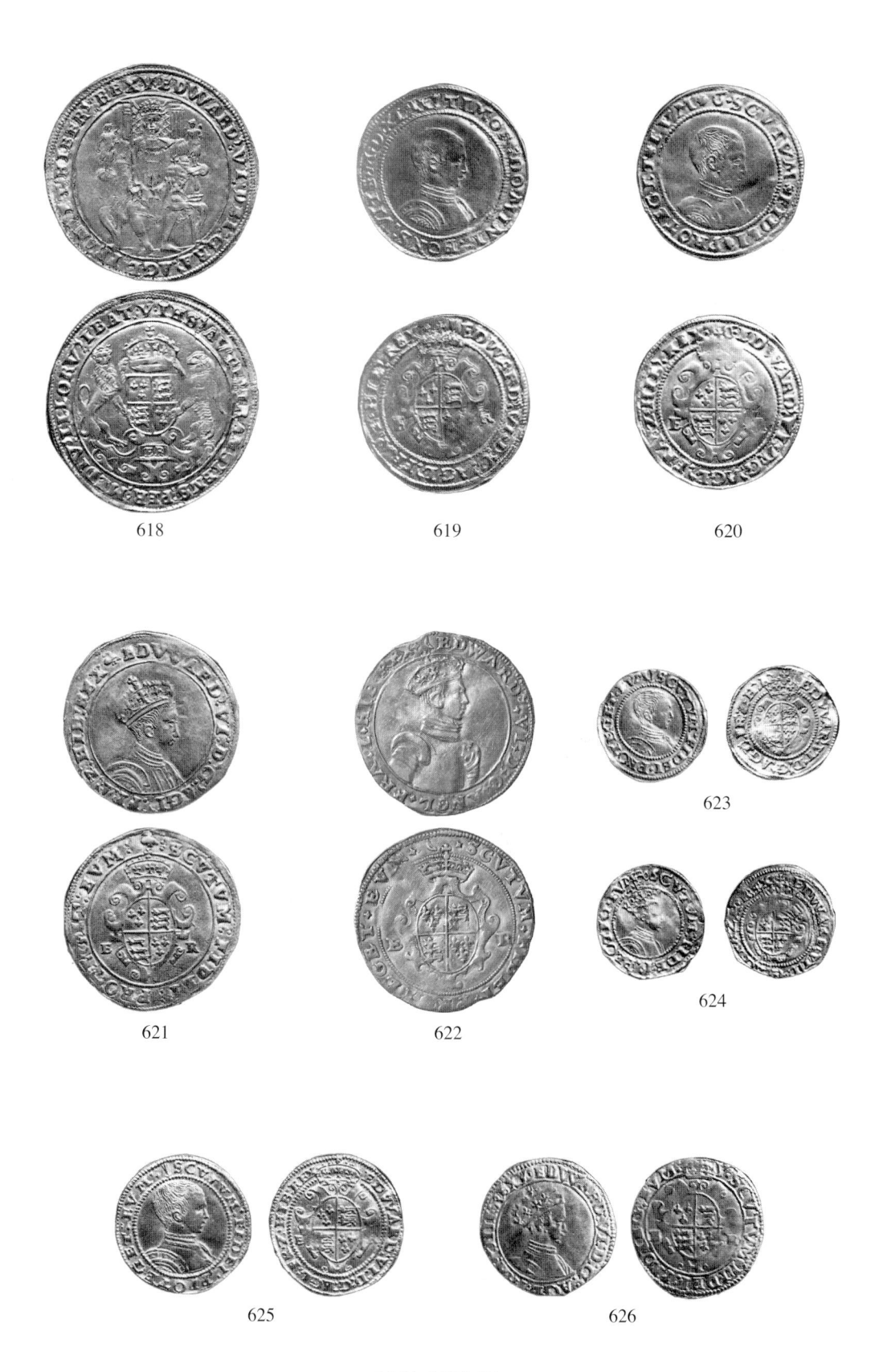

625 626

1544–1551 (3)

PLATE 37

627

628

629

630

631

632

633

1544–1551 (4)

PLATE 38

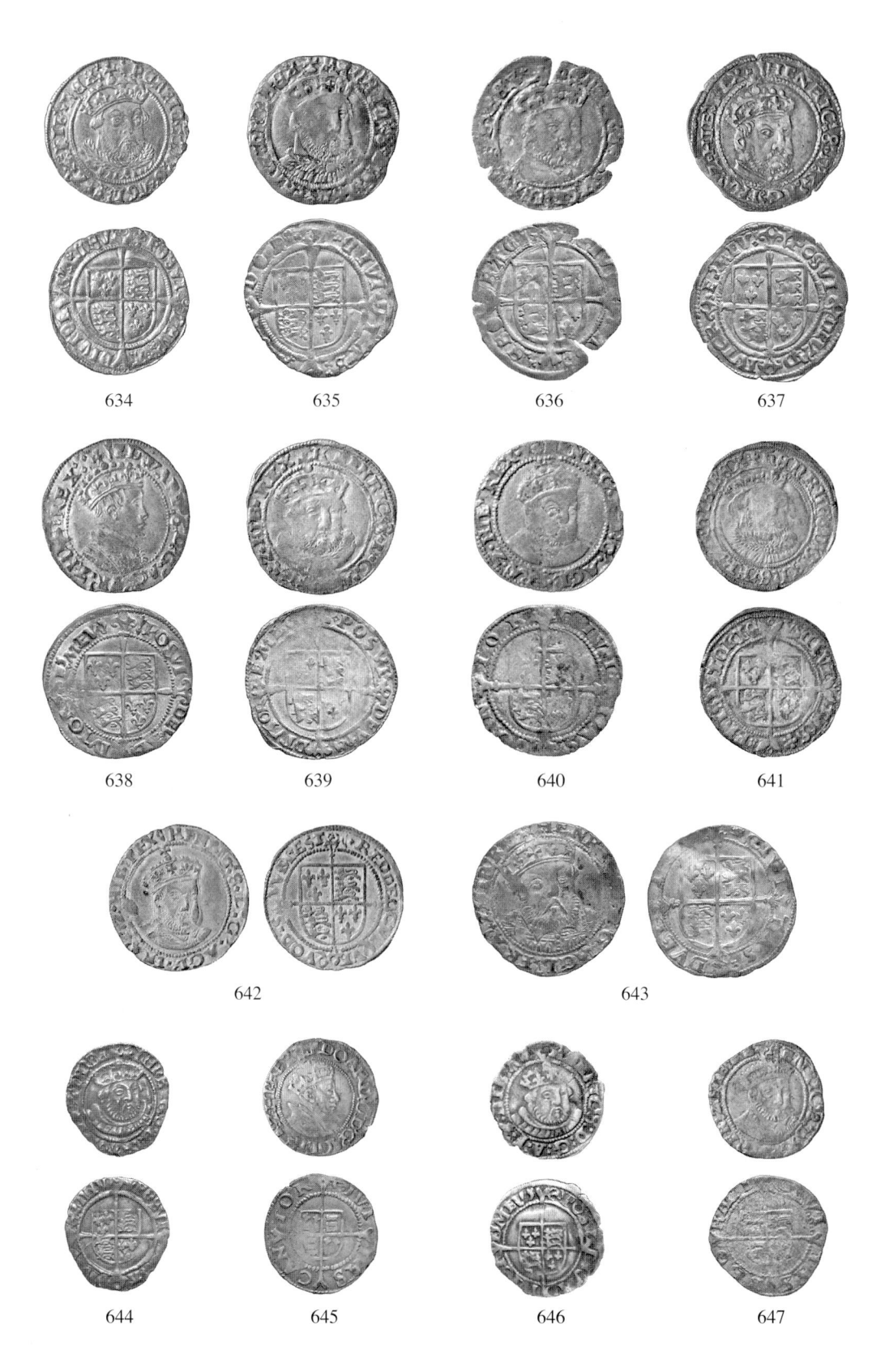

634 635 636 637

638 639 640 641

642 643

644 645 646 647

1544–1551 (5)

PLATE 39

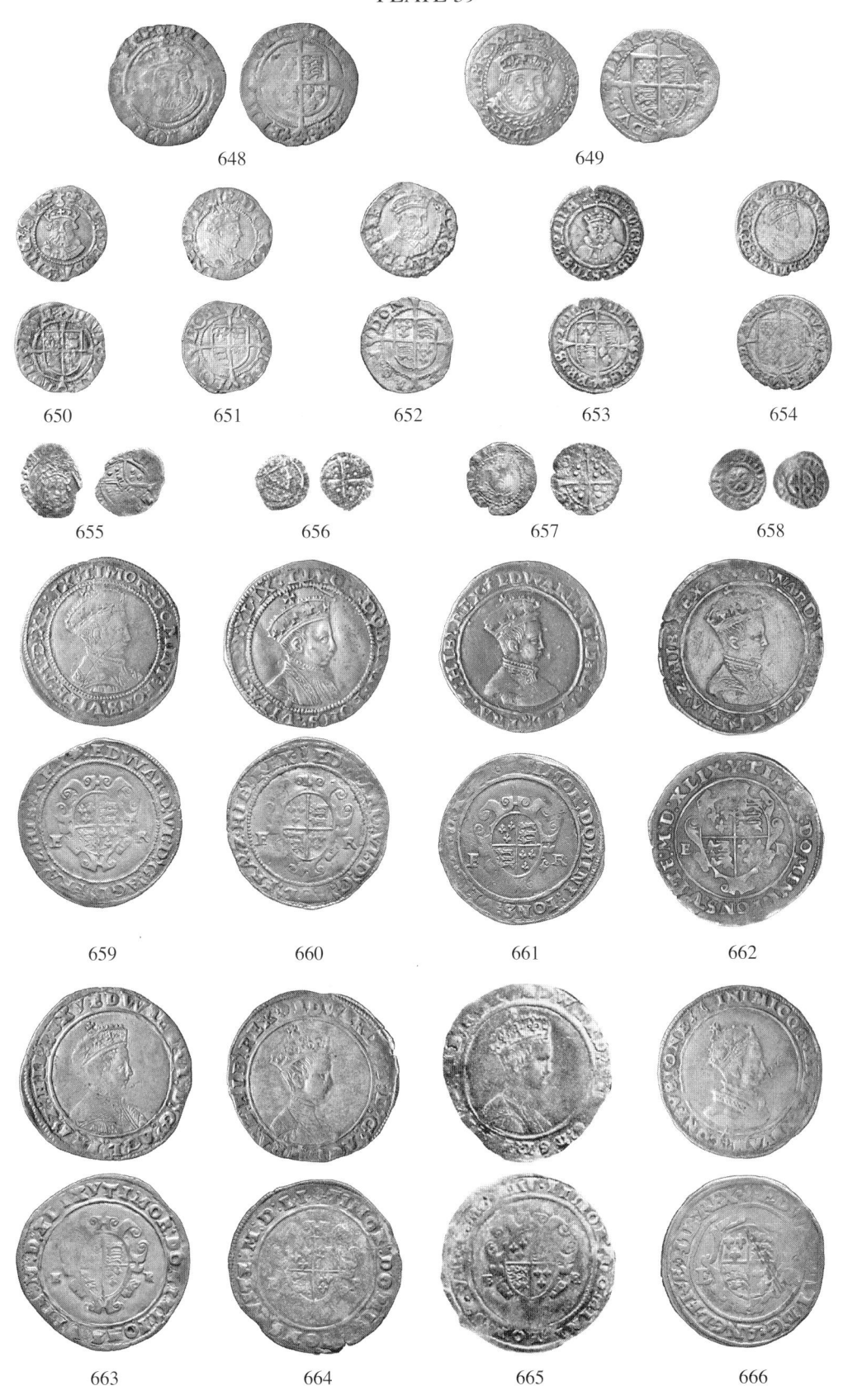

648   649

650   651   652   653   654

655   656   657   658

659   660   661   662

663   664   665   666

1544–1551 (6)